D1566478

An Encyclopedic Dictionary of
MARXISM, SOCIALISM
AND COMMUNISM

Economic, Philosophical, Political and Sociological Theories, Concepts, Institutions and Practices – Classical and Modern, East–West Relations Included

J. Wilczynski
Ph.D., D.Sc.

DE GRUYTER
BERLIN · NEW YORK

Library of Congress Cataloging in Publication Data

Wilczynski, J. (Jozef), 1922–
   An encyclopedic dictionary of Marxism, socialism
   and communism

   1. Socialism—Dictionaries.   2. Communism—Dictionaries.
I. Title
HX17.W54 1981   335'.003 81–1757 AACR2
   ISBN 3–11–008588–7

CIP–Kurztitelaufnahme der Deutschen Bibliothek

Wilczynski, Jozef
An encyclopedic dictionary of Marxism, Socialism and Communism:
economic, philosoph., polit. and sociolog. theories, concepts, institutions
and practices – class. and modern, east-west relations incl./J. Wilczynski.—
Berlin, New York: de Gruyter, 1981.
   ISBN 3–11–008588–7

© J. Wilczynski 1981

First published 1981 by
THE MACMILLAN PRESS LTD London and Basingstoke, and
WALTER DE GRUYTER, Berlin and New York.

Printed in Great Britain

ISBN 3 11 008588 7

Preface

Marxism was originally conceived in the early 1840s and immediately became a controversial body of doctrine, destined to lead to far-reaching intellectual, social and political consequences. After Marx's publication of *Capital* vol. I in 1867, virtually all thought on fundamental social issues has been either in support or in opposition to Marxist postulates and interpretations.

Precisely half a century later, the 'ten days that shook the world' resulted in the first Marxist government being successfully installed in power in Russia. By 1980, the number of countries ruled by Marxist regimes had risen to 25 – Afghanistan, Albania, Angola, Benin, Bulgaria, China (PR of), Congo, Cuba, Czechoslovakia, Ethiopia, the German DR, Guinea-Bissau, Hungary, Kampuchea (DPR of), Korea, Laos, Mongolia, Mozambique, Poland, Romania, the Somali DR, the USSR, Vietnam (PDR of), the Yemen and Yugoslavia. These countries now constitute more than one-third of the world. In addition, there are some 100 Communist parties in the capitalist world, not to mention an even larger number of socialist parties of one description or another.

The ideology ushered in by Marx and further developed by his followers has been eulogized by some as 'the greatest conception in the world. It links world wealth with world welfare' (G. Baker) and offers 'light in the darkness of a depressed world; hope and opportunity for all people; economic wisdom, political salvation, religious practice' (J. W. Bowen). But some others have denounced it as 'a fake, a comedy, a phantom and a blackmail' (B. Mussolini) and as 'the system which is workable only in heaven, where it is not needed, and in hell, where they have got it' (C. Palmer). Whether one agrees with Marxist ideas and Communist practices or not, one thing is certain – they are here to stay and they are commanding increasing interest not only from their supporters, but also from uncommitted observers as well as from enquiring critics.

This *Dictionary* provides a quick reference, explaining doctrines, terms and phrases for the student of the social sciences and the educated or curious public. The scope of the *Dictionary* is indicated by its sub-title. Non-Marxist theories are also considered, if Marxists have a definite view on them. Modern practices in the countries ruled by Marxist regimes are explained and all significant Communist and socialist parties in the world are described in detail appropriate to their importance. Included are also personalities of significant theoretical interest or major political consequence.

The author's aim is to be as objective as is humanly possible, in what is after all the most controversial topic of our times. His task is to be informative and neither propagandist nor destructively critical. But he does not hesitate, still in the informative vein, to highlight the strengths and failings of Marxism, especially in comparison with capitalism.

This *Dictionary* is a product of several years' work carried out at different institutions. The author wishes in particular to thank the Central School of Planning and Statistics, Warsaw, the University of Pittsburgh and Carleton University, Ottawa, for financing or otherwise facilitating his research. He also wishes to acknowledge the untiring assistance given to him by the National Library of Australia and the Bridges Memorial Library of the Royal Military College of Australia. He further wishes to express his appreciation to Mr Alex Ikonnikov, of the Australian National University, for his valuable information and helpful advice.

University of New South Wales   JOZEF WILCZYNSKI
at Duntroon, Canberra

A

Abnormal Surplus Value In Marx's analysis of capitalist production, an abstract concept denoting a kind of monopolistic super-normal profit. Due to competition, the capitalist introduces innovations designed to increase the intensity of work and to reduce the INDISPENSABLE LABOUR-TIME, leading to a higher productivity of labour than in other rival firms. A.s.v. is the main driving force behind technological progress under capitalism.

Above-Compulsory Delivery Under AGRICULTURAL PROCUREMENT, the sale of products to the state over and above the compulsory quota determined by the state. The a.-c.d. is voluntary and generally attracts higher prices than those payable on COMPULSORY DELIVERIES, as an inducement to larger agricultural output and a compensation for higher production costs.

Above-Plan Profit In a Socialist economy, profit achieved by the enterprise over and above that laid down in the plan. A.-p.p. is largely due to the above-normal efforts of the enterprise personnel. As a rule, a proportion larger than that of the PLANNED PROFIT is allowed for the MATERIAL INCENTIVES FUND.

Above-Plan Profit Rate In modern Socialist accounting, the achieved profit rate which actually exceeds the PLANNED PROFIT RATE. It amounts to the overfulfilment of the planned target and usually qualifies the enterprise personnel to additional bonuses on a progressive basis.

Absenteeism Non-attendance at work caused by reasons which may be socially justified (sickness, reasonable personal circumstances, furlough) or not (laxity, wilful absence). A. may be resorted to on an organized basis (especially in capitalist countries) in the form of mass sickness – an industrial tactic where open strikes are not allowed by law, custom or professional pride (police, teaching, government service, and the like). The extent of a. appears to be roughly the same under socialism as under capitalism. But, compared with the West, there are certain distinctive forces, operating in opposite directions. On the one hand, there is a more generous social security system, limited scope for spending incomes for private use, prevalent sellers' markets and longer standard working hours. On the other, there are lower income levels, workers' ownership of the means of production, workers' participation in management and control, state propaganda directed against laxity and social irresponsibility, all of which are further enhanced by SOCIALIST COMPETITION. The Socialist state takes a very serious view of a., regarding it not merely as a private affair, but a matter of considerable social concern. A. reduces output, adversely affects the achievement of targets, which may disrupt planned production flows creating bottlenecks. As such, a. delays the advance to FULL COMMUNISM. In each Socialist country, the labour code provides for penalties for unjustified a., viz. a warning, reprimand, transfer to a less important job, demotion, fines, dismissal and in some extreme cases, corrective labour camps.

1

Absentee Ownership

Absentee Ownership The ownership of income-yielding property (land, buildings or business firms, including shares) where the owner does not reside or work. A.o. has traditionally been identified with land, when historically, the owner would reside in the nearby town, a distant city or abroad. The land was farmed by peasants or tenants paying rent in one form or another which was administered by a professional hired manager. In Latin America approximately nine-tenths of the large landlords are a. owners. Since the end of the 19th c. another type of a.o. became an important feature in mining, industry, commerce, finance, transport and other services. Here firms or large shareholdings are owned by proprietors or dominant shareholders, but otherwise such entities are operated by professional salaried managers. A.o. has been subject to bitter attacks by Marxists for the following reasons: 1. a. owners are idle capitalists, usually receiving high property incomes in the form of rent, interest, profits or dividends; 2. such non-labour incomes constitute the exploitation of those who operate the means of production, i.e. the workers who are the real producers and creators of value; 3. under a. land ownership, whilst income is produced in agriculture it is spent largely in other branches of the economy (or abroad), thereby depressing agricultural investment and progress; and 4. the a. proprietors or shareholders are interested in maximum income for themselves, not in the conditions of work and production, resulting in the neglect of the latter. However, it may be pointed out here that the extent and abuses of a.o. have been somewhat reduced since W.W.I by land reforms, heavy death duties and other taxes, nationalization, industrial legislation and other forms of state intervention.

Absolute Consumer's Sovereignty An economic regime where the 'consumer is absolute king'. It prevails where all economic activities are basically induced by, and geared to, consumers' preferences, whether such preferences are so-cially legitimate or not. In effect, the allocation of resources is basically shaped by consumers through their spending power. A.c.s. was typical of *laissez-faire* capitalism where the extent of monopoly was small and the state refrained from intervening in the economy. Marxists are opposed to a.c.s., as some consumer's preferences are irrational leading to ANTI-SOCIAL CONSUMPTION and could interfere with the planned utilization of resources. See RATIONALIZED CONSUMERS' SOVEREIGNTY.

Absolute Equalitarianism The extreme form of equality amongst persons advocated by some social reformers, especially utopian socialists, Left Communists and impatient radical revolutionaries. On the whole, Marxism rejects a.e. as unworkable and socially detrimental. Stalin dismissed it as a 'petty bourgeois deviation' in his famous Uravnilovka Speech in 1931. The principle was widely discussed in China, especially during the GREAT PROLETARIAN CULTURAL REVOLUTION, when several efforts were made towards a.e. Mao Tse-tung had changing views on a.e., but finally he publicly condemned it in 1972 by reference to practices in the PEOPLE'S LIBERATION ARMY (in 'On Absolute Equalitarianism', embodied in *Five Articles*). It is widely agreed amongst Marxists that even under full communism distribution will not be completely egalitarian, but 'according to needs' (which implies differences from one person to another).

Absolute Ethics The field of ETHICS concerned with immutable and eternal moral standards, which are considered to be universal, irrespective of society's geographical, political and social environment and historical development. The founder of a.e. was H. Spencer (1820–1903), who distinguished it from RELATIVE E. Marxist philosophers reject a.e., regarding it as a logical product of IDEALISM. They insist that there is no such thing as a completely neutral morality independent of the material and social conditions of life, as ethical standards vary geographically, socially and historically, reflecting the interests of different social groups.

Absolute Rent In a Marxian application to the capitalist economy, a form of GROUND RENT appropriated by the landowner. As such, it is an element of SURPLUS VALUE representing the exploitation of agricultural workers, tenants and consumers of agricultural products. A.r., as distinct from DIFFERENTIAL RENT, arises from the monopolistic private ownership of land and from a lower ORGANIC STRUCTURE OF CAPITAL in agriculture than in industry (i.e. amounting to under-capitalization in the former). Consequently, the value of agricultural products is higher than their cost of production. The difference between the two indicates the size of the a.r. Under socialism, as a rule, a.r. does not occur, but where it does it is generally absorbed by the state.

Absolute Surplus Value In Marx's analysis of capitalist production, value created by SURPLUS LABOUR, i.e. value which is produced by the worker as a consequence of the lengthening of the working day and the intensification of labour beyond the INDISPENSABLE LABOUR-TIME (necessary to support the worker and his family at subsistence level). It contrasts with the RELATIVE SURPLUS VALUE.

Absolute Truth In philosophy, truth that is indisputable and cannot be invalidated. In METAPHYSICS, true knowledge is regarded as eternal and immutable and consequently all truth, if it is truth, is absolute. The Marxist approach is different. It views the establishment of truth as a dynamic and historical process whereby the nature of truth differs according to historical circumstances. Thus, normally, truth is relative and only in the ultimate phase of perfection does it become absolute. Marxist philosophers reject the idealist and metaphysical interpretation of truth, regarding it as unscientific and an attempt to replace science with FIDEISM and RELIGION. See also OBJECTIVE TRUTH.

Abstract Art A movement in painting, sculpture and graphics which originated in the West in the early part of the twentieth c. It emphasizes individual feeling, symbolism, escapism and utilitarianism and is opposed to any form of regimentation. It is also known as abstractionism, non-objective art or non-representational art. Some of its supporters have hoped to influence Socialist art by offering it greater freedom, originality and variety. On the whole, the Socialist countries have officially repudiated a.a. as being subjectivist, egotistic, anarchical and reactionary. See CUBISM, EXPRESSIONISM, FUTURISM.

Abstract Labour Marxian term for labour performed in general. It is the productive expenditure of human energy leading to the creation of value, irrespective of its concrete form. As such, it is the common indicator of value constituting SOCIAL LABOUR and contrasts with CONCRETE LABOUR.

Abstraction The process of reasoning consisting in the identification of essential features of objects or phenomena and their relations and the formulation of generalizations, laws and theories. It is important to distinguish between the idealist (bourgeois) and materialist (Marxist) conception of a. Although Marxists recognize the cognitive and scientific value of a., they point to its potential misuse on philosophical grounds. They oppose ascribing an independent real existence to characteristics, relations and generalizations arrived at in the process of a. This in turn would lead to idealist philosophy (IDEALISM) and supernatural religious beliefs. A. may also involve an unrealistic divorce from reality, leading to FORMALISM and sterile speculation, incapable of dealing with social realities.

Academic Socialism A term disparagingly used by revolutionary Marxists to describe the mild version of socialism advocated by intellectuals from the safety and comfort of their academic positions. It is also known as 'armchair socialism' or 'socialism *ex-cathedra*'. A.s. emphasizes theory rather than action and ethics rather than practice. A.s. was originally identified with the ideas propagated in Germany in the second half of the nineteenth century by such thinkers as B. Hildebrandt (1812–78), W. Sombart (1863–1941) and A. Wagner (1835–1917). They argued that socialism could be evolved gradually via peaceful reforms from above without either a class war or violent revolution, utilizing the state as an initiating and unifying force. K. Marx attacked a.s. (in *Critique of the Gotha Programme*) as too timid and too slow. To some extent, a.s. has found support in ECONOMISM, FABIANISM, LEGAL MARXISM, EUROCOMMUNISM, and REVISIONISM.

Academy of Social Sciences The highest institution of party education in the USSR. It is located in Moscow, is attached to the Central Committee of the Communist Party of the Soviet Union and was established in 1946 as an indirect successor to the INSTITUTE OF RED PROFESSORSHIP. It admits only graduate students with experience in party, trade union or government work on the recommendation of higher regional party authorities. Its function is to train ideologically reliable specialists in history, philosophy, politics, political economy, literature, journalism, art, international relations and the critique of capitalism. The course involves a thesis leading to the degree of Candidate of Science (corresponding to Ph.D.) which the Academy is empowered to award.

Accounting Prices See SHADOW PRICES.

Accumulation The term used in Socialist national income accounting, corresponding to the Western concept of investment in its broadest sense. It is that part of national income which is produced but not consumed during the year in question (A = NY − C). Its main purpose is to increase the productive capacity of the economy. According to the official classification, a. consists of: (i) the stock of added fixed

assets in the sphere of MATERIAL PRODUCTION; (ii) the stock of added fixed assets in the NON-PRODUCTIVE SPHERE; (iii) net addition to the stock of circulating assets in the process of production; (iv) net addition to reserves (held idle as an insurance against unexpected contingencies); and (v) the foreign trade balance. In a Socialist economy a. is placed on a planned basis and great importance is attached to a high ACCUMULATION RATE.

Accumulation Rate The percentage ratio of ACCUMULATION (A) to the NET MATERIAL PRODUCT (NMP): a.r. = A/NMP.100. Depending on whether depreciation is deducted or not from accumulation, the a.r. can be calculated on a net or gross basis, the former being the commonly implied rate. The a.r. is determined at the top political level and is quite high, typically in the range of 15–30 per cent (higher than would be the case under capitalism at the same stage of economic development). In the traditional Socialist view, steeped in the EXTENSIVE GROWTH strategy, the level of a.r. determines the rate of ECONOMIC GROWTH.

Action Programme A short name for the 'Action Programme of the Communist Party of Czechoslovakia'. It was a scheme for far-reaching economic reforms adopted by the Central Committee of the Communist Party in April 1968. But it was never implemented, owing to the military intervention by the Warsaw Pact countries (INVASION OF CZECHOSLOVAKIA) and the dismissal of the liberal Communist government. Designed by Ota Sik (Deputy Prime Minister at the time), it aimed to establish a 'New Economic Model', a type of MARKET SOCIALISM in Czechoslovakia. Its main elements were: the decentralization of planning and management; the strengthening of material incentives; the predominantly free market formation of wholesale and retail prices; competition; the self-financing of enterprises and the liberalization of external economic relations.

Activist A person who is active in assisting the implementation of the party policies on a voluntary basis. His activities may be carried on in a political association, an educational institution, a cultural society, a sporting club or some other social organization.

Added Product In Socialist national income accounting, another (less commonly used) term for SURPLUS PRODUCT.

'*Adresnost*' A Russian term which has no exact equivalent in English, used in economic planning to describe the fact that a planned TARGET is specifically 'addressed' to an entity or a group of entities in an explicitly defined class for implementation.

Advertising The application of mass media (press, posters, leaflets, radio, television, cinema) by sellers or their agents to influence potential buyers' preferences as a method of sales promotion. A. can be informative or persuasive. It reaches its highest development and influence in industrialized capitalist countries which are noted for BUYERS' MARKETS, COMPETITION and private profit motivation. In Marxist political economy a. is considered to be largely a waste of resources in the social sense, and moreover, a. agencies are classed as non-productive entities since they do not contribute to MATERIAL PRODUCTION. Marxists see a. in a capitalist market economy as an attempt to overcome the inherent weakness of capitalism's tendency toward over-production in relation to demand, i.e. the insufficiency of the spending power at the disposal of the masses to absorb all the output. A. is motivated by private greed and is often designed to mislead the public, to eliminate rival firms and to establish and defend monopoly. In Socialist planned economies, a. is largely pointless and could be considered harmful. There is no lack of demand, for demand tends to outrun supply, as is evident in the number of prevalent SELLERS' MARKETS. But more importantly, a. could lead to unplanned changes in demand, create bottlenecks and disrupt the economic plan. However, since the mid-1960s, the European Socialist countries have adopted a somewhat more positive attitude to a., as it is realized that a. can perform two useful functions in a planned economy: 1. consumers are able to make more advantageous decisions in spending their income, thereby increasing satisfaction from a given level of income; and 2. judiciously state-conducted persuasive a. can be used as an instrument of 'consumer education' and CONSUMPTION STEERING. Here consumers' preferences are adapted to the socially desired planned patterns of production on the one hand, and to the easy disposal of unwanted stocks of goods on the other, thereby rectifying planners' errors. A. of a kind is also utilized on a systematic and comprehensive basis in the form of PROPAGANDA.

Aeroflot The state owned and only Soviet airline in the country and which is also the largest in the world. It was founded in 1923 and has experienced an impressive development, especially since 1970. In 1978 it operated flights to 3,600 cities and settlements in the USSR, 80 cities in foreign countries, covered over 850,000 km of domestic and international air routes, carried 110m passengers, handled one quarter of all air cargo in the world and treated 100m sq. hectares of agricultural land by aero-chemical methods. It performs more than 100 types of avionic uses in the national economy.

AES In Russian, the abbreviation for *Atomnaya Elektrostantsiya*, meaning atomic power station.

Aesthetics The theory of art concerned with the criteria, characteristics and types of beauty in nature and man-made objects. Ae. has been one of the fields of controversy between materialist (MATERIALISM) and idealist (IDEALISM) approaches to art. This is exemplified by the attacks by V. G. Belinsky (1811–48), N. G. Chernyshevsky (1828–89), N. A.

Dobrolubov (1836–61), V. I. Lenin (1870–1924) and G. V. Plekhanov (1856–1918) against the divorce of art from reality, the ideological neutrality of art, the freedom of creativity and 'art for art's sake' advocated by such idealist philosophers as I. Kant (1724–1804) and G. W. F. Hegel (1770–1831). Marxists regard art as one of the forms of SOCIAL CONSCIOUSNESS, an artistic approach to understanding human reality and social relations. They also consider that the elements of beauty (line, shape, shade, colour, sound) pleasing to man's senses and understanding exist in the object itself, whilst man's subjective appreciation is derivative and secondary, i.e. beauty is objective, belonging to the object and not the beholder's emotional response to his experience. See ART, SOCIALIST REALISM.

AFL-CIO The national trade union organization in the USA and partly covering Canada, formed by the amalgamation of the AMERICAN FEDERATION OF LABOR and the CONGRESS OF INDUSTRIAL ORGANIZATIONS in 1955. It has about 30m. members, embracing some 70 per cent of organized labour in North America. There are a number of important trade unions which are independent, such as the Longshoremen, Mine Workers, Railroad Brotherhoods, and the Teamsters.

African Party for the Independence of Guinea and Cabo Verde (*Partido Africano de Indepêndecia de Guiné e Cabo Verde*) The ruling political party in Guinea-Bissau, whose programme is largely Marxist but disclaims to be a communist party.

African Socialism A general name for the developing mixture of African traditionalism, Western social reformism, classical Marxism and some features of Soviet, East European and Chinese socialism adapted to modern national needs and local conditions. The ideas and practices introduced by Western and Socialist-educated indigenous intellectuals and colonial (mostly French) administrators and settlers have been supplemented or modified by such local traditional quasi-socialist elements as the collective (tribal) ownership of land, co-operative pursuits based on mutual help and obligations, the absence or weakness of the conventional market mechanism, communal living and the persistence of egalitarianism. The development of A. s., going back to the early 1950s, has been linked with national liberation movements against COLONIALISM and NEO-COLONIALISM. The most publicized version of A.s. is TANZANIAN SOCIALISM.

Afro-Asian Journalists' Association A regional INTERNATIONAL COMMUNIST FRONT ORGANIZATION established at the Bandung Conference in April 1963 by the resolution of the Fifth Congress of the INTERNATIONAL ORGANIZATION OF JOURNALISTS in Budapest in August 1962. Its headquarters were originally in Djakarta, but after the abortive communist coup in Indonesia in 1965 its centre of operations moved to Peking.

Afro-Asian People's Solidarity Organization A regional INTERNATIONAL COMMUNIST FRONT ORGANIZATION established in 1958 to strengthen the struggle of the countries of Africa and Asia against imperialism and colonialism and to promote their economic, social and cultural development. From the start, it became strongly influenced by the USSR, China and the United Arab Republic, but since 1967 it has been dominated by the USSR. It claims national committees and affiliated organizations in 75 countries and its headquarters are in Cairo. It regularly publishes *Afro-Asian Bulletin* (monthly) and occasionally *Afro-Asian Publications*, *Afro-Asian Women*, and *Afro Asian Writings* – all in Arabic, English and French.

Afro-Asian Writers' Permanent Bureau A regional INTERNATIONAL COMMUNIST FRONT ORGANIZATION originally set up on the Soviet initiative in Tashkent in 1958; however, the Permanent Bureau was established in Colombo in 1962. Owing to the Sino-Soviet rivalry, two operational centres were subsequently (in 1966) created – the Chinese-dominated one in Peking and the pro-Soviet one in Cairo. The respective factions publish *Call* and *Lotus* at irregular intervals in Arabic, English and French.

Agitation A type of political activity consisting in the persuasive propagation of simple ideas and slogans designed to arouse emotions (rather than to appeal to reason) of a large crowd in order to influence its consciousness and mood in directions desired by the party. A. is usually associated with one simple fact or event that can be easily understood by a large mass of common people. It can be carried on by holding mass meetings, organizing discussion sessions, distributing leaflets and using mass media in one way or another, calculated for more or less immediate reactions. All communist parties have special a. sections, mostly combined with, but sometimes separate from, propaganda. The purpose of a. in capitalist countries may be to cause a state of excitement, discontent, indignation, disruption and even violent action. In the Socialist countries, a. serves the general interests of the party – the indoctrination of the masses, the explanation of the party and state policies, the enlistment of electoral support for the party, a wider participation in state programmes and campaigns and the arousal of anger and hostility against internal and external enemies. In Marxist practice, a distinction is made between a. and PROPAGANDA. Since the mid-1960s, a new view of a. has emerged in the more advanced Socialist countries. The traditional type of crude a. is being discarded in favour of more sophisticated politinformation, designed to influence reasonably well educated and informed mass audiences.

Agitator A person who carries on AGITATION, either on a voluntary or professional basis. The a. differs from the propagandist in that the former uses simple facts or ideas appealing to emotions in order to

excite the common masses for immediate reaction, whilst the latter goes into a more substantive justification appealing to reason and directed at smaller and sophisticated audiences for lasting effects. More recently, the function of the a. has to some extent been taken over by the POLITINFORMATOR.

Agitprop The Russian syllabic abbreviation for the (*Odtel Agitatsii i Propagandy*) Agitation and Propaganda Section. The term was established in Soviet Russia in 1920 when such sections were first created in the Secretariat of the Central Committee of the All-Russian Communist Party (of the Bolsheviks) and lower party organizations. It was responsible for AGITATION, PROPAGANDA and cultural activities for domestic and foreign consumption in accordance with the Party's directives or guidelines. The term A. is no longer used, as the Section was reorganized in the 1930s. Nonetheless, its work is still carried on in the USSR by some 400,000 activists in the field, trained in some 6,000 special schools.

Agnosticism A philosophical theory maintaining that nothing is known beyond material phenomena, as human mind is incapable of the cognition of the world and its laws beyond the limits of sensual experience, i.e. man can know only the features or externals of a thing but not the thing itself. This theory has also been extended to the religious sphere, denying the possibility of knowing the supernatural, and thus suspending judgement on whether god exists or not. The beginnings of a. go back to the ancient times and were contained in sophism and particularly SCEPTICISM. A. was accepted and elaborated upon by D. Hume (1711–76), I. Kant (1724–1804) and A. Comte (1798–1857), and further systematized in the second half of the 19th c., notably by T. H. Huxley (1825–95) who popularized the term after 1869. Although it may appear paradoxical, both Marxism and most religions have rejected a. but, of course, for different reasons. Marxist attacks against a. were led by F. Engels (especially in *Ludwig Feuerbach and the End of Classical German Philosophy*, 1888) and V. I. Lenin (in *Materialism and Empirio-Criticism*, 1909). Engels, Lenin and other communist thinkers argue that a. does not go beyond sensory impressions, it renounces scientific enquiry and logical thinking, is essentially bourgeois and reactionary, diverts the attention of the working class from the cognition of the objective laws of social development and that its acceptance leads to IDEALISM, not MATERIALISM. In DIALECTICAL MATERIALISM the world is postulated as objective and man to be capable of knowing it. It is further stressed that there are no absolute limits to cognition and that all human experience disproves a., since the knowledge of nature and society is constantly being extended through scientific observation and study. To Marxists, the acquisition of knowledge is a dynamic process. Even if there are facts, phenomena or ideas unknown today, they will be discovered by experience and reasoning and verified by PRACTICE in the future. Ideologically, the Marxist rejection of a. implies that there is nothing mysterious, divine or immutable about nature and society. Man is capable of constantly extending his knowledge of and power over them, and in particular, is capable of improving them. Also ATHEISM, EPISTEMOLOGY, POSITIVISM, REFLECTION THEORY.

Agrarianism A movement led by social reformers which first appeared in Western Europe in the middle of the 19th c. and later spread to Eastern Europe and Russia. Its objective was to solve the socio-economic problem in the countryside by creating and strengthening reasonably-sized peasant farms and undertaking certain major tasks (purchases, marketing, etc) on a co-operative basis in order to protect their interests against large landowners, suppliers and traders. These objectives were to be achieved through state-implemented reforms and self-help. Marxists have never accepted this movement as a satisfactory solution, as it was not radical and revolutionary enough and preoccupied too much with property ownership.

Agricultural Circles Voluntary self-governing associations of private farms in Poland for the purpose of mutual help and the growth of agricultural production (80 per cent of agricultural land in Poland is privately owned). They combine the private interest of the peasants with social interest by promoting technological and cultural progress and material well-being in rural areas. A.C. engage in various forms of co-operative activities involving the purchase and use of agricultural machinery, land improvement, the production of building materials and the processing of certain agricultural and pastoral products. In addition to their own resources, they receive support from the state. In the mid-1970s there were 35,000 a.c. embracing 2.5m. members.

Agricultural Commune One of the three types of collective farms in existence in the USSR from 1918 to 1931. It was noted for the highest degree of collectivism, compared with the *TOZ* and the *'ARTEL'*. Not only all the means of production (land, farm buildings, equipment, livestock), but also the means of consumption (dwellings, kitchen, means of transport and most other consumer durables) were collectively owned or shared. Distribution was in accordance with the principle 'FROM EACH ACCORDING TO HIS ABILITY, TO EACH ACCORDING TO HIS NEEDS'. These communities were established by the most revolutionary elements from amongst the rural as well as urban workers (including returned soldiers), mostly in the confiscated estates of the former landowners. The a.c. at first received a good deal of official support and in 1919 a model statute was promulgated to this effect. Some monasteries also converted to the a.c. in order to escape confiscation and persecution. The number of a. c.s increased from 260 in 1918 to 7,600 by 1931 when they constituted 9 per cent of all collective farms. In practice these communes proved inefficient and conflicted with Bolshevik authoritarianism, and after 1931 were transformed into the *artel* system. Ever since, the a. c. has been officially regarded in the USSR as an early and inferior form of agricultural and social organization and attempts to revive them have been described as naive and reactionary. Also COMMUNE, PEOPLE'S COMMUNE.

Agricultural Procurement The system whereby the state purchases agricultural products from collective farms, private farms (where they exist) and individual plot holders at wholesale prices determined by the government. The quantities to be delivered can consist of compulsory quotas and above-compulsory sales, the prices in the latter case being more favourable to the growers. Compulsory deliveries were abolished in the USSR in 1958 and have since been virtually discontinued in other Socialist countries as well. The function of a.p. is to ensure orderly supply of food and other farming products for the population, industry and export, to maintain stable controlled prices and to absorb DIFFERENTIAL RENT thereby financing and otherwise facilitating industrialization. An increasingly important type of a.p. is CONTRACTATION.

Agrobiology The field of biology concerned with the systematic study and management of plant and livestock breeding, claimed to be the science of general biological laws. This term is peculiar to Soviet literature and was popularized by T. D. LYSENKO after 1935, although work along these lines had first been taken up by E. V. Michurin (1855–1935) (MICHURINISM). A. received a good deal of official support from the Soviet government, especially in the 1940s and 1950s for its belief that nature could be transformed on a planned basis. This appeared to be of great ideological and practical significance. In Lysenko's view, a. is a superior sphere of developmental biology, as only it can employ scientific methodology for the planned development of plants or animals consistent with DIALECTICAL MATERIALISM. Like dialectical materialism, a. is concerned with the general laws of development from lower to higher stages and varieties. It also attaches a decisive role to the interrelation of matter between the organism and environment. The rule of the Lysenko-style a. partly contributed to the failures in Soviet agriculture during the early 1960s, and which contrasted with the remarkable successes in Western agriculture made possible by the modern science of GENETICS. Since that time the term a. has been virtually abandoned in favour of 'agricultural biology' and, as a consequence, genetics has in effect been rehabilitated in the USSR.

Agro-industrial Complex A large rural enterprise combining agricultural and industrial activities. It is noted for industrial methods of farming, including the wide application of agricultural machinery and other mechanical and automated devices, artificial fertilizers, large-scale production and strict commercial accounting. There is also industrial processing of farm produce, the exploitation of local resources (brick-making, quarrying, woodworking), simple manufacturing (haberdashery, souvenirs, basketware, pottery) based on local raw materials and the operation of certain service enterprises (power plants, engineering workshops, road-building). Typically an a.-i.c. comprises 5,000-30,000 hectares (12,000–75,000 acres) of land, with some 12,000 persons or 3,000 households. Although the idea of the Socialist a.-i.c. goes back to the 1920s (in the USSR), its systematic development only began in the late 1960s in the more developed European Socialist countries (notably the USSR, Bulgaria, the German DR, Hungary and Czechoslovakia). Ideologically the a.-i.c. is regarded as a step towards Full Communism, in that it enables the equalization of rural and urban, as well as physical and mental, labour and distribution based on the Marxian principle, 'from each according to his ability, to each according to his needs'.

Agro-town (*Agro-gorod* in Russian) An agricultural settlement with the urban amenities of life, viz. paved streets, apartment-type or individual dwellings, electricity, water, modern shops and services and educational and cultural facilities. The idea was first mooted in the USSR in the 1920s, then revived in the late 1940s and has been given serious consideration since the 1960s. In 1968 a scheme was adopted in the Orel region to transform the existing 4,170 villages into 960 agro-towns by the early 1980s. The programme announced in 1971 provides for the reduction of the 704,000 rural settlements in the USSR to 111,000, of which at least 60,000 are to be agro-towns. An a.-t. provides opportunities not only for decentralization but also for the implementation of the Marxian ideal of the equalization of the rural and urban population.

Al-Ansar The military arm of the COMMUNIST PARTY OF JORDAN. It was formed in 1970 and its size is apparently very small.

Albania, People's Socialist Republic of (*Republíca Popullore Socialiste e Shqipërísë*) A small South-Eastern European country, with an area of 28,750 sq. km., a population of 2.7m. in (1978) and ruled by the ALBANIAN PARTY OF LABOUR. The Communist regime emerged in 1944 and became firmly established after the elections of December 1945. To date A. has had about the most dogmatic and Stalinist regime of all the Socialist countries. A. was declared a 'People's Republic' in 1946 and a 'People's Socialist Republic' in 1976 when a new Constitution was adopted. The supreme legislative power rests with the People's Assembly, elected every four years by universal suffrage from a single list of the DEMOCRATIC FRONT, led by the Albanian Party of Labour in whose leadership the effective power is concentrated. During the Sino-Soviet dispute, A. supported China from the end of 1960 to mid-1977. A. ceased participating in the work of the COUNCIL FOR MUTUAL ECONOMIC ASSISTANCE and the WARSAW PACT in 1962, and formally withdrew from the latter in 1968 in protest against the military intervention in Czechoslovakia. During 1977–8 A. broke off friendly relations with China in protest against the 'revisionist' policies of Hua Kuo-feng's regime.

Albanian Party of Labour (*Partia e Punës e Shqipërísë*) The ruling communist party and the only legal political party in Albania. Its origins go back to 1928 when an Albanian Communist Party group was formed in Moscow. In 1941 it adopted the name, the Albanian Communist Party, but changed it to its present form in 1948. Its membership in 1975 stood at over 100,000 (out of the total population of 2,380,000), of whom workers accounted for 38 per cent. The highest authority is the Party Congress, held every five years, which elects the Central Committee (71 full members and 39 candidate members). The effective power rests with the Politburo (13 full members and 4 candidate members) headed by the First Secretary, ENVER HOXHA (1908–   ). It is assisted by two mass organizations – the Union of Albanian Labour Youth (for ages 14–26) which in 1977 numbered 370,000 members, and the Union of Albanian Women. The main Party's publications are: *Zëri popullit* (*People's Voice*), the daily organ of the Central Committee; *Rruga e partisë* (*The Party Road*), a theoretical monthly journal, and *Zëri i rinisë* (*The Voice of the Youth*), the daily organ of the Union of the Albanian Labour Youth.

Algerian Communist Party (*Parti Communist Algérien*) A small illegal party without parliamentary representation, with a pro-Soviet (rather than a pro-Chinese) orientation. It originated in 1920 as a section of the Federation of the French Communist Party, separated in 1935 and became known as the Communist Party of Algeria but changed its name to the present form the following year. Throughout its existence it has operated

10

mostly through left-wing organizations (namely the Socialist Vanguard Party), owing to its several proscriptions, first by the French authorities and after independence (in 1962) by the Algerian Government. Its membership is believed to be about 400 (out of the total population of 17.0m. in 1977). Its organ is *Saut al-Sha'b* (*People's Voice*), published through the Socialist Vanguard Party.

Alienation The estrangement of the worker from his 'true' social being, his family, his colleagues, and his work as a result of unmeaningful and unnatural work. The concept owes its socio-economic connotation to K. Marx, who discussed it in his *Paris Manuscripts* (1844), the GRUNDRISSE (1857–58) and CAPITAL (1867). A. is a consequence of monotonous specialization, the rigid division of labour and the private ownership of the means of production. The worker loses interest in the objects he produces as he no longer has a meaningful relationship with the act or labour of producing the product himself. Consequently, the worker's relationship with the product of his work has a direct bearing on his consciousness. He is also conscious of the fact that he produces the means of labour (capital goods) utilized by the capitalist to replace labour, which leads to the continued expansion of the RESERVE ARMY OF WORKERS. In effect both the goods produced and the capitalist employer become 'alien' to the worker – who thus becomes de-humanized. In a capitalist society a. of a kind also exists between rural and urban, manual and mental and unskilled and managerial workers. In the official Socialist view, a. has been regarded as a phenomenon in pre-socialist societies and not in a communist or socialist society, where the means of production belong to the workers and where there is no class struggle. However, there is a good deal of evidence indicating that a. does reassert itself under socialism. It has manifested itself in the persisting reappearance of poor work discipline, a high labour turnover, the neglect of and damage to socialized property, pilfering in factories and on farms, the embezzlement of public funds, elaborate ways of circumventing laws and regulations, the black market, dissent and conflicts between workers and management, enterprises and bureaucracy and between the individual person and the monolithic and ubiquitous state. A number of thinkers in Yugoslavia as well as in Czechoslovakia and Poland and the USSR have conceded that the abolition of the private ownership of the means of production and the disappearance of the class struggle does not necessarily remove a. The opposite Marxian concept to a. is OBJECTIFICATION.

Allende Principle A basis for international compensation under which a less-developed country has a right to deduct super-normal profits, viz. those in excess of 10 per cent, from the amount payable to the foreign owners of nationalized firms. The principle was first embodied in a Decree issued in Chile in September 1971 when a left-wing coalition government was in power under President S. G. Allende (1908–73), a Marxist who believed that Marxism and democracy were compatible.

'All Power to the Soviets' A slogan of the revolutionary elements in Russia in 1917 which was utilized by the BOLSHEVIKS to their advantage. It was first used by Lenin after his return to Petrograd (now Leningrad) in April 1917 in his APRIL THESES. It was publicly launched by workers and soldiers led by the Bolsheviks in Petrograd and other cities on 20–21 April (3–4 May, New Style Calendar) 1917. After the Bolshevik Party was declared illegal (and Lenin's arrest was ordered) by the PROVISIONAL GOVERNMENT of Kerensky in July 1917, the Bolsheviks temporarily withdrew the slogan. But it was employed by them again after 1 (14 N.S.C.) September when the ALL-RUSSIAN CENTRAL EXECUTIVE COMMITTEE received demands from 126 local SOVIETS to take power. This time the slogan became a revolutionary challenge, calling for armed rebellion against the Provisional Government and the transfer of power to the Soviets, who had a majority. After the arrest of the Provisional Government by the Bolsheviks on 25 October (8 November N.S.C.) 1917, formal power was taken over by the Soviets (GREAT OCTOBER SOCIALIST REVOLUTION).

All-Russian Central Executive Committee The highest executive body with wide legislative, administrative and controlling powers and which existed in the RUSSIAN SOVIET FEDERATED SOCIALIST REPUBLIC during 1917–37. It consisted of over 100 members elected by the ALL-RUSSIAN CONGRESS OF SOVIETS, to which it was responsible. The A.-R.C.E.C. included various non-bourgeois political parties and other groups, but the BOLSHEVIKS constituted the majority. Its highest working body was the Presidium, assisted by the Council of People's Commissars of the R.S.F.S.R.

All-Russian Congress of Soviets A type of parliament of the RUSSIAN SOVIET FEDERATED SOCIALIST REPUBLIC in existence during the first two crucial decades of Soviet power 1917–37. It consisted of deputies representing urban and provincial Soviets (workers' and peasants' representative councils). It met at least once every 1–2 years, but the effective power was exercised by the ALL-RUSSIAN CENTRAL EXECUTIVE COMMITTEE elected by it. In 1937 the A.-R.C. of S. was replaced with the Supreme Soviet of the R.S.F.S.R.

All-Russian Extraordinary Commission See CHEKA.

All-Russian Extraordinary Commission for the Liquidation of Illiteracy A special state agency, established by the RUSSIAN SOVIET FEDERATED SOCIALIST REPUBLIC, in existence during 1920–30. It was responsible for giving basic instruction to illiterate persons between the ages of 8 and 50. At the time of the Bolshevik seizure of power, 85 per cent of the population was illiterate. Its work was continued for some years after 1930 on a smaller scale by the All-Russian Conference on the Liquidation of Illiteracy. An important secondary purpose of the literacy campaign was to increase the capacity of the ex-illiterates for absorbing communist propaganda.

All-Russian Socialist Revolutionary Organization A secret united association formed by Russian revolutionary intellectuals (mostly NARODNIKS) and industrial workers which was active during 1874–75. Its purpose was to develop a unified organization for the overthrowing of the autocratic tsarist regime, by violent methods, if necessary. It originated in Zurich but it concentrated its activities in Moscow (hence, also known as the 'Circle of Muscovites') and other industrial centres in Russia. Its leaders were arrested and severely punished after the 'Trial of the Fifty' in 1877.

All-Union Bureau of Russian Social-Democratic Labour Party An anti-Bolshevik association which operated in the GOSPLAN and other state agencies in the USSR in the 1920s. Its members were determined to restore to prominence the RUSSIAN SOCIAL-DEMOCRATIC LABOUR PARTY, but the group was exposed and liquidated during 1930–31 as a 'counter-revolutionary organization'.

All-Union Central Council of Trade Unions The highest permanent body in the USSR responsible for the control and co-ordination of the activities of trade unions. It consists of more than 400 full-time and candidate members who are elected for four year terms at the trade union congresses. Its PLENUMS take place at least once every six months, whilst the responsibility for the work between the plenary sessions is in the hands of the Presidium elected by it. The Council's main functions are to initiate labour and industrial legislation, to facilitate the implementation of the economic plan and to represent Soviet trade unions abroad.

All-Union Communist Party (of the Bolsheviks) The official name of the COMMUNIST PARTY OF THE SOVIET UNION over the period 1925–52.

All-Union Congress of Soviets The Soviet 'parliament' which existed in the USSR from 1922 to 1936 (previously known as the ALL-RUSSIAN CONGRESS OF SOVIETS). It was, theoretically, the highest organ of state power, but held only 8 meetings during its existence. Its membership consisted of representatives from Soviets (councils) of all the Republics. Its powers included making constitutional changes, admitting new republics to the Union, approving the general principles of economic management and development and planning the state budget. In 1937, when the new Constitution replaced the earlier one of 1922, it was succeeded by the SUPREME SOVIET of the USSR.

All-Union Leninist Communist League of Youth The full name, introduced in 1926 but now obsolete, of the *KOMSOMOL*.

Alternative System Also described as 'alternative society' or 'alternative lifestyle', a vague concept popularized in the West in the 1960s to denote a new social system to replace the modern highly organized industrial consumer society, whether capitalist or communist. The supporters of the a.s. are often either idealist social reformers, hippies, malcontents with Bohemian or artistic inclinations, advocates of counter-culture or dropouts. They often dress in a deliberately unconventional or unkempt manner and usually live apart from the rest of the community on a nomadic or impermanent basis. Although at least implicitly they support egalitarianism, they repudiate both LEGAL MARXISM and revolutionary MARXISM-LENINISM, and are rather inclined to ANARCHISM. They turn to withdrawal, hoping thereby that the existing organized system will disintegrate, but they have not yet produced a consistent and viable alternative model. In the USA, the idea of the a.s. has been loosely associated with the NEW LEFT. By 1970 there were approximately 3,000 communes experimenting with the alternative life style.

Althusser, Louis (1918–) Prominent French Marxist theoretician operating within the FRENCH COMMUNIST PARTY and noted for his structuralist approach to Marxism. Althusser was born in Algeria of French parents, participated in Catholic youth movements and was called up for the military in 1939. He was imprisoned by the Nazis and continued his studies in Paris after the war under the philosopher, Gasten Bachelarch. In 1948 Althusser joined the PCF where he has been one of its central theoreticians to this day. His structural approach rejects Marxism as a humanism, e.g. the link with Hegel, and the work of the young LUKÁCS, SARTRE and Gramsci. Althusser's Marxism is that of a scientific conception of history, a science of HISTORICAL MATERIALISM and a science of society. For Althusser philosophy only identifies concepts, whereas Marxism utilizes the concepts or structures of the forces and relations of production as the driving force of historical change. His major works are: *For Marx* (1965); *Lenin and Philosophy* (1968); *Politics and History* (1972); *Reading Capital* (1965) and *Essays in Self-Criticism* (1974).

Altruism Disinterested concern for the self, in effect placing other people's interest before one's own, the opposite to egoism. In the Marxist view, bourgeois ethics restricts the scope of a. to interpersonal relations, ignoring the class basis of morality and the individual's obligation to society. A. is given considerable attention in Socialist ethics in which individual interest is necessarily linked to social interest. When the two are in conflict the latter is deemed to prevail (the PRIMACY OF SOCIAL INTEREST).

Amah An early feminist emancipation labour movement in China, which originated in the middle of the 19th c. amongst young women of poor families. The a.

hoped to make themselves economically independent rather than be sold by their parents as prostitutes or concubines. They formed a union to earn their living as household servants, swearing themselves to a life of chastity. In some cases, they formed co-operatives and became economically independent. The movement declined with the development of the factory system, as many of the women preferred the freedom and security of factory employment.

American Federation of Labor The largest national trade union organization in the USA from 1886 to 1955, which embraced mostly CRAFT UNIONS. It was noted for moderate policies directed towards extracting maximum material gains for its members through negotiations rather than through disruptive industrial disputes. It also refused to co-operate with the Communist-dominated WORLD FEDERATION OF TRADE UNIONS, which it left in 1949. The A.F.L.'s conservatism drove the more militant unions into forming the CONGRESS OF INDUSTRIAL ORGANIZATIONS during 1935–38. The two bodies were engaged in bitter DEMARCATION DISPUTES until their merger in 1955 (AFL-CIO). At the time of the amalgamation, the A.F.L. had 9.5m. members (compared with C.I.O.'s 6.5m.) and its leader (George Meany) became the overall President.

Amortization The term used in the Socialist countries for the depreciation of fixed assets through wear and tear (physical a.) and for becoming obsolete owing to technological progress (moral a.). For the replacement of the depreciated assets a. quotas, which are treated as a part of production costs, are set aside. A centrally determined proportion of the a. quota is handed over to the higher levels of economic management (branch associations, ministries, the state budget) and the rest is retained in the enterprise a. fund.

Amsterdam International A short name for the INTERNATIONAL FEDERATION OF TRADE UNIONS, which existed from 1919 to 1945 to co-ordinate trade unionism along moderate, social democratic lines.

AMTORG A Russian abbreviation for *Amerikanskaya Torgovlya* (American Trade), a joint US-Soviet trading company established in New York in 1924 (by the amalgamation of two American companies, the 'Products Exchange Corp.' and 'Arcos America'. It also had an office in Moscow and handled most of the US-Soviet trade up to the mid-1930s. But its role declined after 1935, when the Soviet Government decided to conduct trading directly from Moscow.

AN A Russian abbreviation for the identification of different models of aircraft originally designed by O. K. Antonov.

Analysis and Synthesis Methods of study, where a. consists in the decomposition of an object, idea or phenomenon into simple component parts, whilst s. amounts to the combination of such parts into a connected and completed whole. In the Marxist view, the bourgeois approach treats these two methods as mutually exclusive, whilst Marxist DIALECTICS regards them as a complementary unity. Engels stressed (in *ANTI-DÜHRING*) that 'without analysis there can be no synthesis'.

Anarchism A radical doctrine and movement with philosophical, political, social and economic premises, directed against any form of authority imposed from above, especially by the state. It favours voluntary co-operation amongst free individuals and groups on a decentralized basis. Its theoretical bases and programmes of reforms were developed in Europe (especially France, Italy, Spain and Russia) and to a lesser extent in Latin America during the nineteenth century. Its main theorists were W. Godwin (1756–1836), P. J. PROUDHON, K. Schmidt (1806–56), E. Reclus (1830–1905) M. A. BAKUNIN, P. A. KROPOTKIN, L. TOLSTOY and Emma Goldman (1869–1940). There has been a considerable revival of a. since the mid-1960s in association with the NEW LEFT and the radical student movements. There are many versions of a., ranging from peaceful and individualistic types to violent and communistic types. The five major categories are: 1. *Anarcho-individualism*, advocating a return to free natural and competitive economy operated by small independent owners; 2. *Anarcho-co-operativism*, basing social and economic activities on co-operative communities; 3. *Anarcho-syndicalism*, basing social and economic organization, management and pursuits on trade unions; 4. *Anarcho-communism*, postulating the immediate implementation of communism by the elimination of the state and the introduction of free collectivism; 5. *Atheistic a.*, rejecting the church and even the institution of marriage; and 6. *Ethical a.*, postulating high social ethics and the law of charity as the basic regulators of social relations and economic pursuits. Although a. is opposed to capitalism and advocates egalitarianism, Marxism (especially its revolutionary version) is bitterly opposed to it, regarding it as utopian and ineffective. Marxists have denounced a. as a disruptive force in the working class movement and as a petty bourgeois dream appealing to impractical intellectuals, confused youth and to the desperate *LUMPENPROLETARIAT*. Marx, Engels and Stalin, attacked a. in *THE HOLY FAMILY, THE GERMAN IDEOLOGY, POVERTY OF PHILOSOPHY* and *ANARCHISM OR SOCIALISM*. In Russia, anarchists actively participated in the Revolution of 1905–7, the February Revolution of 1917 and the Great October Socialist Revolution of 1917 helping the BOLSHEVIKS. However, during the Civil War (1918–20) anarchists often supported the PETTY BOURGEOISIE and the *KULAKS*. After the KRONSTADT UPRISING of 1921, the anarchists were persecuted and suppressed by the Bolsheviks as counter-revolutionaries.

Anarchism or Socialism A polemical pamphlet written by Stalin, originally published as a series of articles in Georgian papers in Tiflis from June 1906 to April 1907. It was directed against ANARCHISM, and contained an analysis of the revolutionary Marxist alternative. Stalin attacked the anarchists and the MENSHEVIKS for instilling bourgeois ideas into the working class movement. He emphasized that only revolutionary Marxism, a powerful socialist state and the dictatorship of the proletariat could create an ideal society. He further analysed DIALECTICAL MATERIALISM and HISTORICAL MATERIALISM in application to society's development. In this process, Stalin stressed the progressive dynamism of the proletariat and the receding and decaying condition of the bourgeoisie. He rejected the dual interpretation of nature, viz. materialistic and idealistic, in favour of MONISM. He also emphasized the decisive influence of nature and society on human consciousness (not the other way round).

Anarcho-Communism One of the major types of ANARCHISM, originally advocated by the Russian anarchists, Prince P. A. KROPOTKIN (mainly in his book, *The Conquest of Pain*, 1892). The supporters of a.-c. envisage a society formed out of 'associations of working people' and where distribution will be 'according to needs' rather than 'according to work'. They accept the PRIMACY OF SOCIAL INTEREST over INDIVIDUALISM and attach great importance to moral suasion. Consequently, they are opposed to anarcho-individualism and the violent version of anarchism advocated by Bakunin. They disagree with Marxists and insist that in the development of an ideal society there is no need for a long transitional stage with a powerful socialist state, the dictatorship of the proletariat and a disciplined authoritarian Communist party.

Anarcho-Syndicalism One of the major types of ANARCHISM, which attaches crucial importance to trade unions (called 'syndicates' in Latin countries) and strikes as the main or only instruments of the workingmen's struggle for a better society. It is opposed to the bureaucratic state and political action. It originated in the theoretical writings of PROUDHON and BAKUNIN and has achieved its greatest development in France, Italy and Spain. A.-s. is opposed to Marxism, as the latter postulates political struggle and the DIC-TATORSHIP OF THE PROLETARIAT. Marxists describe anarcho-syndicalists as being naive and compromising with the bourgeoisie and, moreover, have accused them of supporting TROTSKYISM and even FASCISM. In 1922 anarcho-syndicalists established the INTERNATIONAL WORKERS' ASSOCIATION in Berlin and issued their manifesto, *Principles of Revolutionary Syndicalism*. The closest version of a.-s. in practical operation is represented by WORKERS' SELF-MANAGEMENT in Yugoslavia. See also INDUSTRIAL WORKERS OF THE WORLD.

Anarchy of Production A phrase often used by Marx (especially in *CAPITAL*) with respect to the peculiarity of economic processes under unrestricted *laissez-faire* capitalism. He attributed it to the greed of capitalists, the blind operation of the market mechanism, cut-throat competition, rapid changes in the methods of production and the absence of economic planning – all leading to uncertainty, crises and fluctuations. Theoretically, the a. of p. should not occur in the Socialist countries owing to central economic planning and the control of the market forces. See also CYCLICAL FLUCTUATIONS.

Angola, People's Republic of (*Republica Popular de Angola*) An ex-Portuguese colony in West Africa, which achieved independence in 1975 and has come to be ruled by a Marxist regime (POPULAR MOVEMENT WORKERS' PARTY), backed by the USSR and Cuba. The country's area is 1,246,700 sq. km. and its estimated population is 6.5m. (1979). After four centuries of Portuguese rule, three national liberation movements, namely, the Marxist Popular Liberation Movement of Angola (*MPLA*), the National Liberation Front of Angola (*FNLA*) and the National Union for the Total Independence of An-

gola (*UNITA*) signed an agreement in Jan. 1975 to proclaim A. an independent country on 11 Nov. 1975. After the declaration of independence, a period of bitter civil war followed during which the Soviet and Cuban backed *MPLA* virtually eliminated the other two South African-backed groups, and by February 1976 assumed effective power. But the latter two groups, which have formed a united front, continue engaging in occasional guerrilla operations. Selective nationalization (especially in agriculture and forestry) and social reforms have been undertaken by the Marxist leadership of President Agostino Neto, in which Soviet, Cuban and East European advisers have played a role. In July 1976 A. joined the COUNCIL FOR MUTUAL ECONOMIC ASSISTANCE and in Oct. 1976 a 20-year Treaty of Friendship with the USSR was signed. The Soviets and Cubans have provided generous military and economic aid. In 1979 there were about 20,000 Cuban troops in the country.

Animism The attribution of spirit to every object which conditions its being, and the identification of a spiritual force in each phenomenon. Marxists recognize that all societies pass through this phase in the lower stage of their cultural development, but this is only indicative of their ignorance and inability to cope with nature. In their view, a. has given rise to RELIGION and (in philosophy) to IDEALISM.

Antagonistic Conditions of Distribution The Marxian view of the maldistribution of national income in non-socialist societies, especially under capitalism. Owing to the EXPLOITATION of the PRO-LETARIAT, the consumption of the masses is depressed, which creates an increasing discrepancy between the production and consumption capacity of the economy. The growth of consumption, necessary to create sufficient demand to ensure full employment, depletes the amount of SUR-PLUS VALUE and, in turn, ACCUMULA-TION. Consequently, the deficiency of demand is a chronic and inherent feature of capitalism, inevitably resulting in unemployment as testified by the RESERVE ARMY OF WORKERS.

Antagonistic Contradiction See CONTRADICTION.

Antagonistic Production Relations A Marxist concept, also known as 'exploitative p.r.', denoting conflicting and insoluble relations between the owners and/or controllers of the means of production on the one hand, and the exploited working class on the other. Owing to the inevitable changes in PRODUCTION FORCES, PRODUCTION RELATIONS should change accordingly, but there is usually a lag in the latter behind the former. This is certainly so in ANTAGONISTIC SOCIO-ECONOMIC FORMATIONS, viz. SLAVERY, FEUDALISM and CAPITALISM. When the adaptation of production relations to the changing level and content of production forces is delayed by the ruling classes for too long, the adjustment is eventually achieved through a violent social revolution. Such a revolution constitutes a qualitative leap, whereby the new production relations replace the old ones to correspond to the new production forces. Communist leaders claim that a.p.r. do not exist in the Socialist countries, owing to the social ownership of the means of production, the absence of exploitation and the pursuit of central economic planning. These three conditions enable the state to make progrressive, immediate and anticipatory adjustments called for by changes in production forces.

Antagonistic Socio-Economic Formations In Marxian terminology, those social systems which are noted for irreconcilable class contradictions stemming from unjust economic relations. Marx (in *A CONTRIBUTION TO THE CRITIQUE OF POLITICAL ECONOMY*) distinguished three a.s.-e.f.: SLAVERY (masters – slaves); FEUDALISM (lords – serfs) and CAPITALISM (bourgeoisie – proletariat). On the other hand PRIMITIVE COMMUNISM, SOCIALISM and FULL COMMUNISM are not regarded as a. s.-e. f.

Anthropologism A philosophical view preoccupied with the nature and role of man as a biological being, emphasizing his material and spiritual unity. The beginnings of a. go back to the ancient Greek philosophers, but in modern times it reached its heyday in the 19th c. through the work of L. FEUERBACH and N. G. CHERNYSHEVSKY. The attitude of Marxist philosophers to a. is mixed. On the one hand, they concede that a. has made an important contribution to MATERIALISM by denying the primacy of IDEAS over MATTER. But on the other, they emphasize that a. was only a limited and weak strain of materialism, as it proved incapable of integrating the theory of cognition with social practice. Consequently – as was pointed out by Engels (in *LUDWIG FEUERBACH AND THE END OF CLASSICAL GERMAN PHILOSOPHY*) and Lenin (in *PHILOSOPHICAL NOTEBOOKS*) – the exponents of a. could not explain the development of societies, the class struggle, class solidarity and social co-operation, which only HISTORICAL MATERIALISM could do.

Anti-charter A public declaration arranged by the Czechoslovak Communist authorities in 1977 condemning CHARTER '77. In a massive campaign through the state media and 'spontaneous' meetings in factories and offices, thousands of signatures were collected from workers. Most of the signatories had not seen Charter '77 as it had been suppressed in Czechoslovakia by the regime.

Anti-clericalism Opposition to CLERICALISM, i.e. attitude or movement critical of the influence of the organized Church and religion in society's public, economic, social and cultural life. Although the origin of a.-c. in the West goes back to the early Middle Ages, its intensity and scope have been greatly enhanced since the Industrial Revolution. In this development, especially since the middle of the 19th c., socialism and revolutionary Marxism have played an active role. See also ANTI-CONFUCIUS CAMPAIGN, ATHEISM, DISCLERICALIZATION.

Anti-colonialism A movement based in Africa and Asia against the political, economic and cultural domination of less-developed and weaker nations by the former imperialist powers and modern industrial expansionist interests in general. It stems from historical grievances, radical feelings, nationalism, social considerations and the like. Marxists have always supported a.-c. with the following considerations in mind: 1. *ideological* (equality of the peoples); 2. *humanitarian* (opposed to exploitation); and 3. *practical* (weakening the capitalist powers' economic, political and military influence in the THIRD WORLD and enticing it towards the Socialist side). At the INTERNATIONAL CONFERENCE OF THE COMMUNIST AND WORKERS PARTIES held in Moscow in June 1969 and attended by Communist leaders representing 75 countries, an anti-colonial declaration was issued in a document entitled: '*Tasks of the Struggle against Imperialism at the Present Stage and the Unity of Action of the Communist and Workers' Parties and all Anti-Imperialist Forces*'. Also AFRO-ASIAN PEOPLE'S SOLIDARITY ORGANIZATION, COLONIALISM, IMPERIALISM, NATIONAL LIBERATION MOVEMENTS, NEO-COLONIALISM.

Anti-Comintern Pact An agreement, entered into by Germany and Japan on 25 Nov. 1930, explicitly directed against international communism (the COMINTERN) and implicitly against the USSR. The official name of the document was '*Agreement against the Third International*'. The Pact was originally signed for 5 years but it was renewed in 1936 and in 1941 and incorporated other states into the agreement. Italy joined on 6 Nov. 1937, Hungary, Manchukuo and Spain in 1939, and during W.W.II Croatia, Denmark, Finland, Romania, Slovakia and the pro-Japanese Chinese Government of Wang Ching-wei also acceded. The Pact was not terminated with the dissolution of the Comintern in 1943, but became void in effect after the defeat of the Axis powers.

Anti-Communism Attitudes, theories, policies and practices hostile to Marxism, and in particular to the Communist regimes in the SOCIALIST COUNTRIES. It can be traced back to the reaction against *THE COMMUNIST MANIFESTO*, the excesses of the PARIS COMMUNE, the COMINTERN and STALINISM. It has become most intense in the richest and most powerful Western countries. A.-c. has been conditioned by: 1. genuine ideological convictions opposed to extreme left-wing movements; 2. the opposition of religious groups, especially the organized churches, to ATHEISM; 3. the propertied classes' fear of losing their privileged position; 4. national resentment against Soviet, Chinese and Vietnamese expansionism, domination or militancy; 5. the pressure from military-industrial establishments in the leading Western countries which stand to benefit from East–West tension; and 6. personal grievances of dissenters and émigrés who have suffered from systematic persecution by militia and secret police. A.-c. has assumed varied forms in domestic and international arenas, namely, the proscription of Communist parties, demonstrations against visiting Communist leaders, boycotts of Socialist-produced goods, violence against Communists, financial blockades, the prohibition of exports of 'strategic' goods and technology to the Socialist countries and military intervention. Also ASSEMBLY OF CAPTIVE EUROPEAN NATIONS, CENTRAL INTELLIGENCE AGENCY, CONTAINMENT POLICY, COUNTER-REVOLUTION, DISSENTERS, INDONESIAN BLOODBATH, INTERVENTION, McCARTHYISM, NON-COMMUNIST MANIFESTO, NORTH ATLANTIC TREATY ORGANIZATION, STRATEGIC EMBARGO, WHITE GUARDS.

Anti-Confucius Campaign A course officially embarked upon by the Maoist establishment in China during 1972–74, calculated to discredit the social philosophy of Confucius inconsistent with MARXISM-LENINISM and otherwise inconvenient to MAO TSE-TUNG and his supporters. Confucius (551–479 B.C.) was a philosopher and a traditionally revered thinker, but in the early 1970s he was officially described as a reactionary and was attacked for: 1. adherence to philosophical IDEALISM; 2. the acceptance of the hierarchical stratification of society; 3. opposition to social change, especially the freeing of slaves; 4. insistence on respect, obedience and loyalty to the rulers, bureaucrats and parents; and 5. his belief in the superiority of mental over physical work. Although the campaign was initiated in the form of historical criticism, it was soon employed to highlight contemporary parallels in order to justify the GREAT PROLETARIAN CULTURAL REVOLUTION and to further discredit LIU SHAO-CH'I and LIN PIAO who were branded as enthusiasts and imitators of Confucius.

Anti-Dühring The short title (and subtitle) of the best known work of F. ENGELS, *Herr Eugen Dühring's Revolution in Science* (1878). It was a profound reply to E. Dühring who had repudiated Marx's *CAPITAL* and instead presented his own, moderate, model of socialism. Engels attacked Dühring's UTOPIAN SOCIALISM and 'petty bourgeois ideology'. A.-D., which has exerted considerable influence on Communist thought and practice, is divided into 3 parts: I. Philosophy; II. Political Economy; and III. Socialism. In it, Engels substantiated three corner-stones of Marxism, viz. dialectical and historical materialism, the Marxist principles of political economy and the theory of scientific socialism (communism).

Anti-economism The ideological position adopted by revolutionary Marxists opposing the ECONOMISM of social democrats and other right-wing socialists who insist that all the problems of the working class can be solved on the economic plane. A.-e. stresses the primacy of politics over economics and opposes OPPORTUNISM, wide disparities in wages and excessive material incentives (favouring MORAL INCENTIVES instead). The first major attack on economism was made by Lenin in 1902 in *WHAT IS TO BE DONE?* A.-e. also played an important part in MAOISM, especially during the GREAT PROLETARIAN CULTURAL REVOLUTION.

Anti-Japanese Red Army University An institution established by Chou En-lai in Yenan in the late 1930s to provide political and military training at tertiary level for middle and high-level Party and military cadres. It was first headed by MAO TSE-TUNG and later by LIN PIAO. The institution attracted many young people from other parts of China. It was terminated after W.W.II.

Anti-Marxism Reaction against the basic philosophical, economic, political and sociological doctrines of KARL MARX, his followers and their practical application in the Socialist countries under Communist regimes. It is partly an aspect of ANTI-COMMUNISM, but it is directed at the most fundamental theoretical tenets, together with their feasibility and implementation in practice. It is partly anti MARXIAN, partly anti MARXIST but is not necessarily anti COMMUNIST. Marxism has been attacked not only by non-communist but also communist thinkers. The non-communist indictment of Marxism includes the following: 1. the idealist thinkers reject DIALECTICAL MATERIALISM and HISTORICAL MATERIALISM as too simplistic and ideologically convenient (e.g. I. Berlin, *Historical Inevitability*, 1954); 2. the economic rationalists believe that in a collectivist economy the rational pricing, accounting and allocation of resources are impossible (e.g. L. v. Mises, '*Economic Calculation in the Socialist Commonwealth*', 1920); 3. the supporters of liberal democracy oppose the Marxist postulate of the DICTATORSHIP OF THE PROLETARIAT, especially its Stalinist version (e.g. G. de Rugiero, *The History of European Liberalism*, 1959); 4. the advocates of economic liberalism identify hierarchical Socialist economic planning with economic totalitarianism (e.g. F. v. Hayek, *The Road to Serfdom*, 1946); 5. humanitarians have accused the Marxist state of de-humanization (e.g. A. Koestler, *Darkness at Noon*, 1941 and R. H. Crossman, *The God That Failed*, 1953); 6. christian thinkers condemn ATHEISM, violence and the abolition of private property

Anti-matter

(e.g. The Papal *Encyclicals* of 1891, 1931, 1961 and J. Maritain, *True Humanism*, 1938). But significantly, some aspects of Marxism have been challenged by idealist or disillusionist communists, too: (a) destructive revolutionism (e.g. E. Bernstein, *Evolutionary Socialism*, 1899); (b) socialist totalitarianism (e.g. K. Kautsky, *Terrorism and Communism*, 1919; (c) the Stalinist type of police state and paranoia (e.g. L. Trotsky, *The Revolution Betrayed*, 1937 and A. Solzhenitsyn, *The Gulag Archipelago 1918–1956*, 1973–76); and (d) the unwieldy power-seeking bureaucracy (e.g. M. Djilas, *The New Class*, 1957, and *The Unperfect Society: Beyond the New Class*, 1969).

Anti-matter A substance consiting of anti-particles or anti-atoms (anti-protons, anti-neutrons). Anti-atoms cannot exist in the space occupied by atoms, as mutual collisions would lead to their annihilation, but a.-m. in isolation from ordinary matter would be stable. The possibility of existence of a.-m. was proved by P. A. M. Dirac in 1928 and further supported by laboratory experiments. Some scientists believe that there may be anti-world in outer space. The concept of a.-m. has become a subject of philosophical and ideological controversy. The supporters of IDEALISM cite a.-m. as evidence of the possibility of the destruction of matter through collision with a.-m., consequently, they maintain that this fact proves that MATTER is secondary and IDEAS are primary. But Marxists, defending MATERIALISM, point out that the very fact of the existence of matter and a.-m. illustrates the dialectical conflict between two opposites, providing support for DIALECTICAL MATERIALISM. Further, this fact indicates that matter is indestructible, for only its forms change, lending support to HISTORICAL MATERIALISM.

Anti-militarism A movement, developed by Marxists and some other social reformers in the four decades preceding W.W.I., directed against the military establishments in the leading imperialist powers (especially Germany, France, Russia, Britain and the USA) and wars as a solution to international conflicts. This was the stand adopted by the SECOND INTERNATIONAL which *inter alia* condemned MILITARISM, the ARMS RACE, war credits, aggressive wars. The Second International instead advocated the replacement of the entrenched military establishments with a popular militia. The most systematic exposition of a.-m. was presented by K. LIEBKNECHT (in *Militarism and Anti-Militarism*, 1907), in which he concluded that militarism would disappear as a matter of historical development. But some other Marxist thinkers such as ROSA LUXEMBURG and V. I. LENIN did not believe that militarism would disintegrate on its own accord or could be eliminated by LEGAL MARXISM, and consequently had to be destroyed by proletarian revolutionary violence. Also PACIFISM.

Antinomy In philosophy, contradiction between two mutually exclusive assertions, yet appearing equally valid. E.g., from the capitalist's standpoint, prices should be increased, but from the workers' point of view they ought to be reduced. The concept of a. was first elaborated upon by I. Kant (1724–1804) who attributed the apparent contradiction to the limitation of human mind and reasoning. Although Marxist philosophers have criticized the concept if it is employed to justify AGNOSTICISM, they have found it useful in DIALECTICAL MATERIALISM. In their view, contradictions in human concepts are a reflection of real contradictions which are basic to the development of nature and society.

Anti-parasite Laws Legislation in the Socialist countries directed against persons who live at the expense of society without legitimate justification. Such persons avoid work without a reasonable excuse, and in order to support themselves they engage in socially unacceptable or plainly unlawful activities, such as the black market, bribery, the embezzlement of public funds, theft and damaging social property. Such behaviour is treated very seriously by the authorities for in Marxist thinking there is no justification for socially irresponsible conduct and economic crimes in a Socialist country (but there is in a capitalist society). A.-p.l. were tightened in the late 1950s and early 1960s in most Socialist countries.

Anti-Party Group The description applied officially in the USSR to a small circle of distinguished Party leaders who opposed KHRUSHCHEV and unsuccessfully attempted to remove him from the Party leadership in June 1957. The Group was critical of Khrushchev's brand of DE-STALINIZATION and the concentration of power in his hands. It included the members of the PRESIDIUM OF THE CENTRAL COMMITTEE OF THE CPSU, viz. N. A. Bulganin, I. M. KAGANOVICH, G. M. MALENK-OV, V. M. MOLOTOV, M. Z. Saburov, D. T. Shepilov and others. After Khrushchev's successful appeal to the extraordinary PLENARY SESSION of the Central Committee, the leading members of the Group were removed from the Presidium, expelled from the Central Committee and stripped of their influential government posts, or demoted or (in the case of Bulganin) severely reprimanded. But none was 'liquidated' in the Stalinist fashion.

Anti-rightist Campaign An official drive in China in 1957–58 against the 'conservative, entrenched and unimaginative' Party leaders, cadres and the non-Party elite. The Campaign was in a sense a radical reaction against the 'HUNDRED FLOWERS' INTERLUDE of April–June 1957. Many Party leaders were purged (but most were rehabilitated later and returned to power). The A.-r.c. was followed by the GREAT LEAP FORWARD and departures from the Soviet model. Anti-rightist charges were revived later during the GREAT PROLETARIAN CULTURAL REVOLUTION.

Anti-Semitism Contemptuous and hostile attitudes towards Jews, which may be re-

flected in various forms of discrimination and even physical violence. Marxism, in principle, is unequivocally against a.-s., treating it as a relic of religious, racial and nationalistic prejudice in pre-Socialist societies. Active a.-s. is outlawed in all the Socialist countries, but in practice one can detect anti-semitic feelings and discrimination owing to the following circumstances: 1. the Jews' devotion to their religion; 2. Jewish solidarity, often transcending working class solidarity; 3. the Jewish prominence in the top Party and government apparatus, universities and the professions, well beyond the Jews' proportion in the total population; 4. the high proportion of Jews in the secret police; and 5. the conspicuous Jewish presence in the private sector, where it exists, and in black market operations. A.-s. was strong in the USSR in the late 1920s, the mid-1930s (during the GREAT PURGES), the early 1950s (the 'DOCTORS' PLOT'), since the late 1960s (continued restrictions on emigration) and on occasions in some Eastern European countries since the mid-1950s.

Anti-social Attitudes A phrase in common usage in the Socialist countries, denoting a mode of thinking and conduct contrary to the social interest. It may be reflected in egoistic behaviour, the violation of the social norms of conduct, nonparticipation in social activities and community work and disrespect or damage of social property.

Anti-social Consumption Consumption which is not in the long-run interest of society, even though it brings immediate satisfaction to individual consumers. Examples are: excessive use of drugs and alcohol; CONSPICUOUS CONSUMPTION; dangerous fast cars; luxuries which the economy cannot afford; consumption derived from the misappropriated assets of the state or other individuals; excessive consumption on the national scale resulting in too low a level of saving and investment, and undesirable imports. The concept is often used in the Socialist countries where it is treated seriously, as it violates the PRIMACY OF SOCIAL INTEREST and interferes with the planned utilization of resources.

Anti-social Profit In general, capitalist profit (PROFIT, CAPITALIST) is regarded by Marxists as anti-social, but the concept has acquired a more specific meaning in application to the modern Socialist economy. In the latter sense, it is that profit which is made either by breaking existing laws and regulations, or achieved illegitimately at the expense of society – be it by socialized enterprises, private firms or individual persons. There are 7 important categories of a.-s.p. in these countries: 1. p. achieved by neglecting social interest (failure to protect or maintain socialized assets and workers' safety); 2. abnormal p. made by large socialized enterprises which are in a position to influence prices by restricting output; 3. p. made by changing the structure of output in an enterprise in favour of the most profitable items, contrary to the mandatory assortment plan laid down by the planning authorities; 4. p. made by falsely classifying the goods produced; 5. p. made by misrepresenting the manipulation of enterprise accounts; 6. p. made possible by bribing officials; and 7. p. made in black markets. Where a.-s.p. occurs legally, it has to be handed over in full to the state budget, and where it occurs illegally those involved are subject to heavy penalties (including imprisonment).

Anti-test Ban Treaty See NUCLEAR TEST BAN TREATY.

Anti 'The Five Styles of Conduct' A campaign staged in China from the end of 1960 to the spring of 1961 to eradicate the 5 attitudes evident in the work of the Party cadres and in their life in the countryside, viz.: 1. the 'communistic' style; 2. the style of 'commanding by force'; 3. the style of 'giving blind commands'; 4. the style of 'being pompous'; and 5. the style of 'being special'.

Antithesis The contrast of ideas expressed by the parallelism of opposite characteristics, facts or developments. Thus the a. of PRIVATE PROPERTY is socialized property, of distribution 'according to work' – 'according to needs'. The concept of a. is most important in Marxist dialectics – the simplified triad of dialectics, THESIS, ANTITHESIS AND SYNTHESIS.

Anti-war Manifesto A declaration made by the International Socialist Conference at Kiental, Switzerland in April, 1916 (KIENTAL CONFERENCE), condemning W.W.I as an imperialist war. It also called on the Socialist parties and the working class to oppose the war and instead turn it into a proletarian revolution. The Manifesto was prepared by the Russian delegation headed by Lenin.

Antonov-Ovseyenko, Vladimir Aleksandrovich (1884–1939) A Russian Marxist who had the distinction of personally arresting the PROVISIONAL GOVERNMENT of A. KERENSKY (but not Kerensky, who had been warned) in the Winter Palace on the night of 25–26 Oct. (Old Style Calendar) 1917. An army officer by training, he joined the RUSSIAN SOCIAL-DEMOCRATIC LABOUR PARTY in 1903. At first, he supported the MENSHEVIKS, but in 1917 he switched to the BOLSHEVIK side and was one of the chief organizers of the GREAT OCTOBER SOCIALIST REVOLUTION. After the Revolution, he held top-level positions in military administration, including the post of the Chief of the Political Administration of the RED ARMY. Ever since the REVOLUTION OF 1905-7, he was closely associated with TROTSKY and when the latter was defeated in 1925, A.-O. lost his post. He was the Soviet representative in the SPANISH CIVIL WAR, but after his return to the USSR he disappeared in Stalin's GREAT PURGES. His name was rehabilitated after the Twentieth Congress of the CPSU in 1956.

Antonov Rebellion Also known as *Antonovshchina*, an anti-Bolshevik armed popular revolt in Soviet Russia, in the Tambov agricultural region (south-east of Moscow, from 1919 to 1921, opposing the

DICTATORSHIP OF THE PROLETARIAT and the forced requisitioning of food. The rebellion was led by A. S. Antonov, a prominent *KULAK*, a representative of the SOCIALIST REVOLUTIONARIES and the chief of the district militia, who at one stage commanded an army of more than 50,000 peasants and Red Army deserters. In spite of the initial widespread popular support, the rebellion collapsed, owing to a series of military defeats and the liberal course adopted by the Soviet regime known as the NEW ECONOMIC POLICY.

Apologetics A disparaging term used by Socialist economists for attempts to provide convenient yet basically unsound theoretical justifications for certain situations, policies or practices. The concept has been used in two different senses: 1. efforts by bourgeois theoretical writers to provide justifications for the existence, operation and perpetuation of the capitalist economic and social system; and 2. endeavours by Socialist economists to justify *ex ante* or (mostly) *ex-post* Party decisions or government policies and practices in ways consistent with Marxism or attempts to sanctify them as 'economic laws of socialism'.

Apoliticism An attitude of indifference to politics and withdrawal from participation in political processes. In the Socialist countries a. is found amongst non-Party members, especially less educated workers, disillusioned intelligentsia, former higher social classes and their descendants. Also included are those who may be interested in politics, but view the policies and practices of the Communist regime with cynicism and experience a feeling of political impotence. The official view is that a. is un-Marxist and anti-social, especially under Socialism, where there is all-pervasive state intervention. In such countries there is a need for cultivating a SOCIAL CONSCIOUSNESS and the transformation of society, and where it is also necessary to protect the system by popular vigilance against internal and external enemies.

Apparatchik A Russian word denoting an official of the Communist establishment in the USSR. It is derived from *apparat*, meaning (Party or state) apparatus. The term is used colloquially, usually with a cynical connotation, symbolizing an active but docile supporter of the Communist Party and the Soviet state.

April Theses A political programme issued by Lenin on 4 (17, New Style Calendar) April 1917 after his arrival in Petrograd (now Leningrad) from Switzerland via Germany. Lenin refused to co-operate with the PROVISIONAL GOVERNMENT (which had emerged out of the FEBRUARY REVOLUTION), indicated his opposition to the continuation of the war, pressed for the peasant occupation of large estates and declared his determination to seize power and establish a DICTATORSHIP OF THE PROLETARIAT. Some of the Bolshevik leaders (notably KAMENEV, RYKOV, STALIN and ZINOVIEV) were at first sceptical of the Bolshevik chances, but the majority of the Party in Petrograd accepted the programme.

A priori, a posteriori The process of reasoning from cause to effect, or from an effect to its cause, respectively, the former being deductive and the latter inductive. The generalization arrived at by the *a priori* method is based on abstract reasoning, which may be highly speculative and geared to one's previous notions, whilst in the *a posteriori* case the conclusion rests on experience and practice. Marxist philosophers recognize the value of the *a priori* reasoning to a point but they stress its limitations and its affinity to IDEALISM. In particular, they reject the contention that man possesses knowledge prior to and independently of experience. They attach greater importance to the *a posteriori* process, as in their view knowledge in all forms and man's capacity to think logically came only after experience through his senses. *A posteriorism* is more consistent with DIALECTICAL MATERIALISM.

Arab Communist Organization An extremist body founded in the early 1970s to replace those Arab Communist parties which the organizers accused of OPPORTUNISM and REVISIONISM. It is based in Lebanon, but it operates in small party units in a decentralized fashion in all the Arab countries. Its members are mostly young (16–24 years), they are critical of both the Chinese and Soviet policies and they advocate radical social and political changes in the Arab world through sabotage and violence.

Arab Socialism A mixture of socialism propagated in most Middle Eastern and North African countries embodying elements of Islam, FABIANISM, POPULISM and state economic planning. Although its beginnings can be traced back to the early part of this century, its substantive development dates from the mid-1950s or later (especially in Algeria, Egypt, Iraq, Libya, Yemen, Syria and Tunisia). A.s. stands for: 1. Islamic religion and ethics; 2. redistribution of land; 3. social welfare programmes; 4. freedom of enterprise; 5. controlled market mechanisms; 6. freedom of trade unions; 7. planned economic development; 8. selective state capitalism; 9. modernization; and 10. Arab brotherhood. The movement is led mostly by Western-educated intellectuals, public servants, army officers and teachers. The two major political parties broadly subscribing to A.s. are the ARAB SOCIALIST UNION and the BA'TH Party.

Arab Socialist Union The ruling political party in Egypt, broadly adhering to ARAB SOCIALISM. It regards itself as the vehicle of the 'Socialist Revolution' in Egypt. Its origin goes back to 1953 when the National Liberation Organization was created by the officers' regime, which had deposed King Farouk in 1952. The NLO was reformed into the National Union in 1957–58 which, in 1962, was transformed into the A.S.U. Since that time the A.S.U. has been the only legal political party in Egypt and an integral part of the state establishment.

Arbitration The method of settlement of an industrial dispute involving labour (employees) and capital (employer) by an impartial body or person. A. may be voluntary or compulsory, but the award handed down is binding on the parties involved. Marxists are generally critical of a. under capitalist conditions. In particular, they object to compulsory a., as in their view: 1. it amounts to interference in the internal affairs of trade unions; 2. trade unions may be involved in costly procedures; 3. awards may lead to conflicts within the working class, as some groups of workers are likely to be adversely affected; and 4. the a. court or commission, however nominally independent it may appear, is still a part of the capitalist state, and as such is not neutral enough to settle disputes between capitalists and workers. In the Socialist countries, there is no a. of industrial disputes, as it is officially assumed that there is no basic conflict between labour and the employer. Moreover, trade unions act as TRANSMISSION BELTS for state policies. But in all these countries (except Yugoslavia) a. has been introduced to settle property disputes between socialized entities (state enterprises, co-operatives, economic associations and various public institutions). A. is compulsory and the parties involved have a choice of arbiters from a state-determined list. A. has been found necessary for protecting the entities operating on the basis of ECONOMIC ACCOUNTING and responsible for the implementation of planned targets. In Yugoslavia, property disputes are handled by economic courts. Most Socialist countries also maintain foreign trade a. courts or tribunals for settling trade disputes with Socialist as well as capitalist partners.

Archangel Expedition The US interventionist armed corps, 5,000 strong, which operated in the coastal region from Archangel to Murmansk in the western part of Arctic Russia during the Bolshevik civil war, 1918–19. The operations of the A.E. were a mixture of conflicting interests and views. Although officially hostile to the

BOLSHEVIKS, the A.E. did not engage in any major confrontation and one of its intended objectives was to counter a possible Japanese move into Siberia. Its casualties (killed and wounded) totalled about 500.

ARCOS A Soviet-owned company which operated in London from 1922 to the mid-1930s, handling Anglo-Soviet trade. Originally established in 1920 as the 'All-Russian Co-operative Society' by a delegation representing the Soviet co-operative movement, in accordance with English law, it was re-named 'A. Ltd' in 1922. It grew into a large organization with affiliates in a number of Western countries. A raid by the English police on A. offices in 1927 led to the breaking off of Anglo-Soviet diplomatic relations (till 1929). A. closed its operations in the mid-1930s, when the Soviet Government decided to conduct trade directly from Moscow.

Argentine Communist Party See COMMUNIST PARTY OF ARGENTINA.

Aristocracy The highest social class in non-Socialist societies which, by virtue of its privileged economic, legal and cultural position, dominated the government, especially before the rise of the BOURGEOISIE. Marxists view the existence of an a. as not only socially unjust, but also as a barrier to social reform, PROLETARIAN REVOLUTION and a possible leading force in COUNTER-REVOLUTION. Some highly-paid labour groups, particularly the exclusive trade unions of the second half of the 19th c. (such as the NOBLE ORDER OF THE KNIGHTS OF LABOR in the USA) and intellectuals have been described as the 'a. of labour' undermining the solidarity of the working class.

Armchair Socialism See ACADEMIC SOCIALISM, UTOPIAN SOCIALISM.

Arms Race A drive by a state or a group of states to surpass or at least equal the actual or potential enemy in basic types of armaments. In the Marxist view, the blame for the a.r. must be borne by the richest and most powerful capitalist countries. The a.r. is peculiar to, and inevitable under, capitalism due to: 1. the pressure by capitalists, especially monopolies, to make larger profits; 2. the desire of the governments to reduce unemployment and thus stay in office under the system of democratic elections; 3. the determination of the right-wing elements to prevent the spread of communism by intimidating the Socialist countries; and 4. the cost of the a.r. is largely disregarded as average per capita incomes are high and are financed by the exploitation of the masses and of the less-developed countries.

Art The expression of creative imagination and emotions in terms of line, form, shade, colour or sound, pleasing to human senses. In addition to its narrow and more common meaning embracing graphics, painting, sculpture and architecture, a. also includes literature, drama and music. One of the well known Marxist contentions is that capitalist a. lacks ideological significance, or at least does not reflect the interests of the masses. Marx (in 'Theories of Surplus Value' written 1861–63) pointed out that 'capitalist production is inimical ... to art and poetry', and Lenin (in 'Party Organization and Party Literature', 1905) concluded that the decadence of capitalist a. reaches its lowest level in the era of imperialism. Other Marxist thinkers have stressed that a. in a given historical period is determined by the material BASE and social relations. Whether in pre-Socialist or Socialist societies, a. serves to protect and perpetuate the existing social order. New and important works of a. have usually been associated with social upheavals. They further maintain that a. should be a faithful reflection of reality, not merely a pursuit for the sake of the artist's expression or beholder's enjoyment. A faithful recreation of reality is essential in order to present a sublime analysis of social relations and give meaningful directions for the transformation of society. Different approaches to a. can be detected in different Socialist countries, especially the two largest ones. Whilst Soviet a. is generally considered to be rather heavy, routinized and somewhat naive, Chinese a. seeks to preserve imagination, myth and fancy. Mao Tse-tung endeavoured to instil revolutionary romanticism into it – a synthesis of 'revolutionary realism', the reproduction of the class struggle and 'revolutionary enthusiasm, vigour and hope'. In contrast to other Socialist countries, Hungary – by the 1972 amendment to her Constitution (of 1949) – guarantees the freedom of pursuit in creative arts. Also AESTHETICS, 'ART FOR ART'S SAKE' CONSTRUCTIVISM, PROLETARIAN ART, *PROLETKULT*, SOCIALIST REALISM.

ARTEL A Russian term meaning 'team', but technically denoting a producer's co-operative of artisans. Its beginnings go back to the 1860s in Tsarist Russia, where it grouped co-operating artisans in small-scale industry, usually in cloth-making, tailoring, craftwork, woodworking and implement-making. Moderate socialists and supporters of POPULISM attached great importance to the *a.* as a vehicle for the social transformation of society. After the Bolshevik Revolution, the *a.* was retained and extended in traditional industries. Like any other socialized enterprise, the a. has to fulfil production plans but enjoys a greater independence than a state-owned enterprise. About 1.5m artisans are associated in *a.* contributing some 5 per cent of the Soviet industrial output. This form of production association also exists in collectivized agriculture, where it is known as an 'agricultural *a.*', where all the means of production (except land, which belongs to the state) are collectively owned and the results are shared by the members according to the work performed. Of the three types of COLLECTIVE FARMS, the agricultural *a.* has been the dominant type in Soviet agriculture since 1930.

'Art for Art's Sake' A principle developed by the French romanticist writer T.

Gautier (1811–72), stressing visual impressions rather than ideas and feelings. In his poem, *Art* (1857) he held that art creates only formal beauty and should not be governed by intellectual, moral or emotional values. Marxism, especially in its official interpretation in the USSR, has been opposed to this principle, maintaining that there is no such thing as neutral art, but that art always serves the interests of the ruling class. Also PROLETARIAN ART, SOCIALIST REALISM.

Assembly of Captive European Nations A political association in the USA representing exiles from Central and Eastern Europe dominated by the USSR and/or ruled by the Communist regimes. The countries or nations represented are: Albania, Bulgaria, Czechoslovakia, Estonia, Hungary, Lithuania, Poland and Romania. It was founded in 1954, following the 'Declaration of Aims and Principles of Liberation of the Central and Eastern European Peoples', put forward by the organizing committee in Philadelphia in 1951. The Secretariat of the Assembly is in New York and its membership of about 170 consists mostly of democratic political leaders, intellectuals, diplomats and trade union leaders.

Associated Labour A general socio-economic term peculiar to the Yugoslav system of self-management. It recognizes the social ownership of the means of production, and the right of the workers to 'associate' themselves for the purpose of economic pursuits using the socialized resources. In this process, the workers have the right to manage their activities related to production as well as the distribution of the income within the legal and socio-economic framework laid down by the state. The power of crucial decision-making within each economic entity, called the 'Basic Organization of Associated Labour', is vested in its WORKERS' COUNCIL.

Atheism The scientific and practical rejection of religion and associated phenomena, especially miracles, life after death and the divine determination of history. The beginnings of a. go back to the ideas of such ancient materialist philosophers as Democritus (c. 460–c. 370 B.C.), Epicurus (c. 341–c. 270 B.C.) and Lucretius (99–55 B.C.). The extension of scientific enquiry and discoveries since the 15th c. have provided further evidence in support of a. from some of the most outstanding men of learning, namely N. Copernicus (1473–1543), G. Galileo (1564–1642), B. Spinoza (1632–77), D. Diderot (1713–84), and (in Russia) M. V. Lomonosov (1711–65), A. N. RADISHCHEV and I. M. Sechenov (1829–1903). But the most radical support for a. has come from Marxists. Pre-Marxist atheists generally explained religion in terms of fraudulence on the part of the clergy, ignorance and the gullibility of the people and thought that religious beliefs could be phased out by education. However, Marxism goes much further. Marx, Engels and Lenin maintained that the origin and types of RELIGION are essentially a product of the material conditions underlying the development of societies. In the Socialist countries, although nominally there is a freedom of religious beliefs and worship, there is also the freedom of atheistic propaganda which is supported ideologically and financially by the state. Marxists hold that the elimination of religion is necessary for social progress and human happiness and that a. can be fully attained only in a Communist society where a high degree of education and harmonious social relations remove the need for religion. Also AG-NOSTICISM, LEAGUE OF MILITANT ATHEISTS, PANTHEISM.

Atlantic to the Urals' Doctrine, 'From the A long-range policy for pan-European unification to embrace Western and Eastern Europe, irrespective of the differences in the social systems. The doctrine was put forward in 1958 by General Ch. de Gaulle, President of the French Republic, to promote peace in Europe, through the elimination of the eastern IRON CURTAIN and the western STRATEGIC EMBARGO. The doctrine has come to be identified with the Western European desire for emancipation from US domination and for the normalization of West–West European relations. To some extent it was favourably received in the East.

August Revolution A show of strength and determination by the VIET MINH in Aug. 1945 to establish an independent and Socialist Vietnam. It began in Cao Bang-Lang Son, a northern zone of Vietnam adjacent to China, as a mild revolt against the Japanese 'protection', a warning against the return of French colonialism and a refusal to support the monarchy of Emperor Bao Dai. On 29 Aug. 1945, 2,000 Viet Minh troops, led by General VO NGUYEN GIAP, marched into Hanoi and Bao Dai abdicated. The latter handed over power to HO CHI MINH who became the first President of the Provisional Government of Vietnam. Following these developments, on 2 Sep. 1945 Ho Chi Minh proclaimed the formation of the Democratic Republic of Vietnam and its national independence. The opposition of the French led to a nine-year war (1946–54) which ended with the Viet Minh's resounding victory at DIEN BIEN PHU in March 1954.

Aurora, The (*Avrora* in Russian) The name of the cruiser in the Imperial Russian Baltic Fleet which participated conspicuously in the two Russian Revolutions in Petrograd (now Leningrad) in 1917. Its crew supported the FEBRUARY REVOLUTION, rebelled against Tsar Nicholas II and took control of the vessel on 28 Feb. (O.S.C.; 13 March, N.S.C.). It played a crucial role in the GREAT OCTOBER SOCIALIST REVOLUTION. On orders from the Petrograd Military Revolutionary Committee, the A. facilitated the military manoeuvres of the RED GUARDS and on 25 Oct. at 9.45 p.m., it gave the agreed signal for the storming of the Winter Palace, in which its crew also took part. Since 1948 the A. has been permanently moored on the Neva River in Leningrad as a revoluntionary monument. It was awarded the Order of the Red Banner in 1927 and the Order of the October Revolution in 1968.

Ausra ('The Dawn' in Lithuanian) A Lithuanian SAMIZDAT journal for counteracting the Soviet distortion of Lithuania's history and providing a critical commentary on Soviet policies. Its first number was published in Oct. 1975 and subsequently has been appearing roughly once a year. It supplements another *Samizdat* publication, *The Chronicle of the Lithuanian Catholic Church*.

Australian Communist Party See COMMUNIST PARTY OF AUSTRALIA.

Australian Labour Party A moderate left-wing political party in Australia, traditionally concerned with the economic betterment of the working population rather than with ideology. Founded in 1901 (with its beginnings going back to 1891), it is the oldest, and in terms of voters, usually the largest party in the country. Its leader, J. C. Watson, became the world's first labour prime minister in 1904. The Party stands for generous social security, the nationalization of key industries, a high level of employment, female and racial equality, a rather independent stance in foreign policy and fairly sympathetic policies towards the Socialist countries. It derives its support mainly from trade unions and a large section of the middle class, especially intellectuals. Throughout its history, it has been mostly in opposition against the coalition of moderate right-wing parties (the Liberal Party and a rural party). After 23 years in opposition it was returned to power in 1972 for 3 years, during which period it embarked on a far-reaching social welfare programme, various social reforms and some changes in foreign policy (notably, Australia's disengagement from the Vietnam war).

Austrian Communist Party See COMMUNIST PARTY OF AUSTRIA.

Austrian Socialist Party See SOCIALIST PARTY OF AUSTRIA.

Austro-Marxism A school of thought in the Austrian Social-Democratic Party in the early part of this century which provided an ideological basis for CENTRISM in the international working class movement. Its main representatives were M. Adler (1873–1937), O. Bauer (1882–1938), K. KAUTSKY, K. Renner (1870–1950) and (for the time) R. HILFERDING. Their ideas were expounded mostly in *Marx-Studien* (*Marxist Studies*), occasional papers edited by Adler and Hilferding from 1904 to 1923, and in a monthly journal *Der Kampf* (*Struggle*) published from 1907 to 1933. In general, A.-M. represented attempts to mediate between Marxist orthodoxy and REVISIONISM. In philosophy, its leading members endeavoured to integrate some elements of NEO-KANTIANISM and EMPIRIO-CRITICISM with traditional MARXISM. A.-M. was critical of dogmatic MATERIALISM and HISTORICAL MATERIALISM, and marginally accommodated religion. In politics, on the whole, it favoured nationalism and cultural freedom, did not object to the Austrian participation in W.W.I and rejected the DICTATORSHIP OF THE PROLETARIAT. Its members were active in forming the SECOND-AND-A-HALF INTERNATIONAL (1921) and later (1923), in its merger with the BERN INTERNATIONAL, was active in forming the LABOUR AND SOCIALIST INTERNATIONAL (a successor to the SECOND INTERNATIONAL) which was opposed to the COMINTERN. The ideas and actions of the members of A.-M. were bitterly attacked by Lenin and other revolutionary Marxist thinkers before, as well as after, the Bolshevik Revolution. The School disappeared after the advent of Nazism in the late 1930s without leaving any successors. It has been described as a 'school of one generation'.

Autarky A policy designed to promote a country's self-sufficiency. It was embraced by the USSR after 1918 when the

STATE FOREIGN TRADE MONOPOLY was introduced. The pursuit of a. was prompted by the desire to become economically independent from the hostile capitalist countries and to facilitate the INSULATION of its domestic markets from foreign markets and consequently simplify its economic planning. After W.W.II a. was utilized by other Socialist countries, imitating the Soviet model. But since the mid-1950s, the Socialist countries have increasingly departed from their previous autarkic policies in favour of a greater participation in the INTERNATIONAL DIVISION OF LABOUR. However, today their policies are still largely oriented towards a. Although these countries as a whole claim 40 per cent of the world's industrial output, their share in world trade is only 12 per cent. Some Socialist economists have accused the leading capitalist countries of a., due to the latter's unnecessary expansion of military production, protectionism, direct state intervention and the various forms of discrimination against the Socialist countries. They further maintain that the consequent losses upon capitalist a. are borne by the working class through higher living costs.

Automation The substitution of self-regulating machinery and other equipment for labour. It is now found in most manufacturing and some service industries in advanced countries. Although the extent of a. is smaller in the Socialist countries than in the West, Communist leaders favour a. on both practical and ideological grounds for the following reasons: 1. a. lightens the burden of physical labour; 2. it makes work safer and cleaner; 3. in some ways, it makes work more interesting; 4. it enables mass production and high labour productivity, and as such it helps the advance of Socialist society towards COMMUNIST CORNUCOPIA: and 5. it is conducive to the equalization of MENTAL AND PHYSICAL LABOUR. From the Marxist view, a. under capitalism is likely to lead to : (a) UNEMPLOYMENT: (b) larger SURPLUS VALUE for capitalists; and (c) ALIENATION.

Automovement See SELF-MOVEMENT.

Autonomous Region, Autonomous Republic Administrative territorial divisions in the USSR based on the nationalities which are too small to qualify for an ordinary region (*Oblast*) or a Union Republic respectively. This statute is supposed to give each entity a measure of autonomy in spite of its small size. There are 8 A. Regions (5 in the RSFSR, 1 in Azarbaijan, 1 in Georgia and 1 in Tadzhikistan), each represented by 5 deputies in the SOVIET OF NATIONALITIES of the SUPREME SOVIET OF THE USSR. As to the A. Republics, there are 20 (16 in the RSFSR, 2 in Georgia, 1 in Azarbaijan and 1 in Uzbekistan) and each is represented by 11 deputies. Although autonomy provides a distinct territorial administration, it is of little consequence as the real locus of power is in the Party apparatus.

Autumn Harvest Uprising An unsuccessful armed revolt led by MAO TSE-TUNG in Sep. 1927 against the KUOMINTANG'S control of the Hunan province in south-east China. He used the 'First Army', consisting of armed detachments of industrial workers, miners, peasants and soldiers, numbering about 5,000 men, against the Comintern's opposition and without the approval of the Central Committee of the Chinese Communist Party. His aim was to establish Communist power in the province but proved to be a dismal failure. At the meeting of the CC in the following November, Mao was severely reprimanded and dismissed from the Party's Politburo.

Aveling, Edward (1851–98) An English Socialist who was the husband of Eleanor Marx, Marx's youngest daughter. Aveling was a member of the Social Democrats' Federation and helped found the Socialist League. He is best known for co-translating Marx's *Das KAPITAL* with Samuel Moore in 1887 and Engels' *Socialism: Utopian and Scientific*.

Average Profit Rate An abstract concept in the Marxian analysis of capitalism to denote the rate of profit which is average for the whole economy over a period of time. It is calculated on a macroeconomic basis, i.e. the percentage ratio of total profits (s) to CONSTANT CAPITAL (c) and VARIABLE CAPITAL (v) engaged in production, i.e. a.p.r.$=s/(c+v)$. In practice, the actual profit rates vary in different branches of the economy and to different degrees. Marx (in *Capital*, vol. I) stressed the tendency for the profit rate to be equalized. This is the case since rivalry and competition involve firms switching from low-profit to high-profit forms of production, i.e. they tend to leave industries with a high ORGANIC STRUCTURE OF CAPITAL and move to those with a low one. There is a long-run tendency for the a.p.r. to decline, which intensifies the EXPLOITATION of the working class and exacerbates capitalist contradictions. The concept of the a.p.r. is in a sense inconsistent with the LABOUR THEORY OF VALUE. Moreover, Marx implicitly abandoned the theory (in *Capital*, vol. III), when he introduced the concept of PRODUCTION PRICE.

B

Backyard Furnaces Small furnaces which appeared in China in the late 1950s for the local production of iron and steel. They were located around villages, in the gardens of schools and houses in towns, and along railway lines. The building of b.f. started with the 'Backyard Iron and Steel Drive' in early 1958, and soon developed on a massive scale during the GREAT LEAP FORWARD. By the end of 1958 over 2m. b.f. had appeared as a result of the work of some 60m. Chinese. The campaign was prompted by: 1. the reaction against the Soviet stoppage of the delivery of large metallurgical plants; 2. the decentralization drive to ease the pressure on the meagre transport facilities; 3. Mao Tse-tung's conviction that the same results could be achieved through mass initiative and enthusiasm, without an institutionalized hierarchical technocracy. In most cases, the cost of the products was very high and the quality very low. In early 1959 the government decided to halt the movement and most of the b.f. were subsequently abandoned.

Bacteriological Warfare The deliberate use of bacteria against an enemy to cause disease in man, animals or plants. It can be waged by infected live carriers or by aerial sprays. The recourse to b.w. was prohibited by the Hague Convention of 1907, and further reaffirmed by the Geneva Convention of 1925. Although b.w. was attempted by Germany and Japan during W.W.II, the greatest publicity was given to that allegedly resorted to by the USA during the Korean War (1950–53). According to unsubstantiated reports, the American troops dropped bacteria-laden bombs on the civilian population which caused epidemics in the Communist-held areas. Some American prisoners of war admitted to the crime, but it is not certain whether their 'confessions' were genuine or a product of BRAINWASHING.

Baghdad Pact A mutual defence agreement originally concluded by Iraq and Turkey in 1955 directed against possible aggression by the USSR. It was open to all the member countries of the Arab League. Pakistan and the United Kingdom also acceded to it and the USA supported it on a selective basis. In 1959 the Pact was replaced by CENTO.

Bakunin, Mikhail Aleksandrovich (1814–76) An outstanding Russian theoretician of ANARCHISM and a revolutionary leader. He was born to a wealthy noble family, but his revolutionary activities abroad resulted in his estates being confiscated. In the 1840s and 1850s, B. participated in the revolutionary movements in central and western Europe. He developed his anarchical views in the 1860s after his escape from Siberia. He advocated ANARCHO-COMMUNISM which stressed: collective ownership; the political, economic and social equalization of classes; absolute individual freedom and the abolition of the state. B. rejected the Marxian postulates of the CLASS STRUGGLE and the DICTATORSHIP OF THE PROLETARIAT. His ideas and activities exerted considerable influence in revolutionary circles in Russia – as represented by NIHILISM and POPULISM – as well as in France,

Italy and Spain. Marx and Engels attacked B. for his 'petty bourgeois radicalism'. The break between Marxists and B. and his followers came in 1872, when B. was prevented from attending the FIRST INTERNATIONAL at The Hague when Marx contrived to expel him on charges of embezzlement. B.'s main works were: *The Social Revolution* (1871), *The State and Anarchism* (1871) and *God and the State* (1877).

Balanced, Proportionate Development See PLANNED PROPORTIONATE DEVELOPMENT.

'Balance of Terror' A phrase coined during the COLD WAR to denote the nuclear threat, to which the world became exposed after the USSR developed its own thermonuclear bomb in 1953, thus matching the USA. The Soviet technical and military capacity was further enhanced by the successful space programme with the launching of the first satellite in 1957.

Balances of the National Economy A tabular representation of the utilization of material, labour and financial resources of a country, showing the sources of supply and planned needs or achieved results. They were first prepared in the USSR for 1923/24, using Quesnay's 'Economic Table' (PHYSIOCRATISM). According to Soviet claims, this pioneering piece of work provided ideas for W. Leontief who invented the INPUT-OUTPUT ANALYSIS.

Balkan Communist Federation A loose international organization in existence from 1920 to 1932 created to consolidate the Communist parties, co-ordinate their activities and create worker-peasant republics in Bulgaria, Greece, Romania and Yugoslavia. It originated from the Balkan Social-Democratic Federation (founded in 1910), which participated in the formation of the COMINTERN in 1919. The B.C.F. was subsequently affiliated to the Comintern. G. M. DIMITROV became a leading spirit in the former and an active leader in the latter. After 1932 the B.C.F. ceased its operations owing to Fascist oppression. But after W.W.II there were attempts to revive it under the name of the BALKAN CONFEDERATION.

Balkan Confederation A scheme for a political and economic association of the 'Balkan and Danubian States' (Albania, Bulgaria, Czechoslovakia, Hungary, Poland, Romania and Yugoslavia), proposed by G. M. DIMITROV and J. Tito in 1947. The plan was frustrated by Stalin in Jan. 1948, who thought it would interfere with his idea of the integration of the European Socialist countries into the Soviet orbit. (On Stalin's initiative, in 1949 the COUNCIL FOR MUTUAL ECONOMIC ASSISTANCE was created for the purpose.)

Baltic Cities Riots Unrest, punctuated with violence amongst workers and housewives, which broke out in the Polish Baltic ports of Gdansk, Gdynia and Szczecin in December 1970. They were caused by substantial increases in food prices, which particularly affected the lower income groups. The riots led to the replacement of the Party leader W. Gomułka by E. GIEREK and some moderate liberalization.

Bamboo Curtain A term, parallel to the IRON CURTAIN, denoting the political and social barrier erected by the Communist regime in China after 1949. It restricted the flow of ideas and people to and from the capitalist world, especially the Western countries. The barrier has been partly dismantled by several developments since 1960, namely China's turn to the West for trade and technology (prompted by the SINO-SOVIET DISPUTE), PING-PONG DIPLOMACY (beginning April 1971), China's admission to the United Nations (Oct. 1971), President Nixon's visit (Feb. 1972) and full diplomatic relations with the USA (Jan. 1979).

Bangladesh Communist Party A description that may have 3 different meanings: 1. the pro-Soviet B.C.P., created in Dec. 1972 as a separate entity from the Pakistan C.P. It is the largest Communist party in Bangladesh, with about 2,500 members, but was proscribed in 1975; 2. the 3 Communist parties whose names include the B.C.P. (viz.: the 'B.C.P.' as under 1. above), the 'B.C.P.-Leninist' (ultra pro-Chinese, founded in 1971) and the 'B.C.P. League' (founded in 1972, advocating 'scientific socialism'); 3. broadly all the Communist parties in Bangladesh, of which there are at least 8, viz.: in addition to the three under 2 above, they are: the Bengali C.P. (it originated in 1971, moderately pro-Chinese); the 'East Pakistan C.P. Marxist-Leninist' (formed in 1966, leaning towards China); the 'East Bengal C.P. Marxist-Leninist' (created in 1968 by those expelled from the 'East Pakistan C.P. Marxist-Leninist' for being too lenient to feudalism); the 'Purba Bangla Sarbohara' (formed in 1971, opposed to factionalism) and the 'Purba Banglar Sammayad Dal' (a radical militant splinter group which separated from the East Pakistan C.P. Marxist-Leninist in 1972). The beginning of the Communist movement in what is now Bangladesh goes back to at least 1928, when the C.P. of India was founded. After independence (1947) and the separation of Pakistan from India, the East Pakistani membership of the C.P. was 12,000; however, the Party was banned from 1954 to 1971. But since 1975 total or partial proscription has followed under the military regime.

Bank of China The bank for foreign trade in the P.R. of China. It was founded in 1908 as China's central bank, but under the Communist regime it has been relegated to handling the country's international payments. Its head office is in Peking and it has four branches abroad – in London, Singapore and two in Hong Kong. It maintains correspondent relations with over 600 foreign banks and has 1,700 branch offices in more than 130 countries.

Banque Commerciale pour l'Europe du Nord (Commercial Bank for Northern Europe) The Soviet-owned bank (in which the French Communist Party is re-ported to have a small share) located in Paris. It was originally founded by the White Russian emigrés in 1921, but was bought by the Soviet Government in 1925. It has grown to become the largest foreign bank in Paris (outranking the Bank of America, the next largest, by two and a half times). Its telegraphic address is the 'Eurobank', which gave the name to the 'Eurodollar' (now 'Eurocurrency') market in the 1950s which, ironically, the Bank has helped develop. The Bank engages in financing East–West trade, operates in the Eurocurrency market, and trains bankers for the USSR, other Socialist countries and some less-developed countries.

Barefoot Doctors Medical workers in China with only rudimentary training in traditional medicine. They are mostly young peasants with an incomplete primary education. They are trained by young qualified doctors and sent to the countryside to attend to the simpler and most common ailments. The provision of b.d. is part of the state campaign to improve health services in rural areas, especially in the PEOPLE'S COMMUNES.

Barone, Enrico (1859–1924) An Italian mathematical economist who *inter alia* made pioneering contributions to the 'COMPETITIVE SOLUTION' and the TRIAL AND ERROR METHOD for a collectivist economy. In his article, 'The Ministry of Production in the Collectivist State' (1908), he maintained that the problem of the organization of production under socialism would not be significantly different – if such production were to be efficient – from that under competitive capitalism. He stressed that such categories as prices, wages, interest, rent, profit and savings must also appear and should be arrived at by a 'trial and error' method. He used a system of simultaneous equations to support his theoretical proposition. Though B. is generally credited as the original contributor, proposed solutions along these lines had been embodied or implied previously in the works of F.v.

Wieser (in *Natürliche Wert*, 1889) and V. Pareto (in *Cours d'économie politique*, 1896–97). Neither B. nor Wieser and Pareto was sympathetic to the cause of socialism.

Base A term introduced by Marx (in CONTRIBUTION TO THE CRITIQUE OF POLITICAL ECONOMY, 1859) for the material basis of society's living. It simply refers to the economic system with its production relations in the material sphere at a given stage of society's development. It is also known as 'substructure' or 'understructure' and contrasts with the SUPERSTRUCTURE (political, legal and cultural ideas and institutions). The b. plays a fundamental role in Marxist ideology, as its nature and its relation to the superstructure determine social development and class relations. The b. is not immutable but it changes historically. At a given stage of development, contradictions emerge between the material PRODUCTION FORCES and the existing PRODUCTION RELATIONS. If this disparity is too great and lasts too long, revolution results. In a capitalist society b. refers to the private ownership of the means of production and the exploitation of hired labour. Under socialism these features are eliminated, thus negating any serious disparities between the b. and the superstructure.

Basel Resolution A declaration made by the Emergency International Socialist Congress held in Basel, Switzerland in Nov. 1912. It appealed to the socialist movements throughout the world to refuse to serve in the impending imperialist war, and instead to take advantage of the confusion and overthrow capitalism.

Basic Economic Law of Contemporary Capitalism A tenet formulated by Stalin in 1952 (in THE ECONOMIC PROBLEMS OF SOCIALISM IN THE USSR, which reads: 'the maximization of capitalist profit through the exploitation, ruin and pauperization of the masses in a given country, the systematic pillage of other nations, especially backward countries and through wars and the militarization of the national economy'. He regarded this 'law' as a distinctive characteristic of capitalism in its 'imperialist stage of development'. He stressed further that the driving force behind modern MONOPOLY CAPITALISM is not merely the AVERAGE PROFIT RATE (as implied by Marx) but *maximum* profit.

Basic Economic Law of Socialism The fundamental principle governing the nature of Socialist production. This 'law' was formulated by Stalin (in *The Economic Problems of Socialism in the USSR*, 1952), who claimed that it was an 'objective law' operating irrespective of human will, once appropriate conditions for its operation were created. He stated the law in the form of a goal: 'the securing of the maximum satisfaction of the constantly rising material and cultural requirements of the whole society through the continuous expansion and perfection of socialist production on the basis of higher techniques'. The law implies that the income of the population grows faster than production, which in turn provides a powerful stimulus to the continued expansion of society's production capacity and ensures continuous full employment. Stalin stressed that the 'law of balanced (or planned), proportionate development of the national economy' is not a basic law of socialism.

Basic Exchange Rate In Socialist practice, the official exchange rate between the domestic and a foreign currency, usually based on the official parity (defined in gold or a key currency) and applicable to visible trade. It is essentially an artificial rate, as it is set at a level grossly exaggerating the value of the domestic currency in relation to convertible capitalist currencies. It is held stable over long periods, irrespective of changing economic conditions. This rate is not relevant in decision-making in foreign trade and its only practical use is in recording the official value of exports and imports of merchandise for statistical purposes. Thus in 1978 the b.e.r. was: in the USSR – 0.67 rouble = US$1.00 (whilst the black market rate was

3.60r. = \$1.00); in Poland – 3.16 zlotys = \$1.00 (compared with the TOURIST EXCHANGE RATE of 31.62z. and the black market rate of 90z. = \$1.00).

Basic Law of the Socio-economic Formation An economic rule formulated by Stalin (in *The Economic Problems of Socialism in the USSR*, 1952) which governs the conditions, processes and directions of development in a particular SOCIO-ECONOMIC FORMATION. The 'law' determines the purpose of production and the means of implementing this purpose, both of which are essentially conditioned by the OWNERSHIP OF THE MEANS OF PRODUCTION and the consequent PRODUCTION RELATIONS. Stalin pointed out that this law is an expression of the thinking and interests of the ruling class which happens to be in power. Each of the 5 socio-economic formations has its own peculiar law, viz.: 1. primitive Communism – the production of the indispensable means of subsistence, using primitive methods on the basis of collective ownership and labour; 2. slavery – the creation of surplus product for masters through conquests and the exploitation of slaves; 3. feudalism – the creation of surplus products for feudal lords through the exploitation of serfs; 4. capitalism – the creation of the maximum possible surplus value for capitalists through the expansion of production, innovations and the increasing exploitation of hired labour and (in the era of imperialism) of colonies and less-developed countries; and 5. socialism – a steady growth and improvement of production on the basis of the social ownership of the means of production for the highest possible satisfaction of the constantly increasing material and cultural needs of the socialist society.

Basic Organization of Associated Labour (*Osnovna Organizacija Udruženog Rada*, in Serbo-Croat) In Yugoslavia, the smallest self-managing work-place, founded in 1971. The creation of the system was a result of the government's concern with the growing size of enterprises (through horizontal and vertical integration) and the consequent diminution of decision-making power at the grass-root level. The B.O.A.L. is found in all types of enterprises engaged in material production or services, including government departments, hospitals, research establishments and various institutions. A B.O.A.L., through its elected WORKERS' COUNCIL, has complete control over the most important questions, including the distribution of profits earned by it. An enterprise may have from 1 to 40 B.O.A.L.s. A small enterprise not only constitutes a B.O.A.L. but its personnel constitute its own Workers' Council. B.O.A.L.s. are encouraged to combine with other B.O.A.L.s. to create 'work organizations' whereupon the latter may form a 'Complex Organization of Associated Labour' (*Složena Organizacija Udruženog Rada*).

Basic Problem of Philosophy A question to which Marxist philosophers attach fundamental importance, viz. the relation of ideas to material existence. It is considered basic, because the way in which all other problems concerned with the world outlook are approached depends on how this relation is resolved and whether idealist or materialist philosophy is accepted as valid. The advocates of IDEALISM insist on the primacy of ideas over the material world. On the other hand, Marxists accept MATERIALISM, postulating that matter and nature are primary whilst ideas, consciousness and spirit are secondary and derived from the material world. This question was fully dealt with by Stalin in *On Dialectical and Historical Materialism* (1938). Marxists are uncompromising on this question, and also reject DUALISM (according to which spiritual and material factors exist separately and independently).

'Basic Principles of the International Socialist Division of Labour' Guidelines for specialization amongst the member countries of the COUNCIL FOR MUTUAL ECONOMIC ASSISTANCE. They were adopted at the 15th Session of the CMEA in Warsaw in Dec. 1961, and further confirmed at the Conference of the Leaders of the Communist and Workers' Parties in Moscow in June 1962. The document, containing about 20 pages divided into 7 chapters, specifies that specialization is to be determined on a planned basis and, in the main, in accordance with the principle of comparative advantage. The member countries undertake to export and import agreed items by entering into firm commitments whereby each member country agrees to pursue a rapid economic development. It is also established that the less-developed member countries are to be assisted by the more developed ones, so that the former's growth rates are faster than the latter's in order to equalize economic levels. It is further stressed that each member country is sovereign and equal to any other.

Basic Wage See MINIMUM WAGE.

Basmachi ('Raiders', in Turkish) Anti-Bolshevik insurgents who operated in Turkestan (central Asia) from 1918 to 1924. They were mostly KULAKS and local nationalists opposing Soviet authority. Although the b. were virtually wiped out or resettled by the mid-1920s, some bands carried on in the mountains up to the early 1930s and again during W.W.II.

Ba'th, Al ('Renaissance', in Arabic) A predominantly moderate socialist Arab party founded in the 1930s. Its general programme is to implement socialism in all Arab lands. Its motto is 'Unity, freedom and socialism – one Arab nation, the bearer of Eternal Mission'. The movement originated in Syria and then spread to most other Arab countries. However, it has suffered from factional conflicts, deriving from differing ideological interpretations and uncompromising personalities. The two traditionally rival centres of its influence are in Damascus (Syria) and Baghdad (Iraq), the former being more radical (almost Marxist).

Batrak A Russian term for 'poor peasants' who worked as agricultural labourers for rich peasants, KULAKS. The b.s typically lived on their employers' farms and were paid in kind (accommodation, food and clothing). After the Bolshevik Revolution, the b.s were immediately embraced as a natural ally of the Soviet regime.

Battle Act A short name for the Mutual Defense Assistance Control Act, passed by the US Congress in 1951 to reinforce the STRATEGIC EMBARGO against the Socialist bloc. Popularly named after Senator L. C. Battle (the author of the Bill), the Act prohibited the export of strategic items to the Socialist bloc from a country receiving US aid, under the penalty of losing that aid. The administration of the Act caused a good deal of adverse reaction amongst recipients against the USA, although the application of the penalty was subsequently moderated by the US President's liberal interpretation of the Act's provisions. The Act was fairly successful at first, but lost its effectiveness after 1960, owing to the economic recovery and strength of Western Europe and the national pride of the capitalist countries in general.

Bavarian Soviet Republic A self-proclaimed independent state in southern Germany controlled by a coalition Soviet Government consisting of Communists and Social-Democrats, in existence from 13 April to 1 May 1919. The Government, based in Munich and at first dominated by Communists, immediately took over the control of large enterprises, nationalized banks, organized a 'Red Army' and created an 'Extraordinary Commission for Combating Counter-Revolution'. However, it did not command wide support from the lower industrial working class and the peasantry. On 27 April, the Communists were ousted from the Government and troops were sent from Berlin and German Provinces to Munich on 1 May. The 'Soviet Government' immediately collapsed, but the 'Red Army' continued fighting till 5 May 1919.

Bay of Pigs (*Bahia de los Cochinos*, in Spanish) The site of an unsuccessful invasion of Cuba on 17 April 1961 by a force of anti-Communist refugees. The landing was planned by the CENTRAL INTELLIGENCE AGENCY in its belief that there would be a general revolt against the F. CASTRO regime. The invaders were immediately and thoroughly routed by the loyal Castro units which killed 60 and captured 1,200 of the invaders.

Bebel, August (1840–1913) A German socialist theoretician and leader who worked for the PARLIAMENTARY ROAD TO SOCIALISM. A joiner by trade, he became a successful manufacturer, yet remained a loyal Marxist of the peaceful evolutionary version (for which Marx and Engels accused him of OPPORTUNISM). B. founded the SOCIAL-DEMOCRATIC WORKERS' PARTY in 1869, which in 1875 he succeeded in uniting with the General Workers' Union into the Socialist Workers' Party (which later became the SOCIAL-DEMOCRATIC PARTY OF GERMANY). He was the editor of the influential newspaper *Vorwärts*, he denounced IMPERIALISM and MILITARISM, helped found the SECOND INTERNATIONAL (1889) and advocated equal rights for women (in *Woman: In the Past, Present and Future*, 1886). He succeeded in having the whole Marxist programme adopted as the policy of the Social-Democratic Party in 1891. He was subjected to harassment and imprisonment by the authorities.

Bednyak ('Poorling', in Russian) A Bolshevik term for a poor peasant with little or no land, working for a middle peasant (*SEREDNYAK*) or a KULAK. The b. class, which before the Revolution constituted 65 per cent of the peasantry, was used by the Bolsheviks as an instrument of class warfare against the rich peasants, until the collectivization drive was completed in the USSR in the late 1930s.

Beehive, The The socialist weekly bulletin published by the London Trades Council from 1862 to 1876, which in the 1860s was a medium for propagating Marxist ideas. Marx unsuccessfully made efforts to gain control of it and turn it into the organ of the FIRST INTERNATIONAL. The bulletin was bought out by a wealthy and influential industrialist and politician, Samuel Morley, in 1868 whereupon it was gradually transformed into a moderate journal. Marx and his followers then boycotted it, made the L.T.C. withdraw its patronage in 1876 resulting in the journal's collapse in 1885.

'Beggars' Communism' A disparaging phrase coined by N. S. KHRUSHCHEV to describe the Maoist insistence on simple subsistence living. It was a reaction against Mao Tse-tung's campaign attacking CONSUMERISM and his attempts to elevate poverty to a virtue and a principle governing the living of the masses.

Behaviourism A major movement in psychology which explains behaviour in biological, chemical, physical and (especially) physiological terms, i.e. as an outcome of the operation of definite laws emphasizing the causal relationship between motives, actions and reactions. B. developed particularly in the USA as a result of ideas originally put forward by J. B. Watson (1873–1958) in his *Behaviourism* (1925). Its exponents maintain that only observable behaviour of man or animal provides a legitimate and scientific basis of study, and rejects or minimizes the method of introspection, consciousness, impression, mental processes, attitudes and values. B. has made a considerable impact on the study of learning, activity analysis, public relations, industrial psychology and sociology. Some economists, especially T. B. Veblen (1857–1929) and W. C. Mitchell (1874–1948), believed that behaviouristic methods could be used to make economics a 'science of the economic behaviour of man' instead of merely a study of the economic equilibrium. Marxists are largely opposed to b., as in their view it reduces psychological processes and behaviour to the physiological-mechanistic

Being and Consciousness

level. In the socio-economic sphere, b. is held to distort the active and DIALECTIC content of interpersonal relations, which leads to DETERMINISM and VULGAR MATERIALISM. They stress that man is not merely a passive possessor and observer of mental states, but also an active and re-active organism in complex relationships with other organisms.

Being and Consciousness Philosophical concepts which play an important part in the different outlooks of bourgeois and Marxist philosophers. In Marxist-Leninist DIALECTICAL MATERIALISM, there is no b. without substance or matter, as the as-sumption to the contrary would mean that b. precedes matter, which would imply that god exists. Instead, Marxists maintain that the sequence of the relation is: nature, matter, b., c., where b. is an exter-nal attribute whilst c. is the highest form of reflection. But external forms of existence may distort the real nature of b. (e.g., the apparent movement of the sun from east to west, reflecting the earth's rotation from west to east). The task of scientific study, as Marx (in *CAPITAL*, vol. 3) and Lenin (in *PHILOSOPHICAL NOTEBOOKS*) held, is to ensure that c. corresponds to b. Dialectical materialism in principle rejects AGNOSTICISM, which isolates c. from b., and vulgar EMPIRICISM, which identifies b. with c.

Belgian Communist Party See COMMUN-IST PARTY OF BELGIUM.

Belgrade Conference An East-West 'Conference on Security and Co-operation in Europe', held in Belgrade from 4 Oct. 1977 to 9 March 1978. It was attended by 1,000 delegates nominated by the Ministries of Foreign Affairs of 35 nations – 8 European Socialist countries (Bulgaria, Czechoslovakia, the German DR, Hungary, Poland, Romania, the USSR, Yugoslavia), 25 West European countries, plus Canada and the USA. Ob-servers from several other countries also attended. The Conference was a follow-up to the HELSINKI CONFERENCE. The

specific questions which were reviewed included *détente* in East-West relations, disarmament and human rights. Three distinct divisions emerged at the Confer-ence – the Soviet bloc (Bulgaria, Czecho-slovakia, the German DR, Hungary, Poland, Romania and the USSR), the NATO group, and the 'Neutral and Non-Aligned Nations' (the last comprising 9 countries, including Yugoslavia). The Communist regimes were attacked by Western and neutral representatives and emigré groups on the violation of human rights, especially in the USSR, Czecho-slovakia, the German DR, Poland and Romania. The Conference achieved little, and it was agreed that the next one should be held in Madrid in 1980.

Belgrade Declaration An understanding published officially in a joint Soviet-Yugoslav statement on 2 June 1955, re-garding the exclusive right of each country to pursue its OWN PATH TO SOCIALISM. The B.D. had been preceded by N. S. Khrushchev's visit to Yugoslavia and a public apology to J. Tito for previous Soviet attempts (under Stalin) to interfere with Yugoslav internal affairs. The B.D. was later reaffirmed by L. Brezhnev when he visited Yugoslavia in Sep. 1971.

Belinsky, Vissarion Grigorievich (1811–1848) An outstanding Russian pre-Marxist materialist philosopher and democratic revolutionary, regarded as the father of the Russian revolutionary intel-ligentsia. His work was directed towards exposing the evils of autocracy, serfdom, clericalism and chauvinistic nationalism. In his philosophical writings, he stressed that man's consciousness and ideas are determined externally – by the material environment, hence his critiques on AG-NOSTICISM and SCEPTICISM. He inter-preted social development as an outcome of contradictions and struggle, leading from lower to higher forms. B. never be-came a revolutionary Communist and is identified by Marxists with UTOPIAN SOCIALISM, despite the respect with which they treat his ideas and work.

Benevolent Capitalism A scornful term applied by radical reformers and revolutionary Marxists to paternalistic capitalism, where the most obvious faults of the system are artificially mended by the government and charitable organizations, but where the social establishment is basically unchanged. The critics of b.c. regard it as a timid and misguided attempt or calculated stratagem, in each case dissipating the energies of social reformers or postponing the PROLETARIAN REVOLUTION. The term is derived from *Our Benevolent Feudalism* (1902), by the American author, W. J. Ghent.

Benin, People's Republic of A country in west-central Africa, 112,000 sq. km., with a population of 3.3m. and ruled by a Marxist regime. It was formerly the French colony of Dahomey, which became independent in 1960 but which took its present official name in Dec. 1975. The country is ruled by the PEOPLE'S REVOLUTIONARY PARTY OF BENIN, is committed to Marxism-Leninism, and has an illegal right-wing opposition party called the Front for the Liberation and Rehabilitation of Dahomey. Effective power is exercised by the National Political Bureau which is a small inner body of the National Council of the Revolution whose 69 members constitute a military government. It has embarked on far-reaching reforms, including nationalization and free, compulsory and secular education.

Beria, Lavrenty Pavlovich (1899–1953) The notorious chief of the Soviet secret service from 1938 to 1953. Of Georgian-Jewish descent, he joined the Bolshevik Party in 1917 and after 1921 worked in the *CHEKA*, the *GPU*, the *NKVD*, the *NKGB* and the *MGB*. He participated in the GREAT PURGES of the 1930s and had his rivals liquidated, including YEZHOV (the chief of the *NKVD* at the time) whom he succeeded in 1938. For the next 15 years he organized systematic and ruthless terrorization of elements inconvenient to the Communist regime in the USSR, as well as in the territories taken over from the Bal-

tic States, eastern Poland, Czechoslovakia and Romania after W.W.II. He also dominated the security organizations in the Eastern European Countries. From 1941 to 1953 he was a Deputy Prime Minister, in 1945 he became a Marshal of the Soviet Union and for a short while after Stalin's death in 1953 he was a member of the COLLECTIVE LEADERSHIP. In the struggle for power that followed, B. was defeated, arrested and shot in June 1953. His liquidation was partly meant to transform the entrenched terrorist *NKVD* into a more moderate state security organization.

Berlin The German capital up to May 1945, since then divided into East and West Berlin, reflecting the political division of Germany and the East-West conflict. From June 1945 to June 1948 the authority over B. was vested in the Allied *Kommandantura*, consisting of the generals commanding the city's 4 zones occupied by France, the UK, the USA and the USSR. After the BERLIN BLOCKADE and the BERLIN AIRLIFT, the USSR withdrew from the *Kommandantura* in June 1949, ending the four-power joint government of the city. After the creation of the GERMAN DR in Sep. 1949, East B. was made its capital (Oct. 1949), whilst West B. was given a special favoured status by the FR of Germany (Oct. 1950) against Soviet and East German opposition. The division of B. into the 2 sectors was further reinforced physically by the construction of the BERLIN WALL by the German DR in Aug. 1961.

Berlin Airlift A massive air transport operation between West Germany and West Berlin maintained by the US forces stationed in West Germany, from March to June 1949 to counteract the Soviet BERLIN BLOCKADE. The B.A. proved successful from the Western powers' standpoint and reflected the US CONTAINMENT POLICY.

Berlin Blockade An embargo placed by the Soviet occupation authorities in East Germany on the surface supply lines from

West Germany to West Berlin between March 1948 and June 1949. The B.B. was the Soviet reaction against Western policies on the German question, in particular the currency reform initiated by the Western allies in West Germany. In June 1948, the Soviets also boycotted the joint military administrative command (*Kommandantura*), established by the 4 occupying powers in June 1945, refusing co-operation in the joint administration of Berlin. The B.B. was frustrated by the BERLIN AIRLIFT. Following the B.B., in Sep. 1949 the Eastern and Western occupational zones of Germany were formed into separate sovereign states, viz. the GERMAN DR and the Federal Republic of Germany, whilst West Berlin was given a special status.

Berlinguer, Enrico (1922–) The leader of the ITALIAN COMMUNIST PARTY. He joined the Party in 1944 and became a member of the Central Committee in the following year and its Secretary-General in 1972. He was also active in the Communist youth movement and from 1950 to 1953 was Chairman of the WORLD FEDERATION OF DEMOCRATIC YOUTH. Since 1968 he has been a member of the Chamber of Deputies in the Italian Parliament and since the mid-1970s one of the most prominent advocates of EUROCOMMUNISM.

Berlin International A colloquial name for the anarcho-syndicalist INTERNATIONAL WORKERS' ASSOCIATION established in Berlin in 1922.

Berlin Method An experimental basis for financial accounting in joint ventures established by the member countries of the Council for Mutual Economic Assistance from 1964 to 1973. It involved agreed procedures for calculating investment costs, current material costs, wages, the distribution of profits and the like. The B.M. aimed at overcoming the problem of the incomparability of prices and unrealistic exchange rates in evaluating each member's contribution to the joint ven-

ture and the consequent entitlement to profits. In 1973 the B.M. was replaced by the VARNA METHODOLOGY.

Berlin Riots Spontaneous unrest in East Berlin lasting 5 days in June 1953 amongst the workers who tried to organize a general strike in protest against oppressive living and working conditions. The riots were swiftly crushed by the East German police and Soviet tanks.

Berlin Wall A stone wall about 3m high constructed by the Communist regime in the GERMAN DR in August 1961 to prevent the escape of East Germans to the West. (Over the period May 1945 to Aug. 1961, 3.7m. persons escaped to the West, threatening a depopulation of the GDR.) The Wall separates the eastern and western sectors of Berlin and it has come to be identified with the most visible and striking evidence of the IRON CURTAIN.

Bern International An international organization founded 3–10 Feb. 1919 at a conference held in Bern, Switzerland by the leaders of the Social-Democratic parties of Argentina, Austria, Bulgaria, Czechoslovakia, Denmark, Finland, France, Germany, Great Britain, Hungary, Italy, the Netherlands, Palestine, Sweden and Switzerland (other countries joined later). It was opposed to the COMINTERN, rejected the postulate of the DICTATORSHIP OF THE PROLETARIAT, favoured democracy and attempted to revive the SECOND INTERNATIONAL. In the eyes of the Comintern, the B.I. represented CENTRISM, OPPORTUNISM and SOCIAL CHAUVINISM. The B.I. held 3 conferences – in Amsterdam (April 1919), Lucerne (Aug. 1919) and Geneva (July–Aug. 1920). Amongst its best known leaders were E. BERNSTEIN and K. KAUTSKY. In Feb. 1921 several European Social-Democratic and Socialist parties created the VIENNA INTERNATIONAL or the SECOND-AND-A-HALF INTERNATIONAL. In May 1923 the B.I. and the Vienna International merged to form the LABOUR AND SOCIALIST INTERNATIONAL.

Bernstein, Eduard (1850–1932) A notable German Socialist and Social-Democratic leader who in his later years turned to evolutionary as opposed to revolutionary socialism. For some years he co-operated with Engels and Kautsky in editing Marx's *Capital*, vol. III, which appeared in 1895. But after Engels' death in the same year, B. repudiated Marxism, in particular its postulate of the CLASS STRUGGLE, the law of the increasing IMMISERATION OF THE WORKING CLASS, the assumption of the inevitability of the BREAKDOWN OF CAPITALISM, the need for a violent PROLETARIAN REVOLUTION and the necessity for the DICTATORSHIP OF THE PROLETARIAT. Instead (especially in *Evolutionary Socialism*, 1899), he advocated a peaceful transition to socialism through gradual reforms initiated by legislation within the framework of the existing system. He predicted that in the event of a proletarian revolution, workers would be unable to govern and would fall prey to dictatorship (which actually happened after the Bolshevik Revolution). Revolutionary Marxists have bitterly attacked B. as the architect of REVISIONISM and OPPORTUNISM. In philosophy, B. was criticized for opposing DIALECTICAL MATERIALISM.

Beveridge Report A comprehensive scheme for social security in Britain prepared by Sir William Beveridge (1879–1963), a British economist, in a document entitled *Report on Social Insurance and Allied Services*, 1942. The scheme sought to remove the causes of poverty 'from the cradle to the grave', largely by a system of national insurance. After the war, the B.R. was used as a basis for far-reaching social security legislation implemented by the Labour Party when it was in power, 1945–50.

Big Bourgeoisie A Marxist term for the upper stratum of the BOURGEOISIE, i.e. those capitalists who own or control large industrial, mining, trading or transport companies, or banks, especially if they constitute MONOPOLIES. B.b. contrasts with PETTY BOURGEOISIE.

Big Brother A concept popularized by George Orwell in his book *1984*, published in 1949. It has come to be identified with the omnipotent and ubiquitous State, especially in the Socialist countries ruled by the Communist parties under the mono-party system of government. The designation is also used in Eastern Europe to allude to the USSR and in the Asian Socialist countries to China.

Big-character Poster (*Tatzu Pao*, in Chinese) Wall poster with prominent letters which can be either handwritten or printed, peculiar to China since the late 1950s. It became a major medium of propaganda first during the 'HUNDRED FLOWERS' INTERLUDE in 1957. The posters proved so effective that the authorities officially adopted them and government offices were instructed to set up special units to prepare them. During the GREAT PROLETARIAN CULTURAL REVOLUTION Mao Tse-tung extolled the b.-ch.p. as a powerful weapon. It was embraced to great effect by the RED GUARDS and CH'EN PO-TA described it as a 'spark igniting the popular movement'. The importance of b.-ch.p. in China's life is reflected in the fact that the 1975 Constitution, under Article 13, guarantees the freedom of expression via this medium. Thus these posters can be put up by individuals to air their private grievances (e.g. against neighbours) or (especially since 1978) by dissidents demanding human rights.

Bilateral Clearing A system of payments between two countries, whereby settlements are effected not by means of a convertible currency but through central institutions in the partner countries (usually central banks). Such an institution makes payments to domestic creditors in domestic currency out of earnings from the partner country. The condition of a satisfactory operation is that the value of the partner countries' deliveries to each other is balanced over an agreed period (usually a year). Interest-free SWING CREDITS provide for temporary imbalances. If there is an outstanding imbalance at the end of the period, it may be settled in gold, convertible currencies, additional deliveries or be transferred to the next clearing period.

Bilateral Justice A phrase sometimes used in support of BILATERAL TRADE. The Socialist countries favour this basis of trade settlement, as it does not leave either partner country with trade surpluses or deficits thus minimizing NON-EQUIVALENT EXCHANGE. At the same time, some Western countries have been unwilling to let the Socialist countries earn trade surpluses for fear of such surpluses being spent in other countries, hoarded, or used for anti-Western economic aid to the Third World.

Bilateral Trade A basis of settling a payment in foreign trade where a country endeavours to balance its export and import in relation to each partner country separately. This may occur when at least one of the countries may not wish either to earn a trade surplus or incur a trade deficit with the partner concerned. The precise form of the settlement is usually prescribed in a bilateral trade and payment agreement. An extreme case of bilateral settlement is a barter transaction, where a certain quantity of goods is exchanged for an agreed quantity of other goods, involving no currency – either as a medium of exchange or as a unit of account. B.t. has been widely practised by the Socialist centrally planned economies with capitalist countries, especially those of the THIRD WORLD. B.t. was first pursued by Western countries in the 1930s (but virtually abandoned after 1958) and by many less-developed countries after W.W.II. In the late 1970s, in addition to the 25 or so SOCIALIST COUNTRIES, there were 30 other nations which had BILATERAL TRADE AGREEMENTS in force.

Bilateral Trade Agreement An agreement between two countries usually concluded for 2–6 years, designed to balance the value of their mutual export and import over annual periods. It typically specifies the overall value of trade, classes of goods, methods of payment, the application of tariffs, the exchange of trade missions and the arbitration of trade disputes. It is a characteristic feature of the Socialist countries' foreign trade amongst themselves and (to a lesser extent) with other nations. A b.t.a. concluded with another Socialist country is quite detailed with definite export and import commitments on each side. But if signed with a capitalist partner, the agreement is less prescriptive, amounting to intentions rather than firm undertakings. Although in many cases a b.t.a. stipulates the bilateral balancing of trade (in value, exports to match imports over a particular period), this condition is no longer strictly observed, especially with capitalist countries. Trade may also be carried on between the two partner countries outside the b.t.a.

Birch Society An anti-communist fraternity in the USA, founded by R. H. W. Welch, Jr. after W.W.II. The Society was named after a Baptist missionary killed by communists in China in 1945. It was quite active in the 1950s and 1960s, mainly through publicizing real or alleged pro-communist sympathies amongst persons in positions of influence. The B.S. aroused considerable adverse public opinion. It has been accused of fascism and unnecessary witch-hunting, and, since the mid-1960s, has lost much of its former influence.

'Birthmarks of the Old Society' A phrase originally used by Marx in the CRITIQUE OF THE GOTHA PROGRAMME (1875) to describe the surviving features of capitalism that would initially exist after the PROLETARIAN REVOLUTION. Marx justified the changeover from capitalism to communism via a transitional period which he designated as SOCIALISM – a new 'society which emerges out of the womb of capitalism and which in every respect bears the birthmarks of the old society'. He regarded capitalism as a necessary historical SOCIO-ECONOMIC FORMATION from which communism can evolve.

BKP Abbreviation for *Bulgarska Kommunisticheska Partiya*, meaning the BULGARIAN COMMUNIST PARTY.

Black Bourgeoisie A satirical and disparaging description used in the USA for the well-to-do blacks in business and the professions who are indifferent to, or critical of, their poor, underprivileged and militant racial fellowmen. The b.b. numbers about 2m., or less than 10 per cent of the black population in the USA. The designation is derived from a book under that title written in 1955 by E. F. Frazier (1894–1962), a black American sociologist.

Black Capitalism A concept popularized in the USA in the 1960s to describe the desire and trend amongst a section of the blacks to acquire capital in its various forms, rather than to engage in militant and destructive activities. The advocates of b.c. see it as a means of raising the economic and social position of the blacks through the control of the means of production and mutual assistance and patronage. Sometimes the concept is used with respect to the BLACK BOURGEOISIE.

Black Congress A critical Bolshevik description of a conference organized by right-wing interests (landlords, industrialists and Orthodox churchmen) held in Moscow from 12 to 14 Oct. 1917 (O.S.C.) to work out a common strategy against the BOLSHEVIKS who were becoming increasingly militant and successful. However, the Congress achieved little, as the Bolsheviks speeded up their operations and seized power 11 days later in the GREAT OCTOBER SOCIALIST REVOLUTION.

Black International A colloquial term sometimes used for the Roman Catholic Church. The designation appeared first in the 1860s when the INTERNATIONAL WORKINGMEN'S ASSOCIATION (the First International) was being organized and founded. Also GREEN INTERNATIONAL, RED INTERNATIONAL, YELLOW INTERNATIONAL.

Blackleg A disparaging name applied to a worker who returns to work before the strike or some other industrial dispute is over. This word can also be used as a verb, to describe the practice of working for a master whose workers are on strike.

'Black Line in Education' A charge officially levelled in China during the GREAT PROLETARIAN CULTURAL REVOLUTION against 'right-wing' educational management and practices. It was claimed that certain opportunist elements opposing Mao Tse-tung laid greater emphasis on the acquisition of competence than on the correct ideological line and that students of poorer social backgrounds were being discriminated against.

Blacklist A term used in industrial relations to denote the practice of proscribing a trade union, a firm or a person as a retaliatory or bargaining weapon. This technique can be resorted to either by an employer or a labour organization.

'Black Thursday' The peak day of the POZNAN RIOTS in Poland, reached on Thursday, 28 June 1956.

Blagoyev Group A Marxist political party in Russia in existence from 1883 to 1887. It was organized by a Bulgarian student, D. Blagoyev (1856–1924) in St. Petersburg (now Leningrad), which he at first called the 'Party of the Russian Social-Democrats'. The Group soon established 15 similar circles for the study of Marxism in the main cities of Russia. In 1885 it established the first Social-Democratic workers' magazine in Russia, called *Rabochy (The Worker)*, of which only 2 issues appeared. The B.G. was subjected to repression by the Tsarist police and broke up in 1887. It gave rise to the RUSSIAN SOCIAL-DEMOCRATIC LABOUR PARTY. Also *TESNYAKS*.

Blanc, Jean J. C. Louis (1811–82) A French social worker, revolutionary, socialist political leader and thinker. He advocated a gradual social transformation mainly through the creation and development of 'National Workshops' aided by the state. He further proposed to replace competition by production and marketing co-operation (in *The Organization of Labour*, 1839). His support of republicanism and criticism of the monarchy (in *History of the Ten Years*, 1841) exerted a great influence in France. B. was a member of the provisional government established in France during the Revolution of Feb. 1848, but in 1870 he opposed the PARIS COMMUNE. Marxists have attacked B. for his assumption of class co-operation (as opposed to class struggle), the paternalistic role of the state and his PETTY BOURGEOIS politics.

Blanqui, Louis Auguste (1805–81) A French revolutionary whose writings on and leadership in insurrections provided a driving force for the radical socialist movement. For his activities, he spent more than 33 years in 30 gaols and became a symbol of martyrdom for the revolutionary cause. He advocated a revolution by a small body of devoted enthusiasts, a short period of dictatorship to subdue the capitalists and to carry out the socialization of industry and services and the establishment of agricultural co-operatives. Marx borrowed some ideas from B. such as the CLASS STRUGGLE, the PROLETARIAN REVOLUTION and the DICTATORSHIP OF THE PROLETARIAT, but rejected others, especially B.'s disregard of the participation by the broad masses. Also BLANQUISM.

Blanquism A school of thought in the socialist movement which originated in France in the mid-19th c. directed towards a revolutionary seizure of power by a small secret elite, consisting of devoted and disciplined intellectuals. The term is derived from L. A. BLANQUI, who led such a group hoping to seize power on behalf of the working class, but without success. Although Marxists took a good deal of interest in B., in general they rejected it, regarding it as too utopian (UTOPIAN SOCIALISM), too elitist, and not broadly

based on the masses. In their view, B. was destined to failure, even if the minority succeeded in overthrowing the existing government.

Blat A slang Russian word for 'pusher' or 'corrupt villain', more specifically denoting a person who illegally engages in the acquisition of scarce commodities in the black market in the USSR. A *b.* can be a private individual engaging in this sort of operation for his own benefit, or a manager of a socialized enterprise seeking to secure urgently needed materials which have not been allocated or delivered to the enterprise. In the latter case, although acting illegally, the *b.* may perform a useful social function. Also *TOLKACH*.

Blonsky, Pavel Petrovich (1884–1941) A Russian educational psychologist and philospher and a founder of the Soviet theory of education. He developed various principles of proletarian education, including the concept of the 'people's labour school' (in *Labour School*, 1919). His ideas influenced the Soviet educational system up to the early 1930s, but then he fell into disgrace.

Bloody Sunday Sunday, 9 Jan. 1905, when a procession of about 150,000 workers in St. Petersburg (now Leningrad) were attacked by police and Cossacks, killing 1,000 and wounding 5,000. The procession, organized by an ambitious priest G. GAPON, was peaceful and a petition was to be presented to the Tsar in the Winter Palace for various reforms. On orders from the Tsar or a minister, the marchers were fired upon by soldiers and cut down by Cossack sabres. The event sparked off the REVOLUTION OF 1905–07. It was later reported by communists that Gapon was a paid agent of the Tsarist police and was instructed to organize the procession as an act of provocation. He was later hanged by the SOCIALIST REVOLUTIONARIES.

B.O.A.L. The English abbreviation of the 'BASIC ORGANIZATION OF ASSOCIATED

44

LABOUR' in Yugoslavia, corresponding to the Serbo-Croat *OOUR* (*Osnovna Organizacija Udruženog Rada*).

Board of Honour A notice board commonly found in the Socialist countries in factories, institutions and farms on which production or other achievements of exemplary workers are publicized. This practice reflects the weakness of material motivation amongst workers and is meant to stimulate interest in maximum performance. Also MORAL INCENTIVES.

Bogdanov, Aleksander Aleksandrovich (1873–1928) A medical man by profession whose original name was A. A. Malinovsky, but who achieved considerable distinction in philosophy and in social, political and cultural work in Russia and abroad. A member of the RUSSIAN SOCIAL-DEMOCRATIC LABOUR PARTY (after 1896), for a time he was associated with the BOLSHEVIKS. But after 1905 he turned to the MENSHEVIKS and a selective REVISIONISM of Marxism. He was one of the organizers of the anti-Bolshevik association and the founder of a school of philosophy, EMPIRIO-MONISM (in *Empirio-Monism*, 1905–06). He was also a creative thinker in the field of organization theory ('organizational dialectic' (in *Tectology*, 1922), which he based on a harmony between society and nature, and not on the class struggle. He wrote a widely studied textbook on Marxian economics (*A Course of Political Economy*, 1910) and contributed significantly to the theory of proletarian culture. B. died after a self-imposed experimental blood transfusion in the Institute for Blood Transfusion, which he had established himself (the first in the world). B. was attacked as a philosophical idealist, revisionist and an anti-Soviet reactionary by Lenin (in *MATERIALISM AND EMPIRIO-CRITICISM*) and by Stalin (in *ECONOMIC PROBLEMS OF SOCIALISM IN THE USSR*). Also BOGDANOVISM.

Bogdanovism A name given to a school of thought in Russia initiated by A. A. BOG-

DANOV concerned with a revision of Marxism. It had many Russian and then Soviet adherents in the first 3 decades of this century. Its objective was to strengthen Marxism by removing some of its inconsistencies and adapting it to modern realities, especially in the fields of aesthetics, education, epistemology, ethics, historiography, logic and sociology. B. was attacked by Lenin and later by Stalin and was officially proscribed by the Soviet regime as REVISIONISM.

Bolivian Communist Party See COMMUNIST PARTY OF BOLIVIA.

Bolshevik The name of the theoretical journal of the Central Committee of the 'Russian Communist Party (of the Bolsheviks)' from 1924 to 1925 and of the 'All-Union Communist Party (of the Bolsheviks)' from 1925 to 1952. Since 1952 the journal has appeared under the title of *KOMMUNIST*.

Bolshevik Revolution A shortened version of the GREAT OCTOBER SOCIALIST REVOLUTION.

Bolsheviks ('Majoritarians', in Russian) A name given to a group of revolutionary Marxists in Russia and for a time in the Soviet Union. The B. emerged from a split in the RUSSIAN SOCIAL-DEMOCRATIC LABOUR PARTY at its Second Congress, on the revolutionary strategy, held in London in 1903. The faction, led by LENIN, advocated an uncompromising course and a violent overthrow of the Tsarist regime by a tightly organized and disciplined revolutionary party, basing its support on the union of workers and peasants. The other faction, led by MARTOV, stood for a gradual evolution by moderate means. The former faction received a majority of votes and became known as the B. (whilst the latter became the MENSHEVIKS), but both remained Marxist. In 1912 the B. established themselves as a separate party – the 'Russian Social-Democratic Labour Party (of the Bolsheviks)'. They overthrew the PROVISIONAL GOVERNMENT of

Kerensky in the GREAT OCTOBER SOCIAL-IST REVOLUTION, also known as the Bolshevik Revolution, with astonishing ease. Although in the CONSTITUENT ASSEMBLY (elected a month after the Revolution) the B. were in a minority with only 25 per cent of the votes, they retained power and in 4 years eliminated all the other parties. The name B. was officially retained until 1952, but it was dropped in that year when the official name of the party was changed to the COMMUNIST PARTY OF THE SOVIET UNION.

Bolshevism A version of Marxism developed by the BOLSHEVIKS, initially under the leadership of LENIN, and hence also called (especially by Stalin) 'Leninism'. The term B. was adopted by Lenin in 1909, although it had been vaguely used for several years before. B. attaches critical importance to the following aspects of the theory and practice of Marxism: the CLASS STRUGGLE; the need for a small tightly and hierarchically organized disciplined party led by professional revolutionaries; the necessity of overthrowing the bourgeois regime in a violent PROLETARIAN REVOLUTION; and, after the seizure of power, the DICTATORSHIP OF THE PROLETARIAT exercised by the Communist party organized on the basis of DEMOCRATIC CENTRALISM. B. may also mean left-wing ideological and political totalitarianism, or the principles, policies and practices followed by the Soviet regime.

Bolshevization A less frequently used term now for SOVIETIZATION.

'Bombard the Headquarters' A slogan in China which initiated the attack by the RED GUARDS against the allegedly conservative or entrenched top Party and Government bureaucracy inc nvenient to Mao Tse-tung during the GREAT PROLETARIAN CULTURAL REVOLUTION. The slogan was written by Mao as a BIG-CHARACTER POSTER and displayed in Peking on 5 Aug. 1966, and subsequently in other parts of China. It was implicitly directed against LIU SHAO-CH'I, Chairman of the Government and Vice-Chairman of the Chinese Communist Party at the time.

Bonus Incentive payment made to individual, or groups of, workers and management in money or kind to promote achievement and over-fulfilment of targets and efficiency. In the European Socialist countries (except Albania), b. funds are derived from enterprise profits, but in China they are earmarked portions of the wage funds. In general a b. represents from 10 to 25 per cent of the base wage or salary.

Booty Capitalism A term used by Max Weber (1864–1920) in his most famous work, *The Protestant Ethic and the Spirit of Capitalism* (1904). It denotes the type of capitalism where wealth was acquired by the financing of wars and the expectation of booty or reparations.

Borba (*Struggle*, in Serbo-Croat) The daily organ of the SOCIALIST ALLIANCE OF THE WORKING PEOPLE OF YUGOSLAVIA. The paper was founded in Feb. 1922 and up to 1952 was the organ of the Communist Party of Yugoslavia and from 1952 to 1954 the organ of the LEAGUE OF COMMUNISTS OF YUGOSLAVIA. Its daily circulation in the late 1970s was 90,000.

Border Areas During the Sino-Japanese War 1937–45, the parts of China which were designated as Communist spheres of influence, as agreed between the CHINESE COMMUNIST PARTY and the KUOMINTANG (previously called 'Special Areas'). The first B.A. so established was the Shen-Kan-Ning B.A., in north-central China. Later more were organized in the north of China and south of the Yellow River. B.A. were distinct from 'Guerrilla Areas', which were completely controlled by the Chinese C.P. The B.A. became not only military springboards for fighting the Japanese armies, but also revolutionary bases in which Communist 'governments' were set up issuing their own currency known as 'Border Currency', 'Border

Notes' or occasionally 'Resistance Currency'. At the end of W.W.II (August 1945) there were 18 Communist governments in the B.A. of various sizes, with 1,200,000 Party Members, 900,000 members of the regular forces and a 2,500,000-strong militia.

'Boring from Within' See ENTRYISM, INTERNATIONAL COMMUNIST FRONT ORGANIZATIONS, POPULAR FRONT.

Borodin, Mikhail Markovich (1884–1951) (original name: M. M. Gruzenberg) A Russian of Jewish descent who distinguished himself in the Russian and international Communist movement. Originally in the Jewish Bund, he transferred his loyalty to the Bolsheviks in 1903. In addition to Russia, he operated in Britain, China, Mexico and the USA. He helped organize the SOCIALIST PARTY OF AMERICA (in 1908) whose left-wing later (in 1919) became the Communist Party of the USA. From 1919 to 1923 he worked as an agent in the COMINTERN and then (1923–27), at the invitation of Sun Yat-sen, acted as the chief political adviser to the Central Executive Committee of the KUOMINTANG in China. His work there was viewed by Stalin as a failure owing to the massacre of the Communist allies by Chiang Kai-shek. After his return to the USSR, B. was demoted several times. He was finally arrested in 1949 in Stalin's anti-semitic drive on the basis of false evidence and died in a Siberian forced labour camp in 1951. After Stalin's death (1953) he was rehabilitated in 1956.

Bottleneck An obstacle critically impeding the planned flow of production. It may be caused by unfulfilled deliveries of indispensable materials or equipment to the enterprise concerned, the shortage of a particular type of skilled labour, unavailability of the relevant technical knowledge and other unexpected changes in the circumstances. The occurrence of a b. is typical of Socialist centrally planned economies, noted for TIGHT PLANNING, the lack of flexibility consequent upon centralized and HIERARCHICAL PLANNING AND MANAGEMENT, and the SELLERS' MARKET.

Bourgeois A Marxist term with a contemptuous connotation, meaning pertaining to, or a member of, the BOURGEOISIE. It also denotes the supporting of the capitalist system and explicitly or implicitly being opposed to socialism and communism.

Bourgeois Democracy A Marxist concept for imperfect democracy under capitalism serving the interests of the BOURGEOISIE, but detrimental to the proletariat. The concept was most thoroughly discussed by Lenin (in *THE STATE AND REVOLUTION* and *The Proletarian Revolution and The Renegade Kautsky*, 1918) who highlighted the following features of b.d.: parliamentary institutions; a multi-party system; free elections based on extended suffrage and the freedom of press and association. Although Lenin recognized these features as improvements over feudalism and aristocratic rule, he pointed out that they essentially were concessions to the liberal section of the bourgeoisie and were of little benefit to the masses. Whilst there may be political democracy for the capitalists there is no substantive democracy for the proletariat and no economic democracy. Marxists in fact denounce such concessions as being inadequate, on the one hand, and a postponement of the PROLETARIAN REVOLUTION, on the other. B. d. contrasts with PEOPLE'S DEMOCRACY.

Bourgeois-democratic Revolution Revolution essentially led by bourgeois interests against feudal or imperialist oppression in order to secure more political rights or national independence. Examples are: the FRENCH REVOLUTION, 1789–99; the REVOLUTION OF 1848–49 in Western Europe, and the REVOLUTION OF 1905–07 and the FEBRUARY REVOLUTION OF 1917 in Russia. In contrast to the previous b.-d.r., those since 1848 have in most cases been noted for considerable

Bourgeoisie

participation by broader masses. However, in the Marxist view, the b.-d.r. is not brought to its logical conclusion, owing to the role of the bourgeois interests which only use the working classes against feudal or imperialist authority in order to achieve limited objectives suited to the BOURGEOISIE. Consequently, revolutionary Marxists insist (especially Lenin in *The Two Tactics of Social-democracy in the Democratic Revolution*) that the b.-d.r. is only a desirable (but not necessarily essential) prelude to the PROLETARIAN REVOLUTION. In Lenin's view the February Revolution and the GREAT OCTOBER SOCIALIST REVOLUTION in 1917 confirmed that historical law in application to Russia.

Bourgeoisie A term commonly used by Marxists to denote the wealthy ruling class in a capitalist society. The term originated in France in the late Middle Ages meaning the urban class of freemen of common birth acquiring wealth in the form of capital (not land). Marx borrowed the term from Pierre Leroux and together with F. Engels gave it a distinct ideological and social connotation (in the COMMUNIST MANIFESTO, 1848). The b. owns the means of production, employs wage labour, appropriates SURPLUS VALUE and as such, exploits the PROLETARIAT. Thus the b. includes the owners of industrial, commercial and financial capital and landowners. Marxists also distinguish between the BIG B. and the PETTY B. but in a broader sense the b. may mean all middle classes, including professions which, although not owning much capital, identify their interests with those of the capitalists. In its broadest meaning, the b. embraces all those persons who support the capitalist system for one reason or another (economic, political, social, religious) and thus are opposed to communism. However, a section of the b. (especially some intellectuals, liberal politicians, social workers and reformers) is not unsympathetic to the proletariat. Hence, the Marxists argue, its support must be cultivated by the communists as it may be of

assistance in the PROLETARIAN REVOLUTION which constitutes the last act ending the rule of the b.

Bourgeoisiefication Another term for *EMBOURGEOISEMENT*.

Bourgeois Nationalism In the Marxist view, an inevitable political feature of CAPITALISM, where chauvinistic and egoistic false PATRIOTISM is generated to suit the interests of the BOURGEOISIE to the detriment of the working classes and weaker countries. Marxists are opposed to b.n., as in their view it diverts attention from the more pressing social issues, enfeebles the CLASS STRUGGLE, leads to IMPERIALISM and international wars, and runs counter to PROLETARIAN INTERNATIONALISM.

Bourgeois Revolution A term used by Marxists with two different meanings. More commonly, it is a shortened version of the BOURGEOIS-DEMOCRATIC REVOLUTION. In its second connotation, it refers to the relentless capitalist revolutionization of the methods and organization of production in quest for profit maximization. As Marx and Engels pointed out (in the COMMUNIST MANIFESTO, 1848), 'The bourgeoisie cannot exist without constantly revolutionizing the instruments of production and thereby the relations of production, and with them the whole relations of society'. It is further held that these rapid and disruptive changes have been peculiar to capitalism since the INDUSTRIAL REVOLUTION, in contrast to the pre-capitalist SOCIO-ECONOMIC FORMATIONS, when methods of production and PRODUCTION RELATIONS remained unchanged over long periods.

Bourgeois Socialism A term of contempt sometimes used by revolutionary Marxists to describe the mild form of socialism within the framework of capitalism, B.s. results as a consequence of OPPORTUNISM and REFORMISM and is a betrayal of true Marxism. Alternatively, b.s. may mean ACADEMIC SOCIALISM or UTOPIAN

SOCIALISM, i.e. socialism as professed by intellectuals, usually of bourgeois background, who put forward idealistic but impracticable models of society and who are completely divorced from the working masses.

Boycott A weapon of industrial or political coercion completely or partly banning economic dealings with the person, firm, institution or country in question. It was originally employed in Ireland as a tactic by peasants and traders in 1880 against a Capt. Ch. Boycott, an agent of an Irish landholder. In its best known form today, b. is resorted to by organized labour as a reserve weapon in support of its demands, or is used against an employer who fails to honour an agreement or infringes upon the rights of his employees. A *primary* b. consists in the withdrawal of patronage from the employer involved and the soliciting of others to do likewise. A *secondary* b. involves a denial of the union's co-operation with any entity dealing with the employer concerned. B. has also been used as a form of political protest against the policies of a particular country or regime. This is illustrated by the pressure exerted by anti-communist elements in the USA during the COLD WAR on traders and shops handling goods imported from the Socialist countries.

Boycottists Name given to the extremist BOLSHEVIKS in Russia who pressed the Social-Democratic deputies elected to the *DUMA* in 1906 to boycott the latter. The B. believed that the participation in parliamentary work would amount to a tacit approval of the Tsarist institutions and the PARLIAMENTARY ROAD TO SOCIALISM. However at that stage, Lenin did not support their stand, preferring to utilize the legal institutions for the time being, thus the B. did not achieve their objective or command a majority following in the Bolshevik faction.

Brainwashing A form of thought control by a superior authority, using sophisticated methods designed to produce attitudes and response suited to that authority. This technique may include talks, group discussions, films, intimidation, flattery, psychological conditioning through diet, fatigue and loneliness and various forms of cruelty. The term was popularized in the USA in the early 1960s as a consequence of the success of the North Korean's indoctrination of American prisoners of war and persuading them to 'confess' to various crimes, including atrocities, BACTERIOLOGICAL WARFARE and the repudiation of their own country. The term has also been applied retrospectively to Soviet techniques applied to accused 'counter-revolutionaries' and deviationists in the MOSCOW TRIALS of the late 1930s.

Branch Associations Intermediate organs of economic management (or administration) found in most Socialist countries. B.a. exist in Czechoslovakia, the German DR, Hungary, Poland and the USSR, whilst in Romania and Bulgaria they are known as 'industrial associations' (or simply 'industrials') and 'economic associations' respectively. Each association embraces enterprises and combines in the same or several related branches of industry. They exercise authority over member entities and have their own funds. Their importance has increased since the ECONOMIC REFORMS resulted in the decentralization of operational responsibilities which previously had been in the hands of state planning commissions and economic ministries. The main tasks of the associations include the co-ordination of activities of the associated enterprises, the implementation of the plans along the most effective lines and the speeding up of innovations.

Brazilian Communist Party (*Partido Communista Brasileiro*) The oldest and principal Communist party in Brazil, originally founded in 1922 as the Communist Party of Brazil. By 1947 it had 150,000 members. In the late 1950s dissenting factions began to emerge, the Party was reorganized and in 1960 assumed its present name. With the exception of short interludes in the 1920s and 1945–47, its operation has been completely banned or restricted. Its membership in 1978 was estimated at 4,000 (when the total population was 115m.). In 1961, pro-Chinese dissidents recreated the C.P. of B. which now has about 1,000 members. There are also other small Communist groups, namely: the Workers' Revolutionary Party (Trotskyite); the Workers' Communist Party (supporting guerrilla activities); the Marxist-Leninist Popular Action Party (organized along traditional Soviet lines); the Revolutionary Brazilian Communist Party; and the Palmares Armed Revolutionary Vanguard. All the Communist parties and groups in Brazil have been proscribed since 1964 whilst their leaders carry on their activities from abroad.

Brazilian Democratic Movement Officially amalgamated opposition front in Brazil. It advocates socialism, mostly in the form of state intervention and the nationalization of key enterprises and is opposed to foreign capital in Brazlian industries. It is nationalistic and on the whole anti-revolutionary.

Breakdown-of-Capitalism Thesis One of the central propositions put forward by Marx in his interpretation of the weaknesses of CAPITALISM and the historical progression to socialism and communism. In his view, there is an inexorable tendency in the capitalist society for: 1. the elimination of smaller firms and craftsmen; 2. the increasing size of MONOPOLIES; 3. the increasing CONCENTRATION AND CENTRALIZATION OF CAPITAL AND PRODUCTION; 4. the increasing RESERVE ARMY OF WORKERS; 5. the increasing severity of crises; 6. the increasing IMMISERATION OF THE PROLETARIAT; 7. the DECLINING PROFIT RATE; and 8. the growth of class antagonisms and other social contradictions in general. These questions were widely debated by Marxists of various shades, particularly in the last two decades before W.W.I. However, some revisionists and moderate Marxists, such as BERNSTEIN

and KAUTSKY, concluded that capitalism would not necessarily lend itself to a clear breakdown. It may be further added that capitalism lends itself to improvements through the growing power of the industrial and political labour movement, reforms and state intervention. Experience over the last century has confirmed some of Marx's tenets (1-4) but not others (5-8).

Brentano, Lujo (1884–1931) A German economist noted for his support of the PARLIAMENTARY ROAD TO SOCIALISM. He came to be regarded by Marxists as one of the most capable representatives of ACADEMIC SOCIALISM. Although he used Marxist terminology, he rejected the Marxian postulate of the CLASS STRUGGLE and instead advocated the organization of reformist trade unions. He also urged far-reaching industrial and social legislation, believing that social justice and harmony could be attained within the framework of capitalism.

Brest-Litovsk Treaty Peace treaty concluded on 3 March 1918 between Soviet Russia on the one hand and Germany, Austro-Hungary, Bulgaria, Turkey and the Ukrainian Republic on the other. The Treaty was negotiated on the initiative of Lenin and Trotsky and was signed on the Soviet side by G. V. Chicherin, the first Soviet Commissar (Minister) for Foreign Affairs. Very harsh conditions were imposed on the Soviet Government which was neither in a position to carry on the war nor believed in its continuation due to its imperialistic nature. The Treaty, which consisted of 14 Articles with Appendices, ceded Poland, the Baltic lands and large portions of Byelorussia and the Ukraine to Germany and Austro-Hungary. The signing of the Treaty evoked strong opposition in Soviet Russia, in particular from the LEFT SOCIALIST REVOLUTIONARIES headed by BUKHARIN who pressed for the continuation of the war as a revolutionary struggle against international imperialism and as a prelude to proletarian revolutions in Western

Europe. The Treaty was repudiated by the Soviet Government on 13 Nov. 1918 after the overthrow of the monarchy in Germany.

Brezhnev, Leonid Ilyich (1906–) Secretary-General of the Communist Party of the Soviet Union, President of the PRESIDIUM OF THE SUPREME SOVIET, Chairman of the Defence Council, Marshal of the Soviet Union. Of a Ukrainian working class background, he joined the KOMSOMOL in 1923 and the Communist Party in 1931, served as a POLITRUK in the RED ARMY 1941–45 (where he reached the rank of major-general), was elected to the CENTRAL COMMITTEE OF THE CPSU in 1952 (of which he became the Secretary in 1956), became a member of the Party's Presidium (now called the Politburo) in 1957 and in 1964 replaced Khrushchev as the FIRST SECRETARY of the CC of the CPSU (which in April 1966 he changed back to the previous designation of 'Secretary-General'). An engineer by training and an outstanding organizer and administrator, with experience in agriculture, heavy industry, military production and the space programme, B. is identified with the new technocracy. In relation to Western countries, he has adopted a moderate line and has made several fruitful initiatives towards strengthening peaceful relations and limiting the ARMS RACE. But he has stressed on several occasions that the relaxation of international tension and PEACEFUL COEXISTENCE do not mean Soviet ideological reconciliation with capitalism and a renunciation of Marxism.

Brezhnev Doctrine A version of the LIMITED SOVEREIGNTY DOCTRINE applied to the Socialist countries, especially the signatories of the WARSAW PACT. The term was coined in the West, after the INVASION OF CZECHOSLOVAKIA in Aug. 1968, attributing the idea to BREZHNEV, the Soviet Party leader. At the Fifth Congress of the POLISH UNITED WORKERS' PARTY in Nov. 1968 he said (to justify the military intervention in Czechoslovakia):

'When external and internal forces hostile to socialism try to turn the development of a given Socialist country in the direction of a restoration of capitalism, when a threat arises to the cause of socialism in that country – a threat to the Socialist community of nations as a whole – this is no longer merely a problem for that nation but a question of common concern to all the Socialist countries' (*Pravda*, 13 Nov. 1968). Some Western specialists see the B.d. as a new formulation of the postulate put forward by Lenin (at the Third International) in 1919 and later insisted upon by Stalin that the first duty of Communists in any country is to protect the USSR. The term and implications of the B.d. are frowned upon in the Socialist countries, the existence of the doctrine is denied and Brezhnev himself officially refuted it (in Moscow on 7 July 1971). The Socialist view is that the B.d. is an invention of Western propaganda, especially in the USA, to justify the TRUMAN DOCTRINE.

Brigade See PRODUCTION BRIGADE.

Brigade of Communist (or Socialist) Labour A title awarded to an outstanding PRODUCTION BRIGADE or other team of workers which has excelled in production and/or social work. This award was introduced in the USSR in 1958 to promote SOCIALIST COMPETITION, and has also been adopted, with some national variations, in most other Socialist countries. In the USSR, before 1958 the title was known as 'Shock Brigade' (SHOCK WORKERS MOVEMENT) or 'Stakhanov Brigade' (STAKHANOV MOVEMENT). In making the award, in addition to work performance, innovations, the acquisition of qualifications and involvement in community work may also be taken into account. The winning brigade is usually awarded a banner on an annual basis and its members may be issued with special certificates and (if won several times) cash prizes. The award is typically administered by trade unions in co-operation with other bodies (such as the Council of Ministers, the Communist Party or a youth organization).

Brigade of Outstanding Quality A title awarded in the USSR to a PRODUCTION BRIGADE or other team of workers for outstanding achievements in the sphere of quality improvement. The award was introduced in 1949 and is administered by trade union authorities in co-operation with other related bodies. Similar awards have been introduced in other Socialist countries, especially since the economic reforms of the early 1960s.

Brigadier Name commonly given in the Socialist countries to the working foreman or the leader of a PRODUCTION BRIGADE. He is usually a highly skilled and experienced worker with an outstanding work record. His responsibilities include the distribution of work tasks in his brigade, the fulfilment of set targets and the prevention of waste.

Brinkmanship An uncompromising or even provocative stand in foreign policy, implicitly or explicitly threatening a resort to devastating war, but stopping short of military action at the verge of the conflict. B. became one of the weapons of the COLD WAR. The term was established in the USA in the late 1950s and popularized by John Foster Dulles (the Secretary of State in the Eisenhower administration) when he publicly conceded in 1956 that the USA had been deliberately pursuing b. in her efforts to stem the expansion of communism. The best example of b. is provided by the US handling of the CUBAN MISSILE CRISIS in Oct. 1962, when President J. F. Kennedy declared a blockade of Cuba and threatened military action against Soviet involvement.

British Labour Party See LABOUR PARTY.

Bronstein, L. D. The original family name of TROTSKY.

Brusnev Group An early Social-Democratic association, led by M. I. Brusnev (1864–1937) in Russia, which propagated Marxism amongst intellectuals and revolutionary workers from 1889 to 1892. It supported the EMANCIPATION OF LABOUR GROUP but was opposed to terror as advocated by some *NARODNIKS*. The B.G. virtually ceased to exist after most of its leaders were arrested and sent into exile in 1892.

B.S.S.D. M.R.B.M. The Russian abbreviation of *Ballistichesky Snaryad Srednei Dalnosti*, meaning 'Medium-Range Ballistic Missile'.

B.T.A. Abbreviation of *Bulgarska Telegrafna Agentsia*, meaning the 'Bulgarian Telegraphic Agency'. Originally founded in 1898, the *B.T.A.* has been transformed into the official state-owned organization for the collection and dissemination of domestic and foreign news. It has agreements with all the leading foreign news agencies in the Socialist as well as capitalist countries. It supplies news to newspapers, radio and television stations at home and abroad.

Bucharest Agreement An arrangement agreed to by the member countries of the COUNCIL FOR MUTUAL ECONOMIC ASSISTANCE at its Eighth Session in Bucharest in June 1958, concerning foreign-trade prices. The arrangement arose out of the fact that, owing to the pricing confusion and the absence of EFFICIENCY PRICES, there was no national price basis acceptable to all members in their mutual trade. The Agreement laid down that mutual-trade prices were to be based on world (capitalist) market prices, averaged over an established period (2–5 years). Such prices, 'cleansed of capitalist fluctuations', were then to be used for the negotiations of contract prices. Appropriate mark-ups to reflect cost conditions in the partner countries concerned were held stable for a number of years so as to coincide with the various five-year plans. The B.A. was in force up to the end of 1974, after which it was replaced by the MOSCOW AGREEMENT.

Bucharest Meeting A conference of delegates of the ruling Communist parties attending the Congress of the Romanian Workers' Party (renamed the 'Romanian Communist Party') in Bucharest in June 1960. The meeting bcame the first open clash between the Chinese and Soviet delegates which developed into the SINO-SOVIET DISPUTE.

Buddhism and Marxism Although the former is a religion and the latter a seemingly incompatible ideology, they approach several political, economic and social problems in similar ways. Both B. and M. are atheistic, recognize virtues in primitive communism, favour pragmatism (as distinct from idealism), strive to be mass movements of the poor, attach importance to the welfare of the masses, and condemn conventional wars. This latter point is explained in terms of greed but both allow wars for idealistic reasons. Both Buddhist monks and Communist Party members are forbidden to accumulate wealth. In the 1920s the Soviets utilized B. as a means of approaching Buddhist national groups in the USSR e.g. the Buryats, the Kalmyks, the Tuvins and the Kirghiz, with considerable success. Since 1962 some elements of M. have been grafted on to B., notably in Burma in the so-called BURMESE ROAD TO SOCIALISM. However, in the USSR after 1929, Stalin reversed the previous policy of religio-ideological assimilation. In China and the DPR of North Korea, Buddhist monasteries were expropriated and for some years the Buddhists were treated as counter-revolutionaries. Critical orthodox Marxists point out that B. and M. are incompatible in several respects, viz.: 1. B. stands for a passive acceptance of reality however socially unjust it may be; 2. B. facilitates the spread and consolidation of feudalism; 3. B. became a spiritual instrument of the subjugation of the masses by the Buddhist hierarchy; 4. B. preaches humility and benevolence to the exploiting classes; and 5. B. quietly accepts the imperialism and colonialism of the European powers.

Budget A statement of the state's revenue and expenditure for the past and the coming year. Compared with a capitalist market economy, the scope of the b. is much greater under Socialist economic planning, but at the same time it is relatively less important as an instrument of economic policy. About two-thirds (about one-half in federal countries, such as the USSR and Yugoslavia and also China) of the national income passes through the b. (if national income is brought to the Socialist basis). At the same time, the b. is subsidiary to the national ECONOMIC PLAN, of which the b. is merely a derived financial expression. The b. and the economic plan are worked out simultaneously by the Ministry of Finance and the State Planning Commission and presented to the Parliament for approval at about the same time.

Budgetary Equalization Settlements Also known as 'budgetary differentials', payments by socialized enterprises to the state budget or payments out of the state budget to the enterprises, when the same product is either bought or sold at different prices. This often occurs in the case of products entering foreign trade. Thus, if the price of the imported goods is lower than that established by the domestic sale price, the proceeds from the price differential are handed over to the state budget, but, if the reverse is the case, then the importing enterprise is paid a subsidy to compensate it for the loss on account of the lower domestic price administered by the state. B.e.s. not only insulate the domestic markets from the foreign markets, but also neutralize the effect of different price levels on enterprises. In the latter case, 'profits' made or 'losses' incurred by an enterprise, as a consequent of price differentiation administered by the state, do not affect the economic performance of the enterprise. Thus the payment of bonuses is based on the effort of the enterprise personnel, not on fortuitous circumstances beyond its control.

Budgetary Financing of Investment The provision of non-returnable and usually interest-free finance to the socialized enterprises. It was the predominant form of investment financing in the Socialist countries under the CENTRALIZED DIRECTIVE SYSTEM OF PLANNING AND MANAGEMENT, noted for detailed plans imposed from above. Although the b.f. of i. is still an important method of financing investment in the case of new enterprises and projects of key importance, SELF-FINANCING economic reforms have assumed greater importance. About one-quarter to one-third of total investment is financed from the state budget (the other two sources being bank loans and the enterprises' own funds).

'Building of Bridges' Policy A new line in US foreign policy in relation to the Socialist countries, announced by President L. B. Johnson on 23 May 1964. It involved a differential approach to the Eastern European countries, the USSR, China and Cuba, so as to encourage the SATELLITE countries to follow more independent and liberal policies. The instruments of encouragement ('bridges') were the extension of trade ties and economic aid, designed to promote national self-assertion and reforms. In spite of some popular appeal of the policy in Eastern Europe, the Communist regimes attacked it as a propaganda move and as a crude scheme for destroying the unity of the Socialist bloc. It represented another version of the KENNEDY DOCTRINE and the DULLES-EISENHOWER DOCTRINE.

Bukharin, Nikolai Ivanovich (1888–1938) An outstanding theoretician of the Bolshevik Party and a prominent political leader in the crucial formative stage of the first Socialist state. He modernized Marxism by making important contributions in the fields of philosophy, political economy, sociology and international relations. His principal works were: *Imperialism and the World Economy* (1915); *Economy of the Transitional Period* (1920); *Programme of the World Revolu-*tion (1920); *ABC of Communism* (1921); *Historical Materialism* (1925); *Road to Socialism and the Peasant-Worker Alliance* (1925); *Economic Theory of Rentiers* (1926); *Poetry, Poetics and the Problem of Poets in the USSR* (1935). He joined the Bolshevik Party in 1906 and was very active as a writer and organizer of Russian Social-Democrats in Western Europe and the USA. He played a prominent part in the Bolshevik Revolution and the consolidation of the Soviet state and economy over the period 1917–29. He was very active in the COMINTERN and became its chairman in 1925. He headed the LEFT COMMUNISTS in opposition to Lenin in 1918, and then led the RIGHT OPPOSITION against STALIN 1928–29. At first he supported Stalin against TROTSKY, but later opposed him for his treatment of the KULAKS and his neglect of the agricultural situation. After 1928 B. was stripped of all his offices, arrested in 1937, put on trial in 1938 as a right deviationist and counter-revolutionary and condemned to death and shot in the same year. Although the charge against him has been officially dropped, he still has not been rehabilitated. His ideas (BUKHARINISM) have never lost appeal to some Marxists as an alternative to Stalinism.

Bukharinism The system of Marxist precepts presented by BUKHARIN in the Soviet Union in the 1920s, especially his doctrine concerning the role of agriculture and incentives in economic development under socialism. It is opposed to extremist and adventurous domestic and international communist policies and to political intriguing and totalitarianism. Instead, it emphasizes moderation, incentives, competition, decentralization and class harmony. As a developmental strategy, B. assigns crucial importance to agriculture as a pre-condition to the development of heavy industry. To implement this Bukharin stressed that the state should pay reasonably high prices for agricultural products and then develop light industry to supply industrial products to agricultural sectors at reasonably low prices. Healthy and prosperous agriculture could then supply agricultural raw materials and provide a sufficiently high level of ACCUMULATION to forge ahead with heavy industrialization. B. was partly utilized during the NEW ECONOMIC POLICY but was abandoned by Stalin with the first Five Year Plan 1928–32. Consequently, the developmental strategy advocated by FEL'DMAN and PREOBRAZHENSKY (opposed to B.) prevailed. However, B. has found a considerable expression in Chinese economic policies at one stage or another, including Mao's ideas expressed in the TEN MAJOR RELATIONSHIPS.

Bukovsky, Vladimir (1941–) One of the best known Soviet DISSIDENTS fighting for HUMAN RIGHTS in the USSR who spent 12 years in prison for his beliefs and activities. A biologist and writer by profession, he was first imprisoned in 1963–64 in a psychiatric ward, and again from 1967 to 1970. In 1970 he appealed to the West to investigate the Soviet practice of confining dissenters in mental institutions. Consequently, he was sentenced to 7 years' imprisonment in a forced labour camp and then exiled for 5 years. In Dec. 1976 he was exchanged in Zurich for a gaoled Chilean Communist leader (Luis Corvalen) and went to live in Britain.

Bulgaria, People's Republic of (*Narodna Republika Bulgariya*) – a medium-sized country in Eastern Europe, with an area of 110,910 sq. km. and a population of 8.8m. (in 1978), and ruled by a Communist party subscribing to Marxism-Leninism. B. has been under Communist control since Sep. 1944 when the Soviet Army entered the country. A Soviet-type constitution was adopted in Dec. 1947, which was replaced in May 1971. The supreme organ of state power is a single-chamber NATIONAL ASSEMBLY of 400 deputies which is elected every five years from a single list of the FATHERLAND FRONT by universal suffrage. Effective power is concentrated in the Politburo of the BULGARIAN COMMUNIST PARTY, headed by its

First Secretary, T. Zhivkov. B. is a foundation member of the COUNCIL FOR MUTUAL ECONOMIC ASSISTANCE and the WARSAW PACT, and has been the most consistent supporter of the USSR.

Bulgarian Communist Party (*Bulgarska Kommunisticheska Partiya*) – the ruling party in Bulgaria subscribing to MARXISM-LENINISM. It can trace its origin back to at least 1903, when the Bulgarian Workers' Social Democratic Party ('Narrow Socialists') was founded. The name B.C.P. was first officially used from 1919 to 1924, but after having been proscribed it was able to operate legally under the name of 'Workers' Party' (1927–34). It then operated illegally as the 'Bulgarian Workers' Party (Communist)' from 1934 to 1948. It came to power in Sep. 1944 with the support of the Soviet Army and the Communist-dominated FATHERLAND FRONT. By 1948 the opposition parties had been dissolved and in Aug. of that year the Social-Democratic Party was forced to amalgamate with the B.W.P.(C.) to form the B.C.P. The Party's membership as of 1976 was 789,800 comprising 9 per cent of the total population. The highest level of authority is represented by the Party Congress, held every 4–5 years, which elects a CENTRAL COMMITTEE which in turn elects a POLITBURO. At the 11th Congress held in 1976, 171 full members and 107 candidate members were elected to the CC. The latter elected a Politburo of 11 members and 4 candidate members headed by the First Secretary, T. Zhivkov. The Congress also elected a Secretariat, which carries on the Party's day-to-day work, consisting of the First Secretary, 6 Secretaries and 4 Members. The Party has always been the most loyal to the Communist Party of the Soviet Union and has consistently supported its leadership in the international Communist movement. The B.C.P.'s. mass youth organization is the 'Young Communists' League, with 1.3m. members. The Party's main regular publications are: *Rabotnichesko Delo* (*Workers' Cause*), the daily organ; *Novo Vreme* (*New Times*), the theoretical monthly journal of the CC; and *Partien Zhivot* (*Party Life*), a monthly journal dealing with Party organization and administration.

Bund Also known as the 'Jewish B.' or the 'Jewish Workers' Union', a Jewish labour and political organization, comprising worker groups in Russia, Poland and Lithuania, in existence from 1897 to 1921. It joined the RUSSIAN SOCIAL-DEMOCRATIC LABOUR PARTY in 1898, withdrew from it in 1903, but joined it again in 1906. It sided with the MENSHEVIKS and opposed the BOLSHEVIKS led by Lenin. In 1917 it supported the PROVISIONAL GOVERNMENT, but later gave qualified support to the Bolsheviks. Under pressure from the Bolsheviks the B. finally dissolved itself in 1921.

Bureau for the Co-ordination of the Chartering of Cargo Ships A cartel-like organization established by the member countries of the COUNCIL FOR MUTUAL ECONOMIC ASSISTANCE in 1963. Its head office is situated in Moscow. It carries on its work now in accordance with the 'Basic Terms for Charter Transactions Concluded amongst the CMEA Member Organizations' adopted in 1976.

Bureaucracy An over-developed and hierarchical class which carries out the policy and administrative responsibilities of public authorities and other large institutions or organizations. It is usually noted for formalistic and slow procedures, excessive preoccupation with the letter rather than the spirit of the law and regulations, indifference of the officials to individual citizens and the public interest in general. The role of b. in society is closely associated with the political, economic and social set-up in force, but it always serves the interests of the ruling class. Marx and Lenin regarded b. as a feature of the developed bourgeois society. After the Bolshevik Revolution, attempts were made to democratize it through workers' participation and 'control from below' (WORKERS' AND PEASANTS' INSPECTO-

RATES). However, experience has shown that b. becomes even more developed under socialism, mainly owing to the SOCIAL OWNERSHIP OF THE MEANS OF PRODUCTION, central economic planning, the predisposition to large organizations for the sake of the economy and the ease of control by the Party and the all-pervading state intervention. The ordinary citizen is in a weak position, as b. represents the ubiquitous and omnipotent totalitarian state. Under developed socialism a new super-bureaucratic elite emerges, known as TECHNO-BUREAUCRACY. Also CADRES, NEW CLASS, TECHNOCRACY.

Burma Communist Party A weak divided and proscribed, but militant party with its origin going back to 1939. In 1946 a split occurred in the Marxist-Leninist faction. One group called itself the 'Communist Party of Burma', popularly known as the 'Red Flag', while the group, known as the Trotsky faction, retained the old name and described itself colloquially as the 'White Flag'. After independence in 1948 both parties went underground and have been proscribed since 1953. After the mid-1960s both turned pro-Chinese in their international orientation. The combined Party membership is about 10,000 (out of the total population of 32.2m. in 1978). The B.C.P. is the larger of the two, occasionally engages in guerrilla actions and illegally operates a radio station situated across the border in China. Also, the BURMESE ROAD TO SOCIALISM.

Burma Socialist Programme Party (Lanzin Party) The only legal political party in the country, created in 1962 by the Revolutionary Council and headed by General U Ne Win. Its ideology is unique, being a conglomerate of Marxism, Buddhism, humanism, Burma nationalism and authoritarianism. It is organized along military lines, exercises tight hierarchical controls, and its 'Programme' includes the SOCIALIZATION OF THE MEANS OF PRODUCTION, CENTRAL ECONOMIC PLANNING and the democratization of social relations along pragmatic lines. In the late 1970s, it had 170,000 full members and 850,000 candidate members. The Party publishes: *Lanzin Tadin* (*Party News*), a fortnightly; *Party Affairs Journal*, a monthly; and *International Affairs Journal*, also a monthly. Also BURMESE ROAD TO SOCIALISM.

Burmese Road to Socialism A curious mixture of Marxism, Buddhism, humanism, Burmese nationalism and authoritarianism intended to speed up the cultural, social and economic development of a traditional society. Marxism was first brought to Burma in the early 1930s when a Burmese thinker, Takin Soe, preached Marxist ideas applying Buddhist terms and interpretation (BUDDHISM AND MARXISM). When U Nu came to power after W.W.II, he gave the country a quasi-socialist Constitution in 1947 and endeavoured to integrate Marxism into the lay ethics of Buddhism. But this was not acceptable to the BURMA COMMUNIST PARTY, which, owing to its militant opposition, was subsequently (in 1953) declared illegal. In 1962 a revolutionary military government came to power headed by General U Ne Win, which, to this day, has ruled the country with a mono-party system vested in the BURMA SOCIALIST PROGRAMME PARTY. During 1962–63 the government proclaimed the 'B.R. to S.', a manifesto consisting of two documents providing an ideological explanation of the new social order. In its implementation, the socialization of land, industry, transport and banking (with an emphasis on foreign-owned property) followed in 1963–64, 1968 and 1971–72, together with the adoption of economic planning. The pace of transformation into a socialist-democratic state accelerated

after 1973 when the country was declared a 'Socialist Republic', a new Constitution was adopted and the BURMA SOCIALIST PROGRAMME PARTY was declared the only legal political party.

Buy-back Agreement One of the forms of INDUSTRIAL CO-OPERATION which has become a peculiarity of East-West economic relations. The Western partner usually supplies equipment, technology or a complete industrial plant to the Eastern partner. In payment the latter makes agreed deliveries of the goods so produced to the Western partner. Thus, in effect, the Western partner 'buys back' the articles produced with its material or technical aid. The Socialist countries favour this form of arrangement, because it enables them to secure Western technology and equipment without having to pay in hard currencies. It also facilitates their entry into the hard-currency markets. In 1978 there were well over 100 such agreements in force between Western and Eastern partners. The USSR, Poland and Hungary are the most active participants in this type of arrangement.

Buyers' Market A situation in the market where the total supply of goods (and services) tends to exceed or grow faster than the total effective demand at existing prices. It is noted for a high pressure to sell, a wide range of goods and services available for sale, and good quality and commercial service. The b.m. is typical of capitalist market economies, and contrasts with the SELLERS' MARKET which prevails in Socialist centrally planned economies.

57

C

Cabet, Etienne (1788–1856) A prominent French utopian communist who was criticized by Marx for not being critical enough of the existing socio-economic environment, for not putting the proletariat in a position of ascendancy and for not advocating a proletarian revolution. His major work was *Voyage en Icarie* (1842).

Ca'canny An industrial tactic of 'go-slow' or 'invisible sabotage' resorted to by organized labour in capitalist countries, designed to keep production down to exert pressure on the employer. The term is of Scottish origin, meaning 'go cautiously', but it is also used in England and the USA.

Cadets See KADETS.

Cadres A term commonly used in the Socialist countries for ideologically reliable and trained personnel with qualities of leadership working in the Party apparatus or carrying out Party policies in other organizations. The term is derived from the French, meaning a 'frame', implying a permanent core staff, around which a complete operational unit can be developed at need. The term was originally adopted by revolutionary Marxists to denote a hard core of militant professional revolutionaries about whom broadly based revolutionary actions could be developed when an opportunity arose. The selection and training of c. is the most basic responsibility of the Communist party. Stalin said in 1935 that c. are the 'commanding staff of the Party' and that 'c. decide everything'. In a vague and broad sense, c. may include all Communist party members as well as other trained administrative personnel with secondary, vocational and tertiary education, working in any organization implementing the policies of the Communist regime.

'Cadres Decide Everything' See CADRES.

Cambodian Communist Party See KAMPUCHEAN UNITED FRONT FOR NATIONAL SALVATION.

Canadian Communist Party See COMMUNIST PARTY OF CANADA.

Capital One of the most basic concepts used by Marxists, to denote the sum of VALUE, or stored-up labour owned by CAPITALISTS enabling them to appropriate SURPLUS VALUE through the exploitation of labour. The ownership of c. is the source of the capitalists' power and the foundation of CAPITALISM. Marx described c. (in *CAPITAL*, vol. I) thus: 'Capital is dead labour, that vampire-like only lives by sucking living labour, and lives the more, the more labour it sucks ... Capital comes dripping head to foot from every pore with blood and dirt'. C. in the hands of the capitalist undergoes three phases of transformation. In the first phase, *money* c. is turned into productive c. which assumes two forms: constant c. (plant, equipment, intermediate products, raw materials) and variable c. (wage payments). During the second phase, the process of production, whilst constant c. merely 'transfers' its value to the new commodity (to the extent of its depreciation), variable c. not only transfers its value (to the extent of the wages paid) but also *creates* extra value to the extent of SURPLUS VALUE. In the third phase, *commodities* are transformed into money c. when sold, at which stage surplus value is realized and appropriated by the capitalist. Etymologically, the term c. is derived from Latin *caput* which in Roman law meant 'the principal sum of a debt' (as distinct from interest). The term was brought to England by the merchants of Lombardy during the Renaissance. In the Socialist countries, the term c. is not used in application to their economies, hence avoiding the implication of capitalism and the consequent exploitation. Instead, ACCUMULATION, investment and 'funds' (e.g. basic f., circulating f., amortization f.) are employed.

Capital Charge A regular levy imposed on socialized industry, and in some cases, on enterprises in some European Socialist countries. It is expressed as an interest rate (the percentage value of the assets in possession) payable, as a rule, quarterly to the state budget. The charge was first introduced in 1953 in Yugoslavia, then in 1964 in Bulgaria, the German DR and Hungary and, in 1966, in Czechoslovakia, Poland and the USSR. However, Bulgaria and Yugoslavia dropped it during the 1970s. Its level is 5 per cent p.a. in the German DR and 6 per cent p.a. in the remaining four countries. The purpose of the c.c. is to induce enterprises to unload unused or under-used assets and utilize those in their possession more intensively. The introduction of the c.c. amounts to an admission that capital is scarce and that it must earn a minimum capital return, indicating the macrosocial opportunity cost.

Capital: Critique of Political Economy The English title of the principal work of K. MARX, originally published in German as *DAS KAPITAL: KRITIK DER POLITISCHEN OEKONOMIE*. The first English translation of vol. I (by S. More and E. Aveling) appeared in 1887 (20 years after the German edition). Volumes II and III, translated by E. Untermann, were published in 1907 and 1909, respectively.

Capital Export In the Marxist view, an inevitable outcome of MONOPOLY CAPITALISM in search of higher profit opportunities than those available domestically. Whilst in a competitive capitalist economy the increased production capacity merely leads to the export of goods, under monopoly capitalism there are surpluses of the proceeds available for investment abroad. C.e. is prompted by four features peculiar to developed capitalism: 1. limited domestic investment opportunities in view of the insufficiency of demand caused by the IMMISERATION OF THE PROLETARIAT; 2. the DECLINING PROFIT RATE at home; 3. the craving for the additional and external creation of SURPLUS VALUE (super-normal profits); and 4. the predisposition of STATE MONOPOLY CAPITALISM to extend and consolidate the political penetration of dependent nations (IMPERIALISM). Communist leaders regard c.e., as traditionally understood, to be immoral and assert that the Socialist countries do not engage in it. Yet most of these countries have made investments both in the West and in less-developed countries in joint or wholly-owned production and marketing ventures, totalling about $1,000m.

Capitalism A social system noted for the ownership of the means of production being concentrated in the hands of private capitalists, based on the private profit motive, a well developed industrial, commercial and financial set-up, the freedom of enterprise, the operation of the market mechanism, competition, individualism and a democratic government based on multi-party politics. The term was popularized with a critical connotation by socialist thinkers of the 19th c. It was first used in French in 1839 by J. J. C. BLANC (in *Organisation du travail*) and only a decade later in German by Marx and Engels (in THE *COMMUNIST MANIFESTO*, 1848). It was first employed by an English writer, W. M. Thackeray, in 1854 (in *The Newcomes*). To Marxists, c. is a SOCIO-ECONOMIC FORMATION which evolved from decaying feudalism and is inevitably bound to be succeeded by SOCIALISM. Although, in their view, c. in its earlier stages performs a useful historical function, it degenerates into a grossly unjust system embodying 'incurable diseases' (as Stalin described them), viz.: the existence of two antagonistic social classes – the BOURGEOISIE and the PROLETARIAT; the exploitation of the latter by the former in the form of SURPLUS VALUE; the intense CLASS STRUGGLE; the unemployed RESERVE ARMY OF WORKERS and the increasing IMMISERATION OF THE PROLETARIAT. Although in Marx's view, c. 'carries the seeds of its own destruction', revolutionary Marxists insist that a PROLETARIAN REVOLUTION is necessary to accelerate the process and shorten the misery of the working class. But evolutionary Marxists hold that c. is flexible enough lending itself to improvement. Moreover, socialism can be achieved by reforms through legislation without a wasteful violent revolution. Also BOOTY C., COLONIAL C., COMMERCIAL C., FINANCE C., IMPERIALISM, INDUSTRIAL C., MONOPOLY C., PEOPLE'S C., STATE C., STATE MONOPOLY C.

'Capitalism in One Country' A phrase coined by an American political scientist, T. McCarthy (in *Ramparts*, May-June 1975) envisaging a possibility of all the countries in the world except the USA becoming socialist. The phrase alludes to Stalin's maxim, SOCIALISM IN ONE COUNTRY. In McCarthy's view, the progressive, political and economic isolation of the USA, evident in the recent past, will continue in the future. But if this continues, the USA will be transformed into a quasi-socialist country itself. He concludes that whilst 'socialism in one country' was possible and its success was historically demonstrated, 'c. in o.c.' is not feasible in the long run.

Capitalist A person who owns CAPITAL and appropriates SURPLUS VALUE (profit, rent, interest) without creating value himself. According to Marx, the c. 'possesses power, not on account of his personal qualities, but inasmuch as he is an owner of capital' (*Manuscripts of 1844*). The c. is the dominating figure in the last pre-socialist socio-economic formation, i.e. CAPITALISM. The term c. was first used in England in 1792, by A. Young.

Capitalist Accumulation See LAW OF CAPITALIST ACCUMULATION.

Capitalist Crises See CRISIS OF CAPITALIST PRODUCTION, CRISIS OF THE WORLD CAPITALIST ECONOMY, GENERAL CRISIS OF CAPITALISM.

Capitalist Division of Labour See DIVISION OF LABOUR.

Capitalist Encirclement A widely held view amongst the Soviet leaders from 1918 to 1945 that the USSR, being surrounded by hostile capitalist states, was in danger of being attacked externally and undermined internally by forces of COUNTER-REVOLUTION. The FOREIGN INTERVENTION of 1918–22, the Western gold and credit blockades against the Soviet Union in the early 1920s and the German attack in 1941 were cited as supporting evidence. The conviction of c.e. was raised by Stalin to that of a doctrine whereupon he used it as a theoretical justification for his policy of SOCIALISM IN ONE COUNTRY and for various terrorist measures. After W.W.II, the US CONTAINMENT POLICY, NATO, the BAGHDAD PACT, CENTO, SEATO and the COLD WAR were interpreted by Soviet propaganda as a continuation of the c.e.

Capitalist Mode of Production The organization and process of production involving PRODUCTION FORCES and PRODUCTION RELATIONS peculiar to CAPITALISM. According to Marxists, the c.m. of p. is noted for: 1. the private ownership of the means of production in the hands of capitalists; 2. the private profit motive; 3. the increasing use of capital; 4. the employment of hired labour by capitalists; 5. the excessive specialization of labour; 6. typically, large-scale production; 7. the ANARCHY OF PRODUCTION, caused by the operation of the market mechanism; and 8. the EXPLOITATION OF LABOUR in the form of SURPLUS VALUE. The c.m. of p. contrasts with the SOCIALIST M. OF P.

Capitalist Profit See PROFIT, CAPITALIST.

Capitalist Roader A derogatory description used in China especially during the GREAT PROLETARIAN CULTURAL REVOLUTION for right-wing Party leaders and anybody opposed to or inconvenient to left-wingers.

Capitalist Survivals Beliefs, attitudes, institutions and practices peculiar to CAPITALISM carried on after the PROLETARIAN REVOLUTION into SOCIALISM. These survivals, which are incompatible with Socialism, may include: 1. the acquisitive instinct; 2. private enterprise, including the black market; 3. the disrespect for collective property; 4. the distinction between mental and physical work; 5. distribution according to work (and not according to need); 6. nationalism; 7. economic crimes; and 8. the state as a means of oppression. Some of the capitalist characteristics cannot be immediately removed as they are 'BIRTHMARKS OF THE OLD SOCIETY'. Moreover, some are deliberately retained by the Communist regime as expedients during the TRANSITIONAL PERIOD and some are passively tolerated because of their widespread continuation, whilst others, although officially suppressed, persist illicitly or illegally. It is vaguely assumed in Marxist doctrine that as the material BASE is changed, the c.s. will completely disappear under FULL COMMUNISM.

Captains of Industry A concept used by socialists and social reformers for the key role played by big businessmen and managers in the industrialized capitalist society. The term was coined by T. Veblen (in *Absentee Ownership and Business Enterprise in Recent Times*, 1923). A parallel term of lower rank, LABOUR LIEUTENANTS, is sometimes used to describe trade union leaders.

Captive Nations A description given to the East European nations (Bulgaria, Czechoslovakia, Estonia, Hungary, Latvia, Lithuania, Poland and Romania) which were brought under the control of Communist regimes with the political and military support of the USSR after 1939. Although these countries have retained their national identities and boundaries, their sovereignty is limited. This is the case owing to the military power, political importance and idelogical leadership of the USSR. The suppression of the HUNGARIAN UPRISING and the INVASION OF CZECHOSLOVAKIA support this fact. Also BREZHNEV DOCTRINE.

Careerism A term used by revolutionary Marxists in application to persons belonging to left-wing political parties subordinating party and social interests to their own ambitions and cravings. C. is considered 'calculated OPPORTUNISM' and generally results in disciplinary action being taken against careerists. Purging from the party ranks is the usual course of action.

Carrillo, Santiago (1915–) The Spanish Communist leader and one of the most forceful exponents of EUROCOMMUNISM. A journalist by profession, he made his name first during the SPANISH CIVIL WAR when in 1936 he succeeded in uniting the Socialist and Communist youth movements in Spain. He became the Secretary-General of the illegal COMMUNIST PARTY OF SPAIN in 1960 operating from Paris. He was released from detention in Dec. 1976 and in the following April, the C.P.S. was legalized. In July of the same year he was elected a deputy to the lower house of parliament. C. has established a reputation for a moderate brand of communism, rejecting the need for a violent proletarian revolution and the dictatorship of the proletariat. He holds that capitalism can be transformed into a socialist society by democratic, parliamentary means. His best known book, *Eurocommunism and the State* (1977) has become a bestseller. But in the same book he also warns against 'salvaging the decadent imperialist

capitalism' and advocates its speedy liqui-
dation. In 1968 he condemned the INVA-
SION OF CZECHOSLOVAKIA by the Warsaw
Pact countries. C. has been attacked by
the ruling Communist parties (except
Romania's) as a renegade.

Cashless Settlements The name given to
the common practice under Socialist
economic planning of settling payments
between socialized entities by debiting
and crediting bank accounts administered
by the State Bank. This method of settlement involves no cash and is similar to
payment by cheque in capitalist
economies. C.s. are compulsory in the
case of most transactions (about 95 per
cent by value) amongst state and co-
operative enterprises, institutions and offices directly operated by public authorities. Only transactions of minor importance involving petty cash are allowed to
be settled in cash. C.s. not only reduce the
cost of administration of payments but
also facilitate public control and minimize
the chance of the embezzlement of funds.

Cash Plan In Socialist economic planning,
the planned forecast of the banking system's cash payments and receipts. It shows
the channels through which currency is *put
into circulation* (wages, payments to farms
for agricultural deliveries, withdrawals
from savings banks, cash social benefits,
the servicing and repayment of state loans,
and the like) and *returns to the banks* (cash
deposits by trading enterprises, personal
deposits in savings banks, personal taxes
etc.). These circuits primarily involve the
population and the private sector where
it exists (farms, workshops, services). Although cash payments amongst the socialized entities are also included, they represent a small proportion (usually one-
tenth or less of the total cash flow), as most
settlements have to be made by cashless
transfers.

Castro, Dr Fidel (1926–   ) The leader of
the Cuban revolution and the Prime
Minister of Cuba. A lawyer by education,
he first devoted himself to revolutionary
activities in 1947. He led the TWENTY-
SIXTH OF JULY MOVEMENT, which by Jan.
1959 had overthrown the corrupt capitalist regime of F. Batista. F.C. became the
Prime Minister in the following month. He
was at first a casual socialist and for a long
time was critical of the Cuban communists. F.C. became a communist only after
he came to power (he considered himself a
Marxist-Leninist for the first time in Dec.
1961), but he insists on his own brand of
communism which has come to be known
as CASTROISM. He has cherished the idea
of spreading his version of revolution to
other parts of Latin America and to Africa, to date with greater success to the
latter (especially in Angola and Ethiopia)
than to the former.

Castroism A brand of revolutionary communist strategy applied originally in Cuba
under the leadership of F. CASTRO. It was
further developed by his supporters, especially E. GUEVARA and R. Debray, and
advocated as a suitable model for other
less-developed countries. In its approach
to the PROLETARIAN REVOLUTION, C. insists on armed struggle by devoted, but not
necessarily tightly organized and disciplined guerrillas, operating independently
from political control (thus being opposed
to DEMOCRATIC CENTRALISM postulated
in MARXISM-LENINISM). In its follow-up
policies, C. emphasizes the need for collectivist agrarian reforms along gradual
and humane lines, the elimination of illiteracy, the SOCIALIZATION of large firms,
the NATIONALIZATION of foreign-owned
capital, an independent foreign policy in
relation to imperialist powers irrespective
of political and economic consequences,
co-operation with the Socialist countries
and assistance to revolutionary movements in less-developed countries. C. has
found many adherents in Latin America
and Africa.

Categories In philosophy, basic logical
concepts reflecting the most general and
essential characteristics and relations of
objects and phenomena. The term was
first applied in its philosophical sense by

Aristotle (in *Categories*). Marxism approaches the study of c. in a different way to that of IDEALISM. Whilst the latter regards c. as *a priori* forms of thinking (i.e. before experience and independent of reality), DIALECTICAL MATERIALISM insists that c. are a reflection of the most general and essential facets of nature and society. Further, c. are considered to be 'dynamic', i.e. responding to historical changes in the material conditions of production. Some of the basic c. of Marxist philosophy are: 1. CAUSALITY; 2. MATTER; 3. the MODE OF PRODUCTION; 4. MOTION; 5. PRODUCTION RELATIONS; 6. REVOLUTION; 7. SOCIO-ECONOMIC FORMATIONS; 8. the BASE and SUPERSTRUCTURE; 9. BEING AND CONSCIOUSNESS; 10. NECESSITY; 11. QUANTITY and QUALITY; and 12. SPACE AND TIME.

Catholicism The largest denomination of the Christian religion, most predominant in Latin America and southern and central Europe, and headed by the Pope in Rome. Marxist critics have attacked C. for: 1. having been the state religion of the European countries under feudalism which it endeavoured to sanctify and perpetuate; 2. having developed its own hierarchy along feudal and monarchical lines; 3. having been the largest landowner in feudal times; 4. having persecuted progressive forces, including scientists and social reformers; 5. having allied itself with the BOURGEOISIE and aided its rule over the PROLETARIAT; and 6. like any religion, being superstitious and reactionary. In particular, C. has been blamed for the open acceptance of the preordained hierarchical social classes, for preaching asceticism, poverty and subordination to workers' exploiters and for manipulating super-natural after-life rewards and fears. C. has also been criticized for instigating opposition to Communist regimes in Eastern Europe and for interfering with elections in other countries. However, it is interesting to note that in the Encyclical Letter of 1967, Pope Paul VI condemned: 1. profit as the key motive power of economic activity; 2. competition as the regulator of economic activity;

and 3. the private ownership of the means of production as the absolute right. Also CHRISTIANITY, POPE JOHN PAUL II.

Causality In philosophy, the attribution of universal interdependence. This is the well established Marxist understanding of the world order, as analysed by Engels (in *ANTI-DÜHRING* and *DIALECTICS OF NATURE*) and Lenin (mainly in *PHILOSOPHICAL NOTEBOOKS*). C. logically derives from DIALECTICAL MATERIALISM, according to which each phenomenon in nature and society is an effect of some cause. Although cause produces effect, the latter is not passive but also acts on the cause. In fact, Marxists stress, a particular phenomenon may be an effect in one situation but a cause in another. The Marxist view is opposed to such Western schools of philosophy as EXISTENTIALISM, IDEALISM, LOGICAL POSITIVISM, PERSONALISM and PRAGMATISM. These schools, in their different ways, deny the existence of objective c., maintain that c. is an *a priori* category independent of consciousness, or that in nature or society there is neither cause nor effect.

CC The abbreviation of the CENTRAL COMMITTEE (of the Communist Party).

CC CPSU The (English) abbreviation of the CENTRAL COMMITTEE OF THE COMMUNIST PARTY OF THE SOVIET UNION.

CCCP — USSR. The Russian abbreviation in *Cyrillic* alphabet of *Soiuz Sovetskikh Sotsialisticheskikh Respublik*, meaning the UNION OF THE SOVIET SOCIALIST REPUBLICS.

CCP The abbreviation of the CHINESE COMMUNIST PARTY.

Ceausescu, Nicolae (1928–) Romanian Communist Party leader and statesman of world standing. He joined the Communist party in 1936 and after W.W.II held several high positions in the Party and the Government. In 1965 he succeeded his mentor Georghiu Dej as Secretary-General of the Central Committee of the Romanian Workers' Party (now the ROMANIAN COMMUNIST PARTY), became the President of Romania in 1967 and in 1969 was appointed the Supreme Commander of the Armed Forces. He has established a reputation for being a skilful champion of Romanian national interests and an astute statesman. He has steered Romania to a neutral position in the Sino-Soviet dispute, reasserted Romania's independent stand in the COUNCIL FOR MUTUAL ECONOMIC ASSISTANCE, extended and strengthened his country's links with Western and less-developed countries and opposed the WARSAW PACT's military intervention in Czechoslovakia in 1968.

Ceiling Prices Prices which are not allowed by the state to rise above a fixed maximum, but are free to fluctuate below that level. They are typical of the Socialist centrally planned economies for specified classes of products (especially raw materials and certain necessities) where the operation of the market is tolerated to the desired limit. C.p. may also be imposed in capitalist market economies in wartime, postwar reconstruction or other national emergencies. C.p. usually lead to black markets in any type of economy.

Cell – or 'Party cell' – a term still sometimes used for the smallest local unit of the Communist party. This designation was officially used in the USSR until 1934, after which it was replaced with the PRIMARY ORGANIZATION, of which (in the late 1970s) there were nearly 400,000, embracing 16.5m. members.

CEMA – or more commonly CMEA, an abbreviation of the COUNCIL FOR MUTUAL ECONOMIC ASSISTANCE.

Censorship The control of expression by an authority, which may involve printed matter (newspapers, periodicals, pamphlets, books), radio, television, motion pictures, theatre and variety performances, exhibitions and even personal mail and telecommunications in domestic as well as external relations. The purpose of c. may be to ensure compliance with the law, the 'reason of the state' and accepted conventions. C. exists, in one form or another, in virtually all countries, and is usually employed consciously or subconsciously to protect the existing beliefs, interests of the state and the social system in force. C. is much more comprehensive, repressive and institutionalized in the Socialist countries than in democratic capitalist nations. The Communist party regards c. as a systematic instrument in the hands of the Socialist state for combating the threat of COUNTER-REVOLUTION and the pursuit of various ideological and political objectives. This is facilitated by state ownership, the strict control of all media and a very well developed administrative and policing network. The administration of c. is usually in the hands of the Ministry of Internal Affairs, or additionally, may be shared by several relevant ministries or special agencies directly responsible to the Council of Ministers and/or the Parliament.

Centner Hundredweight, i.e. 100 kgs (220.46 lbs), a term often used in application to the European Socialist countries.

CENTO The abbreviated form of the Central Treaty Organization, a rather inactive defence pact for mutual security embracing Iran, Pakistan, Turkey and the United Kingdom, with the USA as a member of three of its Committees. It replaced the BAGHDAD PACT in March 1959 and was in existence from that date until March 1979. With its headquarters based in Ankara, its activities were directed towards counteracting Communist (especially Soviet) influence in the region by promoting economic development and by combating subversion.

Central Committee In the Communist Party organization, theoretically the highest organ of power between the Party

64

Congresses. It consists of 'full' and 'candidate' (in some Parties called 'alternate') members. The latter have no voting power and are elected from amongst the most prominent Party members at the PARTY CONGRESS. The C.C. is headed by the SECRETARY-GENERAL (in some Parties called FIRST SECRETARY or Chairman), the highest Party post. The Committee periodically holds PLENARY SESSIONS (as a rule twice a year). But otherwise its policy is carried out by its POLITBURO where the real power rests. The day-to-day work of the C.C. is carried on by the SECRETARIAT and the Control Committee. The C.C. concerns itself not only with the organization of the Party staff, but also with various policy matters of the Socialist state. Thus, in China, at the 11th Congress of the CHINESE COMMUNIST PARTY held in August 1977, of the 1,510 delegates attending (representing 35m. members), 201 full and 132 alternate members were elected to the C.C. The C.C. in turn elected 23 full and 3 alternate members to the Politburo.

Central Committee of the Communist Party of the Soviet Union The highest organ of Party power in the USSR between Party Congresses. Before 1917 the C.C. had hardly existed, but from 1917 to 1934 it wielded a good deal of power and operated along fairly democratic lines. Its role was reduced during the period 1934–53 under Stalin (who liquidated 70 per cent of its members in the GREAT PURGES of the late 1930s). After Stalin's death the importance of the C.C. was enhanced, in particular by its adjudicating role between disputatious factions. This was illustrated in the debate between KHRUSHCHEV and the ANTI-PARTY GROUP in 1957. The C.C. consists of full and candidate members elected at the PARTY CONGRESS. At the 26th Congress, held in March 1976, 287 full and 139 candidate members were elected, out of the total 4,998 delegates (representing 15,700,000 Party members). As a rule, the C.C. meets once in 6 months in a PLENARY SESSION, but otherwise its responsibilities are discharged by three inner bodies elected by the C.C. itself: 1. the POLITBURO, headed by the Secretary-General (L. Brezhnev) plus 15 full and 6 candidate members; 2. the Secretariat, consisting of 6 Secretaries and 5 Members; and 3. the Committee of Party Control. The responsibilities of the C.C, as exercised in particular by its Politburo (the ulimate seat of power) include not only the overall organization and supervision of the Party apparatus, but also establishing policy guidelines for the government and seeing to their broad implementation.

Central Economic Planning The system of managing the processes of production, distribution, consumption and investment in the whole economy by the state rather than through the free market mechanism. It is typical of the Socialist countries, where the general objectives are dictated by the Communist party, to leave the responsibility for the construction of the national economic plan and its implementation to the STATE PLANNING COMMISSION (or whatever its official name in a particular country may be). C.e.p. covers different periods, viz. medium-term (usually 5 years), perspective (15–20 years) and short-term (12, 6, 3 months and even less). It is directed towards a rapid structural transformation of the economy with continuous full employment, high rates of economic growth and the desired distribution of national income in fulfilment of ideological and socio-economic objectives. In contrast to the practice in capitalist countries, economic planning under socialism is more comprehensive and based on the SOCIAL OWNERSHIP OF THE MEANS OF PRODUCTION. Moreover, targets are specific and detailed, defined in physical units and directly (i.e. compulsory) enforceable by law.

Central Executive Committees Executive organs of the CONGRESSES OF SOVIETS at the All-Russian and Republic levels during the two formative decades of building socialism in the USSR, 1917–37. Each C.E.C., elected by its Congress of Soviets to which it was responsible, had legislative, administrative and controlling powers and was dominated by the BOL-SHEVIKS. However, the real power was exercised by its highest working body, the Presidium, which was assisted by the COUNCIL OF PEOPLE'S COMMISSARS. The most important C.E.C. was that at the national level known as the ALL-RUSSIAN CENTRAL EXECUTIVE COMMITTEE. Under the 1937 Constitution, C.E.C. were abolished and their functions were transferred to the SUPREME SOVIET, the PRESIDUM OF THE SUPREME SOVIET and the Council of the People's Commissars.

Central Intelligence Agency A powerful Federal organization in the USA concerned with espionage, counter-espionage and related activities to safeguard and promote the country's military, political, social and ideological interests. The C.I.A. was originally established (in 1947) specifically to handle foreign operations. But after 1964 its activities were extended to handle the detection and suppression of domestic subversion. Headed by the Director (Theodore Sorensen since 1977) and appointed by the President with the approval of the Senate, it operates under the National Security Council and reports directly to the President. The C.I.A. employs over 15,000 full-time, highly trained staff, most of whom have university degrees with 5 per cent holding doctorates, plus thousands of informants and intermediaries. From the Communist point of view, it is the most powerful, militant and sinister counter-revolutionary (COUNTER-REVOLUTION) organization in the capitalist world. Moreover, they see it as being concerned not only with the preservation of the capitalist system but also the suppression of left-wing revolutionary elements and the instigation behind anti-communist activities in capitalist, as well as the Socialist countries. Like its Soviet counterpart, the K.G.B., the C.I.A. has been described as an 'invisible government' and a 'law unto itself'. On several occasions it has seriously embarrassed the US President and the Administration, as well as governments in other countries.

Central Planning Office The name of the state organ for economic planning in Poland during the period 1945–50. It was succeeded by a more powerful body called the State Economic Planning Commission (which in turn was renamed in 1956 the 'Planning Commission Attached to the Council of Ministers').

Centralization and Concentration of Capital and Production See CONCENTRATION AND CENTRALIZATION OF CAPITAL AND PRODUCTION.

Centralized Directive System of Planning and Management The economic regime that prevailed in most Socialist countries before the economic reforms of the early 1960s. Described also as the 'Stalinist model' or as a 'command economy', it was noted for the following main features: 1. the extreme centralization of decision-making (exercised by central planners in the State Planning Commission); 2. the hierarchical character of economic relations; 3. the directive (i.e. compulsory) nature of planned TARGETS and methods of their implementation; 4. TIGHT PLANNING (with no or very low reserves or stocks of inputs); and 5. the central allocation of resources, completely by-passing the market mechanism. Experience has shown that whilst this system may be quite effective in improving a stagnant and backward economy in a relatively short period of time, it is not conducive to efficiency and technological progress in the higher stages of economic development. The system was partly abandoned after the ECONOMIC REFORMS of the 1960s.

Centrism A middle-of-the-road line between extreme left and right-wing factions in a political movement. In Marxist thought and practice, the term originated during the SECOND INTERNATIONAL when, in 1889, K. KAUTSKY took the middle ground between the Left Revolutionaries (inspired by K. LIEBKNECHT, ROSA LUXEMBURG and F. MEHRING) and the advocates of REVISIONISM (represented by E. BERNSTEIN). The centrists were prepared to compromise, believing that a BOURGEOIS-DEMOCRATIC REVOLUTION was essential before a PROLETARIAN REVOLUTION. Revolutionary Marxists identify c. with confused liberalism, exemplifying ideological indecision and timidity and regard it as 'double-faced OPPORTUNISM'.

Centro Internationale Handelsbank A joint East-West international commercial bank established in Vienna in 1974. It is owned by the following 7 partner banks, each holding 14.3 per cent of the joint capital: *Bank Handlowy w Warszawie* (Poland); *Banco di Sicilia* (Italy); *Banco Popular Español* (Spain); *Bank für Wirtschaft und Arbeit* (Austria); BANK OF TOKYO (Japan); *Banque Occidentale pour L'industrie et Commerce* (France) and BENSON, KLEINWORT, LONSDALE (UK). It engages in financing East-West trade and provides advice and other assistance for East-West economic co-operation.

Certificate of Honour A testimonial commonly awarded in the Socialist countries by the authorities to a Leading Worker or an Exemplary Enterprise for outstanding work performance or efficiency. It is also known in some countries as the 'C. of Merit', or the 'Diploma of Honour'. It is one of the means of 'moral' motivation (MORAL INCENTIVES) applied to individuals or groups of workers under the conditions of full employment, well-developed social security and the absence of private enterprise.

Četeka The commonly used abbreviation of *Československá Tiskova Kancellář*, meaning the 'Czechoslovak Press Bureau'. It is the state-owned official news agency in Czechoslovakia, controlled by the Federal Government through its Presidium, for the collection and distribution of domestic and foreign news. It maintains working relations with all the major news organizations in the Socialist as well as capitalist countries.

CGT Abbreviation of *CONFÉDÉRATION GÉNÉRALE DU TRAVAIL*.

Chairman Designation of the highest executive official of the CHINESE COMMUNIST PARTY elected, or rather confirmed, at the Party Congress. The present Ch. is HUA KUO-FENG who succeeded MAO TSE-TUNG in 1976. He is the Ch. of the Party's CENTRAL COMMITTEE, of its POLITBURO and also heads the STANDING COMMITTEE of the Politburo. In most other ruling Communist parties, the post is known either as the SECRETARY-GENERAL, the FIRST SECRETARY, or, in Yugoslavia, as the President.

Chang Ch'un-chiao (1911–) A Chinese Communist leader and politician who played an important role under Mao Tsetung. A journalist by profession, with extreme left-wing tendencies, Ch.Ch.-ch. was one of the leaders of the NATIONAL CULTURAL REVOLUTIONARY GROUP (created in May 1966) and played the leading part in establishing a revolutionary power base in Shanghai during the GREAT PROLETARIAN CULTURAL REVOLUTION. After the G.P.C.R. he joined the leftist group known as the GANG OF FOUR, was elected to the STANDING COMMITTEE of the Politburo of the CCP, was appointed to the post of Director of the General Political Department of the PEOPLE'S LIBERATION ARMY in 1975 and in the same year became Vice-Premier (one of 12) in the State Council (Cabinet). After the assumption of the Party and government leadership by HUA KUO-FENG in 1976, Chang was named a 'KUOMINTANG'S special agent', lost his posts, arrested, publicly tried in Dec. 1980–Feb. 1981 and sentenced to death, which 'may be carried out if he does not repent in two years'.

Charities Institutionalized private or semi-private firms which aim to alleviate poverty. They are well developed in industrialized capitalist countries and are often administered by disinterested professionals in the field. To Marxists, ch. are misguided attempts to remove the symptoms, and not the real causes, of social injustice in the capitalist society. Marx (in THE *POVERTY OF PHILOSOPHY*) regarded them as humiliating to the recipients, tacitly giving approval to the iniquitous distribution of wealth and income, and postponing the need for a PROLETARIAN REVOLUTION. In the Socialist countries as a rule, charities do not exist, as there are no wealthy capitalists and the sources of social poverty have been removed on a systematic basis through the provision of SOCIAL INSURANCE and SOCIAL SECURITY, which are treated as rights and not ch.

Charter '77 An open petition for HUMAN RIGHTS originally put forward by a group of Czechoslovak dissidents in Jan. 1977, which is still supported by dissident and liberal groups in other Socialist countries. The Charter, also described as the 'Human Rights Manifesto', was initiated in Prague in 1976 by Pavel Kohout and signed by 243 Czechoslovak intellectuals, labour leaders and workers. It was published in the Western European press on 6 Jan 1977. Ch. '77 referred to the Human Rights Convention acceded to by the Czechoslovak Government in 1968 which was also confirmed at the HELSINKI CONFERENCE in 1975. The document also listed several cases of the systematic violation of civil liberties, such as the freedom of expression, religion, education and travel. The year 1977 was chosen symbolically, alluding to the year of amnesty for political prisoners declared by Amnesty International. The Czechoslovak Communist Party denounced Ch. '77 as an 'anti-state, anti-socialist and demagogic' statement, 'instigated by anti-communist and Zionist interests'. It in turn countered with its own ANTI-CHARTER. Also CHARTER OF LIBERTY.

Charter of Liberty A public declaration put forward by the Paris Group of exiles from Central and Eastern Europe on 5 Oct. 1977, demanding political and social justice for the European nations under Communist rule. The Charter, set out in 6 chapters and issued in 18 languages, con-demned Communist totalitarianism, the oppression of minorities and the violation of democratic freedoms. It further called for the absolute observance of human rights, the freedom of enterprise, the preservation of traditions, pluralistic democracy, social justice, national sovereignty and the unification and solidarity of all the European countries along co-operative and democratic lines.

Chartism A popular movement for parliamentary reform in Britain, most active from 1837 to 1839 but continuing until 1855. Its name was derived from the 'People's Charter', drawn up by 6 members of the Working Men's Association of London and 6 members of Parliament, and presented to Parliament on 13 May 1839. The charter petitioned for universal male suffrage, the secret ballot, the abolition of property qualifications for voting and for candidates, equal electoral districts, annual Parliaments, and payment to members of Parliament. It carried 1.25m. signatures but was rejected. In the consequent agitation in Nov. 1839, troops fired upon the Chartists, killing 10 and wounding 50. Their leaders were arrested and some were subsequently transported to the penal colonies. Although the movement failed, it aroused widespread interest and represented the first political action in Britain where the working masses put forward their class demands.

Chauvinism An extreme form of NATIONALISM consisting in the exaggeration of the qualities, interests and achievements of one's own nation and the disregard of its faults and failures. It is further reinforced by the belittling, vilification, contempt and even hatred of other nations. In the Marxist view, ch. is a feature of CAPITALISM, especially during the stage of IMPERIALISM. Here, ch. is employed as an instrument designed to set the masses against neighbouring or colonial peoples and to justify military production, wars of aggression and COLONIALISM for the benefit of the national BOURGEOISIE. Marxism is opposed to ch. and stresses the need for a united international brotherhood of working classes. But on occasion, Communist regimes have resorted to chauvinistic methods, especially in defensive wars and wars of national liberation against aggressors.

Cheka The original colloquial name of the Soviet secret police from 1917 to 1922. Also known as *Vecheka* and *Cherezvychaika*, it is an abbreviated form of *Vserossiyskaya Cherezvychainaya Kommissiya Borbie Kontrrevolutsiei i Sabotazhem*, meaning the 'All-Russian Extraordinary Commission for Combating Counter-Revolution and Sabotage'. It was established on the initiative of Lenin in Dec. 1917 (6 weeks after the Bolsheviks came to power) as an organ of the Security Police. F. E. DZIERZHINSKY was appointed its first head. Its activities were directed towards detecting and stamping out counter-revolutionary practices, including anti-Soviet opposition, espionage, sabotage, the embezzlement of public funds, speculation, and the suppression of minority views deviating from the official Bolshevik line. It also administered the censorship of the press. At first the *Ch.* was meant to be temporary and concerned only with preliminary investigations, but it soon acquired the power to arrest, try, imprison and execute. Its terrorist methods became notorious, especially after an assassination attempt on Lenin's life in Aug. 1918. It set up local offices and transport units, recruited special security troops and developed a system of concentration camps. Its functionaries became known as 'Chekists'. The *Ch.* was abolished in Feb. 1922, or rather transformed into the *GPU*.

Cheng Feng The Chinese term for the RECTIFICATION CAMPAIGNS.

Ch'en Po-ta (1904–) Chinese Communist theoretician, historian and an interpreter of Mao Tse-tung's ideas. He served as a Political Secretary to Mao from 1937 to 1956 and was elected to the Central Committee of the Chinese Communist Party in 1937. He was appointed Editor of *Hung-ch'i* (the Party's theoretical journal) in 1958, Deputy Chairman of the State Planning Commission in 1962 and the Rector of Peking University in 1967. From 1959 to 1969 he was a member of the Politburo of the CC of the CCP. Ch.P.-t. played a leading role in the GREAT PROLETARIAN CULTURAL REVOLUTION as a member of the GROUP OF FIVE of which he became the leader. He was ranked fourth in the Party hierarchy (after Mao, Lin Piao and Cho En-lai). He had a close association with LIN PIAO, for which he fell into disgrace with Mao. Ch.P.-t. was denounced at the Tenth Party Congress (in Aug 1973) as an adventurous power seeker and was stripped of his posts.

Ch'en Tu-hsiu (1879–1942) A Chinese intellectual social reformer, Marxist and Communist leader who introduced Mao Tse-tung to Marxism in 1919. Born to a wealthy family and well educated, he became professor of literature at Peking University where he denounced Confucianism, became a Marxist and organized a Marxist study group in 1918. With LI TA-CHAO he is regarded as the co-founder of the CHINESE COMMUNIST PARTY in 1921 and became its first Secretary. He accepted the recommendation of the COMINTERN for collaboration with the KUOMINTANG, but was later blamed for its failure, accused of TROTSKYISM and was removed from the Secretary's post. He then joined the Party's 'Left Opposition' and became critical of the growing authoritarianism in the Party. He was imprisoned by the Nationalist Government in 1932 but was later released to fight the Japanese. He died of poor health in May 1942.

Cherezvychaika Another name for *CHEKA*.

Chernoznamentsy ('Black Flag Bearers', in Russian) The colloquial name of a faction of a Russian anarchical movement. The *C.* existed before and shortly after the

Bolshevik Revolution and advocated an anarchical society achieved by terror and the expropriation of property owners. Those engaged in terrorism, just on principle and without motive, were known as *bezmotivniki*. Their ranks were decimated by the Tsarist police and later by the BOLSHEVIKS.

Chernyshevsky, Nikolai (1828–89) An outstanding early Russian materialist philosopher, revolutionary democrat and utopian socialist, to whose contributions and courage Lenin paid tribute. In his writings on MATERIALISM, Ch. criticized AGNOSTICISM, MACHISM, NEO-KANTIANISM and POSITIVISM. Attacking the exploiting classes in Russia, he pressed for a far-reaching emancipation of peasants. He advocated the reorganization of society on a communal co-operative basis and believed that it was essential to overthrow the Tsarist autocratic rule (in *What Is To Be Done?*, written in prison in 1863). He is regarded by some as the father of Russian NIHILISM. His writings also exerted considerable influence on the development of social-democracy in Russia, an early forerunner of the Communist Party of the Soviet Union. He anticipated the Leninist concept of PARTY-MINDEDNESS (in *Anthropological Principle in Philosophy*, 1875. He was a great Russian patriot who attacked both COSMOPOLITANISM, NATIONALISM and RACISM. He spent over 20 years in Siberia for his revolutionary ideas. Ch. has been criticized by Marxists for a mechanistic approach to philosophy, for being divorced too much from relations of social production and for the impracticability of some of his social theories.

Chervenkov, Vylko (1900–) A distinguished Bulgarian Communist whose ruthless methods took him to the top Party and Government leadership, but later led to his downfall. He joined the Bulgarian Communist Party in 1919 as a founder member and took part in the unsuccessful September Uprising of 1923 to establish Communist rule in Bulgaria. From 1925 to 1944 he was in the USSR. After his return, he led the Bulgarian MUSCOVITES and achieved notoriety for organizing a political show trial in 1949 of his rival T. KOSTOV (later executed). Ch. became the First Secretary of the BCP in 1950 (until 1954) and Prime Minister in the same year (until 1956). The political methods he resorted to and his self-fascination led to his gradual demotion after 1954 and finally to his expulsion from the Party in 1962.

Chervonets The name of one of the monetary units in circulation in the USSR from 1922 to 1947. It was issued as a 'stabilized' currency note equal to 10 roubles, representing the gold content of 7.74234 grammes of fine gold. The designation was officially introduced as a substitute for the ROUBLE which was discredited ideologically and ruined in value by the inflation and hyper-inflation of 1918–24. The name alluded to historical antecedents ('fine gold tenner'), when gold coins bearing that name had been issued in Russia from 1701 to 1867. In 1975, as part of the campaign to inspire international confidence in Soviet currency, the *GOSBANK* minted 250,000 gold coins named *ch.*, with the same gold content as the old *ch.* The Soviet authorities assert that these gold coins are legal tender in the USSR. The coins have been marketed in several Western countries with a good deal of publicity (originally for about $40 each).

Chiang Ch'ing (1913–) Also spelled Jiang Qing, a former actress and the third wife of Mao Tse-tung. She married Mao in 1939 and kept out of politics until 1964. Then she increasingly engaged in the cultural and political upheavals, especially during the GREAT PROLETARIAN CULTURAL REVOLUTION of which she became one of the five leaders in the NATIONAL CULTURAL REVOLUTIONARY GROUP. In 1969 she was elected a full member of the Politburo (being the only woman there), where she pressed for a more radical line in literature, theatre and cinema. She continued her extremist left-wing activities as one of the GANG OF FOUR in Mao's top hierarchy. After Mao's death (Sep. 1976), she was named a 'renegade' and a 'left-wing deviationist' and accused of plotting against CHOU EN-LAI. She was arrested in Oct. 1976, publicly tried in Dec. 1980–Feb. 1981 as a member of the Gang of Four and sentenced to death, which 'may be carried out if she does not repent in two years.'

Chilean Communist Party See COMMUNIST PARTY OF CHILE.

China, People's Republic of (*Chung-hua Jen-min Kung-huo-kuo*) The most populous Socialist country in the world, with an estimated population of over 900m. (in 1979) and an area of 9,561,000 sq. km. The beginnings of the development of Ch. as a Socialist state go back to the early post-W.W.I period when the CHINESE COMMUNIST PARTY was founded in Shanghai in 1921. From 1924 to 1927, on instructions from the COMINTERN, the Communists collaborated with the KUOMINTANG in the first 'united front', but it ended with the massacre of Communists and their sympathizers. The Party was soon reconstructed and a guerrilla force was developed by MAO TSE-TUNG, CHU TEH and CHOU EN-LAI. In 1931, the first CHINESE SOVIET REPUBLIC was created in the province of Kiangsi and a firmer Communist political and military base was developed after the LONG MARCH (1934–35) in the Shensi province. From 1937 to 1945, the Communists again collaborated with the Kuomintang in the second united front against the Japanese invaders. After W.W.II, the Kuomintang's campaign directed towards a complete destruction of the Communist forces developed into a Civil War, 1946–49, which ended with the defeat of Kuomintang's forces on the mainland and the escape of Chiang Kai-shek's regime to Taiwan. On 1 Oct. 1949, the P.R. of Ch. was formally proclaimed, with Mao Tse-tung as the Head of the State. After 1950, Tibet was also incorporated into the P.R. of Ch. The socialization of industry and services, the collectivization of agriculture

and radical social reforms were implemented smoothly and in a relatively liberal manner (compared with the USSR). Economic planning was adopted after 1950, at first imitating the Soviet model. The first Constitution was adopted in 1954 but later replaced by another in 1975. The highest organ of state power is theoretically vested in the NATIONAL PEOPLE'S CONGRESS elected every five years, which meets once a year, but operates expressly under the 'guidance of the Party'. The NPC elects a Standing Committee which convenes the Congress, interprets laws and supervises the work of the STATE COUNCIL (the Government). The ultimate source of power is in the hands of the Chinese Communist Party, but 8 minority parties are formally tolerated which co-operate in a 'united front' under the domination of the CCP (in the National People's Congress). Ideology has conspicuously affected developments in the P.R. of Ch., which, in several cases, led to abrupt turns in policies. These were exemplified by the HUNDRED FLOWERS INTERLUDE (1957), the GREAT LEAP FORWARD (1958–61), the SINO-SOVIET DISPUTE (from 1960 on), the GREAT PROLETARIAN CULTURAL REVOLUTION (1966–69) and the campaign against the GANG OF FOUR. Under HUA KUO-FENG, who succeeded Mao to the Party and Government leadership in 1976, a moderate course has been adopted both in domestic and foreign policies. More attention is being paid to economic commonsense (and less to ideology), the acceleration of technological progress and material incentives and a rehabilitation and revival of private enterprise. A course of *rapprochement* with the West (including the USA) has been pursued, largely for the sake of economic and technical considerations and as a counter to the Soviet threat. In Oct. 1971 the P.R. of Ch. was admitted to the United Nations and full diplomatic relations were established with the USA in Jan. 1979.

China Differential In the administration of the Western STRATEGIC EMBARGO,

71

those items which were barred from being exported to the P.R. of China, the D.P.R. of (North) Korea and the D.R. of (North) Vietnam, but not to the Soviet bloc. Such items appeared on the special 'China List', prepared by the CHIN-COM, created in Paris in 1952, and recommended to the co-operating governments. The Ch.d. was dropped in 1957. But the USA, whose version of the Ch.d. amounted to a virtually complete ban on trade with the 3 countries, continued the differential until 1972 when it was abandoned in application to the P.R. of China.

China's Khrushchev A derogatory description applied by the extremist supporters of Mao Tse-tung to LIU SHAO-CH'I during the GREAT PROLETARIAN CULTURAL REVOLUTION. Liu was accused of rightwing revisionist policies and schemes and an uncritical acceptance of foreign ideas and practices. On these grounds he was identified by his critics with N. S. KHRUSHCHEV.

Chin-Com The abbreviated designation of the 'China Co-ordinating Committee', established by the CONSULTATIVE GROUP in Paris in Sep. 1952. The function of the Ch.-C. was to compile a special 'China List' of recommendations for the co-operating countries' governments on the strategic exports to the P.R. of China, the DPR of (North) Korea and the DR of (North) Vietnam. It supplemented the work of the CO-COM, adding items of lesser technological sophistication, reflecting the lower stage of economic and technological development attained in the Asian Socialist countries as compared with the Soviet bloc. Ch.-C. was dismantled in 1957 when the China differential was dropped by the member countries with the exception of the USA.

Chinese Communist Party (*Chung-kuo Kung-ch'an tang*) The ruling political party in the People's Republic of CHINA, with the largest membership of a political party in the world. It was founded in July 1921 in Shanghai. Its first Congress was attended by 12 delegates, including MAO TSE-TUNG. It is one of the few Communist parties which has not changed its name and, although persecuted up to its seizure of power in 1949, was never illegal. At its second Congress in May 1922, it issued a Marxist 'Manifesto', proclaiming communism to the Chinese people. On orders from Moscow and the COMINTERN, it attempted to co-operate with and infiltrate the KUOMINTANG. However, by 1927, it was almost wiped out by Chiang Kai-shek in a series of massacres. It soon reappeared first in the mountain area of Chingshan, then moved to the Kiangsi province in 1929 (where two years later it founded the first CHINESE SOVIET REPUBLIC) and subsequently, after the LONG MARCH (1934–35), to the Shensi province with its capital at Yenan. During the Sino-Japanese war 1937–45, the C.C.P. collaborated with the Kuomintang in fighting the Japanese, gradually increasing its strength and the area under its control. The Kuomintang's all-out offensive against the Communists in 1945 led to the Civil War, which ended with the defeat of the Nationalist forces on the mainland in 1949. As leader of the C.C.P., Mao proclaimed the People's Republic of China on 1 Oct. By 1978 the Party's membership had grown to 35m. (compared with 17m. in 1961) which is roughly the same as all other Communist parties in the world put together. The highest source of power is the National Party Congress. This Congress is held every 4–5 years, elects the Central Committee, which in turn elects a Politburo and its inner executive body (the Standing Committee). The numerical composition of the highest Party organs elected at the 11th N.P.C. in Aug. 1977, attended by 1,510 delegates (representing 35m. members) was: the Central Committee – 201 full, and 132 alternate, members; the Politburo – 23 full, and 3 alternate, members; and the Standing Committee of the Politburo – 5 members, headed by the Chairman (HUA KUO-FENG) and assisted by 5 Vice-Chairmen (Yeh Chien-ying, Wang Chien-ying, Wang Tung-hsing, TENG HSIAO-P'ING and Li

Hsien-nien). The supporting mass organizations of the C.C.P. are: the Little Red Guards; the RED GUARDS; the Communist Youth League; Poor, Lower, and Middle Peasants Associations; the Militia and the PEOPLE'S LIBERATION ARMY. The Party's main regular publications are: *Jen-min jih-pao* (*People's Daily*), the official daily organ; *Hung-ch'i* (*Red Flag*), the theoretical monthly journal of the CC; and *Chiehfang chun-pao* (*Liberation Army Daily*), the daily organ of the People's Liberation Army.

Chinese People's Political Consultative Conference A type of constituent assembly, but without any powers, in operation in the P.R. of China from 1949 to 1954. It was headed by CHOU EN-LAI as Chairman, with MAO TSE-TUNG as the Honorary Chairman. The Conference resembled an anti-bourgeois 'united front', which was completely dominated by the CHINESE COMMUNIST PARTY but in which representatives of co-operating political parties or groups were tolerated, viz. the Kuomintang Revolutionary Party, the China Democratic League, the China Democratic National Construction Association, the China Association for the Promotion of Democracy, the Chinese Peasants' and Workers' Democratic Party, the Third of September 1945 Society (representing scientists and technicians), the China Chih-kung Party (a 19th c. secret society) and Taiwan Democratic Self-Government League. The Conference assisted with the preparation of the 1954 Constitution. In that year most of its functions were transferred the the newly created NATIONAL PEOPLE'S CONGRESS.

Chinese Red Army See RED ARMY, PEOPLE'S LIBERATION ARMY.

Chinese Socialist Revolution The period of the civil war in China, 1945–49, when the forces of the KUOMINTANG under Chiang Kai-shek were defeated by the Communists led by Mao Tse-tung, at the end of which the People's Republic of China was proclaimed (1 Oct. 1949). The

conditions for the successful Ch.S.R. had been partly prepared by three quasi-socialist revolutions, viz.: *1921–27*, when the CHINESE COMMUNIST PARTY was founded and links were established with intellectuals, the Kuomintang and the COMINTERN; *1927–36*, when the CCP was reconstructed, a guerrilla force was developed, the first CHINESE SOVIET REPUBLIC was created in Kiangsi province in 1931, and when a more solid political and military base was developed in Shensi province after the LONG MARCH; and *1937–45*, when the national liberation struggle against Japanese imperialism was combined with the consolidation of Communist power in the BORDER AREAS. In contrast to the GREAT OCTOBER SOCIALIST REVOLUTION in Russia, the Ch.S.R. originated in the countryside and later moved into the cities. Also, it lasted five years *after* which the central government was set up in the national capital. The success of the Chinese Communists was due to: 1. the apparent absence of opposition from the majority of the population on religious, social and national grounds; 2. the honest, energetic and popularly acceptable administration in the Communist-won areas, contrasting with the ineptitude and corruption of the Nationalist Government; 3. the strong indoctrination and strict discipline of the PEOPLE'S LIBERATION ARMY, in contrast to the weak ideological convictions and widespread demoralization and desertions of the Nationalist forces; and 4. the suitability of the Maoist revolutionary strategy of guerrilla warfare and the social reforms initiated in the areas gained by the Communists. It may be noted here that Mao himself did not regard the Ch.S.R. as a proletarian revolution, but rather a BOURGEOIS-DEMOCRATIC REVOLUTION against feudalism and colonialism.

Chinese Soviet Republic An area in the province of Kiangsi (south-east China) under the rule of the CHINESE COMMUNIST PARTY from Nov. 1931 to Nov. 1934. It was established by the remnants of the CCP (after the massacre by the KUOMIN-

TANG in 1927) who moved to Kiangsi in 1929 led by MAO TSE-TUNG and CHU TEH. The Provincial Government of the Ch.S.R. was headed by Mao and for a time by CHOU EN-LAI in its capital at Zuikin. The Republic was the first attempt in China to establish a Marxist state based on the alliance of peasants and workers who participated in the reforms and administration through 'councils' along SOVIET lines. It embarked on organizing co-operatives, state trading and issued its own currency. The Ch.S.R. was blockaded and attacked several times by the Kuomintang forces and finally routed in Oct. 1934. After this disaster, the Communists and their supporters set out on the LONG MARCH to Shensi province where they established a similar state but on a more solid basis away from the Kuomintang.

Chingshan Mountains The stronghold of the CHINESE COMMUNIST PARTY on the Hunan–Kiangsi border (south-east China) in the 1920s. It was Mao Tse-tung's first model community in China and the first rural revolutionary base in modern history (the name is also spelled Ching Shan, Tsing Shan, Chingkanshan and Ching-kab Shan). From 1922 to 1925, when the Communists collaborated with and attempted to infiltrate the KUOMINTANG, the Ch.M. were kept as a reserve area. After the massacre of the Communists by Chiang Kai-shek's forces in 1927, the remnants (including MAO TSE-TUNG, CHU TEH, CHOU EN-LAI and LIN PIAO) regrouped there, and spread their revolutionary activities to the rural areas where the position of the ruling classes was weak. In 1929 the Communist activities were pushed to Kiangsi province where in 1931 the first CHINESE SOVIET REPUBLIC was established.

Chistka ('purification', in Russian) A Russian term for a purge in the Party membership. It may be a periodical drive to expel or liquidate members who are not zealous enough, lack enthusiasm or loyal-ty, for DEVIATIONISM from the Party line, or for other serious misconducts of one type or another. Under Stalinist rule, the *ch.* assumed the form of a mass liquidation of undesirables, as illustrated by the GREAT PURGES of the late 1930s.

Chornyi Peredel ('*Black Redistribution*', in Russian) A land redistributionist group in Tsarist Russia in the late 19th c. It was a small revolutionary organization of *NARODNIKS*, formed in 1879, after a split in the *ZEMLYA I VOLYA*. The *Ch.P.* continued the programme of its predecessor, but was opposed to terrorism directed at individuals. Amongst its members were such revolutionaries as G. PLEKHANOV and P. Axelrod. It published a bulletin under the same name from 1880 to 1881.

Chou En-lai (1898–1976) A distinguished Communist Chinese leader of Mandarin birth and intellectual background, the first and long-serving Prime Minister of the P.R. of China. He became a Marxist in France in 1914, where he organized a Chinese Communist group. After his return to China, he joined the CHINESE COMMUNIST PARTY in 1922 and (for infiltration purposes) the KUOMINTANG in 1924, and became the Political Director of the Whampoa Military Academy in Canton. He organized a workers' uprising in Shanghai in March 1927 and the following year was elected to the Politburo of the Party's Central Committee, a position which he retained until his death. Although at first he supported the 'erroneous line' of urban revolution, he later joined MAO TSE-TUNG and remained his loyal supporter until the end. In 1931 Chou moved to Kiangsi province, where, at one stage in the CHINESE SOVIET REPUBLIC, he was above Mao as Political Commissar of the Red Army (renamed PEOPLE'S LIBERATION ARMY in 1946). He took part in the LONG MARCH (1934–35) and then (1937–45) actively supported the Nationalist-Communist struggle under Chiang Kai-shek's leadership against the Japanese. After the victorious Civil War of 1945–49, he became the first

Prime Minister (until his death in 1976) and Foreign Minister (until 1958). Chou fully supported Mao in the GREAT PRO-LETARIAN CULTURAL REVOLUTION, but tried to restrain the extremists. Due to his efforts, China was admitted to the United Nations (in Oct. 1971). He also prepared the ground for the normalization of relations with the USA.

Christian Democrats Religiously motivated political parties occupying important positions in the Catholic countries of Western Europe (especially the FR of Germany and Austria) and to a lesser extent in Latin America. They represent a middle-of-the-road stand between the extreme right-wing parties and left-wing socialists, supporting social-welfare programmes, economic planning, co-operation between employers and trade unions, but rejecting socialist egalitarianism, the class struggle, atheism, and communism in general. The movement originated in the 19th c., but it has since broadened its appeal by supporting moderate social reforms and welfare schemes. After W.W.II, ch.d. parties have been in office in several countries (e.g. the Christian Social Party in Austria, the Christian Democratic Union in the FR of Germany, the Christian Democratic Party in Italy and the Popular Republican Movement in France), mostly in coalition with left-wing parties.

Christianity The most widespread religion in the world, claiming 1,500m. adherents or 37 per cent of all religious believers. It falls into the following 3 major divisions: Roman Catholic (over one-half of the adherents); Protestant; and Greek-Orthodox. The latter two consist of several denominations or groups or sects. Although mutually opposed to each other, Ch. and MARXISM (as it exists today) have many elements in common: 1. both have founding fathers (Christ, Marx); 2. both have their definitive books (*Bible, Capital*); 3. both assume that there was originally a fairly equitable society (Garden of Eden, Primitive Communism); 4.

both embody the idea of the original sin or evil (sex, emergence of private property); 5. both favour collective property (Church, society); 6. both involve a regular presence at meetings (church attendance, party meetings); 7. both fight departures from the dogmatic or officially accepted lines (heresies, deviations); 8. both insist on the regular admission of errors against established common codes (confession, self-criticism); 9. both have resorted to punitive expulsion of members (excommunication, party purges); 10. both have staged show trials of inconvenient offenders (Inquisition, Great Purges); 11. both attach crucial importance to a separate system of education (church schools, seminaries, party schools and universities); 12. both have eulogized their own persecuted followers and both have engaged in the persecution of their opponents; 13. both have hierarchical authoritarian organizations; 14. both engage in censorship; 15. both subscribe to internationalism, whilst accepting patriotism; 16. both postulate an eventual reconciliation of evil and inequality (the Last Judgment, the proletarian revolution); and 17. both envisage a better world or society in the future (Paradise, classless society). But Marxists, as exemplified by Engels (in 'Contribution to the History of Early Christianity', *The Peasant Revolt in Germany*) and Lenin (in 'Attitude of the Workers' Party to Religion', 'Socialism and Religion') have attacked Ch. for its: 1. incorporation of the philosophy of IDEAL-ISM into its dogma; 2. acceptance of the existing social system as divinely decreed and immutable; 3. encouragement of escapism and belief in miracles and supernatural saviours rather than of practical revolutionary action; 4. historical support given to the ruling classes under slavery, feudalism and capitalism; 5. advocacy of humility to social superiors and of class harmony; 6. interference in elections, especially directed against Communist parties; and 7. participation in COLONIAL-ISM and IMPERIALISM through missions and the exploitation and demoralization of the native peoples. Also CATHOLICISM,

GOD, PROLETARIAN REDEMPTION, RELIGION, THEOLOGY.

Christian Peace Conference A communist-inspired movement postulating that Christianity and Marxism are reconcilable and complementary in the task of building an ideal society. It was founded in Czechoslovakia in 1958, in response to the overtures from Communist parties that the Christian churches should move into the field of international politics. Many distinguished church leaders took part in the founding Conference and Prof. J. Hromadka, a noted Prague theologian, was elected its first President. The Ch.P.C. has called for the construction of a new society based on social justice, disarmament and the industrialization of the less-developed countries with financial and technical aid from the former colonial and imperialist powers. It has also condemned EXPLOITATION, COLONIALISM, NEO-COLONIALISM and RACISM. The Ch.P.C. claims membership (churches, ecumenical bodies and individuals) in 48 countries. Fourteen of these are Socialist (Benin, Bulgaria, Cuba, Czechoslovakia, Ethiopia, German DR, Hungary, DR of Korea, Mozambique, Poland, Romania, USSR, Vietnam and Yugoslavia – but not China) and included amongst the capitalist countries are Canada, France, FR of Germany, India, Indonesia, Italy, Japan and the USA. Its work is carried on between the 'All-Christian Peace Assemblies' and an 'International Secretariat' aided by six 'Commissions' (Theological, Economy and Politics, Anti-Racism, Youth, Women's Problems, and International Problems). It organizes periodical international conferences in different parts of the world with an emphasis on Africa, Asia and Latin America. The Ch. P.C. publishes: *Peace Courier*, a fortnightly bulletin in English, French, German and Spanish; *Bulletin*, a bi-monthly in English and French; *Perspectives*, a quarterly in English and French and numerous pamphlets and reports. It co-operates with the WORLD PEACE COUNCIL, and like the latter, is regarded in the West as an INTERNATIONAL COMMUNIST FRONT ORGANIZATION.

Christian Socialism A political and social movement which seeks to combine Christian ethics with socialist reform in the interest of social justice and harmony. The movement originated in Britain during the 19th c. but also found parallel development in Austria, France, Germany, the USA and some other Western countries. It supported the development of labour organizations, co-operatives, the extension of education, adult franchise, assistance to the underprivileged, and the elimination of social abuses and injustices. F. D. Maurice, Ch. Kingsley, G. Walter, Henry George and E. Bellamy were amongst its notable adherents. Marx and Engels regarded Ch.s. as a mild middle-class palliative, only detracting the proletariat from the class struggle and the preparation for a proletarian revolution. They referred to it derisively in the *COMMUNIST MANIFESTO* (1848): 'Christian socialism is but the holy water with which the priest consecrates the heart-burning of the aristocrat'. Ch.s. has never gained wide support. Some later Ch. socialists put forward the conception of Christ as an early socialist and revolutionary of compassion (COMRADE JESUS).

Chronicle of Current Events A well-known bi-monthly journal of the Soviet Civil Rights Movement, first published in 1968 by Amnesty International in London. It is translated from Russian after the originals are produced in Moscow and circulated by *SAMIZDAT*. The journal contains details and evidence of the Soviet violations of HUMAN RIGHTS, political and religious persecutions, trials, sentences, labour camps, political 'psychiatric' institutions, protest actions and notes on current underground publications circulated in the USSR. The *Chronicle Archives* is a supplement to the *Ch. of C.E.*, and *A Chronicle of Human Rights in the USSR* also appears quarterly in Russian and English.

Chuchow Model A scheme for the resettlement of youths in special agricultural stations in China, first set up by the Chuchow city factories in conjunction with the neighbouring communes. Its origin goes back to the late 1960s, when some factories in Chuchow established their own schools and then (beginning in 1971) sent their graduates for resettlement in agricultural stations in the surrounding rural areas associated with the factories. The model has been adopted in other parts of China too, in which local factories, communes and government organizations participate. The purpose of the Ch.M. is to develop closer links between urban and rural communities, to promote agricultural production and experimentation of interest to local industries and to induce young people to move to rural areas (RUSTICATION DRIVE).

Chu Teh (1886–1976) The architect of the Chinese Red Army (in 1946 renamed PEOPLE'S LIBERATION ARMY) and a distinguished political leader. He had reached the rank of general before he became a member of the Chinese Communist Party in 1925. After the massacre of the Communists by the KUOMINTANG in 1927, he joined MAO TSE-TUNG in the CHINGSHAN MOUNTAINS, from where they spread their revolutionary activities to other parts of China. Ch.T. became the Commander-in-Chief of the Red Army in the CHINESE SOVIET REPUBLIC in 1931, was one of the leaders of the LONG MARCH (1934–35) and was largely responsible for Communist victories against the Japanese (1937–45) and the defeat of the Kuomintang's forces in the Civil War (1945–49). He was relieved of his command of the PLA in 1934, but was made Marshal the following year. He then occupied several positions of distinction which were of little consequence in the decision-making at the top. In 1954 he was appointed the sole Vice-Chairman of the P.R. of China, which he held till 1959 when he subsequently became Chairman of the Standing Committee of the NATIONAL PEOPLE'S CONGRESS. He maintained close contacts with Soviet and East European Communist leaders in the late 1950s and attended the 20th Congress of the CPSU, including KHRUSHCHEV'S SECRET SPEECH. At that time, Ch.T. ranked fifth in the Party hierarchy.

CIA See CENTRAL INTELLIGENCE AGENCY.

CIO See CONGRESS OF INDUSTRIAL ORGANIZATIONS.

Circulation A Marxist economic term denoting the turnover of capital associated with the process of production. In a capitalist economy, as expounded by Marx (in *CAPITAL*, vol. III), c. takes place in the market, viz. the capitalist using *money capital* purchases *means of production* and *labour*, transforming the latter two into productive capital. This phase is followed by a break in c. after which production yields *commodities*. *Commodity capital* is then realized in the form of a market sale for *money capital*. After this, the cycle of c. is repeated. The two phases of c. are handled by financial and commercial capitalists (the middle phase is handled by the industrial capitalist), whose source of income is SURPLUS VALUE (constituting the exploitation of the workers, the real producers). The process of the c. of capital may start from the production phase, or the latter may be omitted (as in the case of speculation). But in neither case is the nature of money capital or the appropriation of surplus value by the capitalists changed. The term c. is also used, in a general sense, with respect to the circular flow of money, credit and products independent of, or in conjunction with, each other.

Circulating Capital Capital used in the process of production. The amount of c.c. in an enterprise essentially depends on the size of output, thus excluding FIXED CAPITAL. In the Marxian theory of value, c.c. consists of two elements: 1. that portion of CONSTANT CAPITAL which is used to purchase raw materials, fuels and intermediate products; and 2. VARIABLE CAPITAL, i.e. expenditure on wages.

Civil Rights BELGRADE CONFERENCE, CHARTER '77, CHARTER OF LIBERTY, DISSENT, DISSENTERS, HELSINKI CONFERENCE, HUMAN RIGHTS.

Civil War An unorganized internal armed conflict between sections of the population in the same country, as illustrated by the hostilities in the USA 1861–65, Soviet Russia 1918–20, Spain 1936–39 and China 1945–49. Marxists see c.w. as an acute form of class struggle, basically caused by economic considerations, where one social class endeavours to secure political and economic advantages over another.

Class A basic Marxist concept for a large social group, indicating its relation to the MEANS OF PRODUCTION, thus reflecting its source and level of income and its attitude to the SOCIAL SYSTEM in force. For details, BOURGEOISIE, CLASS ANTAGONISM, CLASS COLLABORATION, CLASS CONSCIOUSNESS, CLASS STRUGGLE, CLASSLESS SOCIETY, PROLETARIAT, SOCIAL CLASSES.

Class-against-Class Tactics An ideological and political line pursued by the radical wings of the Communist parties in France and to a lesser extent in Britain, Germany, India, Yugoslavia and some other countries from the mid-1920s to the early 1930s. It was directed against moderate social-democratic and socialist parties, in particular against REVISIONISM and OPPORTUNISM, with the intent of sharpening the class struggle and revolutionary spirit. This line was supported by the COMINTERN in a resolution adopted at its Sixth Congress in 1928. The main form of this resolution was a refusal to co-operate in and out of parliament with non-radical left-wing parties and groups. These groups were declared to be the main enemies of the working class, worse, in fact, than either fascism or Nazism. There were also cases of partial boycotts of socialist and 'deviationist' Communist groups (incl. TROTSKYISM). The c.-a.-c.t. proved a failure, as it increased disunity in the working class movement, reduced the electoral and parliamentary effectiveness of left-wing political parties and indirectly aided fascism and Nazism. Stalin conceded this mistaken approach and total failure, and abandoned it during the mid-1930s.

Class Antagonism Inherent hostility between SOCIAL CLASSES. In the Marxist view, it existed and exists in all ANTAGONISTIC SOCIO-ECONOMIC FORMATIONS, viz. SLAVERY, FEUDALISM, CAPITALISM, and between the 'haves' and 'have-nots' of the MEANS OF PRODUCTION. The 'haves' (masters, feudal lords, capitalists) constitute the ruling class, imposing their will upon and exploiting the 'have-nots' (slaves, serfs, proletarians). C.a. may be hidden or open but generally expresses itself in the latter case through the CLASS STRUGGLE, which may lead to a PROLETARIAN REVOLUTION.

Class Consciousness The awareness and understanding by members or groups of a particular layer of society belonging to a distinct SOCIAL CLASS. The concept is Marxist in origin, expounded particularly by Engels and Lenin who stressed a need for the development of an antagonistic c.c. of the PROLETARIAT against the BOURGEOISIE. In this context, c.c. involves: 1. realization amongst the workers that they constitute a distinct and fraternal social class, both nationally and internationally, and separate from the rest of society; 2. the workers' pride in their belonging to the largest class, united by common problems and a struggle for the just cause; and 3. the conviction that the interests of the proletariat are irreconcilably opposed to those of the bourgeoisie, against which the workers must unite and fight to ensure social justice and to achieve a CLASSLESS SOCIETY.

Class Co-operation Collaboration and harmony between different SOCIAL

CLASSES, implied or advocated by non-Marxists. Revolutionary Marxism opposes c.c. when ANTAGONISTIC SOCIO-ECONOMIC FORMATIONS (slavery, feudalism, and especially capitalism) exist, viewing it as a betrayal and a postponement of the inevitable revolution. Those who tolerate or support c.c. are regarded as being guilty of OPPORTUNISM and REVISIONISM. In the Communist doctrine, c.c. is admissible only as a temporary tactic in the following three exceptional circumstances: 1. people's war against FASCISM; 2. NATIONAL LIBERATION MOVEMENTS against IMPERIALISM; and 3. possibly, in a BOURGEOIS-DEMOCRATIC REVOLUTION, paving the way for a PROLETARIAN REVOLUTION.

Classical Bourgeois Political Economy Name given by the Socialist economists to pre-Marxist economies developed notably by Adam Smith (1723–90), T. R. Malthus (1766–1834), D. Ricardo (1772–1823), J. Mill (1773–1836), J. S. Mill (1806–75) and J. Ch. Sismonde de Sismondi (1773–1842). In the Marxist view, c.b.p.e. was preoccupied with the processes of production and distribution of the BOURGEOISIE, first in relation to FEUDALISM and then the PROLETARIAT. It fell into 2 periods: 1. *LAISSEZ-FAIRE* political economy – up to about 1830, concerned with macroeconomic production relations, maximum economic efficiency and the accumulation of capital, stressing the need for private enterprise, competition and the absence of state intervention; and 2. *VULGAR POLITICAL ECONOMY* – concentrating on the analysis of market processes, largely subjectivist and divorced from social relations, which amounted to the 'apologetics of capitalism'. Marxist political economy drew heavily on several relevant concepts and theories pioneered by the classical economists in the first period, especially the LABOUR THEORY OF VALUE (Ricardo), the IRON LAW OF WAGES (Malthus, Ricardo) and the IMMISERATION OF THE PROLETARIAT (Sismondi).

Classical Marxist Thinkers Those writers who significantly contributed to the development of Marxist philosophical, political, economic and sociological thought, roughly from the early 19th c. to the creation of the first Socialist state in Nov. 1917. The main thinkers were K. MARX, F. ENGELS, ROSA LUXEMBURG, and V. I. LENIN. Those who made substantial contributions included: A. A. BOGDANOV, N. G. CHERNYSHEVSKY, J. DIETZGEN, A. DOBROLUBOV, A. E. HERZEN, R. HILFERDING, K. KAUTSKY, A. LABRIOLA, P. LAFARGUE, K. LIEBKNECHT, F. MEHRING, N. P. OGARIOV, D. I. PISAREV, G. V. PLEKHANOV, A. N. RADISHCHEV, J. K. RODBERTUS and K. A. TIMIRIAZIEV.

Class 'in Itself' and Class 'for Itself' Hegelian concepts adapted and used in classical Marxist terminology (especially by Marx and Engels) to describe two stages of the development of CLASS CONSCIOUSNESS among the working class. The former indicates the earlier stage, when workers become aware of their grievances against capitalists. If they take any action, it is directed against individual employers, not capitalists as a class. In the second stage, class 'for itself', workers become conscious of their class identity (as the PROLETARIAT) and of the unbridgeable antagonism that divides them from the class of capitalists (the BOURGEOISIE). The latter stage is reached as a result of the development of capitalism and corresponding social injustices, when the proletariat increases in size, develops a revolutionary theory, organizes national trade unions and Communist parties, strengthens the bonds of solidarity, accumulates experience in the class struggle and prepares for a PROLETARIAN REVOLUTION.

Classless Society Society noted for the absence of SOCIAL CLASSES, especially of social distinctions based on inequality and antagonistic relations. The concept was popularized by Marx and Engels, but borrowed from FOURIER. In Marxist ideology, a crude c.s. existed in PRIMITIVE

Class Struggle

COMMUNISM, but a fully-fledged c.s. could only be achieved under FULL COMMUNISM. The features of the c.s. to emerge in the future are envisaged to be: 1. the complete absence of the private OWNERSHIP OF THE MEANS OF PRODUCTION; 2. the disappearance of a distinction between rural and urban and between physical and mental labour; 3. the complete emancipation of women; 4. personal income based on the principle, 'FROM EACH ACCORDING TO HIS ABILITY, TO EACH ACCORDING TO HIS NEEDS'; 5. the NEW COMMUNIST MAN, devoid of extreme acquisitive inclinations and imbued with an unselfish social mentality; and 6. in its ultimate form, the elimination of differences between poor and rich regions in the world to ensure a world c.s. Also SINGLE INDUSTRIAL SOCIETY.

Class Struggle (in its extreme form also known as **Class War**) One of the cornerstones of Marxist ideology, explaining the course of history in terms of the struggle between conflicting SOCIAL CLASSES in ANTAGONISTIC SOCIO-ECONOMIC FORMATIONS (SLAVERY, FEUDALISM and especially CAPITALISM). The c.s. as a philosophical notion was first conceived by HEGEL and used in a socialist context by BLANQUI in 1832. But it was MARX and ENGELS who gave it a revolutionary ideological connotation and popularized the use of the term. In the *COMMUNIST MANIFESTO* they said: 'The history of all hitherto existing society is the history of class struggles. Freeman and slave, patrician and plebeian, lord and serf, guildmaster and journeyman – in a word oppressor and oppressed, stood in constant opposition to one another, carried on an uninterrupted, now hidden, now open fight ...' Marxism views the c.s. as an expression of DIALECTICAL MATERIALISM, where contradictions between classes lead to a struggle which is resolved in a synthesis, the process repeating itself as PRODUCTION FORCES change. The class owning the MEANS OF PRODUCTION utilizes the STATE, equipped with instruments of oppression, to maintain its rule over the

exploited class. This rule and exploitation are opposed by the oppressed class in primarily two spheres: 1. *economic* – a struggle for the improvement of the conditions of work and a change in the principle governing the distribution of the fruits of labour; and 2. *political* – a struggle for the seizure and maintenance of political power. In a capitalist society, the c.s. takes place between the PROLETARIAT and the BOURGEOISIE, which in the end must lead to a PROLETARIAN REVOLUTION, the overthrow of capitalism and the DICTATORSHIP OF THE PROLETARIAT. Under SOCIALISM, the c.s. continues, but it assumes new forms: 1. the suppression of the surviving pockets of the bourgeoisie; 2. the extension of the power of the revolutionary proletariat over other classes, including the PETTY BOURGEOISIE and rich peasants; 3. the detection and elimination of counter-revolutionary activities of the old privileged bureaucracy and other specialists, undermining the Socialist state; and 4. the intensification of the struggle against IMPERIALISM and NEO-COLONIALISM in the international arena.

Clericalism Efforts of the well-entrenched churches to subordinate the political, social, economic and cultural activities of a society to the clergy and its teachings. The term was first popularized in France in 1848 as a reaction against the power of the Roman Catholic church. The concept has since been given a broader connotation by Marxists, extending to all churches with established clergy throughout history. Thus c., also described as 'clerical reaction' and 'clerical fascism', has been identified with Greek-Orthodox, Islamic, Protestant and Roman Catholic religions, with its peak having been reached in the late Middle Ages. C. has been accused of conservatism, the perpetuation of hierarchical social stratifications, opposition to left-wing political movements and social reforms, the suppression of indigenous religions in colonial countries (by missions) and participation in COUNTER-REVOLUTIONS. C. has in some cases generated anti-clericalism, directed not necessarily against religion (like ATHEISM), but against the excessive power of the churches and clergy, especially their involvement in politics, education and the economy.

'Closed Shop' By reference to capitalist countries, a place of employment where only persons who are already members of the relevant trade union(s) may be hired. A closed union is a trade union which does not admit any more members or makes it difficult for new members to join. A UNION SHOP is a place of employment in which workers must become union members within a specified period of time. In contrast to the c.s., the u.s. provides freedom to the employer of hiring persons who are not yet trade union members. The purpose in each case, from the union's point of view, is to maintain higher wages and better working conditions by restricting the supply of labour.

CMEA An abbreviation for COUNCIL FOR MUTUAL ECONOMIC ASSISTANCE.

Co-Com The abbreviated form of the 'Co-ordinating Committee', a working body established by the CONSULTATIVE GROUP (high-level diplomats of the leading Western nations represented in Paris) at the end of 1949 to assist in the implementation of the STRATEGIC EMBARGO. The C.-C., which started in Jan. 1950, acts as a forum for discussions and conducting research on the compilation and current revision of lists of items barred from being exported by the member countries (Belgium, Canada, Denmark, France, the FR of Germany, Greece, Italy, Japan, Luxemburg, the Netherlands, Norway, Portugal, Turkey, the United Kingdom and the USA) to the Socialist bloc. It can only recommend its lists to the co-operating governments as it has no power to impose or enforce them. Also CO-COM DIFFERENTIAL, CHIN-COM.

Co-Com Differential Those items on the Western STRATEGIC EMBARGO lists which are barred from being exported from the USA, but not other Co-Com countries (CO-COM) to the Socialist bloc. The strict US lists have typically included 10 per cent more items than the Co-Com lists. In another sense, the C.-C.d. may mean the items which are barred from being exported to the Asian Socialist countries (China, North Korea, North Vietnam) after 1957 from the USA, but not from other Co-Com countries (the USA dropped the differential in application to China in 1972).

Coefficient of the Relative Value of Foreign Currencies Also known as the (currency) 'multiplier', a corrective calculation device, used in most Socialist countries which have official non-equivalent exchange rates. It is fixed periodically by the Ministry of Foreign Trade in relation to the major convertible currencies or currency areas in order to reflect the value of foreign currencies to the Socialist country in question. In fixing the coefficient, the Ministry takes into account such factors as the negotiated (or world market) prices, the degree of CURRENCY TRANSFERABILITY, various terms of dealings and the balance of payments considerations. The official BASIC EXCHANGE RATE multiplied by the coefficient gives an exchange rate (sometimes called a 'shadow exchange rate') which is close to the equivalent level, given the postulated policy objectives.

Coexistence The principle of parallel existence of the capitalist and Socialist systems, based on the mutual renunciation of war as a method of resolving conflicts between the two rival blocs. The principle was first put forward by Lenin in 1921, but up to 1956 it had been understood to be a condition of unremitting political warfare and minimal relations with (industrialized) capitalist nations. The danger of a global nuclear war and the conviction that socialism could succeed in peaceful competition led KHRUSHCHEV to put forward the principle of peaceful c. at the TWENTIETH CONGRESS OF THE CPSU in 1956, which has been implicitly accepted by the

West. C. implies non-interference in each other's internal affairs, equality in political and economic relations, undertakings not to export revolution and counter-revolution, the partial disarmament or at least a slowdown in the arms race and competitive participation in international relations. However, the Communist regimes make it clear that c. does not include peaceful c. in the ideological arena, since the class struggle and the fight for national liberation from imperialist oppression and neo-colonialist domination must continue. Rather, c. is understood to be the peaceful competition in political, social, economic, technological and cultural spheres, which in the long run is bound to demonstrate the superiority of the Socialist system and its ultimate victory. On the other hand, China has attacked the Soviet approach to c., regarding it as a form of REVISIONISM and capitulation. But China in fact put forward its own version of c. with respect to India in 1954 in a document known as the FIVE PRINCIPLES OF PEACEFUL COEXISTENCE. Also SELECTIVE COEXISTENCE.

Cognition The process of the sensory and abstract acquisition of knowledge, the results of which are expressed in concepts, categories and laws. Marxist philosophy regards c. as a reflective process of DIALECTICAL MATERIALISM and HISTORICAL MATERIALISM. According to Lenin (in his *PHILOSOPHICAL NOTEBOOKS*), there are 3 distinct but mutually complementary stages in c. – from concrete sensory perception through reasoning to practical verification. This process develops in a spiral progression where the confrontation of the newly acquired facts with the previously established knowledge leads to the negation of the outdated elements. These in turn no longer satisfy the needs of the new situation at a higher level of knowledge, and so on. There are five distinctive features of c. as viewed by Marxists: 1. it is a complex process in which sensory perception and abstract thinking are mutually complementary and indispensable; 2. c. is a historically continuous process, i.e. constantly developing, verified and proceeding to higher levels; 3. c. is a social process, a result of individual experience in society; 4. c. is a type of human activity, i.e. man plays an active part in transforming OBJECTIVE REALITY into knowledge; and 5. the criterion for the validity of c. is practical, which is both the source and objective of c. Also CONCEPT, EPISTEMOLOGY, PERCEPTION, PRACTICE.

Cold War Hostile policies and practices, but not including open military warfare, pursued by the USA and the USSR against each other after W.W.II. The C.W. was more or less actively supported by other Western and Socialist countries respectively. The term was introduced by B. Baruch, an American politician, in a speech in Columbia (South Carolina) on 16 April 1947 and popularized by an American journalist, W. Lipmann. The methods resorted to in the C.W. included propaganda, psychological tactics, political manoeuvring, economic measures and military threats. More specifically, whilst the West resorted to the CONTAINMENT POLICY, the STRATEGIC EMBARGO, politically-motivated economic aid and the instigation of opposition in Eastern Europe against the USSR, the East engaged in inciting social unrest in the West, subversion, promoting NATIONAL LIBERATION MOVEMENTS in the Third World and obstructing the work of many international organizations. The C.W. proper began with the BERLIN BLOCKADE (March 1948) and virtually ended with the signing of the NUCLEAR TEST BAN TREATY by the USA, UK and the USSR (Aug. 1963). The C.W.'s most 'frigid' stage was reached during the Korean War (1950–53). The Socialist leaders trace the origin of the C.W. to Churchill's speech at Fulton (Missouri) in March 1946, in which he urged an alliance of the USA and the British Commonwealth nations against Soviet expansionism. The prevailing opinion in the West blamed the East and saw the C.W. as an expression of Soviet aggression and obstructionism, Stalin's and Khrushchev's designs to weaken and isolate the Western powers and the Socialist ambition to spread communism.

Collaborationism See MILLERANDISM.

Collective A term commonly used as a noun in the Socialist countries to denote a social group organized on the basis of DEMOCRATIC CENTRALISM, acting in a responsible way in the pursuit of socially acceptable objectives. Thus there may be a production, educational, cultural, sporting or military c., of which the first two are most common. The term is applied approvingly, reflecting the Marxist belief in COLLECTIVISM and the acceptance of the PRIMACY OF SOCIAL INTEREST, as opposed to INDIVIDUALISM and private interest.

Collective Agreement A term used in industrial relations denoting a firm understanding between the organizations representing the employer(s) and trade unions, defining conditions of work and remuneration for individual work accords. In capitalist countries, a c.a. is looked upon as a form of protection of workers' interests secured by organized labour against employers. In the Socialist centrally planned economies, conditions for negotiating a c.a. are laid down by the Council of Ministers, but the c.a. itself is negotiated between the relevant ministry or branch association and the trade union concerned. In practice, the trade union is the passive side since the c.a. is essentially derived from the directive planned production targets. Such an 'agreement' reflects the general line of the state policy, which usually regulates the following: 1. general conditions of employment and work in each socialized enterprise in the industry (vocational training, practical experience, physical and health work environment, and hours of work); 2. wages (standard rates, qualification allowances); 3. benefit entitlements (bonuses, housing and socio-cultural services); and 4. management-worker relations (especially those affecting the fulfilment of targets, methods and organization of work, effi-

ciency, and subsidiary activities and amenities such as canteens, crèches, reading rooms). In general, the Socialist countries subscribe to the 'privileged workers principle', i.e. individual agreements which are less favourable to the workers than is laid down in the relevant c.a. are nullified by the latter.

Collective Anarchism See ANARCHO-COMMUNISM.

Collective Bargaining A description used for the negotiations between a trade union representing the employees and representatives of the management or the employer. C.b. may involve wages, margins (payable for dangerous work, travel time anf fares), hours of work, pensions and other working and remuneration conditions. The term is used in capitalist countries and was popularized by Beatrice Webb after 1891. C.b. is regarded as one of the great achievements of the labour movement, as it gives workers the right to form unions and strengthens the workers' bargaining power. C.b. contrasts with individual b. which prevailed in the 19th c. and before, when attempts at c.b. were regarded as a form of 'conspiracy' and punishable by law.

Collective Consumption SOCIAL CONSUMPTION.

Collective Farm Also known as the 'agricultural production co-operative', a large farm operated by its members collectively. It is the dominant form of agricultural production organization in all the Socialist countries, except Poland and Yugoslavia (in which c.fs. occupy only 1 per cent and 7 per cent of the total agricultural land, respectively). Although, legally, in most Socialist countries land is considered to belong to the state, the management and working of the farm as well as the distribution of its output and income are left to the members. In contrast to the STATE FARM, the members of the c.f. are allowed to live in their own dwellings, are entitled to SUBSIDIARY PLOTS and share in the net income (after costs, taxes, collective needs are met) according to the work units performed. Work is usually organized in specialized PRODUCTION BRIGADES or PRODUCTION TEAMS. There are three types of c.f.: 1. those where land still belongs to individual members but the machinery is collectively owned; 2. integrated c.f., where there is no individual ownership of either equipment or land, but private living and consumption are allowed; and 3. those where all the means of production are socialized and living is communal. The second type is now prevalent, whilst the third category is characteristic of China. Ideologically, it is vaguely envisaged that under FULL COMMUNISM c. f.s will be transformed into state farms. The name of the c.f. in application to the USSR is *KOLKHOZ*. Also *TOZ, ARTEL,* COMMUNE.

Collective Farm Market A relatively free market in the Socialist countries, where collective farmers can sell their privately grown produce on SUBSIDIARY PLOTS. The prices prevailing in the c.f.m. are not fixed by the state, but are free and fluctuate according to the current supply and demand. They are usually much higher than the state-fixed prices administered in shops for the same products. This market is tolerated for a time, as it encourages extra farming production (especially milk and dairy products, meats, vegetables and fruits) and thus helps overcome shortages. It also provides extra income to collective farmers, whose income is below the national average.

Collective Incentives Those incentives for a work entity which are awarded not to individuals but to a group of workers, such as a team, brigade, plant, or enterprise or industry. C.i. are well developed in the Socialist countries, where they are considered to be ideologically superior to individual incentives, as the former cultivates a collective spirit and social responsibility. C.i. may be either material (in cash or kind) or moral (appealing to the group's pride, work satisfaction and comrade-

ship). An example of a moral c.i. for a group would be the honour of being awarded the title of the BRIGADE OF COMMUNIST (OR SOCIALIST) LABOUR, the industry banner awarded to a factory, or the title of 'Exemplary Enterprise'.

Collective Leadership The system in an organization where leadership is shared by a group of persons or, in an extreme case, by all its members. This principle is subscribed to by the Communist parties. Stalin reaffirmed its (theoretical) validity and the CENTRAL COMMITTEE and its POLITBURO are usually cited as exemplifying the rule. However, in practice, a c.l. has often proved unworkable, whereupon the institutional set-up and the acceptance of another principle known as DEMOCRATIC CENTRALISM has resulted in a concentration of authority in one person and, in extreme cases, resulted in a PERSONALITY CULT. The principle of c.l. was reaffirmed after the death of Lenin (1924) and Stalin (1953) and the removal of Khrushchev (1964). Thus, after Stalin's death, the leadership was at first shared by Khrushchev, Malenkov and Bulganin, but KHRUSHCHEV soon emerged as the principal leader, monopolizing the most crucial sources of power – the First Secretary of the Central Committee of the CPSU, the unofficial 'head' of the Presidium of the CC of the CPSU, Chairman of the Council of Ministers (Prime Minister) and Chairman of the Bureau of the CC of the RUSSIAN SOVIET FEDERATED SOCIALIST REPUBLIC. After his removal, the c.l. was shared by Brezhnev (Secretary-General of the CC of the CPSU), Podgorny (President) and Kosygin (Prime Minister). But by 1978 Brezhnev had also become President, Marshal, and the Chairman of the Defence Council. C.l. has also proved unworkable in the mangement of enterprises, where the rule of a one-man authority (exercised by the DIRECTOR) has been firmly accepted, with some qualifying exceptions in China and Yugoslavia.

Collective Management A basis of operation of socialized enterprises and institutions, where management responsibilities are shared collectively by all working members or their elected representatives. C.m. is regarded by Marxists to be ideologically superior to single person management and has been widely experimented with in the Socialist countries. C.m. was introduced in Soviet Russia soon after the Bolshevik Revolution in 1917. However, in most cases, it proved disastrous and was finally abandoned in 1934 in favour of a single-person managerial approach. A version of c.m. is WORKERS' SELF-MANAGEMENT, developed in Yugoslavia and to a lesser extent in Czechoslovakia and Poland.

Collectivism In political, economic and social theory and practice, a system where power, management, administration and the ownership of the means of production are shared collectively in one form or another. Although the doctrine of c. goes back at least to the 18th c., the term was first used in its modern sense in 1835 by J. G. Colins (1783–1859) in *Le Pact Social*, but was popularized only after 1869 by the FIRST INTERNATIONAL. In contrast to INDIVIDUALISM, c. emphasizes the PRIMACY OF SOCIAL INTEREST. There are different degrees of c., ranging from idealistic communities where everything is contributed, provided and shared collectively and where there is no central authority (as exemplified by ANARCHO-COMMUNISM), to a centralized, hierarchical and directive system regulating all aspects of social life. In the Socialist countries, the term c. is often used synonymously with co-operativism. Thus, a distinction is made between collective enterprises and farms (managed and worked by the members on a co-operative basis) and state entities (owned and managed by the state employing wage-earners). In capitalist countries, the term c. is used in a broader sense and may denote any unwelcome form of socialism, state intervention and generous social security.

Collectivization In its general sense the SOCIALIZATION of agriculture, i.e. the expropriation of private owners of land, farm buildings, equipment and livestock, usually without compensation, and the formation of large collective or state farms. But in its narrower (and more appropriate) meaning c. denotes consolidation of peasant holdings into COLLECTIVE FARMS, where land is state or collectively owned and the farm is managed and worked by its members along co-operative lines. C. in this sense is best exemplified by the USSR from 1929 to 1938 when 26,000,000 peasant holdings were forced into 235,000 collective farms. C. is an aspect of the socialization of the means of production, and, consequently, a normal move after the Communist accession to power. Its purpose is to neutralize the power of large landowners and rich peasants, promote social equality, facilitate mechanization, achieve economies of scale, release manpower to industry and to integrate agriculture into economic planning. C. is theoretically voluntary, but in the Soviet case it was crudely imposed from above, resulting in the rich peasants (*KULAKS*) being eliminated in the process. In other Socialist countries, c. has been more or less voluntary or has at least been carried out in a more humane manner.

Colombian Communist Party COMMUNIST PARTY OF COLOMBIA.

Colonial Capitalism A concept first used by Max Weber (1864–1920) in *The Protestant Ethic and the Spirit of Capitalism* (1904–5), to denote the capitalist system where wealth was derived mainly from the exploitation of colonies in the form of cheap raw materials and where lucrative markets are protected for manufacturers. Also COLONIALISM, IMPERIALISM, NEO-COLONIALISM.

Colonialism The economic, political, social and cultural domination of less developed areas by stronger, developed countries. Its history goes back to pre-capitalist times, when its purpose was to obtain slaves, occupy land for settlement and establish trading posts. The nature of

c. changed after the middle of the 19th c., when most less developed countries became systematically subordinate to the leading Western imperial powers. The term has been in common use since the Bandung Conference in 1955, when President Sukarno employed it in its modern sense, in preference to the previously used term, IMPERIALISM. The use of the term c. has been further popularized by the Communist leaders and writers and employed as a propaganda weapon directed against the most powerful capitalist countries. C. has been identified by Marxists with the exploitation of poorer nations (through cheap sources of raw materials and labour and protected markets for manufacturers), the retardation of their economic, social, political and cultural development and the suppression of NATIONAL LIBERATION MOVEMENTS. Conflicting colonial interests have also been blamed for wars between colonial powers (such as the Spanish-American War of 1898, the Russo-Japanese War of 1904–5 and W.W.II). In the Communist view, DECOLONIZATION since W.W.II has not led to the complete disappearance of c., but has re-emerged as NEO-COLONIALISM. Also INTERNAL COLONIALISM.

Combination Acts The legislation passed by the British Parliament in 1799 and 1800 banning the organization of trade unions ('combinations of workers'). The penalties included imprisonment or transportation to penal colonies for any worker who combined with another to secure higher wages or shorter working hours. Owing to widespread industrial unrest and the work of social reformers (especially Francis Place), the C.A. were partly repealed during 1824–25.

Combine See *KOMBINAT*.

Comecon A short version popularly used in the West for the COUNCIL FOR MUTUAL ECONOMIC ASSISTANCE. The abbreviation was originally understood to stand for the 'Communist Economic International', to parallel with such terms as COMINTERN and COMINFORM.

Cominform The commonly used abbreviation in the West for the 'Communist Information Bureau', which was offically designated in Russian as *Informationnoe Biuro Kommunisticheskikh i Rabochikh Party* (Information Bureau of the Communist and Workers Parties), abbreviated to *Informbiuro*. It was established on Stalin's initiative at a meeting of the representatives of the ruling Parties of Bulgaria, Czechoslovakia, Hungary, Poland, Romania, the USSR and Yugoslavia, plus the delegates from the French and Italian Communist Parties in Warsaw in Sep. 1947. In a sense, the C. was an attempt to revive the COMINTERN, but it had a smaller membership and less ambitious objectives. It was essentially a Soviet response to counter the TRUMAN DOCTRINE and the MARSHALL PLAN. The function of the C. was to place the exchange of information amongst the member Parties on a systematic basis and to co-ordinate their activities. Further, Stalin hoped to be able to exercise a tighter control over the European Communist Parties. The headquarters of the C. were first located in Belgrade, but in 1948 they were transferred to Bucharest. In practice the C. was of little worth. Its only significant action was the condemnation of Tito and the Communist Party in Yugoslavia (as it was known then) in June 1948. The corresponding economic boycott was short-lived. The C. became dormant after Stalin's death (1953) and was formally dissolved in April 1956 with Khrushchev's gesture of a reconciliation with Yugoslavia.

Cominformists A small faction of hardline Communists in Yugoslavia which has supported the stand of the COMINFORM in the international Communist movement, including its action against Tito's regime from 1948 to 1953. They have been accused of forming a Communist party to rival the ruling LEAGUE OF COMMUNISTS OF YUGOSLAVIA and of plotting to restore the Stalinist model of socialism. One such group was arrested in Montenegro in 1974, tried and sentenced to imprisonment.

Comintern The commonly used abbreviated form of the Communist International (*Kommunistichesky Internatsional*, in Russian), specifically referring to the THIRD INTERNATIONAL, which existed over the period 1919–43. It was established at its First Congress in Petrograd (now Leningrad) in March 1919 and was attended by LENIN, ZINOVIEV (its first Secretary-General), TROTSKY, BUKHARIN, RADEK and 47 other delegates representing Communist parties in 30 countries. The original purpose of the C. was to promote the international unity of the Communist parties and co-ordinate their activities towards the world proletarian revolution. Lenin saw its function as the 'general staff of world revolution', instrumental in the creation of the 'International Soviet Republic'. Lenin worked out the TWENTY-ONE CONDITIONS OF ADMISSION TO COMINTERN and the principle of DEMOCRATIC CENTRALISM was adopted. The decision of the C. was binding on the member Communist parties, and an International Control Commission was created in 1921 to supervise international Communist discipline. In reality under Stalin, the C. became a tool of Soviet foreign policy, manipulated to protect and further the interests of the USSR. The C. held seven world Congresses in 1919, 1920, 1921, 1922, 1924, 1928, 1935 and then virtually lapsed. Its work was hampered by doctrinal and personality differences. It never achieved much and most of its Soviet and foreign leaders were eliminated during Stalin's GREAT PURGES of the late 1930s. The C.'s main official organ was *COMMUNIST INTERNATIONAL*, published from 1919 to 1943. In May 1943, as a gesture of goodwill to the Western Allies in W.W.II, the C. was formally dissolved by the Presidium of its Executive Committee. Also COMMUNIST YOUTH INTERNATIONAL, *KRESTINTERN*, PROFINTERN, SPORTINTERN.

Comisco An abbreviated form of *Comité International Socialist Consultatif*, meaning the 'Consultative Committee of the Socialist International'. It was a temporary rallying centre of the international socialist organization in existence from Dec. 1947 to June 1951. It was succeeded by the SOCIALIST INTERNATIONAL.

Command Economy Economy noted for a centralized, directive system of planning and management, where targets and even methods of production are imposed on the enterprises from above. Its features include a hierarchical authoritarian structure of the transmission of DIRECTIVES, a central allocation of resources in physical terms, TIGHT PLANNING, BOTTLENECKS, a predominantly BUDGETARY FINANCING OF INVESTMENT (as distinct from SELF-FINANCING), fixed prices over long periods and the minimal use of MATERIAL INCENTIVES. In effect, the system is inflexible, enterprises have little independence, and it is more responsive to bureaucratic commands than to the users' needs. The system prevailed in the European Socialist countries up to the early 1960s (in Yugoslavia up to the early 1950s), but appeared in its extreme form in the USSR under Stalin from 1928 to 1953. The term is sometimes used in application to any economy (incl. capitalist) in wartime.

Commanding Heights A term used in the USSR in the 1920s, especially over the period coinciding with the NEW ECONOMIC POLICY (1921–28). After the economic chaos of WAR COMMUNISM (1917–20) and on Lenin's initiative, relatively free markets and private enterprise were restored to the spheres of agriculture, consumer manufacturing and wholesale and retail trade, as a tactical retreat to reconstruct and strengthen the economy. But the 'construction of socialism' was still continued, and the economy was centrally controlled through such strategic sectors (c.h.) as the socialization of land, heavy industry, the transport and communications network, the credit system and the state foreign trade monopoly.

Commandism A concentration and exercise of power at the centre, best exemplified by a COMMAND ECONOMY. C. leads to BUREAUCRACY and SUBJECTIVISM, the blind execution of orders to curry favour with the higher authorities, inflexibility and the inability to respond easily to changing conditions. It was partly abandoned after the ECONOMIC REFORMS in the European Socialist countries.

Commercial Capitalism In a Marxist interpretation, the early phase of CAPITALISM which appeared in societies which incorporated SLAVERY, FEUDALISM and preceded INDUSTRIAL CAPITALISM. Commercial capital emerges as a result of the circulation of commodities and money, and plays an active role in PRIMITIVE CAPITALIST ACCUMULATION and the development of capitalist production and social relations. C.c. also coexists with industrial and FINANCE CAPITALISM, but unlike finance capital, it does not lead to the creation of VALUE. Consequently, the profit of the commercial capitalist comes from the SURPLUS VALUE created in MATERIAL PRODUCTION.

Commissariat PEOPLE'S COMMISSARIAT.

Commissar A term previously used in the USSR, denoting 'commissioner' or a high-ranking official or bureaucrat. After the Bolshevik Revolution in 1917, government ministers were renamed 'People's Commissars', and were known collectively as the 'Council of People's Commissars'. These designations remained officially in force until 1946. There were also 'military commissars' (up to 1940), who were attached to military units, and were responsible for the political education and reliability of the troops. In addition, there were other officials carrying this designation who were responsible for clearly defined functions or even *ad hoc* tasks.

Committee for Co-operation in Planning Work An organ of the COUNCIL FOR MUTUAL ECONOMIC ASSISTANCE established in 1962 and located in Moscow. Its function is to improve and standardize planning methods so as to facilitate the co-ordination of the economic plans of the member countries and to promote their economic integration. The Committee is attached to the EXECUTIVE COMMITTEE OF THE CMEA and co-operates closely with its Secretariat.

Committee for Scientific and Technical Co-operation An organ of the COUNCIL FOR MUTUAL ECONOMIC ASSISTANCE for the co-ordination and promotion of scientific and technical research and development amongst the member countries. It was originally established in 1962 under the name 'Permanent Committee for the Co-ordination of Scientific and Technical Research', but was reorganized and given its present name in 1971. The Committee is located in Moscow and is attached directly to the EXECUTIVE COMMITTEE OF THE CMEA.

Committee for Social Self-Defence (*Komitet Samoobrony Społecznej*, in Polish) an association originally formed in Poland in 1976 as the 'Workers' Defence Committee', but renamed in Sep. 1977. Its members are Marxists of one type or another, and do not question the existing social system in principle, but only the details of its operation. One of its most prominent members is Professor E. Lipinski, a highly respected economist. Its aims are: 1. to fight unfair reprisals imposed by the authorities for political, philosophical, religious and racial reasons; 2. to ensure the enforcement of guaranteed human rights; and 3. to provide legal, financial and moral aid to persons adversely affected by the encroachment on their rights. It publishes a periodical *The Worker* (*Robotnik*) and co-operates with another group recently formed, the 'Movement for the Defence of Human and Civil Rights' (*ROPCO*), which publishes *Opinion* (*Opinia*).

Committee for State Security (in the USSR) See *KGB*.

Committees of Poor Peasants Local squads consisting of agricultural labourers and poor peasants in the USSR formed by the Bolsheviks in June 1918. The Committees had two functions: 1. to seize land, equipment and livestock belonging to rich peasants (the *KULAKS*) and redistribute it amongst the landless, poor and middle peasants; and 2. to assist the FOOD DETACHMENTS in finding, collecting and confiscating food, especially if hoarded by rich peasants. The Committees were most active in the second half of 1918, when their number reached 105,000, and they redistributed some 50m. hectares of farming land. At the end of that year they were absorbed by the Rural SOVIETS. The Bolsheviks created the Committees as a revolutionary stratagem to gain support from the rural masses and intensify the class struggle in the countryside. After the land was redistributed it was then collectivized (COLLECTIVIZATION).

Commodity In the Marxian political economy, a product of labour for sale in the market. Its distinguishing features are: 1. it is a combination of material qualities and SOCIALLY-INDISPENSABLE LABOUR; 2. it must have use-value, i.e. it must be useful and subject to exchange; 3. c. production implies the division of labour; 4. c. production is the essence of capitalist production, where the market mechanism and private enterprise prevail; and 5. in a capitalist economy, even labour is a c., as it has value and is bought and sold. In the Marxist view, capitalism is unduly preoccupied with c. production (COMMODITY FETISHISM), irrespective of its social use, so long as it is profitable. In a centrally planned Socialist economy, only consumer goods produced for the market and all goods for export are classed as commodities.

Commodity Convertibility See MONETARY AND SUBSTANTIVE CONVERTIBILITY.

Commodity Fetishism A term used by Marx (in *CAPITAL* vol. I, 1867) for the production and exchange of goods motivated solely by profit maximization. He regarded c.f. to be a distinguishing feature of CAPITALISM, where production for sale in the market becomes an end in itself to the disregard of social needs and social justice. In this process, the producer and trader are at the mercy of fluctuating prices and demand. Consequently, commodities predominate and relations amongst commodities dominate relations amongst people. C.f. is also identified with an obsessive striving for money, i.e. in particular for what money can buy, to the exclusion of other values. It is held that in a Socialist economy c.f. disappears, owing to central economic planning, and the removal of the private profit motive and the market mechanism. C.f. must not be confused with the FETISHISM OF OUTPUT, which may occur under Socialist economic planning.

Commodity-Money Relations The Marxist description of market relations, where items are bought and sold in the market at prices more or less reflecting the conditions of supply and demand. C.-m.r. appeared under societies which incorporated SLAVERY and continued under FEUDALISM, but reached their greatest development in the capitalist market economy (CAPITALISM), where consumer goods and services, the means of production (land and capital) and labour become commodities (COMMODITY). When based on the private ownership of the means of production and the market mechanism, c.-m.r. generate contradictions between private and social interests, leading to antagonisms between SOCIAL CLASSES, FLUCTUATIONS, CRISES and the RESERVE ARMY OF WORKERS. These contradictions become particularly acute under MONOPOLY CAPITALISM. In a Socialist centrally planned economy, c.-m.r. do not apply to labour, the means of production and producer goods. They are virtually limited to consumer goods and services sold for private consumption, products sold in foreign markets and to the transactions between state and co-operative producers. Where c.-m.r. do occur in a Socialist economy, they are different from those under capitalism, as they are based on the social ownership of the means of production and central economic planning. Since the ECONOMIC REFORMS of the 1960s (1950, in the case of Yugoslavia), c.-m.r. have been substantially strengthened in the European Socialist countries. However, under FULL COMMUNISM they are expected to disappear, as it is assumed that work and distribution will be governed by the principle 'FROM EACH ACCORDING TO HIS ABILITY, TO EACH ACCORDING TO HIS NEEDS'.

Commodity Theory of Labour Theory reproachfully attributed by Marxists at first to VULGAR POLITICAL ECONOMY and then to bourgeois economics. In their view, the c.t.l. was substantiated in practice by PRODUCTION RELATIONS existing in the capitalist economy. The theory assumes that labour is one of the basic factors or production, i.e. together with land and capital. As such, it is subject to market dealings with supply and demand determining its price in the form of wages (e.g. rent and interest in the case of land and capital). The dispossessed PROLETARIAT has no means of survival except by selling its labour to capitalists who own the means of production. Under these condititions, labour is like a COMMODITY, as it is bought and sold at its price determined by the supply of and demand for labour. As interpreted by some classical economists, this price (wage) is governed by the utility of labour on the one hand, and by its cost of production (reproduction at subsistence level, i.e. the IRON LAW OF WAGES) on the other. Marxists reject the moral validity of the theory, as it amounts to the 'dehumanization' of labour, stressing that labour cannot be placed in the same category as land and capital. It is argued that labour alone is the creator of value, whilst land and capital are merely means of production. To Marxists, the theory amounts to an apologetic justification for the capitalist economic and social system, where the owners of the means of production live by the exploitation of labour.

Common Freight Car Pool An organization established by the member countries of the COUNCIL FOR MUTUAL ECONOMIC ASSISTANCE for operating the joint use of rail freight cars to minimize their empty runs in international and domestic traffic. It was founded in 1963 with its head office in Prague and now has about 250,000 rail cars at its disposal, all contributed by the member countries. The Pool represents collective-use property and no charges are made for using the cars, but penalty levies are enforced for excessive use by a country above its quota.

Common Programme The provisional Constitution proclaimed by the Communist regime in China in Oct. 1949, which was in force until it was replaced by the Constitution of 1954. The C.P. had been formulated and accepted by the CHINESE PEOPLE'S POLITICAL CONSULTATIVE CONFERENCE at its meeting on 21–30 Sep. 1949. The Conference represented all non-bourgeois political parties but was completely dominated by the CHINESE COMMUNIST PARTY. The C.P. set out the general principles to guide the government during the transitional period. It guaranteed the freedom of national minorities, offered to protect the rights of the overseas Chinese, indicated a scheme for the RESOCIALIZATION of the former middle and upper classes, outlined a plan for the modernization of the country and defined the role of the PEOPLE'S LIBERATION ARMY in the task of reconstruction.

Communalism A system of social organization where there are self-governing communities, with a minimum of centralization and external coercion. In each community, most of the activities are regulated by tradition and custom in the spirit of co-operation. The individual is subordinate to the communal interest and at the same time he or she is protected by the community concerned. The concept of c. has been applied mostly to PRIMITIVE COMMUNISM and to communities established along idealistic lines in pre-Socialist

societies. Also COMMUNE, COM-
MUNITARIANISM, PEOPLE'S COMMUNE,
PHALANSTERY.

Communal Property Property which is
freely open to the members of the community on a non-exclusive basis, i.e. the
authority cannot exclude either an individual or a group from using it and no
group or individual can exclude another.
C.p. has always existed in one form or
another in all societies – pre-capitalist,
capitalist and socialist, as exemplified by
parks, roads, rivers, and the like. C.p. of
the MEANS OF PRODUCTION is rare in
capitalist society, but it is complete or
nearly so under PRIMITIVE COMMUNISM
and under socialism (SOCIALIZATION OF
THE MEANS OF PRODUCTION).

Commune In the orthodox Marxist
theory, the highest form of social organization for work and living, where not only
all the means of production (land, buildings, equipment) are collectively owned,
but also the means of consumption (food,
dwellings, means of transport and other
consumer durables) are collectively
shared. It is an organized production and
social community in whose management
all members participate directly, or indirectly through their elected representatives. Members live in communal homes
and share kitchens, laundries, nurseries
and recreation facilities. Work and distribution are based on the idealistic principle, 'FROM EACH ACCORDING TO HIS
ABILITY, TO EACH ACCORDING TO HIS
NEEDS'. The term can be traced back to
the Middle Ages in France, where small
village communities were organized along
communal lines. Similar communities
were developed by religious, socialist or
anarchist idealists in Italy and North and
South America in the 19th c., but were
short-lived. The c. became a favourite
production and social entity in the USSR
after the Bolsehvik Revolution in the
1920s, especially in agriculture (AGRICUL-
TURAL COMMUNE), but was disbanded
after 1931. The most ambitious c. drive

was embarked upon in China in 1958,
where it is known as the PEOPLE'S COM-
MUNE, but which has several characteristics distinct from other c.s.

Communism An ideology postulating full
social equality and a political and
economic system for its implementation as
envisaged by Marxists. Although the idea
of c. goes back to ancient times, the term
itself was first introduced in secret French
revolutionary societies between 1834 and
1839 and was derived from the French
communes or small village communities
which appeared in the Middle Ages
(etymologically, the term can be traced to
the Latin *communis*, meaning 'held or
done in common'). The term entered public use in France in 1841 to denote the
proletarian and militant revision of socialism, whilst in English it appeared first in
1843 (in *New Age*) where it was popularized by the advocates of OWENISM. Marx
and Engels used the designation c. in the
COMMUNIST MANIFESTO (1848) to distinguish their socialism from the UTOPIAN
SOCIALISM of the earlier French and English theorists. More specifically, the concept of c. has since been applied to denote
the following seven different meanings: 1.
the mode of living in idealistic, self-
managed communities, where the means
of production *and* consumption are
shared on a communal basis (more correctly described as COMMUNALISM); 2.
another name for MARXISM, i.e. the complete system of philosophical, political,
economic and sociological concepts, critiques, theories and prescriptions for the
demise of capitalism and the creation of a
communist society; 3. a vague general description of the social system after the
overthrow of capitalism, consisting of two
stages: the lower phase of c. (also called
'socialism') and the higher phase of c.
(also called simply 'c.', or 'full c.'); 4. in its
most appropriate sense as specifically understood by Marxists, the ultimate socio-
economic formation of FULL COMMUNISM,
following the transitional stage of socialism; 5. a totalitarian system of government noted for the supremacy of the state

over the individual, based on the mono-party system of all power exercised by the Communist party, as contrasted with Western parliamentary democracy; 6. the authoritarian political and economic system based on the DICTATORSHIP OF THE PROLETARIAT and a hierarchical structure of authority in force in the present 25 or so SOCIALIST COUNTRIES ruled by the Communist parties which came to power not by democratic elections but imposed by a revolutionary seizure of power or by the domineering support of the USSR; and 7. the extremist militant ideology and policies pursued by the Communist regimes, especially those of China and the USSR, in the international scene, resorting to subversion, terrorism and aggressive wars designed ultimately to destroy capitalism. C. has evoked strong emotional responses and attitudes in its favour and in opposition to it. This is exemplified in the following definitions or characterizations of c.: (a) 'When society can inscribe on its banners, "from each according to his ability, to each according to his needs"' (K. Marx); (b) 'When people become accustomed to the performance of public duties without any specific machinery or compulsion' (V. I. Lenin); (c) 'A mighty, unifying thunderstorm, marking the springtime of mankind' (N. S. Khrushchev); (d) 'A hammer which we use to crush the enemy' (Mao Tse-tung); (e) 'The highest formation of society which replaces the capitalist formation' (*Great Soviet Encyclopedia*); (f) 'Heavens below' (W. H. G. Armytage); (g) 'The opium of the intellectuals' (Raymond Aron); (h) 'The devil's imitation of Christianity (A. W. Tozer); (i) 'An untenable illusion' (Sigmund Freud); (j) 'The corruption of a dream of justice' (Adlai Stevenson); (k) 'Autocracy turned upside down' (Alexander Herzen); (l) 'The type of totalitarianism which consists of three basic factors for controlling the people .. power ... ownership ... ideology' (Milovan Djilas); (m) 'An apostasy from civilization' (J. C. Murray); and (n) 'Treason ... not against governments but against humanity' (Richard M. Nixon).

'**Communism is Soviet power plus the electrification of the whole country**' A slogan coined by Lenin as part of his efforts to establish the State Commission for the Electrification of Russia in 1920 (*GOELRO*).

Communist As an adjective, pertaining to COMMUNISM or to any of the 25 or so Socialist countries ruled by the Communist parties; as a noun, it may mean one who believes in Communism, or one who actively supports Communism, or one who is a member of the Communist party, or (disparagingly) one who holds extremist radical views intolerant of other ideologies and is committed to violent revolutionary action. The term c. was first used in French in 1840 and was introduced in England in the same year by Goodwin Barmby (in *The New Moral World*). Barmby was an advocate of OWENISM who in the following year founded the London Communist Propaganda Society. The term had been well established by the time Marx and Engels had written their most famous joint work in 1848, the *COMMUNIST MANIFESTO*, in which they described the Communists as 'the most advanced and resolute section of the working class parties of every country, that section which pushes forward all others'.

Communist Academy Name of a learned research-propagandist organization in the USSR in existence from 1923 to 1935 for the purpose of promoting DIALECTICAL MATERIALISM, discrediting philosophical IDEALISM and defending MARXISM-LENINISM. The Academy created several specialized institutes and operated under the Central Committee of the RUSSIAN COMMUNIST PARTY (OF THE BOLSHEVIKS) and, after 1925, under the ALL-UNION COMMUNIST PARTY (OF THE BOLSHEVIKS). The C.A. was the successor to the ACADEMY OF SOCIAL SCIENCES (founded in 1918) which was dissolved in 1935 when its institutes were absorbed by the Academy of Sciences of the USSR.

Communist Control Act A law enacted by the US Congress in 1954, directed against the COMMUNIST PARTY OF THE UNITED STATES and its members. The Act, passed at the height of McCARTHYISM, declared the CPUS as 'an instrument of conspiracy to overthrow the Government of the United States' and deprived it of legal rights and privileges normally accorded to other organizations. The Party was denied the right to enter into contracts, thus bringing forth lawsuits for the right to nominate candidates for elections. Although the Act did not make the membership of the Party illegal, its members were subject to the McCURREN-WOOD INTERNAL SECURITY ACT of 1950 and its SUBVERSIVE ACTIVITIES CONTROL BOARD. The C.C.A. was unprecedented in American history, representing the first legal measure preventing the use of the ballot by a political party. Doubts have been expressed about the constitutionality of the Act, resulting in its limited enforcement.

Communist Cornucopia The age of plenty assumed by Marxists to exist when the stage of FULL COMMUNISM is attained in the future. It is envisaged that technological progress combined with the SOCIAL OWNERSHIP OF THE MEANS OF PRODUCTION and ECONOMIC PLANNING will enable the economy to become saturated with production, thus solving the problem of the scarcity of goods and services. There will be total affluence and work and income will be based on the Marxian principle, 'FROM EACH ACCORDING TO HIS ABILITY, TO EACH ACCORDING TO HIS NEEDS'. The term 'cornucopia' is of Latin origin, meaning the 'horn of plenty', referring (in Greek mythology) to the goat Amathea from which Zeus suckled.

Communist Dictatorship See DICTATORSHIP OF THE PROLETARIAT.

Communist Education See INDOCTRINATION, RESOCIALIZATION, SOCIALIST EDUCATION INTERNATIONAL, SOCIALIZATION.

Communist Front A critical description given to an organization not generally being identified as openly communist, but which is manipulated by communists in one way or another. Such an organization may be: 1. either influenced or controlled by communists from outside by using inside officials; or 2. infiltrated by communists; or 3. by establishing a new entity by communists using a name calculated to disguise its real activities and objectives. The term was popularized in the West in the 1930s, after the COMINTERN decided in 1935 to abandon the CLASS-AGAINST-CLASS TACTICS in favour of ENTRYISM and POPULAR FRONTS. Thus, in the USA in the 1950s, at least 100 C.f. organizations were officially identified. Of particular interest are the INTERNATIONAL COMMUNIST FRONT ORGANIZATIONS.

Communist Information Bureau See COMINFORM.

Communist International In its general sense, the term refers to the world Communist fraternity, emphasizing the international character and interests of the working class movement and implying the ultimate ideals of the disappearance of national boundaries under FULL COMMUNISM. More specifically, the term has been used to designate the international organizations established after 1863 for the coordination of the policies of the Communist (or Socialist) parties with a view to world revolution. They are as follows: 1. The FIRST INTERNATIONAL (1864–76); 2. The SECOND INTERNATIONAL (1889–1914) (strictly speaking a SOCIALIST INTERNATIONAL); 3. The SECOND-AND-A-HALF INTERNATIONAL (1921–23); 4. The THIRD INTERNATIONAL (1919–43), better known as the COMINTERN; 5. The FOURTH INTERNATIONAL (1938–   ); and 6. As a consequence of the SINO-SOVIET DISPUTE, the Chinese Marxists have considered launching a Fifth International. In its widest sense, the C.I. may also include the INTERNATIONAL WORKERS' ASSOCIATION (the Berlin International, 1922–33), the COMINFORM

(1947–56) and the INTERNATIONAL CONFERENCES OF THE COMMUNIST AND WORKERS' PARTIES. But in its narrowest and most appropriate meaning, the C.I. denotes the Comintern.

Communist International The official organ of the executive committee of the THIRD INTERNATIONAL, published in Petrograd (in 1924 renamed Leningrad) and then in Moscow from 1919 to 1943. The organ was established by G. R. Zinoviev, its founding editor and the first Chairman of the COMINTERN. It dealt with the theory, strategy and practices of the international Communist movement. It appeared in English, French, German and Russian editions, and for short periods also in Chinese, Czech, Danish-Norwegian and Spanish.

Communist League According to the Communist interpretation, a secret organization of German revolutionaries in Belgium, England, France, Italy and Switzerland, in existence from 1847 to 1852. The beginnings of the C.L. go back to 1834 when a group of German refugee socialists in Paris founded the Exiles' League. However, the more extreme members broke away two years later and created the League of the Just. Some of the latter members then went to London where they formed the Federation of the Just, which in 1840 was transformed into the German Workers' Educational Association, subsequently re-named the Communist Workers Educational Society. The latter group hosted the Second Congress of the C.L. in Dec. 1847 at which Marx and Engels were invited to draw up a declaration setting forth the objectives of the C.L. A declaration was published in Feb. 1848 under the title of the *COMMUNIST MANIFESTO*. Some critical historians maintain that the C.L. was not a real, significant organization, but largely a product of Marx and Engels's wishful thinking, in which casual gatherings of scattered exiles were elevated to the rank of an international Communist association.

Communist Manifesto, The A declaration prepared by MARX and ENGELS at the invitation of the Second Congress of the COMMUNIST LEAGUE in London in Dec. 1847 and which appeared first in Germany (under the title of *Manifest der Kommunistischen Partei*) in Feb. 1848, shortly before the REVOLUTION OF 1848–49. In the same year a Polish version was printed, whilst the first English translation was published in 1850 (by Helen Macfarlane in *The Red Republican*) and the Russian in 1869 (by BAKUNIN in *Kolokol*, in Geneva). *The C.M.* was re-written in 1872 in a more radical version after the experience and failure of the PARIS COMMUNE in 1870–71. *The C.M.* was a pamphlet consisting of four chapters addressed to the workers, written in a simple and challenging style, and constituted the first programmatic statement on modern communism. It contained such basic Marxist propositions as the CLASS STRUGGLE, HISTORICAL MATERIALISM, the DICTATORSHIP OF THE PROLETARIAT, PROLETARIAN INTERNATIONALISM, the SOCIALIZATION OF THE MEANS OF PRODUCTION and the inevitability of the BREAKDOWN OF CAPITALISM. By 1980, *the C.M.* had been translated into 100 languages, appeared in more than 950 editions (470 in the USSR alone, with 27m. copies) and has enjoyed a circulation exceeded by few other publications in world history.

Communist Parties, Non-ruling Those Communist parties which are not in power at the national level. Their total number in the world in the late 1970s exceeded 200 (incl. splinter Parties), i.e. those outside the 25 or so SOCIALIST COUNTRIES. Of the 200, only those in 30 countries can be regarded as significant. The n.-r.C.p. are noted for their differing interpretations of Marxism. Consequently, they follow different programmes and methods to gain power, ranging from orthodox MARXISM, MARXISM-LENINISM and TROTSKYISM, to EUROCOMMUNISM and indigenous blends of traditionalism-communism. The total membership of the n.-r.C.p. in the late 1970s was 4.9m., compared with 66.7m. of the ruling C.p. The 15 largest n.-r.C.p., according to the claimed or estimated membership (incl. splinter parties and groups), by countries is: 1. Italy – 1,800,000; 2. India – 690,000; 3. France – 600,000; 4. Japan – 370,000; 5. Spain. – 300,000; 6. Portugal – 120,000; 7. Chile – 100,000; 8. Argentina – 70,000; 9. Mexico – 60,000; 10. Finland – 48,000; 11. FR of Germany – 40,000; 12. Greece – 30,000; 13. Great Britain – 30,000; 14. Turkey – 25,000; and 15. Austria – 20,000. In the following 27 countries the Communist parties are illegal: Algeria, Bangladesh, Bolivia, Brazil, Burma, Chile, Egypt, El Salvador, Guatemala, Haiti, Honduras, Indonesia, Iran, Jordan, Malaysia, Nepal, Nicaragua, Nigeria, Pakistan, Paraguay, the Philippines, Saudi Arabia, Sudan, Thailand, Tunisia, Turkey and Uruguay.

Communist Parties, Ruling Those Communist parties which are in power, effectively controlling the legislation and governments in their respective countries. This applies above all to the 16 Socialist bloc countries in which the official names of the Communist parties (in descending order of their membership in the late 1970s) are as follows: 1. CHINESE C.P. (35,000,000); 2. C.P. OF THE SOVIET UNION (16,200,000); 3. ROMANIAN C.P. (2,700,000); 4. POLISH UNITED WORKERS' PARTY (2,570,000); 5. SOCIALIST UNITY PARTY OF [EAST] GERMANY (2,080,000); 6. KOREAN WORKERS' PARTY (1,800,000); 7. LEAGUE OF COMMUNISTS OF YUGO-SLAVIA (1,540,000); 8. VIETNAM C.P. (1,530,000); 9. CZECHOSLOVAK C.P. (1,380,000); 10. BULGARIAN C.P. (790,000); 11. HUNGARIAN SOCIALIST WORKERS' PARTY (770,000); 12. C.P. OF CUBA (200,000); 13. ALBANIAN PARTY OF LABOUR (100,000); 14. MONGOLIAN PEOPLE'S REVOLUTIONARY PARTY (67,000); 15. PEOPLE'S REVOLUTIONARY PARTY OF LAOS (15,000); and 16. KAMPUCHEAN UNITED FRONT FOR NATIONAL SALVATION (10,000). In addition there are nine other r.C.p. (as of the late 1970s) which are Communist in one sense or another and whose precise membership is not known; alphabetically arranged they are: 17. AFRICAN PARTY FOR THE INDEPENDENCE OF GUINEA AND CABO VERDE (in the Republic of Guinea-Bissau); 18. CONGOLESE PARTY OF LABOUR; 19. LIBERATION FRONT OF MOZAMBIQUE (also known as *FRELIMO*); 20. MARXIST ALL-ETHIOPIAN SOCIALIST MOVEMENT (in Socialist Ethiopia); 21. Party of People's Revolution (in the P.R. of Benin); 22. POPULAR MOVEMENT WORKERS' PARTY (in the P.R. of Angola); 23. SEYCHELLES PEOPLE'S UNITED PARTY; 24. SOMALI SOCIALIST REVOLUTIONARY PARTY; and 25. YEMENI SOCIALIST PARTY. The combined membership of the 25 r.C.p. in the late 1970s was 66.7m. (compared with 4.9m. of the remaining, non-ruling C.p.). The 25 countries account for 93 per cent of the world's Communist party membership, over 38 per cent of the world's industrial output, 34 per cent of the world's population, about 32 per cent of the world's national income and 28 per cent of the world's area.

Communist Party In the Marxist-Leninist view, the leading ('vanguard') political organization of the working class movement with the mission of overthrowing capitalism (or feudalism) and building SOCIALISM and FULL COMMUNISM. There are different theoretical and practical orientations followed by different C.p.s, ranging from orthodox Marxian to indigenous communism adapted to local conditons, such as CASTROISM, EUROCOMMUNISM, MAOISM, MARXISM, MARXISM-LENINISM, TITOISM and TROTSKYISM. The C.p. is noted for being a highly disciplined organization, more than other political parties and is typically organized along the following lines. There are usually strict and demanding conditions of the admission to full membership (especially in the case of ruling C.p.). Members elect delegates to the PARTY CONGRESS, which is normally held every 3–5 years and is the highest source of authority on major policy issues. The Party Congress elects a CENTRAL

Communist Party of Argentina

COMMITTEE and its chief executive official, the Secretary-General (also called in some Parties the FIRST SECRETARY, or the CHAIRMAN or President). The Central Committee elects an inner top body called the POLITBURO plus the SECRETARIAT and a Control Committee. A C.p. may be in power (COMMUNIST PARTIES, RULING) or not (COMMUNIST PARTIES, NON-RULING).

A note on the location of the Communist parties in each country in this Dictionary. They appear under their official or otherwise formalized names rendered into English where necessary. Virtually all C.p. are shown in this Dictionary, i.e. those of significant countries or where the Party's position is significant in the country concerned. If the caption is not found under the 'Communist Party of [name of the country]' below, it appears under the name of the relevant country (e.g. 'Japan C.P.') or in its adjectival form (e.g. 'Romanian C.P.'). In some cases, the term 'Communist' may not appear in the name of the Party, in which case the Party appears under the concerned country's name or adjective, e.g. 'Polish United Workers' Party', or reference is indicated to the location of the official name (e.g. 'Yugoslav C.P.' LEAGUE OF COMMUNISTS OF YUGOSLAVIA).

Communist Party of Argentina (*Partido Comunista de Argentina*) The largest Communist party in Argentina and the oldest in South America. Its origin goes back to 1918, when a faction of the Socialist Party created the International Socialist Party, but in 1920 it changed its name to its present designation. The programme of the C.P.A. is more socialist than communist in content, and its membership consists largely of the former Peronists. It draws its support mostly from skilled workers and professional people, and has surprisingly little influence on trade unions. The membership of the C.P.A. declined from 150,000 in the mid-1970s to about 80,000 in the late 1970s (when the country's total population was 26,300,000). In its international orientation, the C.P.A. has supported the Soviet line. There are other smaller Communist or Marxist parties, namely: 1. The Social Democratic Party – a moderate, middle-class Marxist party of about 20,000 members); 2. The Socialist Workers' Party – a moderate Marxist party of 15,000 members with Trotskyite inclinations; and 3. The Revolutionary Communist Party – a pro-Chinese party with some 10,000 members. The Socialist Vanguard Party (Marxist-Leninist) and the Peronist Montenero Party (*MONTENEROS*) are also occasionally vocal, but have little effect. Since the military coup in March 1976, all Marxist and terrorist parties and groups have been made either illegal or their activities have been severely restricted.

Communist Party of Australia A very small and insignificant party noted for internal conflicts and splits. It was founded in 1920 under its present name, temporarily changed to the 'United C.P.A.' in 1922 but then reverted to its original name, under which it became affiliated with the COMINTERN from 1922 to 1943. Over the period 1944–51 its name was the 'Australian C.P.' but since that time the original name has been resumed. Its membership is only 1,500 (out of a total population of 14,200,000 in 1978). Although the Party has considerable influence in some large trade unions, politically it has never been of any consequence and has never had a seat in the Federal Parliament. There is an internal split based on the Sino-Soviet dispute. There are several small factional groups: the C.P. of Australia (Marxist-Leninist), founded in 1963; the Socialist Party of Australia, formed in 1971; plus the Socialist Labour League (Trotskyite); the Workers-Students Alliance (Maoist); the International Socialists; and the Melbourne Revolutionary Marxists. The main publications of the C.P.A. are *Tribune*, a weekly and *The Australian Left Review*, a monthly journal. The C.P.A. (M.-L.) publishes *Vanguard* (weekly) and *The Australian Communist* (monthly). There is also an intellectual journal *Arena* (published quarterly).

96

Communist Party of Austria (*Kommunistische Partei Österreich*) A vocal but relatively small political party, with a membership of 20,000 (out of a total population of 7,520,000 in 1978). Founded in Nov. 1918 as the 'C.P. of German Austria', it adopted its present name in the following year. It was illegal during the Nazi rule, 1933–45, but it continued its activities underground. It was quite influential in the first 15 years after W.W.II when it had 1–3 seats in the Parliament. Its role has declined since 1959, when it failed to gain parliamentary representation, having polled only 1–2 per cent of the votes cast in recent elections. Although, on the whole, it has followed a pro-Soviet line, it has suffered from internal struggles between 'dogmatists' and 'revisionists' and from splintering Trotskyite and Maoist factions. In 1970, the pro-revisionist factions (led by F. March and E. Fischer) gave way to the orthodox pro-Soviet forces headed by F. Muhri (Party Chairman) and E. Scharf and W. Wachs (Party Secretaries). The Party now advocates radical nationalization and land reform. The Party publishes a daily organ called *Volkstimme* (*People's Voice*) and a monthly theoretical journal *Weg und Ziel* (*The Road and Goal*).

Communist Party of Belgium (*Parti Communiste de Belgique*) The largest and oldest C.p. in Belgium, with a membership of about 10,000 (out of a total population of 9,850,000 in 1978). Founded in 1921, it operated illegally during the German occupation 1940–45. It has been quite active in the industrial field and at the 1977 elections polled 2.7 per cent of the votes cast and won 2 (out of 212) seats in the Lower House of the Parliament. The Party's regular publications are the daily organ, *Le Drapeau Rouge* (*Red Banner*), a weekly magazine in Flemish, *De Rode Vaan* (*Red Banner*), and a monthly theoretical journal in French, *Cahiers Marxistes* (*Marxist Papers*). There are also several small competing rival groups, especially the 'Marxist-Leninist C.P. of Belgium' (founded in 1962), the 'Re-volutionary Workers' League' (Trotskyite), and the 'All-Power to Workers Group' (with Maoist sympathies), but their combined membership is no more than 2,000.

Communist Party of Bolivia (*Partido Comunista de Bolivia*) A very small and illegal party with a claimed membership of 300 (out of a total population of 6,100,000 in 1978). It can trace its origin to a Trotskyite group founded in 1938 and the 'Party of the Revolutionary Left' formed in 1940. In 1950, a separate entity emerged led by dissidents of the P.R.L., and adopted the present Party's name. Following the Sino-Soviet dispute, the C.P.B. has supported the Soviet line, but several other splinter groups have appeared, such as: 1. the 'C.P. of B. Marxist-Leninist', pro-Chinese; formed in 1965, with about 150 members today; and 2. the original Trotskyite 'Revolutionary Workers' Party'. The latter now operates in three separate factions: the 'National Liberation Army' founded in 1966 under GUEVARA (which in 1975 formed the 'Bolivian Workers' Revolutionary Party'); and the 'Movement of the Revolutionary Left', founded in 1971. All these rival groups are illegal. The only known Communist publication is the illegal *El proletario* (*The Proletarian*), published irregularly by the B.W.R.P.

Communist Party of Brazil BRAZILIAN COMMUNIST PARTY.

Communist Party of Canada A small and uninfluential party with a membership of about 2,000 (compared with a total population of 23,600,000 in 1978). Originally founded as an illegal party in 1921, it operated through a front organization called the 'Workers' Party of Canada'. From 1924 to 1931 the C.P.C. received limited legal recognition, but was again repressed during the period 1931–34. It operated as a legal entity from 1934 to 1940, but then was banned again. It re-emerged in 1943 as the legal 'Labour Progressive Party' and in 1946 reverted to its original name, after which it operated as a fully-fledged legal party. Although its overall impact has been insignificant, it has exerted some influence in several trade unions and local councils, and has been vocal in denouncing US foreign policies and the Canadian involvement in NATO. In its international orientation the C.P.C. has supported the Soviet line. For some years now, the Party's influence has largely been limited to reconciling (and fighting) ideological differences amongst various Canadian Communists and Communist rival groups. The main ones are: 1. The Communist Party of Canada (Marxist-Leninist) – Maoist, with Albanian leanings; 2. The Canadian Communist League (Marxist-Leninist) – pro-Chinese; 3. The Canadian Party of Labour – a Maoist splinter group from the Progressive Workers' Party; 4. The League of Socialist Action – the largest Trotskyite group in Canada; 5. The Workers' League of Canada – the official Trotskyite group affiliated to the FOURTH INTERNATIONAL; and 6. The Revolutionary Marxist Group – a dissident and the most radical Trotskyite association in the country. The Parties above are all quite vigorous in their publication efforts. The C.P.C. publishes *The Canadian Tribune* (a weekly, in Toronto) and *The Pacific Tribune* (weekly, in Vancouver). The C.P.C. (M.-L.) publishes the *Mass Line* (a theoretical journal appearing irregularly), whilst the L.S.A. and L.S.O. publish *Labour Challenge* (a fortnightly) and *Liberation* (a monthly in French) respectively. In addition, *World Marxist Review* now appears in Toronto.

Communist Party of Chile (*Partido Comunista de Chíle*) A proscribed party with a fairly large following and a long chequered history. Its origin goes back to 1912, when the Socialist Workers' Party was founded. It joined the COMINTERN in 1921 and adopted its present name the following year. It was quite influential in Chilean politics from 1938 to 1948, was illegal from 1948 to 1952, but became very active again from 1956 to 1973. In 1969 it joined the 'Popular Unity Front'

and in the following year the leader of the C.P.Ch., Salvador Allende, was elected President of Chile. The C.P.Ch., in coalition with other left-wing parties, became the first Communist party in world history to come to power at the national level, and to rule by democratic means. During 1970–73, it held 24 (out of 150) seats in the Chamber of Deputies and 6 (out of 50) seats in the Senate. It embarked on many far-reaching social and economic reforms. The Party lost power and its leader was assassinated or committed suicide in the military coup of Sep. 1973. Although the C.P.Ch. was declared illegal (together with four other left-wing political parties) the same year, its assets confiscated and some of its leaders imprisoned, it continues to be an active underground organization directed by devoted leaders based abroad. Its peak membership was 200,000 in 1972, but its present number is not known, probably less than a half the peak figure. In the Sino-Soviet dispute, it sided with the USSR. There are also two other active Marxist parties: 1. the Movement of the Revolutionary Left – a terrorist Castroite organization founded by students in 1965; and 2. the Revolutionary Communist Party of Chile created in 1966 by expelled pro-Chinese dissidents from the C.P.Ch. in 1963. The main publications circulated illegally and irregularly by the C.P.Ch. include *Unidad Antifascista* (*Anti-Fascist Unity*) and *Principios* (*Principles*), whilst the M.R.L. publishes a weekly *El Rebelde* (*The Rebel*).

Communist Party of China CHINESE COMMUNIST PARTY.

Communist Party of Colombia (*Partido Comunista de Colombia*) An active, fairly influential and the oldest Communist party in the country. It traces its origin back to 1926, when the Socialist Revolutionary Party was founded. Two years later it joined the COMINTERN. The Party adopted its present name in 1930, but from 1944 to 1947 it operated temporarily under the front name of the Social Democratic Party. Since 1972 it has collaborated with four other left-wing parties in the 'Union of National Opposition' which, during the 1974 general election, won 5 (out of 199) seats in the Lower Chamber and 2 (out of 112) seats in the Senate. In its international orientation, the Party has followed a pro-Soviet line which, since the mid-1960s, has led to the formation of two pro-Chinese splinter groups, viz. the 'C.P. of C. Marxist-Leninist' (and its military arm the 'Colombian Revolutionary Armed Forces') and the 'Independent Revolutionary Workers' Movement'. There is also a small Castroite terrorist group called the 'Communist Liberation Army'. The membership of the C.P.C. is about 12,000 and the total of the other groups is probably 2,000 (the country's total population in 1978 was 25,700,000). The C.P.C. publishes a weekly newspaper *Voz proletaria* (*Proletarian Voice*) and a theoretical journal *Documentos politicos* (*Political Documents*). The C.P.C. M-L. circulates a bulletin called *Revolucion* (*Revolution*).

Communist Party of Cuba (*Partido Comunista de Cuba*) The ruling and the only legal political party in the country. Its origin goes back to 1923, when the Communist Group of Havana was formed. It was reorganized in 1925 under the auspices of the COMINTERN and assumed its present name. The Party was outlawed from 1935 to 1938 and in 1940 merged with the Revolutionary Union Party (created in 1937) to form the Revolutionary Union Communist Party, which then changed its name to the Popular Socialist Party. The latter was declared illegal in 1953 and remained so until the overthrow of Batista's regime in Jan. 1959 by the TWENTY-SIXTH OF JULY MOVEMENT led by Fidel Castro. The successful revolution was carried out by Castro's Movement, without any significant support from the P.S.P. The two were gradually integrated over the period 1960–64 and in 1964 the combined organization was named the United Party of the Socialist Revolution, which in the following year assumed the

present name, the C.P.C. In contrast to other ruling Communist parties, its organization has been rather loose, but it has been held together effectively by the magnetic personality and capable leadership of F. CASTRO. The Party's first Congress as the ruling party was held in Dec. 1975. It was attended by 3,136 delegates (representing 200,000 members) who elected a Central Committee of 112 full and 12 alternate members. The latter elected a Political Bureau of 13 members, including F. Castro as its First Secretary and a Secretariat of 9 members. In its international Communist orientation the Party, after some initial hesitation, has firmly taken a pro-Soviet line. The mass support organizations developed by the Party include the Confederation of Cuban Workers, the National Association of Small Farmers, the Federation of Cuban Women, the Union of Young Communists and the Union of Cuban Pioneers (the last, for children aged 5–14 years). The most important official Party organs are *Granma*, a daily newspaper published by the Central Committee and *Juventud rebelde* (*Rebelling Youth*), a daily newspaper of the Union of Young Communists.

Communist Party of Egypt A very small and illegal party which has never been of any significance in Egyptian political and social life. It was originally founded by a group of Russian Jews, Greeks and Italians in 1921, but has never reached a legal status. Its maximum membership was attained in the early 1960s, but in 1965 the Soviet Government (anxious to improve relations with Egypt) prevailed upon the leadership of the C.P.E. to dissolve the Party and to join the ARAB SOCIALIST UNION (the only legal party). However, it has continued existing underground, with an estimated membership of 1,000 in the late 1970s (when the country's population was 39,600,000). In spite of the mixed Soviet support in the past, the Party has followed a pro-Soviet, rather than a pro-Chinese line.

Communist Party of Great Britain A small party with insignificant political influence, but the oldest and largest Marxist organization in the country with considerable influence in trade unions, some professions and local councils. It was founded in 1920 under its present name and has never been proscribed. Since 1950 it has had no seats in the House of Commons, although it usually polls 0.5 per cent of the votes cast, but (paradoxically), it has one member in the House of Lords. The Party stands for the abolition of the monarchy and of the House of Lords and advocates proportional representation, the breaking up of monopolies, state control of the media, the withdrawal from NATO and its replacement with a collective East-West European security scheme. In 1977 it issued a document called *The British Road to Socialism*, committing itself to the destruction of monopoly capitalism, unity with the LABOUR PARTY, political pluralism and EUROCOMMUNISM. The Party's membership in 1977 was 25,000 (when the country's population was 54,300,000). The highest level of the Party's authority is the Congress, held every other year, which elects the Executive Committee of 42 members. The latter then elects the Political Committee of 16 members and the chief Party officials. As of 1977 Mick McGahey was the Party Chairman, Gordon McLennon its General Secretary and Dave Cook the National Organizer. The Party's main support comes from the trade unions, where Party members sit on virtually every union executive committee. It is also supported by its Young Communist League (founded in 1920) with a membership of 2,800. In the international Communist movement, the Party has followed the Moscow line, although on occasions it has criticized Soviet policies. The Party publishes a daily organ *Morning Star*, a fortnightly magazine, *Comment*, and a monthly theoretical journal, *Marxism Today*. The Y.C.L. circulates *Challenge*, a monthly magazine and *Cogito*, a monthly theoretical journal. In addition to the C.P.G.B. there are numerous other Marxist parties or groups, the main ones being: 1. Communist Party of Great Britain (Marxist-Leninist) – the most important pro-Chinese group led by Reg Birch, with a membership of about 400, publishing its fortnightly organ *The Worker*; 2. INTERNATIONAL MARXIST GROUP; 3. NEW COMMUNIST PARTY; 4. SOCIALIST WORKERS' PARTY; 5. WORKERS' REVOLUTIONARY PARTY; 6. WORKERS' SOCIALIST LEAGUE.

Communist Party of Greece (*Kommounistikon Komma Ellados*) The oldest and main Communist party in the country. Its origin goes back to at least 1920, when the 'Socialist Workers' Party (Communist) of Greece' was founded, but its name was changed to its present designation in 1924. It was declared illegal by the Greek Government in 1936 and by the German occupational authorities in 1940. However, it continued its activities underground and organized a small guerrilla force (the 'Greek Popular Liberation Army'), fighting Germans and Italians. After the withdrawal of the occupational forces, it staged an unsuccessful coup to seize power by force. It continued armed operations after W.W.II and was declared illegal again in 1947. However, it carried on its activities illegally through a legal front organization called the 'United Democratic Left' formed in 1951, which in turn was also banned in 1967. The Party was legalized in July 1974 and has developed a fairly solid foothold in the country. The Party's membership is about 28,000 (of the total population of 9,400,000 in 1978), and at the 1977 general election polled 9.3 per cent of the votes cast and won 11 (out of 300) parliamentary seats. However, an internal split occurred dividing the C.P.G. into the 'C.P.G. – Interior' (with a nationalist and progressive programme, led by C. Florakis) and the 'C.P.G. – Exterior' (strictly subscribing to the Marxist-Leninist line loyal to Moscow, led by F. Drakopoulos). Other splinter groups are: the Panhellenic Socialist Movement (Marxist, but not Leninist); the Organization of Marxists-Leninists (syndicalist);

the Revolutionary Communist Movement of Greece (established by students); the Greek Revolutionary Liberation Front (hardline Stalinist and Maoist outlook); plus several minor Trotskyite, Maoist and anarchist factions. Only the two divisions of the C.P.G. have regular publications: *Avgi (Dawn)*, the daily organ of the C.P.G. – Interior; *Rizospastis (The Radical)*, the daily organ of the C.P.G. – Exterior; and *Kommunistiki Epitheorisi (Communist Review)*, a monthly theoretical journal of the C.P.G. – Exterior.

Communist Party of India The oldest Communist party in India, with a fluctuating influence in the country's politics. Founded in 1925, it was outlawed by the British in 1934 until 1942 when it undertook to support the British war effort. Its effectiveness has been weakened by internal personality differences and ideological splits. In 1964 the left-wing dissidents established the 'C.P.I. (Marxist)' and in 1969 the Maoist extremists formed the 'C.P.I. (Marxist-Leninist)'. Thus, the C.P.I. is now regarded as moderate and pro-Soviet, the C.P.I. (M) – left-wing, independent and neutral, whilst the C.P.I. (M.-L.) – most radical and rejecting parliamentary methods. Their respective memberships in the late 1970s were: about 550,000, 120,000 and 10,000 (compared with the country's total population of 628,000,000 in 1978). During the March 1977 general election for seats in the Lower House (542 seats), the C.P.I. (which had been closely associated with Mrs. Gandhi's Congress Party) suffered a reduction of seats – from 24 to 7, whilst the C.P.I. (M.) gained 22 seats (17 of them in West Bengal). In June of the same year the C.P.I. (M.) came to power for the first time in West Bengal where it won an absolute majority in the State Assembly (178 of the 294 seats). On the other hand, the C.P.I. has had a strong influence in the State of KERALLA. The C.P.I. publishes two daily organs – *Janug (People's Era)* in Hindi and *New Age* in English, and a weekly also in English called *Party Life* (all appearing in New Delhi). The organ of

the C.P.I. (M.) is *People's Democracy* published weekly in Calcutta.

Communist Party of Indonesia (*Partai Komunis Indonesia*) The oldest Communist party in Asia and formerly the largest in the capitalist world, but now an illegal and insignificant organization, largely operating from abroad. It traces its origin to 1914, when Marxist sympathizers formed the Indies Social Democratic Party, renamed the 'C.P. of the Indies' in 1920 which in 1924 was changed to its present designation. In 1926–27 it attempted to seize power by force, but without success. It operated illegally from 1932 to 1949 and during W.W.II joined the national struggle against the Dutch and the Japanese. The peak of the Party's size and influence was reached in the early 1960s, under the leadership of D. N. Aidit, when its membership topped 3.0m., which made it the third largest Communist party in the world (after China and the USSR). The Party staged another coup in Sep. 1965, which failed with most disastrous consequences, including widespread massacres of its leaders, members and sympathizers, persecution and the legal proscription of the Party (GESTAPU AFFAIR). But it has continued its activities underground, directed by Party Committees located abroad – Moscow and Prague (the pro-Soviet faction) and Peking and Tirana (the pro-Chinese line). The estimated Party membership in Indonesia in the late 1970s was 1,000 (when the total population was 146,900,000).

Communist Party of Ireland A very small and politically insignificant party, with members in southern and northern Ireland. Although its origin can be traced back to 1921, it became active only after 1933. It has suffered from internal frictions which, in 1948, led to the formation of the Irish Workers' Party in the south and the C.P. of Northern Ireland in the north. But in 1970 they were reunited under the old name. Its total membership is estimated to be 500, plus about 100 in its youth organization called the Connolly

Youth Movement. In the Sino-Soviet conflict, it has taken the Soviet line. The Party's regular organs are: *Unity* and *Irish Worker*, both published weekly in Belfast and Dublin respectively; there is also a monthly journal, *Irish Socialist* and a quarterly theoretical journal, *Irish Socialist Review*. The C.Y.M. publishes a fortnightly magazine called *Forward*.

Communist Party of Jordan (*al-Hizb al – Shuyu'i al-Urduni*) A very small and illegal party, fut fairly active. It was founded in 1951, but it can trace its origin back to 1943 when the Palestinian National Liberation League was formed. The peak of its influence was reached in the mid-1950s, when it co-operated with the Socialist parties and had a minister in the cabinet in 1956. Its work has been hampered by the hostile attitude of the government and religious interests. The Party was declared illegal in 1957 after its involvement in an abortive coup to overthrow the monarchy. Nevertheless the Party has continued its activities, mostly through legal front organizations. Its membership, consisting mostly of Palestinians, was about 400 in the late 1970s (when the country's population was 2,850,000). It receives support from the Palestinian National Front (an organization representing trade unions and professional associations), but it competes with a rival Marxist group called the POPULAR FRONT FOR THE LIBERATION OF PALESTINE. In its external relations, the Party has supported the pro-Soviet line. In spite of its small size, it publishes three periodicals appearing illicitly and irregularly: a newspaper *al-Watan* (*The Homeland*), a magazine on party organization and activities *al Jamahir* (*The Masses*) and a journal *al-Haqiqah* (*The Truth*).

Communist Pary of Lebanon (*al-Hizb al-Shuyu'i al-Lebnani*) A fairly small party, but significant in Lebanese politics. It originated in 1928 when Lebanese and Syrian Communists formed the Lebanese People's Party. As a result of the emergence of Lebanon and Syria as two separate states in 1941, the L.P.P. also separated in 1944 into two independent parties. Since the mid-1960s the C.P.L. has co-operated with other left-wing political groups and in some elections secured parliamentary representation. The Party participated actively in the civil war in the 1970s against the Christian Phalangist Party. The membership of the C.P.L. is about 2,500 (compared with the country's population of 3,100,000 in 1978). In the Sino-Soviet dispute it has taken the Soviet line. The Party publishes a daily newspaper *al-Nida* (*The Call*), a weekly magazine *al-Akhbar* (*The News*) and a monthly theoretical journal *al-Tariq* (*The Road*).

Communist Party of Malaya A small illegal and now insignificant party with a membership of about 4,000 (the country's population in 1978 was 13,000,000). It traces its origin back to 1928, when the South Seas Communist Party was formed under the auspices of the COMINTERN. Two years later, it adopted its present name. It became active in guerrilla operations, first against the Japanese during W.W.II and then against the British (1957–60) and the ruling conservative Malayian government. It was declared illegal in 1948 and subdued first by the British and then by the Malayan troops. Its effectiveness has been further reduced by internal doctrinal differences and the emergence of rival splinter groups, such as an 'C.P.M. (Revolutionary Faction)' and the 'C.P.M. (Marxist-Leninist)', with about 500 and 200 members respectively. The three Parties participate or support the 'Malayan People's Liberation Army' – scattered guerrilla forces mainly along the Thai border. As the C.P.M. is illegal (like the other groups), its headquarters are located abroad, partly in southern Thailand and partly in southern China. The main medium of communication and publicity are clandestine broadcasts ('The Voice of the Malayan Revolution') from Changsha in southern China. The C.P.M. group in London publishes *The Malayan Monitor and General News* (appearing irregularly).

102

Communist Party of Nepal A small illegal, but active party with a membership of about 6,000 (out of the population of 13,400,000 in 1978). At first its operations were directed from Calcutta, where the Party was founded in 1949. It operated illegally from 1952 to 1956 and was formally dissolved (together with other political parties) in 1960. Although illegal, it has continued its activities with varied tolerance on the part of the government. In 1962 a radical and Maoist rival to the C.P.N. was formed with its headquarters in India, whilst the indigenous C.P.N. still follows a pro-Soviet line.

Communist Party of Pakistan An insignificant party which is very small in size and illegal. Its origin can be traced back to 1928 when it was a component of the COMMUNIST PARTY OF INDIA. It became a separate entity after the partition of the Indian sub-continent in 1947. In 1954 it was declared illegal, but has operated underground through certain left-wing front organizations. The Party has never been large numerically or politically influential. Its strength was further reduced by the secession of Bangladesh in 1971. Its membership in the late 1970s was estimated at 1,500. In the Sino-Soviet conflict, it has recently switched from a pro-Chinese line to a pro-Soviet orientation.

Communist Party of Poland (*Komunistyczna Partia Polski*) A small revolutionary Marxist party which existed in Poland between the two World Wars. It emerged in Dec. 1918 as an amalgamation of the former Social Democratic Party of Russian Poland and the Polish Socialist Party under the name of the 'Communist Workers Party of Poland'. In 1921 it became a section of the COMINTERN and, as a consequence, was declared illegal, but continued its activities underground, mostly through trade unions and other front organizations. In 1925 it dropped 'Workers' from its name and turned its attention towards the 'workers-peasants alliance'. During the GREAT PURGES of the late 1930s in the USSR, many Polish Communist leaders were implicated, tried and most of those who were in the USSR at the time were liquidated (including, W. Bogucki, S. Bobiński, B. Bortnowski, M. Broński, T. Dabał, J. Hanecki, Wiera Kastrzewa, S. Królikowski, S. Pestkowski, E. Próchnik, W. Ulanowski, H. Walecki and A. Warski-Warszawski). On Stalin's orders, the C.P.P. was dissolved by the Comintern in 1938. Those leaders who survived later (in 1942) formed the Polish Workers' Party, the precursor of the present POLISH UNITED WORKERS' PARTY. After the TWENTIETH CONGRESS OF THE CPSU in 1956, a joint Soviet-Polish Party Commission declared Stalin's allegations and the purges of the Polish Communists as groundless, resulting in total rehabilitation.

Communist Party of Spain (*Partido Comunista de España*) An important political party, drawing support from the working as well as the middle classes, with a long tradition of struggle and playing an increasingly active role since its legalization in April 1977. Its origins go back to 1920, when a radical Federation of Socialist Youth adopted the name 'Spanish Communist Party', and the left-wing socialists in the Labour Party of Spain formed the 'Communist Labour Party of Spain'. In the following year, the two parties amalgamated and adopted its present name. The Party was illegal over the period 1939–77, but carried on its activities underground quite effectively from its headquarters in Paris. The Party's membership was 300,000 in 1936 (before the SPANISH CIVIL WAR), 100,000 in 1976 (the largest of any illegal party ever), and 250,000 in 1978 (when the country's population was 37,300,000). The Party is led by S. CARRILLO, its Secretary-General, and Mrs Dolores Ibarruri ('La Passionaria'), its President. At the first parliamentary election since the Spanish Civil War, in June 1977, the Communists polled 9.2 per cent of the votes cast and won 20 (out of 350) seats in the Congress of Deputies and 12 (out of 248) seats in the Senate. The C.P.S. is the third largest party in the

Congress – after the Union of Democratic Centre (with 165 seats) and the SPANISH SOCIALIST WORKERS' PARTY (118 seats). Up to 1968 the C.P.S. had firmly followed a pro-Soviet line but since the INVASION OF CZECHOSLOVAKIA (which the Party condemned), it has steered an independent course. The Party has become one of the most outspoken promoters of EUROCOMMUNISM and describes itself now as 'Marxist, democratic and revolutionary', and no longer 'Marxist-Leninist'. Its main publications are *Mundo Obrero (The Workers' World)*, a daily (appearing irregularly since 1931) and *Nuestra Bandera (Our Flag)*, a monthly theoretical and political journal. In addition to the C.P.S., there are other smaller Marxist parties or groups, the main ones being: the Revolutionary Communist League (Trotskyite); the Patriotic Anti-Fascist Front (Maoist); and the Basque Communist Party.

Communist Party of Thailand An illegal revolutionary party, with substantial influence in some outlying rural areas. It was formally founded by Communist refugees from China and Vietnam in 1942, Declared illegal in 1952, it has continued its activities underground, with varying degrees of intensity at different times. In the early 1960s, it created the Thai People's Liberaton Armed Forces, a guerrilla organization resorting to terrorist activities. The Party and its guerrilla units control some remote rural areas where the population is about 200,000. The membership of the Party, together with its insurgent forces and the local militia, is believed to be about 15,000 (whilst the country's population in 1978 was 45,100,000).

Communist Party of the Netherlands (*Communistische Partij Nederland*) A fairly active and moderate party, with varied influence at different times. Although Communist groups had existed before W.W.I, the Party was formally founded in 1919 as the 'C.P. of Holland', which was changed to its present designation in 1935. The Party advocates the abolition of the monarchy, radical nationalization, the

withdrawal from NATO and a reduction of defence expenditure. Since the mid-1960s it has turned its attention primarily to domestic problems and has adopted an independent line in the Sino-Soviet dispute (the 'new orientation'). There are, however, several dissident Marxist groups, mostly supporting Peking, the best known of which is the 'Netherlands Communist Unity Movement, Marxist-Leninist'. The membership of the C.P.N. in the late 1970s was 12,000 and the N.C.U.M, M.-L. about 2,500 (whilst the country's population in 1978 was 13,950,000). At the 1977 general election, Communists polled 1.7 per cent of the votes cast and won 2 (out of 150) seats in the Lower House. There are two auxiliary organizations supporting the C.P.N: the General Netherlands Youth Organization; and the Netherlands Women's Movement. The Party publishes a daily organ called *De Waarheid (The Truth)* and a bi-monthly theoretical journal, *Politiek en Cultuur (Politics and Culture)*.

Communist Party of the Philippines (*Partido Komunista ng Pilipinas*) An active party with a fairly long tradition of revolutionary struggle. Although its origin can be traced back to 1919, it was formally founded in 1930 and soon after was declared illegal (from 1931 to 1938). It was very active during W.W.II and organized the Anti-Japanese People's Army, popularly known as the HUKS. After the war and after independence in 1946, the C.P.P., especially the *Huks*, continued their struggle, but against the government. After repeated attempts at reconciliation, the Party was proscribed in 1957, but continued its revolutionary activities in several parts of the country. As a result of internal dissent, several rival parties and groups emerged after the late 1960s, such as the 'C.P.P. Marxist-Leninist' and the 'New People's Army'. During the Sino-Soviet dispute, the C.P.N. aligned itself on the Soviet side, whilst most splinter groups favoured a pro-Chinese stand. The Party's membership has been estimated at ranging from 2,000 to 5,000, including guerrilla units. The principal publication of the C.P.P. is *Ang Komunista* (*The Communist*), appearing irregularly, whilst the C.P.P. M.-L. publishes *Ang Bayan* (*The Nation*).

Communist Party of the Soviet Union (*Kommunisticheskaya Partiya Sovetskogo Soiuza*) The ruling and only legal political party in the USSR and the first Marxist party in world history which successfully staged a PROLETARIAN REVOLUTION (in the GREAT OCTOBER SOCIALIST REVOLUTION). It is the ultimate source of policy-making decisions and retains control over their execution in different spheres and at all levels of authority in the country. Its origin goes back to 1898 when the RUSSIAN SOCIAL-DEMOCRATIC LABOUR PARTY was founded. By 1900 a revolutionary left-wing group, the BOLSHEVIKS, emerged within the R.S.-D.L.P which, in 1903, became a majority faction led by Lenin. They conflicted with the MENSHEVIKS who were the minority party. After 1904 the Bolsheviks lost their majority and in 1912 they separated from the Mensheviks and formed a distinct party, the 'Russian Social-Democratic Labour Party (of the Bolsheviks)', which in March 1918 was changed to the 'Russian Communist Party (of the Bolsheviks)'. In 1925, it became the 'All-Union Communist Party (of the Bolsheviks)' and in 1952 took its present title. It has been the only legal political party in the country since 1922, when all other parties were abolished by law. Owing to its pioneering achievements, it won high prestige in the international Communist movement and has served as a model for Marxist-Leninist parties. The Party membership was 8,400 in 1905, 240,000 in 1917, 1,088,000 in 1925, 8,239,000 in 1959 and in 1978 the figure stood at 16,500,000 (whilst the country's population in the latter year was 261,000,000). In 1978 Party members constituted 9 per cent of the adult population. The Party is organized in accordance with the Leninist principle of DEMOCRATIC CENTRALISM. The highest level of authority is the PARTY CONGRESS, now held

every 5 years, which lays down general policy guidelines and elects the CENTRAL COMMITTEE (the Party's highest level of authority between the Congresses) and the CENTRAL AUDITING COMMITTEE. The CC elects two smaller bodies, the POLITBURO and the SECRETARIAT. The Politburo is the supreme policy-making authority and its decisions are unconditionally binding on the Party as a whole. The first Party Congress was held in 1989, the seventh (the first with the Party in power) in March 1918 and the twenty-fifth in March 1976. The Twenty-Fifth Party Congress was attended by 4,998 delegates and elected 187 full and 139 candidate (non-voting) members to the Central Committee. The CC elected 6 full and 6 candidate members to the Politburo and 11 members to the Secretariat headed by the Secretary-General (L. I. BREZHNEV). The Party is run by a quarter of a million full-time professionals on a hierarchical basis, with the lower levels being subordinated to the higher. There are 380,000 'primary Party units' (formerly called 'Party cells') ranging from three to several hundred members, based on the place of employment, rather than on the area of residence. Above them are 'regional committees' in ascending order of authority: 2,810 rural circuits, 448 urban circuits, 760 city committees, 10 district committees, 142 county committees, 6 province committees and 14 union-republic committees (but there is no separate committee for the RUSSIAN SOVIET FEDERATED SOCIALIST REPUBLIC, as it is directly attached to the Central Committee of the C.P.S.U.). Membership rules are very strict. To join, the applicant has to be a Soviet citizen over 18 years of age and be recommended by three members and approved by the district (or city) Party Committee. There is a probationary period of at least one year, during which the 'candidate member' has no voting power and may be refused admission. The C.P.S.U. has a number of auxiliary mass organizations, of which the three main ones are: the *KOMSOMOL* (with over 36m. members); the ALL-UNION CENTRAL

COUNCIL OF TRADE UNIONS (110m. members); and the Soviet Voluntary Society for the Promotion of the Army, Aviation and the Navy (70m. members). The Party has an extremely well-developed publication programme. Its main dailies and periodicals are: *PRAVDA (The Truth)* – the daily organ of the C.P.S.U.; *KOMMUNIST (The Communist)* – the theoretical journal of the C.C. of the C.P.S.U. appearing 18 times a year; *Partynaya Zhizn (Party Life)* – a fortnightly magazine on Party organization and internal affairs; *KOMSOMOLS-KAYA PRAVDA* – a newspaper organ of the *Komsomol*; and *Molodoi Kommunist (The Young Communist)* – a monthly theoretical journal of the *Komsomol*.

Communist Party of the United States of America The largest Marxist party in the country, with virtually no influence in Federal or State politics. It traces its origin to 1919, when the Communist Party of America and the Communist Labor Party were formed. These parties were outlawed in the early 1920s, but they created legal front organizations called the Workers' Party of America (1921) and the United Toilers of America (1922) respectively. However, before that, the United Communist Party was established in 1920. Of the three, the W.P.A. emerged as the most viable and in 1925 it changed its name to the 'Workers' (Communist) Party of Americ.', which in the following year was changed to the C.P.U.S.A. The latter has survived to date, but during a short interval (1944–45), its official designation was the 'Communist Political Association'. Several rival Trotskyite, Maoist and Independent Marxist groups also emerged, the main ones being: the Communist Party (Marxist-Leninist) of the USA (Maoist, formerly the October League); the SOCIALIST WORKERS' PARTY (the main Trotskyite group); the PROGRESSIVE LABOR PARTY (rigidly Stalinist); the REVOLUTIONARY COMMUNIST PARTY (Maoist); and the WEATHERMAN UNDERGROUND ORGANIZATION (Marxist-Leninist). The C.P.U.S.A. itself has followed a pro-Soviet line in its international orientation. Although the Party is not illegal, it suffers from an overwhelmingly hostile public opinion and has no representation either in the Federal or State legislatures. Its membership in the late 1970s was about 18,000 and other groups comprised about 10,000 (whilst the country's total population in 1978 was 218,400,000). The Party's highest level of authority is a Convention held every three years, which elects a Central Committee and a National Council. The 21st Convention held in 1975 elected 96 members to the former and 136 to the latter. Gus Hall was elected the General Secretary and Henry Winston the National Chairman. At the 1976 Federal election, the Communists polled only 0.2 per cent of the votes cast. The C.P.U.S.A. publishes *The Daily World*, appearing five times a week, and *Political Affairs*, a monthly theoretical magazine.

Communist Party of Uruguay (*Partido Comunista del Uruguay*) An active party with significant influence in the country's political life before 1975, but illegal since that time. It was founded in 1920 and in the following year joined the COMINTERN. To varying degrees it has collaborated with several other left-wing political parties and groups in the Left-Wing Liberation Front and in the Broad Front which it formed in 1962. After a right-wing regime took power in 1973, all left-wing political parties were banned. The C.P.U. was banned in Jan. 1975. But the Party continues operating underground and is directed from abroad. Its membership is estimated to be about 6,000 (out of the country's population of 2,830,000 in 1978). The Party's leader, R. Arismedi, is reported to be in Moscow. In its international orientation the Party has supported the Soviet line. It circulates an underground weekly *Carta semana del Partido Comunista (The Weekly News-sheet of the Communist Party)*. Also TUPAMOROS.

Communist Party of Venezuela (*Partido Comunista de Venezuela*) An active and moderate Communist party which has had a chequered history since its foundation in 1931. It has suffered from several official proscriptions (especially in the 1960s) and internal dissent. Its membership in the late 1970s was about 5,000 (when the country's population was 13,100,000). The Party supports a PARLIAMENTARY ROAD TO SOCIALISM and rejects terrorist action. It is influential in the industrial labour movement (viz. the United Workers' Confederation of Venezuela). The Party's daily organ is *Tribuna popular* (*People's Tribune*) and its theoretical journal (appearing irregularly) is *Documentos politikos* (*Political Documents*). There are several other Marxist parties and groups, such as the 'Movement Towards Socialism' (influential in universities and some youth organizations), the 'Movement of the Revolutionary Left' (Marxist-Leninist), the 'Socialist League' (Trotskyite), and the 'New Party' (Maoist).

Communist University A general term for higher educational institutions in the USSR between the two World Wars for the political training of Party leaders. The most famous establishments were the COMMUNIST UNIVERSITY FOR THE TOILERS OF THE EAST, the COMMUNIST UNIVERSITY FOR WESTERN NATIONAL MINORITIES and the SVERDLOV COMMUNIST UNIVERSITY. The present name for the C.U. in most Socialist countries is the ACADEMY OF SOCIAL SCIENCES.

Communist University for the Toilers of the East (*Kommunistichesky Universitet Trudyashchikhsia Vostoka*) A Soviet training centre for Communist cadres, originally meant for the eastern republics of the USSR, but later extended to include Asia, the Middle East and the eastern Mediterranean. It was established jointly by the RUSSIAN COMMUNIST PARTY (OF THE BOLSHEVIKS) and the COUNCIL OF PEOPLE'S COMMISSARS in 1921, with its main campus in Moscow and branches in Baku, Irkutsk and Tashkent. It was closed in 1938. For six years it had two foreign divisions, which were known as the 'Sun

Yat-sen' University for the Toilers of China' (1925–29) and the 'Communist University for the Toilers of China' (1929–38) (the 'S.Y.-S. U.T.Ch' must not be confused with the 'Sun Yat-sen University' in Canton, founded in 1924, reorganized in 1953 and still in operation). During its existence, the University received students of 73 different nationalities and developed a three-year programme, which included party and political education, political economy, trade unions, administration and law. The students were expected to acquire practical experience in agitation and propaganda whilst training. Amongst its most famous lecturers were A. V. LUNACHARSKI and his student HO CHI MINH. From 1927 to 1938 the University published a journal (in Russian) called *The Revolutionary East.*

Communist University for Western National Minorities (*Kommunistichesky Universitet Natsionalnykh Menshinstv Zapada*) A training centre for Party cadres originally meant for minority nationals in the Western USSR (Byelorussians, Estonians, Germans, Karelo-Finns, Lithuanians and Poles), but later also open to other European countries (Bulgaria, Italy and Yugoslavia). It was founded in Nov. 1921 by the decision of the COUNCIL OF PEOPLE'S COMMISSARS and was based in Moscow, with a branch in Petrograd (renamed Leningrad in 1924). It had one- and three-year programmes, with courses on party work, politics, trade unionism, political economy, administration and law. The students were also required to participate in practical work involving agitation and propaganda. Its first rector was J. Marchlewski, a Polish Communist, and its second, Maria Frumkina, was a militant Jewish Bolshevik who was later arrested during the GREAT PURGES and subsequently disappeared. The University was closed down in 1936.

Communist Women's Organization A short-lived international association established by the COMINTERN in 1919 and operated during the early 1920s. Its work was carried on by a Women's Secretariat, which organized several international conferences on women's questions. However, it was not successful outside the USSR and never succeeded in establishing a network of affiliates in other countries.

Communist Youth International A section of the COMINTERN, in existence from 1919 to 1943. It originated from the International Youth Conference held in Bern in April 1915. In 1919 an International Youth Bureau was created in Berlin, consisting of representatives of revolutionary youth organizations from 14 countries. Its headquarters were moved to Moscow two years later. The supreme organ of the C.Y.I. was the Congress, which held six sessions (in 1919, 1921, 1922, 1924, 1928 and 1935). The C.Y.I. was dissolved together with the Comintern in May 1943.

Communitarianism A term applied to the ideas, organization and practices followed in the early forms of communal experiments, usually based on religious principles, especially in the New World in the 19th c. Examples of such socialist or communist fraternities were the Harmonist Community in the USA, founded in 1805 and the New Australia Community in Paraguay which existed in the 1890s.

'Community of Women' Also known as the 'nationalization of women', one of the accusations levelled by right-wing and religious critics against Marxism. The charge was first made in the middle of the 19th c. and renewed after Engels's publication of the *ORIGIN OF THE FAMILY, PRIVATE PROPERTY AND THE STATE* in 1884, where he put forward the thesis of group marriages and MATRIARCHY as features of PRIMITIVE COMMUNISM. It was further repeated after the Bolshevik Revolution, prompted by such Communist practices as collectivization, communal living, FREE LOVE and ATHEISM. Most Marxists have rejected the allegation as unjustified, and in turn de-nounced the bourgeoisie for loose morality and creating conditions for

prostitution. In no Socialist country has the C. of W. been introduced by the authorities, and in fact the Socialist marriage laws and the sexual code appear to be stricter than in most Western countries.

Company Union A local trade union or other association of employees limited to one company or some other employer, not affiliated to any national labour organization. In many cases a c.u. is dominated by the employing firm, where the employer may have initiated it and then financially supported it. The idea of the company-dominated union runs counter to the logic of the industrial labour movement in capitalist countries. Usually, industrial legislation protects workers' organizations against domination by employers.

Comparative Cost Theory A foreign trade theory, originally put forward by the English classical economists (R. Torrens and D. Ricardo), but later developed by other Western economists into an elaborate doctrine. Its central tenet is that countries should specialize in those goods and services in which they have the greatest comparative (not merely absolute) advantage or the least comparative disadvantage, export them and import those in which they have the greatest comparative disadvantage. This basis of the international division of labour ensures the maximum possible gains from foreign trade. The theory is unacceptable to the Socialist centrally planned economies. In its static form, it has been described by the Socialist economists as 'a pseudo-scientific reactionary doctrine' providing an apologetic theoretical justification for the perpetuation of the domination of the less-developed and weaker countries by the rich, industrialized capitalist nations. It is held that the theory may be an acceptable guide to trade between countries at about the same reasonably high level of economic development, otherwise it leads to NON-EQUIVALENT EXCHANGE.

Comparative Economic Systems A phrase with four different meanings: 1. A description and analytical study of different types of economy, concentrating on the differences in the theoretical assumptions, the institutional framework and the processes of decision-making. Typically a number of representative countries today are selected for the purpose (such as the USA, UK, Sweden, India, Yugoslavia, East European countries, the USSR, Cuba and China). As such it is sometimes regarded as an aspect of regional economics. 2. A historical and analytical study of the types of economy in different stages of development in the past as well as today. It may include primitive communism, the ancient slave-based economy, the medieval feudal economy, contemporary subsistence economy, *LAISSEZ-FAIRE* capitalism, fascist economy, mixed economy, directive centralized Socialist planned economy, market socialism, or full communism. 3. A rigorous study of the principles underlying the institutional organization and the operation of the different types of economy. In this case, the approach is via problem areas or some crucial fields of economics, such as the ownership of the means of production, consumption, investment, growth, prices, employment, wages, incentives, services and external economic relations. 4. A scientific study of the methods of comparing and evaluating the objectives, structure, operation and achievements of the different types of economy. There are two schools of thought concerning the methodological scope of the study of c.e.s. The minimalists believe that the analysis should be rigorously objective and as free as possible from value judgments. They stress that the aims of economic systems are outside the realm of economics, and that the economist's task should be limited to identifying the different aims and the most efficient means of their implementation. On the other hand, maximalists maintain that c.e.s. are broader than economics, as their study inevitably involves value judgments. This is particularly so in choosing the criteria for the evaluation of different economic systems, where political,

psychological, social, ethical and technical factors must be introduced. They further point out that most economic variables are an outcome of forces beyond the scope of economic analysis.

'Compass' (*Moked*, in Hebrew) A political organization in Israel consisting of several left-wing groups formed in 1975. It is a by-product of the dissent within the Israeli Communist Party founded in 1948, but tracing its origin to the 'Workers of Zion' formed in 1919. The membership of C. (about 1,000, out of the country's population of 3,700,000) consists almost wholly of Israelis. It rejects Zionist ideology and has a considerable following in the trade unions. It publishes two monthly magazines, *Fray Israel* (*Free Israel*), in Yiddish, and *Emda* (*Position*) in Hebrew. Also NEW COMMUNIST LIST.

Compensation Deals Commercial transactions in international trade, where at least a part of the payment is made in kind. They are widely practised in EAST-WEST trade, mostly on the insistence of the Socialist countries which are short of convertible foreign exchange. A c.d. may be a straight barter transaction (the exchange of goods for goods without using money), or a part of the payment by the Socialist to the Western partner is made in agreed product(s). The Western partner may not necessarily need such products himself, and in most cases he sells his claim to others, usually through specialized 'switch dealers' (SWITCH DEALING). Compensation for transactions involving all trade partners of two countries may be effected through BILATERAL CLEARING, without using currency in inter-country settlements.

Compensation Theory A proposition supported by the leading English classical economists – J. Mill (1773–1836), N. Senior (1790–1864), J. R. MacCulloch (1789–1864), J. S. Mill (1806–1873) and initially by D. Ricardo (1772–1823) – according to which the introduction of machinery in production does not adversely affect the employment of labour. They maintained that the workers released in the mechanized forms of production find employment in machine-building and other ancillary industries. Marx (in *CAPITAL*) and other Marxist thinkers criticized the theory along two lines: 1. the workers displaced by machines cannot find employment in the machine-building industries unless they are re-trained for the new jobs; and 2. mechanization releases more workers than can be absorbed in machine-building, because VARIABLE CAPITAL is transformed into CONSTANT CAPITAL.

Competition Rivalry amongst firms or social groups or individuals, prompted by the desire to attain maximum advantage especially in production, trade or employment. This economic behaviour is generally identified with capitalist free enterprise and is highly regarded by its supporters as a constant spur to production, efficiency and economic progress. Marxists have criticized c. in capitalist economy, especially amongst private firms, as it is directed towards the maximization of profits through: 1. the exploitation of the suppliers of labour, materials and equipment; 2. the sale of products at the expense of other sellers; and 3. the disregard of legitimate social needs. As the capacity to compete differs, the profits attained also differ, which leads to further differentiation amongst capitalists. In the process, some capitalists become richer, whilst others are eliminated with small struggling independent craftsmen. Marx (in *POVERTY OF PHILOSPHY*) said: 'Competition engenders poverty, foments civil war, it disturbs families, corrupts the public conscience ... overturns the notions of equity and justice ... and of morality. It even forces its own destruction'. Socialist economists distinguish between free atomistic c., which existed under *laissez-faire* capitalism in the 19th c., and rivalry amongst monopolies, which is typical of developed capitalism. Whilst the former was conducive to stable prices, technical progress and increasing efficien-

cy (as profits are mostly made by reducing production costs), the latter leads to higher prices and may impede technical progress (as a monopoly in the market forces prices to rise resulting in less pressure for innovation). In the Marxist view, c. reaches its most sinister forms in the era of IMPERIALISM when, according to Lenin (in *IMPERIALISM: THE HIGHEST STAGE OF CAPITALISM*) it results in the following: 1. the prevention of supplies to a rival; 2. the poaching of labour from a rival; 3. interference in the deliveries of components, equipment and the like to a rival; 4. the restriction of the outlets for a rival's products; 5. control of the marketing network normally used by a rival; 6. price undercutting calculated to ruin a rival; 7. the restriction of credit lines to a rival; and 8. the organization of a variety of boycotts calculated to intimidate, weaken or ruin a rival. However, Marxists accept the desirability of SOCIALIST COMPETITION. Also COMPETITIVE SOLUTION, NATURAL SELECTION.

'Competitive Solution' A proposition first put forward by E. BARONE in 1908 (in an article 'The Ministry of Production in the Collectivist Society') maintaining that the organization of production and the utilization of resources in the future collectivist economy should be similar to that under competitive capitalism. This idea was further elaborated upon by several socialist economists in the 1930s, notably O. LANGE. The proponents of this solution reasoned that despite the fact that under collectivism there is no ordinary (private) market for the factors of production (land, capital, and labour), such categories as rent, interest, wages, prices and profits should be reactivated in the interest of rational (most efficient) decision-making. It was further insisted upon that the following two rules, peculiar to the operation of firms under competition, should be observed: 1. the scale of production in each enterprise is to be set at the minimum average cost; and 2. the price of the product is to be fixed at the level of the lowest average cost (so that the marginal cost is equated to the marginal revenue). The optimum levels of the different economic categories could be arrived at by the TRIAL AND ERROR METHOD. The c.s. has never been fully applied in any Socialist economy, except to some extent in Yugoslavia and Hungary (MARKET SOCIALISM).

Complex Labour Another less frequently used term for COMPOUND LABOUR.

Complex Organization of Associated Labour (*Složena Organizacija Udruženog Rada*, or *SOUR*, in Serbo-Croat) In Yugoslavia, a loose group known as the BASIC ORGANIZATIONS OF ASSOCIATED LABOUR, embracing a combine or industry on a federation basis.

Complex Price System A price determination system where price controls and the market mechanism coexist supplementing each other. Also known as the 'flexible p.s.', it has become a feature of most Socialist economies since the ECONOMIC REFORMS of the 1960s, and has been best developed in Hungary and Yugoslavia. Typically, there are four categories of prices: 1. fixed prices, set by the authorities and applying mostly to the necessities and raw materials critical to the cost of living or cost of production; 2. ceiling prices, maximum levels set by the authorities, mostly covering less essential items of household use (these prices are free to fluctuate below the set levels); 3. free-range prices which can move freely within the specified maximum and minimum limits and mostly apply to semi-luxuries; and 4. free prices, determined freely in the market and applicable mostly to luxuries and certain seasonal agricultural products.

Complex Programme A short name for the Complex Programme of Further Intensification and Perfection of Co-operation and the Development of Socialist Economic Integration amongst the Member Countries of the Council for Mutual Economic Assistance. It is an ambitious scheme of accelerated specializa-

tion and technological progress adopted at the 25th CMEA Session in Bucharest in 1971. It sets out objectives, methods and concrete economic and technical targets for all the branches of the economy over long-term periods (up to 1990). The document (as published in Russian) contains 119 printed pages and falls into 17 chapters, each concerned with a different major task or branch of the economy. It specifies a large number of developmental projects of international importance to the member countries. To assist in the implementation of the Programme, 34 international co-ordinating centres, 7 scientific and technical councils, 3 international study groups of scientists, 3 joint laboratories and research-production associations have been established.

Compound Labour A Marxist term for skilled labour, i.e. labour requiring special training which is distinct from SIMPLE LABOUR (unskilled). C.l. is more productive than simple labour, i.e., the former is capable of creating more value per unit of time than the latter can. On these grounds, a differentiation of wages is justified, if the principle of distribution 'to each according to his work' is accepted.

Comprador In its original meaning, a local merchant in a colony performing the function of a middleman between foreign capital and the local market, mostly concerned with buying local materials for foreign producers or traders. Marxists have given the term an ideological connotation, identifying the c. with the era of COLONIALISM and imperialist domination and exploitation. In their view, the c. class constituted the local upper bourgeoisie. This group owed its privileged economic and social position to foreign monopolies, and consequently developed an interest in the preservation of the colonial set-up and the social system associated with it.

Compromise Concession made to an opponent or rival. Revolutionary Marxists are strongly opposed to c., as they identify it with REFORMISM, REVISIONISM and OP-

PORTUNISM. After the split in the RUSSIAN SOCIAL-DEMOCRATIC LABOUR PARTY in 1903, the BOLSHEVIKS often described their moderate rivals, the MENSHEVIKS, as 'compromisers'. This was reaffirmed after the FEBRUARY REVOLUTION OF 1917, when the latter joined the KADETS and gave support to the PROVISIONAL GOVERNMENT.

Compulsory Deliveries A form of the state procurement of agricultural products, which formerly prevailed in the Socialist countries. It involved the legal obligation of the socialized and private farms to supply certain minimum quantities of certain products by specified dates at fixed prices determined by the state. The prices were usually set at very low levels, compared with ABOVE-COMPULSORY DELIVERIES and free market prices. The low prices were designed to absorb the differential rent and prevent excessive consumption by peasants, in the interest of maximum investment in the priority branches of the economy (especially industry and construction). C.d. were first introduced on a systematic basis under socialism in the USSR in 1933, after which 10 to 50 per cent of the agricultural output was disposed of. After W.W.II other Socialist countries introduced the system. After the mid-1950s c.d. were gradually abandoned and the states turned more to incentives (higher prices, CONTRACTION and moral suasion) to encourage agricultural output and sale.

Computational Profit Also known as calculation p., a concept used in some Socialist countries (such as Poland) in economic calculation. It is profit, calculated by the application of an efficiency index, to overcome the distortion of administered prices. This methodology of calculating profitability is used particularly in foreign trade, as domestic prices do not necessarily reflect factor cost and the official exchange rates do not realistically relate to the purchasing power of the domestic currencies compared to foreign currencies. C.p. may be used for compiling a list of exportables in a descending order of profitability, thus serving as a guide to determining the efficiency of foreign trade enterprises and bonuses to personnel.

Comrade Originally, one who shares the same chamber. The term has been adopted by socialists and communists for Party members. In this sense, it came into use towards the end of the 19th c., replacing 'brother', especially in continental Europe. The term was formally introduced first in Germany (*Genosse*) in 1879. In the Socialist countries the term is commonly used in a semi-formal manner as a form of address, in lieu of 'Mr', 'you' or 'Sir'.

Comrade Jesus A phrase used by the socialists before W.W.I, when religious beliefs and particularly Christian ethics were widely accepted by the working class. Jesus Christ was presented by some social reformers as a compassionable leader sympathetic to the underprivileged and oppressed masses. Furthermore, they maintained that if he had lived in the modern industrial age he would have been a socialist. Many Marxists did not object to the phrase, since they saw it as a symbolic bridge from Christian socialism to non-sectarian socialism, which in its logical conclusion would lead to communism.

Comrades' Court A voluntary semi-judicial court found in either a large place of employment, an educational institution, a suburb or village in several Socialist countries. Its jury consists of fellow workers or neighbours elected for a fixed term (usually two years). The system is best developed in the USSR where it was pioneered as a social institution in the spirit of communism. These courts were first established soon after the Bolshevik Revolution in 1917, when the Revolutionary Military Committee ordered open c.c. to be set up in the RED GUARDS units in Petrograd (now Leningrad). The idea appealed to Marxists, who believed that all citizens should participate in some aspect of social management, and represented a step towards the eventual substitution of educational measures for punishment. In the late 1970s there were 280,000 of these courts in the USSR (5,000 in the Moscow area alone). The offences typically dealt with by the c.c. include pilfering, damage to social property, absenteeism, irresponsible acts at work, insults, slander, hooliganism, family conflicts and disturbances in the neighbourhood. The penalty may include a public reprimand, a fine, demotion, overtime work, social ostracism, a term in a corrective labour camp or referral to a proper court. In some Socialist countries (such as Poland) the c.c. is known as a Social court.

Concentration and Centralization of Capital and Production Two related concepts often used in Marxist thought in application to capitalism. The concentration of capital denotes the growth of capital in absolute terms through the addition of profits to the existing stock of capital, and, in a relative sense, results in a faster growth of capital in the hands of the largest firms, so that a larger proportion of the total capital and production in a given industry and the whole economy is controlled by a few large firms or capitalists. Although, in the Marxist view, this behaviour is prompted by COMPETITION, its purpose is in fact to reduce competition and attain monopoly. This trend leads to a change in the ORGANIC STRUCTURE OF CAPITAL, viz. CONSTANT CAPITAL (especially fixed capital), which increases at the expense of VARIABLE CAPITAL (wages). The centralization of capital occurs at the same time and involves the merger of smaller capitalists, firms or the absorption or elimination of smaller entities, so that the increasing amount of capital passes under one control. The emergence and expansion of the 'company' with share capital illustrates this development. The concentration of a large amount of capital under one control enables the expansion of production and innovations. The c. and c. of c. and p. lead to an increasing scale of production and the consequent economies

of scale, increasing specialization and a declining number of capitalists, paralleled by the growing size of the proletariat. These processes produce several contradictions: conflict between the private ownership of capital and the social character of production; the ALIENATION of the workers from the increasingly rich capitalists; rising unemployment (owing to the substitution of capital for labour); and the appearance of monopolies.

Concept An idea or image whereby man, through the process of COGNITION, recognizes the essential features of objects or phenomena. The Marxist approach to the formation of a c. and its relation to reality is opposed to that in philosophical IDEALISM. According to the latter (regarded by Marxists as bourgeois), a c. is divorced from actual reality and is separate from the concrete and the particular, i.e. a c. exists *a priori*, before and independently of human experience. On the other hand, DIALECTICAL MATERIALISM insists that a c. first appears as a product of direct observation or experience, and only then, through abstract thinking, is it advanced to a higher level, when a generalization is made on the basis of the concrete and particular. Dialectical materialism further implies that a c. is not immutable but flexible and dynamic, because natural and social phenomena are interdependent. Changes produce new contradictions, which in turn are resolved at a higher level leading to new concepts. This approach to conceptual formation has an ideological significance for Marxists, implying that society and its thinking develop from lower to higher stages towards FULL COMMUNISM.

Concerted Economy PRECONCERTED ECONOMY.

Conciliation In an industrial dispute, an attempt by an independent conciliator to bring the employer and trade union representatives to the negotiating table to resolve the dispute, possibly by mutual concessions. A conciliator is usually a per-

113

son with a thorough knowledge of the industry concerned, rather than a lawyer. In contrast to ARBITRATION, recommendations made in the course of c. are not binding, unless the parties to the dispute agree to accept them. C. is often favoured as it is usually less time-consuming and less costly than either arbitration or STRIKE.

Concordance of Production Relations with Production Forces LAW OF THE NECESSARY CONCORDANCE OF PRODUCTION RELATIONS WITH THE NATURE OF PRODUCTION FORCES.

Concrete Labour A Marxian term for work actually performed or labour expended on products having USE-VALUE. C.l. assumes different forms according to the worker's occupation and the purpose of the work involved. It is a condition of man's survival and consequently is not associated with any particular social system. C.l. is not the only source of value as it can be expended only in association with the means of production. It contrasts with ABSTRACT 1.; whilst MATERIALIZED 1. contrasts with LIVE 1.

Concrete Truth In philosophy, a valid generalization based on actual historical conditions when a given event or process takes place. So understood, truth is always concrete, as it depends on the existing conditions in time and space. The concept is employed by Marxist philosophers who stress the limitations of such truth and regard it at best as RELATIVE TRUTH. They emphasize that abstract ideas can be misleading, if they are out of a historical context, e.g. the level of science and technology, methods of production and social organization. Thus, such concepts as DEMOCRACY, SOCIAL JUSTICE, PRICE, PROFIT, VALUE have different meanings in different SOCIO-ECONOMIC FORMATIONS, such as CAPITALISM, SOCIALISM, and FULL COMMUNISM. The basic reason for this Marxist philosophical stand is to show that the ideas and the social system developed in capitalism are not ETERNAL TRUTHS,

but only transitional to higher socio-economic formations.

Confédération Générale du Travail (General Confederation of Labour) The central and largest trade union organization in France. Founded in 1895, the *C.G.T.* has traditionally played a considerable role in French economic and political affairs. Its policies have been greatly influenced by the French Communists. In 1921, the Communists precipitated a split (resorting to CLASS-AGAINST-CLASS TACTICS) and formed the *C.G.T. Unitaire* which, in 1923, affiliated itself with the PROFINTERN. However, in 1934, the Communists rejoined the *C.G.T.* in reponse to the policy of the COMINTERN which favoured the anti-fascist POPULAR FRONT. This co-operation greatly increased the membership and national standing of the *C.G.T.*. In 1939 the Communists were expelled from the *C.G.T.* and, in the following year, it was dissolved by the Vichy government.

Conference of the Three Internationals A unique conference held in Berlin in 1922, in which three rival organizations took part, each claiming to represent the international working class movement, viz. the SECOND-AND-A-HALF INTERNATIONAL (which initiated the Conference), the SECOND INTERNATIONAL and the THIRD INTERNATIONAL, better known as the COMINTERN. Its purpose was to unite the three Internationals, or at least to work out a basis for co-operation. However, the differences were too great and hardly any agreement was reached. In the following year, the Second-and-a-Half Int. joined the Second Int. to form the LABOUR AND SOCIALIST INTERNATIONAL (which existed until 1947) whilst the Comintern continued until 1943.

Conflict and Unity of Opposites In DIALECTICS, the interaction between force and counter-force which becomes resolved in a new phenomenon. This process proceeds in cycles in a spiral fashion, and constitutes the essence of SELF-

MOVEMENT and progress. This conception was first put forward by HEGEL and later adopted in Marxist philosophy with certain modifications and a change in emphasis, yielding DIALECTICAL MATERIALISM.

Confucius ANTI-CONFUCIUS CAMPAIGN.

Congealed Labour MATERIALIZED LABOUR.

Congolese Party of Labour (*Parti Congolais du Travail***)** The ruling and the only legal political party in the P.R. of the CONGO. A party claiming to be Marxist-Leninist and committed to SCIENTIFIC SOCIALISM, it replaced the National Revolutionary Party Movement, and was declared the only legal party in Dec. 1970 when the P.R. of the Congo was proclaimed. However, its programme is pragmatic and adaptable. The Party is organized along hierarchical lines in accordance with DEMOCRATIC CENTRALISM. The CENTRAL COMMITTEE elects its Chairman who also becomes the country's President. There was also a Political Bureau, but in Jan. 1976 it was replaced by a 'Special Revolutionary General Staff', where the state's power is concentrated.

Congo, People's Republic of the (*République Populaire du Congo***)** A small country in western central Africa, ruled by the Marxist regime, the CONGOLESE PARTY OF LABOUR. The country has an area of 342,000 sq. km., and a population of 1.5m. (in 1978) and its capital is Brazzaville. Formerly a part of French Equatorial Africa, it achieved independence in 1960. After 1963 its military-supported regime turned to a Marxist programme and developed close relations with the Socialist countries (especially China, Cuba and the USSR). A new Constitution was adopted in Jan. 1970 and in the following December the country was proclaimed a 'People's Republic' and the C.P.L. was proclaimed the only legal political party. The country's President is elected by the Party (and is also the

Chairman of the Party's Central Committee). The government has embarked on a gradual socialization of the means of production and the extension of social services. In Jan. 1976 the President dismissed the Party's Political Bureau and replaced it with a special Revolutionary General Staff. In March of the same year, trade union leaders were expelled from the Party for calling a general strike. In April 1977, the People's National Assembly (which had been elected in 1973 from a single list of candidates prepared by the C.P.L.) was dismissed and the 1970 Constitution was abrogated. However, since that time, the regime has turned to a conciliatory course towards the West, including such countries as France and the USA.

Congress of Industrial Organizations One of the two central trade union organizations in the USA which existed from 1935 to 1955. It originated as the Committee for Industrial Organizations led by John L. Lewis, a breakaway faction expelled from the AMERICAN FEDERATION OF LABOR. The C.I.O. was critical of the A.F.L.'s conservative policies, adopted militant tactics, was prone to strikes (including 'sit-down' strikes) and engaged in radical political campaigns. It was most active amongst industrial rather than craft unions. It never surpassed the A.F.L. in size, but enjoyed a good deal of support amongst the masses of unskilled workers. At the time of its merger with the A.F.L., the C.I.O. had 6.5m. members (compared with the A.F.L.'s 9.5m.).

Congress of Industrialization Name officially given in the USSR to the Fifteenth Congress of the ALL-UNION COMMUNIST PARTY (OF THE BOLSHEVIKS) held in Moscow in Dec. 1927. The theme adopted at this time was accelerated industrialization. It initiated the great industrialization drive under central economic planning and adopted the directives for the first Five-Year Plan, 1928–32.

Congress of the Communist Party PARTY CONGRESS.

Congress of Soviets ALL-RUSSIAN CONGRESS OF SOVIETS, ALL-UNION CONGRESS OF SOVIETS.

Consciousness The awareness of a person's thoughts and feelings, or the knowledge of knowing. The relation of c. to MATTER is one of the fundamental problems of philosophy. In IDEALISM c. is assumed to be primary, whilst matter is considered secondary. On the other hand in the Marxist philosophy of MATERIALISM, c. is regarded as being secondary, derived from matter which exists independently of c. and is the source of sensual perceptions, images and ideas. Marx (in *A CONTRIBUTION TO THE CRITIQUE OF POLITICAL ECONOMY*) stated that: 'It is not consciousness of men that determines their being, but on the contrary, their social being that determines their social consciousness'. Marxist philosophers further maintain that c. is peculiar to human beings and develops in the process of production and social relations in the community. Changes in production and social conditions induce modifications in c., but in turn c. also affects these conditions. The appearance of c. is associated with the appearance of language (LABOUR THEORY OF LANGUAGE DEVELOPMENT). On this question, however, Mao Tse-tung's interpretation is different from the orthodox Marxist position. Whilst Marx argued that changes in c. must be preceded by changes in material conditions, Mao (in 'The FOOLISH OLD MAN') emphasized that man and his c. must be altered first (as soon as possible) to accelerate changes in the material and social conditions – otherwise the revolutionary impulse may not develop, and may weaken (in the form of OPPORTUNISM and REVISIONISM). Thus in Mao's view, in the advanced stage of the process of COGNITION (when ideas are applied and tested in practice), c. creates matter.

Conservatism Political and social ideology defending the existing social order and traditionally accepted values, allowing only such changes which are essential to the desired functioning of existing institutions (such as the state, family, the church). Marxists reject c. on political, social, and economic as well as philosophical grounds, as it is likely to impede progress by interfering with adjustments to the changing material and social conditions of production and living. More fundamentally, DIALECTICIAL MATERIALISM and HISTORICAL MATERIALISM emphasize the successive appearance of contradictions which must be resolved. The longer the readjustments are postponed, the more abrupt and violent the solutions are likely to be.

Conspicuous Consumption Ostentatious purchase, use or ownership of items by a consumer calculated to confirm or enhance his higher social status, even though such items may be not warranted on other grounds. The term was introduced by Thorstein Veblen (in *Theory of the Leisure Class*, 1899). Marxists view c.c. as a form of false escapism stressing class distinction and a logical consequence of capitalism noted for its social stratification and distorted values.

Conspicuous Production A disparaging term sometimes used in the West in application to the Socialist countries, to describe unnecessary and spectacular projects of doubtful economic viability. They are calculated to impress the masses at home and observers abroad. The term appears to have been used first in the USA in the 1950s as a retaliation against the accusation of CONSPICUOUS CONSUMPTION. C.p. may assume the following varied forms: striking designs of products; imposing frontages of factories (PALACES OF LABOUR), location in an unjustifiably conspicuous place; and widely publicized projects. In extreme cases it may be directed towards being the 'largest', the 'longest', the 'most powerful', the 'most modern' or the 'first in the world'. Western critics have attributed c.p. mostly to the USSR. Also GIGANTOMANIA.

Constant Capital In Marx's terminology (in *CAPITAL*, vol. I), that part of capital which in the process of production is in the form of fixed and circulating assets, viz. buildings, machinery, equipment, tools, fuel and power, raw materials and other means of production (as distinct from labour). In the Marxian formula for value ($c + v + s$), it is designated by c, denoting the flow of outlays on non-labour resources and signifying the stock of capital used in the process of production. Marx called it 'constant', because (unlike VARIABLE CAPITAL) its value does not change in the process of production, but is merely transferred to the output produced to the extent of the depreciation of fixed capital and the amount of the circulating assets used up. In capitalist society, c.c. is derived mostly from SURPLUS VALUE and the capitalist, driven by competition, endeavours to invest more and more in c.c. in order to appropriate more surplus value in the future. The substitution of constant capital for variable capital produces two significant social effects: 1. an increase in the RESERVE ARMY OF WORKERS; and 2. the DECLINING PROFIT RATE.

Constituent Assembly A type of revolutionary parliament in Russia, elected on a popular basis in Nov. 1917 (a month after the GREAT OCTOBER SOCIALIST REVOLUTION), but dissolved on 6 Jan. 1918 (Old-Style Calendar). The idea of the C.A. had been first mooted by Russian reformers in the 19th c. and received enthusiastic support from the BOLSHEVIKS in the 1905 and February 1917 Revolutions. Of the 703 deputies elected, the Bolsheviks won only 24 per cent of the vote, whilst the SOCIALIST REVOLUTIONARIES gained 54 per cent, the national minority groups 11 per cent, the LEFT SOCIALIST REVOLUTIONARIES 5 per cent, the Mensheviks 2 per cent, the KADETS 2 per cent and the Popular Socialists 1 per cent. Faced with 76 per cent of the deputies being non-Bolsheviks, Lenin decided not to summon the C.A. The C.A. held one session on 5–6 Jan. 1918, but it refused to pass the Bolshevik proposals. In reply, the Bolshevik Government gave orders to armed sailors to break up the session, and the ALL-RUSSIAN CENTRAL EXECUTIVE COMMITTEE dissolved the C.A. by a decree proclaimed on 6 Jan. 1918 (O.-S.C.).

Constructivism An abstract art movement in architecture, construction and sculpture in the early post-revolutionary period in the USSR. It emphasized functionalism and the aesthetic use of industrial materials, such as metal, wire and glass, in an attempt to reflect the industrial machine age. The theoretical foundations of c. had been developed by V. Tatlin (1875–1956) between 1913 and 1917 under the influence of Picasso and CUBISM. Special attention was given to the expression of the dynamism of the Socialist society in the technological age, as exemplified by the structure of public buildings resembling electric generators, motor vehicles and the like. The most ambitious of the constructivist projects was Tatlin's proposed monument to the COMINTERN in the form of a gigantic perspective steel spiral embodying three geometric figures representing the congresses and other meetings. Most constructivists, including Tatlin, accepted the Party's postulate that c. should serve the Socialist state. The most extreme direction of c. along these lines was PRODUCTIVISM. However, liberal constructivists insisted that art should be free, and some of them, notably the sculptor, Naum Gabo (1890–1977), left the USSR and settled in Germany, France and the USA. Owing to its essentially abstract forms which were not easily comprehended by the masses, by 1920 c. had fallen out of official favour. Although it continued through individual efforts in the 1920s, it received little assistance from the authorities. Its decline was further accelerated by the official turn toward SOCIALIST REALISM.

Consultative Group A policy-consulting body for the STRATEGIC EMBARGO, created in Paris in Nov. 1949. The foundation member countries were Belgium, France, Italy, Luxemburg, the Netherlands, the UK and the USA. Canada, Denmark, the FR of Germany, Greece, Japan, Norway, Portugal and Turkey joined soon afterwards. It involves high-level diplomats representing their respective countries in Paris. It was very active in the 1950s, when it established its two working committees, the CO-COM and CHIN-COM. After 1958 its activities began to decline gradually.

Consumerism Strong pressure by consumers and related interests exerted in the economy and on the authorities to increase the volume, variety and quality of consumer goods and services, even if it involves the curtailment of investment and the rate of economic growth. It is peculiar to capitalist market economies, especially in the West. C. originated in the USA in the 1920s, but more recently it has been associated with consumer protection, e.g. truthful advertising, informative labelling, better health and safety standards, and fair pricing (the movement associated with Ralph Nader). In the Socialist plannned economy, c. is neither allowed to play an important role nor is there much need for it. Total consumption in the economy and its major components are predetermined on a planned basis. Unfair business practices are either absent or can be directly controlled by the authorities. However, the ECONOMIC REFORMS in most European Socialist countries since the early 1960s (and some ten years earlier in Yugoslavia) have facilitated the emergence of c. See also CONSUMER'S SOVEREIGNTY.

Consumers' Co-operative A type of co-operative enterprise in capitalist countries found in distribution, especially retailing, wholesale trade and insurance. Its purpose may be a reduction of living costs, the cultivation of a communal spirit in preparation for socialism or a substitution for socialism. A c.c. is normally operated by hired professionals, with the members benefiting either from lower prices or receiving dividends in proportion to their investment or the value of their purchases.

The system is best developed in Western Europe, but only in a few cases has it proved successful. The oldest, largest and the most successful c.c. is the Co-operative Wholesale Society Ltd, founded in Manchester in 1863. Marxists have mixed feelings on c.c. Although they concede that as a working-class movement it is a commendable struggle against capitalist exploitation, they deny that by itself it can supplant capitalism. In their view, it is not radical enough and adapts its methods to capitalist production and social relations. Lenin, in fact, called it a 'collective capitalist institution'. In the Socialist countries, whilst producers' co-operatives are favoured and fairly well developed, c.c.s are not, as they tend to be largely pointless (except to some extent in Poland and Yugoslavia). Also see ROCHDALE CO-OPERATIVE.

Consumers' Freedom of Choice An allocative and distributive system where the consumer is free to buy what he wishes from amongst the goods and services made available by the authorities. The total volume of the products and their broad structure made available in the market are determined not by consumers' preferences, but by central planners. C.f. of ch. is an intermediate stage between CONSUMER'S SOVEREIGNTY and rationing and is typical of the Socialist centrally planned economies. Consumers' preferences do not determine the allocation of resources, as the latter is in the hands of central plannners ('planner's sovereignty'). The market equilibrium is achieved by the official manipulation of retail prices (in practice the readjustment of TURN-OVER TAXES), so that consumption is adapted to production.

Consumer's Sovereignty A system of the utilization of resources and the distribution of output where the 'consumer is king', i.e. where he is free to buy whatever goods and services he wishes. His preferences also determine total consumption and the allocation of resources, not only for the production of consumer goods, but also indirectly of producer goods. Given the profit motive, producers strive to supply a volume and structure of goods and services that meet consumers' preferences, whereby profits can be maximized. If not, producers suffer losses and are eliminated from the market. ABSOLUTE C. S. can exist only in capitalist market economies. A Socialist economy at best can ensure only RATIONALIZED C.S.

Consumption Fund In Socialist economic practice, that portion of the national income (i.e. NET MATERIAL PRODUCT) allowed for current consumption, as distinct from ACCUMULATION. The c.f. is predetermined in the economic plan and its size depends on the postulated investment and the rate of growth of the national income. The c.f. in its real (material) form has an equivalent in its financial counterpart. It falls into two major components: 1. PRIVATE CONSUMPTION, which is financed out of the private incomes of the population and consists of goods and services, plus the depreciated value of housing during the period in question; and 2. SOCIAL CONSUMPTION, financed out of various social consumption funds and consisting of the cost value of goods and services provided by enterprises, other employing entities and public authorities to the population, completely free or at only nominal charges. In general the Socialist countries reserve 65–85 per cent of their net material product for the c.f., which is roughly 10 per cent less than would be normal in a capitalist market economy at the same stage of economic development.

Consumption of Labour Power A Marxian concept meaning the process of embodying LABOUR POWER into a commodity. Marx described it thus: 'The consumption of labour power is at one and the same time the production of commodities and of surplus value. The consumption of labour power is completed, as in the case of every other commodity, outside the limits of the market or of the sphere of circulation' (*Capital*, vol. I, 1867).

Consumption Steering The adaptation of consumption patterns by the state in pursuit of various policy objectives. It may be prompted by the determination to control ANTI-SOCIAL CONSUMPTION and to guide consumers to new forms of consumption in anticipation of new ideas and developments planned by the state, thereby facilitating the transformation of the economy and society along desired lines. C.s. was practised in Nazi Germany, Fascist Italy, Imperial Japan and many other countries in wartime. More recently it has been practised by less-developed countries. It is also pursued on a more systematic basis by the Socialist centrally planned economies as a matter of normal practice, usually by direct controls and propaganda.

Containment Policy A major direction in US foreign policy after W.W.II, aimed at confining Communism to the existing boundaries of the Socialist bloc. It was first formulated in 1947 by G. Kennan, an authority on Soviet affairs and US Ambassador to the USSR (1952–53). In 1947, the policy was enunciated by President Truman and applied as the TRUMAN DOCTRINE in the form of military aid to Greece and Turkey. The C.P. was based on the conviction that if Soviet and Chinese expansionism was blocked, communism would sooner or later collapse due to its own internal weaknesses, inconsistencies and dissensions. The Policy embodied the following elements: 1. mutual defence alliances with friendly countries, especially on the peripheries of the Socialist bloc; 2. the maintenance of military bases directed against the Socialist countries; 3. an extensive armament programme to act as a deterrent and to enable the USA to negotiate 'from a position of strength'; 4. defensive actions and wars against Communist expansionism (the BERLIN AIRLIFT, the Korean War, the VIETNAM WAR, and naval protection of Taiwan); 5. the STRATEGIC EMBARGO; and 6. a vast programme of economic and technical aid to Western Europe, Japan and many less-developed countries to counteract Communist influence. The C.P. became a major facet of the COLD WAR on the Western side and proved moderately successful for two decades, but was virtually abandoned with the US withdrawal from Vietnam after 1973. Also 'BALANCE OF TERROR', DOMINO THEORY, DULLES-EISENHOWER DOCTRINE, 'ROLLBACK' PROPOSITION.

Contingency A philosophical concept meaning chance or fortuity, employed in the interpretation of phenomena (it is opposite to NECESSITY). There has been a long controversy in philosophy as to whether the processes taking place in nature and society are a matter of c. or necessity. Some philosophers maintain that c. is the rule and some (idealists) that although phenomena have their causation, the causes lie in the supernatural world, not in the material reality. Marxist philosophy, based on MATERIALISM, does not accept c. either in nature or society. It is stressed that all phenomena are governed by definite laws. The material BASE is primarily conditioned by natural laws whilst the SUPERSTRUCTURE mostly responds to changes in the base, but in turn also influences the latter. It is further argued that although an object or a situation may be affected accidentally by external forces, the latter still have their causation and occur according to definite laws.

Continuing Revolution (*Pu-tuan Koming*, in Chinese) A tenet formulated by Mao Tse-tung, postulating the continuation of the PROLETARIAN REVOLUTION and the DICTATORSHIP OF THE PROLETARIAT until the ideal society featured by the NEW COMMUNIST MAN is firmly established. In its final version, the postulate was proclaimed for China in Mao's speech, *SIXTY ARTICLES*, on 28 Jan. 1958, in which he stressed the need for 'striking while the iron is hot', so that revolution would advance from one phase to another 'without interruption'. Mao warned that the Chinese C.R. must not be confused with the PERMANENT REVOLUTION put forward by Trotsky (of whom the Chinese leaders are critical as he was opposed to Stalin).

Contractation A term applied in the Socialist countries to one of the forms of the planned procurement of agricultural products by the state from collective and private farms by negotiation and mutual commitment. The state, usually through the socialized trading or industrial enterprises, concludes contracts with the farms for the production and delivery of an 'agreed' quantity and quality of products at 'agreed' prices and other conditions imposed by the state. The state gurarantees not only the purchase of the products and the prices, but also the provision of the necessary credit and technical assistance. C. is a more liberal form of AGRICULTURAL PROCUREMENT than COMPULSORY DELIVERIES and has greatly contributed to the stability in Socialist agriculture and in the economy in general.

Contracting Reproduction A Marxist concept used in national income accounting to denote a situation in the economy when the total volume of material production is insufficient to sustain current consumption and replace the worn-out means of production. It amounts to a negative rate of investment, i.e. disinvestment (drawing on past accumulation) and is usually associated with or followed by a declining or a negative rate of growth of the national income. C.r. contrasts with EXPANDED R. and SIMPLE R.

Contradiction One of the most fundamental concepts in Marxist philosophy, denoting a conflict of opposing forces, tendencies, interests or thoughts. Marx borrowed the idea (first used in *The Poverty of Philosophy*) from HEGEL and made it the central feature of his HISTORICAL MATERIALISM. The concept was further elaborated upon in its different ramifications by Lenin (in *Philosophical Notebooks*), Stalin (*Dialectical and Historical Materialism*, 1938), Mao Tse-tung (in 'On Contradiction', 1937, and *ON THE CORRECT HANDLING OF CONTRADICTIONS*) and by many others. To Marxists, c. occurs in nature as well as in society and is the very mainspring of existence, development and progress. Abstractly speaking, c. consists in a *thesis* being confronted with an *antithesis* and resolving itself in a *synthesis* ('dialectic triad'). Thus in mechanics, a c. is illustrated by action and reaction, in physics, by positive and negative electric charge, and in politics, by revolution and counter-revolution. In society a c. is exemplified in the CLASS STRUGGLE. This view of development contrasts with the non-Marxist thought on the question, which is preoccupied with harmony and equilibrium. Furthermore, in the Marxist view, a c. may be *primary* (or *basic*), if it is of a major dimension and fundamental (e.g. between the BOURGEOISIE and the PROLETARIAT), or *secondary*, a logical consequence of the former (e.g. between MENTAL AND PHYSICAL LABOUR). When the conflict is irreconcilable, a c. is called *antagonistic*, and can be resolved only in a violent way (e.g. conflicts between nations or social classes in wars or revolutions). C. is *non-antagonistic* when opposing actions or interests can be resolved in a co-operative manner (e.g. between rural and urban workers by mutual concessions and support). Classical Marxist philosophers assumed that antagonistic social contradictions would disappear soon after a victorious PROLETARIAN REVOLUTION, a view which is officially accepted in the Soviet bloc. But Mao Tse-tung argued that such contradictions do continue reappearing even under socialism, and have to be resolved in a CONTINUING REVOLUTION. Also CONTRADICTIONS OF CAPITALIST PRODUCTION, SOCIAL CONTRADICTIONS.

Contradictions of Capitalist Production In the Marxist interpretation, conflicts arising from the private ownership of the means of production and the appropriation of the SURPLUS VALUE by capitalists on the one hand, and the social character of production on the other. The former two lead to the separation, independence and rivalry of individual firms, whilst the latter (noted for the division of labour) links and unites individual enterprises and makes them interdependent. This basic CONTRADICTION is reflected in the conflict between capital and labour. The PROLETARIAT, in order to survive, has to sell its labour power to the capitalist entrepreneurs, but the latter exploit the former by appropriating the SURPLUS VALUE (profits). Thus, there is a contradiction between profits and wages, whereby one is increased at the expense of the other. Another contradiction concerns the size of the workers' consumption. On the one hand, the smaller this consumption is, the larger is the surplus value. But on the other hand, surplus value may be not maximized, as it is realized through sales to consumers, of which the working class constitutes the great majority. Workers enable the capitalists to accumulate capital, but the latter use the very capital created by workers in order to replace labour. This leads to the growing RESERVE ARMY OF WORKERS, a further IMMISERATION OF THE PROLETARIAT, underconsumption, idle resources and further unemployment. Other c. of c.p. include the highly organized and disciplined capitalist firm and the ANARCHY OF THE MARKET, plus the conflict of interests between agriculture and industry, rural and urban population, the BIG BOURGEOISIE and the PETTY BOURGEOISIE, industrial capitalists and the FINANCIAL OLIGARCHY and between developed and underdeveloped countries. These contradictions are considered by revolutionary Marxists to be antagonistic, i.e. irreconcilable, and can only be resolved in a proletarian revolution.

Contribution to the Critique of Political Economy, A A book on which MARX worked during 1857–58 and published in 1859 (under its German title, *Zur Kritik der politischen Ökonomie*). It was his first major work in the field of political economy (previously he had been preoccupied with philosophy and politics). It was an economic groundwork for his most important work, *CAPITAL* (the first volume of which appeared eight years later). Some Marxists regard it as the most fundamental of all his writings (a 'centre-piece'), yet it was his last major work to be published in English translation (first by I. N. Stone in 1904). The book embodies the first systematic exposition and analysis of the Marxian theory of value and monetary theory. In it, Marx in effect became an advocate of the gold standard, regarding gold as the most appropriate commodity for measuring value (i.e. materialized labour). Other major problems which Marx examined included ALIENATION, INDIVIDUALISM and the role of capital and labour in production.

Control by the Rouble (*Kontrol rublom*, in Russian) The exercise of financial control in the economy by banks in the course of credit extension, the regulation of conditions for financial processes and the settling of accounts between enterprises. Although the phrase and practice were established in the USSR (over the period 1930–37), they have become symbolical of financial control in most planned economies, paralleling and reinforcing direct controls over physical flows. The c. by the r. (or by the *koruna, peso* or *renminbi*) is exercised in the following manner. Each socialized enterprise has to have a bank account with one designated branch of the state bank in which it has to keep virtually all its financial resources earmarked for specified purposes (e.g. Wage Fund, Investment Fund, Research and Development Fund, Material Incentives Fund). The withdrawal of money or the settling of accounts are done under the supervision of the bank, the latter being responsible for seeing that the transactions are consistent with social interest and, in particular, are directed to the implementation of the economic plan.

Control Figures A term used in central economic planning, showing the initial plan indicators (targets) postulated by the central planning authority in the process of plan construction. The term was introduced in the USSR in the early 1920s and in July 1924 the Council of Labour and Defence ordered the Central Statistical

Administration to compile a balance of the national economy for 1923–24. The c.f., which may be too ambitious, too modest or inconsistent with the attainment of other targets, are tested for feasibility by being circulated down the hierarchical ladder of planning and management to enterprises. As a result of additional information production capacities, new developments, proposals and counter-proposals, the central body works out the final, internally-consistent plan which then becomes binding.

Convergence Thesis A theory according to which capitalism and socialism are shedding their extreme features, and instead are adopting or developing characteristics formerly peculiar to the other side. The theory implies that the two systems will ultimately 'converge' into one conglomerate, embodying the best elements of its predecessors and few of their weaknesses. The c.t. was first put foward explicitly by Jan Tinbergen in 1961, although the idea can be traced back to the early 1940s. The spheres of convergence include the following: 1. the ownership of the means of production; 2. economic planning and management; 3. banking and finance; 4. incentives; 5. the role of the consumer; 6. prices; 7. the distribution of national income; 8. the social structure; 9. POLYCENTRISM on each side; and 10. increasing commercial, financial, industrial and technological co-operation between capitalist and the Socialist countries. The converging trends are attributed to three autonomous developments, tending to produce similar effects, irrespective of the social system, namely, technological change, industrialization and affluence. Although the c.t. has found many supporters in the capitalist world, it has been officially rejected in the Socialist countries as a wishful desire to rescue capitalism from its inevitable breakdown. Also TRANSIDEOLOGICAL COLLABORATION.

Conversion A Marxian term denoting the transformation of values in the process of production and distribution. Thus, money capital is converted by the capitalist into the means of production (land and capital) and labour, and these, in turn, into commodities, which when sold in the market are converted into money. Then the surplus value, appropriated by the capitalist, is in turn converted into capital, and so on. Also TRANSFORMATION PROBLEM.

Co-operative A term used in two forms. As an adjective, it means pertaining to co-operation, collectivism or undertakings carried out in common; e.g. co-operative housing fund, co-operative producers' union, or co-operative drainage project. As a noun, it means an enterprise operated by a co-operative association of consumers, producers or lenders-borrowers such as a retail store, a workshop, a farm or a housing society. Also see CO-OPERATIVE MOVEMENT, CO-OPERATIVE SOCIALISM, COLLECTIVE FARM.

Co-operative Banks See CREDIT CO-OPERATIVES.

Co-operative Commonwealth The ideal state postulated by the advocates of CO-OPERATIVE SOCIALISM, in which most consumers and producers are organized in collective entities and antagonistic social relations are replaced by co-operative attitudes and ties. It is also the title of a book by Laurence Grönlund (1846–99), an American socialist theoretician of Danish descent: *The Cooperative Commonwealth* (1884).

Co-operative Commonwealth Federation A movement in Canada founded in 1932 for the development of co-operation between farmers and labour, substantially along socialist lines, and with an emphasis on welfare and improved production and social relations. It was the official designation of the democratic socialist party embodying a number of farmer, worker and socialist parties in western Canada and the Canadian Brotherhood of Railway Employees. In 1933, the Federation issued a national programme of reforms, called the 'Regina Manifesto', which advocated economic planning, the socialization of banks, main public utilities and natural resources, a farm stabilization scheme, the development of producer and consumer co-operatives, social security, progressive taxation and employment-creation schemes. The C.C.F. became quite active in politics and in 1944 it governed in Saskatchewan. It also entered Federal elections and in the 1950s polled about 15 per cent of the votes cast. It was also a member of the SOCIALIST INTERNATIONAL. After 1958 it merged with the New Democratic Party.

Co-operative Enterprise A voluntary revolutionary association of persons operating a joint enterprise for the benefit of the members sharing in its net income (and losses, up to their contributed shares), and generally organized along democratic lines. The members contribute shares to the assets of the c.e., and when contributing to its operation, may be either 'active' or 'passive' (or 'sleeping'). The operation and functions of the c.e. depend on the political, economic and social system under which it carries on its activities. In a capitalist society, the c.e. is mostly a defensive association to protect members against monopolistic and monopsonistic firms and the uncertainties of the market. In the Socialist countries, c.es. are encouraged by the state and play an important part in the economy, contributing up to one-fifth of the total production (the balance being represented by the state sector, plus the private sector if it still exists). C. es. participate in the implementation of the economic plan, whereby their operations benefit their members as well as society in general. They also discharge important educational, training, rehabilitation and civic responsibilities. C. es. are best developed in agriculture (AGRICULTURAL CIRCLES, COLLECTIVE FARMS), small-scale industry, retail trade, consumer services and personal and housing finance. In each Socialist country, a 'statute for co-operative enterprises' establishes the national norms. Membership is open not only to individual persons, but also to other enterprises. A c.e. is managed by a 'management board', which is supervised by a 'council' elected by the members at a 'general meeting'.

Co-operative movement A movement consisting of voluntary associations of persons for the pursuit of economic activities on a collective basis for the benefit of the members. It arose in Western Europe (especially in France and Italy) after 1830 as an idealistic experiment and as a form of defence for the interests of the artisans, peasants and other small-scale producers against the disruptive operation of the market, powerful suppliers, traders and banks. Co-operatives may embrace either producers or consumers or, in some cases, both. To promote the c.m., the IN-TERNATIONAL CO-OPERATIVE ALLIANCE was established in 1895, with its headquarters in London. At its 23rd Congress in Vienna held in 1966, it laid down six principles guiding the c.m. in the world. They are as follows: 1. open and voluntary membership; 2. member participation in management and control on a democratic basis ('one person, one vote'); 3. limitation of return on capital contributed by the members; 4. distribution of dividends on an equitable basis; 5. provision of information on the operation of the co-operative enterprise and the co-operative movement in general; and 6. collaboration amongst co-operative enterprises on a local, national and international scale. The c.m. has spread to all parts of the world, irrespective of the stage of economic development and the social system in force. In the Socialist countries, co-operative enterprises have been extended and constitute the so-called 'co-operative sector' (as distinct from the 'state' and 'private' sectors). Although the co-operative sector contributes less than one-fifth of the total production in these countries, it is quite important in agriculture, small-scale industry, retail trade, various consumer services and small-scale savings and credit fields. In addition to economic pursuits, they also engage in various activities of a broader social nature (educational, vocational, cultural, sporting and humanitarian). Most Marxist thinkers regard the c.m. as of a marginal consequence and largely as a transitional stage on the road to full communism. Also see CONSUMERS' CO-OPERATIVE, CO-OPERATIVE SOCIALISM, CREDIT CO-OPERATIVES, PRODUCERS' CO-OPER-ATIVE, ROCHDALE CO-OPERATIVE.

Co-operative Socialism A general term for the theories, experiments and practices designed to develop economic and social organization along co-operative lines, where workers collectively own, manage and operate production and distribution. The doctrine of c.s. was developed towards the end of the 19th c. in Western Europe, especially in Britain, France and Italy. C.s. opposes both capitalism and communism, and instead advocates the mass organization of people in producers and consumers' co-operatives in agriculture, manufacturing, trade, transport, banking and finance. Most Marxist thinkers oppose c.s. for being impractical, utopian and tolerant of the exploiting classes. As such, it detracts a portion of the working class from the class struggle, thereby postponing the proletarian revolution. Lenin described c.s. as a 'collective capitalist institution'.

Co-operativism Another term for CO-OPERATIVE SOCIALISM.

Corporatism An economic, social and political movement, postulating compulsory occupational associations organized into tightly-knit 'Corporations' embodied into the state structure. C. emphasizes co-operation and the mutuality of interests of different social classes and groups. Each Corporation associates employers, employees and representatives with the state, and in turn, the system replaces trade unions, local councils and the parliament. The private ownership of the means of production and the traditional social structure are basically retained. C. has received support from some churches

124

(CLERICALISM) and some authoritarian nationalistic movements as an attempt to stem the spread of socialism and communism. C. prevailed in Fascist Italy (1922–43) and was also introduced partly in Nazi Germany (1933–45) and to a milder degree in Spain and Portugal under the Fascist regimes. C. was embraced in these countries more for political expediency rather than religious and social convictions, and to strengthen the power of the state, rather than improve the economic and social conditions of the working class. The Socialist countries have looked upon c. as one of the worst forms of reactionary capitalism.

Cosmopolitanism Indifference to patriotism, treating national and state institutions as outdated and national traditions and culture as pointless and harmful. Advocates of c. maintain that the only real homeland of man is the whole world. Basically, Marxism is not opposed to c. and in a sense is in its favour as far as the international brotherhood of the working class is concerned. But in practice, the official attitudes in the Socialist countries have been highly critical. C. has come to be regarded, especially in the USSR since 1941, as a reactionary view and practice instigated by the imperialist powers to justify their political, economic and cultural penetration of other countries and to counteract NATIONAL LIBERATION MOVEMENTS. It has also been identified with right-wing CATHOLICISM, ZIONISM and TROTSKYISM. C. is contrasted with PROLETARIAN INTERNATIONALISM, which is claimed to be a harmonious combination of PATRIOTISM and the national interests of the working class with the international solidarity of the proletariat in the world.

Cost of Living Private expenditure per person or household on goods and services customarily accepted as appropriate at a particular stage of economic development. It depends on the volume of the items normally purchased and their prices. The portion of total consumption which is provided free by society, known as SOCIAL CONSUMPTION, does not affect the c. of l. The c. of l. index, which is usually compiled by the authorities, is an important element in wage determination, especially of the minimum wage. Compared with capitalist countries at the same level of economic development, the c. of l. in the Socialist planned economies is lower for, amongst others, the following reasons: 1. the price of goods and services, especially those entering the c. of l., is strictly controlled and reasonably stable; 2. many items entering the c. of l. are subsidized out of the state budget to protect the standard of living of the lowest income groups; and 3. social consumption, which is freely provided by society or at only nominal charges, represents a high proportion of total consumption (typically 20–40 per cent, compared with 5–25 per cent in capitalist countries).

Cost-price of a Commodity In Marx's analysis in application to the capitalist economy, that portion of the VALUE of the commodity representing the capitalist's expenditure on MATERIALIZED LABOUR and LIVE LABOUR embodied in the commodity in question. In Marxian symbols it is represented by $c + v$, i.e. CONSTANT CAPITAL plus VARIABLE CAPITAL (or total value minus SURPLUS VALUE).

Council for Mutual Economic Assistance The organization for economic co-operation embracing the following Socialist countries: Bulgaria; Cuba; Czechoslovakia; the German DR; Hungary; Mongolia; Poland; Romania; and the USSR. Angola (since 1976), Vietnam (1978), Yugoslavia (1964), Finland (1973), Iraq (1975) and Mexico (1975) are also members on a more or less limited basis. The organization is also known as the COMECON, CMEA, CEMA, CEA or *S.E.V* (Russian for *Sovet Ekonomicheskoi Vzaimpomoshchi*) or the 'Soviet bloc common market'. It was founded in Jan. 1949 on the Soviet initiative as a countermove to the MARSHALL PLAN. The Secretariat of the CMEA is located in Moscow, but most of its instrumentalities are found in the (full) member countries' capitals or other cities. The highest policy-making body is the CMEA Session, which meets, as a rule, once a year in the capital city of each member country in rotation. The Executive Committee is the highest permanent organ carrying out the CMEA Session's policy, and is directly assisted by the Secretariat, the Committee for Co-operation in Planning Work, and the Committee for Scientific and Technical Co-operation – all four being situated in Moscow. Next there are 20 specialized 'Permanent Commissions' for: Agriculture; the Chemical Industry; Communications; Construction; Currency and Finance; Economic Questions; Ferrous Metallurgy; Food Processing; Geology; Light Industry; Machine-Building; Non-Ferrous Metallurgy; Nuclear Energy for Peaceful Purposes; Oil and Gas; Radio and Electronics; Standardization; Statistics; and Transport. Their seats are distributed in the member countries' capitals. There are also over 20 other permanent joint specialized organs, scientific institutes, production associations, service organizations and conferences. The CMEA is an economic grouping where co-operation is not shaped by free market forces but rather by planning, formal agreements and commitments. The grouping has made a good deal of progress, particularly since the early 1960s. However, although the CMEA has an impressive institutional framework, its success in promoting specialization and integration has in several ways been limited. The extent of practical achievements in these two directions has been below the levels of what would be economically most beneficial to the grouping as a whole. There were several Soviet attempts to create a supranational authority, but without any success owing to the reluctance of the remaining member countries to forgo their national sovereignties. A supra-national authority would have the power to make majority decisions, whilst under the present set-up the CMEA makes recommendations which become binding on the member country only if it agrees to such

an undertaking. In almost all respects, the CMEA is larger than its Western European counterpart, the European Economic Community. Taking the nine full member countries as a whole, the CMEA represents the following proportions of the world economy: population, 10 per cent, area, 18 per cent; national income, 21 per cent; industrial output, 30 per cent; and foreign trade, 9 per cent. The respective proportions for the EEC (also nine full members) are: 7 per cent; 2 per cent; 18 per cent; 19 per cent; and 34 per cent.

Council of Ministers of the USSR The highest executive and administrative body in the USSR, or simply the 'government'. From 1917 to 1946 it was officially known as the Council of People's Commissars. It is the largest C. of M. in the world, consisting of 95 persons, viz.: the Chairman (or Prime Minister N. A. TIKHONOV; one First Vice-Chairman; five Vice-Chairmen; 59 Ministers; 13 Chairmen of the most important state agencies; the Chief of the Central Statistical administration; and 15 Chairmen of the Republics' Councils of Ministers. It is elected by and responsible to the SUPREME SOVIET OF THE USSR or its Presidium. Theoretically, the C. of M. carries out the laws enacted by the Supreme Soviet, but in practice, it implements the policy of the COMMUNIST PARTY OF THE SOVIET UNION, as virtually all members of the Council are senior Party members.

Council of People's Commissars of the USSR The official name of the highest executive and administrative organ in the USSR from 1917 to 1946, corresponding to the Council of Ministers in other countries. It was first elected and acquired its name at the Second Congress of Soviets in Oct. 1917, immediately after the Bolshevik seizure of power. The term 'People's Commissars' was intended to imply that the Soviet Government was not like the Tsarist or bourgeois 'Ministers' but, rather, working-class appointees. To avoid any frequent misunderstandings in foreign countries, in 1946 the name was changed officially to the COUNCIL OF MINISTERS OF THE USSR.

Councils of the National Economy (in the USSR) See *SOVNARKHOZ.*

Counter-imperialism A term used by R. Lowenthal to describe the new approach by the Socialist countries, especially the USSR, to counter the Western influence in the Third World by linking the latter to the Socialist bloc through lasting economic ties based on the viable division of labour. C.i. dates back to the early 1960s, and contrasts with the previously pursued policy of anti-imperialism which emphasized economic aid and the support of the NATIONAL LIBERATION MOVEMENTS. The new Socialist trade and aid policies are aimed at increasing the economic independence of the ex-colonial countries from the former imperial powers and, at the same time, counteracting NEO-COLONIALISM. The share of the Socialist bloc in the Third World's total foreign trade increased from less than 2 per cent in the early 1950s to more than 5 per cent in the late 1970s.

Counter-insurgency Military operations against subversion or guerrilla warfare. The use of the term is associated with the right-wing ruling regimes, usually supported by Western powers, conducting defensive or annihilating campaigns against left-wing revolutionary forces. Communists denounce c.-i. as: 1. a form of counter-revolution; 2. a pretext for the imperialist powers to interfere in the local affairs of colonial or ex-colonial countries; and 3. an excuse for conducting hostilities against NATIONAL LIBERATION MOVEMENTS.

Counter-planning A term used in some European Socialist countries after the economic reforms of the 1960s. C.-p. is economic planning 'from below', where branch associations and enterprises participate in determining the structure of production according to their own capacity, demand and profitability. C.-p. con-

trasts with the CENTRALIZED DIRECTIVE SYSTEM OF PLANNING AND MANAGEMENT, where plans are worked out in detail by central planners and imposed on the enterprises from above. C.-p. is a feature of decentralization which allows greater initiative and responsibility for the enterprises. It has been practised most in Hungary, Czechoslovakia and Poland.

Counter-purchase See COUNTER-TRADE.

Counter-Revolution A violent struggle directed towards the restoration of the political and social order altered by the revolution. The term was first used during the FRENCH REVOLUTION for the monarchist attempts to restore the *ancien régime.* The designation was later adopted by Marx and other Marxist thinkers to describe violent, as well as peaceful, efforts to undermine the PROLETARIAN REVOLUTION or to overthrow a Socialist or Communist regime. It is in this sense that c.-r. is generally understood today. In DIALECTICAL MATERIALISM, whilst REVOLUTION constitutes the 'thesis', c.-r. represents the 'antithesis'. In this clash, c.-r. is considered to be the reactionary and retrogressive step, bound to lose to the progressive forces of revolution.

Counter-sales See COUNTER-TRADE.

Counter-trade Types of commercial deals where the importer obliges the exporter to accept full or part payment in kind, rather than in foreign exchange. The transaction involving the incidental product to the main deal is then described as a 'counter-sale' by the importer and a 'counter-purchase' by the exporter. It typically covers 10–30 per cent of the payment for the main transaction, but may be as high as 100 per cent. C.-t. is a feature of the Socialist countries' trade with the West (where they offer payment in kind) and with the Third World (where they mostly receive). In many cases, the Western partner, who receives payment in unwanted goods, sells his claim to others through specialized brokers at a discount. Vienna, Zurich, Geneva, Amsterdam and Rotterdam are the main centres for arranging c.-t. transactions. Also REVENGE BARTER.

Counter-urbanization A term sometimes used for the RUSTICATION DRIVE in China.

Countervailing Power A situation in modern democratic society, where powerful groups or interests are inevitably matched sooner or later by restraining or opposing forces, so that potential abuses are mutually checked or neutralized. This proposition was developed by J. K. Galbraith (in *American Capitalism*, 1956) in application to modern capitalism. Thus, monopoly is matched by monopsony, employers (and their associations) by trade unions, monopolistic distributors by consumer societies, private enterprise by nationalized industries and state intervention, and so on. The concept of c.p. has been utilized by the defenders of capitalism, maintaining that capitalist society has an in-built capacity for resolving its contradictions when they arise. Marxists do not accept the validity of this proposition and regard it as a convenient apologetic prop supporting capitalism in its waning stage. They point out that the balance of power is hardly ever 'balanced' (as in the case of monopolistic distributors and consumer societies), and, moreover, ostensibly opposing interests may enter into collusive agreements to defraud the public (e.g. 'sweetheart agreements' between employers and trade unions).

'Coventry, Send to' A phrase used in Britain for the isolation of an individual from the rest of his group as a punishment for his lack of solidarity with the group. Although the origin of this practice is uncertain, it was practised in England in the 19th c. by trade unions to punish workers who failed to support their union's actions or policies (strikes, overtime work, pay).

CPSU abbreviation for the COMMUNIST PARY OF THE SOVIET UNION.

Craft Unions Labour organizations embodying workers of the same occupation or related occupations, irrespective of the type of industry in which they are employed. They usually set minimum trade or professional qualifications for membership. Their power derives from 'exclusive unionism' (restricting the supply of qualified labour). C.u., as a rule, are not as large as INDUSTRIAL UNIONS. Marxists have often been critical of c.u., accusing them of being bourgeois and having a right-wing socialist mentality, removed from the labouring masses (LABOUR ARISTOCRACY).

Creative Marxism The name used by Communists for that version of Marxism which emphasizes a dynamic interpretation and flexible adaptation of Marxist ideas to changing conditons, and discovering new ways and means for advancing Socialist society to full communism. C.M. is against a rigid, dogmatic interpretation of classical Marxism. Marx himself pointed out that his ideas should not become a dogma, but rather guidelines for further development and action. C.M. attaches great importance to the DIALECTIC approach to development, viz. successive clashes between the new and the old, leading to new resolvements. It stresses the unity of theory and practice, the need for continuous action by the working class, the role of creative PROLETARIAN ART and the evolution of the NEW COMMUNIST MAN. The Stalinist exposition of C.M. appeared in the *History of the All-Union Communist Party (of the Bolsheviks): A Short Course* (1938).

Credit Automatism A term used in the Socialist countries for the automatic provision of credit by the state to socialized enterprises. This practice, which appeared in its extreme in the USSR in 1930 and 1931 and in several other Socialist countries in the late 1940s and the early 1950s, was largely conditioned by the PRODUCTIVE CREDIT THEORY. Under this system, suppliers to other socialized enterprises are automatically paid by the state bank upon the delivery of the goods on the strength of the receipts issued by the 'purchasing' enterprise. The payment is ef-

128

fected, irrespective of: 1. the quality and suitability of the goods delivered; and 2. the ability of the purchasing enterprise to pay. The only condition is that the type and quantity of the goods in question must be consistent with the economic plan in relation to the enterprises involved. C.a. has been virtually discontinued in all the Socialist countries, owing to the laxity, irresponsibility and waste that resulted.

Credit Co-operatives Savings and loan associations operated on a co-operative basis. They are found in several Socialist countries, especially China, Czechoslovakia, the German DR and Poland, where they are operated along banking lines and regulated by special legislation. Thus, in Poland during the late 1970s, there were over 1,600 c.c. with some 2,300 branches, agencies and sub-agencies servicing some 3.5m. members. Their function is to provide banking and financial services to co-operative and private farms and small-scale industry in rural as well as urban areas. They collect savings and extend trade, investment and housing loans. Their assets are derived from the members' contributed shares, savings deposits, retained profits and credits from the state bank or agricultural bank. C.c. are considered to be a transitional institution meant to be absorbed by the state-owned banks (as has already occurred in Bulgaria and the USSR).

Credit Plan In Socialist economic planning, the planned amounts of credit to be extended in the economy by the banking system. It also includes the details of the cash deposits by socialized enterprises held in the banks. It usually covers quarterly periods and strictly corresponds to the economic plan. As banks are virtually the only source of finance (as a rule, there are no stock exchanges, finance companies and inter-enterprise finance is not allowed except in Hungary and Yugoslavia), the c.p. is an expedient instrument of the implementation and enforcement of the economic plan along the postulated lines.

Crisis of Capitalist Production In the Marxist interpretation (especially in Marx's CAPITAL, vol. III and Engels's ANTI-DÜHRING, the inevitable tendency for over-production in relation to consumption, caused by the capitalist quest for profit maximization and the exploitation of the working class. Capitalists, driven by greed, rivalry and the DECLINING PROFIT RATE, expand their production capacity in excess of the purchasing capacity of the population, especially of the working proletariat. The working classes, which are the real and only producers, are unable to buy the goods they produce owing to the following: 1. the capitalist appropriation of SURPLUS VALUE and the consequent prevalence of wages at subsistence levels; 2. the replacement of labour with capital, made possible by the accumulation of capital (from the surplus value), which leads to unemployment (the RESERVE ARMY OF WORKERS); and 3. the excessive price setting by monopolies, which inevitably emerge as capitalism develops, reducing the purchasing capacity of the working classes. The c. of c.p. has an unstable cyclical pattern that may develop into an acute depression. Since W.W.I, the c. of c.p. has been further superimposed by the CRISIS OF THE WORLD CAPITALIST ECONOMY and the GENERAL CRISIS OF CAPITALISM.

Crisis of the World Capitalist Economy The Communist view of certain processes in the international scene since W.W.I, leading to the 'decomposition of the world capitalist economic system'. Before W.W.I, Western industrialization, the need for sources of raw materials and markets, the weakness of backward underdeveloped countries and IMPERIALISM resulted in the formation of colonial empires and the internalization of economic relations, encompassing the whole (capitalist) world. But beginning with W.W.I, the system, evolved for the benefit of the imperial powers and monopolies, has been largely eroded by the following developments: 1. the suicidal wars and economic rivalry amongst the leading im-

Critical Realism

perialist powers; 2. the emergence of powerful Socialist countries ruled by Communist regimes, now controlling one-third of the world; 3. the liberation of colonial countries and the consequent reorientation of their economic relations away from the former imperial powers, followed by the adoption of some elements of socialism and economic planning and closer economic links with the Socialist bloc; and 4. the prevalence of protectionism, together with 2 and 3 above, has produced new patterns of the international division of labour, no longer dominated by capitalism.

Critical Realism A philosophical theory that denies the identity of being with consciousness and divorces the subject from the object of COGNITION. In effect, it regards ideas not as a reflection of objective reality, but credits them with an independent existence. The theory reached its peak in the USA in the 1930s through the works of A. O. Lovejoy (1873–1962) and G. Santayana (1863–1952). Marxist philosophers, especially Lenin (in *MATERIALISM AND EMPIRIO-CRITICISM*), have attacked c.r. as a version of bourgeois IDEALISM akin to AGNOSTICISM, and as such irreconcilable with DIALECTICAL MATERIALISM.

Criticism The negative appraisal of human activities or their results from the standpoint of particular criteria, such as ideology, cognition, aesthetics, morality or *praxis*. In Marxist ideology, c. (together with SELF-CRITICISM) is regarded as one of the ways of resolving CONTRADICTIONS, and consequently, is an important driving force of development and progress. Marxists point out that in capitalist societies, c. can only be destructive owing to the antagonistic social relations, and that only socialism provides a sound basis for constructive c. Communist party rules provide for 'criticism from below', which is regarded as a 'creative initiative'. Any Party member has a right to criticize any official at a meeting and may take his views to the top Party authorities. However, in practice, the scope for c., especially of Party policies, is narrowly circumscribed. First of all, no c. of the Marxist ideology is allowed as this would be tantamount to REVISIONISM. Where matters of the Party policies are involved, the principle of DEMOCRATIC CENTRALISM demands that a particular measure can be subjected to c. only at the debating stage. Once a decision has been made by the appropriate authority, c. is no longer permissible. The system of government and administration as it has developed in the Socialist countries, together with the secret police and tight censorship, make it unlikely that ordinary citizens would risk c. Also see CHARTER '77, CHARTER OF LIBERTY, DISSENT.

Critique of the Gotha Programme A study written by Marx in 1875, containing a critical analysis of the draft programme of the German Social-Democratic movement at its Conference at Gotha in 1875. Marx attacked the conciliatory and moderate nature of the programme and described its authors as being petty bourgeois. Instead, he emphasized the need for a well disciplined, tightly organized and devoted revolutionary Communist party and the DICTATORSHIP OF THE PROLETARIAT after the PROLETARIAN REVOLUTION. He also outlined the main features of the transition from capitalism to socialism, and distinguished between 'lower' and 'higher' phases of communism (SOCIALISM and FULL COMMUNISM). The study was not published in Marx's lifetime. It was Engels who arranged for its publication in 1891, in time for the Erfurt Conference of the SOCIAL-DEMOCRATIC PARTY OF GERMANY (ERFURT PROGRAMME).

Crystallized Labour See MATERIALIZED LABOUR.

CTK See ČETEKA.

Cuba, Republic of (*República de Cuba*) A central American country ruled by the

130

Marxist-Leninist COMMUNIST PARTY OF CUBA. The country's area is 114,520 sq. km. and its population is 9,750,000 (in 1978). The country had been ruled by the repressive right-wing regime of President F. Batista which, after a period of revolutionary struggle from 1953 to 1959, was ousted from power by the TWENTY-SIXTH OF JULY MOVEMENT led by F. CASTRO. The Communist regime came officially to power on 1 Jan. 1959. Soon after, far-reaching economic and social reforms were begun, including the expropriation of large landowners, the socialization of industry (foreign capital included) and all-round democratization. The breaking off of diplomatic relations by the USA in Jan. 1961 pushed C. closer to the Socialist countries, especially the USSR. The CUBAN MISSILE CRISIS in 1962 further aggravated US-Cuban relations (for a few years, Cuban-Soviet relations were also marred). An attempt to oust Castro's regime in 1961 (BAY OF PIGS) by Cuban exiles supported by the CIA failed completely. The Communist regime has followed its own brand of Marxism known as CASTROISM. Its attempts to export revolution to other Latin American countries in the 1960s (see E. GUEVARA) failed. But it proved successful in Africa where, in the late 1970s, there were 40,000 Cuban troops and advisers, namely in Angola (25,000), Ethiopia (17,000), Mozambique (1,000), Libya (1,000), Zambia (600), Tanzania (500) and at least five other countries. In 1972 C. was admitted as a full member to the COUNCIL FOR MUTUAL ECONOMIC ASSISTANCE. In Feb. 1976 the first Socialist Cuban Constitution was adopted. The highest legislative organ is the NATIONAL ASSEMBLY OF PEOPLE'S POWER, which elects its permanent executive body known as the State Council and formally appoints the Council of Ministers. The President of the State Council is also the Prime Minister (Dr Fidel Castro). But effective political power is exercised by the Political Bureau of the Communist Party of Cuba, consisting of 12 members headed by its First Secretary (Dr Fidel Castro).

Cuban Missile Crisis A sharp confrontation between the USA and the USSR in October 1962 over the Soviet installation of a nuclear ballistic missile base in Cuba, which took the world to the brink of a nuclear war. The missile installations were discovered by US aerial photography reconnaissance and were reported to President J. F. Kennedy on 16 Oct. 1962, who subsequently declared a 'quarantine' (blockade) of Cuba to prevent further shipments of Soviet weapons, and demanded the removal of the missiles from Cuba under American supervision. This move received support from the Organization of American States and the North Atlantic Treaty Organization. On 28 Oct. 1962, the USSR agreed to the US demands, without consulting the Cuban Government, in exchange for the American undertaking to lift the blockade and guarantee not to invade Cuba, which the USA accepted.

Cubism A school of painting and sculpture which emerged in France between 1906 and 1912 and which played a decisive role in the transformation of graphic arts in the 20th c. Its founders were Pablo Picasso and G. Braque, but the term c. was first used (with a rather derogatory connotation) by a critic L. Vauxcelles in 1908. The distinctive features of c. are the tridimensional cardboard representations, fragmental structural elements, the discontinuity of contours, the absence of perspective and the maximum reduction of form and colour. C. aroused some interest in the early post-revolutionary period in Soviet Russia (although the beginnings of that interest go back to the pre-W.W.I years), as it broke off from traditional bourgeois art. Many exponents, including Picasso, were noted for their left-wing leanings. To a small extent, c. influenced CONSTRUCTIVISM and CUBO-FUTURISM (which had a short life-time in the USSR). But owing to its largely abstract content, not easily comprehended by the masses, c. has never been integrated into PROLETARIAN ART in any Socialist country.

Cubo-futurism A radical and revolutionary literary movement which existed in Russia and then in the USSR, roughly from 1913 to 1930. Inspired by CUBISM and symbolism, c.-f. was a reaction against conventions and traditions and a protest against the 'moral and cultural disintegration of bourgeois society'. The Cubo-futurists, among whom V. V. MAYAKOVKSY was the best known representative, supported the Bolshevik Revolution, regarding it as a prelude to a new social era and a new opportunity for their literary movement. Their peak of influence was reached in 1918–19, when they participated in establishing foundations for PROLETARIAN ART and received support from LUNACHARSKY, TROTSKY and BUKHARIN. But c.-f. soon came into conflict with LENIN who was against the wholesale rejection of the Russian cultural heritage. Many Bolsheviks also attacked the cubo-futurists for their petty bourgeois mentality, individualism and indifference to Marxist ideology. The role of c.-f. gradually declined in the 1920s and, after Mayakovsky's suicide (partly in protest against the regimentation of the Soviet thought and culture) in 1930, it virtually disappeared.

Cult of Personality See PERSONALITY CULT.

Cultural Revolution A Marxist-Leninist term for a radical transformation of attitudes and the cultural development of the masses in its broadest sense, designed to create a new Socialist culture. The concept and the content of the c.r. were first formulated by Lenin at the Third Congress of Soviets in Moscow in 1918, when he warned against the danger of Communist complacency. The main elements of a c.r. are: 1. a selective continuation of the cultural heritage; 2. the elimination of illiteracy; 3. the organization of Communist education; 4. a preferential treatment of the children of industrial workers and peasants for admission to secondary and higher education (and discrimination against or even exclusion of the children of

the former 'exploiting' classes); 5. the creation of the Socialist intelligentsia; and 6. the foundation of a framework for the development of PROLETARIAN ART and the NEW COMMUNIST MAN. The c.r. is regarded as a continuation of the PROLETARIAN REVOLUTION 'from above', generally completed in the Socialist countries in the first 10–15 years following the Communist seizure of power. In the USSR the cadres of teachers, students and other educational and cultural workers sent to the countryside in the 1920s to deal with illiteracy, were called the 'soldiers of culture'. But the popularization of culture led to a drastic reduction of standards. A much more radical and intensive approach to the c.r. was represented by the GREAT PROLETARIAN CULTURAL REVOLUTION in China (1966–69) and the REVOLUTIONIZATION MOVEMENT in Albania (1965–69, 1973–76).

Cultural Revolution Group In China, a radical body consisting of high Party officials responsible for the conduct of the GREAT PROLETARIAN CULTURAL REVOLUTION in the late 1960s. Its beginnings went back to mid-1965, when the Group of Five was formed in Peking headed by Peng Chen to steer the G.P.C.R. But it was not considered radical enough. After Mao Tse-tung returned from Shanghai on 16 May 1966, he prevailed upon the Central Committee of the Chinese Communist Party to dissolve the G. of F. and its organization and replace it with the C.R.G. to be headed by CHEN PO-TA, former Secretary to Mao and Editor of HUNG-CHI. The Group was duly established and its size increased to about 20, including Madame CHIANG CH'ING (the First Deputy Head), Chiang Chun-chiao and Yao Wen-Yuan, all three of whom were later (in 1976) branded, disgraced, arrested and tried in 1980–1 as the members of the GANG OF FOUR.

Culture In its broadest sense, the totality of spiritual and material achievements of society, in particular in such spheres as literature, art, education, philosophy, morality, science, technology, methods of production and the institutions associated with them. According to philosophical IDEALISM, widely accepted in capitalist countries, c. is basically conditioned by consciousness, mind and the activity of gifted persons, and in its essence, is permanent and immutable. But Marxist HISTORICAL MATERIALISM stresses that c. is an outcome of the underlying material conditions of society and the social and political system in force, consequently reflecting the SOCIO-ECONOMIC FORMATION of a particular historical period. Cultural development is governed by the law of the development of the MODE OF PRODUCTION and the LAW OF THE CONCORDANCE OF PRODUCTION RELATIONS WITH THE NATURE OF PRODUCTION FORCES. Thus, Marxists maintain that c. is not a product of conscious activities determined by the will of man, but is largely a result of the operation of objective laws independent of him. As the development of material production is historically continuous, so is cultural development which, on the whole, advances from lower to higher stages. It is further emphasized that in a society with antagonistic class relations, c. is dominated by the ruling class which uses it to justify and consolidate its rule. However, even under CAPITALISM there are elements of proletarian c., reflecting the CLASS STRUGGLE and the aspirations of the working classes. Consequently, after the PROLETARIAN REVOLUTION (as Lenin insisted), the cultural heritage must not be discarded wholesale, but continued on a selective basis and developed into the new SOCIALIST CULTURE.

Currency Transferability A conditional currency convertibility, involving the ability to transfer surplus earnings from one country to another for purchases in a third country, provided that the latter two agree. This feature applies to the TRANSFERABLE ROUBLE, the currency used for multilateral settlements amongst the member countries of the COUNCIL FOR MUTUAL ECONOMIC ASSISTANCE. In the past, many capitalist countries with hard currencies applied this type of restriction on transferability in order to make the Socialist countries spend their export earnings on imports from the same country, and thus achieve the bilateral balance of trade.

Cybernetics A branch of the theory of information concerned with the optimal purposeful steering of complex and dynamic systems. It originated in the USA during W.W.II and is based on modern achievements in mathematics, mechanics, electronics, logic, economics, physiology and other sciences. The practical applications of c. are found in cybernetic machines for steering complex equipment, translations into other languages, the composition of music and other fields. In the Socialist countries up to the late 1950s, especially in the USSR, c. was feared ideologically as a bourgeois challenge to DIALECTICAL MATERIALISM. C. was described as 'reactionary', 'pseudo-scientific', 'anti-humanitarian' and an 'invention of the imperialist utopia to replace thinking human beings with inexorable automatic machines' (M. Rozenthal and P. Yudin, eds, *Kratky filosofsky slovar*, Moscow, 1954). However, since that time the official attitude has changed and c. has come to be embraced as a new instrument for supplementing and strengthening Marxist-Leninist philosophy. C. is now seen as a discipline providing a scientific basis for a systematic extension of AUTOMATION and the optimum development of the interrelations of all the elements of the social system. It is envisaged that c. will radically improve the steering of social processes and will contribute to the evolution of the NEW COMMUNIST MAN.

Cyclical Development of Society, Theory of A doctrine according to which society develops in definite stages, which over very long periods repeat themselves, viz. divine, primitive, heroic, youthful and human (mature), followed by a decline back to its primitive stage, and so on. The theory was originally put forward by G.

Vico (1668–1744) and further developed by F. Nietzsche (1844–1900), O. Spengler (1880–1936) and others. Marxist philosophers reject the validity of the theory, as it implies that capitalism is the highest stage, after which further social progress is impossible. In their view, HISTORICAL MATERIALISM provides the only scientific explanation of the development of society, which is governed by the LAW OF THE CONCORDANCE OF PRODUCTION RELATIONS WITH THE NATURE OF PRODUCTION FORCES. In their interpretation, society develops from PRIMITIVE COMMUNISM, through societies supporting SLAVERY, FEUDALISM, CAPITALISM to SOCIALISM and finally to FULL COMMUNISM.

Cyclical Fluctuations Periodical alternating expansion and contraction in economic activity, especially in production, employment, credit, prices and trade. A complete business or trade cycle may last from 7 to 11 years and typically passes through the following four phases: crisis; depression; revival; and boom. Within these there may be shorter 2–4 year cycles and, superimposed on them, longer cycles of 40–50 years. In Marxist thought, c.f. have received a good deal of attention and are regarded as an inevitable peculiarity of the capitalist economic system, reflecting its inherent CONTRADICTIONS. C.f. have appeared since the Industrial Revolution, first in England in 1825, but after 1857 they became international. Marxists attribute c.f. to the following: 1. the conflict between the increasingly social character of production processes and the private ownership of the means of production; 2. the subordination of production to private profit maximization; 3. an insufficient demand for products owing to the IMMISERATION OF THE PROLETARIAT, the largest social class; 4. variations in the PROFIT RATE and the long-run tendency for the DECLINING PROFIT RATE, basically caused by technological change and the increasing accumulation of capital replacing live labour; and 5. under MONOPOLY CAPITALISM, c.f. are noted for wide vagaries in investment, low prices of inputs (including wages), and high prices of products (thus restricting the demand for them, further accentuating unemployment). Although Marxists have generally claimed that c.f. can be eliminated in the Socialist planned economy, there is evidence of cycles in investment, construction, total production and trade in these countries. This has been demonstrated by a number of Western economists (such as L. J. Brainard, Katherine H. Hsiao, R. Hutchings, B. Mieczkowski, G. J. Staller, J. Stankovsky, and E. Zaleski) as well as several Socialist economists (e.g. A. Bajt, P. Erdös, J. Goldmann, O. Lange, H. Rost and Ma Yin-chu).

Cypriot Communist Party See PROGRESSIVE PARTY OF THE WORKING PEOPLE OF CYPRUS.

Cyrillic Alphabet (*Kirilitsa*, in Russian) A set of letters reputedly invented by St. Cyril (827–69 A.D.) and his disciples in the 9–10th centuries on which the modern Bulgarian, Mongolian, Russian and Yugoslav (partly) alphabets are based. Fashioned on the Greek alphabet at the time, it probably appeared first in northeastern Bulgaria and consisted of 43 letters, most of which also denoted numbers. In Russia the c.a. was radically modified at the beginning of the 18th c., on the orders of Peter the Great, by eliminating some letters and making others more similar to Latin in appearance. The modern Russian alphabet consists of 32 letters.

Czechoslovak Communist Party (*Komnunistická Strana Československa*) The ruling political party in Czechoslovakia, officially adhering to the Marxist-Leninist and pro-Soviet line. It was founded in 1921 under its present name, but was outlawed from 1938 to 1945, first by the Czechoslovak Government and then by the German occupation authorities. It became the dominant political force (but without a majority) after the Soviet liberation of the country in early 1945. In the election of May 1946, Communists polled only 38 per cent of the votes cast. The Party came to undisputed power in the coup of Feb. 1948, when non-communists were ousted from the Government and the multi-party system came to an end. After A. Dubček became the Party's leader in Jan. 1968, liberal reforms were initiated, but the INVASION OF CZECHO-SLOVAKIA in Aug. 1968 and the removal of Dubček in April 1969 put an end to them. Some 350,000 dissident members were expelled from the Party in accordance with the new hardline course which has ruled ever since. The Party's membership in 1976 was 1,383,000, out of the total population of 14,920,000. The highest authority is vested in the PARTY CONGRESS, held every fifth year, which elects a CENTRAL COMMITTEE. The latter elects a Presidium (11 full, plus 2 candidate members) headed by the SECRETARY-GENERAL (G. Husak) and a Secretariat (8 secretaries and 2 members). The Cz.C.P. is supported by three mass organizations: the Revolutionary Trade Union Movement; the Czechoslovak Union of Women; and the Socialist Youth Movement. The main regular Party publications are: *Rudé právo* (*Red Jurisprudence*), the main daily organ; *Tribuna* (*The Tribune*), a weekly theoretical review; *Zhivot Strany* (*Party Life*), a fortnightly review of Party work and organization; and *Mlada fronta* (*The Young Front*), the daily organ of the Socialist Youth Movement.

Czechoslovak Socialist Republic (*Česko-slovenska Socialisticka Republika*) A medium-sized Eastern European Socialist country, with an area of 127,880 sq. km., and a population of 15,150,000 (in 1978), and ruled by a Communist party (the CZECHOSLOVAK COMMUNIST PARTY). After the liberation of the country by the Soviet army (completed in May 1945), state power was exercised by a National Front and a coalition of independent parties, but with the Communists holding the most important portfolios. At the elections of May 1946, although the Czechoslovak Communist Party emerged as the largest single party, it won only 38 per cent of the votes. A coalition government was formed under a Communist Prime Minister (K. GOTTWALD). After the PRAGUE COUP D'ÉTAT in Feb. 1948, non-communists were removed from the government and a new Constitution was adopted in May 1948, which was followed by POLITICAL SHOW TRIALS and purges. Another Constitution was adopted in 1960, amended in Oct. 1968, July 1971 and May 1973. In Jan. 1968 a liberal Marxist, A. DUBČEK, became the Party leader and liberal political and economic reforms were initiated. But the INVASION OF CZECHOSLOVAKIA in Aug. 1968 blocked the reforms, and a repressive regime was re-established after Dubček was replaced by G. Husak in April 1969. On 1 Jan. 1969, the Cz.S.R. became a federal country, with equal rights for the Czech and Slovak peoples. The highest organ of state power is the FEDERAL ASSEMBLY, which elects the President (now G. Husak), who in turn appoints the cabinet and judges to the Supreme Court.

D

Danielson, Nikolai Frantsevich (1844–1918) A Russian economist who was the chief exponent of liberal *NAROD-NISM* and who translated Marx's *Capital* into Russian (and published volumes, I, II and III in 1872, 1875 and 1896 respectively). His liberal *Narodnik* views were presented in *Studies of Our Pre-Reform Economy* (1893). D. maintained extensive correspondence with Marx and Engels and he claimed to be a Marxist. However Engels was sceptical of his version of Marxism. Later Lenin took him to task and attacked him for his lack of appreciation of the role of the industrial proletariat, the class struggle and for his idealization of the peasant communes.

Danish Communist Party (*Danmarks Kommunistiske Parti*) One of the smallest political parties in the country with a membership of 8,000 (out of the country's total population of 5,100,000 in 1978). At the 1977 election, it polled 3.7 per cent of the votes cast and won 7 (of the total of 179) seats in parliament. The party was founded in 1919 as a splinter group of the Social-Democratic Party. During the German occupation 1940–45 it was banned, but it carried on its activities underground. It has followed a pro-Soviet orientation which, in protest, led to the formation of the SOCIALIST PEOPLE'S PARTY in 1958. The Party has a fairly active youth arm called the Danish Communist Youth. The Party's regular publications are: *Land og Folk* (*Country and People*) – the daily organ, *Tiden-Verden Rund* (*Time Round the World*) – the theoretical journal, and *Fremad* (*Forward*) – the organ of the D.C.Y.

Darwinism See SOCIAL DARWINISM

Dashnaks A nationalistic anti-communist party in Armenia which fought the Bolsheviks during the Civil War 1918–20. They used ruthless tactics against Communists, founded an Armenian Government and even took over other parts of Caucasia. However, by the end of 1920, they had been routed by the Bolsheviks, and their leaders were executed or deported to other parts of Soviet Russia.

Das Kapital See KAPITAL, DAS

DDR An abbreviation in German for *Deutsche Demokratische Republik*, meaning the GERMAN DEMOCRATIC REPUBLIC.

Dead Labour Another Marxian term for MATERIALIZED LABOUR (as opposed to live labour).

Deborinism Another, less common term for MENSHEVIKIZING IDEALISM.

Decembrists The anglicized version of DE-KABRISTS.

'Declaration of Sincere Solidarity and Unity in Resistance to the Enemy' A declaration announced by the Central Committee of the CHINESE COMMUNIST PARTY on 23 Sep. 1937, undertaking to co-operate with the KUOMINTANG in the struggle against the Japanese invaders. The Declaration embodied the following resolutions: 1. the pursuit of Sun Yat-sen's THREE PEOPLE'S PRINCIPLES (national independence and interest, democracy, and social justice); 2. the discontinuation of all violent acts and Sovietization aimed at the overthrow of the Kuomintang; 3. the abandonment of the policy of expropriation of landlords' land; 4. the liquidation of the CHINESE SOVIET REPUBLIC (in favour of the 'Special Area Government'); and 5. the reorganization of the Red Army (re-named the National Revolutionary Eighth Route Army) to present a common front with the Kuomintang's Army under Chiang Kai-shek against Japan.

Declaration of the Forty-Six A statement which was signed by TROTSKY and 45 leading Trotskyites and democratic supporters, including defenders of DEMOCRATIC CENTRALISM, and presented to the Central Committee of the RUSSIAN COMMUNIST PARTY (OF THE BOLSHEVIKS) in Oct. 1923. The Declaration was a protest against the growing authoritarianism in the Party and was prompted by the likely change in its leadership in the hope of democratizing the Party (Lenin had been ill for some time and died three months later). The signatories explained that the Party apparatus had developed into a powerful bureaucracy, was intolerant of opposition groups, dominated the ordinary members and was indifferent to the workers' problems. The CC rejected the Declaration, in reply to which Trotsky wrote a pamphlet, *The New Course*.

'Declaration of the Rights of the Toiling and Exploited People' A charter prepared by the Bolshevik regime and submitted to the CONSTITUENT ASSEMBLY on 5 Jan. (18 Jan. N.S.C.) 1918 for ratification. But the C.A., in which the Bolsheviks were in the minority, refused to pass it. In retaliation, the Bolsheviks prevailed upon the ALL-RUSSIAN CENTRAL EXECUTIVE COMMITTEE to dissolve the C.A. and this was done by the decree of 6 Jan. (19 Jan.) 1918.

Declining Profit Rate, Law of One of the key propositions made by Marx (in *CAPITAL*, vol. III), embodying certain fallacies. Marx insisted that in the capitalist economy there is a tendency for CON-STANT CAPITAL (outlays on non-labour means of production) to rise faster than VARIABLE CAPITAL (wages). As only the variable part of total capital produces SURPLUS VALUE, the profit rate on total capital $(s/(c+v))$ must decline, provided that the total rate of exploitation (s/v) remains unchanged. The d.p.r. is indicative of the substitution of capital (originally created by labour) for labour, which leads to unemployment and the increasing IMMISERATION OF THE PROLETARIAT. There are two flaws in Marx's assertion. 1. some studies indicate that since W.W.I the profit rate has not been declining but rather increasing; 2. if the rate of exploitation stays the same (as it does by Marx's assumption), the increasing capital-labour ratio leads to the rising productivity of labour, which must result in either lower prices (more likely in the Marxian framework) or higher wages, i.e. in either case increasing real wages. This is inconsistent with Marx's assertion of the constant rate of exploitation and the increasing immiseration of the working class. Marx could substantiate the d.p.r. only by abandoning his assertion that real wages tend to remain constant.

Decollectivization The transfer of collectivized land to private owners, its previous owners or to the current members of the collective farm, for private farming. Some d. took place in Poland after 1955 and in Yugoslavia after 1951, where the proportion of socialized land declined from 22-23 per cent to 15 per cent.

Decolonization The political, economic and cultural liberation of colonies from the control of the imperial powers. It was most widespread between 1943 and 1964 when 60 colonial countries achieved their independence. In the Communist view, the process of d. has been prompted and facilitated by the following developments: 1. the emergence of the national bourgeoisie, intelligentsia and proletariat as a consequence of commercial and industrial developments in some colonial countries; 2. the weakening of the colonial powers as a result of the world wars; 3. the intensified exploitation of the dependent territories for war purposes; 4. the victory of the Great October Socialist Revolution in Russia in 1917 and the emergence of other Socialist countries after W.W.II, who were all opposed to imperialism and colonialism on ideological and political grounds; and 5. the development of political parties in the colonies which had co-operated with the NATIONAL LIBERATION MOVEMENTS, supported by the Socialist countries. In 1960, on the initiative of the USSR, the General Assembly of the UN made a declaration postulating the right of every nation to be freed from colonial rule. Also see NEO-COLONIALISM.

Decree of Peace The first official act of the Soviet regime, prepared by Lenin and passed by the Second Congress of Soviets on 26 Oct. (8 Nov. N.S.C.) 1917, calling upon the governments and peoples engaged in W.W.I to cease the war and make a just and democratic peace, without annexation or war indemnities. Neither the Central nor the Allied powers responded to it.

Deism A philosophical and religious doctrine maintaining that an impersonal god created the universe, set it into motion and endowed it with the laws of nature, otherwise no intervention in its operation was involved. D., which commanded considerable interest in the 17th and 18th centuries (especially in England and France), was a product of RATIONALISM. D. rejected 'revelation' and 'miracles', the need for church as an intermediary between god and people and religious ceremony, and pressed for the emancipation of learning and morality from religious dogmas. H. Cherbury (1583–1648) held that institutionalized religion was invented by naive and unscrupulous churchmen, and A. A. C. Shaftesbury (1671–1713) pointed out that morality was separate from religion; A. F. M. Voltaire (1694–1778) and J. J. Rousseau (1712–78) held similar views. Marxists regard d. as a compromise between THEISM and ATHEISM and a comfortable reconciliation of science with re-

ligion. However, they conceded that d. proved beneficial to some extent and contributed to the development of MATERIALISM, as it freed some scientific minds from the religious straitjacket.

Dekabrists (or Decembrists) The first liberal revolutionary movement in Tsarist Russia, which in December (*Dekabr*, in Russian) 1825 initiated a series of uprisings against autocracy and monarchy. The movement arose in 1816 as a secret society amongst the gentry and intellectuals, and its leaders included N. Muraviev, K. Ryleiev, P. Pestel and the brothers P. and A. Borisov. The D. programme aimed at replacing absolute monarchy with a democratic republic and the abolition of serfdom. It stressed materialism, humanitarianism, high ethical standards and patriotism. The uprisings were put down swiftly, their five leaders were executed by hanging and over 100 other prominent participants were banished to Siberia. The movement failed because, as Lenin explained later, it was too cautious and not based on the working masses. However, although unsuccessful in the first instance, D., through their materialist philosophy, exerted considerable influence on later generations of Russian revolutionaries.

De Leonites A small socialist movement in the USA active from 1890 to 1914, which advocated militant trade unionism as, ultimately, a means of the revolutionary overthrow of capitalism. The movement was named after Daniel de Leon (1852–1914), an American socialist thinker and journalist, who founded the Socialist Trade and Labor Alliance in 1895 and helped establish the INDUSTRIAL WORKERS OF THE WORLD in 1905. The ideas of D.L. were studied by the BOLSHEVIKS, some of which were later applied in the USSR. De Leon received favourable recognition from Lenin.

Demagogy An unscrupulous political and propagandist method of gaining support from naive listeners, crowds or masses, convenient to the demagogue or his cause. D. resorts to misrepresentation, appeals to flattery, promises, prejudices and suspicions of its audiences or readers, inciting them to action. The charge of d. is freely made in bourgeois-Marxist polemics. Marxists claim d. to be an instrument in the hands of the exploiting classes, manipulated to facilitate and perpetuate their rule by setting different national, racial and religious groups against each other, according to the capitalist time-honoured principle '*divide et impera*'. In the capitalist view, it is the Communist leaders and propagandists who resort to d. to foment class antagonisms and to incite mobs to acts of violence. Also see AGITATION, PROPAGANDA.

Demand Planning See 'PLANNING FROM BELOW'.

De-Maoization The mild process of departure from some forms of ideological extremism and political adventurism associated with MAO TSE-TUNG in favour of an emphasis on moderate economic commonsense and political, economic, technological and cultured co-operation with Western countries. De-M. developed with the assumption of the leadership by HUA KUO-FENG in 1976. The term is used in the West and the USSR, but is frowned upon in China, where it is officially asserted that in spite of some changes, the new policies do not represent a rejection of MAOISM and that Mao's spirit is still revered. De-M. has included such moves as the repudiation of the GANG OF FOUR, a preference for stability against disruptive political and economic policies and practices, some reactivation of private enterprise and a tacit acceptance of profit and material incentives as useful expedients in economic management and development.

Demarcation Dispute In industrial relations in capitalist countries, a disagreement or clash between trade unions (rather than between a union and an employer) on such matters as to which union is entitled to represent workers on a particular question, and which union has the right to perform particular tasks in related types of work. A d.d. is essentially an internal affair of the labour movement, and demarcation strikes are generally considered by the public and employers as petty and selfish, and consequently, in many capitalist countries they are banned. Although d.d. may arise in Socialist countries, they are less acute, are settled by arbitration if necessary, and are certainly not allowed to disrupt work and production.

Democracy Literally, the power or rule by the people, a political system where people directly or indirectly through representatives decide the way they are governed. The term is meant to have a favourable connotation and it has been freely used by individuals and groups in widely differing and even opposing political persuasions. It all depends on how one defines the 'people' and their 'representatives'. Thus, d. existed in ancient Greece (where slavery predominated), amongst feudal lords and in modern times in monarchies (such as the Netherlands) and under Socialism (as in the DPR of [North] Korea). There are three facets of d.: 1. *Parliamentary d.* – universal suffrage, free elections, secret ballot and the multi-party system; 2. *Economic d.* – the absence of inequality in property ownership (e.g. through the socialization of the means of production, the equality of employment opportunity and a reasonable even distribution of personal income); and 3. *Social d.* – class equality, i.e. the absence of domination or exploitation of one social class by another. In the Communist view, capitalist countries can only be bourgeois d., at best parliamentary d. (but it tends to degenerate into STATE MONOPOLY CAPITALISM or FASCISM), but not economic d. or social d. Also BOURGEOIS DEMOCRACY, EXTENSIVE DEMOCRACY, NEW DEMOCRACY, PROLETARIAN DEMOCRACY, SOCIALIST DEMOCRACY, ULTRA-DEMOCRACY.

Democratic Centralism The general principle governing the organization and operation of Marxist-Leninist Communist parties and state administration under socialism, combining centralized hierarchical structure of authority with popular participation and supervision. It is meant to reflect a DIALECTIC (complementary) unity of authority and action 'from below and from above'. The concept was first used by the BOLSHEVIKS at the TAMMERFORS CONFERENCE in Dec. 1905, and Lenin is credited with its elevation to the Party principle when he incorporated it into the Party statutes in 1917. Lenin used the principle to justify the DICTATORSHIP OF THE PROLETARIAT. It was also embodied into the TWENTY-ONE CONDITIONS OF ADMISSION TO COMINTERN and consequently adopted by all Communist parties subscribing to Marxism-Leninism. In application to Party organization and work, d.c. embodied the following elements: 1. all Party organs (officials) from the lowest to the highest are elected democratically; 2. all Party decisions are made by the majority, and the minority is subordinate to the majority, i.e. the Party discipline requires that once a decision is made, it is the duty of all to support it and to implement it the most effective way, no FACTIONALISM being tolerated; 3. all Party organs have to account periodically for their activities to their own organizations and to higher organs; 4. decisions made by the higher organs are binding on the lower Party echelons; 5. all Party organs are obliged to examine carefully the comments and proposals submitted to them by members and other organs and inform them of their decisions; and 6. each Party organ has the right of independent decision-making within the sphere of its competence, provided it is consistent with the general Party line and decisions of higher Party organs. The actual interpretation of d.c. may differ in each Party and country, but on the whole there is much more centralism than democracy in its content. Mao Tse-tung stressed that d.c. may degenerate into a privileged elitist bureaucratic hierarchy interested in preserving the *status quo*, rather than in the CONTINUING REVOLUTION and the rela-

tion 'from the masses to the masses'. In his view, that is what has developed in the USSR since Stalin's death (in 1953).

Democratic Centralists A group in the RUSSIAN COMMUNIST PARTY (OF THE BOLSHEVIKS) who in 1920, whilst accepting the principle of DEMOCRATIC CENTRALISM in Party organization, advocated a greater democratization of economic management. They pressed for the members of the Supreme Council of the National Economy (*VESENKHA*) to be nominated by trade unions, and not by the Party. At the operational level, they demanded that the management of factories be transferred from single managers to trade unions; however, their scheme was not accepted.

Democratic Communism A liberal political and economic system, combining political democracy with a completely socialized economy. It implies the absence of the MONO-PARTY SYSTEM OF GOVERNMENT, of the DICTATORSHIP OF THE PROLETARIAT and of the Stalinist CENTRALIZED DIRECTIVE SYSTEM OF PLANNING AND MANAGEMENT. There has been no case of d.c. operating in practice, but may eventuate either in a Western-style democratic country as vaguely envisaged in EUROCOMMUNISM or in the Socialist countries under FULL COMMUNISM.

Democratic Dictatorship A term used in China to describe the consolidation of power by the CHINESE COMMUNIST PARTY in the workers-peasants alliance over all rival political parties. Although several (eight non-bourgeois) political parties are allowed to exist in the NATIONAL DEMOCRATIC FRONT, their influence is of no consequence, and they are merely tolerated as a democratic façade. In 1926 Stalin used the phrase, the 'Democratic dictatorship of the proletariat' by reference to China, meaning a united national front of the political parties under the leadership of the Chinese Communist Party, directed primarily against imperialism.

Democratic Front (*Fronti Demokratik*) In the PSR of ALBANIA, a political organization resembling a united electoral front, to which all adult Albanians are supposed to belong. It was founded in 1942 and is completely dominated by the Communist party (the ALBANIAN PARTY OF LABOUR. Its President is E. HOXHA, the First Secretary of the A.P. of L. and the Chairman of its Politburo. The D.F. prepares a single list of candidates for elections from amongst the persons nominated by the A.P. of L. The official organ of the D.F. is its daily newspaper called *Bashkimi* (Unity).

Democratic Front for the Reunification of the Fatherland A political mass organization in the DPR of [North] Korea for presenting a united electoral front and supporting the Communist regime in the implementation of its policies. The Front is led and completely dominated by the Communist party, the KOREAN WORKERS' PARTY, but it includes other non-bourgeois parties and organizations, viz. the North Korean Democratic Party, the Chondoist Chongu Party (religious organization supporting the W.P. of K.), the General Federation of Trade Unions, the Korean Democratic Youth League and some other social organizations.

Democratic Socialism A liberal political and economic system combining the elements of DEMOCRACY, the market mechanism, the SOCIAL OWNERSHIP OF THE MEANS OF PRODUCTION and ECONOMIC PLANNING, meant to ensure maximum social welfare and harmonious social relations. It is essentially evolutionary, consisting in the retention of the best elements of capitalism and elimination of its worst abuses and weaknesses on the one hand, and the adoption of the most appropriate features of Socialist economic planning on the other. D.s. has been evolved to varying extents in the Scandinavian countries, Britain, Austria, New Zealand, India and others. It is noted for differences in approach and emphasis ranging from theoretical models of philosophical, moral and political content to practical *ad hoc* economic solutions. Its main elements are: 1. a peaceful, evolutionary (non-revolutionary) transformation of the economy and society via the PARLIAMENTARY ROAD TO SOCIALISM; 2. the selective nationalization of key industries (e.g. iron and steel, energy, transport, communications, banking, insurance) whilst private enterprise prevails elsewhere; 3. a mixutre of centralization and decentralization, their complementary application depending more on practical needs than on ideological dogmas; 4. indicative or orientational, rather than directive economic planning; 5. industrial democracy consisting in considerable worker participation in the management and ownership of the entities of their employment; and 6. the redistribution of national income through highly progressive taxes and death duties and generous social services to reduce social inequalities and maximize social welfare. Revolutionary Marxists are hostile to d.s., regarding it as a compromising palliative still within the framework of capitalism, amounting to OPPORTUNISM and REVISIONISM and only postponing the PROLETARIAN REVOLUTION.

Deng Xiao-Ping The *Pinyin* (phonetic) term of spelling of TENG HSIAO-PING (the spelling version of the latter being based on the Wade-Giles system).

Denikin, Anton Ivanovich (1872–1947) A Russian general of peasant descent who fought on the side of the Whites against the Bolsheviks during the Civil War in Russia, 1917–20. After the FEBRUARY REVOLUTION, he was Deputy Chief of Staff of the Russian Army and he was one of the organizers of the KORNILOV REBELLION in Aug. 1917 to overthrow the PETROGRAD SOVIET. After Kornilov's death, he became the Commander-in-Chief of the Counter-Revolutionary Volunteer Army. In autumn 1918 he occupied Kuban and a large part of the Ukraine, and in June 1919 began an offensive against the Bolshevik forces to occupy Moscow. He was defeated at Orel in October 1919, returned to the Crimea in March 1920, resigned his command in favour of General P. N. WRANGEL and emigrated to Belgium and then to France, where he wrote his memoirs, *History of the Civil Strife in Russia*. D.'s name gave rise to the term popularized by the Bolsheviks, 'Denikinshchina', denoting the counter-revolutionary movement under his leadership without popular support.

Department for International Liaison (*Otdel Mezhdunarodnoi Sviazi*) A division of the COMINTERN for maintaining ties with the affiliated Communist parties. It was created by the decision of the Third Congress of the Comintern in June-July 1921. It had a network of agents all over the world, whose responsibility was to transmit the decisions of various Comintern organs to the appropriate officials in foreign countries, deliver information to the Comintern organs and arrange for financial assistance when and where warranted. It worked under great difficulties as most of its work was of a secret nature.

Department I and II Marxian concepts denoting the division of MATERIAL PRODUCTION in the economy into that of the producer (I) and consumer (II) goods. D. I embraces raw materials (of mineral, plant, animal and industrial origin), components, tools, machinery and other forms of equipment and buildings for production enterprises, whilst D. II involves single-use and durable-use consumer goods including buildings for non-productive purposes (public administration, education, science, culture, social welfare, finance and insurance and defence). In Marxist political economy, the proportion between these two departments is considered to be of a crucial importance in economic growth and it is usally determined and enforced on a planned basis. In the earlier stage of socialist economic development the rate of growth of D. I production should substantially exceed that of D. II production. To this purpose, the

Socialist policy was traditionally directed to reserving relatively high proportions of national income for investment and concentrated on capital-using technological progress. Owing to the rapid growth of D. I production, the Socialist countries have achieved impressive rates of economic growth and have laid down solid bases for continued development, especially in the industrial sphere. The division between D. I and II production is parallel to GROUP 'A' AND 'B' output in industry.

De-Politicization, De-Politicalization The process of the separation of various spheres of society's life (the economy, law, education, science, culture) from politics, especially their liberation from political interference or domination. D. is advocated by objective observers not committed to any particular social system, and it is a reaction against the principle of 'POLITICS IN COMMAND'. Marxists maintain that d. is impossible and insist that political power inevitably determines the development of all other spheres of human activity, whether in a capitalist or a Socialist society. However, there has been some d. in the European Socialist countries since the economic reforms of the 1960s and in China since the death of Mao Tse-tung. The process has gone furthest in Yugoslavia.

Deradicalization Making a person, a group or an institution less radical, extremist or violent, or their becoming less so on their own initiative. The term has been popularized by R. C. Tucker (in *Amer. Pol. Sci. Rev.*, June 1967) in application to Marxist movements, especially the COMMUNIST PARTY OF THE SOVIET UNION, with the following evidence: 1. REVISIONISM initiated by E. BERNSTEIN and the SOCIAL-DEMOCRATIC PARTY OF GERMANY towards the end of the 19th c.; 2. the NEW ECONOMIC POLICY 1921–28; 3. the acceptance by the COMINTERN of the policy of the Popular Fronts in the mid-1930s; 4. the acceptance of co-operation with non-Communist parties in the countries of the Third World; 5. the rejection of the Leninist principle of the inevitability of wars under imperialism at the TWENTIETH CONGRESS OF THE CPSU in 1956; 6. the acceptance of the possibility of a non-violent transition to socialism by parliamentary methods (Twentieth Congress of the CPSU); 7. the acceptance of a new concept of COEXISTENCE, amounting to peaceful competition and active participation, instead of unremitting political warfare or withdrawal (Twentieth Congress of the CPSU); 8. the abandonment of the DICTATORSHIP OF THE PROLETARIAT in the USSR in favour of the 'STATE OF THE WHOLE PEOPLE' (Twenty-Second Congress of the CPSU in 1961); and 9. the development of EUROCOMMUNISM since the early 1970s.

De-Stalinization The hesitant process of selective liberalization in the USSR and most East European countries, following KHRUSHCHEV'S SECRET SPEECH at the TWENTIETH CONGRESS OF THE CPSU in Feb. 1956 denouncing Stalin's crimes and PERSONALITY CULT. The measures were intended to reduce autocratic and arbitrary rule, to reassert SOCIALIST LEGALITY and to restore individual freedom and economic rationality. Many victims of Stalinist persecution were rehabilitated, restrictions on intellectual pursuits were somewhat relaxed, most of Stalin's statues were removed and cities bearing his name were renamed (including STALINGRAD). Electrifying effects occurred in Poland (POLISH OCTOBER) and Hungary (HUNGARIAN UPRISING) and Eastern European countries were accorded greater freedom to pursue their OWN PATH TO SOCIALISM. The ECONOMIC REFORMS of the 1960s were also pursued in the same vein. De-S. is regarded as Khrushchev's greatest achievement in what was a very delicate situation. There has been a reaction against de-S. in the form of RE-STALINIZATION.

Determinism A philosophical doctrine according to which all events and changes in nature, society and thought are determined by causes and are governed by definite laws. D. is based on three principal assumptions: 1. CAUSALITY – that all phenomena have their causes and each cause has its effect; 2. conformity – that all phenomena conforms to the operation of laws; and 3. consistency – that the same causes under the same conditions produce identical effects. There are several schools of thought of d., one of which accepts only 1, another 1 and 2, whilst others subscribe to all three. A version of d. is mechanistic d., the extreme form of which is FATALISM (according to which all future phenomena are predetermined or 'predestined'). D., with some qualifications, is one of the cornerstones of DIALECTICAL MATERIALISM and HISTORICAL MATERIALISM in Marxist philosophy, and has important implications in SOCIAL D. The opposite of d. is INDETERMINISM, accepted in philosophical idealism and most religions.

Deutsch-Französische Jahrbücher **(Franco-German Annals)** The title of what was meant to be a periodical publication for combining left-wing Hegelian radicalism and French socialism. The publication was edited by K. Marx and A. Ruge, but only one issue appeared, in Paris for March 1844. Among others it included two contributions by Marx ('A Critique of the Hegelian Philosophy of Right: An Introduction' and 'On the Jewish Question') and two by Engels ('Outline of a Critique of National Economy' and a criticism of Carlyle). In these articles Marx broke from philosophical IDEALISM. It is through the Annals that Marx and Engels initiated a lifelong collaboration and friendship. Owing mainly to differences on the editorial policy between Marx and Ruge, no further issues appeared.

Development A philosophical concept adopted by Marx from G. W. F. HEGEL, denoting progressive movement or change arising out of CONTRADICTIONS, where a struggle between thesis and antithesis usually leads to a superior solution in the form of synthesis. The driving force of d. is the energy released by the clashes of the opposites. In DIALECTICAL MATERIALISM and HISTORICAL MATERIALISM, this law applies not only to nature but also society. Social d. is regarded as a process determined by the changing conditions of production, proceeding through the CLASS STRUGGLE from one SOCIO-ECONOMIC FORMATION to another, the ultimate stage of which will be a classless society under FULL COMMUNISM.

Development of the Monist Interpretation of History, The One of the major works by G. V. PLEKHANOV, published in 1895 under his assumed name of N. Beltov. The book contains a critical review of pre-Marxian philosophy and sociology and a profound exposition of Marxist DIALECTICAL MATERIALISM and HISTORICAL MATERIALISM, together with a sharp attack against the thought, strategy and tactics of the *NARODNIKS*. The main theme of the book is that matter is primary whilst ideas are secondary and derived from the material world, and that the development of societies is determined by the economic factor. Through this book, Plekhanov exerted considerable influence on the understanding and development of Marxism in Russia before the Bolshevik Revolution. Although he never joined the BOLSHEVIKS and was highly critical of some of their methods, his book has been officially accepted by the Soviet regime as a correct and most valuable presentation of Marxist ideas.

Deviationism A term used in the Communist party vocabulary to denote departure by individual, or a group of members from the official Party line. In this sense, the term appeared first in 1921 in a resolution, 'On the Syndicalist and Anarchist Deviation in the Party', passed by the Tenth Congress of the RUSSIAN COMMUNIST PARTY (OF THE BOLSHEVIKS). It is maintained that in the dialectic process, a given thesis and antithesis can be resolved correctly only in one synthesis, viz. the one officially adopted by the Party. In Marxist-Leninist ideology, there

are two major types of d.: 1. DOGMATISM – the blind application of Marxist theory without reference to actual conditions; and 2. EMPIRICISM – the tendency to ignore Marxist theory and proceed according to practical circumstances at the time (REVISIONISM). D. can occur either to the right ('right d.'), which is known as OPPORTUNISM or to the left ('left d.'), usually identified with ANARCHISM and militant extremism. Unlike FACTIONALISM and SECTARIANISM, d. is not a fully formed movement and it can be corrected. Party discipline requires that offenders be reprimanded and subjected to SELF-CRITICISM, demoted or expelled from the Party. The charge of d. has been resorted to on occasions by unscrupulous Party officials or ordinary members in inner Party struggles to discredit and ostracize inconvenient rivals or personal enemies.

Dialectic, Dialectical Used as adjectives, in philosophy, pertaining to a progressive change in nature, society or thought as a result of conflicts between two opposites, viz. 'conflicts between two opposites'. They can also be synonymous with 'dynamic', or 'complementary'. Although etymologically, the terms go back to ancient Greece (where they meant 'pertaining to argument' or 'skilled in argument'), in their modern sense they were established by G. W. F. HEGEL, from whom Marx borrowed the term and the concept which he adapted to his own needs. The d. method of study consists in the recognition of contradictory elements potentially in conflict with each other yet which constitute a totality.

Dialectic, Dialectics Used as nouns, a major doctrine in philosophy which, historically speaking, has three meanings; 1. in ancient philosophy, the art of discourse and rationalization of truth through the identification and resolution of contradictions; 2. in the German philosophy of IDEALISM in the 19th c. as propounded by G. W. F. HEGEL, the process of development of ideas through the appearance and resolution of opposites; and 3. in Marxist philosophy, the general theory of the development of reality expressed in terms of the emergence and struggle of contradictions. But whilst for Hegel d. was primarily a theory of the development of spirit and reality, with emphasis on the former, Marx (in The *POVERTY OF PHILOSOPHY*) and Engels (in *ANTI-DÜHRING* and *DIALECTICS OF NATURE*) made it a theory of material reality and ideas only derivatively. In their view, Hegelian d. was not scientific and its propositions were essentially applicable to ideas, not to the real world. To Marxists, d. is also a theory of COGNITION and a 'guide to action'. Marxist d. emphasizes that everything in the real world is interdependent and that all objects and phenomena are constantly changing, emerging, disappearing, and as such it has been described as the theory of universal connections. According to Engels, there are three basic laws of d.: 1. *the transition from quantity to quality* – the occurrence of qualitative leaps through the accumulation of quantitative change; 2. *the inter-penetration of opposites* – internal contradictions have their positive and negative sides and the clash between them releases energy. In the process of development, whilst unity is conditional, the struggle is absolute; and 3. *the negation of the negation* – the old gives rise to the new, but the latter itself constitutes a new contradiction and develops its own negation. In addition to the three basic laws, the dialectic process is governed by such categories as the relations between the particular and the general, POSSIBILITY AND REALITY, FORM AND CONTENT, cause and effect and CONTINGENCY and NECESSITY. In the traditional Marxist d., it is held that thesis and antithesis combine into one – synthesis. But Mao Tse-tung gave a different interpretation of this process postulating that instead of 'two combining into one', 'one divides into two' (*'ONE DIVIDES INTO TWO' VS 'TWO COMBINE INTO ONE'* CONTROVERSY). In particular, he stressed that in application to the PROLETARIAN REVOLUTION, synthesis breeds its own antithesis, necessitating another revolution, and so on which, in his view, provides a

philosophical justification for the CONTINUING REVOLUTION. Also DIALECTICAL MATERIALISM, TRAGIC DIALECTICS.

Dialectical Logic In Marxist philosophy, a higher stage of logic going further than FORMAL LOGIC, and as such a conception parallel to DIALECTICAL MATERIALISM. The origin of d.l. goes back to ancient Greece (Heraclitus of Ephesus, 540–480 B.C.), where logic began as a form of polemic, viz. the clash of two opposing views. Dialectical logic questions the fundamental laws of traditional logic such as the law of identity, the law of non-contradiction, and the law of excluded middle, on the grounds that they obstruct an understanding of objects and phenomena in the process of their change and development from lower to higher forms.

Dialectical Materialism The most fundamental doctrine of Marxist philosophy, concerned with the most general laws of change and development in nature, society and thought. It was derived from the philosophical work of Marx (mainly in THE *POVERTY OF PHILOSOPHY*) and Engels (*ANTI-DÜHRING*) and developed further by Lenin (*MATERIALISM AND EMPIRIO-CRITICISM*), Stalin (*ON DIALECTICAL AND HISTORICAL MATERIALISM*) and many others. The expression d.m. was coined by JOSEF DIETZGEN. D.m. is one of three theoretical cornerstones of the Communist movement (in addition to Marxist political economy and scientific communism). It is 'dialectical' because in its approach and the method of study, d.m. attaches crucial importance to the successive and progressive struggle of opposites ('thesis and antithesis') being resolved in synthesis (and thus is opposed to METAPHYSICS); it is 'materialism', because d.m. postulates that MATTER is primary and the material world alone is real, whilst CONSCIOUSNESS, mind, ideas and thought are secondary or simply reflections or derivatives of the material factors (and thus it is opposed to IDEALISM). According to Marxists, d.m. is the only consistent and scientific version of philosophical MATERIALISM, as it constitutes 'the historical synthesis of scientific achievements' (Marx) and 'the generalization of results of particular disciplines' (Engels). As such, it is claimed to be 'living' and 'dynamic', as it changes its form in response to scientific discoveries. D.m. is viewed as not only a theory of knowledge, but also a practical scientific method for the understanding and revolutionary transformation of nature and society. As such, d.m. is a guide to the policies of the working class movement and the strategy and tactics of the Communist parties. Also DIALECTICS, ECONOMIC MATERIALISM, HISTORICAL MATERIALISM, MECHANISTIC MATERIALISM, PHILOSOPHY, VULGAR MATERIALISM.

Dialectics of Nature A collection of philosophical articles written by F. Engels over the period 1873–83, but first published only in 1925 in the USSR. Engels presented a profound philosophical analysis of the history of natural sciences and mathematics from the revolutionary Marxist standpoint, and emphasized that a thorough knowledge of these two disciplines was indispensable to the correct understanding of DIALECTICAL MATERIALISM. He attached great significance to the law of the conservation of energy, described as the 'absolute law of nature' which, he believed, negates the idealistic and theological theories on the doom of the world. Engels also critically examined MECHANISTIC MATERIALISM, METAPHYSICS and MYSTICISM and rejected their validity, as he saw them to be inconsistent with Marxist philosophy. Other major problems analysed included a critical evaluation of Darwin's theory of evolution, the role of labour in the humanization process of man, CONTINGENCY and NECESSITY. Some of Engel's pronouncements on physical laws are rather naive and have been disproved by developments since that time.

Dialectic Triad The Marxist term for the conflict and unity of the elements of change and development, viz. THESIS, ANTITHESIS and SYNTHESIS.

Diamat A syllabic abbreviation for DIALECTICAL MATERIALISM.

Dictatorship of the Proletariat The dictatorial rule by the working class, exercised by the Communist party or rather its top leader(s) following the PROLETARIAN REVOLUTION in the transition from capitalism to socialism or communism. Stalin distinguished three basic elements or objectives of the d. of the p.: 1. the suppression of the former exploiting classes, the defence of the Socialist system against external enemies and the development of links with the working classes of other countries to aid proletarian revolutions; 2. the separation of the working classes from the BOURGEOISIE, to ensure their unification and consolidation and to enlist their full participation in the construction of the Socialist society; and 3. the development of a CLASSLESS SOCIETY. The d. of the p. is based on the MONO-PARTY SYSTEM OF GOVERNMENT, DEMOCRATIC CENTRALISM, an extensive police network and in extreme cases (such as COUNTER-REVOLUTION) a widespread terror. The postulate of the d. of the p. was first put forward by Marx in 1850 (in *The Class Struggles in France*), which he probably borrowed from L. A. Blanqui (1805–81), and further elaborated in *CRITIQUE OF THE GOTHA PROGRAMME.* The first case of the d. of the p. in history was the PARIS COMMUNE (1871). The Soviets proclaimed it in Jan. 1918 when they dissolved the CONSTITUENT ASSEMBLY. By 1936 the d. of the p. in the USSR had been offically transformed into the 'd. of the working class', but in reality from 1934 to his death in 1953 Stalin ruled virtually as the absolute dictator. At the 22nd Congress of the CPSU in Oct. 1961, it was declared that the dictatorship had ceased to be necessary in the USSR in internal relations and it had been replaced by 'a state of the whole people'. But the

Chinese Communist Party attacked the Soviet stand in June 1963, and during the GREAT PROLETARIAN CULTURAL RE-VOLUTION the content of the d. of the p. was strengthened. In fact, in contrast to the 1954 Constitution (in which China was defined as 'a people's democratic state'), the 1975 Constitution describes China as 'a Socialist state of the dictatorship of the proletariat'. One of the distinguishing features of EUROCOMMUNISM is that it concedes that the d. of the p. is no longer relevant or necessary.

Dien Bien Phu A strategic locality in north-western Vietnam (in the province of Lai Chau) made famous by the defeat of the French colonial forces by the Vietnamese Communists. In Nov. 1953 D.B.P. was transformed by the French into a stronghold with a garrison of 15,000 troops commanded by Gen. de Cartries. The People's Army of Vietnam, led by Gen. VO NGUYEN GIAP, attacked the stronghold on 13 March 1954, encircled it and by 7 May 1954 almost completely annihilated the French troops. It was a crucial battle in the history of Vietnam, as the Communist victory forced the French to negotiate at the Geneva Conference in that year, which led to the French withdrawal from Indochina and a *de facto* recognition of the Communist regime in North Vietnam.

Dietzgen, Josef (1828–88) A German worker, Social-Democrat and a self-taught philosopher, who arrived at several basic principles related to DIALECTICS and DIALECTICAL MATERIALISM independently of HEGEL, MARX and ENGELS. D. was the first to coin the expression 'dialectical materialism'. Although a tannery worker, he carried on studies in philosophy, political economy and socialism, which earned him favourable references from Marx, Engels and Lenin. But he also incurred some criticism by them for having made too many concessions to IDEALISM and AGNOSTICISM, and identified CONSCIOUS-NESS with MATTER. D.'s supporters, Machists (including his son Eugen D.),

attempted to create a new philosophical system called 'Dietzgenism' to rival or at least complement Marxism.

Differential Rent In the Marxist interpretation in application to the capitalist economy, the element of SURPLUS VALUE over and above average profit, derived from the private and monopolistic ownership of land of differing productivity (in respect of climate, soil and location). As such, it represents unearned income and constitutes the exploitation of agricultural workers and tenants. Marx distinguished (in *CAPITAL*, vol. III) between d.r.I, which is based on the natural quality of land, and d.r.II, made possible by the differences in land productivity brought about by man-made improvements. In the Socialist planned economy, the problem of the d.r. is approached on a planned basis in the interest of the whole society. D.r.I is fully absorbed by the state in the form of differentiated taxes and procurement prices, while d.r.II is at least partly left to the socialized farms as an incentive for the intensification of farming by their own efforts.

Different Paths to Socialism See OWN PATHS TO SOCIALISM.

Dimitrov, Georgi Mikhailov (1882–1949) An outstanding leader of the Bulgarian and international Communist movement and a devoted disciple and friend of Lenin and Stalin. D. joined the Bulgarian Social-Democratic Party in 1902, out of which under his leadership the BULGARIAN COMMUNIST PARTY developed (established under this name in 1919). In Sep. 1923 he was one of the leaders of an unsuccessful uprising to establish Communist rule in Bulgaria. He was persecuted by the Bulgarian monarchist authorities, sentenced to death twice, but escaped in each case. In the notorious Nazi conspiracy, he was accused of burning down the *Reichstag* in 1933. But his courageous and brilliant defence and his exposure of the anti-communist provocation at the Leipzig

Diploma of Honour (or of Merit)

Trial earned him international fame and acquittal. D. was very active in the COMINTERN, where he worked in its Executive Committee and from 1935 to 1943 was its Secretary-General. He was awarded Soviet citizenship in 1934 and the Order of Lenin in 1945. After 22 years in exile, D. returned to Bulgaria in Nov. 1945. Under his leadership with the Soviet support and resorting to ruthless methods, Communist power was firmly established in Bulgaria by the end of 1947. In 1946 he became the first Prime Minister of the P.R. of Bulgaria and he framed its first Constitution (of 1947). As a Marxist thinker, D. attached great importance to combining theory with practice in the revolutionary movement, emphasizing that practice without theory is 'blind' and theory without practical verification is 'sterile and fruitless'. He promoted the idea of a possible BALKAN CONFEDERATION, to include Bulgaria, Yugoslavia and perhaps other countries. For this and his friendship with Tito, D. lost favour with Stalin, but remained Prime Minister until his death in 1949. In Stalin's campaign in the COMINFORM against Tito and Yugoslavia in 1948, D. stood out as the only Communist leader who refused to support it.

Diploma of Honour (or of Merit) See CERTIFICATE OF HONOUR.

Direct Action In the strategy of the industrial labour movement in capitalist countries, the practice of resorting to strike rather than negotiation, CONCILIATION, ARBITRATION or the PARLIAMENTARY ROAD TO SOCIALISM. A threat of d.a. of a major historical interest was that made by the British Trades Union Congress in 1919, to restrain the British Government from supporting anti-Bolshevik groups during the Civil War.

Direction of Labour The channelling of labour by the state to desired industries, regions or occupations. In democratic capitalist countries, it is resorted to only in national emergencies, such as those associated with war or major disasters. The d. of l. may be administered on a more systematic basis in the Socialist centrally planned economies, but under normal conditions compulsion is avoided, and instead similar effects may be achieved by propaganda and various forms of incentives. However, compulsion is usually applied in the case of Communist party members, certain occupations (such as doctors) and graduates from tertiary institutions in the first year of their employment. Extreme or large-scale cases of the d. of l. are exemplified by the MILITARIZATION OF LABOUR (in Soviet Russia) and the RUSTICATION DRIVE (in China).

Directives A term used in the Socialist countries for mandatory instructions laid down by the Communist party or planning authorities, which are binding down the hierarchical ladder of planning and management. The implementation of d. at the enterprise level is usually conditional to the award of MATERIAL INCENTIVES to the personnel. Economic planning in most Socialist countries is directive, i.e. TARGETS and some other plan indicators are compulsory, contrasting with indicative (or ORIENTATIONAL) planning.

Directive Plan Indicator In Socialist economic planning, a target or constraint laid down by the central authority, which may be defined in the volume, value or structure of output (or production), wage payments, materials used, profit and the like. The d.p.i. is mandatory, the fulfilment or observance of which is usually conditional to the award of bonuses. The number of d.p.i. was quite large under the CENTRALIZED DIRECTIVE SYSTEM OF PLANNING AND MANAGEMENT, but since the ECONOMIC REFORMS of the 1960s (1950s in Yugoslavia) their number has been substantially reduced.

Director The term used in the Socialist countries for the (general) manager of an industrial enterprise, or any large enterprise in construction, transport, communications or trade (there is no relation to the company 'director' in capitalist countries). His appointment is made either directly by, or with the approval of, the local Communist party organ. In most Socialist countries, the rule of one-man management responsibility and power has been firmly established, although the d. is obliged to consult his specialist deputies or departmental managers (chief engineer, chief accountant, senior economist, personnel manager). He is also expected to enlist democratic participation by all workers in one form or another. Thus the principle of DEMOCRATIC CENTRALISM is supposed to be applied in the management of socialized enterprises. The d. is primarily responsible for the preparation and implementation of the enterprise's economic plan. The precise extent of his responsibility and power differs from one country to another. On the whole, it is greatest in the German DR and the USSR and least in China and Yugoslavia.

Director's Fund The name of a fund in socialized enterprises formed out of profits for financing bonuses to the personnel, factory-owned housing, and various social and cultural amenities. The term was used in the USSR up to 1955 and somewhat later in some other Socialist countries, but since that time the designations like the 'Enterprise Fund' or the 'Material Incentives Fund' have become more common.

Discipline Subordination and observance of the norms regulating internal relations or conduct in a particular organization. D. may be either externally imposed or developed from within the individual or group. Marxism, being critical of INDIVIDUALISM, attaches great importance to d., as it has far-reaching social implications. There are different types of d. and the Socialist countries have developed characteristic ways (distinct from those in capitalist countries) in approaching it in specific fields, such as MILITARY DISCIPLINE, PARTY DISCIPLINE, SOCIAL DISCIPLINE, WORK DISCIPLINE.

Disclericalization The emancipation of various spheres of social and individual activity and life from the influence of the organized church and religion. It typically assumes the following steps: 1. the separation of the state from the church; 2. the elimination of the church's legislative, administrative, educational, economic and cultural powers in society; 3. a diminution of the prestige and influence of the clergy and church institutions in society; and 4. the reduction of religious beliefs and practices to the individual and private sphere, and their separation from public and social processes. D. is typical of developed societies as a consequence of scientific, political, social and economic progress, particularly where the power of tradition and vested religious interests is weak and the power of left-wing elements is strong. The beginnings of d. in Europe go back at least to the Renaissance, but several developments since then have radically accelerated its spread, especially RATIONALISM, COMMUNISM, ATHEISM and ANTICLERICALISM in general. D. has been placed on a more systematic basis in the Socialist countries.

Disideologization A decline in ideological fervour, which has set in since the late 1950s, both in the West and (to a lesser extent) in the Socialist bloc. It is also known as 'the end of the age of ideology' or 'anti-ideologism'. This trend has been facilitated by the acceptance of the principle of peaceful COEXISTENCE (after 1956), the virtual discontinuation of the COLD WAR (after 1963), and POLYCENTRISM, i.e. weakening the cohesion and chauvinism of the two rival power blocs, paralleled by increasing TRANSIDEOLOGICAL COLLABORATION. The process has been conditioned by the realization that ideological conflicts are reflections of old prejudices and grievances, and as such are pointless and harmful.

Disinformation A term used in the Socialist countries (especially in the USSR, where it originated as *desinformatsiya*) to describe deliberate misinformation. The

Dissent

term is usually applied to anti-communist reports in capitalist literature on the situation and developments in the Socialist countries.

Dissent In modern sense, minority protest against excessive restrictions on liberties by intolerant conservative or authoritarian governments. The movement began in the early 1950s in the West, and it has developed since both in the West and in the East. In the West, it is identified with the radical NEW LEFT and its leading organ *Dissent* (a bi-monthly published in New York). However, the term d. is now more commonly understood in the context of the Socialist countries, especially Czechoslovakia, the German DR, Hungary, Poland, the USSR, Yugoslavia and more recently China. The beginnings of d. go back to 1953–54, when M. DJILAS published a series of articles in Yugoslavia. D. has become more assertive since the mid-1960s, and has intensified since the early 1970s. Its leading proponents are writers, artists, students and certain minority groups (especially Jews). They press for a greater freedom of expression and religious practice, rights of individuals and national groups. Most of them are not necessarily against the Communist establishment, but rather demand liberal reforms within the framework of the existing system. The forms of protest include underground publications, occasional demonstrations, illegal exhibitions, hunger strikes and appeals to world public opinion. Although d. is fought with determination, the authorities are not as ruthless now as they used to be before the mid-1950s. Also CHARTER '77, CHARTER OF LIBERTY. *CHRONICLE OF CURRENT EVENTS*, HUMAN RIGHTS, DISSENTERS, *SAMIZDAT*.

Dissenters, Dissidents The name given to persons in the Socialist countries (especially in Czechoslovakia, the German DR, Hungary, Poland, the USSR and Yugoslavia) demanding HUMAN RIGHTS. Some of the best known d. are: A. Amalrik (historian, USSR, now living in the West); R. Bahro (writer, now in the West); W. Biermann (poet, GDR, now in the West); V. Bukovsky (sociologist, USSR, now in the West); M. Djilas (writer, Yugoslavia); A. Ginzburg (journalist, USSR, now in the West); P. G. Grigorenko (general, USSR, now in the West); V. Havel (playwright, Czechoslovakia); P. Kohout (writer, Czechoslovakia); E. Lipinski (economist, Poland); A. Medvedev (writer, USSR); A. Michnik (historian, Poland); Y. Orlov (scientist, USSR); A. Sakharov (physicist, USSR); A. Sinyavsky (writer, USSR); A. SOLZHENITSYN (writer, USSR, now in the West) and M. Stern (physician, USSR). The d. have been subjected to surveillance, harassment, frequent interrogations, the loss of employment, isolation in psychiatric institutions, hard labour, deportation and imprisonment. Also see DISSENT.

Distance Theory in Art A principle of artistic creativity expecting the artist to rise above the immediate ideological requirements and to oppose SOCIALIST REALISM. The advocates of the d.t. in a. press for the freedom of thought and expression, and in particular for the freedom from interference by the state or the Party in creative work, so as to enable them to have a sufficiently free perspective in their work. In no Socialist country is this postulate acceptable to the Communist regime, but in Hungary an amendment to the Constitution (of 1949), adopted in 1972, guarantees freedom for creative arts and sciences.

Distribution According to Work See TO EACH ACCORDING TO HIS WORK.

Disutility of Labour A concept which has several meanings: 1. from the employer's point of view – the cost of employing labour, irrespective of the latter's productivity; from the worker's standpoint – the forgoing of leisure time and the affliction, discomfort or inconvenience associated with work; and 2. from the employer's point of view – employment beyond such a level where the marginal cost of labour (additional wages) exceeds the marginal productivity of labour (the consequent additions to production), from the worker's standpoint – work which results in affliction, discomfort or inconvenience exceeding the wage (higher overtime rates, compared with standard rates, are justified on the grounds of the increasing d. of l.). From the macro-social point of view in the Socialist planned economy, there is no d. of l. to justify unemployment, as the state guarantees to provide employment or sustenance to all its citizens, and any additional work constitutes additions to total production. In the Marxist interpretation by reference to Communist society, the concept of the d. of l. will become irrelevant under FULL COMMUNISM, owing to the complete social ownership of the means of production, the absence of exploitation, short working hours, moral (as distinct from material) motivation in work, the prevalence of interesting and light work and, in general, the operation of the principle 'FROM EACH ACCORDING TO HIS WORK, TO EACH ACCORDING TO HIS NEEDS'.

Divergence Thesis One of the theories explaining a tendency in the development of capitalism and socialism, maintaining that the two systems are becoming increasingly divergent. This theory commanded considerable support amongst specialists in East-West relations in the late 1950s and early 1960s and contrasted with the earlier SUBMERGENCE HYPOTHESIS and the CONVERGENCE THESIS that followed it. The supporters of the d.t., encouraged by the policy of COEXISTENCE, maintained that neither side is sufficiently superior to 'submerge' the other. The isolation of the two blocs enforced by the IRON CURTAIN and the STRATEGIC CURTAIN, further enhanced by the COLD WAR, makes them develop along increasingly divergent lines. Propaganda, narrow-mindedness and vested interests on each side, having a stake in tension between the two blocs, further accentuate the differences. As a result many divergencies which were at first imaginary have since materialized as real differences.

Division of Labour A general term for occupational, industrial and territorial specialization, with emphasis on labour as the determining factor of production. In contrast to CLASSICAL BOURGEOIS POLITICAL ECONOMY, which stressed the beneficial effects of the d. of l. on efficiency, Marx and Engels (in *THE GERMAN IDEOLOGY*) treated it critically from the social standpoint. They identified the d. of l. with private property and in fact used the two concepts interchangeably, i.e. in their view the d. of l. between and within the social classes reflects property relations. Marx pointed out (in *The Economic and Philosophical Manuscripts of 1844*) that in ANTAGONISTIC SOCIO-ECONOMIC FORMATIONS, the d. of l. increases the wealth of exploiting (propertied) classes, 'impoverishing the worker and reducing him to a machine'. In a similar vein a century later, in 1944, Mao Tse-tung explained that 'Any specialized skill may be capitalized and so may lead to *arrogance* and contempt of others' (quoted in *LITTLE RED BOOK*). Several Marxist thinkers argued that in the international setting, the d. of l. enables the industrially-developed nations to exploit the poor primary-producing countries through VERTICAL FOREIGN TRADE and NON-EQUIVALENT EXCHANGE. The benefits of the d. of l. are, of course, fully appreciated in the Socialist countries, but Marxist economists emphasize that there it is placed on a centrally planned basis and pursued in the interest of the whole society. The d. of l. amongst the Socialist countries (especially within CMEA) is based on mutually agreed planned specialization and assistance, meant to lead to the balancing out of the economic levels between the less and more developed member countries. Also INTERNATIONAL SOCIALIST DIVISION OF LABOUR, NEW COMMUNIST MAN, OCCUPATIONAL DIVISION OF LABOUR.

'Dizzy with success' A phrase used by Stalin in March 1930 to describe the success of the proceeding COLLECTIVIZATION and the appalling and unnecessary cost of human suffering and widespread waste. In

151

his article under that title, he blamed the officials (mostly industrial workers from the cities) for their 'enthusiasm' and 'misunderstanding of his intentions'.

Djilas, Milovan (1911–) A Yugoslav Communist theoretician, formerly a leading supporter of Tito, but since the early 1950s one of the best known idealist Communist dissenters. He joined the (illegal) Communist Party of Yugoslavia in 1932, became a partisan leader loyal to Tito during W.W.II, a high Party official after the war and Vice-President of Yugoslavia in 1953. In winter 1953–54, he published a series of articles exposing the emergence of a closely-knit elitist bureaucracy, which he described as a group of 'privileged and parasitical tyrants' oblivious of Marxian ideals, and he advocated radical democratic reforms to protect HUMAN RIGHTS. He also published several books abroad in the same vein, viz. *The New Class* (1957), *Land without Justice* (1958), *Conversations with Stalin* (1962), *Unperfect Society* (1969), *Wartime* (1977), *Tito* (1980). He was deprived of his party and Government posts and expelled from the Party in 1954, and spent eight years in prison. Although his writings have caused a sensation in the West, the immediate impact of his ideas in Yugoslavia and other Socialist countries was small. However, he may be regarded as the forerunner of DISSENT in Eastern Europe and the USSR, which has assumed increasing proportions since the mid-1960s and especially since the early 1970s.

Dobrolubov, Nikolai Aleksandrovich (1836–61) A Russian precursor of Marxism, a REVOLUTIONARY DEMOCRAT, an ideologist of peasant revolution and a materialist philosopher, whose contributions were later acknowledged by Lenin. In particular, D. attacked the survival of serfdom in Russia and believed that only a revolution, rather than reforms, could abolish it. He also wrote a vision of a perfect society, free of oppression and exploitation, which he described as an 'ideal republic' and 'sacred brotherhood'.

In his philosophical writings, he regarded the material world as primary, whilst consciousness and ideas were secondary, the former conditioning the latter. He stressed that everything in nature and society is subject to constant change and progressive development. Although a priest by education, he attacked religion as well as agnosticism. He died at the age of 25 from poverty and overwork.

'Doctors' Plot' An alleged conspiracy in 1952–53 by a group of physicians on the Kremlin staff, most of whom were of Jewish descent, to murder top Soviet leaders, including Stalin. The doctors were accused of acting on the orders from the American and British secret service and Zionist organizations. The 'plot' was reported in Jan. 1953 and arrests followed. It was later disclosed, after Stalin's death (5 March 1953), that the charges had been fabricated, the doctors were released as not guilty, but at least one (Y. G. Etinger) had died under interrogation. The complete truth behind the incident is still unknown. But from the available fragmentary information, it appears that the plot had been planned by a group of high-ranking Party officials who enlisted the support of the Kremlin doctors in order to dispose of Stalin before he could carry out his projected purge of the Party hierarchy.

Doctrine of Limited Sovereignty See LIMITED SOVEREIGNTY DOCTRINE.

Dogmatism A blind, uncritical acceptance and application of a doctrine or principles without reference to rational evidence or actual conditions. The term was first applied in a religious context, but since the emergence of the Socialist states after the Bolshevik Revolution in 1917, the inclination to d. has also appeared amongst many other Communist thinkers and policy-makers. In their view, in the works of the classics of Marxism, solutions and parallels can be found to all possible problems that may arise in any situation, despite the fact that neither Marx nor Engels had ever observed a functioning Socialist country (even the development of capitalism as they knew it was vastly different from that of today). D. has often led to embarrassment and waste, especially in the economic sphere, as exemplified at one time or another by the disregard for differential rent, interest and profit in economic management, prejudice against marginal analysis and opposition to cybernetics. Officially, d. has been frowned upon, and it is now postulated that Marxism is not meant to be a rigid doctrine, but rather 'a guide to action' in a dialectical sense (CREATIVE MARXISM). However, there are many forces in the Socialist countries favouring d. – the readiness to defend Marxism against bourgeois attacks, the convenient preference for the well established thought and practice and the fear of being accused of divergence towards the opposite direction, viz. OPPORTUNISM and REVISIONISM.

Dole A colloquial term for unemployment benefit or relief. The term, going back to the 15th c. in England, originally meant a charitable fund left from a bequest for dealing (distribution) to the poor.

Dollar Diplomacy, Dollar Imperialism The phrase d.d. was established under President Taft's administration in the USA (1909–13) and initiated by P. C. Knox in 1910, denoting the American policy of lending to favoured governments to strengthen US political and economic influence. The policy was pursued most vigorously in Central America, the Far East, and Liberia. Although its supporters saw it as a reasonable and peaceful form of expansion to mutual benefit, its critics – especially Marxists – viewed it as IMPERIALISM leading to COLONIALISM and later NEO-COLONIALISM. Khrushchev once described the capitalist world as 'the kingdom of the dollar'.

Domino Theory Assumption made by many US theoretical writers and policymakers, and widely accepted in the capitalist countries in the 1950s and 1960s, to the effect that if one country falls

to Communist control, other countries in the same area will do likewise in successive order, 'like a row of dominoes'. The theory was first publicized by the US National Security Council in 1950 in application to Indochina and became a basis of American policy in South-East Asia up to the early 1970s. In 1956 President D. D. Eisenhower indicated that South Vietnam represented the first, critical domino which later (1964–72) became an object of massive US protection and direct military intervention. To some extent, the theory was proven correct by subsequent developments. With the fall of South Vietnam in 1975, Cambodia and Laos also fell to Communist control.

DO-RO Method An officially supported scheme in Poland to improve the quality of industrial products, mainly by preventing the cumulative effect of faults in the production process. Its name *DO-RO* is derived from *DObra RObota* (meaning a 'well-done job'), alluding to a philosophical and sociological treatise on this question by an eminent Polish social scientist, T. Kotarbiński (*Traktat o dobrej robocie*, 1955). The method relies primarily on self-control by the worker, by appealing to his pride and material motivation. The D.-R.M. has been introduced in a drive to improve the quality of production, as bureaucratic controls, continuous full employment, well-developed social security, the weakness of material incentives and prevalent sellers' markets tolerate and even encourage poor quality. The main elements of the method are derived from the Soviet SARATOV METHOD and the American Zero Defects system.

Double Ten Points A compromise programme of the education of the masses and the cadres, embodying the ideas of MAO TSE-TUNG and LIU SHAO-CH'I put forward during 1963–64. In May 1963, 'Early Ten Points' prepared under Mao's direction were issued, specifying how the education of the masses and the cadres was to be managed in the SOCIALIST EDUCATION MOVEMENT. A modified version, drafted by TENG HSIAO-PING and called 'Later Ten Points', was announced in the following September. In Sep. 1964, Liu Shao-ch'i circulated 'Revised Later Ten Points', with a greater revolutionary and a lesser bureaucratic content. As Liu's revision was not acceptable to Mao, Liu produced a compromise programme based on the drafts of Mao and Teng, calling it D.T.P. However, Mao rejected it as impracticable.

Dov Unit of the social utility of products proposed by S. Strumilin, a Soviet economist, during WAR COMMUNISM (1918–20) as part of his plan to abolish money. The idea was prompted by the Marxian ideal of the NATURALIZATION OF ECONOMIC PROCESSES. *D.* was complementary to *TRED*, a labour unit of value. *D.* is a syllabic abbreviation of the Russian word *dovoltsiviya*, meaning a 'measure of satisfaction'. It was meant to represent the minimal need of food of an average man in one day, amounting to 2,000 calories. The d. was found impractical, and the scheme as suggested by Strumilin was never implemented. Instead, the authorities embarked on a RE-MONETIZATION of the economy in 1921 (with the adoption of the NEW ECONOMIC POLICY).

Down-to-the-Countryside Drive See RUSTICATION DRIVE.

DPR of Korea See KOREA, DEMOCRATIC PEOPLE'S REPUBLIC OF.

***Druzhba* Pipeline** See FRIENDSHIP PIPELINE.

DRV Abbreviation for the Democratic Republic of [North] Vietnam, in existence from 1954 to 1976. In contrast to the Republic of [South] Vietnam, it was ruled by the Communist regime. On 2 July 1976 the DRV officially merged with the RV and formed a unified country of Vietnam (VIETNAM, SOCIALIST REPUBLIC OF).

Dualism A movement in philosophy accepting both material and mental entities as components of existence (and as such it is opposite to MONISM). The best known exponent of d. was R. Descartes (1596–1650), who held that being consists of two independent elements: physical substance and spirit (idea). Marxist philosophy, in particular DIALECTICAL MATERIALISM, rejects d. (and idealism) in favour of materialist monism, insisting that matter is primary whilst ideas only derive from matter and have no independent existence.

Dual Satellitism A term sometimes used for precarious foreign policies of dual alignment in relation to the USA and the USSR (or China). Such a course may be pursued either as a matter of political necessity or economic or military benefit. The term has been applied at one time or another to Finland, India, Pakistan, Romania and Yugoslavia.

Dual Unionism The overlapping of two trade unions in serving a particular group of workers. Although d.u. is sometimes favoured by employers, the trade union movement is, on the whole, against it, as it reduces the solidarity of organized labour, enables the employers to play off one union against another, possibly leading to DEMARCATION DISPUTES.

Dubček, Aleksander (1921–) Czechoslovak Communist leader who attempted political and economic liberalization in 1968 without success, and was later demoted and expelled from the Party. He joined the CZECHOSLOVAK COMMUNIST PARTY in 1939 and during W.W.II was active in the resistance against the Germans. In 1963 he became the leader of the Slovak Communist Party and a member of the Presidium of the Cz.C.P. He was appointed First Secretary of the Cz.C.P. in March 1968 and under his leadership liberal reforms were initiated (ACTION PROGRAMME). But they aroused sharp reaction from other Warsaw Pact countries, which resulted in the INVASION OF CZECHO-

SLOVAKIA in Aug. 1968. He was removed from the Party's leadership in April 1969, was made President of the FEDERAL ASSEMBLY instead, but he lost that position too, and was sent to Turkey as Czechoslovakia's Ambassador in Jan. 1970. He was recalled from that post in June 1970 after his expulsion from the Party and was given a minor post in economic administration.

Dühring, Karl Eugen (1833–1921) A German academic engineer, economist and philosopher, who attracted sharp criticism from Engels. As a philosopher, D. was an eclectic, endeavouring to combine POSITIVISM, MECHANISTIC MATERIALISM and IDEALISM. He exerted some influence on the SOCIAL-DEMOCRATIC PARTY OF GERMANY. He criticized Marx and Engels (in *Natural Dialectics*, 1865, and *Critical History of Political Economy and Socialism*, 1871) for their one-sidedness and extremism, and produced his own model of moderate socialism. D.'s ideas became an object of attack by F. Engels in his best known work, *Herr Eugen Dühring's Revolution in Science* (1878), popularly known as *ANTI-DÜHRING*.

Dulles-Eisenhower Doctrine An anticommunist set of propositions underlying US foreign policy in the 1950s aiming at 'rolling back Communism'. The doctrine was more militant than the previously announced CONTAINMENT POLICY. The fundamentals of the doctrine were first formulated in 1949 by J. F. Dulles, the ideologist of the Republican Party and the Secretary of State in the Eisenhower Administration 1952–59. The doctrine was officially elaborated upon by President Eisenhower in his address to the Congress on 5 June 1957. It embodied such elements as the US offer of economic and military aid to countries suffering from Communist attacks and subversion, and the MASSIVE RETALIATION STRATEGY, with nuclear weapons. The D.-E.D. found its expression in the American intervention in Iran in 1953, Guatemala and South Vietnam in 1954 and Lebanon in 1958.

Duma ('Thinking', in Russian) The Representative Assembly in Tsarist Russia in existence from 1906 to 1917. Its establishment had originally been proposed by M. M. Speransky in his reform programme of 1809. But it was created only by the Manifesto and Statutes of Tsar NICHOLAS II of Aug.–Dec. 1905, in a token response to the public pressure and events of the REVOLUTION OF 1905-7. To distinguish from other types of representation, its full name was State D. (*Gossudarstvennaya Duma*) and its functions were concerned with national legislation, the state budget and the state loans. But the powers of the D. were severely limited. Not only was it based on limited franchise favouring large landowners, but its bills could be vetoed by the State Council (resembling the Upper House) and the Tsar. The consequent widespread dissatisfaction of anti-Tsarist and revolutionary ferments led to the February and October Revolutions of 1917. There were four D. terms – 1906, 1907, 1907–12 and 1912–17. In the Fourth D., completely dominated by right-wing and conservative parties, the BOLSHEVIKS had only six deputies (of the total of 411).

'Dustheap of History' A phrase made famous by L. D. TROTSKY on 25 Oct. (7 Nov. N.S.C.) 1917. It was directed to the MENSHEVIKS and RIGHT SOCIALIST REVOLUTIONARIES, when they were walking out of the Second Congress of Soviets in protest against the Bolshevik seizure of power the preceding night. At that moment Trotsky said, 'Our uprising has succeded. You are torn and disunited castaways ... bankrupts; you are now redundant. Go to the place you belong from now on – to the dustheap of history.'

Dutch Pacifist Socialist Party See PACIFIST SOCIALIST PARTY.

Dutch Party of Labour See PARTY OF LABOUR.

Dynamic Marxists Also known as progressive M. or creative M., those who basically accept most ideas of K. MARX, but interpret them in a pragmatic way, adapting them to changing political, economic, cultural, geographical and historical conditions. They support CREATIVE MARXISM.

Dzierzhinsky, Feliks Edmundovich (1877–1926) Originally a Polish Social-Democrat of landowning family background, who became one of the chief organizers of the Bolshevik Revolution and who later held several top ministerial posts in the Soviet Government. He was exiled several times to Siberia for revolutionary activities and was freed by the February Revolution of 1917. D. was elected to the Central Committee of the RUSSIAN SOCIAL-DEMOCRATIC LABOUR PARTY (OF THE BOLSEHVIKS) in Aug. 1917 and was one of Lenin's closest assistants and friends at the time of the Bolshevik seizure of power in Oct. 1917. In Dec. 1917 Lenin appointed him the chief of the first Soviet secret police organization, the CHEKA (1917–22) and its successor, the GPU (1922–26). He was also People's Commissar (Minister) of Internal Affairs (1919–21), of Transport (1921–24) and the chairman of the Supreme Council of the National Economy (VESENKHA) until his death in 1926. D.'s name is commemorated in the names of several localities and institutions in the USSR, and a monument has been erected to his memory in a square in Moscow (facing the LUBYANKA) and in a square in Warsaw (bearing his name).

Dzhugashvili, Josip Vissarionovich The original family name of J. STALIN.

E

Early Ten Points (of the education of the masses and the cadres in China) See DOUBLE TEN POINTS.

East German Socialist Unity Party See SOCIALIST UNITY PARTY OF GERMANY.

East Germany See GERMAN DEMOCRATIC REPUBLIC.

East-West In its present political connotation, a term introduced after W.W.II to describe the division between the Socialist bloc and the developed capitalist countries. Originally, the term referred to the East (incl. all the USSR) and West European division, but soon it was extended to include all the European and Asian Socialist countries on the one hand and the Western European countries, Canada, the USA, Japan, Australia, New Zealand and South Africa on the other. By this token, Czechoslovakia, the German DR, Hungary and Poland, which traditionally identified themselves with the Western civilization, are now classified as belonging to the 'East', whilst Japan is no longer an Eastern but a Western country in this context. The goods shipped from Japan to Nakhodka are deemed to be moving from the West to the East. However, before W.W.II E.–W. contrasted Oriental countries (incl. Japan), belonging to the Eastern civilization, with most European countries (incl. Czechoslovakia, what is now the German DR, Hungary, Poland, plus Croatia and Slovenia) and North America, belonging to the Western civilization. Between 1833 and 1847, there was a journal published in China called *East-West Magazine*, and at the University of Hawaii there is an East-West Center, both using E.–W. in the pre-W.W.II sense.

ECCI Abbreviation used for the EXECUTIVE COMMITTEE OF THE COMMUNIST INTERNATIONAL (the Russian abbreviation was *IKKI*).

Eclecticism The practice of selecting the most obvious or 'best' element from different theories to form a new doctrine regarded by its creators and supporters as more complete and plausible than the previous 'one-sided' ones. Alternatively, e. may mean selecting only certain aspects of a particular phenomenon in nature or society and interpreting them in the most customary and convincing, popular manner. Marxism is opposed to e., considering it as an unoriginal attempt to combine incongruous and often contradictory views and concepts. In particular, it rejects the eclectic combination of MATERIALISM and IDEALISM in philosophy, as exemplified by Kantianism and MACHISM. OPPORTUNISM and REVISIONISM are also regarded by Marxists as forms of e.

Economic Accountability, Economic Accounting Bases of the financial management of socialized enterprises in the Socialist countries, roughly meaning 'operation on a commercial basis' or 'profit and loss accounting'. The enterprise receives fixed and variable assets from the state and is supposed to carry on its operations on the basis of self-financing and only settles its overall financial balance with the state budget. To this effect, it has its own management empowered to make its own economic decisions, it can enter into economic relations with other entities and it is virtually independent of direct budgetary supervision. Such an enterprise may still receive subsidies from the state budget in the case of PLANNED LOSSES, or other approved exceptional circumstances. In the USSR e.a. is known as *KHOZRASCHET*.

Economic Calculation The determination of the relative scarcity of resources and the valuation of the objectives of economic activity and the cost of achieving them in order to ensure the most efficient pattern of the utilization of resources. The need for e.c. arises from the scarcity of resources in relation to human wants. The aim of e.c. is to achieve the most economical or the most effective substitution of resources and of products. In the capitalist market economy e.c. is basically carried on at the microeconomic level, where firms endeavour to maximize profits on the basis of the market prices and demand. This process is by and large conducive to maximum efficiency. In the Socialist centrally planned economy, e.c. is first carried out at the macroeconomic level (i.e. from the point of view of the economy and society as a whole) at the time of the economic plan using PROGRAMMING PRICES. Although e.c. is also carried on at the enterprise level, it does not necessarily lead to maximum efficiency, owing to the distorted price structure. E.c. under Socialist economic planning does not ensure the most efficient utilization of resources due to the absence of SCARCITY PRICES. Such prices could be obtained either in conventional markets (where there is private ownership of the means of production) or in SHADOW MARKETS, or in simulated markets using computers and ideal information. Also NEO-AUSTRIAN CRITIQUE OF SOCIALISM, NEO-MARXISM.

Economic Chambers In Yugoslavia, associations of enterprises for business co-operation, corresponding to chambers of commerce and chambers of manufacturers combined in capitalist countries. Membership is voluntary but most enterprises belong to them (farms being excluded). Related enterprises are represented in the Chambers as industry committees, and these exist at the provincial, republic and federal levels. The network is headed by the Federal Economic Chamber which, in addition to overall co-ordination, disseminates business information, exerts a moderating influence on price agreements between producers and users, safeguards the interests of the enterprises against the encroachments by the state and supervises the allocation of foreign exchange quotas to importing enterprises.

Economic Crimes A description used in the Socialist countries for serious anti-social offences committed by persons against property. Although Marx and other early idealist Communist writers believed that with the socialization of the means of production, e.c. and even most other crimes would disappear. However, in reality they do exist in all the Socialist countries today and present a continual problem. They include pilfering in factories and on farms, the embezzlement of public funds, the black market, bribery and vandalism. In fact, it appears that there has been a resurgence of e.c. since the late 1950s, as is reflected in the strengthening of legislation against 'property offenders' and 'social parasites' (in the USSR the death penalty for e.c. was reintroduced in 1961). Penalties for e.c. are more severe when social property is involved than in the case of private property.

'Economic Democracy' The title of the programme of the General Trade Union Society of Germany published in 1928, setting out its views on the progress to socialism. Its main objectives were the nationalization of key industries, the creation of industrial associations with trade union participation, far-reaching industrial and social legislation and the development of consumers' co-operatives. The programme implied gradual reforms and it did not envisage any radical changes. It was rejected by revolutionary Marxists who described it as exemplifying RE-VISIONISM and capitulationism.

Economic Determinism A theory according to which society's political, social, intellectual and artistic values, organization and various pursuits are determined by economic factors. It also implies that historical developments are determined by changes in the material sphere. Marxism is noted for its support of e.d., maintaining that the material BASE determines the SUPERSTRUCTURE. There are two schools of Marxist thought on the question. The proponents of 'narrow' e.d. hold that the determination proceeds only in one direction from the material base to the superstructure. In the 'broad' interpretation, which is more commonly accepted, it is conceded that the base is also affected by the superstructure. Marx and Engels stressed that they did not regard the economic factor as the exclusive determinant. They recognized the role of such factors as ideas, personalities and religions, but they attributed only a secondary role to them. On the basis of e.d., Marxists predict the inevitable BREAKDOWN OF CAPITALISM and the victory of communism. Also ECONOMIC DEVELOPMENT, HISTORICAL MATERIALISM, SOCIAL DETERMINISM, SOCIO-ECONOMIC FORMATION.

Economic Development The process of progressive quantitative and structural changes in the economy leading to increases in production and social welfare. It is a broader concept than ECONOMIC GROWTH, but, in addition to the increases in national income, it also encompasses processes of a broader economic and social content of lasting consequence. Marxism attaches fundamental importance to e.d., as in its view it transforms the material BASE, which in turn determines all other phenomena and relations called the SUPERSTRUCTURE. Marxists identify the following crucial processes in e.d.: 1. the

quantitative expansion and qualitative improvement of the means of production (capital and land) and labour, called PRODUCTION FORCES; 2. progressive changes in the methods of production; 3. changes in PRODUCTION RELATIONS; and 4. changes in social relations, the class structure and political, social, moral and religious ideas and institutions. Marxists interpret the whole course of history as being basically conditioned by progressive economic changes, and consequently each major historical stage is noted for its characteristic SOCIO-ECONOMIC FORMATION. In the traditional Marxist theory, e.d. necessarily passes through these stages successively from lower to higher. But according to MAOISM e.d. can proceed in 'leaps', with a possibility of skipping a particular stage.

Economic Epoch See SOCIO-ECONOMIC FORMATION.

Economic Equilibrium A state of balance where, under given conditions, there is a mutual concordance of economic magnitudes (such as production, investment, demand, prices, income), so that there is no tendency amongst the related variables to depart from the existing state. On the whole, in Western economic theory, it has been traditionally assumed that economic processes naturally work towards a harmonious equilibrium and, although disequilibria arise, they are automatically corrected by the market forces. On the other hand, the Marxist view stresses the conflicting processes arising from the more or less continuous clashes of contradictory forces (THESIS, ANTITHESIS and SYNTHESIS). This is so in capitalist market economies, owing to the ANARCHY OF PRODUCTION operating in the uncontrolled market. In the Socialist centrally planned economies, economic processes are shaped on a systematically planned basis. E.e. is considered to exist when there is a concordant operation of all economic variables towards the attainment of social goals embodied in the plan. E.e., so un-

159

derstood by the Socialist economists, implies the maximum implementation of the planned targets under the condition of full employment, i.e. when there are neither shortages nor surpluses of labour, means of production and products.

Economic Growth A continuous increase in production, usually reflected in and measured by the (positive) RATE OF GROWTH of national income. The capitalist and Marxist interpretations of e.g. differ owing to the different approaches to the concept of NATIONAL INCOME. According to the former interpretation, e.g. encompasses not only the production of goods, but also all services as long as they are explicitly or implicitly paid for. On the other hand, Marxists define national income as embracing MATERIAL PRODUCTION only, with the result that the output of non-productive services (i.e. those other than transport, communications and trade) is not included. In the traditional Marxist approach to e.g. emphasis was placed on EXTENSIVE GROWTH, and production in DEPARTMENT I of the economy grew faster than in Department II. However, since the ECONOMIC REFORMS of the 1960s, most Socialist countries have recognized the importance of INTENSIVE GROWTH (increases in productivity) and in some years have planned for the output of consumer goods (especially industrial consumer goods, called GROUP 'B' OUTPUT) to grow faster than that of producer goods (Group 'A' output).

Economic Harmony A concept established by the French economist, F. Bastiat (1801–50) in *Economic Harmonies* (1848). He maintained that, given private property, free enterprise and the unrestricted operation of the market mechanism, economic processes tend towards equalization, harmonious relations and the improvement of the whole of society. His concept reflected the views widely accepted by the supporters of *LAISSEZ-FAIRE* capitalism. Marxists deny the validity of the concept and its underlying conditions. In Marxist philosophy, the essence

of existence is not harmony and equilibrium but conflict, where contradictions (thesis and antithesis) lead to disequilibrium. Thus private property and free enterprise generate ANTAGONISTIC PRODUCTION RELATIONS, the CLASS STRUGGLE and REVOLUTIONS, and the free market mechanism begets the ANARCHY OF PRODUCTION and crises.

Economic Incentives See MATERIAL INCENTIVES.

Economic Interpretation of History See ECONOMIC MATERIALISM, HISTORICAL MATERIALISM.

Economic Law In its most general sense, a regularity, tendency or principle operating in the economic sphere. The Marxist conceptualization of, and approach to e.l. is more complex than is usual in other interpretations. First of all, Marxists distinguish between general e.l., which operate under any economic system, and special e.l. which apply only to a particular SOCIO-ECONOMIC FORMATION. The former is illustrated by the law of SURPLUS VALUE (that labour in addition to INDISPENSABLE PRODUCT also creates SURPLUS PRODUCT) and the law of increasing labour productivity and social development (that the former is a condition of development of the latter in any society). The LAW OF CAPITALIST ACCUMULATION and the law of the DECLINING PROFIT RATE are peculiar to capitalism, whilst the BASIC LAW OF SOCIALISM and the LAW OF PLANNED PROPORTIONATE DEVELOPMENT are applicable to socialism. In the economic practice of the Socialist countries, the attitudes and approach to e.l. have also displayed certain peculiarities. Some early Marxist economists, notably ROSA LUXEMBURG and N. I. BUKHARIN, argued that e.l. would not operate in the Socialist planned economy. But that view was later refuted, amongst others by Lenin and even by Stalin in his later years. The concept of the e.l. has been used in the Socialist countries with the following meanings: 1. as an apologetic justification by economic writers of a current economic policy or practice, by elevating them to the rank of 'laws'; 2. as a legal regulation governing major economic practices applicable to the whole economy; 3. as a normative principle discovered or to be discovered by theoreticians to implement long-run economic objectives ('the purpose of Socialist political economy is to change economic laws, not to adopt them wholesale from the capitalist system'); and 4. as a desirable objective of a crucial, long-run economic and social significance, to which economic policies and practices must be subordinated (e.g. the BASIC ECONOMIC LAW OF SOCIALISM).

Economic Man A model of man whose economic behaviour is assumed to be individualistic and rational and directed towards the maximization of his economic gain or satisfaction at the smallest possible cost. The concept was developed by J. S. Mill (1806–73), although the idea can be traced back at least to Adam Smith (1723–90). This model is not acceptable to Marxists, as in their view it attaches too much importance to subjectively conditioned motives (SUBJECTIVISM), the selfish acquisitive instinct and INDIVIDUALISM in general. As such, it is reflective of the set of values convenient to and accepted by the BOURGEOISIE. The E.M. so understood disregards such human needs as security, membership of a group, social recognition and creativity and thus contrasts with the NEW COMMUNIST MAN.

Economic Materialism A philosophical and social theory maintaining that the economic factor is the only determinant of society's development. The main proponents of this theory were E. BERNSTEIN, M. N. Pokrovsky (1868–1932) and the advocates of LEGAL MARXISM and ECONOMISM, who tried to pass e.m. for a sociological and historical aspect of Marxism. MARXISM-LENINISM is opposed to e.m., regarding it as a one-sided and 'vulgar' interpretation of history and a misrepresentation of Marxian HISTORICAL MATERIALISM. In the Marxist-Leninist interpretation, it is emphasized that although the economic factor is a primary determinant, political and social ideas and institutions also play an important part, and in fact the latter also influence the former. The logic behind this revolutionary Marxist view is to justify the creation of disciplined and devoted Communist parties, consciously working towards the speeding up of the PROLETARIAN REVOLUTION, the subsequent DICTATORSHIP OF THE PROLETARIAT and the planned accelerated advance to FULL COMMUNISM – all of which are regarded as co-determinants of social development.

Economic Normatives A term used in the Socialist centrally planned economies, meaning instruments employed by the state to induce or discourage actions of producing and trading entities and consumers in desired directions. E.n., which contrast with DIRECTIVES, allow greater freedom of decision-making at the microeconomic level and have been substantially extended since the ECONOMIC REFORMS. They include interest rates, depreciation rates, CAPITAL CHARGES, various taxes, quality and novelty mark-ups, trade margins, differentiated wage rates and bonuses.

Economic Plan A formal and consistent document setting out a programme of objectives of economic pursuits and the means of its implementation over a particular period. In a capitalist economy, the e.p. (if there is one at all) is usually expressed in general terms and is not compulsory, so that the market mechnism still basically operates. Under Socialism, the e.p. is prepared ('constructed') more systematically, it is comprehensive and detailed and is mostly directive (compulsory, enforced by legal sanctions). Basically, it replaces the market mechanism, although the market may be tolerated to operate in a restricted fashion in the distribution of labour and consumer goods. As normally understood it covers the whole economy, but there are also regional, branch-of-the-economy and individual enterprises'

161

plans. According to the period covered, there are long-term (15–20 year), medium (5–7 year) and short-term (1–12 month) plans, the medium-term plan being basic (FIVE-YEAR PLAN). The most characteristic feature of the e.p. is its TARGETS and other PLAN INDICATORS. The internal consistency of the e.p. is ensured by MATERIAL BALANCES, but the most effective (or efficient) plan can be arrived at only by OPTIMAL PLANNING. In Yugoslavia, the e.p. is called the SOCIAL PLAN. Also ECONOMIC PLANNING, PLAN IMPLEMENTATION.

Economic Planning The system of managing and administering the economy on the basis of an *ex-ante* ECONOMIC PLAN. E.p. is now practised in most capitalist countries in one form or another and in all the Socialist countries. But it is different under Socialism. As it is based on the SOCIAL OWNERSHIP OF THE MEANS OF PRODUCTION, it is pursued on a continuous, systematic, comprehensive and directive basis. It virtually supplants the market mechanism and it is a vital instrument of the economic and social transformation of the country. Its major objectives include economic stability, FULL EMPLOYMENT and the maximum feasible RATES OF ECONOMIC GROWTH. In each Socialist country, there is a well developed institutional set-up for e.p., headed by the STATE PLANNING COMMISSION (its official wording may differ from one country to another). Socialist e.p. is governed by the following five basic principles or procedures: 1. the formulation of general guidelines by the Communist party; 2. DEMOCRATIC CENTRALISM; 3. the determination of key and secondary priorities; 4. PLAN CONSISTENCY; and 5. financial correspondence to real economic processes, to facilitate control and motivation. E.p. may be pursued on a highly centralized hierarchical and directive basis, or be substantially decentralized, and largely non-compulsory. Historically, there has been a tendency for the former to be replaced by the latter, especially since the ECONOMIC REFORMS. Also CENTRALIZED DIRECTIVE SYSTEM OF PLANNING AND MANAGEMENT, INDICATIVE PLANNING, 'PLANNING FROM ABOVE', 'PLANNING FROM BELOW', SOCIAL PLANNING.

Economic Problems of Socialism in the USSR A short book written by STALIN and published in 1952, six months before his death. It is devoted to some problems of socialist political economy and the transition from socialism to communism. He formulated several economic 'laws' or rather his generalizations and other propositions concerning socialism and capitalism. They are as follows: 1. the BASIC ECONOMIC LAW OF SOCIALISM (increasing wants and increasing capacity of the socialist economy to satisfy them); 2. the law of the PLANNED PROPORTIONATE DEVELOPMENT; 3. the BASIC ECONOMIC LAW OF CONTEMPORARY CAPITALISM; and 4. the LAW OF THE CONCORDANCE OF PRODUCTION RELATIONS WITH THE NATURE OF PRODUCTION FORCES. He also dealt with the following questions: the continued production for the market under socialism; the extent of the operation of the LAW OF VALUE in the socialist economy; the equalization or rural and urban and physical and mental labour; the GENERAL CRISIS OF CAPITALISM; the inevitability of wars amongst capitalist countries; the role of the pacifist movement; contradictions between PRODUCTION FORCES and PRODUCTION RELATIONS under socialism; the objective nature of economic laws and the emergence of two 'parallel markets' (capitalist and socialist) in the international scene.

Economic Reforms A general term for the liberal reforms in the economies of the European Socialist countries except Albania. The reforms began in Yugoslavia in 1950, in the German DR, Hungary, Poland and the USSR in 1962–63 and Bulgaria, Czechoslovakia and Romania in 1967–68. Although there have been occasional anti-reform reactions, the reforms are still continuing, but, at a different pace and time in each country. The common elements of the reforms have been: 1. the replacement of the centralized, directive and detailed system of planning by less prescriptive plans with a greater participation for enterprises; 2. some decentralization of economic management and administration, so that enterprises and branch associations have greater independence of decision-making; 3. the official adoption of PROFIT as the main indicator of enterprise performance; 4. the strengthening of MATERIAL INCENTIVES to labour according to the quantity and quality of work; 5. some reactivation of markets in shaping prices of specified classes of goods and services; 6. the reactivation of financial instruments, especially credit, INTEREST RATES, CAPITAL CHARGES, depreciation allowances and price mark-ups for quality and novelty; 7. the financing of investment predominatly from the enterprises' own liquid funds (SELF-FINANCING) and repayment bank credits, rather than from non-repayable budgetary allocations; 8. liberalization in agriculture, especially the discontinuation of the COMPULSORY DELIVERY OF FARM PRODUCTS to the state, increases in the prices of agricultural products, some DECOLLECTIVIZATION, and better treatment of SUBSIDIARY PLOTS; 9. some reactivation of private enterprise in selected spheres – crafts, market gardening, catering, personal services, retailing; 10. some de-insulation of domestic markets from foreign markets, greater participation in the international division of labour and greater freedom allowed to enterprises engaging in foreign trade. The extent of the reforms in the different countries is indicated in the following descending order: Yugoslavia, Hungary, Czechoslovakia, Bulgaria, Poland, the German DR, the USSR, Romania. China for a long time was highly critical of the reforms in the European Socialist countries, but after the assumption of power by HUA KUO-FENG in 1976, similar reforms have been initiated.

Economic Romanticism A term used by Marxists to describe economic theorizing by idealist social reformers in the first half of the 19th c. on the plight of the impoverished gentry, small producers and the working class as a consequence of the development of the factory system under capitalism. A. H. Müller (1779–1829) in Germany, J. Ch. L. S. de Sismondi (1773–1842) in France and J. Ruskin (1819–1900) in Britain were its chief exponents. They idealized the domestic system and medieval guilds, blamed INDUSTRIAL CAPITALISM for the exacerbation of social conflicts, and consequently advocated measures to impede the CAPITALIST MODE OF PRODUCTION and a return to the pre-capitalist system of production and social relations. E.r. aroused a good deal of interest among anarchists, syndicalists and populists (incl. the *NARODNIKS* in Tsarist Russia). But Marxists rejected e.r. as utopian, because in their view: 1. the capitalist mode of production was historically inevitable; 2. capitalism represented a higher SOCIO-ECONOMIC FORMATION than the preceding systems; and 3. given further development, capitalism would create the conditions of its own destruction and pave the way for socialism. An exhaustive critique of e.r. was presented by Lenin in *A Characterization of Economic Romanticism* (1897).

Economics and Politics In Marxist theory and practice, the two facets of social life which are treated in their mutual interdependence and as an inseparable unity. The economic system constitutes the BASE which determines the political SUPERSTRUCTURE. Politics, being a reflection of the methods of production and other economic relations in a given SOCIO-ECONOMIC FORMATION, is subordinated to the interests of the ruling class. Thus bourgeois p. aims at the perpetuation of the capitalist system and the exploitation of the working class at home and weaker nations abroad. In a Socialist country, politics is directed towards the consolidation and perpetuation of the power of the working class and accelerating the economic and social advancement to FULL COMMUNISM. But if e. and p. are in conflict with each other, the latter has to prevail. Lenin called p. 'the concentrated form of economics' and he insisted that it is the Communist party and the state that determine economic development. An extreme view is represented by Mao Tse-tung's tenet of 'POLITICS IN COMMAND'.

Economism A doctrine advocated by a faction ('Economists') in the RUSSIAN SOCIAL-DEMOCRATIC LABOUR PARTY at the turn of the century, emphasizing that the working class should concentrate its struggle on the economic front for the immediate improvement of its material conditions (higher wages, shorter hours, better working conditions), to the disregard or at least postponement of political action. The term e. was first used and popularized by Lenin, who attacked it in *A Protest by Russian Social-Democrats* (1899) and *WHAT IS TO BE DONE?* (1902). He described it as a form of OPPORTUNISM and REVIONISM, as he considered political struggle and the cause of revolution to be equally or more important. The use of the term was revived by the Chinese Communist Party in 1967, during the GREAT PROLETARIAN CULTURAL REVOLUTION, when a campaign was staged against the pressure for higher wages, bonuses and better working conditions to the disregard of ideological fervour.

Effectiveness A term used to describe microeconomic efficiency in a Socialist centrally planned economy. It is the most efficacious production in a particular enterprise or of a particular product within the framework imposed and regulated from above, in respect of the planned allocation of resources, the pricing of resources and output, wage scales, employment laws and various directive plan indicators. If the factors affecting enterprises were determined in competitive markets, e. at the microeconomic level would correspond to macroeconomic efficiency.

Efficiency Prices Prices which reflect relative scarcities, i.e. cost-preference relations, which as such are conducive to the highest possible economic efficiency (at least in the short run). E.p. exist, as a rule, in capitalist market economies, where the conditions of supply and demand determine prices in the market. The Socialist centrally planned economies have no e.p. in this sense, as free markets do not operate in these countries. Also, most prices are fixed on a planned basis by reference to a variety of considerations, of which scarcity (even if it is known) may be only one of many. E.p. can be arrived at in three types of markets.: 1. the conventional free markets in capitalist countries; 2. trial-and-error SHADOW MARKETS; and 3. computer-simulated markets on a scientific basis with perfect information (which could produce OPTIMAL PRICES). None of these markets fully operates in any Socialist country.

Egalitarianism A social doctrine postulating a political and economic system which would ensure complete or reasonable equality of all the members of society with respect to legal status, human rights, property ownership, income and other significant conditions of life. The doctrine is based on the premise that people are essentially equal, that their needs are similar and that, for the sake of SOCIAL JUSTICE and maximum social welfare, the state should ensure the equality of opportunity and living conditions for its citizens. Amongst the most notable advocates of e. were T. More (1478–1535), C. H. SAINT-SIMON (Saint-Simonism), CH. FOURIER, R. OWEN, K. MARX and F. ENGELS. In general, the scope for the implementation of e. is limited in a capitalist society, owing to the unequal distribution of (private) property, the existence of non-labour incomes, sensitivity to vested interests and INDIVIDUALISM. Although in the popular view communism implies complete equality, most leading Marxist thinkers as well as Communist policy-makers reject its validity or advisability in practice. Marx himself recognized that one person was superior to another, physically or mentally or both. Lenin as well as Stalin opposed the extreme form of e. advocated by LEFT

COMMUNISTS. It has been widely accepted officially in the Socialist countries that under SOCIALISM (the transitional stage to FULL COMMUNISM) differentiation in the occupational status and income is inevitable. In the social interest, e. is vaguely assumed to be achieved under full communism, but even so, distribution will not be totally uniform, rather 'according to needs'. E. is opposite to ELITISM and SOCIAL STRATIFICATION.

Egyptian Communist Party See COMMUNIST PARTY OF EGYPT.

'Eight-Legged Essay' An expression popularized by Mao Tse-tung in his speech ('Oppose the Party "Eight-Legged Essay"') to the Party cadres in Yenan on 8 Feb. 1942. He referred to a pamphlet circulated by an influential group in the Chinese Communist Party, propagating a greater sophistication in literary work along eight lines. Mao's expression alludes to a complicated eight-section diagram which in old China had been used in Confucian dogmatic teachings, in civil service examinations and as a guessing game. It was noted for its complex arbitrary strokes in each section looking ugly and creeping like an octopus. Mao attacked the pamphlet and presented it as a symbol of SECTARIANISM, excessive FORMALISM and SUBJECTIVISM which, in his view, had dangerously crept into the CCP. He described these three vices as 'monsters', 'rats' and 'anti-Marxist', all directed against the FOURTH OF MAY MOVEMENT, 'benefiting only the exploiting classes'. He countered the E.-l.e. with eight indictments: 1. it is empty and long-winded; 2. it is pretentious; 3. it is written at random, without taking its objective into consideration; 4. it is dry and flat in style; 5. it follows pedantic classification; 6. it is irresponsible, harming everybody; 7. it is poisonous to the Party and endangering the revolution; and 8. it is poisonous to the nation.

Eight-point Charter for Agriculture (in China) A programme of the intensification and modernization in Chinese agriculture introduced in the early 1960s, prompted by widespread failures necessitating large imports of grains from capitalist countries. The improvement followed eight lines: 1. irrigation and water conservancy; 2. the rational distribution of fertilizers; 3. soil improvement; 4. the upgrading of seeds; 5. close planting; 6. crop protection against diseases and pests; 7. better farming implements; and 8. adequate field management.

Eighty-per-cent Communism A workable type of the Communist economic and social system advocated by some liberal Marxists, basically Communist but retaining some elements peculiar to capitalism. The proportion of productive capital socially owned, of agricultural land occupied by state and collective farms, of SOCIAL CONSUMPTION in total consumption and of prices fixed by the state would, in each case, be about 80 per cent. The balance would essentially operate like a capitalist market economy, subject to general central control to ensure its operation in conformity with social interest. The supporters of the proposed system believe that it is more realistic and less wasteful than FULL COMMUNISM would be. Marxism-Leninism rejects this idea, regarding it merely as a transitional stage to full communism, or otherwise a form of REVISIONISM.

Eisenachers The colloquial term applied to the members of the SOCIAL-DEMOCRATIC WORKERS' PARTY OF GERMANY, founded at the Conference of the General German Workers' Association at Eisenach in 1869 by left-wingers led by A. BEBEL and W. LIEBKNECHT. In 1875 at the Gotha Congress, the E. reunited with the G.G.W.A. and formed a united party under the name of the Socialist Workers' Party of Germany.

Eisenhower Doctrine See DULLES-EISENHOWER DOCTRINE.

Ekaterinburg Also spelled Yekaterin-

Ekonomsovet

burg, a city in the Ural region of Russia, where NICHOLAS II, the last Tsar, and his family were executed by the Bolsheviks in July 1918. In 1924 the city was renamed Sverdlovsk, in tribute to a Bolshevik revolutionary leader Ya. M. Sverdlov. It is a centre of iron and steel industry and engineering, with a population of 1.1m. (1978).

Ekonomsovet Abbreviation for *Ekonomicheskii Sovet*, in Russian meaning the 'Economic Council'. It was established in 1937 and was the highest economic institution in the USSR. It replaced the Council of Labour and Defence and had authority over the *Gosplan*. The E. was dissolved in 1941.

Electoral Front A general term for electoral co-operation amongst left-wing political parties, which may also include CENTRISM parties or groups not opposed to socialism and communism. It is better known as the POPULAR FRONT or UNITED FRONT.

Electrification The development of the electric power industry and its distribution network in the economy. The crucial role of electricity has been recognized by Communist leaders ever since Lenin's launching of the long-term e. plan in 1921 (*GOELRO*). Lenin popularized the phrase, 'Communism is Soviet power plus electrification of the whole country'. E. has been embraced by the Communist leaders for the following reasons: 1. as the basic element of industrialization; 2. as the symbol of Communist modernization and dynamism; 3. the promotion of literacy and reading capacity for propaganda literature in the long evenings; 4. the dissemination of propaganda through radio, cinema and television; and 5. as an important element of the increasing standard of living. In the USSR, the output of electricity rose from less than 3,000m. kWh in 1916 to 1,300,000m. kWh in the late 1970s. The Soviets have the largest thermal power station in the world – at Krivoi Rog (of 3.0m. kW capacity) and the three

largest hydroelectric power stations in the world – Shushenskoe (6.4m. kW), Boguchansk (6.4m. kW) and Krasnoyarsk (6.0m. kW). The Socialist bloc now generates over 23 per cent of world electric power (compared with its claimed share of 38 per cent of the world's industrial output).

'Elements against the Three' In China during the GREAT PROLETARIAN CULTURAL REVOLUTION, a condemnatory description used by individuals and groups opposing 'Mao Tse-tung, the Chinese Communist Party and socialism'. They were accused of REVISIONISM and even participation in forms of COUNTER-REVOLUTION, and were subjected to public humiliation, cruel repression and other forms of persecution.

'Eleventh Thesis on Feuerbach' The last and most famous proposition postulated by Marx in *THESES ON FEUERBACH*, which reads: 'The philosophers have only interpreted the world in various ways; the point is to change it.' It symbolizes the Marxist insistence on the revolutionary transformation of society.

Elite A 'superior' or privileged group, noted for special qualities such as race, birth, wealth, education occupational status or achievement, regarded as important in a particular society or organization. In Marxist sociology, the term has a depreciative meaning usually applied to the ruling class and separated from the majority of the population, especially the working class. HISTORICAL MATERIALISM treats historical development as a process of struggle for power between the old and new elites, representing different social classes or interests. It may be noted here that each Socialist country has its own e., viz. the top hierarchy in the Party and state apparatus, enjoying a good deal of power and privileges. In addition, there are technocrats and talented and successful professionals, such as top architects, engineers, scientists, writers, actors and so on. Also CADRES, ELITISM.

166

Elitism Social and political theories, views or practices postulating the division of society into the ruling elite and the ruled masses as desirable or at least inevitable, and as such, is opposite to EGALITARIAN-ISM. The supporters of e. argue that different persons are essentially unequal owing to racial, ethnic or class origin or background. Marxism is strongly opposed to e. as it is in conflict with equality and social justice as well as being embraced by the propertied and ruling classes as a convenient justification for the domination of the oppressed masses. But it may be pointed out here that e. is implicitly subscribed to in the Socialist countries, too. Power is basically exercised by the Communist party, 'the vanguard of the working class', to the exclusion of other political parties. In fact, the crucial decisions are made exclusively by the Party's top elite generally known as the POLITBURO, removed from the rank and file of the Party membership and even more so from the rest of the population. This fact was subjected to searching criticism by Mao Tse-tung in the GREAT PROLETARIAN CULTURAL REVOLUTION ('BOMBARD THE HEADQUARTERS') and by M. DJILAS.

Emancipation of Labour Group The first organized Russian Marxist circle and the earliest precursor of the Communist Party of the Soviet Union. The Group was formed by G. V. PLEKHANOV as one of the organizers in Geneva in 1883. Although its leading members were *NARODNIKS*, it soon adopted a Marxist revolutionary programme, translated the works of Marx and Engels into Russian and distributed them in Russia. The Group joined the SECOND INTERNATIONAL in which it opposed the *Narodniks* and REVISIONISM. However, differences began to emerge and most of its active members, including Plekhanov, turned to a moderate course. The E.L.G. participated in the foundation of the RUSSIAN SOCIAL-DEMOCRATIC LABOUR PARTY in Russia in 1898.

Embodied Labour See MATERIALIZED LABOUR.

Embourgeoisement Acquiring characteristics peculiar to the BOURGEOISIE. The term was established by ROSA LUXEM-BURG in *Crisis of Social Democracy* (1916). She referred to the greatly improved material and political conditions of the working class in Britain in the four decades preceding W.W.I which led to its e. and removed the immediate need for a PROLETARIAN REVOLUTION. The use of the term has been extended by revolutionary Marxists to describe the compromising attitudes of the exclusive trade unions and professional associations and social-democrats supporting co-operation with the bourgeois state. More recently, since the ECONOMIC REFORMS of the 1960s, the term has been applied to the general public in the European Socialist countries who are pressing for immediate improvements in living conditions and losing their interest in ideological fervour. The most conspicuous development along these lines is the RED BOURGEOISIE.

Emergence Theory Also known as emergent evolutionism, a philosophical theory of the history of nature, first developed in England in the 1920s (by S. Alexander and C. Lloyd Morgan). In contrast to the Darwinian theory of mechanistic NATURAL SELECTION, the e.t. explains new characteristics and species as products of a sudden emergence without apparent causes, rather than as an outcome of gradual evolution through the elimination of unnecessary features. In Marxist philosophy, the e.t. is rejected as unscientific, akin to AGNOSTICISM, IRRATIONAL-ISM and NEO-REALISM, and as such, inconsistent with DIALECTICAL MATERIALISM. Marxists point out that the e.t. in fact turns to MYSTICISM, as it sees development as a discontinuous process whereby the variety, diversity and complexity of the species are explained by forces beyond man's comprehension.

Empiricism An important movement in philosophy, maintaining that the source of cognition and knowledge of existence (reality) is experience (and consequently is

Empirio-criticism

opposite to both RATIONALISM and IR-RATIONALISM). There are two major variants of e.; *idealistic e.* (represented by D. Hume, E. March and A. A. BOGDANOV) limits experience to the totality of sensory impressions or images, denying that material nature is the basis of experience. On the other hand, *materialistic e.* (F. Bacon, T. Hobbes, J. Locke) emphasizes the role of material nature as the basis of sensory experience. Marxist DIALECTICAL MATERIALISM rejects the validity of the former and gives qualified acceptance to the latter. But in the Marxist view, bourgeois materialistic e. disregards the role of abstraction, ideas and theory in cognition and knowledge (SENSUALISM being its extreme version), whilst dialectical materialism stresses the importance of progression from sensation to reasoning and practical testing or verification, as necessary steps in the process of meaningful experience.

Empirio-criticism An anti-Marxist philosophical movement, emphasizing the role of 'critical experience' or the union of the knowing mind and the known world. It was created in Germany and Austria in the second half of the 19th c. by R. Avenarius (1843–96) and E. MACH, and further supported by the Russian philosopher A. A. BOGDANOV. The founders of e.-c. maintained that the object (the world) is non-existent without the subject (consciousness, sensations) and that there are no objective natural laws, i.e. that sensations are primary whilst the material world is secondary. E.-c. was attacked by Lenin in his major philosophical work *MATERIALISM AND EMPIRIO-CRITICISM* (1909), accusing it of SUBJECTIVISM, FIDEISM and IDEALISM in general. He insisted that MATTER is primary, whilst sensations and ideas are secondary, having been derived from the material world, and that DIALECTICAL MATERIALISM and HISTORICAL MATERIALISM represent the only valid interpretations.

Empirio-monism A variant school of philosophy of EMPIRIO-CRITICISM, em-

phasizing 'uniform experience' and propagated in Russia by A. A. BOGDANOV (mainly in his *Empirio-Monism*, 1905–6). E.-m. attaches central significance to 'collective consciousness' as the creator of nature (in contrast to 'individual consciousness' postulated by R. Avenarius and E. Mach in empirio-critcism). The physical world is understood as 'socially-organized experience of collective mankind'. Lenin (in *MATERIALISM AND EMPIRIO-CRITICISM*) attacked e.-m., describing it as a philosophy of subjective IDEALISM and a desperate search for god.

Empirio-Symbolism A philosophical theory representing a version of EMPIRIO-CRITICISM, developed in Russia by P. Juszkiewicz before W.W.I. It interprets images and concepts in experience as being merely 'symbols', and not reflections of the material world. Marxist philosophy is opposed to e.-s., regarding it as being akin to subjective *IDEALISM* and the HIEROGLYPHIC THEORY OF COGNITION denying the objective reality of the external world. As such e.-s. is in direct conflict with the Marxist REFLECTION THEORY.

Employers and Workmen Act (of 1975) In Britain, the Act of Parliament which recognized the equality of organized capital and labour before law. It is one of the important landmarks in the history of the working class in the West, as it gave workers the power of organizing various actions associated with strikes, including picketing.

Employment Engagement in working capacity directed towards the production of goods or services for remuneration. In its broader sense, it includes all the working population, whether self-employed or as employees, whilst in its narrow meaning only the latter category is understood. In a capitalist market economy, the maintenance of a high level of employment is one of its inherent problems. No capitalist country has had continuous FULL EMPLOYMENT. In the Socialist planned economies, continuous full employment is the rule (with the exception of Yugoslavia), where the rights to e. is guaranteed in Constitutions and where work is regarded as a duty. Owing to central economic planning and the absence of non-labour incomes, frictional unemployment is usually less than 1.0 per cent (compared with about 2.0 per cent in capitalist market economies). Most socialist countries in fact experience shortages of labour.

Energism A philosophical doctrine which rejects the concept of matter, and instead explains existence and phenomena in nature and society in terms of energy and movement. Energy is studied as something subjective and dependent on human consciousness. The doctrine was first formulated by the German Nobel prize-winning chemist, W. Ostwald (1853–1932) in *The Conquest of Scientific Materialism* (1895). In the social sphere, some energetists (such as A. A. BOG-DANOV) explain the transformation of society as an increase or decrease of energy in particular directions. Marxists reject e., considering it reactionary and unscientific and describe it as a version of PHYSICAL IDEALISM, a direct contrast with HISTORICAL MATERIALISM and DIALECTICAL MATERIALISM. Lenin attacked e. in his major philosophical work, *MATERIALISM AND EMPIRIO-CRITICISM*.

Engels, Friedrich (1820–95) A German philosopher, economist, sociologist and military writer, co-founder of SCIENTIFIC COMMUNISM and a devoted friend and collaborator of K. MARX. Born into a well-to-do manufacturing family, he embarked upon a military career in 1841. Despite his resignation in 1842 he continued his military interest (and was nicknamed 'General' by his close friends). He then moved to Manchester, to one of his father's textile factories, and came into contact with the English working class movement. He met Marx through working for the *DEUTSCH-FRANZÖSISCHE JAHRBÜCHER* in Paris in 1844 and often assisted him financially. Together they wrote *The HOLY FAMILY* (in Paris, 1845), directed against the YOUNG HEGELIANS, *The GERMAN IDEOLOGY* (in Brussels, 1845–46), criticizing the philosophy of L. FEUERBACH, M. Stirner, ultra left-wing socialism and Feuerbach's socialist followers and a pamphlet *The COMMUNIST MANIFESTO* (1848). E. participated in the February 1849 uprising in Germany and after its collapse he escaped to Switzerland and then lived mostly in England. He was one of the founders and intellectual leaders of the FIRST INTERNATIONAL. He delivered a moving speech at Marx's burial at Highgate Cemetery in London in March 1883 and prepared volumes II and III of *Capital* for publication. In addition to the joint works already mentioned, E.'s most important publications were: The *Condition of the Working Class in England* (1845); *ANTI-DÜHRING* (1877–78); *DIALECTICS OF NATURE* (1873–83); *ORIGIN OF THE FAMILY, PRIVATE PROPERTY AND THE STATE* (1884); *Socialism: Utopian and Scientific* (1884); and *Ludwig Feuerbach and the End of Classical German Philosophy* (1888).

Enlarged Reproduction See EXPANDED REPRODUCTION.

Enragés ('Madmen', in French) Name given to the reckless revolutionaries led by J. Roux and J. Varlet in the FRENCH REVOLUTION in 1789, who wished to see a more radical upheaval, instead of merely a BOURGEOIS-DEMOCRATIC REVOLUTION. They also pressed for immediate price control and curbs on speculation. Their impact on the outcome of the Revolution was minimal (although at one stage they entered into an alliance with the JACOBINS). The name was revived during the FRENCH STUDENT REVOLUTION in May 1968 by the extremist students at the Sorbonne led by Daniel Cohn-Bendit.

Enterprise A term used in the Socialist countries in lieu of 'firm', denoting an economic entity with a distinct legal and organizational status engaged in the production of goods or services for sale. An e. is headed by a DIRECTOR, is based on the social ownership of the means of production (vested in the state or a co-operative), is responsible for the preparation and implementation of its own plan, carries on its operations on the basis of ECONOMIC ACCOUNTABILITY and is subject to various forms of direction, supervision and auditing by state organs. But otherwise the e. has a good deal of independence and is expected to maximize its profits. Each e. must have an account with one designated branch of the State Bank (or some other specified bank), and most of its financial transactions have to be carried out in CASHLESS SETTLEMENTS. Further, each e. has to operate several earmarked 'funds' supervised by the bank, such as the WAGE FUND, SOCIO-CULTURAL AND HOUSING FUND, MATERIAL INCENTIVES FUND, Reserve Fund. In Yugoslavia the officially accepted name for most enterprises is the BASIC ORGANIZATION OF ASSOCIATED LABOUR.

Enterprise Cost of Production Another, less frequently used, description of PRIME COST.

Enterprise Fund A fund maintained by enterprises in the Socialist countries for financing individual and collective incentives and services to the members of the enterprise (bonuses in cash or kind, housing, child care, social amenities and cultural activities). The E.F. is replenished out of the enterprise's profits according to strict rules laid down by the authorities. The incentive role of the E.F. has been considerably increased since the ECONOMIC REFORMS involved the linking of enterprise profits to bonuses. In some Socialist countries the E.F. may be known as the 'Director's Fund' or 'Material Incentives Fund'.

Enterprise Planning See OPERATIONAL PLANNING.

Enterprise Profit A general term used in Socialist enterprise accounting which denotes that the profit belongs to the enterprise concerned, and not to private capitalist shareholders. Since the ECONOMIC REFORMS in the European Socialist countries e.p. has been accepted as a criterion for enterprise performance and a basis for MATERIAL INCENTIVES to the enterprise personnel. In its more technical sense, e.p. means 'net profit' (after taxes and other compulsory charges are deducted from the GROSS PROFIT).

Entropy A theory proposed by a German physicist, R. Clausius (1822–88) in 1850, asserting that there is a tendency in nature for increasing disorder. Marxism rejects this view, as it implies that the universe will eventually reach a stage of disintegration and collapse. E. is in conflict with DIALECTICAL MATERIALISM, which insists that phenomena occur in an orderly fashion according to definite laws in progressive patterns from lower to higher stages within an infinite time scheme (no beginning and no end).

Entryism A tactic employed by non-ruling Communist parties, whereby Communists infiltrate an organization. In many cases, owing to their superior preparation, devotion and discipline, they come to occupy influential positions. They may destroy the organization or operate it as a Communist 'front organization'. The practice of e. is also known as 'boring from within'.

Epiphenomenalism A psychological and philosophical theory, attributing all mental phenomena to physiological causes in the brain or the central nervous system and denying any effect of the mind on the body. Thus, psychological behaviour is interpreted as a surface appearance ('epiphenomena') of physiological processes. Consequently, the body is viewed as an autonomous system. H. Maudsley (1834–1918) and S. H. Hodgson (1832–1912) were amongst the best known exponents of e. Although e. is sometimes seen as an extreme form of materialism, it is only partly accepted by Marxists. They agree that psychological phenomena are basically determined by physiological processes in the brain and the higher nervous system. But they also insist that the mind interacts with the body whereby the latter is affected by the former.

Epistemology The study of the theory of knowledge concerned with man's capacity for acquiring the knowledge of reality and attaining truth. It is also known as the theory of cognition, the science of knowledge or gneseology. E. may be approached from the standpoints of either IDEALISM or MATERIALISM. In the idealistic interpretation knowledge is either: a reflection of the universal idea (OBJECTIVE IDEALISM); is created in the process of COGNITION (SUBJECTIVE IDEALISM); or it is denied that man is capable of knowing the truth (AGNOSTICISM). Marxism rejects all idealistic interpretations, regarding them as unscientific, reactionary and detached in their knowledge of the external world and its laws. Consequently the idealistic views deny the possibility of improvement of society through development and revolutionary change. On the other hand, DIALECTICAL MATERIALISM insists that matter is real and independent of human consciousness and that sensation and perception are reflections of the material world. Knowledge and truth are products of the development of cognition through well defined stages and tested in practice as the ultimate criterion of truth. In contrast to the earlier versions of materialism, Marxist materialism emphasizes the decisive role of production and social activities in the process of the acquisition of knowledge of nature and society. Also SOCIOLOGY OF KNOWLEDGE, TRUTH.

Equalitarianism A less commonly used term for EGALITARIANISM. But see ABSOLUTE EQUALITARIANISM.

Equality See ABSOLUTE EQUALITARIANISM, EGALITARIANISM, SOCIAL EQUALITY, ULTRA-DEMOCRACY.

Equilibrium Theory of Society A doctrine according to which the laws of equilibrium operating in mechanical engineering can also be applied to social phenomena. The state of equilibrium is considered to be natural and normal, whilst movement and development are temporary and induced by external forces. It is further maintained that social conflicts are atributed to man's struggle with nature. Otherwise, social relations and development are seen as harmonious processes. Some of the leading exponents of this theory were A. Comte (1798–1857), H. Spencer (1820–1903), K. KAUTSKY and A. A. BOGDANOV. The theory also implies that social classes and imperialist powers must inevitably cooperate amongst themselves (ULTRA-IMPERIALISM). The e.t. of s. also maintains that it is natural for capitalism and socialism to coexist peacefully 'in equilibrium' and, moreover, that capitalism can evolve peacefully into socialism without any need for violence and proletarian revolution. The e.t. of s. is rejected in Marxist philosophy and sociology, as it is considered to be mechanistic and reactionary reflecting conservatism and OPPORTUNISM, and as such is inconsistent with Marxist DIALECTICS. Marxists maintain that movement and development are normal and not exceptional. They are inherent in nature as well as in society as a matter of the dialectical process of CONTRADICTIONS. In ANTAGONISTIC SOCIOECONOMIC FORMATIONS, especially CAPITALISM, there cannot be class harmony, as class interests are contradictory and irreconcilable. Societies do not develop by a smooth and harmonious process, but by periodical qualitative leaps and revolutions.

Equimarginal Principle A condition of the maximization of economic gain or welfare ('Pareto optimum'). On the one hand, it presupposes a pattern of the allocation of resources in such a way that the marginal value productivity of each factor is the same in all industries. On the other, the e.p. maintains that the pattern of consumption is such that the MARGINAL UTILITY for all households is the same. The principle implies perfect competion and

CONSUMER'S SOVEREIGNTY. The principle is not applied in the Socialist centrally planned economies owing to: 1. the ideological rejection of the MARGINAL ANALYSIS; 2. the virtual absence of SCARCITY (OR EFFICIENCY) PRICES of the factors of production (especially of non-labour resources); and 3. the virtual absence of free markets where equilibrium could be arrived at or verified. Theoretically, the e.p. could be applied in a Socialist economy under extensive computerization with ideal information, which would enable the determination of relative scarcities and OPTIMAL PRICES in simulated markets.

Erfurt Programme A programme of the SOCIAL-DEMOCRATIC PARTY OF GERMANY adopted at its Congress in Erfurt in Oct. 1891 and accepted up to 1921. It was drafted by K. KAUTSKY and was more Marxist in content than its predecessor, the GOTHA PROGRAMME. The E.P. stressed the role of the party in social progress and postulated universal suffrage, the secret ballot, proportional representation and the payment of the members of parliament. It served as a model for other member parties of the SECOND INTERNATIONAL. But the more radical members of the S.-D.P.G. opposed the Programme for its timidity and slowness and consequently seceded from the Party. Engels attacked the E.P. for embodying elements of OPPORTUNISM, REVISIONISM and its reconciliation with capitalism and the monarchy.

Essaires A colloquial abbreviated designation for the SOCIALIST REVOLUTIONARIES, a small political party in Russia which pressed for social reforms and opposed Tsarist autocracy. The E. played an important part in the February and Bolshevik Revolutions of 1917.

Establishment Economics Another, less frequently used, term for MAINSTREAM ECONOMICS.

Estates Social classes which prevailed during FEUDALISM and whose status was determined not only by occupation and property ownership, but also by law or custom. Each e. had its own legally defined privileges and obligations based on hereditary principles. Thus in feudal Russia (before 1861) there were four e.: 1. the nobility and gentry; 2. the clergy; 3. working townsmen (mainly craftsmen and merchants); and 4. the peasantry. The highest e. was exempt from taxes and corporal punishment, its members could be tried only by their own peers in special courts and were entitled to have estates with serfs. The clergy was also exempt from taxes and other dues. Only the lower e. were subject to taxes. E. survived in Russia in some respects up to the Bolshevik Revolution, but were finally abolished by a Decree of the All-Russian Central Executive Committee and the Council of People's Commissars of 10 Nov. (23 Nov. N.S.C.) 1917. The best known and most clearly defined e. historically were those in France before the Revolution of 1789–99: 1. the clergy; 2. the nobility; and 3. the 'Third Estate' (craftsmen, merchants, peasants, servants). E. contrast with SOCIAL CLASSES peculiar to capitalism and, although differing in economic and social status, are equal before the law. However, some socialist writers have facetiously referred to the PROLETARIAT as the 'Fourth Estate' and to the *LUMPEN-PROLETARIAT* as the 'Fifth Estate'. In Britain trade unions are sometimes described as the 'Fifth Estate'.

Estrangement of the Working Class See ALIENATION

Etatism The involvement of the state (*état* in French) in the economic and social operation of CAPITALISM, to remove its major abuses and weakness and promote stability and higher levels of economic development and social welfare. E. may assume the following forms: 1. a systematic regulation of the economic and social processes by legislative and administrative measures; 2. the nationalization of key industries (especially mining, iron and steel, vehicle-building, railways, airlines, banking, insurance) in many cases establishing state monopoly to the exclusion of private enterprise; 3. the establishment of state-owned corporations to compete with private enterprise; and 4. the operation of social welfare programmes through the redistribution of national income by progressive taxation and extensive social services. However, in each case the basic elements of capitalism are largely retained – the predominantly private ownership of the means of production, the market mechanism and democratic freedoms. The term is of French origin and was established in the 1920s. The opponents of e. have described it as the 'fetishism of the state, where man can hardly breathe'. The extreme cases of e. were represented by FASCISM in Italy (1921–43), Nazism in Germany (1933–45) and the wartime economies of the belligerent Western countries. E. is widely resorted to in the less-developed countries to speed up modernization and economic development and to promote social justice. Revolutionary Marxists are opposed to e. They consider it as a temporary palliative to disguise the fundamental weaknesses of capitalism and as a postponement of the need for PROLETARIAN REVOLUTION. Also STATE CAPITALISM, STATE INTERVENTION, STATE-MONOPOLY CAPITALISM.

Eternal Truths A philosophical concept used in METAPHYSICS, meaning that true facts are immutable. Although Marxism accepts obvious and simple features or facts as e.t. (such as the chemical composition of clearly defined substances), it is critical of such a view in relation to complex forms of existence or phenomena, whether in nature or society. In particular, Marxists stress that in society, the methods of production, social relations and concepts of morality and justice are not permanently fixed but are dynamic, capable of improvement by the process of natural development or revolutionary transformation. Engels (in *ANTI-DÜHRING*) pointed out that both nature and society experience progressive developments, which often invalidate old

truths or render them irrelevant. If development is arrested there is stagnation, which can only be temporary. Also ABSOLUTE TRUTH, RELATIVE TRUTH.

Ethics The science of morality, a major field of philosophy concerned with the study of moral behaviour and mutual obligations involving individuals and social groups, and with the nature of judgments about what is right and wrong. Pre-Marxist e. was preoccupied with eternal norms of conduct accepted as applicable to all persons, social groups, nations and stages of development. This approach is rejected in Marxist e., as developed by Marx, Engels, Trotsky, Lenin and other thinkers. They insist that it is only Marxism that has created a scientific system of e., emphasizing that e. is one of the forms of SOCIAL CONSCIOUSNESS and that morality is conditioned by the class structure of society. Marxism clearly separates e. from religion and stresses that moral norms are not absolute but change historically to suit different social classes. Consequently from the standpoint of Marxist e., the CLASS STRUGGLE, revolutionary violence, the expropriation of private owners (however hard-working and deserving) of the means of production, the DICTATORSHIP OF THE PROLETARIAT and the oppression of the opponents of the Communist rule are all morally good. On the other hand, the PARLIAMENTARY ROAD TO SOCIALISM, REVISIONISM and COUNTER-REVOLUTION are morally wrong. In the Socialist society, Marxist e. attaches great importance to the moral involvement of man in the social transformation of the country, work integrity, group loyalty and SOCIALIST INTERNATIONALISM.

Ethiopia, Socialist A medium-sized country in eastern central Africa (1.0m. sq. km. and 28.8m. people in 1978) ruled by an autocratic monarchist regime up to 1974, but proclaimed a 'Socialist State' in Dec. 1974. Before then the country had traditionally followed a Western right-wing orientation, but the new military regime has committed itself to a revolutionary

Marxist-Leninist line. It soon embarked upon the nationalization of banks, financial companies, insurance, larger industrial and commercial firms, rural and urban land and has made efforts to secularize all schools and develop peasant co-operatives and workers' councils. The Marxist course, internal political opposition (including dissident Marxist groups), secessionist struggle (in Eritrea and Ogaden) and the ambivalent American attitude led the government to seek closer relations with the Socialist countries. The USSR has provided massive military and technical aid, whilst Cuba has sent troops and advisers totalling some 17,000 in 1979. The country is ruled by a military regime (under national emergency conditions), politically representing the MARXIST ALL-ETHIOPIAN SOCIALIST MOVEMENT.

Eugenics A field of biology concerned with the study of the ways of improvement of physical and mental hereditary characteristics of man. The term (meaning 'good breeding') was introduced by F. Galton in 1869 (in *Hereditary Genius*) and was commonly used until 1906, when it was partly replaced by GENETICS. On the whole, Marxists reject e. regarding it as unscientific, reactionary and apologetic. It is seen as an attempt to justify the discriminatory racial, national and social policies of the ruling classes in pre-Socialist societies, and as such it became associated particularly with IMPERIALISM and FASCISM. E. emphasizes that physiological and mental inequalities among people are hereditary, which in turn are explicitly or implicitly used to rationalize the inevitability of the economic, social and cultural class differentiation. Marxism denies the validity of this interpretation, and instead attributes the emergence and existence of the lower social strata to the exploitation by the propertied ruling classes, i.e. to environmental factors. It further maintains that if the environment is changed, man also changes in response to it. Consequently, given appropriate conditions, which can be created by man, a CLASSLESS SOCIETY of equals can be evolved. In the

Marxist view, e. can be recognized as a socially legitimate field of study, if it is directed towards the perfection of human beings by the elimination of hereditary diseases and by the appropriate improvement of the upbringing, living and working environment. Viewed in this light, e. can be instrumental to the evolution of the NEW COMMUNIST MAN.

Eurobank Originally the telegraphic address of the Soviet-owned bank in Paris, the BANQUE COMMERCIALE POUR L'EUROPE DU NORD. It is widely believed that the name 'Eurodollar market' (now the 'Eurocurrency market') was derived from it.

Eurocommunism A liberal version of communism accepted by the leading Western European Communist parties since the mid-1970s, in their conviction that only this form of communism has an electoral chance of success and of implementation in the democratic West. The term was first mentioned by F. Barbieri in *Deutschlandarchiv* of April 1967, but it is commonly thought that the birth of E. was on 15 Nov. 1975, when the French and Italian Communist parties issued a joint declaration on the subject. The leading exponents of E. are G. MARCHAIS, E. BERLINGUER and S. CARRILLO, the leaders of the French, Italian and Spanish Communist parties, respectively. The joint French-Italian declaration of 15 Nov. 1975, described by some as the 'Eurocommunist Manifesto', made the following concessions towards the democratization and humanization of communism: 1. the plurality of political parties and the abandonment of the postulate of the DICTATORSHIP OF THE PROLETARIAT; 2. democratic elections and the democratic parliamentary road to socialism and communism; 3. the right to the existence and activities of opposition parties; and 4. the guarantee of civil liberties – the freedom of thought, expression, religion, the press, assembly, association, demonstration and of foreign travel. Eurocommunist views were further elaborated upon at the Conference of the

29 (East and West) European Communist and Workers' Parties in East Berlin in June 1976 (after two and a half years of negotiations). E. has reserved the right of selective criticism of the policies pursued by the Communist regimes in the Socialist countries, and in particular it regards the Soviet and Chinese policies as reflective of the early and crude stage of communism. The Soviet leadership has condemned E. as reactionary and another form of RE-VISIONISM. However, support for E. has been expressed in Yugoslavia and, although not easily articulated, there are unofficial pro-Eurocommunist sym-pathies in Eastern Europe, especially in Czechoslovakia, Hungary, Poland and Romania.

Eurosocialism A moderate form of social-ism, appropriate to developed democratic countries, and pursued or advocated by the leading socialist and social-democratic parties in Western Europe. The term, pat-terned on EUROCOMMUNISM, came into limited use in the mid-late 1970s, and was first popularized in the SOCIALIST INTER-NATIONAL. E. emphasizes SOCIAL JUSTICE but not complete SOCIAL EQUALITY, it ac-cepts regulated private enterprise and market mechanism, it supports selective RATIONALIZATION and INDICATIVE PLAN-NING and works towards the extension of social welfare programmes. It postulates a democratic party system and the PAR-LIAMENTARY ROAD TO SOCIALISM. It does not necessarily reject co-operation with Eurocommunism, but it is totally opposed to revolutionary Marxism, especially the CLASS STRUGGLE, PROLETARIAN REVOLU-TION and the DICTATORSHIP OF THE PRO-LETARIAT. The leading parties subscribing to E. are: the FRENCH SOCIALIST PARTY, the ITALIAN SOCIALIST PARTY, the LABOUR PARTY OF GREAT BRITAIN, the PARTY OF LABOUR OF THE NETHERLANDS, the SOCIAL-DEMOCRATIC PARTY OF DEN-MARK, the SOCIAL-DEMOCRATIC PARTY OF WEST GERMANY, the Social Democratic Workers' Party of Sweden, the SOCIALIST PARTY OF AUSTRIA and the SPANISH SOCIALIST WORKERS' PARTY.

'Evening out of Economic Levels' One of the objectives embodied in the BASIC PRINCIPLES OF THE INTERNATIONAL SOCIALIST DIVISION OF LABOUR, adopted by the member countries of the COUNCIL FOR MUTUAL ECONOMIC ASSISTANCE at its 15th Session in Dec. 1961. In Article 6, it recognized that, owing to pre-Socialist historical circumstances, different member countries are in different stages of economic development (which is typi-cal of capitalist economies). However, since Socialism demands equality amongst countries and in particular a uniform high standard of living which is aimed to be achieved under FULL COMMUNISM or at an earlier time, the RATE OF ECONOMIC GROWTH in the less developed member countries must be higher than in the more developed ones. This is to be achieved partly by the latter countries extending economic and technical aid to the former. One of the forms of this assistance was the free transfer of technology under the SOFIA RULES.

Evolution and Revolution Two ap-proaches to progressive development car-rying different ideological implications, especially in the social sphere. E. amounts to slow, gradual quantitative changes, whilst r. consists in a sudden, radical qual-itative innovation. In the orthodox Marx-ist view, the evolutionary process al-though important is insufficient to explain the emergence of qualitatively new phenomena, and at the same time denies the need for revolutionary upheavals. DIALECTICAL MATERIALISM is opposed to this monistic interpretation and insists that development is dualistic – both evolutionary as well as revolutionary. Evolutionary changes are continuous, quantitative and cumulative and prepare the ground for a radical qualitative LEAP. The revolutionary leap breaks the con-tinuity and graduality of evolution and constitutes progression from quantity to quality. Whilst the evolutionary move-ment introduces new and minor elements into the old system without destroying it, the revolutionary movement amounts to an upheaval partly or largely destroying the old order. However, liberal Marxism, such as EUROCOMMUNISM and legal Marxism, does not necessarily accept the inevitability of revolutionary upheavals in social progress.

Evolutionary Marxism Liberal, peaceful and gradual Marxism as opposed to revolutionary Marxism, as exemplified in particular by EUROCOMMUNISM, LEGAL MARXISM, REVISIONISM, SOCIAL DEMOCRACY.

Evolutionary Socialism A book published by E. BERNSTEIN in 1899, in which he criticized several fundamental propositions of Marx and outlined a peaceful, PARLIAMENTARY ROAD TO SOCIALISM. He denied that in the capitalist countries, the class conflict was becoming increasingly acute, that the concentration of production was increasing, that the working class was becoming poorer and poorer and that labour was the only creator of value. He rejected the need for a violent proletarian revolution and instead advocated a gradual transition to socialism by legislation, the extension of trade unionism and the development of co-operatives. Lenin attacked Bernstein's book as an example of OPPORTUNISM, REVISIONSIM and a betrayal of Marxism.

Evolution of Man See LABOUR THEORY OF HUMANIZATION.

Exchange One of the phases in the Marxian process of REPRODUCTION (production, distribution, exchange and consumption), consisting in the sale and purchase of goods and services in the market, and with money being typically used as a medium of e. Whilst distribution determines what portions of the national income produced are allocated to the different social classes and individual persons, e. is the actual act of receiving the entitlement. The scope and nature of e. depend on the character of production and the SOCIO-ECONOMIC FORMATION. In a capitalist economy, e. is carried on predominantly amongst private producers on their own account and at their own risk, is subordinate to the private profit maximization and reaches its utmost development in that type of economy. Under Socialist central economic planning, e. is limited only to commodities and services produced for the consumer market, is based on the social ownership of the means of production and is subordinate to planned distribution.

Exchange Rate The price of one currency in terms of another, or the exchange ratio between two currencies. For concepts peculiar to the practice in the Socialist countries, see BASIC EXCHANGE RATE, COEFFICIENT OF THE RELATIVE VALUE OF FOREIGN CURRENCIES, MULTIPLE EXCHANGE RATES, TOURIST EXCHANGE RATE.

Exchange Value A Marxian concept denoting the external expression of value of a COMMODITY either in terms of money or another commodity. E.v. is based on VALUE, but not extrinsic value, because the amount of the SOCIALLY-INDISPENSABLE LABOUR embodied in it is not known precisely and has to be verified by supply and demand conditions. For a commodity to have value, it must have USE-VALUE, of which the appropriate intensity of demand is a necessary condition. As supply and demand operating in the market changes, the e.v. of a commodity fluctuates, increasing or decreasing from the original value. However, in the long run, e.v. approximates value. In Marx's writings, there is a terminological confusion between 'e.v.' and 'value'. In his earlier confused usage (in A CONTRIBUTION TO THE CRITIQUE OF POLITICAL ECONOMY, 1859), by e.v. Marx in fact meant 'value' and contrasted it with 'use-value'. But in CAPITAL (1867–94), more consistently with his presentation of political economy as a whole, he distinguished between the 'e.v.' and 'value' along the lines explained above.

Ex-Com The abbreviated name of the Executive Committee of the SOVIET in Petrograd, which consisted of mostly left-wing MENSHEVIKS and several BOLSHEVIKS, in existence from March to Nov. 1917. It was never elected properly, but more or less appointed itself and then co-opted other activists. Its size rose from about 20 to nearly 100. It was headed by N. Chkheidze and amongst its members at one time or another were A. F. KERENSKY, V. MOLOTOV and A. G. Shlyapnikov. The Ex-Com was an unruly group, but it succeeded in establishing two commissions, one to deal with the procurement and distribution of food and another to deal with military affairs. When the critical moment arrived in Oct. 1917, it proved unwilling and unprepared (virtually by default) to take the responsibility of power which was seized by the Bolsheviks instead.

Executive Bureau of the Presidium of the League of Communists of Yugoslavia The highest permanent Party body and the highest effective seat of political power in Yugoslavia. It consists of 12 members headed by the Secretary (S. Dolanc). It carries out the policy worked out by the Presidium of the L.C.Y. (which has 69 members), a body chosen by the Central Committee (165 members) of the L.C.Y. Together with the Presidium, the Executive Bureau corresponds roughly to the POLITBURO of the CC of the CPSU, or Political Bureaux in some other ruling Communist parties.

Executive Committee of the CMEA The highest executive organ of the COUNCIL FOR MUTUAL ECONOMIC ASSISTANCE, carrying out the general policies laid down at the CMEA Sessions. The Committee, established in June 1962, replaced the 'Conference of the Member Countries' Representatives', and has its seat in Moscow. It is composed of the representatives of the member countries at the level of Vice-Premier, their deputies and advisers (including the Vice-Chairmen of the State Planning Commissions). It meets at least once a quarter to examine proposals from the member governments, the CMEA Permanent Commissions and the Secretariat. The chairmanship of the E.C. is held in rotation by the representative of each member country. The day-to-day work of the E.C. is carried out by three permanent bodies directly attached to it – the Secretariat, the COMMITTEE FOR CO-OPERATION IN PLANNING WORK and the COMMITTEE FOR SCIENTIFIC AND TECHNICAL CO-OPERATION.

Executive Committee of the Communist International The highest level of authority of the Third International (COMINTERN) in existence during the period 1919–43. It was based in Moscow and consisted of several elected Soviet representatives and a representative from each of the major Communist parties outside the USSR. Its first Chairman and Secretary were G. E. ZINOVIEV and K. RADEK, respectively. The Committee initially elected a smaller body called the 'Bureau' later renamed the 'Presidium' (1921). These bodies consisted of from 5 to 30 members. The Committee's routine work was later taken over by the Secretariat established in 1922. In May 1943, on instructions from Stalin, the Presidium dissolved the Comintern (thereby violating its own Constitution) with member Party support.

Existentialism A philosophical doctrine concerned with the problems of the existence of man who is postulated to be an absolutely free individual. E. developed during the 19th c. by S. A. Kiergaard (1813–55) and F. Nietzsche (1844–1900). K. Jaspers (1883–), G, Marcel (1889–1973), M. Heidegger (1889–1976) and J.-P. Sartre (1905–80) were the main exponents of e. during the 20th c. Existentialists emphasize that man in his constant decision-making is guided exclusively by his own 'free will', independent of any circumstances. This makes him 'absolutely responsible' in that no circumstances can be credited or blamed for his acts. Consequently, man is destined to suffer from anxiety, fear and despair. Marxist philosophy is strongly opposed to e. on four major grounds: 1. that it basically subscribes to philosophical IDEALISM and SUBJECTIVISM; 2. that it advocates absolute freedom of the individual, which suits the interests of the strong and the privileged and the exploiting ruling classes, to the detriment of the working class; 3. that it is preoccupied with man as an absolute individual, instead of as a member of society and a product of historical development; and 4. that it is unduly pessimistic, excluding the possibility of social progress through evolution and revolution and the attainment of FULL COMMUNISM. There were attempts by Sartre to reconcile e. (which he described as an 'enclave within Marxism') with Marxist philosophy, but without success.

Expanded Reproduction Marx's term denoting a situation in the economy when the volume of the means of production and of consumption produced during the year in question is greater than the volume used up during a similar period. This occurs when gross investment is greater than depreciation, i.e. net investment being a positive figure amounting to the expansion of the capital stock in the economy. In Marxist political economy, great importance is attached to e.r., as it is considered to be critical to technical and economic progress. It enables the growth of national income in the future, the rising standard of living and the advancement of the Socialist society towards full communism. E.r. contrasts with SIMPLE R. and CONTRACTING R.

Expediters In the Socialist centrally planned economies, middlemen proficient in the ways and means of securing supplies to enterprises not obtainable through regular channels, or when supplies are needed at short notice. E. are paid a recompense for their services. Although their operations are not legal, the authorities in most cases tolerate e. as they perform a useful function in an inflexible bureaucratic system and enable the enterprises to fulfil their production targets on time. In the USSR the e. is colloquially known as the *TOLKACH*.

Exploitation The appropriation of the results of another person's labour. The term is an important concept in Marxist ideology supported by an elaborate social doctrine, including the LABOUR THEORY OF VALUE. The exploiters are the owners of the means of production (historically speaking, masters, feudal lords, capitalists) and the exploited are the propertyless workers (slaves, serfs, wage earners) who have to sell their labour for subsistence. A worker normally produces more value than is necessary for his subsistence and reproduction (the cost of his living and training and that of his immediate family). This excess in ANTAGONISTIC SOCIO-ECONOMIC FORMATIONS (slavery, feudalism and capitalism) assumes the form of SURPLUS VALUE, consisting of profit, rent and interest. The surplus value is extracted from the worker (the real producer) by the economic necessity and, historically speaking, by force, legal sanctions and the institutional set-up (including the free market mechanism). E. is measured by the difference between VALUE and INDISPENSABLE VALUE, or the ratio of the INDISPENSABLE LABOUR TIME to surplus value, or the ratio of surplus value to variable capital (s/v) called the RATE OF SURPLUS VALUE. Although orthodox Marxists apply the fact of e. only to antagonistic pre-socialist societies, it can be argued that e. also exists in the Socialist countries. The occurrence of e. in Socialist countries between man and man is minimal, but it is evident between man and the state where the latter enforces an elaborate institutional set-up maintained by bureaucratic controls. The SURPLUS PRODUCT is extracted by the strict central control of personal income on the one hand, and of retail prices on the other. E. also takes place in international trade between more developed countries and less developed nations in the form of NON-EQUIVALENT EXCHANGE.

Export of Capital In the Marxist view, one of the inevitable features of IMPERIALISM and NEO-COLONIALISM, prompted by the possibility of earning higher PROFIT RATES by political expansion abroad. The apparent surplus of capital in the capital-exporting country is produced by the increasing EXPLOITATION of the proletariat. The e. of c. is also a means of the exploitation of the proletariat, and of the less-developed capital-importing countries in the form of interests and dividends, made possible by local cheap labour and NON-EQUIVALENT EXCHANGE.

Export of Revolution A phrase introduced after W.W.II by opponents of communism in the USA and then popularized in other capitalist countries, accusing the communist regimes of instigating revolutionary movements and subversion in the capitalist world. The first well-known advocate of the e. of r. was TROTSKY in the form of PERMANENT REVOLUTION. The NEW OPPOSITION in the USSR (1924–27), rejecting Stalin's postulate of SOCIALISM IN ONE COUNTRY, also supported the idea of the e. of r. The creation of the COMINTERN and the proclamation of the NEW COMMUNIST MANIFESTO in 1919 represented a more systematic and global approach to the e. of r. After W.W.II the e. of r. has been mostly identified with the Communist regime in Cuba. In the 1960s Cuban agents participated in attempts to overthrow right-wing governments in at least 10 Latin American countries including Bolivia (GUEVARA) and later extended to Asia and Africa. Cuba has been active in at least 16 African countries through either participating in, or consolidating, revolutions, especially in Angola, the Congo, Ethiopia, Guinea, Mozambique, Tanzania and Zambia. In 1979 there were some 40,000 Cuban troops and advisers in Africa. The implicit condition of peaceful COEXISTENCE in Soviet-US relations is the mutual undertaking to refrain from the e. of r., on the one hand, and from the export of COUNTER-REVOLUTION on the other.

Expressionism A movement in the graphic arts, literature, theatre, cinema and music, postulating the liberation of the creative artist from the material environment and its realistic representation, and instead emphasizing the intuitive, spontaneous and explosive expression of meaningful internal images and feelings. E. developed in Germany and then spread to other Western countries in the first three decades of this century. It represented a strong reaction against IMPRESSIONISM and NATURALISM. E. assigned a vital role to art and the artist in the task of the melioration of man by freeing him from national, state, class, religious and family strictures and traditions. Some expressionists identified themselves with LEFT COMMUNISM, otherwise, e. never commanded much interest in the Socialist countries. It has been officially condemned for its SUBJECTIVISM and idealistic, anarchist and utopian premises and implicit opposition to SOCIALIST REALISM.

Expropriation The open transfer of property from one owner to another against the will or interests of its previous owner. The concept of e. occupies an important place in Marxist social doctrine and HISTORICAL MATERIALISM. E. can be effected by legal or administrative measures, or by the ordinary market mechanism. Historically e. assumed the following forms: 1. small-holders expropriated by large landowners; 2. the church and nobility expropriated by the BOURGEOISIE; 3. smaller capitalists expropriated by larger capitalists; 4. the small and large capitalists expropriated by the bourgeois state (usually with compensation to previous owners), leading to STATE MONOPOLY CAPITALISM; 5. after the PROLETARIAN REVOLUTION, the e. of all private owners of the means of production by the Socialist state (as a rule, without compensation); and 6. foreign capital expropriated by domestic capitalists, the bourgeois state or the Socialist state. Also NATIONALIZATION, SOCIALIZATION OF THE MEANS OF PRODUCTION.

Extended Reproduction EXPANDED RE-PRODUCTION.

Extensive Democracy A concept in the form of a slogan used in China during the GREAT PROLETARIAN CULTURAL RE-VOLUTION to denote an active and wide-spread involvement of the masses in pub-lic life, e.g. criticism and supervision of the Party and the State hierarchy through the media. The slogan was popularized by LIN PIAO in his speech at a huge rally in Peking in Nov. 1966. Mao Tse-tung described the content of the slogan as 'the best way for the masses to educate and liberate them-selves'.

Extensive Growth A Marxist concept de-noting increases in production in the economy derived from the quantitative increases in labour and the means of pro-duction (capital and utilized land). The term has been used in the Socialist coun-tries since the mid-1950s, but its origin can be traced back to Marx who disting-uished between extensive and intensive EXPANDED REPRODUCTION (in *Capital*, vol. II). The Socialist development strategy up to the early 1960s was predo-minantly based on e.g., relying heavily on the underutilized reserves of the factors of production. But the developmental strategy based on e.g., although quite suc-cessful up to about 1960 (in most Euro-pean Socialist countries), proved wasteful in several respects, and furthermore was not conducive to technological progress and a rapid growth of productivity. Since the early 1960s the emphasis has shifted to INTENSIVE GROWTH.

Extremist Movements Organizations which resort to violence or in other ways deliberately breaking the law in the pur-suit of extreme left-wing, right-wing, anarchist or nationalist objectives. In the *Annual of Power and Conflict 1975–76*, edited by E. Crozier, 133 significant ex-tremist movements were listed, of which only one was in the Socialist bloc ('Us-tashi' in Yugoslavia). Of the 132 organiza-tions outside the Socialist bloc, 96 were left-wing and of these, 26 were described as 'Marxist' (pro-Soviet), 20 – 'Maoist', 11 – 'Castroite', 6 – 'Anarchist' and 2 – Trotskyte. Of the 96 left-wing organiza-tions, 25 were found in Latin America, 19 in Western Europe, 14 in South-East Asia, 7 in Africa south of the Sahara and 6 in the Arab world.

F

Fabianism A social movement associated with the Fabian Society founded in England in 1884, advocating a gradual and peaceful PARLIAMENTARY ROAD TO SOCIALISM within the framework of the existing capitalist society. The Society's name is derived from Quintus Fabius Cunctator, a Roman general who defeated the invading Carthaginian armies by cautious delaying tactics. Amongst its founders and early members were such intellectuals as G. D. H. Cole, G. B. Shaw, SIDNEY AND BEATRICE WEBB and H. G. Wells. From the start, F. repudiated revolutionary Marxism and instead advocated the extension of public ownership, class co-operation, and an elitist bureaucratic approach to the development of socialism, technical research and publicity. F. has exerted a considerable influence on social thought and policies in Britain. Fabians founded the London School of Economics (1895) and helped found the Labour Party (1900) and draft its Constitution (1918). Revolutionary Marxists have always been hostile to F., in that it amounts to a reconciliation of the working class with the BOURGEOISIE, OPPORTUNISM, and as such is opposed to SCIENTIFIC SOCIALISM. F. has also been attacked for rejecting the CLASS STRUGGLE and HISTORICAL MATERIALISM, showing indifference to pauperism and for supporting IMPERIALISM. F. Engels (in a letter to Sorge in 1893) described Fabians as 'a gang of careerists . . . scared of revolution'.

Factionism A term used in application to differences arising within a Communist party around a controversial question of policy. A faction is an organized group differing with the Party leadership, at the root of which is the different doctrinaire interpretation of general principles or strategies. In the Marxist-Leninist parties, f. is treated more gravely than DEVIATIONISM. Party rules insist that once a decision is made by the leadership in accordance with DEMOCRATIC CENTRALISM, both the majority and the minority are bound to support the decision consistently. F. received early attention in Soviet Russia when the Central Committee of the RUSSIAN COMMUNIST PARTY (OF THE BOLSHEVIKS) adopted a secret resolution in 1920 (made public at the 13th Congress in 1924) to take disciplinary action against the guilty members. Also LEFT OPPOSITION, RIGHT OPPOSITION.

Factors of Production In Western economics, land, labour and capital (basic factors) and sometimes entrepreneurship and technology. Each factor is considered to contribute to production and to be legitimately entitled to its remuneration (wages, rent, interest and profit), which in national income accounting constitute 'factor cost'. The term is not used in Marxist political economy, but the nearest equivalent would be PRODUCTION FORCES. Marxists regard labour as the sole creator of value and thus alone entitled to remuneration, whilst land and capital are treated as the 'means of production'. Entrepreneurship and technology are recognized only to the extent of the work performed, and as such, are partly included in labour.

Factors Theory of Social Evolution An eclectic theory explaining social develop-

181

ment as a result of the mutual interaction of autonomous 'factors' such as geographical environment, politics, morality, science, race, natural selection, competition and the like. The main exponents of this theory were J. M. Baldwin (1861 – 1934), Ch. Darwin (1809 – 82), J. Lamarck (1744–1829), C. L. Morgan (1852–1936), A. R. Wallace (1823–1914) and A. Weismann (1834–1914). Marxists dismiss the theory as both too vague and too mechanistic. They maintain that all aspects of society's life and development such as political organizations, legal systems, social attitudes (called collectively by Marx the SUPERSTRUCTURE) are governed by the material BASE, in particular the MODE OF PRODUCTION of material goods. To some extent the superstructure influences the base.

Factory Acts In its general meaning, labour legislation designed to protect workers' safety, health, working hours and other conditions at work not only in factories but also in other places of employment. In its narrow sense, the term is used historically to describe a series of Acts of the British Parliament in the 19th c. to improve the physical conditions of work in industry (factories and mines). The Acts, passed in 1802, 1833, 1867 and 1891 accorded the following: 1. established the minimum age for the employment of juvenile labour; 2. restricted the employment of women in certain industries (especially mining); 3. limited the hours of work of juvenile workers; and 4. provided government inspection for the enforcement of safety regulations in factories.

Factory Price A term used in the Socialist countries for the industrial producer price, i.e. the price as received by the factory or similar producing enterprise. It is usually fixed on the basis of the average PRIME COST of the enterprises grouped in a particular branch of industry, plus a profit mark-up according to a pre-established scale. F.p. does not include a turnover tax or a subsidy, or a wholesale margin.

'Fair Play for Cuba' Committee A left-wing group active in the USA in the early 1960s which opposed the anti-Castro policies of the US Government and the aid and encouragement given to Cuban exiles. The Committee was incorrectly accused of being communist-controlled, although it naturally received sympathy from the communists. It had no effect on the policies of the Government.

Falling Rate of Profit See DECLINING PROFIT RATE.

Family A social group whose members are linked by marriage, parenthood (or adoption) or kinship. It is a universal social group which appears in all communities at different levels of economic, social and cultural development, despite the different forms it may assume. Marxists stress that the nature, size, organization and functions of the f. are determined by the social systems in force, and that it changes in response to PRODUCTION FORCES and PRODUCTION RELATIONS. Engels (in *The ORIGIN OF THE FAMILY, PROPERTY AND THE STATE*) pointed out that throughout the ages the f. has been a reflected microcosm of contradictions in social development. Thus for example, in a bourgeois society, marriage is not conditioned by mutual compatibility and attraction, but by crude economic calculation which, together with the prevalence of poverty amongst the masses, can lead to prostitution. Marxism is committed to the equality of the sexes and in the Socialist countries women's equal rights and responsibilities are officially accepted as a matter of social justice. The generous social security (maternity leave and allowances, free medical care, child endowment, the provision of crèches in places of employment) and equal employment opportunities provide a sound basis for the development of the f. The Socialist approach to the f. contrasts with that advocated by ANARCHISM which regards the f. as a reactionary social institution, whether under capitalism or socialism.

Fanaticism Uncritical and uncompromising conviction of one's own beliefs or cause, leading to intolerance and even hostile acts against real or imagined opponents. It may be religious, racial, nationalistic, political or ideological in content. In capitalist-Socialist relations, each side has accused the other of f., and each side has been guilty of it; it reached its peak during the COLD WAR.

Fascism A general name for the ideologies, political movements and state systems noted for extreme NATIONALISM, authoritarianism, totalitarianism and MILITARISM. The term is derived from *fasces* (a 'bundle of twigs', in Latin), a symbol of unity, power and obedience in Ancient Rome. F. prevailed in its original form in Italy from 1922 to 1944 under B. Mussolini (an ex-Social Democrat), but it also spread to Germany (as Nazism), Japan, Spain, Portugal, South Africa and to a lesser extent in other countries. Although f. claimed to be anti-capitalist, it has been the object of attack by Marxists on the following grounds: 1. the proscription of Communist parties and persecution of Communists; 2. the rejection of the CLASS STRUGGLE in favour of CORPORATISM (employers, workers and the state co-operating in the same 'corporations'); 3. the oppression of the working class by the dissolution of trade unions; 4. ELITISM steeped in RACISM and authoritarian hierarchical organization; 5. CHAUVINISM, directly opposed to SOCIALIST INTERNATIONALISM; and 6. militant IMPERIALISM, as illustrated by Italian, Japanese and German aggression in the 1930s and W.W.II. In Communist writings, f. has often been referred to as any system opposed to Marxism. Social-democracy has also been described as 'social f.'.

Fatalism A philosophical doctrine maintaining that all future events are predetermined, and consequently cannot be prevented by human endeavour. F. may be conditioned either by religion (such as Islam, Calvinism) accepting divine predestination, or by a particular interpretation of natural laws (as in MECHANISTIC MATERIALISM) attributing future events to the sequence of past causes. In social relations, f. leads to a resigned humility and a passive acceptance of the existing social structure as human efforts to improve it appear to be pointless. Marxist philosophy, whilst subscribing to DETERMINISM, is opposed to f. in all its forms and regards it as a reactionary dogma, conveniently embraced by theocratic or bourgeois ruling classes. Marxists reject the mentality of resignation and hopelessness, and instead emphasize man's freedom of will and the need, ability and effectiveness of human actions in controlling nature and improving society. In particular, they attach great importance to the role of the Communist party in the transformation of the social system into a better society, i.e. FULL COMMUNISM.

Fatherland Front (*Otechestven Front*, in Bulgarian) In the PR of BULGARIA, a mass organization representing the officially accepted political parties and nation-wide social associations acting as a united electoral bloc in support of the Party and Government policies. Its membership in 1977 was 3.8m. out of a total population of 8.8m. It has elected local and regional committees which are co-ordinated by the National Council of Sofia and headed by a member of the Politburo of the BULGARIAN COMMUNIST PARTY (P. KUBADINSKI). The F.F. is completely dominated by the B.C.P., even though it includes the Bulgarian Agrarian People's Union (a remnant of the former Agrarian Party, with a membership of 120,000), trade unions and the Communist youth movement (plus individual citizens). Its most significant function is to prepare a single list of candidates for elections with the pre-approval of the B.C.P. According to official data, 99.9 per cent of the electorate participated at the last general elections of 1976. The F.F. holds a Congress every five years which elects the National Council.

February Revolution of 1917 The revolution in Russia which deposed Tsar

NICHOLAS II and installed a liberal democratic PROVISIONAL GOVERNMENT committed to either a constitutional monarchy or a republic. It began on 23 Feb. (8 March, N.S.C.) 1917 with strikes in Petrograd (now Leningrad), which was the capital of Russia at the time, and other industrial centres. The Provisional Government was formed by the State *DUMA*, first led by Prince Lvov but soon succeeded by A. F. KERENSKY. In Petrograd, SOVIETS OF WORKERS' AND SOLDIERS' DEPUTIES were formed, dominated by the MENSHEVIKS who gave support to the Kerensky Government. The F.R. did not solve Russia's political, social or military problems and the Provisional Government proved weak without a solid popular support. The BOLSHEVIKS regarded the F.R. as a BOURGEOIS-DEMOCRATIC REVOLUTION, merely a stepping stone to a PROLETARIAN REVOLUTION, which indeed followed eight months later (GREAT OCTOBER SOCIALIST REVOLUTION).

Federal Assembly (*Federální Shromádzdeni*, in Czech) In the CZECHOSLOVAK S.R., the federal parliament (which replaced the National Assembly on 1 Jan. 1969), consisting of two equal Chambers. The Chamber of Nations has 150 members, 75 from the Czech Socialist Republic and 75 from the Slovak S.R. The Chamber of the People consists of 200 members elected on a population basis. Both Chambers are elected every five years by universal, equal and secret ballot by citizens aged 18 and over from a single list of candidates prepared by the NATIONAL FRONT dominated by the CZECHOSLOVAK COMMUNIST PARTY. One or more candidates can be nominated for one electoral district. The Chairman of the F.A. at the time of writing was A. Indra, a member of the Presidium (Politburo) of the Central Committee of the Cz.C.P. In addition to being the highest organ of legislation in the country, the F.A. elects the President of the Republic and judges to the Supreme Court.

Federal Assembly (*Savezna Skupština*, in Serbo-Croat) The Yugoslav parliament

consisting of the Federal Chamber and the Chamber of Republics and Provinces. The F.Ch. consists of 220 members, 30 from each of the six Republics and 20 from each of the two Autonomous Provinces (all nominated by the SOCIALIST ALLIANCE OF THE WORKING PEOPLE). The Ch. of R. and P. numbers 88 delegates, 12 from each of the Republican Assemblies and eight from each Autonomous Provincial Assembly, the eight Assemblies sitting in joint session.

Federal Economic Chamber The national organization in Yugoslavia for co-ordinating the activities of ECONOMIC CHAMBERS.

Fel'dman, Grigory Aleksandrovich A pioneering theoretical Soviet economist of the 1920s in the field of economic growth under Socialist central planning. He worked out a simplified model, improving on the Marxian reproduction scheme, to which he attached crucial importance to the activities directed at the creation of new production capacities, i.e. the output of capital goods (as distinct from the activities merely sustaining or utilizing them). In his model, the output of capital goods is a narrower concept than Marx's Department I output, the propensity to save is virtually ignored and there are several limiting (and unrealistic) assumptions. He presented his model whilst working in a subordinate position in the *GOSPLAN,* but it was severely criticized and ignored by Stalin. F. disappeared (probably in the Great Purges of the 1930s). However, ideas along F's lines were in fact applied to the Soviet developmental strategy for three decades without due credit being acknowledged. Later, his original contribution was recognized and his name professionally rehabilitated by the Soviet economists in the 1960s.

Fellow Traveller A term first used in the USSR in the 1920s with respect to a member of the intelligentsia who hesitatingly supported the Bolshevik regime, because other options (Tsarism, anarchism, foreign intervention) were less desirable. After W.W.II, the term was applied in other Socialist countries in the late 1940s to the members of non-bourgeois political parties co-operating with the Communists in the UNITED FRONTS. After the mid-1930s, when the POPULAR FRONTS were created, the description was adopted in capitalist countries but in a rather depreciative sense. It denotes a person or group giving support to the Communist party without actually becoming its member, either being sympathetic to Marxism but not wishing to be subjected to Party discipline, or trying to further his own interests.

Feminism A liberal movement which originated in the second half of the 19th c. directed towards the social, legal and economic equality of women with men. Although Marxism approves of the idea of equality between the sexes, from the start it adopted a negative attitude to the movement on the following grounds: 1. F. originated as an exclusive movement amongst property-owning middle and upper class women, determined to improve their situation and ignoring working-class women; 2. F. has rejected the CLASS STRUGGLE as the road to social justice. Its extremists advocate inter-sex struggle, which would have no place in a CLASSLESS SOCIETY; and 3. communism offers a more effective and lasting basis for complete equality of all women with men.

Fetishism of Commodities See COMMODITY FETISHISM.

Fetishism of Output A phrase used in the Socialist centrally planned economies, denoting obsession amongst enterprises preoccupied with reaching and exceeding quantitative targets, irrespective of the quality and suitability of the products to satisfy society's wants. It prevailed under the CENTRALIZED DIRECTIVE SYSTEM OF PLANNING AND MANAGEMENT before the ECONOMIC REFORMS of the 1960s (before 1950 in Yugoslavia). This was largely due to the faulty system of incentives which rewarded quantity, and not quality or efficiency. The f. of o. led to the piling up of unsaleable stocks of goods, which further aggravated shortages of other goods of the desired assortment and quality.

Feudalism The hierarchical, social and economic system which prevailed in the Middle Ages (especially 11th–17th centuries), based on a lord-vassal relationship, where the right to the possession of land (or some other privilege) was reciprocated by services and subordination. The hierarchical system involved the following classifications: king, overlords, lesser lords, free tenants, villains and cotters (the last two being serfs). Parallel to and supporting this land-oriented structure were merchants, master craftsmen, journeymen, apprentices and servants. The relations between these social classes were legally defined and further enforced by church teachings and by custom. In the Marxist interpretation of history, f. was one of the three ANTAGONISTIC SOCIO-ECONOMIC FORMATIONS which was preceded by slavery and succeeded by capitalism. The social organization and relations under f. are seen as an outcome of the material conditions of production revolving around land, the main means of production and source of wealth at the time. The feudal lords were the ruling and exploiting class, whilst serfs were the lowest class exploited through feudal labour and feudal rent. Owing to commercial and financial developments, the increasing division of labour, the growth of manufacture and towns and the emergence of the burghers' class (rich urban groups), f. was replaced by capitalism and in many cases by bourgeois-democratic revolutions. In Russia, serfdom was formally abolished only in 1861, but the feudal social structure persisted till the Bolshevik Revolution in October 1917.

Feudal Socialism Name given by Marxists to the patronizing version of state intervention towards removing workers' main grievances by introducing reforms, whilst preserving the hierarchical social structure (ARISTOCRACY, BOURGEOISIE, PROLETARIAT) essentially intact. The best known use of the concept was in application to Germany under Bismarck. His social measures were seen by revolutionary Marxists as palliatives, designed to remove the worst abuses of capitalism (by the introduction of the universal male suffrage and some social services), in order to prevent the enlightened segment of the bourgeoisie combining with the proletariat against the aristocracy.

Feuerbach, Ludwig (1804–72) A German philosopher who turned from IDEALISM to MATERIALISM and ATHEISM, and whose ideas attracted the attention of the leading Marxist philosophers. His views were developed in *A Contribution to the Critique of Hegelian Philosophy* (1839) and *The Essence of Christianity* (1841). Although Marxists regard F. as a great pre-Marxist materialist philosopher, they are critical of his complete rejection of Hegelian DIALECTICS, of his contemplative and metaphysical inclinations and of his failure to appreciate HISTORICAL MATERIALISM in relation to social development. His writings were subjected to a thorough examination by Marx (in *THESES ON FEUERBACH*, Engels (*LUDWIG FEUERBACH AND THE END OF GERMAN CLASSICAL PHILOSOPHY*) and Lenin (*MATERIALISM AND EMPIRIO-CRITICISM*).

F Fund (*F. Alap* or *Feilesztési Alap*, in Hungarian) In Hungary under the NEW ECONOMIC MECHANISM, the Enterprise Development Fund. It is one of the major funds in an enterprise into which about four-fifths of the gross profits are channelled (the other being the R FUND, or Material Incentives Fund). The F.F. is subject to a profit tax and a deduction for the Reserve Fund. The net amount is then available for investment purposes according to the decision of the management (not the state).

Fideism A philosophical outlook and a theological doctrine according to which the knowledge of ultimate truths is beyond human reason and is possible only by supernatural revelation and religious faith. Extreme f. relies exclusively on revelation, whilst moderate f. denies the adequacy of scientific cognition. It attaches a decisive role to dogmas and articles of faith in the case of conflicts between religion and science. In Marxist philosophy f. is rejected in its entirety and is identified with extreme philosophical IDEALISM and as a reactionary outlook impeding scientific and social progress.

Fidelismo The brand of Communist ideology and style of government bearing the dominant imprint of Dr Fidel CASTRO in Cuba, especially during the period 1956–68. Its distinguishing features are: 1. reckless guerrilla radicalism, independent of the institutionalized Communist party discipline; 2. largely personal rule by Fidel Castro, who is noted for his magnetic personality commanding utter devotion amongst his immediate colleagues and sub-ordinates. He has wide support in Cuba as well as in Latin America and Africa; and 3. reliance on enthusiasm and *ad hoc* measures dictated more by local conditions than doctrinaire rectitude and practical models developed elsewhere. However, since the late 1960s there have been several important departures from F. in Cuba in favour of Soviet orthodoxy – a moderation of the revolutionary line, a 'de-personalization' drive, a reactivation of material incentives and tightly systematic institutionalized forms of economic planning.

Fi-Fi A colloquial designation of the 'Physical-Financial' planning model in France, first introduced to cover the five-year period 1971–75. It is a computer-programmed model, more systematic than the previous five plans, embodying some 2,000 equations. The emphasis in the model is on detailed structural analyses and economic policy, rather than on projections. It enables both sectoral and overall analyses of the economy.

Fifth Amendment of the US Constitution Adopted in 1791, it stipulates that no one 'shall be compelled in any criminal case to be a witness against himself'. The Amendment was made famous in the 1950s, when investigations of alleged Communists and/or sympathizers were held by the House UN-AMERICAN ACTIVITIES committee. Many refused to answer questions on the grounds that they were maintaining their constitutional right.

Fifth Column Secret agents or an organized force pursuing disruptive or revolutionary activities (espionage, sabotage, popular unrest) to facilitate invasion by the enemy. The term was first used in the SPANISH CIVIL WAR in 1936 by a Nationalist general, E. Mola. He boasted that in addition to his four columns marching to capture Madrid from the Republicans, there was a 'f.c.' consisting of Trotskytes behind the lines subverting the city from within. The description was subsequently applied to any agents of Nazi Germany, Fascist Italy and Imperial Japan secretly operating in other countries. During the COLD WAR, the term was sometimes used in East-West polemics for 'counter-revolutionary' or Communist subversion.

Fifth Estate Name sometimes given to either trade unions (as in Britain) or to the *LUMPENPROLETARIAT* (as in Germany). The other four ESTATES are usually identified (historically) as the titled landowners (nobility and gentry); the clergy, the urban working and lower middle class and the peasantry.

Final Act of the Conference on Security and Co-Operation in Europe See HELSINKI CONFERENCE.

Finance Capitalism In the Marxist interpretation of history, the advanced and degenerate stage of capitalism, following commercial and industrial capitalism, which developed in the Western industrialized countries during the last four decades before W.W.I. It was noted for the rapid expansion of banking, stock exchange and other financial institutions. Domestically, it led to the exploitation and domination of small firms by financial interests and to the fusion of industrial banking capital. Externally, f.c. led to the EXPORT OF CAPITAL and IMPERIALISM. F. c. was also dominated by FINANCIAL OLIGARCHY.

Financial Accumulation In the Socialist enterprise accounting, the monetary difference between total receipts from the sale of goods and services and the PRIME COST of the sold output. F.a. is not the same as SURPLUS PRODUCT, because prices received by enterprises usually deviate from value. Furthermore some forms of the surplus product (especially social insurance, interest on bank credits and most taxes) are treated as prime cost. F.a. is partly channelled to the state budget and partly retained in the enterprise for bonuses to the personnel and the financing of collective incentives and social amenities.

Financial Balances A term used in Socialist economic and financial planning and recording, showing receipts and expenditure in monetary terms. There are six main types of f.b.: 1. the overall state balance embracing all income and expenditure of the state and the socialized entities in the country; 2. the state budget, showing the details of the state's receipts and expenditure; 3. the assets and liabilities of the banking system; 4. the credit plan, showing sources of finance and the distribution of credits; 5. financial balances of the enterprises and institutions; and 6. various 'funds', showing the sources of finance and their disposition (e.g. Investment Fund, Circulating Assets Fund, Technical Progress Fund). F.b. contrasts with MATERIAL BALANCES.

Financial Convertibility MONETARY CONVERTIBILITY.

Financial Curtain Measures taken by the leading Western powers against the USSR after the Bolshevik Revolution (1917) and against other Socialist countries (after 1945), banning the purchase of Soviet gold (up to the mid-1920s) and the extension of long-term credits (exceeding five years) up to the early 1960s. The F.c. paralleled the IRON CURTAIN after W.W.II.

Financial Discipline A term used in Socialist economic accounting and management whereby systematic financial control and high penalties are enforced. F.d. ensures the legality of transactions, integrity, economy, the conformity of operations according to laid-down economic plans and the protection of social property against neglect, damage, embezzlement and the like. F.d. is ensured by the following forms of control: 1. current and periodical control by the chief accountant in each enterprise; 2. current daily control by the banks; 3. periodical scrutiny by local or regional authorities of the enterprises' settlements with the state budget; and 4. periodical or *ad hoc* control by special auditors sent by higher authorities (branch associations or ministries). Also CONTROL BY THE ROUBLE.

Financial Instruments In Socialist economic management and accounting, monetary means of control or influence over economic processes. F.i. include prices, various mark-ups (for quality, novelty), trade margins, interest rates and other credit terms, depreciation allowances, capital charges, fines and material incentives to workers. F.i. are employed by the authorities to induce or discourage enterprises which pursue activities in the most efficient manner and in the best social interest. These instruments have been reactivated in the European Socialist countries since the early 1960s (1950s in Yugoslavia). They have been found to be more conducive to efficiency and are consistent with a greater independence of enterprises than DIRECTIVES.

Financial Oligarchy A Marxist critical description of the small group of the richest capitalists, especially those controlling large amounts of financial resources (o. means 'rule by the few'). F.o. is a feature of FINANCE CAPITALISM and controls much of the industrial capital and production.

Financial Planning The integral part of economic planning in the Socialist countries, consisting in the financial quantification of the means and objectives to facilitate the implementation of an economic plan along desired lines. A f. plan outlines the requisite tasks for financial flows, specifying size, direction and balances at the beginning and end of the planned period. F.p. is essentially concerned with the creation and distribution of financial accumulation and amortization funds on the macro as well as microeconomic scale. F. plans may be either analytical (as guides to the management) or directive-analytical, the latter case being mandatory. To be consistent both internally and with the economic plan, the f. plan must be balanced (FINANCIAL BALANCES).

Finnish Communist Party (*Suomen Kommunistinen Puolue*) Normally the fourth-fifth largest political party in the country, consisting of two independent factions within a formally united front and one of the influential non-ruling Communist parties in the world. It was founded by left-wing Social-Democrats in Moscow in 1918 and remained illegal in Finland up to 1944. But it operated through front organizations and, for a brief interval in 1939–40, it was the ruling party in the Soviet-occupied Terijoki. Under Soviet pressure, the Party was legalized in 1944 and has played an active part in Finnish politics and Finnish-Soviet relations ever since. In the Sino-Soviet dispute, it has followed a pro-Soviet orientation. In 1978 the Party had a membership of 48,000 (when the country's total population was 4,750,000). During the 1975 election it polled 19 per cent of the votes cast and won 40 (out of 210) seats. The Party's daily organ is *Kansan Uutiset* (People's News), whilst *Kommunisti* (The Communist) is its monthly theoretical journal.

Finnish Social-Democratic Party (*Suomen Sosialidemakraattinen Puolue*) The socialist party and the largest political party in the country since the mid-1960s. It was founded in 1899 (but later, its left-wing radical dissidents illegally created the FINNISH COMMUNIST PARTY in Moscow in 1918). The F.S.-D.P. derives its support mainly from the working and middle classes and small farmers. Its membership in the late 1970s was 85,000 and its leader (and former Prime Minister) is K. Sorsa. The Party has pursued a liberal parliamentary road to socialism within an essentially capitalist framework. At the 1975 elections it won 54 (of the 210) seats. The Party's main publications are the daily organ *Suomen Sosialidemokraatti* (Finnish Social-Democracy) and the monthly *Sosialistinen Aikakauslehti* (Socialist Magazine).

First International The popular name of the first international organization of the working class movement under the official name of the 'International Workingmen's Association', based in London 1864–72 and in New York 1872–76. The initiative for its creation came from the English trade union leaders in London, mainly G. Ogden and W. R. Cremer, but K. MARX, F. ENGELS and M. BAKUNIN were also leading participants. The purpose of the F.I. was to provide a permanent co-ordinating organization for the socialist and communist movements in Europe, especially Britain, France, Germany and Italy. A declaration of its principles was prepared by a subcommittee headed by Marx. In 1870, the Russian Section (based in Geneva) was added. The F.I. held seven Congresses – in London (1865), Geneva (1866), Lausanne (1867), Brussels (1868), Basle (1869), London (1871) and The Hague (1872). The Russian anarchist M. Bakunin joined the F.I., according to Marx, with a view to

infiltrating and dominating it. Largely due to Marx's efforts, Bakunin and his anarchist supporters were expelled from the F.I. at its Seventh Congress in The Hague. Its headquarters were then moved to New York, after which it declined and was formally dissolved in Philadelphia in 1876. The F.I. was succeeded by the SECOND INTERNATIONAL (created in 1889).

First of May See MAY DAY.

First Proletariat A colloquial name for the International Social-Revolutionary Party 'Proletariat', the first Polish working class party, founded in Warsaw in 1882. It was also known as the 'Great Proletariat'. Its founder and leader was L. Waryński, who was aided by H. Dulęba, and S. Kunicki. Its objective was to overthrow capitalism and establish socialism with the aid of the peasantry and the left-wing intelligentsia. Its activities extended over Russian Poland and also spread to other parts of Poland occupied by Austria and Germany. Owing to the severe Tsarist repression, the F.P. disintegrated as a party in 1888. It was followed by the SECOND PROLETARIAT.

First Secretary Designation of the highest executive official of the Communist party in six Socialist countries (Albania, Bulgaria, the German DR, Hungary, Mongolia and Poland) and of some non-ruling Communist parties. This designation was also officially used in the USSR after Stalin's death (March 1953) up to April 1966. The F.S. heads both the highest executive body of the Communist party (called the POLITBURO in most ruling parties) and the SECRETARIAT OF THE CENTRAL COMMITTEE. In most cases, he is elected at either the first PLENARY SESSION of the C.C. or after the PARTY CONGRESS, or, in some cases, by the Party Congress itself. In some Communist parties the designation used is SECRETARY-GENERAL, whilst in some, notably the Chinese Communist Party, the Chairman is the highest Party official.

'Five Antis' Campaign

'Five Antis' Campaign An official drive in China in the early 1950s against private enterprise. In particular it was against: 1. bribery; 2. tax evasion; 3. the theft of state property; 4. fraud on government contracts (inferior materials, poor workmanship); and 5. the disclosure of state economic secrets for private gain. The campaign, designed to reduce the power of private merchants and industrialists, was most intense from Oct. 1951 to Sep. 1952. It seriously disrupted commercial and industrial activities in 1952. The campaign was staged mostly in the cities and corresponded to the 'FOUR CLEAN-UPS' in the countryside.

'Five Duties' A term introduced by the Communist Party of Vietnam in 1977, laying down responsibilities for Party members (replacing the previously laid-down 'Seven Responsibilities'). They are: 1. devotion to the Communist cause; 2. to strive for political, ethical and occupational self-improvement through study and training; 3. close rapport and co-operation with the masses; 4. maintenance of Party discipline; and 5. participation in the Party's policies with respect to PROLETARIAN INTERNATIONALISM.

'Five Good' Drive A campaign in China initiated in 1963, requiring PRODUCTION TEAMS to be 'F.G. Teams'. It involved being 'good at': 1. the implementation of the Party's policies; 2. the promotion of political education; 3. the fulfilment of the tasks of collective agricultural and sideline production targets; 4. the most economical execution of tasks; and 5. carrying out other tasks that may be assigned to them by the state.

'Five Major Crimes Committed by Mao Tse-tung' Charges laid in the USSR in 1969, representing the most bitter accusations in the SINO-SOVIET DISPUTE in the sphere of international relations. The five 'crimes' were: 1. frenzied attacks against the USSR and other Socialist countries; 2. venomous attacks against Marxist-Leninist parties; 3. splitting and under-

mining national liberation movements in Asia, Africa and Latin America; 4. provoking a US-Soviet nuclear war; and 5. the diversion of trade away from the Socialist camp in favour of capitalist countries. The charges were formulated in Moscow by a pro-Soviet Chinese Communist leader Wang Ming, described by the Chinese leadership as a 'reactionary', 'revisionist', 'renegade', 'traitor', and a 'lackey of imperialism'.

Five Most Read Articles Five articles written by MAO TSE-TUNG between 1929 and 1945, widely publicized in a pamphlet (of about 15 pages) during the GREAT PROLETARIAN CULTURAL REVOLUTION as a historical and theoretical groundwork for its understanding and development. They were as follows: 1. 'Serve the People' (8 Sep. 1944); 2. 'The FOOLISH OLD MAN WHO REMOVED THE MOUNTAIN' (11 June 1945); 3. 'IN MEMORY OF NORMAN BETHUNE' (21 Dec. 1939); 4. 'On Correcting Mistaken Ideas in the Party' (Dec. 1929); and 5. 'Combat Liberalism' (7 Sep. 1937).

Five Principles of Peaceful Coexistence Five tenets first formulated in an agreement signed by China and India in April 1954, and further confirmed in a joint declaration issued by CHOU EN-LAI and Pandit Nehru in New Delhi later in the same year. The F.P. were: 1. mutual respect for each other's national territory and sovereignty; 2. non-aggression; 3. non-interference in each other's internal affairs; 4. equality and mutual benefit; and 5. peaceful coexistence. Thus, the Principles had been put forward two years before Khrushchev's proposition of peaceful COEXISTENCE in Feb. 1956. The Five Principles were also incorporated in the Bandung Declaration of Asian and African countries in 1955 and endorsed in the Chinese Constitution of 1975.

Five Principles of Socialist Credit A set of rules governing the extension of credit, developed in the USSR after the early 1930s and later adopted by other Socialist

190

countries as a rough guideline. The f.p. specify that credit extended to socialized enterprises must be: 1. planned; 2. specific; 3. secured by a collateral; 4. repayable; and 5. with a fixed period of maturity. In practice, the application of these 'principles' means that once the targets or conditions laid down in the relevant economic plan are satisfied, the applying enterprise is granted the desired credit as a matter of course, which in extreme cases in the past led to CREDIT AUTOMATISM.

Five Pure Classes A designation used in China to describe the five 'legitimate' (non-bourgeois) social classes: 1. workers; 2. poor peasants and lower-middle peasants; 3. soldiers; 4. good Party officials; and 5. revolutionary martyrs (those persecuted by anti-communists). The designation has been in use since the Communist seizure of power in Oct. 1949, but it was popularized during the GREAT PROLETARIAN CULTURAL REVOLUTION and used as a test for the membership of the RED GUARDS.

Five-Year-Plan The medium-term economic plan commonly pursued in the Socialist centrally planned economies. Although there are short-term (1, 3, 6, 12 and 24 month) and long-term (15–20 year) plans, the F.-Y.P. is basic in Socialist economic planning. It embodies not only production targets to be achieved in five years, but also other social goals. Consequently, it is in an effective position to show details of the distribution of national income. The first F.-Y.P. was pioneered in the USSR and covered the period 1928–32. Over the period 1956–65 several Socialist countries experimented with Seven-Year Plans, but have abandoned that idea since, and have reverted to F.-Y.P. (1966–70, 1971–75, 1975–80, 1981–85).

Fixed Capital That portion of capital which consists of the site, buildings, equipment, various installations, tools, instruments and patented technology used in production. It consists of durable-use producer items, as distinct from single-use materials and power (circulating assets). In Marxist usage, f.c. must not be confused with CONSTANT CAPITAL (the latter being a broader concept, including not only f.c. but also circulating assets). In Marx's interpretation, f.c. cannot create VALUE. In the process of production, a portion of f.c. – to the extent of its depreciation – is 'transferred' to the commodities produced (only VARIABLE CAPITAL creates value).

Flexible Price System Another expression for the COMPLEX PRICE SYSTEM.

Fluctuations See CYCLICAL FLUCTUATIONS.

Food Detachments In Soviet Russia under WAR COMMUNISM (1918–20), armed units of workers and peasants operating in the countryside to enforce the Soviet regime's 'food distribution system' to ensure that food supplies reach the urban population. Where necessary, force was used to locate and confiscate food hoarded by peasants, especially by the KULAKS who were hostile to the BOLSHEVIKS. F.d. were disbanded after the advent of the NEW ECONOMIC POLICY in 1921, when private trade in food was restored and higher prices were paid to peasants.

'Foolish Old Man Who Removed the Mountain' A philosophical article written in simple language by Mao-Tse-tung. It was originally published on 11 June 1945 and later in an abbreviated form included in the 'Draft Resolution of the Central Committee of the Chinese Communist Party Concerning Certain Current Problems of Agricultural Labour'. It was also embodied in a pamphlet, *The FIVE MOST READ ARTICLES of Mao Tse-tung* published during the Great Proletarian Cultural Revolution. The article is a parable addressed to the masses to teach them the Maoist approach to the theory of knowledge (EPISTEMOLOGY). It aims to demonstrate that ideas and consciousness create matter, thus seemingly supporting philosophical IDEALISM and differing from the classical Marxist materialism. Mao stressed that ideas are not innate in mind (to this extent agreeing with Marx and Lenin), but come from three kinds of social practice, viz. the struggle for production, the class struggle and scientific experiment. Once the ideas are grasped by the mass of the working people, they turn into a material force, which changes society and the world.

Force The exercise of power to overcome resistance. According to some versions of the theory of f. (such as those put forward by E. DÜHRING and L. GUMPLOWICZ), f. is the direct determinant of the course of history. Marxism is, in general, opposed to this interpretation of history, as it is in conflict with HISTORICAL MATERIALISM, although Marxists do concede that the existence of antagonistic classes has often involved the use of f. The attitude to the use of f. varies according to the different brands of Marxism. Liberal Marxists (such as those representing EUROCOMMUNISM, the PARLIAMENTARY ROAD TO SOCIALISM and REVISIONISM) are opposed to a violent strategy. But revolutionary Marxists, especially those professing CASTROISM, MAOISM, MARXISM-LENINISM, or TROTS-KYISM, insist on the recourse to force in the CLASS STRUGGLE and especially in the PROLETARIAN REVOLUTION. The use of f. in the proletarian revolution is considered necessary in breaking the entrenched bourgeoisie, destroying at least some of the capitalist institutions, combatting COUNTER-REVOLUTION and speeding up the transition to socialism. All this necessitates the DICTATORSHIP OF THE PROLETARIAT. Also EXTREMIST MOVEMENTS.

Forced Labour Camps Concentration camps holding mostly political prisoners with an emphasis on the performance of arduous labour. They were first established on a systematic basis in Soviet Russia by the *CHEKA* in 1919, but reached the greatest development under Stalin. The state security system (at different times known as the *Cheka*, the *GPU*, the *OGPU*, the *NKVD*, the *MGB* and the *KGB*) through the *GULAG* (Main Administration of Corrective Labour Camps) acted as the contractor to the government for work in mining, quarrying, lumbering and building new towns, railways and canals. In 1938, there were 9.0m. people in the Soviet f.l.c., or nearly 9 per cent of the working population. In 1945 the estimated number (including foreigners) was 12–15m. In 1948 at least 125 such camps were identified in the USSR (Karaganda, Kolyma, Norilsk and Vorkuta having been the most notorious). Most of the f.l.c. were situated in the remote and climatically harsh regions. The proportion of forced labour sentences to total sentences in the USSR was 21 per cent in 1927 and had risen to 58 per cent by 1958. F.l.c. contributed considerably to the economic development of the USSR at a low cost to the state. Most of the f.l.c. had been liquidated by 1959, but on a minor scale they have been retained in the form of 'corrective labour camps'. With the spread of DISSENT since the mid-1960s, mental institutions have partly taken the place of the old f.l.c. The estimated number of political prisoners in the USSR in the late 1970s was 1.0–3.0m.

Fordism A system of centralized management of a large industrial capitalist enterprise, originally introduced by H. Ford (1863–1947) in his motor vehicle firm in Detroit. His establishment became a model of scientific and efficient organization and operation in the 1920s. Its distinguishing features were the extreme division of labour and the application of the automatic assembly line, setting the pace for workers' operations. F. attracted the attention of Marxists and became a target for criticism on account of its extreme de-humanization and exploitation of labour, undemocratic management and the reduction of the worker's role to performing repetitive, monotonous tasks at speeds pushed to the limits of human endurance.

Foreign Intervention, The The direct and unsuccessful involvement of the American, British, Czech, French and Japanese troops in Soviet Russia from 1918 to 1922 in support of the anti-Bolshevik forces or for the sake of territorial acquisition. British, French and Japanese units entered Siberia via Vladivostok in Aug. 1918 and defeated the local Bolshevik opposition. The Japanese occupied an area from Vladivostok to China, with a view to its permanent annexation. At the same time the Czech Legion (mostly released prisoners of war), heading for the Western Front via Vladivostok, clashed with the local Bolsheviks, occupied much of Siberia along the Trans-Siberian Railway and linked up with the White army units in the Volga region. The British and French troops aided the White army under A. V. KOLCHAK, but were routed by the Bolsheviks led by M. V. FRUNZE. Foreign troops (together with some of the White Russian elite) were evacuated in 1919 and 1920, and the Japanese were driven out in the East by the Bolsheviks in Oct. 1922. Later, in the 1930s, Stalin used the case of the F.I. together with the CAPITALIST ENCIRCLEMENT as excuses for his dictatorial powers and GREAT PURGES.

Foreign Investment Capital owned by investors resident in another country. It may assume the form of direct investment (the establishment of new plants or the acquisition of local firms) or portfolio investment (bonds, debentures, medium or long-term loans). F.i. has become an important feature of international economic relations since 1870. Historically, f.i. has been typically undertaken by the more developed industrialized capitalist nations (Britain, France, Germany, Belgium, the Netherlands, the USA, Italy, Switzerland and Japan) in primary-producing, less-developed countries. But since the late 1950s, it has been increasingly directed toward other industrialized capitalist countries (especially in Western Europe). Since 1972, some less-developed countries (primarily the oil-exporting countries of the Middle East) have been exporting capital to the richest capitalist countries (the USA and North-Western Europe). In

the late 1970s, the book value of f.i. in the capitalist world exceeded $250,000m. In Marxist thought, f.i. is identified with MONOPOLY CAPITALISM, IMPERIALISM and NON-EQUIVALENT EXCHANGE. Marx (in *CAPITAL*) saw f.i. as an expression of the exploitation of the proletariat at home and of the poorer and weaker countries by the rich, industrialized nations. In this process, he saw monopolies playing the leading role, driven by the DECLINING PROFIT RATE at home and their insatiable greed. Rosa LUXEMBURG (in *Accumulation of Capital*, 1913) highlighted the part played by the exploitation of raw materials and markets in colonies as the new source of capital accumulation for capitalist monopolies. Lenin (in *IMPERIALISM: THE HIGHEST STAGE OF CAPITALISM*) stressed the role of f.i. in the rivalry and wars between imperialist powers. Although the Socialist countries are in principle against f.i., they have in fact developed investments in the capitalist world valued at $1,000m., mostly in (some 700) wholly-owned and JOINT VENTURES for the marketing of their products. Socialist f.i. is important in the CMEA region, mostly in the form of INTERNATIONAL PRODUCTION ASSOCIATIONS.

Foreign Trade Corporations, or F.T. Enterprises In the Socialist countries, enterprises owned by the state and given the exclusive right to export and/or import specified classes of goods. Their number is relatively small – ranging from 5 in Mongolia and 7 in Albania to 56 in Poland and 69 in the USSR. They are usually large entities, and they often enjoy a degree of monopolistic – monopsonistic power when dealing with foreign firms. In some Socialist countries, export-producing and import-using enterprises may be licensed to engage in foreign trade directly, whilst in Yugoslavia any entity (state, co-operative or private) may be licensed to engage in export and (less likely) in import.

Foreign Trade Efficiency Indexes Formulae or coefficients developed in the

Eastern European countries in the 1950s and 1960s for measuring the effectiveness of exports, imports and foreign trade efficiency of investment. Their purpose is to overcome the absence of equilibrium exchange rates and distortions in domestic price structures. In the numerous indexes devised, domestic costs expressed in the national currency are related to the receipts or expenditure of foreign exchange. An example of an index is given below:

$$NfeEx = \frac{C - iS + mC}{FPfe + iSfe} ;$$

$NfeEx$ = net foreign-exchange effectiveness of export;

C = factory cost price (incl. factory profit mark-up, but not including the turnover tax);

iS = value of the imported component supplies used up in the produced article (expressed in domestic currency);

mC = domestic portion of marketing costs (incl. trade and profit mark-ups);

$FPfe$ = net current export price obtainable in foreign markets expressed in foreign exchange;

$iSfe$ = value of the imported component supplies used up, expressed in foreign exchange.

With the aid of the indexes, lists of exportables and importables are prepared in descending order of 'effectiveness'. The authorities decide on the cut-off levels, guided mainly by balance-of-payments considerations.

Foreign Trade Monopoly See STATE FOREIGN TRADE MONOPOLY.

Formalism Preoccupation with form and abstraction, rather than the content of concepts, objects, phenomena, relations and actual artistic representations. The term is used in philosophy, sociology and the arts. The official view of f. in the Socialist countries is negative on the following grounds: 1. being preoccupied with form, it ignores content, amounting to the denial of the unity of FORM AND CONTENT; 2. in sociology, it implicitly accepts bureaucratism, i.e. the mechanistic execution of directives and recommendations handed down from above, irrespective of their applicability to individual practical situations; and 3. in the arts (literature, painting, sculpture, music), f. is associated with 'ART FOR ART'S SAKE' and is antisocial. In the cultural field it fails to carry the message of ideological and social significance to the masses, and as such, is in conflict with SOCIALIST REALISM.

Formal Logic The rigorous study of the laws and forms of thinking. It lays down rules for the correct process of thinking, such as the requirements of clarity, precision, unequivocality and consistency. It is also concerned with the nature of concepts, judgment and methods of reasoning. F.l. is also described as the 'grammar of thinking'. Marxist philosophers accept f.l. as far as it goes, but they do not believe that it goes far enough to provide a sufficient basis for verifiable thinking and cognition. They maintain that f.l. is too elementary and static, treats phenomena outside its mutual relations and interdependence, and disregards change and development. Marx and Engels regarded f.l. as the 'lower mathematics of logic' and contrasted it with DIALECTICAL LOGIC, which they called the 'higher mathematics of logic'.

Form and Content Philosophical concepts the approach to which, and especially to their relationships, determines the philosophical division of IDEALISM and MATERIALISM. In some idealistic and metaphysical philosophical theories, f. and c. are treated as separate and independent. On the other hand in Marxist DIALECTICAL MATERIALISM, they are considered to be interdependent and constituting a unity, c. being primary and dominant over f. Marxist philosophers stress that c. and its development precede

194

and condition f. and its development. But in this process, f. is not passive, as it in turn also influences c., either facilitating or impeding its development. Although f. and c. constitute a unity, sooner or later CONTRADICTIONS appear between them. In the process of development c. comes into conflict with the old f. no longer corresponding to the new c. This struggle is resolved by the old giving way to the new. It may also happen that the new c. may utilize the old f., as is illustrated by Socialist society, which utilizes such old capitalist f.s as money, prices, interest and profit. The separation of f. from c. and the excessive attention given to f. is called FORMALISM, which is rejected in Marxist philosophy.

Forward English titles of German and Russian left-wing newspapers *VORWÄRTS* and *VPERED*, important in the history of the socialist and communist movement.

'Four Bigs' In China, the popular name given to the four freedoms of expression: 1. speaking out freely; 2. airing personal views fully; 3. holding great debates; and 4. writing big-character posters. They are 'guaranteed' to Chinese citizens in the Constitution of 1975 under Article 13. However, the Constitution also lays down the conditions under which the F.B. can be exercised, viz. discipline, centralism, the leadership of the Chinese Communist Party and the dictatorship of the proletariat.

'Four Clean-Ups' A campaign in China directed against economic dishonesty and 'hostile classes' in the countryside, in particular: 1. accounts; 2. warehouses; 3. properties; and 4. work points. The campaign was first staged in the early 1950s, when it corresponded to the 'FIVE ANTIS' CAMPAIGN in the cities. It reappeared in the early 1960s as part of the SOCIALIST EDUCATION MOVEMENT and as a prelude to the GREAT PROLETARIAN CULTURAL REVOLUTION. In addition to the immediate check on honesty, the campaign aimed at detecting people hostile to the Communist regime, especially amongst former landlords, rich peasants and speculators. The drive was an expression of the class struggle, in which the rural masses were to become watchdogs and champions of Socialist integrity.

'Four Firsts' In China, four principles laid down in 1960 to govern INDOCTRINATION in the Chinese army and in society in general. They were first formulated by Marshal LIN PIAO in Sep. 1960 as 'four relations', but soon were rephrased and named the 'F.F.' In terms of priority, they are: 1. the human factor over weapons; 2. political work over other work; 3. ideological study over routine political work; and 4. living ideology over ideas from books. After some revisions by Mao Tse-tung the 'F.F.' were accepted by the Military Affairs Committee and subsequently approved by the Central Committee of the Chinese Communist Party on 21 Dec. 1960. The principles were officially adopted in mid-1963 as part of training in the PEOPLE'S LIBERATION ARMY. They also played an important role during the next decade in industrial and national campaigns under the slogan of 'learn from the PLA'.

'Four Freedoms' The postulate of non-interference in agriculture, first advocated by LIU SHAO-CH'I in 1953 with respect to: 1. renting and selling land; 2. hiring labour; 3. engaging in sideline economic pursuits; and 4. lending money at interest. Liu advocated an equivalent of Lenin's NEW ECONOMIC POLICY, in order to strengthen agriculture before the collectivization drive. MAO TSE-TUNG attacked Liu's proposed course thus halting its implementation. Later, during the GREAT PROLETARIAN CULTURAL REVOLUTION, Liu was branded as a 'capitalist roader', removed from his position of power and expelled from the Party.

'Four Good' Drive An emulation campaign in the PEOPLE'S LIBERATION ARMY in China launched in 1961, which stressed the importance of being good at: 1. political and ideological work; 2. military training; 3. the THREE-EIGHT WORK STYLE; and 4. a sound management of one's living.

'Four Greats' A slogan in China popularized by CHEN PO-TA during the GREAT PROLETARIAN CULTURAL REVOLUTION as part of the PERSONALITY CULT of Mao Tse-tung. Mao was credited with the following four traits of exceptional quality: 1. great teacher; 2. great leader; 3. great supreme commander; and 4. great helmsman.

Fourier, Charles (1772–1837) A prominent French utopian socialist whose ideas, popularized in the second quarter of the 19th c., attracted the attention of K. Marx and other Marxist thinkers. F. maintained that man has 'appetites' which under capitalism become anti-social but, given an ideal society, they could prove to be sources of happiness and assets to society. He developed a vision of the ideal society in which the basic unit of social and production organization would be a PHALAN-STERY, in which there would be affluence, equality and co-operation. He believed that such a society could be evolved peacefully with the co-operation of the capitalists, without a violent revolution. His main works were: *Theory of Four Movements* (1808); *Association of Domestic agriculture* (1822); and *New Industrial Communal World* (1829). F. exerted a great influence over many social reformers. A number of model communities inspired by his ideas were established in Western Europe and North and South America, but with limited success. Although Marx acknowledged F.'s contributions and called him a 'patriarch of socialism', he did not treat them seriously. He identified F.'s proposals with UTOPIAN SOCIALISM, in that they were divorced from practical reality and the working masses.

Fourierism A direction in the French socialist movement widely propagated in the 1830s and 1840s, based on the ideas of CH. FOURIER. It envisaged the replacement of capitalism by a communal type of social organization where a PHALANX would be the basic unit regulating production, distribution and domestic life, planned centrally for the benefit of all people. The Fourierite society would be characterized by reasonable equality – a classless society where differences between physical and mental, and rural and urban, labour would disappear. But distribution would be based according to the amount of work and property contributed. F. was opposed to violence and revolution and placed its hope on persuasion and example. Revolutionary Marxists reject F. as impractical and timid, i.e. exemplifying UTOPIAN SOCIALISM.

'Four Modernizations' National goals as announced by CHOU EN-LAI at the Fourth NATIONAL PEOPLE'S CONGRESS in Jan. 1975 to carry out an all-round modernization of China by the end of this century. The modernization applies to four spheres: 1. agriculture; 2. industry; 3. defence; and 4. scientific and technical set-up. The objective is to modernize China at an accelerated pace, so that by the next century she is equal to the most advanced capitalist countries.

'Four Olds' Campaign In China, a drive launched by LIN PIAO at a Red Guards rally in Aug. 1966 against: 1. old customs; 2. old habits; 3. old thinking; and 4. old ideology. It followed the resolution forced through the Central Committee of the Chinese Communist Party by Mao Tse-tung in May 1966 to 'put destruction first, before construction'. The campaign was one of the important drives during the GREAT PROLETARIAN CULTURAL REVOLUTION, directed against the old surviving order (including books, old art objects, old ways of dress and traditional weddings).

Four Principles of Chou En-lai Four conditions laid down by the Chinese Prime Minister in 1960, binding the Japanese firms which wished to trade with China. The four conditions were: 1. no moral or material aid to Taiwan for military purposes; 2. no heavy investment in Taiwan or South Korea; 3. no supply of arms to the USA in Indochina; and 4. no significant involvement with American companies. These 'principles' were more or less in force for more than 12 years, until they were quietly dropped in early 1973.

Four Rules of Guerrilla Operations The principles of GUERRILLA WARFARE formulated and successfully tested by MAO TSE-TUNG. They are: '1. when the enemy advances, we retreat; 2. when the enemy halts, we harass; 3. when the enemy avoids battle, we attack; and 4. when the enemy retreats, we pursue'.

Fourth Estate A description sometimes applied by socialists in the 19th c. to the PROLETARIAT, by analogy to the 'Third Estate' embracing the bourgeoisie (below the aristocracy and clergy constituting the First and Second Estates) in France before the Revolution of 1789. Occasionally, the term is also used for the 'press'.

Fourth International An international revolutionary Marxist movement, founded by L. TROTSKY and his supporters in Paris on 3 Sep. 1938 as an alternative to the Third International (the COMINTERN) and the LABOUR AND SOCIALIST INTERNATIONAL. The function of the F.I., as stated by Trotsky, is to 'undermine the base of the ruling classes and to prepare for the mobilization of the masses for the revolution'. His TRANSITIONAL PROGRAMME was adopted as a guide. The F.I. has found support mainly in Latin America, Britain, the USA, France and Japan. However, it has never wielded much power, despite the dissolution of the Comintern in 1943, and has seriously suffered from splits. At its Conference in 1946, it re-established the Executive Committee of the International Secretariat in Paris. At its Fourth World Congress in 1954, the movement split into two sections: 1. the *International Secretariat* – which commanded the majority, believed that the USSR would be reformed after Stalin's death and was flexible in its doctrines; 2. the *International Committee* – with a more rigid approach, placed its hopes in the colonial revolutions in the Third World. In 1962 the Latin American Bureau of the I.S. broke away and formed the POSADIST F.I. under the leadership of a Uruguayan J. Posadas and supported by small groups in Belgium, France, the FR of Germany, Italy and Spain. In the following year another splinter group broke away, which later called itself the REVOLUTIONARY MARXIST TENDENCY of the F.I. In 1963 the I.S. changed its name to the United Secretariat, whilst the I.C. virtually disintegrated in 1972. The majority section of the latter formed the International Committee for the Reconstruction of the F.I.

Fourth of May Movement A revolutionary movement in China after W.W.I., directed against foreign imperialist influence, bureaucracy and warlords, which was led by nationalist and communist elements. It originated on 4 May 1919, when students demonstrated against the leading Western powers' 'gift' of China's Shantung Peninsula to Japan. Some of these students later joined the Chinese Communist Party after it was founded in 1921. From the Chinese Communist point of view, the F. of M.M. represented a BOURGEOIS-DEMOCRATIC REVOLUTION, as the national bourgeoisie, the petty bourgeoisie and the proletariat co-operated, with the possibility of creating a UNITED FRONT. However, that possibility did not materialize, as the bourgeoisie and the proletariat separated and followed divergent paths, led by the KUOMINTANG and the CHINESE COMMUNIST PARTY respectively.

'Four Withs' A drive in China in the early 1960s to investigate the abuses of SOCIALIST MORALITY in the countryside. The investigation was carried out directly by judiciary cadres sent to the rural areas who were required to: 1. eat; 2. live; 3. work; and 4. deliberate with poor and lower-middle peasants. In the process, both sides were expected to raise the standards of honesty and morality and expose both lax and corrupt peasants and judicial cadres.

Fractionalism Another, less frequently used, term for FACTIONALISM.

'France of the East' A description sometimes applied to Romania, especially in the 1960s, on account of its independent stand in foreign policy. Like France, Romania is not only a Romance country but also defied the USSR in the COUNCIL FOR MUTUAL ECONOMIC ASSISTANCE and the WARSAW PACT, as France defied the USA in NATO. France withdrew from the military side of NATO in 1967 and Romania refused to participate in the Warsaw Pact's INVASION OF CZECHOSLOVAKIA in 1968.

Fraternal Democrats An international moderate-revolutionary group in London which existed from 1845 to 1853. It was founded by G. J. Harvey (1817–97) and other Chartists supported by emigrés from the Continent. The F.D. represented a wide range of convictions, ranging from extreme left-wing to moderate views, but radical socialists predominated. They adopted a motto 'All people are brothers', and worked towards the international unity and solidarity of the working class. The F.D. attracted the attention of Marx and Engels, who endeavoured to steer their ideas and activities in militant, revolutionary directions.

Fraternity Pipeline A network of international pipelines for supplying natural gas from the USSR to Bulgaria, Czechoslovakia, the German DR, Hungary and Poland. It taps the extensive gasfields in Western Siberia near Orenburg, partly following the same route as the FRIENDSHIP PIPELINE (for oil). The USSR has the largest deposits of natural gas in the world. Also called 'Soyuz Gas Pipeline' or 'Transgas', it was completed in 1979. The Pipeline is 2,750 km long, bridging 150 rivers, rising up to 1,500 m above sea level, 142 cm in diameter, operating under 75kg/sq.cm. pressure and has an annual transmission capacity of 28,000m cu. m of gas.

Fraternization A term used in Socialist and trade union practice with reference to wars, demonstrations and strikes aimed at establishing friendly relations with enemy, soldiers or police against the bourgeois state or capitalists. F. was resorted to on a major scale by the Bolshevik soldiers and their sympathizers in the latter stages of W.W.I with German soldiers as an expression of PROLETARIAN INTERNATIONALISM, but without much response on the German side.

Freedom and Necessity Two philosophical concepts, the relation between which is treated differently in non-Marxist and Marxist philosophy. Whilst f. is associated with human actions, n. is concerned with the laws governing nature and society. In METAPHYSICS, f. and n. are approached as mutually exclusive categories, where some philosphers assume the absolute f. of will (VOLUNTARISM), whilst others maintain that there is no free will, only absolute will (FATALISM). Marxist-Leninist philosophy rejects these two extreme interpretations and treats f. and n. as a dialectic unity, approaching the two categories in their mutual relation conditioning each other. F. is considered to consist not in man's complete independence from natural and social laws, but in the cognition, understanding and utilization of such laws by him. But the laws operate objectively, i.e. independently of man's will, so that n. is primary whilst f. is secondary. Thus n. is viewed as inexorable only if it is unknown, whilst the knowledge of n. enables man to be a master over it. Engels (in ANTI-DÜHRING) pointed out that 'freedom is the appreciation of necessity' and he acknowledged Hegel's discovery of this relationship. The implication of this philosophical attitude is that whilst man has to act within the confines of the material world, he can utilize objective laws to change nature and society.

Free Enterprise The economic order usually identified with capitalism and typically associated with the private ownership of the means of production, the pursuit of private profit, the operation of the market mechanism and the prevalence of democratic freedoms. The term carries an emotive commendatory connotation, by implication contrasting it with state interference, bureaucracy, expropriation and the absence of civil liberties. Marxism is opposed to f.e., as it leads to EXPLOITATION, SOCIAL STRATIFICATION, CYCLICAL FLUCTUATIONS, UNEMPLOYMENT, anti-social production and, in general, the domination of the weak (small firms, the PROLETARIAT) by the strong (MONOPOLIES, the BOURGEOISIE).

Free Love Casual or continuous sexual relations or cohabitation in defiance of religious, legal or social sanctions. Traditionally in Western societies, f.l. has been frowned upon in one way or another, and its extreme condemnation is expressed in Catholic and some Protestant religions. F.l. has usually been advocated by socialist and communistic reformers, beginning especially with Fourier and Saint-Simon in the 19th c. Their view is that male-female sexual relations are a private affair, which should be left to the discretion of the individual persons concerned. Engels (in *ORIGIN OF THE FAMILY, PRIVATE PROPERTY AND THE·STATE*) contended that marriage and family relations in capitalist societies were governed by economic factors. He was in favour of marriage based on love, in which he recognized the importance of sexual gratification. But on the whole, Marxists did not advocate the socially immoral f.l., rather they condemned prostitution and rejected the anti-Marxist accusation of the 'COMMUNITY OF WOMEN'. After the Bolshevik Revolution in 1917, marriage laws in Soviet Russia were liberalized by: less-restrictive divorce laws; the removal of legal discrimination against illegitimate children; the legalization of abortion, and the passing of local laws to allow and encourage f.l. There were also extremists who pressed for the destruction of the traditional family relations. Amongst them was Aleksandra KOLLONTAI who propagated and openly practised casual sex 'for the satisfaction of her biological needs' and the 'good of the revolution'. But Lenin and most Soviet leaders were and still are against f.l. As a consequence marriage laws have been gradually tightened up. Today marriage laws and practices in the Socialist countries are not much different from those in the West, and in some countries (especially China, Poland, Romania and the USSR) sexual morality is stricter than is typically the case in the West.

Free People's State A concept used by Marx (in *CRITIQUE OF THE GOTHA PROGRAMME*) for the socialist state to operate in the transitional period from capitalism to communism. He described it as 'subordinate to the people', and contrasted it with the capitalist state as the 'agent of the bourgeoisie'. In Marx's view, after facilitating the elimination of the remnants of capitalism and the construction of the new ideal society, the state would 'wither away' under FULL COMMUNISM. In actual fact, the Socialist state has become much more powerful, autocratic and intolerant than the bourgeois state, and there appears to be little prospect for the disappearance of the state, even in the oldest Socialist country where the DICTATORSHIP OF THE PROLETARIAT was officially abandoned in 1961.

Free Trade A foreign trade policy based on the absence of state intervention. Its supporters advocate the abolition of (protective) tariffs, licensing, quotas, financial restrictions and exchange control and impositions on imports as well as exports. Historically, f.t. roughly coincided with *LAISSEZ-FAIRE*, and prevailed in some of the leading industrialized capitalist countries from the middle of the 19th c. to the Great Depression of the 1930s. The doctrine of f.t. was first formulated in England at the end of the 17th c. by D. North (in *Discourses upon Trade*, 1691) and further elaborated upon in CLASSICAL

Free Will

BOURGEOIS POLITICAL ECONOMY. Marxists reject f.t. in application to both capitalist and Socialist economies. They emphasize that in capitalist market economies f.t. leads to NON-EQUIVALENT EXCHANGE, where rich, industrialized nations exploit the poor, undeveloped countries. F.t. is completely inconsistent with a Socialist centrally planned economy, where there is STATE FOREIGN TRADE MONOPOLY and where foreign trade is integrated into the national economic plan. The opposite of f.t. is protection.

Free Will In contrast to Western philosophy, Marxism has devoted little attention to this question. Marxist philosophy maintains that all reality and development are governed by the laws of MATTER, which implies DETERMINISM. But at the same time, man can act in a creative manner, especially in the social sphere, and can accelerate certain developments or create certain situations, such as revolutions. Marxists are also opposed to FATALISM as well as VOLUNTARISM, from which it may be deduced that Marxism places f.w. between these two extremes. This assumes that f.w. operates within the constraints of the material world, especially the material conditions of production. Marxist philosophy, however, has been much more concerned with the related problem of FREEDOM AND NECESSITY.

'Free World' A designation of the capitalist world, commonly used in official and anti-communist publications in the USA and to a lesser extent in other Western countries during the COLD WAR. It included all countries outside the bloc of the 12 SOCIALIST COUNTRIES. Cuba was regarded as part of the F.W. up to 1960, and Yugoslavia was sometimes included in it as well. Although in some cases it was not intended, the description carried a favourable emotive connotation of the capitalist world, implying the lack of freedom in the Socialist bloc. Though the implication was correct, the designation was a misnomer as there were several non-Socialist countries which had autocratic and repressive regimes, such as Greece, the Philippines, Portugal, Rhodesia, South Africa and Spain. An examination of the domestic policies and practices from the standpoint of HUMAN RIGHTS in the early 1960s showed that fewer than 25 of the 100 non-Socialist countries would have actually qualified for a truly 'free world' (the USA was not among them).

Frelimo The abbreviated popular form for *Frente de Libertação de Moçambique*, in Portuguese meaning LIBERATION FRONT OF MOZAMBIQUE.

French Communist Party Normally the fourth largest political party in France, the second largest Communist party outside the Socialist bloc and one of the most influential in the capitalist world. It started as a dissident offshoot of the FRENCH SOCIALIST PARTY and it assumed a separate identity as the F.C.P. in 1920. Although it was declared illegal during W.W.II, first by the Vichy Government and then by the German occupation authorities, the Party functioned underground and was most active in the Resistance Movement. After 1972 the F.C.P. co-operated with the French Socialist Party and the Left Radical Party and jointly formulated a 'Common Programme of Government', designed to enable the 'French Left' to win the 1978 elections. However, serious differences reappeared in late 1977 which contributed to the electoral victory of the right-wing coalition in March 1978. At that election, the Communists won 86 seats in the National Assembly or 18.3 per cent of the total. The Party's membership in 1978 was 600,000 (compared with the country's total population of 53,250,000) and its Secretary-General is G. MARCHAIS. It is influential in local government and dominates the *CONFÉDÉRATION GÉNÉRALE DU TRAVAIL*, the largest labour organization. During the Sino-Soviet dispute, the Party generally supported the Soviet line. But it has displayed a good deal of independence, as illustrated by its condemnation

200

of the Soviet invasion of Czechoslovakia in 1968, and its former support of EUROCOMMUNISM. A split in 1964 led to the expulsion of a pro-Chinese group which formed the Federation of Marxist-Leninist Circles. The publications of the F.C.P. include: *L' Humanité* (*Humanity*), a daily; *France Nouvelle* (*New France*), a weekly; *La Terre* (*Land*), a peasant weekly; *Cahiers du Communism* (*Communist Notebooks*), a monthly theoretical journal; *Economie et Politique* (*Economics and Politics*), a bi-monthly journal of political economy; *La Nouvelle Critique* (*New Critical Journal*), a monthly intellectual journal; and *La Pensée* (*Thought*), a bi-monthly philosophical journal.

French Revolution A violent, political, social and economic upheaval in France 1789–99, which abolished the monarchy (and guillotined the king and queen). The Revolution, which became an important landmark in world history, was a subject of study by Marx, Engels, Lenin and Stalin. In their interpretation, it was an inevitable result of the class struggle between the bourgeoisie and feudal absolutism, whereby the old social relations no longer corresponded to the new production forces. The early stage, 1789–92, represented a bourgeois revolution for liberty, based on reason, whilst the latter stage, 1792–99, was a democratic revolution for equality. For a time, the F.R. was supported by peasants, urban workers and the poor (the third group were called the *ENRAGÉS*). Gracchus Babeuf, a utopian revolutionary (1760–97), worked to steer the Revolution towards a communist ideal, but without success (he was guillotined in 1797). The class consciousness of the proletariat was low, was poorly led and was used by the bourgeoisie for its selfish class purposes. In a series of counter-revolutionary moves by the GIRONDINS and the JACOBINS, the bourgeoisie ensured that the F.R. did not develop into a PROLETARIAN REVOLUTION. The F.R. was followed by a bourgeois government and further reinforced by Napoleon's ascension to power in 1799.

French Socialist Party About the third largest political party in France, originally founded in 1905. The F.S.P. adopted its present name in July 1969. The Party advocates economic planning, full employment and gradual nationalization. Its leader is F. Mitterand who, during the 1974 Presidential election, lost to Giscard d'Estaing. At the 1978 election, the F.S.P. won 103 seats to the parliament or 21 per cent of the total votes cast. Although the Party collaborated for some five years with the FRENCH COMMUNIST PARTY and the Left Radical Party, pursuing a 'Common Programme' to win the 1978 election, the alliance broke down in late 1977 resulting in the right-wing coalition (led by Giscard d'Estaing) being returned to power. The main organ of the F.S.P. is a weekly called *L'Unité* (*Unity*).

French Student Revolution of March–May 1968 A series of unsuccessful anti-establishment protests and violent actions by left-wing students (later supported by workers), representing the only revolutionary attempt in a Western industrial country since W.W.II. It started on 18 March as a student demonstration against IMPERIALISM (the US presence in France and the VIETNAM WAR), and soon gathered the support of many other left-wing groups. On 22 March they formed a loose organization called the TWENTY-SECOND OF MARCH MOVEMENT, led by a Franco-German student D. Cohn-Bendit (its members called themselves *ENRAGÉS*). Based at the Sorbonne in Paris, where a 'Student Soviet' was created, the Movement revolted against university authorities. By 10 May the Movement's actions developed into an attempt to overthrow the French Government and the capitalist system. Students in Belgium, Italy and Spain gave sympathetic support and a series of strikes followed all over France (9m. workers on 22 May). The Government, in a sudden move, met all the demands of the trade unions, thereby depriving the Movement of its vital industrial support. By the end of May the revolt collapsed.

3-97.25
Clean

Fretilin

Fretilin (*Frente Revolucionaria de Timor Leste Independente,* in Portuguese) The Revolutionary Front for the Independence of East Timor, a Marxist organization which was active over the period 1974–78. In Aug. 1975, it unilaterally declared the independence of the ex-Portuguese colony and proclaimed the 'Democratic Republic of East Timor' with T. X. D. Amaral as its President. The Indonesian Government intervened with troops, established effective control in Dec. 1975, massacred from 60,000 to 100,000 F. members and suspected sympathisers, accused F. of attempting to establish a satellite Communist country, declared F. illegal and on 17 July 1977 incorporated East Timor as Indonesia's 22nd province. But F.'s armed resistance continued until Dec. 1978. Since that time, some of its leaders have decided to co-operate with the Indonesian Government (incl. T. X. D. Amaral), whilst others have continued their activities opposing Indonesia, in East Timor, Australia, Mozambique and Portugal.

Freudism A doctrine founded by the Australian psycho-analyst Sigmund Freud (1856–1939), maintaining that the subconscious inexorably dominates consciousness through sexual motivation ('libido'). The libido requires an outlet, leading to aggressiveness which, owing to social pressures, is repressed. These psycho-social conflicts determine human behaviour and thought. Marxism is opposed to F. on the following grounds: 1. by attributing the decisive role to the libido, F. ignores the materialist conditioning of human attitudes and behaviour (MATERIALISM); 2. by insisting that the sexual drive begins in early childhood, thereby predetermining adult behaviour, F. in effect, subscribes to FATALISM, which is rejected in Marxist DIALECTICAL MATERIALISM; and 3. F. explains social phenomena and relations (customs, rites, institutions, revolutions, wars) in terms of sexually-conditioned appetites and aggressions, whilst Marxist HISTORICAL MATERIALISM attributes them to the material environment, especially changing PRODUCTION FORCES and PRODUCTION RELATIONS.

'Friendly Firms' A term used in China between 1960 and 1972 for those Japanese firms which met certain conditions of acceptability (mainly the absence of commercial relations with the USA and Taiwan) to the Peking regime for carrying on trade. On the advice of the Japan Communist Party and the Sohyo Federation of Labour, 50 firms (mostly medium and small) were designated as 'F.F.' Many unacceptable Japanese companies established dummy companies to pass for F.F. In 1966, China broke off commercial relations with some F.F. which were supporting the Japan C.P. which was becoming increasingly pro-Soviet. In 1969, 89 per cent of Sino-Japanese trade was conducted through the F.F. The rule of trading with the F.F. was further strengthened in 1970 by the FOUR PRINCIPLES OF CHOU EN-LAI. The insistence on trading through the F.F. was virtually dropped in the early 1970s, owing to China's increasing need for Japanese equipment and technology and her gradual improved political relationship with the USA.

Friendship Pipeline A pipeline network supplying oil from the USSR to other member countries of the COUNCIL FOR MUTUAL ECONOMIC ASSISTANCE. The F.P., which began in 1960, runs from the Volga-Ural oilfields (north-west of Kuibishev) to Mozyr (in Southern Byelorussia). From there, it branches off to the west and north (Friendship I) through Poland (Plock) to the German DR (Schwedt, Leuna, Seefeld). The southern branch leads to Bulgaria, Hungary and Czechoslovakia (up to Záluži, Most). There are also two important branch pipelines on Soviet territory running up to Klaipeda (on the Baltic Sea) and up to Odessa (on the Black Sea). The F.P. is the longest continuous oil pipeline in the world – over 5,500 km. The USSR is the largest oil producer in the world (ahead of the USA since 1974).

202

Friendship University The abbreviated form, now commonly used, of 'Patrice Lumumba People's Friendship University' in Moscow. It is an institution of higher learning providing teaching and research facilities, mainly for students from Africa, Asia and Latin America. It was established in 1960 and named after P. Lumumba, a left-wing pro-Soviet Congolese leader, assassinated in 1961. The University is financed by the Soviet state, there are no fees and is almost wholly residential. It has about 8,000 students from 90 countries (one-third are from the USSR) in eight faculties, the language of instruction is Russian and great importance is attached to practical experience. There is no evidence to suggest that F.U. is deliberately used as a training ground for Communist revolutionaries. One-fifth of all students from the less-developed countries in the USSR are enrolled at the F.U.

'Frogs' (or 'Toads') A derogatory description of the French bourgeoisie used by Marx, Engels and other left-wing German exiles who lived in France and Belgium in the four middle decades of the 19th c.

'From each according to his ability, to each according to his needs' A Marxian principle denoting the policy of work and personal income under FULL COMMUNISM. Although the idea was first put forward by a French utopian socialist, C. H. SAINT-SIMON, it was Marx who elaborated upon it, popularized it and vested it with ideological significance. The principle means that in an ideal society, each person able to work should contribute as much labour to society as he is capable by virtue of his physical and mental capacity. At the same time, his income should not be proportional to his work but according to what he legitimately needs. Under this system a perfectly fit person with outstanding work performance would receive less income from society than a non-working handicapped person. The principle has not been fully applied in any Socialist country yet, but the relatively large and growing SOCIAL CONSUMPTION is meant to implement gradually the second part of it.

'From each according to his ability, to each according to his work' A rule governing work and personal income under socialism, the transitional stage from capitalism to full communism. It essentially means that each able-bodied person in the working age group bracket should work and contribute his utmost according to his capacity and training. At the same time, personal income is differentiated according to the quantity and quality of work performed, which leads to considerable differences in income. The rule was first introduced by Lenin in 1921 with the NEW ECONOMIC POLICY, after the practical failure of the Marxian principle, 'FROM EACH ACCORDING TO HIS ABILITY, TO EACH ACCORDING TO HIS NEEDS'. Later, it was adopted by other Socialist countries. The adherence to the Leninist rule has been further strengthened since the ECONOMIC REFORMS. China, for long opposed to this rule, has decided to re-adopt it and confirmed it in the Constitution of 1975, Article 91. Its application has been strengthened by the HUA KUO-FENG regime.

Front of Socialist Unity (*Frontul Unitati Socialiste*) The political and social organization in Romania for the purpose of rallying mass support to the Communist regime and to assist in the implementation of its policies. It was created in 1968, having replaced the inactive Democratic Front, originally established in 1944 under the name of the National Democratic Front. An important reason for the creation of the F.S.U. was to strengthen further the unity and cohesion of the Romanian people in case of Soviet intervention. The Front includes the ROMANIAN COMMUNIST PARTY, trade unions, professional associations, women's organizations and national minority groups, but is completely dominated by the R.C.P. The F.S.U. encourages mass participation in the discussions of domestic and foreign policies, organizes national campaigns, arranges electoral meetings and prepares a single list of candidates for election to the GRAND NATIONAL ASSEMBLY and to the

People's Councils. At the last general elections (in 1975), according to official returns, 99.9 per cent of the electors voted for the F.S.U. candidates. The F.S.U. works through local and regional committees, co-ordinated by the National Council which is headed by Chairman N. Ceausescu (First Secretary of the R.C.P.).

Front of the Nation's Unity (*Front Jedności Narodu*) The united front of the non-bourgeois political parties and related social organizations in Poland, dominated by the POLISH UNITED WORKERS' PARTY (the ruling Communist party). It was created by the decision of the Central Committee of the P.U.W.P. in 1951 and is based on worker-peasant alliances. Its membership includes the P.U.W.P., the United Peasants Party, the Democratic Party, the Progressive Catholics, the Trade Union Movement, the Co-operative Union, the Women's League, the Students Alliance, the Rural Youth Association and the Scouts. Its function is to give mass support to the Communist regime and help implement its policies, in particular to initiate various national drives and campaigns, organize electoral meetings and prepare a list of candidates for elections. It works through local committees which is co-ordinated by the National Council (of 210 members) headed by the Presidium (of 16 members) and led by a Chairman (a member of the Political Bureau of the P.U.W.P.). There is also a Secretariat of 10 persons. At the March 1976 general election, the numbers of the deputies elected from the single list of candidates were as follows (of the total of 460 seats in the SEJM): P.U.W.P., 261; U.P.P., 113; D.P., 33; and Non-Party, 49. According to official data, 99.4 per cent of the electorate voted for the F.N.U. candidates.

Front Organizations See INTERNATIONAL COMMUNIST FRONT ORGANIZATIONS.

Frunze, Mikhail Vassilevich (1885–1925) A Bolshevik military commander and a Party activist. He participated in the RE-VOLUTION OF 1905–07 and was twice sentenced to death by the Tsarist courts. In 1917, he organized the first units of the RED GUARDS in Byelorussia and directly participated in the GREAT OCTOBER SOCIALIST REVOLUTION. During the Civil War and the FOREIGN INTERVENTION, he was one of the leading commanders of the RED ARMY responsible for the defeat of the counter-revolutionary armies of A. KOLCHAK in Turkestan and P. WRANGEL in the Crimea in 1919. Elected to the Control Committee of the RUSSIAN COMMUNIST PARTY (OF THE BOLSHEVIKS) in 1921, he subsequently became the Chief of the General Staff of the Red Army and the Commandant of the Military Academy (now bearing his name). In 1925 he was appointed Commissar [Minister] for the Army and Navy, replacing the disgraced L. Trotsky. F. also made significant contributions to military theory. After his death, the place of his birth, Pishpek, was renamed in his honour (the capital city of the Kirghiz S.S.R.).

Full Communism According to Marxists, the highest stage of political, economic and social development, to succeed SOCIALISM. F.C. was incidentally described by K. Marx and F. Engels in *THE GERMAN IDEOLOGY* and *THE COMMUNIST MANIFESTO*, by K. Marx in *CRITIQUE OF THE GOTHA PROGRAMME*, by V.I. Lenin in the *THE STATE AND REVOLUTION* and by L. Trotsky in *LITERATURE AND REVOLUTION*. In their vision, F.C. is to be characterized by eight features. 1. the complete socialization of the means of production; 2. the abolition of money; 3. the elimination of market relations; 4. all-round affluence; 5. work and distribution governed by the principle, 'FROM EACH ACCORDING TO HIS ABILITY, TO EACH ACCORDING TO HIS NEEDS'; 6. a CLASSLESS SOCIETY; 7. the WITHERING AWAY OF THE STATE; and 8. the disappearance of political and economic boundaries. Some of these features are mutually inconsistent, such as 2 and 4, and 3 and 7, above. No Socialist country has reached F.C. yet. In Oct. 1961, N. KHRUSCHEV predicted that the USSR (the oldest Socialist country) would start entering F.C. in about 1980. However, owing to the slowdown in the economic growth since that time in the USSR and other Socialist countries, the arrival of F.C. has been delayed. Furthermore, F.C. cannot be completely established as long as there are powerful capitalist states.

Full Employment A situation in the economy when virtually everybody who wants to work can find employment, or when the number of work vacancies is at least equal to registered unemployment. Absolute (100 per cent) f.e. can never exist, due to frictional unemployment. Under Socialism, owing to the social ownership of the means of production and central economic planning, frictional unemployment can be reduced to 0.5–1.0 per cent of the total labour force, whilst in capitalist market economies the proportion is typically 2.0–3.0 per cent. Consequently, f.e. in the Socialist centrally planned economies exists when 99.0–99.5 per cent of the labour force is employed, whilst under capitalism the proportion is 97.0–98.0 per cent. On the whole, the Socialist countries have experienced continuous f.e. (Yugoslavia being the conspicuous exception), whilst capitalist countries usually attain it only in wartime and boom periods.

Functionalism In the ideologically relevant context, it has two different meanings. 1. in Socialist art, architecture and craftwork, the adaptation of the shape of furniture, buildings and other objects to the functions performed by them in practice, rather than an aesthetic expression of 'ART FOR ART'S SAKE'. F. leads to simplicity, logic and easy identification. As such, it is a facet of SOCIALIST REALISM; 2. in sociological systems analysis, f. denotes a modern trend in Western sociology since W.W.I. that is preoccupied with the theoretical and methodological study of the structure of societies as functional units. It has its roots in the social anthropology and ethnology of B. Malinowski (1884–1942), A. R.

Radcliffe-Brown (1881–1955) and others. F. emphasizes the microsocial and macrosocial network of organic links in society, which are treated as functional and self-regulating. Marxist sociologists point out that the systems analysis was first consistently applied by the founders of HISTORICAL MATERIALISM, especially by Marx. Further, they maintain that as the bourgeois analysis is largely static, it is retrogressive compared with the Marxist historical and dynamic approach. Marxists approach the study of society as a process of change through evolution and revolution, in response to the changing PRODUCTION FORCES and PRODUCTION RELATIONS.

Functional Pricing Planned pricing where prices are set at such levels as to perform desired functions. It is commonly practised in the Socialist centrally planned economies in pursuit of such objectives as the saving of particular resources, the promotion of the production of particular articles, the improvement of quality, the adjustment of demand to the predetermined supply, the equalization of personal income (via high prices of luxuries and low prices of necessities) and the attainment of the desired level of saving in the economy. As such, f.p. departs from SCARCITY PRICES and may interfere with the most efficient utilization of resources.

Futurism A movement in the arts (especially literature, painting, sculpture and theatre) which developed in the first quarter of the 20th c., rejecting the past and the traditional forms of art in favour of radical ideas and expression. Extremist futurists declared war on past conventions, describing them as having 'utilitarian cowardice' and 'artistic impotence' and even advocated the destruction of libraries, museums and galleries. F. originated in Italy (where F. T. Marinetti coined the term) and in Poland and Russia. Unlike Italian f., which was nationalistic and later fascist and militaristic, the East European version became proletarian and revolutionary. In Russia, where f. appeared in about 1910, the best known futurist was V. MAYAKOVSKY, who later became the 'poet of the Revolution'. F. received a good deal of support from the early Soviet regime, and played a part in creating the new PROLETARIAN ART. However, Lenin disagreed with the individualistic and anarchistic proclivities of the Soviet futurists and their rejection of traditional culture. Official support was soon withdrawn, especially under Stalin after 1925, and after Mayakovsky's suicide it virtually disappeared. Also CUBO-FUTURISM.

Futurology The scientific study of the future, including the methodology of short-term forecasting and long-term projections. It is concerned with the prospective developments in the availability and utilization of resources, technology, population, political, economic and social developments and international relations. F. assumed rigorous advanced levels in the West in the 1960s with the leading industrialized nations establishing special institutes or study groups for the purpose. F. has been placed on a much more systematic basis in the Socialist countries for two major reasons. 1. Marxism is essentially concerned with the transformation of the existing societies into the future society of FULL COMMUNISM. Moreover, it is claimed that only Marx and Engels discovered the scientific laws of social development; 2. central economic planning requires precise and detailed information on the availability of resources, demographic, technological and social developments in the construction of short, medium and prospective plans, up to 20 years ahead.

G

Gang of Four The group of four high-ranking members of the Chinese Communist Party, active in the cultural field, who formed a 'left opposition' after the GREAT PROLETARIAN CULTURAL REVOLUTION but in 1976–81 were expelled from the Party, arrested and put on public trial. According to Party seniority, they were: 1. WANG HUNG-WEN (Vice-Chairman of the Central Committee of the C.C.P.); 2. CHANG CH'UN-CHIAO (member of the Politburo); 3. CHIANG CHI'NG (member of the Politburo, widow of Mao Tse-tung); 4. YAO WEN-YUAN (member of the Politburo). In the campaign against them from 1975 to 1977, they were accused of: 1. pursuing a counter-revolutionary line in the arts and a revisionist and disruptive course against the party; 2. misrepresenting Mao's directives; 3. scheming to seize power; 4, trying to assassinate Hua Kuo-feng; 5. interfering in the running of the PEOPLE'S LIBERATION ARMY; 6. advocating extreme equalitarianism (the same wage for all industrial workers); and 7. endeavouring to establish ties with the USSR. According to the present regime, they had been attacked by Mao himself, who allegedly coined the description of the 'G. of F.' at a Politburo meeting on 3 May 1975. The G. of F. were arrested on 6–7 Oct. 1976, stripped of their posts, expelled from the Party in mid-July 1977 and closely watched (under house arrest) by the authorities since. They were officially branded as follows: Wang – 'a new bourgeois element'; Chang – 'a Kuomintang special agent'; Chiang – 'a renegade'; and Yao – 'an alien class element'. Publicly tried Dec. 1980–Feb 1981 they were sentenced: Yao – 20yrs, Wang – life imprisonment, Chang and Chiang – death sentences conditionally suspended.

Gapon, Father Georg Apollonovich (1870–1906) A controversial Russian priest who headed a large procession of dissatisfied workers in St. Petersburg (now Leningrad) on 9 Jan. 1905, to present a petition to the Tsar for improved working conditions and liberal reforms. The driving force behind the procession was the Union of Russian Factory Workers, which G. had organized in the preceding year. The event turned into the disastrous BLOODY SUNDAY, when about 1,000 participants were massacred by the Tsarist police and Cossacks (and many more wounded). For obscure reasons G. escaped from Russia after the event, and when he returned in the following year he was murdered. The BOLSHEVIKS described him as a police agent who had deliberately set out to provoke and expose radical elements. Others considered him a genuine reformer with high ideals, but too naïve to be able to cope with complex situations and conflicting revolutionary, religious and reactionary interests.

Gaponade A movement ostensibly representing the working class, but manipulated by the police representing the bourgeois state and establishment. Its purpose is to expose genuine revolutionary leaders, separate them from the working masses by bribery and then turn them into scapegoats for the failures and arrests. The term was originally coined in

207

Russia from the name of Father G. A. GAPON after the events of BLOODY SUNDAY in 1905.

GAZ The Russian abbreviation for the Gorky Motor Works (*Gorkovsky Avtomobilnyi Zavod*). It is used to identify motor vehicles (trucks, vans, passenger cars, incl. the *Chaika* and *Volga*) made at the Works established in Gorky (about 500 km. east of Moscow) in 1932. The present name of the factory dates since 1958, when it replaced the 'Molotov Motor Works'.

Gdańsk Riots Strikes and violence centred in the shipyards in the Polish port and industrial centre of Gdańsk in Dec. 1970. The rioters were not former capitalists, intellectuals or dissidents, or an anticommunist political group, but workers protesting against sharp increases in the prices of food and oppressive working and political conditions. Violence erupted and troops and tanks were sent by the government against the rioters, which led to substantial damage to property and cost 45 lives. The G.R. resulted in the replacement of W. Gomułka's regime with that of E. GIEREK as the leader of the POLISH UNITED WORKERS' PARTY. Similar riots occurred in other Polish cities (BALTIC CITIES RIOTS, SOLIDARITY).

GDR Abbreviation for the (East) GERMAN DEMOCRATIC REPUBLIC.

General Conditions of Delivery A short version of the 'General Conditions of Delivery of Goods between Enterprises of the Member Countries of the Council for Mutual Economic Assistance'. It is a document regulating the practical conduct of trade amongst the CMEA countries, adopted in 1968 and supplemented by several protocols since that time. It consists of 110 paragraphs regulating such questions as the formulation of contracts, the terms of delivery, quality, packaging, technical documentation, guarantees, payment procedures, penalties and the settlement of commercial disputes.

General Crisis of Capitalism A Marxist concept denoting the emergence of fundamental contradictions and the processes of disintegration of capitalism. The g.c. is claimed to emerge in the highest stage of capitalism, viz. IMPERIALISM, and embraces all the major spheres of society's existence, i.e. the economy, politics and ideology. Three phases are distinguished historically in this process: 1. W.W.I. weakening of the imperialist states, the victory of the GREAT OCTOBER SOCIALIST REVOLUTION and the establishment of the first Socialist state in 1917; 2. W.W.II, the defeat of imperialist FASCISM and the formation of ten more Socialist states in Eastern Europe and Asia; and 3. since 1960, the emergence and development of NATIONAL LIBERATION MOVEMENTS the breaking up of colonial empires and the turn of many liberated countries to socialism (nationalization, economic planning, social welfare programmes, and trade with the Socialist bloc). Other features further aggravating capitalist problems are idle production capacity, unemployment, inflation, the struggle for markets and the exacerbation and internationalization of industrial disputes. In the Marxist view, the g.c. of c. creates pre-conditions for PROLETARIAN REVOLUTIONS and must inevitably lead to the world communist system.

General German Workers' Association The first broadly based German working-class organization, founded in Leipzig in 1863, and the first important social-democratic party in the world (from which the present SOCIAL-DEMOCRATIC PARTY OF GERMANY has evolved). It was headed by F. LASSALLE and it included such members as K. MARX, F. ENGELS, A. BEBEL, W. LIEBKNECHT. But the Association suffered from conflicts between Lassalle's right-wing group and the radical revolutionary faction. At the Eisenach Conference in 1869, the revolutionary faction led by A. Bebel and W. Liebknecht established a separate party called the SOCIAL-DEMOCRATIC WORKERS' PARTY, whilst the G.G.W.A. continued as a reformist socialist party co-operating with Bismarck's regime. In 1875 at the Gotha Congress the two organizations agreed to unite, and formed the Socialist Workers' party of Germany.

General line for the transition period of the state A policy direction proclaimed by the Chinese Communist Party and the Government in autumn 1953 and embarked upon in 1954. Its main goals were the extension of the social ownership of the means of production (especially in industry), industrialization (emphasizing heavy and large-scale industry) and the social transformation of China.

General Secretary of the Communist Party See SECRETARY-GENERAL (of the Central Committee of the Communist Party).

General Strike A simultaneous political strike by virtually all the workers in a country, especially those organized in unions. A g.s. is regarded by the advocates of SYNDICALISM as the ultimate weapon for overthrowing capitalism, but not by orthodox Marxists who do not accept it as sufficient and thus no substitute for the PROLETARIAN REVOLUTION. The idea of the g.s. was first popularized by an English trade union leader, William Benbow, in 1832, when he advocated the formation of the GRAND NATIONAL CONSOLIDATED TRADES UNION (which was actually established in 1834) and the staging of a 'grand national holiday of the working class'. There were several attempts to hold a g.s., namely: Russia in 1905; Belgium in 1913; Germany in 1920; Britain in 1926; and France in 1968. However, none was comprehensive and long enough to achieve its broad objectives. The best known g.s. was that in Britain, initiated by the coal miners with promised support from the TRADES UNION CONGRESS. It was declared on 4 May 1926. But the Conservative Government in power (headed by Stanley Baldwin) was able to run essential services by non-union labour, mostly middle-class volunteers and troops. Many trade union leaders and strikers were too

timid and the T.U.C. refused support after 12 May, although the miners continued their strike until August. In the following year, the Baldwin Government passed an Act through Parliament prohibiting general strikes, which remained in force until the Labour Government repealed it in 1946. The only g.s. that has so far occurred in a Socialist country was the HUNGARIAN UPRISING of 1956, which also proved unsuccessful.

Genetic and Teleological Planning Two contrasting approaches to economic planning, the former being more conservative and preoccupied with the continuation of past developments, and the latter emphasizing a rapid transformation of the economy to reach postulated future objectives. The terms were first established in the USSR in the 1920s as the result of a controversial debate on developmental strategies. In the case of g.p., past patterns of the allocation of resources and of the distribution of output and past trends are accepted as basic. The economic plans essentially involve the extrapolation and correction of past developments. It contrasts with t.p., or 'planning by objectives', where planners deliberately set out to change the previous patterns and tendencies and are essentially guided by the desired future. Plans are accordingly constructed with a view to transforming the economy by initiating and accelerating developments in socially desired directions. G.p. is more suited to the early stages of economic development, where planning techniques are simple, where there is a prevalent conservatism and where there is an important sector (such as agriculture or foreign trade) which cannot be easily planned. On the other hand, t.p. is typical of countries with a highly developed and comprehensive system of planning and where the authorities are determined to achieve their social objectives rapidly.

Genetics The field of biology concerned with the study of the transmission of characteristics in living organisms from one generation to another. According to g., characteristics of plants, animals and human beings are products of heredity transmitted through genes ('units of heredity'). The term g. was introduced in 1906 (replacing 'eugenics') by an English biologist, W. Bateson (1861–1920), who is regarded as the founder of g. Others who made the most important contributions included: G. Mendel (1822–84), basic laws of heredity in plants; F. Galton (1822–1911), the application of statistical methods to the study of heredity; A. Weismann (1834–1914), theory of embryonic plasma; and T. Morgan (1866–1945), chromosome theory of heredity. G. has received a stormy and mixed reception from Marxists. After the Bolshevik Revolution, Lenin appointed N. I. Vavilov (1887–1943), a distinguished Russian geneticist, to take charge of all genetic research in the USSR. But his position gradually deteriorated after Lenin's death (1924), as it was soon recognized that g. was in conflict with Marxism. Initially, Marx and Engels had maintained that acquired characteristics could be inherited. Later Soviet leaders (especially Stalin), recognized the significance of this idea in the evolution of the NEW COMMUNIST MAN by the suitable manipulation of the environment. G. also highlighted differences between individuals and implied inherited inequalities between social classes and races. Thus under the Stalinist regime, g. was declared a fascist distortion of science and official support was instead given to MICHURINISM and LYSENKOISM. In 1939, Vavilov was removed from his position of authority (and replaced by T. D. LYSENKO), arrested in 1940 and died in a Siberian forced labour camp in 1942. Opposition to g. in other Socialist countries, although officially evident, was never as strong as in the USSR. However, the uncritical support to Lysenkoism began to be questioned as early as 1951 and after 1956 it became gradually discredited. A *de facto* official acceptance of g. took place in 1965, when the Soviet Government sent a delegation of genericists to an international symposium in Prague (held under the auspices of the Czechoslovak Govern-

ment) to commemorate the centenary of the original appearance of Mendel's pioneering contribution. About 800 geneticists, from both capitalist and Socialist countries attended.

Geneva Agreements A series of international accords and declarations prepared and signed at the Conference on Indochina held in Geneva from 26 April to 2 Aug. 1954. They followed the French defeat by the Communist forces of North Vietnam at DIEN BIEN PHU. There were 12 agreements to this effect: 1. accord on a ceasefire in Vietnam; 2. accord on a ceasefire in Laos; 3. accord on a ceasefire in Cambodia; 4. declaration of the Government of Laos concerning military alliances, foreign military bases and military aid; 5. declaration of the Government of Cambodia concerning people's rights and elections; 6. declaration of the Government of Cambodia concerning military alliances, military bases and military aid; 7. declaration of the French Government concerning the withdrawal of French forces from Indochina; 8. declaration of the French Government concerning the guarantee of independence and sovereignty of Cambodia, Laos and Vietnam; 9. declaration of the American representative explaining the US Government's stand on the Indochina question; 10. final declaration of the Geneva Conference on the Restoration of Peace in Indochina by the representatives of Cambodia, Laos, the D.R. of [North] Vietnam, the R. of [South] Vietnam, the P.R. of China, France, Great Britain, the USA and the USSR – with the legal force as an international treaty; 11. accord on economic and cultural relations between the D.R. of Vietnam and France, concluded in the form of exchange of letters between Pham Van Dong (Vice-premier) and P. Mendès-France (Premier); and 12. to implement the agreements, the creation of an International Supervisory and Control Commission. The USA later declared that as she has not officially participated in the negotiations, she was not bound by the G.A.

210

German Communist Party

Geographical Doctrine in Sociology A doctrine attributing the decisive role in social development to the geographical environment. Its chief exponents were C. L. Montesquieu (1689–1755), H. T. Buckle (1821–62) and L. I. Mechnikov (1838–88). Thus differences between nations and their social systems are explained as a consequence of the differences in climate, soil, physiography, flora and fauna and minerals. Marxist sociology, with the exception of certain obvious qualifications, does not agree with this interpretation. Although Marxists concede the influence of geographical factors on the material conditions of life of societies, they emphasize that their role declines with social development. Whilst the geographical environment remains stable over long periods, societies change fairly rapidly through evolution and revolution. Furthermore, man himself alters the geographical environment. In the Marxist view, fundamental factors governing the development of societies are changes in the MODE OF PRODUCTION. The higher the level of development of PRODUCTION FORCES, the higher the stage of social development, and at the same time the less society is dependent on primary natural conditions. This is particularly so in the Socialist countries, where natural resources are not monopolized by private egoistic owners, but owned by the whole society. This facilitates a planned utilization and adaptation of the geographical environment.

Geopolitics Political theory postulating that the key geographical position of large nations demands (and justifies) the extension of their living space and boundaries at the expense of other peoples. This postulate is based on the extreme acceptance of the GEOGRAPHICAL DOCTRINE IN SOCIOLOGY, where the geographical environment is treated as a critical factor in society's development. The term g. was popularized by R. Kjellén (1864–1922), a Swedish supporter of Pan-Germanism (in *The State and Living Space*, 1917). Other writers who elaborated upon the theory include F. Ratzel (1844–1904) of Germany, A. T. Mahon (1840–1914) of the USA and H. J. Mackinder (1861–1947) of Britain. Marxism rejects g. not only for being unscientific, but above all for being a convenient justification for IMPERIALISM, FASCISM (of the Italian, Nazi, imperial Japanese and South African types) and US expansionism (incl. the LIMITED SOVEREIGNTY DOCTRINE). Marxists point out that the geographical environment is not a decisive factor in social development. The geographical environment is relatively stable, whilst foreign policy changes more rapidly and does so in response to changes in the socio-economic system, conditioned by the MODE OF PRODUCTION.

George, Henry (1837–97) An American economist and a social reformer who criticized capitalism and advocated the complete absorption by the state of the DIFFERENTIAL RENT on the unimproved value of land in the form of a single (and the only) tax (in *Progress and Poverty*, 1879). He believed that the main cause of poverty was the monopolistic ownership of land and steadily increasing ground rent, leading to declining wages and profits (in real terms). He was largely motivated by idealistic religious beliefs and did not press for the nationalization or collectivization of land but wanted to retain private incentives and freedom. Marxists never treated his ideas seriously, regarding them as limited, and he was in fact attacked for his 'petty bourgeois' outlook and religious naivety.

German Communist Party *(Deutsche Kommunistische Partei)* A small, legal political party in the FR of [West] Germany in existence since Sep. 1968. Its origin goes back to 31 Dec. 1918, when the SPARTACUS LEAGUE (formed in 1916 by a left-wing group of the SOCIAL-DEMOCRATIC PARTY OF GERMANY) founded the Communist Party of Germany. In the following month, under the leadership of KARL LIEBKNECHT and ROSA LUXEMBURG, it staged an unsuccessful

211

German Democratic Republic

proletarian revolution. In 1920, the left-wing faction of the Independent Social Democratic Party of Germany merged with the C.P.G. and formed the United Communist Party of Germany, which in turn then dropped the qualification 'United'. The Party was illegal under the Nazi regime 1933–45, but continued its activities underground and abroad. It operated legally from 1945 to 1956, but then went underground again. The G.C.P. was founded in 1968 as a legal party and was joined by many members of the illegal C.P.G. The G.C.P., which has about 40,000 members (of the total population of 61,400,000 in 1979), draws its support from some trade unions, especially the industrial area of the Ruhr (its headquarters are in Düsseldorf) and intellectuals (especially in universities). At the 1976 Federal elections, it polled 0.3% of the votes and won no seats. In its international orientation, the Party has followed a pro-Soviet line. The Party's main regular publications are: *Unsere Zeit* (*Our Times*), a daily; and *Marxistische Blätter* (*Marxist Papers*), a theoretical bi-monthly. It may be added here that the legal G.C.P. as well as the illegal C.P.G. are distinct from the Communist parties in the [East] German DR, called the SOCIALIST UNITY PARTY OF GERMANY, and in West Berlin, bearing the name of the Socialist Unity Party of West Berlin.

German Democratic Republic (*Deutsche Demokratische Republik*) The eastern part of Germany which was occupied by the USSR during 1945–49 but proclaimed an independent state on 7 Oct. 1949, following the BERLIN BLOCKADE and the creation of the Federal Republic of [West] Germany (on 20 Sep. 1949). The area and population of the G.D.R. are 108,178 sq km and 16,750,000 people in 1978 (compared with the F.R.G.'s 248,620 sq km and 61,400,000) and its capital is in East Berlin (whilst that of the F.R.G. is in Bonn). The effective power rests with the SOCIALIST UNITY PARTY OF GERMANY, headed by E. Honecker, the First Secretary. The original Constitution of 1949 was replaced by a new one in 1968 and amended in 1972. The highest formal source of legislative power is the People's Chamber (VOLKSKAMMER), whose work between sessions is carried on by the National Council headed by the Chairman (Willi Stolph). An intensification of the class struggle and socialist construction was announced in 1952. The regime has pursued about the most orthodox Communist policies in the Socialist bloc. It has achieved impressive economic and technical results and the highest standard of living of all the Socialist countries. The G.D.R. was admitted to the COUNCIL FOR MUTUAL ECONOMIC ASSISTANCE in 1950, to the Warsaw Pact in 1955 and to the United Nations in 1973. From the start, the G.D.R. became dependent on the political and military backing, as well as the raw materials and markets, of the USSR. Both regimes have consistently given each other loyal support.

German Ideology, The (*Die Deutsche Ideologie*) A philosophical study written jointly by K. MARX and F. ENGELS in Brussels in 1845–46, but first published in the USSR in 1932. The book contains a further development of philosophical ideas introduced in their previous joint work HOLY FAMILY, together with a critique of the idealism of the HEGELIAN LEFT and the limited materialism of L. FEUERBACH. There is the first systematic exposition of HISTORICAL MATERIALISM, in particular some of the laws of social development and the analysis of the SOCIO-ECONOMIC FORMATIONS. The authors attacked the prevalent 'degeneration' of German philosophy, the hostility of philosophical IDEALISM to the working classes, the passive and metaphysical nature of materialism as propagated by Feuerbach, bourgeois INDIVIDUALISM, the so-called True Socialism, NATIONALISM and PETTY BOURGEOIS attitudes. Further, they put forward the basic foundations of socialism, stressed the need for the cultivation of revolutionary qualities amongst workers, emphasized the need for a PROLETARIAN REVOLUTION as the only way to the construction of a new, ideal society. They also dwelt on the nature of economic laws which they considered as objective categories, independent of human will.

German October A name given to the attempted Communist insurrection in Germany staged in Oct. 1923. It was instigated by the COMINTERN, but met with little popular support in Germany and failed miserably.

German Social-Democratic Party See SOCIAL-DEMOCRATIC PARTY OF GERMANY.

German Socialist Unity Party See SOCIALIST UNITY PARTY OF GERMANY.

Germ Warfare See BACTERIOLOGICAL WARFARE.

Gestapu Affair The unsuccessful coup staged by the COMMUNIST PARTY OF INDONESIA in 1965, and the consequent massacre of Communists. The name 'Gestapu' is derived from *Gerakan September Tiga Pulu*, in Indonesian meaning the 'Thirtieth of September Movement'. It was on the night of 30 Sep. 1965 that the top Communist Party leaders, together with left-wing Army and Air Force officers, attempted to seize power in Djakarta (for the third time in Indonesian history). Six generals were murdered by Communist youths, but the army units led by Gen. Suharto quickly overcame the rebels in two days in the Djakarta area, although fighting continued in the provinces. Anti-communist Muslim youth groups massacred several hundred thousand Communists, mostly Chinese, and 580,000 Indonesians were detained for alleged complicity in the coup. The final sequel to the G.A. was the proscription of the Indonesian Communist Party on 12 March 1966.

Giap Vietnamese general and versatile political leader, whose full name is VO NGUYEN GIAP.

Gierek, Edward (1913–) The Polish Communist party leader who succeeded W. Gomułka in Dec. 1970 as a result of the BALTIC CITIES RIOTS. From 1923 to 1948 he lived in France and Belgium, where he later worked as a coalminer. He joined the French Communist Party in 1931 and the Communist Party of Belgium in 1937. During W.W.II he was active in the Belgian Resistance and among the Polish emigrés he organized an illegal branch of the UNION OF THE POLISH PATRIOTS (based in Moscow and subservient to Soviet policies). He returned to Poland in 1948 and rose rapidly in the hierarchy of the POLISH UNITED WORKERS' PARTY. Elected to the Central Committee in 1954 and to the Party Secretariat in 1956, he was promoted to the Politburo in 1959 and in the 1960s emerged as the Party's leading specialist on economic affairs. Since Dec. 1970, when he became the First Secretary of the P.U.W.P., he has demonstrated a good deal of personal courage, political astuteness and practical economic commonsense in the rather precarious circumstances in which Poland has found herself. He was ousted from power and replaced by S. Kania in the wake of widespread strikes.

Gigantomania Obsession with grand achievements for their own sake, where cost usually exceeds their commonsense usefulness. The term has often been applied to the USSR and sometimes to China, especially in the Stalinist era. G. was officially condemned in the USSR by a Party instruction of 1934, but it persisted and was revived in the early 1950s, especially in the economic field. It was conditioned by the faulty system of investment (free allocation of investment resources to enterprises out of the state budget), the Communist leaders' desire to impress the masses at home and abroad, and to highlight the superiority of communism over capitalism. Thus Soviet leaders and writers like to point out that communism has enabled the USSR to become the largest world producer (ahead of the USA) of black coal, books, bricks, buses, cement, coal, cotton goods, fertilizers, grain harvesters, iron ore, locomotives, manganese ore, metal-working machinery, oil, peat, reinforced concrete structures, steel, steel pipes, sugar, timber (sawn), tractors, window glass and woollen goods. The USSR also has the largest electrode factory (at Novosibirsk), helicopter (V-2), hydroelectric power station (Sayan-Sushenskoe), nuclear reactors construction plant (Volgodonsk), telescope (Mount Zblenchukskaya in the Urals), thermal power station (Krivoi Rog) and truck factory (Kama) in the world, the longest oil pipeline (Friendship) and railway line (T.S.R.) in the world, the tallest earth fill dam (Rogun) in the world, and the most powerful turbo-generator (Kostroma), atomic reactor (Byeloyarsk), icebreaker (*Arktika*) and weapon exploded in world history (nuclear bomb in 1960). A facet of g. were PALACES OF LABOUR.

Girondins A moderate political group prominent in the FRENCH REVOLUTION, who wanted the bourgeoisie to subdue the nobility, but did not wish the power to be shared by urban workers and peasants. The G. opposed the left-wing JACO-BINS, and, rather than allow the Revolution to develop into a PROLETARIAN RE-VOLUTION, they allied themselves with royalists. Lenin, in his confrontation with the moderates in the Russian Social-Democratic Labour Party, especially the MENSHEVIKS, described them as the 'Socialist Gironde'.

Global Income In Socialist enterprise accounting, total receipts of an enterprise. It is smaller than the 'grosss income' by the value of materials purchased from outside. If wages are further deducted, the balance is known as the GROSS PROFIT.

Global Product In Socialist national income accounting, the total value of output in the material branches of the economy (industry, construction, agriculture, transport and communications, trade) in a country over a particular period (usually a

year) at realized prices. When materials used and depreciation are deducted, the balance is the national income as defined by the Socialist method, or better known in Western terminology as the NET MATERIAL PRODUCT. The nearest Western concept to g.p. is the 'gross national product', which excludes materials used, but also includes NON-PRODUCTIVE SERVICES.

Goal Pricing TARGET PRICING.

God To believers, the highest supernatural and the most powerful being, identified with truth, justice and idealism, and the object of religious veneration and worship. Marxism, both in philosophy and in sociology, denies the validity of the existence of g. and emphasizes the negative causes and consequences of the belief in g. Marxists reject the philosophy of IDEAL-ISM, largely because of its implicit or explicit acceptance of the idea of g., whilst MATERIALISM restricts itself to man and his world. The idea of g. is seen as a historical process, reflecting the stage of cultural and social development through: 1. primitive myth; 2. systematized myth; 3. religious dogma; 4. abstract being; and 5. theology (the normative study of g., interpretation, proof, defence). In the Marxist social view, g. is embraced either by the unscrupulous church hierarchy or the ignorant, naïve and the oppressed. To the masses g. is a desperate escape from the hopeless social conditions which in their belief only miracles could change. The belief in g. only makes the masses humble and submissive to the exploiting ruling classes, makes them and conditions them to be reconciled to their fate in expectation of reward after life. Also CHRIS-TIANITY, CHRISTIAN SOCIALISM, DEISM, FIDEISM, GOD-SEEKING, RELIGION, THEISM.

God-Seeking (or God-Constructing, or God-Inventionism) A middle-class religio-socialist movement in Russia after the failure of the REVOLUTION OF 1905–07, endeavouring to reconcile Marxism with religion. It identified god with fair play, social justice, humanity and the dignity of all social classes. The leading exponents of G.S. were V. A. Bazarov (1874–1939), A. A. BOGDANOV (1873–1928), A. V. LUNACHARSKY (1875–1933) and D. S. Merezhovsky (1865–1941). Lenin attacked the movement (in *MATERIALISM AND EMPIRIO-CRITICISM*) as a reaction of despair and a bourgeois attempt to undermine Marxism and the solidarity of the revolutionary working-class movement.

Goelro An abbreviation in Russian of *Gossudarstvennaya Komissiya po Elektrifikatsi Rossy*, meaning the State Commission for the Electrification of Russia. It was established in 1920 to develop power generation and the transmission network on the initiative of Lenin, who said, 'Communism is Soviet power plus the electrification of the whole country'. *G.* immediately produced a plan (on the basis of a scheme prepared by the Tsarist Government during W.W.I) for achieving the task in 10–15 years by the construction of 20 thermal and 10 hydroelectric regional power stations and the necessary transmission lines. It was the first planned effort for the industrialization of Soviet Russia. The Commission was reorganized in 1921 and incorporated into the *GOSPLAN*, which was established in the same year and headed by *GOELRO'S* chairman, G. M. Kzhizhanovsky (an engineer). The *G.* scheme was later embodied into the Five-Year Plans, the original targets implemented ahead of schedule.

Gold Curtain A term sometimes used to describe the Western forms of monetary and financial boycotts and controls against the Socialist countries, especially the ban on the purchase of Soviet gold in the early years following the Bolshevik Revolution. The term parallels IRON CURTAIN. Also FINANCIAL CURTAIN.

Golos Sotsial-Demokrata ('*The Voice of the Social-Democrat*', in Russian.) The main bulletin of the MENSHEVIKS, published outside Russia (in Geneva, then in Paris) from 1908 to 1911. It was edited by

F. T. Dan (1871–1947) and L. MARTOV, The G.S.-D. was directed against the BOLSHEVIKS and Lenin's leadership.

Gorky, Maxim (1868–1936) The assumed pen name of Aleksiei Maksimovich Peshkov, a Russian writer and the initiator of the literature of SOCIALIST REALISM. Of proletarian family background and self-educated. he became interested in *NARODNISM* and embarked upon his literary work in 1892. He joined the revolutionary movement in 1905 and corresponded with Lenin. He advocated a simple ideal society based on justice, love and religion, and for a time was associated with the GOD-SEEKING group. After the Bolshevik Revolution he was very active among writers supporting the Soviet regime. He later developed the idea of REVOLUTIONARY ROMANTICISM and literature based on folklore. In his world famous books and tales, he depicted the feelings and sufferings of the poor and oppressed most perceptively and sympathetically. According to official Soviet sources, he was poisoned by Trotskyites.

Gosbank The syllabic abbreviation in Russian of *Gossudarstvennyi Bank*, meaning the State Bank (of the USSR). It was established (under that name) in 1921 and took over the functions of the People's Bank (founded on 25 Oct. 1917 but dissolved in 1920). The *G.*'s responsibilities include currency issue, the provision of short-term credit, clearing operations in the form of CASHLESS SETTLEMENTS amongst socialized entities, financial control over enterprises (CONTROL BY THE ROUBLE), the collection of savings and the holding of international reserves. Its power has been increased considerably by its exclusive power to extend short-term credit since 1930, its separation from the Ministry of Finance since 1954 and its absorption of the Agricultural Bank, the Central Communal Bank, the Industrial Bank and the Trade Bank during 1956–59 and the Savings Bank in 1963. Its Chairman is an *ex officio* member of the Council of Ministers of the USSR. The *G.*

is the largest bank in the world and is sometimes described as a MONOBANK. In the late 1970s it had 4,430 branches, over 80,000 savings bank offices, operated the accounts of 4,500,000 enterprises and organizations and had outstanding credits in excess of 180,000m. roubles (about $225,000m.). Its operations are regulated by the CASH PLAN and the CREDIT PLAN and are constructed in such a way as to accommodate the economic plan. The only two other banks in the USSR are the INVESTMENT BANK and the Bank for Foreign Trade (*VNESHTORGBANK*), both subordinated to the *G*.

Gosekomsovet The Russian syllabic abbreviation for *Gussudarstvennyi Ekonomicheskyi Sovet*, meaning the State Economic Council. It was the highest organ of economic planning and decision-making in existence over the period 1960–62, which took responsibility for long-term planning from the *GOSPLAN*. In 1962 this responsibility was transferred back to the *Gosplan* and the *G.* was abolished.

Gosekonomkomissiya In the USSR, the abbreviated form of *Gossudarstvennaya Ekonomicheskaya Komissiya*, meaning the State Economic Commission. It was in existence only during 1955–57, when it took over short-term economic planning from the *GOSPLAN*.

Goskhoz A less commonly used term for SOVKHOZ in the USSR, meaning 'State farm'.

Gosplan The syllabic abbreviation in Russian of *Gossudarstvennaya Planovaya Komissiya*, meaning the State Planning Commission (of the USSR). It was established on Lenin's initiative in 1921 when the GOELRO (including its Chairman G. M. Kzhizhanovsky) was transferred to the new body continuing under the same Chairman. At first the *G.* was only an advisory and co-ordinating body, concerned with working out and reconciling directive schemes and CONTROL FIGURES.

But its powers have increased considerably beginning with the first Five-Year Plan (1928–32). The *G.* went through a period of reorganization and limitation of its responsibilities between 1954 and 1966. During 1955–57 its short-term planning functions were temporarily transferred to the *GOSEKONOMKOMISSIYA*, whilst the *GOSEKOMSOVET* handled the long-term planning responsibilities over the period 1960–62. It was again temporarily subordinated to the Supreme Council of the National Economy from March 1963 to Oct. 1965. But since 1962, the *G.* has been responsible for all planning – short-term, medium-term and prospective plans. Under the *G.* there are Republic *Gosplans*, the planning departments of enterprises and state farms, and the *GOSBANK* is virtually subordinated, too. The Chairman of the *G.* (currently N. Baibakov) is an *ex officio* member of the Council of Ministers and is one of its 14 Vice-Chairmen.

Gossnab The abbreviated version in Russian of *Gossudarstvennoe Snabzhencheskoe Upravlenie*, or the State Supply Agency in the USSR. It was an organ of the *GOSPLAN*, in existence from 1948 to the mid-1950s. It was responsible for the distribution of indispensable materials to state enterprises in accordance with the economic plan.

Gosstrakh A commonly used abbreviation in the USSR for *Glavnoe Upravlenie Gossudarstvennogo Strakhovaniya*, meaning the Central Administration of State Insurance. It was established in 1921 and operates under the Ministry of Finance. It administers insurance chiefly in collectivized agriculture and co-operative housing (buildings, equipment, livestock, crops) and various institutions, which is compulsory. It also handles other insurance which is not compulsory (state farms, state enterprises, life insurance).

Gotha Programme A declaration of objectives of the SOCIAL-DEMOCRATIC PARTY OF GERMANY made at its Congress at Gotha in 1875, considered a landmark in the history of the socialist movement. It was mainly based on the ideas of F. LAS-SALLE and included such postulates as universal suffrage, equality before the law in its administration and enforcement, popular education, the extension of rights and liberties and progressive taxation – all to be achieved on a peaceful, parliamentary basis. Marx criticized the Programme as it ignored the need for a PROLETARIAN REVOLUTION and the DICTATORSHIP OF THE PROLETARIAT and described it as 'petty bourgeois nonsense'. His censure was suppressed by the Party leadership at the Congress and it was only after Marx's death that Engels published it in 1891 under the title CRITIQUE OF THE GOTHA PROGRAMME (after the G.P. had been superseded by the ERFURT PROGRAMME).

Gottwald, Klement (1896–1953) Czechoslovak and international Communist revolutionary and Party leader. He was a co-founder of the CZECHOSLOVAK COMMUNIST PARTY in 1921 and its Secretary-General after 1929. From 1928 to 1943 he was a member of the EXECUTIVE COMMITTEE OF THE COMMUNIST INTERNATIONAL and from 1935 to 1943 its Secretary. After the German occupation of Czechoslovakia he went to the USSR and returned in 1945. He soon assumed the leadership of the Cz.C.P. and was active in the organization of the National Front under Communist control. He was Vice-Premier in 1945–46 and Prime Minister in the coalition government 1946–48. After the PRAGUE COUP D'ETAT in Feb. 1948, he became the Prime Minister in the new Communist government. From June 1948 until his death he was President of Czechoslovakia (having replaced E. Beneš).

Goulash Communism A depreciative phrase used by N. S. KHRUSHCHEV (first at the 22nd Congress of the CPSU in Oct. 1961) for a mixture of communism and capitalism which was emerging from the ECONOMIC REFORMS in some Eastern European Socialist countries, roughly cor-responding to TUTTI FRUTTI COMMUNISM. G.c. embodies excessive concessions to consumers' comforts to the disregard of the needs of long-run economic development, ideology and the march to FULL COMMUNISM. (G. in Hungarian means a herdsman's stew made of beef and veal flavoured with paprika).

GPU The abbreviation in Russian of *Gossudarstvennoe Politicheskoe Upravlenie*, literarily meaning the 'State Political Administration'. It was the secret police organization in Soviet Russia established in Feb. 1922 (replacing the CHEKA within the NKVD (People's Commissariat of Internal Affairs). After the country officially became the 'USSR' (in Dec. 1922), the GPU was transferred in 1923 to the OGPU (United State Political Administration) attached to the COUNCIL OF PEOPLE'S COMMISSARS. Although the GPU operated after the internal situation had become normalized, the methods it used to suppress counter-revolutionary activities and dissident opinions were even more notorious than its predecessor, the *Cheka*. The chief of the GPU was F. E. DZIERZHINSKY.

Grand Alliance, The A description applied to the far-reaching co-operation between the Western Allies (especially the USA, Britain and the British Commonwealth countries) and the USSR against the Fascist aggressors (Germany, Italy and Japan) during W.W.II after the German attack on the USSR on 22 June, 1941. The name alludes to the G.A. created by the League of Augsburg in 1686 which included the European states allied against Louis XIV who planned to achieve a complete domination of Europe. There was large-scale American and British economic and military aid to the USSR, the Western Allies took a more tolerant view of Soviet communism, and the USSR decided to dissolve the COMINTERN (in May 1943). Various joint conferences (at Casablanca, Cairo, Teheran, Yalta and Potsdam) brought the two sides together for co-operation purposes. The G.A. began to deteriorate after the war was over, and turned into the COLD WAR.

Grand National Assembly (*Marea Adunare Naţională*) The Romanian parliament, the highest formal source of power. It is composed of 349 deputies elected for a five-year term by universal suffrage from a single list of candidates prepared by the FRONT OF SOCIALIST UNITY (dominated by the ROMANIAN COMMUNIST PARTY). At the March 1975 elections, for the first time, 139 seats were contested by two candidates for each seat, otherwise one candidate for each constituency is still the rule. The Assembly's work is controlled by its Bureau, consisting of a President and four Vice-Presidents.

Grand National Consolidated Trades Union The federation of British Trade Unions founded in 1834, largely due to the efforts of R. OWEN. Its purpose was to embrace all organized labour in Britain and to strengthen its bargaining power with a possible recourse to a GENERAL STRIKE. It soon encompassed half a million workers, but the timidity or ineptitude of some of the union leaders, internal dissensions, the hostility of the employers and the animosity of the government, led to its dissolution in the same year.

'Gravediggers of the Bourgoisie' The Marxist militant description of the PROLETARIAT which is destined by the historical process of evolution and revolution to undermine the BOURGEOISIE and destroy capitalism. The description comes from the *COMMUNIST MANIFESTO*, published by Marx and Engels in 1848, where the last sentence in Part I reads: 'What the bourgeoise therefore produces, above all, are its own gravediggers. Its fall and the victory of the proletariat are equally inevitable'. Also WE'LL BURY YOU.

Great Debate, The Vigorous, controversial and relatively free discussions in the USSR in the 1920s on the strategy for Soviet economic development, especially industrialization. The debate tacitly assumed Stalin's alternative, SOCIALISM IN ONE COUNTRY, raged mainly within the Communist party, reached its peak in the mid-1920s and focused on such questions as the institutional framework, the financing of investment and the pace of industrialization. Two opposing camps emerged. The right-wing group (represented by N. I. BUKHARIN, M. P. Tomsky and many Party bureaucrats associated with the NEW ECONOMIC POLICY) advocated a liberal course, with equal priorities to agriculture and industry. They favoured a moderate rate of investment, emphasis in industrial development on consumer goods, lenient treatment of peasants (including *KULAKS*), strong material incentives and the retention of the market mechanism. On the other hand, the leftists (mainly L. KAMENEV, E. PREOBRAZHENSKY, L. D. TROTSKY and G. E. ZINOVIEV) pressed for accelerated industrialization and more radical measures, especially a high investment rate (mainly by exploiting the peasant), emphasis on heavy industry and a highly centralized and ruthless administrative system. The course finally adopted by Stalin in 1928 (with the first Five-Year Plan) was the leftist alternative, even though he had originally opposed it as a matter of personal rivalry (against Trotsky).

Great Industrialization Drive, The A phrase applied to the planned accelerated development of industry in the USSR over the period 1928–40. The crash industrialization programme, amounting to an 'Industrial Revolution', was achieved at the cost of great suffering of the masses – austerity, long working hours, forced labour and the extravagant use of resources. But it proved successful in that it established a solid foundation for basic industries, especially those related to further industrialization and defence (as W.W.II subsequently proved).

Great Leap Forward The ideologically prompted drive in China over the period 1958–61, initiated by Mao Tse-tung and designed to transform radically the Chinese economy and society towards FULL COMMUNISM. In particular, it was directed towards the formation of large PEOPLE'S COMMUNES, the construction of large-scale projects (especially for water conservancy), the development of local light industries and the opening of small-scale mines and BACKYARD FURNACES. It involved extreme regimentation, a reduction of current consumption, the virtual abolition of material incentives, the emphasis on local effort and self-help and mass propaganda campaigns to develop and sustain enthusiasm. The G.L.F. proved disastrous in the second half of 1958, but was continued in several fields until it was abandoned in 1961. The failure was aggravated by three successive years of natural disasters (1959–61), the sudden withdrawal of Soviet aid (Aug. 1960) and conflicts within the Chinese Communist Party and the Government. The G.L.F. was severely criticized by Western as well as Soviet and East European economists. In the orthodox Communist view, the Leap was based on Mao's erroneous un-Marxian conception of the possibility of 'skipping' certain stages of socio-economic development and defying the law of BALANCED, PROPORTIONATE DEVELOPMENT.

Great October Socialist Revolution The seizure of power in Russia by the BOLSHEVIKS under the leadership of V. I. Lenin in Oct. 1917 (O.S.C.). Also known as the Bolshevik Revolution, it proved to be the first successful PROLETARIAN REVOLUTION and one of the most momentous events in world political and social history, with far-reaching consequences. The G.O.S.R. must not be confused with the FEBRUARY REVOLUTION of the same year, regarded by Marxists as a BOURGEOIS-DEMOCRATIC REVOLUTION, when the Tsar was deposed and a liberal PROVISIONAL GOVERNMENT was established. The G.O.S.R. was accomplished in two weeks, but the actual seizure of power was achieved in one night. After the failure of the KORNILOV REBELLION, the Central committee of the RUSSIAN SOCIAL-DEMOCRATIC LABOUR PARTY (OF THE BOLSHEVIKS), on the initiative of Lenin, decided on 10 Oct. (OLD-STYLE CALENDAR, or 23 Oct., NEW-STYLE CALENDAR)

to depose the Provisional Government of A. F. KERENSKY by force. Two days later, the PETROGRAD SOVIET established a Military Revolutionary Committee. On 24 Oct. (O.S.C., or 6 Nov. N.S.C.) the Bolsheviks completed preparations for the insurrection and Lenin arrived at the Smolny Institute in Petrograd (the capital of Russia at the time, now Leningrad). On the night of 24–25 Oct. (O.S.C., 6–7 Nov. N.S.C.), the Bolsheviks, with the aid of the LEFT SOCIALIST REVOLUTIONARIES, arrested most of the members of the Provisional Government (except Kerensky, who could not be found). The new Soviet Government was set up on 25 Oct. (7 Nov.), headed by Lenin and including L. D. TROTSKY (as Commissar for Foreign Affairs) and J. STALIN (Commissar for National Minorities). It was approved by the Second Congress of Soviets, which met on the same day, in which the Bolsheviks had a majority. In the elections to the CONSTITUENT ASSEMBLY in Nov. 1917, the Bolsheviks secured only 25 per cent of the seats. Faced with defeat in the C.A., the Government dispersed it with the aid of troops and formally dissolved it on 6 Jan. 1918 (O.S.C.) by the decree of the ALL-RUSSIAN CENTRAL EXECUTIVE COMMITTEE. A period of civil war followed, known as WAR COMMUNISM, from which the Bolsheviks emerged victorious in 1921. Tsar NICHOLAS II and his immediate family were executed in July 1918 and in 1922 the RUSSIAN COMMUNIST PARTY (OF THE BOLSHEVIKS) was proclaimed the only legal political party in the country. The other parties, including those which assisted the Bolsheviks to seize and retain power, were dissolved.

Great Patriotic War The Soviet name for W.W.II, from 22 June 1941 (when the USSR was attacked by Germany) to 2 Sep. 1945 (the defeat of Japan). Although seemingly inconsistent with SOCIALIST INTERNATIONALISM, patriotic appeals were made to the Soviet people to defend the motherland against the fascist invaders. On one occasion at least, Stalin even appealed to god for aid.

Great People's Assembly Another, less common, English name for the Mongolian Parliament, better known as the PEOPLE'S GREAT HURAL.

Great Power Chauvinism Marxist accusation directed against the leading Western Powers, and regarded as peculiar to the last stage of capitalism viz. IMPERIALISM. Lenin (in *IMPERIALISM: THE HIGHEST STAGE OF CAPITALISM*) maintained that greed and rivalry among the imperial powers necessarily lead to wars (thereby, disagreeing with Kautsky's peaceful ULTRA-IMPERIALISM). In the USSR, in the early 1920s, there was a group in the Party which pressed for a tight unitary Soviet state and the suppression of national minorities' characteristics. But Stalin opposed it, calling its members 'great power chauvinists'. However, during and after W.W.II, the USSR annexed large areas on the peripheries of the USSR – Karelia (from Finland), East Prussia, Estonia, Latvia, Lithuania, eastern Poland, Sub-Carpathian Ruthenia (from Czechoslovakia), Moldavia and Bessarabia (from Romania), Tannu-Tuva (from Mongolia) and the Kuril Islands and Southern Sakhalin (from Japan). In 1951, it was officially declared in the USSR that the Tsarist conquests in the 18th and 19th c. had been justified as 'Russia had saved those territories from falling to the reactionary imperial powers' (Britain, Persia and Turkey).

Great Proletarian Cultural Revolution The ideological and political struggle launched by MAO TSE-TUNG and his close supporters in China in the latter 1960s. The G.P.C.R. was against right-wing and other factional elements disagreeing with Mao's ideas and practices in the CHINESE COMMUNIST PARTY and the state hierarchy. The name first appeared in the *Army Daily* on 18 April 1966. Officially, the G.P.C.R. lasted from Aug. 1966 (with the launching of the SIXTEEN POINTS PROGRAMME to April 1969, but had been preceded by three years of preparatory drives and was continued along selected lines virtually up to Mao's death in 1976. The G.P.C.R. was a striking expression of Mao's postulate of CONTINUING REVOLUTION. Its general and lasting aim was to revolutionize the attitudes and thoughts of the masses in order to prevent the re-emergence of exploiting classes, the dominance by the Conservative Party bureaucracy and the re-appearance of Communist complacency. There were several overlapping campaigns which were meticulously planned by a special commission of the Central Committee of the C.C.P., which included LIN PIAO, CH'EN PO-TA, K'ANG SHENG, CHIANG CH'ING and CHOU EN-LAI. The main force of the G.P.C.R. were the RED GUARDS and the REVOLUTIONARY REBELS. The chief victims of the Revolution were LIU SHAO-CH'I, P'ENG CHEN, TENG HSIAO-P'ING and some 4.5m Party members. Lin Piao, ultraleftists led by Chen Po-ta and the GANG OF FOUR fell victims after the Revolution. The G.P.C.R. not only produced great political chaos, but also led to far-reaching disruption in education and, more importantly, in the economy. The G.P.C.R. was reminiscent of Lenin's CULTURAL REVOLUTION of the 1920s and Stalin's GREAT PURGES of the late 1930s, but it differed greatly in its approach and methods, and has been criticized by the Communist Party of the Soviet Union and other pro-Soviet Communist parties.

Great Purges The Stalinist wave of terror primarily directed against senior Party, Government and Army members in the USSR over the period 1936–38. The G.P. instituted on the orders from Stalin were carried out by the NKVD under the ruthless direction of N.I. YEZHOV, whilst A. Y. Vyshinsky acted as the Public Prosecutor in the three open TREASON TRIALS. Previous purges in the USSR had mostly involved lesser deviationists and opponents and had been carried out quietly, generally in the form of demotion, ridicule, expulsion, banishment or exile. But the G.P. encompassed many old distinguished Bolsheviks, including trusted colleagues of Lenin, and were pursued by highly sophisticated methods, incl. POLITICAL SHOW TRIALS, and led to an appalling loss of life. There were four distinct purges, each 'legally sanctioned' by a treason trial: Aug. 1936; Jan. 1937; June 1937; and March 1938. The names for the purges were compiled by the *NKVD* in accordance with Stalin's instructions (at least 383 such lists were later officially identified). The accused were summarily sentenced to either death, long terms of imprisonment or hard labour by special committees. Each of these committees consisted of three high officials of the *NKVD* called the *Troika*. Among the victims were N. I. BUKHARIN, L. B. KAMENEV, G. K. ORDZHONIKIDZE, K. RADEK, A. I. RYKOV, Marshal M. N. TUKHACHEVSKY and G. E. ZINOVIEV. L. D. TROTSKY was also tried and sentenced to death *in absentia* (he was murdered in Mexico in 1940, almost certainly on Soviet orders). According to KHRUSHCHEV'S SECRET SPEECH in 1956, out of 87 members of the Central Committee of the ALL-UNION COMMUNIST PARTY (OF THE BOLSHEVIKS), 71 were liquidated and at least 7,000 Party members were killed. Nine-tenths of the officers of senior rank were purged, mostly shot. According to some reports, the total number of victims ranged from 8m. to 10m. The G.P. left Stalin in an indisputable position as the dictator.

Great Society A broad programme of domestic social reforms vaguely outlined by the US President, L. B. Johnson, in 1964–65, promising welfare and human rights to all Americans. This was to be achieved by continuing the 'war on poverty', the improvement of the educational system, the introduction of Medicare, the provision of social security for the aged, the alleviation of housing in slums and fighting racial injustice. Pressing external demands on resources (Vietnam War, foreign aid) seriously impeded the achievement of the g.s. as originally envisaged by social reformers.

Great Terror, The Another description of Stalin's GREAT PURGES of the late 1930s

(also the title of a book by R. Conquest, first published in 1968).

Greek Communist Party See COMMUNIST PARTY OF GREECE.

Greek Democracy Intra upper-class democracy in society supported by a legally, economically and socially subjugated lower class, as in ancient Greece (masters and slaves). The term was sometimes used in the past by the defenders of the social system based on serfdom and slavery, as in post-medieval times in Europe and the United States up to the mid-1860s, before both were finally abolished by law.

Green International A general name for the international organization representing the interests of democratic peasants of eastern and southern Europe, created in 1921 and reconstituted in 1947. As a counter-move to COMINTERN (established in 1919), representatives of Bulgarian, Czechoslovak, Polish and Yugoslav Peasant parties formed the International Agrarian Bureau in 1921, which in the following year organized the International Peasant Union, with its headquarters in Prague. The I.P.U. followed the line of POPULISM, supporting ownership and advocating thorough agrarian reforms, agricultural co-operative organizations for production and marketing, the extension of popular technical education, agricultural modernization, moderate industrialization, social insurance and low tariffs. The Comintern immediately campaigned against the G.I., described it a 'bourgeois-kulak' and 'fascist' organization and in 1923 created a rival body called the International Peasants Council, or KRESTINTERN, based in Moscow. Although K. was a disciplined organization with the full backing of the USSR and the Comintern, it failed to attract international peasant support and was dissolved in 1933, whilst the G.I. continued, albeit on a rather loose and informal basis. After W.W.II, the Communist regimes either incorporated the Peasant parties into the Communist parties, dissolved them altogether, persecuted or retained them as 'democratic' façades in united fronts (in Bulgaria, Czechoslovakia and Poland) completely subordinate to the Communist parties. Many peasant leaders were liquidated or escaped to the West. However, in July 1947, the exiled peasant leaders reconstituted the I.P.U. in Washington. 11 eastern and southern European Peasant or Agrarian parties from the following countries were represented: Albania; Bulgaria; Czechoslovakia; Estonia; Hungary; Latvia; Lithuania; Poland; Romania; the Ukraine; and Yugoslavia. In addition to its headquarters in Washington, it has a European office in Harrow, England. The I.P.U. is headed by an Executive Committee assisted by three research Committees and publishes a quarterly *bulletin* in English and occasional reports and pamphlets.

Grönlund, Laurence (1846–99) A socialist theoretical writer who emigrated from Denmark to the USA (in 1867), whom revolutionary Marxists regarded as a representative of UTOPIAN SOCIALISM. In his books, *Dialogue on the Coming Revolution* (1880), *Our Destiny* (1891) and *The New Economy* (1898), he advocated a gradual, peaceful road to socialism. He supported FABIANISM, and was active in the formation of the Fabian Society.

Gross Agricultural Output In Socialist national income accounting, the total value of output produced by state, collective and private (if any) farms and personal plot holders during a year. The figure does not indicate net production, as it includes depreciation of fixed assets and the value of materials (including power) obtained from other production entities.

Gross Income In Socialist enterprise accounting, the value of net enterprise receipts, i.e. GLOBAL INCOME *minus* the value of materials (incl. power) purchased from outside. It is equal to the gross enterprise profit *plus* wages. Very roughly, g.i. is equal to the value of production (or 'value added') in Western national income

accounting. In some Socialist countries in the past, g.i. was used as an indicator of enterprise performance (but now GROSS PROFIT is used for the purpose).

Gross Industrial Output In Socialist national income accounting, a basic concept indicating the total value of output of manufacturing and mining output of enterprises over a particular period (usually a year). It includes depreciation of fixed assets and the value of the materials and power used, obtained from other enterprises.

Gross Profit In Socialist enterprise accounting, the total profit of the enterprise before taxes and other charges for the state budget and intermediate levels of economic management. It is calculated by deducting materials and power purchased from outside plus wages from GLOBAL INCOME. It is also known as 'social profit' or 'net revenue'.

Gross Profit Rate See PROFIT RATE.

Gross Rentability (Rate) See RENTABILITY.

Gross Social Profit A basic concept used in Socialist national income accounting, embracing the value of output of all enterprises engaging in MATERIAL PRODUCTION over a particular period (usually a year). It includes depreciation.

Ground Rent In Marxian political economy, used in application to pre-Socialist societies to denote that portion of the SURPLUS VALUE which is created by agricultural producers (workers) but appropriated by landowners. Under capitalism, it appears in the form of ABSOLUTE RENT and DIFFERENTIAL RENT.

Group 'A' and 'B' Output In Socialist national income accounting, the classification of industrial output into producer (A) and consumer (B) goods. The division is based either on the types of industrial enterprises according to the purpose of the major portion of their output or (more appropriately) on the immediate purpose for which the goods are destined. G.'A'. includes the output of mineral and industrial raw materials, semi-finished products, instruments, machinery and other types of capital equipment, whilst G. 'B'. consists of finished consumer goods (single-use and durable-use). A distinction is further made between industrial producer goods meant for the production of other producer goods ('A1') and those to be used for the production of consumer goods ('A2'). Traditionally, it was assumed in Socialist economic theory and policy that in a dynamic society (with positive rates of economic growth) G. 'A' output must rise faster than G. 'B' output (and 'A1' faster than 'A2'). However, in recent years that approach has been subjected to a reappraisal, with some practical concessions to G 'B' output. The classification of output into producer and consumer goods on the whole economy scale is called DEPARTMENT I AND II production.

Group Incentives Inducements commonly awarded in the Socialist countries in production or other spheres of activity of social value to a deserving group of persons constituting a team, brigade, plant or an enterprise. The award may be in the form of MATERIAL INCENTIVES (in cash or in kind) or MORAL INCENTIVES (certificate, plaque, banner, order). G.i. may not be as effective as INDIVIDUAL INCENTIVES, but ideologically, they are superior as they cultivate group solidarity and social consciousness combating INDIVIDUALISM.

Group of Five A team of five high Party officials in China, appointed by the Standing Committee of the Politburo of the Chinese Communist Party on the initiative of Mao Tse-tung in mid–1965, to conduct a cultural revolution among the intellectuals. This revolution was a prelude to the GREAT PROLETARIAN CULTURAL REVOLUTION. The Group was headed by P'ENG CHEN (a member of the Politburo, the First Secretary of the Peking Party Committee and the Mayor of Pek-

ing) and his deputy Wu Han and also included K'ANG SHENG. The Group produced two reports in February and May 1966 on the 'Academic' and 'Cultural' situations. However, Mao considered the Group too liberal and not revolutionary enough, and replaced it in May 1966 with the NATIONAL CULTURAL REVOLUTIONARY GROUP, headed by Ch'en Po-ta.

Grundrisse A short title in German of *Grundrisse der Kritik der politischen Ökonomie (Rohentwurf)*. [*Foundations of the Critique of Political Economy (A Rough Outline)*]. It was a voluminous manuscript of K. MARX written during 1857–58 and originally meant to cover the whole field of politcal economy in six volumes. The existence of the manuscript, apparently unknown to F. ENGELS, was first announced in 1923 by D. Rayazanov, the director of the INSTITUTE OF MARXISM – LENINISM in Moscow. Marx gave up the idea of publishing it in the originally envisaged form and turned to writing *Capital*. Instead, he re-wrote volume I between Aug. 1858 and Jan. 1859 and had it published under the title *Zur Kritik de politischen Ökonomie* in 1859, which appeared in English translation only in 1904 (in Chicago) as a *CONTRIBUTION TO THE CRITIQUE OF POLITICAL ECONOMY*. The *G.* was published in Moscow in 1939, with a supplementary volume in 1941, totalling some 1,000 pages, but the edition was small. A German edition was published in East Berlin in 1953. David McLellan, a British authority on Marx, published an edited abbreviated version in English (152 pages) in 1971 under the title *The Grundrisse*, which he described as the 'centrepiece' of Marx's work.

Guerrilla Warfare Small-scale war of attrition by partisans or irregulars against troops superior in numbers and equipment. The term is Spanish in origin (meaning 'little war') and it first crept into international vocabulary during the Peninsular War (1804–14), when small units of Spanish partisans carried on unexpected harassing and sabotage operations against Napoleon's armies. It may be waged by a defeated nation against the occupying power or by a national or social group against the established order, as the only method of survival and overthrowing the oppressive regime. G.w. is approved of in revolutionary Marxist ideology as justified against fascist, imperialist or oppressive bourgeois regimes. G.w. was carried on by the Soviets behind the German lines during the GREAT PATRIOTIC WAR, by TITO, MAO TSE-TUNG, CASTRO, GUEVARA, and HO CHI MINH, each having contributed new strategy and tactics.

Guesdists Followers of J. Guesde (1845–1922), a French revolutionary socialist leader. They were mostly members of the French Workers' Party, founded in 1880 by Guesde in collaboration with P. LAFARGUE. G. were a prominent feature of the French political scene before W.W.I and were commonly regarded to be the most faithful disciples of Marxism. Their Party organ was *Socialiste* (*The Socialist*), which advocated workers' ownership of the means of production by revolutionary methods. During W.W.I, most G. supported the French war effort and rejected Lenin's call for boycotting or disrupting the 'imperialist' war.

Guevara, Ernesto (1928–67) Popularly known as 'Che', a Latin American revolutionary leader of Argentine descent who played an outstanding part in the Cuban Revolution (1958–59), was subsequently Finance Minister in F. Castro's government and lost his life heading a guerrilla force in Bolivia. On the basis of the Cuban experience, he formulated a new approach to social revolution (chiefly in his book *Guerrilla Warfare*, 1961) and became an advocate of the 'export' of the Cuban revolution to other Latin American countries. In defiance of the traditional Marxist-Leninist prescriptions – postulating the revolutionary spontaneity of the industrial working class and a strong disciplined Communist Party – G. contended that it was not necessary to wait until all conditions were ripe for a PROLETARIAN REVOLUTION. He insisted that a

small dedicated guerrilla band could become a nucleus for an insurrection. By gradually gaining sufficient popular support to defeat the armed forces commanded by the ruling base, a revolution could be undertaken in an underdeveloped area such as Latin America and Africa. To this extent, he essentially agreed with Mao Tse-tung (MAOISM), but he questioned the latter's insistence on the absolute supremacy of the political leadership (the Communist party) over guerrilla forces. G.'s ideas caught the imagination of several revolutionary elements in Latin America and Africa who were impatient with the unimaginative and impotent Communist parties. His theory was put to a practical test in Bolivia, where G. himself led a small guerrilla force in 1966–67. However, his venture miscarried due to poor technical and military preparation and the failure to secure support from the local peasantry and the Communist party. G. himself was killed by Bolivian troops (the 'Rangers', trained by US antiguerrilla experts) in Oct. 1967. Nevertheless, G. has become a legendary hero to many revolutionaries all over the world, particularly young and impatient radicals.

GUGB Abbreviation of the Russian *Glavnoe Upravlenie Gossudarstvennoi Bezopasnosti*, meaning the Chief Administration of State Security, which existed within the NKVD from July 1934 to Feb. 1941. Under the GUGB, the Stalinist terror reached its peak and was responsible for carrying out Stalin's GREAT PURGES (1936–38). Its main divisions were the Secret Operations Department, the Economic Dept., the Military Dept. (which supervised Special Sections in the armed forces), the Foreign Dept. (espionage and subversion abroad) and the Special Wing for the Protection of Leaders. In Feb. 1941, the GUGB was transformed into the NKGB, a separate People's Commissariat [Ministry] of State Security.

Guild Socialism A direction in the English trade union movement which developed before W.W.I advocating the transformation of trade unions into production associations ('guilds') to be co-ordinated by a 'federal national guild'. G.s. emphasized democratic participation and decentralization. Guilds, organized by industry or occupations, were supposed to replace private enterprise, on the one hand, and counteract the centralizing and potentially dictatorial tendencies of the state owning the means of production, on the other. The best known proponent of g.s. was G. D. H. COLE (in *Self-Government in Industry*, 1917, and *Guild Socialism Restated*, 1920). G.s. represented a compromise between SYNDICALISM and FABIANISM. Marxists reject g.s., as in their view it by-passes the CLASS STRUGGLE, represents OPPORTUNISM or UTOPIAN SOCIALISM and merely 'disarms' the PROLETARIAT for the benefit of the BOURGEOISIE. Although the Yugoslav system of WORKERS' SELF-MANAGEMENT and the state ownership of the means of production are similar to g.s., the Yugoslavs deny any ideological or historical link to it.

Gulag The Russian abbreviation for the 'Main Administration of Corrective Labour Camps (*Glavnoe Upravlenie Ispravitel'no-Trudovykh Lagerei*). It was the organization in the USSR which administered the FORCED LABOUR CAMPS on behalf of the *NKVD* from 1934 to 1960. At one stage (in 1945) as many as 15m. prisoners were held in its camps. The arbitrary arrests, the cruel treatment of the prisoners by the police and guards, and the shocking living and working conditions prevalent in the camps were first brought to light by the well-known Soviet writer A. SOLZHENITSYN in a three-volume book, *The Gulag Archipelago*, published in the West in English in 1973, 1974 and 1976.

GUM The popular name of the largest department store in the USSR, located in Moscow in Red Square opposite the Kremlin. Its name is derived from the first letters of *Gossudarstvennyi Universalnyi Magazin*, the State Universal Store. It has over 130 departments employing 8,000 persons selling 330,000 different items and serving 200,000 customers daily. Its

ordering system has been computerized since 1969.

Gumplowicz, Ludwik (1838–1909) A pioneering Polish social scientist of Jewish descent turned Christian, who later achieved recognition as an Austrian jurist, sociologist and historian. His theories attracted the attention of Marxists and other social reformers. His ideas were expounded (at first mostly in German and Polish). in *Race and the State* (1875), *Systematic Sociology* (1877), *Racial Struggle* (1883) and *Outline of Sociology* (1885), the last one having been translated into English. Applying the rigorous scientific methodology of A. Comte to Darwin's theory of evolution or the STRUGGLE FOR EXISTENCE, G. developed a naturalistic doctrine of society akin to SOCIAL DARWINISM and SOCIAL DETERMINISM. He gave support to Marxism in some respects but disputed it in others. Not unlike Marx, G.: 1. explained social phenomena in terms of conflicting interactions between social, ethnic and other groups (rather than in terms of the behaviour of persons as individuals) conditioned by economic considerations; 2. interpreted history as a continuous cycle of aggression, subjugation and amalgamation, and social stratification as an inevitable product of the iniquities associated with this process; 3. viewed the development of the state as a vehicle for the exploitation of subjugated groups when the ruling class found it preferable to genocide; 4. pointed out that, historically, the struggle between individuals is replaced by that between ethnic groups, then between the state and social classes, and eventually between nation states; and 5. in view of the universal laws governing the interactions between and within social groups, he believed that the schemes for social reforms put forward by the exponents of UTOPIAN SOCIALISM were futile. But unlike Marx, G. attributed social conflicts not only to material factors, but also to racial and ethnic differences and was sceptical about the possibility of ever developing a harmonious classless society.

H

Hallstein Doctrine A principle applied in the foreign policy of the FR of [West] Germany over the period 1955–67, postulating the non-recognition of the [East] German DR as a separate state and severance of diplomatic relations with the states (the USSR excepted) entering into diplomatic relations with the GDR. By this token, the West German Government wanted to establish that the FR of Germany was the only legitimate successor to Germany and that the reunification of East and West Germany should be achieved under its leadership. The doctrine was formulated by W. Hallstein, Secretary of State (in K. Adenauer's Government) in Dec. 1955. The exception of the USSR was rationalized on the grounds that she was occupying a part of German territory. In pursuit of this doctrine, the West German Government broke off diplomatic relations with Yugoslavia in 1957 and with Cuba in 1963. The H.D. had limited effects and was gradually discontinued after Jan. 1967 when the West German Government established diplomatic relations with Romania and again with Yugoslavia in Jan. 1968 (at that time, the GDR had diplomatic relations with more than 50 states). The application of the doctrine was restricted by W. Brandt (then Foreign Minister) to such cases where the country in question was hostile to the FR of Germany or approved the division of Germany as permanent. The doctrine was officially dropped by W. Brandt when he became the Chancellor in 1969 and was further confirmed in 1972 when the GDR was officially recognized as a separate soverign state.

Hanover Resolution A declaration formulated by the left-wing members of the SOCIAL-DEMOCRATIC PARTY OF GERMANY at its Congress in Hanover in Oct. 1896, rejecting most of the views advocated by E. BERNSTEIN as revisionist and capitulationist.

'Harmonic' Growth RUSH AND HARMONIC GROWTH.

Have-Nots A term used for individuals or social groups owning no means of production (land or capital), and either earning no income or sufficient only for subsistence living. The designation is also applied to the less-developed countries of the THIRD WORLD, where *per capita* national income is very low and close to the bare subsistence level (less than $750 p.a. at the 1975 prices). There are approximately 50 countries in this category. Marxists attribute the existence of the h.-n. to the private ownership of the means of production, the private profit motive, the blind market mechanism, NON-EQUIVALENT EXCHANGE between more-developed and less-developed countries, IMPERIALISM and NEO-COLONIALISM.

Hawthorne Experiment A series of practical studies, originally carried out at Hawthorne near Chicago for a number of years beginning in 1927, on certain obvious factors affecting labour productivity (such as tea breaks, eating at work, the length of the working day, lighting). The experiment was devised and conducted by a group of researchers from Harvard University, headed by E. Mayo (1880–1949) and commissioned by Western General Electric. The studies demonstrated that the key factor in the growth of productivity, disregarded in the originally assumed variables, was human relations among the workers and the treatment they received from their immediate management. The H.E. attracted a good deal of interest among efficiency experts, trade union leaders and social workers. Its methods of investigation and findings, in particular the role of non-material motivation, received a good deal of attention in the USSR, and later in other Socialist countries as well.

Hayek, Friedrich August von (1899–) See NEO-AUSTRIAN CRITIQUE OF SOCIALISM.

Hegel, Georg Wilhelm Friedrich (1770–1831) The greatest German philosopher of idealism and dialectics. His main works were: *The Phenomenology of Spirit* (1807); *The Science of Logic* (1812–16); *The Encyclopedia of The Philosophical Sciences* (1817); *The Philosophy of Right* (1821), *Lectures on the History of Philosophy* (1833–36), *Philosophy of History* (1837) and *Aesthetics* (1837–42). He exerted a great deal of influence not only on the philosophical establishment of his time, but also on the founders of Marxist philosophy, viz. K. Marx and F. Engels. As students, they temporarily belonged to the HEGELIAN LEFT, but soon left it as they disagreed with several fundamental propositions of Hegel's philosophy. Their attitude to H.'s philosophical system was as follows (as reflected in their joint works, *The HOLY FAMILY* and *THE GERMAN IDEOLOGY*): 1. they accepted H.'s DIALECTICS, i.e. the theory purporting to explain development as a continuous struggle of contradictions, where quantitative changes lead to qualitative transformation; 2. but they rejected H.'s IDEALISM in favour of MATERIALISM. They disagreed with H.'s insistence that spirit and consciousness, and not matter and nature, are the primary factors in development and history. Engels described Hegelian philosophy as 'materialism upside down'; 3. they also attacked H. for his support of the modern state, the acceptance of wars and contempt for the proletariat.

Hegelian Left A school of German philosophers who, while basically accepting Hegel's philosophy, gave it a liberal-socialist interpretation. It was most influential in the 1830s and 1840s, and its leading proponents were B. Bauer (1809–82), E. Bauer (1820–86), D. E. Strauss (1808–74), A. Ruge (1802–80), M. Stirner (1806–56) and initially, also L. FEUERBACH. The H.L. or 'Young Hegelians', played down Hegel's 'absolute idea', and instead postulated 'self-knowledge' as the highest form of existence, which they identified with the intelligentsia and the state. The Left Hegelians saw the Prussian king as the embodiment of the ideal of Plato's enthroned philosopher and the Prussian state as the best vehicle for implementing liberal social reforms. They rejected religion, identifying it with the uneducated superstitious masses. Marx and Engels were also members of the H.L. in the early 1840s but, when in 1842 the H.L. failed to live up to its expectations they criticized it (especially in the years 1843–46) for its contemptuous interpretation of the role of the proletariat and for favouring social reforms through the bourgeois state within the existing framework of capitalism. The only major element of the H.L. which appealed to them was its rejection of Hegel's philosophy of religion.

Hegelian Right A school of German philosophy which accepted the philosophical system of G. W. F. HEGEL its entirety, including his philosophy of religion, civil society and the state. The H.R. was most influential in Germany in the 1820s and 1930s. Marx and Engels regarded it as ultra-conservative and reactionary, worse than the HEGELIAN LEFT.

Helsinki Conference A short name for the international 'Conference on Security and Co-operation in Europe' held in Helsinki in 1975, which was concluded with the signing of the 'Final Act' on 1 Aug. 1975. The theme of the H.C. was a *détente* in East-West relations in general. The Eastern delegates stressed the need for accepting the existing political division and boundaries in Europe as permanent and a condition of stability, while the Western side dwelt mainly on human rights. Most of the time was spent on the need to protect civil liberties in accordance with the aims and principles of the Charter of the United Nations, of the Universal Declaration of Human Rights and various international conventions on the subject. The 'Final Act of the Conference on Security and Co-operation in Europe' was signed by 33 East and West European nations, plus Canada and the USA. But it has no international legal force, as it was not eligible for registration under Article 102 of the U.N. Charter. Nevertheless, the H.C. has proved to be a landmark in the history of East-West relations. Each side often refers to the Final Act, in particular to its violations by the other side. The charges have mostly been made by the Western side and dissident groups in the East against the Communist regimes, in particular such signatories as Czechoslovakia, the German DR, Hungary, Poland, Romania and (especially) the USSR for violating human rights (censorship, persecution of dissenters, discrimination against minorities, restrictions on religious worship, travelling and emigration). The H.C. was followed up by the BELGRADE CONFERENCE in 1977. Also CHARTER OF LIBERTY, CHARTER '77, DISSENT, HUMAN RIGHTS.

Helsinki Group An association of DISSENTERS in the USSR, founded by Dr. Yuri Orlov after the HELSINKI CONFERENCE in 1975. Its aim is to protect and enforce HUMAN RIGHTS in the USSR guaranteed by the Soviet Government as a signatory of the Final Act of the Conference on Security and Co-operation in Europe. The Group publicizes cases of the violation of human rights and participates in *SAMIZDAT* publications. For his activities, Orlov was sentenced in May 1978 for 7 years of hard labour in a prison camp to be followed by 5 years of exile.

'Hero of Socialist Labour' A title and order awarded to individual persons in the USSR for outstanding achievements in economic, scientific and cultural fields. The award was instituted in Dec. 1938 and is formally made by the PRESIDIUM OF THE SUPREME SOVIET. The order is in the form of a five-pointed star with raised hammer and sickle in the centre.

'Hero of the Soviet Union' The highest title of honour awarded in the USSR for outstanding services to the Soviet state, involving a heroic act by an individual or a group; instituted in 1934, it is awarded with the order of the 'Golden Star'.

Herzen, Alexander Ivanovich (1812–70) A Russian REVOLUTIONARY DEMOCRAT, materialist philosopher and writer, who contributed substantially to the development of the early revolutionary movement in Tsarist Russia. In his most important work, *Letters on the Study of Philosophy* (1845–46), he attacked the philosophy of IDEALISM, especially that of HEGEL. He advocated linking MATERIALISM with the idea of development, natural studies with philosophy and theory with practice. The failure of the REVOLUTION OF 1848-49, which he witnessed in Paris, made him pessimistic toward the revolutionary capacity of the proletariat. Instead, he turned to the IDEALIST CONCEPTION OF HISTORY and UTOPIAN SOCIALISM. He then advocated the distribution of land in Russia to peasants and was one of the founders of *NARODNISM*, which Marxists regarded as a 'petty-bourgeois solution'. At one stage, H. also turned to ANARCHISM as propounded by BAKUNIN. But later (in 1869) he disassociated himself from Bakunin's group during the FIRST INTERNATIONAL and sided with Marx. H. was also one of the early pioneers of the idea of SOCIALIST REALISM in art. Although Lenin acknowledged H.'s contributions, he said that Herzen advanced to the precincts of DIALECTICAL MATERIALISM, but halted before HISTORICAL MATERIALISM.

Hess, Moses (1812–75) A German communist who introduced communism to the HEGELIAN LEFT. Hegel was a close friend and collaborator of MARX and participated in the early congresses of the

FIRST INTERNATIONAL. He contributed to the *RHEINISCHE ZEITUNG* and the *DEUTSCH-FRANZÖSISCHE JAHRBÜCHER* and was a follower of Feuerbach along with Marx.

Hierarchical Planning and Management

The economic system under which directives and other instructions are handed down the hierarchical ladder of economic authorites. In the Socialist centrally planned economies, the different levels of the authorities involved in descending order are: the Communist party (laying down the most general and crucial guidelines for the economic plan); the State Planning Commission; the economic ministries; branch (or 'industrial' or 'economic') associations; and finally enterprises. Dealings between enterprises are not direct or 'horizontal', but 'vertical', i.e. via higher organs of authority. This pattern of economic decison-making prevailed in its extreme form under the CENTRALIZED DIRECTIVE SYSTEM OF PLANNING AND MANAGEMENT, before the economic reforms of the 1960s and best exemplified the Stalinist model in the USSR. Although it may be effective in a backward economy needing a rapid structural transformation and accelerated development, it has proved wasteful and unwieldy in higher stages of economic and social development. That system has been at least partly abandoned in favour of HORIZONTAL PLANNING AND MANAGEMENT.

Hierarchical Stratification

The division of society into social classes in descending order from the highest to the lowest according to some criterion, such as property ownership, income, education, occupational status, or race. Such an arrangement may be sanctioned by law (as under feudalism or Nazism), custom (castes in old India) or established by economic status. Marxism in theory rejects any form of social stratification. In the Socialist countries, three social classes are generally recognized, viz. workers, peasants and intelligentsia, but it is claimed that they are parallel, vertical divisions, none of whom enjoys a privileged status. However, in practice, hierarchical horizontal strata can be identified, viz. the Party and State elite, technocrats, successful professionals, skilled workers and at the bottom the unskilled agricultural labourers.

Hieroglyphic Theory of Cognition

One of the idealistic theories in philosophy, according to which sensory perceptions and images are not faithful reflections of objects but only conventional symbols ('hieroglyphs'), devoid of any similarity to the actual external world. The theory was widely discussed in Russia before W.W.I by its main exponents, G. V. PLEKHANOV and I. Isaakovna Axelrod (1868–1946). It is opposed to the Marxist interpretation of COGNITION known as the REFLECTION THEORY. Lenin attacked the h.t. of c. in his *MATERIALISM AND EMPIRIO-CRITICISM*.

Hilferding, Rudolf

(1877–1941) One of the leading theoreticians of AUSTRO-MARXISM, a leader of the Social-Democratic movement in Germany and the Minister of Finance in two German Social-Democratic governments in 1923 and 1928. He supported Marx on the LABOUR THEORY OF VALUE and attacked the Austrian MARGINAL ANALYSIS. His most important contribution to Marxism was his *Finanzkapital* (*Finance Capital*) (1910), in which he showed that the banks' increasing control over industry led to monopoly, cartelization, imperialism and war. He further reasoned that the contradictions produced by the dictatorship of finance capital must lead to a proletarian revolution and the dictatorship of the proletariat. His study of the concentration and centralization of finance capital led him to the idea of a super state bank, which could be employed to regulate the whole economy on a centrally planned basis, where money would play only a secondary role and prices would be used merely as a tool for the desired distribution of national income. From 1907 to 1915 H. was the political editor of *VORWÄRTS!* and chief editor of *Freiheit* (organ of the Independent Social-

Democrats). He fled from Germany after Hitler's accession to power in 1933 and died in prison after his capture by the Gestapo in Paris in 1941.

Hired Labour In Marxist political economy, workers deprived of the ownership of the means of production and compelled to sell their services ('labour power') to capitalists. H.l. is the object of capitalist exploitation (to the extent of the SURPLUS VALUE) and as such is a feature of CAPITALISM. In the Socialist countries h.l. survives only in the private sector where there are limitations to the number of hired workers one can employ, and where there are heavy progressive taxes on the wages paid.

Histmat A colloquial syllabic abbreviation for HISTORICAL MATERIALISM.

Historical Epoch A less frequently used term for SOCIO-ECONOMIC FORMATION.

Historical Idealism See IDEALIST CONCEPTION OF HISTORY.

Historical Materialism One of the four cornerstones of Marxism (the other three being dialectical materialism, the labour theory of value and the postulate of the class struggle). H.m. is a philosophical, economic and sociological doctrine, also known as the materialist interpretation (or conception) of history. It essentially consists in the application of DIALECTICAL MATERIALSIM to explain historical events, processes and developments in society. It emphasizes the role of basic material human needs, the development of PRODUCTION FORCES and changing PRODUCTION RELATIONS as the fundamental determinants of the course of history and progress. At a given stage, the expansion and improvement in the means of production (land and capital) and labour lead to CONTRADICTIONS with the existing property and production relations, inducing ALIENATION and CLASS STRUGGLE. The accumulation of these contradictions sooner or later precipitates a REVOLUTION

consisting in the transformation of not only the material BASE but also the non-economic SUPERSTRUCTURE. Marx regarded revolutions as indispensable vehicles of progress. Historically, he distinguished six 'socio-economic formations', viz. PRIMITIVE COMMUNISM a society based on SLAVERY, FEUDALISM, CAPITALISM, SOCIALISM and (in the future) FULL COMMUNISM – each representing a higher stage compared with the preceding one. H.m. is opposed to the IDEALIST CONCEPTION OF HISTORY and the INDIVIDUALIST INTERPRETATION OF HISTORY.

Ho Chi Minh (1890–1969) Vietnamese Marxist-Leninist revolutionary leader and an organizational genius, whose lifelong struggle led to the establishment of the Communist regime in North Vietnam and later the reunification of Vietnam under Communist leadership. His name, which he assumed after 1940 (meaning 'He Who Enlightens'), was the third he used (after 'Nguyen That Than' and 'Nguyen Ai Quoc'). Largely self-educated, ambitious and patriotic, he lived and studied in Europe from 1911 to 1925, mostly in France, Britain and the USSR. He was one of the founders of the French Communist Party, when it split from the French Socialist Party in 1920. In 1923 he studied at the COMMUNIST UNIVERSITY FOR THE TOILERS OF THE EAST in Moscow and became active in the COMINTERN. After his return to Asia in 1925, he temporarily became a translator to M. M. BORODIN in Canton. In 1930 Ho founded the Communist Party of Indochina, to which the present VIETNAM COMMUNIST PARTY is an indirect successor. After the failure of an uprising against the French in 1940, he escaped to China, where in 1941 he founded Vietnamese guerrilla units called the VIET MINH, to liberate Vietnam from both the French and the Japanese. After the surrender of the Japanese in 1945, Ho proclaimed the establishment of the Democratic People's Republic of Vietnam. But he had to wage a guerrilla war against the French, who were finally defeated at DIEN BIEN PHU in 1954. His government actively supported VIET CONG guerrillas in South Vietnam after 1964, in which the HO CHI MINH TRAIL played a very important role. In addition to the Party Chairmanship, he was also President of the DPR of Vietnam. He died in March 1969, six years before the reunification of North and South Vietnam. The former capital of South Vietnam, Saigon, was renamed Ho Chi Minh City in 1976.

Ho Chi Minh City The largest city of the SR of Vietnam, with a population of 1.7m. in the late 1970s. It was formerly called Saigon and the capital of the Republic of [South] Vietnam. The present name was officially adopted by the decision of the National Assembly of the SR of V. in July 1976 as a tribute to HO CHI MINH, the North Vietnamese Communist leader and the architect of the reunification of Vietnam.

Ho Chi Minh Trail A carefully camouflaged route of infiltration and supply, which led from North to South Vietnam and played a crucial role in the VIETNAM WAR. It was 400 km. long, leading from North Vietnam through south-eastern Laos to north-western South Vietnam and consisted of four major supply lines running across rugged and inaccessible terrain and involving underground tunnels and depots. Although it was a frequent target of American bombing during the Vietnam War, it was never blocked for any appreciable period of time. The Trail was named after HO CHI MINH, the North Vietnamese Communist statesman who led the struggle for the reunification of North and South Vietnam under Communist direction.

Holy Family: or Critique of 'Critical Critique', The A philosophical study written by K. Marx and F. Engels in 1845 (originally in German). It was their first joint work and was directed against the HEGELIAN LEFT and the philosophy of HEGEL in general. Humorously presented, it specifically singled out the Bauer brothers and their faithful followers grouped around the *Allgemeine Literatur-Zeitung (German Literary Review)*. The authors attacked the philosophy of IDEALISM, MECHANISTIC MATERIALISM, PERSONALITY CULT represented by the 'critically thinking individuals', and at the same time emphasized the great potential of the PROLETARIAT and its historic mission in social development. Lenin described the book as a groundwork of 'philosophical materialism' and 'revolutionary socialism'.

Homo Communistis Plenus, Homo Novus Sinicus, Homo Novus Sovieticus Alternative Latin designations for the ideal of the NEW COMMUNIST MAN.

Horizontal Co-production A form of INDUSTRIAL CO-OPERATION where each partner engages in the production of components or assemblies of about the same level of technological content and are mutually supplied on a systematic basis. Each partner then assembles the complete product which may be marketed separately or jointly. In their relations with the West, the Socialist countries prefer this type of industrial co-operation (rather than VERTICAL CO-PRODUCTION), as it is conducive to the equality of the partners and to the transfer of advanced Western technology.

Horizontal Planning and Management As opposed to HIERARCHICAL PLANNING AND MANAGEMENT, a decentralized system under which enterprises have a substantial degree of freedom in planning, negotiating and conducting their activities directly with other enterprises. The role of higher authorities is limited to establishing general guidelines and intervening directly when social interest demands it. This approach has been a feature of the Socialist countries since the ECONOMIC REFORMS, Yugoslavia and Hungary being the best examples.

'Hot Line' Direct telecommunication link between the top leaders of the USA and the USSR, terminating in the White

House and the KREMLIN. A need for it became apparent in the context of an imminent nuclear attack by error and was particularly prompted by the CUBAN MISSILE CRISIS of 1962. The H.L. was established on the basis of a 'Memorandum of Understanding', signed in Geneva by the US and Soviet representatives.

How to be a Good Communist A well-known book by LIU SHAO-CH'I in China, originally published in 1939 and later republished with minor changes in 1962. Among the themes treated were 'left opportunism' and 'intra-party struggle'. It was a prescribed text for the Party cadres during the 'rectification campaign' of 1942–43. In March 1967, the book became an object of attack by Mao Tse-tung and his organizers of the GREAT PROLETARIAN CULTURAL REVOLUTION. The book was described as a 'poisonous weed' and was criticized on the grounds that it ignored the CLASS STRUGGLE and the DICTATORSHIP OF THE PROLETARIAT, encouraged an uncritical acceptance of orders from the hierarchy and promoted INDIVIDUALISM and self-cultivation.

'How to Spend the Other Eight Hours' Campaign A widely publicized drive launched in China in the early 1960s setting down guidelines for the socially-acceptable use of leisure time by peasants, workers, soldiers and intellectuals. The guidelines included the following exhortations: 1. study the works and poetry of Mao Tse-tung; 2. keep fit by engaging in gymnastics every day; 3. tell and listen to revolutionary stories and contrast the misery of the past with the happiness of the present; 4. engage in hearty conversations with your friends to cultivate social outlook; 5. keep your dwellings tidy; 6. wash clothes regularly; and 7. look after your children.

Hoxha, Enver (1908–) The Albanian Communist leader and statesman, noted for his inflexible interpretation of MARXISM-LENINISM and autocratic rule. A teacher by education, he led the national liberation struggle between 1939–44. He founded the Albanian Communist Party in 1941 (in 1948 renamed the ALBANIAN PARTY OF LABOUR) and became its Secretary-General in 1943 (the post was renamed 'First Secretary' in 1954). He was also Prime Minister and Supreme Commander of the Albanian Forces from 1944 to 1954. His Stalinist rule is made possible through several key positions he maintains, namely, the First Secretary of the A.P. of L., President of the General Council of the DEMOCRATIC FRONT and Member of the Presidium of the People's Assembly (parliament).

Hsin Hua The old version (according to the Wade-Giles system) of spelling XIN HUA, the Chinese name of the official New China News Agency.

Hua Kuo-Feng (1922–) The Chinese Communist leader and statesman, who succeeded CHOU EN-LAI and MAO TSE-TUNG in 1976. During the Civil War 1946–49, he fought against the KUOMINTANG and in the next 12 years occupied a variety of administrative posts in the province of Hunan. In 1958 he became its Vice-Governor and proved most active and capable in carrying out land and economic reforms. As a member of the CHINESE COMMUNIST PARTY up to 1971, he worked in the provincial Party apparatus where he reached the position of the Secretary for Hunan in 1959 and was elected to the Party's Central Committee in 1969. He rose rapidly in the Party and Government hierarchy after his transfer to Peking in 1971. He was elected to the Politburo of the CCP in 1973 and two years later was appointed Minister of Public Security. After Chou's death, he became Vice-Premier in Jan. 1976 and three months later became Prime Minister and Vice-Chairman of the CCP. In the following October, he was elevated to the Chairmanship of the Party's Central Committee and of its Military Committee (thus succeeding to Mao's posts). Hua has established a reputation for sound administration, moderation, pragmatism, shrewd tactics and the appreciation of the need for political stability, rapid modernization with the aid of Western technology and economic commonsense. In Sept 1980 he resigned his post of P.M. in favour of Zhao Ziyang.

Huks The colloquial name for the Communist-controlled guerrilla force in the Philippines. It is an abbreviation of *Hukbo ng Magappalya ng Bayam* or *Hukbalahab*, meaning 'People's Liberation Army'. Its origin goes back to 1942 when it was an anti-Japanese guerrilla organization. After the war it refused to be disbanded and surrender its weapons. The H. were proscribed in 1948, but the enforcement of the law was held out till 1957, when it (together with the COMMUNIST PARTY OF THE PHILIPPINES) was outlawed. The H. have continued their terrorist and extortionist activities against the rich and the supporters of NEO-COLONIALISM. After the split in the C.P. of the P. in 1969, the pro-Chinese faction formed the 'New People's Army' as its military arm, into which most of the H. were absorbed. The N.P.A. has adopted MAOISM and Lin Piao's revolutionary strategy. It has become quite active in local government and has established communal farms and workshops. The Soviet-oriented faction formed the 'National Army' which has managed to retain some H. The total number of the H. is estimated to be 2,000 (as of the late 1970s).

Humanism An intellectual and moral outlook and movement assigning the highest importance to man, who is credited with the right to full development, dignity and the master of his own destiny. The term was introduced in the 19th c., at first in application to the Renaissance in Western Europe in the 14th and 15th centuries as a reaction among intellectuals against the feudal and religious establishment which had subordinated man to authoritarianism and dogma. Marxists are critical of pre-socialist h., as in their view it was elitist and excluded peasants and the urban masses. Contrasted with traditional h. is

'socialist' or 'proletarian' h., which emphasizes the liberation of the working man of all races and nationalities from capitalist exploitation, discrimination and oppression. The basic propositions of socialist h. as seen by Marx, Engels and Stalin are: 1. private ownership of the means of production by capitalists is the chief barrier to the development of human happiness; 2. the social class which can remove the obstacles to the development of human dignity and happiness is the working class, and can only achieve this by a proletarian revolution; 3. the highest form of h. is a harmonious classless society, where differences between rural and urban, physical and mental, and labouring and managerial occupations are eliminated; and 4. socialist h. postulate the all-round development of all the members of society, the avoidance of excessive specialization and the ultimate abolition of coercion (the state). The critics of revolutionary Marxism point out that ideological intolerance, the DICTATORSHIP OF THE PROLETARIAT, the FORCED LABOUR CAMPS or mental institutions for dissenters, the denial of HUMAN RIGHTS and the growing power of bureaucracy and technocracy, all represent negations of h. Some liberal Communist leaders have pressed (unsuccessfully) for 'SOCIALISM WITH A HUMAN FACE'.

Humanité, L' (*Humanity*, in French) The daily organ of the FRENCH COMMUNIST PARTY since 1920. It was founded by a moderate socialist leader, J. L. JAURÈS, in 1904 as the organ of the FRENCH SOCIALIST PARTY which he edited until his death in 1914. Its publication was suspended in 1939, but appeared illegally in Paris 1940–44. Its daily circulation is about 200,000.

Humanization of Industrial Relations The improvement of human relations in the entities of employment, especially between workers and management. The Socialist countries attach considerable importance to this problem on the grounds of ideology, social ethics and labour productivity considerations. It assumes the following three forms: 1. workers' participation in management and control; 2. protection and improvement of the conditions of work; and 3. social and cultural activities, embracing managerial, specialist and unskilled personnel outside working hours (social functions, picnics, theatre parties, excursions), designed to develop better personal relations in a more relaxed atmosphere. The extent and success of these arrangements vary from one Socialist country to another and from one place of employment to another. China and Yugoslavia appear to be leading in this field.

Human Rights Civil liberties or freedoms of citizens from the encroachment by the state, explicitly guaranteed by law or implied in the absence of restricting laws. The commonly accepted h.r. include the freedom of speech, press, worship, association, peaceful demonstration and travel, the absence of discrimination on the grounds of beliefs, race, nationality and sex, and the right to education, the privacy of home and correspondence and to protest. Although in the Socialist countries h.r. are usually guaranteed constitutionally, the guarantees are vague. Their interpretation may be subordinated to the 'higher interests of the Socialist state' where there are no independent courts or where there is no machinery or easy procedures for the enforcement of the guarantees. Thus, in the new Soviet Constitution of Oct. 1977, it is stated that 'the citizens' exercise of their h.r. must not harm the interests of society, the state or other individuals'. Political persecution, escapes to capitalist countries and h.r. movements in the Socialist countries provide evidence of these phenomena. Also BELGRADE CONFERENCE, CHARTER OF LIBERTY, CHARTER '77, DISSENTERS, HELSINKI CONFERENCE, MOSCOW HUMAN RIGHTS COMMITTEE, *SAMIZDAT*.

'Hundred Flowers' Interlude A short period of intellectual freedom in China, which lasted from the end of April to early June 1957. The 'H.F.' 'campaign' was launched by Mao Tse-tung who invited criticisms of Party policies by anticommunist intellectuals, with the well-known slogan from Chinese classical history, 'Let a hundred flowers bloom and a hundred schools of thought contend'. It was prompted by the post-Stalin 'thaw' in the USSR and Eastern Europe and Mao's desire to improve the Party's style of work and image. The liberalization move had been planned earlier in Mao's 'secret speech' (to a closed session of the Supreme State Conference in Peking) on 27 Feb. 1957, entitled ON THE CORRECT HANDLING OF CONTRADICTIONS AMONG THE PEOPLE. It was published only after the Interlude and in an amended form. The response, although slow at first, was extraordinary and the Party leadership became alarmed. The 'thaw' was stopped after 8 June 1957, when a warning editorial appeared in the *People's Daily*. A reaction came in early July 1957, known as the ANTI-RIGHTIST CAMPAIGN and the 'Hundred Flowers' came to be described as 'poisonous weeds'.

Hungarian People's Republic (*Magyar Nepkotarság*) A medium-sized country in Eastern Europe ruled by the HUNGARIAN SOCIALIST WORKERS' PARTY. Its area is 93,030 sq. km. and its population is 10.7m. (1978). Formerly a monarchy under a fascist regime, it was proclaimed a 'People's Republic' on 1 Feb. 1946. After a period of participation in two coalitions 1944–48, the Hungarian Communist Party (as it was then known) eliminated or absorbed other left-wing parties by intrigues and terrorist tactics and became the undisputed ruling party. Economic planning was adopted in 1947 and the socialization of banks and industry was carried out during 1947–48. This was followed by general collectivization over the period 1948–62. After Stalin's death (March 1953), a liberal Prime Minister was appointed, I. NAGY, who was later removed by the Communist establishment in 1955. In the following year (Oct.–Nov.), the HUNGARIAN UPRIS-

ING broke out, directed against Soviet domination and the subservient local Communist leadership. The new coalition government led by I. Nagy decided to withdraw Hungary from the WARSAW PACT and appealed to the United Nations for the protection of its neutrality. But the Uprising was crushed by the Soviet tanks. A pro-Soviet regime was re-established under J. KÁDÁR, which at first took severe reprisals against the liberal elements, but later adopted a moderate course and cautious liberalization. Major economic reforms were embarked upon in 1968, emphasizing the role of the market and profit, with considerable success. As a result, Hungary has come to be regarded as the most liberal Socialist country next to Yugoslavia. A Soviet-type Constitution was adopted in Aug. 1949 and amended in April 1972. The highest formal source of power is the NATIONAL ASSEMBLY, consisting of 352 deputies elected by universal adult suffrage for five years from a single list of candidates prepared by the PATRIOTIC PEOPLE'S FRONT.

Hungarian Socialist Workers' Party (*Magyar Szocialista Munkáspárt*)The ruling Communist party in Hungary with a long revolutionary tradition. Its origin goes back to March 1918, when the Communist Party of Hungary was created as a section of the RUSSIAN COMMUNIST PARTY (OF THE BOLSHEVIKS). However, at the end of the same year it became a separate national organization. During March–August 1919, the C.P.H. was the ruling party in a left-wing coalition which proclaimed the HUNGARIAN SOVIET REPUBLIC. The Party was declared illegal immediately after the defeat of the H.S.R. and was dissolved by the COMINTERN in 1922, after which it remained largely dormant until the later stages of W.W.II. It re-emerged in 1944 as the Hungarian Communist Party in the areas liberated from the Germans. It initiated the formation of the National Independence Front, in which the Social-Democratic Party, the Smallholders Party, the National Peasants Party and the Democratic Urban Party

participated. After its failure at the Nov. 1945 elections (when the Smallholders Party won 57 per cent of the votes), the H.C.P. organized a left-wing coalition bloc in opposition, which polled 61 per cent of the votes at the Aug. 1947 elections. In June 1948, the H.C.P. merged with the Social-Democratic Party and formed the Hungarian Workers' Party. Other political parties were infiltrated and eliminated by 1949. During the HUNGARIAN UPRISING in 1956, the Party's name was changed to its present designation. In 1978 the Party's membership stood at 770,000, out of a total population of 10,700,000. Its subsidiary mass organization is the Communist Youth League, which has approximately 800,000 members. The top level of the Party's authority is the Congress, held every four years. The 1975 Congress elected a Central Committee of 125, which in turn elected a Political Committee consisting of 13 members plus two 'additional' members. The latter (in most other Socialist countries known as the 'Politburo') is headed by the Party's First Secretary (J. KÁDÁR) and is the highest effective policy-making body in the country. There is also a Secretariat (First Secretary plus six members) and a Control Committee (of 24 members). The Party's main regular publications are: *Népszabadság* (*People's Daily*), the daily organ; *Pártélet* (*Party Life*), a monthly journal on Party organization and work; and *Társadalmi szemle* (*Social Review*), a theoretical monthly.

Hungarian Soviet Republic A Marxist state which existed in Hungary from 21 March to 1 Aug. 1919. A Revolutionary Government (later called the 'Council of People's Commissars') was formed by the Socialist Party of Hungary (a merger of the Communist Party of Hungary and the Social-Democratic Party). Although the Prime Minister was S. Garbai, the real leader was a revolutionary Marxist, Béla Kun, who was 'People's Commissar for External Affairs'. On 25 March, a Decree was issued to form the Red Army of Hungary, and on the following day the nationalization of industry, transport and banks was decreed. Large estates were nationalized on 3 April. An eight-hour working day and universal social insurance were introduced and a Constitution was adopted. Armed attacks by Romanian and Czechoslovak troops and nationalist forces led to the collapse of the H.S.R. Political power was seized by a right-wing government headed by M. Horthy and G. Karólyi de Nagykarolyi.

Hungarian Uprising An unsuccessful popular revolt in Hungary from 23 Oct. to 14 Nov. 1956 against Soviet political, military and economic domination and the rigid pro-Soviet Communist regime. The Uprising began with a students' demonstration in Budapest, demanding the following: 1. the reinstatement of a liberal Communist leader I. NAGY to the Prime Ministership (to replace M. RÁKOSI); 2. the removal of Soviet troops from Hungary; and 3. a changeover to a multi-party system of government. The firing by police upon the demonstrators aroused public sympathy, and workers, soldiers and other members of the public joined the insurrection throughout the country A general strike was declared to last until the Soviet troops left the country. On 30 Oct., a Socialist coalition government was formed under the leadership of I. Nagy who, on 1–2 Nov. appealed to the United Nations to guarantee Hungary's neutrality upon her withdrawal from the WARSAW PACT. The USSR denounced the Uprising as a 'COUNTER-REVOLUTION' and sent more troops, including tanks, to Budapest, thus ending the insurrection. By 14 Nov., I. Nagy had taken refuge in the Yugoslav Embassy in Budapest, but was tricked into leaving it (on 22 Nov.), arrested, taken to Romania and executed. A repressive Communist regime was reimposed under J. KÁDÁR. The methods resorted to by the Soviets and the Hungarian Stalinists caused profound and widespread indignation in the non-Communist world.

Hung-Chi (*Red Flag*, in Chinese) The theoretical organ of the Central Committee of the Chinese Communist Party. It appears monthly in Peking and its publication is supervised by the Propaganda Department of the C.C. of the C.C.P.

Hural A short name for the Mongolian parliament, officially known as the PEOPLE'S GREAT HURAL.

Husák, Gustav (1913–) A Czechoslovak Communist leader and statesman. He joined the Slovak Communist Party in the early 1930s, became a lawyer and a champion of Slovak rights and was active in the Communist resistance movement during W.W.II. In 1945, he was elected to the Central Committee of the CZECHOSLOVAK COMMUNIST PARTY, but was later imprisoned for 'bourgeois-nationalist deviations' (1954–60). After his release he supported A. DUBČEK and his reforms and became Vice-Premier (April 1968 – Jan. 1969). After the INVASION OF CZECHOSLOVAKIA (in Aug. 1968) he was appointed to the Executive Committee of the Presidium of the C.C. of the Cz.C.P. (Sep. 1968 – April 1969) and made Commander-in-Chief of the People's Militia. In April 1969, he replaced Dubček as the First Secretary of the Cz.C.P. (re-named Secretary-General in 1971) and in May 1975 was appointed the President of Czechoslovakia.

Hyndman, Henry Mayers (1842–1921) An English journalist by profession who became a Marxist writer and Socialist leader. He popularized the ideas of Marx, Engels and Lassalle and was opposed to British imperialism. His main writings include *The Historical Basis of Socialism in England* (1883), *The Economics of Socialism* (1890), *The Commercial Crisis of the Nineteenth Century* (1908) and *A Record of an Adventurous Life* (1911). In 1881 (together with William Morris) he founded the Social Democratic Federation, which had a Marxist programme. He was later the Chairman of the British Socialist Party which succeeded the S.D.F.

I

I.B.E.C. Abbreviation for the INTERNATIONAL BANK FOR ECONOMIC CO-OPERATION.

Iceberg Thesis A conviction held by some Marxists and non-Marxists that under normal conditions only about 3 per cent of the population ('the tip of the iceberg') is ideologically and idealistically inclined, constituting the vanguard of social progress. The remaining 97 per cent are basically interested in their own private material pursuits. Marxists, however, point out that human nature can change with the modified environment and, through PROPAGANDA and AGITATION, the proportion of the ideologically active population can be doubled. It is interesting to note that the membership of the Communist parties in the Socialist bloc as a whole represents 6 per cent of the population.

Icelandic People's Alliance PEOPLE'S ALLIANCE OF ICELAND.

I.C.F.T.U. INTERNATIONAL CONFEDERATION OF FREE TRADE UNIONS.

Idealism One of the two main divisions of philosophy (the other being materialism), maintaining that ideas (thought, reason, spirit, god) are primary, whilst matter is secondary and derivative from ideas. Consequently, ideas are active and creative, independent of the material world, the latter being considered passive, dependent, created by god or human mind. There are many schools of idealist philosophy, ranging from extreme OBJEC-TIVISM, as represented by Plato (427–347 B.C.) and G. W. F. HEGEL to extreme SUBJECTIVISM, identified with G. Berkeley (1684–1753) and D. Hume (1711–76). Some of the best known idealistic theories which have received critical attention from Marxist philosophers include AGNOSTICISM (I. Kant, 1724–1804), EMPIRIO-CRITICISM (E.MACH), HIEROGLYPHIC THEORY OF COGNITION (I. Isaakovnna Axelrod, 1868–1946), IRRATIONALISM (F. Nietzsche, 1844–1900), METAPHYSICS (B. Spinoza, 1632–77), POSITIVISM (A. Comte, 1798–1857) and THEISM (E. H. Gibson, 1884–). Marxism rejects i. and instead accepts MATERIALISM as the ultimate explanation of existence. Its criticism is particularly directed to objective i. which has always been associated with the religious outlook of the world ('god created the world out of nothing'). In the Marxist view, i. has been a product of the separation of mental from physical work and the appearance of exploiting classes. I. is regarded as unscientific, as it separates the process of cognition from reality and practice. The age-long controversy between i. and materialism, going back to ancient times, has reflected the class struggle between regressive and progressive forces. I. was attacked by Marx and Engels in their joint works *The HOLY FAMILY* and *The GERMAN IDEOLOGY*, by Plekhanov in *The Development of the Monist View of History* (1895) and by Lenin in *MATERIALISM AND EMPIRIO-CRITICISM*.

Idealist Conception of History Philosophical and sociological theories re-

garding spirit, ideas, theories, consciousness and views as the basic and independent determinants of the development of
societies. These theories, like IDEALISM,
fall into two categories – objective and
subjective. The former attributes historical development to the 'absolute idea' or
god, as represented by HEGEL. The latter
explains the course of history in terms of
the will, motives and opinions of the individuals, and was supported by the
HEGELIAN LEFT in Germany and NAROD-
NISM in Russia. Marxists are totally opposed to the i.c. of h., as in their view: 1. it
exaggerates the role of spiritual and intellectual forces to the disregard of material
factors and the methods of production; 2.
it assigns the dominant role to individual
persons (messiahs, thinkers, kings, con-
querors, heroes and other 'men of destiny'), ignoring the role of the masses; 3.
it implies that historical events are a product of favourable or adverse accidents
and not governed by objective laws of
social development; and 4. it assumes that
social progress can be achieved merely by
improving the education of some individuals, thus rejecting the need for the
class struggle and the revolutionary transformation of production relations and the
social structure. The Marxist interpretation of history is embodied in HISTORICAL
MATERIALISM.

Idealistic Incentives Another description
for the more commonly used term MORAL
INCENTIVES.

Idealist Monism MONISM.

Ideas Notions or conceptual knowledge
conceived by the human mind. Their conditioning and emergence are the subject of
controversy between Marxist and non-
Marxist philosophers. In non-Marxist
philosophy, i. are regarded as primary
phenomena, independent of the material
environment and the class structure. An
extreme case of the idealist view are the
so-called INNATE I., formulated by
Plato (427–347 B.C.), R. Descartes
(1596–1650) and I. Kant (1724–1804),

viz. those which are presumed to exist
independently of any experience what-
soever (god, concepts of time, space,
geometry). Marxist materialist philosophy
is opposed to this interpretation, maintaining that i. in fact constitute reflections
of reality in man's consciousness and are
indicative of man's relation to his environment. Furthermore, Marxists stress that in
a class society, i. are class-conditioned and
represent material interests of the social
classes. Marx and Engels in fact went
further and stated that 'The ruling ideas of
each age have ever been the ideas of its
ruling class' (in *The Communist Manifesto*). I. can be *progressive*, reflecting new
economic and social forces, and *reactionary*, when they portray the economic and
social establishment in decay resisting
change. New i. occur and develop only
when the stage of the material development of society is such that it places new
tasks before it, and consequently new i.
are indispensable to social progress.

Identity A concept denoting absolute
similarity (in the qualitative sense) or
equality (quantitatively). I. can be *formal*,
when two objects or phenomena have a
specific property in common, or *material*,
when two concepts equally apply to the
same thing. One of the pre-Marxist interpretations of i. was that of HEGEL (in
The Science of Logic, 1812–16), in whose
view the law of i. contains only 'formal,
abstract and incomplete truth'. He insisted that truth is complete only in the
'unity of identity with difference' i.e. the
unity of contradictions. Although the
Marxist view of i. is largely derived from
Hegel, most Marxist (in contrast to some
Mensheviks) philosophers are opposed to
the extreme identification of CONTRADIC-
TIONS, such as peace and war, the
bourgeoisie and the proletariat or life and
death, as they are mutually exclusive.
Marxists, as exemplified by Engels (in
DIALECTICS OF NATURE) approach i. in a
dynamic manner, emphasizing that in nature nothing is immutable, so that no object or phenomenon remains identical to
itself through time.

Ideology A term which appeared first during the French Revolution (1789–99) and was elaborated upon by Destut de Tracy (1755–1836), who defined it as the 'science of ideas'. However, the concept soon came to acquire a more specific meaning, viz. that of a system of ideas, outlooks, attitudes and emotions of a particular social group. I. usually has its own philosophy from which distinctive political, economic, social and cultural views derive. It may be fragmentary or complete, closed or open, and explicitly or implicitly embodies certain desired objectives, thus basically conditioning most activities of the group. In the Marxist view, i. is not neutral. I. is always associated with a particular social class in four ways: 1. it stems from the historical conditions of life; 2. it is biased, reflecting the interests of the social class concerned; 3. it performs important social functions, by increasing the cohesion of the class and assisting the class in improving or defending its position in society; and 4. depending on the social class, whether exploiting or exploited, i. may play a retrogressive or progressive role. An extreme stand was adopted by Lenin (in *WHAT IS TO BE DONE?*) who insisted that there were only two ideologies – bourgeois and proletarian, and that mankind had not devised a 'third'. Marxists regard a particular i. as 'scientific' if it is consistent with the theoretical assumptions underlying the activities of progressive social forces. In their view, only Marxism can provide such assumptions. At the same time, the development of science must be conditioned by progressive social forces and their interests. They reject the postulate of freeing science from i. (considering it 'false consciousness'), and they dismiss claims by some Western philosophers of the inevitability of DISIDEOLOGIZATION.

Il The Soviet abbreviation for the models of military and civilian aircraft designed originally under the direction of S. V. Ilyushin (1894–   ).

Illegitimate Profits ANTI-SOCIAL PROFITS.

Ilyn, V. One of the early assumed names of V. I. Ulyanov, better known as V. I. LENIN. His first major book, *The Development of Capitalism in Russia* (1899) was published under this pen name.

Immiseration of the Proletariat A Marxian concept denoting the increasing impoverishment of the working class, as CAPITALISM passes from lower to higher stages of economic development. This is one of the fundamental propositions in Marx's economic and social doctrine, embodied mainly in *CAPITAL*, vol. I. It is also known as the 'law of the increasing misery (or 'pauperization') of the proletariat'. The designation 'i'. owes its popularization to J. Schumpeter, who gave the original Marxian term (in German) *Entlendung* its new English version. In Marx's contention, the greater the social wealth, the greater is the CONSTANT CAPITAL, and the faster its growth the greater is the size of the PROLETARIAT and the RESERVE ARMY OF WORKERS. The operation of the 'law' is inexorably associated with the LAW OF CAPITALIST ACCUMULATION, the increasing ORGANIC STRUCTURE OF CAPITAL and the law of the DECLINING PROFIT RATE. Marx's theorizing about the i. of the p. is about the most fallacious of his 'laws'. Contrary to his predictions, the standard of living of the working classes has vastly improved, especially in the most developed capitalist countries. The defenders of Marx maintain that he was right if we consider the relative position of the working class, i.e. it has not improved as much as that of the BOURGEOISIE. However, this assertion cannot be proven by statistical evidence, as the opposite appears to be the case.

Imperative Planning Another designation of the CENTRALIZED DIRECTIVE SYSTEM OF PLANNING AND MANAGEMENT.

Imperialism A major concept in Marxist political science, political economy and sociology, identified with the highest stage of capitalism. The traditional Marxist interpretation of i. is based on Lenin's

Imperialism

IMPERIALISM: THE HIGHEST STAGE OF CAPITALISM, which drew heavily from R. Hilferding's Finance Capital (1910) and Rosa Luxemburg's Accumulation of Capital (1913). Lenin described i. as the 'monopoly stage of capitalism . . . parasitic and decaying'. He distinguished five characteristic features: 1. concentration of production and expansive and vicious competition; 2. finance capitalism, where banks are transformed into omnipotent monopolies in the financial market; 3. capital export to economically under-developed countries, and their parasitic exploitation; 4. a division of domestic and foreign markets by monopolies and inter-national cartels into more or less exclusive preserves; and 5. a complete division of the less developed world into spheres of economic and political exploitation furth-er contributing to the struggle between the imperialist powers on the instigation of monopolies. I., Lenin stressed, leads to the extreme exacerbation of capitalist contradictions, i.e. increasing conflicts between monopolized and non-monopolized industries, accelerated de-velopment in some spheres and retarda-tion in others, the growing exploitation of poor nations by the rich countries, inten-sified rivalry leading to wars among the imperialist powers, and the widening rift between capital and labour forced beyond the bridging point. He also blamed i. for ideological opportunism in the labour movement whereby the monopolies' vast profits are used to corrupt skilled workers and labour leaders to undermine the unity of the working class. Lenin's analysis of i. led him to the formulation of a new view of the PROLETARIAN REVOLUTION. He em-phasized that owing to the differing rates of the maturation of the conditions neces-sary for such a revolution, it was imposs-ible to achieve it on a world-wide scale at once, therefore the process would have to be gradual, starting with 'socialism in one country or a few at the most'. Since the 20th Congress of the CPSU in 1956 the official view of i. has been somewhat mod-ified in the USSR. It was pointed out at the Congress that owing to the disintegration of the colonial empires, the growing strength of the Socialist camp and the existence of nuclear weapons and inter-continental ballistic missiles, a new situa-tion had arisen in the international scene. It was no longer valid that the decaying capitalist powers would resort to war as a matter of course, therefore Lenin's theory, while applicable to the First and Second World Wars, is no longer relevant. K. NKRUMAH, the Ghanaian left-wing leader (deposed in 1967), known as the 'Black Lenin', wrote NEO-COLONIALISM, THE LAST STAGE OF IMPERIALISM (1965) with the intent of continuing Lenin's analysis. Nkrumah's point is that in this stage, ex-colonial powers endeavour to retain their influence in the politically lib-erated countries by indirect means, such as the extension of economic aid, and the imposition of Western patterns of con-sumption, education and culture. Since the disappearance of the colonial empires, the meaning of i. has been extended to describe any undue control or influence exercised by a large country over a smaller one. As such, the concept has been occa-sionally used in application to the USSR and the P.R. of China. Examples of this would be the USSR annexing eastern Po-land in 1939, Bessarabia and northern Bukovina in 1940 (from Romania), Es-tonia, Latvia and Lithuania in 1940, Karelia in 1940 (from Finland), Tannu-Tuva in 1944 (from Mongolia), the Sub-Carpathian Ruthenia in 1945 (from Czechoslovakia), East Prussia in 1945 (from Germany) and Karafuto and Kurile Islands in 1945 (from Japan). The Soviet military intervention in the German DR in 1953, Hungary in 1956 and Czecho-slovakia in 1968 also illustrate the USSR's determination to preserve Eastern Europe as her exclusive sphere of influ-ence. The Sino-Soviet rift in the Socialist camp and in the Third World, whereby local ideological and political allegiance are being sought, has also been described as a version of i. Some African leaders have openly expressed their opposition to the 'white and yellow imperialists'. Also BREZHNEV DOCTRINE, COLONIALISM,

COUNTER-IMPERIALISM, NEO-COLONIAL-ISM, SATELLITE COUNTRIES, ULTRA-IMPERIALISM.

Imperialism: The Highest Stage of Capitalism One of the most important works of V. I. LENIN, written in Switzerland in 1916 and published in 1917. The book was meant to be a supplement to Marx's *CAPITAL*, in which Lenin deduced the principles governing the development of IMPERIALISM, which he called the 'last parasitic and putrid' stage of capitalism. He identified and analysed five characteristics of i.: 1. the replacement of competition in the early phase of capitalism by the CONCENTRATION AND CENTRALIZATION OF PRODUCTION and MONOPOLY CAPITALISM; 2. the exacerbation of the rivalry among powerful monopolies, the increasing ANARCHY OF PRODUCTION, the growth of banking, financial companies, stock exchanges and of a FINANCIAL OLIGARCHY, and the fusion of industrial and financial capital; 3. the EXPORT OF CAPITAL to the less developed countries with cheap labour and raw materials, leading to COLONIALISM and rivalry amongst the imperialist powers; 4. the formation of international cartels by national monopolies, dividing the world market into exclusive spheres of exploitation, and resulting in an insatiable greed further aggravating a rivalry leading to the breakdown of the cartels; and 5. the direct involvement of the capitalist states assisting the national monopolies in their struggle for world markets, leading to the imperialist division of the world among the main imperial powers, thus creating conditions for imperialist wars, into which almost all capitalist nations are dragged. Lenin attacked Kautsky's idea of ULTRA-IMPERIALISM and emphasized that there was no possibility of the imperialist powers forming a friendly world imperial coalition and that imperialist wars were inevitable. He further analysed the process of the exploitation of the working classes in the colonies as well as in the imperialist countries. The large profits made by the monopolies enable them to bribe the labour leaders and upper-grade workers in order to undermine the solidarity of the working class movement. In the last chapter, Lenin concludes that the antagonistic class contradictions aggravated by i. must inevitably lead to the BREAKDOWN OF CAPITALISM. But he stressed that the uneven economic and social development in different capitalist countries makes some more mature for a PROLETARIAN REVOLUTION than others. Consequently, it is unlikely that such a revolution will be successful in all countries at once.

Impoverishment of the Working Class IMMISERATION OF THE PROLETARIAT.

Imprekorr A syllabic abbreviation of *Internationale Presse Korrespondenz*, in German, meaning the 'International Press Correspondence'. It was a press agency established by the COMINTERN in 1921 and supervised by the EXECUTIVE COMMITTEE OF THE COMMUNIST INTERNATIONAL. Owing to persecutions, its base had to be moved several times – Berlin (1921–23), Vienna (1923), Berlin (1923–34), Basel (1935–39) and finally Stockholm (1939–53). It also published bulletins in Czech, English, French and Spanish. In spite of the dissolution of the Comintern in 1943, *I.* continued its activities until 1953.

Incentives A general term for various forms of motivation applied to workers to promote higher performance and efficiency. Owing to the virtual absence of private enterprise, continuous full employment (except Yugoslavia) and generous social security, the Socialist countries have had to develop elaborate systems of i. to induce workers to greater effort and the implementation of the planned targets along desired lines. The following are types of i.: 1. MATERIAL I. and MORAL I.; 2. INDIVIDUAL I. and COLLECTIVE I.; and 3. specialized i. (awarded for a narrowly defined achievement, such as quality improvement or the saving of power) and SYNTHETIC I. Marxism attaches great importance to moral and collective i. It is envisaged that under FULL COMMUNISM material i. will disappear.

Incitative Planning A term sometimes used to describe a mild form of economic planning, where targets or broad objectives are achieved by a well developed system of incentives, rather than by DIRECTIVES. I.p. goes further than INDICATIVE PLANNING in actively promoting the implementation of the plan along desired lines. The authorities primarily resort to taxes, subsidies, credit, price mark-ups and price mark-downs, bonuses to workers, financial penalties and moral motivation, to carry out their plans. Thus, targets and other objectives are achieved largely through the market. The system is considered to be consistent with decentralization and the independence of enterprises. Since the ECONOMIC REFORMS of the 1960s, i.p. has been developed best in Yugoslavia and Hungary, to a moderate extent in Bulgaria, Czechoslovakia and Poland, and to a lesser extent in other Socialist countries.

Independent Labour Party A socialist party founded in Britain in Bradford in 1893 under the leadership of Keir Hardie and Tom Mann. It aimed at increasing labour representation in local government and in Parliament, independently of the Liberals and Conservatives. It has never directly played any important role in British politics, but it was instrumental in organizing the early LABOUR PARTY (in 1906). The I.L.P. has advocated the public ownership of all the means of production, the establishment of workers' councils in all workplaces and the complete unilateral disarmament of both conventional and nuclear weapons. It opposed Britain's participation in W.W.I. and W.W.II. It was disaffiliated from the Labour Party in 1932. Its membership continued to decline, from 3,000 in 1948 to about 300. Most of its disillusioned former members joined the Communist, Trotskyite, anarchist or other radical groups.

Indeterminism A philosophical doctrine maintaining that the normal course of events is not necessarily determined by any causes or laws, especially in the social sphere. As such, it is opposed to DETERMINISM. I. emphasizes 'absolute free will', i.e. human actions are interpreted as not necessarily being dependent on anything. It rests on three basic propositions: 1. not every phenomenon has its cause; 2. not all phenomena are governed by laws; and 3. the same conditions do not necessarily produce the same phenomena. Marxists reject i., regarding it as a natural derivative of IDEALISM and RELIGION. They consider absolute free will as an apologetic justification for the anarchy of bourgeois INDIVIDUALISM and the right of the ruling classes to exploit the working class. In their view, i. negates the historical laws of social development through different SOCIO-ECONOMIC FORMATIONS, the BREAKDOWN OF CAPITALISM and its inevitable replacement by socialism and full communism. The doctrine is inconsistent with HISTORICAL MATERIALISM.

Indexes of the Effectiveness of Investment Formulae for calculating the efficiency of investment projects from the standpoint of particular objective(s). These indexes are widely used in the Socialist centrally planned economies to enable the selection of the most desirable projects. The term 'effectiveness' is more appropriate than 'efficiency', owing to the distortion of prices which do not necessarily reflect scarcity. There are a large number of the indexes to suit particular purposes and some are quite complex. The two main types are: 1. 'Index of the time recoupment' (or 'of the pay-off period'), in which the capital cost is related to the operating cost of the old and proposed investment project:

$$T = \frac{I_2 - I_1}{C_1 - C_2}$$

T = time of recoupment
I_1 = investment outlay incurred on the existing plant

I_2 = investment outlay on the proposed project

C_1 = annual operating cost of the existing plant

C_2 = annual operating cost of the proposed project

The shorter the period of recoupment, other things being equal, the more preferable is the proposed project. If the period of useful life of the proposed project exceeds the time of recoupment T, the contemplated modernization is economical. The degree of efficiency is indicated by annual savings in operating costs (C_1-C_2) multiplied by the period of the excess life of the project.

2. 'Synthetic index of investment effectiveness', in which investment outlay is related to the value of production:

$$sIe= \frac{\frac{1}{T}I(1-d.f)- Cn.vc}{Vn.vp}$$

sIe = the synthetic index of investment effectiveness

I = investment outlay

d = the coefficient of discount indicating annual losses caused to the economy during the period of construction of the investment undertaking and usually fixed for the whole economy (e.g. 0.20 in Hungary)

f = the freeze period, i.e. the number of years necessary to complete the investment project

Cn = the total cost of exploitation of the project, including maintenance and repairs during the whole period n

vc = the coefficient of cost variation during the period of exploitation

Vn = the total value of production in the entire period n

vp = the coefficient of production variation during the period of exploitation

Indian Communist Party COMMUNIST PARTY OF INDIA.

Indian National Congress The oldest and one of the largest socialist political parties in India. Founded in 1885, it split into factions (Moderates and Extremists) in 1907 and again, in 1969, into Conservatives and Progressives. The latter, called the I.N.C. – P., has been led by Mrs Indira Gandhi. It was continuously in power for 30 years after independence (1947). At the general elections in March 1977, the representation of the I.N.C. – P. in the Lower House was reduced from 355 to 153 (out of the total of 542) seats, and power went to the Janata Party (271 seats) and the Congress for Democracy (28 seats). The I.N.C. – P. is committed to a casteless and classless society, based on the principle of social, economic and political justice, including equality of opportunity and freedom to work. In its programme it advocates a peaceful PARLIAMENTARY ROAD TO SOCIALISM, the public ownership of key industries and services, the development of co-operatives in industry and agriculture and a neutral foreign policy.

Indian Socialist Party SOCIALIST PARTY OF INDIA.

Indicative Planning Economic planning where tasks (targets) are defined in general terms and are not directive, i.e. not compulsory for enterprises and other entities, especially outside the state sector. It is common in some capitalist market economies and was first applied in France after W.W.II. An i. plan above all shows the intended expenditure of the state, including nationalized industries, and the desired directions of economic and social development. The state, it is assumed, is in a better position to anticipate future developments and considers its duty to initiate and promote such developments in society's interest. The plan provides valuable information to individual industries and firms for their investment. The state may use various weapons of economic policy (fiscal, monetary, administrative) to promote or discourage certain developments, essentially through the market. I.p. is more than mere forecasting, but not as definite and mandatory as socialist CENTRAL ECONOMIC PLANNING. Also INCITATIVE PLANNING, ORIENTATIONAL PLANNING.

Indifferentism A term used in the Socialist countries to describe the attitude of indifference to social problems and developments. It can be directed against the old system and values, which is not officially frowned upon, or against the new regime which is of course condemned. In the latter case, i. may be conditioned by noisy and crude Communist propaganda, the excesses of the zealous Party cadres and may be an expression of impotence, hopelessness and ALIENATION in general.

Indirect Colonialism Another term used in the Socialist countries for NEO-COLONIALISM.

Indirect Labour Costs A euphemistic phrase used in the Socialist countries to placate orthodox Marxists steeped in the LABOUR THEORY OF VALUE. It was coined by V. V. Novozhilov, one of the outstanding pioneers of OPTIMAL PLANNING in the USSR, who postulated that the use of non-labour resources (land and capital) in production should be paid for explicitly or implicitly in the form of DIFFERENTIAL RENT and CAPITAL CHARGES, to ensure the most efficient utilization of all resources. This view is rationalized on the grounds that a withdrawal of capital or land amounts to increases in (direct) labour costs, i.e. the substitution of labour for non-labour resources.

Indirect Planning Non-directive economic planning which allows for the operation of the market mechanism and decentralization. The term has been used in application to Yugoslavia (after 1950), Hungary (after 1967) and other Socialist countries which have embarked upon the ECONOMIC REFORMS since the early 1960s. The main features of i.p. are: 1. an overall economic plan prepared for the whole economy by the central planning authority through the process of PLANNING FROM BELOW; 2. non-compulsory established targets; 3. state reliance on various financial incentives and penalties to induce the implementation of the tasks along the desired lines; and 4. enterprises have a good deal of independence and are in a position to respond to changes in market forces. Under this system, short-run partial equilibria are ensured by the market mechanism, mostly through changes in prices affecting supply and demand. Long-run imbalances are corrected by the plan and financial instruments wielded by the state flexibly.

Indispensable Labour A Marxian term denoting that portion of the total labour performed which is devoted to earning the subsistence, maintenance and reproduction of a worker and his family employed in MATERIAL PRODUCTION. The balance of the labour performed is called SURPLUS LABOUR. The value of i.l., also known as 'necessary labour', is indicated by the value of the INDISPENSABLE PRODUCT or the wages received by the worker. Marx developed this concept in *CAPITAL*, vol. I.

Indispensable Labour-Time In Marxian terminology, that portion of the work day which is necessary to create such an amount of production (INDISPENSABLE PRODUCT) that is sufficient to support a worker and his family at subsistence level. The remaining portion of the total work day Marx called the 'SURPLUS LABOUR-TIME'.

Indispensable Product In Marxian political economy, that part of the value of production created by the worker which is necessary to provide subsistence living for him and his family, i.e. indispensable for the reproduction of his LABOUR POWER. The remaining portion of the total product created by the worker is called the SURPLUS PRODUCT. In the Marxian formula of VALUE, $c+v+s$, i.p. is indicated by v, i.e. wages paid. The concept of i.p. is also used on the macroeconomic scale in national income accounting, meaning the total wage bill of the manpower employed in the sphere of MATERIAL PRODUCTION. The share of the i.p. in national income tends to decline historically, owing to the increasing ORGANIC STRUCTURE OF CAPITAL. The term i.p. is usually applied to capitalism, whilst under Socialism the description PRODUCT FOR ONESELF is preferred.

Indispensable Social Labour SOCIALLY-INDISPENSABLE LABOUR.

Individual Consumption PRIVATE CONSUMPTION.

Individual Incentives Incentives which are awarded to individual persons, commonly administered by the state in the Socialist countries, to promote better performances in socially desirable directions. They can be awarded either as MATERIAL INCENTIVES (in cash or in kind) or as MORAL INCENTIVES (certificates, pennants, entry in the factory 'roll of honour', medals, publicity through the media and the like). Ideologically i.i. are considered to be less desirable than COLLECTIVE INCENTIVES.

Individualist Interpretation of History A theory attributing historical events and development to outstanding individuals, e.g. leaders, heroes, thinkers, writers, inventors, administrators and the like. By implication, the theory ignores or denies the role of economic factors, changes in climate and physiography, religion, divine causation, fatalism etc. in the course of history. Among the exponents of this view were two Russian philosophers, P. L. Lavron (1823–1900) and N. K. Mikhailovsky (1824–1904), who were advocates of NARODNISM. Having accepted the i.i. of h., the Narodniks (especially those who joined the NARODNAYA VOLYA) resorted to the tactics of individual terror as a revolutionary method of struggle against the autocratic and repressive Tsarist regime in Russia. The theory is rejected by

Marxists, whose interpretation of history rests on HISTORICAL MATERIALISM. In particular, they object to the view that the masses cannot play any significant role in determining historical developments. In their view, the theory explains history in terms of accidents, it negates the possibility of a revolution being initiated by the masses, and has been used as a bourgeois justification for conquests, IMPERIALISM and FASCISM. The best known Marxist attacks against the i.i. of h. were made by Lenin (in *What the 'Friends of the People' Are and How They Fight the Social-Democrats*, 1894), Plekhanov (*Our Differences*, 1885) and Stalin (*Anarchism or Socialism*, 1906–07).

Individualism Social, economic and political attitudes or philosophy assigning priority to the views, interests and behaviour of individual persons. The individual is regarded as an end in itself and society is considered to have no reality in itself and no interests or objectives apart from the individuals composing it. In particular, i. is against state intervention in the affairs of individual persons. I. has been associated with capitalism, especially *LAISSEZ-FAIRE*, and the writings of Adam Smith (1723–90), J. Bentham (1748–1832), J. S. Mill (1806–73) and H. Spencer (1828–1903). But the term itself was first used in English in 1835 by H. Reeve, when he translated de Tocqueville's *De la démocratie en Amerique* (*Democracy in America*). Marxism, in opposing i., assigns priority to COLLECTIVISM and society, postulating the PRIMACY OF SOCIAL INTEREST. I. is regarded as one of the basic weaknesses of capitalism, leading to egoism, differences in the private ownership of property, cut-throat rivalry and anti-social behaviour. Mao Tse-tung, in a discourse 'On Correcting Mistaken Ideas in the Party' (written in Dec. 1929), highlighted the following six evils of i. by reference to the Chinese Red Army (as it was then known): 1. the repudiation of criticism within and without the Party and the Army, thereby corroding fighting capacity; 2. the 'small-group mentality', to the neglect of broad social interest; 3. the 'employee mentality', where members of the Army feel responsibility only to their immediate individual superiors, and not the Revolution and the State; 4. pleasure-seeking, avoiding more arduous tasks which may be of great benefit to society as a whole, in favour of private comfort; 5. passivity, or indifference to social work when immediate individual interest is absent; and 6. the desire to leave the Army in order to do easier and materially more rewarding work in civilian life.

Individual Plots SUBSIDIARY PLOTS.

Indoctrination The inculcation of a belief or IDEOLOGY designed to impose a complete and uncritical acceptance, to the disregard of critical consideration. The term has a pejorative connotation in the West, whilst in the Socialist countries it is hardly used. I. may also mean the introductory preparation of a new member to the thinking, customs and practices of a particular social group. I. is carried on in the Socialist countries on a systematic and scientific basis. In the armed forces, for example, one-third of the time is devoted to i. Also AGITATION, BRAINWASHING, PROPAGANDA, RESOCIALIZATION, SOCIALIZATION.

Indonesian Bloodbath A widespread massacre of Communists by the right-wing elements in Indonesia during the GESTAPU AFFAIR in the latter part of 1965. Led by the loyalist armed forces and extreme Mahommedan groups, the attackers decimated the COMMUNIST PARTY OF INDONESIA, which had 3m members. (the largest Communist party outside the Socialist bloc at the time). The number of the Communists killed was officially estimated at 87,000, but unofficial estimates place the figure between 150,000 and 300,000. Among those massacred was D. N. Aidit, the leader of the C.P.I. and a large number of Chinese. In addition, at least 120,000 persons, allegedly members of the C.P.I., were imprisoned in 300 special gaols and camps. The C.P.I. was declared illegal and its remaining members

were removed from public institutions and the army. As a result, the military regime of General. T. T. J. Suharto was firmly established and left-wing elements were virtually eliminated from Indonesian political life.

Indonesian Communist Party COMMUNIST PARTY OF INDONESIA.

Industrial Capital A concept used in Marxian political economy in application to industrially-developed capitalism. I.c. is concentrated in the hands of private industrial capitalists and is viewed as a circular flow assuming three successive phases: monetary capital; production capital; and commercial capital. In its narrow meaning, it refers solely to industry, but in its broad connotation it includes all capital involved in MATERIAL PRODUCTION. In the Marxist interpretation of history, in the stage of MONOPOLY CAPITALISM i.c. merges with finance capital (represented by large banks and various finance companies) leading to FINANCE CAPITALISM.

Industrial Capitalism The economic system noted for highly developed manufacturing industries, owned by private capitalists who dominate the economic, political and social scene. In the Marxist interpretation of history, it is also seen as one of the stages of development of capitalism, following COMMERCIAL CAPITALISM, but preceding FINANCE CAPITALISM. I.c. can be roughly identified with the Industrial Revolution in the West. It developed first in Britain between 1783 and 1870 and several decades later in other leading Western countries, namely, France after 1830, the USA after 1843, Germany after 1850, Sweden after 1868 and Japan after 1878. In the Marxist view, i.c. was associated with a BOURGEOIS-DEMOCRATIC REVOLUTION, when the industrial BOURGEOISIE finally established itself, in collusion with or to the exclusion of the feudal aristocracy, as the dominant ruling class. I.c. produces an industrial PROLETARIAT, the exploited social class destined to overthrow capitalism in a PROLETARIAN REVOLUTION.

Industrial Co-operation Co-operation between independent enterprises associated with industrial production. It involves reciprocally matching or joint pursuits in such fields of interest to the partners as research and development, know-how, the training of specialists, investment, manufacturing, the construction of projects for third parties and marketing. I.c. is more systematic and lasting than ordinary trading relations. It has become a feature of East–West economic relations since the early 1960s (since the mid-1950s in Yugoslavia). The total number of East–West i.c. agreements in force in the late 1970s exceeded 2,000 with the annual value of deliveries arising out of them being $1,500m. Enterprises in Hungary, Czechoslovakia, Bulgaria and the German DR (roughly in that order of participation) on the eastern side and those in the FR of Germany, Sweden, Italy and Switzerland on the Western side, are the most eager co-operants. I.c. must not be confused with JOINT VENTURE.

Industrial Democracy A broad term applied in capitalist countries to WORKERS' PARTICIPATION.

Industrialization The process of development of manufacturing industries and the necessary supporting branches of the economy at an accelerated rate. I. leads to profound economic, technical, socio-political and cultural changes in society. It may be a gradual process, brought about by favourable historical, geographic and social conditions, as was the case of the Industrial Revolutions in the leading Western countries, or it may be a deliberately planned development induced or imposed 'from above', as in most Socialist countries (Czechoslovakia and the German DR being exceptions). I. has been a focus point for Marxist analysis. The early Marxist thinkers believed that a PROLETARIAN REVOLUTION could occur only in industrialized countries (they were later proven wrong). After the seizure of power, the Communist regimes assigned top priority to i. for the following reasons:

1. to develop more balanced economic structures (virtually all had been backward agricultural countries); 2. to become independent of the capitalist world for the export of raw materials and the import of manufactures; 3. to develop a solid military-industrial base in order to defend socialism and support revolutionary movements in capitalist countries; 4. to ensure full employment by creating new jobs in industry; 5. to raise labour productivity and advance the Socialist society towards FULL COMMUNISM, a precondition of which is all-round affluence; 6. to enlarge the industrial working class, the mainstay of Communist power; and 7. to demonstrate the superiority of Socialism as being capable of achieving i. in a relatively short period of time and relying on individual efforts. In capitalist countries, i. began mostly in light industries (textiles and other consumer goods) in response to market forces. The Socialist i. strategy, on the other hand, follows a planned pattern with identifiable established stages, where at first heavy industry (iron and steel, heavy engineering, machine construction) and the necessary infra-structure receive priority. Light industries and the technologically most sophisticated lines of development receive attention at a later stage. In the leading Western countries i. was financed by the exploitation of the working class, the colonies and by the inflows of capital and war reparations. On the other hand, Socialist industrialization has been financed on a centrally planned basis, by eliminating the high incomes of the former bourgeoisie and the strict control of total consumption. Also INDUSTRIAL CAPITALISM, CAPITALIST ACCUMULATION, PRIMITIVE SOCIALIST ACCUMULATION.

Industrial Party A secret anti-Bolshevik organization which operated in the USSR during 1926–31. According to the official Soviet version, it was financed by the White Russian interests in Paris and engaged in sabotage and other counter-revolutionary activities in several industrial centres. A POLITICAL SHOW TRIAL was held in 1930, known as the I.P. Trial, and the organization was eliminated in 1930–31.

Industrial Reserve Army Another Marxian expression for unemployment in industry, also known as the RESERVE ARMY OF WORKERS.

Industrial Revolution An accelerated and profound transformation of production originating from the handicraft domestic system and progressing to large-scale mechanized production in factories owned by a newly-emerged capitalist class. The term is applied to the far-reaching changes in the methods and organization of production not only in industry but also in the whole economies of the leading Western countries from the end of the 18th c. to the 20th c. For example: England, 1783–1842; France, 1830–1910; USA, 1843–1910; Germany, 1850–1910; Sweden, 1868–1930; and Japan, 1878–1940. Marxists attach special significance to the I.R. in the form it occurred in the capitalist countries for the following reasons: 1. the financing of the I.R. was made possible by capitalist exploitation (slave trade, colonies, the urban and rural proletariat); 2. there was a cheap supply of labour to the factories, owing to the preceding agrarian and agricultural revolutions and the BOURGEOIS-DEMOCRATIC REVOLUTIONS (which had transformed serfs into free workers); 3. cheap labour was further accentuated by the growing RESERVE ARMY OF WORKERS, consequent upon mechanization and the increasing productivity of labour; 4. there was the development of the world market supplying cheap raw materials and absorbing vastly increased industrial production, in which COLONIALISM and IMPERIALISM played an important role; 5. there was a rapid accumulation of capital and its concentration in the hands of a smaller and smaller capitalist elite, dominating the economic, political and social scene; and 6. there was the rise and progressive expansion of the industrial proletariat which became increasingly conscious of being exploited and alienated from the capitalist system. The congregation of workers in factories (as distinct from peasants and craftsmen living and working in isolation under the domestic system) and the oppressive working and living conditions in the cities facilitated discussions of common grievances, the formation of trade unions, strikes and revolutionary activities. Marx and Engels thought that the I.R. was a necessary precondition to the PROLETARIAN REVOLUTION but the events in Russia in 1917, Mongolia in 1921–24, in Eastern Europe in 1944–45, in China in 1945–49 and in Cuba in 1956–59 disproved that view. Although the term is not generally applied to the Socialist countries, the I.R. may be said to have begun with the adoption of systematic economic planning (five-year plans, following the initial post-revolutionary reconstruction), e.g. in the USSR in 1928, the Eastern European countries (except Czechoslovakia and the German DR) and China in 1951. Although Communism was born as a protest against the I.R., the Communist regimes in the Socialist countries immediately became champions of INDUSTRIALIZATION.

Industrial Society SINGLE INDUSTRIAL SOCIETY.

Industrial Unionism A basis of the organization of trade unions according to the type of industry (as distinct from CRAFT UNIONS or occupational or professional associations). In the case of i.u. efforts are made to include all the workers employed in a particular industry, firm or plant, irrespective of their skill, occupation or position. I. unions are usually larger and more militant than craft unions. Marxists favour i.u. because it is more conducive to EGALITARIANISM, a keener community spirit, and facilitates social and political meetings.

Industrial Workers of the World An American revolutionary labour organization which emphasized industrial action in its strategy. It was founded in Chicago in

1905 by E. V. Debs, W. D. Haywood and D. De Leon, as a reform movement, committed to the unification of skilled and unskilled workers into 'one big union'. Its members were nicknamed 'Wobblies'. Their principal weapons were the general strike, mass sabotage and passive resistance, all of which never developed into political action. The movement adopted SYNDICALISM and later, after 1908, ANARCHO-SYNDICALISM. Although it engaged in class struggle, it rejected violence against persons. The heyday of the movement was the period from 1910 to 1920, when it staged several sensational strikes (1913 and 1919) and organized anti-war demonstrations. It was also involved in the formation of the Communist Party of the USA (founded in 1919). Organizations similar to the I.W.W. were also created in Australia and in Scotland. However, their impact was rather short-lived and eventually they disbanded in the early 1920s.

'Infantile Communism' A term introduced by Lenin to describe LEFT COMMUNISM, which he regarded as immature and impracticable. It was derived more from a naïve enthusiasm than from a profound understanding of the problems and consequences involved. He attacked it in a pamphlet, *The Infantile Disease of 'Left Communism'* (1920).

Infinite and Finite Two opposite concepts in philosophy, which are given different interpretations by non-Marxists and Marxists. In non-Marxist metaphysical philosophy, the i. and f. are treated as two mutually exclusive categories. On the other hand, Marxist materialist philosophy regards them as a mutually linked dialectical unity. Engels (in *DIALECTICS OF NATURE*) argued that the i. exists only through f. forms of matter. The material world is i. in space, time, variety and quality, but at the same time it is a totality and unity of developing f. material elements. The i. carries internal contradictions, as it embodies f. components which are not merely a sum total of the static elements, but a dynamic unity where the

elements are constantly changing, developing, and are disappearing whilst others are emerging. Thus the i. and f. constitute contradictions which exist only in mutually intertwined relations.

Inflation A situation in the economy noted for the persistent rise in the general price level and the consequent decline in the purchasing power of money. I. has been of great concern to social reformers, as it produces adverse social effects on people with fixed incomes and on workers since wage increases usually lag behind price increases. Marxists have traditionally identified i. with capitalist economies and attribute the following causes of i. to the inherent defects of capitalism: 1. excessive credit expansion in efforts to maintain higher levels of economic activity and to insure continuous full employment; 2. budgetary deficits caused by financial mismanagement and the reluctance to increase taxation, owing to the fear of possible adverse electoral reaction; 3. continued over-development of the non-productive sphere as a cure for unemployment; 4. unscrupulous increases in prices by monopolies in their quest for maximum profits; 5. conflicts between capital and labour, leading to costly industrial disputes and waste which are passed on by the capitalists to the public in higher and higher prices; and 6. over-expansion of international liquidity through the irresponsible US balance-of-payments deficits calculated to finance the American economic and military domination of the world (foreign investment, the Eurodollar market, wars and 'neo-colonialism' in general). Although official statistics suggest there has been virtually no i. in the Socialist countries, in reality there has been continuous *suppressed* i. of a peculiar type which is known as SOCIALIST INFLATION.

Informburo The Russian version of the COMINFORM.

Inheritance The acquisition of assets in the form of tangible property, money or rights through bequest. It may be strictly regulated by custom, so that neither the testator nor the legatee have any freedom of disposing of it. This is typical of primitive and traditional societies. More commonly, they are free to dispose of the assets involved to whoever they wish, which is the usual practice in developed capitalist countries. Marxists regard i., whether in a society that accepts SLAVERY, under FEUDALISM or CAPITALISM, as not only socially unjust but also perpetuating the existing unequal distribution of property. As most property also yields income, i. also perpetuates differences in income. In the Socialist countries, as a rule, the means of production cannot be inherited by private persons as they are socialized. But they can be inherited in the private sector, where i. still exists. I. is also possible in the Socialist countries with respect to personal effects, houses, subsidiary plots, cash, savings bank accounts and government bonds. In China, whilst the 1954 Constitution explicitly guaranteed the i. of property, the Constitution of 1975 does not.

'In Memory of Norman Bethune' One of the 'FIVE MOST READ ARTICLES' during the GREAT PROLETARIAN CULTURAL REVOLUTION, written by Mao Tse-tung on 21 Dec. 1939. This article extolled individual devotion, self-sacrifice and international revolutionary solidarity. N.B. was a member of the Communist Party of Canada who was sent to China in 1938 to fight against the Japanese. He met Mao and worked as a doctor, treating soldiers and civilians with utmost dedication to the Chinese cause and the underprivileged. He died a martyr at his post in 1939.

Innate Ideas In philosophy, ideas which, according to some theories, exist in human consciousness, irrespective of sensory experience. This view was first propounded by Plato (427–347 B.C.) and later elaborated upon and supplemented by St. Augustine (345–430). R. Descartes (1596–1650), G. W. Leibnitz (1646–1716) and. I. Kant (1724–1804).

Descartes maintained that the concepts of god and abstract geometrical figures represent i.i. According to Leibnitz, i.i. are inherent in the human soul, not as ready tested concepts, but as general attitudes and principles. Kant postulated time, space and causality as *a priori* forms of knowledge. To Marxist philosophers, i.i. are wild speculations, typical of IDEALISM and completely inconsistent with MATERIALISM. According to DIALECTICAL MATERIALISM, all ideas without exception are reflections or generalizations of sensory experience of the real world.

Inner Party Democracy One of the rules supposedly governing intra-Communist party relations. It is meant to ensure: 1. the election of officials to various party bodies; 2. the obligation of party officials to provide reports to the party membership concerned; and 3. a reasonable allowance of CRITICISM and SELF CRITICISM within the party. However, in practice, i.p.d. is narrowly circumscribed and can be over-ruled by authoritarianism, embodied in the party principle of DEMOCRATIC CENTRALISM. This is particularly the case in the ruling Communist parties which enforce very strict party discipline, do not tolerate 'destructive criticism' and do not allow the formation of FACTIONS within or without the party.

Input-Output Analysis The mathematical and economic study of the flows of input (materials, power, semi-finished products) and output (final products) between the branches of production, i.e. the suppliers and recipients of goods. It is the basic technique employed in the preparation of plans in centrally planned economies, while in market economies it can be used in national income accounting and in estimating the efficiency of production. The inventor of this technique was an American economist of Russian descent, W. W. Leontief. In 1931, Leontief utilized the 'Economic Table' of F. Quesnay (PHYSIOCRATISM), the ideas of E. Walras, and the BALANCES OF THE NATIONAL ECONOMY in the USSR for 1923/24 to work out i.-o. tables for the American economy for 1919–29. The i.-o.a. had originally been rejected in the USSR, largely on ideological grounds, until it came to be recognized in the West. But the USSR claims that the technique is a Soviet invention based on Marx's theory of reproduction. The first stage in this analysis is the preparation of an i.-o. table for the economy (or its division) usually covering an annual period, better known in Socialist economic planning as INTER-BRANCH BALANCES. Such a table consists of: 1. vertical columns, showing the material inputs comprising the supplies received from the domestic branches of the economy and those from imports, plus the value added (wages, depreciation and the surplus product); and 2. horizontal rows, setting out the distribution of the output produced by each branch to all other branches of the economy and for export. Each column carries the name of a branch of the economy which is repeated in the same sequence in the rows. The i.-o. table for the whole economy is composed of four quarters: Division I (upper left) specifies inter-branch balances, shaping the material structure of production costs and forming the basic division of the table; Division II (upper right) represents the distribution of final production among final recipients (including productive investment); Division III (lower left) sets out the composition of the SURPLUS PRODUCT in different branches of production; and Division IV (lower right) may be used for representing the redistribution of income (shown in Division III) through the budget or some other form of redistribution, or may be left blank. The second stage in the i.-o.a. is concerned with the calculation of the coefficients of production costs, of investment and of the surplus product, using the data from the tables. The third stage is directed to the analysis of the relationships between gross output and net production and between the prices of the products and their added value. In this process, the coefficients arrived at in the second stage are employed. A valuable mathematical aid to the i.-o.a. is LINEAR PROGRAMMING applied in OPTIMAL PLANNING.

Institute of Marxism-Leninism (*Institut Marksizma-Leninizma*) A research institute in the USSR located in Moscow and attached to the CENTRAL COMMITTEE OF THE COMMUNIST PARTY OF THE SOVIET UNION. It is the best known and the largest institution of this type in the world. In addition to research, it is concerned with the preparation and editing of Communist literature, especially Marxist classics, documents of the Party congresses and conferences, plenary meetings of the Central Committee, the Party history, and labour movements, their leaders and collaborators. The Institute is also responsible for the collection and care of documents of historical value on Marxism, which are housed in the Central Party Archives. The Institute has a fairly long history. In 1920 the Party established the Marx-Engels Institute and in 1923 the Lenin Institute. In 1931 the two institutions were merged into the Marx-Engels-Lenin Institute. Later, Stalin was included in the title, but in 1953 his name was dropped. The present name was adopted in 1956.

Institute of Red Professorship (*Institut Krasnoi Profiesury*) A training institute for CADRES, Party activists and teachers of the social sciences in higher educational establishments in the USSR. It was in existence during 1921–31 and was created on the initiative of Lenin, in order to place the education of leaders and teaching on a solid Marxist basis. The Institute was reorganized in 1931 and replaced by the following eight specialized Institutes: 1. Agriculture; 2. Historical Studies; 3. Party History; 4. Philosophy; 5. Literature; 6. Political Economy; 7. Soviet Constitution and Law; and 8. World Economy and Politics. Soon after, Institutes for Natural Sciences and for Technology were added. In 1938 all the Institutes were wound up.

Institutionalism A doctrine in Western

economic thought (especially in the USA) in the first three decades of this century, emphasizing the role of norms and principles (or 'institutions') governing the operation of an economy. The 'institutions' which received particular attention included ownership, the inheritance of property, the distribution and redistribution of national income, the division of labour, vocational training and promotion. It is emphasized that institutions critically influence the relative position of the different social classes, the structure of production and the directions of development. Some of the most prominent exponents of i. were T. Veblen (1857–1929), J. R. Commons (1862–1945) and W. Mitchell (1874–1948). I. has been subjected to a critical examination in the Socialist countries, especially the USSR. Steeped in HISTORICAL MATERIALISM, the participants to the controversy have pointed out that there are no universal economic laws and that i. is too simplistic and static. In their view, institutions are too varied in time and space, reflecting different material conditions in different regions and countries, to provide a reliable basis for generalizations. Further, the institutions themselves are subject to changes according to the stage of development of PRODUCTION FORCES and PRODUCTION RELATIONS. Although institutionalists attach great importance to the role of the state, Marxists regard this approach as petty bourgeois in motivation and content, only delaying the need for a proletarian revolution.

Institutionalization of the Revolution The stabilization of the revolutionary process within the created framework of the Party and state institutions. It implies dogmatism, a bureaucratic hierarchical structure, inflexibility and a considerable degree of conservatism – as distinct from adventurism, anarchism and extremism. The phrase was first applied to the USSR under Stalin in the 1920s and was identified with 'SOCIALISM IN ONE COUNTRY' and opposed to LEFT COMMUNISM and PERMANENT REVOLUTION.

Instrumentalism A philosophical and social doctrine treating human thought and will as primary elements and emphasizing ideas, concepts and theories as man's instruments in the pursuit of world order and development. I. identifies reality with the idealistic conception of experience. It owes its origin to the American philosopher and educationist John Dewey (1859–1952), and it is related to PRAGMATISM. Instrumentalists treat any fact or phenomenon as useful in the given circumstances, consequently, success justifies the means. Marxists have attacked i. as subjectivist, identifying it with IDEALISM. By its very nature, i. negates the existence of matter as objective reality and consequently it is inconsistent with DIALECTICAL MATERIALISM, HISTORICAL MATERIALISM and the postulate of the CLASS STRUGGLE. Marxists further point out that i. does not treat ideas as a reflection of human consciousness in the material world and its natural laws of development, but identifies reality with the idealistic conception of experience.

Instruments of Labour In Marxist political economy, the most decisive component of the MEANS OF LABOUR. The forms and complexity of the means of labour vary greatly, depending largely on the stage of the economic development of society, ranging from simple tools, implements and hand-operated machines to power-driven machinery and automated machines and equipment. In the Marxist view, the invention, making and use of the i. of l. became a decisive factor in the rise of man above animals (LABOUR THEORY OF HUMANIZATION). Marxists maintain that the i. of l. are the most dynamic element of PRODUCTION FORCES. Historically, all changes in production, and consequently in society, always originated from the improvement in the i. of l. Marx (in *CAPITAL*, vol. I) stressed their importance in the development of society and pointed out that the differences between the SOCIO-ECONOMIC FORMATIONS consisted not in what each formation produced, but how and with what i. of l. man engaged in production.

Insulation of Domestic from Foreign Markets The economic policy and practice typical of the Socialist centrally planned economies where the domestic market is shielded from disruptive changes in foreign countries. It is maintained by the state strictly controlling exports and imports, maintaining stable domestic prices which are divorced from world market prices, administering artificial and in many cases MULTIPLE EXCHANGE RATES and restricting foreign travel. The effect of the fluctuating prices in foreign markets is neutralized by BUDGETARY EQUALIZATION SETTLEMENTS.

Intellectualism A doctrine in philosophy and psychology, attributing a decisive role to intellect. It has a long history, going back to Plato (427–347 B.C.), R. Descartes (1596–1650) and A. Comte (1798–1857). I. identifies truth, which can be discovered only by intellect, with goodness – justice, virtue, and propriety. Marxism is critical of i. on the following grounds: 1. i. treats cognition as a purely intellectual process, divorced from practice; 2. it assumes truth to be absolute and eternal, whilst Marxists regard truth as relative, depending on the stage of the development of PRODUCTION FORCES and the SOCIO-ECONOMIC FORMATION; and 3. in the social sphere, i. is not sufficient and in fact may be harmful, as is historically illustrated by UTOPIAN SOCIALISM. I. must be backed by action, otherwise it is sterile.

Intelligentsia A designation commonly used in the Socialist countries to denote the social class consisting of persons with tertiary or vocational secondary education (writers, scientists, doctors, lawyers, teachers, engineers, technicians, managers, Party cadres, higher state officials, students). I. is one of the three social classes recognized in these countries, ranked after workers and peasants. It constitutes about one-fifth of the total population, the proportion being lower in the less developed Socialist countries (such as Albania, China and Cuba) and higher in the advanced ones (Czechoslovakia, the German DR and Hungary). The term i. was first introduced into Socialist terminology in Eastern Europe, Russia and Latin America in the middle of the 19th c. to describe that portion of the educated middle class which participated in revolutionary politics and supported the proletarian stand in the class struggle. But later the term was broadened to include all educated class. After the communist seizure of power in Russia and Eastern Europe, the former i. fell into three groups. Some gave unqualified support to the Communist regime, most adopted a neutral attitude, whilst others continued to oppose it. Much of the Communist leadership at the time of the Communist takeover was in fact recruited from the i. The i. has never emerged as an identifiable class in developed capitalist countries, where the nearest comparable strata are intellectuals (smaller in extent than the i.) and the middle class (broader than the i.). In pre-Socialist societies, the i. is usually recruited from, and identifies itself with, the BOURGEOISIE. But under Socialism varied links are developed between the i. and the urban and rural working class. They are facilitated by the extension of educational opportunity (deliberately favouring the children of the working class and peasants), the expansion of the professions, the Party apparatus and of the state administration, and rapid economic development necessitating the growth of productive and non-productive services. The role of the i. has been substantially reduced in China, a country with a long tradition and respect for intellectuals. This was most conspicuous during the GREAT PROLETARIAN CULTURAL REVOLUTION.

Intensive Growth A Marxist term for a developmental strategy, where increases in production are derived mainly from a more intensive utilization of the existing resources. It enables rapidly rising efficiency, so that the growth of national income is achieved mostly or wholly from increasing productivity, and not merely from the extension in the volume of the resources (labour, capital, land). The concept of i.g. is derived from Marx's analysis of production processes, in which he distinguished between 'intensive' and 'extensive' reproduction (in *CAPITAL*, vol. II). Most Socialist countries have turned to i.g. since the early 1960s, as the strategy of EXTENSIVE GROWTH (followed previously) had proved ineffective in the higher stages of economic development. The strategy of i.g. emphasizes technological progress (incl. automation), industrial, occupational and regional specialization, scientific management, the economies of scale, the improvement in the quality of resources and a greater participation in the international division of labour.

Intensity of Labour The degree of physical or mental exertion in work performance. It can be measured by the productivity of labour, the degree of fulfilment of work norms, fatigue, accidents, occupational diseases, the ageing of the worker and the like. The subject of the i. of l. has received a good deal of attention from Marxists, who regard it as being dependent on the socio-economic formation, the state of technology and the organization of production. In their view the i. of l. increase as capitalism proceeds from lower to higher stages of economic development. In order to maximize their profits, capitalists resort to various forms of innovation and the lengthening of the working day, to which they are further prodded by COMPETITION and the DECLINING PROFIT RATE. The intensification of labour is pursued on a more systematic basis in FORDISM, TAYLORISM and similar efficiency schemes. The increasing i. of l. under capitalism, in their view, generates ALIENATION among the workers, which sooner or later must lead to the BREAKDOWN OF CAPITALISM. Contrary to the assertions by Communist leaders, the i. of l. in the Socialist countries is quite high. This is conditioned by the ambitious developmental programmes, designed to accelerate the rate of economic growth, the high

production targets set in the plans and the staging of production campaigns (e.g. BRIGADES OF COMMUNIST LABOUR, STAKHANOVISM, SUBBOTNIKS). The evidence of the high i. of l. having an adverse effect is illustrated by the BALTIC CITIES RIOTS, BERLIN RIOTS, GDANSK RIOTS, PILSEN RIOTS and POZNAN RIOTS.

Inter-Branch Balances An elaborate input-output table, employed in Socialist economic planning, showing the flows of materials and products from the supply to the recipient branches of the economy. The table resembles a chessboard divided into horizontal rows, representing the branches in their supplying capacity, and vertical columns, specifying the recipient branches. The names, numbers and sequences of the branches in the rows correspond to those in the columns. What is the final output of a particular branch becomes the input for other (recipient) branches. The main purpose of the preparation of i.-b.b. is to ensure the internal consistency of the economic plan, so that the implementation of the plan is feasible and there are no BOTTLENECKS or unavoidable idle resources. Also INPUT-OUTPUT ANALYSIS, MATERIAL BALANCES.

Interest Income yielded by capital or a regular payment made by the debtor to the creditor for the use of monetary capital. Marx described i. as the 'price of loanable funds'. To Marxists i. appears first of all to be an element of SURPLUS VALUE (in addition to rent and profit), accruing to CAPITALISTS, and indirectly stemming from the exploitation of labour. The institution of i., especially if its rate exceeds the cost of administration of lending and repayment (above 1–3 per cent p.a.), leads to unjustified non-labour income, enhances capital accumulation of capitalists, and thus contributes to SOCIAL STRATIFICATION. After the Communist regimes came to power in the Socialist countries, i. was virtually abolished. Budgetary allocations of finance to socialized enterprises were interest-free and non-repayable, at least for investment purposes. Although interest was charged on bank credits, the rate was very low, usually below 2 per cent p.a., and was treated as the cost of administering banking services. Interest was also paid on savings bank deposits (3 per cent p.a.). However, since the ECONOMIC REFORMS in the European Socialist countries in the 1960s, the role of i. has been greatly enhanced with a view to promoting the most effective patterns of investment at the enterprise level. I. rates are used flexibly, their average level has been increased substantially (to roughly 6 per cent p.a.) and they are highly differentiated – up to 20 per cent p.a. (and in some cases even more).

Intermediate Level of Economic Management A description used in the Socialist countries for the organs of economic management, below the State Planning Commissions and 'economic' Ministries, but above the enterprises. These organs are known as 'Industrial Branch Associations' in the German DR and Poland, 'Economic Associations' in Bulgaria, 'Centrals' in Romania and 'Chambers of Industry, Transport, Commerce', etc. in Yugoslavia. The i.l. of e.m. is largely a product of the ECONOMIC REFORMS of the 1960s in the European Socialist countries and aimed at decentralization. It relieves central authorities of many details of economic administration and management, and at the same time assists, coordinates and supervises the activities of the enterprises within particular branches. These organs of management are best developed in the German DR, Poland and Romania, and have proved more effective than regional decentralization, experimented with in the USSR (1957–65) and the German DR (1961–65).

Internal Colonialism The exploitation of minority nationalities or certain regions. The term has been applied to the 'Celtic fringe' in Britain, the 'South' in Italy and the USA, and the Asian part of Tsarist Russia and later of the USSR.

Internal Exports A description used in the European Socialist countries, where the state sells articles in special shops to foreign or domestic holders of hard currencies. Such articles are usually of high quality and are not normally available for sale domestically for soft currencies. The countries which are most active in this line of business are (with the names of the retail outlets in brackets): Bulgaria (*Corecom*); Czechoslovakia (*Tuzex*); the German DR (*Intershops*); Hungary (*Elektroimpex, Intertourist, Konsumex*); Poland (*Pewex, PKO* agencies); and the USSR (*Beriozka*).

International A German organization of left-wing Social-Democrats in existence from March to Dec. 1915. It organized anti-war demonstrations and propaganda and published a bulletin under the same name, to which K. LIEBKNECHT and ROSA LUXEMBURG contributed. From 1916 on, it became the SPARTACUS LEAGUE, the nucleus of the Communist Party of Germany (founded in 1918).

International, The (anthem) *INTERNATIONALE.*

International Agrarian Bureau GREEN INTERNATIONAL.

International Alliance of Social-Democrats An anarchist group formed by the Russian revolutionary M. A. BAKUNIN (together with E. Recluse and A. Richard) in Geneva in 1868. It was to join the FIRST INTERNATIONAL (founded in 1864) as an independent organization; however, the General Council of the First International, urged by Marx, insisted on its dissolution and transformation into a section of the F.I. But the I.A.S.-D. secretly continued its activities, with a view to infiltrating the General Council of the F.I. At the Congress of the F.I. in The Hague in 1872, Bakunin and his supporters were expelled. But they did not recognize the validity of the decision and continued holding Congresses of their own 'International'. They exercised a good deal of influence, especially in Italy and Switzerland, and to a certain extent, in Spain, France and Belgium.

International Association for Cultural Freedom An independent international association of writers, scholars, scientists, artists and men of public affairs for the purpose of defending intellectual freedom against infringements, especially Communist regimes. It sponsors conferences, seminars and publishes journals and magazines in English, French, German, Spanish and other languages. It has publicized such violations of freedom as the HUNGARIAN UPRISING of 1956, the INVASION OF CZECHOSLOVAKIA in 1968 and the persecution of DISSENTERS in the Socialist countries. It is financed by the Ford Foundation and grants from West German and Italian foundations.

International Association of Democratic Lawyers An INTERNATIONAL COMMUNIST FRONT ORGANIZATION for the promotion of contacts and co-operation among left-wing lawyers and their organizations. It was founded in Paris in 1946. Its membership consists of organizations and correspondents in 65 countries, including most of the Socialist countries, except Czechoslovakia, comprising about 25,000 lawyers. It has been active as a Socialist spokesman in peace campaigns and maintains close ties with the WORLD PEACE COUNCIL. The Association has a permanent Secretariat in Brussels, engages in research on legal problems and publishes a half-yearly journal called the *Review of Contemporary Law*. The Association supported the Stalinist line against Yugoslavia and was expelled from that country in 1949, but has rejoined it since.

International Bank For Economic Cooperation A banking institution established by the member countries of the COUNCIL FOR MUTUAL ECONOMIC ASSISTANCE in 1963, to facilitate payment settlements and provide short-term and medium-term credits for trading purposes. Its head office is in Moscow and one of its ambitions is to place payments among the member countries on a multilateral basis by means of the TRANSFERABLE ROUBLE. In several respects it corresponds to the International Monetary Fund in the capitalist world under the auspices of the United Nations. The I.B.E.C. began to raise finance in the Eurocurrency market in 1972 and accepts deposits in hard currencies from capitalist banks. It has extensive connections in the capitalist world and its Charter provides for the possible membership of capitalist countries. Its capital and reserves make it about the 150th largest bank in the world. About one-third of its operations are carried on in convertible currencies.

International Brigades Volunteer armed units fighting on the side of the Republican 'People's Army' during the SPANISH CIVIL WAR (1936–38) against the Nationalist forces led by Gen. Franco supported by Fascist Italy and Nazi Germany. There were six brigades: Anglo-American; Austro-German; Balkan-Czechoslovak; French; Italian; and Polish, totalling 35,000 men. Organization and transportation were undertaken by the COMINTERN, using national Communist parties as its agents. Among the leading organizers were P. TOGLIATTI, P. Nenni and L. Longo, from Italy, and J. Broz (later known as TITO), of Yugoslavia. Other national leaders included H. Beimler (of Germany), R. Fox (of England), M. Stern (of Austria), K. Świerczewski (of Poland) and M. Zalka (of Hungary). The failure of the People's Army and of the I.B. was partly due to Stalin's sudden discontinuation of supplies at the time when Germany and Italy were stepping up theirs. After the defeat, many Republican and I.B. leaders escaped to the USSR, where most of them perished in Stalin's Purges.

International Brotherhood An international anarchist group founded by M. A. BAKUNIN in Florence in 1864 and subsequently reconstituted in Naples in 1868. It maintained a revolutionary terrorist programme called *REVOLUTIONARY CATECHISM*, prepared jointly by S. NECHAYEV and Bakunin. The I.B. postulated that labour alone had the right to determine the economic and social organization and activities in society. Society should be organized into independent communes, linked in loose national federations, and co-ordinated on the international scale by experienced revolutionary anarchists. The Brotherhood rejected the state and other institutions of authority, including religion. Although the I.B. was at first supported by a few anarchists in 11 countries, it never had a wide following, except in southern Italy.

International Centre for Scientific and Technical Information An organization established in 1971 by the member countries of the COUNCIL FOR MUTUAL ECONOMIC ASSISTANCE. It is located in Moscow, but is based on the member countries' national networks of information. The Centre maintains a uniform system of scientific and technical information which it makes available to the national entities of the member countries, it supplies experts on the organization of scientific and technical information, runs training courses for specialists and engages in research on information theory and practice.

International Communist Front Organizations Entities which although do not include 'Communist' in their official name, support or directly pursue pro-Communist policies. They are either organizations specifically established by Communists for the above purpose, or are existing entities that have been infiltrated by them. In each case such organizations are used as fronts to mislead the public or evade anti-communist legislation. They first appeared after the Bolshevik Revolution through the efforts of the COMINTERN, viz. the INTERNATIONAL ORGANIZATION FOR AID TO REVOLUTIONARIES (1922–47), and the INTERNATIONAL PEASANTS' COUNCIL (1923–33), the PROFINTERN (1921–37) and the RED SPORT INTERNATIONAL (1921–35). In the mid-1930s, the Comintern turned to the POPULAR FRONTS, but later in the 1950s the USSR officially abandoned the tactics of 'boring from within'. Since W.W.II, 13 important i.c.f.o. have been established. They are 1. the CHRISTIAN PEACE CONFERENCE (founded in 1958, with its Secretariat in Prague); 2. the INTERNATIONAL ASSOCIATION OF DEMOCRATIC LAWYERS (1946, Brussels); 3. the INTERNATIONAL FEDERATION OF RESISTANCE MOVEMENTS (1951, Vienna); 4. the INTERNATIONAL ORGANIZATION OF JOURNALISTS (1946, Prague); 5. the INTERNATIONAL RADIO AND TELEVISION ORGANIZATION (1946), Prague); 6. the INTERNATIONAL UNION OF STUDENTS (1946, Prague); 7. the WOMEN'S INTERNATIONAL DEMOCRATIC FEDERATION (1945, East Berlin); 8. the WORLD COUNCIL OF CHURCHES (1948, Geneva); 9. the WORLD FEDERATION OF DEMOCRATIC YOUTH (1945, Budapest); 10. the WORLD FEDERATION OF SCIENTIFIC WORKERS (1946, Paris); 11. the WORLD FEDERATION OF TEACHERS' UNIONS (1946, Prague); 12. the WORLD FEDERATION OF TRADE UNIONS (1945 Prague); and 13. the WORLD PEACE COUNCIL (1950, Helsinki).

International Communist League (*Liga Comunista Internacionalista*) A small Trotskyite revolutionary organization in Portugal working towards a government by workers. According to its programme, workers' militia replace the police and the army. It is affiliated to the FOURTH INTERNATIONAL.

International Confederation of Free Trade Unions An international organization of free and democratic trade unions opposed to both Communist domination and imperialist aggression by any nation. It was founded in London in Dec. 1949 by delegates representing 70 trade union organizations in 53 capitalist countries, as a reaction to the Communist domination of the WORLD FEDERATION OF TRADE UNIONS (founded in 1945). The I.C.F.T.U. is an indirect successor to the

INTERNATIONAL FEDERATION OF TRADE UNIONS. The I.C.F.T.U. headquarters are located in Brussels, but there are also branch offices in Geneva and New York and a regional office in Djakarta. The highest level of authority is the Congress, which is held every four years, and which elects an Executive Board and a General Secretary. The membership of the I.C.F.T.U. consists of 120 affiliated national trade union organizations in 88 non-Socialist countries, representing 56.2m. trade unionists. It works towards the improvement of working conditions, full employment, universal social welfare programmes, high standards of living and a world-wide system of collective security. The I.C.F.T.U. has a consultative status with ECOSOC, FAO, IAEA, IMCO, UNCTAD, UNESCO, UNICEF and UNIDO. It publishes *International Trade Union News* (fortnightly), *Economic and Social Bulletin* (bi-monthly), *Free Labour World* (bi-monthly), *Yearbook of the International Free Trade Union Movement*, and various reports and pamphlets.

International Conferences of the Communist and Workers' Parties Irregularly held meetings of the leaders of the Marxist parties for the purpose of inter-party co-operation, the exchange of views and experience and the discussion of controversial problems of the international Communist movement. The Conferences carry on the co-ordinating work previously performed by the FIRST INTERNATIONAL, the SECOND INTERNATIONAL, the COMINTERN and the COMINFORM. But in contrast to the previous organizations, the Conferences are less formal and do not attempt to impose majority (or Soviet) decisions on the participating Parties. The need for the Conferences was felt after the formal dissolution of the Cominform in 1956. The first meeting was held in Nov. 1957 in Moscow, when 64 Marxist parties participated, followed by those in Nov. 1960 (in Moscow, with 81 Parties attending) and in June 1969 (in Moscow, 75 Parties attending). Similar Conferences have also been arranged on a European scale – one at

Karlovy Vary (Czechoslovakia) in April 1967 and another in East Berlin in June 1976. The questions which were considered at these Conferences included: 1. NATIONAL LIBERATION MOVEMENTS; 2. COLONIALISM and IMPERIALISM; 3. disarmament and world peace; 4. DOGMATISM; 5. revisionism; 6. 'OWN PATHS TO SOCIALISM'; 7. peaceful COEXISTENCE; 8. SINO-SOVIET DISPUTE; 9. the VIETNAM WAR; 10. the Israeli-Arab conflict; 11. EUROCOMMUNISM; and 12. the unity of the Socialist countries. At the first two Conferences (of 1957 and 1960), it was agreed and reaffirmed that all Communist and Workers' Parties are equal to each other and independent in their internal policies and the choice of their 'own paths to socialism' and to revolution.

International Co-operative Alliance An organization for the promotion of the co-operative movement throughout the world, and in particular for fostering links among co-operative societies, both nationally and internationally. It was founded in 1895, and its headquarters are in London, with two regional offices in New Delhi and Moshi (Tanzania). It also maintains a representative office at the United Nations in New York, having a consultative status with ECOSOC, FAO, IAEA, ILO, UNESCO, UNICEF and UNIDO. Its membership consists of 673,080 co-operative societies (comprising 326m. members) in 60 countries, including 8 socialist countries (Bulgaria, Czechoslovakia, the German DR, Hungary, Poland, Romania, the USSR and Yugoslavia). Its highest authority is the Congress of delegates from the affiliated organizations held every four years. It elects a Central Committee of some 150 members from among the nominees of the member organizations, which in turn appoints an Executive Committee (of 15 members). In addition there are several 'Auxiliary Committees', viz. for Insurance, Banking, Workers' Production Societies, Agricultural Co-operatives, Fisheries, Housing, Wholesale and Retail Trade, and also a Women's Advisory Council. At its 23rd

Congress in Varna (Bulgaria), the Alliance laid down the following six guiding principles for co-operative enterprises: 1. open membership; 2. democratic management; 3. limitation of interest payments on contributed capital; 4. division of profits on a democratic basis and for the benefit of all members; 5. educational and promotional work to explain the features and rules of co-operation; and 6. collaboration among co-operative entities locally, nationally and internationally. The I.C.A. publishes *Review of International Co-operation* (bi-monthly) in English, French, German and Spanish, *Co-operative News Service* (monthly) in English, *Consumers' Affairs Bulletin* (monthly) in English and French, plus a dozen other publications.

International Corporation for Yugoslavia A Yugoslav-capitalist investment company for financing ventures in Yugoslav industry, agriculture and tourism. It was established in 1969 by 13 Yugoslav banks (including the National Bank, the Belgrade Bank, the Ljubljana Bank, the Yugoslav Agricultural Bank and the Yugoslav Investment Bank), and 42 capitalist banks and financial institutions, including the International Finance Corporation (United Nations), the Amsterdam-Rotterdam Bank (Netherlands), the Banco di Napoli (Italy), the Deutsche Bank (FR of Germany), Girard Co. (USA) and the Kuwait Investment Co. Its financial head office is in London, but its administrative headquarters are now in Zagreb.

International Council of Social-Democratic Women The co-ordinating body for women's organizations of the political parties affiliated to the SOCIALIST INTERNATIONAL. It links organizations in 33 (mostly Western) countries totalling 2.0m. members. No Socialist country is a participant. The Council was founded in July 1955 as the successor to the INTERNATIONAL SOCIALIST WOMEN'S SECRETARIAT and its seat is in London. The Council's official perodical publication is *Bulletin*,

appearing monthly in English and German.

International Division of Labour Specialization in production and consequent trade among capitalist and the Socialist countries, as well as between them. It commands a number of advantages for the participating countries, creates a better basis for the utilization of resources and leads to faster developments, greater productivity and higher standards of living. In this process, Marxists, in accordance with HISTORICAL MATERIALISM, emphasize the influence of the stage of development of the PRODUCTION FORCES and PRODUCTION RELATIONS on the direction and content of the i.d. of l. Historically, they see four major stages: 1. specialization and exchange between pastoral and agricultural tribes; 2. specialization and trade between countries, concentrating on handicrafts (clothing, implements, ornaments), food and raw materials; 3. capitalist specialization and trade, especially since the Industrial Revolution, involving large-scale production, world-wide markets and the division of the world into rich industrialized nations and poor underdeveloped primary-producing countries. This stage is also associated with COLONIALISM, the EXPORT OF CAPITAL from more developed to less developed countries, IMPERIALISM and NON-EQUIVALENT EXCHANGE. The capitalist i.d. of l., as it has historically developed, only accentuates the differences in the stages of economic development and perpetuates the division between the industrialized, rich and powerful nations and agricultural poor, backward and weak countries; and 4. the international Socialist d. of l., based on the social ownership of the means of production, carefully planned specialization among the member countries and firm commitments on exports and imports agreed in advance. Since W.W.II the i.d. of l. has been noted (as Stalin concluded) for two 'parallel world markets' – capitalist and Socialist, each governed by its own peculiar laws. Since the mid-1950s, the Socialist countries have abandoned their previous policies of AUTARKY and have been increasingly turning to the i.d. of l. As a result, trade betwen capitalist and the Socialist countries has been expanding faster than either intra-capitalist or intra-Socialist foreign trade.

Internationale The anthem of the international proletariat. It was originally written in 1887 by a French transport worker and poet, Eugène Pottier (1816–87), who had been a member of the INTERNATIONAL WORKINGMEN'S ASSOCIATION and of the PARIS COMMUNE. The first verse begins with the words, 'Arise, you wretched of the earth, Arise you who are starving. . . .' The song challenges the workers of the world to unity and action. The tune was composed in 1888 by a Belgian industrial worker, Pierre de Geyter (1848–1932), from the French city, Lille. The song became the international anthem of the SECOND INTERNATIONAL and of the COMINTERN, and has been translated into most languages. Over the period 1921–44 it was also the national anthem of the USSR, where it was colloquially known as 'Stalin's song'. It is still sung at international Communist demonstrations and rallies, and also at the end of the INTERNATIONAL CONFERENCES OF THE COMMUNIST AND WORKERS' PARTIES.

International Federation of Christian Trade Unions An organization founded in 1920, basing its policies and activities on general Christian principles. Its headquarters were in Brussels, but it also had regional offices in Africa, Asia and Latin America. It refused to co-operate with Communist-dominated trade union organizations, incl. the WORLD FEDERATION OF TRADE UNIONS. In 1968, 11 international occupational associations and national trade union organizations in some 60 countries were affiliated to it, comprising over 6m. trade unionists. In that year, at its 16th Congress in October in Luxemburg, it decided to broaden its appeal to other religiously oriented trade unions and changed its name to WORLD CONFEDERATION OF LABOUR.

International (Free) Federation of Deportees and Resistance Internees An organization created in Nov. 1951 by the opponents of the Communist domination of the INTERNATIONAL FEDERATION OF RESISTANCE MOVEMENTS. Its head office is in Paris and it embraces affiliated associations in 10 non-Socialist countries (Austria, Belgium, Denmark, France, the FR of Germany, Israel, Italy, Luxemburg, the Netherlands and Spain), plus Czechoslovak and Polish associations in exile.

International Federation of Resistance Movements An INTERNATIONAL COMMUNIST FRONT ORGANIZATION based in Vienna, established in June 1951 to promote ties and co-operation among the former members of the Resistance during W.W.II. It is a successor to the International Federation of Former Political Prisoners of German Concentration Camps (founded in Paris in 1947). In the late 1970s, it had about 3m. full members in 22 countries affiliated to it through 45 associations. Of the 22 member countries, 12 were capitalist (in Western Europe, plus Israel) and 8 were Socialist (Albania, Bulgaria, Czechoslovakia, the German DR, Hungary, Poland, Romania and the USSR). Most of the affiliated associations are left-wing and have expressed the Socialist approach to East–West relations and peace, such as the approval of the North Korean action in the Korean War 1950–53 and the condemnation of the West German membership of the NATO. The Federation's activities have been mostly directed to giving support to another international Communist front organization, the WORLD PEACE COUNCIL. In Nov. 1951, the opponents of the Communist domination of the I.F.R.M. formed the INTERNATIONAL (FREE) FEDERATION OF DEPORTEES AND RESISTANCE INTERNEES.

International Federation of the Socialist and Democratic Press An organization for commercial technical and editorial co-operation among publishers, printers and editors of moderate and conservative socialist newspapers founded in 1953. It has about 100 affiliated associations, linked to the political parties supporting the SOCIALIST INTERNATIONAL, all located outside the Socialist bloc. It also co-operates with the INTERNATIONAL CONFEDERATION OF FREE TRADE UNIONS. The I.F.S.D.P. is headed by an Executive Committee, its Secretariat is in Bad Godesberg (FR of Germany) and it holds Conferences every other year. The Secretariat publishes a *Handbook of the Socialist Press*, at intervals of several years.

International Federation of Trade Unions An organization in existence during 1919–45 for the purpose of promoting the policies on the industrial front of the Social-Democratic parties which belonged to the SECOND INTERNATIONAL. In particular, it pressed for the development of international social legislation, international struggle against militarism and reactionary groups, and advocated international action by trade unions in pursuit of its objectives. The Federation was founded at a Congress in Amsterdam by the reformist representatives of trade unions in Austria, Belgium, Czechoslovakia, Denmark, France, Norway, Sweden, Switzerland, the United Kingdom and the USA. In the year of its foundation (1919) it claimed 24m. members in 28 countries. It exerted considerable influence in the international trade union movement between the two world wars. It refused to be dominated by the COMINTERN and did not co-operate with *PROFINTERN*. During W.W.II the I.F.T.U. was virtually dormant and was formally dissolved in 1945. It was indirectly succeeded by the INTERNATIONAL CONFEDERATION OF FREE TRADE UNIONS (founded in 1949).

International Institute of Economic Problems of the World Socialist System A scientific institute based in Moscow, established in 1971 under the auspices of the COUNCIL FOR MUTUAL ECONOMIC ASSISTANCE. Its function is to study theoretical and practical problems associated with the

development of economic co-operation among the member countries. Since 1976 it has given more attention to practical issues, especially problems submitted by the CMEA organs and national authorities. The Institute is headed by a Director, who is Professor Y. S. Shiryaiev, a well known Soviet economist and authority on Socialist economic integration.

International Investment Bank A banking institution based in Moscow, founded by the member countries of the COUNCIL FOR MUTUAL ECONOMIC ASSISTANCE in 1971. It extends medium and long-term credits for investment projects of collective importance to the member countries. It also administers aid to less-developed countries of the Third World. Its foundation capital is 1,071m. transferable roubles, contributed by the 10 member countries on the basis of their exports in mutual trade. By 1978 the Bank had extended loans for 61 projects and the total of its outstanding credit was 825m. tr. r. The Bank extends credit partly in convertible capitalist currencies. Beginning in 1973 it began raising finance in the Eurocurrency market. In recent years it has established close links with a number of state banks and regional development banks in Africa, Asia and Latin America.

Internationalism Ideological, political and social stance expressing itself in a tendency towards closer relations, co-operation and friendship among nations, whose dignity and distinctive features are taken for granted. Marxism has always been identified with i., regarding workers of all nations as constituting a single class struggling against property-owning classes and nationalistic imperialism. Although Marxists are opposed to both CHAUVINISM and COSMOPOLITANISM, they are not necessarily against PATRIOTISM. Also PROLETARIAN INTERNATIONALISM.

Internationalists A name given to those members of the SECOND INTERNATIONAL who condemned W.W.I as an imperialist war, and urged that the working class turn it into a civil war and a proletarian revolution. V. I. LENIN, K. LIEBKNECHT, ROSA LUXEMBURG and G. E. ZINOVIEV were among the leading i. The term was first applied to the ZIMMERWALD LEFT at the ZIMMERWALD CONFERENCE in Aug.–Sep. 1915 and the KIENTAL CONFERENCE in April 1916.

International Labour Assistance An organization based in Bonn for providing relief to, and facilitating rehabilitation and resettlement of, victims of political and social disturbances and persecution, in particular refugees from Eastern Europe opposed to Communist domination and violations of democratic principles and human rights. It was founded in 1950 under the name of the 'International Socialist Aid' but in the following year it adopted the designation of the I.L.A. Its membership came from seven West European countries (Austria, Denmark, France, the FR of Germany, Italy, Norway and Switzerland). It continued its operations until 1974.

International Labour Organization A major international institution, concerned with the broadly understood improvement of the conditions of work and living throughout the world and the elimination of social injustice. It was originally established in 1919 by the Versailles Treaty as an autonomous organ affiliated to the League of Nations. In 1946 it became a specialized agency of the United Nations. Its headquarters are in Geneva (but during 1940–48 it operated from Montreal) and it has an external office in New York and a number of regional offices. Its top organs are the International Labour Conference, composed of national delegations normally meeting once a year, the Governing Body, functioning as an executive council, and a permanent secretariat called the International Labour Office. The membership of the I.L.O. embraces 135 countries, including all the Socialist countries, except Albania and the DPR of Korea. The USA withdrew in Nov. 1977. The I.L.O.'s objectives are: 1. full employment; 2. the suitability of employment to workers according to their skills and personal preferences; 3. appropriate vocational training; 4. fairness of treatment of all workers in respect of working conditions and pay; 5. the extension of social security; 6. protection of life and health of the workers; and 7. availability of proper nutrition, housing and recreation to the workers. The main practical function of the I.L.O. is to conduct discussions and recommend measures, including minimum norms, known as 'Conventions', to the governments to improve working and living conditions. After the ratification by the member government, the latter is obliged to implement the Conventions and report to the I.L.O. The Conventions adopted in the past (about 140 so far) are known as the 'International Labour Code'. The I.L.O. publishes a wide range of reports, documents and studies of specific labour problems and in addition the following periodicals: *International Labour Review* (monthly); *Legislative Service* (bi-monthly); *Official Bulletin* (quarterly); and *Yearbook of Labour Statistics*.

International Marxist Group A small but active British Trotskyite revolutionary organization, affiliated to the United Secretariat of the FOURTH INTERNATIONAL. The Group's membership in the late 1970s was about 1,200. Its secretariat is in London and it publishes a bulletin *Socialist Challenge* (which replaced the *Red Weekly*) and a journal *International Socialist Challenge*. The Group periodically engages in well chosen single-issue campaigns of social or international significance.

International Meetings of the Communist and Workers' Parties INTERNATIONAL CONFERENCES OF THE COMMUNIST AND WORKERS' PARTIES.

International Monopolies Large firms or organizations being virtually the only sellers of a particular product or service, operating in more than one country. The term appears in classical Marxist literature, while nowadays the designation 'multinational (or 'transnational') corporations' is more commonly used. An extreme case of i.m. is represented by international cartels, associating national and i.m. for the purpose of the restriction of production, the division of the world market into exclusive spheres of exploitation and the maintenance of agreed high selling prices. I.m. became an early object of attack by Marxists, who regard them as peculiar and inevitable features of capitalism in its higher stages of development (MONOPOLY CAPITALISM). In their view, i.m. are a logical and inexorable consequence of the CONCENTRATION AND CENTRALIZATION OF CAPITAL AND PRODUCTION. The expansion into other countries is prodded by the economies of large-scale production, competition, the need for large markets and cheap sources of raw materials and the law of the DECLINING PROFIT RATE. Although most i.m. are privately owned, in the modern era of STATE MONOPOLY CAPITALISM there are also state-owned i.m., such as British Steel (UK), Ente Nazionale Idrocarburi (Italy). Renault (France) and VÖEST-Alpine (Austria). I.m. have become important agents of IMPERIALISM, exercising a good deal of economic and political influence in the era of COLONIALISM and NEO-COLONIALISM and impeding the industrialization of less-developed countries. Further, they are charged with earning abnormal profits, exploiting not only the working classes in their parent countries but also in foreign (especially poor less-developed) countries. A portion of these profits is used to bribe labour leaders inducing them to OPPORTUNISM and the betrayal of the working class cause. I.m. received some attention from Marx and Engels, but more systematic analyses were advanced by R. Hilferding (in *Finanzkapital*, 1910), Rosa Luxemburg (*The Accumulation of Capital*, 1913), V. I. Lenin (*IMPERIALISM: THE HIGHEST STAGE OF CAPITALISM*, 1917) and K. Nkrumah (*Neo-Colonialism: The Last Stage of Imperialism*, 1965).

International Organization for Aid to Revolutionaries An INTERNATIONAL COMMUNIST FRONT ORGANIZATION, which existed from 1922 to 1947 and provided financial, moral and political aid to participants in revolutionary anti-fascist struggles and victims of repression in capitalist countries. It was established as a union of several associations formed in different countries after W.W.I (such as the old Bolsheviks, former political prisoners of war) under the leadership of a Polish Communist, J. B. MARCHLEWSKI, and worked closely with the COMINTERN. It was also known as the 'International Red Aid'. In 1934 it claimed 12m. members (one-half of whom were in the USSR) in more than 50 countries. It was headed by an Executive Committee in Moscow, in which different national sections were represented. Special street concerts and collections were held on 'Red Aid Day' (18 March), the anniversary of the founding of the PARIS COMMUNE in 1871. The finance raised was used to aid the victims and their families, provide legal aid and publicize political persecutions in capitalist countries.

International Organization of Journalists An INTERNATIONAL COMMUNIST FRONT ORGANIZATION for the promotion of co-operation and ties among journalists, associations and individual journalists. It was founded in 1946 in Copenhagen, as the successor to the International Federation of Journalists (created in Paris in 1926) and the International Federation of Journalists of the Allied or Free Countries (formed in London in 1941). At first, the I.O.J. included associations from both capitalist and the Socialist countries. But beginning in 1947 (at its Congress in Paris), the Organization became dominated by Communists and their sympathizers, and its headquarters were moved to Prague. In protest, many associations from non-Socialist countries withdrew and recreated the International Federation of Journalists at a conference in Brussels in 1952. During the Korean War (1950–53), the I.O.J. became the mouthpiece of the Socialist side, criticized the United Nations intervention and publicized atrocities and the BACTERIOLOGICAL WARFARE allegedly carried on by the USA. In the 1960s it organized several schools in Eastern Europe and Africa for training journalists from less-developed countries. The membership of the I.O.J. is open to national associations and groups of journalists as well as (since 1950) to individuals engaged in journalism. It claims a membership of 150,000 in 58 countries, including all the Socialist countries with the notable exception of Yugoslavia. In addition to occasional reports and pamphlets, it publishes two journals, *Information Bulletin* (fortnightly) in Arabic, English, French, Russian and Spanish, and *The Democratic Journalist* (monthly) in English, French, Russian and Spanish.

International Peasants' Council The governing body of the Peasants' International (*KRESTINTERN*), created in Moscow in Oct. 1923 on the initiative of the COMINTERN. Its purpose was to organize support for the international Communist movement among small farmers and agricultural labourers, especially in Eastern Europe and Latin America. It was a counter to the moderate and democratic International Agrarian Bureau (created in 1919) which organized the GREEN INTERNATIONAL. T. Dąbał, a Polish Communist, led the I.P.C. up until 1929. Although the I.P.C. worked with great determination, it failed as a rival to the Green International and was dissolved in 1933. Dąbał was executed during Stalin's GREAT PURGES in 1937.

International Peasant Union GREEN INTERNATIONAL.

International Production Associations in CMEA Enterprises in the member countries of the COUNCIL FOR MUTUAL ECONOMIC ASSISTANCE, owned or at least operated by more than one country. These Associations usually involve joint research and development, trade, and are concerned with the joint extraction or production of raw materials or manufacturing. There are about 20 such associations in CMEA. Some are financed by the state budgets of the partner countries, such as 'Interelektro' – founded in 1973 and based in Moscow, for the manufacture of electrical equipment owned by Bulgaria, Czechoslovakia, the German DR, Hungary, Poland, Romania and the USSR. Others are operated as enterprises along ordinary commercial lines. The textile machinery manufacturer, 'Intertextilmash', was also founded in 1973, based in Moscow and owned by the same countries. Other examples are: 'Agromash' (Budapest, horticultural machinery); 'Haldex' (Katowice, coal waste extraction); 'Interchim' (Halle, light chemicals); 'Interpodshypnik' (Warsaw, bearings); and 'Intransmash' (Sofia, intra-factory transport equipment). The Associations are considered as a step towards collective property on an international basis and towards SOCIALIST INTERNATIONALISM. But their development has been hampered by the distorted price structures, unrealistic exchange rates and the absence of a convertible currency in the CMEA.

International Radio and Television Organization An INTERNATIONAL COMMUNIST FRONT ORGANIZATION, concerned with the exchange of information and programmes for international understanding and co-operation in the sphere of radio and television. It was founded in 1946 in Brussels under the name of the International Broadcasting Organization (meant to succeed the *Union Internationale de Radiodiffusion* created in 1925), but its name was changed to the present form in 1959. Although at first many countries participated, it soon became dominated by Communists. Western members left it and joined the European Broadcasting Union or 'Eurovision' (established in 1950) based in Geneva, to which 71 capitalist countries and Yugoslavia now belong. The seat of the I.R.T.O. is in Prague and its membership includes broadcasting associations in the

11 Socialist bloc countries (Albania, China and Yugoslavia excepted), Finland and 5 less-developed countries (Algeria, Egypt, Iraq, Mali and Sudan). I.R.T.O.'s publications include *Radio and Television* (bi-monthly), in English, French, German and Russian, and *O.I.R.T. Information* (monthly), in French.

International Red Aid INTERNATIONAL ORGANIZATION FOR AID TO REVOLUTIONARIES.

International Shipowners' Association A cartel-like organization established in 1970 under the auspices of the COUNCIL FOR MUTUAL ECONOMIC ASSISTANCE, with its head office in Gdynia (Poland). Its function is to maintain agreed levels of freight rates, prevent cut-throat competition among members, to take common action against discriminating capitalist shipowners and to facilitate technical and operational co-operation in general. Its membership is also open to private capitalist companies. Thus, although its members are state shipping enterprises of the CMEA countries (Bulgaria, Cuba, Czechoslovakia, the German DR, Hungary, Poland, the USSR and Yugoslavia), India also participates in the scheme. The I.S.A. co-operates closely with another CMEA entity, the BUREAU FOR THE CO-ORDINATION OF THE CHARTERING OF FREIGHT SHIPS, is a member of the Baltic and International Maritime Conference Documentary Council, and also has a consultative status with the Intergovernmental Maritime Consultative Organization and the UNCTAD.

International Socialist Aid An international organization created in Strasbourg in 1950 to assist East European political refugees of democratic persuasion. In 1951 its name was changed to INTERNATIONAL LABOUR ASSISTANCE.

International Socialist Bureau The permanent executive and information organ of the SECOND INTERNATIONAL, which operated from 1900 to 1915 from its seat in Brussels. At one stage (from 1905 on) Lenin was a member in the capacity of representative of the RUSSIAN SOCIAL-DEMOCRATIC LABOUR PARTY.

International Socialist Division of Labour International specialization and trade among the SOCIALIST COUNTRIES. Although it is carried on within the broad framework of the INTERNATIONAL DIVISION OF LABOUR, it has acquired distinct characteristics of its own. It has emerged since W.W.II and is based on the SOCIAL OWNERSHIP OF THE MEANS OF PRODUCTION, CENTRAL ECONOMIC PLANNING, and detailed and binding TRADE AGREEMENTS and TRADE PROTOCOLS. The i.s.d. of l. is best developed among the member countries of the COUNCIL FOR MUTUAL ECONOMIC ASSISTANCE (founded in 1949), where it has advanced through several stages. Over the period 1949–62, the emphasis was on inter-branch and intra-branch specialization since that time. In the 'BASIC PRINCIPLES OF THE INTERNATIONAL SOCIALIST DIVISION OF LABOUR', it is stressed that in contrast to the capitalist international division of labour, specialization and trade among the CMEA countries promote broad all-round development and lead to the 'EVENING OUT OF ECONOMIC LEVELS' among the member nations. At first (1949–53), the basic vehicle of specialization were bilateral agreements, through which it was hoped to influence national economic plans. However, since then, the co-ordination of national economic plans has become the main instrument. An important stage is represented by the COMPLEX PROGRAMME, adopted in 1971. There is, however, much reluctance and even opposition to specialization, especially among the less developed member countries (Angola, Bulgaria, Cuba, Mongolia, Romania, Vietnam), which would first like to develop reasonably balanced economic structures before turning to specialization.

International Socialists of Great Britain A small but active revolutionary group which existed before Dec. 1976. It was Trotskyite-oriented, but left the FOURTH INTERNATIONAL in the early 1950s. It was based in London and its membership was about 3,500. It advocated workers' control and extra-parliamentary action. It derived support mainly from sections of industrial unions, teachers and government officials. The I.S. were also known as 'Cliffeites' after Tony Cliffe who became their leader in 1971. In Dec. 1976 the group decided to broaden its activities and public appeal, and was transformed into the SOCIALIST WORKERS' PARTY as a more radical alternative to the Labour Party.

International Socialist Women's Conference The name given to the anti-war meeting held in Bern (Switzerland) in March 1915, organized on the initiative of the Russian Socialist women's groups. The Conference was attended by 25 delegates representing Social-Democratic women's associations in Britain, France, Germany, Italy, the Netherlands, Poland, Russia and Switzerland. Among the most active organizers were NADEZHDA KRUPSKAYA (Lenin's wife) and CLARA ZETKIN. The Conference considered a draft resolution, submitted by the Russian delegation, condemning W.W.I as an imperialist war. The resolution also called for turning the war into a civil war and a proletarian revolution. But the resolution was partly opposed by the centrist (majority) group and only the first portion was adopted. Similar conferences, on a broader basis, were held in 1916, viz. the ZIMMERWALD CONFERENCE and the KIENTAL CONFERENCE, also in Switzerland.

International Socialist Women's Secretariat A co-ordinating office of Women Socialist groups affiliated to, or supporting, the SECOND INTERNATIONAL. The Secretariat was founded in 1907 in Stuttgart and formally existed until 1955, when it was reconstituted as the INTERNATIONAL COUNCIL OF SOCIAL-DEMOCRATIC WOMEN.

International Soviet Republic The idea of an international Socialist community, entertained by some Bolshevik leaders after the successful GREAT OCTOBER SOCIALIST REVOLUTION in 1917. The most prominent visionaries of the I.S.R. were G. E. ZINOVIEV, Chairman of the EXECUTIVE COMMITTEE OF THE COMMUNIST INTERNATIONAL (1919–26), and L. D. TROTSKY, advocate of the PERMANENT REVOLUTION. They believed that the Bolshevik rule would not survive in Russia, unless proletarian revolutions also occurred in Western Europe. Zinoviev prepared a plan for spreading revolution by means of war and in May 1919 predicted that all Europe would become Communist. However, although three national 'Soviet Republics' were proclaimed in 1919, namely the BAVARIAN S. R., the HUNGARIAN S. R. and the SLOVAK S. R. (a similar attempt was also made in Berlin), the revolutions failed within months. In a sense the COMINTERN approximated the I.S.R., in that the affiliated national Communist parties were merely 'Sections' of the Comintern. The Soviet Party and State establishment gave up the idea of carrying a revolution by force of arms to other countries, especially after Stalin came to power in 1924 and the policy of SOCIALISM IN ONE COUNTRY was adopted. Both Zinoviev and Trotsky were soon ousted from the position of influence and were ultimately executed (in 1934 and 1940 respectively).

International Tribunal for War Crimes An informal tribunal established by the British philosopher Bertrand Russell in 1966 to examine witnesses and other evidence relating to the alleged war crimes in Vietnam. The Tribunal consisted to some well-known and respected personalities from different countries. After its two sessions, in May 1967 in Stockholm and Nov. 1967 at Roskilde near Copenhagen, it declared the US Government to be guilty of crimes against peace and the people in Vietnam. The Governments of Australia, South Korea, New Zealand, the Philippines and Thailand were also condemned as accessories to the crimes. In 1970 the Tribunal also found the US Government guilty of aggression in Cambodia and previously in Laos.

International Union of Students An IN-TERNATIONAL COMMUNIST FRONT OR-GANIZATION for the promotion of friendship and co-operation among students, irrespective of race, creed and economic circumstances. It was founded in Nov. 1945 on the initiative of the British 'National Union of Students' which approached student associations in capitalist and the Socialist countries. The founding Congress was held in Aug. 1946 in Prague, where its headquarters are located. But it soon became dominated by left-wing elements, especially Communists. About 90 student organizations from 84 countries are affiliated to it, including all the Socialist countries. Most of its members, 10m. in all, are from the latter countries. The I.U.S. holds a Congress every three years, at which an Executive Committee is elected (which meets at least three times between the Congresses). Its regular publications include *World Student News*, a monthly magazine in English, French, German and Spanish, and *News Service*, a fortnightly news-sheet in Arabic, English, French and Spanish.

International Women's Secretariat A bureau established in Moscow in 1920 under the auspices of the COMINTERN to guide the work of women's organizations and groups associated with the Communist parties affiliated to the Third International. Its Secretary was CLARA ZETKIN. The Secretariat's activities varied, but on the whole it achieved little, owing to disagreements and the small numerical size of the interested women.

International Workers' Association A revolutionary organization founded in Berlin in Dec. 1922 by the supporters of ANARCHO-SYNDICALISM, in protest against the Bolshevik persecution of anarchists and the Soviet domination of the Third International (the COMINTERN). Its name alluded to the INTERNATIONAL WORKINGMEN'S ASSOCIATION (or the

FIRST INTERNATIONAL 1864–76). The I.W.A. was also known as the 'Berlin International of Trade Unions' or simply the 'Berlin International'. It acted as a co-ordinating centre for anarcho-syndicalist groups in Argentine, Chile, Denmark, France, Germany, Mexico, Portugal, Spain, Sweden, Switzerland, Uruguay and emigré Russian anarcho-syndicalists. In its manifesto, 'Principles of Revolutionary Syndicalism', it formulated an anarcho-syndicalist programme of 'libertarian syndicalism', postulating a gradual transition from capitalism to liberal communism, free from state coercion and the dictatorship of the proletariat. It also rejected nationalism, militarism and political tactics, and instead advocated industrial action and the transfer of production and public functions in society to trade unions. At the height of its influence in 1928, the I.W.A. had 3m. members. But it declined in the 1930s, owing to the repressive fascist and Nazi movements and the rise of other international trade union organizations after W.W.II (INTERNATIONAL CONFEDERATION OF FREE TRADE UNIONS, World Confederation of Labour, World Federation of Trade Unions).

International Workingmen's Association An organization founded in London in 1864 to act as a co-ordinating international body for the working class movement. It later became known as the First International. Its origin goes back to 1862 when at a public meeting in London, arranged by G. Odger (President of the London Trades Council) and W. R. Cremer (Secretary of the Masons' Union), a resolution was passed to establish a permanent association linking workers' organizations in England, France, Germany and Italy. An organizing committee was formed, which included the two trade union leaders and K. MARX. Marx also served on a sub-committee which drafted the objectives and the organization of the future body. The Association held its first Congress in London in 1865 and elected a General Council. A programme was adopted that was more moderate than that proposed by Marx. The Association then became a battleground between the adherents of Marx's communism and the followers of the anarchist M. A. BAKUNIN. The latter was eventually expelled at the last Congress in The Hague in 1872. The seat of the General Council was then transferred to New York. But owing to the demoralization following the failure of the PARIS COMMUNE, the I.W.A. became dormant and was formally dissolved in 1876. It was followed by the SECOND INTERNATIONAL (founded in 1889).

International Working Union of Socialist Parties The full official name of the SECOND-AND-A-HALF INTERNATIONAL (1921–23).

Intershops A network of state-owned retail outlets in the German DR engaging in INTERNAL EXPORTS, i.e. selling superior consumer goods to foreign and domestic holders of hard currencies. Such goods are either imported from the West, or are produced domestically for export, but are not normally available for sale for East German marks.

Intervention, The A short name given in the USSR for the military intervention by several capitalist countries in the Russian Civil War 1918–20 (FOREIGN INTERVENTION).

Intourist The state-owned enterprise in the USSR with a monopoly of arranging foreign travel to and from the USSR. It was established in 1929 with its head office in Moscow. It has branches in most major cities of the USSR and has entered into contractual relations with more than 700 foreign travel agencies.

Intuitionism A school of thought in philosophy attaching crucial importance to intuition as a source of cognition and knowledge. I. ignores the role of the senses and reasoning as a means of arriving at the truth. The main exponent of this view was a French philosopher H. Bergson (1859–1941). Marxism is strongly op-

posed to i., regarding it as reactionary and a version of philosophical IDEALISM. DIALECTICAL MATERIALISM denies the existence of intuition as an inborn capacity for cognition.

Invasion of Czechoslovakia The military intervention by the Warsaw Pact countries (Bulgaria, the German DR, Hungary, Poland and the USSR, but not Romania) in Czechoslovakia, which began on the night of 20–21 Aug. 1968. It was a reaction against the liberal and democratic reforms initiated under the leadership of A. DUBČEK and the alleged Czechoslovak leanings to the West. In Jan. 1968 Dubček replaced A. NOVOTNY as the Communist Party leader and two months later Gen. Svoboda replaced Dubček as the President of the Republic, while O. Cernik became the Prime Minister. The most determined proponents of the I. of Cz. were the USSR, the German DR and Poland, which considered the MANIFESTO OF THE TWO THOUSAND WORDS as a counter-revolutionary challenge to the Communist rule not only in Czechoslovakia but also in other Warsaw Pact countries. Dubček and Cernik were arrested and taken to the USSR. Soviet-Czechoslovak negotiations followed in Moscow (23–26 Aug. 1968), which resulted in a 'compromise'. The two Czechoslovak leaders were released but the liberal reforms were dropped and the 'temporary presence' of the Warsaw Pact forces was legalized. In April 1969 Dubček was replaced as the Party's First Secretary by G. HUSÁK and in Jan. 1970 Cernik was replaced as Prime Minister by L. Štrougal. In May 1969 an amnesty was proclaimed for those who had illegally left Czechoslovakia and who returned within a specified period. The I. of Cz. violated the Czechoslovak-Soviet Treaty of Friendship and Alliance of 1943, the Charter of the United Nations (Article 2) and the Soviet Government's Declaration of 30 Oct. 1956. The invasion caused widespread indignation throughout the world and was also condemned by many Communist parties outside the Socialist bloc. It has been interpreted by some

Western commentators as the practical
expression of the BREZHNEV DOCTRINE.

Investment As understood in the Socialist
planned economies, outlays on fixed assets directed to the modernization, reconstruction or the creation of new projects.
The assets classed as i. refer not only to the
productive sphere (industry, construction,
agriculture, transport and communications, and trade) but also to those in the
NON-PRODUCTIVE SPHERE (housing public
administration, schools, hospitals, cultural
centres and the like). As in capitalist
countries, i. can be calculated on a gross
basis (including depreciation) or a net
basis (involving only additions to the existing fixed assets). In the Socialist countries,
i. (whether on the macro or microeconomic scale) is determined on a
planned basis and is not subject to such
wide fluctuations as in capitalist market
economies. In Marxist political economy,
great importance is attached to the distinction between productive and non-
productive i. The former includes i. in the
sphere of MATERIAL PRODUCTION, whilst
the latter embraces i. in NON-PRODUCTIVE
SERVICES. Only 'productive' i. is regarded
as increasing the production capacity of
the economy and thus directly contributing to the growth of NATIONAL INCOME (as
defined in Socialist national income accounting). For this reason, productive i.
has received priority over non-productive
i. I. is a narrower concept than ACCUMU-
LATION.

Investment Ceiling A term used in the
Socialist planned economies for the maximum investment outlay set by a planning
authority which must not be exceeded
during the period in question. This level is
calculated by reference to the general directives laid down at the top political level,
technical norms and material and labour
costs.

Investment Cycle This term, used in the
Socialist planned economies, has two different meanings. 1. In the operational
sense, it denotes the period of implemen-

tation of an investment project from the
initial to the final stage. The average
period in the Socialist countries is about
three years. There has been a tendency for
the i.c. to be excessive, due to the poor
preparation of the investment plans, unexpected bottlenecks in the supply of the
allocated materials, equipment and technologies and insufficient managerial discipline. The extended i.c. increases the
freeze period of the resources and thus
leads to a lower efficiency of the economy.
2. In a broader sense, i.c. means a useful
life period of an investment project after
which it is replaced as being no longer
economical. In this sense, other things
being equal, the longer the useful period
of exploitation, the more effective the investment outlay is. However, technological progress may render the originally envisaged i.c. shorter, as new equipment and
technologies may be relatively more effective. There is evidence that the Socialist
countries have been experiencing
economic fluctuations caused by i.c. due
to investments in certain key industries
having been made in the past at about the
same time. Subsequent replacements also
have to be made at about the same time,
producing recurring investment highs and
lows in certain industries.

Investment Slip A concept used in Socialist economic planning for that portion of
the outlay on a particular investment project which was not completed in the preceding planned period, which then has to
be finished and financed in the following
period. I.s. is common in the Socialist
countries owing to unforeseen circumstances, poor preparation of the investment plans, slack work discipline and
bottlenecks in the supply of the necessary
materials and equipment.

'Invisible Hand' The system of shaping
economic activities by the anonymous
market forces. The term was first applied
by Adam Smith (in *The Wealth of Nations*) in 1776. The 'i.h.' is a symbol of the
automatic operation of the market
mechanism, implying competitive, free

and private enterprise and the absence of state intervention. Under this system, each consumer and producer is 'led by an i.h.' to respond to economic conditions and changes, which cannot be influenced by an individual. The 'i.h.' contrasts with Socialist CENTRAL ECONOMIC PLANNING, where the state consciously makes decisions in defiance of the market forces, so that in effect the central planning authority becomes the 'visible hand'.

Iraqi Communist Party (Al-Hizb al-Shuy'i al-Iraqi) A small, fairly moderate party following a pro-Soviet orientation. Its origin goes back to 1934, when a 'Committee for Struggle against Imperialism' was formed, which in the following year adopted its present name. It operated underground from 1949 to 1960, was partly legalized in 1960 and fully in 1973. Its membership is about 2,000, out of the country's population of 12,300,000 (in 1978), and is larger than its Communist rival, the 'Party of People's Unity'. Although the I.C.P. is small in absolute numbers, it is one of the most influential Communist parties in the Middle East. Since 1973 it has been co-operating with the ruling conservative faction of the BA'TH PARTY. The I.C.P.'s regular publications include: *Tariq al-Sha'b* (*People's Road*), a popular daily; *Ittihad al-Sha'b* (*People's Union*), the Party's daily newspaper; *al-Fikr al-Jadid* (*New Thought*), a cultural weekly; and *al-Taqafah al-Jadihah* (*New Culture*), a literary political weekly.

Iron Curtain The Western name for the barrier to travel and communication erected by the European Socialist countries after W.W.II to insulate themselves from the capitalist world physically and ideologically. The most visible element of the I.C. is the BERLIN WALL. The term I.C. is commonly attributed to W. Churchill, who first publicly used it in a speech at Fulton in the USA on 5 May 1946 (considered by some as the beginning of the COLD WAR), but in fact it has a longer ancestry. In this sense the term was first employed in Nazi Germany towards the

end of W.W.II by L. Schwerin von Krosigk (Finance Minister) towards the end of 1944 and then by J. Goebbels (Propaganda Minister) in Feb. 1945. But its appearance can be traced even further back, when L. Nikulin, writing for the *Literaturnaya gazeta* (*Literary Gazette*) in Jan. 1930, accused the leading capitalist countries of having erected an i.c. to prevent the 'fire of Communism' spreading to the capitalist world. The barrier erected by Communist China has been given the name the BAMBOO CURTAIN. It may be noted here that the West has erected several economic barriers against the East, viz. the GOLD CURTAIN, Strategic Curtain (STRATEGIC EMBARGO) and TECHNOLOGICAL CURTAIN.

Iron Law of Wages A theory according to which wages tend to oscillate around the subsistence level, a level where the supply of labour is equated to the demand for labour. If wages rise above this natural level, workers will tend to have larger families, the death rate will tend to fall and consequently the supply of labour will increase, which will depress wages, and vice versa. The essence of this theory was first formulated by T. R. Malthus (1766 – 1834) and D. Ricardo (1772 – 1823), while F. LASSALLE (1825 – 64) coined this popularly accepted phrase and further elaborated on its implications. Lassalle argued that any efforts by trade unions or the political labour movement to raise wages were pointless in the long run, as they would counter the inexorable laws of supply and demand. Classical Marxists used the i.l. of w. as an argument against capitalism, maintaining that the only hope for the working class to rise above the subsistence level was communism. The 'law' has been completely discredited in the developed capitalist countries, where wages have increased vastly in the last century and yet the population growth has tended to decline. The rise in the level of wages has been due to the increasing productivity of labour, the effectiveness of the industrial and political labour movements and state intervention.

Irrationalism A view in the theory of knowledge and in social theory, according to which human cognition and actions are not necessarily governed by reason, but by factors which are not logically motivated or rationally explainable (as such it is opposite to RATIONALISM). I. denies the capacity of the human mind and science to arrive at TRUTH, and instead emphasizes the role of the will, instincts, intuition, subconsciousness, revelation and mysticism. The main exponents of i. were A. Schopenhauer (1788–1860), F. Nietzsche (1844–1900), H. Bergson (1859–1941) and B. Russell (1872–1970). Marxism is strongly opposed to i., regarding it as an extreme version of philosophical IDEALISM, and in effect subscribing to superstitions, religion, fanaticism and backwardness. Marxists point out that i. appeals to those social groups in despair, especially in crises, and the existing social order. Thus, it provides little hope for the working class. I. rejects HISTORICAL MATERIALISM, the possibility of the sensory cognition of reality and reasoning and the advisability of organized action by the working class to improve its social position.

Iskra (*Spark*, in Russian) An underground newspaper of the Russian revolutionary movement, established by Lenin in 1900. It was the first Russian Marxist newspaper directed at the masses. It was printed abroad (e.g. in Leipzig) and smuggled into Russia. Its motto was, 'The spark shall ignite the flame' (a phrase which is attributed to Pushkin, who was one of its sympathizers). In its early years, *I.* provided a unifying platform for different Marxist groups within and without Russia. After the split in the RUSSIAN SOCIAL-DEMOCRATIC LABOUR PARTY in 1903, Lenin lost the control over *I.* and it passed into the hands of the MENSHEVIKS, after which its influence declined.

Israeli Communist Party 'COMPASS', NEW COMMUNIST LIST.

Italian Communist Party (*Partito Communista Italiano*) The second largest political party in Italy and the largest Communist party outside the Socialist bloc. It is the seventh largest in the world (after China, the USSR, Romania, Poland, the German DR and the DPR of Korea). Its membership in the late 1970s was 1,800,000 (compared with the country's total population of 57,000,000) and it is one of the most influential non-ruling Communist parties in the world. It was founded in 1921, but its origin goes back to at least 1892, when the ITALIAN SOCIALIST PARTY was created. Communists within the Party exerted a good deal of influence. After a period of persecution by the Fascists 1923–26, it was declared illegal. But it continued its activities underground, directed by its leaders who moved to France and then (in 1939) to the USSR. The Party was legalized in 1943 and has become increasingly stronger ever since. It is organized into 11,000 local sections, grouped into 93 provincial federations and co-ordinated by 20 regional committees. At the national level it is headed by the Central Committee, consisting of 177 members elected at the Party Congress held every four years, which in turn elects a Directorate (of 33 members) and a Secretariat (of 8 members). The Party's Secretary-General is E. BERLINGUER and its President is L. Longo. Although on occasions it has co-operated with the Italian Socialist Party, in the past it has refused to participate in coalition governments, even though it is usually the second largest party in the parliament. At the 1976 general elections, it polled 34 per cent of the votes cast and won 228 (of the 630) seats in the Chamber of Deputies. But in recent years it has embraced EUROCOMMUNISM and may join a coalition in the future. In its international orientation, the party has followed a mildly pro-Soviet or independent line. Its mass support organizations include the Italian General Confederation of Labour (with some 3,850,000 members), the National League of Co-operatives (2,450,000 members), plus the Union of Italian Women, the Italian Communist Youth Federation, the Association of Democratic Lawyers and the Association of Democratic Journalists. The Party pursues a vigorous publishing programme. The most important regular publications are: *L'Unitá* (*Unity*), the Party's daily organ; *Rinascitá* (*Rebirth*), a weekly cultural magazine; *Critica Marxista* (*Marxist Critique*), a theoretical bi-monthly; and *La Nuova Rivista Internazionale* (*The New International Review*), a quarterly journal of international affairs. In addition to the I.C.P., there are at least a dozen small Marxist or revolutionary groups, the main ones of which are: Workers' Vanguard (founded in 1971, with some 25,000 members); Proletarian Democracy (founded in 1977); Continuing Struggle (founded in 1968); the RED BRIGADES; Armed Proletarian Units; the 'Communist Party of Italy (Marxist-Leninist)'; the 'Organization of the Communists of Italy (Marxist-Leninist)'; and Workers Autonomy.

Italian Socialist Party (*Partito Socialista Italiano*) The third largest political party in Italy (after the Italian Christian Democratic Party and the Italian Communist Party). It was founded in 1892, but has suffered from internal differences and splits. In 1921 its left-wing group established the ITALIAN COMMUNIST PARTY, and in 1947 its right-wing faction, opposing collaboration with the I.C.P., formed the Italian Workers' Socialist Party. In 1952 the I.W.S.P. merged with other minor political groups to form the Italian Social Democratic Party. The latter rejoined the I.S.P. in 1966, but then in 1969 another split followed. The I.S.P. is committed to a moderate socialist programme, less radical than that of the I.C.P., but more reformist than the course followed by the Italian Christian Democratic Party. The best known publication of the I.S.P. is *Avanti* (*Forward*), its daily organ.

'It is Right to Rebel' One of the best known slogans formulated and popularized by Mao Tse-tung. He first put it forward at a rally in Yenan on 21 Dec. 1939, when he said: 'Marxism consists of thousands of truths, but they all boil down to one sentence, "It is right to rebel". For thousands of years, it had been said that it was right to oppress, it was right to exploit, and it was wrong to rebel. This old verdict was only reversed with the appearance of Marxism'. Mao employed the slogan to justify not only a BOURGEOIS-DEMOCRATIC REVOLUTION and a PROLETARIAN REVOLUTION, but also a rebellion against the entrenched and conservative Party bureaucracy. After the failures of the GREAT LEAP FORWARD, Mao lost a majority support in the top Party establishment. This slogan, together with 'BOMBARD THE HEADQUARTERS', was freely used during the GREAT PROLETARIAN CULTURAL REVOLUTION to reassert Mao's authority.

Izvestiya (*The News* or *Gazette*, in Russian) The official daily organ of the Soviet Government, published by the PRESIDIUM OF THE SUPREME SOVIET OF THE USSR. It was founded on 28 Feb. (O.-S.C., or 13 March N.-S.C.) 1917 as the organ of the PETROGRAD SOVIET OF WORKERS' AND SOLDIERS' DEPUTIES. In the summer of 1917 it was adopted as the organ of the Central Executive Committee of all Soviets, when it fell under the control of the MENSHEVIKS. It became the official gazette of the Soviet Government soon after the Bolshevik Revolution in Oct. 1917. The headquarters of *I.*, originally in Petrograd (now Leningrad), were transferred to Moscow in March 1918. *I.* carries the full text of the laws, decrees, notices about official appointments, changes in government machinery, pronouncements on official policies and the work of the Soviets, including those at the local level. *I.* is printed in 40 Soviet cities and its daily circulation is 9.0m. copies (the second largest in the country, after *PRAVDA*).

J

Jacobins A left-wing political group active during the FRENCH REVOLUTION (1789–99), which pressed for far-reaching political and social reforms in the spirit of socialism and the complete elimination of the monarchy and the nobility. Its name was derived from St. Jacob's monastery, where the group held its meetings. The party became increasingly radical under its leader M. Robespièrre. In 1791 it had 136 deputies in the Legislative Assembly (which numbered 745 in all). In contrast to their moderate rivals, the GIRONDINS, the J. favoured limitations on personal freedom and private enterprise, pressed for the centralization of authority, price controls and the mobilization of the whole society. The J. exercised dictatorial powers in France from 31 May 1793 to 27 July 1794 and resorted to unnecessary terror. However, the alarmed bourgeoisie ousted the J. from power with the support of the populace. They continued to exist until 1799 with limited success and were finally abolished after Napoleon's coup that same year. At the time of the split in the RUSSIAN SOCIAL-DEMOCRATIC LABOUR PARTY in 1903 into the BOLSHEVIKS and MENSHEVIKS, Lenin compared the former to the J. (and the latter to the Girondins). The modern Marxist view of the J. is that they represented a revolutionary group of the bourgeoisie which, when necessary, allied itself with the working class, but without really having convinced the latter of their proletarian programme.

Japanese Communist Party (*Nihon Kyosanto*) An influential and usually the third largest political party in Japan (after the Liberal Democratic Party and the JAPAN SOCIALIST PARTY). Its membership in the late 1970s was 380,000 (out of the total population of 115,400,000 in 1978). At the 1976 general elections it polled 10 per cent of the votes cast and won 17 of the 511 seats in the Lower House of parliament. The Party was founded in 1922, but had to stay underground until its legalization in 1945. Its influence grew remarkably after W.W.II and in the late 1940s it had 15 per cent of the seats in the Lower House. The Party's activities have been largely directed against American domination and imperialism and Japanese monopoly capital. Since 1961 the Party has followed a moderate course, professing a peaceful PARLIAMENTARY ROAD TO SOCIALISM, has become sympathetic to EUROCOMMUNISM since the mid-1970s and after 1976 no longer described itself as 'Marxist-Leninist'. It has concentrated on domestic issues and in the Sino-Soviet dispute it has adopted an independent line. The Party's highest source of authority is Congress held every two years, which lays down the general policy guidelines and elects a Central Committee which in turn elects a Presidium, a Standing Committee (the latter exercising real power), a Secretariat and Control and Auditing Commissions. At the 14th Party Congress in Oct. 1977, 141 full and 54 alternate members were elected to the C.C., which elected the Presidium of 40 members, the Standing Committee headed by the Chairman (K. MIYAMOTO), the Secretariat Central Control Commission (for Party discipline) and the Central Auditing Commission (for finance). The Party has fairly solid support from several mass organizations, such as the Democratic Youth League (about 200,000 members). But its influence in trade unions is patchy. The largest trade union organization, the Sohyo Federation of Labour, is loyal to the Japan Socialist Party. The J.C.P. operates a well developed and successful publications programme. Its main regular organs are: *Akahata* (*Red Flag*), a daily newspaper; *Sekai Seiji Shiryo* (*Documents of World Politics*), a fortnightly bulletin; and *Zenei* (*Vanguard*), a monthly theoretical journal. In addition to the J.C.P., there are other Marxist or revolutionary groups, the main ones being: the 'Voice of Japan' (pro-Soviet); the 'Japan Communist Party (Left)', pro-Chinese; the 'Fourth International Group', Trotskyite; the 'Japan Communist Revolutionary Party'; and the 'Japan Labour Party'.

Japan Socialist Party (*Nihon Shakaito*) One of the two largest political parties in Japan (the other being the Liberal Democratic Party). It was originally founded in 1901, but was soon dissolved and went underground. It reappeared in 1945, with a moderate programme of a gradual transformation of Japan into an egalitarian society by parliamentary means. In 1947 it won the largest number of seats in the Diet and its leader, Katayama Tetsu, became Prime Minister in a coalition government. The Party has suffered from internal dissent and a split between gradualists (friendly to the USA) and revolutionaries (anti-American, some leaning towards the USSR and others to China and Maoism). The Party has a fairly solid support from most trade unions, including the Sohyo Federation of Labour (the largest trade union organization in the country, with a membership of 4.5m.) and from some sections of the middle class. At the 1976 general elections, it won 123 (of the 511) seats in the Lower House and continues to be the main opposition party in the Diet.

Jaurès, Jean Léon (1859–1914) A French socialist political leader, philosopher and historian, who became known as a Marxist revisionist. He led the right wing of the FRENCH SOCIALIST PARTY before W.W.I and earned the nickname of 'The Incorruptible'. He rejected HISTORICAL MATERIALISM and was opposed to the revolutionary road to socialism. He advocated the liberation of mankind from political authoritarianism, exploitation, colonialism and wars. He had a vision of society based on justice and harmonious relations. He helped found a socialist newspaper *L'HUMANITÉ* in 1904 (of which he was its editor until his death), which after 1920 became the organ of the French Communist Party. J. was assassinated by a French chauvinist (R. Villaine) on the eve of W.W.I.

Jen-min Jih-pao (*People's Daily*, in Chinese) The official daily organ of the Central Committee of the Chinese Communist Party. It was founded in 1948 and its publication is supervised by the Propaganda Department of the CC of the CCP. Its daily circulation in 1979 was reported to be 3.5m.

Jen Min-pi Another transliteration of REN-MINBI, the official Communist name of the currency unit in China.

Jevons, William Stanley (1835–1882) An English philosopher and political economist, whose opposition to Marx's LABOUR THEORY OF VALUE was based on the MARGINAL UTILITY theory. His principal work was *The State in Relation to Labour* (1882).

Jewish Doctors' Conspiracy See 'DOCTORS' PLOT'.

John Birch Society An extremist right-wing anti-communist association in the USA, founded by R. H. W. Welch in 1958. It is named after an American soldier and evangelist, who had been killed in China during the Communist advance in Aug. 1945 and who was later described as the 'hero of the Cold War' and 'the first casualty of W.W.III'. The Society's headquarters are in Belmont, Mass., and its claimed membership is 100,000 concentrated in New England, southern California and several southern states. The Society's objectives and strategy are embodied in its *Blue Book*. Its activities have been directed not only against Communists but also Jews and Negroes. Its founder at one stage accused former US Presidents, D. Eisenhower, H. Truman and F. D. Roosevelt as 'Communist agents'. The Society's peak of influence was reached in the early 1960s, but has since declined. It publishes a monthly journal, *Bulletin*, for its members, and a magazine, *American Opinion*, appearing 11 times a year, for the wider public.

John Paul II See POPE JOHN PAUL II.

Johnson's Doctrine The ideas, assumptions and objectives which conditioned US policy towards the Socialist bloc under the Administration of President L. B. Johnson. Enunciated on 23 May 1964, it represented a more active and elaborate form of the preceding KENNEDY DOCTRINE, and was directed towards establishing closer contacts with most Socialist countries, on the one hand, and weakening the cohesion of the Socialist bloc, on the other. It embodied the scheme of 'building bridges' to Eastern Europe and a differentiated treatment in trade and aid of the Socialist countries according to the degree of their Communist militancy, attitude to the West and the defiance of the USSR. The doctrine also envisaged an active US intervention against Communist insurgency threatening the independence of non-communist regimes, as illustrated by US involvement in the VIETNAM WAR and several conflicts in Latin America. Its application also led to the strengthening of NATO, especially the role of the FR of Germany. The doctrine became a target of bitter attack not only by Communist regimes, but also by several capitalist nations, such as France, Pakistan and Sweden.

Joint Institute for Nuclear Research A scientific establishment concerned with theoretical research and experimentation in the field of atomic energy primarily for peaceful purposes. It is operated jointly by Bulgaria, Czechoslovakia, the German DR, Hungary, the DPR of Korea, Mongolia, Poland, Romania, the USSR and Vietnam. China also participated up until 1969. The Institute was established on the basis of an agreement concluded in March 1956 and is located at Dubna, 130 km. north of Moscow (where the Soviets had built their first proton accelerator in 1949). The Institute includes departments of theoretical physics, high energy, nuclear problems and neutron physics.

Joint State-Private Enterprises Entities which were formed in Communist China in the 1950s in industry, commerce and banking as a step towards the socialist transformation of the economy. At first, in the early 1950s, they were limited to small individual undertakings, but after 1955 the partnerships were extended to cover whole branches of industry and other divisions of the economy. Capital was jointly owned and the private partner earned dividends of up to 5 per cent p.a., but in OVERSEAS CHINESE INVESTMENT CORPORATIONS the return was 8 per cent p.a. The former owners of the firms usually retained their positions as managers or specialists. The objectives, which prompted the formation of the partnerships, were to extend the state sector, prevent private speculation and profiteering, enforce price stability, facilitate economic planning and train state managers utilizing private expertise. Most of these enterprises were later completely taken over by the state, especially during the GREAT PROLETARIAN CULTURAL REVOLUTION.

Joint Venture A term used for an integrated enterprise jointly owned and managed by capitalist and Socialist parent enterprises. A j.v. is distinct from an industrial co-operation in that the latter involves no joint ownership and mangement and no joint sharing of risk. In the late

Jordanian Communist Party

1970s, there were about 500 capitalist-Socialist ventures in operation, two-thirds of which were located in the capitalist world. The rest were located in six Socialist countries – Cuba, Hungary, Poland, Romania, Vietnam and Yugoslavia (the only Socialist countries allowing foreign ownership of capital within their borders). In 1967, Yugoslavia became the first country to allow capitalist investment, while the other five countries followed suit since 1972.

Jordanian Communist Party See COMMUNIST PARTY OF JORDAN.

Journey from St. Petersburg to Moscow, A The first Russian revolutionary book, written by a nobleman A. N. RADISHCHEV, which he published anonymously at his own expense in 1790. The book represented profound criticism of the exploitation of peasants, serfdom and the Tsarist autocratic bureaucracy. Radishchev attributed those evils to the faulty legal and social system and called for radical agrarian and political reforms. The book was read by Empress Catherine II, who, outraged by it, sentenced Radishchev to death. This was commuted to imprisonment in Siberia for 10 years. Radishchev later committed suicide. The English translation of the book appeared in 1958.

Jugobanka The commonly accepted name for the Yugoslav bank of foreign trade, with its head office in Belgrade. It was founded in 1955 under the name of *Jugoslovenska Banka za Spoljnu Trgovine*, but its name was simplified to J. in 1971. It is one of the most dynamic Socialist banks operating outside Yugoslavia. In the late 1970s it had branches or representative offices in Amsterdam, Berlin (West), Chicago, Düsseldorf, Frankfurt, Hanover, London, Mannheim, Milan, New York, Nuremberg, Stuttgart, Teheran, Toronto, Tripoli (Libya), Vienna, and also in Moscow and Prague.

July Manifesto A proclamation made by the Polish Committee of National Liberation in Chelm Lubelski (eastern Poland) on 22 July 1944. It defined the principles of the new socio-political order in Poland, indicated the need for alliance with the USSR and intimated democratic elections and a new Constitution. It was the first political and legal declaration of the Soviet-backed self-styled Polish authority on Polish territory, thereby defying the legal Polish Government-in-Exile in London. The Manifesto also outlined some specific reforms, viz. the immediate reorganization of agriculture, the state management of large enterprises and banks, radical industrial legislation, generous social security and free education at all levels. The J.M. marked the beginning of the Communist regime in Poland and 22 July has since been observed as a national holiday.

July 26 Movement TWENTY SIXTH-OF-JULY MOVEMENT

Junius One of the assumed names of ROSA LUXEMBURG. She used it when she wrote a pamphlet in prison in 1916 entitled *The Crisis of Social-Democracy*.

276

K

Kádár, János (1912–   ) A Hungarian Communist leader and statesman of peasant background. He was one of the founders of a revolutionary youth organization in 1931 and in the same year joined the (illegal) Communist Party of Hungary (as it was known then). He was active in the anti-fascist resistance during W.W.II, was elected to the Party's Central Committee in 1942 and in the following year became its Secretary. After the war, he was elected to the Party's Political Bureau and in 1948 was appointed the Minister of Internal Security, thereby replacing L. Rajk, his rival for whose arrest and execution K. was partly responsible. In 1951 he was imprisoned and tortured, but was released and rehabilitated in 1954. He became the Party Secretary in 1956 and during the HUNGARIAN UPRISING (Oct.–Nov. 1956) initially sided with the liberal regime of I. NAGY. However, he soon reversed sides, supported the Soviet armed intervention, succeeded I. Nagy as Prime Minister and the First Secretary of the HUNGARIAN SOCIALIST WORKERS' PARTY. Although at first his regime was unnecessarily vindictive and repressive (which included execution of 'counter-revolutionaries', I. Nagy included), after 1961 he responded to the public mood and successfully embarked on several far-reaching reforms in the spirit of liberalization and social reconciliation.

Kadets Members of the Constitutional-Democratic Party which existed in Russia from 1905 to 1920. The term was used colloquially and was derived from *Konstitutsionno-Demokraticheskaya Par-*

tiya, founded in Oct. 1905, after the revolutionary unrest following BLOODY SUNDAY. The K. were 'revolutionary democratic liberals', mostly representing the progressive middle class who advocated a constitutional monarchy, the division of large estates among the peasants, regarded strikes as the main weapon of political action, but otherwise did not favour socialism. After the GREAT OCTOBER SOCIALIST REVOLUTION in 1917, they opposed the BOLSHEVIKS and assumed the name of the 'People's Freedom Party, which Lenin described as the 'General Staff of the Counter-Revolution'.

Kaganovich, Lazar Moysevich (1893–?) A Jewish shoemaker who became a Soviet revolutionary leader and statesman and a loyal supporter of Stalin. He joined the Bolshevik faction of the RUSSIAN SOCIAL-DEMOCRATIC LABOUR PARTY in 1911, participated in the GREAT OCTOBER SOCIALIST REVOLUTION (1917) and the Civil War (1918–20). In 1918 he was appointed to the ALL-RUSSIAN CENTRAL EXECUTIVE COMMITTEE. He was People's Commissar (Minister) for Transport (1935–44) and Vice-Premier (1938–57) and a member of the State Defence Committee during W.W.II. He held several senior posts in the Party including that of First Secretary of the Ukrainian C.P. (1930–52) and in 1957 was elected to the Presidium (now called the Politburo) of the CC OF THE CPSU. After the death of Stalin (March 1953), K. was one of the three most important members of the collective leadership (with G. Malenkov and V.Molotov). K.'s membership in the ANTI-

PARTY GROUP, his opposition to DE-STALINIZATION, and Khrushchev's rise to power eventually resulted in the latter's expulsion from the Government, the Party Presidium and finally from the Party. According to some reports he subsequently died in mysterious circumstances in the early 1960s, but his death has never been officially announced.

Kalecki, Michał (1899–1970) An outstanding Polish Marxist economist and statistician who made substantial contributions to the theory of economic growth and equilibrium, especially under Socialist economic planning. He was an engineer by trade and a self-taught economist. He antedated Keynesian theory by a year when in 1935 he independently formulated rigorous causal relations between production, investment, profitability and employment. But unlike Keynes, K. stressed the distribution of national income and the contradictions of the capitalist system, expressing themselves in cyclical fluctuations. K. also developed a dynamic theory of capitalist economic growth, in which he stressed that the decisive role in the development of the capitalist economy in the long run is played not by endogenous conditions, but by semi-exogenous factors such as innovations and discoveries of new sources of raw materials. K.'s theories basically derive from Marx's interpretation of the process of REPRODUCTION and Rosa Luxemburg's analysis of ACCUMULATION. K. may be said to have created a complete school of economic growth under Socialist economic planning. His ideas have been widely accepted in the Socialist countries as well as further afield, including the leading Western countries. In his approach he may be criticized for overestimating the role of the extension of resources in economic growth, as distinct from productivity increases (EXTENSIVE GROWTH, INTENSIVE GROWTH). K. went to Britain in 1936 where he worked at the University of Cambridge. During W.W.II he carried out research projects for the British Government. He returned to Po-

land after the war and became Professor of Economics in 1956. He acted as an economic adviser not only for the Polish Government, but also for Israeli (1951), Indian (1959–60) and Cuban (1961) governments. His main publications are: *Theory of Economic Dynamics* (English ed. in 1954, followed by a Polish ed. in 1958) and *Outline of the Theory of Growth of the Socialist Economy* (1963).

Kalinin, Mikhail Ivanovich (1875–1946) A Soviet revolutionary leader and statesman who was the formal head of the Soviet state from 1919 to 1946. Of peasant background, he joined the RUSSIAN SOCIAL-DEMOCRATIC LABOUR PARTY in 1898 (when it was founded), and after the factional split in 1903, supported Lenin thereby becoming a BOLSHEVIK. He was active in the REVOLUTION OF 1905-07 and later was one of the founders of *PRAVDA* (in 1912) and a contributor (up to 1917). K. participated in the GREAT OCTOBER SOCIALIST REVOLUTION, subsequently served as Mayor of Petrograd (now Leningrad), and was elected to the Party's Central Committee (1919) and to its Politburo (1925). From 1919 to 1922 he was the Chairman of the ALL-RUSSIAN CENTRAL EXECUTIVE COMMITTEE, of the All-Union Central Executive Committee between 1922 and 38 and the Supreme Soviet of the USSR from 1938 to 1946. K. was one of the few old Bolsheviks who favoured a moderate, right-wing approach to agriculture and industrialization and managed to survive Stalin's purges. His name has been commemorated in a number of geographical features, the main one being Kaliningrad (previously Königsberg, in former East Prussia).

Kamenev, Lev Borisovich (1883–1936) A Soviet revolutionary, diplomat and writer. He joined the RUSSIAN SOCIAL-DEMOCRATIC LABOUR PARTY in 1901, took the side of the BOLSHEVIKS at the time of the split in 1903 and was one of the close associates of Lenin in Switzerland before the Revolution. In 1917 he was elected to the Central Committee of the

Bolshevik Party. At first, together with G. E. ZINOVIEV, he opposed Lenin's idea of an armed coup believing that revolution could not succeed in just one country. After the October Revolution, he was appointed Chairman of the ALL-RUSSIAN CENTRAL EXECUTIVE COMMITTEE, but in Nov. 1917 he was removed from the post for patronizing right-wing SOCIAL RE-VOLUTIONARIES and MENSHEVIKS. Together with Zinoviev and TROTSKY (whose sister he married) he led the Party's LEFT OPPOSITION, formed in 1925. He was temporarily removed from the Party (in 1927) and appointed Soviet Ambassador to Italy and later the first Director of the Marx-Engels-Lenin Institute (now INSTITUTE OF MARXISM-LENINISM). After the death of S. M. KIROV, K. (together with Zinoviev) was arrested in 1934 and executed in 1936 for alleged anti-Soviet activities (including 'plotting to assassinate Stalin').

Kampuchea, People's Republic of A small country in south-east Asia, of 181,000 sq. km. and 8,850,000 inhabitants (1978), ruled by a Communist regime. After a long period of monarchical rule, the Kingdom of Cambodia became the Khmer Republic in Oct. 1970. A period of civil war followed in which government forces supported by the USA and the Republic of [South] Vietnam fought the North Vietnamese and the Khmer Rouge. Although the North Vietnamese and US troops withdrew in 1973, the civil war continued until April 1975 when the Communists eventually gained power. A new regime, controlled by the Kampuchean Communist Party and backed by China, was established. Initially it was led by a figurehead, Prince Sihanouk, but later real power was assumed by Pol Pot and Ieng Sary. The country was thrown into self-imposed isolation, marked by massive shifts of population from the cities to the rural area and widespread terror in which about one million people were reported to have been massacred. A Communist opposition emerged called the KAMPUCHEAN UNITED FRONT FOR NATIONAL SALVATION, which,

with massive Vietnamese military support, ousted Pol Pot's regime in a civil war from Dec. 1978 to Feb. 1979. The new regime, headed by Heng Samrin, has the backing of Vietnam and the USSR. But the armed guerrilla units of the Khmer Rouge still continue their resistance along the eastern border.

Kampuchean United Front for National Salvation The ruling Communist regime in the People's Republic of KAMPUCHEA. It can trace its Communist origin back to 1930, when the Communist Party of Indochina was founded. A specifically regional party was formed in 1951 and named the People's Party of Khmer. As it was proscribed first by the French and then the Cambodian authorities, the P.P.K. operated underground and through front organizations. It became increasingly revolutionary and established a military arm called the Khmer Rouge. In 1970 the P.P.K. changed its name to the Khmer Communist Party and embarked upon a long struggle against the conservative regime of Lon Nol. It seized power in April 1975 and changed its name to the Kampuchean Communist Party. It followed a pro-Chinese orientation, but otherwise kept aloof from the international Communist movement. The Party's crude policies and widespread massacres led to the emergence of a Communist opposition encouraged by Vietnam. With the Vietnamese military support the regime of Pol Pot was ousted from power between Dec. 1978 and Feb. 1979 and the K.U.F.N.S. took over. But Pol Pot, supported by the loyal guerrilla units of the Khmer Rouge, continued resistance in areas along the Thai border. In its international orientation, the K.U.F.N.S., led by Heng Samrin, pursues a decidedly pro-Soviet line.

K'ang sheng (1899–1975) A prominent Communist Chinese revolutionary and one of the most loyal supporters of Mao Tse-tung. A son of a wealthy landowner, he joined the Chinese Communist Party in 1925 and was elected to its Politburo in 1945. He was one of the few Chinese

Communist leaders who widely travelled abroad and maintained contacts with other Communist parties. K. came into the public limelight during the GREAT LEAP FORWARD and again during the GREAT PROLETARIAN CULTURAL REVOLUTION, both of which he actively supported. He established a reputation for thoroughness and ruthlessness (and was sometimes described as 'China's Beria'). K. was a member of the GROUP OF FIVE, created on instructions from Mao in 1965 (of which K. was the most rebellious member) and in turn of the NATIONAL CULTURAL REVOLUTIONARY GROUP which replaced it in May 1966. In 1969 he was elected to the Standing Committee of the Politburo, the highest effective policy-making body in China.

Kantorovich, Leonid Vitalevich (1912–) An outstanding Soviet mathematical economist. He became Professor at the University of Leningrad in 1934. When commissioned to solve a complex transport scheduling problem in 1939, K. discovered the method of linear programming, long before its (independent) formulation by G. B. Dantzig in the West in 1947. But K.'s contributions in this field remained unrecognized for a long time in the USSR. In 1949 he was awarded the STALIN PRIZE for his contribution to functional analysis. His work or linear programming and economic models was first recognized in the West. In his best known work, *The Best Use of Economic Resources* (originally published in Russian in 1959 and in English translation in 1965) he perfected the techniques of linear programming in relation to the optimal utilization of resources and outlined a methodology for arriving at scarcity factor prices (OBJECTIVELY DETERMINED VALUATIONS) under Socialist economic planning. He was criticized by many orthodox Marxist economists for his implied rejection of the LABOUR THEORY OF VALUE. Nevertheless, the significance of his work was officially recognized and he (together with N. S. Nemchinov and V. V. Novozhilov) was awarded the LENIN PRIZE in 1965, the highest scientific award in the USSR. K. was also awarded the Nobel Memorial Prize in Economics in 1975.

Kao Kang (1902?–1954?) A Chinese Communist revolutionary and economist, who favoured economic commonsense rather than ideological rectitude. He belonged to the 'Old Guard' of Chinese Communists who distinguished himself in the 1930s, during the Sino-Japanese War (1937–45) and in Manchuria after the war. In 1952 he was elected to the Politburo and became the first Chairman of the State Planning Commission. He disagreed with Mao Tse-tung over some fundamental issues on economic development and management. He fell out of favour with Mao and reportedly committed suicide before the formal dismissal from his post.

Kapital, Das: Kritik der Politischen Oekonomie See CAPITAL: *Critique of Political Economy*. The original title in German of the main work by K. MARX. Volume I, the most important of all volumes, was published in Hamburg in 1867, while volumes II and III, edited by Engels, appeared posthumously in 1885 and 1894 respectively. Marx's remaining manuscripts, collected and systematized by Kautsky over the period 1905–10 under the title *Theories of Surplus Value* and first published in 1955, are sometimes regarded as vol. IV (but are not a proper part of the title set). The first translation of vol. I appeared in Russian in 1872, in French in 1875, in Polish in 1884 and in English in 1887 (*CAPITAL*). It has been translated at least into 40 other languages and has become the 'bible of Marxism' and an inspiration to Communist thinkers and many social reformers throughout the world. It is one of the crucial books in the history of human thought, as virtually all writings in the field since its publication have either been in its support or criticism. The work is the best known indictment of CAPITALISM, presented in a rigorous ('scientific' according to Marxists) manner. Marx analysed the processes of capitalist production and the creation and distribution of capital. The main points of his analysis are directed at the exploitation of the PROLETARIAT by the CAPITALISTS, the CONCENTRATION AND CENTRALIZATION OF CAPITAL AND PRODUCTION, capitalist CRISES, social CONTRADICTIONS and ALIENATION – the evils which must inevitably lead to the BREAKDOWN OF CAPITALISM. To the disappointment of many thinkers, the work does not provide a positive blueprint for an ideal Communist society, but merely a negative analysis of capitalism at its worst, as Marx knew it at the time.

Kapitalistate A concept attributed to an American Marxist, James O'Connor, denoting modern capitalism dominated or supplemented by indirect and direct state intervention. The term alludes to the original title (in German) of Marx's main work *KAPITAL*, and is a modernized version of the Marxist notions of STATE CAPITALISM and STATE MONOPOLY CAPITALISM. The function of the modern state is seen as protecting rather than curbing the institution of private property and the power of the propertied classes. K. is also the title of a hardline Marxist journal established by a group of American, British and German Marxists (including O'Connor) in 1973, to supplement the classical Marxist theory of the capitalist state. It originally appeared in West Berlin, but since 1974 it has been published, irregularly (roughly once a year), in San Francisco by the 'San Francisco Bay Area Kapitalistate Group'.

Kardelj, Edward (1910–79) A Yugoslav Communist leader and the chief theoretician of the LEAGUE OF COMMUNISTS OF YUGOSLAVIA. He joined the Communist Party of Yugoslavia (as it was known then) in 1927 and lived in the USSR from 1934 to 1937. During W.W.II, he was one of the chief partisan leaders in Slovenia and became one of the closest associates of TITO. After the war K. drew up the first Communist Yugoslav Constitution (modelled on Stalin's Constitution of 1936), which was adopted in Jan. 1946. Later he was appointed a Vice-Premier (1953–63) and

Minister for Foreign Affairs. He emerged as chief theoretician and advocate of the specifically 'Yugoslav road to socialism'. His main works (in Serbo-Croat) are: *Towards New Yugoslavia* (1946); *Socialist Democracy in Yugoslav Practice* (1954); *Problems of Our Socialist Construction*, in 5 vols (1954–64); *Problems of Socialist Policy Towards Agriculture* (1959); and *Socialism and War* (1962), also published in French and English translations.

Karl Marx Medal The highest award of the Academy of Sciences of the USSR for outstanding achievements in the field of social sciences, especially Marxist theory.

Katyn A village in the western USSR, 10 km. west of Smolensk, near which in a forest about 8,000 Polish officers were murdered in 1940 or 1941. The officers were prisoners of war taken by the Soviet troops which invaded eastern Poland in Sep. 1939. The mass graves were discovered by Germans who announced the discovery in April 1943, alleging that the crime had been committed by the Soviets in 1940, and invited investigation by an independent body of experts. The Polish Government-in-Exile in London approached the International Red Cross to examine the German allegations. All the evidence available at the time indicated that the massacre had been carried out in 1940, before the German occupation of the area. The Soviet Government denied this and used the move by the Polish Government as a pretext for breaking off diplomatic relations. Several attempts have been made since the war by the Polish groups in exile and by other bodies in the West to re-examine the crime, but the Soviet Government has refused permission to carry out investigations on the location.

Kautsky, Karl (1854–1938) One of the most influential socialist thinkers who, although at first a Marxist, was opposed to the revolutionary road to socialism. He was born in Prague, joined the Austrian Social-Democratic Party in 1874, later became a Czechoslovak citizen, but worked mostly in the German socialist movement. He moved again to Austria, 1924–38, but after the Nazi takeover he went to the Netherlands, where he died in the same year. He first met Marx and Engels in 1879, with whom he was closely associated till their deaths. In 1883 he founded and became the editor of *Neue Zeit* (*New Times*), a German Social-Democratic paper in which he opposed the REVISIONISM of E. BERNSTEIN. K. helped Engels in editing volumes II and III, and vol. IV largely on his own, of Marx's *Capital*. K. never accepted Marxism in full. He first rejected HISTORICAL MATERIALISM and the postulate of the DICTATORSHIP OF THE PROLETARIAT. At the controversial founding Congress of the SECOND INTERNATIONAL in 1889, at which he emerged as the most authoritative participant, he adopted a centrist stand and endeavoured to reconcile the right-wing group inspired by E. Bernstein and the left-wing faction led by K. LIEB-KNECHT, ROSA LUXEMBURG and F. MEHRING. In 1891 K. prepared the draft of the ERFURT PROGRAMME for the Social-Democratic Party of Germany, which was attacked by Engels as representing OPPORTUNISM and REVISIONISM. After the split in the RUSSIAN SOCIAL-DEMOCRATIC LABOUR PARTY in 1903, K. supported the MENSHEVIKS against the BOLSHEVIKS, and became a pacifist in opposition to Lenin's idea of a world civil war and Trotsky's PERMANENT REVOLUTION. In contrast to Lenin, K. maintained that imperialism did not necessarily lead to wars and advanced the concept of ULTRA-IMPERIALISM. He frequently criticized Lenin's policies after the Bolshevik Revolution for their unnecessary intolerance, cruelty and extremism, and similarly he adopted a negative attitude to the attempted Communist revolution in Germany in 1919. Lenin attacked K. (in *Proletarian Revolution and the Renegade Kautsky*, 1918) as a traitor to the Marxist cause. K. exerted great influence on the labour movement in central Europe both as an organizer and (particularly) as a theoretician. His main

works (originally published in German) are: *Thomas More and His Utopia* (1887); *Precursors of Modern Socialism* (1895); *The Agrarian Question* (1899); *The Social Revolution* (1903); *The Road to Power* (1909); *Internationalism and War* (1913); *The Origins of Christianity* (1914); *The Dictatorship of the Proletariat* (1918); *Terrorism and Communism* (1919); *The Labour Revolution* (1925); and *The Materialist Conception of History* (1927).

Kautskyism A less frequently used term for CENTRISM, of which K. KAUTSKY was the best known representative in the SECOND INTERNATIONAL.

Kennan Doctrine See CONTAINMENT POLICY.

Kennedy Doctrine A body of principles and assumptions which governed the anti-communist policies pursued by the US Administration under President J. F. Kennedy during 1961–63. It aimed at combating world communism by political, economic and ideological means, while military confrontation was relegated to the last resort. The doctrine emphasized peaceful tactics and replaced the DULLES-EISENHOWER DOCTRINE. At the same time the doctrine of MASSIVE RETALIATION was discarded and US military involvement in fighting communism was limited to local anti-guerrilla operations. The K.D. stressed peaceful engagement and assumed the possibility of settling East-West conflicts by non-military means.

Kerala A state of 39,000 sq. km. and 25m. people in south-western India, noted for the Communist prominence in local politics since 1957. It is the first state in world history where a Marxist government came to power by democratic elections. In 1957 the COMMUNIST PARTY OF INDIA won 60 of the 126 seats in the local parliament and with the support of the Independents, formed a government headed by E. M. S. Namboodiripad. In its two years in office, it carried out some far-reaching economic and social reforms. Owing to the pressure from right-wing parties and the national government, the Communists were ousted from power in 1959. A Communist coalition was returned to power in the 1967 elections. At the general elections to the Lower House of the Indian Parliament (542 seats) in March 1978, K. elected four deputies representing the Communist Party of India (the other three were elected by Tamil Nadu).

Kerensky, Aleksandr Fiodorovich (1881–1970) A Russian moderate socialist and Prime Minister, whose government was overthrown by the Bolsheviks in Oct. 1917. A lawyer by profession, he had frequently defended revolutionaries in Tsarist political trials. From 1912 on he was a deputy in the DUMA, where he led the SOCIAL REVOLUTIONARIES and then during W.W.I – the *TRUDOVIKS*. After the FEBRUARY REVOLUTION OF 1917, he accepted the post of the Vice-Chairman of the PETROGRAD SOVIET of Workers and Soldiers' Deputies, joined the PROVISIONAL GOVERNMENT as the Minister of Justice and then became Minister of War and the Navy. On 7 July (O.-S.C.) he became Prime Minister replacing Prince G. E. Lvov. He supported Russia's continued participation in W.W.I and after the failure of the KORNILOV REBELLION (Sep. 1917) proclaimed the Russian Republic, with himself as the President and Commander-in-Chief of the armed forces. He was opposed to a violent revolution and took several measures against the BOLSHEVIKS. He was one of the most eloquent speakers in Russian history, established a reputation for fair dealings, but proved too mild to cope with the great upheavals dominated by ruthless elements and unscrupulous men. Just before the outbreak of the GREAT OCTOBER SOCIALIST REVOLUTION on 24 Oct. 1917 (O.-S.C.), he left Petrograd (now Leningrad) for the front. The Bolsheviks arrested the members of his Government and seized power under the leadership of Lenin in less than two days. After several attempts to oust Lenin and the Bolsheviks from power, K. left Russia in May 1918.

He lived in Paris till 1940 and then in New York until his death (on 11 June 1970). His major publications (in English) include: *Prelude to Bolshevism: The Kornilov Revolt* (1919); *The Catastrophe* (1919); *The Crucifixion of Liberty* (1934); *Russia and History's Turning Point* (1965); and *The Kerensky Memoirs* (1966).

Ketteler, Wilhelm Emanuel von (1811–77) An early theoretician of the Catholic social movement in Germany. He was a Jesuit bishop active in politics, who fought for the independence of the church from the state. He advocated an improvement in the conditions of the working class and pressed for advanced social reforms in accordance with Roman Catholic doctrine. He urged his church authorities to establish co-operative societies to be financed by the church, independently of the state. He also pressed for far-reaching industrial and social legislation, ahead of his time. In his writings he highlighted the moral weaknesses of *laissez-faire* economy, the operation of which, in his view, could be improved only by the application of Christian ethics. His pioneering ideas were embodied in three books (in German), which aroused wide interest at the time: *Crucial Questions of Our Times* (1849); *The Labour Question and Christianity* (1864); and *Liberalism, Socialism and Christianity* (1871).

KGB (abbreviation in Russian of *Komitet Gossudarstvennoi Bezopasnosti*, meaning the 'Committee for State Security') The Soviet secret service organization, which is the largest organization of its kind in the world. It is believed to consist of 50,000 highly trained, disciplined and devoted professionals, plus about one million agents in the USSR and abroad. It was established under this name in March 1954, when it was separated from the *MVD* and made directly responsible to the Council of Ministers and the Party's Politburo (its Chairman being a member of both). It is a successor to the *MVD* (1953–54), the *MGB* (1946–53), the

NKGB (1941–46), the *NKVD* (1934–41), the *OGPU* (1922–34), the *GPU* (1922) the *CHEKA* (1917–22). Its responsibilities include: 1. the protection of state military secrets and political and economic information; 2. intelligence work (research, collection of data and dissemination to appropriate authorities); 3. the supervision of all Soviet nationals at home and abroad; 4. the detection and suppression of counter-revolutionary thought and activities; 5. the operation of the network of open and secret agents at home and abroad; and 6. the promotion and control of subversive activities abroad, closely cooperating with foreign Communist parties and other left-wing organizations.

Kharkov Incentive Scheme A method of linking bonuses to workers with enterprise profits, originally put forward by E. G. LIBERMAN, Professor of Economics at the Kharkov Technical University in the USSR. Although the principle of making bonuses dependent on enterprise profits was officially accepted by the Soviet Government in 1962 and gradually incorporated into the Soviet economic system, the K.I.S. was never implemented in the form originally advocated by Liberman, as it proved unworkable under Soviet institutional and economic conditions.

Khmer Rouge Communist armed forces originally formed in Cambodia in the 1950s and now still partly found in the P.R. of KAMPUCHEA. In the past, the K.R. operated as illegal guerrilla units (before 1970 and since Feb. 1979) and as the legal military arm of the Khmer Communist Party (1970–75) and of the Kampuchean C.P. (1975–79). Since the overthrow of the regime of Pol Pot in Feb. 1979, the K.R. has carried on guerrilla operations against the regime of Heng Samrin, who heads the KAMPUCHEAN UNITED FRONT FOR NATIONAL SALVATION, in the western borderland area adjacent to Thailand, receiving support from China.

Khozraschet A syllabic abbreviation in Russian for *Khoziaistvennyi raschet*, meaning 'economic accountability'. It is a basis of financial management of enterprises in the USSR, whereby enterprises carry on profit-and-loss accounting and are expected to be self-supporting and as efficient as possible. This system was introduced in the USSR in 1929. Enterprises which operate on this basis are: 1. independent legal entities, capable of entering into contracts with other entities on equal terms; 2. responsible for the resources allocated to them or acquired in the course of their legitimate business operations; and 3. free from direct budgetary control. Virtually all Soviet socialized enterprises (as distinct from public institutions) are on *k*. In the case of those entities which carry on economic activities but are not on *k*., their profits and losses are directly absorbed by the state budget.

Khrushchev, Nikita Sergevich (1894–1971) A distinguished Soviet Party leader and politician who emerged after Stalin as the dominant figure in the USSR. Born to a poor Ukrainian peasant family, he worked as a swineherd, coalminer, blacksmith and locksmith. He joined the Bolsheviks in 1918 and fought in the Civil War, 1918–20. From 1932 to 1938 he worked as Secretary in the Moscow Party Organization, was used by Stalin in various purges and effectively directed the construction of the Moscow underground railway. In 1934 he was elected to the Party's Central Committee and in 1939 to the full membership of the Politburo. He took an active part in the Great Patriotic War campaigns and reached the rank of lieutenant general. After Stalin's death, he successfully disposed of the ANTI-PARTY GROUP in 1955, became the Party's First Secretary and in 1958 the Prime Minister. At the height of his career, he held four top positions in the country: 1. First Secretary (now called Secretary-General) of the CC of the CPSU; 2. the unofficial head of the Presidium (now called the Politburo) of the CC; 3. Chairman of the Council of Ministers of the USSR (Prime Minister); and 4. Chairman of the Bureau of the Party's CC of the RUSSIAN

SOVIET FEDERATED SOCIALIST REPUBLIC. In Feb. 1956, he denounced Stalin for his unnecessary terror and personality cult (KHRUSHCHEV'S SECRET SPEECH). Under his leadership, in addition to DE-STALINIZATION, the USSR embarked upon far-reaching educational and economic reforms (which included the acceptance of profits after Sep. 1962) and signed the NUCLEAR TEST BAN TREATY (in 1963). K. accomplished one of the most difficult tasks that a leader may face in an autocratic state, viz. he initiated new directions of development along liberal lines, without losing control of events in the face of potentially explosive events at home and abroad. In foreign relations, he initiated the policy of peaceful COEXISTENCE (in 1956) and during the CUBAN MISSILE CRISIS (in 1962) he rose to the situation by avoiding a global nuclear war. K. was removed from power by his Party colleagues in a bloodless coup in Oct. 1964 while he was away from Moscow. But he showed no public resentment in the remaining years of his life.

Khrushchevism A term used by the Chinese Maoists to symbolize the Soviet distortion of Marxism that took place in the USSR and some other European Socialist countries when N. S. KHRUSHCHEV was in power. The features attributed to K. included REVISIONISM (especially the adoption of the profit criterion and emphasis on material incentives), the neglect of ideology, OPPORTUNISM, hierarchical elitist bureaucracy, SOCIAL IMPERIALISM, reconciliatory concessions and collusive policies in relation to the Western powers.

Khrushchev of China A derogatory description by Maoists of LIU SHAO-CH'I, especially by the radicals during the GREAT PROLETARIAN CULTURAL REVOLUTION in China. Like N. S. KHRUSHCHEV, Liu was accused of REVISIONISM, OPPORTUNISM and the betrayal of Marxism in general.

Khrushchev's Secret Speech A bitter attack by N. S. KHRUSHCHEV, then First Secretary of the CC of the CPSU, in his speech 'On Personality Cult and Its Consequences' against Stalin at the TWENTIETH CONGRESS OF THE CPSU in Feb. 1956. The speech lasted six hours and was delivered on 24 and 25 Feb. to a select group of 140 delegates (out of the 1,436 attending the Congress). His speech was not published in the USSR at the time, but its text was supplied to other Communist parties and soon found its way to the West. K.'s denunciation of Stalin and his rule dwelt on the disregard of SOCIALIST LEGALITY, dictatorial Party administration and departure from the principle of COLLECTIVE LEADERSHIP, the abuse of power for personal ends, the PERSONALITY CULT and unnecessary terrorism. When the essence of the speech became known, it caused a great sensation throughout the world. K. further elaborated publicly upon his disclosures at the 22nd Party Congress in Oct. 1961. Most observers within, and especially outside the USSR gave credit to K. for his personal courage and capable handling of the sensitive question long overdue for re-examination. But Stalinist diehards charged him with the initiation of discordant ferments in the Socialist bloc and the international Communist movement. They also accused him of excessive condemnation of a leader under whom the USSR had made outstanding economic and social achievements, defeated German invaders and helped save the world from fascism.

Kibbutz Co-operative farming settlement in Israel based on the collective ownership of all the means of production and consumption, the collective organization and operation of production and services (housing, transport, education, culture, entertainment) and the shared responsibility for virtually all aspects of the members' needs. It professes adherence to the Marxian principle of work and distribution, 'FROM EACH ACCORDING TO HIS ABILITY, TO EACH ACCORDING TO HIS NEEDS.' K.'s were developed after 1908 by Jewish immigrants from Europe who were socialists and advocates of ZIONISM, largely as a form of defence against cheap Arab labour. In the late 1970s, there were about 250 k.s in Israel, embracing over 100,000 people, or 3.5 per cent of the total population in the country. Although in several respects the k. resembles a Socialist COLLECTIVE FARM, it differs from the latter in that: 1. k.s were largely established by immigrant labour and financed by aid from international Zionist organizations; and 2. a k. operates in a basically capitalist economy under market conditions.

Kiental Conference An international socialist conference held at Kiental, a village in western Switzerland south of Lake Thun, from 24 to 30 April 1916. It was attended by 43 delegates from Austria, France, Germany, Italy, Norway, Poland, Portugal, Russia, Serbia and Switzerland. It followed the ZIMMERWALD CONFERENCE of Aug. 1915. At the K.C. the ZIMMERWALD LEFT had 12 delegates and gained a stronger position than at the Zimmerwald Conference. However, most of the delegates supported CENTRISM. The topics discussed included the ways of ending the war, the attitude of the working class to the peace settlement and the PARLIAMENTARY ROAD TO SOCIALISM. The K.C. adopted the ANTI-WAR MANIFESTO, submitted by the Russian delegation headed by Lenin.

KIM A Russian abbreviation for *Kommunistichesky Internatsional Molodezhi*, meaning the COMMUNIST YOUTH INTERNATIONAL (in existence from 1919 to 1943).

Kim Il-Sung (1912–) The North Korean Communist leader and statesman, Chairman of the KOREAN WORKERS' PARTY and President of the Democratic People's Republic of [North] Korea. Born to a middle-class family, he migrated to Manchuria in 1926, formed a Communist Youth League in 1927, joined the (illegal) Korean Communist Party (at the time part of the Chinese Communist Party) in 1931

and organized and led the Korean People's Revolutionary Army fighting the Japanese. During W.W.II he received military and political training in the USSR, participated in the Battle of Stalingrad in 1942 and reached the rank of captain in the Soviet army. He returned to North Korea in 1945 with the Soviet occupational forces and with Soviet support ruthlessly eliminated non-communist parties, united the existing three Communist parties into the Korean Workers' Party, of which he became Chairman in the same year. From 1948 to 1952 he was Prime Minister and in 1950 he became Commander-in-Chief of the Korean armed forces (and later was promoted to Marshal). In 1956, he crushed the opposition in the K.W.P. which pressed for de-Stalinization. His austere, ruthless and capable rule since that time has led to his PERSONALITY CULT. In 1972 he was appointed to the post of President of the Republic. In the Sino-Soviet dispute, although at first supporting China, he has adopted a shrewd independent course of 'national identity' (*Juche*). He placed some of his relatives in high positions in the Party and state hierarchy, including his son Kim, Chong-il.

Kirov, Serghiei Mirovich (1886–1934) A prominent Bolshevik who in his later years became critical of Stalin's policies. He appeared to be gaining increasing support but was assassinated. He joined the RUSSIAN SOCIAL-DEMOCRATIC LABOUR PARTY in 1904 and was one of the leading figures in the GREAT OCTOBER SOCIALIST REVOLUTION and the following Civil War. In 1923 he was elected to the Central Committee, in 1930 to the Politburo, and from 1925 to his death held the important post of the Secretary of the Leningrad Party Committee. He was assassinated by a young Communist on 1 Dec. 1934, probably on Stalin's secret instructions. The assassination was taken by Stalin as a pretext for promulgating the KIROV LAW, which was followed by unprecedented repression culminating in the GREAT PURGES and the *YEZHOVSHCHINA*.

Kirov Law Also known as Lex Kirov, a colloquial name for a legal act proclaimed in the USSR on 1 Dec. 1934 which required the courts and police to deal with the 'enemies of the people', especially involving cases of terror, speedily and summarily. It also specified that death sentences be carried out immediately. Thus the defendants were precluded from the possibility of appealing against their sentences. The law was named after S. M. KIROV, who was assassinated on the same day, probably on Stalin's orders. The K.L. became one of the characteristics of the GREAT PURGES which followed in the next four years.

Knights of Labor A shortened name for the NOBLE ORDER OF THE KNIGHTS OF LABOR.

Knights of St. Crispin A semi-secret union of shoemakers in the USA in the second half of the 19th c., noted for right-wing reactionary attitudes, on the one hand, and hostility to the introduction of machinery, on the other. Its first active lodge was established in 1867 and by 1870 it had 600 lodges with 50,000 members. After several disastrous strikes and the recession of 1873, the union declined. It was dissolved in 1878 and most of its remaining members joined the NOBLE ORDER OF THE KNIGHTS OF LABOR. Although Marxists applauded the union's strike actions and tight organization, they regarded it as an early misguided form of the labour movement, with PETTY BOURGEOIS policies designed to establish an aristocracy of labour.

Knowledge Ideas and facts acquired by the human mind in the process of COGNITION and thinking. Marxist philosophers insist that the human brain, consisting of highly organized matter, is capable of knowing the world and the laws governing its existence and operation. They view k. as a product of man's confrontation with OBJECTIVE REALITY, i.e. the active reflection of the material world, purposive thinking geared to human needs and, most

importantly, verified by practice. Marxists identify eight significant steps in the acquisition of k. They are: 1. sensation; 2. perception; 3. idea formation; 4. conceptualization; 5. appraisal; 6. inference; 7. hypothesis; and 8. theory. Also EPISTEMOLOGY, REFLECTION THEORY.

Koba One of the assumed names of J. V. Dzhugashvili, better known as J. STALIN.

Kolchak, Aleksandr Vasilievich (1873–1920) A Russian admiral and one of the organizers of the COUNTER-REVOLUTION against the Bolsheviks during the Civil War, 1918–20. He had distinguished himself in the Russo-Japanese war in 1905 and then in W.W.I. After the FEBRUARY REVOLUTION OF 1917, he was sent by the PROVISIONAL GOVERNMENT to the USA and Japan for discussions concerning the Russian participation in W.W.I. After his return in Nov. 1918, he became the Minister for War in the counter-revolutionary All-Russian Provisional Government in Ufa. Following a military coup against the A.-R.P.G. in Dec. 1918, K. proclaimed himself supreme ruler of Russia. His government was recognized by Britain, France, Italy, Japan and the USA. He led counter-revolutionary forces in the Urals and Siberia which advanced up to the Volga, leaving a trail of 'white terror'. He suffered several defeats from the Red Army after April 1919 and in Jan. 1920 he was succeeded by Gen. A. I. DENIKIN. K. was captured by the Czech Legion in Jan. 1920 and handed over to the Bolsheviks who shot him in Irkutsk the following month.

Kolkhoz The Russian abbreviated form for collective farm (*kollektivnoe khoziaistvo*). It is a type of production organization in Soviet agriculture (and fishing). These farms were first established in 1918, but a systematic collectivization drive did not take place until 1929. During 1950–53 a large number of *k.* were consolidated into larger entities and in the following decade the less successful *k.* were transformed into state farms (*SOVKHOZ*). *Kolkhozes* now occupy about one-half of agricultural land in the USSR and contribute some two-thirds of the total agricultural output. In 1976 there were 28,000 *k.*, on the average having 6,500 hectares and 5,000 head of livestock each. Each *k.* is a self-contained farming community. Legally, land belongs to society, but it is 'leased' to the members and the remaining means of production (buildings and equipment) and output belong to the members collectively. Members have a right to occupy SUBSIDIARY PLOTS (up to 0.5 hectare), can own private assets in the form of dwellings, indispensable farm buildings and implements and livestock (and, of course, personal and household effects). The *k.* is operated on a self-management basis. The general meeting of the members, or their representatives, elects a management board, headed by a chairman whose work is supervised by an elected auditing committee. There may also be other auxiliary committees for specific purposes (all governed by the *Kolkhoz* Statute of Nov. 1969). Remuneration is based on the quantity and quality of work performed (WORK-DAY UNIT). The gross income of the *k.* is distributed as follows: taxes and other payments to the state budget; the investment fund; collective needs (social security, contingencies, culture, and entertainment); and the balance is distributed as personal income.

***Kolkhoz* Market** One of the forms of retail trade in the rural areas of the USSR, in which members of the *KOLKHOZ* sell privately-grown produce on SUBSIDIARY PLOTS. Other types of persons who may participate in these dealings are workers on state farms and people living in the surrounding towns. It is a relatively free market, as prices are not fixed by the state but are set according to supply and demand. However, the state can affect the prices by influencing supply and demand and by changing the official prices in state retail trade. The items subject to dealings in the *k.*m. are fruit, vegetables, milk products, meat and various handicraft articles

made privately by the collective farmers or other persons living in the district.

Kolkhoznik Member of a collective farm (*KOLKHOZ*) in the USSR.

Kollontai, Aleksandra Mikhailovna (1872–1952) A prominent Russian social reformer, champion of women's rights and Soviet diplomat. A daughter of a Tsarist general, she joined the revolutionary movement at the end of the 19th c. as an agitator of women's rights and advocate of FREE LOVE. After the Revolution of 1905 she joined the MENSHEVIKS and from 1908 to 1917 she lived in exile (Europe and the USA). In 1915 she joined the Bolsheviks, returned to Russia after the FEBRUARY REVOLUTION OF 1917 and was soon elected to the Central Committee (the only woman on it). She participated in the GREAT OCTOBER SOCIALIST REVOLUTION and thereafter held several government posts and was active in the COMINTERN. She became the first People's Commissar (Minister) of Social Welfare and then was appointed to the ALL-RUSSIAN CENTRAL EXECUTIVE COMMITTEE – in spite of her previous Menshevik association and her links after the Revolution with LEFT COMMUNISM (1918) and WORKERS' OPPOSITION (1920). She also became the head of the Women's Section in the Bolshevik Party. But her advocacy and open practice of free love 'for the good of the Revolution' became an embarrassment to the Party leadership. From 1923 on she served in the Soviet diplomatic corps and attracted world attention as a capable ambassador to Sweden, 1930–45.

Kolokol (*The Bell*, in Russian) An important revolutionary bulletin published by Russian émigrés in London and Geneva between 1857 and 1867. It was founded by A. I. HERZEN, edited by him and by N. P. OGARIOV. It appeared first monthly and then fortnightly and was smuggled into Russia illegally. The bulletin was directed against Tsarist autocracy, publicized abuses by the Tsarist government and police (including various secret documents) and was a vehicle for populist and Marxist ideas. *K.* came to be highly regarded among revolutionary and liberal-minded Russians at home and abroad. Lenin later described it as 'the forerunner of the workers' press'.

Kombed Russian syllabic abbreviation for *Komitet Bednoty*, meaning COMMITTEE OF POOR PEASANTS.

Kombinat A term first introduced in the USSR in the 1930s to describe an industrial enterprise consisting of several plants usually located in different places, linked by common management and organized on a complementary basis. A vertical *k.* is one where separate establishments concentrate on different stages of production of basically the same article – from the processing of raw materials to the manufacture of the final product (typically found in the iron and steel industry). A horizontal *k.* exists where separate plants engage in the manufacture of different products from basically the same type of raw materials or using the same or similar technology (mostly found in the chemical industry). In Yugoslavia the term *k.* is sometimes used for a vertically integrated entity in rural areas engaging in agricultural production and/or livestock raising and also in the processing of the farming produce involved (and in some cases producing other manufactures from the locally available materials). In most other Socialist countries, this type of enterprise is known as the AGRO-INDUSTRIAL COMPLEX. In a loose sense, a *k.* may mean any large multi-plant industrial enterprise. In Poland, since 1972, the term *k.* has been replaced by 'Big Industrial Organization' (*Wielka Organizacja Przemysłowa* or *WOP*).

Kommunist The theoretical organ of the CC OF THE CPSU, published in Moscow and appearing 18 times a year. It was initiated by Lenin in 1915, when one issue appeared. But continuous publication began in 1924 under the title of *Bolshevik*, which

in 1952 was changed to *K.* The journal is concerned with the current problems of Marxist-Leninist theory, Party history, the international labour movement and the ideological aspects of arts and literature, indicating the official Party line. Articles are contributed by distinguished Party members and academics and by leaders of foreign Communist parties, including those from capitalist countries. The journal's circulation is 850,000 copies per issue.

Kompartia, *Kompartiya* A syllabic abbreviation colloquially used in the European Socialist countries for the 'Communist party'.

Komsomol The Communist mass organization in the USSR for young people of ages from 14 to 28. The name is a syllabic abbreviation of *Vsesoiuznyi Leninsky Kommunistichesky Soiuz Molodezhi*, meaning the All-Union Leninist Communist League of Youth. It was originally founded in Nov. 1918 on Lenin's initiative under the name of the Russian Communist League of Youth. After Lenin's death (Jan. 1924), its designation was changed to the Russian Leninist Communist League of Youth and two years later to the All-Union Leninist Communist League of Youth, but in practice the shortened name *K.* has been used. The main function of *K.* is to educate the youth 'in the spirit of communism, patriotism and internationalism'. It also participates in various campaigns – cultural, social and economic, including the construction of projects of national importance. Thus the city of Komsomolsk (in south-eastern Siberia), founded in 1932 and now having a population of over 250,000, was built initially by *K.* members. *K.* members also serve as leaders and advisers for the PIONEERS (10–14 age group). *K.* carries on extensive publication and propaganda work. Its main organ is *KOMSOMOLSKAYA PRAVDA*, but it publishes 150 other newspapers, about a dozen periodicals and in addition some 350 books and pamphlets each year, totalling about 23m. copies annually. *K.*

has the right to initiate legislation at different levels. The organization of *K.* is similar to that of the Communist Party of the Soviet Union (Congress, Central Committee, Bureau, Secretariat, Auditing Committee). In the late 1970s, the membership of *K.* was 36m., which constituted 20 per cent of the persons in the eligible age group. In the international scene, *K.* is affiliated to the WORLD FEDERATION OF DEMOCRATIC YOUTH.

Komsomolets, Komsomolka Male and female members of *KOMSOMOL*, the Communist League of Youth in the USSR.

Komsomolskaya Pravda (*The Communist Youth Truth*, in Russian) The daily official organ of the Central Committee of *KOMSOMOL*, the Communist League of Youth in the USSR. It was founded in 1925 and its main functions are to facilitate the education of the youth along Communist lines, as established by the Communist Party of the Soviet Union. It indicates the official line and is particularly directed against DEVIATIONISM and DISSENT. The paper's daily circulation exceeds 10m. copies.

Konstantinov, Fedor Vasilevich (1901–) A leading Soviet philosopher and ideologist, noted for his orthodox expertise in the fields of HISTORICAL MATERIALISM and the theory of indoctrination and social development. He joined the Bolsheviks in 1918 and later studied at the INSTITUTE OF RED PROFESSORSHIP where he completed his studies in 1932. He became Professor of Philosophy in 1934, and then Editor of *VOPROSY FILOSOFYI*, the leading Soviet journal of philosophy (1952–54), Rector of the ACADEMY OF SOCIAL SCIENCES (1954–55), Head of the Department of Propaganda and Agitation in the CC OF THE CPSU (1955–58) and Editor-in-Chief of *KOMMUNIST* (1958–62). In 1962 he was appointed Director of the Institute of Philosophy of the Academy of Sciences of the USSR. His main publications (all in Russian) are: *The Meaning of Personal Property and Work under Socialism*

(1938); *Historical Materialism* (1950); *Fundamentals of Marxist Philosophy* (1958); and he also edited *Historical Materialism* (1951) and *Philosophical Encyclopedia* (1957).

Korea, Democratic People's Republic of (*Chosun Minchu-chui Inmin Kongwaguk*) A country in East Asia ruled by a Communist party (KOREAN WORKERS' PARTY), with an area of 121,250 sq. km. and a population of 17.0m. (in 1978). Korea was formerly a Japanese dependency, but at the Cairo Conference in 1943 a decision was made by Britain, China and the USA that K. should be independent. This was further confirmed at the YALTA CONFERENCE (Feb. 1945). Owing to disagreements between the USA and the USSR, the country was divided into two zones, with the 38th parallel to be the demarcation line. The Japanese were driven out of North Korea in Aug. 1945 which was occupied by Soviet troops who formed a Communist-dominated government. In July 1946 left-wing political parties, dominated by the North Korean Communist Party and led by KIM IL-SUNG, formed the United Democratic Patriotic Front. In Sep. 1948 the D.P.R. of K. was formally declared as a sovereign state north of the 38th parallel, with its capital in Pyongyang (while in the south the Republic of Korea was proclaimed in the same year, with its capital in Seoul). By that time, Communist power had been firmly consolidated and Soviet troops left the country. The socialization of industry, transport banking and foreign trade was carried out in 1946 and economic planning was introduced in 1947. The confiscation of large and all foreign landholdings was effected in 1946, and full-scale collectivization was completed between 1954 and 1958. The industrialization drive began in 1957. A Constitution was adopted in Nov. 1948, subsequently replaced by that of 1972. The ultimate source of power is formally vested in the SUPREME PEOPLE'S ASSEMBLY, elected on a universal, direct, equal and secret ballot basis. But effective power is in the hands of the Party's Political Committee of 15 members headed by Chairman (KIM IL-SUNG). Although there are two other non-bourgeois political parties represented in the DEMOCRATIC FRONT FOR THE REUNIFICATION OF THE FATHERLAND, the latter is completely dominated by the Korean Workers' Party. The North Korean attempts to reunite Korea by a massive attack on South Korea led to the Korean War (June 1950 – July 1953), during which the United Nations supported the leading Western powers in defending S.K. The boundary was eventually restored along the 38th parallel. In 1972, secret talks between the two countries were held to seek reunification by peaceful means.

Korean Workers' Party (*Choson Nodondang*) The ruling Communist party in the Democratic People's Republic of [North] Korea. The Party's origin goes back to 1918, when the Korean People's Socialist Party was founded in Soviet Russia in Khabarovsk. In the following year it changed its name to the Korean Communist Party and moved its seat to Vladivostok. In 1925 it transferred its headquarters to Seoul but, as an illegal organization, it was soon eliminated by the Japanese. Its remnants were absorbed by the Chinese Communist Party in Manchuria. After the Soviet occupation of North Korea (Aug. 1945), the K.C.P. was legalized (Oct. 1945) and its name was changed to the North Korean C.P. (Dec. 1945). The returned Communists from China and from the USSR formed Communist parties of their own, which in turn were amalgamated with the N.K.C.P. in June 1949 under its present name and under the leadership of KIM IL-SUNG. The Party's highest formal source of power is the National Party Congress held every 4–5 years, at which the main Party organs are elected. The Fifth N.P.C. elected a Central Committee of 117 full and 55 alternate members and a Political Committee of 15 full and 12 candidate members. The Political Committee, headed by the Chairman (Kim Il-Sung) is the real

seat of power. The Party draws its mass support from the General Federation of Trade Unions (2.0m. members), the League of the Working Youth (2.7m. members), the Union of Agricultural Working People and the Democratic Women's Union. There are two political parties which are tolerated in the DEMOCRATIC FRONT FOR THE REUNIFICATION OF THE FATHERLAND, viz. the North Korean Democratic Party, and the Chondoist Chongu Party (a religious group supporting the regime). They pose no threat to the K.W.P. which completely dominates the Front. The membership of the K.W.P. is estimated at 1,800,000 (for 1978), compared with the country's total population of 17,020,000. The Party's main daily and periodical publications are: *Rodong Sinmun* (*Labour Daily*), the daily organ; and *Kunraja* (*Labourer*), the monthly theoretical organ of the Central Committee. The League of the Working Youth publishes a daily, *Rodong Chongyon* (*Working Youth*).

Kornilov Rebellion An unsuccessful attempt in Russia in Aug. 1917, led by General L. G. Kornilov (son of a Cossack officer), to remove the PROVISIONAL GOVERNMENT of A. F. KERENSKY in order to establish a right-wing military dictatorship. The march led by K. to seize the capital, Petrograd (now Leningrad), failed for two main reasons: 1. mass desertions from his army and a collapse of discipline; and 2. the mobilization of RED GUARDS by the PETROGRAD SOVIET for the protection of the city. The failure of K.'s design turned out to be a major factor in enhancing the power of the BOLSHEVIKS. To gain support of the left-wing elements, Kerensky released TROTSKY and several other Bolshevik leaders from confinement, whereupon the Bolsheviks then gained control of the Red Guards. Kornilov was removed from his command by the Provisional Government. But during the Civil War following the Bolshevik Revolution, he organized a counter-revolutionary force in the Caucasus where he was killed by the Bolsheviks in March 1918.

Korsch, Karl

Korsch, Karl (1886–1961) An outstanding German Marxist theoretician who, like the young LUKÁCS, was influenced by the success of the GREAT OCTOBER SOCIALIST REVOLUTION and the failure of the brief revolutions in the West in 1919. Korsch came from a middle-class background, was a student of law and joined the GERMAN COMMUNIST PARTY (KPD) in 1920. His *Marxism and Philosophy* (1923) (similar to Lukács' *History and Class Consciousness*) was criticized for its comment on Marx's debt to HEGEL, its criticism of Engels' excessive mechanical DIALECTICAL MATERIALISM and the need for a developed proletarian consciousness via an understanding of DIALECTICS. Korsch was expelled from the KPD as a consequence in 1926 and left Germany in 1933 for America, where he settled. His other main work is *Karl Marx* (1938).

Kostov, Traicho (1897–1949) A Bulgarian activist in the international Communist movement and statesman. He joined the Bulgarian Communist Party in 1920, participated in the anti-fascist uprising in 1923, became a member of the Central Committee of the BCP in 1931, editor of *Rabotnichesko delo* (*Workers' Cause*) – organ of the CC of the BCP, and the Party Secretary. During W.W.II he organized resistance against the monarchy and fascism. After the war, he became a Vice-Premier and proved to be one of the most active and capable leaders in the postwar reconstruction and the Socialist transformation of Bulgaria. However he fell victim to intrigues by the Moscow group led by V. CHERVENKOV. K. was falsely accused of treason, pronounced guilty in a show trial and executed in Dec. 1949.

Kosygin, Aleksiei Nikolaievich (1904–80) A Soviet Communist leader and statesman, by his background identified with the new technocracy. He joined the Red Army in 1919 (at the age of 15) and the ALL-UNION COMMUNIST PARTY (OF THE BOLSHEVIKS) in 1927. He was elected to the Party's Central Committee in 1939 and to the Politburo in 1948. From 1959 to 1960 he was a Vice-Premier and from 1964 to 1980 the Prime Minister (having replaced Khrushchev), collaborating with Brezhnev. K. has a strong background of economic administration. A graduate of a textile college, he was very active in the co-operative movement and for a short period, 1959–60, was Chairman of the *GOSPLAN*. He established a reputation for sound administration and economic commonsense. He resigned in Oct. 1980 due to ill health and was succeeded by N. A.Tikhonov.

Krasnaya Zvezda (*Red Star*, in Russian) The daily organ of the Ministry of Defence of the USSR. It was founded in 1924 and now appears as a newspaper, with a daily circulation of 2.5m. copies. It features articles on all aspects of Soviet military theory and practice. It concentrates on the latest developments and also devotes considerable space to the role of the military in Soviet society and the building of communism.

Kremlin The original fortified inner part of Moscow and, since March 1918, the seat of the Soviet Government. The K. became a residence of the Muscovite princes in the 14th c. First built in 1156, it represents some of the best examples of Russian architecture and houses the most valuable historical objects and works of art. Party Congresses and important state functions take place in the K. The May Day parade is held along its walls facing RED SQUARE and LENIN'S MAUSOLEUM. Metaphorically, the K. is identified with the Soviet establishment, in particular the autocratic rule imposed by the Bolsheviks.

Krestintern A syllabic abbreviation of the Russian *Krestiansky Internatsional*, meaning the Peasants' International. It was also known as the Red Peasants' International, to distinguish it from the GREEN INTERNATIONAL. The *K.* was founded in Moscow in Oct. 1923 as a revolutionary organization on the initiative of the COMINTERN and chiefly by the efforts of a Polish Communist, T. Dąbał, who became its Vice-Chairman. The function of the *K.* was to counteract the influence of the Green International, and in particular: 1. to develop access to small farmers and landless farm workers and integrate them into the Communist movement, especially in Eastern Europe and Latin America; and 2. to co-ordinate the activities of peasant organizations in order to achieve 'workers' and peasants' government'. The organization of the *K.* was patterned on that of the Comintern. But although the *K.* was to hold congresses every two years, it held only one conference in 1927 and never achieved any significant influence. It virtually ceased its activities in 1933 and its work was passed on to the *PROFINTERN* (itself disolved in 1937). The *K.*'s leaders (including Dąbał) were eliminated by Stalin in the GREAT PURGES and it was formally dissolved by the Comintern in 1939.

Krokodil (*The Crocodile*, in Russian) The leading Soviet satirical magazine, now appearing three times a month. It was initiated in 1922 as a weekly supplement to a newspaper *Workers' Gazette*. Among its contributors were such well-known personalities as V. V. MAYAKOVSKY, I. G. Erenburg and L. TOLSTOY. The circulation of *K.* is about 2.5m. copes per issue.

Kronstadt Uprising An anti-Bolshevik rebellion at Kronstadt, a naval base guarding Petrograd (now Leningrad), which occurred 7–18 March 1921. The garrison of the base (14,000 strong) sympathized with the strikes and demonstrations by Petrograd workers and protested against food shortages, political restrictions and the MILITARIZATION OF LABOUR. Influenced by the advocates of ANARCHISM and LEFT COMMUNISM, the garrison demanded the removal of the Bolsheviks from the PETROGRAD SOVIET and pressed for liberal economic and political reforms. The uprising was ruthlessly crushed by the Bolsheviks in a military expedition led by TROTSKY and TUKHACHEVSKY, and the survivors were summarily shot or imprisoned. However, Lenin recognized the basic causes of the rebellion and attempted to rectify them by embarking upon the NEW ECONOMIC POLICY in Aug. 1921.

Kropotkin, Peter Alekseievich, Prince (1842–1921) A Russian army officer, geographer and politician, but best known as the founder and theoretician of ANARCHO-COMMUNISM. He was sympathetic to the Russian peasantry and critical of the Tsar and nobility. Imprisoned for his efforts to organize workers, he escaped to Western Europe in 1876 where he wrote extensively on ANARCHISM. He stressed the role of mutual help and co-operation in the evolution of societies and disagreed with Darwin's theory of evolution, the STRUGGLE FOR EXISTENCE. K. insisted that man is by nature co-operative, if left alone by the state. He worked out a model of a communist version of anarchism, in which he combined the principle of the absolute freedom of the individual with the communal ownership of the means of production and consumption. He saw the future ideal society as a union of spontaneously formed independent production associations. Unlike his countryman, BAKUNIN (who postulated violent action), K. stressed peaceful propaganda. He thought that a changeover from capitalism to stateless communism was possible, which could be achieved by a revolution. His main publications (mostly in French) were: *Words of a Rebellion* (1885); *The Conquest of Bread* (1892); *Anarchism: Its Philosophy and Ideals* (1896); and *Mutual Aid: A Factor in Evolution* (1902). Although K. returned to Russia in 1917, he was disillusioned with the Bolsheviks and the DICTATORSHIP OF THE PROLETARIAT. K.'s views have come to be respected by social reformers in many parts of the world, including the most conservative Western countries.

Krupskaya Academy of Communist Upbringing A secondary teachers' college which was in existence in Moscow from 1923 to 1935 (and in Leningrad from

1934 to 1935). It was named after NADEZHDA K. KRUPSKAYA, Lenin's wife and a noted educationist. It was open to the members of the Communist party and of the KOMSOMOL with completed secondary education. Its function was to train secondary school teachers of the social sciences, i.e. those related to ideology. The course extended over four years and included general studies, specific teaching subjects and political indoctrination. In 1935 it was restructured and renamed the Krupskaya Communist Pedagogical Institute.

Krupskaya, Nadezhda Konstantinovna (1869–1939) Lenin's wife and a loyal participant in his revolutionary activities, social worker and educationist. She turned to revolutionary work as a teacher and propagandist among the workers in St. Petersburg (now Leningrad). She met Lenin in 1894 when she was 25 (two years older than him). Arrested for revolutionary activities, she asked to be sent to Siberia to join Lenin exiled in Sushenskoe, where they married in 1896. She joined the RUSSIAN SOCIAL-DEMOCRATIC LABOUR PARTY soon after its foundation in 1898 and took part in the REVOLUTION OF 1905–07. She assisted Lenin in editing revolutionary literature, engaged in educational work and developed a Marxist theory of education through work and vocational training (in *Popular Education and Democracy*, 1917). After the Bolshevik Revolution in 1917, K. became one of the leading organizers of adult education. She was also a co-founder of the Communist youth organization called the PIONEERS. In 1927 she was elected to the Party's Central Committee and later to the PRESIDIUM OF THE SUPREME SOVIET. After her death (in Feb. 1939) her ashes were buried in the Kremlin Wall, near LENIN'S MAUSOLEUM.

Kulaks (literally 'fist', in Russian) A term applied by the Bolsheviks to the rich landowning and labour-employing peasants in Russia and the USSR. They were regarded as members of the property-owning and employing class opposed to Communism. They were distinguished from the SEREDNYAKS (middle peasants) and the BEDNYAKS (poor peasants). The k. became the object of exploitation and persecution by the Bolsheviks and were finally eliminated as a class in Stalin's ruthless COLLECTIVIZATION drive, 1929–35, which, in turn, caused great dislocation and a loss of efficiency in Soviet agriculture.

Kulakization A term sometimes used in Cuba, Poland and Yugoslavia to describe the process of enrichment of workers-peasants in these countries. Such persons own small or medium farms, and in addition go to work in nearby towns. By deriving their income from two different sources, they are quite prosperous and subsequently are accused of having 'petty bourgeois' mentalities.

Kultprop A Russian syllabic abbreviation for *Otdel Kultury i Propagandy Leninizma*, meaning the Department of Culture and the Propagation of Leninism. It was a section of the Secretariat of the ALL-UNION COMMUNIST PARTY (OF THE BOLSHEVIKS) in the USSR from 1934 to 1939. Its task was to work out tactics for shaping public opinion in favour of Marxist attitudes and the policies followed or intended by the Soviet regime.

Kun, Béla (1886–1939) A Hungarian journalist and Communist leader. He joined the Hungarian Social-Democratic Party in 1902 and, when a prisoner of war in Russia in 1916, joined the RUSSIAN SOCIAL-DEMOCRATIC LABOUR PARTY. In 1918 he fought in the Russian Civil War on the side of the Bolsheviks and organized the Hungarian section in the RUSSIAN COMMUNIST PARTY (OF THE BOLSHEVIKS). After his return to Hungary, he was one of the founders of the Communist Party of Hungary which became the ruling party in the HUNGARIAN SOVIET REPUBLIC from March to Aug. 1919. K. was the virtual leader of the revolution and in the revolutionary government was Minister for

Foreign Affairs and a member of the Political Council. After the collapse of the H.S.R., he went to the USSR where he participated in the establishment of the COMINTERN and became a member of the EXECUTIVE COMMITTEE OF THE COMMUNIST INTERNATIONAL. While in the USSR, he organized and supervised anti-fascist resistance in Hungary. During Stalin's GREAT PURGES he was falsely accused and arrested in 1937 and executed in Nov. 1939. K. was rehabilitated after the TWENTIETH CONGRESS OF THE CPSU in 1956.

Kuomintang (National People's Party, in Chinese) A basically right-wing political party in China, founded by Sun Yat-sen in 1912, with which the CHINESE COMMUNIST PARTY co-operated at times but which was finally driven out of the Chinese mainland to Taiwan in 1949. At first, the K. pursued liberal and patriotic policies. It was reorganized in 1924 and with the assistance of the CCP was transformed into a revolutionary mass party, embracing the national bourgeoisie, peasants and workers to fight the warlords. On orders from the COMINTERN, Communists also participated but their party retained its separate identity. After the first revolutionary civil war, 1924–27, the right-wing faction in the K., under Chiang Kai-shek, took control and turned against the Communists, which ended in a series of massacres of the Communists and their sympathizers. The second revolutionary civil war followed, 1927–37, during which the remnant Communist groups were pursued (who escaped in the LONG MARCH to Yenan, 1934–35). The Japanese invasion of China forced the K. to co-operate with the Communists (largely on the latters' initiative) in the war against the Japanese (1937–45). Occasional armed actions were resorted to against the Communists, especially in the years 1939–43. After the war, the K. again embarked upon the destruction of the Communist forces, which resulted in the third revolutionary civil war, 1946–49. But this time the K. forces were defeated, some of who defected to the Communist side while the remnants fled to Taiwan. The K. has never recognized the Communists regime and for a long time was determined to re-establish its rule on the mainland. According to Communist sources, during the period of the K.'s rule 50m. Communists and their supporters were unnecessarily killed.

Kunmz The abbreviation of *Kommunistichesky Universitet Natsional 'nykh Menshinstv Zapada*, in Russian meaning COMMUNIST UNIVERSITY FOR WESTERN NATIONAL MINORITIES.

Kutv The abbreviation of *Kommunistichesky Universitet Trudiakhshchikhsia Vostoka*, in Russian meaning COMMUNIST UNIVERSITY FOR THE TOILERS OF THE EAST.

L

Labour Purposeful human activity directed to the satisfaction of human wants. It is a central concept in Marxist ideology, defined by Marx as 'a process in which both man and nature participate and in which man of his own accord initiates, regulates and controls the material reactions between himself and nature' (see *CAPITAL*, vol. I). Engels described l. as 'the basis and condition of human existence', 'it has raised man above animals' and is a 'basic factor ... in determining human personality' (in *Part Played by Labour in the Transition from Ape to Man*, written in 1876, first published in German, in 1896). L. is also regarded as the only or essential creator of value, as is postulated in the LABOUR THEORY OF VALUE. But Marx and Engels distinguished between l. and work, the former involving the process of the creation of EXCHANGE VALUE (products for sale in the market), while the latter consisting in the production of USE VALUE (products for consumption). Marxists further stress that the forms and content of l. are subject to historical changes according to the MODE OF PRODUCTION and the social conditions under which it is performed. Under capitalism, l. is essentially hired l. where the worker sells his L. POWER like a commodity and is exploited in the process by the capitalist. On the other hand, it is argued, in a Socialist economy there are no antagonistic classes, l. ceases to be a commodity, exploitation is eliminated and l. is utilized on a planned basis. The term l. is sometimes used symbolically in capitalist countries to represent the working class, as distinct from 'capital' identified with the property-owning and employing class. Also see below, and ABSTRACT L., COMPOUND L., CONCRETE L., HIRED L., INDISPENSABLE L., LIVE L., MATERIALIZED L., PRICE OF L., PRIVATE L., PRODUCTIVE L., SIMPLE L., SOCIAL L., SOCIALLY-INDISPENSABLE L. TIME, SURPLUS L.

Labour, Abstract See ABSTRACT LABOUR.

Labour and Socialist International An international organization of moderate socialist and social-democratic parties, created in Hamburg in May 1923. It was an amalgamation of the BERN INTERNATIONAL and the SECOND-AND-A-HALF INTERNATIONAL, which decided to join forces to continue as a successor to the SECOND INTERNATIONAL. The headquarters of the LSI were at first in London (up to 1926), then in Zurich (up to 1935) and later in Brussels (up to 1940). It was dormant during W.W.II, but in 1947 it was revived as the COMISCO (Consultative Committee of the Socialist International), which in 1951 became the SOCIALIST INTERNATIONAL.

Labour Aristocracy A concept used by Marxists in application to capitalist countries to describe the upper stratum of workers receiving above-average incomes or enjoying other special privileges, and whose mentality is closer to that of the BOURGEOISIE than of the PROLETARIAT. It includes sections of skilled workers and the bureaucratic elements of trade unions, co-operatives and social-democratic parties who, to protect their privileged positions, are opposed to the CLASS STRUG-

GLE. The early examples of l.a. in this sense were the KNIGHTS OF ST. CRISPIN and the NOBLE ORDER OF THE KNIGHTS OF LABOR. L.a. has been viewed as a deliberate product of bourgeois bribery, designed to separate the more capable workers and labour leaders from the working class movement and revolutionary struggle. Lenin accused the l.a. of OPPORTUNISM and REFORMISM.

Labour Book, Labour Card A record of basic personal details, educational qualifications, vocational training and employment, commonly issued to workers in the Socialist countries. The document is normally held in the personnel office of the employing entity and is returned to the worker concerned when he leaves his employment. It was first introduced on a systematic basis in the USSR in 1939.

Labour Code A set of regulations specifying rights and duties of the management and workers in the field of work in enterprises. The Socialist countries approach the l.c. on a more systematic basis than is usually the case in capitalist countries. Each enterprise has its own l.c., worked out by the general manager in consultation with the workers' council or trade union, which then becomes legally binding on both sides. A l.c. may lay down such conditions as: 1. the principles governing the organization and operation of the enterprise, especially management-workers relations; 2. the distribution of work time in the enterprise, its plants and of its workers in relation to their responsibilities; 3. the system of reporting and justifying absence from work; and 4. penalties for persons offending the l.c.

Labour Colony A refuge for the unemployed, usually operated by a charitable body. It made its appearance in the half century preceding W.W.I and later reappeared between the two world wars, especially in Britain, North America and Australia. It provided temporary accommodation and other aid for the unemployed. Unlike a colony organized on the

principle of COMMUNITARIANISM, l.c.s had no reformist ambitions but rather endeavoured to remove the most glaring symptoms of capitalism.

Labour Co-operative See WORK CO-OPERATIVE.

Labour Day A holiday falling on a work day, usually a Monday or a Friday, to celebrate an important achievement of organized labour. The actual date differs from one year to another and from one country to another. Thus in Canada and the USA it is celebrated on the first Monday in September and in New South Wales on the first Monday in October. However, labour movements in many capitalist and in all the Socialist countries celebrate MAY DAY – 1 May – irrespective of the day of the week.

Labour Discipline See WORK DISCIPLINE.

Labour Front A slogan popular in some capitalist countries (especially the USA), calling for the unity of the labour movement in its dealings with employers and the state. It implies 100 per cent union membership and co-operation among different working class organizations when negotiating with capital and the authorities.

Labourites A description applied to the members of the Labour Party in Britain and sometimes in Australia and New Zealand.

Labour Legislation See FACTORY ACTS.

Labour Lieutenants A description sometimes used for labour leaders, especially influential officials of large trade unions. The term appears to have been coined in the USA by Marcus A. Hanna (1847–1904), a successful businessman and employer, to parallel the term CAPTAINS OF INDUSTRY. The description l.l. implies that in a modern capitalist economy labour leaders are in a less commanding position than big business leaders.

Labour Party The main left-wing political party in Great Britain and one of the two major political parties (the other being the Conservative Party) in the country. It originated from the trade union movement and the political and social reforms in the latter part of the 19th c. Founded in 1900 as the Labour Representative Committee, it assumed its present name in 1906. It has traditionally followed a moderate course, lacking a strong theoretical commitment and has been noted for pragmatism and the acceptance of a peaceful, evolutionary and PARLIAMENTARY ROAD TO SOCIALISM. It has hardly ever collaborated with the Communists, and cooperated with the government's war effort (incl. W.W.I, W.W.II and the Korean War). It has also supported the British participation in NATO, though not enthusiastically, and condemned the Soviet invasion of Czechoslovakia in 1968 (as well as the US involvement in Vietnam). When in office after W.W.II (1945–51, 1964–70, 1974–79), it introduced far-reaching social welfare programmes and economic measures which substantially increased state intervention (nationalization, price controls, incomes policy, subsidization). However, it has not always received support from the trade unions. This is evident in some of the serious industrial disputes that have marred its periods in office.

Labour Party of New Zealand A moderate socialist party and one of the two major political parties in the country (the other being the National Party). It was founded in 1916 and its support comes mainly from industrial and white collar workers and Maoris. Although it temporarily collaborated to some extent with the Communists in the 1930s and 1940s, it has traditionally pursued a peaceful and PARLIAMENTARY ROAD TO SOCIALISM. When it was in office, especially 1957–60 and 1972–75, it extended state intervention in the economy together with generous social welfare schemes.

Labour Power A Marxian concept denoting the physical and mental capacity of the worker to perform labour to earn his subsistence. It is only a potential force, not actual work. Marx explained: 'The capitalist buys labour power in order to use it, and labour power in use is labour itself. The purchaser of labour power consumes it by setting the labourer to work.... The value of labour power is determined, as in the case of every other commodity, by the labour-time necessary for the production, and consequently also reproduction, of this special article' (see *CAPITAL*, vol. I). Also CONSUMPTION OF LABOUR POWER, VALUE OF LABOUR POWER.

Labour, Price of A concept used by Marx and Engels, which they defined as: 'The cost of production of a workman is restricted, almost entirely, to the means of subsistence that he requires for his maintenance, and for the propagation of his race.' (See *COMMUNIST MANIFESTO*.)

Labour Process A Marxian description of production and the creation of value. Marx identified three elements in the l.p.: 1. personal activity by the worker; 2. the object of the work; and 3. the means of production (land and capital) used by the worker. (See *CAPITAL*, vol. I).

Labour Reserve Army See RESERVE ARMY OF WORKERS.

Labour Theory of Abstract Thought The Marxist explanation of the origin and development of human intellectual powers. According to Marxism, thought derives from MATTER, and is not independent of it, and further, the capacity for abstract thinking has developed from the labour process. Work generated such elements of thought as memory, foresight, insight and reasoning. Abstract thinking has been associated with the development of language (see LABOUR THEORY OF LANGUAGE DEVELOPMENT), and language itself has facilitated the development of SOCIAL LABOUR and abstract thought. The capacity to think can be regarded as a general tool of labour. Thinking advanced to higher levels when special-purpose tools were invented. Thus, according to Marxists, thought has evolved out of the social background created by labour and cannot be divorced from the historical stage in which society is found. The supporters of philosophical IDEALISM disagree with the Marxist interpretation of thought development. In their view, abstract thought can be pure, independent of matter and labour. Also LABOUR THEORY OF HUMANIZATION.

Labour Theory of Humanization The Marxist theory explaining the evolution of humans from apes in terms of working for a living, involving the making and use of tools and weapons. The theory, which is opposed to the assumption of divine creation, is the cornerstone of HISTORICAL MATERIALISM and Marxist SOCIOLOGY. Darwin's general explanation of the evolution of man from ape did not completely satisfy Marx and his followers. The Marxist solution to the problem was provided by Engels in *Part Played by Labour in the Transition from Ape to Man* (written in German in 1876, first published in 1896). He reasoned that labour was the basic and most distinctive feature of humankind, and work and its results were responsible for the transformation of the primate into the human. The biological changeover to the upright posture freed fore-limbs, but it is only labour that transformed them into human hands, which are not only an instrument of labour but also its product. The growing complexity of labour and its concomitant language (see LABOUR THEORY OF LANGUAGE DEVELOPMENT) led to the enlargement of the brain and thinking (see LABOUR THEORY OF ABSTRACT THOUGHT). The theory explains the process of transition from the primate to man as a facet of the struggle for survival in nature under changed conditions and rationalizes the development of all abilities peculiar to man and superior to apes in terms of labour. It also provides explanations for further development of humanity – specialization, the increasingly

complex social organization and civilization in general. Thus in the Marxist view, it is not reason (as some philosophers hold) or soul (as theologians insist), but the capacity to turn some of man's energy into the means of producing other useful objects that distinguish him from animals. The theory has been largely rejected in non-Marxist thought, which has advanced theories of the bigger brain, brighter intellect and biological change instead.

Labour Theory of Language Development The Marxist explanation of the evolution of speech, attributed to social (co-operative) labour. The origin of language is seen in the need for the exchange of ideas by man in the process of earning his living, in particular making tools and weapons and organizing production. To start with, language registered and preserved the results of thinking in words and sentences, enabling the exchange of ideas among men. Speech served as a medium of communication in communal living and co-ordination between labourers, thus joint social and working activities led to a further development of speech. Language proved necessary not only for carrying on the work but also for showing, explaining and delegating work tasks to the members of the team or community. According to some Marxists, such as N. Y. Marr (1865–1934), language may reflect the class struggle, in that different social classes may speak different languages or dialects (see MARRISM). Stalin (in 'On Marxism and Linguistics', 1950) maintained that in the future, by a dialectic process, different languages would gradually coalesce into one international language, which would be achieved under FULL COMMUNISM. Although the l.t. of l.d. may explain changes in a particular language, it provides no explanation of the origin of speech and of different languages. Many animals noted for co-operative work habits, such as ants, bees and beavers, have not developed speech.

Labour Theory of the Evolution of Man See LABOUR THEORY OF HUMANIZATION.

Labour Theory of Value The Marxist doctrine of prices, according to which value is determined by the SOCIALLY-INDISPENSABLE LABOUR TIME embodied in the product and that individual market prices are, on the whole, proportionate to values. Value is represented in the well-known Marxian formula $c + v + s$ (see CONSTANT CAPITAL, VARIABLE CAPITAL, SURPLUS VALUE). Marx discussed the l.t. of v. mainly in *CAPITAL*, vol. I and III, but he himself had borrowed the idea from D. Ricardo (who had expounded it in 1817) and which had been supported by most British economists up to about 1870. However, Marx and later Engels gave the theory their own social interpretation, mainly in order to demonstrate the capitalist exploitation of labour and to enhance the theoretical role of the working class in the economic processes. The theory became one of the cornerstones of Marxist ideology applied to mid-19th c. capitalism. It rests on several simplifying, and not necessarily realistic, assumptions, viz.: pure and perfect competition; constant costs at any level of output; the homogeneity of labour; and the uniform ORGANIC STRUCTURE OF CAPITAL in all the branches of production. The theory has been subjected to severe criticism. It disregards the role of non-labour factors of production and underestimates the part played by the demand side in price formation. There is a lack of consistency in Marx's analysis. In *Capital* vol. III, in contrast to vol. I, he implied that constant capital (like variable capital) was capable of creating value (as distinct from transferring value); in effect, Marx abandoned the theory. Marx himself probably realized that to demonstrate exploitation under capitalism, it was not necessary to have the l.t. of v., as exploitation could in fact be demonstrated by the inferior bargaining power of labour compared with the capitalists'. However, Marx was probably not satisfied with the latter explanation, as the strengthening of labour's bargaining power (through trade unions) would imply that exploitation could be removed within the framework of capital-ism which, he insisted, must be destroyed. There has been a protracted controversy ever since 1917 as to whether the l.t. of v. is applicable to the Socialist planned economy. Ideologically and in principle the theory is accepted as valid, but to avoid the implication of exploitation under Socialism, surplus value is described as 'net product' or 'surplus product'. But in practical price management and economic planning, the theory is disregarded. In each Socialist country there is a TWO-TIER PRICE SYSTEM and further, each tier may be administered under the COMPLEX PRICE SYSTEM, where different degrees of price stability and flexibility are allowed to different categories of products. In intra-Socialist foreign trade, capitalist world market prices are accepted as the starting basis for negotiation. Also see EXCHANGE VALUE, VALUE.

Labour Time A Marxian concept denoting the period during which a worker expends his labour in production. It is measured in hours, days, weeks, and emphasizes the quantity of time spent rather than quality of the work performed. Marx explained that the socially-indispensable l.t. was that required to produce an article under normal conditions of production and with the average degree of skill and intensity prevalent at the time (see *CAPITAL*, vol. I). Under capitalist production conditions, l.t. consists of INDISPENSABLE L.T. and SURPLUS L.T., but under Socialism, where theoretically there is no exploitation, the respective components are called 'Labour Time for Oneself' and 'Labour Time for Society'.

Labour Turnover The mobility of labour from one entity of employment or another, usually measured as a percentage ratio of persons changing employment during the year to the total working force. L.t. differs from one branch of the economy to another and from year to year. Experience shows that in the Socialist countries it is not significantly higher or lower than in the capitalist world. It typically ranges from 5 to 20 per cent in both economies.

Labriola, Antonio (1843–1904) A socialist leader and the first Marxist theoretician and propagandist in Italy. Professor of philosophy at the University of Rome, he was a co-founder of the ITALIAN SOCIALIST PARTY in 1892. His philosophical views gradually changed from Hegelianism to Marxism and his main contributions were in the field of HISTORICAL MATERIALISM. He rejected ECONOMIC DETERMINISM and stressed the need for 'open Marxism', responsiveness to new scientific discoveries and adaptability to changing practical conditions. His main works were: *Against a Return to Kant* (1873); *Questions of the Philosophy of History* (1887); *On Socialism* (1889); *On Historical Materialism* (1896); and *Discourses on Socialism and Philosophy* (1897).

'Lada' The simplified name of the Soviet passenger car for export, domestically known as the *ZHIGULI*. The name L. has been chosen because it is short and easily pronounced and written in all languages, whilst *Zhiguli* is difficult to pronounce (as in Scandinavian languages) or has uncomplimentary meanings (as e.g. 'counterfeit' in Arabic, 'pimp' in French, 'vomiting' in Polish). The L. is produced at the Volga Automatic Works at Togliattigrad, constructed by Fiat of Italy during 1967–70, where 800,000 vehicles are produced annually. The L. is essentially based on the Fiat 124, but it has a stronger body and undercarriage and comes in several models. The L. is marketed in more than 50 foreign countries, including such motor car manufacturing countries as Britain, Canada, the FR of Germany, New Zealand, Sweden and the USA.

Lafargue, Paul (1842–1911) A French Marxist active in the French and international working class movements. He became acquainted with Marx in 1865 in London and married his second daughter, Laura, in 1868. He joined the FIRST IN-TERNATIONAL in 1866 and was active in the PARIS COMMUNE of 1871. Together with J. Guesde (1845–1922), he organized and led the French Workers' Party in 1880 and jointly founded its organ *Revue Socialiste*, later renamed *Socialiste* (1885–1904). He actively participated in politics and wrote several works on Marxist philosophy, ethics, religion and sociology, including *Idealism and Materialism in the Interpretation of History* (1895) and *The Problem of Cognition* (1910). He committed suicide together with his wife in 1911.

Laissez-faire ('Let things alone', in French) An extreme form of CAPITALISM based not only on the private ownership of the means of production, but also on the complete freedom of enterprise, competition, private profit and virtually no state intervention. This system first appeared in Britain towards the end of the 17th c. as a reaction against the mercantilist state control of the economy. But its philosophy was worked out by the French physiocrats (see PHYSIOCRATISM) and the British exponents of CLASSICAL BOURGEOIS POLITICAL ECONOMY. They maintained that economic activities are determined by objective economic laws which activate self-regulating processes, such that if everyone seeks his own advantage society as a whole would attain maximum benefit. The system reached its greatest development in the most advanced capitalist countries of Western Europe and North America in the 19th c. *L.-f.* began to decline after 1870 and was virtually abandoned after W.W.I for STATE INTERVENTION. The Marxist view is that *l.-f.* replaced mercantilism because the latter no longer suited the interests of the BOURGEOISIE. Marx's condemnation of capitalism was essentially directed at *l.-f.* capitalism during its peak period of development.

Lange, Oskar Ryszard (1904–65) An outstanding Polish socialist economist, social reformer and political leader. He joined the Polish Socialist Party in 1928 and supported its left wing. He went to

Britain and the USA on scholarships, 1934–37, and from 1938 to 1945 was professor of economics and statistics at the University of Chicago. After W.W.II he supported the Communist regime in Poland and occupied a number of high-level positions in the diplomatic service, academia, economic planning, the party and government. L. was Polish Ambassador to the USA (1945–48), a member of the Central Committee of the POLISH UNITED WORKERS' PARTY, Professor of Economics at the Central School of Planning and Statistics in Warsaw (1949–56) and its Rector (1952–55), Chairman of the Economic Committee of the Council of Ministers (1952–62) and Chairman of the Economic Commission for Europe (1957–59). He also advised Ceylon (now Sri Lanka), India, Iraq and the United Arab Republic (now Egypt) on economic planning. His scholarly interests included political economy, socialist economic planning, statistics, econometrics, cybernetics and sociology. He first established his international scholarly reputation in 1936–37, when in an article, 'The Economic Theory of Socialism' (published in the *Review of Economic Studies*, London), he refuted the thesis that a rational system of a socialist economy was impossible. He convincingly showed that rational prices were possible under Socialist economic planning and further outlined the basic features of MARKET SOCIALISM which could be superior to capitalism (see SHADOW MARKET, TRIAL AND ERROR METHOD). His main service to econometrics and cybernetics came in 1958 when, in the face of ideological constraints, he demonstrated that these two disciplines were in fact not inconsistent with Marxism and could be of great value to Socialist economic planning. His major works include: *Price Flexibility and Employment* (1944); *Theory of Statistics* (1952); *Introduction to Econometrics* (1958); *Political Economy* (1959); *Theory of Reproduction and Accumulation* (1961); *Optimal Decisions* (1964); and *Introduction to Economic Cybernetics* (1964).

Language See LABOUR THEORY OF LANGUAGE DEVELOPMENT.

Lao-dong A Communist Chinese term for physical labour to which considerable ideological importance is attached. In the official view, it is highly desirable for non-manual workers to take up physical labour, as it involves them socially and politically with ordinary labourers and peasants. *L.-d.* is expected from the CADRES. All students normally have to spend a part of their vacations working in communes or in factories, and army officers, up to the rank of general, usually have to serve one month a year as privates. The *l.-d.* campaign was first embarked upon in 1957 during the GREAT LEAP FORWARD, and reached its peak during the GREAT PROLETARIAN CULTURAL REVOLUTION (1966–69).

Laos, People's Democratic Republic of A small country ruled by a communist regime in South-East Asia, with an area of 235,700 sq. km. and a population of 3,550,000. It is bordered by China, Vietnam, Kampuchea, Thailand and Burma. Formerly a French dependency and then an independent kingdom, it went through a period of civil war from 1953 to 1974. In the two decades of the strife, Communist insurgents called the PATHET LAO, assisted by the VIET MINH of North Vietnam, fought the royal establishment supported by Thai mercenaries and US advisers and equipment. In 1974 the two sides agreed to form a coalition government which was immediately dominated by two Communist groups: the Patriotic Front of Laos (and its military arm, the Pathet Lao) and the People's Party of Laos. The two groups merged and created the PEOPLE'S REVOLUTIONARY PARTY OF LAOS which adheres to Marxism-Leninism, and which in Dec. 1975 proclaimed the P.D.R. of L. Far reaching reforms were immediately embarked upon and economic planning was adopted to speed up development. However, the country lacks stability owing to the serious conflicts among the pro-Chinese, pro-Soviet and pro-Vietnamese forces.

Lassalle, Ferdinand (1825–64) An outstanding German socialist regarded as one of the theoretical founders of socialism and a leading organizer of the labour movement in Germany. He was considered by Marxists to be a reformist. Born to a wealthy family, he became a lawyer, but turned to socialism in the late 1840s. He met Marx, contributed to the *NEUE RHEINISCHE ZEITUNG* and participated in the REVOLUTION OF 1848–49. He turned against the liberal bourgeoisie and in 1863 helped found the GENERAL GERMAN WORKERS' ASSOCIATION (which led to the formation of the SOCIAL-DEMOCRATIC PARTY OF GERMANY). He once said that all social classes, except the working class, were reactionary. L. was opposed to the CLASS STRUGGLE and strikes and was convinced of the validity of the IRON LAW OF WAGES. Instead, he emphasized the need for political action and the PARLIAMENTARY ROAD TO SOCIALISM. He advocated the organization of the economy into cooperative production associations under the auspices of the state to replace private enterprise. He supported the national ambitions of Germany and preferred to collaborate with the monarchical government (under Bismarck) pursuing right-wing reactionary and imperialist policies. His best-known publications were *Heraclitus the Obscure* (1857) and *The System of Acquired Rights* (1861). He died in a duel over a woman.

Later Ten Points (of the education of the masses and the cadres in China) See DOUBLE TEN POINTS.

Law A term that is used in two different senses in the ideological context. 1. *A principle regulating the relation between cause and effect.* While in philosophical IDEALISM a l. is treated in a subjectivist and voluntaristic light (SUBJECTIVISM, VOLUNTARISM), Marxism – in accordance with its philosophy of MATERIALISM – regards a l. as an objective relation independent of the human will. However, Marxists emphasize that while all laws of nature are immutable, some social laws are universal

and others change according to the MODE OF PRODUCTION. Thus the LAW OF THE CONCORDANCE OF PRODUCTION RELATIONS WITH THE NATURE OF PRODUCTION FORCES is a universal l., while the LAW OF COMPETITION AND THE ANARCHY OF PRODUCTION is peculiar only to capitalism, and the law of PLANNED PROPORTIONATE DEVELOPMENT is applicable to socialism. Some laws under socialism are formulated as merely desired objectives, to which other developments should be subordinated or which should condition other developments, as illustrated by Stalin's 'law of the constantly rising material and cultural requirements of the whole society' (BASIC ECONOMIC LAW OF SOCIALISM). 2. *A norm enacted by legislature.* Marxists regard laws in this sense as an expression of the will of the ruling class, designed to protect and strengthen existing social relations and institutions which are convenient to it. The implementation of the l. is ensured by the force of the state power. Marx and Engels pointed out (in the *COMMUNIST MANIFESTO*): 'Your legal enactments are raised to the level of law only by the will of your class, the will which represents the material interests of your class'. Marxists maintain that laws and the whole legal set-up cannot exist in themselves, that is, in isolation from the social system in force. It is further pointed out that l. has no ethical value in itself. It is officially admitted that under socialism l. is an instrument of state power designed to ensure the dictatorship of the proletariat and the perpetuation of communism.

Law No. 3. A proclamation made by Dr. F. Castro on 10 Oct. 1958 giving the right of landholding to each Cuban peasant. The Law had further widespread support in the countryside for Castro's revolutionary TWENTY-SIXTH OF JULY MOVEMENT and its assumption of power in Jan. 1959.

Law No. 120 A law in Czechoslovakia guaranteeing HUMAN RIGHTS to its citizens. It embodies two International Covenants on Human Rights originally accepted by the Czechoslovak Republic in

Law of Balanced Planned Development

Oct. 1968 and later, after the HELSINKI CONFERENCE, ratified by the Czechoslovak Federal Assembly in Nov. 1975. Czechoslovak DISSENTERS and the framers and supporters of CHARTER '77 have based their claim to greater personal freedom on the fact that the Communist regime does not honour its own laws, i.e. there are sufficient laws in Czechoslovakia to protect human rights, but the government chooses not to observe and enforce them.

Law of Balanced Planned Development See PLANNED PROPORTIONATE DEVELOPMENT.

Law of Capitalist Accumulation One of the laws originally formulated by K. Marx (in *CAPITAL*, vol. I) and later supplemented by Rosa Luxemburg (in *Accumulation of Capital*, 1913) concerning the transformation of a portion of SURPLUS VALUE into new capital. In Marxist ideology, the law is regarded as the main driving force of capitalism, responsible for SOCIAL STRATIFICATION, the IMMISERATION OF THE PROLETARIAT and IMPERIALISM. C.a. induces the CAPITALIST MODE OF PRODUCTION, and competition further drives the capitalist to innovations and a larger scale of production, leading to the CONCENTRATION AND CENTRALIZATION OF CAPITAL AND PRODUCTION and to monopolies. This also leads to the increasing RESERVE ARMY OF WORKERS, since CONSTANT CAPITAL tends to grow faster than VARIABLE CAPITAL. Rosa Luxemburg pointed out that in a closed capitalist economy the scope for appreciable c.a. was limited. Consequently, in a dynamic developed capitalist economy, the bourgeois state is impelled to favour military production and resort to the penetration or conquests of weaker nations (see COLONIALISM), where surplus value can be realized and appropriated by capitalists (through low prices of raw materials and high prices of final products).

Law of Combined Development A belief held by some Marxists (including Lenin and Trotsky) that a particular country can experience several lines of economic and social development, each with a different degree of advancement. Thus the peasantry may be still in the medieval stage, the bourgeoisie in the mercantilist phase, while the proletariat may be developing along the lines of industrial capitalism. This situation apparently existed in the pre-revolutionary Russia. Invoking the l. of c.d., Trotsky (in *History of the Russian Revolution*, 1932–34) explained why, contrary to Marxist tenets, a successful proletarian revolution had occurred in a backward agricultural country like Russia.

Law of Competition and of the Anarchy of Production According to Marxists, the inevitable economic feature of capitalism, where the production of the products are shaped spontaneously in the unruly market among rival participants without planning. The operation of the law is basically attributed to the contradiction between the social character of production (involving the division of labour and co-operation) and the private ownership of the means of production. The latter, prompted by private profit, drives the producers to individualism, independence and rivalry. The operation of the law is best reflected, in the Marxist view, in periodical over-production and crises.

Law of Diminishing Returns An economic law according to which after a stage each successive addition to a particular factor of production results in a less than proportional increase in output. In effect, efforts to increase production inevitably lead to increasing unit costs (declining marginal product or increasing marginal cost). The law was formulated by classical economists in Western Europe in the 18th and 19th c. (by A. R. Turgot, T. R. Malthus, D. Ricardo, L. M. Walras, V. Pareto and others). It was first discussed in reference to agriculture, but was extended to all branches of production. The law received a good deal of attention from classical Marxist economists, especially Marx, Engels (mostly in mutual correspondence) and Lenin (in *The Agrarian Question and the 'Critics of Marx'*, 1901). Although they conceded its possible applicability in static conditions, they rejected its validity in a changing progressive economy. They, and later Socialist economists, also pointed out that average outlays of materialized and live labour (per unit of output) have been decreasing with expanding production, which is made possible through scientific and technical progress. On these grounds, Marxist economists largely reject the concept of scarcity. In their view the assumption of the fixity of 'other factors of production' is not justified in the long run. Marxists regard the l. of d.r., as formulated by the bourgeois economists, as a convenient theoretical justification for the inequality of income, especially the poverty of the working class.

Law of Distribution According to Work See DISTRIBUTION ACCORDING TO WORK.

Law of Increasing Proletarian Misery See IMMISERATION OF THE PROLETARIAT.

Law of Planned Proportionate Development See PLANNED PROPORTIONATE DEVELOPMENT.

Law of Primitive Socialist Accumulation See PRIMITIVE SOCIALIST ACCUMULATION.

Law of the Concordance of Production Relations with the Nature of Production Forces One of the Marxist laws of socio-economic development, emphasizing the link between the two sides of the MODE OF PRODUCTION. The law was first formulated by Marx (in a letter to P. V. Annenkov in Dec. 1846) and further elaborated upon by Lenin and Stalin as constituting a foundation for HISTORICAL MATERIALISM. The mode of production is determined by the character of production forces which shape the corresponding production relations among the members of society. If production relations correspond to the level of development of the production forces, the development of the approp-

riate SOCIO-ECONOMIC FORMATION proceeds smoothly. If not, the maladjustments are in due time rectified by a revolutionary upheaval. The law applies to pre-Socialist as well as Socialist societies. But in the former, vested private interests tend to impede the adaptation of production relations to the changing character of the production forces, which generates antagonistic contradictions leading to revolutionary situations. On the other hand, Marxists claim that under Socialism there are no antagonistic social classes, and that necessary readjustments are made on a systematic planned basis removing the need for social upheavals.

Law of the Concordance of the Superstructure with the Material Base A Marxist law of social development, according to which the SUPERSTRUCTURE (legal, political, moral and cultural institutions and social consciousness) is essentially determined by the material BASE (factors and methods of production). Changes in the character of PRODUCTION FORCES and the techniques of production necessarily bring about readjustments in the non-material organization and activities of society, which may lead to a new SOCIO-ECONOMIC FORMATION. Under capitalism, the material base gives rise to the bourgeois state and law, bourgeois morality and philosophy, bourgeois culture and other associated bourgeois institutions. In contemporary Socialist societies, characterized by the social ownership of the means of production, the superstructure corresponding to the material base includes such elements as Marxist ideology, the mono-party system of government, the Socialist state, economic planning, Socialist morality and (culturally) SOCIALIST REALISM. In a class society, Marxists claim, the dominant role in the superstructure is played by those ideas and institutions which represent the interests of the ruling class. These elements of the superstructure play an important part in preserving and strengthening the social relations as they are, in order to ensure the continuation of the existing socio-economic formation. Consequently, to some extent the superstructure also exerts some influence over the material base.

Law of the Declining Profit Rate See DE-CLINING PROFIT RATE, LAW OF.

Law of the Development of the Mode of Production See MODE OF PRODUCTION.

Law of the Increasing Misery of the Pro-letariat See IMMISERATION OF THE PRO-LETARIAT.

Law of the Priority of Growth of Depart-ment I One of the laws in the Marxist theory of development applied to capital-ist as well as the Socialist economies, pos-tulating a faster expansion of output in the branches producing the means of produc-tion (DEPARTMENT I) than in those pro-ducing the means of consumption (DE-PARTMENT II). In the Marxist view, this is essential if: 1. the rate of growth of nation-al income is to increase, the capital-output ratio being constant; and 2. the rate of growth of national income is to be main-tained at a constant level while the capital-output ratio increases. In such cases, in-vestment must expand faster than con-sumption. An expression of the adherence to this law in the Socialist countries has been the restriction of current consump-tion in favour of high and rising propor-tions of national income channelled to investment. Several modern Socialist economists have questioned the universal validity of this 'law'. They maintain that while the observance of the law may be desirable in the early stages of economic development, the adherence to it may be unnecessary or even harmful once a reasonable level of development is at-tained. High rates of growth of national income may be generated by a faster growth of Department II than of Depart-ment I.

Law of the Transformation of Quantita-tive Changes into Qualitative Develop-ment See QUALITATIVE DEVELOPMENT AND LEAPS.

Law of Uneven Development An economic law attributed by Marxists to capitalism, which states that different countries develop at different rates and consequently reach the stage of maturity for a PROLETARIAN REVOLUTION at differ-ent times. The uneven incidence of economic development applies to differ-ent firms, branches of the economy and whole nations, as under the conditions of private enterprise they have different capacities of adaptation to changes in technology and market demand. There-fore some entities develop faster and often at the expense of others through cut-throat competition. The disparities in de-velopment become most striking in the era of IMPERIALISM, owing to the CONCEN-TRATION AND CENTRALIZATION OF CAPI-TAL AND PRODUCTION, the growth of MONOPOLIES, the exploitation of colonies and the 'imperialist wars' (W.W.I and W.W.II). On the basis of the analysis along these lines, Lenin argued (in *IM-PERIALISM: THE HIGHEST STAGE OF CAPITALISM*) that it was futile to wait until all countries were ready for a PRO-LETARIAN REVOLUTION. He indicated that there was a possibility of the victory of revolution initially in one or only a few countries. The uneven development of the remaining countries, he further argued, would prevent capitalist nations uniting and attacking the successful Communist regimes. Similarly, in the 1920s, Stalin attacked Trotsky's idea of PERMANENT REVOLUTION. The former maintained that SOCIALISM IN ONE COUNTRY (in the USSR) could be successfully established and defended, even if no other countries were mature enough for it.

Law of Value The Marxist doctrine of long-run prices, according to which value is determined by average SOCIALLY-INDISPENSABLE LABOUR (materialized and live), even though individual prices may deviate in the short run. This law, formulated by Marx (in *CAPITAL*, vols I and II), is deemed to be applicable to commodity production (i.e. goods pro-duced for the market), irrespective of the social system in force. The law, according to Marxists, plays a strategic role in the capitalist market economy as: 1. it operates spontaneously – and not only in the market for products, but also in the market for the means of production (land and capital) and labour; 2. it regulates the division of labour in society; 3. it subordinates the structure of production and directions of development to the whimsical market forces; 4. it induces the CONCENTRATION AND CENTRALIZATION OF CAPITAL AND PRODUCTION in certain industries; 5. it eliminates those producers who are unable to follow and anticipate the anarchical market mechanism, which results in bankruptcies (especially of small, struggling firms and craftsmen) and unemployment; 6. it creates powerful material motivation for innovations and technological progress in general; 7. it operates in the most distorted fashion under MONOPOLY CAPITALISM, where monopolists manipulate prices (usually fixing them above PRODUCTION PRICES), restrict output and earn more than the AVERAGE PROFIT RATE; and 8. it leads to the extension of the markets domestically as well as internationally, and in the past was indirectly responsible for colonialism and inter-imperial wars. The question of the applicability of the law to the Socialist planned economy has been a subject of great controversy among Marxists. The operation of the law in the USSR was officially denied up to 1941. During the following decade it was held among the Soviet economists that the law functioned under socialism, but in a 'transformed' manner. Stalin (in *Economic Problems of Socialism in the USSR*, 1952) criticized the existing view and pointed out that if an economic law operates, it does so 'objectively', irrespective of human will. But he restricted the functioning of the law to the sphere of private consumption. There has been a lively discussion on the law since the mid-1950s in all the Socialist countries, with views ranging from its complete rejection to its entire acceptance. In economic planning and development strategies, little notice has been taken of

the l. of v. In fact neither enterprise accounting nor the national statistical systems are geared to the recording of production data in Marxist value terms. The existence of different types of prices (COMPLEX PRICE SYSTEM, TWO-TIER PRICE SYSTEM), the BUCHAREST AGREEMENT, the MOSCOW AGREEMENT and the existing pricing confusion, all indicate that the application of the l. of v. in the Socialist economic practice is neither possible nor desirable, at least at this stage.

Law of Variable Returns LAW OF DIMINISHING RETURNS.

Laws of Supply and Demand Law explaining causal relationships between the supply of, and demand for, goods and services on the one hand, and prices on the other, and vice versa. Thus increased supply, all things being constant, normally leads to lower prices, increased demand – to higher prices, as lower prices tend to reduce supply but expand demand. These laws operate in free markets and are important elements in a capitalist private enterprise economy. In a Socialist centrally planned economy, these laws operate only in free markets where they are still tolerated: 1. in the local markets for privately grown and traded produce and craftwork (*KOLKHOZ MARKET*); and 2. in a modified form, in the consumer goods market, where the freedom of consumer's choice is accepted and the authorities are anxious to maintain market equilibrium (i.e. to avoid shortages and surpluses). The laws do not operate in the 'organized markets' for producer goods, the output and distribution of which are determined directly by economic planning. Since the economic reforms (in Yugoslavia in the early 1950s and in other European Socialist countries in the 1960s), the role of the l. of s. and d. has been extended, especially in Yugoslavia and Hungary.

Lazarus Layers A term sometimes used by social reformers and Marxists to describe the poorest sections of society under capitalism. These include servants, casual labourers, beggars, the unemployed and the homeless, slum-dwellers and the under-privileged in general. The term is derived from Lazarus, a biblical character symbolizing a destitute beggar. Marxists regard L.l. as being peculiar to pre-Socialist societies noted for the private ownership of the means of production, concentrated in the hands of the higher social classes, the exploitation of labour and the absence or inadequacy of social welfare schemes.

League of Communists of Yugoslavia (*Savez Komunista Jugoslavije*) The ruling and the only legal political party in Yugoslavia and the eighth largest Communist party in the world (after those of China, the USSR, Romania, Poland, the German DR, the DPR of Korea and Italy). Its origin can be traced back to 1918, when the Yugoslav Section of the RUSSIAN COMMUNIST PARTY (OF THE BOLSHEVIKS) was formed in Soviet Russia by former prisoners of war. At the unification congress held in Belgrade in 1919 the Socialist Workers' Party was founded (which included both socialists and communists), but in the following year its name was changed to the Communist Party of Yugoslavia, and then in 1952 to its present designation. The Party and its military arm, the 'Partisans', led by J. TITO, played an important part in the resistance against the German and Italian invaders and the puppet government created by the occupying powers. After the war it took over power, having ruthlessly eliminated the opposition – the right-wing *Chetniks* led by D. MIHAJLOVIĆ. In 1978 the League's membership stood at 1.6m. (compared with the country's total population of 22.0m.). The highest formal level of the League's authority is the Congress, held roughly every four years, at which the main League's organs are elected. The 11th Congress, held in June 1978 and attended by 2,291 delegates, elected a Central Committee of 165 members. The latter elected a Presidium of 24 (formerly 69) members headed by President (J. Tito), the latter constituting the real seat

of power in the country. The League exercises its political and social influence in the country largely through a type of electoral front, the SOCIALIST ALLIANCE OF THE WORKING PEOPLE OF YUGOSLAVIA, the largest political organization in the country, with 8.6m. members. The League's mass organization for the young people (14–27 years) is the League of Socialist Youth of Yugoslavia, embracing more than 3.5m. members (60 per cent of those eligible). The official regular publications of the L.C.Y. are: *Borba* (Struggle), the daily organ of the S.A.W.P.Y.; *Komunist*, the weekly organ of the Central Committee of L.C.Y.; and *Socijalizam* (Socialism), a bi-monthly theoretical organ of the C.C. of the L.C.Y.

League of Militant Atheists An organization which existed in the USSR from 1925 to 1943 for the purpose of disseminating anti-religious propaganda and promoting ATHEISM. It also engaged in various provacative actions to justify the persecution of priests and believers and the closing down of churches. It was headed by the Central Council which published *Antireligioznik* (*The Godless Man*) from 1926 to 1941. The League was revived after W.W.II under the less demagogic name of the All-Union Society for the Dissemination of Scientific and Political Knowledge, which in 1960 began publishing *Science and Society*.

League of Russian Revolutionary Social Democrats Abroad A semi-revolutionary association of Russian moderate socialists, which existed in Western Europe from 1894 to 1905. The League was established by the EMANCIPATION OF LABOUR GROUP, it was active among Russian political emigrés especially in England and Switzerland and published its own bulletin called *Rabotnik* (*The Worker*). Although the League at first cooperated with Lenin after 1900, it became increasingly preoccupied with the economic improvement of the working class in Russia, and less interested in a violent revolutionary programme. After the split in the RUSSIAN SOCIAL-DEMOCRATIC LABOUR PARTY in 1903, it supported the Menshevik faction.

League of Struggle for the Liberation of the Working Class A short-lived revolutionary association in Russia, in existence in 1895–96. It was organized by Lenin assisted by N. KRUPSKAYA (who later became Lenin's wife) in St Petersburg (now Leningrad), but it soon spread its activities to other leading industrial cities of Tsarist Russia. It had a nucleus of a Communist party, with a Secretary-General (Lenin), a Central Committee, a disciplined membership with a militant outlook, and was in close touch with the masses. The League staged several industrial actions, including a successful strike in St Petersburg in 1896. Its strength was weakened after 1895 when Lenin was arrested and exiled to Siberia. The League represented the first attempt in Tsarist Russia to combine Marxist propaganda with organized work among workers, and as such may be regarded as the forerunner of the Communist Party of the Soviet Union.

League of the Just A secret socialist society of German émigré workers in Belgium, Britain, France, Italy and Switzerland, which was active in the 1840s. In 1847 Marx and Engels joined its Brussels branch, ousted the existing leader (Wilhelm Weitling), reorganized it and renamed it the COMMUNIST LEAGUE. Later in that year at a meeting of the reconstituted League in London, Marx and Engels were commissioned to prepare a declaration of its objectives. The declaration, prepared in German and published in Feb. 1848, was the *COMMUNIST MANIFESTO*.

'Leaning to all Sides' A phrase used in China to describe the policy of the regional diversification of Chinese foreign trade after 1960. The policy was a reaction against the 'LEANING TO ONE SIDE' drive over the period 1949–60 and amounted to a substantial diversion of trade towards Western and less-developed countries. The main reasons for this reversal of the previous policy were: 1. the SINO-SOVIET DISPUTE; 2. the need for large grain imports, which could be obtained only from capitalist countries; 3. the need for more advanced equipment and technology, which could be obtained only fom the West; and 4. the desire to extend closer political and economic relations with the countries of the Third World. While in the early 1950s four-fifths of China's foreign trade was with the Socialist bloc, by the late 1970s the proportion declined to one-fifth.

'Leaning to one Side' A slogan underlying the foreign trade policy in China over the period 1949–60. The policy was first foreshadowed by Mao Tse-tung in a statement 'On the People's Democratic Dictatorship' in June 1947, when it was clear that the tide of the Civil War had turned in the Communists' favour. The adoption of this policy was prompted by several circumstances, viz.: 1. the ideological affinity with other Socialist countries engendered by a successful revolution in China; 2. Soviet credits and technological aid extended to China on generous terms; 3. the COLD WAR in East–West relations; and 4. the Western STRATEGIC EMBARGO, which was particularly severe in relation to China. L. to o.s. enabled China to benefit from the economic support by the European Socialist countries without having to join the CMEA, which might otherwise have impeded Chinese ambitions for self-sufficiency. The peak of the policy was reached during the Korean War in 1952 when nearly 80 per cent of China's foreign trade was with other Socialist countries. This proportion began to decline after 1955 and was later accentuated by the Sino-Soviet dispute. In 1961 the policy was replaced by the phrase 'LEANING TO ALL SIDES'.

Leap An important concept in the Marxist philosophy of history, denoting a sudden change from one state, form or motion to another, either in nature or society. The idea was originally advanced by HEGEL, but received an elaborate ideological interpretation from PLEKHANOV (in *Development of the Monist View of History*, 1895) and Stalin (in *Foundations of Leninism*, 1924). The l. occurs as a result of a gradual accumulation of hidden quantitative changes released suddenly in a breakthrough, leading to a new qualitative state or motion. The main ideological significance of this concept is that it rationalizes the need for a revolutionary change from one social system to another. Consequently, in order to replace capitalism by socialism, a PROLETARIAN REVOLUTION is unavoidable, making the PARLIAMENTARY ROAD TO SOCIALISM, REFORMISM and REVISIONISM in the ultimate analysis insufficient, and in fact retrogressive. Leaps apply only to pre-Socialist societies, where there are antagonistic class relations, impeding quantitative and qualitative adjustments to the changes in the material conditons of production. Once the exploiting classes are eliminated under Socialism, progress can be continuous and gradual, facilitated by central economic planning. Thus it is maintained that the transition from Socialism to Communism will not be effected by a l. but will take place gradually in a peaceful manner. The supporters of METAPHYSICS disagree with the Marxist view, and emphasize that the transition from one qualitative state to another is evolutionary, not revolutionary, and without leaps. C. Linnaeus (1707–78), a Swedish botanist, formulated the well-known principle, '*Natura non facit saltum*' (Nature does not proceed by leaps).

Leap Forward See GREAT LEAP FORWARD.

'Learn from Tachai' Campaign See TACHAI CAMPAIGN.

'Learn from Taching' Campaign See TACHING CAMPAIGN.

'Learn from the PLA' Campaign A movement launched in China in Feb. 1964 by Mao Tse-tung to emulate the PEOPLE'S LIBERATION ARMY, anticipating the Great Proletarian Cultural Revolution. The Campaign was prompted by Mao's determination to strengthen his position in the showdown with rival political leaders. Through the Campaign he was assured that the PLA was on his side and that it was becoming very influential. The Campaign involved the formation of 'political departments' in factories, communes and educational establishments, which were not only patterned on the PLA but were also manned by PLA personnel. These departments were concerned with political control and propaganda. The Campaign also included such drives as the 'FOUR FIRSTS' and the THREE-EIGHT WORKING STYLE.

LEF A Soviet futurist literary group which existed from 1923 to 1930. Its name was derived from *Levyi Front Iskusstv*, meaning the Left Front in the Arts. Its main initiator was an outstanding Russian revolutionary and futurist poet V. V. MAYAKOVSKY. The group (to which B. L. Pasternak also belonged at one stage) published a literary journal also called *LEF* from 1923 to 1925 and *Novyi LEF* (New Lef) in 1927–28, each of which was a mouthpiece of FUTURISM in the service of political and social objectives of the Soviet government. The *LEF* exerted great influence during a formative phase of Soviet art. In 1929 the *LEF* was transformed into the *REV* (*Revolutsionnyi Front Iskusstv*, Revolutionary Front in the Arts).

Left A term describing an ideology, a person, a group or a political party, ranging from moderate socialist to radical and revolutionary communist. The designation, which is used both as an adjective and a noun, was introduced during the French Revolution in May 1789, at the first joint meeting of the Estates General. At that session, the Third Estate (bourgeoisie) were placed to the left of the presiding king (while the nobility sat on the king's right). This arrangement was meant to identify the L. with the 'residual', 'odd' or 'sinister'. The term has also been used in the Socialist countries for extreme Communists, more radical than the policy line accepted by a Party's majority (LEFT COMMUNISM, LEFT OPPOSITION). In capitalist countries the L. is identified today with: 1. political, economic and social reforms in favour of greater equality and popular participation; 2. substantial state intervention in the economy, including nationalization; 3. the provision of generous social welfare by the state; 4. the separation of the church from the state and the latter's involvement in education; 5. internationalism, as distinct from nationalism; and 6. the acceptance of violence as a legitimate means of achieving political objectives. The L. is contrasted with the RIGHT and CENTRISM.

Left Communism, Left Communists Names given to the extreme faction in the Bolshevik party before and especially after the October Revolution of 1917 in Russia. The tendency to L.C. can be traced back to 1903 in the form of the opposition to Lenin's leadership and pressure for more radical action. In 1909 Lenin managed to have the 'Left Fools' expelled from the Bolshevik faction. During W.W.I a new group of L.C. emerged, led by N. I. BUKHARIN, favouring a total world revolution and the continuation of the war against Germany. Although the L.C. became largely passive during War Communism (1918–20), they renewed their activities in 1921 (when they partly contributed to the KRONSTADT UPRISING) and in 1923 (anticipating Lenin's death). L.C. were: 1. politically–anarchistic; 2. in state and Party administration – anti-authoritarian; 3. in economic affairs – democratic and participatory, but opposed to the NEW ECONOMIC POLICY; 4. in the military sphere – militant and favouring guerrilla warfare; and 5. in foreign relations – extremely internationalistic and anti-nationalistic. They also pressed for a complete destruction of the bourgeois cultural heritage, the abolition of money, the immediate 'withering away'

of the state, law, family and school. Lenin and especially Stalin were strongly opposed to L.C. Stalin took severe measures against them. First he contrived to expel them from the Party at the 15th Congress in Dec. 1927. Virtually all of them were eliminated in the GREAT PURGES of the late 1930s. It is interesting to note that many ideas and practices of Soviet L.C. later resurfaced in China as MAOISM, especially during the GREAT PROLETARIAN CULTURAL REVOLUTION.

Left Communist Party [of Sweden] (*Vänsterpartiet Kommunisterna*) A fairly influential political party in Sweden. Its membership in the late 1970s was about 15,000 (out of the country's total population of 8,300,000). At the 1976 general elections it polled 5.0 per cent of the votes cast and won 17 (of the 349) parliamentary seats. Its origin goes back to May 1917, when the left-wing faction withdrew from the Social Democratic Party and created the Left Social Democratic Party. Four years later it changed its name to the Swedish Communist Party and joined the COMINTERN. After several splits, it finally adopted its present name in 1967. In 1973, an old splinter Maoist group of the S.C.P. calling itself the Communist League/Marxist-Leninist appropriated the old name of the S.C.P. The highest source of authority of the L.C.P. is the Congress held every three years, which elects a Party Board (the official name of the Central Committee since 1964) of 35 members. The P.B. then elects an Executive Committee of eight members headed by the Party leader (Lars Werner). The Party has a small support organization, the Communist Youth, but has no control over the Federation of Trade Unions. In the international Communist movement, the L.C.P. supports the Peking line. Its main publications are: *Norskensflamman* (*The Blaze of Northern Lights*), the Party's daily organ; *Ny Dag* (*New Day*), issued twice a week; and *Socialistik Debatt* (*Socialist Debate*), a theoretical quarterly journal. The S.C.P. publishes a weekly organ called *Gnistan* (*Spark*).

Left Front of Art A radical anti-bourgeois movement in art which existed in Russia from 1913 to 1930 and which came into conflict with Bolshevik thinking and policies. Its vanguard was a literary group led by the poet V. V. MAYAKOVSKY, which emerged in 1913 as a revolt against literary conventions, authoritarianism in life and art, and bourgeois traditions and values. Although anarchistic in outlook, the group welcomed the Bolshevik Revolution which offered prospects for the realization of their version of PROLETARIAN ART. However, after an initial period of mutual co-operation, Lenin rejected the left extremist attacks on the Russian cultural heritage. The Soviet regime found most representatives of this form of art too difficult to regiment in line with official policies. In some respects their art was too abstract and too difficult to be understood by the masses. The L.F. of A. was given support by the LEFT COMMUNISTS (incl. Trotsky and Bukharin) and for a time by LUNACHARSKY. After Lenin's death (1924), the Soviet regime took stronger measures against the movement, which virtually disappeared after the death of Mayakovsky in 1930 (who committed suicide). Also CUBO-FUTURISM, SUR-REALISM.

Left Hegelians See HEGELIAN LEFT.

Leftist, Left-wing General descriptions for persons, groups or political parties professing, advocating or pursuing ideas or programmes peculiar to the LEFT. The label may cover social democrats, legal Marxists, liberal Marxists, socialists, revolutionary communists, left communists, anarchists and any radicals and extremists in general.

Leftist Radicalism A term sometimes used to describe an extreme political ideology or programme, designed to transform society to SOCIALISM, COMMUNISM or ANARCHISM in a relatively short period of time through revolutionary measures. It may be motivated by sincere ideological convictions, or political irresponsibility, or an obsessive pursuit of power.

Left Opposition The name of a faction largely representing LEFT COMMUNISM in the RUSSIAN COMMUNIST PARTY (OF THE BOLSHEVIKS), re-named the ALL-UNION COMMUNIST PARTY (OF THE BOLSHEVIKS) in 1925, in existence in the 1920s in the USSR. The faction emerged first as a group of members in the Moscow Party organization in late 1923 when it became evident that Lenin would soon die. The L.O. was led by TROTSKY, who was later (in 1926) supported by KAMENEV and ZINOVIEV. It was alarmed at the growing authoritarianism in the Party and the concentration of power in Stalin's hands. Also, Stalin's postulate of SOCIALISM IN ONE COUNTRY was in opposition to Trotsky's ambition for the PERMANENT REVOLUTION. By shrewd moves on the part of Stalin and his supporters, by the mid-1930s the L.O. had been eliminated. In 1924 the 13th Party Congress approved strong disciplinary measures against FACTIONALISM. Trotsky was gradually stripped of his posts and expelled from the Party in 1927, exiled in 1929 and finally assassinated (almost certainly on Stalin's orders) in 1940. Kamenev and Zinoviev were arrested in the GREAT PURGES and executed in 1936.

Left Socialist Party [of Denmark] (*Venstresocialisterne*) A radical left-wing splinter party, founded in 1967 as a result of internal ideological conflicts in the SOCIALIST PEOPLE'S PARTY. At the 1975 general elections, it won 2.1 per cent of the votes cast and won 4 deputies in the 166-seat Parliament.

Left Socialist Revolutionaries The left-wing faction of the SOCIALIST REVOLUTIONARY PARTY in Russia which separated from the right-wing faction after the FEBRUARY REVOLUTION OF 1917. During the most critical period in 1917, the S.R. gave support to the BOLSHEVIKS. The LSR established themselves as an independent party in Dec. 1917, but were eliminated as a party by the Bolsheviks in 1922. The Revolutionaries actively participated in the Great October Socialist Revolution, in which they supported Lenin. They were influential among middle peasants and after the Revolution controlled the People's Commissariat (Ministry) for Agriculture. With the Soviet Government in agreement they pressed for the immediate distribution of large estates to the peasants without compensation to the landlords. However, they gradually withdrew their support from the Bolsheviks after the BREST-LITOVSK TREATY (3 March 1918). The LSR then joined the anti-Bolshevik opposition (represented by J. K. Savinkov, Mariya Spiridonova, B. D. Kamkov and A. Gotz) and turned to LEFT COMMUNISM and ANARCHISM. In July 1918 they unsuccessfully attempted a coup and assassinated the German Ambassador, W. Mirbach. By the end of 1922 they had been eliminated as a political force.

Legal Marxism A political movement initiated among Russian intellectuals in the 1890s, which advocated a non-revolutionary PARLIAMENTARY ROAD TO SOCIALISM. The movement was led by P. STRUVE and was inspired by his book *Critical Observations on the Economic Development in Russia* (1894), which identified such personalities as N. Berdiaiev, S. Bulhakov and M. Tugan Baranovsky. In contrast to revolutionary Marxism, the advocates of L.M. publicized their views in legally acceptable literature and endeavoured to pursue their objectives by legal means. Lenin and other BOLSHEVIKS turned against L.M., regarding it timid in tactics, liberal-bourgeois in content, unrealistic in the long run and a postponement of the need for a PROLETARIAN REVOLUTION. After the Revolution of 1905–7, most representatives of L.M. became KADETS.

Legal System The totality of legal norms and institutions established or recognized by the state, designed to preserve law, order and justice. The Marxist view of the l.s. is that it is an instrument in the hands of the ruling class, primarily evolved to safeguard its interests. The l.s. is determined by the SOCIO–ECONOMIC FORMATION. Accordingly, five main systems can be distinguished historically: communal; slave; feudal; capitalist; and socialist.

Lenin, Vladimir Ilyich (1870–1924) The leader of the first successful proletarian revolution in world history, the architect of the first Socialist state, the designer of the Marxist-Leninist Communist party, the founder of the Third International and, next to Marx, the greatest Marxist theoretician. He was born to a middle-class family (his father was a school inspector) and his original name was V. I. Ulyanov. His older brother (Alexander) was executed in 1887 for his alleged part in the assassination of Tsar Aleksander III. L. studied law at Kazan University, was expelled for radical views, but completed his degree externally at the University of St Petersburg (now Leningrad) in 1891. In 1895 L. united several Marxist groups into the LEAGUE OF STRUGGLE FOR THE LIBERATION OF THE WORKING CLASS. He was arrested for revolutionary activities in the same year and was deported to Siberia in 1897 (to the village of Sushenskoe), where he was joined by N. KRUPSKAYA, whom he married there. In 1900 he was released and went abroad, where he founded the first Marxist newspaper, *ISKRA* (*Spark*). In 1903 at the 2nd Congress of the RUSSIAN SOCIAL-DEMOCRATIC LABOUR PARTY held in London, a split occurred between the revolutionary Marxists led by L., who subsequently became known as the BOLSHEVIKS, and the moderate Marxists, known as the MENSHEVIKS. In 1905 L. founded the Bolshevik organ *VPERED* (*Forward*) directed primarily against the Mensheviks. He was one of the leaders in the REVOLUTION OF 1905–07 against Tsarist oppression. In 1912, through L.'s efforts, the Bolshevik faction became a separate party and adopted the name of the Russian Social-Democratic Labour Party (of the Bolsheviks). At the outbreak of W.W.I, L. was arrested by the Austrian police in Poland, but was later released and went to Switzerland. There (in 1916) he worked out the theoretical possibility of a successful proletarian revolution in one country with little industrialization. After the FEBRUARY REVOLUTION OF 1917, L. and his close collaborators left Switzerland in a sealed train across Germany and arrived in Petrograd in April 1917, where he immediately issued the APRIL THESES postulating another 'proletarian' revolution. L. successfully led the GREAT OCTOBER SOCIALIST REVOLUTION on 24–25 Oct. (OSC, or 6–7 Nov. NSC) 1917 and on the following day became the Prime Minister of the first worker-peasant state in world history. Under his leadership a highly disciplined Communist party was evolved, organized on the basis of DEMOCRATIC CENTRALISM and exercising the DICTATORSHIP OF THE PROLETARIAT. Due to his efforts in 1919 the COMINTERN was established, designed to unify the world Communist movement and protect the first Socialist state. After several years of ill-health L. died on 21 Jan. 1924, at the age of 53. His body was embalmed and enshrined in what is now known as LENIN'S MAUSOLEUM in Red Square along the Kremlin Wall in Moscow. His main works which cover philosophy, ethics, politics and economics, are: *What the 'Friends of the People' Are and How They Fight the Social-Democrats* (1894), directed against the NARODNIKS; *What Is To Be Done?* (1902), directed against ECONOMISM; *ONE STEP FORWARD, TWO STEPS BACK* (1904), embodying the principles of Party organization and the dictatorship of the proletariat; *Two Tactics of Social-Democracy in the Democratic Revolution* (1905), presenting the foundations of revolutionary tactics; *MATERIALISM AND EMPIRIO-CRITICISM* (1908), an exposition of DIALECTICAL MATERIALISM and HISTORICAL MATERIALISM; *IMPERIALISM: THE HIGHEST STAGE OF CAPITALISM* (1916), a theoretical explanation of the emergence and abuses of COLONIALISM and IMPERIALISM; *PHILOSOPHICAL NOTEBOOKS*, embodying attacks on IDEALISM, RELIGION and a further exposition on dialectical materialism; *The STATE AND REVOLUTION* (1917), dealing with the dictatorship of the proletariat, and the transition from capitalism to socialism and then to communism; and *Left-Wing Communism: An Infantile Disorder* (1920), directed against extremist Communists, anarchists and opponents of Party authoritarianism.

Lenin Commemoration Party Enrolment A week of national tribute to Lenin following his death on 21 Jan. 1924. It assumed the form of an open invitation by the RUSSIAN COMMUNIST PARTY (OF THE BOLSHEVIKS) to join the Party. Although group applications were permissible, each applicant was considered on an individual basis at open Party meetings. A quarter of a million persons responded, of whom 240,000 were admitted for membership.

Leningrad The second largest city in the USSR with a population of 4 million (in the late 1970s), and the original centre of the first successful proletarian revolution in world history which installed the Soviet regime in power. It was originally founded by Peter the Great in 1703 as St. Petersburg on the marshlands in the Gulf of Finland to serve as the 'window into Europe'. It was the capital of the Russian Empire from 1712 to 1918, but in 1914 its name was Russified to Petrograd (Peter's City). Lenin's arrival from Switzerland in a sealed German train in Petrograd on 4 April 1917 (OSC) led to the successful GREAT OCTOBER SOCIALIST REVOLUTION on 24–25 Oct. (OSC, 6–7 Nov. NSC) of the same year. Lenin became the undisputed leader of the new Soviet regime. The country's capital was moved to Moscow in March 1918 and, after Lenin's death (Jan. 1924), Petrograd was renamed L. In addition to the October Revolution, L. was the site of the revolt of the DEKABRISTS in 1825, BLOODY SUNDAY in 1905, the FEBRUARY REVOLUTION IN 1917 and was besieged by the Germans from 1941 to 1944 (leaving 1 million dead).

Leningrad Case An intriguing affair in the Leningrad organization of the ALL-UNION

314

COMMUNIST PARTY (OF THE BOLSHEVIKS) in 1948–49, which resulted in the death of a large number of top Party leaders associated with it. It began in Aug. 1948, with the sudden death in suspicious circumstances of A. A. ZHDANOV, the chief of the Leningrad Party organization, a Politburo member and the prospective successor to Stalin. Most of his associates were subsequently ousted from their positions and executed for various trumped-up charges, including N. A. Voznesensky (Chairman of the *Gosplan*), A. A. Kuznetsov (Secretary of the Central Committee), M. I. Rodionov (Chairman of the Council of Ministers of the RSFSR) and P. S. Popkov (Secretary of the Leningrad Party Committee). The complete truth behind the L.C. is not known, but at the TWENTIETH CONGRESS OF THE CPSU in 1956 and the Twenty-Second Congress in 1961 three main culprits were officially mentioned: L. P. BERIA; his accomplice V. S. Abakumov (who was executed in 1954); and G. M. MALENKOV, who had been Z.'s chief rival for the Leningrad post (which he obtained after Z.'s death) and Stalin's office (which he also partly succeeded in obtaining).

Leninism An extension of MARXISM evolved by LENIN, largely on the basis of Russian and Soviet conditions and experience and of world developments after the death of Marx (1883) and Engels (1895). L. can have two meanings: those elements of Marxist theory and practice specifically developed by Lenin himself; or the interpretation of Lenin's contributions as a complementary continuation of classical Marxism in which case it is more appropriately called MARXISM-LENINISM. The term L. was first used in the USSR after Lenin's death (1924), but since Stalin's death (1953) it has been replaced, in official terminology, by Marxism-Leninism. Stalin described L. as 'Marxism in the era of imperialism and proletarian revolution' (*Problems of Leninism*, 1924). In this entry we shall concentrate on the narrow meaning of L., while Marxism-Leninism is dealt with elsewhere. L. is a revolutionary doctrine of philosophical, political, social and pragmatic content. Its theoretical framework was worked out by Lenin between 1902 and 1923 (for his works, see LENIN). Although L. was developed in Russia and the USSR in the last two decades of Lenin's life, the actual Soviet model of L. was distorted after his death by STALINISM, thus linking it to MAOISM and the NEW LEFT. L. may be reduced to 10 basic elements or propositions. 1. it is not enough to rely merely on HISTORICAL DETERMINISM, since it is essential for the working class to accelerate the course of events in preparation for the PROLETARIAN REVOLUTION; 2. SOCIAL CONSCIOUSNESS must be brought to the proletariat from outside by devoted and sympathetic intellectuals; 3. the working class must be led by a highly disciplined Communist party, organized on the principle of DEMOCRATIC CENTRALISM and headed by devoted full-time professional revolutionaries; 4. revolution must be organized and co-ordinated from above by fearless and uncompromising professionals. Spontaneous, isolated revolts and strikes by individual trade unions for higher wages and better working conditions are insufficient and may, in fact, be harmful; 5. a bourgeois-democratic revolution is only a step towards the PROLETARIAN REVOLUTION; 6. a proletarian revolution can succeed in a few countries, or even one unindustrialized country; 7. the Party tactics must be flexible and practical, which in certain circumstances may necessitate ideological retreats; 8. a peaceful coexistence of countries with different social systems is possible, but the ultimate and inevitable victory of communism must not be lost sight of; 9. liberation movements in colonies must be linked with the class struggle in the imperialist exploiting countries to defeat IMPERIALISM; 10. the working class must not participate in wars which are of the imperialist type. However, its participation is justified in revolutionary civil wars, fighting COUNTER-REVOLUTION and in wars of national liberation from imperialist domination.

Lenin International Peace Prize A high Soviet award made for outstanding services in the cause of international peace. Its full official title is: the 'International Lenin Prize for the Preservation of Peace between Nations'. It was established by the SUPREME SOVIET OF THE USSR on 6 Nov. 1956 and is awarded annually by the Lenin Peace Prize Committee which is attached to the Supreme Soviet. It is awarded each year to 3–5 persons 'irrespective of their race, nationality, political views or religion'. The presentation includes a Certificate, a Gold Medal with an imprint of Lenin's portrait and a cash award of 25,000 roubles. About 95 per cent of the prizes so far have been awarded to non-Soviet citizens. Among the recipients were: N. S. Khrushchev (1958); Sukarno (1959); R. Nehru (1960); K. Nkrumah and P. Picasso (1961); and Angela Davies and K. Menon (1977–78).

Lenin Prizes The highest Soviet awards for outstanding services to science, technology, the arts, the construction of Communism and to persons who receive the titles of the 'HERO OF SOCIALIST LABOUR' and the 'HERO OF THE SOVIET UNION'. The prizes may be awarded to civilians and to military personnel. They were instituted in 1925, but between 1939 and 1956 they were known as Stalin Prizes. Proposals for the awards are considered by a Committee for Lenin Prizes attached to the Council of Ministers of the USSR and the Central Committee of the CPSU. However, the prizes are awarded formally by the SUPREME SOVIET OF THE USSR. Unlike some other Soviet awards, L.P. are conferred on a particular person only once. The recipient is given the title of the 'Laureate of the Order of Lenin' and the award is made on the anniversary of Lenin's birthday, 22 April. Formerly about 50 prizes were awarded annually, but now 30 awards are made every other year.

Lenin's Mausoleum The Soviet shrine containing the embalmed body of V. I. LENIN located in Red Square near the Kremlin Wall in Moscow. L.M. was designed by A. V. Shchusev and a permanent solid structure (replacing the original wooden one) was built in 1930 of granite, marble, labrador and porphyry. After Stalin's death (March 1953) his body was also enshrined in the Mausoleum, but was removed in 1961 as part of DE-STALINIZATION. Each year hundreds of thousands of people visit L.M. Foreigners are given favoured treatment in the queues. Guards see to it that the visitors are orderly and conduct themselves in a respectful manner.

Lenin's Scheme for Co-operative Agriculture A plan worked out by Lenin in the years 1919–23 for the transformation of private peasant holdings into large-scale socialized farms managed and operated along co-operative lines. He regarded it as an essential element of the construction of Communism in the USSR. The scheme was based on the following principles and realities: 1. a worker–peasant alliance is necessary for the construction of Socialism in the countryside; 2. the socialist transformation of agriculture must be carried out under the conditions of the DICTATORSHIP OF THE PROLETARIAT; 3. as peasants are largely PETTY BOURGEOIS in mentality, the initiative and administrative machinery for COLLECTIVIZATION must come from outside, viz. the Communist Party and the state; 4. collectivization must be carried out not by the expropriation of peasants by force, but by voluntary association; 5. peasants must be provided with sufficient material motivation to induce them to form or join collective farms; 6. the development of collective farms must be paralleled by STATE FARMS, the relative importance of each depending on historical, geographical, economic, social and political considerations; 7. the state must provide sufficient investment resources and appropriate industrial back-up to facilitate large-scale mechanized progressive farming; and 8. the socialist transformation of agriculture must be integrated into the general development of the economy, in particular

316

accelerated industrialization. L.s. for c.a. was not implemented in the USSR in the humanitarian manner as postulated by Lenin and has occurred in other Socialist countries.

Lenin's Testament The political will left by LENIN concerning the Party leadership and policy directions after his death. The Testament was prepared during his illness in 1922–23 (he died in Jan. 1924) and included critical notes on BUKHARIN, STALIN, TROTSKY and other top-ranking Bolsheviks as prospective leaders of the USSR. Of all, he was most critical of Stalin and, in a special postscript circulated to his colleagues, he insisted that Stalin be removed from the powerful post of the Party's Secretary-General. Stalin saw to it that L.T. was not published in the USSR, either in Lenin's or Stalin's lifetime. But it was made public in the West after Lenin's death and in the USSR after Stalin died, viz. at the TWENTIETH CONGRESS OF THE CPSU in 1956.

Leroux, Pierre (1797–1871) A French socialist thinker who claimed that he was the original inventor of the term 'socialism' in 1832, contrasting it with 'individualism'. He subjected capitalism to severe criticism and up to 1831 adhered to Saint-Simonism. Later he developed his own model of socialism, in which, among other things, he advocated the reorganization of agriculture into communal Christian associations. His ideas were studied by Marx and Engels (he also lived in England as an exile), but they classified him as an impractical dreamer and criticized his schemes as UTOPIAN SOCIALISM.

Less-developed Countries Economically underdeveloped countries, considered as such by their low *per capita* incomes – roughly less than US$1,000 at 1975 rates. They are also known as 'Third World' countries, i.e. other than the developed capitalist countries and the Socialist bloc. The l.-d.c. represent 48 per cent of the area of the world, 45 per cent of its population but only 14 per cent of its total income and 8 per cent of its industrial output. Marxists attribute the economic underdevelopment of these countries to: 1. the persistence of antiquated social relations (feudalism included), enforced by legal, religious and customary norms; 2. the private ownership of the means of production, concentrated in the hands of the exploiting classes disinterested in and even opposed to changes in the social system which may threaten their privileged position; 3. the persistence of corrupt bureaucracy in collusion with the privileged exploiting classes; 4. the lack of educational and occupational opportunities for the masses, whose energies and talents are under-utilized; 5. the anarchical operation of the market mechanism, which leads to the uneven development of non-socialist economies; 6. the absence or insufficiency of state intervention and economic planning; and 7. exploitation by developed capitalist countries through COLONIALISM, NON-EQUIVALENT EXCHANGE and foreign investments.

'Let a hundred flowers blossom' See HUNDRED FLOWERS INTERLUDE.

L'Humanité See HUMANITÉ, L'.

Liberalism A political, economic and social doctrine, according to which the unrestricted freedom of individuals in pursuing their affairs is conducive to social harmony and the maximum wellbeing of society as a whole. It reached its peak of acceptability in Western Europe and North America in the 19th c. It arose as a reaction against feudalism, state absolutism and mercantilism. In politics, l. stood for the freedom of political convictions, association, press, religion and residence, while in the economic sphere it pressed for free enterprise, unrestricted competition, the free market mechanism, free trade and the elimination of state intervention. Revolutionary Marxists have always been critical of l. In their view, 1. is the ideology of the BOURGEOISIE which, although at first a reaction against authoritarianism, later became increasingly reactionary in order to protect the interests of the propertied and professional classes to the detriment of the working class. The democratic freedoms and the unrestricted right to acquire, own and dispose of property, instead of liberating people in effect introduces new constrictions operating to the disadvantage of the PROLETARIAT. After the Communist seizure of power in the present Socialist countries, Communist leaders (notably Lenin, Stalin and Mao Tse-tung) found l. inconsistent with, and indeed inimical to, PARTY DISCIPLINE, the DICTATORSHIP OF THE PROLETARIAT, the SOCIAL OWNERSHIP OF THE MEANS OF PRODUCTION, CENTRAL ECONOMIC PLANNING and the acceleration of ECONOMIC DEVELOPMENT. Mao stated (in 'Combat Liberalism', 1937): 'But liberalism rejects ideological struggle and stands for unprincipled peace, thus giving rise to a decadent, philistine attitude and bringing about political degeneration in certain units and individuals in the Party and the revolutionary organization'.

Liberation Doctrine In US foreign policy towards communism, the name of the most aggressive programme which emerged from the Democratic and Republican Conventions in 1952 (at the height of the Korean War). The promoters of the L.D. (such as J. Burnham) did not think that the CONTAINMENT POLICY led to any solution. Instead, they advocated positive measures to induce ferments in the Socialist bloc, especially in Eastern Europe, in order to liberate the subjugated countries from Soviet domination and the clutches of international communism. The failure of the USA to provide aid to anti-communist elements in the HUNGARIAN UPRISING demonstrated the bankruptcy of the doctrine.

Liberation Front of Mozambique (*Frente de Libertação de Moçambique*) Also popularly known as *FRELIMO*, the ruling Marxist-Leninist party in the People's Republic of MOZAMBIQUE. It was founded in 1962 through an amalgamation of three left-wing nationalist groups, viz. the African Union for Independent Mozambique, Democratic National Union of Mozambique, and the Mozambique African Nationalist Union. From 1964 to 1974 it engaged in struggles against Portuguese rule, which led to the declaration of independence in June 1975. The Front is organized on the basis of DEMOCRATIC CENTRALISM and, although it claims to be Marxist-Leninist, disclaims to be Communist. At its 3rd Congress in Feb. 1977, a Central Committee of 67 members was elected, which in turn selected a Political Committee of 10 members, the real seat of political power in the country. The Front's leader is also the country's President. In its programme, the Front has announced far-reaching reforms along socialist lines. There is an illegal opposition party in the country represented by the Revolutionary Party of Mozambique. In the international arena, the Front has adopted a pro-Soviet line.

Liberation Movements NATIONAL LIBERATION MOVEMENTS.

Liberman, Evsei Grigorevich (1897–) A Soviet economist who achieved fame by economic reforms in the USSR, advocating in particular the adoption of profit as the main indicator of enterprise performance and the basis for bonuses to workers. He became Dean of the Faculty of Economics and the Organization of the Machine-Building Industry at the Kharkov Institute of Engineering and Economics in 1947 and Professor of Engineering Economics in 1963. His advocacy of the adoption of the profit criterion to stimulate efficiency and economic growth can be traced back at least to 1946. He wrote a doctoral thesis in this field in 1957, but official interest in his proposals came only in 1962 when his article ('Plan, Profit, Bonus') was published in *PRAVDA* (9 Sep. 1962). His proposals were formulated in a more systematic manner and experimented with under the name of the KHARKOV SYSTEM. After some years of experimentation, the Soviet Government decided in 1965 to adopt profit as an indicator of enterprise performance and a basis for material incentives to labour. Although L.'s ideas have not been implemented in the form and detail he advocated, he is identified (especially in the capitalist world) as a symbol of Soviet economic reformism. L. himself denied that the adoption of his scheme amounted to the abandonment of planning and a return to capitalism, as Socialist profit is quite different from capitalist profit.

Liebknecht, Karl (1871–1919) A German radical left-wing Marxist and a leader of the German Socialist Republic proclaimed in Nov. 1918. A lawyer by profession, he gained recognition by defending revolutionaries. In 1907 he helped found the first Socialist Youth International and was elected its first leader. Together with ROSA LUXEMBURG he led the left-wing faction of the SOCIAL-DEMOCRATIC PARTY OF GERMANY. He strongly opposed MILITARISM and the German participation in W.W.I. Largely to this purpose, he organized the SPARTACUS LEAGUE in 1915, for which he was imprisoned for the remaining part of the war. After his release in Nov. 1918 he proclaimed the German Socialist Republic and by the beginning of 1919 had transformed the Spartacus League into the Communist Party of Germany. He subsequently led a Communist uprising in Berlin in Jan. 1919, but was arrested and murdered (together with Rosa Luxemburg) by a right-wing gang of ex-army officers (*Freikorps*).

Liebknecht, Wilhelm (1826–1900) A German labour leader and one of the founders of the SOCIAL-DEMOCRATIC PARTY OF GERMANY. He participated in the REVOLUTION OF 1848/49 in Germany and became an associate of Marx and Engels in London (in 1850). He joined the GENERAL GERMAN WORKERS' ASSOCIATION in 1863, but disagreed with its leader F. LASSALLE. In 1869, together with A. BEBEL, he established the Social-Democratic Workers' Party, helped the unification of the G.G.W.A. and the S.-D.W.P. into the Social-Democratic Party

of Germany (in 1890) and edited its organ *VORWÄRTS!*. He participated in the work of the FIRST INTERNATIONAL and the SECOND INTERNATIONAL. He was the father of KARL LIEBKNECHT.

Li Fun-ch'un (1899–1975) A Chinese Communist leader and one of the foremost economists under Mao Tse-tung. One of the earliest members of the Chinese Communist Party, he was elected to its Central Committee in 1934 and its Politburo in 1956. He received his economic training in France and the USSR and on many occasions was involved in commercial negotiations with the USSR (in the late 1940s and the 1950s). He replaced KAO KANG as the Chairman of the State Planning Commission in 1954. He decentralized industrial development by locating manufacturing industries closer to the sources of raw materials (rather than in the centres of population). He also put forward the policy of WALKING ON TWO LEGS. Li became a trusted friend and adviser of Mao and played a prominent part in the early stages of the GREAT PROLETARIAN CULTURAL REVOLUTION.

Li Li-san (1896–1967) An early Chinese Communist leader who, in contrast to Mao Tse-tung and the COMINTERN, emphasized the role of cities and the industrial workers in the revolutionary strategy for China. He gained his education in France (1919–21), became a member of the Executive Committee of the Red International of Labour Unions (the PROFINTERN) at its Congress in Moscow in 1925, and in 1927 was elected to the Central Committee of the CHINESE COMMUNIST PARTY. He reached the peak of his influence in the C.C.P. in 1928–30. At that stage Li was considered a rival to Mao for the Party leadership. He was a left extremist and almost a fanatic. During this period Mao co-operated with him. At the insistence of the Comintern, supported by the Soviets and Mao (who saw his own strength in the countryside), Li was accused of adventurism and DEVIATIONISM, removed from the Party leadership in

1931 and went to live in the USSR (till 1945). After W.W.II he returned to China and was appointed Deputy Chairman of the Chinese Federation of Trade Unions (1948–53) and Minister of Labour (1949–54).

Limited Sovereignty Doctrine A view held in some circles in the big powers (especially the USA and the USSR) postulating the control over certain external and internal policies in the 'protected' countries. It was first put forward under this name in the USA in 1947 as a corollary of the TRUMAN DOCTRINE and further restated in 1970. It is held that where the USA has accepted the responsibility of protection against communism, the countries concerned should accept US control of their external and internal policies relevant to the problem of security. The doctrine was widely discussed in the West during the COLD WAR, but was rejected (especially by France). After 1968, a similar tenet to the L.S.D. has emerged in the WARSAW PACT, especially in the USSR, under the name of the BREZHNEV DOCTRINE.

Limiting (or Marginal) Exchange Rate An operational and flexible exchange rate periodically fixed in some Socialist countries whose currencies are noted for unstable exchange rates. It shows the ratio of the domestic currency to a foreign currency, corrected by the COEFFICIENT OF THE RELATIVE VALUE OF FOREIGN CURRENCIES, above which exports are not permitted and below which imports are not allowed, as in the given domestic costs and the balance-of-payments situation trade is not adequately gainful. In other words, beyond the l.e.r. the earnings of a unit of foreign currency from exports and the savings of domestic resources from imports are not economical in the circumstances. The considerations taken into account in altering the l.e.r. are changes in foreign prices, domestic prices, real wages, the structure of production and other factors affecting the balance of payments. A higher l.e.r. would be fixed if a balance-of-

payments deficit is expected, as such a rate would make an additional parcel of exportables profitable and would also stimulate import replacement.

Linear Programming A basic method of mathematical programming for finding optimal static solutions by the determination of the minimum or maximum function of a set of variables:

$$z = c_1 x_1 + c_2 x_2 + \ldots c_n x_n$$

assuming that the variables

$xj > o$ with given constraints

$$a_{i1} \times_1 + a_{i2} X_2 + \ldots a_{in} x_n \,(>, = \leqslant); \, b,$$

$i = 1, 2 \ldots m$ (where a, b, c are parameters). L.p. has important applications in the construction of economic plans, especially in OPTIMAL PLANNING. Thus there may be n economic processes in which m goods are involved (some of which may be inputs whilst others final products). The quantity of each good involved in the j-th process is proportional to the intensity of the process Xj (the intensity of the j-th $= 1$ process when the quantities of the goods involved are correspondingly equal: $a_{1j}, a_{2j}, \ldots a_{mj}$). Each process entails costs, which is proportional to the intensity of the process equal to c_j when the intensity of the j-th process $= 1$. For each linear function the initial stock m or output requirements b are given. The essence of the technique of l.p. was first discovered by a Soviet economist L. V. KANTOROVICH in 1939, when he developed a mathematical model for the Organization and Planning of Production at the enterprise level. But the significance of his discovery remained unrecognized in the USSR until its independent discovery by G. B. Dantzig and T. C. Koopmans in 1947 in the USA and its increasing applications in the West. Also INPUT-OUTPUT ANALYSIS.

Link A term used in the USSR for PRODUCTION TEAM, a sub-unit of PRODUC-

TION BRIGADE. A l. is headed by a link-leader.

Lin Piao (1910–71) A Chinese Communist military and political leader, at one stage officially accepted as the successor to Mao Tse-tung. Lin joined the Chinese Communist Party in 1925 and became active in the Communist uprisings of 1927 initiated by the COMINTERN. A graduate of the Whampoa Military Academy in 1926, he proved a resourceful and successful military commander and played a distinguished part in the LONG MARCH (1934–35), the anti-Japanese campaign (1937–45) and the Civil War (1946–49). During the Korean War he commanded the Chinese Red Army of Volunteers (1950–53). He was created Marshal and elected to the Politburo in 1955, became a member of the STANDING COMMITTEE of the Politburo of the CCP in 1958 and Minister of Defence in 1959. In 1965 he carried out major reforms in the PEOPLE'S LIBERATION ARMY, including an order abolishing ranks. In the following year he popularized the Maoist theory of revolution (see LIN PIAO THEORY OF REVOLUTION). By Aug. 1966 he had emerged as second to Mao in the Party hierarchy and at the 9th Party Congress in April 1969 he was named Mao's successor. He played the leading role in the GREAT PROLETARIAN CULTURAL REVOLUTION, in which he enlisted an enthusiastic support of the P.L.A. However, although unknown for a long time, differences arose between him and Mao. After an unsuccessful attempt to seize power, he tried to escape to the USSR expecting to win Soviet support, but died in a plane crash in mysterious circumstances over Mongolia on 13 Sep. 1971. At the 10th Party Congress in Aug. 1973, CHOU EN-LAI described L.P. as 'a bourgeois careerist, conspirator, counter-revolutionary, double-dealer, renegade and traitor' and 'a capitulationist to Soviet revisionist social imperialism'.

Lin Piao Theory of Revolution A theory expounded by LIN PIAO in China in 1965, according to which the countryside alone can provide the revolutionary basis from which the PROLETARIAN REVOLUTION can successfully spread to the cities and industrial areas. By the same token, a proletarian revolution in the poor, less-developed world (Africa, Asia and Latin America) can be carried to the rich industrialized West (Western Europe, North America and Japan) to complete the victory of world communism. The theory is an extension of the revolutionary ideas and practice of MAO TSE-TUNG. At that time Lin Piao fully supported Mao. His theory was one of the opening signals for the GREAT PROLETARIAN CULTURAL REVOLUTION.

L'Internationale See *INTERNATIONALE*.

Liquidationism A minor left-wing movement in Russia before and after W.W.I, which advocated the liquidation of the revolutionary working-class movement and the Bolshevik Party itself. The term was first applied by the BOLSHEVIKS in about 1908 to the proposal by the moderates in the RUSSIAN SOCIAL-DEMOCRATIC LABOUR PARTY led by A. N. Portresov. The aim was to liquidate illegal party organizations and turn to LEGAL MARXISM instead. The Liquidators also pressed for three freedoms – the freedom of labour to organize, the freedom of speech and the freedom of the press. In their strategy of the PARLIAMENTARY ROAD TO SOCIALISM, they emphasized the development of trade unions, co-operative workers' educational associations and other institutions and related activities within the framework of the existing social system. They publicized their views in a newspaper *Nasha Zarya* (*Our Dawn*). Their views were shared by the representatives of CENTRISM in the Second International led by Kautsky. L. was strongly opposed by the leading Bolsheviks and in 1912 induced Lenin to declare the Bolshevik faction in the R.S.-D.L.P. as a separate party. After the Bolshevik Revolution in 1917 and following the Civil War (1918–20) arguments were again raised within the RUSSIAN COMMUN-IST PARTY (OF THE BOLSHEVIKS) in favour of liquidating the Party. The proponents maintained that the Revolution had recti-fied the wrongs of the preceding social system and consequently the Party was no longer historically necessary. They also pointed out that the liquidation of the Party would represent a step towards the Marxian postulate of the WITHERING AWAY OF THE STATE. Needless to say, these ideas were rejected by Lenin and especially Stalin. It was the Liquidators who were later liquidated (in the GREAT PURGES of the 1930s).

Lishenets ('Deprived one' or 'Prostrate', in Russian) A political term applied in the USSR after the Bolshevik Revolution to a member of the former exploiting classes who were disfranchized by the Soviet re-gime. The label was officially dropped after the adoption of the new Constitution in 1936.

'Listy' Group, The A small, loose associa-tion in Western Europe of Czechs and Slovaks who supported the liberal reforms in Czechoslovakia in the 1960s and who left the country after the INVASION OF CZECHOSLOVAKIA in Aug. 1968. The Group, formed in 1970, is clustered around *Listy* (*News*), a bi-monthly journal published in London, and circulated not only in the West but also (mostly) in Czechoslovakia. Jiri Pelikan is the pub-lisher of the *Listy* and a central figure in the Group. Its members are social demo-crats, socialists and liberal Marxists and, in general, keep aloof from other Czecho-slovak refugees noted for anti-communist feelings. The Group aims to inform the public in Czechoslovakia, and in the West, about the relevant and current develop-ments in Czechoslovakia and the world, highlighting abuses and persecutions by the Communist regime.

Li Ta-chao (1888–1927) An early Chin-ese Marxist and a co-founder of the Chin-ese Communist Party in 1921. He partici-pated in the democratic Revolution of 1911–13, after W.W.I became the direc-tor of the library at Peking University and was active in organizing Marxist youth groups. Li was one of the leaders of the FOURTH OF MAY MOVEMENT in 1919 and two years later, with CH'EN TU-HSIU, co-founded the C.C.P. In 1923, he became a member of its Central Committee. He supported the Party's collaboration with the KUOMINTANG under Sun Yat-sen in the years 1923–24 and was elected to its Central Executive Committee. In 1924 Li led the delegation of the C.C.P. to the COMINTERN. In 1927 he was arrested and executed on the orders of a warlord.

Literaturnaya Gazeta (*Literary News*, in Russian) The weekly organ of the WRITERS' UNION OF THE USSR published in Moscow. It was founded in 1929 and has become the leading Soviet literary and socio-political periodical. In contrast to the major official journals, *L.G.* is moder-ate and sometimes unexpectedly liberal in its publication policy. Its weekly circula-tion in the late 1970s was 1,600,000 copies.

Little Long Marches Group processions and individual walks by young people in China, especially the RED GUARDS, during the GREAT PROLETARIAN CULTURAL RE-VOLUTION. The marches were initiated by LIN PIAO in Nov. 1966 in order to relieve the pressure on railways and to temper the young people in the hardships of revolu-tion, as their elders had done in the LONG MARCH of 1934–35. It was typical for young people to march in groups mostly towards Peking, wearing red armbands, carrying flags, large pictures of Mao Tse-tung and waving the LITTLE RED BOOK and reciting passages from it.

Little Red Book A book of quotations from the writings of MAO TSE-TUNG. The booklet, which has red covers, contains 426 quotations, three-quarters of which are from the pre-1949 period. Only 21 sayings date from the post-1958 period. It is claimed that the ideas embodied in it are applicable to virtually all situations and can inspire people to profound thinking and good deeds. It was usually carried and prominently displayed by the RED GUARDS during the GREAT PROLETARIAN CULTURAL REVOLUTION. The initial reason for this was that in Peking the control of the Press and Propaganda Department of the central Party apparatus was in the hands of Mao's opponents, who refused to publish a criticism of themselves and restricted the printing and distribution of Mao's works. Its publication and distribution was undertaken by the PEOPLE'S LIBERATION ARMY. By Sep. 1976 (when Mao died) 750m. copies of the *L.R.B.* had been printed in various languages.

Little Yellow Books A colloquial name given to the first study published by Lenin in 1894 consisting of three pamphlets bound in yellow covers. The study, *What the 'Friends of the People' Are and How They Fight the Social-Democrats*, contains an attack against the *NARODNIKS*, who were described as double-faced and who in reality were working against the interests of the common people. Lenin saw the liberal ideas propagated by them as the main obstacle to the spread of Marxism in Russia. Only pamphlets 1 and 3 have survived.

Litvinov, Maksim Maksimovich (1876–1951) The best known Soviet diplomat between the two world wars and a supporter of Soviet co-operation with Britain, France and the USA against Nazi Germany. He joined the RUSSIAN SOCIAL-DEMOCRATIC LABOUR PARTY in 1898 (when it was founded) and was active in the revolutionary movement in Russia as well as in exile. He represented the BOLSHEVIKS in the INTERNATIONAL SOCIALIST BUREAU in 1912 and after the October Revolution in 1917 he became Soviet Ambassador in London. From 1921 to 1930 he served as Deputy Commissar for Foreign Affairs and then, between 1930–39, he was Commissar (Minister). In the Party hierarchy, he was a member of the Central Committee from 1934 to

1941. During W.W.II he was again Deputy Commissar for Foreign Affairs (under V. M. MOLOTOV) and Soviet Ambassador to Washington (1941–43).

Liu Shao-ch'i (1898–1973) A distinguished Chinese Marxist theoretician, trade union leader and statesman who, after 1965, was branded by Mao Tse-tung as a revisionist and deprived of all his posts. The son of a peasant, he won a scholarship in 1919 to study in Moscow. He joined the CHINESE COMMUNIST PARTY when it was founded in 1921, was elected to its Central Committee in 1927 and to its Politburo in 1931. He participated in the LONG MARCH (1934–35) as a Political Commissar and soon established a reputation as the Party's leading theoretician. After W.W.II he was active in the trade union movement. In 1959 Liu succeeded Mao as President of the P.R. of China, retained his post as the Party's First Vice-Chairman and was named the successor to Mao Tse-tung as the Party leader. He became the leading opponent of MAO TSE-TUNG, especially of his adventurous policies initiated during the GREAT LEAP FORWARD. Instead, Liu was in favour of adopting economic reforms along the lines advocated by E. G. LIBERMAN in the USSR, stressing the extension of material incentives and the primacy of sound economic management. During the power struggle which began in 1965, L. was attacked as 'China's Khrushchev', a 'renegade, traitor and scab' and 'a lackey of the Kuomintang and imperialism'. By 1969 he had been relieved of all his posts and expelled from the Party. He died of cancer four years later. He was rehabilitated in 1980.

Live Labour In Marxian political economy, the indispensable element in any process of production. It involves a purposeful expenditure of physical and mental human energy, which is gradually embodied as new value in a product, thus becoming MATERIALIZED LABOUR. In the process of production l.l. utilizes the OBJECTS OF LABOUR (raw materials and semi-finished components) and the MEANS OF LABOUR (tools, machinery, equipment, land) and creates a new product. Although for practical purposes l.l. is often measured by wages, it also includes SURPLUS VALUE (under capitalism) or SURPLUS PRODUCT (under socialism).

Location Theories Theories formulating the principles governing the distribution and specialization of production in a country or the world. The traditional approach in capitalist free enterprise economies was to leave the process to the market mechanism and competition. In such a case, the regional location of a particular type of industry and the consequential territorial division of labour were essentially determined by maximum private profitability, i.e. where there was the most economical access to the input and output markets. In some cases an industry developed in a particular area by a historical accident, but because of inertia the industry continued its growth even where the original justification disappeared or was no longer relevant. The Socialist location theory stresses the role of social cost-benefit considerations, where short-run microeconomic advantages are subordinated to macrosocial interest in the long run. Socialist economists point out that the capitalist approach in the past led to distorted regional patterns of development (LAW OF UNEVEN ECONOMIC DEVELOPMENT), isolated pockets of affluence, slums, pollution and INTERNAL COLONIALISM. In their view, the location of production and the consequent distribution of labour should not be left to chance or to unstable market mechanisms, but be placed on a centrally planned basis where long-run costs and benefits to society as a whole can be taken into account. Transport and traffic, pollution, crowding, social life, employment opportunities, reasonably even economic structures are some of the factors to be taken into consideration in the overall evaluation. Modern theories of location in the West in fact recognize these facts and to that extent may be regarded as departures from the traditional capitalist approach in favour of Socialist thinking.

Lockout A temporary shutdown of a plant on the employer's initiative, thereby depriving workers of employment. It corresponds to the STRIKE initiated by workers. A l. can occur only in a non-Socialist economy. It can be resorted to as a form of retaliation against a strike (or the threat of a strike) or as a method of strengthening the employer's bargaining power in reducing wages or imposing certain other conditions of work. A l. is more likely to appear in times of recession (when there is unemployment) than in times of full employment. On the whole, a l. is less likely to occur than a strike.

Loco-Focos A colloquial name given in the USA in 1895 to the radical wing of the Democratic Party of New York, and for some time afterwards to any member of the Democratic Party. L.-F. stood for equal rights and social justice. The name was derived from resourceful members' use of matches (newly invented and called L.-F.) to rekindle light in the meeting hall maliciously extinguished by their political opponents.

Logic The science of the forms and laws of thinking. There are ideological differences in the approach to l. In the philosophy of IDEALISM, l. considers the forms and laws of thinking independently of the real world where l. has its own transcending reality. On the other hand, Marxism treats the forms and laws of l. as a reflection of OBJECTIVE REALITY in the subjective consciousness of man. Lenin (in *PHILOSOPHICAL NOTEBOOKS*) pointed out that l. is not merely a science of the external forms of thinking but also of the laws of development of all material, natural and spiritual facts. Hence, Marxist l. is sometimes described as 'materialist' l. Marxists maintain that idealistic l. does not link, but rather separates man from nature. They also see an ideological significance in the distinction between FORMAL LOGIC and DIALECTICAL LOGIC.

Logical Positivism A philosophical current of thought representing subjective idealism, which had its origin in the West (at first in Vienna) in the 1920s. Some of its best known representatives include R. Carnap (1891–1970), S. L. Frank (1877–1950), K. R. Popper (1902–), B. Russell (1872–1970) and M. Schlick (1882–1936). The exponents of l.p. deny the existence of the external world independent of human consciousness. Marxist philosophers are opposed to l.p. regarding it as anti-materialist and in effect favourably disposed to religion, as it recognizes MYSTICISM as a method of cognition and approaches the laws and forms of logic in a trite manner. Lenin subjected l.p. to severe criticism in his *MATERIALISM AND EMPIRIO-CRITICISM*.

Logistic In philosophy, a version of symbolical (or mathematical) logic employing mathematical symbols and methods, thereby extending the sphere of FORMAL LOGIC beyond traditional syllogistic reasoning. Its main exponents were R. Carnap (1891–1970) and B. Russell (1872–1970). Marxist philosophers have adopted a negative view of l.s regarding it as a metaphysical distortion of mathematical logic and utilizing it as a weapon of attack against DIALECTICAL LOGIC. They consider it as an extreme version of FORMAL LOGIC, divorced from reality and practical verification.

Lomonosov, Mikhail Vassilievich (1711–65) A pioneering and versatile Russian scientist and materialist philosopher. He became professor of chemistry in the Academy of Sciences in St Petersburg (now Leningrad) in 1745 and 10 years later founded the University of Moscow (bearing his name since 1940). He was the first Russian scientist awarded the title of 'Academician'. He first discovered and experimentally proved the law of the conservation of matter and movement, was the founder of physical chemistry, established the first chemical laboratory in Russia, worked out the first systematic treatment of Russian grammar and was also a poet (Pushkin said that 'L. himself is a university'). L. is regarded by

the Soviets as the true son and great man of the Russian proletariat. L. was born to a peasant family and laid down the foundations for the philosophy of MATERIALISM and DIALECTICS and was critical of the church.

Long March A long trek of the Chinese Red Army from Jui-chin in south-west China to YENAN, in the province of Shensi in north central China. The March lasted from Oct. 1934 to Oct. 1935. It was a feat of great endurance unparalleled in military history. The March was provoked by the attacking superior forces of the KUOMINTANG, which directed its attack against the supply bases of the Red Army of the CHINESE SOVIET REPUBLIC in Kiang-si, Hunan and Hupei provinces and endeavoured to encircle and annihilate the main Communist force. The main portion of the Red Army marched 12,000 km., having crossed 18 mountain ranges and 24 rivers, took 62 cities, fought through 12 provinces occupied by hostile warlords and in addition fought constant battles with the pursuing Kuomintang forces. Much of the success of the March was due to the military leadership and resourcefulness of CHU TEH. After some ideological disputes during the March, Mao Tse-tung emerged as the Communist leader, when new Party officials were elected at the Conference at Tsun-i in Jan. 1935. Of the original 100,000 troops that set out on the March, only 20,000 arrived at the chosen destination.

Longuetites Moderate French socialists who followed the ideas pioneered by Charles Longuet (1833–1903). Longuet adopted the anarchism and socialism of PROUDHON, married Marx's eldest daughter Jenny (in 1872) and turned to Marxism. He was a member of the FIRST INTERNATIONAL (1866–67) and during the siege of Paris 1870–71 was one of the leaders of the PARIS COMMUNE, commanding a battalion of the National Guards against the Germans. But later (after 1880) he turned away from revolutionary Marxism. His followers adopted a pacifist stand during W.W.I and although in principle they supported the Bolshevik Revolution, they rejected the DICTATORSHIP OF THE PROLETARIAT. L. participated in the formation of the SECOND-AND-A-HALF INTERNATIONAL (in 1920).

Loyalty Oaths Declarations on oath required by the US authorities from individuals that they have not advocated the violent overthrow of the government nor belonged to any organization advocating such an overthrow. They were administered in one form or another in critical periods of American history (the War of Independence, the Civil War, W.W.I, the 'Red Scare' of the 1920s), but their widest and most systematic application was during the COLD WAR and was directed against Communists and their sympathisers. Public employees, members of the defence forces, attorneys, teachers and recipients of government benefits (such as students) had to swear the oaths. In 1970 the requirement was dropped in application to federal employees and students. Also McCARTHYISM.

L-T Agreement A short title for the Liao-Takasaki Memorandum Trade Agreement, concluded between China and Japan covering the period 1963–67. The Agreement was jointly announced by Liao Ch'eng-chih (President of the China-Japan Friendship Association in China) and Takasaki Tatsunosuke (a prominent political figure in Japan) on 9 Nov. 1962. It marked the second wave of Sino-Japanese trade expansion, the initiative for which had been taken by CHOU EN-LAI in 1960 (the first drive for the expansion of the Sino-Japanese trade covered the period 1953–57 and involved barter agreements). The L.-T.A. was subsequently renewed in 1968.

L-T Trade In Sino-Japanese economic relations, trade which was conducted under the L-T Agreement, signed in 1962 and covering the five-year period 1963–67. L-T.t. followed a period of stagnation in trade between the two countries from 1957 to 1962. Under the L-T AGREEMENT, Japanese exports to China increased eight times and Japanese imports from China seven times. But in spite of this trade expansion, China's share in Japan's trade was still low, viz. only 3.2 per cent in the peak year (compared with 17 per cent over the period 1930–39). L-T.t. continued after 1967 when the Agreement was renewed in 1968 for another five-year period. However, much of Sino-Japanese trade was conducted outside the scope of the L-T Agreement.

Lubomudry ('Friends of Wisdom', in Russian) A learned society for the promotion of philosophical and literary studies in Russia in the 19th c. The society was founded by the middle-class youth in Moscow in 1823. Among its most prominent members were V. F. Odoyevsky, I. Kireyevsky, D. V. Vienietvinov and S. P. Sheviriov. It accepted the philosophy of IDEALISM, MYSTICISM and revelation. Its activities were largely directed against MATERIALISM and revolutionary ideology, including the ideas of the DEKABRISTS. Although it was dissolved in 1825, it was revived a few years later, after the elimination of the Dekabrists and the intensification of Tsarist oppression, especially in the 1830s and 1840s.

Lubyanka The colloquial name used in the USSR for the secret police (*KGB*) and prison in central Moscow. It is situated in the block adjacent to the street and square originally bearing the name of *L.*, before they were changed to Dzierzhinsky street and square (named after the first chief of the *CHEKA*).

Luddites A loosely organized movement in England in the second decade of the 19th c. opposed to the introduction of machinery in industry, as it deprived men of work. The L. went about destroying and damaging machines in 1811–12 in the counties of Leicester and Nottingham and again in 1816 in Lancashire and Yorkshire. The employers and the establishment regarded these actions as mad and applied a derogatory name to them, derived from Ned Ludd, a village idiot in Leicestershire.

Ludwig Feuerbach and the End of Classical German Philosophy A book written by F. ENGELS and published in 1888. It is a concise and popular exposition of the development of Marxist philosophy, in particular the basic tenets of DIALECTICAL MATERIALISM and HISTORICAL MATERIALISM. Engels attacked the idealistic DIALECTICS of HEGEL and metaphysical materialism of L. FEUERBACH, a German philosopher contemporary to Marx and Engels. Engels further analysed what he called the 'basic law of philosophy', viz. the relation of ideas to being and consciousness to reality in nature, emphasizing that the approach to the relation between these phenomena determines which PHILOSOPHY is accepted – IDEALISM or MATERIALISM. Engels attacked AGNOSTICISM and stressed that man was capable of knowing the real world, in which the crucial part is played by practical experience.

Luhanga See TANZANIAN SOCIALISM.

Lukács, Georg (1885–1971) Hungarian Marxist theoretician and one of the most prominent theorists of Marxist thought this century. Łukács came from a fairly wealthy Jewish family and studied in Germany and Austria-Hungary until the end of World War I where he was influenced by NEO-KANTIANISM. He joined the HUNGARIAN SOCIALIST WORKERS' PARTY in 1918 and was Minister for Education under BÉLA KUN in the short-lived HUNGARIAN SOVIET REPUBLIC in 1919. After the collapse he moved to Vienna where he published his famous essays, *History and Class Consciousness* (1923). In 1929, Lukacs moved to Moscow and worked in the Marx-Engels-Lenin Institute (INSTITUTE OF MARXISM-LENINISM) and stayed until 1957 when he returned to Budapest. Lukacs, like LABRIOLA, evaluated Marx via the latter's debt to Hegel and by

criticizing Engels' *ANTI-DÜHRING*, the *DIALECTICS OF NATURE* and the REFLECTION THEORY of knowledge. In *History and Class Consciousness* he dealt with reification (the thinking or converting into a material thing), the dialect of subject and object as a totality substantiating the unity of THEORY AND PRACTICE gleaned form Marx's 'ELEVENTH THESIS ON FEUERBACH'. His other major works were: *Lenin* (1924); *The Historical Novel* (1937); *Goethe and His Age* (1947); *The Young Hegel* (1948); *Studies in European Realism* (1948); *Aestetics* (1963); and *Solzhenitsyn* (1970).

Lumpenproletariat ('Ragged proletariat', in German) A Marxian term denoting the worst elements ousted from different social classes and reduced to poverty by the conditions peculiar to capitalism. The term was first used by Marx and Engels in the *COMMUNIST MANIFESTO* in 1848, to include demoralized paupers maintained by private charity, beggars, thieves, bandits, prostitutes and the like. The *L.* is not necessarily the poorest stratum of society and does not include the genuinely unemployed, invalids and old age pensioners. While most advocates of ANARCHISM regard the *L.* as the most revolutionary group in society, Marxists disagree and treat it with contempt, as in their view the *L.* is too unstable, too demoralized and too eager to sell itself to the highest bidder, i.e., usually the BOURGEOISIE. The term was revived by Marxists in the 1930s in application to Germany, where in their view Nazi gangs were recruited from the *L.*, facilitating Hitler's rise to power.

Lumumba, Patrice (1925–61) A Congolese moderate left-wing political leader, who founded and led the Congolese National Liberation Movement in 1957. In 1960, he became the Prime Minister of an independent Congo (Kinshasa). As a result of the secession of Katanga and intrigues by his political enemies (chiefly Moise Tsombe and General S. S. Mobutu), *L.* was ousted from his post and murdered in Jan. 1961. In his struggle he endeavoured to combine national liberation from the colonial status with social reforms and alliances with the Socialist countries. In tribute to his high-principled struggle, the Soviet Government decided in 1961 to establish the Patrice Lumumba People's Friendship University in Moscow, now popularly known as the FRIENDSHIP UNIVERSITY.

Lunacharsky, Anatoly Vassilevich (1875–1933) A Soviet political leader, playwright and literary critic and philosopher. He became active in the revolutionary Social-Democratic movement in Russia in the 1890s and in 1903 joined Lenin's Bolshevik faction. He subsequently contributed to revolutionary periodicals in Russia and abroad, namely *PROLETARY*, *VPERED* and *NOVAYA ZHIZN*. After the FEBRUARY REVOLUTION OF 1917, he returned to Russia and participated in the GREAT OCTOBER SOCIALIST REVOLUTION. From 1917 to 1929 he was Commissar (Minister) of Education in the RUSSIAN SOVIET FEDERATED SOCIALIST REPUBLIC, where he directed the development of the new Socialist education and culture. L. is one of the best representatives of Marxist AESTHETICS. His ideas were published in *Outlines of Positive Aesthetics* (1904), *Marxism and Aesthetics* (1905) and *Socialism and Education* (1908). He was the main proponent of SOCIALIST REALISM in art and was opposed to the principle of 'ART FOR ART'S SAKE', but was against depraving art for propaganda purposes and persuaded Lenin to preserve pre-revolutionary art. L. was removed from the government in 1929 and turned to scholarly and diplomatic pursuits. He became a member of the Academy of Sciences of the USSR in 1930 and in 1933 was appointed Soviet envoy to Spain. L.'s other publications include *History of the Western European Literature* (1925), *Literary Profiles* (1925) and *Studies in Criticism* (1925).

'Lunatic Fringe' A term first used by Theodore Roosevelt, the conservative US President (1901–12) as a derogatory description of protesters, demonstrators and social reformers, whom he considered sincere and devoted, but at the same time naive, eccentric, impractical, crazy, fanatical and violent. Marxists disagreed with that interpretation, regarding such people as the revolutionary *avant-garde*, whose activities lead to qualitative leaps (LEAP) and social progress.

Lushan Resolution A declaration made in China in Aug. 1959 concerning the principle to govern the remuneration of commune members. It revoked the rule of full commune ownership of property when production teams were given ownership of small plots of land and minor agricultural implements. The L.R. reaffirmed and formalized the previously announced WUCHAN RESOLUTION.

Luxemburg, Rosa (1870–1919) A radical left-wing socialist leader and an outstanding theoretician of revolutionary Marxism, active in the Polish and German working-class movements. Born in Poland of Jewish descent, she took part in subversive activities in Poland and Russia after 1886. She went through a token marriage to a German, Gustav Luebeck. On the strength of this marriage she escaped imprisonment and in 1899 emigrated to Germany. Between 1904 and 1914 she was a member of the International Bureau of the SECOND INTERNATIONAL. She spent several years in Russian and German prisons, including four years (1915–18) for inciting the German youth to oppose W.W.I. She was active in the left-wing faction of the SOCIAL-DEMOCRATIC PARTY OF GERMANY and collaborated with K. LIEBKNECHT in organizing the SPARTACUS LEAGUE (in 1915) and later the Communist Party of Germany (1918). R.L. was one of the leaders in the Socialist Republic of Germany (proclaimed in Berlin by K. Liebknecht in Nov. 1918). In Jan. 1919, together with K. Liebknecht, she led a Communist-inspired uprising among workers in Berlin, but was murdered, along with Liebknecht, by a right-wing gang of ex-officers. R.L. is regarded as one of the greatest Marxist theoreticians after Marx, Engels and Lenin. In her *Accumulation of Capital* (1913), she supplemented Marx's writings by analysing the role of military production, colonies and imperialism in the revitalization of capitalism and as sources of capital accumulation. Her other works include: *Development of Industry in Poland* (1898); *Social Reform or Revolution?* (1900); *General Strike, the Party and Trade Unions* (1906); and *Crisis of Social-Democracy* (1916).

Lysenko, Trofim Denisovich (1898–1976) A prominent Soviet biologist and one of the most controversial scientists of this century, who endeavoured to steer agricultural research into politically expedient and ideologically acceptable, but scientifically dubious channels. The son of a Ukrainian peasant, L. was an early advocate of MICHURINISM. He skilfully exploited the official suspicion of the laws of heredity and of GENETICS, and constructed his own theory of 'phasic development', especially for plant physiology. He developed a methodology for the pre-treatment of seeds before sowing (VERNALIZATION) and maintained that plant development, like human development, could be shaped predictably by appropriate control of the environment, whereby characteristics could be inherited. L. had a meteoric rise after 1932 under Stalin's patronage, as the former's method promised to revolutionize grain farming in the USSR. Further, his methodology appeared to offer applicability in the development of NEW COMMUNIST MAN. In 1935 L. replaced N. I. Vavilov (a geneticist of world standing) as President of Lenin's All-Union Academy of Agricultural Sciences. In 1939, L. became a member of the Academy of Sciences of the USSR and from 1948 to 1957 ruled as the supreme authority in the USSR on practical and theoretical AGROBIOLOGY. In the view of most scientists, even in the USSR, L. caused long-lasting damage to Soviet biology, genetics and agriculture. During 1956–58 pressure

was applied on L. to resign from the Presidency of the L.A.-U. A.A.S. and by 1964 he was removed from virtually all his other posts. Subsequently, he has been described by some scientists as a crank and charlatan. His peculiar brand of biology and the methods he resorted to have come to be known (especially in the West) as LYSENKOISM. L.'s main publications include: *General Results of Work on Vernalization* (1932); (with L. I. Prezent), *Plant Breeding and the Theory of Phasic Development of Plants* (1935); *Agrobiology* (1943); and *Heredity and Variability* (1943). He also founded a journal, *Vernalization (Yaravizatsiya)* in 1932.

Lysenkoism A description given to the ideas, methods and practices of doubtful scientific validity, developed by T. D. LYSENKO in the field of AGROBIOLOGY. L. was officially supported by the Soviet Government before 1957. The term is used in the West, not in the USSR, where a less compromising designation is common, viz. MICHURINISM. L. was an example of 'un-science', in which the achievements of modern GENETICS and biological science in the West as well as in the USSR were ignored, then rejected. Misguided official support was given to half-truths, which appeared ideologically attractive. L. discarded the Mendelian law of heredity and the Western concept of genes (MENDELISM, WEISMANNISM-MORGANISM). Instead L. placed complete faith in environmental factors, insisting that desirable characteristics in plants could not only be developed under controlled conditions but also subsequently inherited. It was claimed that L. was an extension of Darwin's theory of NATURAL SELECTION. In his endeavours in the scientific field, Lysenko tried to emulate Marxist theorizing on the plasticity of human nature (that man is a product of material and social environment). The Soviet scientists who were openly critical of L. were removed from the position of influence. Some were later tried and disappeared in the Stalinist purges. Some of the propositions put forward by Lysenko can be neither proved

Lysenkoism

nor disproved. However, he was further accused of resorting to inethical methods in his scientific reports to the authorities. More seriously, the official interference in the directions of scientific research and development caused a setback to the study of Soviet genetics for a quarter of a century.

M

Mably, Gabriel Bounot (1709–85) A French historian, philosopher and economic writer, whose ideas on egalitarianism and UTOPIAN SOCIALISM were studied and quoted frequently by Marx. M. saw the origin of social inequality and injustice in the emergence of PRIVATE PROPERTY which replaced PRIMITIVE COMMUNISM. To establish an ideal society, it would be necessary to abolish the institution of private property and ensure guaranteed minimum income to all. However, he was opposed to a violent revolution and instead advocated the development of education and high morality as the most appropriate ways for changing the social system. But he himself was rather pessimistic about the chances of success. His writings include: *Doubts* (1768); *How to Describe History* (1773); *Principles of Law* (1776); and *Principles of Morality* (1784).

Macculloch, John Ramsey (1789–1864) A Scottish economist who was studied by Marx. His principal work was *The Principles of Political Economy* (1830).

MacDonald, James Ramsey (1866–1937) A British socialist who in 1924 became the first Labour Prime Minister, but after 1931 reneged from the socialist Labour Party principles. He joined the INDEPENDENT LABOUR PARTY in 1894, was a co-founder of the LABOUR PARTY in 1900 and led the latter in the House of Commons from 1911 to 1914. As he was opposed to the British participation in W.W.I, he had to resign the leadership. After the war, he was against the British participation in the Russian Civil War (INTERVENTION, THE). He was Prime Minister as the leader of the Labour Party and under his leadership the USSR was extended official recognition by Britain. In 1931 he formed a coalition government in which Conservatives had the majority, and so in effect betrayed his own party. He finally resigned his position in 1935 and died two years later. His publications include: *Socialism and Government* (1909); *The Socialist Movement* (1911); *Parliament and Revolution* (1919); *Parliament and Democracy* (1919); and *Policy for the Labour Party* (1920).

Mach, Ernest (1838–1916) An Austrian physicist and philosopher, advocate of IDEALISM and SUBJECTIVISM, who consequently became a target for Marxist attacks. M. held that sensory impressions are primary elements and regarded objects and phenomena as 'complexes of impressions', and consequently denied the existence of external reality without human consciousness. He further maintained that sense impressions are neutral, neither material nor ideal. Marxists accused M. of extreme ECLECTICISM, PHYSICAL IDEALISM and FIDEISM, and of being hostile to DIALECTICAL MATERIALISM and HISTORICAL MATERIALISM. Lenin attacked M. in *MATERIALISM AND EMPIRIO-CRITICISM*. M.'s main works are *The Analysis of Impressions* (1885) and *Cognition and Error* (1905).

Machine-Tractor Stations State centres for agricultural machinery located in rural areas in the USSR in existence from 1928

Machism

to 1958. They were operated like enterprises (on the basis of commercial accounting) through the hiring out of tractors, other agricultural machinery and the
necessary skilled operators to COLLEC-
TIVE FARMS. M.T.S. were utilized by the
Soviet regime with three objectives in
mind: 1. economizing agricultural
machinery and thereby minimizing investment in agriculture; 2. extracting a high
proportion of surplus from collective
farms; and 3. supervising the collective
farms and enforcing their adherence to
state policies (which was ensured by a
'Political Section' in each M.T.S.). In 1957
there were 7,900 M.T.S., each on average
serving six collective farms. In 1958
M.T.S. were transformed into technical
repair stations and most of their machinery was sold to the collective farms. In
1961, the T.R.S. were also abolished, and
their functions taken over by the farms
themselves. Other Socialist countries,
especially the less-developed ones, have
also adopted, and still maintain, the Soviet
idea of the M.T.S. China began establishing them after 1950. The Party conservatives have favoured their continuation,
but left-wingers have been pressing for
their transfer to the collective farms and
(after 1958) the communes. Despite the
drive during the GREAT LEAP FORWARD
for the dissolution of the M.T.S., many
new ones have since been established.

Machism The subjective idealist school of
philosophy, founded by E. MACH. It is better known as EMPIRIO-CRITICISM which
was attacked by Lenin.

**Macroeconomic and Microeconomic
Analysis** MICROECONOMIC AND MAC-
ROECONOMIC ANALYSIS.

Mainstream Economics Also called establishment economics, a term popularized in
the USA in the 1960s for traditional
Western economics concerned with the
operation of the market mechanism, the
price system, Keynesianism, equilibrium,
marginal analysis, microeconomic efficiency and individualism. It is preoccupied

with economic analysis to the neglect of
social and political factors involved, and
takes the existing economic system for
granted, as natural and universal. M.e.
contrasts with NEW POLITICAL ECONOMY,
POLITICAL ECONOMICS, POLITICAL
ECONOMY, RADICAL POLITICAL ECON-
OMICS and SOCIAL MARKET ECONOMY.

Major Proportions in the Economy A
phrase used in Socialist CENTRAL
ECONOMIC PLANNING, referring to the division of national income and its major
components into different uses. The following proportions are generally considered to be 'major': 1. the division of
NATIONAL INCOME between consumption
and investment; 2. the division of investment between the PRODUCTIVE SPHERE
and the NON-PRODUCTIVE SPHERE; 3. the
distribution of investment among different branches of the economy (e.g. heavy
industry, chemical industry, light industry,
agriculture, transport); 4. the regional distribution of investment; and 5. the division of consumption between PRIVATE
CONSUMPTION and SOCIAL CONSUMPTION.
The determination of the m.p. in the e. is
strategic to the directions of economic and
social development, in particular to the
RATE OF GROWTH of NATIONAL INCOME.
This determination in the Socialist centrally planned economies is not left to the
market mechanism, but made at the top
political level and then used as the basis
for medium and short-term economic
plans.

Makhaiskyism, Machajskism A current of
thought in the RUSSIAN SOCIAL-
DEMOCRATIC LABOUR PARTY before
W.W.I, which was critical of the INTEL-
LIGENTSIA assuming the leadership of the
working class. The proponent of this view
was J. W. Machajski (1867–1926) (spelt
J. V. Makhaisky in transliteration from
Russian), a Polish Socialist active in the
Polish and Russian labour movements.
This attitude was supported mostly by
anarchists. The followers of M. held that
the intelligentsia was a parasitic social
class which, using its superior instruments

332

of labour (professional knowledge), exploited the labouring class. They further argued that the greatest enemy of the proletariat was the Marxist intelligentsia. The ideas along these lines were propagated in the movement's organ *Professional Worker*, founded in 1898. Lenin and most BOLSHEVIKS were opposed to M., describing it as reactionary, irresponsible and damaging to the working class cause. In their view, M. was a version of ECONOMISM, endeavouring to restrict the working class movement to the industrial sphere (higher wages, better working conditions), which should be in the hands of the trade union leaders.

Makhnoism, Makhno Movement A nationalistic movement in the Ukraine during the Civil War (1918–21), which was anarchistic, anti-Tsarist, anti-Bolshevik and led by N. I. Makhno (1884–1934). Makhno was converted to ANARCHISM in 1905 and participated in a number of terrorist actions against Tsarist authorities, for which in 1907 he was sentenced to life imprisonment. Released after the FEBRUARY REVOLUTION OF 1917, he at first led a guerrilla unit fighting Germans. After the October Revolution, the supporters of M. co-operated with the anarchist organization in the Ukraine called the *Nabat* and fought against the counter-revolutionary forces (the Whites), thereby siding with the Bolsheviks. Then the movement turned against the Soviet regime, but was defeated by the Red Army in 1921. Makhno managed to escape with the remnants of his units to the West.

Maksimalists Radical adherents of quasi-anarchism and LEFT COMMUNISM, who were active in the Russian and then Soviet political scene from 1904 to 1920. They emerged from among the ranks of the SOCIALIST REVOLUTIONARIES in 1904. They created the 'Union of Socialist Revolutionary Maksimalists' at a conference in Abo, Finland in Oct. 1906, in which M. I. Sokolov and V. V. Mazurin played a prominent part. In their programme, they insisted on the immediate implementation of the 'maximum' reforms as put forward by the Socialist Revolutionary Party, viz. the simultaneous socialization of land and industry. During and after the REVOLUTION OF 1905–07, they resorted to terrorism and robbery as a method of agitation, calling it 'expropriation'. They were criticized by Lenin for being irresponsible, too undisciplined and too far removed from the masses to be of real progressive use to the revolutionary Marxist movement. They co-operated with the Bolsheviks in the seizure of power in the October Revolution of 1917. But in April-May 1918 they participated in anti-Bolshevik insurrections in Izhevsk and Samara. They were opposed to the DICTATORSHIP OF THE PROLETARIAT, the centralization of administration and the BREST-LITOVSK TREATY with Germany. The M. disintegrated as a group after 1920, when most decided to join the RUSSIAN COMMUNIST PARTY (OF THE BOLSHEVIKS).

Malenkov, Georgi Maksimilianovich (1902–) Soviet Party and political leader who, for a short period, succeeded Stalin as Prime Minister. M. joined the RUSSIAN COMMUNIST PARTY (OF THE BOLSHEVIKS) in 1920, became a member of its Central Committee in 1939, a Secretary of the C.C. 1939–53 and after 1946 a member of the POLITBURO (and later the PRESIDIUM). He held the office of a Vice-Premier from 1946 to 1953 and after Stalin's death (March 1953) became Prime Minister. For a short while in 1953 he was also the Party's FIRST SECRETARY, but was soon succeeded by N. S. KHRUSHCHEV. M. then was demoted to a Vice-Premiership and Ministry of Electric Power (1953–57), removed from his positions by pressure from Khrushchev and stripped of his Party offices as a member of the ANTI-PARTY GROUP. M. was subsequently charged for his complicity in the LENINGRAD CASE. He retired from public life in 1963.

Malthusianism A doctrine put forward by T. R. Malthus (1726–1834) in his *Essay* *on the Principle of Population* (1798), maintaining that while population tends to grow in a geometric progression (1, 2, 4, 8 ...) the means of subsistence increase only in an arithmetic progression (1, 2, 3, 4 ...). Malthus held that this disproportion is an inexorable natural law, conditioned by the LAW OF DIMINISHING RETURNS, explaining the impoverishment of the working class. He argued that the solution lay with the proletariat itself. As remedies, he favoured checks on the growth of population – positive restraints (misery, famines, epidemics, violence, wars) and preventive restraints (late marriages, chastity, birth control). M. was directed in the first instance against the theorists of UTOPIAN SOCIALISM, such as W. Godwin (1756–1836), which blamed capitalism for the poverty of the masses. Although Marx disagreed with utopian socialists on many counts, he agreed with them on M. and pursued its condemnation much further (in *Theories of Surplus Value* (1863), and *CAPITAL* vol. I). He called M. 'a libel on the human race' and stressed that it was an apologetic doctrine constructed for the convenience of the ruling bourgeoisie to provide a theoretical justification for the continuation of the poverty of the working class. He rejected the validity of the law of diminishing returns in the long run and pointed out that technological progress may enable a faster expansion of agricultural production than the growth of population. He further argued that over-population was not a product of a universal and immutable law, but merely a consequence of the capitalist mode of production, under the social system which had become obsolete and was impeding further progress. M. was also attacked by other social reformers, including H. GEORGE and K. KAUTSKY. However, the policy in China, restraining the growth of population through strict morality, late marriages and birth control, to some extent indicates practical Marxist deference to M.

Man See NEW COMMUNIST MAN.

Managed Capitalism The transformed capitalist system as it has evolved in most Western countries, as exemplified by Australia, Britain, France, New Zealand and Sweden. M.c. has developed ways and means for the minimization of the worst abuses of *LAISSEZ-FAIRE* capitalism and extreme INDIVIDUALISM, associated with the concentration of private property, the market mechanism, the private profit motive and the uneven distribution of national income. The features of m.c. include: 1. the nationalization of key firms or industries; 2. a highly professionalized, disciplined and hierarchical public service; 3. monopoly control; 4. the rise of the non-owning, salaried managerial class; 5. national employers' federations and manufacturing associations; 6. workers' participation in the management and ownership of companies; 7. powerful trade unions; 8. the growth of left-wing political parties and radical groups; 9. highly progressive income and inheritance taxes; 10. extensive social welfare programmes; and 11. increasing state participation in economic, social and cultural fields, favouring socialism and lower income groups. In general, Marxists do not agree that m.c. provides the solution to the ills of capitalism, but merely delays the need for a PROLETARIAN REVOLUTION.

Managerialism A feature of highly developed capitalism, where managers of large firms and banks dominate the economic and social scene. This question was first highlighted by a former Trotskyite, James Burnham (in *Managerial Revolution*, 1941). From the ideological point of view, m. entails two phenomena: 1. the separation of control from ownership – professional managers in most cases are no longer owners of the firms which they manage and are not necessarily recruited from the propertied classes. Consequently, modern capitalism is no longer dominated by capitalists; 2. the power elite – managers have emerged as a new elite which, because of its professionalism and its exercise of far-reaching powers over manpower and other resources, is no better and in fact more intolerable than the capitalists. Marxists are critical of m., maintaining that it has not changed capitalism in substance, as top managers are often shareholders and identify themselves with higher social classes, not with the proletariat. Further, m. does not remove EXPLOITATION. Yet, there has been a similar development in the Socialist countries, especially in the more developed ones, in the form of TECHNOCRACY.

Manifesto of Freedom and Democracy A public declaration promulgated by the JAPAN COMMUNIST PARTY in 1976, guaranteeing HUMAN RIGHTS and democratic freedoms should the country come under its administration. The Manifesto is regarded as the first major expression of EUROCOMMUNISM in Japan.

Manifesto of the Chinese Communist Party A declaration of general objectives drawn up at the Second National Party Congress held in Shanghai in July 1922. It proclaimed that the ultimate task of the C.C.P. was to organize workers and peasants to wage the CLASS STRUGGLE, to establish the DICTATORSHIP OF THE PROLETARIAT, to abolish the PRIVATE OWNERSHIP OF THE MEANS OF PRODUCTION and gradually to attain FULL COMMUNISM. It stressed that the immediate enemies of the Chinese working class were capitalist imperialists, the feudal lords and bureaucrats. But there were no references to agrarian reforms or a proletarian revolution.

Manifesto of the 2000 Words A public declaration issued in Prague on 27 June 1968 addressed to workers, peasants, professional groups, scientists and artists, appealing for support to the liberal movement in opposition to the Communist dictatorship. The *Manifesto* was written by L. Vaculik, signed by 70 intellectuals and workers, and was sent by the Czechoslovak Pen Club as a telegram to the International Pen Club in London (of which Czechoslovakia is a member). It was also published in *Literarni Listy* (*Literary News*), Prague, 27 June 1968. The *Manifesto* produced spontaneous popular response and support, but was thwarted by the INVASION OF CZECHOSLOVAKIA in Aug. 1968.

Manual Labour See MENTAL AND PHYSICAL LABOUR.

Maoism A version of Marxism developed by MAO TSE-TUNG reflecting Chinese conditions and experience. The term was first introduced in the USA (by the Harvard scholars C. Brandt, J. K. Fairbank and B. Schwartz), but is not used in China where the 'Thoughts of Mao Tse-tung' is the nearest equivalent. M. as a distinct doctrine evolved between the 8th (1956) and 9th (1969) Congresses of the CHINESE COMMUNIST PARTY. Although based on MARXISM, M. differs from it, and indeed Mao himself on one occasion warned against the uncritical adoption of Marxism 'as a piece of Western culture'. The main distinctive elements of M. are: 1. peasantry and revolution – it is possible to carry out a proletarian revolution based on peasants and the countryside finally engulfing the cities; 2. revolutionary stages – revolution must be carried out in two stages: (a) the nationalist stage, where the proletariat must ally itself with the national bourgeoisie against feudal hierarchy and foreign domination; and (b) the socialist or class war stage, when the working class eliminates the bourgeois elements from power and establishes the DICTATORSHIP OF THE PROLETARIAT. 3. guerrilla warfare – the most appropriate method of the CLASS STRUGGLE to wring power from the well entrenched and equipped bourgeoisie; 4. the PARLIAMENTARY ROAD TO SOCIALISM – acceptable only as a tactical expedient; the Communist party must still have its own military arm, whether legally permitted or not; 5. man vs. equipment in revolutionary wars – ideological indoctrination, disciplined manpower and youthful enthusiasm count far more than military equipment, however plentiful and sophisticated; 6. the primacy of practice over theory – practical verification is the ultimate test for ideas and principles, while theorizing alone is barren; 7. developmental leaps – a new society can skip historical stages and advance to a higher SOCIO-ECONOMIC FORMATION without having to recapitulate all the stages traversed by more developed societies; 8. thought reform – to consolidate revolution and prevent REVISIONISM and the revival of bourgeois mentality, people's minds must be changed in RECTIFICATION CAMPAIGNS and CONTINUING REVOLUTION; 9. the division of labour – excessive specialization leads to SOCIAL STRATIFICATION and is not conducive to EGALITARIANISM and all-round development of personality and personal happiness; 10. manual and mental labour – manual labour is ideologically superior and intellectuals, professional men and students must be induced or forced to engage periodically in physical work in order to keep close to the masses; 11. moral and material incentives – moral incentives to labour are superior to material incentives and the latter must be gradually eliminated; 12. politics and economics – when economic interests are in conflict with political considerations, politics must win over economics; 13. bureaucratism – bureaucracy, especially the top hierarchy, is inimical to Continuing Revolution and is prone to complacency and revisionism; 14. self-reliance – in both revolutionary wars, NATIONAL LIBERATION MOVEMENTS and ECONOMIC DEVELOPMENT, the working class or society must essentially rely on its own efforts, rather than sustained foreign aid; 15. peaceful coexistence with imperialist powers – it is condemned, as it leads to complacency, revisionism and the betrayal of revolution and Marxist ideals. M. has been attacked by the Soviet leadership and is regarded as an immature form of socialism, akin to LEFT COMMUNISM. As such it is viewed as a distortion of MARXISM-LENINISM and a contribution to the disunity of the international Communist movement. But M. has been favourably accepted in many less-developed coun-

tries and by some radical groups in the West. Also SINIFICATION OF MARXISM, DEMAOIZATION.

Mao's Bible A colloquial name given to the *LITTLE RED BOOK*, representing extracts from different writings and speeches of MAO TSE-TUNG.

Mao's Swim A historic swim by MAO TSE-TUNG on 16 July 1966, when he swam 15 km. downstream in 65 minutes. The swim, which was given a good deal of publicity in and outside of China, signified Mao's political comeback during the GREAT PROLETARIAN CULTURAL REVOLUTION and was meant to demonstrate that he was healthy and fit to conduct campaigns.

'Mao's Thoughts' A general description for the aphorisms, mottos, precepts and principles of philosophical, political, aesthetic and military content from the writings and speeches of MAO TSE-TUNG. They have been published in China since 1949 under different titles and in many editions, according to the type of readers aimed at (masses, cadres, intellectuals, foreigners), viz. *Quotations from Chairman Mao Tse-tung, Selected Readings, Selected Works* and the *LITTLE RED BOOK*. M.T. have been published in hundreds of editions, totalling hundreds of millions of copies, in more than 30 languages (incl. Arabic, French, Greek, German, Portuguese, Russian, Spanish, Swahili, and also in Braille). M.T. became compulsory reading in China in the 1960s (especially during the GREAT PROLETARIAN CULTURAL REVOLUTION) for the members of the PEOPLE'S LIBERATION ARMY), the Party and educational establishments.

Mao Tse-tung (1893–1976) Also spelt Mao Dzedong, an outstanding Chinese Communist leader, one of the great theoreticians of Marxism and the founder of the People's Republic of China. He has been variously described as a Chinese nationalist, a revolutionary, an intellectual, an idealist, a military tactician, a skilful politician, a poet and a shrewd determined peasant. A son of a middle peasant, he had little formal education. He was introduced to Marxism in 1919 when he met CH'EN TU-HSIU. Mao was one of the 13 founding members of the CHINESE COMMUNIST PARTY in 1921. Two years later, he was elected to the Party's Central Committee and appointed the director of its Organization Department. In 1926 he formulated his thesis (in 'On the Social Classes in China') that the Chinese peasantry was not only the largest but also the most reliable ally of the urban workers. Together with CHU TEH he founded the Chinese Red Army for use in guerrilla warfare. When the CHINESE SOVIET REPUBLIC was founded in Nov. 1931, M. became its Chairman. During the LONG MARCH (1934–35), there were several contenders for the leadership of the C.C.P. (in the early 1930s Mao was in fact subordinate to CHOU EN-LAI), but M. emerged as the Party leader at a Conference held at Tsun-i in Jan. 1934. Under his leadership the C.C.P. co-operated with the KUOMINTANG in the war against the Japanese invaders (1937–45). The 1930s and 1940s were the most fruitful years for M.'s philosophical, political and military writings. After W.W.II (in summer 1946), the Kuomintang embarked upon the destruction of M.'s strongholds, but by Oct. 1949 his forces had defeated the Nationalist armies on the mainland. On 1 Oct. 1949, M. proclaimed the P.R. of China and took over the Presidency of the Republic and the Chairmanship of the National Defence Council (in addition to the retained Chairmanship of the Party). Although he first supported the policy of close co-operation with the USSR ('LEANING TO ONE SIDE'), after 1956 he became increasingly critical of the Soviet leadership, and in particular its failure to acknowledge him as Stalin's successor to the patronage of the world Communist movement. M.'s GREAT LEAP FORWARD (1958–59), representing a conspicuous departure from the Soviet model and amounting to a dismal failure, not only aroused Soviet hostility but also internal opposition from the Party hierarchy. The opposition was led by LIU SHAO-CH'I who became President of the Republic in 1959 and heir-apparent to M. After several propaganda campaigns to reassert his authority and counteract REVISIONISM, M. launched the GREAT PROLETARIAN CULTURAL REVOLUTION, which he staged successfully with the aid of the People's Liberation Army led by LIN PIAO. By the autumn of 1968 M. routed his conservative Party opponents, reasserting his authority. Liu Shao-ch'i was ousted from power and replaced by Lin Piao as President and successor to M. Lin Piao himself, in his bid for power, later turned against M., but after an unsuccessful coup Lin died in an air accident in Sep. 1971. Owing to his deteriorating health, after May 1971 M. stopped appearing in public, although he continued receiving selected foreign dignitaries. He died on 9 Sep. 1976 and was succeeded by HUA KUO-FENG. M.'s writings were mostly in the form of short articles written at different times, but later were published as collections on major themes, viz.: *Selected Works* (5 volumes); *Four Essays on Philosophy*; *Poems*; *Selected Military Writings*; FIVE MOST READ ARTICLES; the LITTLE RED BOOK; and *A Critique of Soviet Economics*. Also MAOISM, MAO'S SWIM, 'MAO'S THOUGHTS', DE-MAOIZATION.

March 22 Movement See TWENTY-SECOND OF MARCH MOVEMENT (in France).

Marchais, Georges (1920–) The leader of the FRENCH COMMUNIST PARTY and former representative of EUROCOMMUNISM. Of working-class origin and a former metal worker active in the trade union movement, M. is highly regarded as a tough and capable administrator with Soviet sympathies. He joined the F.C.P. in 1947, became a member of its Central Committee in 1956, of its Political Bureau in 1959 and the Party's Secretary-General in 1974. He has also been a deputy to the National Assembly since 1973. Recently he has departed with E. BERLINGUER and S. CARILLO, as an advocate of Eurocom-

337

munism. M.'s main publications are: *What Is the French Communist Party?* (1970); (co-authored) *Communists and Peasants* (1972); *Democratic Challenge* (1973); *Policy of the French Communist Party* (1974); and *Crisis* (1975).

Marchlewski, Julian Baltazar (1866–1925) A Polish economist, writer and international Communist leader. He was active in the FIRST PROLETARIAT and other workers' organizations before W.W.I. He spent most of his time abroad and contributed widely to left-wing newspapers and journals and represented the Social-Democratic Party of Poland and Lithuania in the SECOND INTERNATIONAL. He was also prominent in the German left-wing socialist movement, was one of the founders of the SPARTACUS LEAGUE in 1916 and was arrested by the German police. In a German-Soviet exchange of prisoners he went to Soviet Russia in 1918 and was immediately elected to the ALL-RUSSIAN CENTRAL EXECUTIVE COMMITTEE and in the following year participated in the organization of the COMINTERN. In 1922 M. was a co-founder of the Communist University for Western National Minorities, of which he became Rector. In the same year he acted as the chief organizer of the INTERNATIONAL ORGANIZATION FOR AID TO REVOLUTIONARIES and became its first Chairman. He died in Italy where he was sent by the Soviet Government for medical treatment. His main publications include: *Political Economy: What It Is and What It Teaches* (1902); *Workers' Struggle Under Tsardom* (1905); *Polish Bourgeois Ideas on the Agrarian Question* (1908); *Socialism and War in Theory and Practice* (1915); *Communists and Agricultural Labours* (1919); and *The Agricultural Question and the Socialist Revolution* (1926).

Marcuse, Herbert (1898–1979) A German radical socialist philosopher who lived mostly in the USA. He left Nazi Germany in 1933 and in 1934 accepted a research position at Columbia University.

He settled down in the USA where he held several research and academic posts, including chairs at Harvard and the University of California. He described himself as a Marxist, but not Communist and has been widely regarded as the philosophical leader of the NEW LEFT. M. had a strong stand against modern industrial civilization and mentality and advocated a new radical society governed through an intellectual elite. He also attacked the Stalinist distortions of Marxism-Leninism, maintaining that the working class is no longer a revolutionary force, whether under capitalism or socialism, and hence the leadership should be assumed by the radical intelligentsia to build the ideal society. In his view, there are now four revolutionary driving forces in the world: NATIONAL LIBERATION MOVEMENTS; Marxist SYNDICALISM; under-privileged groups in rich countries; and radical intellectuals. His main publications are: *Reason and Revolution* (1941); *Eros and Civilization* (1955); *One-Dimensional Man* (1964); *The End of Utopia* (1967); *Negations* (1968); *Protest, Demonstration, Revolt* (1968); *Soviet Marxism* (1968); *Critical Interruptions* (1970); *Counter-revolution and Revolt* (1972); and *Studies in Critical Philosophy* (1972).

Marginal Analysis The application of incremental or decremental magnitudes, as distinct from averages and totals, in economic studies. The methods of m.a. were first developed by several schools of CLASSICAL BOURGEOIS POLITICAL ECONOMY in Austria, England, Switzerland and the USA by such economists as K. Menger (1840–1921), V. Jevons (1835–82), L. Walras (1834–1910) and J. B. Clark (1847–1938). The systematic study of m.a. began in the 1870s and revolutionized Western economic theory. It was first applied to the study of utility (MARGINAL UTILITY), but was then extended to studies of cost, profit, propensity to consume and propensity to save. Marxists have traditionally favoured average and total magnitudes and have adopted a critical attitude to m.a. on the grounds that it implied an attack on Marx's analysis of value (as presented in *CAPITAL*, vol. I), that it was too formal and largely subjectivist. In the theory of production and distribution m.a. involves the valuation of non-labour factors or production, and as such is in conflict with the LABOUR THEORY OF VALUE. It is mainly on these grounds that there was official opposition to mathematical economics in the Socialist countries up to the late 1950s, as it involved marginal calculations. However, O. LANGE, L. KANTOROVICH and other Socialist economists convincingly demonstrated that the utilization of m.a. did not amount to the rejection of Marx and the acceptance of bourgeois economic theory. Since the late 1950s, m.a. has been applied in economic planning, especially in the studies of optimization, which involves the substitution of one factor for another (or one product for another) until the maximum total effect or equilibrium is attained.

Marginal Utility The amount or degree of satisfaction achieved from the consumption of an additional unit of a product or service. Normally, m.u. declines with additional units consumed. A consumer attains maximum satisfaction by spending his income up to the point where his m.u. is equal to the price and when his marginal utilities of the goods and services purchased are proportional to their prices. The concept was analysed in the 1870s, discovered or rediscovered by V. Jevons, C. Menger and L. Walras (some 10 years after the appearance of Marx's *Capital*, vol. I).

Market A network of dealings between buyers and sellers, where prices are determined by demand and supply. The emergence of markets is a product of the division of labour and the development of capitalism. The role of the m. is greatest under *LAISSEZ-FAIRE* capitalism, where the free market mechanism provides signals for producers and consumers and more or less regulates the operation of the economy. The role and operation of the m. under capitalism have been subjected to severe criticism by Marxists on the following grounds: 1. it is undemocratic, as persons and interests with greater spending ('voting') power exercise a disproportionate amount of influence; 2. demand and supply, as registered in the m., do not fully reflect social interests, since they do not sufficiently activate some forms of socially-desirable production (e.g. books, educational, health and defence services) and unduly induce the supply of anti-social items (drugs, firearms, damaging luxuries); 3. the m. enables the 'exploitation hat trick' of the PROLETARIAT by the BOURGEOISIE domestically and of the less-developed by the more-developed countries (through NON-EQUIVALENT EXCHANGE); 4. under MONOPOLY CAPITALISM, the m. is manipulated by unscrupulous monopolies; 5. the m. mechanism does not ensure continuous FULL EMPLOYMENT; 6. the functioning of the m. is noted for wide fluctuations, leading to the ANARCHY OF PRODUCTION; and 7. the operation of the m. leads to uneven development within a country, especially between different countries (see LAW OF UNEVEN ECONOMIC DEVELOPMENT). Under Socialism the m. is largely supplanted by central economic planning. However, to some extent the m. also exists in the Socialist countries, mostly in the sphere of consumer goods, where the suppliers are socialized entities and prices are regulated by the state ('organized markets'). But private markets still survive, viz. local markets for privately grown produce in rural areas (KOLKHOZ MARKET). In Poland and Yugoslavia, where about 85 per cent of farming land is still privately owned, there is also a market for land which is officially acknowledged.

Market Communism A concept seldom used, compared with MARKET SOCIALISM, to denote a modified model of FULL COMMUNISM (see EIGHTY PER CENT COMMUNISM) where some 20 per cent of total production would be determined and distributed in relatively free markets. The market would regulate the production of those goods and services which are noted for changing fashions, the sophistication of design and of quality, and where personal attention to customers is highly desirable.

Market Socialism An economic system characterized by a substantial operation of the market mechanism, moderate economic planning and the predominantly social ownership of the means of production. Although some of its ideas can be traced back to E. BARONE, O. LANGE is regarded as the real founder of the model in the late 1930s. The main elements of m.s. are: 1. land and capital are basically socialized; 2. all factors of production are assigned SCARCITY PRICES, arrived at in conventional markets or SHADOW MARKETS; 3. there is freedom of occupation and place of employment; 4. the market equilibrium is maintained according to supply and demand, but the latter two may be influenced by the state where social interest demands it; 5. in general, prices are determined or influenced by the market according to supply and demand by the TRIAL AND ERROR METHOD; 6. the managers of enterprises endeavour to maximize profits as in a competitive market economy, by producing such levels of output in each enterprise at which marginal cost is equated to the given state determined market price (which is also equal to marginal cost and the lowest average cost); and 7. consumers are free to maximize their income and satisfaction, so that there is CONSUMERS' FREEDOM OF CHOICE (but not necessarily CONSUMERS' SOVEREIGNTY). Versions of m.s. have been introduced in Yugoslavia since 1950 and in Hungary since 1968, and were tried in Poland in 1956 and in Czechoslovakia in 1967–68. M.s. is regarded by some socialists and idealist intellectuals in many countries as an ideal economic system. The supporters of the CONVERGENCE THESIS view it as a coalescence of capitalist market economies and the Socialist planned economies. But Marxists consider it as an essentially transitional stage to FULL COMMUNISM.

Marković, Svetozar (1846–75) A Serbian revolutionary democrat and materialist philosopher, who endeavoured to combine national liberation in the Balkans with far-reaching social reforms. Partly educated in Russia, he studied the works of Marx and Engels and participated in the activities of the FIRST INTERNATIONAL (within the Russian Section). He advocated extended patriarchal families and village communes as the basic institutions for the transformation of any society to socialism. In philosophy, he insisted that matter is primary, while ideas are secondary and derived from the material world, that development in nature is essentially dialectic, and he attacked religion as it conflicted with science. He analysed these questions in his *Laws of Realism in Science and Life* (1871–72). His other publications include *Singing and Thinking* (1868); *Realism in Poetry* (1870) and *The Awakening of Serbia* (1872).

Marquetalia One of the best known 'Communist Republics' in existence in Colombia from 1949 to 1965. It was established by Charro Negro (an official of the COMMUNIST PARTY OF COLOMBIA), in the mountain region embodying parts of Huila and Tolima Provinces (southwestern Colombia) with the aid of the local peasantry. The 'Republic' managed to defy the authority of the central government in Bogota and introduced a number of reforms along populist lines. But the central government, with the aid of US advisers and equipment, stepped up its campaign against M. in 1962, killed Negro (in the same year) and by 1966 terminated the 'Republic' and eliminated its leaders.

Marrism Theoretical propositions put forward by N. Y. Marr (1865–1939), a Soviet linguist of Scottish-Georgian descent. Marr claimed that his theories were an extension of Marxism in the field of linguistics; however, they were subsequently rejected in the USSR as unscientific and anti-Marxian. He denied the validity of the 'ancestral language theory', widely accepted in the West, which attributed the development of different languages from a common origin (such as Indo-European) along increasingly divergent lines. As a counter to what Marr called an 'antiquated bourgeois linguistic theory', between 1924 and 1929 he launched a 'social theory of language' (which he at first called 'Japhetic t. of l.). He maintained that the factors responsible for the origin and development of languages were the labour process, the changing methods of production and social organization, that languages developed along convergent lines from simpler to more complex and that language and thought followed separate paths of development. In language development he saw a reflection of the social structure and the class struggle, insisting that in this process there were definite stages of 'dialectical leaps' (the 'stadial theory') corresponding to SOCIO-ECONOMIC FORMATIONS, and identified language as part of the SUPERSTRUCTURE and even a means of production. In his view, languages of all nations will eventually develop into one international language based on world communism. On these grounds, Marr concluded that language development conformed to Marxist DIALECTICAL MATERIALISM and HISTORICAL MATERIALISM. These ideas were further developed by his supporters, especially in the Marr Institute of Language and Thought, which was established in Leningrad. However, many Soviet linguists, such as B. Serebrennikov, dismissed M. as pure speculation without factual proof. It is interesting to note that even Stalin considered himself competent enough to engage in the controversy. In *Pravda* (20 June 1950), he denied that language was part of the superstructure, that it was class oriented, that it could be separated from thought, and that it developed by dialectical leaps. Moreover, he described Marr as 'a simplifier and vulgarizer of Marxism'.

Marshall Plan The popular name for the European Recovery Program, which constituted economic aid from the USA to Western Europe over the period 1948–52. It was formulated by G. C. C. Marshall (1880–1959), the then US Secretary of State, and was one of the forms of implementing the TRUMAN DOCTRINE. The total value of the aid was over $16.4 billion, mostly in (90 per cent) non-repayable grants. The scheme proved to be extremely successful and a turning point in the recovery of the war-affected Western European countries. Under this plan, an offer was also originally made to the European Socialist countries, with strings attached. But the USSR regarded the M.P. as a method of strengthening anti-Communist forces in Europe. Althougn Czechoslovakia and Poland were keen to participate in the M.P., Stalin prevailed upon them to abstain. As a counter-move the COUNCIL FOR MUTUAL ECONOMIC ASSISTANCE was established in 1949.

Martov, L. (original name Tsederbaum, Yulii Osipovich) A Russian socialist of Jewish descent and one of the leaders of the MENSHEVIKS. He joined the LEAGUE OF STRUGGLE FOR THE LIBERATION OF THE WORKING CLASS in 1895 and then the RUSSIAN SOCIAL-DEMOCRATIC LABOUR PARTY. At the Second Congress of the R.S.-D.L.P. in 1903 he opposed Lenin, criticizing him for his autocratic and intolerant approach to party organization. M. participated in the REVOLUTION OF 1905–07, and later, during the ZIMMERWALD CONFERENCE (1915) and the KIENTAL CONFERENCE (1916), he advocated CENTRISM. He returned to Russia with Lenin in the sealed German train in April 1917 and, although he supported the Bolshevik seizure of power, he opposed Lenin's dictatorship of the proletariat and the Red Terror. At the same time M. was opposed to the White COUNTER-REVOLUTION and the INTERVENTION (by Western countries). He emigrated to Germany in 1920, founded a Russian bulletin for the émigrés, *Sotsialistichesky vestnik* (*Socialist Courier*) and participated in the SECOND-AND-A-HALF INTERNATIONAL.

Marx, Karl (1818–83) The founder of international communism, an outstanding theoretical writer in the fields of philosophy, political economy, politics and sociology, and one of the most influential thinkers of all time. One third of the world has based its social system on his ideas. He developed DIALECTICAL MATERIALISM and HISTORICAL MATERIALISM, first postulated the CLASS STRUGGLE, PROLETARIAN REVOLUTION and the DICTATORSHIP OF THE PROLETARIAT as necessary steps in the progress to a CLASSLESS SOCIETY and FULL COMMUNISM. In his ideological framework, M. shrewdly combined classical German philosophy, classical British political economy and French socialist doctrines and revolutionary experience. Born in Germany to a middle-class family of Jewish descent, he first studied at the University of Berlin and then obtained a doctorate in philosophy at Jena (in 1841). In 1842 he became the editor of the *RHEINISCHE ZEITUNG*, an organ of the radical middle class in the Rhineland region, which in 1843 was closed down by the authorities for its revolutionary line. In the same year he married Jenny von Westphalen and moved to Paris, where he edited the *DEUTSCH-FRANZÖSISCHE JAHRBÜCHER*. In 1844, M. met F. ENGELS who became his devoted collaborator, friend and on occasion, financial patron. They both wrote *The HOLY FAMILY* (1845) and *The GERMAN IDEOLOGY* (1845–46). In 1846 he was forced to leave France and went to Brussels where he published *The POVERTY OF PHILOSOPHY*. In 1847 the COMMUNIST LEAGUE commissioned him and Engels to write its programme which was produced and published (first in German), in Feb. 1848 under the title of *The COMMUNIST MANIFESTO*. In 1849 M. went to London which became his permanent base till his death. In 1859 he published his first systematic exposition of the theory of value and other economic principles, *A CONTRIBUTION TO THE CRITIQUE OF POLITICAL ECONOMY*. Eight years later, volume I of *Capital* (*Das KAPITAL*, in German) appeared, his greatest work and one of the most influential books ever published. In 1864 M. (and Engels) helped found the INTERNATIONAL WORKINGMEN'S ASSOCIATION in London, which became a landmark in the history of the international working class movement. But M. was later instrumental in its dissolution when he could not control it. After the failure of the PARIS COMMUNE in 1871, he immediately wrote *The Civil War in France*, which represented revolutionary lessons for his followers. In 1875 he wrote another revolutionary work, the *CRITIQUE OF THE GOTHA PROGRAMME*. Among the foreign languages he commanded was Russian and he was thus very pleased when *Capital*, Vol. I. appeared in Russian (in 1872), the first foreign translation. M. had never anticipated that the first Socialist state based on his ideas would be successfully established in a backward, agricultural country. M. spent most of his life in poverty and exile and was rather difficult and intolerant in his personal relations (Engels excepted) but was a devoted family man. He died in London on 14 March 1883 and was buried in Highgate cemetery: Engels gave the funeral oration. Also MARXISM.

Marxian Pertaining directly to K. MARX, and in particular to the ideas contained in his writings (it differs from MARXIST).

Marxian Value Ratios Fractional relations indicated by different elements in Marx's theory of value: $c+v+s$, where c = CONSTANT CAPITAL, v = VARIABLE CAPITAL and s = SURPLUS VALUE (these components of value represent flows; if a stock is meant, then the symbols are capitalized). The three significant M.v.r. are: 1. s/v = the rate of surplus value, or the rate of exploitation (roughly the capitalist's profit per worker). 2. C/Y = capital stock per worker, or 'capital-labour ratio', or better known in Marxian terminology as the ORGANIC STRUCTURE OF CAPITAL. 3. $s/C + v$ = the rate of profit, i.e. surplus value per unit of capital plus labour cost (the profit maximizing guide to the capitalist, better than s/v).

Marxism The theory and practice of the revolutionary working class movement as originally propounded by K. MARX, other classical Communist thinkers (especially, F. Engels, Rosa Luxemburg and V. I. Lenin) and extended by later interpreters of Marx in adaptation to specific conditions. M. is a self-contained and a complete philosophical, political, economic and sociological system, explaining the basic principles and practices governing natural phenomena, human life and social development. It is largely a conglomerate of Hegelian dialectical logic, Feuerbach's materialism, Ricardian political economy, French revolutionary experience and Western humanism. The main elements of M. are: 1. DIALECTICAL MATERIALISM; 2. HISTORICAL MATERIALISM; 3. the LABOUR THEORY OF VALUE; 4. the theory of SURPLUS VALUE and of the EXPLOITATION of the PROLETARIAT by the BOURGEOISIE; 5. the postulates of the CLASS STRUGGLE, PROLETARIAN REVOLUTION, DICTATORSHIP OF THE PROLETARIAT and the SOCIALIZATION OF THE MEANS OF PRODUCTION; and 6. the acceptance of economic determinism, that societies develop towards higher SOCIO-ECONOMIC FORMATIONS, the ultimate goal being FULL COMMUNISM (to be characterized, among other things, by a CLASSLESS SOCIETY, the abolition of money, the disappearance of market relations, all-round affluence, 'FROM EACH ACCORDING TO HIS ABILITY, TO EACH ACCORDING TO HIS NEEDS', and the WITHERING AWAY OF THE STATE). M. has come to represent a wide range of doctrines and views, not only those left by Marx but also contributed by his many followers who have supplemented or qualified Marx's ideas, viz. ARAB SOCIALISM, BURMESE ROAD TO SOCIALISM, CASTROISM, EUROCOMMUNISM, KAUTSKYISM, LENINISM, MAOISM, MARXISM-LENINISM, STALINISM, SYNDICALISM, TANZANIAN SOCIALISM, TITOISM and TROTSKYISM. Marx and his non-dogmatic followers stress that the only orthodox element in M. is its method, not the acceptance of any particular tenet or solution ('Marxism is not a dogma, but a guide to action'). In fact Marx himself denied that he was a 'Marxist', i.e. admitting that there might be other legitimate interpretations of the ideas he raised, different from his own. M. has come to be accepted as the basic social creed in the 25 SOCIALIST COUNTRIES ruled by Marxist governments, constituting one-third of the world (as of 1979).

Marxism-Leninism The theory and practice of Marxism as developed and applied by Lenin under Soviet conditions. It embodies the elements of classical MARXISM and of LENINISM. Officially, the term appeared in the USSR after Stalin's death (1953), although unofficially the use of the designation can be traced back to at least 1928. However, its use up to the late 1950s had a chequered history and was fraught with ideological perils. Since then, prodded by the SINO-SOVIET DISPUTE, the term has been employed by the Soviet leadership to indicate the correct line for the international Communist movement, as distinct from the 'deviationist' Marxist movements. In its essence, M.-L. is taken in the USSR to embody three major ingredients: 1. Marxist-Leninist philosophy (DIALECTICAL MATERIALISM and HISTORICAL MATERIALISM); 2. Marxist-Leninist political economy (CAPITALISM, IMPERIALISM, SOCIALISM); and 3. SCIENTIFIC COMMUNISM (the strategy and tactics of the international Communist movement, including the postulates of the CLASS STRUGGLE, PROLETARIAN REVOLUTION and the DICTATORSHIP OF THE PROLETARIAT). M.-L. is claimed by the Soviet leadership to have universal applicability and to be a flexible, dynamic and progressive ideology, continually developing and adaptable to changing conditions. By its critics, M.-L. has been variously described as an ideological justification for power politics, a doctrine for the legitimization of the Soviet regime in the USSR, an institutionalized messianic ecclastistical establishment, a closed system unable to depart from its institutionalized and obsolete dogmas, and a betrayal of the original Marxist ideal. About three-quarters of the

Communist parties in the world today class themselves as M.-L.

Marxism-Leninism-Stalinism A term used at the height of Stalin's PERSONALITY CULT 1945–55, to describe the Soviet version of MARXISM as developed by LENIN and STALIN in the USSR. After KHRUSHCHEV'S SECRET SPEECH in Feb. 1956, 'Stalinism' was dropped as part of the DE-STALINIZATION.

Marxist (commonly spelt with the capital letter, but unlike MARXIAN). Pertaining to the system of precepts and practices generally accepted by the followers of K. Marx and developed into MARXISM. Such tenets may be embodied in the works of Marx himself or in their subsequent interpretations and adaptations to suit specific political, geographical, cultural and historical conditions.

Marxist All-Ethiopian Socialist Movement The ruling united front of Marxist parties and groups in Socialist Ethiopia. The Movement was officially created in Feb. 1977 and was established by the Dergue, a left-wing revolutionary 'Armed Forces Co-ordinating Committee', which heads the present military regime. As reported in 1978, the Movement's top organs were a Central Committee of 32 members and an inner Politburo called the 'Standing Committee', consisting of 16 members. There are several underground Marxist groups operating in different regions of Ethiopia which are opposed to the M.A.-E.S.M. and its military regime.

Marxist Dialectical Method DIALECTIC, DIALECTICAL MATERIALISM, DIALECTICS.

Marxist Ethics ETHICS.

Marxist Linguistics LABOUR THEORY OF LANGUAGE DEVELOPMENT, MARRISM.

Marxistology A systematic study of propositions, ideas and doctrines postulated, supported or propagated by Marxist thinkers of various shades in such spheres as PHILOSOPHY, ETHICS, POLITICS, POLITICAL ECONOMY, SOCIOLOGY and the natural sciences.

Marxology A systematic study of theories, concepts, practices and postulates embodied in the writings of K. MARX (as distinct from other Marxist thinkers). The level of the study implied is advanced, as carried on by philosophers, political scientists, economists, sociologists and artists. The term is also used in two other meanings: 1. it refers to the revived study of Marx's ideas and precepts as he understood them and wanted them applied in practice (as distinct from subsequent additions, revisions and distortions by other Marxist theoreticians and leaders). The term in this sense came into use in the West in the 1960s, with the revival being described (by Sidney Hook) as the 'Second coming of Marx'; 2. in the Socialist countries, the term is sometimes used derogatively, referring to the study of Marxism in the capitalist world, designed to distort and discredit the policies and practices pursued by the Communist regimes as irrational, impractical or inconsistent with Marx's original ideas.

Masses A term commonly used by Marxists to describe workers and peasants, especially in capitalist countries, emphasizing their large numbers in relation to the elitist bourgeoisie. The m. usually constitute three-quarters of the total population. The classical Marxist thinkers identified the m. with the social class which is exploited, oppressed, uneducated and unorganized. Lenin in his writings and speeches emphasized that by virtue of their numbers, their vast store of energy and talent and being the sole creators of material production, the m. are the 'true makers of history' – especially if they are made class-conscious. However, in practice, neither Lenin nor Stalin took much notice of the m. when it came to policymaking and top-level administration and management. The Communist party can be seen as an elite apart from the populace. The party as well as the state are organized on a hierarchical basis with a great concentration of power at the top. Stalin said in 1935 that 'cadres are the commanding staff of the Party' and 'cadres decide everything'. A greater role is accorded to the m. in MAOISM. Mao Tse-tung was critical of the Party bureaucracy and identified himself with the masses, which he was fond of describing as 'the real heroes' and embodying 'boundless creative power'. The Maoist fascination with the m. was reflected in the frequent mass campaign (as exemplified by the GREAT PROLETARIAN CULTURAL REVOLUTION).

Massive Retaliation Strategy The US defence policy announced in 1951 by J. F. Dulles, Secretary of State in President D. D. Eisenhower's Administration. The strategy was directed against the Socialist bloc, especially the USSR and China. It gave new emphasis to the possible use of atomic weapons on a large scale, from bases in the USA as well as on the fringes of the Socialist bloc, as a deterrent to would-be attackers. The strategic thinking was based on the conviction that conventional ground combat with Communist forces, especially in Asia, provided no solution. It was also assumed that a strike by the East would not cripple the US ability to retaliate decisively. The M.R.S. replaced the more aggressive policy, the 'sword and shield' strategy, but was eventually replaced in 1957 by the 'gradual deterrence strategy'.

'Mass Line' Movement A campaign promoted by the supporters of Mao Tse-tung in China which emphasized the role of the masses in decision-making and control, as a means of counteracting the emergence of elites and privileges. It reached its extreme form during the GREAT PROLETARIAN CULTURAL REVOLUTION. The Movement assumed several forms: a propaganda drive among workers to make them aware of the danger of a hierarchical power structure; periodical assignment of managerial staff to menial tasks in their enterprises; the requirement that students engage in manual vacation work in the countryside or factories; and the abolition of ranks in the army.

Mass Society A term used in the West to denote the new society shaped by large-scale industrialization, mass production, standardized products, mass media and stereotyped ways of living. It is pointed out that the modern m.s. is a vast improvement for the masses that emerged from the Industrial Revolution in the 19th c. as Marx knew it. The m.s. is characterized by the submergence of individualism in the process of the increasing socialization. Similarly, differences between social classes are becoming obliterated and obsolete. The champions of the m.s. emphasize its liberation from traditional strictures, its high living standards, the wide range of interests and entertainment made possible by affluence, media and travel. But Marxists maintain that modern capitalism, far from solving its traditional problems is actually aggravating or creating a number of problems, such as the monotony of work, faceless workers, hardly any scope for creativity and ever-present alienation.

Master Programme A short name for the Master Programme of Socialist Economic Integration for 1976–80, adopted by the member countries of the COUNCIL FOR MUTUAL ECONOMIC ASSISTANCE. The M.P. was further supplemented by the Co-ordinated Plan of Multilateral Integrative Measures of the CMEA Member Countries for 1976–80. The M.P. was primarily concerned with the construction and development of major industrial complexes designed to meet the needs of all its participants in respect of such products as asbestos, ferro-alloys, gas, iron, nickel, pulp and certain types of machinery and equipment. The estimated cost of those complexes was 9 billion transferable roubles.

Material and Technical Base of Socialism An economic concept commonly used in the Socialist countries, denoting the economic capacity of Socialism for progress and its eventual advance to FULL COM-

MUNISM. It embraces the size and extent of the utilization of natural resources, the size and quality of labour, the volume and structure of capital, the organization of production and subsequent production relations and the level and improvement of technology. It is pointed out by Communist leaders that the m.t.b.s. inherited from the capitalist regime was noted for its antiquated production relations (with the qualified exception of Czechoslovakia and the German DR), low technology and predominantly backward agricultural structure. Since the Communist takeover, rapid industrialization has become the top policy objective. The most important element of the m.t.b.s. is machine-building, as it is strategic to the improvement of the quality of labour and methods of production, the advancement of the structure of the economy to higher levels and an increase in efficiency.

Material Balances The system of balancing the sources of supply and the allocation of material production. It is the basic method used in Socialist central economic planning, first introduced in the *Gosplan* in the USSR during the 1920s. For the economic plan to be internally consistent, the planned supply from all sources must be balanced with the planned demand from all users. M.b. are prepared at the national, ministry, branch, enterprise and regional levels. Owing to the Marxist preoccupation with material production and the complex price structure (not necessarily reflecting scarcity), production flows are detailed in physical units. At the national level, the source (or input) side of the m.b. consists of stocks at the beginning of the planned period, and planned production and imports. Utilization (output) consists of specified deliveries to producing enterprises, supplies for current consumption, reserves, losses, exports and stocks at the end of the planned period. In their final form, the national m.b. are broken down along the hierarchical levels of planning and management. The responsibility for the collection of data and the co-ordination of the balances

in their final form, as well as their correction in response to changing conditions, rests with the STATE PLANNING COMMISSION.

Material Incentives A concept commonly used in the Socialist countries to describe special rewards in money or kind to workers according to the quantity and quality of work performed or economies achieved. In addition to the differentiation of standard wage rates, they include bonuses or other benefits to individual workers or groups of workers out of the MATERIAL INCENTIVES FUNDS. The practice amounts to the acceptance of the principle of distribution of personal income 'to each according to his work' (as distinct from the Marxian ideal of 'to each according to his need'). M.i. have been substantially strengthened in the European Socialist countries since the ECONOMIC REFORMS of the early 1960s (since 1950 in Yugoslavia), owing to the decline in the effectiveness of MORAL INCENTIVES. M.i. have been linked to enterprise PROFIT. The Chinese Communist leadership has, on the whole, been highly critical of m.i. and has instead largely relied on moral motivation. The drive against m.i. was most pronounced during the GREAT PROLETARIAN CULTURAL REVOLUTION. The GANG OF FOUR, in fact, advocated the same wage for all industrial workers. However, under HUA KUO-FENG, the principle 'to each according to his work' has been firmly readopted. Ideologically m.i. are regarded as transitional, to be applied under socialism but to disappear under FULL COMMUNISM, giving way to moral incentives.

Material Incentives Fund A fund administered by enterprises in the Socialist countries for the payment of bonuses to individual workers and/or collectively to a group of workers in money and/or in kind. The Fund is now (since the ECONOMIC REFORMS) maintained out of enterprise profits. Typically 5–15 per cent of enterprise gross profits are allowed into the Fund. It is usually distributed in the following forms: 1. cash bonuses to individual workers or teams of workers, or uniformly to all workers in the enterprise; 2. the financing of the construction and repairs of houses, owned by the enterprise; 3. the financing of various services to the enterprise personnel, such as free excursions, grants for the maintenance of reading rooms and community rooms, assistance to the child-minding sporting and entertainment facilities associated with the enterprise concerned; 4. free tickets to theatres, matches etc; and 5. emergency aid.

Materialism In philosophy, one of the two fundamental directions of thinking, according to which MATTER is primary, is the true reality and everything immaterial either does not exist or is secondary, deriving from matter. M. insists that there is only one reality – the material world – its existence is independent of man's consciousness or will, thus, there is no supernatural world or its claimed creator – god. M. contrasts with IDEALISM. (Philosophical m. is a distinct concept from m. in the moral sense since neither m. nor idealism in philosophy involve ethical value judgments). The beginnings of m. go back to ancient times in China, Babylon, Egypt and Greece. But qualitatively, new developments came only during the 17th–19th centuries, emphasizing different forms of m., in the works of F. Bacon (1561–1626), T. Hobbs (1588–1679), B. Spinoza (1632–77), J. Locke (1632–1704), M. V. LOMONOSOV, A. N. RADISHCHEV, L. FEUERBACH, V. G. BELINSKY, A. I. HERZEN, N. G. CHERNYSHEVSKY, N. A. DOBROLUBOV and others. In the early 1840s, m. attracted the attention of K. MARX and F. ENGELS, but in their view all conceptions of m. up to that time had been simplistic, static, inconsistent, incomplete and unscientific representations of the real natural world and society. To overcome these claimed shortcomings, they developed DIALECTICAL MATERIALISM and HISTORICAL MATERIALISM, which have become the basic foundations of Marxist ideology. They maintained that it is the material world, expressed through man's activity in the changing methods of production and production relations in society, that shapes the nature of man and the whole social structure of any socioeconomic formation. Marxists emphasize that the m. of Marx and Engels was not a mere continuation of traditional m., but a 'qualitative leap' in the development of human thought. They also add that Marxist m. provides the philosophical foundation for ATHEISM, REVOLUTION and social progress from one SOCIO-ECONOMIC FORMATION to another leading to FULL COMMUNISM. To Marxist philosophers, only m. can provide the true understanding of nature, society and change, and the correct answer to the eternal philosophical problem: the relation between being and consciousness. They believe that m. has basically played a progressive role in the development of philosophy, usually representing the world outlook of the enlightened and dynamic groups or social classes. In their view, while idealism has usually favoured conservatism, religion and superstition, m. has exerted a positive influence on scientific and social progress. Also ECONOMIC M., EMPIRIO-CRITICISM, MECHANISTIC M., NATURAL M., VULGAR M.

Materialism and Empirio-criticism A major philosophical treatise by V. I. LENIN, published in 1908 and directed against the EMPIRIO-CRITICISM of E. MACH and his Russian followers. The book also embodies additions to Marxist DIALECTICAL MATERIALISM and HISTORICAL MATERIALISM in the light of subsequent scientific and social developments. L. carried out analytical critical analyses of AGNOSTICISM, EMPIRIO-MONISM, EMPIRIO-SYMBOLISM, FIDEISM and PHYSICAL IDEALISM. He stressed the importance of OBJECTIVE TRUTH and PRACTICE as criteria of truth, and made some new applications of dialectical materialism to the Marxist theory of COGNITION. L. also discussed the need for PARTY-MINDEDNESS in philosophy and militant and uncompromising attitudes against deviations from revolutionary Marxism.

Materialist In philosophy, pertaining to MATERIALISM. As used by Marxists, it may also mean anti-speculative, atheistic, economic, empirical, realist and Marxist.

Materialist Interpretation of History HISTORICAL MATERIALISM.

Materialist Logic See LOGIC.

Materialist Monism See MONISM.

Materialist Understructure See BASE.

Materialized Labour In Marxist political economy, past labour embodied in raw materials, capital goods and consumer goods. In the Marxian formula for VALUE ($c + v + s$), m.l. is represented by c. It contrasts with LIVE LABOUR (v), the direct expenditure of labour. If used in production, the value of m.l. is transferred to the new product. The higher the productivity of live labour, the more m.l. it is capable of transferring to the new product per unit of time.

Material Production In Marxist political economy, production contributed in the PRODUCTIVE SPHERE, viz. industry, construction, agriculture and forestry, transport and communications, trade and other minor material pursuits (fisheries, hunting, gathering, laundrying, research and development). Services (transport, communications, trade, research and development) are included in m.p. only to the extent that they contribute to the value of tangible products (i.e. representing the continuation of the process of production). Such services are called 'material services' or 'productive services' (and contrast with NON-PRODUCTIVE SERVICES). In Socialist national income accounting, only m.p. contributes to national income (NET MATERIAL PRODUCT) and the RATE OF GROWTH.

Material Reserve Norm See NORMATIVE MATERIAL STOCKS.

Material Services A less commonly used Marxist term for PRODUCTIVE SERVICES.

Mathematical Economics The application of advanced mathematical methods to economics. The beginnings of m.e. in the West go back to the mathematical school of the 1870s (primarily the Lausanne School of L. Walras and V. Pareto). The development of econometrics since the 1920s (beginning with R. Frisch) has further extended its scope. M.e. has assumed new levels of importance since the early 1950s. In the Socialist countries for a long time there was little interest in m.e., mainly due to official scepticism and opposition on ideological grounds. Mathematical methods involve MARGINAL ANALYSIS and the valuation of non-labour factors of production and further, in conjunction with computers, they demonstrate errors of judgment. The official attitude in the USSR and the Eastern European countries began to change after 1956, when mathematical methods, econometrics and electronic computers began increasingly to accord official blessing and encouragement. Some outstanding contributions have been made, particularly in Hungary, Poland and the USSR. Some works have been translated into Western languages, such as those by L. V. KANTOROVICH, J. Kornai, O. R. LANGE, V. S. Nemchinov, V. V. Novozhilov and W. Trzeciakowski. Advanced mathematical methods, aided with computers, are revolutionizing the whole system of planning and management, in particular the working out of optimal solutions and OPTIMAL PLANS. The mathematization of economic analysis and planning in the Socialist countries is sometimes described as the 'new Socialist economics'.

Matriarchy Social organization in which the mother is the head of the family and where women play the dominant role. One of the contentions of Marxist HISTORICAL MATERIALISM, mainly contained in F. Engels's *ORIGIN OF THE FAMILY, PRIVATE PROPERTY AND THE STATE*, is that m. was a feature of the first socio-economic formation, PRIMITIVE COMMUNISM. This was due to the existing mode of production peculiar to that formation. Under the conditions of group marriage, typical of early societies, the father of the children was unknown, while the mother brought up the children. Consequently, only the maternal line of kinship was recognized. After marriage, the wife remained with her tribe which her husband joined. Women were not only the heads of the household but also engaged in agricultural activities, while the men engaged in hunting (not a reliable source of subsistence). At this stage, the means of production were held collectively by the tribe. The role of women was changed with the rise of pastoral activities as the main source of subsistence and men came to own the instruments of production, domestic animals and slaves. This led to the gradual economic and social subordination of women to men under PATRIARCHY. On the other hand, the opponents of Marxism maintain that the original form of social organization was patriarchy, which from the start was associated with the private ownership of property.

Matrix of Inter-branch Balances A table consisting of horizontal rows and vertical columns of figures showing flows of inputs and outputs of the producing and recipient branches of the economy in a systematized pattern. If each branch produces one article, the table is called the MATRIX OF SQUARE BALANCES If the rows indicate products and the columns indicate production inputs, the matrix can be either square or rectangular. The m. of i.-b.b. is designed to ensure the internal consistency of the national economic plan and constitutes the upper left quarter of the BALANCES OF THE NATIONAL ECONOMY.

Matrix of Square Balances A simplified input-output table, showing the flows of materials and products from the supplying to the recipient branches of the economy in a systematized pattern. The matrix is the most basic technique used in Socialist economic planning. In the BALANCES OF

THE NATIONAL ECONOMY it appears as the upper left quarter. Its main purpose is to ensure the internal consistency of the economic plan. It looks like a chessboard, with vertical columns setting out the recipient branches and horizontal rows specifying how much in the way of supplies they receive from the different supplying branches. The matrix is 'square' if it is assumed that each supplying branch, specified in horizontal rows, produces one article. If more than one article is produced the table becomes a 'm. of rectangular b.'.

Matter One of the basic concepts in philosophy referring to material objects (atoms, molecules, cells, plants, animals, humans) and the most fundamental element of MATERIALISM. Materialist philosophers differ in detail on the nature and change of m. In Marxist philosophy, it is accepted that only DIALECTICAL MATERIALISM provides the correct interpretation. The main Marxist treatment of m. is contained in F. Engels' ANTI-DÜHRING and DIALECTICS OF NATURE and V. I. Lenin's MATERIALISM AND EMPIRIO-CRITICISM. Marxist philosophers regard m. as an OBJECTIVE REALITY, independent of man but which he perceives with his senses. There is only one world consisting of m. and all phenomena are attributable to m. in its continuous change. M. has universal attributes common to all material objects (such as movement, time, space and conformity to natural laws) and specific features peculiar only to some material objects (life, consciousness, thinking). M. is eternal, i.e. it can neither be created nor destroyed quantitatively, but can assume different forms, states, shapes and contents. Marxists attach great importance to the kinetic theory of m. (constant transformation of m.) in its three basic stages: inorganic; organic; and social (the last one embracing man and society). Marxist materialist philosophy insists that m. is primary, while FORM, IDEAS and spiritual phenomena are secondary, derived from m. and having no independent existence without m. But Mao

349

Maximalists

Tse-tung departed from the traditional Marxist interpretation and advanced the idea (in 'FOOLISH OLD MAN') that through the power of man's will, 'consciousness can be transformed into matter'.

Maximalists See MAKSIMALISTS.

Mayakovsky, Vladimir Vladimirovich (1893–1930) An outstanding Russian poet, revolutionary, one of the founders of FUTURISM in Russia and one of the leading proponents of SOCIALIST REALISM in art. He organized support among writers, actors and painters for revolution and the Soviet regime. His creative work was directed at the masses, in particular the popularization of revolutionary ideals. In 1923 he was a co-founder and editor of a futurist literary group called the *LEF*, which published a literary journal under the same title. After Lenin's death (Jan. 1924), M. came into conflict with Stalinist policies on art. His disillusion, together with his tragic personal affairs, led him to suicide on 14 May 1930.

May Day A holiday celebrated on the 1 May by the international working class movement, as an expression of its solidarity in the form of mass demonstrations, processions and other activities. The decision to introduce M.D. celebrations was taken at the founding Congress of the SECOND INTERNATIONAL in Paris in 1889. The date of the 1 May was chosen to commemorate the beginning of a strike by American workers in Chicago in 1886, ruthlessly handled by the employers and the authorities, for an eight-hour working day. The first M.D. celebrations were held in 1890, and their scope and intensity were on many occasions enhanced by events affecting the international labour movement (such as the REVOLUTION of 1905–07, the Civil War in Russia 1918–20 and the POPULAR FRONT in the 1930s). Since W.W.II the importance of M.D. has declined. In the USA the 1 May was proclaimed by the New York City as the Loyalty Day, and this was later confirmed on a national basis by President D. Eisenhower in 1955. In the Socialist countries M.D. is a state holiday celebrated on a mass scale. The most impressive M.D. celebration is held in Red Square in Moscow, usually featuring a display of modern weapons.

May 4 Movement FOURTH OF MAY MOVEMENT (in China).

May 7 Cadre School SEVENTH-OF-MAY CADRE SCHOOLS (in China).

Mazzini, Giuseppe (1805–1872) A prominent Italian politician, journalist and democrat who led the national liberation movement. Mazzini opposed the Bonapartist invasion of Italy, contributed to the support of the FIRST INTERNATIONAL but later became critical of it and the PARIS COMMUNE. He is best known for his political journalism (the journal *Young Italy* was set up in 1831) which eventually led to his exile in Britain where he became acquainted with Marx.

McCarthyism An anti-communist campaign in the USA in the early 1950s, led by Senator Joseph R. McCarthy. M. was instigated by the revelations of espionage in government service (such as the Hiss Affair), the Korean War (1950–53) and the COLD WAR in general. The campaign assumed several forms, such as the unnecessarily harsh Congressional investigations into the lives of public employees (by a Senate Committee headed by McCarthy protected by parliamentary immunity), the imposition of LOYALTY OATHS, the passage of anti-communist legislation (such as the McCURRAN-WOOD INTERNAL SECURITY ACT of 1950) and the surveillance of scientists, academics, teachers, students and others. M. approached extremist hysteria, conditioned by an exaggerated fear of communism and by political opportunism, and fostered widespread suspicion and distrust. M. subsided after 1954, when McCarthy himself was investigated on the initiative of the Department of the Army.

350

McCurran-Wood Internal Security Act A piece of legislation passed by the US Congress in 1950, directed against the Communist party depriving its members of government employment and making them liable to internment in the case of a national emergency. It also deprived aliens of entry to the USA if they had been Communists. The Act established the Subversive Activities Control Board for the enforcement of the legislation.

Means of Consumption A Marxist term for single-use and durable-use consumer goods, as exemplified by foodstuffs, beverages, clothing, furniture, dwellings. The m. of c. in the Socialist countries constitute about 70 per cent of the NET MATERIAL PRODUCT and are sold to the population through the retail market (PRIVATE CONSUMPTION) or provided free or at below-cost prices (SOCIAL CONSUMPTION). The m. of c. contrast with the MEANS OF PRODUCTION.

Means of Labour In Marxist political economy, the material factors of production, viz. capital and land used by labour in production and applied to the OBJECTS OF LABOUR (products of nature and other raw materials, semi-finished products). Specifically, the m. of l. include implements, tools, machinery, equipment, farm and factory buildings, warehouses, shops, roads, canals, railways, communications, pipelines, agricultural land, forests, sites and fishing grounds. The most important components of the m. of l. are considered to be INSTRUMENTS OF LABOUR. In contrast to the objects of labour, the m. of l. participate in several production processes until such means are depreciated or scrapped. In the process of production a portion of the value of the man-made m. of l. is transferred to the article produced.

Means of Production An important term used in Marxist political economy, embracing the MEANS OF LABOUR (capital and land) and the OBJECTS OF LABOUR (raw materials and semi-finished products). The most important m. of p. are the INSTRUMENTS OF LABOUR (implements, tools, machinery, equipment). Although the m. of p. are indispensable in the process of production, they are incapable of creating value, which only labour can accomplish. The ownership of the m. of p. is of crucial importance in different SOCIO-ECONOMIC FORMATIONS, as it determines PRODUCTION RELATIONS. In the Marxist view, in antagonistic socio-economic formations (slavery, feudalism, capitalism) the m. of p. are predominantly owned on a private basis, which typically leads to EXPLOITATION, while under Socialism the basic m. of p. are socially-owned, which removes the possibility of (private) exploitation. In Western economics, instead of using the concept of m. of p., the 'factors of production' is used, embracing land, capital, labour and entrepreneurship (and, more recently, technology).

Mechanism In philosophy, another term for MECHANISTIC MATERIALISM.

Mechanistic Materialism In philosophy, one of the extreme doctrines of MATERIALISM, attributing all natural phenomena to the operation of the laws of mechanics. It explains development as increases, decreases, repetitions, and movements in terms of the transposition of matter in space, all in response to external stimuli ('the collision of external forces'). M.m. thus negates the internal sources of change, the qualitative nature of development from simpler (lower) to more complex (higher) forms. The beginnings of m.m. can be traced back to Democritus (460–370 B.C.) in ancient Greece, but its greatest development occurred in England, France and the Netherlands during the 17th and 18th c. The leading exponents were T. Hobbes (1588–1679), R. Descartes (1596–1650) and B. Spinoza (1632–77). In the early 1840s, Marx and Engels examined m.m. and found it to be 'a lower stage' of the development of materialist philosophy. They argued that m.m. disregarded the internal sources of the transformation of matter and societies

351

(SELF-MOVEMENT) and saw the possibility of qualitative leaps in development from lower to higher forms in nature as well as society. Instead, they developed DIALECTICAL MATERIALISM, which expressed their materialist interpretation of history (HISTORICAL MATERIALISM) more satisfactorily. There was a revival of m.m. in the USSR in the 1920s, led by L. I. Axelrod (1868–1946) and A. M. Deborin (1881–1963) and supported by Trotskyites and Bukharinists. However, they were condemned by Lenin and Stalin as anti-Marxist and supporters of MENSHEVIKIZING IDEALISM.

Medibank, Medicare See SOCIALIZED MEDICINE.

Mehring, Franz (1846–1919) A German revolutionary Marxist, writer, philosopher and one of the leaders of the left-wing faction in the SOCIAL-DEMOCRATIC PARTY OF GERMANY. He turned to Marxism in the 1880s, joined the S.-D.P.G. in 1891 and became the editor of its theoretical organ, *Die Neue Zeit*. In his historical and philosophical writings, he opposed MECHANISTIC MATERIALISM, ECONOMIC MATERIALISM, IRRATIONALISM, NEOKANTIANISM, REVISIONISM and the principle of 'ART FOR ART'S SAKE'. He also held that morality is not neutral, but is conditioned by the social environment, especially in the interest of the ruling class.

Mendelism An early school of thought in GENETICS, pioneered by an Austrian monk, G. Mendel (1822–84) in the 1860s and rediscovered in 1900. On the basis of his experiments with peas, Mendel formulated the basic laws of heredity, viz. the probability of occurrence of parental characteristics in precise mathematical terms. He also concluded that hereditary characteristics do not depend on the acquired changes in organisms or on the environmental conditions. M. was attacked by Marxist biologists, especially K. A. TIMIRIAZIEV, I. W. MICHURIN and T. D. LYSENKO, who argued that it was not a biological but a statistical theory. In their

view, M. did not identify the real laws of heredity, but merely replaced real biological research with formalistic mathematical methods of investigation. As such, M. negates the possibility of improving organisms and denies the very nature of development. The official Soviet policy rejected M. up to the late 1950s while supporting MICHURINISM and LYSENKOISM. However, after Lysenko's methods and claims were discredited between 1956 and 1964, M. was rehabilitated, opening a new era for Soviet genetics. In 1965, to commemorate the centenary of the original publication of Mendel's findings, a symposium was organized in Prague and Brno under the auspices of the Czechoslovak Government, in which some 800 geneticists, from capitalist and Socialist countries, participated. Also NATURAL SELECTION, WEISMANNISM-MORGANISM.

Menshevik Internationalists The group of radical MENSHEVIKS who were inclined to agree on many questions with the BOLSHEVIKS and were mostly associated with the paper *NOVAYA ZHIZN*. During W.W.I (like the Bolsheviks) the M.I. opposed Russia's participation in the war and demanded immediate cessation from the war 'without annexation and indemnities', wishing to turn it into a proletarian revolution. They were led by L. MARTOV, P. Axelrod and T. Dan. The M.I. took this stand at the ZIMMERWALD CONFERENCE (Aug. 1915) and the KIENTAL CONFERENCE (April 1916), both held in Switzerland. After W.W.I some M.I. (incl. Martov) participated in the organization of the SECOND-AND-A-HALF INTERNATIONAL.

Menshevikizing Idealism A philosophical direction pursued by a number of MENSHEVIKS in the USSR in the late 1920s and early 1930s, who rejected Bolshevik additions to Marxist philosophy. The expression was coined by Stalin in 1930. The group was led by A. M. Deborin (1881–1963), hence 'Deborinism', which is another term for M.i. The movement was directed against the Leninist and Stalinist distortions of the original Marxist philosophical line by a strong Party orientation adopted by the ALL-UNION COMMUNIST PARTY (OF THE BOLSHEVIKS). M.i. also rejected the philosophical validity of the Bolshevik methods under Soviet conditions and was opposed to the distortion of the science of genetics by MICHURINISM. Instead, the members of the group advocated a moderate version of Marxist philosophy as accepted by the SECOND INTERNATIONAL. They were also inclined to embody some elements of Hegelian IDEALISM and to de-emphasize MATERIALISM in favour of MECHANISTIC MATERIALISM. The Soviet leadership condemned M.i. as anti-Marxist and anti-Party. Owing to Stalinist repression, M.i. disappeared by the mid-1930s, but Deborin himself managed to escape persecution.

Mensheviks ('Minoritarians', in Russian) Originally members of the moderate wing of the RUSSIAN SOCIAL-DEMOCRATIC LABOUR PARTY, who advocated LEGAL MARXISM and ECONOMISM and a gradual and humanitarian process to socialism in Russia. They emerged as a distinct faction at the Second Congress of the R.S.-D.L.P. in London in 1903, when a split occurred between the M. (who at the time were in a minority) and the BOLSHEVIKS (who commanded a majority). The M. were led by L. MARTOV, G. W. PLEKHANOV, L. TROTSKY, P. B. Axelrod (1850–1928), A. N. Potriesov (1869–1934) and I. Dan (1871–1947). A. BEBEL and K. KAUTSKY also supported the M. After the split, the M. took over ISKRA (the Party's newspaper founded by Lenin) and took control of the Party's Central Committee. The M. remained in the R.S.-D.L.P., but most were ousted by the Bolsheviks in 1912 who re-named the Party the Russian Social-Democratic Labour Party (of the Bolsheviks). In contrast to the Bolsheviks, the M. did not believe that the Russian workers and the peasants were ready for a proletarian revolution. They were opposed to Lenin's personal domination of the Party and to the postulate of the DICTATORSHIP OF THE PROLETARIAT. In-

stead, the M. practised collective leadership and admitted dissent within their ranks. During W.W.I, the M. were divided on the question of the Russian participation in the war. The OBORONTSY group supported the war effort, while the other section followed the line of MENSHEVIK INTERNATIONALISM, opposing the war and wishing to turn it into a proletarian revolution. The influence of the M. increased after the FEBRUARY REVOLUTION OF 1917. Together, with the SOCIALIST REVOLUTIONARIES, they commanded a majority in most SOVIETS OF WORKERS' AND SOLDIERS' DEPUTIES. In Aug. 1917, the M. organized a moderately successful unification conference of several Social-Democratic groups. Although the M. were in a position to assume power in Russia, they hesitated and the Bolsheviks took the initiative and seized power with remarkable ease in the GREAT OCTOBER SOCIALIST REVOLUTION. After the Revolution, the M. assumed the role of a 'legal opposition'. But in June 1918, the M. were expelled from the ALL-RUSSIAN CENTRAL EXECUTIVE COMMITTEE, and for the next three years existed as a semi-legal group. In 1921 the Soviet Government declared the M. an illegal group. Some M. then decided to co-operate with the Bolsheviks and attained high positions in the Soviet hierarchy. However, most of the leading M. and activists were dismissed from their positions of influence, were tried for treason (beginning in 1931), exiled, imprisoned or executed. Before the Stalinist repression (in the early 1920s) many M. went to Berlin and then to Paris after the Nazi takeover.

Mental and Physical Labour Two forms of labour the distinction between which, in the Marxist view, is of considerable ideological importance. The distinction is regarded as not only a consequence of the division of labour, but largely a product of the appearance of the private ownership of the means of production (PRIVATE PROPERTY) and the consequential SOCIAL STRATIFICATION. The distinction has led to antagonistic social relations, owing to

353

the exploitation of physical labourers not only by property owners but also by mental workers. Under capitalism, which has made mechanization possible, the machine does not necessarily lighten the burden of physical labour but is in fact applied to enslave most labourers, transforming them into appendages of machines. According to revolutionary Marxists, only a PROLETARIAN REVOLUTION can genuinely remove the contradiction between m. and p.l. Although under Socialism the distinction still partly exists; it is not antagonistic but merely associated with the division of labour. As a logical corollary to MATERIALISM Marx, and more recently Maoists (*LAO-DONG*), regard physical labour as the true characteristic of man, while mental work is secondary or removed from the real material world. Under FULL COMMUNISM, the distinction will virtually disappear and most workers will be engaged in both.

Meritocracy A term used in Western sociology to indicate that under modern capitalism higher social classes are not based on the ownership of wealth, but on personal abilities and effort, i.e. on merit. It is pointed out that this system is fair and democratic, is not hereditary and provides opportunities to the lower classes for SOCIAL PROMOTION. At the same time, individuals of poor calibre born to higher social classes are reduced to lower orders. Consequently, this upward and downward social mobility ensure social justice and removes the need for the CLASS STRUGGLE and PROLETARIAN REVOLUTION. Marxist critics reject this interpretation of m. on the following grounds: 1. m. exists within the framework of capitalism, where the means of production are still owned mostly by capitalists; 2. those born to higher social classes have better opportunities for developing their abilities through costly training than the offspring of the poor; 3. those born to higher social classes also have a better chance of securing higher positions by better connections and, if not elsewhere, at least in the entities which they own or control; and 4. m. still ack-

nowledges the inevitability of hierarchical SOCIAL STRATIFICATION.

Meslier, Jean (1664–1729) A French priest who became a materialist philosopher, atheist and a communist thinker. In his 'Testament', which was found after his death, he condemned religion, the church hierarchy and the existing exploitative feudal system. He traced all injustice and other evils in his contemporary society to the private ownership of property, whereby kings, nobility and the church appropriated virtually all wealth, leaving toil, misery and suffering to the dispossessed masses. He further saw religion as a device for instilling blind obedience and superstition in the minds of the common people in order to ensure the stability and preservation of the existing social system. He insisted that men are essentially equal and advocated a federation of communistic fraternities, in which all members would work and benefit equally from the fruits of their labour. In his philosophical views, he identified nature as the only reality which is governed by its own inherent laws, and consequently, he concluded that there is no supernatural world. The early Marxists studied his ideas with interest, but found several of his precepts unacceptable. They discarded his metaphysical materialism in philosophy and classed his model of the ideal society as naïve and impractical, typical of UTOPIAN SOCIALISM.

Metamorphosis of Commodities TRANSFORMATION OF COMMODITIES.

Metaphysics In philosophy, the science of being, concerned with the study of matter, reality, mind and appearance. The term was introduced by Aristotle (384–322 B.C.) to designate his books 'after physics', dealing with philosophy. Other leading exponents of m. were St Thomas Aquinas (1229–74), R. Descartes (1596–1650), B. Spinoza (1632–77), D. Hume (1711–76), I. Kant (1724–1804) and G. W. F. HEGEL. Marxist philosophers interpret m. in their own way, identifying it with the predisposition to be preoccupied with individual and isolated aspects of nature and phenomena, to the virtual exclusion of their inter-relations, movement and change. Consequently, they use it in a depreciative sense, with the marginal exclusion of Hegel. They further attack m. for treating nature as static and stagnant, regarding development as mere quantitative processes caused by external forces and ignoring qualitative changes induced by inherent contradictions and conflicts. As such, they consider m. to be a philosophical instrument defending capitalism as a natural and eternal social system, thereby directed against revolutionary Marxism. In their view, only DIALECTICAL MATERIALISM provides the correct interpretation of natural and social phenomena. The main attack on m. is found in F. Engel's ANTI-DÜHRING.

Mexican Communist Party (*Partido Comunista Mexicano*) A relatively small political party in Mexico, but the main Communist group in the country, which is legal and now pursues a pro-Soviet line in the international Communist movement. Its origin goes back to 1919, when several Communist circles were formed, but officially it was founded in 1920 after which it joined the COMINTERN. In 1940 there was a split, which led to the formation of the Worker Peasant Party of Mexico, but which later merged with the Socialist People's Party in 1963. In the same year, the pro-Chinese dissidents were expelled from the M.C.P. who then founded the Bolshevik Communist Party of Mexico. There are also other Communist groups, including the International Communist Group (Trotskyite), the Socialist League (also Trotskyite) and the Twenty-Third of September Communist League (guerrillas). The membership of the M.C.P. is about 5,000 (of the country's total population of 66 million in 1978), mostly drawn from among the educated middle class rather than workers and peasants. Although the Party is legal, it is of no electoral consequence, as it does not have the legal minimum membership of 65,000

to enter candidates at elections. The Party's publications include: *La Voz de Mexico* (*Voice of Mexico*), its daily organ; *Oposición* (*Opposition*), a weekly; and *Nueva epoca* (*New Era*), a theoretical journal.

Mexican Popular Socialist Party See POPULAR SOCIALIST PARTY OF MEXICO.

Mexican Revolutionary Institutional Party See REVOLUTIONARY INSTITUTIONAL PARTY (of Mexico).

Mezhrabpom The abbreviation of *Mezhdunarodnaya rabochiya pomoshch*, in Russian meaning WORKERS' INTERNATIONAL RELIEF.

Mezhrayonka A small left-wing movement in St Petersburg (later renamed Petrograd, now Leningrad) and Moscow which made several attempts over the period 1913–17 to unite different groups of the RUSSIAN SOCIAL-DEMOCRATIC LABOUR PARTY. The name is derived from *Mezhraionnaya Organizatsiya*, in Russian meaning Inter-District Organization. Its members were called *Mezhrayontsy*. Among them were pro-Bolshevik Mensheviks, Bolshevik conciliators, middle-of-the-roaders and Trotskyites. A. V. LUNACHARSKY, L. D. TROTSKY, A. A. Ioffe and M. S. Uritsky were at one stage or another among the most active participants. The group published a magazine *VPERED*. The M. had considerable influence on women workers and the armed forces and carried on propaganda against the Russian participation in W.W.I. It was very active in 1917 after the FEBRUARY REVOLUTION. In Aug. most members joined the Bolshevik party and took part in the GREAT OCTOBER SOCIALIST REVOLUTION.

MGB (abbreviation in Russian of *Ministerstvo Gossudarstvennoi Bezopasnosti*, meaning the Ministry of State Security) In the USSR, the government department responsible for the secret service from 1946 to 1953. It continued the work of the

NKGB (People's Commissariat for State Security) after the People's Commissariats were re-named as Ministries in 1946. The *MGB* was headed by L. BERIA, was placed in charge of atomic research and played a major role in the SOVIETIZATION of the Eastern European countries and China. Its most notorious assignment of repression was associated with the DOCTORS' PLOT before Stalin's death (in March 1953). After it was revealed that the affair had been a frame-up, the *MGB*'s leadership was purged (including Beria, who was executed). The *MGB* was dissoived in 1953 and its functions were temporarily transferred to the *MVD* (Ministry of Internal Affairs) and in March 1954 to the *KGB* (Committee for State Security). The latter no longer has a Ministry status but is attached directly to the Council of Ministers.

Michurin, Ivan Vladimirovich (1855–1935) A prominent Soviet biologist who was opposed to Western GENETICS (especially MENDELISM and WEISMANNISM-MORGANISM) and who steered Soviet biology along lines consistent with Marxism. Of limited formal education, M. had carried on horticultural experiments before the Bolshevik Revolution of 1917 and received no financial support or recognition from the Tsarist regime. After the Revolution, he became an enthusiastic supporter of DIALECTICAL MATERIALISM and the Soviet regime. In the development of species, he ascribed critical importance to the interrelationship between living organisms and their environment. He devised his own methods for controlling the development of plants by manipulating the environmental (as distinct from hereditary) factors. He developed about 600 new varieties of fruit trees and shrubs. M. enjoyed generous support from the Soviet regime, not necessarily because of any outstanding scientific achievements on his part, but because he was a Communist and a practical horticulturist of great promise to Soviet agriculture and Marxist ideology. He dominated agricultural research and biological thinking in

the USSR up to the mid-1930s. In the West, M. was regarded as a well-meaning and personally honest, but rather naïve and limited scientific worker. His particular brand of biology came to be known as MICHURINISM, which was largely discredited in the USSR after the late 1950s. His *Selected Works* were published in four volumes in 1948.

Michurinism The field of biology developed by I. V. MICHURIN in the USSR, emphasizing the decisive importance of environmental factors in the development of organisms, especially in horticulture. M. embodied three basic elements: 1. the theory and methods of artificial hybridization; 2. the theory and methods of controlled development of organisms via environmental factors; and 3. the theory and methods of artificial selection. M. dominated Soviet AGROBIOLOGY under Stalin, as it was seen as a basis for radically improving the productivity of agriculture. Its Marxist approach offered a possibility of transforming nature and evolving a NEW COMMUNIST MAN. The Soviet regime regarded M. as a higher stage of development of the Darwinian theory of NATURAL SELECTION and the Lamarckian theory of inheritance of acquired characteristics, consistent with the Marxist-Leninist conception of DIALECTICAL MATERIALISM. M. emphasized the interdependence of organic matter and the non-organic environment, which according to Michurin constitute a dialectical unity. The driving force in the developmental process is the contradiction arising from the conflicting exchange of matter between the organism and the environment (assimilation, dissimilation), which amounts to a dialectical struggle between the old and the new. The basic factors in the change of species are the variety and variability of the environment and the inherited mutations induced by the environment. Consequently, the hereditary capacity of an organism is a historical compound of previous generations which passed through the changing environment. M. rejected the concepts of the gene and chromosome, the foundations of WEISMANNISM-MORGANISM. An offshoot of M. was LYSENKOISM. M. was never treated seriously in the West, although it must be recognized that it contributed considerably to the improvement of Soviet horticulture. But from the scientific standpoint it was rather naïve and was responsible for limiting the development of Soviet genetics for some two or three decades. By the mid-1960s, M. had been largely discredited.

Microeconomic and Macroeconomic Analysis Two opposite approaches to the study of economic magnitudes and processes, which may be pursued in economic theory and policy. The microeconomic approach is directed to the analysis of individual persons, enterprises, industries and processes, while macroeconomic studies dwell on aggregates, constituting the whole branch of the economy, the country as a whole or the world economy in general. These two different aspects of economic analysis traditionally received different emphases in capitalist and Socialist economies. Under *LAISSEZ-FAIRE* capitalism, microeconomic units and processes occupied the centre of attention of economic theorists and policy makers. On the other hand, in classical Marxist economic theory and later under CENTRALIZED DIRECTIVE SYSTEM OF PLANNING AND MANAGEMENT, the whole economy and society constituted the starting point of analysis and emphasis. The different approaches simply reflected the traditional capitalist preoccupation with individual interest (INDIVIDUALISM) on the one hand, and the Marxist insistence on the PRIMACY OF SOCIAL INTEREST. However, there have been far-reaching departures under each system from their original approaches. In capitalist economies, there has been a growing interest in macroeconomic theoretical and policy studies, as exemplified by the turn to the general equilibrium theory, initiated by the Lausanne school (L. Walras and V. Pareto) towards the end of the 19th c., and the Keynesian revolution initiated in the late 1930s. In the Socialist coun-

tries, the theorists and even policy makers have been increasingly concerned with the improvement of the efficiency of enterprises and the welfare of the consumers, especially since the ECONOMIC REFORMS of the 1960s.

Middle Class A sociological concept used mostly in application to industrialized capitalist countries to denote the social stratum above the working class but below the upper class. In its modern sense, it has evolved from the wealthy merchant class which later, under the impact of the Industrial Revolution, developed into the BOURGEOISIE (capitalists), living in the cities. Industrialization and the growing complexity of the economy has added small industrialists, owners of small and medium-scale firms, plus intellectual and other professional groups, salaried employees of industrial, commercial, financial and public service entities (white-collar workers), skilled artisans and prosperous farmers to the m.c. The rising per capita incomes and the increasing equalization and democratization in most Western countries have led to a great expansion of the m.c., absorbing large proportions of the working and upper classes. Some sociologists believe that the future POST-INDUSTRIAL SOCIETY will be what traditionally was known as the m.c. The term m.c. is not used in application to the Socialist countries. The designation INTELLIGENTSIA is the nearest equivalent.

Midszenty, Jozsef (1892–1975) A Hungarian Catholic leader who fought for religious freedom and became a symbol of courage and determination in the struggle against communism. He was ordained in 1915, became a Papal Prelate in 1937 and in Sep. 1945 was appointed Cardinal on the strength of his anti-fascist record. M. became a most determined opponent of the Communist encroachment on religious freedom and the role of the church in Hungary. He was arrested in Dec. 1948 and in Feb. 1949 in a spectacular POLITICAL SHOW TRIAL, and was charged with treason, espionage and foreign currency speculation. He was sentenced to life imprisonment, which was later commuted to house arrest. He was released during the HUNGARIAN UPRISING in 1956. After its failure he sought asylum in the US Legation in Budapest, where he spent 15 years, refusing opportunities for safe passage to the West. Following an agreement between the Vatican and the Hungarian Government, he was released in 1971, went to Rome, and then to Vienna where he died in May 1975. He disagreed with the Vatican's policy of accommodation with the Communist regimes in Eastern Europe. M. earned the admiration of many throughout the world. But some sympathetic critics thought that he could have rendered better service to the cause of freedom and the church by a more diplomatic posture to co-operate with other anti-communist forces and to find some form of accommodation with the Communist regime. His *Memoirs* were published in the USA in 1974.

MiG The name of the Soviet fighter aircraft, designed by A. I. Mikoyan and M. I. Gurevich. Originally constructed during 1939–40, it was soon improved and used during W.W.II as the fastest and most effective aircraft of its kind in the world. A number of different models followed and its excellence was further proved during the Korean War (1950–53).

Mihajlović, Draža (1893–1946) A Yugoslav general, guerrilla leader, a right-wing nationalist statesman and the chief opponent of Tito in W.W.II. M. became colonel in 1940 and after the invasion of Yugoslavia by Germany and Italy in 1941, organized and led the right-wing guerrilla forces, called the *Chetniks*. They fought not only the foreign invaders but also the Croats and Communists. His campaigns were quite effective, and as a result he was appointed War Minister in the Yugoslav Government-in-Exile in 1942. Although at first he received Allied supplies, from 1944 onward pressure from Tito and Stalin deprived M. and his *Chetniks* of this support. Later he was dismissed from the Ministry. He lost much of his following, was captured by Tito in March 1946 and tried for alleged treason and collaboration with the enemy. In spite of wide sympathetic support all over the world, he was executed in July 1946.

Militant League of Atheists See LEAGUE OF MILITANT ATHEISTS (in the USSR).

Militarism The excessive influence of the military in society and the glorification of war as a method of settling major conflicts and maintaining national vigour. The term gained its currency in France and England in the 1850s. The Marxist attitude to m. has varied, reflecting the complex ideological and practical considerations involved, but always condemnatory if appearing under capitalism. Marx, and especially Engels (in *ANTI-DÜHRING*) regarded war as a natural method of tackling fundamental social problems and as an inevitable concomitant of class rule, which would disappear only under FULL COMMUNISM. ROSA LUXEMBURG, K. LIEBKNECHT and V. I. LENIN saw m. as a logical result of capitalism in its imperialist stage – a method resorted to domestically to suppress proletarian movements and internationally to dominate colonial countries and fight other imperialist powers for the benefit of monopolies. Later Marxist writers have pointed out that m. reached its highest development under FASCISM in order to strengthen the single party system, to control labour organizations and to fight aggressive wars. One of the proclaimed tasks of Marxism and of the Communist parties is ANTI-MILITARISM. It is claimed that m. cannot occur under Socialism. The SECOND INTERNATIONAL declared that the universal popular militia was the answer to m. After the Communist seizure of power in the Socialist countries, military establishments were immediately recreated, along proletarian lines, for suppressing COUNTER-REVOLUTION and for defence against actual, possible or imagined attack by capitalist countries. In modern Marxist theory, three types of m. are distinguished

– conservative, counter-revolutionary and revolutionary. Also GUERRILLA WARFARE, MILITARIZATION OF LABOUR, MILITARIZATION OF THE ECONOMY, MILITARY-INDUSTRIAL COMPLEX, NATO, WAR, WARSAW PACT.

Militarization of Labour The policy followed by the Soviet regime during WAR COMMUNISM (1917–21) applying military methods to the organization of labour and work. The idea was advanced by M. V. FRUNZE and to some extent supported by L. D. TROTSKY. It was prompted by the weakness of managerial authority, the lack of private motivation and the disintegration of the old labour discipline. The m. of l. assumed the following forms: 1. restrictions were placed on the choice of occupation and the place of employment; 2. manpower was organized for the 'labour front'; 3. workers were classed as 'soldiers', who were not permitted to desert their employment; 4. 'shock brigades' were posted to critical 'battle fronts', to ensure the achievement of crucial production targets; 5. workers were partly or largely paid in rations, rather than in money; and 6. labour victories were celebrated when the postulated production targets were reached.

Militarization of the Economy The subordination of the economy to military purposes. In its extreme form, it appears in wartime, especially in the case of a total war, when far-reaching government intervention in the form of the administrative allocation of resources, direction of labour, wage and price controls and the rationing of consumer goods are involved. W.W.II illustrated the m. of the e. in the belligerent countries. But owing to the social ownership of the means of production and central economic planning, a Socialist economy lends itself to the changeover much better than a capitalist market economy, as was illustrated by the USSR after the German attack in June 1941. The phrase is also applied by Marxists to the leading capitalist powers, in whose view the latter are noted for the following characteristics: 1. the existence of MILITARY-INDUSTRIAL COMPLEXES which exert great economic and political influence; 2. high proportions of national income devoted to military expenditure; 3. the recourse to large military production and large standing armies as devices for the maintenance of higher levels of employment; 4. the state financing of research and development largely directed to military uses; 5. the ARMS RACE; and 6. opposition to DISARMAMENT.

Military Discipline The system of controls and self-restraint typically applied in the armed forces. As traditionally understood, its main elements are: 1. a hierarchical arrangement of authority, the basic distinction between officers, non-commissioned officers and non-ranking soldiers; 2. obedience to higher ranks; 3. the saluting of officers by all subordinates; and 4. a substantial differentiation of pay and privileges according to rank. As such, the armed forces have traditionally been organized along extremely undemocratic lines, largely reflecting social stratification, especially in capitalist countries, but generally regarded as essential for military effectiveness. Under Socialism, there has been a far-reaching democratization and proletarianization of the armed forces. At times, there were attempts to abolish officer ranks and saluting (e.g. in the USSR between the two World Wars and in China during the GREAT PROLETARIAN CULTURAL REVOLUTION). However, the Communist regimes attach great importance to m.d. Even Mao Tse-tung (in 'On Correcting Mistaken Ideas in the Party', 1929) strongly opposed ABSOLUTE EQUALITARIANISM in the army. But the traditional Prussian-type of absolute and undemocratic discipline is rejected in favour of ideologically acceptable methods, relying more on INDOCTRINATION, the basis of recruiting (especially officers) and social responsibility. Also MILITARY OPPOSITION, *POLITRUK*, SOVIET ARMY.

Military-Industrial Complex An informal establishment involving vested military, governmental and private industrial interests, dominating the economic and political scene in the country. The expression was established by President D. D. Eisenhower in 1961 upon his retirement, as a warning against the growing and excessive militarization of society in the USA. Similar establishments may be detected in other leading Western powers, especially Britain, France and the FR of Germany. Marxists have used this fact as further evidence of MILITARISM, which they consider to be inevitable under MONOPOLY CAPITALISM. Communist leaders maintain that a m.-i.c. cannot develop in a Socialist country, as under Socialism there is no profit motive behind military production, and military expenditure is not necessary to achieve high levels of employment. However, there is evidence of the existence of m.-i. establishments in the Socialist countries. In the USSR, where 10 per cent of the GNP is spent for military purposes and military manpower exceeds 3.6m., there are at least eight industrial ministries coordinated by the Ministry of Defence Industries, plus various ancillary industries. About one-tenth of the members of the Central Committee of the CPSU are military personnel. Stalin had a military rank of Generalissimo and Brezhnev, in addition to being the Secretary-General of the CPSU and President of the Supreme Soviet, holds the rank of Marshal of the Soviet Union. The prestige of the military profession is very high and military leaders exert considerable influence through the Party and the government over political, economic and social policies.

Military Opposition In Soviet Russia, a reaction from anarchists and LEFT COMMUNISTS during 1918–19 against the Bolshevik restoration of strict military discipline in the RED ARMY. In particular, the opposition was directed against the employment of ex-Tsarist officers, officially termed as 'military specialists', to enforce the traditional form of army discipline. However, TROTSKY (the founder of the Red Army) was determined to re-

establish strict discipline and on his initiative the M.O. was reprimanded at the 8th Party Congress in March 1919 for being misguided and anti-social.

Militia A term commonly used in the Socialist countries for police. The term m. is preferred to make it distinct from the capitalist set-up where police is regarded as an agency of the bourgeois state, largely directed against the working class. Originally, the less militant Marxists saw the m. as the popular, voluntary defence force, to replace the traditional military establishments as evolved under capitalism. Declarations to this effect were made by the SECOND INTERNATIONAL before W.W.I. The first Socialist m. was created in Soviet Russia in Nov. 1917. Most other Socialist countries followed suit soon after the Communist seizure of power. The Socialist m. is organized and operated to some extent along military lines, more so than is typically the case in capitalist countries. A good deal of attention is given to recruiting to secure a large proletarian core. The m. performs the conventional police functions such as the maintenance of law and order, the issue of identity cards and passports, traffic control, the prevention and detection of crime and the protection of socialized property. It is an instrument of the Socialist state and the main agency for the enforcement of the dictatorship of the proletariat.

Mill, John Stuart (1806–1873) A prominent British liberal philosopher and economist who was criticized by Marx for being a supporter of the bourgeoisie. His principal works were *System of Logic* (1843); *Principles of Political Economy* (1848); *On Liberty* (1859) and *Utilitarianism* (1863).

Millerandism A term contemptuously used by Marxists for socialist members of parliament collaborating with bourgeois government, especially if offered ministerial posts, thereby betraying the revolutionary cause. The term is derived from A. Millerand (1859–1943), originally a radical who was elected to the French Parliament in 1885. He later turned right-wing against his former comrades, held several ministerial posts after 1889, then became Premier and finally President of the Republic (1920–24). His disloyalty was widely discussed in the French Socialist Party and by the SECOND INTERNATIONAL.Collaborationism, ministerialism, or participationism are also used instead of M.

Minimum Wage The lowest wage rate paid to the least skilled labourer working under normal conditions. It may be fixed by law, by custom, or by negotiations between employers and employees or their representatives. It is not necessarily a subsistence wage. The m.w. changes historically and varies geographically, according to the capacity of the economy to pay and current economic policies. The first legal m.w. was introduced in 1894 in New Zealand, followed by Australia in 1907. In the USA, some States initiated a m.w. in 1912. M.w. legislations were commonly passed in Western countries between the two World Wars and in a number of less-developed countries after W.W.II. The m.w. is important as the starting base for working out other wage rates according to qualifications, responsibility, experience or the working conditions of the workers involved. In the Socialist countries the m.w. is fixed on a centrally planned basis and is commonly 45–55 per cent of the average wage in the economy. Other wage rates are also set by the state but, in general, the long-run policy is to raise the m.w. faster than the average wage, in the interest of the gradual equalization of personal income.

Ministerialism See MILLERANDISM.

'Minority is sometimes right' A well-known slogan coined by Mao Tse-tung and widely used during the GREAT PROLETARIAN CULTURAL REVOLUTION in China in order to justify his postulate, 'IT IS RIGHT TO REBEL'. The slogan was directed against the top bureaucratic Party establishment, where Mao lost majority support after the GREAT LEAP FORWARD (hence his related slogan 'BOMBARD THE HEADQUARTERS'). The slogan was also an expression of the ANTI-CONFUCIUS CAMPAIGN, as Confucius had insisted on respect and obedience to authority.

Mir An old Russian name for village commune, going back to the 16th c. It was a peasant community which managed its own affairs, at first under manorial, and after 1861 state, supervision. A *m.* regulated the use of communal arable land and pastures and until 1903 was collectively responsible for paying taxes. Some Russian Marxists before the Revolution, especially the *NARODNIKS*, considered the institution of the *m.* with favour. After the Bolshevik Revolution in 1917 the *m.* facilitated the collectivization of agriculture.

Mises. L.v. NEO-AUSTRIAN CRITIQUE OF SOCIALISM.

Mixed Economy A term used in the West to describe a basically capitalist market economy with substantial state intervention, in which some key industries and services are nationalized and there is indicative or orientational economic planning. Although the market mechanism is retained, its operation is corrected by various forms of state intervention, such as price and wage controls, marketing schemes for primary products, indirect taxes, subsidies, ceilings on profits and the like. Examples of countries with a m.e. are Britain, France, Italy and the Scandinavian countries. In a general sense, no economy today is of a pure system type i.e. either entirely a *laissez-faire* private enterprise free market economy or a completely socialized centralized, directive planned economy. Hence, to some extent any economy nowadays is a m.e.

Miyamoto, Kenji (1908–) The Japanese Communist leader noted for his independence in the international Communist movement and his contributions to Marxist thought. He joined the JAPAN COMMUNIST PARTY in 1931 (illegal at the time), was elected to its Central Committee in 1933, became its Secretary in 1958 and Chairman of the Presidium of the C.C. in 1970. He was imprisoned from 1933 to 1945 for his illegal Communist activities. Under his leadership, the J.C.P. has pursued an independent course from Moscow (since 1964) and Peking (since 1966). Domestically, his stand has been increasingly liberal and anti-revolutionary and he is now regarded as one of the leading advocates of EUROCOMMUNISM. He is also regarded as the intellectual leader of the Party, having made a number of important contributions to the theory, policy and practice of the Communist movement in Japan, viz. *Problems of Democratic Advance Towards Freedom and Independence* (1949), *Twelve Years' Letters* (1952), *Prospects of a Japanese Revolution* (1961), *The Path of Our Party's Struggle* (1961), *Actual Tasks and the Japan Communist Party* (1966), *The Road Towards a New Japan* (1970), *The Standpoint of the Japan Communist Party* (1972) and many others.

MKBS A Russian abbreviation corresponding to ICBM in English, for *Mezhkontinental'nyi Ballistichesky Snaryad*, meaning Intercontinental Ballistic Missile.

Mob An unstable crowd of common irresponsible people who can be manipulated by agitators for a mass disturbance ('mob action', 'mobocracy'). The term is derived from 'mobile' (crowd) and it appears to have been used first in England in 1734, by conservative elements. But its wider popular use dates after the middle of the 19th c.

Mode of Production One of the basic concepts in Marxist ideology, emphasizing the material, technical and social sides of production and distribution, reflective of the stage of economic and social system in force. The concept was introduced by Marx in *A CONTRIBUTION TO THE CRI-*

TIQUE OF POLITICAL ECONOMY, published in 1859. The m. of p. is determined by PRODUCTION FORCES and PRODUCTION RELATIONS, i.e. it represents a DIALECTICAL unity of material and human elements of production. Changes in production forces (increases in the size of the factors of production, improvements in their quality as well as the methods of production) lead to the modification of relations between employers and employees and between different social groups. The transformation may be gradual and evolutionary if the ruling class is weak or finds it expedient to allow the new relations to develop. But more commonly, the ruling class opposes modifications in production relations, in spite of changes in production forces, so that the adjustment has to be eventually made through a violent revolutionary LEAP. Historically, Marx distinguished five m. of p. corresponding to the socio-economic formations, viz. (in their ascending order): 1. PRIMITIVE COMMUNISM; 2. SLAVERY; 3. FEUDALISM; 4. CAPITALISM; 5. SOCIALISM (to be followed by FULL COMMUNISM).

Molotov, Viacheslav Mikhailovich (original name: V. M. Skriabin) (1890–) A Bolshevik leader, writer, statesman and diplomat, noted for his loyalty to Stalin. M. joined the RUSSIAN SOCIAL-DEMOCRATIC LABOUR PARTY in 1906 and in 1912 participated in the founding of *Pravda* and became its editor. He was one of the members of the Party's Military Revolutionary Committee which directed the military moves during the GREAT OCTOBER SOCIALIST REVOLUTION in 1917. He rose rapidly in the Party hierarchy. M. attained the post of the Secretary of the Central Committee in 1921, became a member of the Politburo in 1926 and later of the Presidium from 1952 on. He held the position of the Prime Minister of the USSR from 1930 to 1941, the Commissar (Minister) for Foreign Affairs from 1939 to 1949 and participated in the Teheran (1943), Yalta (1945) and Potsdam (1945) Conferences. M. was one of Stalin's earliest and most faithful supporters. From

1953 to 1956 he was Minister for Foreign Affairs, when he opposed KHRUSHCHEV and the Soviet reconciliation with TITO. M. was removed from his post in 1956 and expelled from the Party in June 1957 as a member of the ANTI-PARTY GROUP. He was then sent to Mongolia as Soviet Ambassador (1957–60) and then to Vienna as Soviet permanent representative with the International Atomic Energy Agency (1960–61). In 1961 he was further denounced by Khrushchev as an accomplice in Stalin's GREAT PURGES. But in spite of demands for his punishment he escaped further penalties and retired from public life.

Moncada Operation A daring and suicidal attack on 26 July 1953 by F. Castro's rebel force on the Moncada Fort (situated on the outskirts of Santiago, in south-eastern Cuba), an armed stronghold of the dictatorial right-wing regime of President Batista. The plan included the following tasks: 1. to disarm the 1,000 soldiers garisoned in the Fort; 2. to occupy the barracks; 3. to capture the rifles, machine guns, tanks, armoured trucks and ammunition; 4. to seize the radio station in Santiago and call upon the people of Cuba to support the rebels against Batista; and 5. to proclaim a programme of economic reforms (mainly workers' participation in the management and profits of enterprises. FIDEL CASTRO and his brother Raul had a force of 200, mostly students and graduates in their 20s. Militarily the attack largely proved a failure, followed by severe reprisals by the Batista forces, involving some 20,000 victims. The Castros escaped by sheer luck. But politically, the M.O. produced a great impact on public thinking and became the 'opening chapter of the Cuban Revolution'. It gave rise to the TWENTY-SIXTH OF JULY MOVEMENT, which appealed to the imagination of revolutionary and nationalistic elements.

Monetary and Substantive Convertibility The capacity of a currency held by a non-resident to be exchanged through ordinary commercial channels and without loss into another, hard currency, gold or for goods and services in the country of the currency concerned. Alternative terms which have been used are 'financial' or 'commercial' (for monetary) and 'commodity' or 'goods' (for substantive) convertibility. The distinction between these two aspects of currency convertibility is important when comparing Western hard currencies and Socialist soft currencies. Normally m.c. also implies s.c. But it is possible to think of situations where the former exists without the latter, and vice versa. In capitalist market economies the term 'convertibility' is commonly used in the monetary sense. S.c. is usually automatic, i.e. the foreign possessor of the currency in question can buy whatever goods and services are available in the country concerned, or order them to be produced. In such a case the government allows their unrestricted export (barring abnormal situations). In fact the government is anxious to promote exports and does so in a variety of ways. On the other hand, in a Socialist centrally planned economy there is no freedom of taking products out of the system, even if there were m.c. None of the Socialist currencies is convertible either in the monetary or substantive sense.

Money A commonly accepted medium of exchange (or 'circulation', in Marxist terminology) which also performs the functions of a unit of account (or 'value'), a store of value, a standard for deferred payments and (in the case of some currencies) a means of international payment settlements. Marxists regard m. as a historical phenomenon, its forms, functions and role reflecting the stages of economic and social development. In Marxist political economy, in accordance with the LABOUR THEORY OF VALUE, a distinction is made between the 'value of m.' and the 'purchasing power of m.'. The former is determined by the SOCIALLY-INDISPENSABLE LABOUR embodied in the product expressed in m., while the latter is indicated by the actual price of the commodity prevailing in the market at the time. Marx was critical of the role of m. under capitalism. He viewed m. as an instrument enabling exploitation and undermining social morality. He said (in *On the Jewish Question*, 1844): 'Money degrades all the gods of mankind and turns them into commodities. . . . It has robbed the whole world of both nature and man of its original value.' After the October Revolution in 1917 there were Bolshevik attempts to abolish m., or at least base it on social criteria (*DOV*, *TRED*), but in both cases without success. M. has been retained under socialism as an expedient during the transitional stage to full communism. But its role has been reduced to a subordinate position (excepting the consumer goods market), as the most crucial economic processes are determined directly by economic planning in physical terms. It is vaguely envisaged that under FULL COMMUNISM m. will disappear, when work and income will be governed by the principle 'from each according to his ability, to each according to his needs'.

Mongolian People's Republic (*Bügd Nayramdakh Mongol Ard Uls*) The second oldest Socialist country (after the USSR), ruled by a Communist party (MONGOLIAN PEOPLE'S REVOLUTIONARY PARTY) since 1924. A Chinese province, 1691–1911 and 1919–21, known as Outer Mongolia, Mongolia was under Russian protection from 1911 to 1919 and declared its independence on 5 Nov. 1921. Since that time M. has been closely allied with the USSR. A Communist regime was proclaimed on 26 Nov. 1924 allied to and aided by the USSR. Collectivization was completed in the late 1950s and all land is now socialized. The country's area is 1,565,000 sq. km. and its population is 1,550,000 (in 1978). In 1962 a treaty was concluded with China settling border disputes and in the same year the M.P.R. joined the COUNCIL FOR MUTUAL ECONOMIC ASSISTANCE. According to the country's Fourth Constitution (of 1960), the state power is vested in the PEOPLE'S GREAT HURAL (modelled on the Supreme Soviet of the USSR), which

elects its Presidium, the Council of Ministers and members of the Supreme Court. However *de facto* power is exercised by the Politburo of the Mongolian People's Revolutionary Party led by Y. Tsedenbal.

Mongolian People's Revolutionary Party (*Mongol Ardyn Khuv'sgalt Nam*) The ruling and the only legal political party in the MONGOLIAN PEOPLE'S REPUBLIC. Its origin goes back to 1921, when the Mongolian People's Party was founded in Soviet Russia, but adopted its present name in 1924 when the Communist regime was firmly established. The Party has received support from the Communist Party of the Soviet Union and its predecessor and has consistently supported the Soviet line in the international Communist movement. The Party's membership in the late 1970s was 67,000 (compared with the country's total population of 1,550,000). The highest source of the Party's authority is the Congress which is held every fourth year. The 17th Party Congress, held in June 1976, elected a Central Committee of 91 full and 61 candidate members, which in turn elected a Politburo of 7 full and 2 candidate members, headed by the First Secretary (Y. Tsedenbal). The Party receives its mass support from the Pioneers and the Revolutionary Youth League. The Party's publications include: *Ünen* (*Truth*), the daily organ of the Party as well as the Government; *Namyn Amdral* (*Party Life*), a monthly journal on Party theory and practice; *Ediyn Dzasag* (*Political Economy*), the economic organ of the Central Committee; *Pionyeriyn Unen* (*Pioneer's Truth*), the organ of the Pioneer Organization; and *Dzaluuchuudyn Ünen* (*Young People's Truth*), the organ of the Revolutionary Youth League.

Monism A view in philosophy which identifies all existence with only one primary element and thus contrasts with DUALISM. There are two versions of m. – idealist and materialist. Idealist m. regards ideas as the essence of all phenomena. The best known proponent of this view was HEGEL.

On the other hand, materialist m. insists that matter is the ultimate and immanent feature of all existence. Marxist philosophers reject the validity of idealist m., identifying it with a justification of superstition, RELIGION and CLERICALISM. They counterpose DIALECTICAL MATERIALISM as the only philosophical m. that can be scientifically supported. They stress that the world is essentially material and all phenomena are in fact traceable to changing matter. Marxist thinkers have also extended m. to the social sphere, maintaining that the development of societies is in fact determined by the MODE OF PRODUCTION of material goods.

Monobank A term applied to the state bank in a Socialist centrally planned economy, where such a bank combines central banking functions with commercial banking. As such, it is virtually the only banking institution in the economy, being the 'centre of cash, credit and control', with the possibility of some clearly defined functions being delegated to specialized banks. The m. system prevailed in several Socialist countries before the ECONOMIC REFORMS, and was associated with the CENTRALIZED DIRECTIVE SYSTEM OF PLANNING AND MANAGEMENT. Also *GOSBANK*, PEOPLE'S BANK OF CHINA.

Mono-party System of Government A political order where only one party is the source of political power by virtue of its being the only legal party in the country or by virtue of its indisputable control of a 'coalition'. This system prevails under FASCISM or in the Socialist countries. The first m.-p.s. of g. under Socialism was introduced in Soviet Russia in 1922 when all other political parties than the RUSSIAN COMMUNIST PARTY (OF THE BOLSHEVIKS) were abolished. In most Socialist countries the Communist party is the only legal party, such as Albania, Cuba, Hungary, Mongolia, Romania, the USSR and Yugoslavia. Although in several Socialist countries (notably Bulgaria, China, Czechoslovakia, the German DR, DPR of Korea, Poland and Vietnam) other non-bourgeois parties are tolerated for one expedient reason or another, effective power is still exercised by the Communist party, usually through the UNITED FRONTS. The m.-p.s. of g. in the Socialist countries is the logical expression of the DICTATORSHIP OF THE PROLETARIAT.

Monopolies A term applied to large private firms or inter-firm agreements (cartels, trusts) being the only or dominant sellers of particular goods or services. M. have become a feature of developed capitalist economies, especially in Western Europe, North America and Japan. In their modern form, they began to appear towards the end of the 19th c., especially in manufacturing industries, mining, transport, trade and banking. M. have attracted criticism from Marxists who see them as a reflection of the CONCENTRATION AND CENTRALIZATION OF CAPITAL AND PRODUCTION and an inexorable development in higher stages of industrial and finance capitalism. The evils attributed to m. by them include: 1. the socially unjustified concentration of private wealth; 2. the ruthless exploitation of the masses through high prices, the restriction of output and the monopsonistic control over wages; 3. the bribery of labour leaders and highly skilled workers and professionals to captivate them to the bourgeois side, thereby undermining the solidarity of the working class; 4. interference in the flow of capital from less to more profitable branches of the economy (ORGANIC STRUCTURE OF CAPITAL); 5. the despoliation of natural resources and environment; 6. indifference and even opposition to the utilization of inventions; 7. the instigation of the ARMS RACE; 8. the domination of the state apparatus for their own benefit (STATE MONOPOLY CAPITALISM); 9. opposition to disarmament; and 10. the exploitation and economic and social retardation of less-developed countries. Marx had not anticipated the possibility of mitigating or removing the abuses of m. through state action in the form of anti-monopoly legislation, the control of banks, excess profit taxes and nationalization. But the Socialist economies are also noted for the existence of m., although they are not privately owned. The Socialist m. are a consequence of the consolidation of the former private firms into larger socialized enterprises, the absence of competition, administrative expediency, GIGANTOMANIA and the like.

Monopoly Capitalism A Marxist concept applied to the stage of developed capitalism which is dominated by privately owned MONOPOLIES. M.c. began to emerge in the leading Western countries (especially Britain, France, Germany and the USA) after 1870 and replaced competitive capitalism. M.c. is characterized by the CONCENTRATION AND CENTRALIZATION OF CAPITAL AND PRODUCTION in a few big firms, cartels or trusts allied with big banks. M.c. is a product of the great improvement in the level and quality of PRODUCTION FORCES, made possible by scientific and technical progress, but at the same time it is noted for its outdated and acutely ANTAGONISTIC PRODUCTION RELATIONS. The increasing disparity between the two and the growing antagonism between the PROLETARIAT and BIG BOURGEOISIE breed the DIALECTIC conditions for a PROLETARIAN REVOLUTION and the breakdown of capitalism. Rosa Luxemburg (in *The Accumulation of Capital*, 1913) and V. I. Lenin (in *IMPERIALISM: THE HIGHEST STAGE OF CAPITALISM*) linked m.c. with IMPERIALISM as the last stage of capitalist development. After 1930, m.c. further developed into STATE MONOPOLY CAPITALISM.

Monteneros ('Black Mountaineers', in Spanish) An extremist illegal guerrilla movement in Argentina, consisting mostly of young men and women of middle class background, fighting against capitalism, authoritarianism and US imperialism. They represent a curious mixture of Argentine folklore nationalism, modified by ANARCHISM, orthodox MARXISM, TROTSKYISM and MAOISM, but their leaders disclaim foreign links. Originally, the

M. were left-wing radicals in the Peronist movement, then in 1969 were organized as a Peronist terrorist group. In 1972 they joined another guerrilla group, the Revolutionary Armed Forces, but by 1975 they had been expelled and declared illegal (together with other left-wing extremist groups, viz. the Workers' Revolutionary Party and the People's Revolutionary Army). The M. operate mostly in urban areas (like the TUPAMAROS in Uruguay) and obtain their funds mostly from armed bank robberies and kidnapping ransoms. Since 1977 they have de-emphasized their terrorist activities and regrouped into a quasi-political movement. In April 1977 they established the Montenero Peronist Movement in exile based in Rome, professing a mild democratic line (its leader being A. E. Firmenich).

MOPR Abbreviation in Russian of *Mezhdunarodnaya Organizatsiya Pomoshchi Revolutsionerom*, meaning INTERNATIONAL ORGANIZATION FOR AID TO REVOLUTIONARIES.

Moral Incentives Rewards of nonmaterial content provided to the managerial personnel and workers appealing to their idealistic motivation. The concept was considered by Marx who attached great importance to them and believed that in an ideal society they should replace MATERIAL INCENTIVES. The Socialist countries have developed various schemes for promoting responsiveness to, and the effectiveness of, m.i., regarding them ideologically superior to material incentives. M.i. may be designed to appeal to the workers' ideological conviction, social consciousness, patriotism, occupational pride, a sense of satisfaction from the work performed, comradeship, and reputation in the eyes of workmates, the family and society. The awards are not made in money or kind, but in the form of boards and books of honour displayed in factories, pennants, badges, medals, orders, appearance on television or radio, invitation to join the Communist party, or some other form of public recognition. M.i. may be awarded to individual workers, or collectively – to a team, brigade or the whole enterprise. M.i. reached their highest pitch in China, especially during the GREAT PROLETARIAN CULTURAL REVOLUTION. But in the European Socialist countries they have been de-emphasized since the ECONOMIC REFORMS of the 1960s.

Morality Attitudes and rules of human conduct defining what is good and bad, in particular ideals and obligations governing relations between persons and between persons and society. In the philosophy of IDEALISM, m. is essentially regarded as being of universal applicability, irrespective of the conditions of human life. On the other hand Marxist philosophers, such as F. Engels (in *ANTI-DÜHRING*), stress that although there are some norms of behaviour which are universal (such as veracity, respect for one's parents, courage), m. is basically a social phenomenon determined historically. It is subject to modifications according to the changing forms of social organization and the economic BASE. In a class society, m. is class conditioned and the prevailing m. is that of the ruling class imposed on the exploited class. Consequently, there are differences between primitive, feudal, bourgeois and SOCIALIST MORALITY.

Morganism See WEISMANNISM-MORGANISM.

Moroccan Communist Party (*Parti Communiste Morocaine*) A very small party which has had a chequered history. It originated as the Moroccan section of the French Communist Party in 1931, was broken up by the French authorities in 1939, but was recreated in 1943 when it assumed its present name. The Party was proscribed again from 1952 to 1956. When Morocco achieved independence its status was legalized, but three years later was dissolved by the Moroccan Government. It re-emerged in 1974 under the name Progress and Socialism as its legal front organization. Its membership is

about 500 (as of the late 1970s, when the country's total population was 19,000,000). The Party has pursued a pro-Soviet line in the international Communist movement. The Party's regular publication is a weekly organ called *al-Bayan* (*The Bulletin*).

Morris, William (1834–96) An English poet, writer, painter architect and the originator of GUILD SOCIALISM. As an idealist, he attacked the factory system and advocated a collective ownership of the means of production and a return to medieval manual craftsmanship. His main works on social questions were: *Art and Socialism* (1884); *True and False Society* (1885); *Useful Work and Useless Toil* (1885); and he co-authored with E. Belfort Bax, *Socialism: Its Growth and Outcome* (1896).

Moscow Agreement An agreement concluded by the member countries of the COUNCIL FOR MUTUAL ECONOMIC ASSISTANCE in Jan. 1975 on a new basis for determining prices in intra-CMEA foreign trade, supplementing the BUCHAREST AGREEMENT. The new contract prices, instead of being fixed for five years coinciding with five-year plans, are changed annually and are based on average world market (capitalist) prices over the preceding three and, after 1976, five years. The aim is to gear intra-CMEA foreign trade prices closer to world market levels, owing to inflationary price increases since the early 1970s, especially for fuels and most raw materials in capitalist markets.

Moscow Declaration An agreement proclaimed at the conference of the 13 ruling and 51 other Communist parties in Moscow in Nov. 1957, which was largely a compromise between the Soviet and Chinese views. The Declaration condemned REVISIONISM and OPPORTUNISM, but conceded the possibility of a peaceful transition to socialism, as distinct from a violent proletarian revolution. Although the COMMUNIST PARTY OF THE SOVIET

UNION was acknowledged as the paceset-
ter in the international Communist movement, the CHINESE COMMUNIST PARTY demanded equal share in the leadership. The
Chinese delegation, led by Mao Tse-tung,
disagreed on whether the peaceful transition was to be a 'tactical' or 'strategic'
retreat. The Chinese memorandum agreed only to a tactical interpretation to
'enable the Communist parties of the
capitalist countries to sidestep attacks on
them ... and to win over the masses'. It
further insisted that Communist parties
must establish autonomous sources of
power whether legal or not. The Yugoslav
delegation did not sign the Declaration as
the latter singled out revisionsim ('right-
wing opportunism') as the main danger to
the international Communist movement.

Moscow Human Rights Committee A
group founded in Nov. 1970 by Soviet
dissenters, V. Chalidze, A. Sakharov and
A. Tverdokhlebov. Its activities are directed towards the promotion of freedom
of speech, press, assembly, association
and movement and against persecution in
prisons, labour camps and mental institutions. Its scope of operation is severely
limited and concentrates on the exposure
of illegal ill-treatment and the publicity of
arbitrary and repressive actions by various
state organs.

Moscow International A colloquial description which was sometimes used for
the COMINTERN (1919–43), in contrast to
the AMSTERDAM I., BERLIN I. and VIENNA I.

Moscow Line A colloquial term for the
orientation of the Communist parties supporting the COMMUNIST PARTY OF THE
SOVIET UNION as the leader and interpreter of the Marxist doctrine on an international scale. Of the 90 significant Com-
munist parties in the world in 1978, 50
clearly followed the M.L. while a further
12 were neutral or independent. The rul-
ing Communist parties supporting the
M.L. are those of Angola, Bulgaria, Cuba,
Czechoslovakia, Ethiopia, the German
DR, Hungary, Mongolia, Mozambique,
Poland, Vietnam and Yemen (South).
Among the non-ruling ones included are
those of Algeria, Argentina, Chile,
Denmark, Egypt, Finland, France,
Great Britain, Greece, India, Iran, Iraq,
Morocco, Norway, Portugal, Sudan,
Switzerland, Syria, Tunisia, Turkey,
Uruguay and the USA. The other
orientation is the PEKING LINE.

Moscow Narodny Bank A Soviet-owned
bank, located in London. It is the oldest
and second largest Socialist bank in the
capitalist world. Originally established by
Russian Co-operative Societies in 1916, it
was taken over by the Soviet Government
in 1919. Its net assets in 1976 amounted to
$2,550m. and ranked the 234th largest
bank in the capitalist world. It has established wholly-owned subsidiaries in
Beirut (in 1966) and Singapore (in 1971)
and a representative office in Moscow (in
1975). It engages in financing East-West
trade by extending loans not only to British and Soviet trading entities in their
mutual trade, but also to other Socialist
traders. It also manages and subscribes to
bond issues floated by Socialist and
capitalist entities, handles Soviet gold
sales in London and trains bankers for the
USSR and occasionally for other Socialist
or less-developed countries. Also BAN-
QUE COMMERCIALE POUR L'EUROPE DU
NORD.

Moscow Statement A communique issued
at the Conference in Moscow attended by
delegates of 81 Communist parties in Nov.
1960. The Conference was concerned
with the role of the COMMUNIST PARTY OF
THE SOVIET UNION and the CHINESE COM-
MUNIST PARTY in the international Communist movement. But the Statement did
not embody any solutions – it merely acknowledged the existence of unresolved
problems. It brought the SINO-SOVIET DIS-
PUTE into the open and recognized the
conditions of POLYCENTRISM.

Moscow Treaty Another name for the
NUCLEAR TEST BAN TREATY.

Moscow Trials Name given to the three public TREASON TRIALS held in Moscow 19–24 Aug. 1936, 23–30 Jan. 1937 and 2–13 June 1938. The M.T. exemplified the POLITICAL SHOW TRIALS, calculated by Stalin to prove publicly the guilt of 54 defendants of treason by sham judicial procedures, in order to eliminate real and potential opposition to his rule by terror. The M.T. were compared by its critics to the Inquisition conducted by the Catholic Church in the Middle Ages.

Mosfilm The Moscow Studio for Artistic Films, being the largest film studio in the USSR. The name is derived from the full Russian equivalent, *Moskovskaya Kinostudiya Khudostvennykh Filmov.* Originally established in 1929 as *Soyuzkino,* its name was changed to *Moskinokombinat* in 1934, but in the following year it adopted its present designation. M. is not concerned with films of purely documentary or propaganda nature, but concentrates on major motion pictures requiring top artistic talent and usually large financial and other resources. It has co-operated with several leading Western film companies, such as Columbia Pictures and Paramount in shooting the $25m. picture 'Waterloo' (to which M. contributed $10m.).

Most, Johann Josef (1846–1906) A German Socialist who turned to ANARCHISM and finally emigrated to the USA. Expelled from Germany, he went to England in 1878, where he established an anarchist paper *Die Freiheit* (*Freedom*) and continued his anarchist agitation advocating violence. Marx was critical of his activities and described him as 'conversant with revolutionary phraseology, but lacking revolutionary backbone'. M. was expelled from England in 1882 and went to the USA, where he continued his paper in New York. He became a notorious proponent of anarchist violence, for which he was imprisoned in 1901.

Motion In philosophy, a change or becoming, involving space and time. There are two contrasting views of m. In the philosophy of IDEALISM, m. is interpreted as being non-material and explained in terms of ENERGISM. Thus, according to idealists, the non-material energy of m. of the photon found in an atom can change into matter, viz. electron and positron, and vice versa. Some idealists attribute the ultimate source of m. to god. In the Marxist philosophy of MATERIALISM, m. is identified with matter. Engels (in *DIALECTICS OF NATURE*) defined m. as the 'mode of existence of matter', and Lenin (in *PHILOSOPHICAL NOTEBOOKS*) said that 'not only is matter unthinkable without motion, but motion is also unthinkable without matter'. In the Marxist view, the source of m. is found in the matter itself in the form of CONTRACTIONS, i.e. the struggle of opposites, and consequently there is no need to invoke divine power to explain m. To Marxist philosophers, photons, electrons and positrons are forms of matter and in the state of m. They regard m., like matter, as eternal which can not be created or destroyed. They distinguish six basic forms of m.: 1. intra-atomic (electrons, protons, positrons); 2. mechanical (change in space); 3. physical (molecular m. reflected in heat, vibrations, electromagnetic waves); 4. chemical (combination of atoms, disintegration); 5. organic (growth, decay of organisms); and 6. social (changing socio-economic formations, class struggle). Each of these forms of m. is considered to be governed by its own laws and may change into one another. M. is one of the most fundamental notions in Marxist ideology, employed to negate divine creation and causation and to explain evolutionary and revolutionary social processes.

Movement for the Defence of Human and Civil Rights A group of dissenters and critical Marxists in Poland formed in March 1977. In Poland it is mainly known as *ROPCO*, being an abbreviation of *Ruch dla Obrony Praw Cywilnych i Obywatelskich.* The Movement publishes a bulletin *Opinia* (*Opinion*), highlighting cases of political, religious and racial persecution, breaches of guaranteed freedoms and over-zealous officials. It cooperates with the COMMITTEE FOR SOCIAL SELF-DEFENCE.

Mozambique, People's Republic of A Socialist country in south-eastern Africa ruled by a Marxist-Leninist party, the LIBERATION FRONT OF MOZAMBIQUE (*FRELIMO*). The country's area is 784,960 sq. km. and its population 9,900,000 (in 1978). It was formerly a Portuguese colony (for four centuries), which achieved independence in June 1975, mainly by the efforts of *FRELIMO*. The regime immediately embarked on far-reaching nationalization (land, banking, major services), the secularization of education and a social security programme. In foreign policy, a pro-Soviet course has been adopted and the country has received substantial aid from the USSR and China. A Constitution was adopted on Independence Day (25 June 1975), which declares that *FRELIMO* is the 'directing power of the state and society'. The President of the Republic is also the leader of *FRELIMO*.

MPLA Popular Liberation Movement of Angola. See POPULAR MOVEMENT WORKERS' PARTY.

M-T Agreement A short name for the Memorandum Trade Agreement, which was concluded by Chinese and Japanese delegations in 1968 to provide a basis for mutual trade not handled by the Japanese FRIENDLY FIRMS. It was signed by negotiators of high rank on both sides, but did not constitute an official agreement between the two governments. The Agreement was a successor to the L-T AGREEMENT and, although it originally covered one year, it was subsequently renewed for another year. The proportion of Sino-Japanese trade conducted under the M-T A. represented only 11 per cent (while 89 per cent was handled by the Friendly Firms).

MTI The commonly used abbreviation

for the Hungarian Telegraph Agency (*Magyar Tavirati Iroda*). It is the official, state-owned instrumentality, with the exclusive right of collecting and distributing domestic and foreign news.

MTS Abbreviation for MACHINE-TRACTOR STATIONS.

Multi-angular Deals A phrase used in Socialist foreign trade as an improvement on BILATERAL TRADE and a step towards MULTILATERAL TRADE AND PAYMENTS. M.-a.d. involve partners from at least three different countries. Payment settlement is achieved not bilaterally but in the circuit of the three or more partners. Typical m.-a.d. in the past involved the following countries: Finland – Poland – USSR; Czechoslovakia – Vietnam – Japan; and FR of Germany – German DR – Denmark.

Multilateral Trade and Payments A system of international trade under which trade surpluses earned in one country (or a group of countries) can be used to offset deficits with another (or several countries). It is typical of the trade of the developed capitalist countries and usually presupposes convertibility of the currency (or currencies) used in settling balances. Only multilateralism can ensure the most gainful flow of trade. This usually happens through the purchasing of imports from the cheapest source and selling exports in the most profitable markets. Most of the Socialist countries' trade with the capitalist world is now on a multilateral basis, using Western currencies. Although only about one-tenth of trade among the member countries of the COUNCIL FOR MUTUAL ECONOMIC ASSISTANCE is on a truly multilateral basis, attempts are being made to extend gradually this basis of settlement in the future. To this effect, the member countries established the INTERNATIONAL BANK FOR ECONOMIC CO-OPERATION in 1963. The TRANSFERABLE ROUBLE is used as a means of settling intra-CMEA payments.

Multinational Enterprises in CMEA IN-
TERNATIONAL PRODUCTION ASSOCIA-
TIONS IN CMEA.

Multiple Exchange Rates Different official rates of exchange of a national currency compared to a foreign currency according to the type of domestic and/or foreign
entity (commercial enterprise, tourist),
the type of transaction (export, import,
visible, invisible, capital) or the type of
commodity (primary, manufactured,
scarce, abundant). Although some
capitalist (especially less-developed)
countries resort to them, the m.e.r. are
more systematically applied by the Socialist centrally planned economies, where
such rates above all reflect distorted
domestic price structures in relation to
world market prices. Up to seven different
exhange rates were administered in the
past by some Socialist countries. However, there has been a tendency towards
evolving single exchange rates. Since
1961, non-commercial (tourist) rates
have been abandoned in the USSR and
Yugoslavia.

Muscovites Those non-Soviet Communists who spent the greater part of W.W.II
in the USSR. The term is particularly applied to those pro-Soviet leaders from
Eastern Europe, North Korea and China
who after their return to their home countries with the Soviet troops, were in conflict with the NATIONAL COMMUNISTS.
Among the best known M. were: B. Bierut
(of Poland); V. CHERVENKOV; K. GOTT-
WALD; KIM IL-SUNG; LI LI-SAN; 1. NAGY;
Anna Pauker (of Romania); M. RÁKOSI;
W. ULBRICHT; and YANG HSIEN-CHEN.

Mutual Assured Destruction (MAD) An
expression introduced by the US strateg-
ists in the early 1960s to describe the
nuclear stalemate reached by the USA
and the USSR. Owing to the large arsenal
of nuclear weapons at the disposal of each
side, no move is open to either adversary
without suicidal consequences to the attacking side.

**Mutual Defense Assistance Control Act
of 1951** See BATTLE ACT.

MVD (abbreviation of *Ministerstvo Vnutriennykh Diel*, in Russian meaning Ministry of Internal Affairs – The ministry responsible for state security (police) and
related internal affairs in the USSR. It
succeeded the NKVD in 1946, when the
People's Commissariats were re-named
Ministries. In 1953, after Stalin's death
the MVD was also responsible for the
secret service (when the MGB was amalgamated with it). In 1962, under
Khrushchev, the MVD was dissolved and
replaced with decentralized departments
in Union Republics in charge of police. In
1965, the former MVD was re-established
under the name of the Ministry of Law and
Order and finally, in Nov. 1968, re-named
again the MVD, which is still in existence.
However, it is no longer concerned with
the secret service. The MVD was taken
over by the KGB after 1953, the latter
being attached not to the MVD but directly to the Council of Ministers of the USSR.

Mysticism In philosophy, a view based on
the conviction of the possibility of man's
spiritual communication with god or other
supernatural phenomena. All religions
embody elements of m. Marxist
philosophers do not treat m. seriously, as
they regard it as irrational and a version of
IDEALISM, completely inconsistent with
MATERIALISM. They further see reactionary social implications in m. Historically,
m. has become, in their view, a way for the
exploited classes to escape from their
misery, oppression and search for
consolation and miracles from the supernatural world.

N

Nagasaki Flag Incident An event which occurred in Nagasaki (Japan) at the Philatelic Exhibition in 1958, when a Japanese citizen removed the flag of the P.R. of China from the flag pole. The Peking Government took a very serious view of the action and demanded an official apology from the Japanese Government. The latter refused on the grounds that it did not recognize the Peking regime. In retaliation the Chinese Government drastically curtailed trade with Japan from $140m. in 1957 to $22m. in 1959.

Nagy, Imre (1896–1958) A Hungarian Communist leader and statesman of peasant parentage, who was executed by the Communist regime for his role in the HUNGARIAN UPRISING. He joined the illegal Communist Party of Hungary (as it was known at the time) in 1921, but between 1930 and 1944, lived in the USSR where he was engaged as an agricultural economist. After his return to Hungary in 1944, he became the Minister for Agriculture and was responsible for the radical transformation of Hungarian agriculture. He became Prime Minister in June 1953 and the chief advocate of the NEW COURSE of far-reaching liberalization. But due to Soviet pressure and his political enemy, M. RÁKOSI, in April 1955 he was stripped of all his State and Party posts for his 'right-wing deviationism'. During the demonstrations in Oct. 1956, which led to the HUNGARIAN UPRISING, popular demand led to his becoming Prime Minister again and chief spokesman for the continuation of the New Course and the withdrawal of Hungary from the WARSAW PACT. After the Uprising was crushed by the Soviet military intervention, N. asked for and received political asylum in the Yugoslav Embassy in Budapest. N. was later given a safe conduct guarantee by the Soviet army, but the assurance was broken and he was abducted by force. At a secret trial, in which he courageously refused to plead guilty, he was sentenced to death for 'treason' and executed in June 1958 (either in Hungary or in the USSR).

Naïve Realism In philosophy, the name of the simplest version of direct REALISM, commonly shared by ordinary people as a matter of spontaneous reaction to nature and reality. It is sometimes described as 'an innocent prejudice of the simple man that has to be overcome if philosophical progress is to be made'. Some philosophers supporting IDEALISM, such as G. Berkeley (1684–1733) and E. MACH, believed that an ordinary man is guided only by his impressions and it does not matter to him whether objects exist in reality or not. Marxist philosophers, such as Lenin (in *MATERIALISM AND EMPIRIO-CRITICISM*), dispute this interpretation, maintaining that the common people are spontaneously convinced of the existence of reality beyond their consciousness and independently of it. They further emphasize that n.r., being based on spontaneous subjective impressions, is not a scientifically founded materialist outlook. Moreover, they maintain that only DIALECTICAL MATERIALISM can provide a solid scientific basis for a consistent philosophical world outlook.

Nan-Ch'ang Insurrection An uprising of several left-wing army groups of Chiang Kai-shek's National Liberation Army against the KUOMINTANG Government in China in Aug. 1927. The Insurrection, involving some 30,000 Communists and their sympathizers led by CHOU EN-LAI and CHU TEH, broke out in Nan-ch'ang (the capital of Kiang-si province, in south-eastern China) on 1 Aug. 1927, which is regarded as the foundation day of the Chinese Red Army. Although the uprising failed miserably, the best combat units survived, which provided a tough and competent nucleus for the Communist army. The surviving Communist groups then moved southward, were confronted and routed again by the Nationalists at Swatow and subsequently fled to the CHINGSHAN MOUNTAINS, which became the Communist revolutionary base.

Narkompros A syllabic abbreviation of *Narodnyi Komissariat Prosvetleniya*, in Russian meaning the State Commissariat for Enlightenment. It was the colloquial name for the Ministry of Education and Culture, headed by A. V. LUNACHARSKY, in Soviet Russia over the period 1917–21. It was preoccupied with the introduction of new standards and the control of literature, fine art, museums, theatres performing arts and all aspects of education.

Narodnaya Volya (Peoples's Freedom or People's Will, in Russian) A terrorist revolutionary organization of the NAROD-NIKS in Tsarist Russia which emerged in 1879 as a result of a split in *ZEMLYA I VOLYA* (Land and Freedom). In its programme the *N.V.* advocated the overthrow of the Tsarist autocracy in favour of a democratic parliament elected by universal suffrage, substantial freedom for local government, the distribution of large estates to peasants and workers' ownership of large enterprises. In contrast to *Zemlya i Volya*, the *N.V.* did not advocate the abolition of the state. The *N.V.* had a membership of about 400 led by A. Zhelyabov (son of a serf but with a university education) and published two jour-

nals, *Narodnaya volya* (1879–85) and *Rabochaya gazeta* (*Workers' News*) (1880–81). In Aug. 1879 the Executive Committee of the *N.V.* sentenced Tsar Aleksander II to death, which was successfully carried out (by a Polish member) on 1 March 1881. The repression that followed led to the elimination of the *N.V.* Lenin's elder brother, Alexander Ulyanov, was among those who attempted to revive the organization. He participated in an unsuccessful assassination attempt on Tsar Aleksander III in 1887 but was caught and hanged. The terrorist work was later carried on by SOCIALIST REVOLUTIONARIES.

Narodnik Communists A small political group formed in Soviet Russia by the LEFT SOCIALIST REVOLUTIONARIES in July 1918, after the assassination of the German ambassador by LEFT COMMUNISTS in July 1918. It included former Narodniks and Bolsheviks and attempted to control terrorist activites. The group later joined the RUSSIAN COMMUNIST PARTY (OF THE BOLSHEVIKS).

Narodniks Early anarcho-socialists in the Russian revolutionary movement in the last four decades of the 19th c., who emphasized the role and interests of the peasantry in social organization and development. Their movement, called NARODNISM, came into conflict with Marxism and attracted criticism from Engels (in *On Social Relations in Russia*, 1875), Lenin (in *What 'Friends of the People' Are and How They Fight the Social Democrats*, 1894) and later the hostility of the BOLSHEVIKS. N. lost their popular support and influence in the revolutionary movement after the foundation of the RUSSIAN SOCIAL-DEMOCRATIC LABOUR PARTY in 1898, especially after the rise of the Bolsheviks in 1903, although they later reappeared as KADETS and SOCIAL-IST REVOLUTIONARIES.

Narodnism (*Narodnichestvo,* in Russian) A pre-Marxist revolutionary movement in Russia in the latter part of the 19th c., which emphasized the interests of the peasantry. It developed in the 1860s and 1870s, but declined after the formation of the RUSSIAN SOCIAL-DEMOCRATIC LABOUR PARTY in 1898, although it lingered on as a political force until 1920. The term comes from *narod*, in Russian meaning the 'common people', which at that time referred to the rural masses. 'Populism' is sometimes used as an alternative English designation. N. originated among the intellectuals with (mostly) anarchist inclinations who were led by M. BAKUNIN, N. F. DANIELSON, P. L. Lavrov (1823–1900) and P. N. TKACHEV. N. advocated the overthrow of the Tsarist autocracy, pressed for a democratically elected parliament, decentralization of administration and the consequent greater role for local government, the redistribution of land owned by the gentry and nobility to peasants, workers' ownership of factories, radical modernization of agriculture, and opposed the development of industrial capitalism. N. saw the village commune as the pivot of social organization and progress. But after 1880, N. turned partly to liberalism and tended to favour the interests of the richer peasantry. There were a wide range of views among the adherents of N. The most active protagonists formed a secret revolutionary organization *ZEMLYA I VOLYA* (Land and Freedom) in 1861/62, which in 1876 split into *CHORNYI PEREDEL* (Land Redistribution Group) and *NARODNAYA VOLYA* (People's Freedom). N. accepted the INDIVIDUALIST INTERPRETATION OF HISTORY. Extremists in their revolutionary struggle with Tsarist oppression resorted to individual terror. The supporters of N. joined the FIRST INTERNATIONAL. The ideology and programme of N. attracted criticism from Marxists, especially from Engels (in *On Social Relations in Russia*, 1875), Plekhanov (in *Our Differences*, 1885) and Lenin (in *What the 'Friends of the People' Are and How They Fight the Social-Democrats*, 1894, and *The Development of Capitalism in Russia*, 1899). The main features of N. (which were unacceptable to Marxists) were: 1. the course of history is not determined by social classes or the class struggle, but outstanding individuals who are followed by the populace; 2. although there were some traces of industrial capitalism in Russia, it would never fully develop under Russian conditions, consequently there was no chance of an industrial proletariat to emerge as a significant social class; 3. the proletariat is not an important dynamic force in a revolution, but rather an inert mass and a 'historical misfortune'; and 4. the main socialist base and the real revolutionary force in Russia is the peasantry led by intellectuals and rural communes. Marxists accused N. of: philosophical eclecticism (favouring POSITIVISM and NEO-KANTIANISM); contempt for the masses, regarding them incapable of an independent and creative movement; neglect of the material conditions of political and social development; serving the interests of rich peasants (*KULAKS*); and advocating UTOPIAN SOCIALISM.

Narodnoe Dyelo (Russian for 'People's Cause') The journal of NARODNISM, representing the Russian Section of the FIRST INTERNATIONAL, which was published in Geneva from 1868 to 1870. Its first issue was prepared by BAKUNIN, who favoured ANARCHISM. However, in its later issues, the journal opposed anarchism, as well as liberal reformism and panslavism, and eventually gave its support to Marx and Engels instead of Bakunin, but did not follow the Marxist line completely. Its editor was N. I. Utin, Secretary of the Russian Section of the F.I., who was assisted by J. L. Dmitrieva and A. W. Korwin-Krukowska.

National Assembly (*Narodno Sobranie*) In Bulgaria, the unicameral parliament consisting of 400 deputies. The deputies are elected by universal and secret ballot for five years from a single list prepared by the FATHERLAND FRONT. At the May 1976 general elections, the BULGARIAN COMMUNIST PARTY won 272 seats, the Bulgarian Agrarian People's Union 100 seats and the non-party elements 28 seats.

National Assembly of People's Power In Cuba, the highest formal organ of state power with constituent and legislative authority, consisting of 481 deputies elected by the Municipal Assemblies of People's Power for a term of five years. Its functions include the enactment and modification of legislation, the discussion and approval of economic and social development plans and the state budget, certain key state appointments, the supervision of the government and other main organs of the state and the preparation and approval of constitutional reforms. The Assembly normally meets twice a year. Decisions in most cases are made by a simple majority vote. The Assembly's governing body and one which discharges its functions between sessions is the Council of State, consisting of 30 members headed by a President (who is also the Head of State).

National Assembly of the Hungarian People's Republic (*Országgyülés*) The Hungarian unicameral parliament, consisting of 352 deputies elected by direct universal suffrage for a term of four years. The deputies are elected from a list prepared by the PATRIOTIC PEOPLE'S FRONT, where 318 constituencies are contested by one candidate in each case and 34 constituencies by two or more candidates. The Speaker of the Assembly (A. Apró) is also a member of the Politburo of the HUNGARIAN SOCIALIST WORKERS' PARTY.

National Assembly of the SR of Vietnam (*Quoc Hoi*) The unicameral parliament in the unified Republic, consisting of 492 deputies (249 representing the North and 243, the South). The candidates are nominated by the approved political parties, revolutionary mass organizations and ethnic and religious groups (but 113 seats are uncontested). The Assembly elects its permanent executive body called the Standing Committee which consists of 20 members headed by a Chairman (Truong Chinh, who is also a member of the Politburo of the VIETNAM COMMUNIST PARTY). The Assembly meets, as a rule, twice a year, while between sessions its functions are performed by the Standing Committee.

National Communists Name vaguely applied to those Communists whose loyalty rests first with their own country and only then with the international Communist movement. They also refuse to follow either the MOSCOW LINE or the PEKING LINE. The term was first applied to the Yugoslav Communists, who in 1948 openly baulked against Soviet domination under Stalin (TITOISM). The name was also applied in the early post-W.W.II period to those Communists who had been active during W.W.II in their own countries fighting German, Italian and Japanese fascism and occupation, as distinct from the MUSCOVITES (who had spent that period in the USSR).

National Cultural Revolutionary Group (*Wen-ge*, in Chinese) A radical vanguard of the GREAT PROLETARIAN CULTURAL REVOLUTION in China, created in May 1966 by the Politburo of the Chinese Communist Party on the initiative of Mao Tse-tung. It replaced the GROUP OF FIVE, which was 'not revolutionary enough' and was led by CHEN PO-TA. The N.C.R.G. included CHANG CH'UN-CHIAO (who played the leading role in establishing a new power base in Shanghai), CHIANG CH'ING (Mao's wife, associated with the rebel RED GUARDS), K'ANG SHENG (the rebellious former member of the Group of Five), YAO WEN-YUAN and several writers on the editorial board of HUNG-CHI (*Red Flag*), the Party's theoretical journal.

National Democratic Front A general name in China for the united electoral coalition of the non-bourgeois political parties since 1949. It has included the China Association for Promoting Democracy, the China Chih Kung Tang, the China Democratic League, the China Democratic National Constructional Association, the China Peasants' and Workers' Democratic Party, the China San Society, the Kuomintang Revolutionary

National Economic Plan

Committee and the Taiwan Democratic Self-Government League. The Front, which acts as a democratic façade, has an advisory role and has been completely dominated by the CHINESE COMMUNIST PARTY. The Front had its formal representation in the CHINESE PEOPLE'S POLITICAL CONSULTATIVE CONFERENCE from 1949 to 1954, and since that time in the NATIONAL PEOPLE'S CONGRESS (both being rubber-stamp Chinese parliaments). The designation is also used to describe the two-periods of co-operation between the Chinese Communist Party and the KUOMINTANG, from 1924 to 1927 and from 1937 to 1945.

National Economic Plan See ECONOMIC PLAN.

National Front of Democratic Germany (*Nationale Front des Demokratischen Deutschland*) The Communist-controlled electoral alliance of the officially approved political parties and other social organizations in the GERMAN DR. The Front is dominated by the SOCIALIST UNITY PARTY OF GERMANY, but four other non-opposition political parties participate, viz. the Christian Democratic Union, the Democratic Peasants' Party, the Liberal Party, and the National Democratic Party (they have nothing to do with similar parties in the FR of Germany). In addition, the Democratic Women's League, the Free German Trade Union Federation, the Free German Youth, and the German League of Culture are represented. The Front prepares a joint programme and a list of candidates for elections held every five years. At the 1976 general elections, out of a total of 500 seats in the *VOLKSKAMMER*, the S.U.P.G. won 127 and the four other political parties won 45 each. The balance 193 was shared by the remaining organizations. According to official data, 99.9 per cent of the electorate voted for the candidates put forward by the Front.

National Front of the Czechoslovak Socialist Republic The popular alliance uniting the officially approved political parties and main social organizations to provide electoral, moral and practical support to the Party and Government policies. It is indisputably dominated by the CZECHOSLOVAK COMMUNIST PARTY, but also embraces other non-bourgeois legal organizations, viz. the Czechoslovak People's Party, the Czechoslovak Socialist Party, the Revolutionary Trade Union Movement, the Slovak Freedom Party, the Slovak Reconstruction Party and the Socialist Union of Youth. According to official figures, at the 1976 general elections, 99.9 per cent of the electorate voted for the N.F. candidates.

National Income A general term used in both capitalist and the Socialist countries to describe the net value of production in a country over a particular period, usually a year. But while the capitalist coverage includes all the goods and services as long as they are paid for, the Socialist concept covers only material production, i.e. goods and material services, viz. those contributed by industry, construction, agriculture, transport, communications and trade. The Socialist N.I. is more appropriately described as the NET MATERIAL PRODUCT at realized prices. As a rough guide, to bring a capitalist N.I. figure to the Socialist basis, reduce the former by one-fifth and increase the Socialist figure by one-quarter to bring it to the capitalist basis.

Nationalism Attitudes and policies which emphasize the interests of one's own nation above, or at least disregarding, other nations. N. may assume different forms, ranging from aggressive IMPERIALISM and intolerant CHAUVINISM to national assertiveness and isolationism. Communist views and practices have varied. The early Marxist thinkers, such as K. Marx and Rosa Luxemburg, were opposed to n., regarding the national states as bourgeois creations, prone to aggression and international wars leading to IMPERIALISM. Instead, they advanced the ideal of PRO-

LETARIAN INTERNATIONALISM. But some Marxists, such as the majority in the SEC-OND INTERNATIONAL and the exponents of AUSTRO-MARXISM, maintained that nations were worth preserving and could make valuable contributions to proletarian development and culture. Lenin, although basically adhering to the principle of SOCIALIST INTERNATIONALISM, saw a role for nations and was sympathetic to national minorities, especially to NATIONAL LIBERATION MOVEMENTS. After the German attack on the USSR in June 1941, the Soviet regime to some extent rehabilitated Soviet n. calling it PATRIOTISM. The latter has been accepted by other Socialist countries as a highly desirable version of n. Some critical observers of Communist policies and practices since W.W.II maintain that n. has in fact come to triumph over communism. L. Lengel (in a book significantly entitled *Nationalism: The Last Stage of Communism*, 1969), in quoting the cases of China, Czechoslovakia, Hungary, Romania and Yugoslavia, pointed out that national sentiments and interests keep on reasserting themselves against internationalism. In Marxist ideology, however, it is assumed that eventually (under FULL COMMUNISM) nation states, together with national boundaries, will disappear.

Nationalization The acquisition of private assets by the nation (state), normally with full or partial compensation to their previous owners (domestic or foreign). In contrast to SOCIALIZATION, the term n. is normally used in application to capitalist countries. N. usually involves entities which are considered to be of key importance or concern to the nation, such as staple minerals, the power supply, railways, shipping, air transport, communications, banking, iron and steel and the marketing of certain products. N. leads to the establishment of a state sector, strengthens the effectiveness of state intervention and facilitates economic planning. N. is one of the principal objectives of left-wing political parties in the capitalist world. However, communist leaders

view n. not as a welcome development but as an attempt to prop up ailing capitalism and as evidence of contradictions producing new contradictions between the private and public sectors. N. in the countries of the Third World is viewed with favour insofar as it is directed against foreign monopolies and a step towards economic planning and the socialist road to development.

Nationalization of Women See 'COMMUNITY OF WOMEN'.

National Labour Union The first national trade union organization in the USA, established in Baltimore in Aug. 1866. It had been prompted by employers' efforts to check unionization and was founded by A. C. Cameron (1834–1901). Its membership rose from 60,000 to 300,000 owing to the campaigning efforts of W. H. Sylvis. The N.L.U. pressed for an eight-hour day. It was partly successful when the Congress passed a law in 1868 applicable to certain federal government employees. But due to internal differences on the role of women and Negroes in the labour movement, the N.L.U. disappeared in 1872.

National Liberation Front of South Vietnam A revolutionary political and military organization established in Dec. 1960 to fight the right-wing government in South Vietnam and foreign intervention to achieve the reunification of South Vietnam with North Vietnam under a Communist regime. It united different subversive and terrorist groups, including the VIET CONG, which were formed into a highly disciplined and effective force. The Committees of the N.L.F.S.V. performed the functions of several government ministries, implementing social reforms and administering areas under its control. The Front was backed by the Democratic Republic of [North] Vietnam, providing training advisers, equipment and (at a later stage) military units. It also received generous aid from China, the USSR and East European countries. The Front fought not only the South Vietnamese government forces, but also those of the USA (which in mid-1968 reached 545,000 troops), Australia, New Zealand and several other countries (totalling some 60,000). The victories of the N.L.F.S.V. were largely due to the strategies planned by General VO NGUYEN GIAP. It handled peace negotiations over the period 1967–69, known as the PARIS PEACE TALKS, until the Provisional Revolutionary Government was formed in June 1969. When the latter formally took over power from the South Vietnamese Government on 30 April 1975, the N.L.F.S.V. immediately declared its allegiance to it and co-operated during the transitional period until the proclamation of the unified country, the S.R. OF VIETNAM, on 2 July 1976.

National Liberation Movements A designation commonly applied by Marxists to the efforts of the colonies and other dependent countries to achieve independence from imperialist domination and exploitation. At the height of IMPERIALISM, before W.W.I, more than two-thirds of the world area was in this category. Widespread and systematic n.l.m. began only after W.W.II, especially after the mid-1950s. N.l.m. were first sanctioned by the FIRST INTERNATIONAL and were then explicitly insisted upon in the TWENTY-ONE CONDITIONS OF ADMISSION TO COMINTERN, adopted in 1921. But the most complete Marxist statement was contained in the document known as the 'Theses on the National and Colonial Question', proclaimed by the 6th Congress of the COMINTERN in 1928, in which the proletariat was urged to support the nationalistic bourgeoisie in the n.l.m. In fact n.l.m. have been generally led by nationalistic middle and upper class elements, in which left-wing groups have participated. Marxists view n.l.m. as a step in the socialist revolution, starting with the BOURGEOIS-DEMOCRATIC REVOLUTION, but which in due course must lead to a PROLETARIAN REVOLUTION, led by a Communist party, at first in coalition with other left-wing parties and then under its exclusive control. The Socialist countries, especially China and the USSR, support n.l.m. on the following grounds: 1. in accordance with Marxist social theory, any oppressed, exploited or underprivileged nation is morally entitled to political, economic and cultural self-determination; 2. n.l.m. lead to the elimination of imperialism, the highest and the most degenerate stage of capitalism; 3. liberation leads to the political, economic and strategic weakening of the most powerful capitalist nations opposed to the Socialist countries; 4. support to the n.l.m. is conducive to gaining goodwill and co-operation in the Third World, thereby weaning the liberated countries away from the capitalist camp; and 5. active support to the n.l.m. assists the local Communist parties and may be instrumental in the local adoption of the socialist road to economic and social development.

National People's Congress In China, 'the highest organ of state power under the leadership of the Chinese Communist Party' (Article 16 of the 1975 Constitution). It is a unicameral parliament, consisting of deputies elected for five years on the basis of democratic consultation among provinces, autonomous regions, major municipalities, the armed forces, parties allowed in the NATIONAL DEMOCRATIC FRONT and the Overseas Chinese groups. In addition some patriotic personnages may be specially invited to become deputies. The N.P.C. is supposed to meet at least once a year, but in practice this rule has not been observed. The N.P.C. replaced the CHINESE PEOPLE'S POLITICAL CONSULTATIVE CONFERENCE in 1954. The First, Second, Third, Fourth and Fifth Congresses were held in 1954, 1959, 1964, 1975 and 1978 respectively. The Fifth N.P.C. held from 26 Feb. to 5 March 1978 was attended by 3,456 delegates. Between sessions the functions of the N.P.C. are performed by the Standing Committee of the N.P.C. The powers of the N.P.C. have been reduced from 19 under the 1954 Constitution to 5 as specified by the 1975 Constitution. These now include: the enactment of laws; the election of the Standing Committee of the N.P.C.; the appointment and removal of the Prime Minister and members of the State Council (the Cabinet) on the recommendation of the Central Committee of the Chinese Communist Party; and the approval of the national economic plan, the state budget, the final state accounts and changes to the Constitution.

National Plan of Socio-economic Development The official name given to the economic plan in Poland since 1971, replacing the previous official designation, the National Economic Plan.

National United Front The mass political organization in the SR of Vietnam embracing various approved political parties and groups to provide electoral and moral support to the Communist regime. It was organized in 1976 by North Vietnam's National Fatherland Front and the National Liberation Front of South Vietnam and formally launched in Jan. 1977. It is dominated by the VIETNAM COMMUNIST PARTY, but also includes the Vietnam Democratic Party (a middle-class party founded in North Vietnam in 1944), the Vietnam Socialist Party (representing intellectuals, originally founded in Hanoi in 1951) and the Vietnam Alliance of National Democratic and Peace Forces (established by the National Liberation Front of South Vietnam in 1968). In addition, other non-opposition political groups and religious organizations are also represented.

NATO Abbreviation for the NORTH ATLANTIC TREATY ORGANIZATION.

Natolin Group A high-level fraternity of Stalinist diehards in Poland who in 1956, contrary to the majority in the POLISH UNITED WORKERS' PARTY and the liberal mood of the public, opposed DE-STALINIZATION, political liberalization and economic reforms. The Group held its meetings in an old palace situated in Natolin, a distant suburb of Warsaw.

Natural Economy A subsistence type of economy where production and distribution are carried on for the direct satisfaction of the wants of the producers themselves. As a consequence, there is no need for money and trade. It is the only form of production and distribution under PRIMITIVE COMMUNISM, but may also appear to some extent in other socio-economic formations, especially SLAVERY and FEUDALISM. A n.e. may have several features favoured by Marxists, such as the collective ownership of the means of production, communal living and the absence of money and exploitation. But it is not accepted as an ideal, as a n.e. is typically stagnant and dominated by custom, religious norms and conservatism. Marxist HISTORICAL MATERIALISM implies continuous change in the MODE OF PRODUCTION and attaches great importance to economic progress and social advancement to all-round affluence, eventually leading to FULL COMMUNISM. Also NATURAL LAWS, NATURALIZATION OF ECONOMIC PROCESSES.

Naturalism A philosophical theory attributing the development of society to the laws of nature, viz. climatic conditions, geographical environment, plant and animal life, racial characteristics of the people and the like. In literature and art, n. emphasizes the faithful reproduction of natural objects and phenomena and the most sordid aspects of life. N. was developed in the 18th and 19th c. and was based on the acceptance of NATURAL LAWS as determining factors in economic and social development. The main exponents of n. were D. Hume (1711–76), H. Spencer (1820–1903) and G. Santayana (1863–1952). Marxists have mixed views on n. On the one hand, they concede that it has rendered some service to MATERIALISM in philosophy and REALISM in literature and art. But on the other, they emphasize that n. ignores other laws governing the life and development of societies, such as the LAW OF THE CONCORDANCE OF PRODUCTION RELATIONS WITH THE NATURE OF PRODUCTION FORCES and the LAW OF UNEVEN ECONOMIC DEVELOP-MENT. They further stress that in literature and art n. is barren and vulgar, monotonous and unsophisticated and without any ideological interpretation and message.

Naturalization of Economic Processes An ideal advocated by some socialist and communist theoreticians (such as K. Marx and S. Strumilin) urging the abolition of money in favour of accounting and distribution in natural units, such as kilogrammes, litres, work hours and the like. Systematic attempts in this direction were made in the USSR between 1917 and 1922, when large proportions of taxes and wages were raised or paid in kind and the value of money was undermined by inflationary issues and periodical cancellations of bank notes. Schemes were also prepared to base income and distribution on work units and units of satisfaction, called *TRED* and *DOV*. In Marxist ideology, it is vaguely assumed that the n. of e.p. will prevail under FULL COMMUNISM.

Natural Laws, Theory of A philosophical view developed in the 17th and 18th c. according to which economic, social and other processes are essentially governed by the laws of nature. Its best known exponents were H. Grotius (1583–1645), W. Petty (1623–87), J. Locke (1632–1704), Ch. Thomasius (1655–1728) and was later supported by the proponents of PHYSIOCRATISM and *LAISSEZ-FAIRE* capitalism. The turn to n.l. was a reaction against the artificial authority and oppression imposed by the feudal system and monarchies and was a warning against the introduction of 'human laws'. Although Marxists partly accepted this view, they rejected the idea that economic and social life were governed by immutable laws outside the sphere of human activities. They stress that neither economy nor society are static. In addition to universal scientific laws, economic and social development are determined by changes in PRODUCTION FORCES and PRODUCTION RELATIONS, which historically have led to dif-

ferent SOCIO-ECONOMIC FORMATIONS. Consequently, capitalism is not a natural and eternal economic and social order, but a stage in development.

Natural Materialism A common view held by natural scientists that the external material world exists and finds its reflection in human consciousness. This belief is based on spontaneous observation and is not necessarily steeped in philosophical MATERIALISM. According to Marxists, this is a predominant and natural impression of those who study natural laws. This unintentionally and impartially acquired view provides further evidence of the primacy of MATTER over IDEAS, and consequently of the validity of materialism, as opposed to IDEALISM. However, Lenin (in *MATERIALISM AND EMPIRIO-CITICISM*) pointed out that ideologically n.m. was too naïve and could be easily attacked unless grounded in DIALECTICAL MATERIALISM.

Natural Philosophy A field of philosophy preoccupied with the explanation of natural phenomena and their interdependence. Its main development took place in Germany in the 17th-19th centuries. It relied more on mere observation and deduction than on scientific experimentation. Its chief exponents were G. W. Leibnitz (1646–1716), I. Kant (1724–1804), G. W. F. HEGEL, F. W. Schelling (1775–1854) and L. Oken (1779–1855). Marxists have acknowledged some contributions by natural philosophers, especially their advanced study of natural phenomena beyond mere description and attempts to explain nature and development. But otherwise, n.p. became a target for attack by the early Marxist philosophers such as F. Engels (especially in *LUDWIG FEUERBACH AND THE END OF CLASSICAL GERMAN PHILOSOPHY*). They regard it as speculative and unscientific, attributing the ultimate world order to mysterious and supernatural forces. In the Marxist view, there is no need for a separate philosophy of nature. But there is a need for the theoretical study of the natural process, in which the methodology of

DIALECTICAL MATERIALISM should be applied.

Natural Selection A theory of evolution put forward by Ch. Darwin and A. R. Wallace independently in 1859, according to which the organisms with more advantageous characteristics in relation to the environment tend to survive better, and thus are more likely to reproduce and transmit their characteristics to subsequent generations. The theory recognizes the great diversity of individual organisms, the inheritance of variant characteristics and emphasizes the STRUGGLE FOR EXISTENCE and the 'survival of the fittest'. The capacity of adaptation to the environment may be physiological, anatomical or behavioural. The modern emphasis is on the selection of groups rather than of individuals. Although Marx almost dedicated the first volume of *Capital* to Darwin, Marxists have been somewhat sceptical of the theory of n.s. and its social validity on the following grounds: 1. it was based on COMPETITION in the struggle for life; 2. it represented an attempt to explain and justify the existing capitalist social order thus helping the BOURGEOISIE remain in power; 3. it was directed against the interests of the exploited lower social strata living in poverty; and 4. it implicitly subscribed to MALTHUSIANISM. A Soviet biologist, T. D. LYSENKO, limited the role of competition only to inter-species rivalry and maintained that intra-species relations are based on co-operation.

Nazism An extreme version of FASCISM, which prevailed in Germany under Hitler from 1933 to 1945.

Necessary Labour INDISPENSABLE LABOUR.

Necessary Labour-Time INDISPENSABLE LABOUR-TIME.

Necessity One of the basic concepts used in philosophy to denote a situation where, given certain conditions (causes) a phenomenon occurs irrespective of all other circumstances. The origin of the concept goes back to Aristotle (384–322 B.C.), but was later developed by G. W. Leibnitz (1646–1716) and I. Kant (1724–1804). N. contrasts with CONTINGENCY and has been a subject of controversy among different schools of philosophy especially in nature and society. The extreme doctrines of n. are FATALISM and MECHANISM, which attribute all phenomena to causation based on inexorable laws, thus denying the possibility of fortuitous occurrences. Some idealist philosophers attribute causation not to the laws of material nature, but to supernatural forces. The concept of n. plays an important part in Marxist philosophy, but its interpretation is rather complex. Basically, Marxist philosophers (such as Marx and Engels) maintain that n. and not chance, fatalism or mechanism prevail in nature and society. According to DIALECTICAL MATERIALISM, the development of phenomena inherently derives from the mutual interdependence of cause and effect, i.e. CONTRADICTION. The contradictions and the consequent phenomena and developments take place irrespective and independently of the will and consciousness of man. In particular Marxists insist that the development of society from one stage to another is conditioned by changes in the material BASE. The ANTAGONISTIC SOCIO-ECONOMIC FORMATIONS (slavery, feudalism and capitalism), the CLASS STRUGGLE and REVOLUTION are all matters of n., not of chance. But at the same time, dialectical materialism does not negate the possibility of fortuitous occurrences. The latter are thought to arise exogenously as a matter of n. from the given causal situation and are subject to the statistical laws of probability. Consequently, in the Marxist (in contrast to the metaphysical) view, n. and contingency are not necessarily mutually exclusive concepts, but are linked dialectically, fortuity supplementing n. The causal concept of n. has led Marxists to the conviction that nature and (especially) society can be influenced by man to his benefit.

Nechayev, Sergei Gennadevich (1847–82) A Russian anarchist revolutionary who advocated, and personally participated in, terrorist activities. After his first escape to Switzerland in 1869, he collaborated with M. A. BAKUNIN and jointly prepared the *REVOLUTIONARY CATECHISM*. He returned to Russia in the same year and organized nihilist terrorist groups called the People's Avenge. In 1872 he had to flee from Russia again but was arrested by the Swiss police, extradited to Russia in 1873 and died in prison nine years later.

Negation A philosophical concept introduced by HEGEL and employed in DIALECTICS. In the process of n. any characteristic or phenomenon develops its own opposite, so that an old quality sooner or later gives rise to a rival, new quality producing a contradiction. Marx adopted the concept in his DIALECTICAL MATERIALISM and made it one of the foundations of Marxist ideology. Lenin later added than n. is not necessarily destructive (if it is, he called it 'black n.'), as in most cases it is a factor of development, where positive elements may be retained.

Negation of the Negation A philosophical proposition introduced by HEGEL in the DIALECTIC process of development. The old quality is negated by its opposite, the new quality, thus constituting the first negation. However, the superceded quality does not remain in its original form but, by another process of negation, develops into the next stage, the n. of the n. Marx, Engels and other classical Marxist philosophers adopted the concept from Hegel, but gave it a materialist content and stressed its dynamic aspect of development. However, as Engels and Lenin insisted, neither negation nor the n. of the n. in dialectics amounts to the total denial or rejection of the old. Thus, socialism is basically a negation of capitalism, yet the former also embodies the best elements of the latter (capital equipment, production technology, cultural achievements). Stalin (in *Dialectical and Historical Materialism*,

1938), to avoid using Hegel's term, advanced substitute designations, viz. 'move from a lower to a higher phase' or 'move from the simple to the complex'.

Neo-Austrian Critique of Socialism Economic and political criticism by distinguished ex-Austrian (later American) economists against the Socialist system, between 1920 and (approximately) 1965. The economists concerned and their main contributions in the field were: F. A. Hayek (*The Road to Serfdom*, 1946); L. Mises ('Economic Calculation in the Socialist Commonwealth', 1920); and J. Viner ('International Relations between State-Controlled National Economies', 1944). The critique focused on three major problems: 1. irrationality – it was maintained that, owing to the absence of the private ownership of the means of production and of the market mechanism, the Socialist centrally planned economy could not know and have scarcity prices. Without such prices and the profit motive, the rational conduct of the economy (ensuring maximum efficiency) is impossible; 2. autarky – state foreign trade monopoly and central economic planning inevitably lead to restrictions on foreign trade, as foreign trade represents an element of uncertainty beyond the control of the planners. This must eventually lead to the virtual elimination of foreign trade; and 3. political and economic enslavement – the dictatorship of the proletariat exercised by the Party elite, ideological intolerance, the centralized, directive system of planning and management and the ubiquitous all-powerful state reduce democratic freedoms and the individual dignity of man. Consequently, the road to socialism is in fact a 'road to serfdom'. The cause of socialism was taken up by a number of Marxists or socialist thinkers. Among them were: M. Dobb (*Collectivist Economic Planning*, 1935); O. Lange ('The Economic Theory of Socialism', 1936–37, and 'Computer and the Market', 1965); and I. Vajda (*The Role of Foreign Trade in a Socialist Economy*, 1965). They pointed out that rational economic calculation and management were possible under socialism by the application of the TRIAL AND ERROR METHOD OF PRICE DETERMINATION, the COMPETITIVE SOLUTION and the utilization of computers in price determination and management. Similarly, the gains from foreign trade are fully appreciated under socialism, to which the departures from autarkic policies since the early 1950s attest. De-Stalinization, economic reforms and other liberal moves since the mid-1950s indicate that authoritarianism is not necessarily concomitant with socialism.

Neo-classical School of Bourgeois Economics An important stage in the development of Western ('bourgeois') economic theory following CLASSICAL BOURGEOIS POLITICAL ECONOMY, extending from about 1870 to 1925. W. Jevons (1835–82) is regarded its founder, but its most prominent exponent was A. Marshall (1842–1924). The School represented an attempt to reconcile the theory of MARGINAL UTILITY with the marginal cost analysis in the formation of prices and partial equilibrium. Marxist economists from the start adopted a critical attitude to the School, regarding it as a further bourgeois departure from classical political economy. They objected to the application of marginal analysis with respect to both demand and supply and to the inclusion of non-labour and market determined incomes (rent, interest, normal profit) as cost components. On the other hand, they acknowledged the School's recognition of objective factors in price formation, i.e. those determining costs (as distinct from subjective utility considerations). The School's preoccupation with perfect atomistic competition was also viewed with favour, as it implied the rejection of monopoly and a more even distribution of income.

Neo-collectivism A term sometimes used in capitalist countries for a modified version of COLLECTIVISM, allowing limited private ownership of the means of produc-

tion. The advocates of n.-c. would like to see all heavy industry, key industries, essential utilities, services and wholesale trade, together with a proportion of land (for experimental stations and model farms) socially-owned. But at the same time they favour small-scale industry to be basically operated by owner-workers and their families, such as craft and art workshops, restaurants, retail shops, medium-size farms and personal services (hairdressing, tailoring and fashion entities).

Neo-colonialism The reappearance of COLONIALISM after the formal political liberation of former colonies or other dependencies of imperial countries. The term is often used in the Socialist countries and in the THIRD WORLD. The use of the term is directed against the continued domination and exploitation of the less-developed countries by the rich and powerful industrialized nations of the West. In this interpretation n.-c. involves: 1. the economic penetration of the liberated countries by Western monopoly capital (especially multinational corporations); 2. conditional economic aid and bribery convenient to the donor countries; 3. the maintenance of military bases by Western powers; and 4. the continuation of the pre-liberation bureaucracy, social structure and political system with which Western powers ally themselves against left-wing elements. The term has also been applied to the expanding Soviet influence, especially in Africa.

Neo-criticism Another term for NEO-KANTIANISM.

Neo-Hegelianism A philosophical movement in three stages which sought to reinterpret and supplement the philosophy of G. W. F. HEGEL with respect to: 1. his natural philosophy and his philosophy of right; 2. his early theological critiques; and 3. his *Phenomenology of Spirit* and Marxism. The first revival reached its high point in Britain, America and Italy before W.W.I. Its main exponents were T. H. Green (1836–1882), F. H. Bradley

(1846–1924), J. Royce (1855–1916), J. Dewey (1859–1952), G. Gentile (1875–1944) and B. Croce (1866–1952). The second revival was centred in Germany, also just before W.W.I. It was a consequent of NEO-KANTIANISM and W. Dilthey's (1833–1911) interest in Hegel's early theological critiques. The third and most important revival occurred in France between the world wars and in the late 1940s and 1950s. Its main contributors were Jean Wahl (1888–1972), Alexandre Kojève (1902–1968) and Jean Hyppolite (1907–1968) who stressed the existential, dialectical and historical content in Hegel's *Phenomenology*, respectively. The latter two emphasised Marx's debt to Hegel.

Neo-Kantianism A philosophical movement roughly between 1860 and 1914 which became quite influential in Germany, Austria, Italy and Russia. It represented an attempt to link the philosophical tenets of I. Kant (1724–1804) with modern achievements in physical and social sciences, focusing attention on the theory of knowledge and value. N.-K. was initiated by H. L. von Helmholtz (1821–94) and F. A. Lange (1828–75), and included such exponents as H. Cohen (1842–1918), O. Liebmann (1840–1912), G. N. Bulgakov (1871–1944) and P. B. STRUVE (1870–1944). Although some of its advocates were socialists, n.-K. was critical of Marxism and it inspired REVISIONISM, AUSTRO-MARXISM and LEGAL MARXISM. N.-K. greatly influenced the thinking of the SECOND INTERNATIONAL, when some of its leaders (especially E. BERNSTEIN, K. KAUTSKY and M. Adler) sought to integrate it with Marxism. The Marxist criticism of n.-K. dwelt on its IDEALISM, SUBJECTIVISM, FIDEISM, AGNOSTICISM and the negation of objective laws in social development. In the Marxist view, n.-K. developed into an even more reactionary philosophical movement called NEO-HEGELIANISM.

Neo-liberalism A revived version of economic LIBERALISM which developed after W.W.II in the most developed capitalist countries (especially the FR of Germany). Its initiator appears to be W. Lipmann (in *An Inquiry into the Good Society*, 1938). Among its main exponents are L. Erhard and E. Heuss (of the FRG), F. A. Hayek and L. Robbins (of the UK), M. Friedman and G. Haberler (of the USA) and J. Rueff (of France). N.-l. is opposed to excessive state intervention and nationalization and attaches prime importance to the market mechanism, scarcity prices, the most efficient utilization of resources, free enterprise and democratic freedoms. It has found its best practical expression in the SOCIAL ECONOMY of the FR of Germany. Although the policies of n.-l. have proved quite successful, Socialist economists view it critically as a reactionary outlook. They attribute the practical success in the postwar period more to historical circumstances than to its inherent merits as a viable alternative to Socialist economic planning.

Neo-Marxism A term for the up-dated version of MARXISM, more suited to practical needs and modern political, social economic and scientific developments beyond the knowledge and experience of the CLASSICAL MARXIST THINKERS. The first wave of n.-M. appeared roughly between 1930 and 1955 and focused on economic theory, mostly directed to the working out of a more rigorous economic model of development and a rational allocation of resources in a collectivist planned economy. The main contributors to this improvement on Marx were the Western liberal Marxists: M. Dobb, O. Lange, P. Sweezy and Joan Robinson. The second wave of n.-M. has been preoccupied with political, management, administrative and economic policies and was prompted by the TWENTIETH CONGRESS OF THE CPSU in 1956 and the ECONOMIC REFORMS since the early 1960s. Its main departures from orthodox Marxism are: 1. there can and should be peaceful COEXISTENCE between the Socialist and capitalist states; 2. wars, while still possible, are no longer necessary even though IMPERIALISM still exists in one form or another; 3. the abandonment of the DICTATORSHIP OF THE PROLETARIAT is possible before the complete victory of communism (STATE OF THE WHOLE PEOPLE); 4. the PARLIAMENTARY ROAD TO SOCIALISM is feasible, as parliaments can be turned from the agencies of bourgeois democracy into instruments of proletarian will; 5. the co-operation of Communist parties with other political parties even under bourgeois leadership is acceptable in the case of NATIONAL LIBERATION MOVEMENTS; 6. in OPTIMAL PLANNING, non-labour factors of production (land and capital) are recognized as having scarcity value, consequently, rent and interest can be treated as components of costs; and 7. PROFIT is accepted as an important criterion of enterprise performance. Also EUROCOMMUNISM, REVISIONISM.

Neo-positivism A modern movement in philosophy according to which positive knowledge alone (made possible by exact sciences) can provide a reliable basis for the philosophical understanding of the world. It is also known as logical positivism or logical empiricism. Although its roots go back to the 19th c., n.-p. developed in the 1920s in Austria and Germany, and then spread to other Western countries, especially Britain and the USA. It draws on modern logic, mathematics and the natural sciences. Its main exponents were R. Carnap, O. Neurath and M. Schlich. According to n.-p., cognition is restricted to only what can be expressed in language, especially in the terminology of physics. Its adherents regard previous philosophy as unscientific, as in their view it was preoccupied with insoluble unscientific questions, such as the world outlook and the existence of god and ideas. Marxist philosophers are critical of n.-p. and consider it a retrogressive development from the standpoint of social philosophy. To Marxists the problem of the world outlook is of fundamental importance in educational and cultural processes, it shapes human behaviour and activities and consequently determines the directions and pace of social, cultural and political developments in the modern world.

Neo-realism A direction in Western philosophy which had begun before W.W.I and was developed in the 1920s by S. Alexander (1859–1938), N. Hartmann (1882–1950), E. B. Holt (1873–1946), W. P. Montague (1873–1953), G. E. Moore (1873–1958), F. J. E. Woodbridge (1867–1940) and others. N.-r. is opposed to IDEALISM and emphasizes 'commonsense'. It is preoccupied with the theory of COGNITION and identifies being and consciousness as a unity, thereby subscribing to MONISM. It thus denies the validity of DUALISM as well as MATERIALISM (in particular the REFLECTION THEORY). Marxist philosophers, although accepting some of the propositions of n.-r. directed against idealism, reject its monistic approach and regard the movement as disguised philosophical idealism. In their view, n.-r. reduces being to sensory impressions, thereby identifying them as primary elements of nature, where even illusions and hallucinations are identified with truth. Lenin attacked some aspects of n.-r. in *MATERIALISM AND EMPIRIO-CRITICISM*. Some adherents of n.-r. branched off to INSTRUMENTALISM, LOGICAL POSITIVISM and SEMANTIC PHILOSOPHY.

Neo-Thomism The official philosophical doctrine of the Catholic church based on the writings of St. Thomas Aquinas (1225–74) and revived in an up-dated form after the Encyclical Letter of Pope Leon XIII in 1879. It achieved its greatest influence in the Catholic countries of Europe (especially Italy, France and Spain), Latin America and also in the USA. Marxist philosophy identifies n.-T. with the extreme version of IDEALISM and further regards it as the most extreme bourgeois philosophical movement in the 'era of imperialism' directed against DIALECTICAL MATERIALISM and HISTORICAL MATERIALISM. In the Marxist view, n.-T. is a weapon wielded by the Vatican which has allied itself with the most reactionary elements in the leading Western powers in order to retain the traditional social *status quo* at home as well as in the ex-colonial countries and to oppose the progressive forces associated with Marxism and socialism.

NEP Abbreviation of *Novaya Ekonomicheskaya Politika* (in Russian), meaning NEW ECONOMIC POLICY.

Net Financial Accumulation One of the alternative terms for PROFIT used in application to the Socialist planned economies. The purpose is to avoid the implication of exploitation which, in the Marxist view, is associated with (capitalist) profit.

Net Material Product The concept used to describe specifically the national income calculated on the Socialist basis, i.e., embracing MATERIAL PRODUCTION only. It represents the net value (i.e. excluding depreciation) of goods and productive services produced over a particular period (usually a year) expressed at REALIZED PRICES (not at factor cost). It is calculated as the sum of wages paid in the sphere of material production plus the value of the SURPLUS PRODUCT. The branches of the economy contributing to the n.m.p. are: 1. industry; 2. construction; 3. agriculture; 4. transport and communications; 5. trade; and 6. other branches (forestry, fisheries, hunting, gathering, laundrying, etc). As the concept excludes the so-called NON-PRODUCTIVE SERVICES, the figure of the n.m.p. is on the average one-fifth smaller than the national income calculated by the Western method (more than one-fifth in the case of a more developed country and less than one-fifth if the country in question is less developed).

Net Material Product Distributed A basis of Socialist national income accounting, showing the utilization of the NET MATERIAL PRODUCT, including 'losses of the economy' and the 'foreign balance' (the balance of payments on current account). Heavy borrowing increases the size of the n.m.p.d., compared with the n.m.p. produced.

Net Material Product Produced The concept of national income normally implied in Socialist national accounts. It embraces the total value of MATERIAL PRODUCTION net of depreciation over a particular period (usually a year) at REALIZED PRICES, where 'losses of the economy' and the 'foreign balance' are not taken into account. It roughly indicates the 'value added' on the macroeconomic scale.

Net Product In Socialist national income accounting, that portion of MATERIAL PRODUCTION which is created in a particular productive enterprise, branch of industry or a branch of the economy. It roughly corresponds to 'value added', as understood in Western national income accounts. Thus, the concept excludes the value of materials used (obtained from outside the entities in question) and the wear and tear of durable equipment (depreciation) in the process of production. It is calculated by deducting the value of materials used (including power), services obtained from outside and depreciation from the Global Product (i.e. roughly the gross value of output). The n.p. is expressed at current REALIZED PRICES. Historically, before the early 1960s, the term n.p. was also used in a vague sense for enterprise profit, to avoid the implication of exploitation associated with capitalist profit.

Net Product for Society In Socialist national income accounting, that portion of the NET MATERIAL PRODUCT which is not distributed in wage earnings to the work force in MATERIAL PRODUCTION (although it is created there). It embraces the wage earnings of the work force in the NON-PRODUCTIVE SPHERE, SOCIAL CONSUMPTION and INVESTMENT. The remaining portion of the Net Material Product is called 'net product for oneself'.

Net Profit In modern Socialist enterprise accounting, the amount of profit which is left in the enterprise after taxes, capital charges, differential payments and other compulsory levies are deducted from the

GROSS PROFIT. The n.p. is also known as 'enterprise profit' and is used for self-financed investment (as distinct from budgetary allocations), reserve funds and MATERIAL INCENTIVE FUND(S).

Net Profit Rate See PROFIT RATE.

Net Rentability See RENTABILITY.

Neue Rheinische Zeitung (*The New Rhineland Newspaper,* in German) A revolutionary-democratic newspaper, subtitled the 'Organ of Democracy', edited and published by Marx in Cologne from 15 June 1848 to 19 May 1849 (except from 25 Sep. to 17 Oct. 1848). It was meant to be a continuation of the RHEINISCHE ZEITUNG (edited by Marx in 1844–45) and initially supported the radical liberals. Marx published the *N.R.Z.* upon returning to Germany from Paris, following the outbreak of the Revolution of 1848. The *N.R.Z.* is generally regarded as the first genuine revolutionary Marxist newspaper, to which F. Engels, W. Wolff, F. Lassalle and other social reformers and thinkers contributed. It had about 6,000 subscribers. The newspaper became an object of repression by the authorities and was ordered to be closed down, and Marx was again sent into exile. The last issue of the paper (19 May 1849) was published in red. Its short-lived continuation sub-titled 'Political and Economic Review', also edited by Marx and assisted by Engels, appeared as a monthly from Jan. to Sep. 1850.

Neutral Money The concept of money as having no influence on economic processes, so that the latter are viewed as essentially the same as in a money-less economy. This view was accepted by most classical and neo-classical economists, whereby money was regarded merely as a 'veil' of real economic processes. Opposed to it was the 'capital-creation' view, put forward by J. Law (1671–1729), according to whom, the creation of money increased capital and national wealth. In the modern Socialist view, and in application to centrally planned economies, the view of money is twofold. On the one hand, it is postulated that money should have no spontaneous influence on real economic processes, as the latter should be determined directly by central planning in physical terms. It is further stressed that money is not an object of consumption and it does not directly participate in MATERIAL PRODUCTION. It cannot replace consumer goods, the means of production or labour, and cannot in its own right create real elements in production processes. Money ought to be utilized only to accommodate the predetermined real flows and enable economic discipline through financial accounting. But on the other hand, it is recognized that money, through its purchasing power over resources and products and its influence on prices and incomes, affects production and distribution. Thus, it can either distort or correct economic processes.

New Class The term used by M. DJILAS (in *The New Class,* 1957) for the Communist elite in Yugoslav of privileged Party officials, ranking bureaucrats, managers of state enterprises and top professionals, all owing their success and power to the existing regime.

New Communist List *Reshima Kommunistit Hadasha* (in Arabic, or *Rakah* for short). The largest Communist group in Israel, active among the Arabs. It was formed in 1965, when the Arab members and some Jews left the Israeli Communist Party. The membership of the N.C.L. is estimated at about 1,000.

New Communist Man A model of the member of society whom Marxism envisages to be typical under FULL COMMUNISM. The ideal is assumed to be: 1. ideologically conscious; 2. honest and courageous; 3. law-abiding; 4. divorced from the crude acquisitive instinct; 5. subordinating his own individual desires and private interests to the needs and interests of society; 6. respecting and protecting social property; 7. socially co-operative (not alienated); 8. noted for all-round occupational and recreational interests (not narrowly specialized); 9. wholeheartedly responding to the Marxian principle 'from each according to his ability, to each according to his needs'; and 10. internationally minded. Marx (in a letter to Engels, dated 7 Aug. 1866) and Engels (in *DIALECTICS OF NATURE*) rejected the idea of the rigidity and immutability of human nature and values ('society makes man what he is, not vice versa'). They held that man is a product of economic and social environment and that it is possible to perfect him by appropriate improvements in his working, living and cultural conditions. While the class struggle brings out the worst in man, in a CLASSLESS SOCIETY man will be capable of ideal behaviour. Some other Marxist thinkers and reformers have stressed the plasticity of human nature and insisted that acquired characteristics are inheritable and can be transmitted to later generations (AGROBIOLOGY, LYSENKOISM, MICHURINISM, SOCIALIZATION). The model of the N.C.M. has been given different emphasis at different times, as reflected in the concepts of New Socialist Man, New Soviet Man, Homo Novus Sinicus and Full Communist Man. Stalin (in *Works*, 1946–48) wrote of 'a man of special mold', and believed that Soviet citizens had all the potential for becoming social ideals, providing a model for other nations. Mao Tse-tung stressed the need for CONTINUING REVOLUTION in order to evolve 'selfless equals' with the 'all-round development of personality and occupational interests'. So far there is little evidence of the N.C.M. having developed as a universal phenomenon in any Socialist country. Even in the oldest Socialist country (the USSR), the incidence of crime, juvenile delinquency, alcoholism, slovenly work habits and craving for material incentives suggest that the average Soviet man is not much different from the average man in the capitalist world.

New Communist Manifesto A term which has been used to describe two different documents. 1. The declaration issued at the First Congress of the COMINTERN in Moscow in March 1919, which called for a world proletarian revolution. It indicated the forms which such a revolution might assume, it was signed by Lenin and endorsed by the representatives of the national Sections of the Third International. 2. More commonly the description is applied to the 'Declaration of the Representatives of the 81 Communist and Workers' Parties' in Moscow in Dec. 1960. Its main conclusions and postulates were: (a) the losing fight of imperialism with socialism; (b) the disintegration of the world capitalist system; (c) the continued development and strengthening of the Socialist bloc; (d) the condemnation of wars initiated by capitalist countries; (e) the need to avoid a global nuclear war; (f) the historial necessity of peaceful coexistence between socialism and capitalism; (g) the need for complete disarmament; (h) the acceleration of processes of DE-COLONIZATION; (i) aid to NATIONAL LIBERATION MOVEMENTS; (j) the acceptance of the possibility of a peaceful transition to socialism (as distinct from a violent proletarian revolution); (k) the necessity of meeting violent resistance to socialism with force; (l) the condemnation of Yugoslav OPPORTUNISM and REVISIONISM; (m) the need for a Communist ideological offensive.

New Communist Party In Britain, a hardline splinter group of the COMMUNIST PARTY OF GREAT BRITAIN formed as a separate party in July 1977. It emerged mainly as a reaction against the C.P.G.B.'s 'British Road to Socialism', which the N.C.P. regards as a mild social-democratic compromise, not Communist. The Party rejects EUROCOMMUNISM, postulates the DICTATORSHIP OF THE PROLETARIAT and follows the Moscow line. Its leaders are Sid French and Jean Geldart and its membership is about 800. The Party publishes *The New Worker*.

New Course A term applied to the period of liberalization in Hungary after Stalin's death (March 1953) under the leadership of I. NAGY who became Prime Minister in that year. Many political prisoners were freed, writers and other intellectuals were accorded considerable freedom of expression, compulsory collectivization was stopped and priority was assigned to consumer goods. But by April 1955, the Party establishment under Soviet pressure intervened. I. Nagy was dismissed from all his government and party posts for 'right-wing deviationism'. The popular dissatisfaction with the ending of the N.C. led to the HUNGARIAN UPRISING in 1956. The term is also the title of a pamphlet written by L. D. Trotsky in 1923, *The New Course*, urging the democratization of the RUSSIAN COMMUNIST PARTY (OF THE BOLSHEVIKS), in opposition to the growing authoritarianism in the Party.

New Culture Movement A period of quasi-Marxist reaction against the Confucian philosophy of life and aristocratic cultural patterns in China from 1916 to 1919. The Movement strove to integrate revolutionary social consciousness with aesthetic values and harness art as an instrument of social change. It was initiated at Peking University by CH'EN TU-HSIU.

New Democracy A concept popularized by Mao Tse-tung (in *On New Democracy*, 1940) in application to China beginning with the FOURTH OF MAY MOVEMENT in 1919. By 'old democracy' Mao understood the socio-political situation in China between 1842 (the Opium War) and 1919, when the proletariat had hardly been a political force and when it had participated in revolutions (such as that of 1911) as a follower of the bourgeoisie. But after 1919 the Chinese proletariat became socially conscious enough and spurred by the Great October Socialist Revolution in Russia to command a growing and independent political force with a revolutionary programme. This development found its expression in the foundation of the CHINESE COMMUNIST PARTY in 1921. N.D. also embodied the progressive national bourgeoisie which had patriotic and anti-imperialist sentiments, and consequently, revolutionary qualities (in con-

trast to the Russian bourgeoisie, which had been more akin to the Chinese *big* bourgeoisie). Thus in Mao's view, N.D. represented 'the joint dictatorship of all anti-imperialist and anti-feudal elements led by the proletariat'.

New Democratic Culture A concept used by Mao Tse-tung (in *New Democratic Culture*, 1940) in application to the new direction in Chinese culture that developed in association with NEW DEMOCRACY beginning with the Fourth of May Movement in 1919. Mao said that 'a given culture is the ideological reflection of the politics and economy of a given society'. He contrasted the N.D.C. with the Chinese imperialist culture shaped by 'foreign imperialists', 'shameless Chinese toadies' and 'semi-feudal worshippers of Confucius'. He further stressed that the N.D.C. was a product of the new ideology, constituting contributions of the new revolutionary forces – the proletariat, the petty bourgeoisie and the national bourgeoisie, all guided by the CHINESE COMMUNIST PARTY.

New Democratic Party A type of social-democratic party in Canada broadly subscribing to SOCIAL DEMOCRACY, advocating extended economic planning, broadened social security, internationalist foreign policy and opposing nuclear weapons. It was founded by the CO-OPERATIVE COMMONWEALTH FEDERATION and the Canadian trade union movement in 1961. It has grown to become the third largest political party in Canada.

New Eastern Policy An English phrase sometimes used for *OSTPOLITIK*, the West German policy of rapprochement with the Eastern European countries.

New Economic Mechanism (or Model) A general designation for the new economic system that has emerged in the European Socialist countries since the early 1960s as a result of the ECONOMIC REFORMS. But more specifically, it is applied to the Hungarian economy since the far-reaching and successful liberal reforms of 1968. These reforms extended the role of the market and local initiative, viz. greater independence of enterprises, the acceptance of profit as the main criterion of enterprise performance, the strengthening of material incentives to labour and the reactivation and flexible use of financial instruments (interest rates, credit, price mark-ups and mark-downs, and the like).

New Economic Policy (*Novaya Ekonomicheskaya Politika*, in Russian) A practical restoration of private enterprise and the market mechanism in the Soviet Union over the period 1921–28. It was initiated in practice in March but officially announced in Aug. 1921. It followed the period of WAR COMMUNISM and constituted a tactical retreat in order to reconstruct the economy dislocated and exhausted by W.W.I and the Civil War and to prepare for the subsequent industrialization drive (beginning with the first Five-Year Plan, 1928–32). The N.E.P. was initiated by Lenin himself who responded to the pressure from the RIGHT OPPOSITION. The Policy embodied the following elements: 1. a far-reaching restoration of private farming (which greatly improved the position of the *KULAKS*; 2. the replacement of compulsory deliveries of farm products by liberal taxes; 3. the restitution of small and medium industrial enterprises (employing less than 20 persons) to their previous owners; 4. the liberalization of private wholesale and retail trade; 5. currency stabilization (1924–25); 6. the participation of foreign capital in the exploitation of Soviet natural resources; and 7. the retention of the COMMANDING HEIGHTS under state control and ownership (key industries and services, banks, foreign trade and all land remained socialized). The dictatorship of the proletariat was also retained and strengthened by the abolition (in 1922) of all political parties other than the Communist Party. By 1924 three-quarters of all trade was in private hands and by 1928 the pre-W.W.I production level had been reached. In some isolated areas, the N.E.P. was carried on into the 1930s but finally discontinued in 1936. A kind of N.E.P. was also pursued in China over the period 1961–64, following the disasters of the GREAT LEAP FORWARD.

New Economics, The The title of a book first published in Russian in the USSR by E. A. PREOBRAZHENSKY. Its sub-title was *An Experiment in Theoretical Analysis of the Soviet Economy*. The book embodied some profound new ideas on the principles of economics under Socialist conditions. In particular, Preobrazhensky expounded the methodology of Soviet economics, the law of PRIMITIVE SOCIALIST ACCUMULATION, Socialist planning and the LAW OF VALUE. His book represented an attack against right-wing economists, especially N. I. BUKHARIN who at that time was supported by Stalin (both Preobrazhensky and Bukharin later perished in Stalin's purges because of their right-wing views). The book appeared in English translation in 1965, as it was believed that Preobrazhensky's ideas were becoming relevant to the problems of less-developed countries.

New Harmony A pilot idealistic colony initiated and financed by R. OWEN in Indiana (USA) in 1825. Its purpose was to develop the model of a happy, efficiently operating community along lay communistic lines, as distinct from religious premises. For this purpose he purchased property from a communist religious sect and endeavoured to enlist its support. But owing to different views on religion and personal conflicts, the experiment failed and its promoter returned to Britain.

New Left An eclectic and heterogeneous neo-Marxist political movement best developed in the USA, emphasizing civil rights, direct participatory democracy, SYNDICALISM, PACIFISM and RADICALISM. At the same time, it is opposed to the traditional social order in leading capitalist and the Socialist countries, in particular extreme social inequalities, racial discrimination, military-industrial complexes, imperialism, authoritarian bureaucracy, state capitalism, Stalinism and ideological dogmas. Among its best known professing organizations were the STUDENTS FOR DEMOCRATIC SOCIETY, the Student Non-Violent Co-ordinating Committee, the Black Panther Party and the Negro Civil Rights Movement. The N.L. emerged in the late 1950s among younger academics and students, reached its peak of publicity development and influence in the late 1960s and declined in the early 1970s. Its leaders maintain that the working class succumbed to *EMBOURGEOIS-MENT*, is no longer a significant revolutionary force and the intellectuals must provide the new revolutionary thrust. They also stress that the acceptance of material progress is to a large extent in conflict with other human priorities. Ideologically, the N.L. has been inspired by the '3M's' – MARX, MAO TSE-TUNG and MARCUSE and by 'Caguho' – CASTRO, GUEVARA and HO CHI MINH. It was further intensified by the NATIONAL LIBERATION MOVEMENTS, the VIETNAM WAR and the GREAT PROLETARIAN CULTURAL RE-VOLUTION. The methods of the N.L. have ranged from a complete withdrawal from the existing society and protests to direct action, the destruction of property and violence. In contrast to the OLD LEFT, the N.L. is noted for a wide range of conflicting ideological views, a lack of discipline, unco-ordinated activities, the instability of leadership, rather adventurous attitudes and the absence of a clear programme of reforms for an ideal society. The N.L. has received a mixed reception in the Socialist countries. On the one hand, it is welcome by dissidents and liberal Marxists opposed to authoritarianism, Party repression and the disregard of human rights by the Socialist states. Up to a point, the Communist regimes view it favourably as it is weakening the leading Western powers and creating revolutionary situations. But otherwise, the Communist leaders reject it, as in their view the N.L. represents REVISIONISM. They deny the disappearance of the revolutionary spirit among the working classes and the class struggle in capitalist countries. Also FRENCH STUDENT REVOLUTION, STUDENT POWER.

New Long March A phrase used in China, alluding to the LONG MARCH, to describe the Party's long-run drive for the modernization and accelerated development of the Chinese economy up to the year 2000. The drive, accepted by the regime of HUA KUO-FENG as the main general objective, implies a greater emphasis on economic and technological tasks than was the case under Mao Tse-tung.

New Man NEW COMMUNIST MAN.

New Opposition A group of Party and Government officials, led by KAMENEV, TROTSKY and ZINOVIEV in the USSR from 1924 to 1927 opposing Stalin's ideas and his rise to power. The N.O. was against Stalin's policy of SOCIALISM IN ONE COUNTRY, unimaginative and shifting practices and the concentration of political power in his hands. It was also opposed to the centralized, hierarchical structure of Party organization. However, the N.O. did not receive much support from the Party. In Oct. 1927, Trotsky and Zinoviev were removed from the Central Committee and then expelled from the Party in Nov. Trotsky was subsequently exiled (and assassinated in Mexico in 1940), while Kamenev and Zinoviev tried to compromise with Stalin, but then fell victim to Stalin's GREAT PURGES and were executed in 1936.

New People's Army An illegal left-wing guerrilla movement in the Philippines, based in the mountains of the Isabela Province and also operating in Mindanao and Sulu. By official estimates, it has a guerrilla strike force of 2,000, 5,000 combat support troops and 50,000 loosely organized partisans. However, the N.P.A. claims to have 20,000 regulars, 100,000 combat support troops and a 'civilian mass base' of 150,000–500,000. It collaborates with Moslem insurgents in the south of the country.

New Political Economy A general term for the type of post-industrial economy which has emerged in the leading Western countries since W.W.II. It is noted for public-private partnership, involving active collaboration with government, large companies and universities and the obliteration of the differences between public and private sectors. Its main features are: 1. widespread state intervention in all the phrases of social, economic and scientific life (not necessarily involving nationalization); 2. the public use of the private sector (the mutual sharing of authority, large government contracts for equipment and research) and the acceptance that a complete domination of the economy by the state is inconsistent with efficiency, freedom and maximum social welfare; 3. the paternalistic involvement of the government (the subsidization of agriculture, the financing of research and development, aid to ailing private industries employing large numbers of workers, and the provision of generous social welfare programmes); 4. powerful interest groups influencing public opinion and the government (organized labour, environmentalists, military-industrial complexes, professional bodies); 5. non-exclusive public service relying for the expertise and cooperation of universities and professional bodies; and 6. pre-occupation with the quality of life and 'universal entitlement'.

New Right A term sometimes used to describe the conservative views and activities of loose groups in the USA during the 1960s, favouring the retention and strengthening of the traditional social order. It is implicitly directed against the NEW LEFT, subversive infiltration and international communism. The movement embraces diverse groups. It can be regarded as a continuation of McCAR-THYISM. Among its supporters are the JOHN BIRCH SOCIETY, the Minutemen and the Christian Anti-Communist Campaign.

New Socialist Man, New Soviet Man NEW COMMUNIST MAN.

New Socialist Economics The new approach to the study of political economy as a science in the European Socialist countries (except Albania) since the mid-1950s. Previously, Socialist political economy was not a respectable discipline, as it had been commonly accepted that 'the victory of the working class revolution constitutes the last act of political economy as a science' (Rosa Luxemburg). The rejuvenation of economics had been facilitated by Stalin's death (1953), the relaxation of censorship, increasing contacts with Western economic thought, the application of mathematical methods and computers to economic analysis and planning, the ECONOMIC REFORMS of the 1960s and the growing appreciation of the need for economic efficiency to attain the goals of FULL COMMUNISM. The term 'economics', as distinct from POLITICAL ECONOMY is commonly used now in most Socialist countries, especially when referring to objective and rigorous studies.

New-style Calendar The basis of recording dates in accordance with the Gregorian Calendar, i.e. that prevailing outside Russia and, since 14 Feb. 1918, in Soviet Russia and the USSR. It is 13 days ahead of the OLD-STYLE CALENDAR which was repealed by the decree of the Soviet Government of 26 Jan. 1918 (O.-S.C.) when it advanced the date of 1 Feb. (O.-S.C.) to 14 Feb. (N.-S.C.) 1918.

New Unionism The inclusion of unskilled and semi-skilled workers in trade unions, in contrast to OLD UNIONISM where mainly skilled workers were admitted. N.U. became most obvious in Britain from 1889 to 1900. It developed along similar lines in other industrialized countries somewhat later. The vastly increased mechanization and rationalization and the consequent mass production, associated with the growth of unskilled and semi-skilled workers in industry, involved the exclusion of the latter from trade unions, i.e. their inclusion was no longer in the interest of the labour movement. The new trade unions developed into 'inclusive unions', typically organized on an industrial (as distinct from craft) basis. They became larger, accumulated larger financial resources, had a more proletarian outlook and their strikes often proved more effective, compared with their predecessors. N.U. also took interest in international co-operation among national trade unions. Although Marxists welcomed N.U. as a road towards a PROLETARIAN-IZATION of trade unions, they were soon disappointed with their preoccupation with the improvement of wages and working conditions, to the neglect of political and revolutionary objectives.

Nicholas II, Nicholai Aleksandrovich (1868–1918) The last Tsar of Russia who ruled from 1894 to 1917 and was executed by the Bolsheviks. He was an autocratic and inflexible ruler, an opponent of reforms and of the freedom of national minorities, and a firm supporter of imperialism. He married a German princess, Alexandra (a granddaughter of Queen Victoria) who fell under the spell of the unscrupulous monk, Rasputin. Before W.W.I, N. allied Russia on the side of the British-French *Entente* which later fought the Central Powers (Germany and Austria). He assumed the supreme command of the armed forces in 1915. After the FEBRUARY REVOLUTION OF 1917, he was forced to abdicate (March 1917, O.-S.C.) and was imprisoned by revolutionary authorities, first in Tsarskoe Selo, then in Tobolsk and finally in Ekaterinburg (in the Urals). By a decision of the revolutionary Ural District Soviet, N. and his family were shot in a cellar near Ekaterinburg (now Sverdlovsk) on 16 July 1918 (N.-S.C.).

Night of the Barricades One of the most dramatic stages of the FRENCH STUDENT REVOLUTION in Paris. The barricades were erected on the night of 10–11 May 1968 against the police by the members of the *Syndicat National de l'Enseignement Supérieur*, a radical trade union of French University teachers, led by its Secretary A. Geismar and supported by D. Cohn-Bendit.

Nihilism (from Latin, meaning 'nothing-ness') An extreme form of ANARCHISM developed in Russia in the second half of the 19th c., according to which there is nothing to be gained or learnt from the existing and previous societies, consequently all historically established standards and values should be rejected. The term owes its origin to the Russian writer, I. S. Turgenev (in *Fathers and Sons*, 1862). Nihilists directed their energies to the overthrow of the Tsarist establishment and organized several assassination attempts, one of which (on Tsar Aleksander II, in 1881) succeeded. They were commonly described as persons 'without principles and scruples' but were favourably regarded by revolutionary elements (including some Marxists) in Russia and elsewhere. Owing to the severe repression after 1881, n. virtually disappeared and its objectives were partly pursued by anarchists and Marxists.

NKGB Abbreviation of the Russian *Narodnyi Komissariat Gossudarstvennoi Bezopasnosti*, meaning People's Commissariat of State Security. It was an organ of political state security in the USSR having succeeded the *GUGB* in Feb. 1941, which was part of the *NKVD*. The *NKGB* was separated from the *NKVD* temporarily in 1941 and permanently from April 1943. In 1946, when the People's Commissariats were re-named Ministries, the *NKGB* became the *MGB* (*Ministerstvo Gossudarstvennoi Bezopasnosti*). The *NKGB* carried on the work of its predecessors, but during the war it relaxed its internal pressure on the population. However, it became notorious for its harsh treatment of the national groups suspected of disloyalty to the Soviet state and was responsible for mass deportations of ethnic Germans, the Balkans, the Chechens, the Crimean Tartars, the Ingushi, the Kalmyks and the Karachi. It also engaged in the elimination of undesirable elements and collaborators with the enemy in Soviet-occupied territories and screened demobilized prisoners of war and other Soviet citizens who at some stage had been outside Soviet control.

Nkrumah, Kwame (1909–72) A Ghanaian left-wing political leader described as a 'Marxist socialist' and the 'Black Lenin of Africa'. Educated in Britain and the USA, he later led the liberation movement in the Gold Coast and became the first Prime Minister and President of Ghana (1957–66). He also emerged as one of the leading spokesmen against COLONIALISM and NEO-COLONIALISM and was a champion of pan-Africanism. In his administration, he followed the principle of DEMOCRATIC CENTRALISM and became a virtual dictator. He also initiated several social reforms and an industrialization programme. While on a state visit to China in 1966, he was ousted from power in an army coup supported by right-wing elements and European and American interests. He then lived in Guinea, where he acted as the Co-Head of the State and later died of cancer in Bucharest. Among his publications are: *Towards Colonial Freedom* (1947); *Neo-Colonialism: The Last Stage of Imperialism* (1965); *Handbook of Revolutionary Warfare* (1968); and *The Class Struggle in Africa* (1970).

NKVD The abbreviation in Russian of *Narodnyi Komissariat Vnutriennykh Del*, meaning People's Commissariat for Internal Affairs (or simply the Ministry of the Interior). It existed in the Soviet Union from 1917 to 1924 and from 1934 to 1946. But the notoriety of the *NKVD* derived from its function as the organ of state security and secret service from 1922 to 1924 and especially from 1934 to 1943. In this capacity, it replaced the *OGPU*, but its powers were extended to include the control of all places of detention, including the corrective labour camps, the ordinary police and civil registry offices. It was headed, among others, by G. G. YAGODA (1934–36), N. I. YEZHOV (1936–38) and L. P. BERIA (1938–43). Its division specifically concerned with state security and the secret service was the *GUGB* (Chief Administration of State Security). It also had

a Special Board, which had the right to pass administrative sentences of up to five years (in practice up to 25 years) in exile or corrective labour camps. The accused had no right to defence counsels and sentences were passed in absentia. Among its tasks carried out were Stalin's GREAT PURGES (1936–38). But public reaction was so strong (Party members included) that Stalin accused the *NKVD* of deliberate sabotage, purged its top leadership in Dec. 1938 and replaced Beria with Yezhov as its head. The *NKVD* then organized the deportation of inconvenient elements from the territories annexed in 1939–40 (Poland, Romania, Lithuania, Latvia, Estonia, and Finland). During W.W.II it had special Blocking Units, operating behind the front line to prevent regular troops from retreating. In 1941, the state security function of the *NKVD* was briefly separated and taken over by the *NKGB*. The separation was made permanent in April 1943. In 1946 when the People's Commissariats were changed to Ministries, the *NKVD* was renamed the *MVD*.

Noble Order of the Knights of Labor An industrial trade union in the USA founded by U. S. Stephens (1821–82) in 1869 which developed into a rallying national labour organization. At first it existed as a secret society, but came into the open in 1878. In its membership, which reached over 700,000, were skilled and unskilled workers, as well as employers, supporting its advocation for class collaboration. It was most successful among miners and railway workers, but was criticized for its unnecessary strikes, many of which had been badly planned. Marxists were critical of the organization for its conciliatory attitude to capitalism, claiming that it was dominated by the 'aristocrats of labour' (highly skilled and well paid workers) and was reconciled to capitalism. Its importance declined with the rise of the AMERICAN FEDERATION OF LABOR (founded in 1886) and was further aggravated by internal conflicts, which led to the Knights' disintegration in 1893.

Nominalism A medieval philosophical theory according to which only individual objects are real, consequently, general concepts do not exist but are merely names for concrete individual items. Its chief exponents were Roscelin (1045–1120), Duns Scotus (died in 1308) and W. Ockham (died about 1349). Marx and Engels regarded n. with favour (in The HOLY FAMILY), as in their view it represented the first expression of MATERIALISM in the Middle Ages, recognized the primacy of material objects and the derived nature of ideas, and as such questioned the thesis in scholastic theology of divine intervention in nature. However, other Marxist philosophers became critical of n. as it later developed into SEMANTIC PHILOSOPHY.

Nominalist Theory of Money A theory maintaining that money is an abstract category and, in whatever form, is merely a token servicing what really matters, viz. real goods and services. The theory also maintains that it is not money but real resources and products that constitute wealth. The theory was originally put forward by G. Berkeley (1684–1753) and J. Steuart (1712–1780) as a reaction against the bullion theory of money and the mercantilist view that only precious metals are natural money. The n.t. of m. became an early object of interest to Marxist economists. On the one hand, they agree that paper money and bank money do not constitute wealth – only assets embodying past labour do. But on the other hand, they object to treating money as an abstract category separate from economic processes. Marx (in CAPITAL, vol. I and III) regarded commodity money, including gold and silver, as forms of wealth, because they embodied past labour. He also attacked nominalists for divorcing money from actual economic relations since they exist in different stages of economic and social development.

Non-antagonistic Contradiction A concept used in Marxist DIALECTICS, where contradictions or opposites can be resolved in the ordinary course of events as a matter of evolution, without a major clash via a revolution. The n.-a.c., which contrasts with the antagonistic CONTRADICTION, is said to exist in a non-antagonistic socio-economic formation such as socialism, where owing to the social ownership of the means of production there are no fundamental conflicts between social classes, and consequently no class struggle. By virtue of the extensive powers of the state, including central economic planning, the government can take measures to facilitate and anticipate adjustments which may be necessary owing to the changing nature of PRODUCTION FORCES, which necessitate concordant adaptations in PRODUCTION RELATIONS.

Non-commercial Exchange Rate The exchange rate administered by some Socialist countries (e.g. Albania, Bulgaria, Czechoslovakia, Hungary, Poland, Romania) in application to foreigners as tourists, diplomats, business travellers and the like, when exchanging their currencies for the Socialist currency and vice versa. It is more favourable to foreigners than the official BASIC EXCHANGE RATE applied in commercial (visible trade) transactions. The higher n.-c.e.r. is meant to reflect the higher level of RETAIL PRICES compared with PRODUCER PRICES. Thus, in Czechoslovakia at the end of 1978, the official basic exchange rate was 5.15 korunas to US$1.00 while the n.-c.e.r. was 9.01 korunas. The respective figures (to US$1.00) in Poland were 3.99 and 30.99 zlotys and in Romania 4.47 and 12.00 lei.

Non-Communist Manifesto The expression used by an American economist W. W. Rostow (1916–) as the sub-title in his notable book *The Stages of Economic Growth* (1960). He maintained that from the economic and social perspective, societies pass through the following consecutive stages: 1. the traditional society; 2. preconditions for take-off; 3. take-off; 4. drive to maturity; 5. economic maturity; and 6. high mass consumption. Consequently, Rostow argued that the Marxist theory of the SOCIO-ECONOMIC FORMA-TIONS (1. primitive communism; 2. slavery; 3. feudalism; 4. capitalism; 5. socialism; and 6. communism) is not valid, and in particular that capitalism must inevitably be replaced by socialism and communism. He further stressed that technological progress necessarily leads to similar methods and organization of production, similar industrial relations and a similar mentality, irrespective of the political system in force. The N.-C.M. also rejects the notion that the economy as a sector of society and economic advantage as a human motive are necessarily dominant, especially in the higher, affluent stages of social development. The N.-C.M. has been attacked by Marxists as another attempt at a theoretical rescue of capitalism from its inevitable breakdown. They point out that capitalism and socialism are becoming increasingly divergent, irrespective of rapid technological progress.

Non-equivalent Exchange A Marxist concept to describe exploitation in trade between more developed and less developed countries. It was introduced by Marx in *CAPITAL*, vol. I. He argued that goods produced by more developed countries, equipped as they are with more and better capital and technology, embody less SO-CIALLY-INDISPENSABLE LABOUR than those produced by backward nations. Moreover, owing to restrictive practices by national and international monopolies, world market prices are further artificially raised for the benefit of more developed countries. At the same time, using their superior bargaining power, industrialized countries pay prices below international values. Modern Socialist economists have added the emergence of discriminatory economic groupings in Western Europe as further accentuating the inequality of exchange. Consequently, in the Socialist view, capitalism inexorably leads to a disparity in terms of trade in favour of the more developed capitalist countries at the expense of less advanced economies, be they capitalist or socialist. To avoid exploitation in international trade, countries

with more efficient labour should pay more for goods imported from less developed countries than for similar goods obtained from domestic production. The argument of n.-e.e. has been used by Romania and Yugoslavia to oppose greater integration in the CMEA until the levels of economic development in the member countries become reasonably even. Some Western right-wing economists have argued that East-West trade is noted for n.-e.e. in the sense that the East exploits the West. They point out that the Socialist countries receive much more in technology than they pay at world market prices. Furthermore, Western earnings from the East are worth less in actual purchasing power to Western traders since they have no free access to the Socialist market and the Socialist currencies are inconvertible.

Non-objective Art ABSTRACT ART.

Non-productive Accumulation A Marxist economic term denoting that portion of ACCUMULATION (roughly investment) which is directed to the NON-PRODUCTIVE SPHERE for fixed assets. It is measured by expenditure on housing for the population, on administrative, educational, cultural and sporting facilities and on defence installations and material. N.-p.a. does not directly contribute to the growth of MATERIAL PRODUCTION (national income by the Socialist method), but is essential for the public administration of the economy and the provision of various facilities and services for the public. About one-quarter of the total accumulation is usually spent on n.-p.a. in the Socialist countries (which is on the whole lower than in capitalist market economies), but the proportion is expected to rise in the future with rising per capita incomes.

Non-productive labour In Socialist economic terminology, labour performed outside the PRODUCTIVE SPHERE, i.e. labour directed to the provision of NON-PRODUCTIVE SERVICES. N.-p.l., although essential, does not contribute directly to

MATERIAL PRODUCTION and, consequently, to the national income as understood in Socialist national accounts. Roughly one-fifth of the labour foce in the Socialist countries is engaged in n.-p.l. in this sense. In a broader sense, with reference to capitalist countries, Marxists regard those forms of labour non-productive which result from the irrationality of the system of production, unnecessary luxuries (especially CONSPICUOUS CONSUMPTION), speculative pursuits, election campaigning, missionary work, persuasive (as distinct from informative) advertising and the like.

Non-productive services A concept important in Socialist national income accounting. It denotes those activities which do not directly contribute to material production, even if they are paid for. Generally, they are the following eight branches of the economy: 1. public administration and justice; 2. education, science and culture; 3. health, social welfare, entertainment and sport; 4. banking, finance and insurance; 5. local government and housing administration; 6. defence; 7. political, social and religious activities; and 8. other minor services (postal and communication services, private travel, tourism, personal services, etc.). In capitalist national income accounting (which is also accepted by the United Nations agencies) such services constitute part of the national income as long as they are paid for.

Non-productive Sphere In Socialist national income accounting, that portion of the economy which does not directly contribute to MATERIAL PRODUCTION but is concerned with the provision of NON-PRODUCTIVE SERVICES. Owing to the Socialist preoccupation with material production (which alone contributes to NATIONAL INCOME as defined by the Socialist method), the n.-p.s. in the Socialist countries is rather underdeveloped. On the average, it roughly represents one-fifth of the total economy, judging by the proportion of the total work force employed. But the proportion has been rising, reflecting higher stages of economic development being attained in the more advanced countries and is likely to be one-half in the future, as in developed capitalist market economies.

Non-Proliferation Treaty NUCLEAR NON-PROLIFERATION TREATY.

Non-socialized Sector A designation officially used in the Socialist countries for the private sector, where the ownership of the means of production is in private hands. It is smallest in the USSR and Mongolia (the only Socialist countries where all land is socialized), and largest in Poland and Yugoslavia where about 20 per cent of material production is contributed by the private sector. In the latter two countries the n.-s.s. is particularly important in agriculture, where more than 80 per cent of farming land is privately owned and worked. But even in the USSR private (officially 'subsidiary') plots contribute 27 per cent of agricultural output. The n.-s.s. outside agriculture embraces private artisans, workshops, restaurants, local transport, repair facilities (shoes, clothing, domestic appliances), laundries, fashion shops, hairdresser's salons and similar personal services. In most cases, owners and workers are synonymous and there are severe restrictions on the employment of hired labour. The n.-s.s. is limited to those spheres where the state has proved incapable and in general to the branches of the economy of low priority and of local significance. There are several forms of discrimination against the n.-s.s., viz. heavy taxes, uncertain supplies of materials and equipment, unavailability of bank credits, frequent petty controls and intimidation by bribe-seeking officials. The n.-s.s. has been reactivated somewhat in the European Socialist countries (Albania excepted) since the ECONOMIC REFORMS of the 1960s (some ten years earlier in Yugoslavia).

Norm A term used in the Socialist countries for a rule specifying the length of working time indispensable under normal conditions for the production of one unit of an article, or the number of units of output to be produced in a specified period of time. A n. may also apply to the permissible quantity of raw materials, power, etc. that can be allowed under normal conditions to produce a given quantity of output. Performance better than the n. usually entitles the worker to a bonus. A n. is laid down by the state in consultation with the trade union concerned and is based on the past records of performance. Norms are changed periodically taking account of technological progress and the availability of modern equipment. The n. system has been found expedient under Socialist economic planning, owing to continuous full employment, well developed social security and a preoccupation with planned production targets.

Normative Costs In Socialist economic terminology, costs estimated by the state on the basis of NORMS, as a guide to the planning authorities and enterprises in the allocation of materials and production targets. N.c. are calculated from current norms of material, fuel, power and labour utilization, the depreciation of fixed assets and data on the organization of production and available technologies.

Normative Economics A term used in the West for the study of economics, where the economist's value judgments are introduced, usually from the standpoint of macrosocial interests. It is preoccupied with what the economy and economic processes ought to be according to social norms, rather than with what the economic realities are. N.e. postulates that political, social and moral considerations should be taken into account to correct the operation of the economy in the interest of the long-run maximization of social welfare. As such, n.e. constitutes a departure from traditional capitalist economics based on the private ownership of the means of production, the operation of the market mechanism and the maximization of private profit. In a sense n.e.

represents a step towards socialism. N.e. contrasts with positive e., where economic studies are concerned with the economic facts and activities as they are in practice which, in turn, may be used to make fairly reliable predictions on the consequences of changes in policies or other circumstances. Also NEW POLITICAL ECONOMY, POLITICAL ECONOMICS, POLITICAL ECONOMY.

Normative Material Stocks In Socialist economic planning, the level of reserves of raw materials and components allowed to enterprises, considered necessary for the continuation of production. These norms are quite strict under a CENTRALIZED DIRECTIVE SYSTEM OF PLANNING AND MANAGEMENT where the system of incentives to enterprises and their personnel is such that enterprises press for the largest possible allocations of materials and the lowest possible imposition of production targets. The uncertainty of allocations and the reappearance of BOTTLENECKS impel enterprises to hold larger stocks than are necessary under normal conditions ('precautionary motive'). Yet, abnormal stocks further enhance shortages and reduce the rate of economic growth. Since the ECONOMIC REFORMS, the norms of material stocks have played a smaller role, owing to the introduction of CAPITAL CHARGES applicable to circulating assets in most European Socialist countries and the acceptance of PROFIT as a criterion of enterprise performance.

Normative Planning CENTRALIZED DIRECTIVE SYSTEM OF PLANNING AND MANAGEMENT, ECONOMIC PLANNING, NORMATIVE ECONOMICS.

Normative Work-hour In Socialist economic practice, the amount of work to be performed under normal conditions in an hour. This norm may apply to a worker, a machine or a production unit. In laying down the n.w.-h., the authorities take the following considerations into account: 1. the worker's qualifications; 2. appropriate facilities supplied to the worker; 3. the worker's reasonable application to work, under the assumption of the standard work day (say eight hours) and the standard work week (say 40 hours); 4. the organization of work (in relation to superiors, subordinates and other workers); and 5. the appropriate utilization of the equipment at the disposal of the worker. The n.w.-h. system is widely used in the Socialist planned economies to ensure uniformity in the whole economy, to promote work discipline, to ensure a reasonable effort of labour, and to provide a basis for the evaluation of performance for material incentives.

North Atlantic Treaty Organization A collective military and political pact originally concluded on 4 April 1949 in Washington by Belgium, Canada, Denmark, France, Iceland, Italy, Luxembourg, the Netherlands, Norway, the United Kingdom and the USA, subsequently also joined by Greece, Portugal, Turkey (Feb. 1952) and the FR of Germany (Oct. 1954). France withdrew from the military part of the alliance in July 1966 and Greece, partly, in 1974. N.A.T.O. was established on the initiative of the USA during the Cold War. It is directed implicitly against the European Socialist countries, especially the WARSAW PACT (founded in 1955). The supreme organ of N.A.T.O. is the North Atlantic Council, assisted by three specialized committees (Challenge of Modern Society, Nuclear Defence Affairs, and the Nuclear Planning Group). The permanent executive and administrative organs are the Executive Council and the International Secretariat located in Brussels (in Paris before 1967). Purely military affairs are handled by the Military Committee, consisting of the 14 commanders-in-chief of the member countries' armed forces (Iceland excepted, as she has no military establishment). N.A.T.O. maintains three main commands: 1. SHAPE (Supreme Headquarters Allied Powers Europe, located at Casteaux, Belgium); 2. CHANCOM (Channel Command, at Portsmouth, Britain); and 3. SALLAND

(Supreme Allied Command Atlantic, at Norfolk, Va., USA). As of 1977, the total manpower in the armed forces of the N.A.T.O. countries was 4,820,000 (plus 5,200,000 estimated reservists) equipped with 11,000 main battle tanks and 3,300 tactical aircraft. N.A.T.O.'s combat manpower in Europe at this time was 1,190,000. The respective figures for the Warsaw Pact were: 4,750,000 (plus 5,150,000); 27,200; and 5,000. N.A.T.O. is regarded by the Socialist leaders as the most powerful counter-revolutionary military organization in the capitalist world whose purpose is to: 1. prevent left-wing elements coming to power in the member countries; 2. to rearm the FR of Germany; 3. to consolidate and perpetuate the US domination of Western Europe; and 4. to provide an aggressive military and political force against the USSR and other Warsaw Pact countries.

Norwegian Communist Party (*Norges Kommunistiske Parti*) The main Marxist party in the country which, although small in absolute membership (2,500, out of the country's total population of 4,050,000 in 1978), has been quite active and fairly influential. It usually co-operates electorally with the Socialist People's Party and the Democratic Socialists. It won 10 (of the 155) seats in the Lower House at the 1973 election, which was later reduced to 2 at the 1977 elections. The Party was founded by a dissident group of the Norwegian Labour Party in 1923 and soon joined the COMINTERN. During the German occupation, 1940–45, it operated underground and after the German attack on the USSR in June 1941, it participated in the anti-German resistance. The Party's official organ is the weekly, *Friheten* (*Freedom*), which takes a pro-Soviet line. It has suffered from several splits and is rivalled by several Communist groups, viz. the Norwegian Communist Workers' (Marxist-Leninist) Party, the Norwegian Communist Youth League, the Socialist Youth League and the Socialist Youth League (Marxist-Leninist).

Norwegian Labour Party (*Norske Arbeider Parti*) One of the most successful moderate socialist parties in the capitalist world. Since W.W.II it has been in power for all but seven years and at the 1977 elections increased its number of seats in the 155-seat Lower House from 62 to 76 (while the Socialist Left Party lost 15 of its previous 16 seats). The N.L.P. has been the largest political party in the country (the next largest is the Conservative Party). In its long periods in office, it greatly extended state intervention in the economy and implemented far-reaching social reforms, especially generous social welfare programmes and nationalization.

Not Guilty The title of the shortened report, published in London in 1937, of the investigation of the Stalinist allegations in the MOSCOW TRIALS (Aug. 1936 and Jan. 1937) of Trotsky's instigation of subversive activities in the USSR from abroad. The title of the full report, also published in London in 1937, was: *The Case of Leon Trotsky: Report of Hearings and Charges Made against Him in the Moscow Trials.* The investigation was carried out in London between 10 April and 7 Sep. 1937 by an international commission chaired by the respected American philosopher John Dewey (1859–1952) and consisted of nine other members, including a legal counsel. The commission found the allegations unsubstantiated and declared Trotsky as no more than a reasonable dissident. In the same year, Trotsky published (in English): *The Revolution Betrayed: What Is the Soviet Union and Where Is It Going?*

Novaya Zhizn (*New Life*, in Russian) The first legal Bolshevik daily paper published in Tsarist Russia. It was printed in St Petersburg (now Leningrad) from 27 Oct. to 3 Dec. 1905 (O.-S.C.). Lenin became its editor in Nov. 1905 and gave it a more revolutionary tone and helped its daily circulation reach 80,000 copies. The paper was subjected to severe censorship and more than half the number of issues (15 out of 27) was confiscated. The paper was finally suspended and after the illegal publication of the 28th issue, Lenin had to flee the country.

Novosti A short name in Russian for *Agenstvo Pechati Novosti*, meaning News Press Agency. It is the official Soviet agency founded in 1961 for the dissemination of information abroad (corresponding to TASS, which is concerned with domestic issues). It has its own publishing house, which engages in producing books, pamphlets, brochures, etc. in Russian and in some 60 foreign languages, which are distributed in over 110 countries. It maintains contacts with news agencies in more than 70 countries.

Novotny, Antonin (1904–) A Czechoslovak Communist leader and statesman. A founding member of the CZECHOSLOVAK COMMUNIST PARTY in 1921, he rose to important Party positions in the 1930s, continued his (illegal) work under German occupation and spent four years in the German concentration camp at Mauthausen. After W.W.II he was elected to the Central Committee of the Cz.C.P. and in Feb. 1948 was a prominent figure in the PRAGUE COUP D'ETAT. In 1951 he became a secretary of the Central Committee, a member of the Party's Presidium and two years later, he became the Party's First Secretary. After the death of President A. Zapotocky in 1953, he was appointed President of the Republic. During the PRAGUE SPRING, as a Stalinist hardliner he lost his position as First Secretary in Jan. 1968 to A. DUBČEK and two months later, resigned from other Party posts and the Presidency (in the latter post he was succeeded by L. Svoboda).

NTS A Russian anti-Communist organization operating in Western Europe which has been officially described by the Soviets as the chief enemy of the Soviet regime. The letters stand for *Narodno-Trudovoi Soiuz*, in Russian meaning People's Labour Alliance. It was originally founded by White Russian émigrés in the 1930s and its ranks were later increased by émigrés during and after W.W.II. Its present headquarters are found in Frankfurt/M in the FR of Germany. It is vaguely committed to the restoration of a non-Communist regime in a strong private-enterprise Russia. The *NTS* maintains links with dissident groups in the USSR and publishes a newspaper called *Posev (Call)*. In its programme, it presently advocates: 1. the immediate release of all political prisoners in the USSR; 2. the observance of HUMAN RIGHTS, including the full implementation of the Final Act of the HELSINKI CONFERENCE; 3. the discontinuation of the occupation of the Eastern European countries; 4. the replacement of the Soviet Constitution by a new democratic constitution, the separation of the state from the party and the abolition of the secret political police (*KGB*); and 5. the de-politicization of education and culture.

Nuclear Non-Proliferation Treaty An inter-governmental agreement concluded in the first instance by the United Kingdom, the USA and the USSR on 1 July 1968 for 25 years, limiting the transmission and use of nuclear weapons and other offensive nuclear devices. The Treaty became effective when ratified by 43 countries including the three original powers. By March 1978, 101 states signed and ratified the Treaty while 43 did not. The following Socialist countries are not party to the Treaty: Albania; Angola, China; Cuba; DPR of Korea; Mozambique; and the DPR of the Yemen. In the case of Kampuchea, Laos and Vietnam, the Treaty was entered into by pre-Communist regimes and it is not certain if the present regimes consider themselves bound by it. Among the non-Socialist countries the following are not party to the Treaty: Bangladesh; Brazil; Egypt; France; India; Israel; Pakistan; South Africa; Spain; Tanzania; and Turkey. The Treaty allows the signatories to carry on research, development, production and utilization of nuclear energy for peaceful purposes.

Nuclear Test Ban Treaty A treaty concluded by the United Kingdom, the USA and the USSR and signed in Moscow on 15 Aug. 1963, agreeing not to test nuclear weapons in the atmosphere, outer space and under water. However, underground testing was not banned. It was subsequently signed by more than 100 other countries, with the conspicuous exception of China and France. The Treaty represents an important landmark in East-West relations in that it constitutes the first successful attempt to limit the nuclear arms race and is regarded as marking the virtual end of the COLD WAR. The N.T.B.T. was further supplemented by the NUCLEAR NON-PROLIFERATION TREATY of 1968.

O

OAS Anti-Communist Declaration See
PUNTA DEL ESTE DECLARATION.

Objectification A Marxian economic and
philosophical concept denoting the embodiment and realization of labour. In the
economic sense, o. means the process of
transmitting labour, i.e. value into OB-
JECTS OF LABOUR. Under ideal social conditions the worker identifies himself with
the products of his work. O. thus becomes
a symbol of man's struggle for the mastery
of nature and his social destiny. In the
Marxist view, only communism can ensure
the intimate subject-object relation
through socially-controlled labour, which
is conditional to humanism. Marx pointed
out (in *Paris Manuscripts of 1844*) that
'The objectification of human existence,
both in practical and theoretical contexts,
means making man's senses human as well
as creative, corresponding to the vast rich-
ness of human and natural life'. The concept which is opposite to o. is ALIENATION,
identified by Marxists with capitalism.

Objective In philosophy, an inherent
quality that exists independently of
human consciousness, understanding or
will. The concept is basic to MATERIALISM
and consequently, important in Marxist
philosophy. O. is contrasted by Marxists
with 'subjective' (referring to man's perceptions, ideas and knowledge) which
merely reflect the external objective
world.

Objective Idealism A variant of the
philosophy of IDEALISM attributing the
essence of existence not to the subjective

consciousness of the individual (as SUB-
JECTIVE IDEALISM does), but to some mys-
tical 'absolute entity', 'world reason' or
'universal will'. They are credited with
'objective' existence, i.e. independent of
human consciousness or will, so that
phenomena are governed by laws interpreted as an expression of world reason
embodied in nature and society. O.i. has
nothing in common with OBJECTIVE REAL-
ITY in the Marxist philosophy of materialism, the former being unequivocally rejected as anti-scientific and an expression
of supernaturalism and THEISM.

Objectively Determined Valuations The
concept used by L. V. KANTOROVICH (in
*The Best Use of Economic Resources,
1959*) for the valuation of all resources,
including non-labour factors of production (land and capital) in the construction
of the economic plan to ensure the most
efficient allocation of resources. They are,
in fact, scarcity prices and can be derived
from the OPTIMAL PLAN. Different resources are assigned coefficients indicating their contribution (productivity) to the
attainment of the optimal plan. The application of the o.d.v. enables such a pattern
of the utilization of resources which ensures maximum production or maximum
social welfare from a given volume of
resources, or which can achieve given objectives with the minimum outlay of resources. O.d.v. are also described as optimal programming prices or simply optimal
prices.

Objective Reality A philosophical view
identifying the existence of matter and

nature separately and independently from man's consciousness. This view is basic to MATERIALISM which regards the material world as being governed by definite laws, independent of man's will, as primary. This approach is accepted in Marxist philosophy which treats perceptions and ideas as secondary, being reflections of and derivations from the o.r.

Objective Truth In philosophy, truth derived from the objective world of matter and nature, representing a faithful reflection of OBJECTIVE REALITY. O.t. exists independently of human understanding or will and can be verified by practice and the laws of nature. The concept of o.t. is one of the fundamental propositions in philosophical MATERIALISM, and consequently accepted by Marxist philosophers. This view, however, is opposed by AGNOSTICISM, IDEALISM, MACHISM, PHYSICAL IDEALISM and SUBJECTIVISM, according to which there is no o.t. but an idealistic organization of experience and consciousness. Lenin defended the validity of o.t. (in *MATERIALISM AND EMPIRIO-CRITICISM*). He pointed out that man's ideas derive from objective reality and that they cannot appear independently of the latter, and further that the o.t. of the existence of the material world before the appearance of man on earth cannot be disputed.

Objectivism In philosophy, a theory postulating an objective approach to cognition and understanding, which attributes objective validity to the ideas so arrived at and thus regards the mind as being capable of attaining real truth. In this sense, it is opposite to SUBJECTIVISM, SCEPTICISM and PHENOMENALISM. O. may also denote an objective method of study of historical events and social phenomena, not biased by ideological partiality. It is the second meaning of o. that has attracted the attention of Marxist philosophers, which they categorically reject and contrast with PARTISANSHIP and party-mindedness. Although they concede the objective nature of the physical sciences, they point out

that the social sciences inevitably have a class character, as truths established in the latter sphere are usually consistent with the interests of a particular social class but not another. Thus, Marxists emphasize that while the bourgeois interpretation of history and society attempts to conceal its bias through pretended o., Marxism openly advocates the application of the postulate of party-mindedness to the analysis and presentation of historical, social, political and aesthetic facts and phenomena.

Objects of Labour In Marxian political economy, materials on which man works using the MEANS OF LABOUR in the process of production. O. of l. include natural resources (soil, mineral deposits, forests, wild animals, water, fishing grounds), raw materials and semi-finished products. When the process of production is completed, the o. of l. become finished products.

Oborontsy (Defenders, in Russian) The moderate section of the MENSHEVIKS, who supported Russia's participation in W.W.I as a legitimate war of national defence. They were led by A. N. Potresov (1869–1934) and followed the general line accepted by most European socialist parties and the majority in the SECOND INTERNATIONAL. The *O.* were opposed by the INTERNATIONALISTS.

Obshchina A type of peasant commune in Tsarist Russia occupying arable land, which was periodically redistributed to the members on an egalitarian basis. Some social reformers including Marxists, saw the *o.* as a survival of PRIMITIVE COMMUNISM and others (especially the NARODNIKS), as a transitional stage to ideal socialism in the future. *O. land* legally belonged to the Tsar, but allocated plots were privately managed and worked. Non-arable land (pastures, forests, lakes, rivers) were not subject to distribution but were communally held under the control of the *MIR*. After 1905, legislation was passed to enable communal peasants to convert their share into private property. By 1914 one-third of the peasants had done so.

Occultism Belief in the existence of hidden supernatural forces in nature, with which only chosen persons can communicate. It is associated with some religions and its origins go back at least to the early Middle Ages. Marxism regards o. as about the most extreme and reactionary form of philosophical IDEALISM, employed by the ruling classes and naïve elements in capitalist countries to divert the attention of the exploited classes away from their plight. It is also held that o. is used as a weapon of weakening the class consciousness of the workers and their capacity to improve the social system.

Occupational Division of Labour Specialization among persons according to the type of training and skill involved or the type of work performed. It contrasts with the industrial and territorial divisions of labour. Marxist economists and sociologists identify the extreme o.d. of l. with developed capitalism where, in their view, the most interesting remunerative occupations are reserved for the ruling classes, while the working classes are usually reduced to the most arduous, manual and routinized occupations noted for low pay, monotony and boredom, leading to ALIENATION. Marx and Engels (in The *GERMAN IDEOLOGY*) envisaged that in an ideal society there would be typically a 'universal man' of many skills and occupations. Such a model man would engage in different types of work – manual, mental and creative. Under FULL COMMUNISM the o.d. of l. would virtually disappear. This ideal was developed in some detail by Mao Tse-tung in a speech before the Supreme State Conference on 28 Jan. 1958. Also DIVISION OF LABOUR, LABOUR, NEW COMMUNIST MAN, RUSTICATION DRIVE in China.

October Revolution A short name for the officially designated GREAT OCTOBER SOCIALIST REVOLUTION in Russia in 1917.

Octobrists A right-wing party in Tsarist Russia which supported the interests of landowners, bureaucracy and rich traders. They were opposed to the KADETS (who pressed for land redistribution), while politically favouring a constitutional monarchy with a strong central government responsible to the Tsar himself. The O. party was founded in Nov. 1905 and took its name from the Tsarist decree of Oct. 1905 establishing the DUMA (Tsarist parliament). O. is also the name of an organization in the USSR for the youngest children (in emulation of the Great October Socialist Revolution).

Ogariov, Nicholai Platonovich (1813–77) A Russian revolutionary thinker and poet of aristocratic background, who was active in the reform movement from 1830 to the 1860s. He was a close collaborator of A. I. HERZEN with whom he co-edited *KOLOKOL* and other revolutionary publications. O. advocated the emancipation of the serfs and supported communal agriculture, such as peasant *ARTELS*. At the same time, he was a staunch opponent of Tsarist autocracy and the entrenched bureaucracy. In the early 1860s O. was one of the leaders of a secret group called *ZEMLYA I VOLYA*, for which he formulated a programme of action. In his philosophical writings, he was a materialist, opposed idealism and was one of the forerunners of HISTORICAL MATERIALISM.

OGPU Abbreviation of *Obiedinionnoe Gossaderstvennoe Politicheskoe Upravlenie*, in the USSR meaning United State Political Administration. It was a political security organization established in Dec. 1922 to which the *GPU* (separated from the *NKVD*) was transferred in 1923. The *OGPU's* responsibility was to combat political counter-revolution, economic sabotage, espionage and organized terrorism. The main objects of its repression were the nobility, intellectuals, landowners, the clergy, former White Army Officers, the WHITE GUARDS, the KULAKS and the MENSHEVIKS. During the collectivization drive, 1929–33, it was also concerned with its enforcement. The chief of the *OGPU* was F. DZIERZHINSKY up to 1926 and then V. R. Merzhinsky until 1934. The *OGPU* was attached to the Council of People's Commissars, but in 1934 it was absorbed by the *NKVD*. The *OGPU* developed a formidable and very well equipped force of about 750,000 carefully selected persons.

Okhrana (Protection, in Russian) The name of the secret police in Tsarist Russia developed after 1880. It was under the control of the Department of Police of the Ministry of Internal Affairs. It employed a wide network of informers and agents who infiltrated revolutionary organizations as members. The *O.* was abolished by the Provisional Government after the FEBRUARY REVOLUTION OF 1917. However, by the end of the same year after the GREAT OCTOBER SOCIALIST REVOLUTION, the Bolsheviks created an even more ruthless secret police organization, the *CHEKA*.

OLAS ORGANIZATION OF LATIN AMERICAN SOLIDARITY.

Old Bolsheviks A group of early BOLSHEVIKS who had become prominent in the Communist movement before the Great October Socialist Revolution, but almost all of whom were eliminated in Stalin's GREAT PURGES of 1934–38. After the FEBRUARY REVOLUTION OF 1917, most of them (including Stalin) opposed the *APRIL THESES*, i.e. Lenin's drive for a PROLETARIAN REVOLUTION (as distinct from the bourgeois-democratic February Revolution) in favour of a support to the PROVISIONAL GOVERNMENT. Among the O.B. executed in Stalin's purges were BUKHARIN, KAMENEV, ORDZHONIKIDZE, RYKOV, TUKHACHEVSKY and ZINOVIEV.

Old Hegelians Another description of Right Hegelians, supporters of the HEGELIAN RIGHT.

Old Left A general term current in the 1960s applied to the supporters of traditional Marxism, socialism or communism. The O.L. was preoccupied with ideology rather than action and was committed to centralized and disciplined party organization. In general, it also accepted the Soviet interpretation of MARXISM-LENINISM. It contrasted with the NEW LEFT.

Old-Style Calendar The calendar in force in Russia up to 14 Feb. 1918, which was 13 days behind the Gregorian Calendar prevailing in the rest of the world since 1582. The O.-S.C. was based on the Julian Calendar, which Russia had introduced in 1699 thereby replacing the Muscovite Calendar. The O.-S.C. was repealed by the Soviet Government by the decree of 26 Jan. 1918 (O.-S.C.) which fixed 1 Feb. 1918 (O.-S.C.) as 14 Feb. 1918 (New-Style Calendar). Thus the revolutionary events in Russia before 14 Feb. 1918 as officially recorded in fact occurred 13 days later by the reckoning followed in most other countries. Consequently, the February Revolution broke out on 23 Feb. (O.-S.C.) or 8 March (N.-S.C.) 1917, the October Revolution on 24–25 Oct. (O.-S.C.) or 6–7 Nov. (N.-S.C.) 1917 and the Constituent Assembly was dissolved on 6 Jan. (O.-S.C.) or 19 Jan. (N.-S.C.) 1918.

Old Unionism The early type of trade unions which were organized on a craft basis and aimed at a restriction of the membership to maintain their wages at higher levels than they thought would be possible otherwise. Such unions were typically small, conservative in outlook and had little sympathy for their unskilled fellow workers. O.U. was a feature of the earlier stages of industrialization and was the prevalent form of labour organization up to the end of the 19th c., but has since given way to NEW UNIONISM. The Amalgamated Society of Engineers (established in 1851) in England illustrated O.U. Marxists were highly critical of O.U., describing it as the 'aristocracy of labour', reconciled to the existing social system and unconcerned about the plight of the unskilled proletariat.

'One divides into two' vs 'two combine into one' Controversy A philosophical controversy on contradictions in China between MAO TSE-TUNG and YANG HSIEN-CHEN. Mao, in his papers written in 1937 and 1957, maintained that CONTRADIC-TIONS are a dynamo of history and each contradiction takes the form of a division of 'one into two'. In the ensuing struggle each of the two conflicting elements to some extent tends to assume the nature of the other, whereupon the conflict is resolved in a synthesis. This dialectic process is repeated and represents a permanent struggle – a microcosm of CONTINUING REVOLUTION. Mao stressed that the unity of opposites is temporary. On the other hand Yang, in his teachings at the Higher Party School after 1955, adopted a stand along the lines more akin to Marx and Engels. He reasoned that although there are opposites in the contradiction, they have an element in common which is more lasting than what divides them. Thus Yang stressed that the two opposites inevitably unite into one element without struggle and that reunification, rather than division, is the natural order in nature and society. Thus, Yang's conviction was that the essence of the dialectic process is a quest for reconciliation and unity, while Mao emphasized conflict and struggle. However, Yang's ideas were declared 'noxious weeds of bourgeois and revisionist humanism', and as such counterrevolutionary.

One Step Forward, Two Steps Back A pamphlet written by Lenin in 1904, in which he laid down theoretical foundations for the organization of the Communist party. This study was directed against the MENSHEVIKS who, after having gained control of ISKRA, campaigned for a liberal and democratic type of party organization along the lines laid down by the SECOND INTERNATIONAL. On the other hand, Lenin stressed the need for a rather exclusive, highly disciplined and tightly knit hierarchical organization of devoted professionals to act as the vanguard of the working class. The party policy objectives were to be laid down at Party Congresses, while the Central Committee was to act as the top executive body responsible for the implementation of the objectives and providing continuity between the Party Congresses. He further postulated that once the party assumed political power, it was to exercise the DICTATORSHIP OF THE PROLETARIAT. The organization of the COMMUNIST PARTY OF THE SOVIET UNION as well as other Communist parties accepting MARXISM-LENINISM is based on Lenin's original blueprint.

One, Two, Three A slogan introduced by Chang Chun Automotive Works in China during the GREAT LEAP FORWARD in 1957. It was popularized by Mao's regime to symbolize three facets of industrial relations as components of the CONTINUING REVOLUTION. 'One' stood for the principle of 'All old rules and regulations should be reviewed in the light of new experience'. 'Two' alluded to the postulate of 'Workers should participate in management, and managers should engage in manual labour'. 'Three' referred to the rule of 'Workers, technicians and administrative cadres should unite and work as a team'.

On Khrushchev's Phoney Communism and Its Historical Lesson for the World An article written by Mao Tse-tung and published in HUNG-CHI in July 1964 and in English translation in *Peking Review* dated 17 July 1964. It was the ninth comment written in response to the open letter of the Central Committee of the Communist Party of the Soviet Union of July 1963. In the article, Mao attacked liberalization and the ECONOMIC REFORMS in the USSR initiated under N. S. KHRUSHCHEV. Mao also dwelt on the danger of similar ideas and practices infiltrating China, which in his view would amount to the betrayal of Marxism and a restoration of capitalism.

On Marxism and Linguistics A book written by Stalin in 1950, in which he attacked MARRISM and presented a view of language development consistent with DIALECTICAL MATERIALISM and HISTORICAL MATERIALISM. Stalin denied that languages belonged to the SUPERSTRUCTURE and that its development reflecting class relations was an instrument of the class struggle and proceeded in revolutionary leaps. He maintained that language directly reflected changes in production, that it developed continuously in an evolutionary (not revolutionary) fashion, that there was a mutual correspondence in the development of language cognition and thought, and that in the future languages would gradually merge into a common language in the communist society.

On Ten Major (or Great) Relationships See *TEN MAJOR RELATIONSHIPS.*

On the Correct Handling of Contradictions Among the People The title of an article written by Mao Tse-tung in 1957, emphasizing the importance of MORAL INCENTIVES and the justification of rebellion if it serves the masses. It also includes an analysis of the problems of the transitional period to communism, especially highlighting the conflicts between democracy and bureaucracy and between leaders and followers. Later, Mao endeavoured to resolve these problems in the GREAT PROLETARIAN CULTURAL REVOLUTION.

OOUR Yugoslav abbreviation in Serbo-Croat of *Osnovna Organizacija Udruženog Rada*, meaning BASIC ORGANIZATION OF ASSOCIATED LABOUR.

Open Shop A term used in capitalist countries to denote the ability of the employer to hire labour irrespective of trade union membership. This practice was the rule in the earlier stages of the labour movement and worked to the advantage of the employers, who in case of strikes could hire non-union labour as strike-breakers. It tended to weaken the bargaining power of trade unions and the unity of the working class in general. O.s. contrasts with CLOSED SHOP.

Operational Planning A term used in the Socialist countries for planning at the enterprise level. In Socialist practice, it typically embraces three constituents: 1. an overall plan, embodying targets and methods of their implementation for the enterprise as a whole; 2. interdepartmental plans, showing the tasks and ways and means of their achievement in individual departments of the enterprise; and 3. intra-departmental plans, specifying tasks for individual sections or teams within each department. In its narrow meaning, o.p. is understood to involve only 2 and 3, and covers annual, quarterly, monthly and even shorter periods. The shorter the period, the more detailed and specific the plans become. O.p. focuses on the practical production processes, in particular the sequence of the operations, dates, stocks of the necessary materials, and modifications of the methods of implementation in the light of changing conditions.

Opium of the People A phrase first used by Marx (in *Towards a Critique of Hegel's Philosophy of Right: Introduction*, 1844). His point was that RELIGION is preached by naïve believers, manipulated by the ruling classes and its effect is the emasculation of the underprivileged. The latter are made to forget their exploitation and plight and instead accept them with humility, looking for consolation in the promised paradise after life. Thus religion is an antidote to the development of proletarian consciousness and revolutionary action.

Opportunism The selfish habit or policy of adapting one's actions and loyalties (if any) to changing circumstances for the sake of convenience. The term was first used by a French writer in 1876 and applied to L. Gambetta, a French Republican leader, who sought compromise with the moderates when right-wingers were influential in parliament. Some years later the label was adopted by revolutionary Marxists and has been employed widely ever since for various forms of comprom-

Opposites

ise in application to working class leaders and groups who subordinate ideological rectitude and class interests to some current advantage, implying co-operation with the bourgeoisie. In this sense, the term was first used by F. Engels in 1879 in a letter to A. BEBEL. O. may have different facets: 1. renunciation of the revolutionary road to socialism; 2. attempts to secure some rights or improvements by parliamentary action; 3. the repudiation of the postulate of the CLASS STRUGGLE; and 4. the rejection of the idea of SOCIALIST INTERNATIONALISM in favour of chauvinistic NATIONALISM, including imperialist wars. So understood, o. is most common among the LABOUR ARISTOCRACY, and was favoured by the majority in the SECOND INTERNATIONAL (represented by CENTRISM and social-democratic parties). Also ECONOMISM, EUROCOMMUNISM, FABIANISM, MILLERANDISM, REFORMISM, REVISIONISM.

Opposites The two essential elements in the philosophy of DIALECTICS. To Marxists, the struggle of o. constitutes the very essence of development in nature, society and human thought. Examples of o. in this sense are: action and reaction; positive and negative electric charges in physics; association and dissociation in chemistry; plus and minus in mathematics; the bourgeoisie and the proletariat; revolution and counter-revolution; induction and deduction. The struggle between opposites provides the driving force for progressive development (SELF-MOVEMENT), which disposes of the need to have god as the abstract explanation for movement and growth. Through the resolvement of the problem of o., new and progressive forces struggle with old and retrogressive forces. This process in the social sphere is called the CLASS STRUGGLE, which is the conflict and clashes between antagonistic social classes – the oppressed and exploited class against the ruling, exploiting class.

Opposition A general term applied to the different groups within the RUSSIAN COMMUNIST PARTY (OF THE BOLSHEVIKS) who in the early and mid-1920s opposed the centralization of power, especially in the hands of STALIN after he became the Party's Secretary-General in 1922. There was no other legal opposition in the country after 1922, when all the political parties other than the Communist party were abolished. The different opposition groups within the Party were: LEFT OPPOSITION, TROTSKYISM, the WORKERS' OPPOSITION; the Moscow Opposition and the Bolshevik Leninists. Few of the members of the O. survived after Stalin's victory in the late 1920s (GREAT PURGES).

Optimal Planning Procedures and methodology involved in the preparation of optimal plans, i.e. those which are not only internally consistent (feasible) but also the most effective from the standpoint of given objectives. It involves such a pattern of resource allocation which ensures maximum production from the given volume of resources, or the attainment of the given objectives (such as material production, social welfare), with the minimum outlay of resources, or both. Interest in o.p. in the Socialist countries began in the late 1950s and was facilitated by the official acceptance of mathematical economics, the development of computers and the need for INTENSIVE GROWTH. The process of o.p. necessitates the calculation of opportunity costs (feedback costs), which involves the scarcity valuation of all resources (including non-labour factors of production, i.e., capital and land) and marginal analysis. To construct o.p., optimal prices are necessary, which can only be derived from the former. This can be achieved, at least theoretically, by the process of reiteration, necessitating perfect information and a vast number of calculations involving simultaneous equations. O.p., so far, has proved to be practically impossible. But partial optimization plans have been constructed (covering a branch of industry, a region, or foreign trade) in some of the most advanced European Socialist countries (Czechoslovakia, the German DR, Hungary, Poland, and the USSR).

408

Optimal Prices A term used in Socialist economic planning for a price structure that best satisfies a given criterion, or that is most conducive to the attainment of a particular objective. The criteria or objectives may be: scarcity; the maximization of production; the most desirable level of ACCUMULATION; social justice and the like. Most commonly, o.p. denote the ideal price structure derived from the optimal plan, which ensures the maximum feasible national income from a given volume of resources or one ensuring the minimum outlay of resources to attain the postulated volume of national income. For this type of optimum pricing KANTOROVICH used the concept of OBJECTIVELY DETERMINED VALUATIONS.

Order No. 1 See SOVIET ORDER NO. 1.

Order of Lenin See LENIN PRIZES.

Ordzhonikidze, Grigory Konstantinovich (1886–1937) A distinguished OLD BOLSHEVIK who perished in mysterious circumstances during the GREAT PURGES. O. joined the Bolsheviks in 1903 and was elected to the Party's Central Committee in 1912. He participated in the REVOLUTION OF 1905–07 and the GREAT OCTOBER SOCIALIST REVOLUTION in 1917. After the Revolution, he held several important positions in the Soviet hierarchy, including the posts of the Chairman of *VESENKHA* (1930–32) and People's Commissar for Heavy Industry. He was always regarded as Stalin's faithful supporter, but was forced by Stalin to commit suicide.

Organic Law (of the Central People's Government) A document embodying 31 Articles adopted by the CHINESE PEOPLE'S POLITICAL CONSULTATIVE CONFERENCE, convened by the Chinese Communist Party on 21 Sep. 1949 (nine days prior to the formal proclamation of the People's Republic of China). The O.L., together with the COMMON PROGRAMME (also adopted at the same Conference), became the basis of the first Constitution of the PR of China adopted by the first NATIONAL PEOPLE'S CONGRESS on 20 Sep. 1954.

Organic Structure of Capital In a Marxian application to capitalism, the relation of the value of CONSTANT CAPITAL (c) to VARIABLE CAPITAL (v), if that ratio reflects the TECHNICAL STRUCTURE OF CAPITAL. There are considerable differences in the o.s. of c. in different industries, reflecting the level of technology and differences in the natural conditions of production. Owing to competition and technical progress the ratio tends to increase, which leads to the DECLINING PROFIT RATE, UNEMPLOYMENT and increasing EXPLOITATION of the working class. Marx's recognition of the differences in the o.s. of c. in different industries and his insistence that the PROFIT RATE is the same in all industries resulted in an inconsistency in his interpretation of the LABOUR THEORY OF VALUE (in *CAPITAL*, vol. I), viz. that market values of various commodities do not correspond only to the value of LABOUR TIME required to produce them. For this reason, Marx later (in *Capital*, vol. III) attributed a value-creation capacity (as distinct from value transmission) to constant capital as well by introducing the concept of PRODUCTION PRICE.

Organic Theory of Society A theory according to which the structure and development of society are reflections of the biological organism. The founder of this theory was H. Spencer (1820–1903), but some of its aspects were further developed by A. Schaefle (1837–1903), F. Nietzsche (1844–1900), A. A. BOGDANOV and others. The exponents of the theory hold that there are three sets of organs in living organisms, viz. feeding, distributive and digestive, which are paralleled in society by workers, traders and capitalists, respectively. Consequently, capitalism is a natural social system. Marxists strongly attacked the theory as reactionary, denying the antagonistic struggle between labour and capital and further implying that capitalism is an eternal and immutable social system conforming to natural biological laws.

Organization of Associated Labour A concept peculiar to Yugoslavia, denoting the basic unit of the Yugoslav economic and social order. Its distinguishing features are: 1. the means of production are (as a rule) socially owned, but are leased to the workers; 2. the workers have the right to use the socially-owned resources on the basis of self-management, including both production and distribution; and 3. the o. of a.l. can be either an enterprise (engaging in economic activities) or an institution. The Yugoslavs see this system to be more conducive to the dignity, freedom and creativity of workers than the STATE CAPITALISM of the Soviet type.

Organization of Latin American Solidarity (*Organización Latinoamericana de Solidaridad*) An organization founded on 16 Jan. 1966 in Havana for the co-ordination of revolutionary activities in Latin America along Cuban lines. The O.L.A.S. represents a counter-body to the anti-communist and US-dominated Organization of American States and the PUNTA DEL ESTE DECLARATION. At the O.L.A.S. Conference in July-Aug. 1967 in Havana, a Declaration was formulated proclaiming that the revolutionary struggle was the only way of solving economic and social problems in Latin America.

Organization of Solidarity of the Peoples of Africa, Asia and Latin America A loose alliance founded at the first Tricontinental Conference in Havana on 12 Jan. 1966 for the co-ordination of struggle against IM-PERIALISM, COLONIALISM and NEO-COLONIALISM. The Organization is based in Havana and publishes *Tricontinental Bulletin* (in English, French and Spanish) and *Tricontinental Review* (in English, French, Italian and Spanish).

Orgburo A shortened form of *Organizatsionnoe Buro* in Russian meaning Organization Bureau. It was founded in March 1919 as one of the three inner bodies (together with the Politburo and the Secretariat) of the Central Committee of the RUSSIAN COMMUNIST PARTY (OF THE BOL-SHEVIKS). The responsibility of the O. was to supervise the procedures involved in Party organizations and the distribution and assignment of the personnel to different offices and functions. After Stalin became the Party's Secretary-General in 1922, the Secretariat took over several powers of the O., which was eventually abolished in 1952. There was also an O. in the COMINTERN which was concerned with the supervision of the CADRES in the member Communist parties throughout the world, directed the activities of the Comintern's AGITPROP and also controlled personnel affairs in various auxiliary organizations.

Orientational Planning A liberal, moderate form of economic planning under Socialist conditions, less detailed and mandatory than the CENTRALIZED, DIRECTIVE SYSTEM OF PLANNING AND MANAGEMENT, but more systematic and prescriptive than INDICATIVE PLANNING. The term was popularized by O. ŠIK who saw o.p. during the PRAGUE SPRING as the appropriate type of planning for Czechoslovakia under liberal communism, intermediate between the Hungarian and Yugoslav models. Under o.p., the state limits itself to determining certain MAJOR PROPORTIONS IN THE ECONOMY and where necessary to initiating key developmental projects, while enterprises experience operational freedom. To induce the latter to implement the broad objectives laid down, the state relies basically on various types of incentives and disincentives through the market rather than DIRECTIVES.

Origin of the Family, Private Property and the State, The One of the most original works of F. ENGELS, written in 1884, dealing with the nature of primitive society and its ideological implications. He examined the history of the family and marriage among ancient Greeks, Romans and German tribes and concluded that their forms were determined by the development of the methods and conditions of production. He maintained that in the earliest primitive society MATRIARCHY (not PATRIARCHY) was the basic form of social organization. In this social structure there was no private property, no state and no social classes. He then stressed that it was only the increasing specialization and the growth in the productivity of labour that led to trade, the private acquisition of property, the appearance of patriarchy, the disintegration of the tribal form of living and the emergence of social classes. The consequent class conflicts necessitated the creation of the state as an instrument of the protection of the richest and strongest ruling class. Ever since, the state has been used as an institution of control and oppression of the weaker and exploited classes. Thus, economic and political power were combined, reinforcing each other. The main point which Engels endeavoured to establish is that private property, social classes and the state are only historical phenomena. Moreover, a classless society without an oppressing state is feasible, as illustrated by PRIMITIVE COMMUNISM. Some Marxists later pointed out that there were two weaknesses in Engels's analysis: 1. his historical classification of social development into wild, barbarian and civilized stages, which he borrowed from L. H. Morgan (1818–81), was inconsistent with HISTORICAL MATERIALISM; and 2. his insistence that, in addition to the mode of material production, kinship and tribal continuity determined social development.

Orwell, George (1903–50) An English adventurer, libertarian and writer on socialism. He first served in the British colonial administration in Burma and then fought in the SPANISH CIVIL WAR on the Republican side. He published *The Road to Wigan Pier* (1937), a book on radical politics, and *Homage to Catalonia* (1938), which commented on issues involved in the Spanish Civil War. But he gained fame for his two satirical books on the inconsistencies and abuses of the Soviet system: 1. *Animal Farm* (1946) – in which he used animals to represent different Soviet leaders and groups and in which he coined the phrase 'all animals are equal, but some are more equal than others'; and 2. *1984* (1949) – in which he presented a perceptive description of the dictatorship exercised by the omnipotent and ubiquitous Soviet state, revealed cynical manipulators and popularized several terms and phrases, such as 'Big Brother is watching you'.

Ospaaal A Spanish abbreviation for the ORGANIZATION OF SOLIDARITY OF THE PEOPLES OF AFRICA, ASIA AND LATIN AMERICA.

Ostpolitik ('Eastern Policy', in German) Name for the reorientation in the foreign policy of then FR of [West] Germany in favour of a rapprochement with the East European countries, initiated in 1966 by Kurt Kiesinger, the country's Chancellor from Oct. 1966 to Oct. 1969. He included the offer of negotiating practical measures for the improvement of personal, economic and cultural relations with the GERMAN DR (but not its formal diplomatic recognition) and the intention to establish full diplomatic relations with the East European governments, regardless of the HALLSTEIN DOCTRINE. The West German Government also declared that it was prepared to conclude treaties renouncing the use or threat of force with the USSR and its East European allies (incl. the GDR). A new phase in *O.* was announced by Chancellor W. Brandt in Oct. 1969. In Aug. 1970 an agreement was concluded in Moscow between the FRG and the USSR on the mutual renunciation of force. Four months later, an agreement was signed with Poland on the mutual normalization of relations, including a *de facto* recognition of the Oder-Neisse (Odra-Nysa) border. Similar agreements were concluded with Czechoslovakia in 1973 and with Bulgaria, the GDR and Hungary in 1974.

Ost-West Handelsbank (East-West Commercial Bank, in German) The wholly owned Soviet bank located in Frankfurt/M. It was founded in Nov. 1971, with the following shareholdings:

the *GOSBANK* – 55 per cent; the *VNESH-TORGBANK* – 30 per cent; and three foreign trade corporations: *Exportles* (export of forest products) – 5 per cent; *Promsyrioimport* (import of industrial raw materials) – 5 per cent; and *Tekhmashimport* (import of machinery and technical equipment) – 5 per cent. The Bank engages in wide-ranging banking activities, financing not only Soviet-West German trade but also East-West trade in general and foreign trade of capitalist countries. It also has a special role in financing Soviet diamond exports to West Germany and extends credits to jewellers. In addition, it handles Soviet gold sales.

Otzovists (Recallists, in Russian) A radical group within the Bolshevik faction of the RUSSIAN SOCIAL-DEMOCRATIC LABOUR PARTY active from 1905 to 1912. They opposed Lenin's decision of having Bolshevik deputies in the DUMA (the Tsarist parliament, introduced in 1905) for propaganda purposes. The *O.* wanted to recall them and also pressed for the withdrawal of Party support to trade unions which ignored political action and which were exclusively concerned with the improvement of their material conditions.

Overseas Chinese Investment Corporation A state investment agency in China which accepts foreign exchange from Chinese residents abroad and arranges for its investment in local undertakings of national importance. These companies were first established in 1952 and developed on a larger scale after 1957. The investment funds remain the property of the overseas investor and can be recouped after 12 years. The investor receives a dividend of 8 per cent p.a., which is more than the return on capital owned by the local investors (about 5 per cent p.a.) where it is still tolerated. As a rule, one-half of the dividend proceeds earned by the overseas investor can be transmitted abroad (with the permission of the authorities). If the overseas investor returns to China and looks for employment, he is given priority in the enterprises financed by his capital.

The overseas investors are encouraged to reinvest their dividends as well as the principal.

Owen, Robert (1771–1858) A successful, self-made British industrialist, philanthropist and versatile social reformer. In his textile mills in New Lanark (Scotland), he reduced working hours (from 14 to 10.5 a day), improved working conditions and established a model school and a child care centre. He then turned from philanthropy to communistic ideas and in 1825 established a model community called NEW HARMONY in the USA, which was a failure. After his return to Britain, he turned to the co-operative movement and trade unionism. He was the main organizer of the National Equitable Labour Exchange (a co-operative organization founded in 1832) and the GRAND NATIONAL CONSOLIDATED TRADES UNION (1934), which although it soon failed later developed along solid and lasting lines. In his philosophical outlook, O. was a materialist and believed that man could be improved if the material conditions in which he lived and worked were improved. To this effect, he favoured communal ownership of the means of production and the development of a classless, efficient society based on co-operation and social justice, rather than competition and elitism. O.'s ideas and practical efforts attracted the attention of Marxists, especially Engels. Although O. was commended for his philanthropy and pioneering reforms, he was criticized for his rejection of the postulate of the CLASS STRUGGLE and the revolutionary road to the transformation of society. He was also attacked for his leniency towards the BOURGEOISIE which he expected to take up the leadership in reforming capitalism gradually. Marxists identify O.'s ideas and actions with UTOPIAN SOCIALISM. Also OWENISM.

Owenism A term used by Marxists to describe the English version of UTOPIAN SOCIALISM, as propounded or implied by R. OWEN, mostly over the period 1820–50. O. was based on the communal ownership of the means of production, social justice, equality, universal civic education and co-operation among different social classes. The transformation of society was to be gradual and peaceful, mainly by the development of co-operative enterprises and communistic colonies, planned and administered efficiently on a central basis. Although O. sought to secure the co-operation of the BOURGEOISIE, it implied that the working class led by social reformers and intellectuals could carry out the transformation. O. aroused a good deal of interest in Britain and the USA, but Marxists regarded it as too timid, too slow and unworkable in practice.

Ownership of the Means of Production The ultimate legal capacity to control the use of and derive income from, land and/or capital. The m. of p. may belong to private individuals, to groups, institutions, social classes or the state. Marxists emphasize that the o. of the m. of p. is a historical phenomenon where the nature of the ownership determines PRODUCTION RELATIONS and SOCIAL STRATIFICATION. They identify the private o. of the m. of p. with ANTAGONISTIC SOCIO-ECONOMIC FORMATIONS (slavery, feudalism, capitalism) and the fundamental cause of social injustice. Private ownership in fact arose out of the development of the m. of p., which led to the appearance of SURPLUS VALUE and its appropriation by the owning social groups. Private ownership may be derived from one's work or from hired labour, but it is only the latter and inheritance that are responsible for large properties. Although under capitalism workers are legally free, they are economically compelled to sell their labour to capitalists. In non-antagonistic socio-economic formations (PRIMITIVE COMMUNISM, SOCIALISM, FULL COMMUNISM) there is SOCIAL O. OF THE M. OF P., usually associated with central economic planning where economic processes are subordinated to the interest of the whole society. Also COMMUNAL PROPERTY, CAPITALISM, STATE MONOPOLY CAPITALISM, WORKERS' SELF-MANAGEMENT.

Own Path to Socialism The freedom of each Communist party or country to choose the form of transition from capitalism to socialism according to national, historical and other circumstances. In the traditional Marxist-Leninist interpretation, the transition to socialism was to be via a violent revolution with the USSR deemed to be the most suitable model to imitate the construction of the Communist society. This interpretation was first questioned by TITO, which led to his break with Stalin and the expulsion of Yugoslavia from the COMINFORM. But the Soviet-Yugoslav reconciliation agreement of July 1955 represented the first implicit abandonment of the traditional Soviet view. The O.P. to S. was officially conceded by KHRUSHCHEV at the TWENTIETH CONGRESS OF THE CPSU in Feb. 1956. This declaration became part of the DE-STALINIZATION and led to POLYCENTRISM and ECONOMIC REFORMS along different lines in each European Socialist country (except Albania).

Ozerki Conference A meeting of the Bolshevik deputies to the DUMA (Tsarist parliament introduced in 1905) held on 2–4 Nov. 1914 regarding the Party's attitude to Russia's participation in W.W.I. The Conference was held secretly at Ozerki, a village near Petrograd (the latter now Leningrad). The participants discussed Lenin's views on the war and agreed with him that Russia should not have entered the war, that the working class should refuse to carry on what was described as an imperialist war and should turn it into a military defeat, civil war and a PROLETARIAN REVOLUTION. The Tsarist police, having been tipped off by an informer, arrested the participants and exiled them to Siberia.

P

Pacifism A movement opposed to wars and other violent forms of settlement and instead advocates peaceful solutions to problems between nations and social classes. Although the term conveys a favourable meaning, the movement has become a target for ideological controversy, with both Marxists and anti-Marxists advocating peace are considered naïve, misguided tions. In the Marxist view, peace propagated by capitalist countries is hypocritical, directed to two objectives: 1. the retention of the existing social system for the benefit of the bourgeoisie; and 2. the preservation of the international status quo between the imperialist or neo-colonialist powers on the one hand, and the colonial or economically dependent nations on the other. Well-meaning individuals advocating peace are considered naïve, misguided or traitors to the cause of social and international justice. To Marxists wars are still justified in three cases: in defence against imperialist or fascist aggression; NATIONAL LIBERATION MOVEMENTS; and fighting COUNTER-REVOLUTION. They insist that to ensure lasting peace, efforts should be directed to the elimination of EXPLOITATION and domination, both in domestic and international relations. But at the same time the Socialist countries do not reject p. and recognize that in any war the main brunt is borne by the masses. Socialist p. is directed against imperialist wars, aggressive wars (especially if waged against a Socialist country) and a nuclear war. But in capitalist countries, the Socialist peace campaigns are largely seen to be cynical, considering that in Korea, Vietnam, Laos, Kampuchea, Angola, Ethio-

pia and elsewhere the attackers were or are Communists, with the active support from other Socialist countries. National liberation movements in Hungary (1956) and Czechoslovakia (1968) were ruthlessly suppressed by Communist military intervention, and subversive and terrorist activities in capitalist countries are initiated and carried on mostly by Communists. The WORLD PEACE COUNCIL is regarded as an INTERNATIONAL COMMUNIST FRONT ORGANIZATION.

Pacifist Socialist Party (*Pacifistich Socialistische Partij*) A minor left-wing political party in the Netherlands, postulating the inseparability of PACIFISM and socialism. It calls for the comprehensive socialization of the economy, the elimination of the last traces of imperialism and colonialism, disarmament and the development of the United Nations into a world government with wide-ranging powers. The Party was founded by a splinter faction of the PARTY OF LABOUR and is Marxist-oriented. Its organ is a daily newspaper *Het Vrije Volk* (*Free People*), published in Amsterdam.

PAI Abbreviation in Polish of *Polska Agencja Interpress*, meaning Polish Interpress Agency. Founded in 1967, it is state-owned and its function is to assist the Polish Press Agency (*PAP*) in issuing foreign language bulletins and aiding foreign journalists.

Palaces of Labour An expression of GIGANTOMANIA and SOCIALIST REALISM in the lavish construction of factories and other places of work in some Socialist countries (especially the USSR) in the 1950s. This practice was based on the conviction that the architectural expression of the Socialist society, where there are no palaces for capitalists, had to find its outlet in the p. of l. for workers. In accordance with this thinking, planners made extravagant provisions for space per worker, halls for meetings, reading rooms, recreation facilities, impressive frontages, embellishments of ideological content, extensive storages, depots and courtyards. Enterprises encouraged this practice as investment was allocated to them free from the state budget. However, by 1960 this practice had been found wasteful and has been largely (but not completely) abandoned since, in the interest of economy and investment efficiency.

Palach, Jan A Czechoslovak student who on 1 Jan. 1969 set himself on fire publicly in Prague, in protest against the Soviet military intervention (INVASION OF CZECHOSLOVAKIA) and the erosion of HUMAN RIGHTS.

Palach Press A Czechoslovak news agency in exile, established by the 'LISTY' GROUP in London in 1970. The P.P., named after J. PALACH, collects news and documents from Czechoslovakia and other parts of the world and supplies it to the bi-monthly journal, *Listy* (*News*), now also published in London.

Panhellenic Socialist Movement (*PASOK*) A fairly influential political party in Greece, formed by dissenters from the COMMUNIST PARTY OF GREECE in 1974. The Movement regards itself Marxist, but not Leninist, and is anti-Soviet, anti-NATO and anti-EEC. It stands for far-reaching nationalization, agricultural co-operatives, a wide range of health services and the abolition of private schools.

Panlogism A philosophical theory identifying being with thinking, and attributing all development in nature and society to the logical and rational world spirit or world mind (*Welt Geist*). Its main exponent was G. W. F. HEGEL. Marxist philosophers regard p. as a version of IDEALISM, and as such inconsistent with MATERIALISM. They maintain that all world phenomena occur in accordance with objective natural and social laws of development. In their view DIALECTICAL MATERIALISM provides a valid and sufficient explanation of development, without the need for a supernatural rationalization.

Pannekoek, Anton (1873–1960) A Dutch Marxist theoretician who advocated council communism and the mass strike. Pannekoek was a prominent professor of astronomy before he took a post as a teacher at GERMAN SOCIAL DEMOCRATIC PARTY college in Berlin. He was a close collaborator with Herman Gorter (1863–1927) a Dutch poet and founder of an anti-Bolshevik Communist Party. Pannekoek and Gorter were advocates of the mass strike and the conscious raising of the proletariat through the CLASS STRUGGLE. Although Pannekoek was a member of the left-wing in both the GERMAN COMMUNIST PARTY and the Dutch Communist he criticized the Bolsheviks for accepting a policy of working within traditional western labour organizations and for its dictatorial character. LENIN in turn criticized this approach in his *Left-Wing Communism: An Infantile Disorder* (1920). Pannekoek's other main critiques were directed at R. HILFERDING and O. Bauer, the Austro-Marxist economists, and R. LUXEMBURG'S breakdown theory of capitalism. He wrote extensively for *Die Neue Ziet* (KAUTSKY'S journal), and his *The Tactical Difference within the Workers Movement* (1909) and *Marxism and Darwinism* (1909) were a systematic analysis of the class struggle in human society as a social development and an historical exposition of the role of man within the development of socialism, respectively.

Panpsychism A variant theory of ANIMISM applied to philosophy, according to which all matter, both organic and inorganic, is physical and all natural phenomena have a capacity for psychical reactions. G. T. Fechner (1801–87), R. T. Lotze (1817–81), J. Royce (1855–1916) and A. N. Whitehead (1861–1947) were among the modern exponents of what is a very old theory. In Marxist philosophy, p. is rejected as a view akin to IDEALISM. It is pointed out that psychic processes, if they occur, are conditioned by physiological factors and consequently can be explained more convincingly and scientifically in terms of MATERIALISM.

Pantheism A philosophical doctrine according to which god is one eternal absolute Being, a primary impersonal element and one who is inherently and universally present in nature (material objects), not external to it. The main exponents of p. were G. Bruno (1548–1600), J. Böhme (1575–1624), B. Spinoza (1632–77), J. G. Fichte (1762–1814) and G. W. F. HEGEL. The attitude of Marxist philosophy to p. is twofold. On the one hand, p. is favourably received as far as it identifies matter as being conditional to existence and rejects god as a supernatural being. But on the other, p. is considered, especially as developed more recently by bourgeois philosophers, as basically another proposition of IDEALISM postulating the existence of god.

PAP Abbreviation in Polish for *Polska Agencja Prasowa*, meaning the Polish Press Agency. It was created in Oct. 1945, replacing *Polpress* (established by the pro-Soviet authorities in March 1944). *PAP* is the official, state-owned press agency serving as the basic source of domestic and foreign news and information for the Polish press, radio and television. It maintains 16 branches in Poland and over 20 foreign correspondents, and in addition has working relations with more than 25 news agencies in the Socialist and capitalist countries. It is aided by two subsidiary agencies, *CAF* (*Centralna Agencja Fotograficzna*, Central Photographic Agency) established in 1951, and *PAI* (*Polska*

Agencja Interpress, Polish Interpress Agency), founded in 1967.

Paper Tiger A term of contempt popularized by Mao Tse-tung for the leading Western powers, especially the USA, and 'reactionaries' in general. Mao used the term first in Yenan in Aug. 1946 in an interview with Louisa Strong (a US journalist) when she mentioned that the USA had an atomic bomb. The implication of this epithet is that although Western powers may be very well supplied with military equipment and technology, their ideological indoctrination and fighting quality are very low, and yet in modern warfare men are more important than equipment. That assertion, entertained by the Chinese leadership since the Korean War (1950–53) contrasts with the Soviet view which is more cautious when it comes to the US military capabilities. But the Chinese leaders have considered Soviet attitudes and policies in relation to the USA as too timid and accommodating.

Paraguayan Communist Party (*Partido Comunista Paraguayo*) A small illegal political party with some of its leaders operating from abroad. It was founded in 1928, proscribed in 1936 and has been illegal ever since except for a few short periods. Its membership is estimated at 3,000 (compared with the country's total population of 2,850,000 in 1978). The Party split in 1963, when a small pro-Chinese group formed the Paraguayan Leninist Communist Party. Both parties are still illegal, but operate underground – the P.C.P. from Buenos Aires and the P.L.C.P. from Montevideo. The P.C.P. is hostile to the USA and imperialism, advocates the immediate distribution of large estates and is opposed to dictatorship. It publishes a newspaper called *Adelante* (*Forward*).

Parasite A term used by Marxists to describe a person or group who does not work in a legitimate occupation but lives off the back of those who do. The term was at first applied to absentee landlords and capitalists, but is now applied to juvenile delinquents, vagrants, habitual absentees from work, speculators, embezzlers and the like in the Socialist countries. The 'p' problem has become acute since the late 1950s, when the ANTI-PARASITE LAWS were introduced and strengthened.

Paris Commune An armed uprising of the working class people and the first communist government in history, which operated in Paris from 18 March to 28 May 1871 (following the Franco-Prussian War). After the defeat of Napoleon III at Sedan in 1870, the newly formed Provisional Government of National Defence (under A. Thiers) created the National Guard for the defence of Paris besieged by the Prussians. All men, including civilian workers, were supplied with arms and artillery bought from public subscriptions. But after the capitulation by the Provisional Government, the workers created the Central Committee of National Guard in mid-February 1871, which became the first proletarian revolutionary government in world history to direct the struggle against political and economic repression by the P.G.N.D. The C.C.N.G. seized power (18 March) and held general elections during which the Commune Council of 90 members was elected. The Council consisted of two main factions – the radical revolutionary Blanquists (who held the majority) and the moderate Proudhonists. The majority prevailed and a DICTATORSHIP OF THE PROLETARIAT (combining legislative, executive and judicial powers) was established with a government of 10 ministries, which immediately embarked upon extensive reforms. The P.C. had an international character and included Belgians, Germans, Hungarians, Italians, Poles and other nationalities in addition to the French. The Provisional Government attacked Paris from Versailles with the support from the German army, and by 18 May the P.C. was defeated. 30,000 *communards* were killed in action and subsequently 50,000 were arrested (including 1,725 foreigners) of which 13,000 were imprisoned or deported and 17,000 shot.

The achievements and mistakes of the P.C. became a subject of study by Marx (in *The Civil War in France*, 1871) and served as a case study for Lenin's model of the dictatorship of the proletariat (in *The STATE AND REVOLUTION*).

Paris Peace Talks Periodical negotiations carried on in Paris between the parties to the VIETNAM WAR, attempting to find a political solution to the hostilities. An agreement to initiate the talks was reached on 3 April 1968 and the first (preliminary) meeting was convened on 13 May 1968, but the actual talks began in Jan. 1969. There were four parties to the talks – the DR of [North] Vietnam, the USA, the National Liberation Front of South Vietnam, and the Republic of [South] Vietnam. The talks were carried on irregularly up to March 1972 and were then broken off by the USA (in retaliation for new attacks by the DR of Vietnam). The talks were resumed in July 1972 until a ceasefire agreement was signed on 27 Jan. 1973 by the four parties.

Parliamentarism A system of government based on elected parliaments, through which the majority party determines current administration and major social changes (if any). P. is best developed in democratic capitalist countries where there is a multi-party system, universal suffrage, regular elections every 3–5 years (or less) and where the government is selected from the parliament and is responsible to it. P. has not received much favour from Marxists. Marx himself was contemptuous of 'parliamentary cretinism' under capitalism where, as he saw it, parliament becomes an instrument of the bourgeois domination of the whole society. He thought that after the proletarian seizure of power there would be no need for p. as the proletariat would legitimately constitute the whole society. Lenin devoted even more attention to it (in *The State and Revolution*, 1917; *The Proletarian Revolution and the Renegade Kautsky*, 1918; and *Left-Wing Communism – An Infantile Disorder*, 1918). He

417

described p. under socialism as historically anachronistic in the context of the DIC-TATORSHIP OF THE PROLETARIAT. P. was also rejected by the COMINTERN at its Second Congress in 1920. But to some extent p. was rehabilitated at the TWEN-TIETH CONGRESS OF THE CPSU in 1956, when it was conceded that in some capitalist countries the working class could utilize parliaments as a suitable channel for improving the conditions of the working class. Also LEGAL MARXISM, PARLIAMEN-TARY ROAD TO SOCIALISM.

Parliamentary Road to Socialism A non-revolutionary and gradual approach to building socialism in a country where the already established political institutions, e.g. legislative bodies, multi-party elections and liberal laws, are used by either a communist or socialist party to gain power. The parliamentary road to socialism does not involve a violent PRO-LETARIAN REVOLUTION or the subsequent DICTATORSHIP OF THE PROLETARIAT. Early advocates of the parliamentary road to socialism were the FABIANS, E. BERNS-TEIN, and those Labour and Socialist Parties in the West that support SOCIAL DEMOCRACY. Today, the Communist parties in the West, with the recent exception of the FRENCH COMMUNIST PARTY, support the parliamentary road to socialism via EUROCOMMUNISM. The leading parties here are the ITALIAN COMMUNIST PARTY led by E. BERLINGUER, the COMMUNIST PARTY OF SPAIN, led by S. CARRILLO and the COMMUNIST PARTY OF GREAT BRI-TAIN. Also, PARLIAMENTARISM, REFOR-MISM and REVISIONISM.

Particular and the General In philosophy, based on materialism, the two concepts are seen as a DIALECTIC complex, viz. in their contradiction and mutual inter-dependence. Marxist philosophers stress that both the individual and the general are reflections of the objective material world. Although the material world consists of particular objects and phenomena, they do not exist in isolation but constitute elements of groups and types, etc. With-

out the existence of the particular, there can be no general concepts, and at the same time the particular cannot exist without the context of the general. From this position, Marxists reject the independent existence of ideas, including god.

Partisanship A philosophical approach emphasizing the inevitability of a social class bias in the understanding and interpretation of existence and phenomena in nature and society. This approach, which is opposite to OBJECTIVISM, is one of the fundamental propositions postulated in Marxist philosophy, with the consequent implications for history, political science and sociology. Marxist philosophers maintain that in a class society any ideology, and consequently, any philosophy, is an expression of the interest of one social class or another, hence, basic philosophical controversies essentially reflect the class struggle. Thus, IDEALISM and METAPHYSICS are products of BOURGEOIS thinking and are employed to justify such phenomena as RELIGION, IMPERIALISM, RACISM and EXPLOITA-TION. But more importantly, Marxist philosophy, based as it is on DIALEC-TICAL MATERIALISM and HISTORICAL MATERIALISM, must actively represent the interests of the PROLETARIAT and guide its thinking and actions towards the destruction of capitalism and the construction of socialism and communism. The basic ideas of p. were developed by Lenin in *The Economic Content of Narodnism* (1895) and *MATERIALISM AND EMPIRIO-CRITICISM*. An applied aspect of p. is PARTY-MINDEDNESS.

Partisans of Peace An international Communist movement, active during 1946–50, which worked towards the preservation of peace and the prevention of W.W.III. They held their first World Congress in April 1949 in Paris, and those who were refused entry to France – in Prague, where a World Peace Committee was elected. At their second Congress, in Warsaw in Nov. 1950, the WORLD PEACE COUNCIL was founded to continue their work on a wider and more systematic basis.

Party A political organization representing the views and interests of a particular social group or class. The p. structure, membership and discipline differ according to ideological, historical, national and social circumstances. In general, p. organization is the most liberal and least coercive in democratic capitalist countries, and most tightly structured, disciplined and elitist in totalitarian fascist nations. Marxists attach great importance to the COMMUNIST PARTY as the vanguard of the working class. Marxism-Leninism postulates a hierarchically structured and highly disciplined p. organized in accordance with DEMOCRATIC CENTRALISM with a hard core of devoted full-time professionals. Its task is to develop CLASS CONSCIOUSNESS, lead the working class to the PROLETARIAN REVOLUTION, direct the construction of socialism under the conditions of the DICTATORSHIP OF THE PROLETARIAT, exercised by the Party itself, and attain FULL COMMUNISM.

Party Cell A term officially used in the USSR until 1934 for the lowest unit of Party organization. The term has been replaced since by 'Primary Organization'.

Party Central Committee See CENTRAL COMMITTEE.

Party Congress An official major conference of the Communist party delegates, under normal conditions meeting every 3–5 years. Between Congresses, Party Conferences may be held. A P.C. usually elects the CENTRAL COMMITTEE, the Secretary-General and an Auditing (or Control) Committee. The P.C. is theoretically the highest level and source of Party authority, laying down major policy objectives to be carried out by the Party organs. Between the Congresses the Central Committee is the highest authority. In practice, the P.C. has become a rubber stamp for the decisions submitted by the highest Party organs. A P.C. is given its consecutive number name. Thus, the CPSU treats the Congress of the RUSSIAN SOCIAL-DEMOCRATIC LABOUR PARTY, held in Minsk in March 1898 as its First P.C. Its last Congress (at the time of writing), held in March 1976, was known as the Twenty-Fifth Congress, and was attended by 4,998 delegates representing 15,694,000 members. The First Congress of the Chinese Communist Party was held in 1921 and the last one, the Eleventh Congress in Aug. 1977, was attended by 1,510 delegates representing 35m. members.

Party Discipline The norms and code of conduct prevailing in a particular political party in relation to its members. In general, the more radical and more elitist (or privileged) the party and the more hierarchical its structure, the stricter the discipline. Of all the significant political parties, the COMMUNIST PARTY subscribing to MARXISM-LENINISM is noted for the strictest p.d. Party rules insist on absolute ideological devotion, the conscientious execution of Party decisions and other duties assigned by appropriate Party officials, and high moral standards. P.d. is ensured first of all by the cultivation of internal consciousness through INDOCTRINATION, regular Party meetings, CRITICISM, SELF-CRITICISM and the development of the spirit of Party comradeship. Admission to the Party is on a selective basis; new members may be admitted only on the sponsorship of two existing members (usually of at least two years' standing). The Party rules provide for various forms of disciplinary action against offending and indifferent members, including expulsion irrespective of the position held. Periodical PURGES of Party members and leaders are carried out. The drive for p.d. reached its peak in the USSR under Stalin in the 1930s in the GREAT PURGES. Strict p.d. was also insisted upon in the national Sections of the COMINTERN in accordance with Lenin's TWENTY-ONE CONDITIONS OF ADMISSION TO THE COMINTERN, which again reached its peak in the 1930s, when Stalin eliminated a large

Partyinost

number of foreign Communist leaders who were in the USSR.

Partyinost A Russian term which has no perfect linguistic equivalent in English, but its nearest renditions are PARTISAN-SHIP and PARTY-MINDEDNESS.

Party Line The term usually applied to the strategy and tactics laid down by the leadership of the Communist party by the majority in the POLITBURO or the CENTRAL COMMITTEE. The p.l. is usually publicized and disseminated in the Party's official daily and periodical publications. The p.l. usually refers to some major controversial question, such as the interpretation of Marx or other Marxist theoreticians, directions of social and economic development, major reforms, international issues and relations with other Communist parties. Once determined by appropriate procedures, the p.l. is binding on all members, including the minority. Attempts to question or undermine the p.l. may be taken as DEVIATIONISM and FACTIONALISM, in which case disciplinary action is usually taken against the offenders. In the international Communist movement, up to 1956 the p.l. of the CPSU was usually regarded as mandatory for other Communist parties. But since that time in domestic policies the principle of taking one's OWN PATH TO SOCIALISM has been accepted. The SINO-SOVIET DISPUTE has led to the emergence of two different p.l. – the MOSCOW LINE and the PEKING LINE.

Party-mindedness A Marxist term denoting the spirit and zeal of Communist party members and of the authorities in the Socialist state guided and motivated by Party objectives and principles. Although the idea of p.-m. had been anticipated by N. G. CHERNYSHEVSKY in 1860 (in *Anthropological Principle in Philosophy*), the original term, *partyinost* in Russian, was established by Lenin in 1895 (in *The Economic Content of Narodnism* and later in *MATERIALISM AND EMPIRIO-CRITICISM*). P.-m. implies that a Party member judges thinking, social problems and ac-

tions from the standpoint of the Communist party and identifies himself with official Party views and policies. The development of p.-m. in the Socialist countries is the explicit responsibility of the Communist party and the Socialist state. Some of its means and expressions are executed through INDOCTRINATION, PROPAGANDA, mass campaigns and SOCIALIST REALISM. The philosophical justification for p.-m. is found in PARTISANSHIP.

Party of Labour (*Partij van de Arbeid*) In the Netherlands, a moderate and influential socialist party. It was formed in 1946 by an amalgamation of the former Social Democratic Workers' Party with left-wing Liberals and progressive Catholics and Protestants. Its programme emphasises democratic socialism, substantial social welfare benefits, the reduction of defence expenditure and favours Dutch membership in the EEC. It is the second largest political party in the country and at the 1974 general elections won 21 (of 75) seats in the First Chamber and 43 (of 150) seats in the Second Chamber, thus becoming the leading government party. Its publications include a fortnightly bulletin *Roos in de Vuist* (*Rose in the Fist*) and two monthlies, *Partijkrant* (*Party Bulletin*) and *SenD* (*Socialism and Democracy*).

Party of Labour of Switzerland (*Partei der Arbeit der Schweiz*) The main Communist party in the country with a moderate to small influence, which has been declining in recent years. Its origin goes back to 1921 when the Communist Party of Switzerland was founded. It was declared illegal in 1940, but was revived in 1944 under its present name. The Party's membership is about 5,000 (compared with the country's population of 6,400,000 in 1978). At the 1975 general elections, it polled 2.5 per cent of the votes and won 4 (of 200) seats. At the Party's 10th Congress in June 1974, a Central Committee of 50 members was elected, plus a Secretariat of 5 members and Politburo of 14 members. In the international Communist movement, it has followed a pro-Soviet line. Its main

420

published organs are: *Voix Ouvrière* (*Workers' Voice*), a daily appearing in Geneva; *Vorwärts* (*Forward*), a weekly appearing in Basel; and *Il Lavoratore* (*The Worker*), a weekly appearing in Lugano. There are at least two other rival Communist parties: the Swiss Popular Party (created in 1967 and which has a pro-Chinese orientation) and the Marxist Revolutionary League (founded in 1969 and representing a revolutionary Trotskyite group).

Party of Russian Social-Democrats See BLAGOYEV GROUP.

Party of the People's Freedom See KADETS.

Party of the People's Will See NARODNIKS, NARODNISM.

Party Secretariat See SECRETARIAT OF THE CENTRAL COMMITTEE OF THE COMMUNIST PARTY.

Party Secretary In the Communist party, the chief executive official, whether at local, regional or national level. He is appointed by and directly responsible to the next higher level of the Party authority. The most important p.s. is the SECRETARY-GENERAL, or the FIRST SECRETARY of the Central Committee.

Parvus ('Small One', in Latin) An assumed name of I. Helpland (1869–1924), a Russian socialist of German descent who contributed articles to Marxist newspapers and periodicals, including ISKRA. He was a close collaborator of L. D. TROTSKY with whom he sought to unite the Bolshevik and Menshevik factions in the RUSSIAN SOCIAL-DEMOCRATIC LABOUR PARTY after its split in 1903. He was keenly interested in the international Communist movement and held that imperialism had greatly contributed to the emerging solidarity of the working class in different countries. He further advocated the EXPORT OF REVOLUTION, which later led Trotsky to the formulation of PERMANENT REVOLUTION.

Pathet Lao The military arm of the PEOPLE'S REVOLUTIONARY PARTY OF LAOS. It appeared first during 1944–45 but extended its operations only after 1954. It had operated in the mountain regions of the country, in Vientiane and Lua Prabang before the Communist seizure of power in Dec. 1977. It has also been active in the north-eastern region of Thailand, where it has provided leaders, training facilities, financial support and weapons to local insurgents.

Patriarchy A system of social and economic organization in primitive societies, characterized by the dominant position of man (*pater*, 'father' in Latin) in the tribe. P. was noted for the existence of private property – land, domestic animals, buildings, implements, weapons and slaves. P. contrasted with MATRIARCHY. The historical stage when p. appeared is a subject of ideological controversy. In the traditional interpretation commonly accepted in the West, p. was the original form of social organization. Consequently, the institution of private property and its private inheritance is a natural social phenomenon going back to the very dawn of man's history or pre-history. It is also pointed out that at no stage was matriarchy a universal form of social organization. It existed only among some of the most primitive races, while p. prevailed elsewhere. In the Marxist view, expounded exhaustively first by Engels (in *The ORIGIN OF THE FAMILY, PRIVATE PROPERTY AND THE STATE*), p. was not the original social unit, but developed only after matriarchy. It emerged from the social division of labour, when pastoral and craft pursuits were separated from agriculture and became the domain of man. In effect, trade developed, wealth increased, private property appeared and slavery emerged. In p., monogamy or polygamy replaced polyandry, the father of the children was known, property was inherited by his children (usually sons) and man became the dominant sex in economic and other activities. Woman thus became an object of exploitation.

Thus, Marxists stress that p. and the institution of private property and the exploitation of slaves and women was only a historical stage which followed PRIMITIVE COMMUNISM, the original socio-economic formation.

Patrice Lumumba People's Friendship University FRIENDSHIP UNIVERSITY, located in Moscow. (Not to be confused with 'Patrice Lumumba Institute of Political Science' in Nigeria, founded by the Socialist Workers' and Farmers' Party, a Marxist party in the country).

Patriotic People's Front (*Hazafias Népfront*) The united electoral front in Hungary, embracing non-opposition elements. It was founded in 1954, having replaced the Hungarian People's Independence Front (created in 1949). It is completely dominated by the HUNGARIAN SOCIALIST WORKERS' PARTY, but includes other non-opposition groups, viz. trade unions, peasants, women and the youth movement. The Front administers the lists of candidates for national and local elections on the basis of nominations at public meetings. There are 3,692 local P.P.F. committees, with a total membership of 116,000. More than one candidate is permitted to stand in a constituency, but to be elected an absolute majority is necessary (more than 50 per cent of the votes cast). To be placed on the list, the candidate must support the P.P.F. At the 1975 general elections, of the 352 constituencies 34 had more than one candidate, and according to official statistics 99.6 per cent of the electors voted for the candidates put forward by the P.P.F. General elections are held every five years. The Front's official publications are: *Magyar Nemzet* (*The Hungarian People*), daily; *Szabad Föld* (*Free Soil*), weekly; and *Népfront* (*Patriotic Front*), monthly.

Patriotism Love of one's country based on historical, cultural and social heritage. P. has been a subject of ideological controversy. In the traditional capitalist view, p. has usually been an expression of NATIONALISM, and as such contrasting with COSMOPOLITANISM and INTERNATIONALISM. The Marxist view of p. has been rather complex. Traditionally, Marxism has emphasized SOCIALIST INTERNATIONALISM. But after the establishment of the first Socialist state in the USSR and later in other Socialist countries p. has been accorded qualified rehabilitation. Marxists maintain that p. is a historical phenomenon and assumes a different content in different SOCIO-ECONOMIC FORMATIONS. Under capitalism, it is held, the BOURGEOISIE regards itself alone as the nation and manipulates p. as an instrument of the development of nation states. Historically, this led to IMPERIALISM and ruling class co-operation in the suppression of working class movements in different countries. True p., according to Marxists, can be developed only by the working class, which opposes not only imperialism but also CHAUVINISM and cosmopolitanism. P. received unprecedented attention in the USSR during W.W.II. In fact, the Soviet war against the 'fascist and imperialist invaders' (Germany, Italy and Japan) during 1941–45 is officially called the GREAT PATRIOTIC WAR.

Pauperism The state of misery among the poorest groups in society, caused by the absence or insufficiency of income or property. P. has been generally identified with capitalism, as a consequence of the concentration of property in the hands of the capitalists, the bourgeois EXPLOITATION of the working masses, UNEMPLOYMENT and the *LAISSEZ-FAIRE* policy of governments neglecting social security. Also IMMISERATION OF THE PROLETARIAT, *LUMPENPROLETARIAT*, POVERTY.

Pauperization Plan A critical term used in South Vietnam to describe the central government policies laid down in the 1976–80 Five Year Plan in the SR of Vietnam. The Plan is seen as a P.P. in two respects: 1. the extremely favourable exchange rate between the North and the

South Vietnamese currencies for the benefit of the North; and 2. the large flow of raw materials, food and other consumer goods from the South to the North. The Plan is officially justified on the grounds that the North contributed considerably more to the postwar reconstruction of the South, the standard of living is still higher in the South and the overall national interest demands a greater uniformity throughout the reunified country.

Pavlov, Ivan Petrovich (1849–1936) An outstanding Russian physiologist, who made substantial discoveries in the fields of blood circulation, digestion, the nervous system and brain structure. His greatest contributions were made in the understanding of higher nerve functions in animals and men which established foundations for the physiological explanation of psychological reactions (as illustrated by his famous experiments with dogs, stimuli, food and saliva). In his researches he emphasized the role of the environment and conditioned reflexes. The Communist Party and the Soviet Government gave P. full moral and financial support, as his work fitted in very well with Marxist philosophy (in particular DIALECTICAL MATERIALISM) and offered a promise of evolving the NEW COMMUNIST MAN. In turn, P. supported the Soviet regime in all the ways he could. The Academy of the Sciences of the USSR published his *Collected Works* in four volumes in 1951–52.

PAX A lay organization of Catholic activists in Poland supporting the Communist regime and participating in the development of a Socialist society. It was founded in 1945, adopted its name in 1947 and in 1949 established its own publishing house under the same name. It is involved in political, social and cultural work and is supported by the Communist regime. It publishes several periodicals, including *Słowo powszechne* (*The Common Word*), *Kierunki* (*Directions*), and *Życie i myśl* (*Life and Thought*). P. is seen by many Catholics as an institution undermining the traditional role of the Catholic Church in Poland.

Peaceful Coexistence See COEXISTENCE.

Peaceful Transition to Socialism A gradual changeover from capitalism to socialism, involving the PARLIAMENTARY ROAD TO SOCIALISM or LEGAL MARXISM. This possibility was conceded by the Communist Party of the Soviet Union at its TWENTIETH CONGRESS in 1956, which became an important ideological breakthrough. It was further confirmed in the MOSCOW DECLARATION of 1957, but the Soviet and Chinese delegations disagreed as to whether the principle of p.t. to s. was to be 'strategic' or 'tactical'. Although the Chinese delegation (headed by Mao Tse-tung) signed the Declaration, in a privately circulated memorandum it stated that the principle be accepted only as a tactical manoeuvre, to enable the Communist parties in capitalist countries to sidestep attacks on them on this issue. The memorandum further stressed that the Communist parties should at the same time develop armed sources of power, with or without a concurrent legal and peaceful struggle. The acceptance of the p.t. to s. is also an important feature of EUROCOMMUNISM.

Peace is indivisible A motto coined by M. LITVINOV in the mid-1930s as the Soviet delegate to the League of Nations. He urged the democratic capitalist powers to join the USSR in forming a bloc against the fascist threat (of Germany, Italy and Japan) to world peace. He emphasized that the threat was very serious, demanding a collective approach by all the endangered countries without exception, irrespective of their ideological differences. The motto also implied that in internal national relations, all political parties should combine into POPULAR FRONTS against fascist or fascist-sympathizing parties.

Peace Manifesto A declaration made at the INTERNATIONAL CONFERENCE OF THE

COMMUNIST AND WORKERS' PARTIES in Moscow in Nov. 1957, which was attended by Communist leaders representing 64 countries. The P.M. was addressed to 'people of good will throughout the world' calling for the end to the COLD WAR and the ARMS RACE and for the liberation of colonies and other dependent peoples.

Peace Power Grid The interconnected electrical power system embracing the European CMEA countries (Bulgaria, Czechoslovakia, the German DR, Hungary, Poland, Romania and the USSR) between the rivers Elbe, Dnieper and Danube. It is also known as the *Mir* P.G. or the Central Electric P.G. The linking began in 1960 and the network now includes at least 15 international transmission ·lines. The central administration, which is computer-controlled, is found in Prague and the combined power capacity of the Grid exceeds 60,000 MW. The interconnected network enables a member country to draw on another member country's power. This reduces the need for reserve capacity, as the peak consumption of power appears at different times in individual countries. The Grid also provides for coping with power breakdowns in the member countries.

Peak of Communism The highest mountain summit in the USSR, in the Pamirs, 7,495m. a.s.l. The first man to have ascended it was E. M. Abalakov in 1933. It is permanently covered with snow and icefields. Before the Revolution, its name was Mount Garmo, but since then the latter name has been transferred to a neighbouring lower mountain, previously unnamed. The P. of C. was first known as Mount Stalin, but after Stalin's death its name was changed to its present designation.

Peasant (or Rural) Idiocy A conception held by early Marxists (including Marx himself) in the latter half of the 19th c., implying the revolutionary uselessness of the peasantry, in contrast to the industrial working class. Peasants were regarded as basically petty bourgeois in outlook, conservative, bound by religion, basically docile, suspicious and too difficult to indoctrinate and organize, owing to territorial dispersion and the low level of education. This view has largely been proven to be unfounded. There were several peasant revolts in Europe including Russia; the first successful proletarian revolution occurred in a predominantly backward agricultural country (Russia) and the Chinese Communist movement was based and developed in rural areas.

Peasants Working farmers particularly in traditional societies, with less advanced agriculture. From the standpoint of Marxism, p. are often noted for PETTY BOURGEOIS mentality and are not as revolutionary and amenable to Communist ideology as industrial workers are. However, because p. represented large proportions of the total population in virtually all the countries when the Communists seized power (and still do), the Communist regimes immediately sought to forge worker-peasant alliances as their mainstay of power. In Communist practice, p. were divided into the following four strata, according to the size of their land holdings and income: landless agricultural labourers; poor; middle; and rich. Rich p. became an object of oppression and elimination, especially in the USSR. The Soviet terms for the four classes of p., in official use from 1917 to the mid-1930s were: *BATRAK*; *BEDNYAK*; *SEREDNYAK*; and *KULAK*.

Peasants International See GREEN INTERNATIONAL, *KRESTINTERN*.

Peking Line Alignment in the international Communist movement supporting MAOISM and acknowledging the pre-eminence of the CHINESE COMMUNIST PARTY (rather than the Communist Party of the Soviet Union). The concept became established in the capitalist world in the early 1960s, after the emergence of the SINO-SOVIET DISPUTE. Of the 90 significant national Communist parties in the world in the late 1970s, those in six countries clearly support the P.L: Burma; Hong Kong; Malaysia; Singapore; Sri Lanka; and Thailand. In addition there are splinter or factional groups in 20 countries (the MOSCOW LINE is supported by some 50 parties). In the remaining 14 countries a neutral or independent line is followed.

P'eng Chen (1902–) A Chinese Communist leader who became a victim of the GREAT PROLETARIAN CULTURAL REVOLUTION. He joined the Communist Youth League in 1922 and the CHINESE COMMUNIST PARTY in 1935, became a political commissar in the Chinese Red Army in 1937 and headed the Central Party School in Yenan from 1938 to 1942. After the proclamation of the P.R. of China in Oct. 1949 his activities took him to Peking, where in 1950 he took over the leadership of the Federation of Trade Unions and from 1955 to 1966 he was the First Secretary of the Peking Municipal Committee of the C.C.P. In mid-1965 he was put in charge of the GROUP OF FIVE to conduct a cultural revolution among the intellectuals, which he did not pursue zealously enough to satisfy Mao Tse-tung. P'eng was attacked by Mao in late 1965 and after April 1966 he lost his posts. Rehabilitated in 1978 he was subsequently co-opted to the C.C. of the C.C.P., elected to its Standing Committee and appointed Chairman of the legal Commission of the National People's Congress.

Peonage A form of labour servitude, where a worker in debt pays off his debt to his creditor-employer until the debt is discharged. The term is generally used in application to the Latin American countries, mostly in rural areas. Marxists regard p. as a primitive form of exploitation approaching serfdom or even slavery.

People's Alliance (*Attydubandalagit*) In Iceland, an influential socialist electoral front, describing itself as a 'Marxist political party'. Its membership is estimated at 2,500, of the total population of 220,000 and since W.W.II it has polled from 10 per cent to 20 per cent of the votes cast. It draws its support mainly from trade unions and radical intellectuals. It advocates nationalization, generous social benefits, the withdrawal of the NATO bases and a policy of neutrality. Its origin goes back to 1921 when a radical left-wing faction of the Social-Democratic Party joined the COMINTERN. Formally, the faction seceded from the S.-D.P. in 1938 and merged with the Communist Party of Iceland (founded in 1930) to form the United Socialist Labour Party. In an effort to form a popular electoral front in 1956, the Communists joined with the left-wing members of the S.-D.P. to create the P.A. It has maintained good relations with the USSR, but in the Sino-Soviet dispute it adopted a neutral stand. The Alliance publishes a daily organ called *Thodviljin* (*Nation's Will*).

People's Army (*Armia Ludowa*, in Polish) An underground military organization, mostly known as *AL*, created by a decree on 1 Jan. 1944 issued by the Home National Council collaborating with the Soviet regime, in defiance of the Polish government-in-exile in London. The purpose of the P.A. was to bring various left-wing partisan and other resistance groups together and carry on the underground struggle against Germany. The creation of the P.A. was largely a political move to rival the well-developed Home Army (*Armia Krajowa*, or *AK*) loyal to the government based in London. The Maximum size reached by the P.A. was 60,000, compared with the Home Army's 300,000. The P.A. from the start was dominated by the Communist party (called at that time the Polish Workers' Party), which attached great importance to ideological indoctrination. On 21 July 1944 the P.A. was integrated with the Polish Army (initially created in the USSR) and formed the Polish Armed Forces, which became the mainstay of the Polish Communist regime. During the Warsaw Uprising (1 Aug. – 2 Sep. 1944) the Communist controlled P.A., under Soviet direction, refused to help the Home

Army fighting a desperate battle against Germany.

People's Bank of China The central bank of the PR of China, with its head office in Peking. It operates more than 34,000 branches and agencies throughout the country, and also has a branch in Hong Kong supervising a dozen Chinese-owned or controlled banks in the Colony. The P.B.C. is the largest bank in the world in terms of the persons employed (over 500,000).

People's Capitalism A social system where a large proportion of national wealth is widely diffused to the working people or is held by the democratic state, sufficient to ensure social justice. Under this system, democratic freedoms, private enterprise and the operation of the market mechanism are retained. State involvement in the economy and social processes is considerable, but the state does not represent the interests of a particular (ruling) social class, rather of the whole society. P.c. has been advocated for a long time by Social-Democratic parties and it is often claimed that it has been largely achieved in the most progressive and affluent Western European countries. Thus, the existing p.c. is contrasted with the 19th c. capitalism that Marx knew. Marxism-Leninism rejects the validity of p.c. as a sufficient solution to the inherent weaknesses of capitalism. Marxists point out that the capitalist framework is still basically retained, there is still a high concentration of property in the hands of the rich, there are great differences of personal income and the antagonistic class relations fundamentally remain.

People's Chamber The English version of *VOLKSKAMMER* (the East German parliament).

People's Commissar The official designation introduced by the Bolsheviks after the Revolution for government ministers, to indicate that the new government was different from the Tsarist establishment.

Thus, the Council of People's Commissars replaced the Council of Ministers. As the designation caused confusion among foreign dignitaries, in 1946 the term was changed back to 'Minister'.

People's Commissariat The official name of the government ministry or department in the USSR from 1917 to 1946. A P.C. was headed by a People's Commissar. Owing to the greater Soviet involvement with foreign governments after W.W.II the Soviet regime reverted back to the pre-revolutionary designations of 'Ministry' and 'Minister'.

People's Commune A multi-purpose social organization developed in the People's Republic of China. It represents a combination of a production unit, state administration and a more or less self-contained community. Rural communes were first established in 1958 by consolidating 10–30 collective farms (of some 5,000 households with about 20,000 persons) in each case into larger entities. By the end of the year, 99 per cent of the rural households were amalgamated. In addition to farming pursuits, a p.c. normally engages in extractive, construction and industrial activities according to the local conditions, such as fishing, timber cutting, mining, quarrying, the building of roads, dams, bridges, irrigation facilities, dwellings, a simple processing of the local farming products and the manufacturing of implements, household effects and more complex items. These activities are usually carried on off-season when there is little or no agricultural work. To some extent a p.c. resembles an AGRO-INDUSTRIAL COMPLEX in the European Socialist countries. Considerable importance is attached to communal living which is promoted to varying degrees by communal mess-halls, nurseries, laundries and by educational, cultural, sporting and entertainment programmes. It is also a unit of military organization. A p.c. is administered by a management committee headed by the chairman who is also the local chief executive representa-

tive of the state. The committee is responsible for overall planning, co-ordination
and the provision of major facilities of
communal importance such as tractors,
pumping stations and industrial plants.
Otherwise, most means of production are
concentrated in the hands of brigades.
Below are teams representing operational
units which are also responsible for minor
items of equipment. Each brigade is usually a separate accounting entity and handles its own acquisitions and sales. Its gross
income is normally distributed for the following purposes: 1. payment for materials
and power used; 2. its own investment
provision; 3. the commune investment
fund administered by the management
committee; 4. the socio-cultural fund; 5.
the social provident fund; and 6. the wage
fund. Wage payments are based on the
quantity and quality of work of the teams
and of the individual members, but great
importance is attached to MORAL INCEN-
TIVES. Urban communes began to be established on a wider scale in 1960. They
may include workshops, factories and various service establishments (especially
canteens, restaurants, tailor and repair
shops, and hairdressing salons), in many
cases employing mostly women. An urban
c. is administered along similar lines to a
rural c., but if there are any factories they
usually enjoy a good deal of independence
from the communal management committee. Ideologically, a c. is regarded as a
basic unit of social organization instrumental in advancing socialist society to
FULL COMMUNISM by the transformation
of collective into all-people's ownership of
the means of production and by speeding
up progress in the methods of production,
education, social relations and communist
morality in general. However, in practice
the success of the communes has been well
below original expectations and in many
cases they have proved a complete failure.
A large number had to be disbanded during the crisis of 1959–61, following the
GREAT LEAP FORWARD. There has been a
shift of emphasis to agricultural pursuits.
A good deal of responsibility and power
has been transferred from brigades to
teams. Work groups and a more liberal
treatment has been accorded to individual
(private) plots. There are now over
70,000 communes in which more than
100m. families live.

People's Daily The English title of JEN-
MIN JIH-PAO.

People's Democracy The term first used
by the Soviets after W.W.II for the political and social system in other Socialist
countries of Eastern Europe and Asia, to
indicate that ideologically it was a lower
stage than the 'Socialist' democracy in the
USSR. The distinguishing features of p.d.
as understood now are: 1. united (or patriotic, national or people's) electoral
fronts led and dominated by Communist
parties, exercising different forms of the
dictatorship of the proletariat; 2. universal, equal and direct voting rights by secret
ballot; 3. economic democracy in the
sense that the means of production have
been socialized and private large capitalists have been eliminated; and 4. a well
developed social security which, together
with the universal right to work and continuous full employment, have removed
poverty and uplifted the standard of living
of the lowest social strata. In the prevailing Western view, p.d. does not meet the
basic requirements for democracy because: 1. there is no multiple-party system
as power is concentrated in the Communist party. In effect (though not necessarily
in name) there is a MONO-PARTY SYSTEM
OF GOVERNMENT; 2. the DICTATORSHIP OF
THE PROLETARIAT is undemocratic; 3.
elections are not free as candidates not
approved by the Communist party are not
allowed to stand; 4. LAW is not the basis of
the political and social order, as it is regarded to have no ethical value in itself,
but is explicitly employed to serve the
interests of only one political party; and 5.
HUMAN RIGHTS are violated, even though
formally guaranteed.

People's Democratic Dictatorship A version of the DICTATORSHIP OF THE PRO-
LETARIAT officially adopted in most East-

ern European countries, PR of China, DPR of Korea and PR of Mongolia. In contrast to the Soviet political, economic and social system, p.d.d. allows the existence of other non-bourgeois political parties under the so-called UNITED FRONT (led and dominated by the Communist party). P.d.d. is regarded as an early, transitional stage towards an exclusive mono-party system of government. The phrase was popularized by Mao Tse-tung in a document he prepared himself, *On People's Democratic Dictatorship*, in 1949 before the official proclamation of the PR of China on 1 Oct. 1949.

People's Front A term sometimes applied to a loose collaboration in capitalist countries among different organizations representing the interests of the working class in its broad sense, embracing industrial workers, peasants, clerical employees, and small businessmen. In contrast to the POPULAR FRONT, RED FRONT and the UNITED FRONT, the P.F. usually implies co-operation on a problem of common concern. Marxists are, in general, contemptuous of this type of action, as in their view it only helps remove the worst features of capitalism, thereby delaying the need for a PROLETARIAN REVOLUTION.

People's Great Hural In the MONGOLIAN PEOPLE'S REPUBLIC, a unicameral parliament, consisting of 354 deputies, the highest formal source of state power. The deputies are elected for a term of four years from a single list of candidates approved by the MONGOLIAN PEOPLE'S REVOLUTIONARY PARTY. Every candidate is elected unopposed and, according to official figures, 99.9 per cent of the electors vote for them. The executive body of the P.G.H. is the Presidium consisting of a Chairman (Y. Tsedenbal, who is also the Party leader), a Vice-Chairman, a Secretary and five other Members.

People's Guards (*Gwardia Ludowa* or *GW*, in Polish) An underground military organization in Poland, created by the Communist party in March 1942, as an ideological counter to the Home Army (loyal to the Polish government-in-exile in London). The activities of the P.G. focused on two objectives: 1. resistance to the German occupational forces; and 2. the development of a military arm of the Communist party in a bid to seize power after the defeat of Germany and forestall the reinstatement of a non-Communist government. In 1943, the P.G. had about 60 partisan units, a small fraction of what the Home Army had. After 1 Jan. 1944, the P.G. were integrated with the PEOPLE'S ARMY, of which they became the main constituent.

People's Liberation Army The official name of the Chinese army controlled by the Communist regime. Its origin goes back to 1927, when several units, led by CHOU EN-LAI and CHU TEH, rebelled against the KUOMINTANG and formed the Chinese Red Army, the military arm of the CHINESE COMMUNIST PARTY. It fought against the Kuomintang forces and then against Japan (1937–45). In 1946 it assumed its present name. The mission of the P.L.A. has always not only been to defend the country but also to implement domestic Party policies. It played a dominant role in the civil war in 1946–49, the seizure of power and the proclamation of the PR of China. It also played a prominent part during the GREAT PROLETARIAN CULTURAL REVOLUTION in 1966–69, under the leadership of LIN PIAO. In terms of manpower, the P.L.A. is the largest armed force in the world, consisting of 3,625,000 regulars (plus 300,000 in the navy, 400,000 in the air force, not to mention the Reserve Army and para-military forces).

People's Political Consultative Conference A conference of political parties and other groups opposed to Chiang Kai-shek's regime held in Peking on 30 Sep. 1949. It was chaired by Mao Tse-tung and can be regarded as the predecessor of the NATIONAL PEOPLE'S CONGRESS. Four social classes were represented at the Conference – the working class, peasantry, the middle class and the national bourgeoisie, who were deemed to constitute the 'people' led by the Chinese Communist Party. The Conference examined Mao's document *On the People's Democratic Dictatorship* and on its basis issued the ORGANIC LAW and the COMMON PROGRAMME, which served as the bases for the formation of the Chinese Communist Government and China's first Constitution adopted by the first National People's Congress in 1954. The proclamation of the PR of China was officially made on the day following the conference (1 Oct. 1949).

People's Revolutionary Party of Benin (*Parti Révolutionnaire Populaire de Benin*) – a small Marxist-Leninist party in the People's Republic of Benin (before Dec. 1975 known as Dahomey). The Party was founded in Dec. 1975, when the name of the country was changed and when the Party absorbed the National Council of Revolution. It is the only legal political party in the country organized on the basis of DEMOCRATIC CENTRALISM and its Marxism is adapted pragmatically to local conditions. The Party's Central Committee plays a leading role in the government. The latter has established close relations with the Socialist countries, especially China and the DPR of Korea. There is an illegal opposition party called the Front for the Liberation and Rehabilitation of Dahomey.

People's Revolutionary Party of Laos (*Phak Pasason Pativat Lao*) The ruling political party subscribing to Marxism-Leninism in the People's Democratic Republic of LAOS. The Party's origin goes back to 1930, when the Communist Party of Indochina was founded, within which, in 1934, the Restoration Party of Laos was formed. Towards the end of W.W.II the latter created a military arm called the PATHET LAO. After some reorganization, in 1955 a Marxist-Leninist People's Party of Laos was established, which by the early 1970s came to dominate Laotian

politics. In 1975 it changed its name to its present designation and in Dec. of the same year seized power in a coup. The Party's membership is about 15,000 (compared with the country's population of 3,550,000, as of 1978). The Party has endeavoured to steer a neutral course in the Sino-Soviet dispute, but there have been conflicting internal conflicts between pro-Soviet, pro-Kampuchean and pro-Chinese factions.

People's University A residential, tertiary educational institution for peasant youth developed in the Scandinavian and East European countries in the 19th c. The idea of the p.u. was worked out by a Dane, N. F. S. Grundtvig, and the first institution of this type was established at Rödding (North Schleswig, Denmark). The teaching programme at a typical p.u. included history, literature and natural sciences and a good deal of emphasis on cultural and social activities. The development of the idea of the p.u. attracted a good deal of interest not only among social reformers but also Marxists. To some extent the idea of a p.u. has been applied in various models of the COMMUNIST UNIVERSITY in the Socialist countries.

Perception In philosophy, the discovery by means of the senses, aided by past experience and thinking, of the existence and characteristics of the external world. The concept of p. is interpreted differently in the two opposite divisions of philosophy, IDEALISM and MATERIALISM, and consequently has become an object of ideological controversy. On the whole, idealists consider p. as being primary in relation to the objects perceived, maintaining that the material world is a creation of our p. On the other hand, materialism views p. as a direct reflection of the material objects and phenomena, irrespective of man's consciousness. P. is seen as a reflection of the object as a whole and its relation to other objects, thus it is contrasted with impression, which is the reflection of a particular property or quality of an object.

Permanent Bureau of the CC The top policy-making body of the Central Committee of the ROMANIAN COMMUNIST PARTY. This inner body was created in 1974 and consists of five members headed by the Secretary-General (N. Ceausescu). It has no equivalent in other ruling Communist parties. It is concerned with economic policy, especially external economic relations. Together with the POLITICAL EXECUTIVE COMMITTEE OF THE CC of the RCP it corresponds to the POLITBURO in the Communist Party of the Soviet Union.

Permanent Revolution In a general sense used by revolutionaries, the view that modern societies achieve democracy and socialism through two major revolutions, viz. a BOURGEOIS-DEMOCRATIC REVOLUTION, a PROLETARIAN REVOLUTION, followed by further revolutionary changes. But in its better known sense, it means the EXPORT OF REVOLUTION to other countries, so that revolutionary processes continue supporting each other until the whole world is engulfed. The theory of the P.R. was developed by TROTSKY in *Our Revolution* (1906) and *Permanent Revolution* (1930). He was inspired by F. MEHRING, PARVUS, LASSALLE, and MARX, but the idea can be traced back further to L. Blanqui (1805–81). The theory is Trotsky's most distinctive contribution to the Marxist doctrine and is sometimes taken as synonymous with TROTSKYISM. Trotsky pressed for the implementation of his postulate of the P.R. soon after the October Revolution in Russia in 1917, maintaining that the defeat of capitalism was possible only by the continuation of the revolution in other countries, whereby capitalist institutions and values could be destroyed to make it easier to develop a new social system. He also believed that the revolution could not succeed in one country alone, especially in Russia, a country that was considered to be less mature for a revolution than the industrialized countries of Western Europe. It appears that Trotsky convinced Lenin, and the COMINTERN was established in 1919 largely on this principle. The postulate of the P.R. was attacked by Stalin, especially after Lenin's death (Jan. 1924), who put forward the idea of SOCIALISM IN ONE COUNTRY instead. In this contest, Trotsky's postulate of the P.R. was rejected by the Party majority. Trotsky was subsequently expelled from the Party (1927), exiled (1929) and assassinated (1940). The idea of the P.R. is similar to, but not identical with, Mao Tse-tung's CONTINUING REVOLUTION.

Personalism A philosophical movement based on the acceptance of personality as the primary reality and the spiritual determinant of being. It treats nature as a complex of spirits, where the spiritual element constitutes the basic driving force of physical as well as biological phenomena. Development in nature is seen as proceeding according to preordained order, conditioned by supernatural powers. God is accepted as the highest form of personality, endowed with reason and will, who created the world. In order to improve the social system, it is necessary to perfect personality, especially the soul. Among the main exponents of p. were B. P. Bowne (1847–1910), E. S. Brightman (1884–1953), E. Mounier (1905–50) and L. V. Stern (1871–1938). Marxist philosophy is strongly opposed to p., regarding it as one of the extreme forms of IDEALISM accepting the basic precepts of religion, thus being inconsistent with MATERIALISM. Marxist philosophers point out that the primary element of being is MATTER, and personality is a product of the natural and social environment. The social system can be improved by perfecting the production and living conditions of people. It is society that determines personality, not the other way round.

Personality Cult An exaggerated view of a leader's ability and importance, elevating him to a god-like stature. The concept is usually identified with the autocratic rule by STALIN and the immense adulation accorded to him, especially after W.W.II. To some extent, the p.c. was, or has been, also associated with MAO TSE-TUNG, HO CHI MINH, E. HOXHA, KIM IL-SUNG and J. B. TITO. It is also an expression of the view that the course of history is determined by heroes, while the masses are essentially passive. The factors which enable the emergence of the p.c. in the Socialist countries include the DICTATORSHIP OF THE PROLETARIAT, the MONO-PARTY SYSTEM OF GOVERNMENT, the complete state control of the media and the ubiquitous and ruthless police system. The term p.c. was first popularized in the USSR after the TWENTIETH CONGRESS OF THE CPSU in 1956, when Stalin was condemned for the monopolization of power in defiance of the principle of COLLECTIVE LEADERSHIP, his violation of SOCIALIST LEGALITY and his unnecessary atrocities (KHRUSHCHEV'S SECRET SPEECH). The p.c. is inconsistent with the Marxist doctrine on the subject, as expounded by Engels (in a letter to H. Starkenburg of 25 Jan. 1894) and Plekhanov (in *The Role of the Individual in History*, 1898). The so-called 'great men' are a product of the material and social environment and it is society that makes men, not vice versa. Marxism also stresses that the masses are capable of embarking on a proletarian revolution and no leader could win without their active participation.

Personal Plots See SUBSIDIARY PLOTS.

Perspective Plan Long-term economic plan covering 15–20 years ahead. As such, it is set out in terms of broad objectives (while short-term and medium-term plans are more specific). A p.p. is mostly concerned with the expected or desired technological developments and the ways and means of making long-term adjustments.

Peruvian Communist Party (*Partido Comunista Peruano*) A small, disunited and partly illegal party. It began as the Peruvian Socialist Party, founded in 1928, but changed its name to the P.C.P. in 1930. Although it became quite active soon after W.W.II, it was declared illegal in 1948 and remained so until 1956. It was revitalized in 1963, but soon split into two factions – a larger pro-Soviet group and a smaller but more radical pro-Chinese fraternity (but both using the same name of the P.C.P.). The membership of the former in the late 1970s was 2,000 and of the latter about 1,200 (compared with the country's total population of 16,800,000). Most of the Communist support comes from workers, some professional groups and students, while peasants are hardly affected at all. The pro-Soviet faction publishes a weekly, *Unidad* (*Unity*), while the pro-Chinese group publishes *Bandera roja* (*Red Flag*), a news-sheet appearing irregularly.

Peterloo A massacre in St Peter's Fields (near Manchester) on 16 Aug. 1819 of English workers who demonstrated against the Corn Laws (i.e. high prices of grains), unemployment, starvation and the destitution of the working class in general. The massacre was carried out by the mounted police on instructions from the Tory government. After the incident, the local labour organization sent a letter to the government congratulating it on its victory, following Waterloo, 'at Peterloo'.

Petöfi Circle A patriotic technical intelligentsia group in Hungary which came into prominence during the HUNGARIAN UPRISING of 1956. It demanded political freedom and an end to censorship, the secret police and autocratic and crude cultural policies. The Circle was named after S. Petöfi, the prominent Hungarian national poet. Petöfi was a youthful revolutionary who served in Kossuth's army as aide-de-camp to Gen. Behm during the Revolution of 1848 and who fell at the Battle of Segesvár against Tsarist Russia.

Petrashevtists A middle-class circle, led by M. V. Butashevich-Petrashevsky (1821–66), in mid-nineteenth century Russia which campaigned for the emancipation of the peasants, the abolition of servitude, the liberation of women and other liberal reforms. They were also opposed to RELIGION and MYSTICISM and instead accepted philosophical MATERIALISM. The P. were mostly intellectuals of a humble social background (known as the *RAZNOCHINTSY*), but did not have a clear programme of action. They fell into two groups – a moderate faction, which concentrated on discussions and propaganda, and a revolutionary group, which advocated violent action. The P. were suppressed by the Tsarist police in 1849 and Petrashevsky was sentenced to death (later commuted to life exile in Siberia). Marxists acknowledged the contribution of the P. to the early reform movement in Russia. But they regarded them as basically an expression of the bourgeois-democratic movement, rather dilletantish in their approach and an example of UTOPIAN SOCIALISM.

Petrograd ('Peter's Town', in Russian) The name of the capital city of Russia over the period 1912–18 and the site of the GREAT OCTOBER SOCIALIST REVOLUTION of 1917, in which the PETROGRAD SOVIET played a crucial part. Before 1912 the city's name was St Petersburg (founded by Peter the Great on swamps in 1703) and after March 1924 it was renamed Leningrad.

Petrograd Soviet A council of workers' and soldiers' deputies established in Petrograd (now Leningrad) on 27 Feb. (O.-S.C.) 1917, on the day when the Tsarist regime was overthrown in the FEBRUARY REVOLUTION. The P.S. became the main rival source of power challenging the PROVISIONAL GOVERNMENT. Under pressure from the BOLSHEVIKS, the P.S. issued the SOVIET ORDER NO.1 (on 1 March 1917), preventing the DUMA committee from using the Petrograd garrison against the rebellious Bolsheviks and other opponents of the Provisional Government. Although the Bolsheviks were at first in a minority, by Sep. 1917 they came to dominate the P.S. (with the aid of the LEFT SOCIALIST REVOLUTIONARIES). During the GREAT OCTOBER SOCIALIST REVOLUTION (24–25 Oct. 1917) the Bolsheviks used the Military Revolutionary Committee of the P.S. (created on 12 Oct. 1917) as their base for directing the seizure of power from the Provisional Government, which put them in a position to enlist the support of the Petrograd garrison.

Petty Bourgeois A Marxist term pertaining to the PETTY BOURGEOISIE.

Petty Bourgeois Anarchism A label applied by revolutionary Marxists to the movement among the ultra-liberal lower middle class, advocating far-reaching personal freedom, reasonable equality and, above all, the destruction of the state as an instrument of oppression (whether in the hands of the BIG BOURGEOISIE or the Communist party). The father of this movement was P. J. PROUDHON. P.b.a. is against the CLASS STRUGGLE, REVOLUTION and the DICTATORSHIP OF THE PROLETARIAT, and instead advocates a gradual transformation of society 'from below' and the retention of small private property and the development of group ownership. From the standpoint of MARXISM-LENINISM, p.b.a. vacillates too much to be of any revolutionary value and historically, in Russia, was classed as counter-revolutionary.

Petty Bourgeois Democrats Liberal socialists, mostly embracing the lower middle class and intellectuals, opposed to extremism. The description was used by Lenin at a Party meeting in Moscow on 27 Nov. 1918 in application to the MENSHEVIKS and the SOCIALIST REVOLUTIONARIES.

Petty Bourgeoisie A label popularized by Marx and Engels and commonly used in Communist terminology, roughly denoting the lower middle class ('small capitalists'). The p.b. is a social class between the industrial workers and the capitalist middle class owning some property. It includes small manufacturers, workshop owners, small landowners and shopkeepers. Lenin and Stalin included well-to-do peasants as well in this category. This class is hardworking and resourceful and its ambition is to rise to the ranks of the BOURGEOISIE and the BIG BOURGEOISIE. The outlook of the p.b. is rather conservative, but it is capable of becoming revolutionary. Consequently, Marxists treat it as a potential ally in the early stages of the socialist revolution.

Petty Bourgeois Socialism A phrase used by revolutionary Marxists to describe the type of socialism advocated by the PETTY BOURGEOISIE, which is opposed to the dominance by the BIG BOURGEOISIE as well as to the PROLETARIAN REVOLUTION and the DICTATORSHIP OF THE PROLETARIAT. It essentially reflects the interests of the lower middle class which suffers from the power and growth of big business, but does not wish to be completely dispossessed and reduced to the PROLETARIAT. P.b.s. favours substantial state intervention, especially in the form of anti-monopoly legislation and control, a return to quasi-medieval production organization and the development of co-operative production, banking and marketing. The main representative thinkers of p.b.s. were J. BLANC and P. J. PROUDHON in France, and J. F. Bray (1804–95), J. Gray (1798–1850) and W. Thompson (1785–1833) in Britain. Marx and Engels attacked p.b.s. as one of the less desirable versions of UTOPIAN SOCIALISM. In their view, p.b.s. was not radical enough in that it merely wanted minor reforms, basically within the framework of capitalism, disregarding the interests of the proletariat.

PGR Polish abbreviation of *Państwowe Gospodarstwo Rolne*, meaning STATE FARM.

Phalanstery, Phalanx Two central features of the social and economic organization in the ideal future society envisaged by CH. FOURIER. In his model a phalanstery occupied about a square mile, with farm common buildings on its outskirts. The buildings were to include workshops, a communal dining hall, a school, a crèche, recreation facilities and private dwellings. The phalanstery was to be occupied by a phalanx, a basic unit of social organization consisting of about 1,800 persons – a number sufficient to encompass a reasonable range of human capacities, and yet not too large for harmonious fraternal communal life. The phalanx was to consist of about 8–10 series, each series subdivided into 24–32 groups and each group to consist of seven or more persons. Fourier and his supporters believed that this organization would combine the advantages of community life with individual freedom and privacy. Furthermore, work would become interesting and creative as it would include both farming and industrial activities. Each member would engage in that type of work for which he or she is best fitted by training, ability and interest. Marx and Engels dismissed these ideas as impractical, exemplifying UTOPIAN SOCIALISM, not providing real solutions to social problems in the industrial age.

Phalanx Socialism A harmonious version of social organization proposed by CH. FOURIER, the main features of which were to be PHALANSTERY and the PHALANX.

Phenomenalism An idealistic philosophical theory, according to which COGNITION is limited only to phenomena (appearances and events), while the real existence of objects is beyond human cognition. The basis of p. can be found in I. Kant (1724–1804), who maintained that phenomena were complexes of human impressions. Marxist philosophers consider p. as a version of SUBJECTIVE IDEALISM, contradictory to DIALECTICAL MATERIALISM. They emphasize that there is no barrier between phenomena and real existence, and that the latter can be known by man through practice, such as his material production activities.

Phenomenology A school of philosophy preoccupied with the study of the phenomena of pure transcendental consciousness in their relation to ideas representing objects. Phenomena are seen as being independent of man's perceptual experience and based on man's intellectual intuition. This school of thought was founded by a German philosopher, E. Husserl (1859–1938) who was greatly influenced by F. Brentano (1838–1917). P. is rejected in Marxist philosophy as a reactionary theory belonging to SUBJECTIVE IDEALISM and in opposition to DIALECTICAL MATERIALISM. Orthodox Marxists point out that p. reduces itself to idle philosophical speculation, completely divorced from natural and social reality. It is also anti-social as it diverts human attention away from the real problems of life and science and, like its related theory of EXISTENTIALISM, leads to the demoralization of social consciousness. The French phenomenoloist, M. Merleau-Ponty (1908–61), in his *Humanism and Terror* (1947) and *Adventures of the Dialectic* (1955), criticized the Stalinist terror and examined the problem of violence in Marxist theory put into practice, respectively.

Philanthropy See CHARITIES.

Philosophical Notebooks A collection of philosophical contributions written by LENIN over the period 1914–16 in Berne which, although originally not meant for publication, were published in 1929–30. They embody critical notes and significant Marxist generalizations from his study of some philosophical works, especially K. Marx, F. Engels, *The HOLY FAMILY*, L. FEUERBACH, *Lectures on the Nature of Religion*, G.W.F.HEGEL, *The Science of Logic*, *Lectures on the Philosophy of History* and *Lectures on the History of Philosophy*, F. LASSALLE, *Philosophy of Heraclitus the Dark of Ephesus* and Aristotle, *Metaphysics*. Lenin's most significant contribution in the *P.N.* is considered to be his analytical exposition of materialist DIALECTICS. The *P.N.* also include notes on natural philosophy, a critique of IDEALISM as presented by Hegel, of the HEGELIAN LEFT, of Feuerbach's MATERIALISM and Kant's AGNOSTICISM,

the part played by CONTRADICTION in SELF-MOVEMENT and other philosophical interpretations in support of SCIENTIFIC SOCIALISM and PARTY-MINDEDNESS.

Philosophy Literally (in Greek) the 'love of wisdom', the area of human thought on the most general principles concerning the world's existence, man's relation to it and human thought. P. is the oldest learned discipline, going back to the ancient times (especially in China and Greece). Up to the 19th c. it guided and interpreted all other sciences and was sometimes described as the 'science of sciences' or the 'science above all other sciences'. P. is noted for a large number of different doctrines, theories, directions, schools and views, many being inconsistent with each other. But basically, two opposing divisions emerged in ancient times and have continued ever since, viz. IDEALISM and MATERIALISM. This division is conditioned by the opposite approach to the 'basic problem of p.', viz. the relation of IDEAS to MATTER. Idealism regards CONSCIOUSNESS and thought as primary. On the other hand, materialism treats BEING and reality as primary, while ideas, consciousness and thought are secondary, derived from the material world. Beginning in the early 1840s, p. has become an ideological battleground between Marxism and capitalism. Marx and Engels, in *The HOLY FAMILY* (1845) and *The GERMAN IDEOLOGY* (1846), attacked idealism as the p. of priests, exploiters and imperialists. Most Marxist philosophers ever since have taken the stand that p. cannot be neutral and above ideology and the class struggle, but must be employed as a 'theoretical weapon steering the strategy of the revolutionary proletariat' (PARTISANSHIP). It is postulated that only materialism can provide the correct philosophical basis for the understanding of all the fundamental issues in nature and society. It is further insisted that DIALECTICAL MATERIALISM and HISTORICAL MATERIALISM have proved radical 'leaps' in the history of p., rendering non-Marxist p. anachronistic.

Photosynthesis The process of assimilation by plants of carbon dioxide with the aid of solar energy (infra and ultra red rays) and chlorophyll. Discovered by a Dutch botanist, I. Ingenhousz (1730–99) and further explored by many other scholars, including K. A. TIMIRIAZIEV and I. V. MICHURIN, Marxists have embraced p. as an example of the transformation of energy. In their view, p. lends support to the philosophy of MATERIALISM, thereby negating VITALISM, which further proves that plant species are not only a product of heredity, but more importantly of environmental factors. Consequently, plants, like human beings, can be improved by changing the environment appropriately.

Phuoc Quoc ('National Restoration', in Vietnamese) An anti-Communist movement in South Vietnam, which has emerged since the Communist takeover in 1975. The movement does not appear to be nationally co-ordinated, but rather limited to five areas: 1. in the Hao Hao villages in the Mekong Delta, along the Kampuchean border; 2. the Montagnard communities in the Lam Dong province; 3. the Catholic villages of the Ho Nai region, north of Ho Chi Minh City (formerly Saigon); 4. the people of Cao Dai in the Tay Ninh province; and 5. the nationalist groups of the Hue and Quang Nam region.

Physical Balancing A technique applied in Socialist CENTRAL ECONOMIC PLANNING. It consists in the construction of economic plans in such a way that the inputs of enterprises are balanced with the outputs of other enterprises using physical units of measurement, such as weight, number, length, capacity and the like. Under this system, there is no need for prices, therefore, a plan can be kept consistent throughout its implementation. But the system is not conducive to the most efficient allocation of resources. For this reason, there is a tendency in the more advanced Socialist countries to express input-output flows in value terms. Also

MATERIAL BALANCES, OPTIMAL PLANNING.

Physical Idealism A term introduced by Lenin (in *MATERIALISM AND EMPIRIOCRITICISM*) to describe those philosophical schools which, using the new discoveries in the physical sciences in the latter part of the 19th c. and the early years of the 20th c., endeavoured to discredit MATERIALISM in the cause of IDEALISM. The main argument of p.i. was that matter could disappear and could be created, as demonstrated by the discoveries in atomic physics, viz. photons could become electrons and positrons, and vice versa. Quantum theory and relativity theory have also been employed to support idealism against materialism. Some of the exponents of this movement included N. Bohr, W. Heisenberg and C. Schroedinger. Lenin described p.i. as a subjectivist-idealistic movement seeking to reconcile science with religion, prompted by reactionary class interests. He pointed out that there was no question of matter disappearing or appearing, but rather its dialectical transformation from and into the forms unknown before. Philosophical materialism, in his view, is not concerned with matter as it had been known to scientists before (perceptibility to senses, gravitation, inertia), but the characteristics of being OBJECTIVE REALITY outside our consciousness.

Physical Labour See MENTAL AND PHYSICAL LABOUR.

Physiocratism An early French school of classical political economy, founded in the 1750s by F. Quesnay (1694–1774) regarding commercial agriculture as the only source of value. The Physiocrats distinguished three social classes in relation to production and distribution: 1. the productive class – farmers, the only class creating surplus product; 2. the appropriating class – property owners, royal and aristocratic households, officials, clergymen and others engaging in nonproductive services; and 3. the sterile class – those engaged in industry, receiving raw materials from the productive class and creating only the value that they consume in the form of subsistence from the farmers. These relations were represented in Quesnay's two 'Economic Tables' (1758, 1768). P. was in favour of *LAISSEZ-FAIRE* and FREE TRADE. Marx and Engels thoroughly studied p. and accepted it in some respects but condemned it in most others. They agreed with the idea of material production as the only source of value and wealth and commended Quesnay on his pioneering model of the REPRODUCTION of social capital. They also acknowledged his exposure of the exploiting class and utilized his ideas in their economic and social theories. But they pointed out that p. in fact represented an ideological expression of the interests of the farming bourgeoisie, basically interested in the retention of the existing social system and opposed to state intervention in production and trade. At the same time, the role and interests of the workers and peasants were conveniently ignored. In examining Quesnay's notion of surplus value, Engels (in *ANTI-DÜHRING*) pointed out that interests and profit were also forms of surplus value, appropriated by the exploiting groups.

Piatiletka Another form of the English spelling of *PYATILETKA*.

Picketing The main measure applied by workers during an industrial dispute (especially a STRIKE) to make it effective internally and externally. The strike committee places guards in and around the place of employment to ensure that: 1. all the workers join the strike; 2. no strike breakers enter the establishment; and 3. maximum publicity is given to win the support of the public (including dissuading customers from entering the firm's premises). The term was first used in this sense by Baron Bromwell in England in 1867, although its origin can be traced back to the middle of the 18th c.

Piecework Wages A basis of the remuneration of workers, according to the quantity of the output produced or the number of tasks performed. In general, this basis is applied where employees work individually, or at least the contribution of each worker is clearly identifiable. Traditionally, organized labour has regarded p.w. with suspicion as they lead to cut-throat competition among workers, sweated labour, wide disparities in wage earnings and are inimical to workers' solidarity. In capitalist countries, before W.W.I., some two-thirds of the manual workers were paid by p.w., but the proportion today is about one-third. Marx (in *CAPITAL*, vol. I) said that p.w. were 'most in harmony with the capitalist mode of production'. In the Socialist countries, p.w. were commonly applied up to the late 1950s, when two-thirds of all the work force was remunerated on this basis. P.w. paid to teams and other groups of workers have been considered ideologically superior to individual p.w. But p.w. encourage a poor quality of output and a wasteful use of materials. Since about 1960, there has been a tendency for p.w. to be replaced by TIME WAGES. Today, roughly one-third of the work force is on p.w., roughly the same proportion as in capitalist countries.

Pilsen Riots A little publicized revolt by workers in the industrial city of Pilsen (Plzen) in Czechoslovakia in June 1953, in protest against oppressive working and living conditions. The riots involving workers as they did, and not former capitalists, or dissidents or intellectuals, were directed against the Stalinist regime in the wake of Stalin's death (March 1953).

Ping Pong Diplomacy An expression applied to the Chinese overtures in the early 1970s towards the improvement of Sino-American relations, to which the US Government responded favourably. The p.p.d. was initiated in April 1971 when China invited an American team to play table tennis in China, which was accepted and reciprocated. The p.p.d. is an example of linking politics with sport for constructive purposes. The Chinese initiative was prompted by four major considerations: 1. the determination to give more attention to external relations, in contrast to the previous preoccupation with domestic policies; 2. the need to search for potential allies against the USSR; 3. the desire to speed up the American disengagement from Asia; and 4. the eagerness to develop a wider diplomatic recognition of China in the world by softening American opposition.

Pink, Pinko Slang terms used by radicals for a left-wing inclined person, too timid or not resourceful enough to declare openly his views and back them up with action. The colour allusion is to 'imperfect red'. Also 'RADISH COMMUNISTS'.

Pinyin ('Phonetic spelling', in Chinese) The new system of spelling Chinese words in other languages, introduced by the Chinese authorities as from Jan. 1979. *P.* more closely approximates spoken Chinese than, for example, the previously commonly accepted English spelling version called the WADE-GILES SYSTEM. *P.* better indicates the voiced consonants, so that the previously rendered 'k', 'p', 't' and 'ts' are now 'g', 'b', 'd' and 'dz', respectively. The 'ch' and 'hs' are now rendered as 'j' and 'x'. Thus, such well established names as Chiang Ch'ing, Hong Kong, Hua kuo-feng, Mao Tse-tung, Peking, Teng Hsiao-ping are now rendered in *P.* as Jiang Qing, Xiong Gong, Hua Guofeng, Mao Dzedong, Beijing and Deng Xiaoping.

Pioneers The Communist organization in the USSR for children aged 10–15. Although membership is not compulsory, most children belong to it. The organization, founded in 1924, is supervised by the COMMUNIST PARTY OF THE SOVIET UNION and is meant to prepare boys and girls for membership of the *KOMSOMOL*. The purpose of the *P.* is to inculcate some Communist ideals into children at an early age and extend their civic education through interesting participatory activities, such as festivals, camps, sport gatherings and well publicized projects of local and national importance.

Pisarev, Dimitr Ivanovich (1840–68) An outstanding Russian materialist philosopher and revolutionary democrat. He also came to be recognized as a champion of the oppressed working class and a precursor of Russian Marxism. In his short lifetime, he made important contributions in several fields of thought and in the mid-1860s emerged as the intellectual leader of the REVOLUTIONARY DEMOCRATS. He called for the overthrow of the monarchy and advocated industrialization as a road to the democratic transformation of Russia and to social justice. In philosophy and sociology, he continued in the vein of the materialist thought of N. CHERNYSHEVSKY. P. reasoned that MATTER is indestructible, eternal and infinite in spite of its different forms of appearance, and further, that it is primary while ideas are secondary and derived from it. He also held that art, like ideas, is a form of reflection of reality. In political economy, he supported the LABOUR THEORY OF VALUE and the economic interpretation of history (HISTORICAL MATERIALISM). P. was hailed by Marxists as a progressive social thinker and a genuine social reformer. But he was criticized for the metaphysical elements in his philosophy and failure to see the social significance of music, sculpture and painting. P.'s life ended tragically by drowning, at the age of 28. His main works were: *Scholasticism of the Nineteenth Century* (1861); *Thoughts on the History of Labour* (1863); *Progress in Fauna and Flora* (1864); *Heinrich Heine* (1867); and *The French Peasant in 1789* (1868).

PLA Abbreviation for the PEOPLE'S LIBERATION ARMY (of China).

Plan See ECONOMIC PLAN.

Plan Consistency A term used in central economic planning for a co-ordination of inputs and outputs, and their appropriate synchronization, of different enterprises so that the overall plan is feasible, ie within the possibility of practical implementation. The central problem is that the targets set must be within the capacity of the enterprises for fulfilment, i.e. must be backed up by appropriate fixed assets, deliveries of materials and power at the right time with the availability of the necessary labour. If the plan is not consistent, BOTTLENECKS appear, leading to a chain reaction of non-fulfilment. P.c. does not necessarily guarantee the optimal performance of a plan (OPTIMAL PLANNING).

Plan Co-ordination A planning procedure consisting of an arrangement of targets and other tasks that are mutually consistent, and consequently, are conducive to the fulfilment of the plan and to a smooth economic development. P.c. is carried on at different levels of management, branches of industry, and ministerial and national levels, but the ultimate responsibility rests with the STATE PLANNING COMMISSION. P.c. is essential owing to the many entities involved, complex objectives and conflicting interests. The main technique employed in p.c. is the method of MATERIAL BALANCES.

Plan Fulfilment See PLAN IMPLEMENTATION.

Plan Guidelines In socialist economic planning, a set of general indicators and recommendations for medium-term and short-term plans worked out by the State Planning Commission, in consultation with the ministries and regional authorities and discussed with and passed by the Council of Ministers. P.g. are usually concerned with investment, the maintenance of fixed assets, innovations, export and import. The guidelines provide a basis for the disassembly of the overall planned tasks at different levels of economic administration and management. On the basis of the p.g., proposed plans are coordinated by the State Planning Commission and finally a national ECONOMIC PLAN is reached.

Plan Implementation The fulfilment of TARGETS and other tasks by specified dates, as laid down in the ECONOMIC PLAN.

The first condition of p.i. is PLAN CONSISTENCY. Since p.i. at micro as well as macro levels is conditional to a smooth pace of economic development, there are institutionalized procedures for ensuring its orderly achievement. Firstly, there is current or operational control of the plan in the course of its fulfilment. One of the purposes of this control is to identify appearing or potential BOTTLENECKS and provide for immediate remedies. Secondly, there is the final control at the end of the planned period. Its purpose is to enforce discipline among the different levels of economic management and to enable appropriate steps to be taken in the next planning period. There are also indirect methods of control, such as the examination of the documents of deliveries and the payments made through the banking system. The highest levels of control of p.i. are the State Planning Commission, the Ministry of Finance, the Auditor-General and finally, the Parliament.

Plan Indicators, Plan Indices Other terms for planned TARGETS.

Planned Losses Those deficits at the macroeconomic or enterprise level which are allowed to arise as a result of the relevant prices being maintained by the state below production costs. P.l. are a regular feature in the socialist centrally planned economies, where PRODUCER PRICES are generally set at average (rather than marginal) cost levels for particular branches or industry, with the understanding that individual enterprises within each branch will probably differ in their efficiency. P.l. are compensated for by state subsidies paid to approved enterprises. But the latter may still be able to pay bonuses to their personnel for reasonable effort in the circumstances.

Planned Profit The profit target which an enterprise is expected to achieve in a planned economy under normal conditions over a given period. P.p. is laid down in the plan based on the authorities taking differential advantages and disadvantages into account. The attainment of the p.p. level is usually conditional to the allocation of a portion of the enterprise profit to the MA-TERIAL INCENTIVES FUND. If the p.p. is under-fulfilled or over-fulfilled, the proportion of the enterprise profit allowed for the incentives is reduced or increased respectively on a progressive basis.

Planned Profit Rate The PROFIT RATE which is worked out by a planning authority in the socialist countries and then becomes a directive, i.e. its fulfilment is conditional to the award of material incentives to the enterprise personnel. This rate may be different for each enterprise to reflect its differential advantages or disadvantages and, consequently, to impel each enterprise to do its best in the circumstances. If this is followed consistently, bonuses paid in less and in more favoured entities are likely to be about the same. The p.p.r. contrasts with the ABOVE-PLAN PROFIT RATE.

Planned Proportionate Development In its full version it is known as the law of the p.p.d. of the national economy (other translated forms of the p.p.d. are balanced proportionate d. and proportionate planned d.). It is one of the vague socialist 'economic laws', which has emerged from the observed practice of central economic planning. It purports to govern the allocation of resources on a planned basis in such a pattern that enables the implementation of social objectives in the most effective way on the macroeconomic scale. In particular, it involves: 1. the development of all major branches of the economy, even though the rate of growth of each may be planned to differ and vary; 2. the utilization of all human, natural and man-made resources (implying full employment) in accordance with the postulates of maximum economy and efficiency; 3. the planning of such a structure of production that ensures harmonious and effective development of the economy in accordance with the changing character of the factors and methods of production; and 4. the rational territorial distribution

of production within the economy as well as in relation to other (especially co-operating socialist) countries. Socialist economists stress that in a capitalist economy the proportions are likely to be irrational and anti-social, owing to the private profit motive, anarchical market forces and disruptive competition. The law was popularized by Stalin (in ECONOMIC PROBLEMS OF SOCIALISM IN THE USSR). But, contrary to the insistence by some Soviet economists, Stalin denied that it was the BASIC ECONOMIC LAW OF SOCIALISM, since in contrast to the latter, it does not embody the purpose for which economic development is pursued.

Planning See ECONOMIC PLANNING.

'Planning from Above' The basis of ECONOMIC PLANNING typical of the CENTRALIZED DIRECTIVE SYSTEM OF PLANNING AND MANAGEMENT, where targets and even methods of their implementation are handed down the hierarchical ladder. Enterprises have little independence and adopt a passive attitude, not conducive to innovations, the optimum structure of production and efficiency. This basis of planning prevailed in the socialist countries in its extreme in the 1950s (except in Yugoslavia) but has been partly abandoned since the ECONOMIC REFORMS in favour of PLANNING FROM BELOW.

'Planning from Below' Liberal economic planning introduced in some European Socialist countries as a result of the ECONOMIC REFORMS. Under this partly decentralized system, enterprises and intermediate levels of economic management become initiating or crucial elements in the planning process, while the role of the central planning authority is concentrated on the co-ordination and reconciliation of the plans initiated. A compromise approach is for the intermediate organs of economic management to issue orientation plans to enterprises and with the latter submitting counter-plans. The mutually agreed plans are then passed on to the ministries and finally to the central planning authority. 'P. from b.' is partly geared to the market and is sometimes described as 'demand planning'.

Planning Horizon A term used in the Socialist countries for the period covered by the economic plan. A short-term plan embraces 3, 6 and 12 months, a medium-term plan – 5 years (in some cases 4 or 7 years) and a long-term (also called perspective) plan – 15–20 years. The longer the p.h., the less detailed and prescriptive the plan is.

Planometrics (also **Planimetrics**) A branch of econometrics (mathematical and statistical economics) concerned with the methodology of constructing economic plans, especially working out the OPTIMAL PLAN with the aid of modern mathematical methods and computers. P. is best developed in Czechoslovakia, the German DR, Hungary, Poland and the USSR. But the term is more commonly used in the West than in the socialist countries.

Plebeians' Union A secret revolutionary and patriotic organization formed in Poznan by W. M. Stefański in 1842–43 for the purpose of national liberation and establishing a socialist society in Poland. It formulated an elaborate programme of social reforms, viz. a democratic government, reasonable social equality, a guaranteed right to work and the transformation of large estates into co-operative farms. The Union aimed at achieving its objective through an armed uprising combined with a social revolution. After the arrest of its leaders by the Prussian authorities in 1845, the P.U. ceased to exist in name, but its remaining members joined another secret organization, called the Polish Democratic Society.

Plekhanov, Georgi Valentinovich (1856–1918) The first and greatest Marxist in Russia before Lenin, a social reformer and literary critic. His working life fell into three periods: from 1873 to 1883, P. was a NARODNIK; from 1883 to 1903,

he was an orthodox Marxist; and from 1903 to 1918, he was a Menshevik. As an émigré in Switzerland after 1880, he organized the first Russian Marxist association, the EMANCIPATION OF LABOUR GROUP in Geneva in 1883 in opposition to NARODNISM and REVISIONISM. At the Second Congress of the RUSSIAN SOCIAL-DEMOCRATIC LABOUR PARTY in London in 1903, P. chaired the meeting siding with the MENSHEVIKS against Lenin and the BOLSHEVIKS. From then on, he opposed Lenin's violent revolutionary line, approved of the Russian defensive participation in W.W.I and did not play any important part in the October Revolution of 1917. In philosophy, P. was a materialist and was opposed to the idealistic conception of art, including the principle of 'ART FOR ART'S SAKE'. Lenin accused P. of the retention of some elements of idealism in his philosophy, the excessive role assigned by him to the geographical environment in social development, bourgeois liberalism, OPPORTUNISM and his lack of appreciation of the peasantry as a revolutionary force. P. made important contributions to Marxist theory and even Lenin described his works as the best exposition of Marxism on the international scale. P.'s main works are: *Socialism and Political Struggle* (1883); *The Development of the Monist View of History* (1895); *Essays on Historical Materialism* (1896); *The Materialist Conception of History* (1897); and *The Role of the Individual in History* (1898).

Plenary Session, or **Plenum** The meeting of a particular body in its full complement, as distinct from its inner working committees. The terms are mostly used by reference to the meeting of the full Central Committee (not merely of its Politburo or Secretariat) of the Communist party. A p.s. is held immediately after the CENTRAL COMMITTEE is elected at the PARTY CONGRESS and then at least once every six months. As a rule the decisions made at the p.s. are more important than those handled at the meetings of its inner bodies. The p.s. of the C.C. in the USSR played a very important part up to the early 1950s. Between 1917 and 1952 it elected the POLITBURO and between 1919 and 1952, the ORGBURO.

PLO Palestine Liberation Organization POPULAR FRONT FOR THE LIBERATION OF PALESTINE.

Pluralism A philosophical view according to which anything that exists consists of a multitude of beings independent of each other. The main exponents of this view were G. W. Leibnitz (1646–1716) and W. James (1842–1910). P. is opposite to MONISM. Marxist philosophy regards p. as one of the expressions of IDEALISM, opposed to MATERIALISM. While p. implies harmony, Marxism emphasizes the struggle of the opposites in the DIALECTICAL process.

Pluralistic Society A society noted for the existence of many independent associations, institutions, pressure groups and firms with mutually interacting positive and negative influences. According to this conception, the political and social organization and changes therein are products not of one but of many complex forces. In industry, the concept implies a condition where trade unions, management and the state play an active, complementary role. The term was first applied at the beginning of this century (by A. de Tocqueville) to the United States. The proponents of this conception (such as G. D. H. Cole, H. J. Laski and R. H. Tawney) maintain that the multiplicity of interests produces a COUNTERVAILING POWER and balancing pressures protecting society against the unscrupulous preponderance of a few powerful groups or arbitrary state power. The model of the p.s. has been virtually rejected by orthodox Marxists, the NEW LEFT and fascists.

Plutocracy ('moneyed power', in Greek) A political and social system noted for the domination of the state and society by the rich, especially banking and financial interests and big business in industry and trade. The term is sometimes used by Marxists contemptuously to describe the upper class in the most industrialized capitalist countries by virtue of its wealth (as distinct from the titled aristocracy of blood).

Plzen Riots See PILSEN RIOTS.

Poland See POLISH PEOPLE'S REPUBLIC.

Polish Communist Party See COMMUNIST PARTY OF POLAND, POLISH UNITED WORKERS' PARTY.

Polish October A liberal reaction against the Stalinist regime and austerity in Poland in Oct. 1956. The Party leadership was taken over by W. Gomulka, a 'National Communist' who was released from arrest and replaced E. Ochab. The ferment had been prompted by the denunciation of Stalin at the TWENTIETH CONGRESS OF THE CPSU in Feb. 1956 and the consequent DE-STALINIZATION. Several reforms were initiated, led by intellectuals and supported by public opinion, which were fed by patriotism and a craving for greater freedom. Although the position of the intellectuals, the Catholic Church and peasants was improved and the worst abuses by the secret police were somewhat reduced, after 1957 a slow return to authoritarianism set in.

Polish People's Republic (*Polska Republika Ludowa*) A medium-size country in Eastern Europe (312,680 sq km and 35.0m people in 1978), ruled by the Communist party (officially described as the POLISH UNITED WORKERS' PARTY). The origin of the Communist regime goes back to W.W.II during which the Soviet government sponsored the UNION OF POLISH PATRIOTS, the Polish Workers' Party and a Polish army in the USSR. The U.P.P. proclaimed itself the National Council in Dec. 1943, which on 28 June 1944 created the Provisional Government of National Unity nominally representing five 'anti-fascist' political parties, in defiance of the legal Polish government-in-exile in London. Under Soviet pressure, the P.G.N.U. was recognized by the Western powers in

Polish Thaw

July 1945 and after a period of SOVIETIZA-TION, secret police terror and faked elections (in Jan. 1947), the Communist regime was firmly established. A Constitution was adopted in July 1952 replaced by another in Feb. 1976, stressing Poland's special relationship with the USSR. The highest formal source of power is vested in the *SEJM*, a unicameral legislature elected from a single list of candidates prepared by the FRONT OF THE NATION'S UNITY. Effective power is exercised by the Polish United Workers' Party, especially its Political Bureau headed by the Party's First Secretary (S. Kania, since Sept. 1980). The P.P.R. is unique in several respects as a socialist country because of: 1. the strong national and patriotic tradition; 2. the historical animosity to and distrust of Russia and the Bolsheviks; 3. the continued existence of other political parties (the United Peasants Party and the Democratic Party), which at the 1976 elections won 146 (of the 460) seats; 4. the dynamic intelligentsia, with a long tradition of Western learning and culture; 5. the indomitable Catholic Church commanding widespread respect and support, further enhanced by the election of a Polish Cardinal to the Papacy in 1978 (POPE JOHN PAUL II); and 6. predominantly private farming, where over 80% of agricultural land is still in private hands.

Polish Thaw A short period of liberalization in Poland in 1955–56, after Stalin's death (March 1953) and KHRUSCHEV'S SECRET SPEECH (Feb. 1956). Its high points were the POZNAN RIOTS (June 1956) and the POLISH OCTOBER (1956).

Polish United Workers' Party (*Polska Zjednoczona Partia Robotnicza*) The ruling Communist party in the POLISH PEOPLE'S REPUBLIC. It can trace its origin to the FIRST PROLETARIAT, created in 1882. But as a Communist party of independent Poland, it was founded in 1919 under the name of the Communist Workers' Party of Poland by the merger of the Social-Democratic Party of Poland and Lithuania and the left-wing faction of the Polish Socialist Party. The C.W.P.P. was illegal but operated underground and in 1921 joined the COMINTERN. In 1925 it adopted the name of the COMMUNIST PARTY OF POLAND, but by Stalin's orders it was dissolved by the Comintern in 1938. Revived in Moscow and Warsaw in 1942 as the Polish Workers' Party, it became the leading political force in creating the Soviet-backed Polish Communist regime, in defiance of the Polish government-in-exile in London. Under Communist pressure, the Polish Socialist Party merged with the P.W.P. in Dec. 1948 to form the P.U.W.P. Ever since its inception, the Party has stood unconditionally for collaboration with the CPSU and the USSR in general. Although the remnants of other non-bourgeois political parties are tolerated (in the FRONT OF THE NATION'S UNITY), the P.U.W.P. is unquestionably the dominant political force. The Party's membership in 1977 totalled 2,573,000, which makes it the fourth largest communist party in the world (after those of China, the USSR and Romania). The highest level of the Party's authority is the Congress, held every fifth year, which elects the Central Committee. However, actual power is concentrated in its Political Bureau, headed by the Party's First Secretary (S. Kania); and consists of 13 members and 3 candidate members with administrative responsibilities held in the hands of the Secretariat (8 secretaries and 2 members). The P.U.W.P. is directly supported by a number of mass organizations, including Trade Unions, the Association of Polish Lawyers, the Association of Polish Journalists and the Federation of the Socialist Union of Polish Youth. The official organs published by the P.U.W.P. include *Trybuna ludu* (*People's Tribune*), a daily newspaper; *Chłopska droga* (*Peasants' Road*), a fortnightly aimed at the peasants; *Życie partii* (*Party Life*), a monthly journal on the Party's organization and practice; and *Nowe drogi* (*New Paths*), a monthly theoretical journal.

Politburo (or less appropriately, **Polit-bureau**) The supreme Party policy-making body in the USSR, being a shortened version of *Politicheskoe Buro* (Political Bureau). It was created by Lenin in 1917, but was formally sanctioned at the 8th Party Congress in March 1919, as one of the three inner bodies of the CENTRAL COMMITTEE (i.e. the ORGBURO and the SECRETARIAT). The power of the P. declined under Stalin, as he preferred to make decisions on his own or in small groups of top Party leaders. During 1952–66, the P. was officially known as the Presidium. The P. is elected by the Central Committee at the Party Congress, directs the work of the C.C. between its Plenary Sessions, which are unconditionally binding on the COMMUNIST PARTY OF THE SOVIET UNION as a whole. As elected at the 26th Party Congress in March 1976, the P. consists of 16 full (voting) members and 6 candidate members, headed by the Secretary-General (L. I. BREZHNEV). In other socialist countries the term POLITICAL BUREAU is more commonly applied.

Political Bureau A term applied to the top policy-making body of the Communist party, constituting an executive elite of its CENTRAL COMMITTEE. The P.B., together with its leader (called the Secretary-General or the First Secretary), is elected by the Party's Central Committee at the Party Congress, but in the case of some parties it may be elected by the Party Congress itself. The size of the P.B. ranges typically from 10 to 25, of whom usually two thirds are full (voting) members and one-third-candidate (or alternate) members. In the case of the Chinese Communist Party, the respective numbers are 17 and 4 and in the case of the Communist Party of the Soviet Union, 16 and 6. Normally, the P.B. exercises power between the PLENARY SESSIONS of the Central Committee. The P.B. represents a great concentration of political power in a small elite whose decisions are binding on the party membership as a whole. The P.B. in each Communist party is patterned on the Soviet POLITBURO. In Czechoslovakia and Yugoslavia the P.B. is officially known as the Presidium (and in the USSR from

1952 to 1966). In the Romanian Communist Party there are two inner bodies of the Central Committee corresponding to the P.B. – the PERMANENT BUREAU OF THE C.C. (5 members) and the POLITICAL EXECUTIVE COMMITTEE OF THE C.C. (37 members).

Political Economics A term used by the radical NEW LEFT, emphasizing the study of economic facts, problems, processes and organization from the political and social standpoint. The term has been well established in the USA by the UNION FOR RADICAL POLITICAL ECONOMICS. Although related to POLITICAL ECONOMY, p.e. differs in that it is essentially applicable to capitalist countries and is much more explicitly conditioned by politics. While conventional Western economics is directed towards economic rationality, efficiency and harmonious processes tending towards equilibrium, p.e. is preoccupied with economic decision-making, power relations in the economy, conflicts between different interests and social justice. P.e. insists that there is nothing immutable about the economic system which is necessarily modified by changing methods of production and relations between social classes. The supporters of p.e. maintain that conventional economics (MAINSTREAM ECONOMICS) has simply become an apologetic discipline, in defence of the existing capitalist system. Thus, they stress that economic development, investment, pricing, inflation and unemployment are not merely economic but also political in content. To ensure social justice, economic decision-making must be politically motivated and influenced by political authorities.

Political Economy A term which has come to be applied by Marxists and other left-wing radicals to economics, emphasizing the study of economic relations and laws governing production, distribution, exchange and consumption at different stages of society's development. The term p.e. was first used by A. de Monchréstien (in *Traité de l'économie politique*) in

Political Executive Committee of the CC

France in 1613 to show that his book was concerned only with state economic management. In England, the term was established by James Steuart (*Inquiry into the Principles of Political Economy*) in 1767. Marx borrowed the term from previous writers (his main work, *Capital*, published in 1867, carried the sub-title, *Critique of Political Economy*) and since then the description has been commonly used in Marxist literature. Since the publication of A. Marshall's *Principles of Economics* (1890), the term 'economics' has become firmly established in English-speaking countries, while the designation p.e. has been generally reserved for the classical and Marxist treatments of economics. Marxists view p.e. in a historical setting, as in their view the subject matter of p.e. and economic laws reflect the nature of the OWNERSHIP OF THE MEANS OF PRODUCTION, the character of PRODUCTION FORCES and PRODUCTION RELATIONS. They deny that p.e. should be a neutral science of purely economic content. Marx called p.e. 'the most moral of all sciences'. An extreme view was taken by ROSA LUXEMBURG (in *Introduction to Political Economy*, 1925) who declared that under socialism there would be no economic laws as the proletarian revolution constitutes 'the last act of political economy as a science'. The NEW LEFT, since the early 1960s, has given p.e. a new shade of meaning, stressing the need for humanism and ethical standards in the study of p.e., rejecting both the traditional Western preoccupation with the functional study of economics and the Stalinist CENTRALIZED DIRECTIVE SYSTEM OF PLANNING AND MANAGEMENT. Also NEW POLITICAL ECONOMY, NORMATIVE ECONOMICS, POLITICAL ECONOMICS, VULGAR POLITICAL ECONOMY.

Political Executive Committee of the CC
An inner top policy-making body of the Central Committee of the ROMANIAN COMMUNIST PARTY. It consists of 25 full (voting) members, mostly including government ministers and leaders of mass organizations, plus 15 alternate members.

It is headed by the Secretary-General of the Central Committee (N. CEAUSESCU). The P.E.C. was originally created in 1965 when N. Ceausescu came to power, in order to ensure the predominance of his supporters in the Party's ruling body. Together with the PERMANENT BUREAU OF THE C.C., it constitutes the real seat of power in Romania. The P.E.C. and P.B. taken together correspond to the POLITBURO (in the USSR) or the POLITICAL BUREAU in most other socialist countries.

Political Officer A type of public relations officer attached to a unit in the armed forces in the Socialist countries responsible for ideological indoctrination and political security. In the USSR he is known as the *POLITRUK*.

Political Section A term well established in the USSR for the Party representation attached to larger organizations of critical ideological importance, to ensure that the activities of their rank and file conform to Party ideology and current policies. The system was first introduced in the Red Army in 1918 and was greatly expanded during the GREAT PATRIOTIC WAR (1941–45), where the political officer is known as the *POLITRUK*. In the 1930s, p.s.s were also introduced in MACHINE-TRACTOR STATIONS and in state farms. Similar sections also exist in other Socialist countries.

Political Show Trials Public trials of persons accused of political crimes by the regime in power. They are given wide publicity by the state in order to expose persons, interests or ideologies inconvenient to the government or leader in power, usually resorting to questionable judicial procedures. P.s.t. have been staged at one time or another in most countries, including Western democracies. But in their extreme form p.s.t. have been generally identified with the Communist regimes, who held them under the guise of legality to set public opinion against the defendants and their cause and to suppress systematically the opposition. These trials were developed quite early in the USSR, often designed to dramatize political campaigns. They were first directed against bourgeois elements, then non-Bolshevik Marxists (Mensheviks, Trotskyites) and then against distinguished OLD BOLSHEVIKS inconvenient to Stalin. They are exemplified by the SHAKHTY TRIAL (March 1928), the INDUSTRIAL PARTY trial (Nov.–Dec. 1930), the Trials of former Mensheviks (March 1931) and the TREASON TRIALS (1936–38). Other Socialist countries copied the Soviet practice as is evident in the late 1940s and the early 1950s. They were mostly directed against non-Communist leaders, but some distinguished Communists also fell victim to them, namely D. MIHAJLOVIĆ (July 1946) in Yugoslavia, Cardinal J. MIDSZENTY (Feb. 1949) and L. Rajk (Oct. 1949) in Hungary, K. Xoxe (June 1949) in Albania, T. KOSTOV (Dec. 1949) in Bulgaria and R. SLANSKY (Nov. 1952) in Czechoslovakia.

Political Socialization A term used in the Socialist countries to describe the process of the inculcation and assimilation of political ideas, values and attitudes, especially those laid down by the Communist party. Also RESOCIALIZATION, SOCIALIZATION.

Political Strike A stoppage of work by organized labour resorted to as a means of achieving political objectives, such as influencing elections, intimidating or discrediting anti-labour opponents, exerting pressure on legislative bodies undermining or destroying the existing political and social system. The extreme form of the p.s is a GENERAL STRIKE. The use of the p.s is favoured by Communist extremists in capitalist countries, provided it is directed by the Communist party. The p.s is absolutely illegal in the Socialist countries and in some capitalist countries. In the latter countries the p.s is frowned upon by the public more than the genuine strike of economic justification. However, it may

be argued that most strikes have political implications.

Political Thinking A term used in the Socialist countries to describe the involvement of an individual or group in the social and political life of the Party and the state. It may assume not only intellectual but also practical forms and is officially identified with civic responsibility and ideological astuteness. According to HISTORICAL MATERIALISM, p.t is class-conditioned. The official Socialist view is that it should be based on MARXISM-LENINISM and loyalty to the Party and the working class.

Politics The art and science of government, concerned with the form of state administration, the party system and relations between different social groups, nations and states. Marxism, in accordance with HISTORICAL MATERIALISM, emphasizes the class character and the changing nature of p. Whilst domestically the basic content of p. is seen as consisting of inter-class relations, externally p. is concerned with relations between the rich and the poor nations, between imperialist and colonial or ex-colonial countries, and between capitalist and the Socialist states. It is further maintained that political authority is derived from the control of the means of production, giving the ruling class the most basic source of power. Thus, Marxists treat p. as an arena of the CLASS STRUGGLE or class rule with respect to the ownership of the means of production, distribution and the maintenance of the existing system of production and social relations. For these reasons Lenin (in 'Once again on Trade Unions', 1921) described p. as 'the concentrated expression of economics'. Although political ideas, institutions and policies are determined by the material BASE, they are not regarded as passive but in turn exert influence on the economy. But although economic developments create conditions for changes in the political system, the latter is not modified automatically, but is changed by progressive social groups – either gradually (evolution) or by qualitative leaps (revolution). One of the well established postulates of Marxism is the primacy of politics over economics, when the two come into conflict with each other.

'Politics in Command' The principle of the primacy of politics over other spheres of social endeavour, such as economics, law, education, literature and art. The phrase was popularized by Mao Tse-tung during the GREAT LEAP FORWARD 1958–60 and then formally appeared in his *Sixty Articles*. The idea itself had been introduced by classical Marxists, especially by Lenin (in *Once again on Trade Unions'*, 1921), but was embraced in its extreme form by Stalin and then even more so by Mao. The principle implies that although the political SUPERSTRUCTURE is first of all conditioned by the material BASE, the political system has a decisive influence over the economy and other aspects of society's life by impeding or promoting their development. It is political power that enables the ruling class – be it feudal, bourgeois or proletarian – to establish and maintain its dominance and rule. The primacy of politics is particularly important to the working class, as only through political power can it establish socialism and advance to full communism. The opposite concept to 'p. in c.' is DE-POLITICIZATION, which has been attempted to some extent in Yugoslavia.

Politinformator Political propagandist employed by the Communist Party in the USSR for more sophisticated audiences. This system is administered by the Propaganda and Agitation Section of the Party Secretariat. The p. contrasts with the AGITATOR, the latter generally being an ordinary worker concerned with mass audiences of the common people and employing simple ideas and more demagogic methods. The p. system was introduced by the resolution of the 23rd Party Congress in April 1966, based on the view that in the advanced socialist society the public is more educated and well informed. Consequently, a more sophisticated approach is needed, requiring professional men such as political scientists, sociologists, economists, executives and cultural specialists. In 1968 there were 600,000 p., which increased to over 2,000,000 in the late 1970s.

Politruk In the Soviet armed forces, a Party official responsible for political instruction and reliability of the troops. *P.* is a syllabic abbreviation in Russian of *Politichesky Rukovoditel* ('Political Leader'). He is usually attached to a company (about 150 troops). The presence of the *p.* caused resentment among military commanders and Marshal G. K. ZHUKOV abolished the system in 1957. After his dismissal in Oct. 1957 it was re-established. The institution of *p.* is an expression of a long established principle in the Socialist armed forces of the subordination of the military to the political leadership and the Party's ultimate control.

Polycentrism In an ideological and political sense, a situation where there are several centres of leadership or power. The term was first introduced by P. TOGLIATTI in June 1956 after KHRUSCHEV'S SECRET SPEECH (Feb. 1956) denouncing STALINISM and allowing each Communist party to pursue its OWN PATH TO SOCIALISM. Togliatti's point was that the Soviet model should no longer be binding on other communist parties. P. in the world Communist movement is manifested by the existence of CASTROISM, EUROCOMMUNISM, MAOISM, MARXISM-LENINISM, TITOISM, TROTSKYISM and other Marxist models. The term p. has also been applied to the disintegration of Western unity since the mid-1960s, formerly impelled in one way or another by the USA.

Pope John Paul II (1920–) The leader of the Roman Catholic Church and the Bishop of Rome, elected on 16 Oct. 1978. His original name was Karol Wojtyła, born to a humble family in Poland, where even under communism some four-fifths of the population are practising Catholics. He was ordained a priest at the age of 26, became the Archbishop of Cracow at 42 and the Cardinal of Poland at 47 (in 1967). In addition to Polish, he is fluent in Latin, Italian, English, French and German (but not Russian) and did two years of doctoral work in Rome. His election to the Papacy created a world sensation. He is the first non-Italian pope since 1522, the first pope from Poland and indeed the first from a Socialist country, and the first pope to have visited a communist-ruled country (Poland, in June 1979). Although his appointment must have placed the Communist leaders in Eastern Europe and the USSR in a rather embarrassing position, most sent their congratulations to him on his elevation to the office (incl. L. I. BREZHNEV and E. GIEREK). The Soviet Foreign Minister (A. Gromyko) paid him a personal visit in the Vatican on 24 Jan. 1979. Some observers view his appointment as heralding a new era for churches in Eastern Europe and perhaps for East-West relations. The Pope is opposed to Marxism as a solution to human problems and in his inaugural speech he highlighted his goal of 'full communion' with other Christians (alluding to his opposition to 'full communism'). He has a reputation for moderate conservatism in the matter of doctrine, but has become a champion of underprivileged people and nations.

Popular Democratic Front for the Liberation of Palestine An extremist Marxist-Leninist organization, influenced by CASTROISM and MAOISM, consisting of Palestinian and Jordanian Arab revolutionaries. It was formed in 1968 by the extreme left-wing faction of the Popular Front for the Liberation of Palestine and is led by Nayaf Hawatmeh (a Jordanian Marxist philosopher). The Front has about 200 members, periodically engaging in guerrilla activities and is believed to be financially assisted by China. In practical terms, the influence of the P.D.F.L.P has been negligible, but it has had some propaganda effect on the Marxist movement in the Arab world.

Popular Front A type of UNITED FRONT or coalition of left-wing political parties by reference to the period of 1934–41. The term was coined by M. Thorez, the leader of the French Communist Party. A P.F. involves electoral and parliamentary cooperation among Communist, Socialist, Social-Democratic and in some cases, Liberal and Radical parties. Although orthodox communist parties are normally against a P.F., as in their view it leads to compromises, OPPORTUNISM and REVISIONISM, the COMINTERN sanctioned the idea of the P.F. at its 17th Congress in 1935, mainly to stem the advance of FASCISM and Nazism. The first P.F. was in power in France (1934–38), followed by Spain (1935–36), Chile (1938–41) and some other countries. The P.F. did not survive due to the constant pressure against them from not only right-wing parties but also from the Communists as well.

Popular Front for the Liberation of Palestine An Arab Marxist-Leninist-Maoist revolutionary organization directed against Israel as an imperialist state and against capitalism in the Middle East. It was founded by G. Habbash in 1967 and its membership includes intellectuals, students and some peasantry. It is organized as an armed guerrilla force, at first based in Jordan then in Lebanon, and resorts to terrorist methods. It receives aid in money and military equipment from the USSR and China, as well as from rich Arab states. The political side of its activities is controlled by the Arab Workers' Socialist Party formed in 1970. The P.F.L.P. has become more moderate since its extremist faction joined the POPULAR DEMOCRATIC FRONT FOR THE LIBERATION OF PALESTINE in 1968.

Popular Movement Workers' Party The ruling Marxist-Leninist party in ANGOLA. It traces its origin to 1956 when the Popular Liberation Movement of Angola (MPLA) was created absorbing the Communist Party of Angola. During 1974–77 the MPLA emerged as the dominant political and military force in the country. Its success was largely due to Soviet advisers, arms and finance and Cuban military support (some 15,000 troops). In Dec. 1977 the MPLA adopted its present name.

Popular Socialist Party of Mexico A Marxist-oriented political party, about the third largest in the country, with a membership of about 60,000 (compared with the country's population of 65,700,000). It was founded in 1947 as the Popular Party, but in the following year adopted its present name. Its strength was enhanced in 1963 when it amalgamated with the left-wing Worker-Peasant Party of Mexico. It draws its support mainly from middle-class intellectuals, students and trade unions. In its programme, it advocates moderate socialism, emphasizing a more even distribution of wealth. Although in the past it usually had some representation in parliament, at the last general election in 1976, it lost all 10 of its previously held seats. The Party has followed a pro-Soviet line.

Populism A Westernized term for NARODNISM in Russia, an early version of the Marxist movement which emphasized the interest of the peasantry, from the late 1860s to the early 1880s.

Populist Socialists A Westernized name for the Russian political group better known as the TRUDOVIKS. They were in existence before the October Revolution of 1917 and emphasized social justice for the peasantry along socialist lines.

Poputchiki ('Fellow Travellers', in Russian) Name given to those Soviet writers during the decade of 1917–26 who, while nominally supporting the Bolsheviks, insisted on the freedom of creative arts. Among its representatives were B. L. Pasternak (Nobel Prize winning author of *Dr Zhivago*), B. Pilniak, K. A. Fiedin and some members of CONSTRUCTIVISM and the *LEF*. They soon attracted unfavourable attention from the Soviet regime and the RUSSIAN ASSOCIATION OF PROLETARIAN WRITERS. Owing to repression, the *P.* had

disappeared by 1932 when the UNION OF SOVIET WRITERS was established.

Portuguese Communist Party (*Partido Comunista Portuguesa*) A fairly influential Marxist-Leninist political party, with a membership of 115,000 (of a total population of 10,300,000 in 1978) and 40 (of the 263) seats in the Lower House of the Parliament (after the 1976 elections). Founded in 1921, it was outlawed several times and operated underground between 1926 and 1974. It co-operated in the successful overthrow of the authoritarian government of M. Caetano in April 1974 and has participated in government ever since. The highest source of the Party's power is its Congress. The 7th Congress in Oct. 1974 (the first legal Congress since 1926) attended by 1,000 delegates, elected a Central Committee of 10 members with the latter selecting a Secretariat of 4 members. The Party's Secretary-General is Alvaro Cunhal. Its official organs are *Avante* (*Forward*), a daily newspaper and *O Militante* (*The Fighter*), a bi-monthly theoretical journal. The Party has followed a rather orthodox pro-Soviet course and is, on the whole, opposed to EUROCOMMUNISM. There are 12 other non-united Communist-oriented groups, including the International Communist League (Trotskyite) and the Popular Democratic Union (Maoist). There is also a military-terrorist organization, the Armed Revolutionary Action, controlled by the P.C.P.

Portuguese Socialist Party (*Partido Socialista Portuguesa*) One of the largest political parties in the country (the other being the Social Democratic Party). It was founded in 1973 as a successor to the former Portuguese Socialist Action. The Party, led by Dr M. Soares, advocates the nationalization of the means of production and a classless society to be gradually achieved by democratic means. At the 1976 elections the Party polled 34 per cent of the votes cast and formed a minority government with M. Soares as Prime Minister. The Party's official organ is a weekly called *Portugal Socialista* (*Socialist Portugal*). The Party has two supporting organizations, the Popular Socialist Front and the Socialist Left Movement, and is affiliated to the SOCIALIST INTERNATIONAL.

Posadist Fourth International A Trotskyite international communist movement, mainly operating in Latin America. It emerged in 1962, when the Latin American Bureau of the International Secretariat of the FOURTH INTERNATIONAL, led by Juan Posadas, broke away. It bases its hopes on the inherent instability of capitalism and favours a nuclear war from which, it is contended, socialism would emerge victorious. The movement also has had some supporters in Belgium, Britain, France, the FR of Germany, Italy and Spain. Although it first operated almost exclusively in the countryside in South America, after the late 1960s it moved into urban areas.

Positivism A major philosophical and sociological movement in the 19th and 20th c., attaching crucial importance to 'positive' facts which can be observed and tested empirically, as distinct from abstract deductions. Positivists emphasize that man should accept the world as nature shows it to be in man's experience, and further, that society and its development are based on natural laws or conform to them. The term was first used by C. H. SAINT-SIMON, but A. Comte (1798–1857) is commonly regarded as the founder of p. Among other positivists are R. Avenarius (1843–96), A. A. BOGDANOV and E. MACH. Positivists maintain that p. is above the conventional philosophies of IDEALISM and MATERIALISM. They argue against the need for philosophy, or at least to restrict its scope to insignificance. Marxists are bitterly opposed to p. In their view, it embodies elements of AGNOSTICISM, CRITICAL REALISM, FIDEISM and SUBJECTIVE IDEALISM, and denies the objective laws of nature, in effect, defending capitalism. According to p., Marxist sociologists point out, contradictions

under capitalism derive from psychic conflicts, the solution to which is not the overthrow of the capitalist system, but the adaptation of human consciousness to the existing capitalist order. The best known Marxist critique of p. was presented by Lenin in MATERIALISM AND EMPIRIO-CRITICISM, in which he stressed the need for philosophy as the most general explanation of existence and a guide to other disciplines and revolutionary action.

Possibilists A group of moderate socialists, formed in France in 1879, opposed to revolutionary methods and favouring a gradual transition to socialism by postulating objectives which were realistic and 'possible' for achievement. Their leaders were P. Brousse and B. Malon. In 1882 they created a party called the Federation of Socialist Workers, which Marxists described as exemplifying OPPORTUNISM and a betrayal of the proletarian cause. In 1890, the F.S.W. lost its support to the GUESDISTS.

Possibility and Reality In DIALECTICAL MATERIALISM, two opposite but related concepts important in the process of development. Marxist philosophy interprets nature and society as being in constant change from the old and receding to the new and progressive. In this process, the new does not become reality immediately but emerges at first as a possibility. However, unlike FATALISM, Marxist HISTORICAL MATERIALISM regards the development of the possible into the real as a DIALECTICAL struggle between opposites, not as an automatic process. This struggle may result in either an advance or a retreat, depending on a variety of circumstances, among which man's activities often play a crucial part. This philosophical proposition has important ideological implications in social development. Thus, although the development of capitalism creates favourable conditions for a progressive advance to socialism, the privileged entrenched capitalist class impedes or prevents such a change. Consequently, to turn p. into r., it is imperative for the working class, and in particular its vanguard, the Communist party, to speed up the transition, if necessary through a proletarian revolution.

Post-industrial Society See SINGLE INDUSTRIAL SOCIETY.

Postulate of Distance in Art See DISTANCE THEORY IN ART.

Potemkin The name of a battleship in the Russian navy based in the Black Sea, which became famous for its's crew's participation in the REVOLUTION OF 1905–07 against the Tsarist autocracy. The act was unprecedented in Russian history and its example was followed 12 years later by the crew of the *Aurora* in the October Revolution.

Poverty The deficiency of income or property, with the consequent inability of the person to satisfy his most basic needs of food, clothing and shelter. Marxists attribute p. to the faulty social system, responsible for such causes as the concentration of wealth in the hands of a privileged class, the great disparity in the distribution of income, inability to ensure continuous full employment, the absence or inadequacy of social security and, in general, various forms of exploitation of some social groups by others. According to classical Marxist thinkers, of all the socio-economic formations, capitalism is noted for the greatest extent and degree of exploitation, especially in its later stages of development when the IMMISERATION OF THE PROLETARIAT is critical. But some Marxist thinkers have discerned a positive effect of p. under capitalism which is of ideological significance. Marx (in *Manuscripts of 1844*) said that p. drives people to a greater class unity and Mao Tse-tung pointed out in 1958 that 'poverty gives rise to the desire for change, the desire for action and the desire for revolution'.

Poverty of Philosophy One of the earliest philosophical works written by K. MARX in 1846/47, in which he formulated his first scientific approach to a critique of economics. It was written in French and was primarily directed against *The System of Economic Contradictions or the Philosophy of Poverty* published in 1846 by P. J. PROUDHON, a French philosopher, economist and anarchist. Marx attacked Proudhon's acceptance of the institution of private property and proposals for co-operative production and trade. Marx denied that Proudhon's schemes would ensure social justice and all-round affluence and regarded them as petty bourgeois tinkerings still within the framework of capitalism. While Proudhon saw only despair in poverty, Marx viewed poverty as a dynamic force which would lead to the breakdown of capitalism. In contrast to Proudhon, Marx perceived a great potential and historic mission in the PROLETARIAT and attached critical importance to the CLASS STRUGGLE and the need for revolutionary action. Marx also presented a critique of the philosophical IDEALISM of G. W. F. Hegel and contrasted it with his own DIALECTICAL method based on MATERIALISM.

Poznan Riots A revolt by the workers in Poznan, in Western Poland in June 1956 against oppressive political, working and living conditions. The peak was reached on Thursday 28 June, which came to be known as 'Black Thursday', with a loss of lives and substantial damage to property. The riots had been prompted by the popular reaction against Stalinism, initiated by KHRUSHCHEV'S SECRET SPEECH in Feb. 1956, and represented a prelude to the POLISH THAW.

Practice An important category in Marxist philosophy, especially in the theory of knowledge and of social development. P. is regarded as the ultimate criterion or test of truth. The concept of p. is viewed broadly and consists, primarily, of all activities associated with production – the basis of society's existence. The importance attached by Marxists to p. is a logical consequence of the acceptance of philosophical MATERIALISM and supporting the working class and manual labour.

P. is seen by Marxist philosophers (as reflected in the writings of Marx, Engels, Lenin and Mao Tse-Tung) to be inextricably linked to theory. The two are regarded as a DIALECTICAL unity in mutual interaction, with p. being the decisive element, without which there can be no scientifically tested theory. At the same time, valid theory becomes a guide to p. In the course of events, theory may become outdated in the light of new practical evidence. This contradiction must be resolved by updating the theory in accordance with the new tests of p. This cycle is repeated in the progressive advancement to higher levels of knowledge.

Pragmatism A major philosophical doctrine according to which the truth of a concept, law or theory must be tested by its practical and useful bearing on human interests, i.e. a generalization is acceptable only if it is conducive to the promotion of man's life and his interests. P. does not recognize objective laws governing the world in their own right, rather it emphasizes subjective human experience as the only valid reality. The founder of p. was Ch. Peirce (1839–1914), but its most influential exponents were W. James (1842–1910), J. Dewey (1859–1952), G. Papini (1861–1956) and F. Schiller (1864–1937). Although surprising in several respects, Marxist philosophers have adopted a highly critical view of p., regarding it as subjectivist, unscientific and reactionary, akin to EMPIRIO-MONISM, INSTRUMENTALISM, INTUITIONISM, IRRATIONALISM, MACHISM and VOLUNTARISM, all inconsistent with MATERIALISM, They stress that the criterion of usefulness has been considered by pragmatists from the standpoint of the BOURGEOISIE, not the PROLETARIAT. It is further held that p. has been employed to justify aggression, imperialism and the suppression of progressive ideas in the name of expediency.

Prague Agreement on Non-commercial Exchange Rates An accord concluded by the member countries of the COUNCIL FOR MUTUAL ECONOMIC ASSISTANCE in Prague in 1963, concerning the rates of exchange in mutual non-trade transactions. It was agreed that the rates of currency exchange would be based on the purchasing power parity geared to retail prices (not producer prices or wholesale prices used in visible trade). For this purpose, an internationally agreed 'consumption basket' was chosen. The composition of the 'basket' was subsequently (in 1971) updated with respect to quantity and quality, services included. Since that time, several member countries in bilateral agreements have further modified their bases for exchange rates. In 1971 these facts were taken into account and a new coefficient of conversion to the TRANSFERABLE ROUBLE was introduced.

Prague Coup d'Etat The Communist takeover of the government in Czechoslovakia in Feb. 1948. The Coup was like a palace revolution, limited to the capital city, without any significant turmoil in the rest of the country. Until that time, Czechoslovakia had had a democratic coalition government within the framework of a United Front, in which non-bourgeois political parties were represented, but in which the CZECHOSLOVAK COMMUNIST PARTY had no majority. The Coup had been prompted by the declining public support for Communists and the approaching general elections in spring 1948. Using the Ministries of the Interior (controlling police and secret security organs) and of Information (both headed by Communists) to its advantage, the Cz.C.P. resorted to both constitutional and unconstitutional methods, to which it was prodded by the USSR. In spite of President Beneš's appeal for co-operation within the framework of the United Front, the Party's Political Bureau prevailed upon him to dismiss non-Communist ministers (except J. Masaryk and V. Šrobár) and to appoint Communists instead with K. Gottwald as Prime Minister. The Coup succeeded and left a tragic reminder, when J. Masaryk committed public suicide on 10 March 1948 in protest against the 'rape of Czechoslovak democracy'.

Prague Spring

Prague Spring A period of liberal reforms in Czechoslovakia from 5 Jan. (when A. DUBĆEK succeeded A. NOVOTNY to the Party leadership) to 20 Aug. 1968 (the INVASION OF CZECHOSLOVAKIA). In April, the Party proclaimed the ACTION PROGRAMME of political, economic and cultural reforms, with a view to transforming the country gradually into a political democracy with a market economy, based on 'SOCIALISM WITH A HUMAN FACE'. In June, the prominent reform leaders announced the MANIFESTO OF THE 2,000 WORDS. There was an explosion of liberal enthusiasm, especially among the intellectuals and patriotic elements. However, there were internal dissensions in the Party and a campaign mounted by the Communist parties of the German DR, Poland and the USSR frustrated the liberal developments. The military intervention by the Warsaw Pact forces on the night of 20–21 Aug. 1968 terminated the P.S.

Pravda (*'The Truth'* in Russian) The daily organ of the Central Committee of the Communist Party of the Soviet Union. It is printed in 42 cities, has a daily circulation of 11m. copies and maintains a network of over 40 foreign correspondents. The newspaper carries the official pronouncements of the Soviet Party leadership on domestic and foreign questions. *P.* was initiated by Trotsky, its first editor in Vienna, but was effectively founded in St Petersburg (now Leningrad) in 1912, with its first issue printed on 5 May. Under Stalin at this time, the paper became the organ of the Bolsheviks in order to develop 'revolutionary consciousness'. It suffered from severe censorship, confiscation and its staff were victimized. Lenin took over the editorship in April 1917 (after his return from Switzerland), but its continuous publication did not begin until 9 Nov. 1917 (O.-S.C.). The name of the paper was thought of by Trotsky, who edited the paper under this title at first in Lvov, then in Vienna from 1905 to 1912. But its editorial board was infiltrated by the Bolsheviks (notably L. KAMENEV who

brought it under Bolshevik control. The Slovak Communist Party publishes a paper under the same title in Bratislava (in the Latin alphabet, not Cyrillic).

Pre-capitalist In Marxist terminology, belonging to a SOCIO-ECONOMIC FORMATION preceding capitalism, viz. FEUDALISM, SLAVERY and PRIMITIVE COMMUNISM. The historical period implied in the Western countries is roughly that before the agrarian, commercial and industrial revolutions of the 18th–19th centuries.

Preconcerted Economy A term originally used in France for an economy subject to non-directive, INDICATIVE PLANNING. The economic plan is worked out under the auspices of the Planning Commissariat by the main bodies concerned with its implementation, viz. trade union confederations, employers' associations, national enterprises, farmers' organizations and planning experts. Directions of development and major objectives are embodied in the plan largely by agreement among the executors of the plan.

Preformation See PREFORMISM.

Preformism A philosophical and biological doctrine, according to which all the characteristics in adult organisms are predetermined (preformed) in a minute form in the reproductive cells, either by divine intervention or by heredity. Living organisms are seen as undergoing quantitative growth, without any development of new characteristics. P. appeared first as a religious doctrine in the 16th c. and later (in the 19th and 20th c.) found expression in Epigenesis, EUGENICS and GENETICS. Among the leading exponents of p. were M. Malpighi (1628–94), A. von Haller (1708–77), G. W. Leibnitz (1646–1716) and W. Roux (1850–1924). Marxism has rejected the validity of p. in whatever form, treating it as a version of idealism completely opposed to DIALECTICAL MATERIALISM. Marxists point out that although living organisms have certain inherent characteristics, the latter can be modified by environmental factors. Consequently, organisms not only grow quantitatively but also develop qualitatively into something new. The qualitative development of organisms can be influenced by man through controlling the environment in appropriate directions. This belief found its expression in the USSR in MICHURINISM and LYSENKOISM (which have been been largely discredited since the late 1950s).

Preobrazhensky, Evgeni Alekseievich (1886–1937) A Bolshevik Party official and economist who made pioneering contributions to the theory of economic development under Soviet conditions. He joined the Bolshevik faction of the RUSSIAN SOCIAL-DEMOCRATIC LABOUR PARTY in 1903. In 1920 he was appointed as one of three Party Secretaries and in the following year became co-editor of *PRAVDA*. He distrusted the market mechanism, opposed the NEP and was highly critical of the enrichment of the *KULAKS*. From 1923 on he provided theoretical economic ideas for the LEFT OPPOSITION led by Trotsky, Zinoviev and Kamenev). He advocated accelerated industrialization with an emphasis on heavy industry, to be financed primarily by forced savings in agriculture (by setting appropriate prices for agricultural and industrial products). In this connection, he developed the concept of PRIMITIVE SOCIALIST ACCUMULATION. But in the mid-1920s his ideas did not suit Stalin and in 1927 P. was expelled from the Party. In 1929 P. 'confessed' his errors, broke with Trotskyism and was temporarily readmitted to the Party. But later he was expelled again and finally perished in Stalin's GREAT PURGES, in 1937. And yet, beginning in 1928, Stalin adopted virtually all of P.'s ideas on economic development, but resorted to a more ruthless treatment of the *KULAKS* and other peasants than P. had envisaged. P.'s most notable book was THE NEW ECONOMICS: *An Experiment in Theoretical Analysis of the Soviet Economy* (1925). His other publications include: *Problems of Monetary Policy*

(1921); *Paper Money in the Age of the Proletarian Revolution* (1921); *Morals and Class Norms* (1923); and *Theory of the Declining Currency* (1930).

Pre-parliament (*Predparlament,* in Russian) The Provisional Council of the Republic of Russia created by the All-Russian Central Executive Committee of the SOCIALIST REVOLUTIONARIES and MENSHEVIKS at the All-Russian Democratic Conference held in Petrograd (now Leningrad) from 14 to 22 Sep. 1917 (O.-S.C.). It was intended to represent the nation until the convocation of a Constitutional Assembly and aimed at forestalling a proletarian revolution in Russia. The P. had about 600 delegates and was hesitant to give support to A. F. KERENSKY. It met on 7 Oct. 1917 (O.-S.C.), but the Bolsheviks decided to boycott it. On 24 Oct. 1917 (O.-S.C.) they sent their troops and dispersed it never to meet again.

Presidium (sometimes also spelled Praesidium) The top policy-making body in some Communist parties, viz. Czechoslovakia and Yugoslavia, in Romania before 1965 and in the USSR from 1952 to 1966. The P. is the inner elite of the CENTRAL COMMITTEE and it is usually elected at the Party Congress at the first PLENARY SESSION of the C.C. In other Communist parties the P. is known as the POLITBURO or the POLITICAL BUREAU.

Presidium of the CC of the CPSU The top policy-making body of the Central Committee of the Communist Party of the Soviet Union from 1952 to 1966. It replaced, and has been succeeded by, the POLITBURO. The Presidium had 25 full (voting) and 11 candidate members and was smaller in size than the Politburo before Stalin's death, but larger than the present Politburo.

Presidium of the Supreme Soviet of the USSR The inner and permanently functioning executive organ of the SUPREME SOVIET OF THE USSR. It replaced the CENTRAL EXECUTIVE COMMITTEE in 1936.

The Presidium is elected from among the deputies at a joint meeting of the two Chambers of the Supreme Soviet and consists of one President, one First Vice-President, 15 Vice-Presidents (one from each Union Republic), one Secretary and 21 Members. It meets formally every other month, carrying on the work of the Supreme Soviet between the latter's plenary sessions. It has the power of issuing decrees, modifying laws and establishing or abolishing government departments. Its chairman (L. Brezhnev, since June 1977) also acts as the ceremonial head of state and is the President of the USSR, signing legislative acts and treaties, presenting orders and higher medals and receiving diplomatic representatives.

Price The monetary expression of the value of a resource, commodity or service. In a free market economy under perfect competitions, p. is determined by supply and demand and ensures market equilibrium. According to the Marxist theory of VALUE, P. should correspond to the quantity of SOCIALLY-INDISPENSABLE LABOUR embodied in the product. Marx (in *CAPITAL*, vol. I) said, 'price is the money-name of the labour realized in a commodity'. But in practice, p. is rarely equal to value, whether under capitalism or socialism. In a capitalist market economy, p. reflects scarcity and changes according to the whimsical forces of supply and demand, or is monopolistically manipulated (by restricting supply and exploiting inelastic demand), or in some cases, artificially fixed by the authorities. But Marx maintained that p. still oscillates around value, sometimes being higher and in some cases falling below value. In the Socialist centrally planned economies, neither PROGRAMMING PRICES, PRODUCER PRICES, or RETAIL PRICES are set by reference to the labour content, but are planned by reference to a variety of practical objectives or functions (the desired distribution of national income, the postulated level of savings, social justice, the regulation of profitability of enterprises and equilibrium in the market). Consequently, under

socialism, p. fixing is not governed by value as defined by Marxists. At one stage, in the 1930s (in the USSR) V. MOLOTOV forbade economists to discuss p. because he rationalized that pricing was a question of politics, not of economics. Also EXCHANGE-VALUE, PRODUCTION PRICE.

Price of Labour See LABOUR, PRICE OF

Price of Production See PRODUCTION PRICE.

Prices and Incomes Policy An expression first established in Britain in 1965, to describe the government's efforts to delay increases in prices and wages. The objective was to achieve stabilization by co-ordinating increases in prices and incomes with the growth of productivity, involving restraint by both employers and employees. To implement this policy Prices and Incomes Boards were established. The policy has not proved successful, although it has exerted some restraining influence. Similar policies have been adopted in some other capitalist countries with varying degrees of success. But this policy is pursued on a much more systematic basis in the Socialist centrally planned economies with great effectiveness, owing to the governments' direct and wide-ranging powers over prices, wages and production and living costs.

Price Scissors A term applied to the relation between the prices of agricultural and industrial products. This relation and changes in it have far-reaching economic and social consequences on the well-being of the rural and industrial population, the level of savings and the distribution of national income in general. Traditionally, in the Socialist countries, especially in the USSR under Stalin, the prices of agricultural products payable to farms were fixed at unduly low levels while those of industrial products were at artificially high levels by the addition of heavy TURNOVER TAXES. The purpose was to keep the consumption of the peasants low, secure cheap food for the industrial workers, low-cost raw materials for the state and to maintain high levels of saving to finance accelerated industrialization (PRIMITIVE SOCIALIST ACCUMULATION). However, since about 1960, the prices of agricultural products have been raised several times in relation to industrial products, so that the price disparity is not as wide now as it was before. This was done mainly to encourage larger agricultural output and reduce the need for the subsidization of the less endowed farms.

Primacy of Politics See INDOCTRINATION, POLITICAL SECTION, POLITICS IN COMMAND, *POLITRUK*.

Primacy of Production A concept to which Marxists attach considerable importance, attributing the decisive role to (material) production in the economic and social life of any society. Although production, exchange, consumption and accumulation are all interdependent, production plays the crucial part. Marx insisted that production determined consumption (not the other way round). It is further stressed that the p. of p. is realized in different ways in the two opposing social systems. Under capitalism, the immediate objective of production is profit. On the other hand, in a Socialist planned economy, production is directly subordinated to the needs of the whole society, with a view to securing the maximum rate of growth of production, while profit – if it is employed – becomes a means towards the attainment of that objective.

Primacy of Social Interest The principle accepted in the Socialist centrally planned economies, according to which if there is a conflict between private preferences and the long-run interest of society as a whole, the latter prevails. The judgment of the Communist party, the government or the planning authority are officially accepted as reflecting social interest, rather than individual consumers, enterprises or institutions.

Primary Party Organization (*Partiynaia yacheika*, in Russian) The present (since 1934) official name of the lowest unit of organization of the COMMUNIST PARTY OF THE SOVIET UNION. Before 1934 it was known as the Party cell. The P.P.O. must have at least three members and typically exists in factories, farms, institutions, military units, and so on. The next higher Party organization is the Bureau, comprising more than 10 members.

Prime Cost In Socialist economic accounting, those outlays which are explicitly incurred by the enterprise (not necessarily the state or society). It is also known as the 'enterprise's own cost'. It consists of the materials used (including fuel, power, lighting), wages and salaries, social insurance, payments for services obtained from outside, depreciation, repairs to plant and interest on bank credit. As a rule, CAPITAL CHARGES (on capital in the possession of the enterprise) are not regarded as cost (Hungary being an exception), but are deducted from enterprise gross profits.

Primitive Accumulation A Marxist concept, denoting the initial accumulation of capital in economically backward countries by private capitalists or the state, subsequently enabling accelerated industrialization. The term was introduced by Marx in application to capitalism before the Industrial Revolution, and in this sense is known as PRIMITIVE CAPITALIST ACCUMULATION. The concept was later applied by E. PREOBRAZHENSKY in the USSR in the 1920s to the Socialist planned economy, which he called PRIMITIVE SOCIALIST ACCUMULATION.

Primitive Capitalist Accumulation The accumulation of wealth by capitalists before the Industrial Revolution which subsequently enabled the CAPITALIST MODE OF PRODUCTION, rapid industrialization and a further growth and concentration of capital in the hands of the bourgeoisie. The concept owes its origin to Marx (in *CAPITAL*, vol. I) and Engels (in *ANTI-DÜHRING*), mainly by reference to Britain. They identified the beginning of p.c.a. with the separation of small producers (peasants, craftsmen) from the means of production, when the latter were appropriated by the propertied classes – masters, feudal lords or other large landowners, traders, usurers, bankers and monarchs. P.c.a. was accompanied by a radical increase of HIRED LABOUR, whose only means of sustenance was its sale of labour to property owners and other capitalists. The forms or means of p.c.a. included enclosures, expropriation of church property, the ruler's farming out of his tax collection to private interests, lending at exorbitant interest rates, speculation, protectionism (especially exclusive charters to big trading companies), slave trade, piracy and colonial conquests. In Western Europe, p.c.a. occurred mostly during the 16th–18th centuries and later in other parts of the world.

Primitive Communism In Marxist ideology, the first (earliest) SOCIO-ECONOMIC FORMATION, where the MODE OF PRODUCTION was based on the communal ownership of land and other means of production and where the products of common labour were distributed according to needs. However, there was some private property – tools, weapons and personal effects. The concept of p.c. in the ideological context was introduced by Marx, but a more profound analysis was carried out by Engels (in *ORIGIN OF THE FAMILY, PRIVATE PROPERTY AND THE STATE*). The communist (or communal) nature of ownership, work and living was attributed to the primitive methods of production and adversities faced in coping with natural elements. P.c. was also noted for the absence of money, prices, exchange, the market, competition, hired labour, social stratification and the state. Engels, and later Stalin, maintained that the original unit of social organization was based on MATRIARCHY, while PATRIARCHY came later and became associated with private property. Marxists emphasize that the original and natural form of socio-economic organization was p.c., hence communism is a natural system for human society. But most non-Marxist sociolog-

ists and anthropologists disagree, stressing that primitive societies are noted for a wide variety of social organizations, of which p.c. and matriarchy are only one.

Primitive Socialist Accumulation A high level of forced savings extracted from the population, especially the peasants, in a backward country in transition from capitalism to socialism, designed to finance rapid INDUSTRIALIZATION. The idea and the term were introduced by E. PREOBRAZHENSKY in the USSR in the early 1920s. Paralleling the Marxian concept of PRIMITIVE CAPITALIST ACCUMULATION, Preobrazhensky reasoned that accelerated industrialization was imperative for the survival of the Soviet regime and the construction of communism. But he emphasized that it required a radical expansion of investment in order to: 1. repair the damage to the economy inflicted by W.W.I. and the Civil War; 2. finance the capital-intensive infra-structure and heavy industry; and 3. ensure a faster growth of the state sector compared with the private sector. This required an unprecedented high level of planned domestic saving as most sources typical of primitive capitalist accumulation were absent in the USSR. In a backward undeveloped country, where agriculture is the main source of wealth, peasants (who constituted some 85 per cent of the Soviet population) were the obvious potential providers of saving, thus it was essential to restrict their current consumption. This was to be achieved by fixing prices of agricultural products payable by the state to the farms at very low levels and, at the same time, setting the prices of industrial products at artificially high levels. Other related measures to be resorted to included a severe restriction of luxuries, a planned neglect of the NON-PRODUCTIVE SPHERE, strict controls over travel (especially abroad) and a virtual prohibition of the import of consumer goods. Preobrazhensky's proposals were supported by the LEFT OPPOSITION (headed by Trotsky), but were rejected by Lenin and Stalin. BUKHARIN called them 'the military-feudal exploitation of the peasantry'. However, after having eliminated both the Left Opposition and the RIGHT OPPOS- ITION (led by Bukharin), Stalin adopted the principle of p.s.a. in 1928 almost to the letter and in fact went to greater extremes than envisaged by Preobrazhensky, which resulted in the virtual extermination of the *KULAKS*.

Principles of the International Socialist Division of Labour See INTERNATIONAL SOCIALIST DIVISION OF LABOUR.

Priority In Socialist economic planning, preference given in the allocation of re- sources and the implementation of plan- ned targets to industries, products, methods of production and distribution according to a scale established by higher authorities. P. is observed in making deci- sions involving alternatives, especially when resources are scarce or unexpected difficulties arise in the course of plan im- plementation. Historically, in the socialist countries, p. was accorded to industry rather than agriculture, to heavy rather than light industry, to the technologically most progressive branches of industry rather than the traditional ones, and to producer rather than consumer goods.

Private Consumption That part of total consumption which is paid for out of the consuming households' own earnings on the basis of the freedom of choice. P.c. is more important in a capitalist market economy, where it typically constitutes 85–95 per cent of total consumption. Under socialism, where it is viewed as less desirable than SOCIAL CONSUMPTION, it represents 65–80 per cent of total con- sumption. Its share is to be reduced to below 50 per cent under full communism.

Private Enterprise An essential feature of CAPITALISM, generally associated with FREE ENTERPRISE, PRIVATE PROPERTY, the private profit motive, the operation of the MARKET MECHANISM, COMPETI- TION, HIRED LABOUR and INDIVIDUALISM. None of these features is consistent with

Marxist ideology where p.e. has become an object of attack. Marxists emphasize that p.e. generates anti-social effects, such as great disparities in the ownership of wealth and the size of personal income, SOCIAL STRATIFICATION, ANTAGONISTIC PRODUCTION RELATIONS, greed and self- ishness. In the Socialist countries, p.e. has been largely, but not completely, elimi- nated in the process of the SOCIALIZATION OF THE MEANS OF PRODUCTION and the adoption of economic planning. However, p.e. still plays a considerable part in all the Socialist countries, especially in Poland and Yugoslavia. But its scope has been reduced to marginal spheres, viz. small- scale farming, handicrafts, restaurants, transport, retail shops and some personal services where individual attention is im- portant (hairdressing, tailoring, beauty care, etc.). The ECONOMIC REFORMS in the European Socialist countries since the early 1960s (some 10 years earlier in Yugoslavia) have created more favoura- ble conditions for p.e. But it is envisaged that p.e. will disappear completely under FULL COMMUNISM. Also NON-SOCIALIZED SECTOR.

Private Labour A term used in the Social- ist countries for labour applied to the pri- vately owned MEANS OF PRODUCTION and carried on under the conditions of PRI- VATE ENTERPRISE on one's own initiative, account and risk. P.l. is carried on inde- pendently of, but not in complete isolation from, other private and socialized produc- ers. Such labour is not socially planned but governed by the uncertain market. The fruits of p.l. may not find buyers if the market (i.e. the public) does not verify the need for such products, leading to private losses. P.l. is part of a broader concept, viz. SOCIAL LABOUR, under any social system.

Private Plots A colloquial term for SUB- SIDIARY PLOTS.

Private Property The ownership of assets by private individuals, as distinct from the SOCIAL OWNERSHIP OF THE MEANS OF PRO- DUCTION. The origin and extent of p.p. are a subject of ideological controversy. Marxists, such as Engels (in *ORIGIN OF THE FAMILY, PRIVATE PROPERTY AND THE STATE)*, deny that the institution of p.p. goes back to the origin of man and that it is natural and inevitable. They view it as a historical phenomenon peculiar to some socio-economic formations, but not to others. They emphasize that the original social system, PRIMITIVE COMMUNISM, was noted for communal ownership, when MATRIARCHY prevailed, and only personal effects were privately owned (some implements, weapons, clothing, adornments). P.p. appeared only with the development of PATRIARCHY and reached some extreme forms under SLAVERY when p.p. was held not only in land and man-made assets, but also in slaves who could be traded and even killed. The same occurred under FEUDALISM, except that serfs could not be killed. But the greatest development of p.p. has taken place under CAPITALISM, where a propertyless proletariat has emerged and has become the largest social class. Under socialism, p.p. in the means of production (land and capital) is virtually non-existent, except the small private sector where it is still tolerated. But the p.p. of personal effects, houses, own savings and the like is retained. Marxists have traditionally attributed all social evils to the institution of p.p. – greed, exploitation, social classes, crime, wars, etc. Also NON-SOCIALIZED SECTOR, 'PROPERTY IS THEFT'.

Private Sector a less commonly used term in the socialist countries than the NON-SOCIALIZED SECTOR.

Privatization The transformation of social property or an organization into a private entity or at least in such ways as to be of benefit to exclusive private groups. The term is widely used in Yugoslavia by the critics of the SELF-MANAGEMENT SYSTEM, where socialized property (land, capital) is handed over (leased) by the state to the ORGANIZATIONS OF ASSOCIATED LABOUR. The latter, under self-management, exploit such resources for the benefit of their own members. As the quality and quantity of such resources differ, considerable disparities of personal income have emerged.

Pro-Chinese Line (or Orientation) See PEKING LINE.

Procurement Prices Prices paid in the Socialist countries to farms and subsidiary plot holders for agricultural products delivered to the state. P.p. in the past were very low compared with free (or black) market prices. The aim of that policy was to restrict the peasants' current consumption, minimize the cost of acquisition of food and raw materials to the state to keep the cost of living of the urban population low and to provide high levels of saving to finance accelerated industrialization. P.p. were differentiated, enabling the state to absorb the DIFFERENTIAL RENT. Prices payable for COMPULSORY DELIVERY were much lower than those for ABOVE-COMPULSORY DELIVERY. The latter prices were meant to encourage production on less productive land where production costs are higher, or otherwise where extra effort is needed to produce additional output. Since the late 1950s, the level of p.p. has been raised substantially in relation to industrial prices in most socialist countries and compulsory deliveries have been abolished. P.p. have been largely replaced by CONTRACTATION PRICES.

Producer Price A term used in the socialist planned economies to denote the price paid to a producing enterprise by wholesale trade or by other producing enterprises. P.p. usually remains stable over long periods (5–15 years). This price does not include a wholesale trade margin (if it does it becomes a wholesale price) nor a turnover tax. P.p. contrasts with RETAIL PRICE and in the Socialist countries the two levels are usually insulated and may move independently.

Producers' Co-operative An economic organization or an enterprise associating small producers to protect or otherwise enhance their interests. There are many forms of p.c., varying from completely independent individual producers co-operating only in some respects (purchases of materials or equipment, the construction of buildings, land improvement, marketing) to completely integrated and jointly owned enterprises. P.c. mostly operate within agriculture, fishing and handicrafts, in both capitalist and socialist countries. Under Socialism, the co-operative sector is one of the socialized divisions of the economy (the other being the state sector). A p.c. in agriculture is called a COLLECTIVE FARM. A p.c. does not include consumers (a CONSUMERS' CO-OPERATIVE does). Also CO-OPERATIVE ENTERPRISE, INTERNATIONAL CO-OPERATIVE ALLIANCE.

Product Buy-back, Product Pay-back A type of counter-delivery commonly practised in East-West INDUSTRIAL CO-OPERATION. The supplier of equipment or the licenser (usually the Western partner) accepts payment from the recipient (usually the Eastern partner) in the form of the goods produced with the aid of the initial delivery. In some cases, the counter-delivery may also include non-resultant goods. The deal is of benefit to both sides – the Western partner finds a market for its equipment and technology, and at the same time he may be assured of cheap components or complete products (especially if they are labour-intensive). The Socialist partner economizes hard foreign exchange, obtains superior technology and has a channel for introducing its products in hard-currency areas.

Product for Oneself In Marxist national income accounting, that portion of the NET MATERIAL PRODUCT which is directly distributed in the form of wages and salaries to the workforce employed in the sphere of MATERIAL PRODUCTION. P. for o is smaller than the INDISPENSABLE PRODUCT, as the latter also includes a portion of social consumption – that which is indispensable to maintain (feed, clothe, house, educate and train) and reproduce the workforce employed in material produc-

tion. The balance of the p. for o. is termed the PRODUCT FOR SOCIETY.

Product for Society In Marxist national income accounting, that portion of the NET MATERIAL PRODUCT which is distributed to the workforce employed in the NON-PRODUCTIVE SPHERE, plus that which is devoted to various social uses, viz. social consumption and investment. The remaining portion of the net material product is known as PRODUCT FOR ONESELF.

Production The process of creation of products (goods and services) capable of satisfying human wants. The Marxist conception of p., expounded by Marx (mainly in CAPITAL, vol. I), is in several ways different from the usual Western interpretation and it emphasizes the following features. 1. P. in any society and in all historical stages is social in character, being a condition of survival of society and entailing social interrelations in the form of the division of labour and exchange. 2. P. comprises only the creation of material products contributed in the following branches of the economy: agriculture, industry, construction, transport and communications, trade and other minor branches (forestry, fishing, hunting, etc.), while non-productive services (even if they are paid for) do not constitute p. 3. From the point of view of social relations, p. has two distinct aspects: society's relation to nature (PRODUCTION FORCES) in the struggle with which it obtains material goods, and intra-societal PRODUCTION RELATIONS. The two sides represent a unity called the MODE OF PRODUCTION. 4. In accordance with the philosophy of HISTORICAL MATERIALISM, p. is subject to constant development originating from changes in production forces, especially the INSTRUMENTS OF PRODUCTION. A change in the mode of production leads to a transformation of the social system. 5. P. consists of the means of production (raw materials, machinery, equipment, buildings) comprising DEPARTMENT I, and of the means of consumption constituting Department II. A condition of the growth

of p. (known as EXPANDED REPRODUC-
TION) is a faster growth of Department I
than of Department II p. 6. While under
capitalism the main driving force behind
p. is private profit, in a Socialist economy
social needs and planning become the
mainspring of p. 7. P. in a socialist
economy is noted for its planned, orderly
and continuous development under the
conditions of full employment, while in a
capitalist market economy p. is subject to
fluctuations, disruptive crises and periodical or continuous unemployment.

Production Brigade A large basic production unit of workers or peasants in a socialized factory or farm in the Socialist countries. A p.b. usually has from 40 to 80
persons, but in China it is typically much
larger, and is headed by a BRIGADIER.
Where necessary, it is divided into smaller
groups for distinct tasks or locations called
links (in the USSR) or production teams
(in China). There has been a lively controversy in China since the GREAT LEAP
FORWARD as to whether the p.b. or the
PRODUCTION TEAM should be the basic
production unit in PEOPLE'S COMMUNES.
On the whole, p.b.s have lost some of
their power to production teams.

Production Forces In Marxist political
economy, the MEANS OF PRODUCTION
(especially the man-made instruments of
production) and LABOUR POWER applied
in the process of MATERIAL PRODUCTION.
Of all the p.f., the INSTRUMENTS OF
LABOUR are considered to be the most
decisive element in production, as the development of p.f. is always initiated by
improvements in such instruments and,
consequently, determine the level and
character of society. The Marxist concept
of p.f. stresses the technical side of material production which, in a sense corresponds roughly to the Western concept of
the FACTORS OF PRODUCTION.

Production Price A Marxist term for the
transformed version of the VALUE OF A
PRODUCT. It was introduced by Marx in
CAPITAL, vol. III in a rather confusing

departure from his concept of value,
thereby, virtually abandoning the
LABOUR THEORY OF VALUE. P.p. embodies three elements: the cost of CON-
STANT CAPITAL c (materials and the depreciation of fixed assets); VARIABLE CAP-
ITAL v (wages); and the AVERAGE PROFIT
RATE based on *full* cost $(s/(c+v))$, that is
$c+v+s/(c+v)$. In a capitalist market
economy, the profit rate differs from one
branch of the economy to another because, although the RATE OF EXPLOITA-
TION is approximately the same, the OR-
GANIC STRUCTURE OF CAPITAL (c/v) differs from one branch to another. The less
advanced the branch (i.e. the lower c in
relation to v) the higher the profit rate.
Only where the organic structure of capital happens to be average for the economy
is the p.p. equal to value. Owing to the
different degrees of competition, p.p. may
be higher in some branches and lower in
other branches than value. But the sum of
all products in the market expressed in
p.p. equals their total value. P.p. is typically higher than value in monopolized industries, but usually lower in agriculture.
The price reforms in the European socialist countries since the early 1960s have
been geared more to p.p. than to value.

Production Relations One of the two crucial elements in Marxist ideology, which
together with PRODUCTION FORCES determine the MODE OF PRODUCTION. The concept was first introduced by Marx (in *A
CONTRIBUTION TO THE CRITIQUE OF
POLITICAL ECONOMY*). Stalin (in
*ECONOMIC PROBLEMS OF SOCIALISM IN
THE USSR*) identified three factors governing p.r.: 1. the form of the ownership of
the means of production; 2. the position of
different social groups in production; and
3. the pattern of the distribution of production and income. Most Marxists stress
that p.r. are an essential twin element
constituting a dialectic unity in the mode
of production and may either facilitate or
impede the progressive development of
production forces. The concept of p.r. emphasizes the social aspect of production in
the process of exchange and income dis-

tribution, especially the relationship between the owners of the means of production and the management on the one hand, and the workers on the other. Changes in p.r. are conditioned by changes in production forces, but the adjustment of the former to latter tends to lag behind. This lag is more acute in ANTAGONISTIC SOCIO-ECONOMIC FORMATIONS, owing to the opposition of the ruling classes as they feel threatened in their privileged position. When the necessary adjustment is artificially held up for too long, a qualitative leap has to occur periodically which may assume the form of a violent social revolution. It is claimed that under Socialism the contradictions that may arise between production forces and p.r. are not antagonistic owing to the social ownership of the means of production. Furthermore, economic planning enables the state to take appropriate measures well ahead or immediately where necessary to remove the contradictions that may arise between the new production forces and the old p.r. But some Marxist thinkers, such as A. A. BOGDANOV and N. I. BUKHARIN, discounted the role of p.r. and identified the mode of production with production forces, their organization and technology.

Production Team A sub-unit of the PRODUCTION BRIGADE for tasks of a distinct nature or for work in a distinct location in a socialized factory or farm in the Socialist countries. A p.t. is headed by a team leader who works out the details of the tasks to be performed and assigns them to individual workers. The p.t. is a crucial feature in PEOPLE'S COMMUNES in China in which the team typically represents a village or some 390 households and about 20 hectares of land. The p.t. has gained in importance since the GREAT LEAP FORWARD at the expense of the production brigade. Experience has shown that if the calculation of work points and the distribution of income is in the hands of the p.t. it has a greater incentive effect on the members. Attempts made during the GREAT PROLETARIAN CULTURAL RE-VOLUTION to return the accounting function to the production brigades have been condemned as a 'left-wing adventurist line'. In the new Chinese Constitution (of 1975), under Article 7, the p.t. is specified as the basic accounting unit.

Productive In Marxist economic terminology, contributing to MATERIAL PRODUCTION. In contrast to Western national income accounting, most services (those excepting transport, communications and trade) – even if paid for – are considered as 'non-productive'.

Productive Accumulation In Socialist terminology, that portion of ACCUMULATION (roughly meaning investment) which is directed to the fixed assets in the PRODUCTIVE SPHERE, i.e. towards the maintenance and expansion of MATERIAL PRODUCTION. P.a. is indicated by the investment expenditure for productive purposes in industry, construction, agriculture, transport and communications, trade and other minor spheres of material production. The Socialist countries spend about three-quarters of their total accumulation for productive purposes (higher than is usually the case in capitalist market economies). P.a. contrasts with NON-PRODUCTIVE ACCUMULATION.

Productive Consumption A Marxist term for the use of the means of production (raw materials, components, semi-finished products and the depreciation of fixed assets) in the process of MATERIAL PRODUCTION. P.c. consists merely in the transfer of value, not the creation of value, as only live labour can.

Productive Credit Theory A theory according to which credit flows reflect the circulation of real products, assuming that credit is conducive to monetary equilibrium, smooth economic development and price stability. It is also known as the 'real bills theory' and its origin goes back to ADAM SMITH (1723–90) after which it was further developed by the Banking School in England during the 19th c. Although the theory was virtually discarded a century ago, it was utilized in the USSR in the early 1930s and later in other Socialist countries. Not only is it consistent with the Marxist emphasis on material production, but it also assigns a passive role to money. The acceptance of the theory in its extreme form led to the so-called 'automatic crediting', which was practised in the USSR during 1930–31 and in several other Socialist countries in the late 1940s and early 1950s. Under that system, suppliers were automatically paid by the bank upon the delivery of goods, irrespective of the quality and suitability of the goods delivered and the buyers' ability to pay. This practice was an extreme reflection of the long-standing conviction that under Socialism there is no scope for credit to regulate independently economic processes. As 'credit automatism' encouraged irresponsibility on the part of both producers and buyers and led to obvious waste, it was soon abandoned.

Productive Funds In Socialist economic terminology, capital used for MATERIAL PRODUCTION. In enterprises, they include funds used for financing fixed and working capital. They exclude expenditure for workers' amenities even though they are owned by the enterprises (such as child care centres, dwellings for the workers, holiday homes).

Productive Labour In Marxist economic terminology, labour performed in the following sphere of MATERIAL PRODUCTION: agriculture; industry; construction; transport; communications; trade; and other minor branches (forestry, fishing, hunting, gathering, laundrying and the like). P.l. can be physical or mental. In general, the work force engaged in NON-PRODUCTIVE SERVICES is regarded as non-productive labour. However, in recent years a number of socialist economists have disagreed with the above traditional Marxist view and have favoured the treatment of the non-productive services provided they are paid for (as p.l.), which is practised in Western economics.

Productive Services In Socialist economic terminology, those services which directly contribute to MATERIAL PRODUCTION and, consequently, to the NET MATERIAL PRODUCT. They include transport (including water supply and sewage), communications, trade and certain other minor services (publishing, film making, mechanical and automatic data processing, laundrying). P.s. contrast with NON-PRODUCTIVE SERVICES.

Productive Sphere In Marxist terminology, the division of the economy contributing directly to MATERIAL PRODUCTION and, consequently, to NATIONAL INCOME (as calculated by the Socialist method). It comprises the following branches of the economy: 1. those contributing tangible products, viz. agriculture, forestry, fishing, hunting, gathering, industry (including mining) and construction; and 2. those rendering productive services, i.e. representing a continuation of the production process, viz. transport (including sewage and water supply), communications, trade, publishing, film-making, data processing, laundrying and other minor services.

Productivism A small, extremist movement in art in the USSR rejecting traditional forms and instead emphasizing current practical collective needs of the working class, conducive to the growth of production and new ideas serving the socialist state. The movement was founded in 1920 by A. M. Rodchenko (1891–1956) and his wife Varvara Stepanova (1894–1958). It began as a school of CONSTRUCTIVISM in the extreme spirit of SOCIALIST REALISM. P. calls for the abolition of virtually all previous art forms in architecture, painting, sculpture, graphics and interior decoration, which it regards as a bourgeois falsehood, destructive of human thought. The movement reached its peak of popular appeal in the early 1920s, but was never officially accepted in full and is of little consequence today.

Profintern A syllabic abbreviation of the Russian *Profsoiuznyi International*, meaning the Trade Union International. It was an international organization in existence from 1921 to 1937, based in Moscow, uniting revolutionary trade unions. Its objective was to organize the workers of the world for the overthrow of capitalism and to establish socialist governments. It was specifically directed against the moderate and independent INTERNATIONAL FEDERATION OF TRADE UNIONS, popularly known as the Amsterdam International. Although nominally independent of the COMINTERN, the P. was created (and dissolved) by it and was dominated by Communists. At least 46 countries were represented in P. including the USSR, Belgium, Canada, Chile, China, Colombia, Czechoslovakia, France, the Netherlands and Yugoslavia, but (with the exception of the USSR) none of these representations were national. The P. held five Congresses, all in Moscow (in 1921, 1922, 1924, 1928 and 1930), but never commanded wide support or achieved any significant results. Attempts to create a common central organization with the I.F.T.U. failed.

Profit, Capitalist One of the three main elements of SURPLUS VALUE, appropriated by the industrial and commercial capitalist and the main target of the Marxist critique of CAPITALISM. According to Marx (mainly in *Theories of Surplus Value* (1861–63) and CAPITAL and his followers, c.p. is the chief form of the EXPLOITATION and IMMISERATION OF THE PROLETARIAT and the ultimate source of egoism, the concentration of property in private hands, wide income disparity, SOCIAL STRATIFICATION, UNEMPLOYMENT, crises, crime, COLONIALISM and wars. C.p. is also regarded as the obsessive mainspring of economic pursuits, where social interest is subordinated to private greed. C.p. arises from the fact that workers create more value for their employing capitalist than they are paid in wages. The lower the ORGANIC STRUCTURE OF CAPITAL (capital-labour ratio), the higher the profit rate, since LIVE LABOUR alone can create value. Although the Marxist condemnation of c.p. was largely justified

under *laissez-faire* capitalism before W.W.I, some of the abuses associated with c.p. have been eliminated or have otherwise disappeared, owing to various forms of state intervention (highly progressive income taxes and death duties, the control of monopolies, price controls, separation of ownership from control, the rising power of trade unions, the growing pressure of public opinion and decolonization).

Profit, Socialist A concept used by modern Marxists in application to a Socialist planned economy, to avoid the implication of EXPLOITATION identified with capitalist profit (PROFIT, CAPITALIST). Before the ECONOMIC REFORMS of the early 1960s, the use of the term profit was avoided relating to a Socialist economy. Other descriptions were preferred, such as net income, net product, net revenue, residual balance or remainder, or if employed at all it was shown in inverted commas. In spite of ideological prejudice, profit has been adopted in most socialist countries since the early 1960s as an important indicator of enterprise performance and a basis for material incentives to workers. In this respect, the ideas of E. LIBERMAN have played an important part. But Socialist economists point out that s.p. is different from capitalist profit in that: 1. it is not a goal but a means, linking the interest of the enterprise and its workers with that of society; 2. it is not an objective category but a flexible instrument, as the state by virtue of its control over costs and prices can shape the patterns of profitability irrespective of the enterprises' activities; 3. it is not necessarily indicative of efficiency on the macroeconomic scale, as Socialist prices are not usually scarcity prices; 4. it does not necessarily determine the allocation of resources at the macroeconomic level, as central planners are usually guided by other objectives as well; 5. it cannot be increased by reducing the enterprise's output to the level where marginal cost is equal to marginal revenue, as in most cases prices are fixed or regulated by the state; 6. it cannot lead to large disparities of personal income and social differentiation, as bonuses are distributed only to the workers who have helped create the profits; and 7. it does not condition the Socialist export of capital as, if it does occur at all, it is motivated by political or humanitarian considerations and not by profitability differentials between domestic and foreign investment.

Profit Rate This concept has two meanings: one as used by Marx in application to capitalism and the other applicable to modern Socialist economies. In Marxian political economy it denotes the relation between SURPLUS VALUE (s), i.e. roughly profit, the total capital outlay, viz. constant capital (c), i.e. outlays on materialized means of production, and variable capital (v), i.e. wages: p.r. $= s/c+v$. Surplus value, assuming constant capital (and methods of production) unchanged, depends on the rate of exploitation of labour (s') and the number of workers employed, viz. $s = s'\ v$. The p.r. is essentially governed by the relation of constant to variable capital or, as Marx called it, the ORGANIC STRUCTURE OF CAPITAL. The higher the share of constant capital in total capital, the lower the p.r. By the same token, as the share of constant capital rises the p.r. falls. The share of constant capital is lower in backward industries (and countries) and higher in more developed ones. There is a natural tendency in the technological age for the share of constant capital to increase both in the backward branches (especially) and in the economy as a whole. Marx concluded (in *CAPITAL*, vol. III) that the p.r. was the motive power of capitalist production, but that at the same time it differed in different branches and that on the whole, the average p.r. tends to fall, which leads to vicious COMPETITION. The share of constant capital is particularly low in agriculture so that the p.r. is higher there than in industry. The equalization of the p.r. is prevented by the private ownership of land, as marginal land is not utilized unless it brings in positive rent. On the basis of these deductions, Marx formulated his LAW OF THE DECLIN-

ING P.R. As under capitalism, the p.r. governs production and investment. The factors which operate in depressing the p.r. also contribute to capitalist contradictions. In application to the modern socialist economy, the p.r. means a percentage ratio of profit to total assets. It is calculated according to the following formula:

$$\text{P.r.} = \frac{Os - pK - D + S + B - Cc - iP}{cA + fA} 100;$$

Os = output actually sold (at producer prices)
pK = prime cost of the output sold
D = differential payments to the state budget (according to the advantages possessed by the enterprise)
S = subsidies received from the state
B = balance of losses and profits on operations outside normal production
Cc = capital charges on fixed assets in possession
iP = illicit profit (achieved in ways conflicting with existing regulations or otherwise damaging to social interest)
cA = value of circulating assets
fA = value of fixed assets

The p.r. has become the most important profit standard in most European Socialist countries since the late 1960s. Compared with other profit standards (the profit mass, rentability and gross income), the p.r. best indicates changes in the improvement or deterioration in enterprise efficiency (or performance). The p.r. can be calculated on a net basis, when it is known as the net p.r., or simply the p.r. as shown in the above formula where net profit is related to total assets. This form of p.r. is used for comparing the profitability (or performance) of different enterprises in the same branch of industry. If gross profit (ie before taxes, capital charges, differential payments and similar levies) is related to total assets, then the indicator is known as the gross (or social) p.r. and is used to compare the effectiveness of asset utilization in different branches of industry or the economy.

464

Profit-sharing A term which has acquired several meanings, in most cases representing a departure from pure capitalism and in one case, as a quasi-capitalist move. Forms of p.s. are as follows: 1. in capitalist firms, participation by workers in the distribution of profits, either in the form of bonuses or dividends from the shares allocated to them; 2. in partnerships or co-operative firms, participation by members in the profits of the jointly owned, operated or patronized venture; 3. in the Socialist countries since the ECONOMIC REFORMS, workers' participation in enterprise net profits in the form of MATERIAL INCENTIVES according to the profitability of their enterprise. A portion of the net profit is placed in the MATERIAL INCENTIVES FUND from which bonuses are paid to the workers who have contributed to the profit. Most Marxists are opposed to p.-s. in capitalist countries, as in their view it leads to sweated labour, acts as a worker-disciplining device and it props up capitalism, merely delaying the need for a proletarian revolution.

Programming The application of mathematical methods to the solution of complex problems, especially in economic planning to achieve optimal effects. P. in the more advanced Socialist countries (Czechoslovakia, the German DR, Hungary, Poland, and the USSR) began in the late 1950s and has been facilitated by the development of computers and electronic data processing. In application to economic planning, p. proceeds in two stages: 1. the construction of internally consistent plans, given certain constraints; and 2. the selection of the optimal plan, ie one which ensures maximum effects from the given volume of resources, or one which enables the achievement of the postulated effects with the minimum outlay of resources. At first p. was linear, ie applying to static conditions. More recently non-linear p. is employed to provide optimal solutions under changing conditions.

Programming Prices Prices applied by the central planning authority in determining the allocation of resources at the planning stage according to macrosocial cost-benefit considerations. For a long time in the past, in Socialist economic planning, prices were either disregarded (in physical planning) or PRODUCER PRICES were used. In recent years, attempts have been made to work out optimal prices by mathematical methods with the aid of computers. Such prices approach SCARCITY PRICES, in which non-labour resources are also subjected to scarcity (or productivity) valuation.

Progress Development from lower to higher stages or from simpler to more complex forms. In accordance with HISTORICAL MATERIALISM, Marxism regards advances in the MODE OF PRODUCTION as the basic carrier of p. Associated with it is the struggle of the dynamic and forward-looking social class against conservative and reactionary forces. As viewed by Marxists, the essence of p. is the struggle of opposites – the new and vigorous with the old and obsolete. Marx (in *THE POVERTY OF PHILOSOPHY*) summed up: 'No antagonism – no progress.' Marxist philosophers and sociologists emphasize that an important part in p. is played by REVOLUTION, which is regarded as a qualitative leap. Societies develop from lower to higher SOCIO-ECONOMIC FORMATIONS and CAPITALISM will inevitably be replaced by SOCIALISM and the latter by FULL COMMUNISM. Marxists reject the theory of the CYCLICAL DEVELOPMENT OF SOCIETY.

Progressive Labor Party of America A small militant ultra-leftist party in the USA formed in 1965 by the extremists expelled from the COMMUNIST PARTY OF THE USA in that year. The membership of the P.L.P.A. is estimated at about 1,000. At first the Party's general orientation was strongly Maoist, but since 1971 it has become rigidly Stalinist, although its two Maoist groups (the Revolutionary Union and the October League) are still influential. It is now critical of both Soviet and

Chinese policies and of 'US–Soviet imperialism'. The Party publishes a news-sheet in English and Spanish, *Challenge/Desafio*, and a theoretical journal, *Progressive Labor*.

Progressive Party of the Working People of Cyprus (*Anarthotikon Komma Ergazomenou Laou Tis Kiprou*) An influential Marxist-Leninist political party and the oldest and the most disciplined party in the country. It was founded secretly under the name of the Communist Party of Cyprus in 1926 and was proscribed by the British authorities from 1931 to 1941 and then from 1955 to 1959. The Party was legalized when the country achieved its independence in 1959. Its membership is quite large, about 11,000 (compared with the country's population of 650,000). It has a strong influence in trade unions and draws support from the United Democratic Youth Organization, the Pan-Cypriot Confederation of Women's Organizations and the Pan-Cypriot Peace Council (affiliated to the WORLD PEACE COUNCIL). At the 1976 elections, the Party polled 30 per cent of the votes cast and won 9 (of the 35 Greek Cypriot) seats. In the international Communist movement, the Party has supported the Moscow line but is opposed to violent action. The Party's publications include: *Kharavyi* (*Dawn*), a daily newspaper; *Neoi Kairoi* (*New Times*), a weekly magazine; and *Theoretikos Demokratis* (*Theoretical Democrat*), a theoretical journal appearing irregularly.

Proletarian Pertaining to the PROLETARIAT.

Proletarian Art A term introduced first in Russia before W.W.I, then firmly established in the USSR after the October Revolution of 1917 and later adopted in other Socialist countries. P.a. denotes a movement in art (architecture, cinema, literature, music, painting, sculpture and theatre) which gives expression to the aspirations, struggles and everyday activities of the working people and to Communist ideology in general. P.a. is opposed to 'ART FOR ART'S SAKE' and formalistic art (especially CUBISM, FUTURISM and IMPRESSIONISM), and instead is guided by SOCIALIST REALISM. Marxists maintain that art, like any other ideology, is conditioned by the economic BASE and reflects the interests of the different classes in a class society. Under Socialism, art becomes an ideological weapon in the hands of the proletariat, 'shielding it from the decadent bourgeois art' and is directed towards the consolidation of power of the socialist state and the propagation of Communist ideals. Also ART, CONSTRUCTIVISM, PRODUCTIVISM, *PROLETKULT*.

Proletarian Cultural and Educational Organization See *PROLETKULT* (in the USSR).

Proletarian Democracy A form of SOCIALIST DEMOCRACY which exists in a Socialist country during the TRANSITION FROM CAPITALISM TO SOCIALISM under the conditions of the DICTATORSHIP OF THE PROLETARIAT exercised by the Communist party. Marx, and especially Lenin (in *The Proletarian Revolution and the Renegade Kautsky*, 1918) were strongly opposed to parliamentary democracy. Although in all Socialist countries parliaments are in existence, their role is more formal than real and in effect meant to legitimize and support the Party's policies on crucial issues. At the elections the voters have no choice of candidates beyond the single list prepared by the Communist party or the Communist dominated UNITED FRONT. Yet Lenin maintained that p.d. in Soviet Russia was 'a million times more democratic than the most democratic republic'.

Proletarian Internationalism The solidarity of the workers in different countries among whom it is postulated there can be no conflicts once their common interests are clearly perceived and who constitute a single class united by their struggle against the bourgeoisie and imperialism. The theoretical foundations of p.i. were first outlined by Marx and Engels in *THE COM-MUNIST MANIFESTO*, emphasizing the community of interests of the PRO-LETARIAT in different countries epitomized in the slogan, 'Proletarians of all lands, unite!' P.i. became the guiding principle of the international working class movement and found its institutional expression in the FIRST INTERNATIONAL, the SECOND INTERNATIONAL, the SECOND-AND-A-HALF INTERNATIONAL, the COMINTERN and the FOURTH INTERNATIONAL. After W.W.II co-operation among the working classes of the socialist countries has assumed the form of SOCIALIST INTERNATIONALISM.

Proletarianization A term used by Marxists with reference to capitalist countries to describe the process of the loss of the means of production by small producers, craftsmen, peasants and traders and their consequent impoverishment. This process was best exemplified during the development of capitalism in the 18th and 19th centuries in the West, when the operation of the unrestricted market mechanism, competition and the private profit motive inexorably impelled the concentration of property in the hands of the BOURGEOISIE. As a result, small-scale independent firms were bought out or made bankrupt by big business and landowners and the small men had to join the ranks of the PROLETARIAT.

Proletarian Majority A concept introduced by classical Marxists emphasizing that in the capitalist society the PRO-LETARIAT is by far the largest social class, larger than the BOURGEOISIE and, consequently, by a truly democratic system of election, political power should be in the hands of the working class. Marx and Engels (in *THE COMMUNIST MANIFESTO*) stressed that all previous social movements in history were minorities, while 'The proletarian movement is the self-conscious, independent movement of the immense majority in the interest of the immense majority'. After the PRO-LETARIAN REVOLUTION, power should be completely monopolized by the proletariat in the form of the DICTATORSHIP OF THE PROLETARIAT and the non-proletarian minority should be completely subordinated to the ruling majority. The term has also been applied to the BOL-SHEVIKS (Majoritarians in the RUSSIAN SOCIAL-DEMOCRATIC LABOUR PARTY), the POPULAR FRONTS (of the 1930s) and the UNITED FRONTS (after W.W.II).

Proletarian Redemption A tenet held by some Marxists, especially in the USSR, attributing historic mission to the suffering PROLETARIAT of the emancipation of the masses from bourgeois domination and exploitation. Under Stalin, the USSR was seen as the spearhead of p.r. with the Soviet victories over the Fascist invaders in the latter stages of W.W.II and the liberation of Eastern Europe cited as practical evidence.

Proletarian Revolution The violent overthrow of bourgeois power by the working class to abolish capitalism and establish the DICTATORSHIP OF THE PROLETARIAT. The p.r. is also known under the broader term of the socialist revolution and contrasts with the BOURGEOIS–DEMOCRATIC REVOLUTION. The need for the p.r. was first substantiated by Marx and Engels in *THE GERMAN IDEOLOGY* (1846) and then by Marx in *The Class Struggles in France* (1850), but they derived the idea from A. Blanqui who had put it forward in 1832. The classical founders of Marxism postulated the p.r. to be necessarily violent for two major reasons: 1. they assumed that no social class in power voluntarily surrenders its privileged position; and 2. they thought it was desirable and even necessary to destroy the preceding state apparatus to pave the way for the dictatorship of the proletariat and new social and property relations. Since Marx, views on the conditions under which a p.r. could succeed have greatly broadened. Marx (as well as Engels and Trotsky) thought that the p.r. could succeed only if the proletariat rose against the capitalist rule in most or all industrialized countries. However, Lenin argued (in *IMPERIALISM: THE*

HIGHEST STAGE OF CAPITALISM) that the p.r. was initially feasible in a few countries, or even one, and further stressed that it was unlikely for a p.r. to succeed in all countries at the same time owing to the different stages in their economic and political development. Lenin also believed that the p.r. did not have to be Europe-centred but could occur in Asia ('the road to Western Europe leads via Peking'). Up to the late 1940s it had been generally accepted that a successful p.r. could originate only in the cities. But Mao Tse-tung (MAOISM), and the Chinese revolutionary developments culminating in 1949, demonstrated that a p.r. could develop in the countryside first and then 'engulf the cities'. Mao Tse-tung also put forward the thesis that a p.r. could first spread in underdeveloped countries and then engulf Western Europe and North America. The Cuban experience of 1956–59 (CASTROISM), confirmed Mao Tse-tung's ideas and further introduced new elements in thinking on the p.r. It was shown that a small guerrilla band operating in the countryside, even without initial wide popular support, could gradually inspire a revolutionary movement leading to a successful p.r. and that the p.r. should be similarly exported to other countries. On the other hand, the TUPAMAROS have attached greater importance to the urban nucleus of the revolutionary movement. Another question tht arises in the process of a p.r. is the relation between the political leadership and the guerrilla force. Lenin and Mao Tse-tung emphasized the need for the absolute supremacy of political control (i.e. by the strong, disciplined Communist party) over the armed insurgent units. On the other hand, GUEVARA insisted on freedom from such control to enable the guerrilla force to operate flexibly and in accordance with local conditions.

'Proletarians have nothing to lose but their chains. They have a world to win' A well-known slogan written by Marx and Engels in the final paragraph of THE COMMUNIST MANIFESTO (1848).

'Proletarians of all lands, unite!' A slogan of the international solidarity of the PROLETARIAT formulated by Marx and Engels in 1848 for the COMMUNIST LEAGUE and appearing as the concluding sentence in THE COMMUNIST MANIFESTO (in some translations it is rendered as 'Workers of all lands, unite!'). In the countries ruled by Communist parties where the proletariat no longer exists, the slogan is 'Workers of all lands, unite' (which appears as a motto on the coats of arms of the USSR and its constituent Republics).

Proletariat In Marxist terminology, one of the two basic social classes of capitalism (the other being the BOURGEOISIE). The p. consists of workers and other low income groups deprived of the means of production and consequently forced to sell their labour power to capitalists for survival. The term is derived from the Latin which in ancient Rome denoted the class owning nothing but offspring (*proles*). Although in English the term can be traced back to 1663, in its modern connotation it was established by Marx (first in 1844 in the DEUTSCH-FRANZÖSISCHE JAHRBÜCHER). The exploited p. is essentially international, as its interests are very similar in whatever country it is (PROLETARIAN INTERNATIONALISM). Owing to its size, capacity for organization and militant attitudes, classical Marxist thinkers recognized the p. as a truly revolutionary class, with a historic mission of transforming mankind into an ideal society. Classical Marxists identified the p. with the industrial working class, but later, especially in China, Mao Tse-tung insisted that poor and even middle peasants also constituted the p. The term p. is not, as a rule, applied to the Socialist countries after the transitional period from capitalism to socialism is over. Instead the descriptions 'the working class' and then, 'the state of the whole people', are used (the respective dates for the introduction of these designations in the USSR were 1936 and 1961).

Proletarskaya Revolutsiya (*The Proletarian Revolution*, in Russian) A journal which appeared in the USSR from 1921 to 1941, dealing with the history of BOL-SHEVISM and the GREAT OCTOBER PRO-LETARIAN REVOLUTION. It was published by *Ispart* (Commission for the History of the Russian Communist Party (of the Bolsheviks) and the October Revolution), set up in 1920.

Proletary (*The Proletarian*, in Russian) An illegal organ of the RUSSIAN SOCIAL-DEMOCRATIC LABOUR PARTY, published in Geneva from May to Nov. 1905 (26 issues in all) and smuggled into Russia. It was edited by LENIN, assisted by LUNACHARSKY and V. V. Vronsky. Under the same title another illegal journal was published by the Moscow and St Petersburg Committee of the R.S.-D.L.P. from Sep. 1906 to Dec. 1909. It was printed first in Finland then in Geneva and Paris. In all, 50 issues appeared and Lenin was also its editor.

Proletkult A syllabic abbreviation in Russian of either *Proletarskaya Kultura* (Proletarian Culture) or *Proletarskaya Kulturno-Prosvetitelnaya Organizatsiya* (Proletarian Cultural and Educational organization). It was a mass organization for the development and popularization of proletarian culture and education in Russia and the USSR from 1917 to 1932. It was established soon after the FEBRUARY REVOLUTION OF 1917 to work out a model of a distinctive proletarian culture and methods for its development and dissemination. Its most prominent theoretical leaders were A. A. BOGDANOV, P. I. Lebediev-Polansky, A. V. LUNACHARSKY and V. F. Pletnikov. Its theatre section was led by G. M. Eisenstein. The *P.* was dominated by leftist extremists who rejected traditional Russian culture to the annoyance of Lenin and later Stalin. Although at first it was independent of the Soviet Government and the Communist Party, in 1919 it was placed under the control of the People's Commissariat of Education, subordinated to trade unions in 1925 and finally abolished in 1932.

Proletkultovtsy A Russian name for the memebers of the *PROLETKULT*, especially those who rejected all previous achievements in Russian culture. The group was led by A. A. BOGDANOV and was soon condemned by Lenin and later by Stalin who favoured selective retention of progressive elements of the previous cultural heritage.

Propaganda Persuasive and explanatory activities designed to shape public opinion in directions desired by the state, party or other organization. The Marxist theory on the subject was first formulated by PLEKHANOV and later accepted and popularized by Lenin. Considerable significance is attached to the distinction between p. and AGITATION. P. consists in a presentation of many ideas or problems which are then thoroughly explained and rationalized in a manner appealing to reasonably intelligent or informed individual persons or small groups. Thus, in comparison with an agitator, a propagandist or POLITINFORMATOR must be fairly well educated and aim at more lasting effects on those he addresses. The aim of p. is not so much to call for immediate action through emotions, but rather to cultivate certain attitudes, opinions and convictions through reason. Marxists point out that p. is conditioned by the historical and social development of societies and has a class character. P. has been resorted to by the ruling classes to impose their ideas on society or by the oppressed classes to arouse their CLASS CONSCIOUSNESS. P. has attained unprecedented levels of sophistication and effectiveness with the development of the modern mass media (press, radio, cinema, television, theatre), the control of which gives the ruling class a powerful advantage over other classes. The authorities in the Socialist countries have a very elaborate machinery for conducting p., not only domestically, but also abroad, directly or through INTERNATIONAL COMMUNIST FRONT ORGANIZATIONS. The PERSONALITY CULT of Stalin, Mao Tse-tung and Kim Il-Sung has been described by Western observers as the greatest triumph of Socialist p.

'Propaganda by Committal' (or 'By Deed') A slogan postulating terrorist acts as the best method of publicizing ANARCHISM and highlighting the faults of oppressive regimes. The slogan was approved at the Congress of Anarchists, held at La Chands-de-fonds in Switzerland in 1879, and adopted in practice by a Russian revolutionary terrorist organization called *NARODNAYA VOLYA* in the late 1870s and early 1880s.

Property See NATIONALIZATION, OWNERSHIP OF THE MEANS OF PRODUCTION, PRIVATE PROPERTY, 'PROPERTY IS THEFT', SOCIAL OWNERSHIP OF THE MEANS OF PRODUCTION.

'Property is theft' A famous phrase popularized by the French anarchist thinker, PROUDHON, in answer to the rhetorical title of his book *What Is Property?* (1840). The phrase has often been misinterpreted by extremists. Proudhon, in fact, defended and even idealized private property in the hands of the 'owners-workers' as an individual right, as long as it was associated with social responsibility.

Proportionate, Planned (Balanced) Development See PLANNED PROPORTIONATE DEVELOPMENT.

Pro-Soviet Line See MOSCOW LINE.

Protestantism The description of several denominations of the Christian religion which emerged from the Reformation of the 16th c. directed primarily against the Catholic Church. On the whole, Marxists are less critical of P. than of Catholicism and most other religions. In their view, P. was a progressive social force which challenged FEUDALISM and serfdom and in several ways led to BOURGEOIS-DEMOCRATIC REVOLUTIONS. However, P. also facilitated the accumulation of capital, industrial revolutions with their adverse effects on the working class, the

development of capitalism and the supremacy of the BOURGEOISIE opposed to revolutionary movements. Thus, in the Marxist view, although P. was at first a progressive force in a truly DIALECTICAL manner, it later degenerated into a reactionary multiple institution, impeding futher social progress. P., like other religions, propagates faith in god and in supernatural forces and its extreme persuasion, Calvinism, preaches predestination – all fundamentally inconsistent with DIALECTICAL MATERIALISM.

Protracted War The concept, tactics and strategy of a long irregular war, whereby a large but backward populace may defeat ? well equipped and organized non-proletarian force. The idea was first developed by Mao Tse-tung in a series of lectures, entitled 'On Protracted War', delivered at the Yenan Association for the Study of the War of Resistance against Japan from 26 May to 3 June 1938. China's war against Japan (1937–45) and the VIETNAM WAR (1960–73) are cited as examples. The features of a p.w. are: guerrilla warfare against a well-equipped enemy which cannot use its technical superiority; 2. the political and patriotic indoctrination of the proletarian forces; 3. the avoidance of battle when the enemy attacks with superior forces; 4. counter-attack by the proletarian forces when and where the enemy is least prepared; and 5. using the countryside as the main theatre of the counter-offensive by the proletarian forces while the cities are engulfed in the final stages of the p.w.

Proudhon, Pierre Joseph (1809–65) An outstanding French social thinker and reformer opposed to the BIG BOURGEOISIE and one of the founders of ANARCHISM. He believed that capitalist society could be improved by self-help among the workers and through financial support from the enlightened wealthy and the government. To this effect, he endeavoured to establish a 'Central Credit Bank' and 'Exchange Banks', without success. He is well known for his aphorisms, 'PROPERTY IS THEFT' and 'universal suffrage is counter-revolution'. But his main philosophical and sociological ideas are contained in *The System of Economic Contradictions or the Philosophy of Poverty* (1846). P. was attacked by Marx (mainly in the *POVERTY OF PHILOSOPHY*) for PETTY BOURGEOIS ANARCHISM and UTOPIAN SOCIALISM. In particular, P. was accused of: 1. advocating timid reforms within the existing framework of capitalism; 2. seeking to preserve the institution of private property; 3. belittling the role of the industrial working class; 4. opposing the CLASS STRUGGLE; 5. rejecting the DICTATORSHIP OF THE PROLETARIAT; and 6. distorting DIALECTICS by idealism and thereby opposing DIALECTICAL MATERIALISM. P. and his supporters were defeated by Marx and his followers in the FIRST INTERNATIONAL.

Provisional Government In Russia, the government formed in Petrograd (now Leningrad), after the FEBRUARY REVOLUTION OF 1917 and then overthrown by the Bolsheviks in the October Revolution eight months later. It was created by the Provisional Committee of the DUMA after the abdication of Tsar NICHOLAS II and his brother in March 1917. The P.G. was composed of liberals and moderate socialists, without the extreme right and left (Bolshevik) parties. It was first headed by Prince G. Lvov and then, from 8 July (O.-S.C.) by A. F. KERENSKY. Lenin, after his return from Switzerland in April, branded it as 'capitalist' and 'imperialist', after which it was under constant attack from the PETROGRAD SOVIET. In the insurrection led by Lenin on 24–25 Oct. (O.-S.C., or 6–7 Nov. N.-S.C.) 1917, the P.G. (except A. F. Kerensky and G. N. Prokopovich) was arrested by the Bolsheviks and on the following day the PROVISIONAL WORKERS' AND PEASANTS' GOVERNMENT was set up.

Provisional Workers' and Peasants' Government The first Soviet government formed in Russia immediately after the successful GREAT OCTOBER SOCIALIST REVOLUTION, having replaced the PROVI-SIONAL GOVERNMENT headed by A. F. Kerensky. The P.W.P.G., headed by V. I. Lenin, was formally created by the Second ALL-RUSSIAN CONGRESS OF SOVIETS in Petrograd (now Leningrad), in which the Bolsheviks had a majority, on 26 Oct. (O.-S.C., or 8 Nov. N.-S.C.) 1917. It was meant to be a temporary arrangement until the convocation of the CONSTITUENT ASSEMBLY. The latter was convened on 5 (18) Jan. 1918, but refused to co-operate with the P.W.P.G., whereupon the Bolsheviks dissolved the C.A. and proclaimed the DICTATORSHIP OF THE PROLETARIAT. The name of the P.W.P.G. was changed by the Third All-Russian Congress of Soviets on 18 (31) Jan. 1918 to the Workers' and Peasants' Government of the Russian Soviet Republic.

Psychological School of Bourgeois Economics The name applied by Marxists to a direction in Western economic theory emphasizing the role of subjective considerations in the determination of value and prices. The school, which emerged in Vienna in the last quarter of the 19th c., was founded by K. Menger (1840–1921) and included E. Böhm-Bawerk (1851–1917) and F. Wieser (1851–1926). It explains utility exclusively in terms of psychological attitudes, attributes greater satisfaction to present consumption compared with that in the future (thereby justifying interest rate), is the most extreme advocate of marginal analysis (in particular insisting that the MARGINAL UTILITY of products declines) and views the equalization of marginal utilities of the different products acquired (proportional to their prices) as a condition of equilibrium (optimum). Marxists regard the p.s.b.e. as a reaction against the LABOUR THEORY OF VALUE and as an apologetic movement for capitalism, resorting to unscientific speculations and divorcing man from his social context. The Marxist economic theory emphasizes the cost side in the determination of value expressed in terms of labour and in average magnitudes, focuses attention on society rather than on individuals and rejects time preference as a justification for interest which is SURPLUS VALUE appropriated by capitalists.

Psychological School of Sociology A movement among some sociologists attributing a decisive role to human psychology (temperament, feelings, cravings, prejudices) in the determination of society's political and social life and development. G. Tarde (1843–1904) of France was one of the founders of the movement. The school assigns great importance to the ideas and personality of great thinkers and leaders, who exert charismatic influence on the populace, thereby ensuring social orderliness and stability. Revolts and revolutionary movements by the lower social orders are explained in terms of unhealthy subconscious drives and psychotic aberrations. Marxist thinkers regard the p.s. of s. to be unscientific, reactionary, directed against HISTORICAL MATERIALISM and an apologetic attempt to justify the capitalist social system as natural and immutable. In their view, the school accepts the division of society into elites and the masses to be inevitable and eternal with the latter being devoid of creative initiative.

Psychological Warfare A description given in the Socialist countries to the campaign embarked upon by the USA and other leading Western powers against the Socialist bloc and Marxism after the failure of the COLD WAR during the early 1960s. It has also been described as ideological warfare, political war, the war of nerves and the war of words. From the Socialist point of view it is calculated to change the ideological convictions and political allegiance of the world public from that of socialism and communism to that of capitalism and the West. The methods resorted to include propaganda, economic threats and bribery, espionage, the arms race and the instigation of nationalism and separatism in the socialist bloc. The Socialist countries can be equally blamed for resorting to p.w. against the leading Western nations using similar methods.

Psycho-physical Parallelism A theory in psychology and physiology maintaining that both mental and physical (neurological) processes in human beings are more or less equally important in determining behaviour, but independent of each other. The original exponents of this theory were R. Descartes (1596–1650) and G. W. Leibnitz (1646–1716). Marxists deny the validity of this interpretation and insist that physiological processes are primary while psychological behaviour is secondary and derived from the former. They further state that to some extent psychological processes also influence physiological conduct and that as p.-p.p. postulates an independent existence of ideas from matter, it denies the fact that consciousness is a reflection of reality. Consequently, Marxists maintain that the p.-p.p. accepts some tenets of philosophical IDEALISM and, as such, is inconsistent with MATERIALISM.

Psychology The science of mental processes and phenomena, involving perception, memory, thinking, feelings, will, joy, anxiety, fear and hate. As in PHILOSOPHY, there are two diametrically opposed approaches to p. which have developed since the middle of the 19th c. and which reflect fundamental ideological differences. The idealistic approach treats psychological behaviour as a purely subjective and introspective process in isolation from material conditions. The Marxist approach to p. is materialist, in accordance with DIALECTICAL MATERIALISM and HISTORICAL MATERIALISM and assumes that the psyche is a product of matter at its high level of development and organization. Marxists attach crucial importance to physiological causation, treating psychological phenomena as epiphenomena (surface appearances), which are secondary and as such cannot be studied scientifically. The brain, the higher nervous system and conditioned reflexes assume the focus of Marxist psychological studies, based mainly on the findings of such physiologists as I. P. Pavlov and I. M. Shechenov. It is further maintained that man's p. is a result of his consciousness shaped by work. Pavlov pointed out that the advance from the ape's p. to human p. began with the qualitative transformation of the brain cortex under the impact of the mental processes associated with labour, requiring the invention, use and perfection of tools and weapons together with co-operation and organization. Great importance is also attributed to environmental factors. Psychological behaviour is essentially regarded as a product of the development of the life of higher organisms evolved in the process of interactions between human beings and their social and physical environment. Consequently, it is held that human p. changes historically in response to the changing economic and social factors. By the same token, man's p. differs today from one society to another, Marxists also maintain that in a class society human p. also develops a class character. Under Socialism, the state utilizes p. in the educational, cultural and political spheres as a means of INDOCTRINATION in its efforts to evolve the NEW COMMUNIST MAN.

Public Order Maintenance Stations Civic centres in the USSR concerned with the prevention of social offences and lawbreaking. At the beginning of 1978 there were over 20,000 such centres in the country. Their work is carried out mostly by local social workers and other responsible citizens, representing the state, local organizations and the public. It is directed mainly at potential or actual juvenile delinquents, drunkards, vagabonds, parents neglecting their children and 'social parasites'. Interviews, warning, supervision and advice are the main methods attempted, but referrals to public institutions or courts may also be used.

Public Ownership A term usually applied in capitalist countries to describe the ownership by federal, state or local authorities of land, industrial and commercial undertakings, banks, insurance companies and various 'public utilities' (transport, communications, electricity, water supply,

sewage and the like). P.o. may be either acquired by NATIONALIZATION or by the creation of new entities in particular fields, either in competition with, or to the exclusion of, private enterprise. P.o. is advocated by left-wing political parties and various social reformers. Its purposes may be: 1. the public control of undertakings of crucial importance to the nation, as in the fields of defence, transport, communications and the like to provide reliable output or service; 2. competition to private enterprise, where otherwise a private monopoly may prevail; 3. a step towards socialism and the ultimate socialization of all the means of production; and 4. an aid to economic planning, as public undertakings may be given directions to implement the postulated planned targets. The description used in application to the socialist countries is the SOCIAL OWNERSHIP OF THE MEANS OF PRODUCTION.

Punta del Este Declaration An antiCommunist resolution passed at the Seventh Session of the Ministers for Foreign Affairs of the member countries of the Organization of American States at Punta del Este, Uruguay, on 31 Jan. 1961. Only the Cuban representative (O. Dorticos) spoke against the resolution. The O.A.S. was founded in 1948 and came to include the USA and 20 Latin American republics. Its major problem has always been communist infiltration. The Declaration was prompted by the success of the Cuban revolution and the growing appeal of CASTROISM in Latin America. It was stressed in the Declaration that communist philosophy and practices were irreconcilable with the existing political and social system prevailing in both Americas. The Declaration represented a determined effort directed against the EXPORT OF REVOLUTION. In 1962, Cuba was expelled from the O.A.S. A counter-move to the P.d.E.D. was the formation of the ORGANIZATION OF LATIN AMERICAN SOLIDARITY in 1966 on Cuba's initiative.

Pure and Simple Unionism An industrial labour movement pursuing purely

Pure Art

economic and practical gains for its union members to the disregard of political, social and other objectives. The phrase was popularized by Samuel Gompers, one of the founders of the AMERICAN FEDERATION OF LABOR and its first Chairman (1886–1924, except 1895). Under his leadership this principle was adhered to with considerable benefit to the members. Revolutionary Marxists condemn this form of unionism, regarding it as opportunistic and reconciled to capitalism. Lenin used the term ECONOMISM in application to Russian p.s.u., which is opposite to SOCIAL UNIONISM.

Pure Art See 'ART FOR ART'S SAKE'.

Purge A term peculiar to Communist parties to denote the expulsion of undesirable members from the Party, which may be followed by a show trial, imprisonment, execution, exile and sometimes rehabilitation. This practice was developed by the Bolsheviks before W.W.I, but was perfected after the Revolution. In Russian, it is known as *chistka* (purification). The p. was first officially sanctioned in Lenin's TWENTY-ONE CONDITIONS OF ADMISSION TO THE COMINTERN in 1920, was further reiterated at the Tenth Congress of the RUSSIAN COMMUNIST PARTY (OF THE BOLSHEVIKS) in 1921 and has become an accepted procedure in all communist parties. The most notorious p.s were those carried out under Stalin in the 1930s, known as the GREAT PURGES.

Pusher See *BLAT*, EXPEDITER, *TOLKACH*.

Pu-tuan Koming The Chinese name of the CONTINUING REVOLUTION.

Pyatiletka The Russian colloquial form of *Pyatiletnyi Plan*, meaning Five-Year Plan. The five-year plans in the USSR covered the following periods: 1928–32; 1933–37; 1938–42 (interrupted in June 1941 by the War); 1946–50; 1951–55; 1956–60 (abandoned in 1957); 1959–65 (Seven-Year Plan); 1966–70; 1971–75; and 1976–80

Q

Qualitative Development and Leaps In philosophy, the Marxist view of quality as a dynamic process, analysed mainly by Engels (in *DIALECTICS OF NATURE*) and Stalin (in *Dialectical and Historical Materialism*, 1938). Quality is regarded not as a static characteristic, but a product of evolutionary qualitative changes and sudden major qualitative leaps. Thus, historically, the different SOCIO-ECONOMIC FORMATIONS are considered by Marxists to represent differences not merely of degree but of kind. In ANTAGONISTIC SOCIO-ECONOMIC FORMATIONS, the greater the accumulation of the underlying changes held back by the reactionary ruling class, the greater and more explosive is the (revolutionary) qualitative leap from the obsolete to the new social system. Marxists reject the interpretation of the changes in quality as a result of quantitative growth or decrease, pointing out that by this metaphysical explanation nothing basically new could appear in the world, unless one accepts divine intervention. It is further pointed out that, in accordance with Marxist DIALECTICS and HISTORICAL MATERIALISM, a q.d., although progressive, is not smooth and continuous, but discontinuous and saltatory (steplike). Q.d. and l. take place not only in nature and in thought, but also in society. In the latter, they are basically determined by changes in the MODE OF PRODUCTION. The Marxist conception of q.d. and l. is employed as a theoretical justification for rejecting the peaceful PARLIAMENTARY ROAD TO SOCIALISM and REFORMISM, and instead favouring a PROLETARIAN REVOLUTION as the more appropriate venue for social progress.

Quality In philosophy, the distinguishing characteristic of an object or phenomenon. Marxist philosophers view q. as an inherent property, and consequently reject the mechanistic theories reducing all diversity to quantitative differences. They also reject the idealistic classification and separation of quality into primary qualitative properties (size, weight, shape, movement, etc.) and secondary qualitative features (colour, sound, smell, taste, touch). This approach, in their view, leads to the negation of the objective existence of secondary and even primary qualitative characteristics and denies their unity. As a matter of DIALECTICS, Marxists stress the qualitative differences rather than common characteristics. In their view, this approach is essential in cognition and the scientific pursuit of knowledge. The rejection of this approach, they point out, leads to subjectivist and idealistic conceptions, whereby qualitative differences of objects are products of impressions experienced by the subject. Q. is approached in its dynamic context by Marxists who stress the constant change and development in nature and society.

Quality Marks A device used in several Socialist countries to improve the quality of production by awarding q. classifications to producing enterprises. Such classifications may bear the grades of I, II, III or Q, 1, 2 or A, B, C, depending on the country and whether the products involved are consumer or producer goods. Grade I, Q or A usually denotes world quality standards. Q.m. entitle the producer to special profit mark-ups and act as a form of advertising. Q.m. are resorted to

475

owing to the usual disinclination of the producers to devote too much attention to quality as there are SELLERS' MARKETS, a well developed social security and virtually no private enterprise.

Quantity In philosophy, an attribute or experience that can be quantified or at least comparatively expressed as more or less, an increase, a decrease or a part within a whole. This concept is usually considered in relation to QUALITY. In METAPHYSICS, q. is regarded to be basic and quality to be secondary, as the latter is considered to be derived from the former, viz. development proceeding quantitatively within the limits of the same quality. In Marxist philosophy, in accordance with DIALECTICS and HISTORICAL MATERIALISM, q. and quality are treated as a dialectic unity, mutually influencing each other. But although q. is regarded as primary, greater significance is accorded to quality. Development – whether in nature, thought or society – is conceived as not merely quantitative but also as essentially qualitative. Quantitative growth or decline are considered as a preparation of the necessary conditions for qualitative leaps. Thus, an increase in PRODUCTION FORCES (especially the instruments of production) may enable better methods of production, which in turn necessitates new PRODUCTION RELATIONS. But, as is likely in ANTAGONISTIC SOCIO-ECONOMIC FORMATIONS, the reactionary ruling class impedes change in production relations, the quantitative changes accumulate and finally, through a revolution, a qualitative leap occurs.

Quantity Theory of Money The theory according to which the general price level (p) and, consequently, the value of money, depends on the quantity of money in circulation (m) and its velocity of circulation (v) in relation to the volume of transactions (t) in the economy. The theory proceeds from the equation of exchange represented by the formula $mv = pt$. It was first put forward by the early English classical economists (D. Hume, D. RICARDO, and J. S. Mill) and later developed further by I. Fisher and others. Marxists have adopted a critical attitude to the theory from the start. Marx (in *A CONTRIBUTION TO A CRITIQUE OF POLITICAL ECONOMY*) contended that the theory implied that money entered into circulation without value and goods without prices and that only after mutual confrontation were prices and the value of money established. Instead, he maintained that the value of money was predetermined by the SOCIALLY-INDISPENSABLE LABOUR embodied in the products exchanged for money and, further, that the level of prices determined the amount of money in circulation. Consequently, changes in the quantity of money in circulation are an effect not a cause of change in the value of products and the price level. Marxists also distinguish between the value of money (predetermined by the socially-indispensable labour expressed in monetary terms) and the purchasing power of money (indicated by the actual prices at which commodities are bought and sold for money in the market). The theory appears to be inapplicable to the Socialist centrally planned economy. A study carried out in Hungary indicated that in fact mv did not equal pt.

'Quarantine' Term used by the US President, J. F. Kennedy, at the time of the CUBAN MISSILE CRISIS in Oct. 1962 for the American blockade of Cuba, aimed at preventing the supply of Soviet weapons. The USSR was warned not to break the blockade as it could lead to war.

R

Rabkrin A syllabic abbreviation in Russian of *Raboche-Krestiyanskaya Inspektsiya*, meaning WORKERS' AND PEASANTS' INSPECTORATES (established by Lenin in 1919).

Rabochy (*Worker*, in Russian) The first Social-Democratic newspaper in Russia, published in St Petersburg (now Leningrad) by the BLAGOYEV GROUP in 1885, of which only two numbers appeared. Its purpose was to disseminate Marxist ideas and to act as the Group's organ. It was discontinued owing to Tsarist repression. Later, under the same name, a newspaper was published by the Central Committee of the RUSSIAN SOCIAL-DEMOCRATIC LABOUR PARTY in Moscow between August and October 1905.

Racism A system of views and practices based on the assumption that races naturally differ in quality – not only physically, but also intellectually, morally and socially – and consequently, some races are 'superior' while others are 'inferior'. It involves prejudice and discrimination against other races or racial groups or distinct nationalities, especially if they are in minority or otherwise in a weak position. R. may be combined with CHAUVINISM and goes back to ancient times. Historically, the evidence of r. can be found in master-slave, feudal lord-serf and imperial-colonial relations. R. appeared in its extreme and most systematic forms in Nazi Germany and imperial Japan and is still in force under apartheid in South Africa. It is also evident in various discriminatory policies and practices (immigration, education, employment, residential areas and the like) in Australia, Britain, the FR of Germany, Israel, the USA and other countries. Marxism unequivocally condemns r. and explains it as a convenient reactionary theory to justify the domination and exploitation of minority or weaker racial groups. The emergence and persistence of r. are attributed to four basic reasons: 1. economic exploitation; 2. a convenient scapegoat for social problems; 3. the division of the oppressed to facilitate their domination; and 4. colonialism. Marxists point out that r. is grossly inconsistent with equality, justice and human dignity and that there are no biological grounds for classifying some races as superior and others as inferior. R. amounts to the acceptance of the view that the class structure of society in the world is preordained and immutable. R. must inevitably lead to antagonistic social relations, which may have to be ultimately resolved in a CIVIL WAR, PROLETARIAN REVOLUTION or a war of national liberation.

Radek, Karl (1885–1939) A Communist leader of Jewish-Polish descent who achieved prominence in the Polish, German, Russian and Soviet working class movements. He joined the Polish Social-Democratic Party in 1902, was active in trade unionism and became a successful political writer. Exiled for revolutionary work, he continued his activities in Germany (1908–13), and then in Switzerland where he collaborated with Lenin, and with whom he travelled in the sealed German train to Russia in April 1917. He then joined the Bolshevik Party and worked in Soviet diplomacy. He was a co-founder of the German Communist Party in Dec. 1918. From 1919 to 1924 he was a member of the Central Committee of the RUSSIAN COMMUNIST PARTY (OF THE BOL-SHEVIKS) and of the Presidium of the Executive Committee of the COMINTERN. In 1920, he became Secretary of the Comintern's Executive Committee and in 1925 Rector of the COMMUNIST UNIVERSITY FOR THE TOILERS OF THE EAST. R. supported Trotsky against Stalin, for which he was expelled from the Party in 1927, but after he had written a flattering pamphlet on Stalin he was reinstated in 1930. During the GREAT PURGES, R. was arrested (in 1937), tried, sentenced to imprisonment and died in a Siberian concentration camp in 1939.

Radicalism Convictions and actions directed towards far-reaching immediate, but not necessarily revolutionary changes in the existing political and social institutions. By the derivation of the word, r. (*radix*, in Latin meaning the 'root') insists on fundamental reforms going to the very roots of the system. The term is used mostly in Western countries where radicals have been described as 'rebels with a vision of a perfect social order' (R. C. Tucker). The degree of extremism of r. has differed in different countries. Originally, in 19th c. France, r. was inspired by the FRENCH REVOLUTION and denoted the insistence on drastic changes in the social system. But in England and the USA, r. has usually implied social reformism of a selective or utopian type associated with liberalism. Although in some cases, r. is used to denote right-wing extremism (e.g. the radical right in the USA), in most cases it implies left-wing militancy. In some instances, r. has been identified with Marxism, but the term is not used by Marxists in application to the Socialist countries. R. flourishes best in Western democracies, where there is freedom of expression and association and scope for social improvement.

Radicalization The process of becoming radical or more radical (RADICALISM), involving militant pressure or action for fundamental reforms. The term became well established in the West in the late 1960s, mostly by reference to students, certain academics (especially teaching political science, economics, sociology, philosophy) and various left-wing movements.

Radicalization of the Masses A movement spearheaded by revolutionary Marxists in the 1920s and supported by the COMINTERN (at its Sixth Congress in 1928), designed to make the working class in the capitalist countries more radical. It assumed three forms: 1. the refusal of the Communist parties to co-operate with socialist, social-democratic and centrist parties and groups in elections and in parliament; 2. a shift from the PARLIAMENTARY ROAD TO SOCIALISM to the CLASS STRUGGLE, including CLASS-AGAINST-CLASS TACTICS; and 3. the appointment of younger militants to top positions in the Communist parties. The drive was most influential in France during 1927–33, but with disappointing results. By the mid-1930s it had been abandoned in favour of the POPULAR FRONTS. The movement was revived to some extent after W.W.II, but again largely abandoned in favour of EUROCOMMUNISM. The r. of the m. was an important feature of the GREAT PROLETARIAN CULTURAL REVOLUTION in China.

Radical Political Economics A movement in Western economics, which first emerged in the USA in the mid-1960s and spread to most other developed capitalist countries. In the USA, it is represented mainly by the UNION FOR RADICAL POLITICAL ECONOMICS and the NEW LEFT. Among the best known Western exponents of r.p.e. are P. Baran, R. S. Franklin, H. Magdoff, E. Mandel, Joan Robinson, H. Sherman, P. Sweezy and E. Wheelwright. The followers of r.p.e. include older as well as younger economists, wholly or partly inspired by Marx. They still employ the traditional tools and methods of bourgeois economic analysis. But, although they accept some elements of Marxist political economy, they are critical of many aspects of the CENTRAL-IZED DIRECTIVE SYSTEM OF PLANNING AND MANAGEMENT in the Socialist countries, particularly of the Stalinist model. R.p.e. is largely directed against traditional establishment or MAINSTREAM ECONOMICS, as the latter is considered to be incapable of coping with such major problems as unemployment, inflation, alienation, racism in the market place, monopoly power, abuses by the multinational corporations, the depredation of environment, the neglect of public utilities and the like. With regard to its scope, r.p.e. covers such major areas as: 1. the structural transformation of society; 2. economic planning; 3. the relationship between political and private economic power; 4. wealth and income distribution; 5. mass participation in decision-making; and 6. foreign domination by the leading powers.

Radical Socialists The name of a political party in France, left of centre, which was a major political force in the 1930s and which has exerted considerable influence since W.W.II. They are staunchly republican, but contrary to their original programme have become rather moderate and are now described as 'neither radical nor socialist'.

Radishchev, Aleksander Nikolayevich (1749–1802) One of the earliest revolutionary thinkers in Russia, whose ideas and courageous conduct provided inspiration to the Russian reformers and revolutionaries, including the DEKABRISTS, RAZNOCHINTSY, the NARODNIKS and Lenin. Although a member of the nobility, he attacked serfdom and autocracy in Tsarist Russia (mainly in *A JOURNEY FROM ST PETERSBURG TO MOSCOW*), for which by the direction of Catherine II he was sentenced to death, later commuted to 10 years of banishment in Siberia. He also made pioneering con-

tributions to materialist philosophy (in *Man: His Mortality and Immortality*, 1809) by attacking IDEALISM and MYSTICISM and putting forward ideas anticipating HISTORICAL MATERIALISM. He emphasized the natural racial equality of peoples, opposed slavery (as it existed in the USA) and class exploitation (especially of peasants by landlords). In his other writings he raised some novel ideas on economics and education. After his release from Siberia he continued campaigning for political and social reforms, but encountered bitter opposition from the nobility and the bureaucratic establishment, and in desperation committed suicide. Before his death he remarked: 'Posterity will avenge me'.

'Radish Communists' A derogatory label once applied by Stalin to the Chinese Communists, implying that they only appeared to be Communists on the surface, but in fact were petty bourgeois and nationalistic.

Rákosi, Mátyás (1892–1971) A Hungarian communist leader and statesman, who dominated the national scene in the first eight crucial years of the Communist regime in Hungary (1945–53). He became a founding member of the Communist Party of Hungary when he was a prisoner of war in Russia in 1918. In the same year he returned to Hungary and in 1919 became the Minister for Socialist Production in the HUNGARIAN SOVIET REPUBLIC. After its collapse, he worked for the COMINTERN, was imprisoned several times and in 1940, in an exchange arrangement, he was allowed to emigrate to the USSR. He returned to Hungary, heading the MUSCOVITES with the Soviet troops in 1944 and became the Party Secretary. With the aid of the secret police, he embarked on a systematic SOVIETIZATION of Hungary, ruthlessly eliminated opposition political parties as well as many of his Communist rivals. He became a symbol of unbending Stalinism and subservience to Moscow. After Stalin's death (March 1953) he gradually lost power and on Soviet advice was removed from the Party leadership in '1956. He was accused by his former colleagues of serious errors of economic judgment, the violation of SOCIALIST LEGALITY and of establishing a PERSONALITY CULT. During the HUNGARIAN UPRISING in 1956 he fled to the USSR where he died in Feb. 1971.

Rappists Members of the Russian Association of Proletarian Writers (in Russian *Rossiiskaya Assotsiatsiya Proletarskikh Pisatieli*) which existed in the USSR from 1925 to 1932. Although mostly of non-proletarian background, the R. were supporters of the Soviet regime and worked towards the Bolshevization of literature. They treated literary work as a form of participation in the class struggle and were opposed to *POPUTCHIKI* (fellow travellers). *R.A.P.P.* was established by the All-Union Conference of Proletarian Writers in 1925 and was designed to unite different literary groups and to reflect official policy on literary work. It published two organs: *On the Literary Post* and *RAPP*. But by 1930 the R. had been described by Stalin as 'simplifiers' and 'vulgarizers' of Marx. They were further accused of the misunderstanding and misinterpretation of Marxism, either because of their bourgeois background or because of poor education. *R.A.P.P.* was dissolved by the ALL-UNION COMMUNIST PARTY (OF THE BOLSHEVIKS) in 1932 and most R. became members of the WRITERS' UNION OF THE USSR (created at the same time).

Rate of Exploitation In the Marxian analysis of the exploitation of labour under capitalism, the percentage ratio of the SURPLUS LABOUR TIME (s, represented by the capitalist's profit) to the INDISPENSABLE LABOUR TIME (v, represented by the subsistence wage actually paid). In Marx's symbols it is expressed as s/v 100, and is also known as the 'rate of surplus value'. Thus, if the total working day is 12 hours and the worker creates production equivalent to his subsistence wage (necessary to maintain and reproduce labour) in 8 hours, the r. of e. is $4/8 \times$

$100 = 50\%$. The r. of e. differs from one form of production to another, owing to the differing ORGANIC STRUCTURE OF CAPITAL (capital-labour ratio) and the fact that prices depart from the values of commodities. The more machinery is used in production, the higher the rate of exploitation, as it now takes less time to produce the worker's means of subsistence. There is a tendency for the equalization of the r. of e., owing to competition among workers to move from industries with high rates of surplus value to those with low rates.

Rate of Growth An economic concept denoting the percentage increase in production compared with the preceding year or some other period. It usually means the r. of g. of NATIONAL INCOME of a country over an annual period. The concept as used in the Socialist planned economies refers to the NET MATERIAL PRODUCT, not Gross Domestic Product, Gross National Product, or Net National Product at Factor Cost. The Communist regimes attach great importance to the maximum feasible r. of g. and on the whole attain higher rates than capitalist countries. Over the period 1950–78, the average annual r. of g. based on official statistics was 7 per cent in the socialist bloc, compared with 4 per cent attained in the capitalist world. However, owing to the peculiarities of the socialist national income accounting, the socialist r. of g. usually embodies an (unintended) upward bias estimated to be from one-quarter to one-third, in comparison with the capitalist rates based on Western national income accounting. If adjustments are made to eliminate the bias, the average socialist rate over the period works out at 5 per cent or from one-fifth to one-quarter above the capitalist rate.

Rate of Profit See PROFIT RATE.

Rate of Surplus Value A concept established by Marx with reference to capitalism, indicating the relation (ratio) of SURPLUS VALUE (s) to VARIABLE CAPITAL (v), i.e. roughly total profits to wages. In

Marxian symbols the r. of s.v. is expressed as $= s/v$. In Marxist economic theory, the only source of surplus value is hired labour. No other factor of production, not even materialized labour (fixed assets, raw materials, semi-finished components), can create value. Materialized labour can only be transferred to the new product (PRODUCTION PRICE). Consequently, CONSTANT CAPITAL (c in the Marxian formula for value, $c + v + s$) is not included in the denominator. The r. of s.v. is different from the PROFIT RATE as in the latter, constant capital c is included in the denominator. The r. of s.v. also shows the relation between the SURPLUS LABOUR TIME and INDISPENSABLE LABOUR TIME, and as such, it also indicates the RATE OF EXPLOITATION of productive labour.

Rationalism A movement in philosophy which reached its greatest development in the 19th c., recognizing reason as the basis of cognition and human activities. The founders of modern r. were R. Descartes (1596–1650) and B. Spinoza (1632–77). In the 18th and 19th c., r. was also applied to the social sphere. Rationalists highlighted the inconsistencies and failures of the existing social institutions and pressed for a new rational social order. R. is opposed not only to IRRATIONALISM and DEISM but also to EMPIRICISM, and insists that sensory experience is accidental, biased and, consequently, misleading. It is reason alone that can enable the understanding of existence. Although Marxists regard r. as an improvement on deism and irrationalism, they disagree with its rejection of sensory experience in the process of cognition, as this stand leads to IDEALISM, thus conflicting with DIALECTICAL MATERIALISM. They point out that the pursuit of KNOWLEDGE and TRUTH involves both sensory experience and abstract reasoning, with the final test of true knowledge being practice. They also stress that irrational factors play a part in human behaviour. Further, social, economic and cultural developments in society are not necessarily determined by rational factors. To improve society, it is not enough to think out theories and models, however rational they may be, as this would lead to utopianism (UTOPIAN SOCIALISM).

Rationalized Consumers' Sovereignty A consumer regime under which the state intervenes to correct consumers' preferences in order to prevent anti-social consumption. The state determines MAJOR PROPORTIONS IN THE ECONOMY, including the proportion of total production allowed for current consumption, private and social consumption and the scale of priorities for the development of the different branches of the economy. But otherwise, the structure of production of consumer goods is shaped by the planners according to consumers' preferences as long as they are not in conflict with social interests. This system typically prevails in the Socialist planned economies. In some respects it is slightly more liberal than the system based on the CONSUMERS' FREEDOM OF CHOICE. The rationalization of consumers' preferences is pursued by a combination of direct controls and propaganda directed towards CONSUMPTION STEERING.

Rational Prices Prices which are not arbitrary but are determined according to some judicious criterion. In capitalist economics, scarcity – as revealed by the forces of supply and demand operating in the market – is generally accepted as the only legitimate criterion, as it reflects cost-preference relations and is conducive to the most efficient utilization of resources and output. By this thinking, Socialist prices are regarded as irrational, as they are not formed in free markets. However, such an assertion is too sweeping. Socialist prices are not arbitrary, but are set at levels to promote socially important objectives, such as the desired level of ACCUMULATION, SOCIAL JUSTICE, the absorption of DIFFERENTIAL RENT and the promotion of the development of certain industries in desired directions (TARGET PRICING). Price setting along these lines is quite legitimate in the context of the social system in force. As such, Socialist prices have a rationality of their own, even though they may appear irrational from the point of view of scarcity and narrowly defined economic efficiency.

Raznochintsy ('of various social classes', in Russian) Intellectuals and professional workers of humble social background who emerged in Russia in the 19th c. as a result of changing social and economic conditions. They came from the peasantry, the urban working class, the white-collar working group and impoverished gentry and clergy. Although educated, they suffered from various restrictions, lived in poverty and provided the backbone of the revolutionary movement in Russia, especially in the period 1850–80. The *R*. were opposed to Tsarist autocracy and feudalism and advocated the abolition of serfdom and the improvement of the conditions of the rural masses. They exerted considerable influence on the development of NARODNISM especially *ZEMLYA I VOLYA*. Many *R*. became REVOLUTIONARY DEMOCRATS.

Reactionary A term often employed by Marxists to describe persons or groups or classes defending the existing exploiting social order and opposing progressive forces working towards a better social system. The concept is derived from Marxist DIALECTICS, according to which if there is action it is opposed by reaction. A r. may be a liberal, social democrat, conservative, or fascist, or in general, anybody who opposes Socialist or Communist ideology or activities. In the Socialist countries, the label of r. may be applied to any dissident deviating from the official Party line (especially to the right) or one who endeavours to restore the old order. In the latter case, he is also known as a counter-revolutionary (COUNTER-REVOLUTION).

Real Bills Theory of Credit See PRODUCTIVE CREDIT THEORY.

Realism In philosophy, an epistemological theory, maintaining that only OBJEC-TIVE REALITY can be known and that the latter exists independently of man's will and consciousness. R. emerged in Britain and the USA in the early years of the 20th c. as a reaction against IDEALISM. Among its early exponents were S. Alexander (1859–1938), W. James (1842–1910), G. E. Moore (1873–1958) and B. Russell (1872–1970). R. is opposite to SUBJEC-TIVE IDEALISM and represents a version of philosophical MATERIALISM. Although essentially materialistic, r. is not fully accepted by Marxist philosophers. Although they agree that reality has its own existence independently of human consciousness, they reject the possibility of cognition independently of man. They maintain that nothing in nature (e.g. minerals) or society (e.g. production relations) can be known without human experience and practice. Engels (in *DIALECTICS OF NATURE*) described r. as an attempt to 'smuggle materialism on the one hand, while rejecting it on the other'. Also CRITICAL REALISM, NEO-REALISM, SOCIALIST REALISM.

Realized Prices A term used in Socialist national income accounting for the calculation of the NET MATERIAL PRODUCT. R.p. are those received by enterprises for final products and material services. While final producer goods and MATERIAL SERVICES are valued at PRODUCER PRICES, close to what is called factor cost in capitalist national income accounting, in the case of consumer goods official retail prices (including turnover taxes) are taken into account. R.p. do not correspond to market prices as understood in capitalist national income accounting, as market prices are subject to various forms of control, hence they are generally below free market prices.

Rectification Campaigns (*Cheng Feng*, in Chinese) A term peculiar to the Chinese communist practice for education, re-education or indoctrination in the spirit of Chinese communism or in accordance with current Party policies ('rectification' in Latin means 'placing along straight, correct lines'). The term r. was first used in 1929 by Mao Tse-tung in application to recruits accepted by the Chinese Communist Party. There were several r.c. in China on a wide scale, viz. of 1942–43 (the Sinification of the MUSCOVITES), 1950, 1951–54 (a purge of 10 per cent of Party members), 1957 (to 'weed out poisonous weeds' after the 'HUNDRED FLOWERS' INTERLUDE), 1963 (emphasis on SELF-CRITICISM) and 1966–69 (the GREAT PROLETARIAN CULTURAL REVOLUTION).

Red A colour ideologically associated with communism. It may mean a communist, a member of a communist party, a Russian, a Soviet citizen, a Chinese communist and is also used as an adjective. R. has been for a long time associated with bloodshed, and by the 17th c. the r. flag had been used as a symbol of defiance and battle. As a symbol of revolution, r. was first publicly used during the FRENCH REVOLUTION (1789–99) and then by the PARIS COMMUNE (1871) and the Bolsheviks in the October Revolution (1917). To Marxists, r. symbolizes the suffering of mutineers against oppression and augurs the dawn of the new social order (in Russian r. implies beauty, *krasnyi* meaning red and *krasivyi* beautiful). The opponents of communism, on the other hand, use the term disparagingly, identifying it with violence and bloodbaths.

Red Academy A general colloquial term for the highest party educational institution at the postgraduate level in most Socialist countries. It is or has been known as the Red University, Institute of Red Professorship, Academy of Social Sciences, or the Higher School of Social Sciences. It is usually attached to the CENTRAL COMMITTEE of the Communist Party and is empowered to award higher degrees. Its main purpose is to train Marxist teaching staff for higher educational institutions and personnel for higher party positions requiring advanced theoretical background. Admission is by strict selection, the usual pre-condition being a degree in philosophy, political economy or

history and experience in party or government work. The course takes 1–3 years and normally involves a thesis. The oldest and best known R.A. is the ACADEMY OF THE SOCIAL SCIENCES of the USSR.

Red Aid See INTERNATIONAL ORGANIZATION FOR AID TO REVOLUTIONARIES.

Red Army A shortened name for the Workers' and Peasants' Red Army in Soviet Russia and then the USSR from 1918 to 1946. It was formally founded by the COUNCIL OF PEOPLE'S COMMISSARS in Jan. 1918 (three months after the Bolshevik Revolution), but in practice it was created by TROTSKY after he became the Commissar for War in March 1918. Initially, the R.A. consisted of ex-Tsarist officers and RED GUARDS, but it was soon developed into a broadly based proletarian army, which by 1920 had reached 5.5m. Saluting and the term 'officer' were abolished soon after the Revolution, but the former was reintroduced in 1941 and the latter in 1943. The name of the R.A. was officially changed in 1946 to the Soviet Army. The designation of R.A. was also used in China from 1927 (NAN-CH'ANG INSURRECTION) to 1945. By the end of W.W.II it had 1m. men and was better led and disciplined than the Kuomintang's National Liberation Army. The name of the Chinese R.A. was changed in 1945 to the People's Liberation Army.

Red Banner of Labour, Order of A Soviet civilian order awarded to individuals, enterprises and other organizations for distinguished economic or scientific services to the USSR. It is in the form of a badge showing a red banner and an inscription 'USSR' and 'Workers of All Lands, Unite'.

Red Banner, Order of A military order in the USSR for conspicuous bravery, which can be awarded to all ranks in the Soviet armed forces, other citizens and to military units. It was instituted by the Presidium of the Central Executive Committee of the USSR in 1924. It is oval in shape with an emblem consisting of a hammer and sickle and a red banner, bearing an inscription, 'Workers of All Lands, Unite'.

Red Board Another name for the BOARD OF HONOUR.

Red Bourgeoisie A colloquial term used in the European Socialist countries, denoting the new emerging elite of well-to-do higher party officials, technocrats and successful professionals, all owing their privileged position to the Communist regime. In a narrower sense, the label is applied to privileged young people studying at tertiary and vocational institutions or leading comfortable idle lives, made possible by their well-to-do and influential parents or relatives. Recognizing this problem, KHRUSHCHEV proposed a radical reform of the Soviet educational system, whereby students in secondary schools were to be required to work in productive enterprises while in secondary training and before proceeding to higher education. The main purpose of the reform was to break down the emergent class distinctions and to prevent well-to-do parents from conferring career advantages on their children. But due to strong opposition from different quarters, the proposed scheme has never been fully implemented. Also *EMBOURGEOISEMENT*.

Red Brigades (*Brigate Rosse*, in Italian) An extremist left-wing terrorist group in Italy founded by R. Curcio in 1969, determined to undermine the capitalist establishment by violent means. The R.B. achieved public notoriety after their kidnapping of A. Moro, President of the Christian Democratic Party and former Prime Minister, in Rome in March 1978. In a 'trial' they sentenced him to death for 'counter-revolution' and 'crimes against the interests of the working people', and shot him on 9 May 1978.

Red Channels An expression used in the USA in the 1950s by supporters of McCAR-THYISM and by other opponents of communism, to denote the real or imagined network of communist infiltration in the country.

Red Commander A term which appeared in the RED ARMY after the October Revolution of 1917, to describe that class of senior officers who rose from the ranks by virtue of their working class background and political reliability, and not necessarily their professional competence. The r.c. contrasted with the ex-Tsarist officer, who was professionally competent but not necessarily politically trustworthy and capable of commanding respect from his proletarian subordinates.

Red Director The general manager of a socialized enterprise in a socialist country, the implication being that he owes his appointment more to his working class background and political reliability than to professional competence. The term came into use in Soviet Russia in the early 1920s, after the socialization of industry and the lack of properly trained and experienced senior executives. The designation used today is simply DIRECTOR.

Red Flag The English translated title of *HUNG-CH'I*, the official monthly theoretical organ of the Chinese Communist Party.

Red Front In party politics, a type of UNITED FRONT where there is close electoral and parliamentary collaboration between the Communist party and other left-wing political parties under Communist domination.

Red Guards (*Krasnogvardiytsy*, in Russian) Detachments of armed workers or ex-servicemen led by the BOLSHEVIKS in Russia and then in Soviet Russia. They first appeared during the REVOLUTION OF 1905–07 and consisted mainly of militant factory workers. The description 'Red' alluded to BLOODY·SUNDAY and revolutio-

nary bloodshed. The R.G. played a prominent role in the GREAT OCTOBER SOCIAL-
IST REVOLUTION of 1917. The backbone
of the force were the Petrograd R.G.,
numbering nearly 40,000 men, who were
instrumental in the Bolshevik seizure of
power. There were 200,000 R.G. in other
urban centres of Russia at the time. The
R.G. were opposed by the WHITE
GUARDS. The R.G. provided a nucleus of
the proletarian military establishment and
by May 1918 they were incorporated into
the RED ARMY.

Red Guards, in China (*Hung-wei Ping*, in
Chinese) Name given to the militant un-
armed youth groups, mostly consisting of
secondary and post-secondary school students during the GREAT PROLETARIAN
CULTURAL REVOLUTION. The first R.G.
were formed at a school attached to Tsing-
hua University in May 1966. In Aug. 1966
Mao Tse-tung reviewed 1.0m R.G. on
parade in Peking and by 1969 there were
several million R.G. units in the country.
Their membership was limited to the
youth of proletarian background viz. children of industrial workers, poor peasants,
revolutionary cadres and of revolutionary
martyrs. They were modelled on the first
Chinese Red Army units (created in
1927) and the PEOPLE'S LIBERATION
ARMY. The R.G. wore red armbands with
the *H.-w.P.* initials, marched carrying a
red flag and Mao Tse-tung's LITTLE RED
BOOK, from which they recited passages at
the slightest opportunity. Mao and LIN
PIAO encouraged them to take matters
into their own hands. The role of the R.G.
was to eliminate the old bourgeois remnants in Chinese culture and administration, which they did with reckless enthusiasm, disrupting the educational system, transport and normal life in general.
They were reprimanded on several occasions and finally a drastic clampdown had
to be applied by the authorities during
1968–69. A large number of R.G. were
sent to the countryside as part of the RUS-
TICATION DRIVE, to learn by working with
peasants and engage in the construction of
various projects.

Red Hundreds Armed units of revolutionary peasants who participated in the RE-
VOLUTION OF 1905–07 in southern Russia.
Their greatest achievement was the armed
uprising in Avkhasia (in the Caucasus
Mountains), Nov.–Dec. 1905, which was
organized by the Bolsheviks led by
ORDZHONIKIDZE. At one stage the R.H.
seized power in the region and established
a proletarian authority. Although the uprising was crushed by Tsarist troops, isolated revolutionary detachments continued their activities up to mid-1907.

Red International A colloquial general
term for any of the seven Internationals –
the FIRST INTERNATIONAL (1864–76), the
COMINTERN (1919–43), the COMMUNIST
YOUTH INTERNATIONAL (1919–43), the
SPORTINTERN (1921–35), the KRESTIN-
TERN (1921–37), the PROFINTERN
(1921–37) and the FOURTH INTERNA-
TIONAL (1938–). Sometimes the de-
scription R.I. is specifically applied only to
the Comintern. The R.I. is contrasted with
the BLACK INTERNATIONAL, the GREEN
INTERNATIONAL and the YELLOW INTER-
NATIONAL.

Red International of Labour Unions PRO-
FINTERN.

Redistribution of National Income The
transfer of purchasing power from higher
to lower income groups by means of progressive taxes and death duties on the one
hand and social services on the other. Its
purpose is to reduce the disparity of personal income in society and thereby increase the level of social welfare as a
whole. This policy is based on the acceptance of the principle of the diminishing
utility of money, so that the rich lose less in
satisfaction in forgone income and property than the poor gain in satisfaction from
the social services. This practice is carried
on in both capitalist and Socialist countries. But it is pursued on a more systematic basis under socialist central economic
planning where: 1. the social ownership of
the means of production facilitates the
transfer; 2. the objective of the equaliza-

tion of personal income is treated more seriously; and 3. the redistribution is planned in such a way as to ensure the necessary level of saving to support the postulated investment programme in the interest of accelerated economic development.

Red Peasants International A colloquial English description of the KRESTINTERN.

'Red Peril' A term first used in Western Europe between the two world wars referring to the Communist threat. The threat was believed to come from two sources: 1. internally – from the local Communist parties, instigating destructive strikes and weakening governments; and 2. externally – from international communism, viz. the COMINTERN and the USSR. The 'r.p.' scare was largely fanned out by right-wing extremists, especially fascists and Nazis as a justification for strong nationalistic and reactionary regimes.

Red Rebels A less common name for REVOLUTIONARY REBELS (in China).

Red Regiments Army units consisting of East and Central European Communists which were formed in Soviet Russia during 1918–20, with the purpose of carrying the proletarian revolution to their countries and establishing Soviet Republics. At that time, there were more than 3m. foreign prisoners of war and refugees in Soviet Russia. Stalin, in co-operation with the COMINTERN, formed National Commissariats (Estonian, Finnish, Hungarian, Latvian, Lithuanian, Polish and Slovak) to organize national R.R. An Estonian R.R. marched with the Bolsheviks in late 1918 to Estonia. Several Hungarian R.R. slipped through to Hungary where they helped establish the HUNGARIAN SOVIET REPUBLIC (March–July 1919) and to Slovakia in mid-1919 to give support to the SLOVAK SOVIET REPUBLIC (June–July 1919). Five Polish R.R. marched to Poland in early 1919 during the Russo-Polish War (1919–20) to assist the Soviet Red Army and establish a Polish Soviet

Republic (which failed dismally). Nowhere did the R.R. achieve any lasting effects, and all the national Soviet Republics that were established soon collapsed.

Red Republic The name given to the first communist regime in history, in existence in Paris from March to May 1871, better known as the PARIS COMMUNE.

Red Saturday Another, colloquial name for *SUBBOTNIK* (in the USSR).

Red Scare A wave of anti-communist hysteria in several Western countries, especially Germany and the USA, over the period 1918–20. It was prompted by such events and developments as 1. the success of the GREAT OCTOBER SOCIALIST REVOLUTION in Russia in 1917; 2. the Bolshevik victories over the White armies in the Civil War (1918–20); 3. the savage pursuit and elimination of counter-revolutionaries by the *CHEKA*; 4. Trotsky's call for the PERMANENT REVOLUTION (EXPORT OF REVOLUTION); 5. the formation of the COMINTERN in 1919; 6. the mushrooming of communist parties in the capitalist world; 7. the creation of national RED REGIMENTS in Soviet Russia (1918–20); 8. the Soviet offensive against Poland (1920); 9. the establishment of Soviet Republics in Bavaria, Hungary and Slovakia in 1919; 10. the failure of the FOREIGN INTERVENTION; and 11. widespread communist-inspired strikes in the leading capitalist countries.

Red Sport International The English colloquial name for the SPORTINTERN.

Red Square The central square in Moscow and the main place in the USSR for MAY DAY celebrations, military parades, and other important public functions. Its origin goes back to the middle of the 12th c. and by the mid-17th c. it was known as the 'colourful market place' (*Krasivaya Ploshchad*). Since the Bolshevik Revolution it has become known as *Krasnaya Ploshchad* (Red Square). The R.S. is flanked by the KREMLIN and LENIN'S

MAUSOLEUM, the State Historical Museum, *GUM* department store and the Cathedral of St Basil the Blessed.

Red Star, Order of A Soviet military order awarded to the members of the armed forces and organizations for outstanding services to the defence of the USSR in peace or in wartime. It is in the form of a five-pointed star, red enamelled, showing an armed soldier with a hammer and sickle emblem below and an inscription, 'Workers of All Lands, Unite'.

Red Sunday See BLOODY SUNDAY.

Red Trade Union International A name sometimes used colloquially for the Red Labour Union International or the PRO-FINTERN.

Reflection Theory The materialist theory of cognition, according to which human sensory experience, concepts and all other knowledge are basically a reflection of the objectively existing reality. The r.t. is one of the fundamental doctrines in Marxist philosophy and was outlined by Marx (in *CAPITAL*, vol. I) and further developed by Lenin (in *MATERIALISM AND EMPIRIO-CRITICISM* and *PHILOSOPHICAL NOTEBOOKS*). In contrast to the idealistic theories of knowledge (such as AGNOSTI-CISM, EMPIRIO-MONISM, HIEROGLYPHIC THEORY OF COGNITION, LOGICAL POSITIV-ISM and PHYSICAL IDEALISM), the r.t. regards ideas as merely 'matter transmitted to human mind and transformed there' (Marx). In accordance with DIALECTICAL MATERIALISM, the external world is credited with its own existence, independent of human consciousness. Impressions are viewed as reproductions of real phenomena and processes in nature and society. The Marxist exponents of the r.t. (in contrast to earlier materialist interpretations) also emphasize that reflection in mind is not a passive photocopy but an active and dynamic reflective process in human consciousness, dialectically contradictory and subject to continuous development. Mind is considered to have its own laws of pur-posive development because man thinks and acts to satisfy his needs.

Reformism A Marxist concept for attitudes and activites in the labour movement directed towards minor and gradual reforms within the framework of capitalism, without basically changing its exploitative nature. R. represents the main ideological difference between revolutionary communism and evolutionary socialism. R. is opposed to the CLASS STRUG-GLE, the PROLETARIAN REVOLUTION and the DICTATORSHIP OF THE PROLETARIAT as the means of achieving an ideal society. Instead, it accepts the PARLIAMENTARY ROAD TO SOCIALISM, industrial action through trade unions, CO-OPERATIVISM and NATIONALIZATION. R. is associated with the ideas popularized by E. BERN-STEIN in the 1890s and later by K. KAUT-SKY. Whilst r. and the related concept OPPORTUNISM emphasize the domestic and practical side, REVISIONISM is more concerned with theory, especially in the international context.

Reign of Terror A term usually applied to the extremist phase of the FRENCH REVOLUTION (1789–99) against the arbitrarily suspected enemies of the new Republican regime. The R. of T. was unleashed by the JACOBINS led by G. J. Danton, M. F. I. Robespièrre and J. P. Marat, and lasted two years, 1793–94. Thousands of nobles and moderate Republicans (GIRONDINS) were judged and sentenced to death by the Committee of Public Safety, including Louis XVI (21 Jan. 1793) and Marie Antoinette (16 Oct. 1793). At the height of the R. of T. Marat was assassinated in July 1793 and Danton and Robespièrre were executed in April and July 1794, respectively. The excesses of the extremists subsequently prejudiced the proletarian cause and power was firmly assumed by the bourgeoisie through the Directory in 1795.

Relative Ethics A philosophical approach to ETHICS, emphasizing that ethical standards are not absolute and immutable, but differ from one society to another, from one social group to another and change historically from one period to another. The idea of r.e. was originally associated with H. Spencer (1820–1903), who distinguished it from ABSOLUTE ETHICS. From the mid-19th c. on, Marxist philosophers have embraced r.e. because it fits consistently into DIALECTICS and HISTORICAL MATERIALISM. The Marxist treatment of r.e is preoccupied with the sources of ethical standards, the description and analysis of different codes of conduct among different peoples and social groups and in different historical periods. The Marxist interpretation stresses that moral norms are an element of the SUPERSTRUCTURE in society, are fundamentally conditioned by the material BASE, and like the latter, also change historically. Ethical standards inevitably have a class character, as the concepts of good and bad differ and vary. Marxists distinguish between religious, feudal, bourgeois, proletarian, socialist and communist ethics. Thus Socialist ethics is opposed to the exploitation of man by man, acquisitive proclivities, racism and chauvinism. Instead, it emphasizes moral motivation in work, social interest, SOCIALIST INTERNATIONALISM and SOCIALIST MORALITY in general.

Relative Surplus Population A Marxian term (discussed in *CAPITAL*, vol. I) in application to capitalist countries, to denote the unemployed work force and their families. It includes the population deprived of the means of subsistence owing to seasonal, frictional and structural unemployment and those who are handicapped and are unable to work. This population represents only a relative surplus owing to the deficiencies of capitalism (at the time of Marx) which cannot ensure continuous full employment and provide the necessary social benefits. Also MALTHUSIANISM, RESERVE ARMY OF WORKERS.

Relative Surplus Value A concept used by Marx (in *CAPITAL*, vol. I) in application to capitalism, referring to the proportion represented by SURPLUS VALUE created by the worker in the SURPLUS LABOUR TIME compared with the INDISPENSABLE LABOUR TIME. The r.s.v. tends to rise owing to technological progress and the consequent growth of labour productivity. This results in the shortening of the indispensable labour time in relation to the surplus labour time. Thus, in a workday of 10 hours, if the worker produces goods equal in value to his subsistence wage in 4 instead of 5 hours, the r.s.v. increases from 50 per cent to 60 per cent.

Relative Truth A philosophical concept denoting truth which is incomplete, i.e. partial or valid only at a particular time and, as such, is opposite to ABSOLUTE TRUTH. The concept is important in Marxist philosophy, which treats the establishment of truth as a dynamic, historical pursuit. Marxist philosophers stress that the process of COGNITION is infinite, like the development of nature or society. At each stage of the development of science and learning, human knowledge is determined by the existing level of technology, methods of production and social organization. Consequently, the truths established by science at a given stage must not be regarded as complete and final ('absolute') truths, as they are relative only to the particular stage requiring further perfection. Thus, changes in historical conditions inevitably lead to a reformulation of truths and only the sum of relative truths ultimately leads to the absolute truth.

Relativism In philosophy, a theory maintaining that all knowledge is relative to man's mind, i.e. human knowledge is limited in relation to the total potential knowledge owing to the limitations of our cognition. R. is also known as the relativity of knowledge and is identified with W. Hamilton (1788–1856), who based much of his thinking on I. Kant (1724–1804) and A. Comte (1789–1857). The theory was further developed by J. S. Mill (1806–73). Although to some extent the theory is accepted by both bourgeois and Marxist philosophers, the interpretation of the limitations to human cognition has been a subject of ideological controversy. From the position of IDEALISM, cognition is essentially subjective and in a sense arbitrary, as ideas exist separately from reality or reality exists only as far as it is known or conceptualized. This interpretation leads to AGNOSTICISM, SCEPTICISM and PHYSICAL IDEALISM. On the other hand, DIALETICAL MATERIALISM views cognition as a process of reflection of reality in mind, and to this extent it is possible to arrive at absolute knowledge. However, Marxism views the acquisition of knowledge as a historical process, conditioned by the stage of development of the material BASE and the consequent SUPERSTRUCTURE. Although a body of knowledge may appear to be valid and advanced at the time, in fact it is only relative, as its validity may become questioned in the light of subsequent developments. Consequently, at any particular stage, we usually know only the RELATIVE TRUTH, in our progress towards the ABSOLUTE TRUTH.

Religion A system of beliefs, practices and institutions expressing the acceptance and veneration of supernatural forces. R. is usually steeped in a doctrine and sustained on an organized basis through a church. R. is a fairly universal phenomenon appearing in almost all societies at different stages of economic, political, social and cultural development. There are four major r. – Christianity, Islam, Buddhism and Brahmanism, most of which fall into a number of denominations, sects and other organized and informal creeds and cults. R. is fundamentally incompatible with Marxist philosophy. Marxists identify r. with philosophical IDEALISM as r. is based on supernatural forces, the separation of such beliefs from the material world. As such, r. is inconsistent with DIALECTICAL MATERIALISM. They deny that r. is eternal and immutable, and, instead, see it as a historical phenomenon conditioned by the material BASE. Marx (in *Towards a Critique of Hegel's 'Philosophy of Right': Introduction*, 1844) pointed out that, 'man

makes religion, religion does not make man'. The original source of religion is attributed to the inability of primitive man to understand the forces of nature and his impotence in coping with it. Consequently, man ascribed supernatural powers to such forces. Later, in class societies, r. was embraced both by the ruling and by the oppressed classes – the former to legitimize and perpetuate their privileged position and the latter to find consolation hoping for miracles or paradise after life. Marx (*ibid.*) said, 'Religion is the opium of the people'. Thus, r. is seen to be inimical to social progress and in particular to be cultivating humility, docility and resignation among the oppressed and preventing them from taking their destiny into their own hands by seizing political power. Classical Marxists envisaged that after the proletarian seizure of power r. would disappear. In reality, even in the oldest Socialist country, the USSR, r. has survived and churches are quite active. It may be argued that while condemning religion, Marxism itself has developed into a kind of r. (as illustrated by reference to CHRISTIANITY). Also ATHEISM, DEISM, FIDEISM, GOD, LEAGUE OF MILITANT ATHEISTS, PAX, PROLETARIAN REDEMPTION, THEISM.

Remonetization The process of the reintroduction of money in the economy. The term is particularly applicable to the USSR over the period 1922–34, following the disastrous consequences of the attempts to abandon money after the Revolution in favour of the NATURALIZATION OF ECONOMIC PROCESSES. Stalin described the dream of a money-less economy as 'a left-wing nonsense'. Many socialist economists now believe that the Marxian postulate of the abolition of money under FULL COMMUNISM is not feasible.

Renegade A term sometimes employed by revolutionary Marxists against evolutionary Marxists, especially those guilty of OPPORTUNISM, REFORMISM, REVISIONISM and even CENTRISM. The term denotes a turncoat, a deserter of principle and a traitor to the communist cause. The most notable r.s in this sense were A. Millerand (MILLERANDISM) and K. KAUTSKY (Lenin wrote a book, *The Proletarian Revolution and the Renegade Kautsky*, 1918).

Renminbi (People's Currency, in Chinese) The official name of the currency unit in the PR of China, divided into 100 fen. It officially replaced the pre-communist unit, *yuan*, after Dec. 1949, but the latter is still colloquially used. It is also spelled *Ren Min-bi* or *Jen Min-bi* and is abbreviated *RMB*. Officially the *RMB* is regarded as a reliable and stable currency, as it is supported by the political and economic power of the state. But in reality, it is a 'soft' currency not of international consequence. At the end of 1978, its official rate of exchange to US$1.00 was 1.67 *RMB*. Since 1969, the Chinese authorities have made several efforts to strengthen the *RMB* in international dealings and it is now used by some less-developed countries in international settlements. Its value has been rising in relation to other currencies. Its black market rate to US$1.00 was 20.00 *RMB* in 1962, 4.00 in 1969 and 2.00 in 1978.

Rent In Marxian terminology applicable to capitalism, one of the three elements of SURPLUS VALUE (the other two being interest and profit). R. is a form of non-labour income ultimately appropriated by the landowner. As it does not represent remuneration for labour, r. constitutes the exploitation of agricultural labourers and consumers. There are two kinds of r., ABSOLUTE R. and DIFFERENTIAL R.. In the Marxist view, as land is not a product of labour it should receive no remuneration, and consequently, r. must not be treated as cost, even in a socialist planned economy.

Rentability (or r. rate) An economic term used in the Socialist countries. In its broadest sense, it may simply mean being economically advantageous from the so-

cial point of view (even though attained at a microeconomic loss), or profitable. In the past, to avoid using the ideologically objectionable term 'profit', r. was occasionally employed as an alternative name for the partial profit rate (the percentage ratio of profits to fixed costs), or even for the (complete) profit rate (the percentage ratio of profits to fixed and circulating assets). However, in its modern meaning, r. denotes the percentage of ratio of profit to the PRIME COST (materials used, wages, depreciation and interest on bank loans): $R = P/pK$ 100. R. may be applied to individual products, or enterprises, or branches of the economy, or the whole economy. But its greatest practical use is to measure enterprise performance. R. can be calculated on a gross or net basis. In the gross rentability rate, also known as social rentability, gross profit is related to prime cost. There has been a tendency in the European socialist countries since the mid-1960s to replace r. with the PROFIT RATE.

Reproduction An important economic term used in the Socialist countries to denote the continuous process of production in the economy, roughly corresponding to the Western concept of economic growth. The term r. was introduced by Marx (in *CAPITAL*, vol. II), who analysed the complete process of the utilization and replacement of the means of production and labour in the whole economy, involving PRODUCTION RELATIONS, MATERIAL PRODUCTION, distribution, exchange and consumption. In the replacement process, he analysed AMORTIZATION (depreciation), PRODUCTIVE CONSUMPTION and consumption by the population. Marx was inspired by Quesnay's *Tableau économique* (1758) (PHYSIOCRATISM), but developed his own methods of analysis. R. may be such that it results in a positive, zero or negative accumulation (net investment). In Marxist terminology, they correspond to EXPANDED R., SIMPLE R. and CONTRACTING R., respectively. Marx's theory of r. was far ahead of contemporary thinking on the macro-economic process of growth and ante-dated non-Marxist analysis in the field by some 50 years. The knowledge of the Marxian theory of r. enabled M. KALECKI to put forward a model of economic growth in 1935, independently and a year ahead of Keynes.

Reserve Army of Workers Also known as the industrial reserve army, a concept established by Marx (in *CAPITAL*, vol. I) by reference to capitalism. It denotes a pool of unemployment which, although fluctuating, has a tendency to increase due to technological progress, as increasing mechanization and more efficient methods of production lead to redundant labour. Marx saw the r.a. of w. as an inevitable and indispensable feature of capitalism. The unemployed workers weaken the bargaining power of the workers remaining in employment, which helps maintain work discipline and tends to depress wages to the bare subsistence level. The increasing exploitation of labour and the curtailment of consumption of the working class enable high accumulation of capital by the bourgeoisie. This leads to additional investment in labour-saving machinery and processes, causing further redundancies. However, Marx's view has become rather dated. Experience over the past 100 years has shown that technological progress does not necessarily depress employment, as released labour finds employment in new industries. Furthermore, increasing labour productivity leads to the shortening of working hours.

Resocialization A sociological term denoting the process of the transformation of society or individuals to a new set of attitudes, values and social conduct by the new regime in power. It differs from SOCIALIZATION in that r. applies mostly to adults. Although r. occurs in all dynamic societies, it is pursued on a more extensive and systematic basis in the Socialist countries, where the state educational and cultural apparatus together with the state-owned media are employed by the Communist regime to transmit new philosophical, political, sociological, moral and economic ways of thinking, expression and behaviour. The methods of r. include AGITATION, PROPAGANDA, and mass campaigns directed against individualism, nationalism, fascism and imperialism. Instead the Socialist countries aim at developing the PRIMACY OF SOCIAL INTEREST, SOCIALIST MORALITY, PATRIOTISM and SOCIALIST INTERNATIONALISM. Two stages are distinguished in Socialist r.: 1. revolutionary r. – immediately after the Communist assumption of power, noted for the more or less forcible insistence on open and enthusiastic support for the new regime; and 2. continuing r. – less overt but more subtle and pervasive indoctrination to legitimize and perpetuate the communist leadership and rule. Also BRAINWASHING, CULTURAL REVOLUTION, RECTIFICATION CAMPAIGN.

Re-Stalinization Reversion to STALINISM after the fall of Khrushchev from power in the USSR in 1964, a process opposite to DE-STALINIZATION. The term r.-S. is applied to the partial rehabilitation of Stalin, the reversal of liberal reforms in the USSR and Eastern Europe and tighter Soviet domination of the WARSAW PACT and the COUNCIL FOR MUTUAL ECONOMIC ASSISTANCE.

Retail Prices Prices charged to final consumers in retail outlets and in contrast with wholesale or PRODUCER PRICES. In the Socialist countries, r.p. embody turnover taxes and a retail trade mark-up. These two elements account for the difference between wholesale and r.p. In these countries a good deal of importance is attached to the level of r.p. On the one hand, they are set at such levels as to ensure a sufficient level of ACCUMULATION for financing investment in the interest of high rates of economic growth. This is achieved by adding heavy TURNOVER TAXES to wholesale or producer prices of industrial products, especially of luxuries and semi-luxuries. On the other hand, the socialist state sets the r.p. of necessities at low levels to safeguard the minimum standard of living of the lowest income groups.

This is done by omitting turnover taxes and, in some cases, by subsidizing necessities, so that the r.p. of the latter are below producer prices.

Réunion Communist Party (*Parti Communiste Réunionais*) A small but fairly influential party with a membership of about 2,000 (compared with the country's population of 500,000 in 1978). It was originally founded as a section of the Federation of the French Communist Party in 1949, but it became a separate party under its present name in 1959. The Party controls the largest trade union (the General Confederation of Labour of Réunion) and is influential in local government as well as in the General Council (parliament). It follows an independent line in the international communist movement and its official organ is a daily newspaper called *Témoignages* (*Testimonies*).

Revenge Barter, Revenge Counter-sales Terms invented in Western Europe in the early 1970s to describe the practice of Western traders, importing goods from the Socialist countries and insisting on counter-purchases, i.e. that the Socialist exporter agrees to accept part or whole payment in the goods offered by the Western importer. This amounts to the reversal of the traditional practice of the Socialist countries' insistence on counter-sales to the Western exporters of goods to the socialist country.

Revised Later Ten Points (of the education of the masses and the cadres in China) See DOUBLE TEN POINTS.

Revisionism A denunciatory term used by revolutionary Marxists for that course in the international working class movement which consists in the revision of the fundamental principles of Marxism in order to adapt to changing circumstances. R. is opposed to the dogmatic and inflexible acceptance of the classical Marxist theory and instead emphasizes the need for CREATIVE MARXISM. The founder of r. was the German Marxist E. BERNSTEIN who, in

the 1890s, turned from revolutionary Marxism. His views were expressed in his book, *Evolutionary Marxism* (1899), which was followed by K. KAUTSKY and his polemic, *The Labour Revolution* (1925). R. presupposes a possibility of a peaceful transition to socialism through industrial action, the PARLIAMENTARY ROAD TO SOCIALISM and reforms, retaining democratic freedoms and institutions. R. rejects the need for the CLASS STRUGGLE, the PROLETARIAN REVOLUTION and the DICTATORSHIP OF THE PROLETARIAT. Revisionists maintain that there is no need for violence, as the historical process will naturally develop from capitalism into socialism. R. is also highly critical of the LABOUR THEORY OF VALUE, especially the non-recognition of the contribution of non-labour resources to production and the consequential faulty socialist pricing. Revolutionary Marxists regard r. as a 'theoretical disarmament of the workers', a 'betrayal of Marxism', and a 'selfish schism' responsible for the disunity in the working class movement. Revisionists are described as 'agents' and 'lackeys' of the bourgeoisie interested in the salvation of capitalism by socialist devices. The main Marxist criticism of r. is contained in Lenin's writings, viz. 'Marxism and Revisionism' (1908), 'Controversial Questions' (1913) and *Proletarian Revolution and the Renegade Kautsky* (1918). In the TWENTY-ONE CONDITIONS OF ADMISSION TO THE COMINTERN (approved in 1920) the Communist parties applying were required to renounce r. Mao Tse-tung said in 1957 that r. was not a socialist but a capitalist line.

Revolution A radical and fundamental change in thought, system of government or mode of production, as exemplified by the scientific and technical revolution (of the 1950s), the French Revolution and the Industrial Revolution. However, Marxists usually identify r. with a violent political and social upheaval replacing one outdated and decaying social order by another progressive and dynamic order. The basic reason for r. is considered to be economic. It usually occurs in ANTAGONISTIC SOCIO-ECONOMIC FORMATIONS when outdated PRODUCTION RELATIONS obstruct further development of PRODUCTION FORCES (i.e. the outdated ruling class refuses to give up its privileged position). In application to modern times, Marxists distinguish between a BOURGEOIS-DEMOCRATIC R. and a PROLETARIAN R.. They consider r.s as highly desirable historical events, constituting qualitative leaps from lower to higher stages, where power is seized by the stronger progressive classes from the obsolete and reactionary classes. Marx (in *The Class Struggles in France*, 1850) called r. 'locomotives of history', and Mao Tse-tung (in his concept of the CONTINUING REVOLUTION) held that r. is a long process taking place in various stages and that each successive stage is essential for the transition to the next. Also COUNTER-REVOLUTION, REVOLUTIONARY MARXISM, REVOLUTIONARY SITUATION.

Revolutionary (or less commonly, Revolutionist) As a noun, a person devoted to the overthrow of an existing social order in a violent way by REVOLUTION. The designation is usually applied to left-wing radicals, especially those subscribing to revolutionary Marxism, REVOLUTIONARY SYNDICALISM, ANARCHO-COMMUNISM and NIHILISM. The extreme model of a r. is the professional r. This idea was first developed in Russia in the latter half of the 19th c. by M. BAKUNIN, S. NECHAYEV and P. TKACHEV, and later embraced by Lenin. In their view, a revolution could be carried out by a small group of such revolutionaries. Bakunin and Tkachev, in *REVOLUTIONARY CATECHISM*, described the ideal r. as a superman, who has no property, no loyalties except the revolution and who is subject to no moral strictures.

Revolutionary Catechism, The The title of a pamphlet written by two Russian revolutionary anarchists, M. BAKUNIN and S. NECHAYEV in 1869 and circulated in European revolutionary circles in the latter part of the 19th c. *The R.C.* was based on the *Programme of Revolutionary Action* drafted earlier in that year by S. NECHAYEV and P. N. TKACHEV and was an expression of violent ANARCHISM and NIHILISM. It also spelled out the functions and qualities of a model revolutionary. This ideal type was described as a professional in his pursuit who has no property and no identity of his own, who is bound by no existing legal, moral or sentimental norms and who is absolutely devoted in thought and action to revolution by any means, however extreme.

Revolutionary Committees In China, committees established during the GREAT PROLETARIAN CULTURAL REVOLUTION to represent the revolutionary elements in society. They were first created in spring 1967 and mushroomed into a comprehensive network at all levels of public adminstration from local to provincial, but not at the central level. Each R.C. consisted of representatives of Party CADRES, the PEOPLE'S LIBERATION ARMY and 'the masses'. For this reason, the R.C. were also described as 'the three-in-one' alliance. In 1969 another 'three-in-one' principle was added, viz. the representation of the younger, middle and older generations. The purpose of the R.C. was to control local affairs, overriding the existing People's Councils in such ways as to promote the Cultural Revolution and, in particular, to prevent the emergence of elites in public administration. At the height of the G.P.C.R., the R.C. virtually became the only active political organization in the entire country. The R.C. have been retained since the G.P.C.R. as a permanent feature, having replaced the People's Councils and are now elected at People's Congresses at each level of administration. At first the P.L.A. membership was dominant, but since the fall of LIN PIAO in 1971 the military representatives have been phased out.

Revolutionary Communist Party In the USA, the largest Maoist group with an estimated membership of 2,000 in the late

1970s. Before 1973, it was known as the Revolutionary Union. It is contemptuous of the COMMUNIST PARTY OF THE UNITED STATES, regarding it as too timid, opportunistic and revisionist. The programme of the R.C.P. provides for an armed seizure of power by the working class. The Party publishes a monthly bulletin called *Revolution*, appearing in Chicago with a circulation of some 15,000 copies. Its youth affiliate organizations include the Revolutionary Student Brigade and Youth in Action.

Revolutionary Defeatism A slogan invented by Lenin before W.W.I calling for the defeat of one's own country to provoke a civil war and a PROLETARIAN REVOLUTION. His argument was that the proletariat in each country must first of all fight its own bourgeoisie. Consequently, in time of war, the working class should refuse to support its own country's war effort, thereby causing a defeat of its military forces and establishment. The consequent unpopularity of the ruling class creates a REVOLUTIONARY SITUATION for the proletariat to seize state power.

Revolutionary Democrats Theoretical and practical social reformers in Europe in the 19th c., who campaigned for greater social equality and the abolition of the last vestiges of feudalism by revolutionary action combined with the development of bourgeois democracy. For a time, Marx was a R.D., but in 1843 he turned to revolutionary communism (as is evident from his work on the *DEUTSCH-FRANZÖSISCHE JAHRBÜCHER*. The term was more specifically applied to the radical movement in Russia, led by V. G. BELINSKY, N. A. DOBROLUBOV, N.P. OGARIOV and D. I. PISAREV.

Revolutionary Dictatorship of the Proletariat See DICTATORSHIP OF THE PROLETARIAT.

Revolutionary Institutional Party (*Partido Revolucionaria Institucional*) A moderate socialist party in Mexico with wide popular support. It was founded in 1928 under the name of the National Revolutionary Party, but adopted its present name in 1946. The Party is broadly based on moderate left-wing elements, representing three main sections of society, viz. the working class, small farmers and peasants and the middle class. The Party has often been in power and its present leader (1981) is J. L. Portillo, President of Mexico.

Revolutionary Marxism See MARXISM, MARXISM-LENINISM.

Revolutionary Marxist Tendency A small Trotskyite group which left the International Secretariat of the FOURTH INTERNATIONAL in 1963. It favours a selective adaptation and updating of the original Trotskyite strategy and tactics in the struggle for world revolution.

Revolutionary Rebels In China, the main adult agents of the GREAT PROLETARIAN CULTURAL REVOLUTION, who largely competed with the RED GUARDS (mostly youth and children) and opposed their excesses. R.R. were formed into R.R. Organizations by local Party officials, mostly in industrial and mining centres and to a lesser extent in the countryside. This was done in order to enlist worker and peasant support against the Red Guards (mostly enthusiastic, but irresponsible teenagers). R.R.O. were authorized to be formed by Mao Tse-tung and first appeared on the scene in Oct. 1966. They largely took over the function of the Party committees, state organs and enterprise management boards. In Jan. 1967, 11 R.P.O. led by the Shanghai Workers' Revolutionary Rebel Headquarters took control of local administration to restore order in Shanghai and the surrounding district. At about the same time R.R. came to control the All-China Federation of Trade Unions and its organ, *Workers' Daily*. Mao saw the R.R. as his 'agents of power seizure at the base' against the opposition of the Party bureaucratic establishment. The R.R. soon displaced the Red Guards as the main force during the G.P.C.R., but later their effectiveness weakened due to factional splits (e.g. the Anti-revolutionary Rebels). This lack of discipline and inability to carry out administrative tasks led to the formation of REVOLUTIONARY COMMITTEES beginning in spring 1967.

Revolutionary Romanticism A term to describe the idealization of the PROLETARIAN REVOLUTION and the revolutionary transformation of society in the TRANSITION FROM CAPITALISM TO SOCIALISM and then to FULL COMMUNISM. The idea of r.r. was developed by M. GORKY (among others) in the USSR. The movement became an integral part of SOCIALIST REALISM in art. Both Stalin and Mao Tse-tung embraced it enthusiastically and made some theoretical contributions to it.

Revolutionary Situation A Marxist concept denoting conditions in society ripe for a PROLETARIAN REVOLUTION. The term was popularized by Lenin. In its broadest classical sense, a r.s. was supposed to occur only in the industrialized countries, with a large and militant industrial proletariat. However, the first successful proletarian revolution occurred in a backward agricultural country led by intellectuals and a small industrial working class. In China, it actually occurred in the countryside first, relying overwhelmingly on peasants. In a narrower sense, a r.s. indicates more specific circumstances, such as when the ruling exploiting class can no longer maintain law and order along the traditional lines and when the discontent and unrest of the masses reach high levels, sufficient for widespread violent action.

Revolutionary Socialists See SOCIALIST REVOLUTIONARIES.

Revolutionary Syndicalism A working class movement attaching crucial importance to the revolutionary role of the trade unions in overthrowing capitalism and developing and administering a new, ideal society. The movement emerged in Italy towards the end of the 19th c. and spread to several West European countries, especially France and Spain. R.s. insists that all the working class population should be organized into labour unions (syndicates), which should be headed by a central coordinating federation or council. The notable feature of the programme of r.s. is the GENERAL STRIKE intended to isolate and cripple capitalists and bring down the bourgeois state. The strike would be followed by extensive economic and social reforms. Thereafter, the economy would be administered by labour unions to be grouped into federations according to the major branches of the economy. R. syndicalists differ as to the form of the central power. Some favour the abolition of the central state authority altogether, while others would tolerate a state authority to be exercised by a national (or world) trade union council. R.s. attaches little importance to political revolutionary action and is opposed to the Marxist-style monoparty system of government and the DICTATORSHIP OF THE PROLETARIAT. Marxists reject r.s. and describe it as a petty-bourgeois, semi-anarchist trend (Lenin, *Marxism and Revisionism*, 1908).

Revolutionary Vigilance A term used by revolutionary Marxists to denote the need for constant preparedness to defend revolutionary theory, as expounded by Marx or in Marxism-Leninism, in order to safeguard the achievements of the PROLETARIAN REVOLUTION, to identify and neutralize class enemies and to detect and destroy COUNTER-REVOLUTION. The idea of r.v. goes back to the 17th c., but Marxism has vested it with unprecedented significance and importance. In Marxist DIALECTICS, any progressive idea or action normally brings forth an opposite reaction, which also applies to ideological relations between socialism and capitalism. In particular, the bourgeoisie, endeavouring to protect or regain its privileged position, resorts to a variety of tactics and strategies in order to undermine Marxist theory and the Communist regimes in power. Of particular concern to Marxists are OPPORTUNISM, REFORMISM, REVISIONISM.

Revolution Betrayed, The One of the best known books written by L. D. TROTSKY, subtitled *What Is the Soviet Union? Where Is It Going?*, first published in 1937. It is an elegant and eloquent indictment of BOLSHEVISM as distorted by Stalin. Trotsky analysed the emergence and power of the Communist elite in the USSR and attacked the idea of the DICTATORSHIP OF THE PROLETARIAT which, in his view, naturally leads to a degeneration of Marxism. He pointed out that after 20 years of Bolshevik power in the USSR, the state instead of 'withering away' had grown into an 'unheard of apparatus of compulsion', and socialism had in fact been supplanted by STATE CAPITALISM.

'Revolution from above' A phrase used by Marxists as applied to radical and far-reaching changes initiated by the communist leadership or the state, not by the masses. It was employed by Stalin to describe the first Five-Year Plan (1928–32) and the collectivization drive (1929–38) in the USSR. 'R.f.a.' contrasts with a PROLETARIAN REVOLUTION initiated by the masses. Mao Tse-tung described the GREAT PROLETARIAN CULTURAL REVOLUTION as a 'revolution from below' (because it was largely carried out by the masses and was directed against the top bureaucratic Party and State establishment opposed to Mao).

Revolutionization Movement A description given to the CULTURAL REVOLUTION in Albania. The R.M. was officially pursued over the period 1966–69 (coinciding with the GREAT PROLETARIAN CULTURAL REVOLUTION in China). Then, after a period of relaxation 1970–72, it was resumed in Feb. 1973 on a more intensive and systematic basis. In a narrower sense, the term is applied only to this second period, which lasted up to 1975.

Revolution of 1848–49 Widespread unrest and revolts in Europe against monarchist establishments, the exploitation of the working classes and poverty, accentuated by the preceding depression and national oppression. The Revolution started with a peaceful middle-class and working-class demonstration in Paris in Feb. 1848, against which monarchist troops opened fire, after which the bourgeoisie revolted, declared a Republic and installed a Provisional Government. This was followed by an attempt at a proletarian uprising in June 1848, directed against the dissolution of the National Workshops (initiated by a government decree of Feb. 1848, intended to provide a guarantee of the right to work), which was suppressed at the cost of 15,000 lives. In Austria, the peasantry rose against feudal landowners, in Germany riots occurred in the Rhineland (in which Marx participated) and in Britain, the Chartists again pressed for parliamentary reform. Croats, Czechs, Danes, Hungarians, Irish, Poles, Romanians and Serbs rioted against the monarchy and national oppression. In Austria, Metternich was turned out of power, Emperor Ferdinand abdicated and Hungary achieved self-government. In Denmark, Ferdinand III was forced to agree to a democratic parliamentary constitution. From the Marxist point of view, the R. of 1848–49 was almost wholly bourgeois or bourgeois-democratic, whereby power shifted from the high aristocracy (kings, princes, counts, prince-bishops) to the BIG BOURGEOISIE (industrial and commercial capitalists and bankers). The working class in the end suffered and gained little or nothing economically. Although immediately fruitless from the proletarian standpoint, the Revolution went down in history as a 'Spring of the Peoples' and the 'roots of other revolutions'.

Revolution of 1905–7 In Russia, liberal and working-class revolts in some of the main cities, especially in St Petersburg (now Leningrad) against Tsarist oppression. The Revolution followed the defeat of Russia in the Russo-Japanese War 1904–5, which was attributed to Tsarist mismanagement. The highlight of the Revolution was BLOODY SUNDAY (9 Jan. 1905) when a peaceful procession of workers and peasants in St Petersburg were massacred by the police and troops. Strikes, demonstrations and violence followed in several cities and the crew of the battleship POTEMKIN mutinied. Revolutionary workers' councils, called SOVIETS, made their first appearance towards the end of 1905. Trotsky and, to a lesser extent, Lenin, were among the organizers. An armed uprising took place in Moscow in Dec. 1905. The riots and unrest continued, but by 1907 they were ruthlessly suppressed. The Stolypin Reaction, 1907–10, followed (named after the Tsarist Minister who directed it). Although the Revolution was crushed, it gave practical experience to revolutionaries and created the institution of the Soviet which, in 1917, played a crucial part in the Bolshevik Revolution.

Revolutions of 1917 Two revolutions in Russia – a BOURGEOIS-DEMOCRATIC REVOLUTION, i.e. the FEBRUARY REVOLUTION, and a PROLETARIAN REVOLUTION, i.e. the GREAT OCTOBER SOCIALIST REVOLUTION.

Revtribunal A shortened version in Russian of *Revolutsionnyi Tribunal*, meaning Revolutionary Tribunal. It was a special type of court in existence in Soviet Russia from 1917 to 1922 for handling counter-revolutionary cases. These courts were established in the main cities and provincial towns.

R Fund The name of the Sharing or MATERIAL INCENTIVES FUND in Hungarian enterprises since the economic reforms of 1968. The Fund, called in Hungarian *Részesedési alap* (Sharing Fund) is derived from enterprise profits. One-fifth of the balance-sheet profits are normally placed into the (taxable) R Fund. The Fund is taxed on a progressive basis (rising from 40 per cent to 70 per cent), which is called the profit tax, then a deduction of 12.5 per cent is made for the Reserve Fund and further, a wage-increase tax is applied on a progressive basis. From the net R.F. bonuses are paid to the enterprise personnel.

Rheinische Zeitung (*Rhineland Gazette*, in German) A daily newspaper printed in Cologne from 1 Jan. 1842 to 31 March 1843 to which Marx contributed articles and then became its editor. The paper was an organ of the Rhineland bourgeoisie and dealt with politics, trade and industry. Its readership opposed the Prussian nobility and pressed for liberal political reforms. Under Marx's editorship the paper became quite radical and suffered from the Prussian censor's cuts and was then permanently suspended. The paper was revived by Marx and some of his supporters during the Revolution of 1848 under the title of NEUE RHEINISCHE ZEITUNG, but was soon closed down by the authorities.

Ricardian Socialism A social movement in Britain, based on the ideas of D. RICARDO (1772–1823) in the first half of the 19th c., which aimed at a peaceful socialist transformation of society. The movement was sustained mostly by intellectuals, who based their programme on the classical political economy of D. Ricardo, the utilitarianism of J. Bentham and the social reformism of R. OWEN. The main exponents of R.s. were the communists W. Thompson and J. F. Bray and J. Gray and T. Hodgkin, identified with the middle-class socialists. In their writings, they carried out a thorough criticism of capitalism with respect to the ownership of property, the organization of production, distribution, the class structure and the role of the state. Although R.s. did not achieve much in practice, it provided many ideas for Marx, Engels and other classical Marxist thinkers, despite their dismissal of R.s. as mere UTOPIAN SOCIALISM.

Ricardo, David (1772–1823) A major British political economist who was examined by Marx. Ricardo's LABOUR THEORY OF VALUE, although an influence on Marx, was criticized for its support of the bourgeois social order. His principal work was on the *Principles of Political Economy and Taxation* (1817). Also, RICARDIAN SOCIALISM.

'Riddle wrapped in a mystery inside an enigma' A phrase pronounced by W. Churchill in a broadcast on 1 Oct. 1939, which he prefaced with a comment. 'I cannot forecast to you the action of Russia' (alluding to Stalin's policy of SOCIALISM IN ONE COUNTRY).

Riga and Yalta Groups Two opposed schools of thought in post-W.W.II US foreign policy towards the USSR. The R.G., represented by George F. Kennan, advocated a containment policy. It based its judgment on the reports of the US diplomatic mission in Riga in the 1920s, according to which the Soviet ideological fervour and commitment to the world communist revolution made the USSR an aggressive world power, not interested in peaceful coexistence. The Y.G., whose most prominent spokesman had been F. D. Roosevelt, believed that the USSR was basically not different from any other world power and was guided in her foreign policy by a variety of considerations, of which ideology was only one. Consequently, accommodation with the Soviets by diplomatic means was possible and advisable. The view of the R.G. appealed to President Truman more convincingly and it is this group that shaped US policy towards the USSR after 1946. This was expressed in the CONTAINMENT POLICY, the MARSHALL PLAN and the TRUMAN DOCTRINE.

Right An ideological and political term, meaning conservative, supportive of higher social classes, conventionally respectable and in general, opposed to the LEFT. The term was introduced in this sense during the FRENCH REVOLUTION in May 1789, at the first joint meeting of the Estates-General, when the nobility were seated to the right of the presiding king, implying the correct and respectable estate. The label of 'r.' is also used within the labour movement, especially by communists, for ideas, individuals or groups which are not radical enough and who favour gradualism, OPPORTUNISM, REFORMISM and REVISIONISM. Also, see the four entries below.

Right Hegelians HEGELIAN RIGHT

Rightist Socialists A description used by communists for those Marxists or social reformers who oppose revolutionary or SCIENTIFIC SOCIALISM, support the PARLIAMENTARY ROAD TO SOCIALISM, REFORMISM and REVISIONISM. The theoretical founders of R. Socialism were E. BERNSTEIN and K. KAUTSKY, while among recent thinkers, H. MARCUSE is included. Revolutionary Marxists regard R.S. as 'pseudo-socialists' and traitors to the Marxist cause, responsible for the disunity in the labour movement resulting in the 'disarmament of the working class' in its struggle with the bourgeoisie and imperialism. R.S. have also been accused of COSMOPOLITANISM and OPPORTUNISM and have been described as 'perverse defenders of capitalism' and even 'counter-revolutionaries'. In party politics, R.S. have been identified with CENTRISM, CHRISTIAN SOCIALISM, DEMOCRATIC SOCIALISM and SOCIAL DEMOCRACY.

Right (or Rightist) Opposition A term used in the USSR and the COMINTERN between the two World Wars for the group within the Bolshevik Party which 'deviated' from the majority to the 'right', by opposing hard line policies and extremism and advocated co-operation and compromise with non-communists. In particular, the R.O. pressed for humane and conciliatory policies towards peasants, including the *KULAKS*, the continuation of the NEW ECONOMIC POLICY and the strengthening of material incentives. The R.O. was led by N. I. BUKHARIN, A. I. RYKOV and M. P. Tomsky, reached its peak of prominence in 1928–29 and was against the LEFT OPPOSITION. The R.O. was eliminated by Stalin and most of its leaders and supporters were eliminated in the GREAT PURGES of the 1930s (Tomsky committed suicide).

Right Socialist Revolutionaries The moderate wing of the SOCIALIST REVOLUTIONARIES in Russia in 1917. They became an identifiable separate group after a split in the Socialist Revolutionary Party, which occurred after the FEBRUARY REVOLUTION when left-wingers formed a separate party calling themselves the LEFT SOCIALIST REVOLUTIONARIES. The remaining members continued under the old name, but the L.S.R. and the Bolsheviks critically described them as R.S.R. Whilst the L.S.R. gave support to the BOLSHEVIKS, the latter sided with the MENSHEVIKS.

Right-wing (or Right or Rightist) Social-Democrats A critical description applied by Lenin's supporters to the moderate faction of the RUSSIAN SOCIAL-DEMOCRATIC LABOUR PARTY. After the split in the latter in 1903, the R.-W.S.-D. – who happened to be in the minority at the time – became known as the MENSHEVIKS (while Lenin's faction became the BOLSHEVIKS).

Rochdale Co-operative The most common type of a consumer co-operative, originally founded at Rochdale, Lancashire in England, in 1844 by the Rochdale Society of Equitable Pioneers. The original R.C. reached 45,000 members and its capital was over £500,000. The features of the R.C. were: membership is open to all; each member has one vote (irrespective of the number of the shares he holds); goods are sold for cash; and profits are distributed to members up to an agreed ceiling (usually representing 4 per cent return on the stock held). The R.C. movement spread to many other parts of the world and in 1895 the INTERNATIONAL CO-OPERATIVE ALLIANCE was established in London to promote and co-ordinate the movement.

Rodbertus (or Rodbertus-Jagetzow), Johann Karl (1805–1875) A Prussian landowner, lawyer and economist, who is credited with having antedated many of Marx's ideas. He developed the LABOUR THEORY OF VALUE (beyond D. Ricardo's contribution) and saw the basic cause of poverty in the unjust division of national income not in the uneven distribution of

property. He proposed that personal income be based solely on the amount of labour contributed. He regarded capitalism as a transitional stage to an ideal society, but favoured a peaceful, gradual PARLIAMENTARY ROAD TO SOCIALISM, rather than a violent PROLETARIAN REVOLUTION. His works – *Claims of the Working Class* (1837), *Towards the Understanding of Our Economic Conditions* (1842) and *Light on the Social Question* (1875) – exerted considerable influence on contemporary socialist thought. But Marx and Engels were critical of his ideas, regarding them as impractical and amounting to ACADEMIC SOCIALISM. Engels, moreover, accused R. of plagiarizing Marx.

'Rollback' Proposition A political and military idea put forward by J. F. Dulles (the US Secretary of State) in 1954 to oust communist regimes from power in Eastern Europe, China and North Korea by force if necessary and to confine communism only to the USSR. There has never been any serious attempt to put this proposition into practice, of which the HUNGARIAN UPRISING and the INVASION OF CZECHOSLOVAKIA provided testing evidence.

Romanian Communist Party (*Partitul Comunist Român*) The ruling and the only legal political party in the Socialist Republic of ROMANIA. Founded in 1921, it operated illegally up to 1944 when, due to Soviet pressure, it was legalized and admitted to the left-wing coalition government. During the following three years it eliminated other political parties and, in 1948, the socialists were forced into a merger with the Communist Party to form the Romanian Workers' Party, which became the only legal political party in the country. In 1965, the R.W.P. reverted to its original name of the R.C.P., when the official designation of the country was changed from the People's Republic to the Socialist Republic. This occurred after N. CEAUSESCU became the Party's

Secretary-General in March 1965. The Party's membership in the late 1970s was 2,700,000 (out of the country's total population of 21,800,000), which makes it the third largest Communist Party in the world (after China and the USSR). The highest formal source of the Party's power is the Congress, held every five years which, in contrast to most other communist parties, also elects the Secretary-General. The 11th Congress held in Nov. 1974 re-elected N. Ceausescu as the Secretary-General and elected a Central Committee of 205 full and 156 alternate members. The C.C. elected a Secretariat of 7 members, a Political Executive Committee of 23 full and 12 alternate members and a PERMANENT BUREAU of 5 members (headed by N. Ceausescu). The Party's mass support organizations are the Union of Communist Youth, the Union of Communist Student Associations, the Pioneers and the National Council of Women. The official Party publications include: *Scînteia* (*The Spark*), the official daily organ of the Central Committee; *Era socialista* (*Socialist Era*), a theoretical fortnightly journal; and *Munca de pardid* (*Party Work*), a fortnightly bulletin on Party organization and activities. The U. of C.Y. publishes a daily newspaper called *Scînteia tineretului* (*The Spark of Youth*). In the international communist movement, the R.C.P. has pursued a neutral line, endeavouring to maintain good, but non-committal, relations with all ruling parties, including the Communist Party of the Soviet Union, the Chinese Communist Party, the League of Communists of Yugoslavia and the Albanian Party of Labour.

Romanian Workers' Party The official name of the ROMANIAN COMMUNIST PARTY between Feb. 1948 (when the Romanian Communist Party merged with the Socialists) and July 1965 (when Romania changed her official designation from the People's Republic to the Socialist Republic, after N. CEAUSESCU became the Party's Secretary-General in March 1965).

Romania, Socialist Republic of (*Republica Socialistă România*) A medium-size East European country (237,000 sq. km. and 21,800,000 inhabitants in 1978), ruled by the ROMANIAN COMMUNIST PARTY under a mono-party system. R. was a monarchy up to mid-1947, but before the end of W.W.II King Michael had turned to the USSR against Nazi Germany. He formed a coalition government of non-bourgeois and anti-fascist parties in 1944. After the war, the socialization of the means of production and the SOVIETIZATION of the political system followed. By the end of 1947 King Michael was forced to abdicate. In Jan. 1948, a People's Republic was proclaimed and in the same year the socialists were forced to merge with the Communist Party, while all other political parties were dissolved by law. Since 1956, R. has pursued an increasingly independent line from the USSR in the COUNCIL FOR MUTUAL ECONOMIC ASSISTANCE and in foreign policy in general. R. was the only Warsaw Pact country which refused to participate in the INVASION OF CZECHOSLOVAKIA (and hence, has been described as the 'FRANCE OF THE EAST'). The country's present Constitution was adopted in Aug. 1965, having replaced that of Sep. 1952. The highest formal organ of state power is the unicameral GRAND NATIONAL ASSEMBLY elected for five years from a single list of candidates drawn up by the FRONT OF SOCIALIST UNITY. Effective power, however, rests with the POLITICAL EXECUTIVE BUREAU and the PERMANENT BUREAU OF THE CENTRAL COMMITTEE of the Romanian Communist Party headed by its Secretary-General (N. Ceausescu since March 1965).

Rouble (less commonly, **Ruble**) The currency unit in the USSR, divided into 100 kopeks. The origin of the term can be traced back to the 13th c. when it meant 'a cutting' (*rubai*) of a silver bar. After the Bolshevik Revolution in 1917, the Soviet regime tried to discredit the r. by inflation and hyperinflation and to replace it physically and in name by the *SOVZNAK* and the

CHERVONETS. There was also a plan to introduce labour (*TRED*) and satisfaction (*DOV*) as units of account. But, by the monetary reform of 1924, the r. was officially and firmly re-established. Officially, the value of the r. is defined in gold (0.987412 gramme of fine gold). According to the official exchange rate in 1978 1.00 r. was equal to US$1.33 but its black market value was in fact only $0.25. The r. is a soft, inconvertible currency of hardly any international consequence. The Soviet r. must not be confused with the TRANSFERABLE ROUBLE.

Rousseau, Jean-Jacques (1712–78) One of the leading French philosophers, social critics and moralists of the Enlightenment. Rousseau's appraisal of man in his world, as expressed in his most famous work, *The Social Contract* (1762), was considered too idealistic and utopian by Marxists. It was criticized for not coming to grips with the plight of the PROLETARIAT in the social conditions set forth. His other main works were *Discourse on Inequality* (1755), *Emile* (1762) and *Confessions* (1781–88).

RSFSR The abbreviation of the RUSSIAN SOVIET FEDERATED SOCIALIST REPUBLIC.

RSDLP The abbreviation of the RUSSIAN SOCIAL-DEMOCRATIC LABOUR PARTY.

RSDLP (B) The abbreviation of the RUSSIAN SOCIAL-DEMOCRATIC LABOUR PARTY (OF THE BOLSHEVIKS).

Rugged Individualism An expression used by Herbert Hoover as the Presidential candidate of the Republican Party in Oct. 1928 in New York. He used it in a laudatory sense, referring to the success of American r.i. in the past and contrasted it with STATE INTERVENTION and state aid. The phrase was largely discredited during the Great Depression of 1929–33, when the individualist USA had an unemployment rate of 25 per cent and while the state interventionist USSR had labour shortages. Also INDIVIDUALISM.

Ruling Communist Parties See COMMUNIST PARTIES, RULING.

Rural Drive In China, see RUSTICATION DRIVE.

Rural Idiocy See PEASANT IDIOCY.

Rural-Urban Contradiction In Marxist ideology, the antagonistic relations between rural and urban population and interests. Marxists attribute this contradiction to the institution of private property and the consequent exploitation and emergence of social classes, which reach their most acute forms under capitalism. There is: 1. the concentration of land in the hands of large landowners at the expense of poor and landless peasants; 2. a steep rise in the prices of agricultural products (owing to marginal cost pricing) which hits the industrial proletariat; and 3. the consequent rise in GROUND RENT, a form of SURPLUS VALUE appropriated by landowners. Furthermore, the monopoly of land ownership impedes the flow of capital to agriculture, resulting in backward and arduous methods of production and low productivity. The urban bourgeoisie exploits the rural population with high industrial prices, high profit mark-ups by commercial firms (dealing with small unorganized agricultural producers) and high interest rates charged by banks. In the Marxist view, only socialism and, especially, communism can remove the otherwise inherent r.-u.c. through the socialization of land, industry, trade, banking, the state absorption of DIFFERENTIAL RENT, the state control of agricultural prices, mechanization, automation and the development of AGRO-INDUSTRIAL COMPLEXES. It is envisaged that under FULL COMMUNISM the rural-urban differences will disappear, creating a CLASSLESS SOCIETY.

Rush and Harmonic Growth Two terms established by a Hungarian economist, J. Kornai (in *Rush versus Harmonic Growth*, 1972), referring to two different strategies of economic development under Socialist economic planning. R.g. denotes accelerated economic development via selected manufacturing industries, sustained by heavy investment outlays almost 'at any cost'. It aims at rapid increases in material production and 'harbours competitive spirit'. The acceleration of growth becomes the main objective of the long-term plan and fetishism for its own sake. R.g. was best exemplified by the Stalinist industrialization drive. On the other hand, h.g. consists in economic development pursued on a broad front, avoiding disproportions and imbalances in the economy. Long-term plans are shaped to suit the many-sided human wants. But, as Kornai points out, harmony is not a clearly objective category free from value judgment. Moreover, harmonic proportions are not valid once and for all, but change according to changing technical relations and human needs, resulting in h.g. as a dynamic strategy incompatible with inflexibility and rigid proportions. In general, r.g. may be appropriate to the earlier stages of economic development, while h.g. is preferable in more advanced economies.

Russian Association of Proletarian Writers (*Rossiyskaya Assotsiatsiya Proletarskikh Pisateli*, in Russian) Also known as *RAPP* and its members as Rappists, a political literary organization in the USSR created at the All-Union Conference of Proletarian Writers in Jan. 1925. It was the first large organization of Soviet writers, combining smaller groups which emerged soon after the Bolshevik Revolution. The Association pursued an ideologically hard line, reflecting the official policy, treating literature as a form of participation in the class struggle and directing its efforts against fellow travellers (*POPUTCHIKI*). It was officially dissolved in 1932, when the WRITERS' UNION OF THE USSR was established and absorbed the former members of the R.A.P.W.

Russian Communist League of Youth A mass youth organization established in Nov. 1918 on Lenin's initiative for young people, roughly for ages 14 to 26, to serve mainly as a training ground for future Communist Party officials. It replaced the Russian Socialist League of Working Youth (created in 1917). The organization of the R.C.L.Y. was modelled on, and its activities subordinated to, the RUSSIAN COMMUNIST PARTY (OF THE BOLSHEVIKS). After Lenin's death (Jan. 1924), the name of the League was changed to the Russian Leninist Communist League of Youth, and today it is known as the *KOMSOMOL*.

Russian Communist Party A vague name and, strictly speaking, incorrect in this form. It can be any of the following precise designations: the ALL-UNION COMMUNIST PARTY (OF THE BOLSHEVIKS) (1925–52); the COMMUNIST PARTY OF THE SOVIET UNION (since 1952); the RUSSIAN COMMUNIST PARTY (OF THE BOLSHEVIKS) (1918–25); the RUSSIAN SOCIAL-DEMOCRATIC LABOUR PARTY (1898–1912); or the RUSSIAN SOCIAL-DEMOCRATIC LABOUR PARTY (OF THE BOLSHEVIKS) (1912–18).

Russian Communist Party (of the Bolsheviks) The official name of the COMMUNIST PARTY OF THE SOVIET UNION from March 1918 to Dec. 1925. It replaced the RUSSIAN SOCIAL-DEMOCRATIC LABOUR PARTY (OF THE BOLSHEVIKS) and then was succeeded by the ALL-UNION COMMUNIST PARTY (OF THE BOLSHEVIKS). Headed by Lenin (up to 1924) and then by Stalin, the R.C.P.(B) guided the destinies of the new Socialist state in its formative stage through the period of WAR COMMUNISM (1918–20), the radical socialization of key industries and initiated the NEW ECONOMIC POLICY. In 1920, on its initiative, the DICTATORSHIP OF THE PROLETARIAT was proclaimed and, in 1922, the R.C.P.(B) was declared the only legal political party in the country with all other parties being abolished.

Russian Marxism A term sometimes used for BOLSHEVISM or MARXISM-LENINISM.

Russian Revolution A general name which may have three different meanings:

1. the political and social upheaval from Feb. 1917 to the end of 1920, from which the communist regime emerged triumphantly. During that period the Tsarist government was deposed, a liberal Republican government was eliminated, the counter-revolutionary forces were defeated, the foreign interventionist troops were forced out and the Soviet regime was firmly established; 2. the overthrow of the capitalist regime in Russia in 1917 in two stages – the BOURGEOIS-DEMOCRATIC REVOLUTION, better known as the FEBRUARY REVOLUTION (when the PROVISIONAL GOVERNMENT replaced the Tsarist regime of NICHOLAS II) and the PROLETARIAN REVOLUTION, better known as the GREAT OCTOBER SOCIALIST REVOLUTION (when the Soviet Government led by V. I. Lenin replaced the moderate Provisional Government of A. F. KERENSKY); and 3. in its narrowest and most commonly understood sense, the Great October Socialist Revolution, when the BOLSHEVIKS seized power from the Provisional Government of Kerensky on 24–25 Oct. 1917 (O.-S.C.) in the capital of Russia, viz. Petrograd (now Leningrad).

Russian Social-Democratic Labour Party The political party in Tsarist Russia in existence under this name from 1898 to 1912, to which the COMMUNIST PARTY OF THE SOVIET UNION traces its origin. It was formally created at its first Congress in Minsk in March 1898. It was established illegally, largely by the former members of the EMANCIPATION OF LABOUR GROUP (founded by PLEKHANOV in 1883), the LEAGUE OF STRUGGLE FOR THE LIBERATION OF THE WORKING CLASS (founded by Lenin in 1895) and other reformist groups. Although a Central Committee was elected, it was immediately arrested (incl. V. I. LENIN, N. KRUPSKAYA and L. MARTOV). In 1900 the Party began publishing its organ ISKRA in exile. The Party split at its second Congress, which was held in Brussels and London in July–Aug. 1903, into the BOLSHEVIKS (led by Lenin) and the MENSHEVIKS (led by Plekhanov). Although a formal reunifi-

cation of the two factions was agreed upon at the Party's fourth Congress in Stockholm in April 1906, each retained its separate identity of views. At a Conference in Prague in 1912, on Lenin's initiative, the Mensheviks were excluded from the Party and the Bolsheviks adopted a modified name, viz. the Russian Social-Democratic Labour Party (of the Bolsheviks). The R.S.-D.L.P. continued to exist largely in name, patronized by the Mensheviks and was formally dissolved in 1922.

Russian Social-Democratic Labour Party (of the Bolsheviks) The official name of the Russian Communist Party from 1912 to 1918 and the Party which carried out the first successful PROLETARIAN REVOLUTION in world history, viz. the GREAT OCTOBER SOCIALIST REVOLUTION of 1917. The name was adopted at a Conference in Prague in 1912 when, on the initiative of Lenin, the MENSHEVIKS were excluded from the Party. The BOLSHEVIKS, led by Lenin, discarded the existing name, the RUSSIAN SOCIAL-DEMOCRATIC LABOUR PARTY, to indicate that their party was a truly revolutionary Marxist party, not to be sidetracked by moderate evolutionary Marxists and revisionists. In the same year, the Party began to publish its organ PRAVDA in St Petersburg (now Leningrad). During W.W.I the Party participated in the ZIMMERWALD CONFERENCE (1915) and the KIENTAL CONFERENCE (1916), both in Switzerland. Although the Party participated in the FEBRUARY REVOLUTION OF 1917, it pressed for a *proletarian* revolution, especially after Lenin's arrival from Switzerland in April 1917 and his declaration of the *APRIL THESES*. The R.S.-D.L.P.(B) was instrumental in organizing the SOVIETS OF WORKERS' AND SOLDIERS' DEPUTIES, which the Bolsheviks soon came to dominate. On 10 Oct. 1917 (O.-S.C.) the Central Committee of the R.S.-D.L.P.(B) made a final decision to organize an armed insurrection and seize power from the PROVISIONAL GOVERNMENT (led by Kerensky). On 12 Oct. the PETROGRAD SOVIET created a Military Revolutionary

Committee in which the Bolsheviks gained a majority. Aided by other left-wing groups, on the night of 24–25 Oct. 1917 (O.-S.C.) the R.S.-D.L.P.(B) seized power from the Provisional Government which was arrested. On the following day, Lenin formed a nucleus of the Bolshevik Government which was sanctioned by the Second Congress of Soviets. After the Revolution, the Party initiated the socialization of the means of production, the conclusion of the BREST-LITOVSK TREATY and organized the armed struggle against counter-revolutionary elements in the civil war that followed. At its seventh Congress, in Petrograd in March 1918, the Party changed its name to the Russian Communist Party (of the Bolsheviks).

Russian Soviet Federated Socialist Republic (*Rossiyskaya Sovetskaya Federativnaya Sotsialisticheskaya Respublika*, in Russian) The largest and oldest of the 15 Union Republics in the USSR. It occupies most of the middle and northern European USSR and virtually all of Siberia and the Far East, stretching from the Baltic Sea to the Pacific and the Arctic oceans and embracing more than 100 nationalities. It constitutes 76 per cent (17.1m. sq. km.) of the USSR's area and 53 per cent (138.6m. in 1978) of the country's population. The Republic's capital is Moscow and administratively is divided into 16 autonomous republics, 5 autonomous regions, 10 national areas, 6 territories (*Krai*) and 49 provinces (*Oblast*).

Rustication Drive A large-scale movement of middle school graduates from urban areas to the countryside in China, launched by Mao Tse-tung in 1968. It is also known as 'counter-urbanization' and reflects the Chinese Communist leadership's links with the rural areas. The R.D. represents a reversal of the usual trend of the rural exodus that is typically associated with classical industrialization. The R.D. was in fact attempted first in the 1950s but on a smaller and less systematic scale. The purpose of the R.D. has been both ideological and economic: to prevent the emergence of 'an angry and bourgeois-minded educated class' in urban areas; to strengthen urban-rural ties; and to promote the development of the countryside, including industrialization along decentralized lines. The emphasis is on practical work, learning from peasants and on simple communal life. Although officially 'voluntary', a good deal of state and Party coercion has been applied. At one stage, some 50,000 Party cadres were sent to supervise the resettlement process, work and study. By the late 1970s some 15m. youth had been resettled in rural areas. But the drive has become unpopular, many youths have illicitly returned to their urban homes and the authorities have had to adopt a more liberal attitude in the late 1970s.

Rykov, Aleksei Ivanovich (1881–1938) A Soviet Communist leader and writer who succeeded Lenin as Prime Minister. R. joined the RUSSIAN SOCIAL-DEMOCRATIC LABOUR PARTY in 1899 and then the BOLSHEVIKS. He participated in the REVOLUTION OF 1905–07, but otherwise spent most of the pre-W.W.I years abroad. R. was one of the conciliators who endeavoured to reconcile the Bolsheviks to the MENSHEVIKS, but without success. In spite of his differences with Lenin on several issues, R. occupied high positions in the Party and Government after the October Revolution of 1917. He was COMMISSAR for Internal Affairs (1917), Chairman of the Supreme Council of the National Economy (*VESENKHA*) (1918–20, 1923–24), Vice-Premier (1921–24) and Prime Minister (1924–30). In the late 1920s, he was identified by Stalin as one of the leaders (together with BUKHARIN) of the RIGHT OPPOSITION, which was critical of Stalin's accelerated industrialization and compulsory collectivization. R. was stripped of his Party and Government posts in 1929, but after his recantation in the same year he was partly restored to his previous prominence in the Government (as Commissar for Communications). But he fell victim to Stalin's GREAT PURGES after he was expelled from the Party in 1937 and accused of Trotskyite plotting. He was sentenced to death as a traitor in March 1938 and executed.

S

Sabotage One of the extreme weapons of industrial dispute resorted to by workers, deliberately failing to carry out normal tasks, damaging their employer's assets, or preventing the implementation of the employer's project. S. may also be employed as an instrument of subversion or indirect political and military warfare. S. may be passive (by deliberate omission) or active (deliberate commission). It is believed that s. was first resorted to by French syndicalists towards the end of the 19th c. by throwing clogs (*sabot* in French) into machines, to cause jamming. Moderate trade unions generally reject s. despite its illegality. However, prosecutions are most difficult, especially in capitalist democratic countries. In the Socialist countries, s. is banned in any form and is treated very seriously by the authorities, especially if socialized property is damaged.

Saint-Simon, Claude Henri (1760–1825) An outstanding early socialist theoretician of noble descent (count), who renounced his title during the French Revolution and later died in abject poverty. His thought and writings were directed towards the elimination of poverty and to the material and cultural uplifting of the proletariat. He pressed for the right as well as the universal obligation to work. His ideas attracted the attention of the early Marxists, and Engels described him as the 'most erudite and all-round mind of his time'. They paid tribute to him for his idealistic humanitarianism, his approach to social history as a progressive development (akin to HISTORICAL MATERIALISM) and

his scheme for a scientifically planned industrial economy. The principle to govern work and distribution under FULL COMMUNISM, 'FROM EACH ACCORDING TO HIS ABILITY, TO EACH ACCORDING TO HIS NEEDS', usually attributed to Marx, had in fact been first put forward by S.-S. But otherwise Marxists consider S.-S.'s ideas impracticable, exemplifying UTOPIAN SOCIALISM and inconsistent with SCIENTIFIC SOCIALISM. In his vision of the ideal society, S.-S. was reconciled to the institutions of private property and social classes. He also believed in class harmony, rejecting the postulate of the CLASS STRUGGLE and a PROLETARIAN REVOLUTION. Although he viewed the proletariat sympathetically as a suffering class, he did not regard it as a viable political force capable of staging a successful revolution. His main works were: *Report on the Science of Man* (1813); *On the Industrial System* (1821); *Industrialists' Catechism* (1823–24); and *The New Christianity* (1825).

Sakharov, Andrei (1921–) An outstanding Soviet nuclear physicist who has become one of the leading dissenters, criticizing the Soviet regime for the Communist Party's authoritarianism, elitism, religious persecution and the disregard for HUMAN RIGHTS. He is regarded as one of the fathers of the Soviet hydrogen bomb, became a full member of the Academy of Sciences of the USSR at an unprecedented age of 32 and was awarded the STALIN PRIZE, Order of Lenin (LENIN PRIZES) and the ·HERO OF SOCIALIST LABOUR·. In 1966 he protested against

506

RE-STALINIZATION, in 1968 he published a pamphlet in the West called *Peaceful Coexistence and Intellectual Freedom*, in 1970 he formed a Human Rights Committee in Moscow and in 1974 his supporters in the West published his views in *Sakharov Speaks*. S. has been removed from the nuclear programme and has been persecuted in various minor ways but, owing to his immense international stature, the authorities have been hesitant to take more drastic action against him.

SALT Abbreviation for the STRATEGIC ARMS LIMITATION TALKS.

Samizdat ('self-publishing', in Russian) Underground or restricted private publishing in the USSR, which appeared first in this sense in 1958 and has developed into a remarkable network, especially since the late 1960s. *S.* is carried on mostly by DISSIDENTS on behalf of human rights and religious or national groups. There are now more than 30 known periodical publications in Russian, other national languages, as well as some Western languages, as exemplified by: *Ausra (Dawn,* in Lithuanian), *Christian Movement,* CHRONICLE OF CURRENT EVENTS, *Chronicle of Human Rights in the USSR, Informational and Judicial Literature, Informatsionnyi Biuleten (Information Bulletin), Novoe Russkoe Slovo (New Russian Word), Russkaya Mysl (Russian Thought), Socio-Political Literature, The Ukrainian Herald.* Some of these periodicals are reproduced in the USSR and some in the West. Their content varies from newsletters, literary contributions, political writings, trial transcripts, petitions to open letters. Soviet citizens are legally permitted to engage in *s.*, but there are certain coincidental prohibitions making it virtually illegal (e.g. ban on the acquisition of duplicating facilities, using printing equipment and operating printeries).

Samokritika The Russian term for SELF-CRITICISM.

San Ping Policy The Chinese name for the policy of monetary stabilization pursued in Communist China in the early 1950s, better known descriptively as the THREE BALANCES POLICY.

Sans-culottes The most active and easily manipulated proletarian elements who rebelled against the aristocracy during the FRENCH REVOLUTION. The term in French means 'without breeches', as they wore long trousers in contrast to the knee-length breeches worn by the aristocrats.

San-zi Yi-pao Policy A liberal economic trend in China in the early 1960s, better known as THREE FREEDOMS AND ONE RESPONSIBILITY.

Saratov Method The best known system of quality control in the USSR, designed to improve the quality of workmanship and ensure faultless production. The method, devised by an engineer, B. A. Dubovikov, was first introduced in a machine-construction factory in Saratov (situated on the middle Volga) in the late 1950s. The method has been widely adopted since the early 1960s in many other factories in the USSR, largely through the Party apparatus (rather than the ordinary administrative network). Its main elements are: 1. meticulous preparation of faultless technical designs and documentation, covering the whole cycle of production; 2. quality self-control by the worker himself; 3. emphasis on the immediate identification and elimination of the causes of faulty work to prevent the cumulative effect of deficiencies; 4. the stimulation of workers' interests by moral and material incentives (not by direction and punishment); and 5. combining production and quality control in the same process.

Sartre, Jean-Paul (1905–1980) Outstanding French philosopher, critic, playwright and novelist who attempted a synthesis of MARXISM with EXISTENTIALISM. Sartre was born in Paris of a middle-class family and was related to Albert Schweitzer. His philosophy, as expressed in his most famous work, *Being and Nothingness* (1943), was based on Husserl's PHENOMENOLOGY and Heidegger's EXISTENTIALISM. In this work, freedom and choice were central to Sartre's situating man's existence and essence on human reality. After World War II he founded the journal *Les Temps Modernes* (*Modern Times*) with his life-long companion Simone de Beauvoir and M. Merleau-Ponty and moved toward Marxism. He loosely allied himself with the FRENCH COMMUNIST PARTY from 1944 to 1968. However, he attacked STALIN's *Dialectical Materialism* in his *Materialism and Revolution* (1946) and the Soviet suppression of the HUNGARIAN UPRISING in his *The Ghost of Stalin* (1956). But Sartre's Marxism expressed itself forcefully in *The Communists and the Peace* (1952) which supported the FCP, North Korea and criticized capitalism, especially in the United States and France. He was also very outspoken on his opposition to the French involvement in Algeria. Sartre's most important exposition on Marxism was *The Critique of Dialectical Reason* (1960). Here he attempted to strengthen the Marxist theory of knowledge (DIALECTICAL MATERIALISM) with existentialism, critical thinking, anthropology and history, not dogmatic dialectics. Sartre's other major works were *The Transcendence of the Ego* (1936), *Nausea* (1938) and Search for a Method (1957). Also SARTRISM.

Sartrism A term sometimes used for EXISTENTIALISM of the version propounded by J.-P. SARTRE (1905–80), a French socialist philosopher and playwright.

Satellite A term which was often used in the West during the COLD WAR for an East European country (Bulgaria, Czechoslovakia, the German DR, Hungary, Poland and Romania), alluding to their uncritical acceptance of the USSR's leadership and domination.

Savings and Credit Co-operatives See CREDIT CO-OPERATIVES.

Scarcity Prices Prices reflecting relative scarcity, i.e. cost-preference relations. Such prices are normally determined in free markets by the interplay of supply and demand and as such are typical of capitalist market economies, not Socialist centrally planned economies. S.p. are conducive to the market equilibrium and the most efficient utilization of resources. But the structure of s.p. may not be in the best social interest, as they do not necessarily reflect social cost-benefit relations and various external economies and diseconomies. Thus, high s.p. of necessities weigh relatively heavy on lower income groups, while low-priced luxuries benefit mostly higher income groups. S.p., theoretically, can also be arrived at in SHADOW MARKETS on a planned basis with the aid of electronic computers (OPTIMAL PRICES), but so far the task has proved impossible in practice. Ideally, s.p. should govern the allocation of resources (as PRODUCER PRICES or wholesale prices), while RETAIL PRICES should reflect social cost-benefit considerations (which can be achieved by indirect taxes or TURNOVER TAXES on the one hand and subsidies on the other).

Scepticism A critical philosophical stand, doubting the possibility of knowing the truth and of acquiring complete true knowledge of the world. S. also disputes the validity and value of commonly accepted moral standards. As a matter of principle, sceptics emphasize that any object or phenomenon can be subjected to doubt by two opposed views. Among the exponents of this stand were Pirron (circa 360–270 B.C.), its founder, R. Descartes (1596–1650), D. Hume (1711–76), E. MACH and B. Russell (1872–1970). In Marxist philosophy, the attitude to s. is varied. On the one hand, s. is evaluated positively, as it rejects the outright acceptance of religion and the human capacity to know ABSOLUTE TRUTH at a particular stage of historical development. In general, it has paved the way for materialist philosophy. But on the other hand, s. is attacked as a stagnant and even reactionary doctrine, reconciled to the existing state of knowledge and social relations. Marxist philosophers maintain that s. leads to AGNOSTICISM, NIHILISM and the denial of the possibility of scientific and social progress. They also emphasize, in accordance with DIALECTICAL MATERIAL-ISM and HISTORICAL MATERIALISM, that the real world can be known progressively through scientific enquiry and practice. Furthermore, social relations can be improved by active involvement in – not indifference to and abstention from – social processes, including the class struggle and revolutions.

Scientific Communism, Scientific Socialism Terms introduced and discussed by Marx and Engels (in their jointly written *The GERMAN IDEOLOGY*, in Marx's *The POVERTY OF PHILOSOPHY* and in Engels's *Socialism: Utopian and Scientific*, 1880), to distinguish their revolutionary proletarian ideology from UTOPIAN SOCIAL-ISM and its predecessors. They called it 'scientific', because in their view it has solid scientific foundations supported by the laws of social development and provides well-founded theoretical precepts for guiding the PROLETARIAT in replacing capitalism with SOCIALISM and ultimately FULL COMMUNISM. The main theoretical foundations of s.c. are: 1. DIALECTICAL MATERIALISM; 2. HISTORICAL MATERIAL-ISM; 3. the LABOUR THEORY OF VALUE; 4. the postulates of the CLASS STRUGGLE, PROLETARIAN REVOLUTION, the DIC-TATORSHIP OF THE PROLETARIAT and ultimately, a CLASSLESS SOCIETY. Later Marxist thinkers, especially Lenin, Stalin and Mao Tse-tung, further developed s.c. on the basis of actual experience in the USSR, China and other Socialist countries.

Scissors Crisis The situation in the market in the USSR during 1922–24, when the state administered very high prices on industrial products and very low prices on agricultural products. Owing to the adverse effects on agriculture, the peasants withheld their produce from the market

creating a crisis. The RIGHT OPPOSITION, led by BUKHARIN, advocated a reduction in the level of industrial prices (which Stalin supported at the time), but PREOB-RAZHENSKY urged the continuation of that policy to finance accelerated industrialization. Stalin, who came to power after Lenin's death (Jan. 1924), supported Bukharin at the time and some concessions to the peasants followed. But later, Stalin reversed his previous stand and switched over to Preobrazhensky's strategy. In the end both Bukharin and Preobrazhensky were executed in the GREAT PURGES.

SD Abbreviation for SOCIAL DEMO-CRACY.

SDS Abbreviation of STUDENTS FOR A DEMOCRATIC SOCIETY (in the USA).

SEATO Abbreviation of SOUTH-EAST ASIA TREATY ORGANIZATION.

Second-and-a-Half International An international moderate socialist organization representing CENTRISM, in existence over the period 1921–23. It was created in Vienna in Feb. 1921 and opposed both the right-wing opportunism of the BERN IN-TERNATIONAL (founded in Feb. 1919 and which identified itself as the successor to the SECOND INTERNATIONAL) and the revolutionary line of the Third International (the COMINTERN, founded in Petrograd in March 1919). It was also known as the Vienna International or the International Working Union of Socialist Parties. It was opposed, in particular, to the postulates of the CLASS STRUGGLE, violent PRO-LETARIAN REVOLUTION, the DICTATOR-SHIP OF THE PROLETARIAT, and represented the moderate socialist parties or groups in Austria, Belgium, Britain, Germany, Greece, Poland, Spain, Romania, the USA and several other countries, as well as some Russian MENSHEVIKS and SOCIALIST REVOLUTIONARIES. The Third International declared the Second International 'dissolved' and its successor organizations as 'null and void'. The S.-a.-

a.-H.I. was meant to be a temporary body to enable the formation of a unified organization of the international working class and, to this effect, initiated a CONFERENCE OF THE THREE INTERNATIONALS in 1922, but without success. In May 1923, the S.-a.-a.-H.I. merged with the Bern International and formed the LABOUR AND SOCIALIST INTERNATIONAL as the successor to the Second International.

Secondary Boycott A tactic resorted to by trade unions in industrial disputes in capitalist countries, refusing to co-operate with or patronize anyone dealing with the employer directly involved in the dispute. A s.b. can be more effective than a primary BOYCOTT (directed against the employer only), but in most countries the former is outlawed. The s.b. is illegal in all the Socialist countries.

Second International An international socialist organization which was active from 1889 to 1914 and finally lapsed in 1919. It was created on the initiative of the German Socialist Party (SPD) (later the SOCIAL-DEMOCRATIC PARTY OF GERMANY) at a congress in Paris as a successor to the FIRST INTERNATIONAL (dissolved in 1876) and maintained an International Socialist Bureau in Brussels and (from 1914) in The Hague. On the whole, the S.I. supported a gradual, evolutionary and PARLIAMENTARY ROAD TO SOCIALISM. But it became a battleground between different opposing factions of MARXISTS, POSSIBILISTS and supporters of CENTRISM and loyal NATIONALISM. The S.I. disappointed revolutionary Marxists, including the Leninist group, who pressed on several occasions to condemn and take action against OPPORTUNISM, REFORMISM and REVISIONISM as well as participation in the 'imperialist' W.W.I. Among the most prominent leaders of the S.I. were A. BEBEL, W. LIEBKNECHT, E. BERNSTEIN and K. KAUTSKY. At a conference in Lucerne in 1919, it was decided to revive the S.I., but the Third International (the COMINTERN) – which was created by Lenin in the same year – declared the S.I. 'dissolved'.

However, the S.I. was re-established in Vienna in 1921 as the SECOND-AND-A-HALF INTERNATIONAL which, in 1923, after having merged with the BERN INTERNATIONAL, became known as the LABOUR AND SOCIALIST INTERNATIONAL, later (in 1947) revived as the SOCIALIST INTERNATIONAL.

Second Proletariat A colloquial name for the Social-Revolutionary Party Proletariat, which operated as a working-class organization in the Russian part of Poland from 1888 to 1893. It was also known as the Small Proletariat and carried on in the tradition of the FIRST PROLETARIAT (or Great Proletariat). The S.P., formed on the initiative of L. Kulczycki and M. Kasprzak, stressed self-government for Poland and recourse to terrorist action. Its activities were directed from two centres – one in Poland and another abroad. The S.P. disintegrated as an organization in 1893 and most of its members joined the Polish Socialist Party.

Secretariat of the Central Committee of the Communist Party A permanent Party organ responsible for carrying out the decisions and day-to-day work of the Central Committee. The S. is elected at the first PLENARY SESSION of the C.C. and consists of the SECRETARY-GENERAL (or in some parties, known as the FIRST SECRETARY) and several Secretaries. The S.-G. is the highest Party official, usually the chairman of the POLITBURO and the most powerful person in a country ruled by a C.P. Some of the Secretaries are also members of the Politburo. The S. determines the appointment of senior CADRES and, by virtue of this function, its power is greatly enhanced. The S. is divided into a number of departments, such as propaganda, economic affairs, defence and relations with other communist parties. For an example, SECRETARIAT OF THE CC OF THE CPSU.

Secretariat of the Central Committee of the Communist Party of the Soviet Union One of the top Party organs which has come to play a powerful role, not only in the Party, but also in the country in general. The institution was established by the decision of the 8th Party Congress (March 1919) to carry out the decisions of the CENTRAL COMMITTEE and the ORGBURO. The S. directs the work of the entire Party machine on a day-to-day basis. It developed into a crucial Party body under Stalin, who was appointed Secretary-General and headed the Orgburo, mainly through its function of appointing senior CADRES, approving delegates to the Party Congresses and controlling the appointment of other important officials outside the Party. The S. is headed by the Secretary-General (known as the First Secretary over the period 1953–66), viz. L. I. BREZHNEV (since 1964). The S. also has four Secretaries and five Members, all of whom, like the S.-C., are elected by the Central Committee at its first PLENARY SESSION at the Party Congress. The S.-G. is the chairman of the Politburo and the four Secretaries are also members of the Politburo. The S. is organized into departments, each concerned with a major sphere of the country's affairs.

Secretary-General The official designation of the highest official of the Communist Party in most Socialist countries, notably in Cuba, Czechoslovakia, Kampuchea, DPR of Korea, Laos, Romania and the USSR. Strictly speaking, the S.-G. is the top executive officer of the Central Committee's SECRETARIAT. The designation was first introduced in the RUSSIAN COMMUNIST PARTY (OF THE BOLSHEVIKS) in 1922 with Stalin as its first holder. The S.-G. is usually also the chairman of the POLITBURO and is not only the most powerful person in the Party but also in the country if the Communist Party is the ruling party. The S.-G. is elected by the Central Committee at its first PLENARY SESSION at the Party Congress, but in the case of the Romanian C.P., he is elected by the Party Congress itself. The position is designated as First Secretary in Albania, Bulgaria, the German DR, Hungary, Mongolia and Poland, Chairman in China and President in Yugoslavia.

Secret Speech on Stalin See KHRUSHCHEV'S SECRET SPEECH.

Sectarianism In Marxist terminology, attitudes and actions of Party members leading to the emergence of narrow groups deviating from the official Party line and policies and separated from the masses. S. was discussed as a problem in the working class movement by Lenin (in *Left-Wing Communism: An Infantile Disorder*, 1920), attributing it to DOGMATISM and the inflexible interpretation of Marxist thought. He insisted that Party members should follow the official line and the Party itself should be prepared to adapt Marxist principles flexibly to changing conditions and, if necessary, make tactical concessions to win the masses. However, he warned that to avoid s. Party members must not turn to OPPORTUNISM and REVISIONISM.

Sejm The unicameral parliament in the POLISH PEOPLE'S REPUBLIC, elected by universal, equal, direct and secret ballot by citizens, 18 years of age and over, for a term of four years. The institution originally emerged in the 15th c. For historical reasons the name has been retained under the Communist regime. The S. is the highest formal organ of state power in the country, which in 1947 replaced the National Council. There are 460 deputies, elected from a single list of candidates prepared by the FRONT OF THE NATION'S UNITY, dominated by the Communist Party (POLISH UNITED WORKERS' PARTY). However, other non-opposition parties and groups are also represented. At the March 1976 general election, the P.U.W.P. gained 255 seats, the United Peasants Party – 117 seats, the Democratic Party – 39 and non-party groups (including various religious bodies) – 49 seats. The powers of the S. include constitutional changes, current legislation and the approval of the state budget and the national economic plan. The S.'s executive body is the Presidium, consisting of the Marshal of the S. and two Vice-Marshals and is assisted by an advisory committee called the Convention of Seniors and Chancellery (secretariat).

Selective Coexistence A term sometimes used in the East and the West for an expedient qualification of the policy of COEXISTENCE. In the East it is stressed that peaceful coexistence applies only to the practical field, viz. trade, technological, scientific and financial relations and the avoidance of a global nuclear war. But it does not include ideological concessions, compromise or the renunciation of local wars of national liberation on the part of Socialist countries. In the West, especially in the USA, it has been accepted in official circles that the policy of peaceful coexistence should not be pursued on the whole front, but selectively, according to the best interests of the Western alliance, implying a flexibility of approach at different times. In particular, it involves the differentiation of treatment of different Socialist countries, according to their current foreign policies and historical circumstances (especially in relatiqn to China, Cuba, the DPR of Korea, Romania, the USSR, Vietnam, and Yugoslavia).

Self-criticism A Marxist term denoting a critical evaluation of one's own attitude or action and the admission of one's own errors inconsistent with communist ideology and current party policy and practice. The term is used in application to party members, especially officials and groups. The importance of s.-c. in the working class movement was first indicated by Marx (in *The Eighteenth Brumaire of Louis Bonoparte*, 1852). S.-c., together with CRITICISM, is regarded as an essential element in the progressive DIALECTIC process of resolving CONTRADICTIONS which are bound to arise in changing circumstances. S.-c. became an established feature of the RUSSIAN COMMUNIST PARTY (OF THE BOLSHEVIKS) after the KRONSTADT UPRISING (March 1921). The rules of all Communist parties provide explicitly for s.-c. It is considered that s.-c. is an effective method of fighting DEVIATION-

ISM, FACTIONALISM and REVISIONISM, counteracts self-adulation and conceit among party officials and brings the CADRES closer to the rank and file of the party membership and public in general. In extreme cases, s.-c. may assume a public self-abasement session and has been a feature of many POLITICAL SHOW TRIALS. Some critics of Marxism view s.-c. as a form of religious confession and penitence borrowed from the Christian religion. Also BRAINWASHING, INNER PARTY DEMOCRACY, PARTY DISCIPLINE, THOUGHT REFORM.

Self-Financing In Socialist economic practice, the financing of investment out of the enterprises' own profits, which has assumed considerable importance in the European Socialist countries since the economic reforms of the 1960s. Roughly one-half of total investment in these countries is now financed in this way. S.-f. is conducive to a greater independence of enterprises, in contrast to the BUDGETARY FINANCING associated with central controls and various imposed conditions.

Self-Movement A philosophical conception according to which there is constant change in nature and society, which is attributed to endogenous causation. The conception has become central thesis in DIALECTICAL MATERIALISM, which maintains that natural and social development is a process fed by the struggle of internal CONTRADICTIONS of phenomena. Thus, Marxists are opposed to the idea of exogenous and even mechanistic causation. They discard the theory that changes in nature derive from an initial 'big push' by god at the time of the 'creation' of the world (as held by I. Newton), or from the reservoir of energy infused by god (as argued by R. Descartes) or from the struggle of contradictions external to the movement in question (as maintained by MECHANISTIC MATERIALISM). S.-m. in SOCIAL DEVELOPMENT does not imply automatic changes independent of man, but a process where persons, groups, classes and nations play active roles in resolving contradictions.

Sellers' Market A market situation where there is a persistent excess of demand over the supply of goods (and services) at existing prices, leading to shortages. In effect a s.m. is noted for the privileged position of producers over distributors and of the latter over buyers, which finds its expression in queues, long waiting lists, low quality goods and poor commercial service. Past experience shows that a s.m. is typical of a Socialist planned economy, for which there are many deep-rooted contributing causes. On the demand side, they include planning for high rates of economic growth (necessitating unduly large resources), the tendency of wage funds to exceed the supply of consumer goods, the excessive growth of SOCIAL CONSUMPTION and the relatively faster growth of income of lower income groups. At the same time, the supply tends to be insufficient due to low or no reserves, BOTTLENECKS, unfulfilled targets, the reluctance of the authorities to allow more resources to distribute, strictly controlled imports and the priorities given to exports. The official determination to prevent prices from rising accentuates the situation and does not favour appropriate readjustments on the part of buyers and sellers. S. markets are not as 'deep' now as they used to be in the past. It is possible now, that a Socialist centrally planned economy is capable of evolving BUYERS' MARKETS.

Semantic Philosophy A branch of philosophy concerned with the study of the sense and significance of words. It is related to LOGICAL POSITIVISM and NOMINALISM and has exerted some influence on linguistic, legal and ethical theories. In s.p., general concepts are considered to be merely conventional designations and combinations of sounds, not meaning or reflecting anything real. S.p. reached its greatest development in Britain, Germany and the USA in the 18th–20th c. Among its exponents were J. Locke (1632–1704), G. W. Leibnitz (1646–1716), G. Berkeley (1685–1753), J. Bentham (1748–1832), J. S. Mill (1806–73) and C. K. Ogden (1889–

1957). S. philosophers maintain that philosophical errors and political conflicts can be ultimately traced to the imperfection of language. Marxist philosophers are highly critical of s.p., which they describe as bourgeois, reactionary, subjectivist and steeped in IDEALISM, incompatible with MATERIALISM. In particular, they are opposed to the s. analysis of words and sounds, disregarding their materialist background and practical experience. They further reject the thesis that class conflicts and other social and political ills are due merely to the semantic shortcomings of the language. Instead, they stress that the cause and effect are reverse, viz. social and political problems are basically caused by the imperfect economic BASE which leads to misunderstanding and communication gaps.

Sensualism A philosophical doctrine which flourished in the 18th and 19th c., according to which sensory experience is the only source of cognition. There are several different interpretations of this process, but the sensualist philosophers fall into two broad categories. Some see the impressions in a human mind to be subjective and having existence in their own right, as represented by G. Berkeley (1684–1753), D. Hume (1711–76), I. Kant (1724–1804) and A. A. BOGDANOV. Others, represented by C. A. Helvetius (1715–71), P. H. Holbach (1723–89) and L. FEUERBACH, maintain that impressions are objectively produced in our mind by external objects and phenomena. Marxist philosophy rejects the first interpretation, as it leads to IDEALISM, whereby ideas are attributed existence independent of the external world. But Marxists give qualified acceptance to the second version, as it treats sensory experience as a reflection of the objective external world and, consequently, amounts to materialist s. However, Marxist philosophers point out that in contrast to the view held by some sensual materialists, the process of cognition does not stop at that stage, as sensory perception is only the first phase in the process. Sensory data are then transformed through abstract thinking into generalizations, and further tested in practice, so that sensory experience, theoretical deduction and practical testing represent a complete DIALECTIC unity in the process of the acquisition of knowledge.

Serednyak A Bolshevik term used from 1917 to the mid-1930s for a middle peasant, owning roughly from 5 to 15 hectares of land. The *s.* ranked between the *BEDNYAK* and *KULAK*. The *S.* usually worked his land himself (together with his family) and in some cases hired *BATRAKS* (agricultural labourers) or *bednyaks*. The Soviet regime classed the *S.* as belonging to the PROLETARIAT and he was treated leniently as an element of the workers-peasants alliance (while the *kulaks* were classed as belonging to the exploiting class).

Serfdom In the Marxist theory of HISTORICAL MATERIALISM, the feature of FEUDALISM, a socio-economic formation which followed slavery but preceded capitalism. S. prevailed in the Middle Ages and in central and eastern Europe and Russia up to the late 19th c. The serfs constituted the class exploited by the feudal lords (the ruler, nobility, gentry, church). There were different degrees of s., ranging from complete serfs (who belonged to the lord) to villeins (bound to the soil or bound to performing certain duties). Unlike a master, in the case of slaves, a lord had no right to kill his serf. Exploitation, i.e. the appropriation of the SURPLUS VALUE of the serf's labour, was realized through legal norms, customary lord's rights and serf's obligations. The development of cities and the consequent increase in the demand for agricultural products often involved serfs in longer working hours and the conversion of rent into obligatory labour, thus intensifying their exploitation. The legal abolition of s. did not improve the economic situation of the peasant until he was given a legal right to own the land he occupied or worked.

Services Economic activities which do not

directly result in MATERIAL PRODUCTION. In Western national income accounting, all services which are paid for, in addition to the annual value of the owner-occupied dwellings, are treated as part of the national income and regarded as products of tertiary industries (in contrast to primary and secondary industries). In Socialist national income accounting, a distinction is made between PRODUCTIVE S. and NON-PRODUCTIVE S. The former – comprising transport, communications trade and certain other minor services – are included in the national income (called the NET MATERIAL PRODUCT) to the extent that they represent an indispensable continuation in the process of material production. Therefore, private travel, mail and telecommunications and the financial handling of trade transactions are excluded. These and all other services, being nonproductive in the Marxist sense, are not considered to be contributing to the Socialist defined national income. However, in recent years, some socialist economists (especially in Eastern Europe) have been advocating a revision of the traditional Marxist classification, in favour of the Western approach (accepted by the United Nations).

S.E.V. C.M.E.A., i.e. an abbreviation of the Russian *Sovet Ekonomicheskoi Vzaimpomoshchi*, meaning the COUNCIL FOR MUTUAL ECONOMIC ASSISTANCE.

'Seven Black Elements' Seven types of people in the CHINESE COMMUNIST PARTY who were considered to be anti-social by the supporters of Mao Tse-tung during the GREAT PROLETARIAN CULTURAL REVOLUTION. They were: 1. former landlords; 2. former rich peasants; 3. former capitalists; 4. rightists; 5. counter-revolutionaries; 6. social parasites (avoiding work); and 7. black market gangsters. A campaign was launched against them by the Thought Reform Teams and Leadership Core Groups within the REVOLUTIONARY COMMITTEES, which reached its peak in late 1968. The purpose of the campaign was to purge the Party ranks to ensure a truly 'revolutionary party based on Mao Tse-tung's thought'. The campaign was marked by confusion, including heated arguments about classifications and reclassifications, which were often based on personal grievances and a lack of information, caused by the destruction of the dossiers during the Cultural Revolution.

'Seven Guarantees' Seven social safeguards ensuring a minimum standard of living allowed to the members of the better situated PEOPLE'S COMMUNES in China, when the economic situation warrants it. They include: 1. food; 2. clothing; 3. medical care; 4. housing; 5. maternity payment; 6. marriage allowance; and 7. burial allowance. Some people's communes are permitted to provide TEN GUARANTEES.

Seventh-of-May Cadre Schools Special schools established in China during the GREAT PROLETARIAN CULTURAL RE-VOLUTION for younger bureaucrats in China (Party and state officials, army officers and managers) to re-educate them along Maoist proletarian lines and bring them closer to the masses. The name derives from a directive to this effect issued by Mao Tse-tung on 7 May 1966. The first experimental School was created by a Revolutionary Committee in Heilungkiang province (north-eastern China) two days later. The Schools were established by factories, various educational establishments, offices and shops located in the countryside. The courses conducted ranged from a few months to a few years, the participants lived in and the objective was to consolidate the social unity of the town and country. The main features of the Schools were: 1. the study of Marxism-Leninism and Mao's thought and the critical evaluation of LIU SHAO-CH'I and CAPITALIST ROADERS; 2. CRITICISM and SELF-CRITICISM sessions aimed at humbling the participants; 3. the development of habits of simple living; 4. strict social (not necessarily militaristic) discipline; and 5. emphasis on physical labour.

Seventy Points Programme, or Seven Points Charter for Industry In China, a detailed scheme of economic development with an emphasis on industrialization along liberal and efficient lines, specifying 70 features put forward by LIU SHAO-CH'I in 1962. It was a reaction against Mao Tse-tung's adventurist policies of the GREAT LEAP FORWARD. The Programme emphasized strict industrial discipline, material incentives, the primacy of economic commonsense and rejected the Maoist postulate of POLITICS IN COMMAND in economic development. The scheme was supported by a group within the Party establishment but was attacked by Mao and was never fully implemented.

Seven-year Plan A medium-term plan for economic development covering seven (instead of the more conventional five) years. The seven-year period was experimented with in the USSR and some East European countries covering the years 1959–65. However, it has not been repeated and, since 1965, these countries have reverted to five-year plans. A s.-y.p. was adopted by the DPR of Korea for the period 1978–84 (following a six-year plan 1972–77).

Sexism Differentiation between men and women with the implied discrimination against women. It may be found in education, vocational training, employment and cultural social and family life. Marxism took an early stand on s., regarding it as a form of exploitation of women by men, typical of pre-socialist societies and convenient to the ruling classes. The Socialist countries have embarked on the wide-ranging equalization of the sexes as a matter of social ethics and practical considerations to captivate women to the Marxist cause. Their economic, political and legal status has been raised by generous social services (child endowment, maternity allowance, paid pregnancy and child-birth leave), priority given to the production of household labour-saving devices (washing machines, cleaning equipment, processed foods), public catering, child care centres, legalized abortion, easy divorce and economic independence from men. Equalization along these lines is also typical in the affluent industrialized countries. The emphasis on absolute sex equality in the Socialist countries has produced several controversial effects, such as female labour in heavy manual employment (construction sites, lumbering, mining), the instability of family life, juvenile delinquency and the like.

Shadow Exchange Rate See COEFFICIENT OF THE RELATIVE VALUE OF FOREIGN CURRENCIES.

Shadow Market An artificial market where SHADOW PRICES are estimated by imputation taking social cost-benefit considerations into account, or where supply and demand are simulated on a centrally planned basis guided by similar considerations. As such, a s.m. is considered to be superior to a conventional commercial market, as the latter operates erratically causing disruptions, registering only private cost and benefit and, in general, producing anti-social effects. The concept of the s.m. was first established by O. LANGE in the late 1930s, as a method of arriving at RATIONAL PRICES of the factors of production by the Central Planning Board in a collectivist economy, where there is no private ownership of the means of production and no conventional market mechanism. He proposed to establish and administer rational prices by a process of successive approximations (TRIAL AND ERROR METHOD) on the basis of the information available to the C.P.B. concerning the actual and socially desirable supply and demand conditions. This process would ensure a market equilibrium and the full employment of labour. The model, as he envisaged, has been applied only to a limited extent. In a sense, central planners, when working out the national economic plan and its current revisions in the process of plan implementation, operate in a s.m. But it is a crude s.m., owing to the lack of ideal information. The advo-

cates of OPTIMAL PLANNING believe that a centrally-administered extensive information network based on high-memory computers will enable a scientifically-simulated market in the future. So far, it has proved possible only on a limited, partial scale.

Shadow Prices Notional prices which are not established and used in conventional commercial markets, but are derived artificially and used as accounting prices. They are arrived at either by correcting the ordinary market prices by the process of successive approximations, or computationally with the aid of high-memory computers. In each case, social cost-benefit considerations are taken into account. The idea of s.p. was introduced and substantiated first by O. LANGE in the late 1930s, to demonstrate that a collectivist economy could derive rational prices of the factors of production in SHADOW MARKETS. There are three types of s.p.: 1. those produced by researchers in capitalist market economies, who correct the free market prices by imputing social costs and benefits, not otherwise registered by the free market mechanism; 2. those in the Langian sense, determined in a collectivist economy through the Central Planning Board by the TRIAL AND ERROR METHOD on the basis of the available information of the actual and desirable supply and demand; 3. PROGRAMMING PRICES, crudely worked out by central planners in the Socialist countries to reflect the scarcity of the factors of production and applied in the economic plan in the interest of the most effective allocation of resources under given constraints; and 4. OPTIMAL PRICES, or ideal prices, derived from the optimal plan through the process of iteration using complete data supplied by a centralized, comprehensive information network based on high-memory computers (so far applied only on a partial basis in the more advanced European socialist countries).

Shakhtyntsy In Soviet usage, specifically the defendants in the SHAKHTY TRIAL, but in general anybody in the official view sabotaging industrial development in the USSR under the first three five-year plans (1928–41).

Shakhty Trial A show trial of some 300 mining engineers and workers staged in the coal mining city of Shakhty in the Donets Basin in the USSR in 1928. The trial was well publicized and was the first of several similar trials directed against 'bourgeois' specialists during the Soviet CULTURAL REVOLUTION. The defendants were charged with 'wrecking the coal industry' and were alleged to be sympathetic to the former owners of the mines and foreign commercial and military interests. Five of the defendants were executed and most others were sentenced to imprisonment of varying terms. The S.T. was later described by outside observers as 'a dress rehearsal for the Great Purges of the 1930s'.

Shanghai Massacre A large-scale treacherous massacre of tens of thousands of workers, warlords and foreign sympathizers in Shanghai on 12 April 1927 by Chiang Kai-shek's troops and thugs recruited from the underworld. Before the massacre, some 600,000 workers through strikes and armed revolt had driven out the warlords and their troops from Shanghai in order to help the approaching Nationalist army of the KUOMINTANG led by Chiang. The S.M. is still shrouded in mystery. Although Chiang was later reprimanded by both the *Kuomintang* and Stalin, no action was taken against him. Nor was the Communist regime, after its seizure of power in 1949, willing to allow the erection of a monument to commemorate the victims.

Shchekino Experiment A widely publicized experiment initiated at the Shchekino Chemical Combine in the USSR in 1967 to spur enterprises to raising their efficiency by minimizing their employment. The savings achieved by labour retrenchments, while maintaining or increasing production, were then partly shared by the remaining personnel. The experiment proved successful and the approach was widely adopted in the USSR, as well as in some Eastern European countries. However, its advocates have been disappointed with the rather indifferent support from the governments. This can be explained by the latters' fear of excessive rises in income, threatening a disruption in the consumer goods market and a large labour turnover of less efficient workers.

Shock Brigade See SHOCK WORKERS' MOVEMENT.

Shock Workers' Movement A state-organized drive in the USSR initiated in 1927 to implement the most critical elements of the crash programme of industrialization established in the five-year plans. The emphasis was on efficiency, the immediate rectification of BOTTLENECKS and the achievement of maximum output in general. By 1934, 5m. industrial and transport workers had been drawn into the movement. The most outstanding workers were awarded the title of 'Shock Worker' and groups of workers – 'Shock Brigade'. The S.W.M. reached its peak of intensity during the first five-year plan (1928–32) which, largely thanks to the movement, was completed in virtually four years. In the mid-1930s, the S.W.M. was succeeded by the STAKHANOV MOVEMENT. Similar drives have been pursued in other Socialist countries at one time or another.

Show Trials POLITICAL SHOW TRIALS.

Shuliatikovism A derogatory term first applied by PLEKHANOV to the version of HISTORICAL MATERIALISM as presented by Russian social-democrat, writer and philosopher, V. Shuliatikov (1872–1912). In the official Soviet view, Shuliatikov's doctrine is noted for oversimplification and misinterpretation, exemplifying VULGAR MATERIALISM and VULGAR SOCIOLOGISM. This is the case because he deduces ideological phenomena directly from the material BASE and denies a certain measure of independence for science, philosophy, literature and art.

Šik, Ota (1919–) A Czechoslovak economist who was the main driving force behind the proposed liberal economic reforms in Czechoslovakia in the late 1960s. A loyal Communist leader (member of the Party's Central Committee and its Economic Committee, 1962–69), he was a member of the State Planning Commission, Director of the Institute of Economics of the Czechoslovak Academy of Sciences (1963–68) and Deputy Prime Minister in 1968. He was the most outstanding advocate of combining planning with the market mechanism, which he believed could usefully supplement each other in peaceful coexistence within a socialist framework. Unlike A. DUBČEK, O.S. went into exile after the INVASION OF CZECKOSLOVAKIA and settled down in Switzerland (where he took a lecturing position at the University of St Gallen). He was deprived of his Czechoslovakian citizenship in 1970. His main publications are: *Economics, Interests Politics* (1962); *Economic Planning and Management in Czechoslovakia* (1965); *Plan and Market under Socialism* (1965); *Money and Socialism* (1966); *On the Question of Socialist Commodity Relations* (1968); *Facts about the Czechoslovak Economy* (1969); *Democratic and Socialist Planned and Market Economy* (1971); *Czechoslovakia: The Bureaucratic Economy* (1972); *Structural Changes in the Economic Systems in East Europe* (1972); *The Third Way* (1972); *Towards an Economy Without the Dogma* (1974); and *The Communist Power System* (1976).

Simple Labour In Marxian terminology, unskilled labour of the lowest degree of productivity. The concept is important in the measurement of the value of labour performed, as s.l. is taken as the lowest common denominator. The opposite concept is COMPOUND LABOUR (skilled labour of different degrees, a multiple of s.l.). In the construction of wage scales in the

socialist countries, the relation between s.l. and the highest classification of compound labour is roughly in the ratio of 1 : 2.5.

Simple Reproduction A Marxian term applied to the situation in the economy when the volume of producer and consumer goods produced is equal to their volume used during the year in question. It means that net investment is nil, the capital stock in the economy is unchanged and the rate of growth of the national income is usually zero (unless efficiency increases). S.r. is identified with economic stagnation, when investment and consumption policies in the Socialist countries are directed towards EXPANDED REPRODUCTION. In technical Marxian terms, s.r. occurs when there is: 1. an equality of VARIABLE CAPITAL (v) and SURPLUS VALUE(S) in DEPARTMENT I and of CONSTANT CAPITAL (c) in Department II; 2. an equality of total production in Department I and of constant capital in both Departments; and 3. an equality of total production of Department II and of variable capital plus surplus value combined.

Simulated Market See SHADOW MARKET.

Single Industrial Society A concept put forward by Western philosophers, sociologists and economic historians, denoting a reasonably uniform society which develops in the post-industrial era. It is understood as a middle class society (not unlike a classless society), which naturally develops in higher stages of economic development noted for affluence, irrespective of the political system in force. The post-industrial era is described by Z. Brzezinski as the 'technotronic age' and by W.W. Rostow as the 'age of mass consumption'. The s.i.s. has been given different designations by different thinkers, viz. 'industrial society' by R. Aron, the 'new industrial state' by J. Galbraith, the 'post-industrial society', by D. Bell, the 'super-industrial society' by A. Toffler and the 'optimum regime' by J. Tinbergen. The proponents of the idea of the s.i.s. maintain that scientific and technological progress is neutral and inevitable and produces similar patterns of organization, occupations, mentality and attitudes in all developed societies. The s.i.s. is already developing in the more affluent capitalist countries. Consequently, to attain the Marxian ideal of a classless society in the West it is no longer necessary to proceed via the class struggle, proletarian revolution and the dictatorship of the proletariat. Revolutionary Marxists have described the conception and rationale of the s.i.s. as 'wishful thinking' and 'utopian'. The Communist parties in the Socialist countries have rejected the idea in application to capitalist countries regarding it as a 'passing fashion among the bourgeois pseudo-thinkers'.

Sinification of Marxism The interpretation and modification of Marxist ideas and precepts in adaptation to Chinese conditions and developments. It has been largely conditioned by Mao Tse-tung's determination to rationalize his strategy in the Chinese revolution and to provide a distinct model of Marxism – more suited not only to China, but also to other economically less-developed societies of Asia, Africa and Latin America. The origin of the S. of M. can be traced to Mao's arguments with LI LI-SAN in the late 1920s. The latter advocated dogmatic Marxian approach to the revolution via the industrial urban working class, while Mao stressed the importance of the countryside and peasants. In the 1930s the S. of M. was largely reduced to Mao and his supporters' struggle against the pro-Soviet faction in the Chinese Communist Party. In 1938, Mao openly denied the relevance of 'abstract Marxism' to the Chinese realities, and emphasized that the Chinese revolution could be led only by the Chinese (and not the Soviets, even though he had a great respect for Stalin as a leader in the USSR). Three years later, Mao pointed out (in 'Reform Our Study', May 1941) that the universal truth of Marxism-Leninism must be combined with the actual practical lessons provided by the Chin-

ese revolution. In 1957, the Chinese leadership decided to depart from the Soviet model of industrialization. They turned to the policy of WALKING ON TWO LEGS and in the following year Mao issued his *SIXTY ARTICLES*. A more radical campaign for the S. of M. has been prompted by the SINO-SOVIET DISPUTE since 1960. The S. of M. is epitomized in the 15 major distinctive features of MAOISM.

Sino-Soviet Dispute The ideological and leadership conflict between the CHINESE COMMUNIST PARTY and the COMMUNIST PARTY OF THE SOVIET UNION, each utilizing its state machinery in the process. The origin of the dispute goes back to at least 1956 when the Chinese Communist leaders repudiated Khrushchev's declaration of peaceful COEXISTENCE and the denunciation of Stalin at the TWENTIETH CONGRESS OF THE CPSU, without previously consulting the Chinese Party leadership (i.e. Mao Tse-tung). In June 1959, the USSR refused to supply nuclear materials and technology to China (thereby breaking the Sino-Soviet Treaty of Oct. 1957) and in Aug. 1960 all Soviet technical specialists were recalled from China. The dispute came into the open at the conference of Communist Party delegations attending the Congress of the Romanian Workers' Party (as it was then known) in Bucharest in June 1960, when bitter mutual accusations were exchanged in front of other delegates. The divergence was further formalized in the MOSCOW STATEMENT of Nov. 1960. In 1962 the two Parties began to denounce each other in the international arena and each intensified its efforts to canvass the support of other Communist parties. Of the 100 significant national communist parties in the world in 1978, 50 clearly supported the CSPU, 7 supported the CCP, 5 were neutral, 8 followed an independent line and the rest were split. Also MOSCOW LINE, PEKING LINE, SINIFICATION OF MARXISM.

Sismondi, Jean Charles Sismonde de (1773–1842) A Swiss economist and one of the early critics of capitalism, whose ideas attracted a mixed reception from Marx, Engels and other classical Marxist thinkers. S. was a firm believer in the LABOUR THEORY OF VALUE, but his main interest was directed at the weaknesses of capitalism and how it could be improved. He reasoned that competition and technological progress in a capitalist society inevitably lead to the elimination of small producers and declining living standards of the masses, which in turn causes economic crises threatening the breakdown of the system. As a solution, he advocated far-reaching state intervention. Although classical Marxists agreed with his acceptance of the labour theory of value and his criticism of capitalism, they rejected his proposed solutions as utopian, representing ECONOMIC ROMANTICISM. His main publications were: *Commercial Wealth or Principles of Political Economy* (1803) and *New Principles of Political Economy* (1819).

Sixteen Points Programme A document drafted under Mao Tse-tung's personal direction and adopted by the Central Committee of the Chinese Communist Party on 8 May 1966 as a guide to thought and action in the GREAT PROLETARIAN CULTURAL REVOLUTION. The Programme exhorted the cadres to embark on an aggressive and imaginative campaign against bourgeois, bureaucratic, complacent and reactionary elements in order to transform China into a new proletarian society. It consisted of 16 articles bearing the following headings: 1. A new stage in the socialist revolution; 2. The main current and the twists and turns; 3. Put daring above everything else and boldly arouse the masses; 4. Let the masses educate themselves in the movement; 5. Firmly apply the class line in the Party; 6. Correctly handle contradictions among the people; 7. Be on guard against those who brand the revolutionary masses as counter-revolutionaries; 8. The question of cadres; 9. Cultural revolutionary groups, committees and congresses; 10. Educational reform; 11. The question of

criticising by name in the press; 12. Policy towards scientists, technicians and ordinary members of working staffs; 13. The question of arrangements for integration with the Socialist Education Movement; 14. Take firm hold of the revolution and stimulate production; 15. The armed forces; and 16. Mao Tse-tung's thought is the guide to action in the Great Proletarian Cultural Revolution.

Sixteenth of May Movement In China during the GREAT PROLETARIAN CULTURAL REVOLUTION, a counter-revolutionary organization in Peking, led by a group of high-ranking officials in the Party and Government, drawing support from young people, some ultra-left and other groups allegedly of bourgeois background and mentality. It was headed by Yao Teng-shan, the expelled Chinese Ambassador to Indonesia. The S.M.M. endeavoured to undermine the authority of Mao Tse-tung, the Central Committee of the Chinese Communist Party, the PEOPLE'S LIBERATION ARMY and of the REVOLUTIONARY COMMITTEES. Its principal objective was to oust CHOU EN-LAI from power. It was named after the date of its formation and issue of the *May Circular* on 16 May 1966, when Mao returned to Peking, dismissed the existing GROUP OF FIVE headed by P'ENG CHEN and replaced it with a more radical organization, the CULTURAL REVOLUTION GROUP headed by Ch'en Po-ta. At first the S.M.M. was secret, but in 1967 its activities were brought into the open.

Sixty Articles A directive of the Chinese Communist Party, designated *Sixty Articles on Work Methods* and signed by Mao Tse-tung on 31 Jan. 1958, calling for a radical acceleration of China's economic development. The directive initiated the GREAT LEAP FORWARD and embodied 60 *Articles*, mostly directed against the Soviet model of economic development in favour of the indigenous strategy suited to Chinese conditions as interpreted by Mao. The directive emphasized enthusiasm, spontaneity and LEAPs in economic development (as distinct from Stalin's PLANNED PROPORTIONATE DEVELOPMENT), decentralization, self-reliance, local initiative, Party control at all levels ('POLITICS IN COMMAND') and the CONTINUING REVOLUTION.

Slansky, Rudolf (1901–52) A Czechoslovak communist of Jewish descent who reached the position of Secretary-General of the Central Committee of the CZECHOSLOVAK COMMUNIST PARTY, 1945–51, but was executed in the following year. He joined the Cz.C.P. in 1925, became a member of its Politburo in 1929 and, in 1944, as one of the MUSCOVITES, led a Communist uprising in Slovakia. In Feb. 1948, as the Party's Secretary-General, he organized armed demonstrations of the Workers' Militia in support of the Communist takeover (PRAGUE COUP D'ETAT). But in 1951, he was charged with TROTSKYISM, TITOISM and ZIONISM, stripped of his offices, arrested, sentenced to death as a traitor in the following year and executed in Dec. 1952. He was partly rehabilitated in 1963.

Slavery The condition of ownership of a person which usually involves the master's right to buy, sell and even kill his slave. In the Marxist interpretation of history, s. is regarded as the first ANTAGONISTIC SOCIO-ECONOMIC FORMATION, where the means of production (land and capital) and labour were owned by the members of the ruling class. S. as a social and economic institution emerged after PRIMITIVE COMMUNISM and was widespread in ancient Rome, Greece, the Middle East, East Africa, India and China. In addition, s. appeared in the later stages of primitive communism in some Asian societies and later on a minor scale under FEUDALISM and CAPITALISM (especially in the USA). S. represented the first systematic form of EXPLOITATION of man by man and slowed down progress in the methods of production (owing to the cheapness of labour). But s. gave rise to specialization, trade and money. It also necessitated the institution of the state as the coercive machinery for

the protection of the masters – the first ruling class. Marxists interpret the slave revolts, which periodically broke out, as the first attempts at PROLETARIAN REVOLUTIONS. But the revolts failed sooner or later, owing to the lack of CLASS CONSCIOUSNESS on behalf of the slaves and the absence of a well organized party commanding the support of the exploited classes. Critics of Soviet communism have pointed out that the FORCED LABOUR CAMPS, especially under Stalin, represented a form of s.

Slovak Soviet Republic A short-lived Communist regime which proclaimed an independent Soviet state on 19 June 1919, but was suppressed in the following month by the Czechoslovak government. The S.S.R. was created under the impact of the successful GREAT OCTOBER SOCIALIST REVOLUTION in Russia in 1917. It was directly aided by the local Red Guards, those peasants rebelling in some districts against the large landowners, Soviet volunteers and a Hungarian RED REGIMENT. Antonin Janousek became the Prime Minister. After the swift suppression of the regime, many Slovak Communists participated in the foundation of the CZECHOSLOVAK COMMUNIST PARTY in 1921.

Smersh ('Death [to Spies]', in Russian) The state security system in the Soviet armed forces during W.W.II (1942–46). It replaced the Special Sections administered by the Military Department of the Chief Administration of State Security (*GUGB*), which was the state security division of the PEOPLE'S COMMISSARIAT of Internal Affairs (*NKVD*). The main functions of *S.* were: 1. military counterespionage; 2. political supervision of the armed forces; 3. political surveillance of Soviet troops abroad; 4. elimination of any political opposition in Soviet-occupied territories; and 5. 're-education' of Soviet citizens who had been 'infected by undesirable ideas' when outside Soviet control. In discharging its responsibilities, *S.* employed special Blocking Units, operating behind the front lines to bar

Smith, Adam

troops from retreating and resorted to mass arrests, deportations to Siberia and summary executions.

Smith, Adam (1723–1790) One of the most prominent classical political economists whose work MARX examined fairly thoroughly. Smith, who was Scottish, was able to observe the effects of the Industrial Revolution in Britain and comment on the inner mechanics of industrial CAPITALISM. His greatest work, *An Inquiry into the Nature and Causes of the Wealth of Nations* (1776), has a marginal comment on ALIENTATION whereby the industrial PROLETARIAT became estranged from their work and themselves. Marx was critical of Smith for his appraisal of the LABOUR THEORY OF VALUE as a given situation in an unquestioned social structure.

Social Accounting Service (*Služba Drustvenog Knjigovodstva*, in Serbo-Croat) The system of public financial control and discipline of socialized enterprises and other public entities in Yugoslavia. Up to 1963, public auditing had been carried out by banks, but in that year accounting and control functions were separated from the banking system and transferred to 380 S.A.S. offices. The system is nationwide, operating under the auspices of the Federal Government. The S.A.S. has the power of initiating legal proceedings against offending entities and, in case of financial difficulties, to block their funds and permit payments to creditors according to an established priority.

Social Catholicism A doctrine which acquired some popularity in several Western European countries (especially France and Germany) in late 19th and early 20th c., emphasizing social co-operation based on Christian ethics and community interests betweem employers and employees. It rejected the postulates of CLASS STRUGGLE, PROLETARIAN REVOLUTION and the DICTATORSHIP OF THE PROLETARIAT. Instead, it advocated CORPORATISM, i.e., confederations of employers and emp-

loyees with mutual responsibilities. S.C. was strongly supported by the Catholic Church, which laid down the principles of S.C. in two papal encyclicals, viz. *Rerum Novarum* by Pope Leo XIII in 1891 and *Quadragesimo Anno* by Pope Pius XI in 1936. Marxists have rejected S.C., objecting to its religious association, the idea of class harmony and the retention of the capitalist system. S.C. has never had any significant social impact, but its idea of corporatism and the anti-communist stance were to some extent embraced by FASCISM in Italy, Portugal and Spain and Nazism in Germany.

Social Chauvinism A conception established by Lenin (in 'Collapse of the Second International', 1915, and 'The Tasks of the Proletariat in Our Revolution', 1917) denoting the collaboration of the socialist parties with the bourgeoisie and the government and supporting imperialist wars in the name of national defence. Lenin insisted that W.W.I was an imperialist war and that the working class should refuse to support the bourgeois governments in fighting and trying to win the war. Instead, he advocated that the proletariat should aim at the defeat of the bourgeois military involvement, thereby creating a REVOLUTIONARY SITUATION, and transform the war into a civil war and a PROLETARIAN REVOLUTION. He branded the collaborating socialist leaders as 'narrow-minded or opportunistic social chauvinists', who in their naïvety or private interest supported the exploiting ruling class to the detriment of the long-run interest of the working class movement.

Social Classes An important sociological and ideological concept, denoting hierarchically stratified groups in society with respect to property ownership, income, type of employment and cultural attainments and interests. Traditionally, upper, middle and lower s.c. have been distinguished, with sub-divisions within each. The origin of and the relations between s.c. command focal interest in Marxist ideology. In accordance with HISTORICAL

522

MATERIALISM, s.c. are seen as an historical outcome of the relation of people to the means of production (land and capital) and of the division of labour, where one class may exploit another. In capitalist society, Marx distinguished between two basic and antagonistic s.c., viz. 1. the BOURGEOISIE (capitalists) and 2. the PROLETARIAT (urban workers and poor peasants). In addition, he identified lesser s.c. with varying degrees of loyalty to one or the other basic s.c.: 3. landlords; 4. PEASANTS and tenant farmers; 5. the PETTY BOURGEOISIE (small businessmen); 6. the intelligentsia (professionals and other white-collar workers); and 7. the *LUMPENPROLETARIAT* (drifters, prostitutes, most criminals and various demoralized elements). In the Socialist countries, it is claimed that the exploiting classes have been eliminated and that under socialism there are three non-antagonistic, 'vertical' s.c., viz. workers, peasants and the intelligentsia, the last one being very largely recruited from the other two. Under FULL COMMUNISM, even the vertical class distinctions are expected to disappear, leading to a CLASSLESS SOCIETY. The critics of the Communist regimes, however, point out that hierarchically stratified s.c. have always existed in the Socialist countries. Moreover, social distinctions are in several ways becoming accentuated. There is the party elite which, although legally not owning the means of production, exercises ultimate control over them and wields effective power, usually aloof from the masses and the rank and file Party membership. Furthermore, peasants have always been at the bottom of the social ladder, in relation to incomes, influence and the social prestige of the intelligentsia, especially technocrats and top professionals (successful actors, architects, artists, bureaucrats, engineers, managers of large enterprises, scientists and writers.) Also FIVE PURE CLASSES, NEW CLASS, UTILITY THEORY OF THE UPPER SOCIAL CLASS.

Social Conflict ANTAGONISTIC CONDITIONS OF DISTRIBUTION, ANTAGONISTIC PRODUCTION RELATIONS, ANTAGONISTIC SOCIO-ECONOMIC FORMATIONS, CLASS STRUGGLE, PROLETARIAN REVOLUTION, SOCIAL CONTRADICTIONS.

Social Consciousness In Marxist ideology, the totality of society's philosophical, moral, political, legal, cultural and religious attitudes, views and theories. S.c. is regarded as part of the SUPERSTRUCTURE and, as such is determined by the material BASE. In accordance with DIALECTICAL MATERIALISM, the economic conditions of life are primary, while consciousness is secondary, a reflection of matter and nature in the human mind. When the material base changes, s.c. is transformed accordingly. But at the same time, Marxism stresses the importance of new progressive ideas, so that s.c. also plays a part in the development of the material base. S.c. must not be confused with CLASS CONSCIOUSNESS.

Social Consumption That portion of total consumption which is provided by society free of charge, or at charges well below cost. It is also known as collective, public, residual or other c. S.c. is very well developed in the Socialist countries, where it typically constitutes 20–35 per cent of total consumption, compared with 5–15 per cent in most capitalist countries. The Socialist state attaches great importance to s.c., as it represents distribution in accordance with the Marxist principle 'according to needs'. The Socialist state is committed to the gradual expansion of s.c. to well over 50 per cent and, under FULL COMMUNISM, theoretically to nearly 100 per cent. S.c. consists of public child care, education at all levels, complete health care, pensions, housing, communal feeding, special holidays, transport, entertainment and cultural services. It is financed out of the state budget, social insurance funds, communal resources and profits from enterprises and farms earmarked for the purpose. S.c. contrasts with PRIVATE CONSUMPTION.

Social Contradictions A Marxist term for conflicting relations between social classes or groups. S.c. are regarded by Marxists as one of the principal driving forces behind social progress. There are two types of s.c. 1. Antagonistic s.c. exist between exploiting and exploited classes, where the former appropriate SURPLUS VALUE created by the latter. They appear in antagonistic socio-economic formations, viz. SLAVERY, FEUDALISM and CAPITALISM and, as a rule, can be resolved only by a revolutionary overthrow of the ruling class. 2. Non-antagonistic s.c. are those which do not require a fundamental transformation of society, but can be resolved on a peaceful planned basis. They occur in the Socialist societies, mostly as a matter of historical survival from the previous social systems. The main s.c. of this nature are those between the rural and urban population.

Social Cost The all-inclusive cost which is borne by society, not merely by individual consumers or producers. In Marxist terminology, it involves all the outlays of SOCIAL LABOUR, both materialized and live, necessary to produce a particular output. It is identified with the (social) value of production and, in Marxian terms, is expressed by the formula, $c + v + s$, where c represents constant capital (materialized labour), v – variable capital (wages) and s – surplus value (profit). On the other hand, the net value of production is represented by $c + v$. The aggregate s.c. in a given period is equal to the gross social product. In application to an individual product, the s.c. refers to the average necessary outlay of social labour, taking the whole economy into account at the existing level of technology.

Social Court See COMRADES' COURT.

Social Credit Movement A Movement initiated by C. H. Douglas (1878–1952), an Anglo-Scottish engineer, with a view to increasing the spending power of the masses. Its proponents held that although technological progress enables the growth of production, the lower income groups (the masses) do not have enough purchas-

ing power to buy the output owing to the excessive monopolistic prices and the uneven distribution of national income. As a remedy, Douglas advocated three basic measures to be taken by the state: 1. to control the monetary system appropriately; 2. to distribute social credit in the form of a 'national dividend' to every person; and 3. to prevent inflation by fixing 'just' prices. The movement also stressed the role of technocrats in social decision-making (rather than politicians and businessmen). It achieved its greatest popularity in Canada (especially in Alberta), other British Commonwealth countries and the USA. In Alberta, the Social Credit Party won provincial elections on this platform in 1935. The idea spread to other parts of the country, but achieved little success elsewhere.

Social Darwinism A sociological doctrine according to which superior individuals, classes, nations or races deservedly survive and become dominant, while the less superior are eliminated or become subservient. The doctrine is based on Ch. Darwin's theory of NATURAL SELECTION (in *On the Origin of Species by Means of Natural Selection, or the Preservation of Favoured Races in the Struggle for Life,* 1859), which was originally conceived for the animal and plant kingdom. The doctrine of s.D. was first put forward by H. Spencer (1820–1903) in *Social Statics* (1850) and *Man versus the State* (1884), who assumed that the Darwinian biological laws of the STRUGGLE FOR EXISTENCE also applied to mankind and social relations. W. Bagehot (1826–77), L. GUMPLOWICZ, O. Ammon (1842–1916), B. Kidd (1858–1916) and others added further elaborations. They distinguished between intra-class, inter-class, international and inter-racial relations. The doctrine accepts the existence of hierarchical social classes as natural, while improvidence and pauperism among the lowest classes are regarded as a reflection of their biological inferiority. On these grounds Spencer was opposed to state intervention and social welfare programmes, as they would interfere with the natural struggle for existence, would protect the inferior elements at the expense of the superior ones and would only lead to the physical and mental degeneration of society. Marxists have, naturally, strongly condemned the doctrine as unscientific and reactionary, calculated to provide an apologetic justification for the existing unjust social system under capitalism. In their view, biological laws that may or may not be valid in animal and plant life should not be conveniently transferred to the social sphere. Man is a product of the material and social environment, not the other way round. Given a fair chance and suitable conditions, the so-called lower social classes could prove their equality to the task as any other privileged social group. The most natural social state is a CLASS-LESS SOCIETY, as it originally existed under PRIMITIVE COMMUNISM. Modern socialism strives to evolve a civilized, classless society under FULL COMMUNISM.

Social Democracy A moderate or right-wing direction in the working class movement. It emerged towards the end of the 19th c., when social-democratic parties appeared in most European countries, vaguely subscribing to Marxist ideas and propagating the transformation of capitalism to socialism. Among them was the RUSSIAN SOCIAL-DEMOCRATIC LABOUR PARTY, illegally established in 1898, to which the COMMUNIST PARTY OF THE SOVIET UNION traces its origin. The movement became international and in 1889, largely on the initiative of the German Socialist Party (SPD), these parties created the SECOND INTERNATIONAL. But, at the turn of the century, splits began to appear between the moderate and revolutionary factions. The former, using the old name or calling themselves 'socialist' or 'labour' parties, adopted a peaceful reformist PARLIAMENTARY ROAD TO SOCIALISM. The latter turned to revolutionary Marxism or 'scientific socialism', emphasizing the CLASS STRUGGLE, PROLETARIAN REVOLUTION and the DICTATORSHIP OF THE PROLETARIAT and established separate 'communist' parties. The split was further aggravated by the different attitudes to the impending war (W.W.I), the former supporting the national war effort, while the latter condemned it as imperialist and called for its transformation into a civil war and revolution. After the victory of the proletarian revolution in Russia in 1917, the rift between the two orientations widened and became irreconcilable. The peaceful and evolutionary direction of s.d. recreated the Second International in the form of the BERN INTERNATIONAL (1919) and formed the SECOND-AND-A-HALF INTERNATIONAL (1921), both of which merged and created the LABOUR AND SOCIALIST INTERNATIONAL (1923). The revolutionary parties under Soviet leadership created the Third International in 1919 (the COMINTERN). Today, s.d. in the labour movement prevails in virtually all countries outside the Socialist bloc and has proved to be the strongest and the most successful in Western Europe. It cooperates internationally in the SOCIALIST INTERNATIONAL.

Social-Democratic Deviationism A phrase applied by the BOLSHEVIKS to the MENSHEVIKS after March 1918, when the RUSSIAN SOCIAL-DEMOCRATIC LABOUR PARTY (OF THE BOLSHEVIKS) was renamed the RUSSIAN COMMUNIST PARTY (OF THE BOLSHEVIKS). As the Bolsheviks were firmly in power, public disagreement with official Party policy was regarded by them as 'deviationism'. After 1922, when the Russian Social Democratic Labour Party was legally dissolved, the phrase was applied to TROTSKYISM and its opposition to Stalin's policy of SOCIALISM IN ONE COUNTRY.

Social-Democratic Party (*Socialdemokratiet*) The largest single political party in Denmark, with an impressive record of achievement in the Danish social reform movement. It was founded in 1871 and its majority adherence to the peaceful and gradual PARLIAMENTARY ROAD TO SOCIALISM made its radical faction leave

Social Democratic Party of America

and form the Danish Communist Party in 1919. The S.D.P. draws its support mainly from the industrial working class and has had long terms in office, but has also been in opposition. It advocates extensive social security, economic planning and full employment, and is a member of the SOCIALIST INTERNATIONAL. The Party's official organ is a daily called *Aktuelt (Current Events).*

Social Democratic Party of America A small political party organized by E. V. Debs in the USA in 1897, patterned on the rising SOCIAL DEMOCRACY in Europe. Its immediate purpose was to unite the militant industrial labour movement with the political socialist movement. In 1900, the S.D.P.A., together with the militant faction of the Socialist Labour Party, formed the SOCIALIST PARTY OF AMERICA.

Social-Democratic Party of Germany (*Sozialdemokratische Partei Deutschlands*) A moderate socialist party in the FR of [West] Germany, normally the largest political party in the country and one of the earliest and most influential social-democratic parties in the world. Its beginnings go back to 1868, when the disciples of Marx formed the SOCIAL-DEMOCRATIC WORKERS' PARTY. It assumed its present name in 1890. It grew remarkably by its own membership and the absorption of other left-wing groups. By 1914 it had become the largest social-democratic party in the world. Although it had begun as a Marxist party, its majority turned to the PARLIAMENTARY ROAD TO SOCIALISM. Before and during W.W.I it gave support to the German war effort and the monarchist regime. The Party was the largest political party in the Weimar Republic and, after Hitler's accession to power, it was the only party which opposed the Enabling Bill of March 1933. Banned under the Nazi rule (1933–45), it was revived in 1945, both in East and West Germany. In the East in 1946, it was forced into a merger with the Communist Party of Germany to form the SOCIALIST UNITY PARTY OF GERMANY. In West Ger-

many, the S.-D.P.G. was weak at first and functioned as an opposition party. Then, in its Godesberger Programme, it publicly abandoned Marxism in favour of the democratic welfare state based on regulated private enterprise and the market. It co-operated in coalition with other left-wing parties (1966–69) and since that time has been the governing party in coalition with the Free Democratic Party. The S.D.P.G. derives its support mainly from industrial areas and stands for a strong central government, mild economic planning, competition, generous social security and democratic freedoms. Its membership is nearly 1.0m. Under its former leader Willy Brandt, it normalized its relations with the East European countries (*OSTPOLITIK*), which has been successfully continued under his successor, Helmut Schmidt. The Party is opposed to communism and has been one of the most active members of the SOCIALIST INTERNATIONAL.

Social-Democratic Party of Switzerland (*Sozialdemokratische Partei der Schweiz*, in German, and *Parti Socialiste Suisse*, in French) A moderate socialist party and the largest single party in the country. Founded in 1870, it is one of the oldest social-democratic parties in the world. It supports far-reaching state intervention in the economy and a generous social welfare programme and has been quite influential in the implementation of these objectives. But it is strongly opposed to communism and is a member of the SOCIALIST INTERNATIONAL. At the 1975 general elections, it won 55 (of the 97) seats in the National Council and 17 (of the 44) in the Council of States.

Social-Democratic Workers' Party (*Socialdemokratiska Arbetarepartiet*) The largest or the second largest party in Sweden and one of the most successful social-democratic parties in the world. It was founded in the 1880s and, after the mid-1930s, dominated the Swedish political scene for four decades. While in office, it introduced liberal economic planning, far-

526

reaching equalization of personal income, generous social benefits and various forms of regulation of private enterprise. But it refrained from excessive nationalization. Largely due to its policies, Sweden has become a progressive democratic welfare state, regarded as a model by many social reformers. Although not Marxist, the Party has, in general, co-operated with communists (LEFT COMMUNIST PARTY). In international relations, it has consistently pursued a policy of neutrality, but belongs to the SOCIALIST INTERNATIONAL. After its long stay in office, the Party was defeated in the 1976 elections. Its main publications are *Aftonbladed* (*Evening News*), a daily organ appearing in Stockholm, and *Arbetet* (*Labour*), another daily organ published in Malmö.

Social-Democratic Workers' Party of Germany One of the first significant Marxist parties in world history. It was founded by the GENERAL GERMAN WORKERS' ASSOCIATION at its conference at Eisenach in July 1869, hence, its members became known as 'Eisenachers'. The leading founders were A. BEBEL and W. LIEBKNECHT, who led the left-wing faction. In 1875, at a congress held at Gotha, the two organizations decided to merge and created a new party called the 'Socialist Workers' Party of Germany' (which, in 1890, became the SOCIAL-DEMOCRATIC PARTY OF GERMANY, still in existence).

Social Democrats In general, supporters of SOCIAL DEMOCRACY after W.W.I and, in particular, members of social-democratic parties, critical of traditional *laissez-faire* capitalism, advocating a peaceful and gradual PARLIAMENTARY ROAD TO SOCIALISM and opposed to revolutionary Marxism. Before W.W.I, s.d. were identified with the left-wing movement dissatisfied with capitalism and ranged from evolutionary compromising Marxists to radical revolutionary Marxists. The division was exemplified by the RUSSIAN SOCIAL-DEMOCRATIC LABOUR PARTY (founded in 1898) in which, beginning in 1903, two opposing factions

emerged – the moderate MENSHEVIKS and the revolutionary BOLSHEVIKS. The central organ of the R.S.-D.L.P. from 1908 to 1917 was called *Sotsial-Demokrat* (*Social Democrat*).

Social Determinism A sociological theory according to which society's existence and development are determined by identifiable external factors, independent of man himself. This theory is opposed to FATALISM, divine intervention and voluntaristic causation. Instead, s.d. attaches a crucial role to the laws of nature and geographical environment (physiography, soil, climate, fauna, flora). S.d. is associated with ideas put forward by Ch. L. Montesquieu (1689–1755), H. T. Buckle (1821–62) and J. A. Gobineau (1816–82). The Marxist attitude to s.d. is twofold. On the one hand, in accordance with HISTORICAL MATERIALISM, Marxist philosophers agree that material factors play an important primary part and that society develops in predictable stages, as is illustrated by successive SOCIO-ECONOMIC FORMATIONS. But on the other hand, they regard it largely to be metaphysical and utopian. They deny the mechanistic operation of natural laws in society, as man's actions may neutralize, postpone or accelerate certain social processes, so that in effect, it is impossible to predict how or when a particular social phenomenon materializes. Thus, they emphasize that, although capitalism will be succeeded by socialism, the time and methods are not predetermined and 'each generation forges its own destiny'. It is still up to the working class to speed up the changeover, if necessary, by a violent revolution. In social development, there are reactionary forces of the ruling classes which usually employ all the means at their disposal to prevent changes threatening their privileged position.

Social Development In general, changes in society leading to more varied and improved political, economic and cultural conditions of life. The concept is based on the conviction that societies pass from

Social Differentiation

simpler to more complex stages, similar to living organisms, where increasing specialization of functions is associated with more varied structural patterns. The question of s.d. is of great interest in Marxist ideology, which emphasizes a progressive social transformation from lower to higher forms of social organization and social relations (as distinct from social change, commonly used in Western sociology). In this transformation, Marxism identifies two different processes, viz. evolutionary and revolutionary, both of which constitute a mutually complementary DIALECTIC unity. Evolutionary changes are regarded to be quantitative in character and gradual, providing an indispensable basis and stage for revolutionary 'qualitative leaps'. Without the former, the latter has no chance of success. Thus, REVOLUTION creates a new basis for higher s.d. The Marxist theory of s.d. is based on DIALECTICAL MATERIALISM and HISTORICAL MATERIALISM, emphasizing continuous struggle and contradictions in three spheres: (a) between man and nature, especially involving labour and the development of PRODUCTION FORCES; (b) between new production relations resting on the new material BASE and the old non-material SUPERSTRUCTURE. In the historical process of s.d., Marxists distinguish six socio-economic formations: 1. historical process of s.d., Marxists distinguish six socio-economic formations: 1. PRIMITIVE COMMUNISM; 2. SLAVERY; 3. FEUDALISM; 4. CAPITALISM; 5. SOCIALISM; and 6. FULL COMMUNISM. They identify four 'laws of s.d.': 1. general laws operating in all historical stages (e.g. the LAW OF THE CONCORDANCE OF PRODUCTION RELATIONS WITH THE NATURE OF PRODUCTION FORCES); 2. laws operating only in some socio-economic formations (e.g. the law of the CLASS STRUGGLE as a driving force in ANTAGONISTIC SOCIO-ECONOMIC FORMATIONS); 3. laws peculiar to a particular socio-economic formation (e.g. the law of the DECLINING PROFIT RATE under capitalism); and 4. laws operating over short periods in a particular socio-economic formation (e.g. the law

of DISTRIBUTION ACCORDING TO WORK under socialism. Also SOCIAL DARWINISM, SOCIAL ENGINEERING, SOCIAL PLANNING, SOCIO-TECHNICS.

Social Differentiation The existence of different social groups and SOCIAL CLASSES, each of a different SOCIAL STATUS, as indicated by SOCIAL DISTANCE, usually implying hierarchical SOCIAL STRATIFICATION. S.d. in its extreme forms is found in what Marxists call antagonistic socio-economic formations (SLAVERY, FEUDALISM and CAPITALISM). S.d. also exists in the Socialist countries, but is more related to occupation, personal abilities and effort, and not inherited or based on property ownership or some other privileges conferred by law or custom.

Social Discipline A system of norms regulating the social behaviour of individuals and groups in society. These norms are enforced by externally imposed formal sanctions (laws, regulations, the informal pressure of public opinion) and self-discipline emanating from the individuals or groups themselves. In Marxist ideology today, s.d. assumes a very important place, owing to the accepted principle of the PRIMACY OF SOCIAL INTEREST and the relegation of INDIVIDUALISM to a subordinate position and even its suppression. In this process, the Socialist state, under the guidance and watchful eye of the Communist party, plays an active and ubiquitous part, shaping social conduct in accordance with current policy requirements and with a long-run view to evolving an ideal CLASSLESS SOCIETY and a NEW COMMUNIST MAN.

Social Distance The social gap separating individuals, groups or classes. The concept was introduced by the German sociologist G. Simmel (1858–1918) in *On Social Differentiation* (1890). S.d. may be measured quantitatively (by differences in property ownership, income, formal education) or qualitatively (by differences in occupational position, race, religion, ethical standards, cultural interests, ideological views). The social separation may be either imagined or real and may be further enforced by legal sanctions. In general, the greater the s.d., the less sympathy, understanding and interaction there is between the entities of different SOCIAL STATUS. The theory of s.d. has received a good deal of attention from Marxists in their analysis of SOCIAL STRATIFICATION in class societies, especially in antagonistic socio-economic formations – SLAVERY, FEUDALISM and CAPITALISM. S.d. may be a result of unilateral rejection (usually of a lower by a higher class entity) or mutual repudiation. A manifestation of s.d. of a fundamental nature in the capitalist society is ALIENATION.

Social Engineering Practical policies concerned with systematic solutions of specific social problems or the steering of the development of society into desired patterns or directions. S.e. is preoccupied with social structure (rather than social functions) and the creation of new forms and patterns (rather than adapting the existing ones). Different social groups and institutions and their intricate intra- and inter-relations are not treated as natural and rigid, but as flexible elements and phenomena which can be shaped in the interest of social harmony. S.e. utilizes sociological principles, but emphasizes their practical applications on a planned basis with the aid of modern media, quantitative techniques and governmental and semi-public institutions. Some believers in s.e. maintain that it is desirable and possible to develop technology separate from social philosophy and sociology to tackle problems on an *ad hoc* practical basis. The idea of s.e. can be traced back to ancient times, but in its modern form it is associated with such Western thinkers as L. F. Ward (1841–1913), R. Pound (1870–1964), G. Myrdal (1898–), K. Popper (1902–) and others. The term s.e. is no longer in common use by sociologists, who prefer more specific designations, such as SOCIAL PLANNING and applied sociology. In the socialist countries the term SOCIO-TECHNICS is preferred.

Social Equality A state of relations in society noted for the absence of privileged groups, where there is equality of opportunity and everybody enjoys the same material and cultural conditions for satisfying his or her needs. The view and content of s.e. largely depend on the social system in force. Historically, there was a retrogressive development in this respect from PRIMITIVE COMMUNISM to SLAVERY, but then a progressive development from FEUDALISM to CAPITALISM and SOCIALISM. In a capitalist society, although there is generally equality of the citizens before the law, there is no economic equality owing to the unequal distribution of (private) property, the existence of non-labour incomes and insufficiently developed social welfare programmes. The Marxist approach to s.e. is more radical and systematic, emphasizing both political and economic e., and equal rights as well as equal duties. The Marxist arguments in favour of s.e. are as follows: 1. e. is not only a moral ideal but also an essential element of communism; 2. a precondition for s.e. is the abolition of exploitation of man by man and the elimination of social classes in favour of a CLASSLESS SOCIETY; 3. a redistribution of wealth and income does not permanently ensure s.e., hence the SOCIALIZATION (not merely nationalization) of the means of production is essential; 4. in the transition from capitalism to full communism, exploitation of man by man is eliminated and the Leninist principle of work and remuneration, 'FROM EACH ACCORDING TO HIS ABILITY, TO EACH ACCORDING TO HIS WORK' is applied; and 5. under FULL COMMUNISM work and income will be based on the Marxian principle, 'FROM EACH ACCORDING TO HIS ABILITY, TO EACH ACCORDING TO HIS NEEDS'. Furthermore, the differences between manual and mental and between rural and urban labour will disappear. Consequently, there will be a classless egalitarian society. However, Marxism rejects the postulate of ABSOLUTE EQUALITARIANISM, even under full communism. The degree of s.e. reached in the Socialist countries so far is surprisingly

Social Evolution

low. Income differentiation is quite wide and in each Socialist country an elite has emerged, privileged in one way or another. More determined efforts have been made in China to achieve greater s.e. This was most pronounced during the GREAT PROLETARIAN CULTURAL REVOLUTION. Also *URAVNÍLOVKA*.

Social Evolution SOCIAL DEVELOPMENT.

Social Fascism A derogatory term commonly applied by communists between the two World Wars to the social-democratic and socialist parties in capitalist countries, as exemplified best by Italy, Germany and Spain. It was claimed that such parties were renegades to true 'scientific' socialism and their views and practices were irreconcilable with those of the Communist parties. Consequently, the latter should not seek UNITED FRONTS with other left-wing parties as a matter of principle and public demonstration to the electorate. The term was first established in the German Communist Party, which coined a popular slogan 'Kick the little social fascists out of the kindergarten'. It then appeared in the documents of the COMINTERN, but was popularized by Stalin in the early 1930s. The term was discarded after the mid-1930s when Stalin accepted the desirability of the POPULAR FRONTS in the face of the real threat of fascism.

Social Group A general term for an identifiable section of society with a feeling of community of ties or interests. A s.g. may be set apart from other groups by virtue of a distinctive geographical location, employment, beliefs, cultural interests, common grievances or some historical antecedents. The s.g. is a crucial object of interest in Marxist sociology, which attaches great importance to the study of social harmony, SOCIAL STRATIFICATION, the social transformation of capitalism into socialism and then to full communism and the PRIMACY OF SOCIAL INTEREST. In contemporary Socialist sociology a small s.g. embraces from 3 to 20 members who are

linked by personal and informal bonds of friendship (e.g. a family, a circle of peers). A large s.g. is generally noted for the absence of close personal bonds, nevertheless, its members are conscious of their separate identity as a group. The size of these groups varies widely, the largest being the SOCIAL CLASS.

Social Imperialism A critical term used in China since 1960 for the authoritarian bureaucratic and expansionist policies of the Soviet leadership ('Socialism in words, imperialism in deeds'). The USSR is identified as STATE MONOPOLY CAPITALISM and, as such, is subject to the 'objective laws of imperialism' striving for world domination. Mao Tse-tung said towards the end of the Vietnam War in 1974 (in *Theory of the Differentiation of the Three Worlds as a Major Contribution to Marxism*) that US imperialism had been declining and had largely become a spent force. But he stressed that the 'Soviet revisionist clique' had stepped in and steered the USSR towards s.i., as manifested by military bases in Asia and Africa, naval expansionism, large sales of weapons, military advisers and collusion with the USA on the division of the spheres of influence.

Social-Industrial Complex A concept introduced by J. O'Connor (in *The Corporations and the State*, 1974) to denote a form of industrial organization under capitalism, where the state actively utilizes the nation's resources in pursuit of social objectives on the advice of social reformers. There could be two variants with respect to the ownership of the means of production – either privately owned (predominantly by large companies) or nationalized (state capitalism). The concept is characteristic of the NEW POLITICAL ECONOMY.

Social Inequality Differences between individuals within social groups with respect to property ownership, income, privileges, responsibilities and the like. Although Marxism concedes that inequality may be partly justified on the grounds of inborn individual differences and effort, s.i.

530

caused by differences in the private ownership of the means of production is grossly unjust and morally repugnant. Differences in property ownership lead to SOCIAL STRATIFICATION, where most of the wealth is concentrated in the hands of a relatively small elite which, thereby, enjoys high incomes and exercises or manipulates political power. Extreme class differences are typical of the antagonistic socio-economic formations – SLAVERY, FEUDALISM, CAPITALISM. However, it may be pointed out that considerable s.i. also exists in the Socialist countries, not only between individuals but also between the party elites, technocrats and top professionals on the one hand, and peasants, unskilled workers and dissident groups on the other. But it is claimed that these differences are survivals from capitalism and will be eliminated in the CLASSLESS SOCIETY under FULL COMMUNISM.

Social Inertia Passive attitude and indifference among individuals or social groups to the existing situation in society. It is a concept to which Marxist sociology attaches considerable significance. S.i. is mostly caused by external factors (such as political terror, the lack of education, unemployment, poverty and the pressure of traditionalism) which deprive certain social groups of the opportunity for social action. Alternatively or additionally, there may be a faulty social organization inhibiting social initiative in work and various cultural activities affecting society. There may also be subjective causes deriving from personal traits and adverse personal experience. S.i. can occur under any social system, but in the Marxist view it is more widespread in antagonistic socio-economic formations – SLAVERY, FEUDALISM and CAPITALISM – especially if the underprivileged classes are devoid of CLASS CONSCIOUSNESS and are unorganized to change the social system. S.i. is also typical among the former exploiting classes in the Socialist countries in the early stages of Communist rule, especially after the failure of a COUNTER-REVOLUTION.

Social Insurance State-established contributory protection against the loss of income from work that may affect the insured. In the Socialist countries, s.i. covers persons who are employed in the socialized sector and is financed out of the contributions paid as a rule by the employing entity (and not the insured employee). This system is at least partly administered by trade unions and provides cover against accidents at work, illness, maternity and old age. There is normally no provision made for unemployment, except in Yugoslavia (where unemployment since 1965 has ranged from 5 per cent to 10 per cent), because the right to work is guaranteed and there is no involuntary unemployment of any significant duration. S.i. differs from SOCIAL SECURITY.

Socialism In its most general sense, a political and economic system emphasizing SOCIAL JUSTICE maintained by the state or other working class institutions. In English, the term first appeared in 1827 in the *Co-operative Magazine* (founded by the London Co-operative Society in 1824), which was well established in the 1830s to describe the reformist ideas of R. OWEN. P. LEROUX claimed to be the original author of the term (in French) in 1832 which he used as a concept opposite to INDIVIDUALISM. There are many variants of s., ranging from theoretical models of UTOPIAN SOCIALISM, peacefully reformed democratic capitalism to a highly authoritarian system established by a violent proletarian revolution and administered under the conditions of the dictatorship of the proletariat. Marx and Engels used the term first in *The COMMUNIST MANIFESTO* and Marx elaborated on it as a social system in the *CRITIQUE OF THE GOTHA PROGRAMME*. By 1924 a British social scientist, D. F. Griffith (in *What Is Socialism?*), had been in a position to compile over 260 definitions of s. S. has been variously described depending largely on the political convictions of the speaker or writer. In the eyes of its enthusiastic beholders, s. has been described as: 1. 'To me s. is the practical expression of Christ's teaching' (Ch. G. Ammon); 2. 'S. is the conception of a new society based on freedom, equality and comradeship' (W. H. Ayles); 3. 'S. is the greatest conception in the world. It links world wealth with world welfare' (G. Baker); 4. 'S.: Light in the darkness of a depressed world; hope and opportunity for all peoples; economic wisdom, political salvation, religious practice' (J. W. Bowen); 5. 'S. is not so much a doctrine as a faith, and not something that exists, but something that is growing in the minds of men' (G. D. H. Cole); 6. 'S. is science wedded to art. It is navigation of social currents by the liberated soul of man' (R. W. Sorensen); 7, 'S. is a system of social economics based on the desire to create and to serve rather than to possess and to be served' (M. Sparkes); and 8. 'S.: The triumph of common sense. Man, once the slave of nature and later of the machine, becomes the master of both' (M. Starr). But there are many critics whose views of s. are exemplified by the following verdicts: 1. 'The combination of religious sentimentality, industry, insanity and moral obliquity' (F. J. C. Hearnshaw); 2. 'A system which is workable only in heaven, where it isn't needed and in hell where they have got it' (C. Palmer); 3. 'The survival of the unfit' (E. Hubbard); 4. 'The rabble of socialists, the apostles of Chandola who undermine the working man's instincts . . . who make him envious and teach him revenge' (F. W. Nietzsche); 5. 'A fake, a comedy, a phantom and a blackmail' (B. Mussolini); and 6. 'All s. involves slavery' (H. Spencer). In Marxist ideology, the concept of s. has a more specific meaning, viz. the stage following capitalism in the transition to full communism. Marx also called s. 'the lower phase of communism'. In this sense, s. is noted for the following features: 1. the predominantly SOCIAL OWNERSHIP OF THE MEANS OF PRODUCTION; 2. the absence of exploitation of man by man; 3. economic planning supplanting or supplementing the market mechanism; 4. DEMOCRATIC CENTRALISM and the leading role of the Communist party; and 5. DISTRIBUTION ACCORDING TO WORK

(rather than needs). Being a transitional stage, s. 'still stamped with the birthmarks of the old society' (as Marx said in *CRITIQUE OF THE GOTHA PROGRAMME*) retains several elements of capitalism. They are: 1. some private ownership of land and capital and to this extent of private enterprise; 2. the prominence of co-operative enterprises in some spheres of activity (farming, small-scale industry, consumer credit); 3. the persistence of non-antagonistic social classes – workers, peasants, intelligentsia; 4. the selective retention of the market mechanism; and 5. the existence of a powerful socialist state, at least in the early stages of s. exercising the DICTATORSHIP OF THE PROLETARIAT. But even Marxists differ on the most appropriate form of s. in practice, as is indicated by the different models represented by CASTROISM, EUROCOMMUNISM, MAOISM, MARXISM-LENINISM, TITOISM. All the countries ruled at present by Communist regimes are still in the stage of s. and describe themselves officially as 'Socialist' (not 'Communist') countries. According to a prediction by N. S. Khrushchev in 1961, the phase of s. in the USSR (the oldest socialist country) would last up to 1980 at least (after which the country would start entering the phase of communism). But owing to the Soviet economic setbacks since that time, the socialist phase will in fact be much longer. Also EUROSOCIALISM, OWN PATH TO SOCIALISM, SOCIAL DEMOCRACY, SOCIALIST INTERNATIONAL.

Socialism *Ex Cathedra* See ACADEMIC SOCIALISM.

Socialism In One Country A well-known slogan authored by STALIN in support of the domestic strengthening of socialism in the USSR, in opposition to Trotsky's postulate of carrying the revolution to other countries (PERMANENT REVOLUTION). Up to 1920 it had been widely accepted by the Soviet leadership that the revolution could not survive in Soviet Russia alone and Trotsky's line appeared to be sensible. But the failures of attempted revolutions in Eastern and Western Europe gave Stalin an opportunity to undermine the credibility and standing of his gifted rival. Stalin used the phrase first in Dec. 1920, although the idea itself had been mooted by him as early as Aug. 1917. However he explained the ramifications of the slogan fully on 3 Nov. 1926 in 'Reply to the Discussion on the Report on "The Social-Democratic Deviation in Our Party"'. In the ensuing struggle after Lenin's death (Jan. 1924), Trotsky and his line had been defeated by 1928, when Stalin launched the first five-year plan as the most monumental expression of his strategy. The slogan caught the fancy not only of most Soviet leaders but also of the populace at large and inspired the population with patriotic and missionary enthusiasm and zeal. Also ·CAPITALISM IN ONE COUNTRY'.

Socialism, Scientific See SCIENTIFIC SOCIALISM.

'Socialism With a Human Face' A phrase popularized by A. DUBČEK who, as First Secretary of the Czechoslovak Communist Party, led the liberal reform movement in 1968 (PRAGUE SPRING). The phrase symbolized a popular reaction against the prevailing austerity under the preceding regime of A. NOVOTNY, noted for the suppression of HUMAN RIGHTS. Owing to the INVASION OF CZECHOSLOVAKIA, the ideal of 's.w. a h.f.' was never put into practice. The Hungarian leaders, who embarked on liberal reforms in the same year and with remarkable success, like to point out: 'We did not talk about "s.w. a h.f.", we simply put it into effect'.

'Socialism Without Doctrine' A description sometimes applied to the working class movement in Australia and New Zealand, where organized labour has been preoccupied with practical improvements in the conditions of life, to the disregard of virtually any form of socialist theory. The phrase was first applied in a book published in French in 1901 (*Le socialisme sans doctrines*) by A. Metin, a French socialist who had visited Australasia on a travelling fellowship and

who later became Minister for Labour. The book was translated into English and published only in 1977, under the title of *Socialism Without Doctrine*. In contrast to many other countries, the Australian and New Zealand labour movements have in most cases willingly co-operated with the 'bourgeois' state and have been remarkably successful in the settlement of industrial disputes, minimum wages, rising living standards of the working class and generous social welfare programmes.

Socialist Alliance of the Working People of Yugoslavia (*Socialistički Savez Radnog Naroda Jugoslavija*) A mass organization concerned with the building of socialism in Yugoslavia and, in particular, performing the function of a united electoral front and giving support to the Communist regime. It replaced the People's Front in 1953 and its membership in the late 1970s stood at 11.1m. (while the country's total population was 22.0m.). The Alliance controls electoral procedures and its most important function is the preparation of the list of candidates for Federal and Republican elections. It is completely dominated by the LEAGUE OF COMMUNISTS OF YUGOSLAVIA. According to official returns, 85–90 per cent of the electors vote for the candidates nominated by the Alliance. Its highest formal source of authority is the Congress, but between the Congresses power rests with the Federal Conference which elects the Presidency (of 49 members) and the Executive Committee (19 members). The statutes of the Alliance were liberalized in 1966 and the organization is now less centralized, more responsive to local views and needs and is less subservient to the regime than similar organizations in other Socialist countries. The official organ of the Alliance is a daily newspaper, *Borba* (*Struggle*).

Socialist Bloc A term widely used during the COLD WAR, especially in the 1950s, for the continuous Euro-Asian area ruled by Communist parties embracing the 12 allied socialist countries, viz. Albania, Bulgaria, PR of China, Czechoslovakia, the

[East] German DR, Hungary, the DPR of [North] Korea, Mongolia, Poland, Romania, the DR of [North] Vietnam and the USSR. Most specialists in the field believe that the term is no longer appropriate, owing to the breakdown of the former monolithic unity of the Socialist community caused by the SINO-SOVIET DISPUTE and other divergencies and conflicts. Nevertheless, the term is in use, vaguely denoting all the countries under Communist rule. In its broadest sense today, the s.b. embraces not only the 12 Socialist countries but also South Vietnam (part of the unified country of the SR of Vietnam), Kampuchea, Laos, Yugoslavia, Cuba; Angola and Mozambique are sometimes also added. In this broad sense, the s.b. constitutes the following percentages of the world: industrial output – 35 per cent; population – 33 per cent; national income – 30 per cent; area – 27 per cent; and foreign trade – 12 per cent.

Socialist Bourgeoisie RED BOURGEOISIE, BOURGEOIS SOCIALISM.

Socialist Competition In the Socialist countries, a mass movement to stimulate workers to better performances, such as the fulfilment and over-fulfilment of targets, economies in the use of materials and power, the improvement of quality and higher productivity of labour in general. The beginnings of s.c go back to the *SUBBOTNIKS* in Soviet Russia in 1919, followed on a more systematic basis by the SHOCK WORKERS' MOVEMENT after 1926 and STAKHANOVISM after 1935. Other Socialist countries have adopted similar forms of s.c. The turn to the state promoted s.c. has been prompted by the widespread predisposition to complacency and apathy, conditioned by the virtual absence of private enterprise, limited scope for individual initiative, continuous full employment and generous social security. S.c. is based on the premise that rivalry is a natural human instinct, which should be harnessed to social benefit and is encouraged among individuals, teams, brigades, enterprises, and institutions. The driving

forces in s.c. are mainly MORAL INCENTIVES, appealing primarily to non-material idealistic convictions and sentiments, social recognition, professional pride, patriotism, the desire to surpass capitalist countries and the like. Achievement certificates, factory banners, rolls of honour, titles, medals and orders, supplemented with material rewards, are an integral part of s.c. The responsibility for s.c. in the economic field is usually entrusted to trade unions, although the state often directly assists in particular campaigns. S.c. has also been extended to education and culture.

Socialist Countries Countries ruled by Communist or Marxist regimes under a mono-party system of government. In the late 1970s there were 25 such countries. Of these, 14 had become socialist before 1960 (in brackets the year of the establishment of effective Communist power), viz.: P.S.R. of ALBANIA (1946); P.R. of BULGARIA (1946); P.R. of CHINA (1949); R. of CUBA (1959); CZECHOSLOVAK S.R. (1946); [East] GERMAN D.R. (1945); P.R. of HUNGARY (1945); D.P.R. of [North] KOREA (1946); MONGOLIAN P.R. (1924); POLISH P.R. (1947); S.R. of ROMANIA (1946); UNION OF THE SOVIET SOCIALIST REPUBLICS (1917); S.R. of VIETNAM (1954, 1976); and S.F.R. of YUGOSLAVIA (1945). In the following 11 countries Communist or Marxist regimes came to power since 1970: D.R. of AFGHANISTAN (1978); P.R. of ANGOLA (1975); P.R. of BENIN (1975); P.R. of the CONGO (1970); S. ETHIOPIA (1974); P.R. of GUINEA-BISSAU (1972); P.R. of KAMPUCHEA (1975); LAOS P.D.R. (1975); P.R. of MOZAMBIQUE (1975); SOMALI D.R. (1976); and P.D.R. of the YEMEN (1970).

Socialist Culture Culture evolved in the SOCIALIST COUNTRIES under the guidance of Marxist parties, where it is regarded as an integral part of the social and political system. Its distinctive features are: 1. it develops after the PROLETARIAN REVOLUTION, in the context of the SOCIAL OWNERSHIP OF THE MEANS OF PRODUCTION and the DICTATORSHIP OF THE PROLETARIAT; 2. it does not discard all pre-revolutionary culture, but continues or assimilates proletarian and national elements to the extent that they are consistent with Marxist ideology and objectives; 3. it is open to all members of the Socialist society and their participation and active involvement in all spheres of culture are encouraged; 4. its roots are widely and firmly embedded in the broad masses of people, reflecting their attitudes, aspirations, creative work and social life in general; 5. although it is intolerant of non-communist ideologies, it is liberal to national and racial minorities; 6. its major developments in each Socialist country are centrally planned in each country under the guidance of the Communist party; and 7. its ultimate purpose is to assist in the evolution of the NEW COMMUNIST MAN and facilitate the advance of the Socialist society to FULL COMMUNISM.

Socialist Democracy A term used in the Socialist countries for their version of democracy, emphasizing social justice and, as such, considered to be superior to BOURGEOIS DEMOCRACY. In their official interpretation, the distinguishing significant characteristics of s.d. are: 1. a social system created by the people for the people; 2. universal, equal and direct suffrage by secret ballot, with nearly 100 per cent of the voters participating in elections; 3. the absence of exploitation of man by man, of hierarchical social classes and of antagonistic class relations; 4. freedom from social insecurity (unemployment, old age, illness and poverty in general); 5. the equality of rights and duties of all nationalities (including various minorities); and 6. national sovereignty and equality in international Socialist organizations (such as CMEA, IBEC, PEACE POWER GRID), noted for the absence of supra-national organs of compulsion. However, there are certain features of the Socialist governments and societies which constitute denials of democracy, such as: (a) the MONO-PARTY SYSTEM OF GOVERNMENT (exercised or dominated by the Communist party); (b) the acceptance of the principle of the DICTATORSHIP OF THE PROLETARIAT; (c) the overwhelming domination of society's activities, thought and life by the all-powerful and ubiquitous state; (d) violations of HUMAN RIGHTS; (e) the existence of horizontal social classes (the party elite, technocrats, successful professionals, unskilled workers, and peasants); and (f) the effective domination of smaller Socialist nations by the two big powers (the USSR and China), as illustrated by the Soviet military intervention in Hungary (1956) and Czechoslovakia (1968) and the Chinese military intrusion into Vietnam (1979).

Socialist Education International An organization in existence from 1922 to 1933 with headquarters in Vienna for the promotion of education along middle-of-the-road socialist lines. In 1923 it joined the LABOUR AND SOCIALIST INTERNATIONAL continuing the tradition of the SECOND INTERNATIONAL. The S.E.I. acted as a co-ordinating centre for socialist educational associations and youth and children organizations, mostly in European countries. It published a journal, in German, *Sozialistische Erziehung* (*Socialist Education*).

Socialist Education Movement A mass campaign in China, launched by Mao Tse-tung in Sep. 1962 to rectify bureaucratic and corrupt practices which had apparently developed during the 'three hard years' of 1957–60. To guide the Movement, three important directives were passed by the Central Committee of the Chinese Communist Party: 1. the EARLY TEN POINTS (May 1963) – to strengthen the collective spirit of peasants fighting INDIVIDUALISM; 2. DOUBLE TEN POINTS (Sep. 1963) – to eliminate illegal practices, especially among the lower cadres; and 3. Twenty Three Points (Jan. 1965) – aimed against CAPITALIST ROADERS. The campaign was directed mainly to the countryside, but it also spread to some industrial cities. A prominent part in the S.E.M. was played by the PEOPLE'S LIBERATION ARMY, designated as a model to learn from.

Socialist Emulation An aspect of SOCIAL-IST COMPETITION intended to promote the fulfilment and over-fulfilment of targets and other tasks of social importance. The first s.e. campaign was staged in the USSR during the first Five-Year-Plan (1928–32) to implement it in four years and to raise labour productivity. S.e. is aimed at PRO-DUCTION TEAMS, PRODUCTION BRIGADES, COLLECTIVE FARMS and regions. They are exhorted to imitate the example of the best and to excel. The party, trade unions, professional associations, youth organizations and the state with its media are all drawn into s.e. In addition to achieving specific major tasks, s.e. is also meant to develop a new idealistic attitude to work in order to transform it from burden and affliction to privilege, honour and heroism.

Socialist Group Capitalism A description of the practice in some Socialist countries (especially Czechoslovakia, Hungary and Yugoslavia), where socialized enterprises can invest in other socialized entities. The shareholding enterprises then participate in the management and profits of the joint-stock entity. In Yugoslavia, enterprises additionally float debentures to raise capital, which may be subscribed to not only by socialized entities but also by private individuals and firms. This, in fact, is a type of capital market.

Socialist Inflation A term used to describe inherent and suppressed inflation under the conditions of the social ownership of the means of production and central economic planning. Theoretically, there should be no inflation, as the state has sufficient powers to ensure a continuous balance between production and spending on a planned basis and to prevent price increases. Official statistics indicate that in the past there was reasonable price stability in most Socialist countries, with only 1–3 per cent annual inflation. But its degree was, and still is, much greater, as manifested by acute SELLERS' MARKETS, queues, long waiting lists for certain con-sumer durables (such as cars) and black markets. The purchasing power of money in private hands in terms of land and capital is nil (except the private sector where it is still tolerated), as the socialized means of production cannot be bought and sold privately. The degree of inflation has increased since the early 1970s under the impact of capitalist inflation. In Yugoslavia, even by official statistics, the rate of inflation since the mid-1960s has averaged more than 15 per cent p.a.

Socialist International A loose international organization of social-democratic and socialist parties for the exchange of views and the promotion of co-operation. It was established in Frankfurt/M in 1951 as a continuation of the LABOUR AND SOCIALIST INTERNATIONAL (created in 1923) and as a successor to the SECOND INTERNATIONAL (founded in 1889). The membership of the S.I. consists of 56 affiliated parties, with a total of 80.5m. individual members (in 1978) in 52 non-Socialist countries. The S.I. is opposed to Marxism of the type pursued by the Communist regimes in the Socialist countries. Both Western and less-developed countries of the Third World are represented in its membership, plus the parties in exile of the following countries: Bulgaria; Czechoslovakia; Estonia; Hungary; Latvia; Lithuania; Poland; Romania; and Yugoslavia. But the greatest influence in the S.I. has been exercised by the parties of Denmark, France, the FR of Germany, Great Britain, Italy, the Netherlands and Sweden. The activities of the S.I. are guided by a Council (elected by a Congress held every three years), which appoints a Bureau and a Secretariat, the latter being situated in London. The official organ of the S.I. is a bi-monthly *Socialist Affairs*, published in London. There are several related organizations operating under the auspices of the S.I., notably the INTERNATIONAL CONFEDERA-TION OF FREE TRADE UNIONS and the IN-TERNATIONAL COUNCIL OF SOCIAL-DEMOCRATIC WOMEN.

Socialist International Enterprises See MULTINATIONAL ENTERPRISES IN CMEA.

Socialist Internationalism A term often synonymously used with PROLETARIAN INTERNATIONALISM. But while the latter is mostly applied to the international solidarity of the proletariat before it seizes power, S.i. emphasizes the international outlook and co-operation among the SOCIALIST COUNTRIES, especially among the ruling Communist parties. There are different aspects and manifestations of s.i. viz. the BREZHNEV DOCTRINE, the COUNCIL FOR MUTUAL ECONOMIC ASSISTANCE, the INTERNATIONAL CONFERENCES OF THE COMMUNIST AND WORKERS' PARTIES, and the WARSAW PACT. The term s.i. is also used in the West for international co-operation among the socialist and social-democratic parties in the capitalist world, especially within the framework of the SOCIALIST INTERNATIONAL.

Socialist Labour International A less commonly used name for the LABOUR AND SOCIALIST INTERNATIONAL.

Socialist Labour League A British Trotskyite group reconstituted in Nov. 1973 as the WORKERS' REVOLUTIONARY PARTY.

Socialist Labour Party of America A small, moderately radical left-wing party in the USA. It began as the Workingmen's Party of America in 1877, but assumed its present name in 1890 and adopted a revolutionary programme under the leadership of Daniel Leon in the 1890s, emphasizing industrial action. In 1900, a moderate group left the Party and participated in the creation of the SOCIALIST PARTY OF AMERICA. Although, on many occasions beginning in 1892, it ran candidates for presidential elections, it polled marginally in the popular vote and won no electoral votes. The Party's official organ is *Weekly People*.

Socialist Legality A concept used in the Socialist countries and which has had several different meanings. The term was first established in the USSR in the 1930s, as a formal concept of justification of the expedient enforcement of Stalin's arbitrary rule on the basis of established legal procedures and the judicial machinery in force. Since his death (1953) s.l. has come to denote the 'rule of law', i.e. the strict and impartial administration and enforcement of justice and the observance of laws by citizens in accordance with legally established statutes, implying the absence of illegal arrests, secret trials and the abuse of power by police. This meaning is now widely accepted in all the Socialist countries, subject to the recognition of the leading role of Marxist ideology and the Communist party in society. The Socialist legal system is openly acknowledged as an instrument of the Socialist state in its task of consolidating the power of the working class and constructing a Communist society. Socialist legislative bodies, courts and police are explicitly or implicitly required to support official and general party policies.

Socialist Mode of Production The MODE OF PRODUCTION (i.e. the unity of resources and production relations) applicable to the socio-economic formation known as SOCIALISM and, in practice, prevailing in the socialist countries. It is based on the following characteristic features, distinct from capitalism: 1. the predominantly SOCIAL OWNERSHIP OF THE MEANS OF PRODUCTION; 2. CENTRAL ECONOMIC PLANNING; 3. the PRIMACY OF SOCIAL INTEREST (as opposed to the private profit motive, or even the microeconomic interest of individual socialized enterprises); and 4. the planned application of instruments designed to subordinate economic processes to the 'optimal satisfaction of material and cultural needs of society at its given stage of development'. With the development of the s.m. of p., the role of the working masses advances from passive executors of decisions by central planners to active participants in decision-making processes (as is best illustrated by WORKERS' SELF-MANAGEMENT in Yugoslavia).

Socialist Morality The system of moral standards and behaviour of individuals and groups officially accepted by Marxists or developed in the Socialist countries. S.m. combines the universal code of morality applicable to any society irrespective of its social system (e.g. respect for one's parents, truth, courage) with the ethical values, norms and conduct deriving from Marxism and developed in actual proletarian and socialist political, economic and social practice. Marxist ethics rejects the view that morality is neutral and that the same standards are universally applicable to all societies at all times. Although Marxists concede that in some respects there are common moral norms, each social class develops its own morality which changes with the material conditions of life, the control of political power and the pattern of social relations. S.m. is conditioned by the CLASS STRUGGLE and is subordinated to the interests of the working masses and, as such is distinct from, and opposed to, bourgeois morality. Thus, the victory of the proletarian revolution and the abolition of the private ownership of the means of production introduces new forms of social values and human relations, namely the PRIMACY OF SOCIAL INTEREST as opposed to bourgeois egoistic INDIVIDUALISM. Other features of s.m. are: the respect for socialized property; civic obligation to work ('from each according to his ability'); contempt for 'social parasites'; preparedness to fight for social justice and Marxist ideology; and the feeling of brotherhood of the working masses throughout the world in the spirit of SOCIALIST INTERNATIONALISM, irrespective of race, nationality, creed and cultural qualities.

Socialist Party of America A small left-wing party in the USA founded in 1900 by splinter groups from the Social Democratic Party of America and of the SOCIALIST LABOUR PARTY OF AMERICA. In addition to political activity, the Party emphasized industrial action and advocated women's suffrage, old age pensions, unemployment, accident and health insurance, better working conditions and the public ownership of key services. The effectiveness of the Party was weakened by internal conflicts between moderates and radicals. The latter, after the successful Bolshevik Revolution in 1917, advocated a similar revolutionary strategy and tactics for the USA. The extremists were defeated in 1919 and formed the COMMUNIST PARTY OF THE USA and the Communist Labour Party. In 1957, the S.P.A. united with the Social Democratic Federation and formed the Socialist Party – Social Democratic Federation, which joined the SOCIALIST INTERNATIONAL.

Socialist Party of Austria (*Sozialistische Partei Öesterreichs*) The largest political party in the country, representing most workers and the lower middle class. At the 1979 elections, the Party polled 51 per cent of the votes cast and won 95 seats in the 183-member parliament, being its fourth consecutive victory. The Party's programme includes the nationalization of key industries and services, indicative economic planning, generous social benefits and neutrality in foreign policy. B. Kreisky is the Party Chairman and the Federal Chancellor and F. Marsch is the Party Secretary. The Party is a member of the SOCIALIST INTERNATIONAL.

Socialist Party of Great Britain A small Marxist party which advocates the democratic control of all the means of production and distribution. Its Secretary-General is K. Knight and the Party publishes *Socialist Weekly*.

Socialist Party of India A small moderate radical party, founded in 1971 as a result of the amalgamation of the Praja Socialist Party, the Indian Socialist Party and the Samyukta Socialist Party. It favours a peaceful revolutionary class struggle, including civil disobedience, to develop a democratic socialist society. It presses for land reform and the nationalization of key industries.

Socialist Patriotism See PATRIOTISM.

Socialist People's Party (*Socialistisk Folkeparti*) In Denmark, a small but active, moderately radical party formed in 1958 by a splinter group of the DANISH COMMUNIST PARTY in protest against the Soviet armed intervention in Hungary in 1956. It advocates far-reaching economic and social reforms, opposes the Danish membership of NATO, the EEC and favours an independent line in foreign policy. It suffered from a split in 1967, when its more radical members formed the Left Socialist Party. At the 1975 elections, the S.P.P. won 9 (of 166) seats in the Lower House.

Socialist Profit See PROFIT, SOCIALIST.

Socialist Realism The officially accepted major artistic movement pioneered in the USSR and, to varying degrees, supported in other Socialist countries as well. It emphasizes the recreation or interpretation of real life and problems in society, comprehensible and meaningful to the masses in literature, theatre, cinema, music, painting sculpture, architecture and engineering. The best known pioneering representatives of s.r. in the USSR were MAYAKOVSKY and Sholokhov. S.r. is regarded as 'the reflection of reality in its revolutionary development', i.e. both an expression and an instrument of the ideological and cultural transformation of society on the road to communism. S.r. is opposed to ABSTRACT ART, FORMALISM and 'ART FOR ART'S SAKE', all of which are considered to be 'bourgeois' and 'decadent'. S.r. is based on the Marxist philosophical conviction that existence does not consist in subjective ideas (IDEALISM), but in OBJECTIVE REALITY, assuming reality exists independently of the artist. Consequently, artistic representation should reflect real life and common people. But the artist should go further – not only should he interpret the real world, but also endeavour to change it by moralizing. The term s.r. appeared first in *IZVESTIYA* of 5 May 1932 in the editorial contributed by its editor I. M. Gronsky (but it is not certain who coined it first).

The conception and role of s.r. were developed and put into practice by STALIN, ZHDANOV and GORKY and parallels Lenin's REFLECTION THEORY and his PARTY-MINDEDNESS in all spheres of life. The doctrine of s.r. was officially promulgated in the USSR in 1934. S.r., in its extreme form, has been embraced in China through the Constitution of 1975. Under Article 12 it is stated that 'Culture and education, literature and art, physical education, health, work and scientific research must serve proletarian politics, serve the workers, peasants and soldiers and be combined with productive labour'. The Western critics of s.r. have described it as a form of 'persuasive commercial art', designed 'to sell an ideology which otherwise would not be bought'. S.r. amounts to an artistic straitjacket, paralyzing truly creative art. Non-conformists are persecuted, as is illustrated by such outstanding writers as B. Pasternak and A. SOLZHENITSYN. Also ART, PROLETARIAN ART, REVOLUTIONARY ROMANTICISM.

Socialist Revolution PROLETARIAN REVOLUTION.

Socialist Revolutionaries A Russian political party in existence from 1902 to 1918, which was supported mainly by peasants and urban working classes. It emerged in 1902 as a united organization of different groups of NARODNIKS in Russia and abroad. Their programme, announced at the first Party Congress in 1905 (in Finland), called for the overthrow of the Tsarist autocracy, to be replaced with a democratic federal republic (with a strong local government), the socialization of land, a liberal nationalities policy, the separation of the state from the church, free secular education and the abolition of the regular armed forces. In their political strategy, they relied heavily on individual terror (including assassination) and largely disregarded the involvement of the masses. Continuous ideological dissensions between the left and right-wing leaders marked the history of the S.R. as a party.

In 1906, the right-wing faction established a separate party called the People's Socialist Labour Party, while the left-wing group became known as the MAXIMALISTS who gravitated towards ANARCHISM and advocated the creation of an anarcho-communist Toilers' Republic. During W.W.I., a moderate faction of the S.R. called the Defenders (*OBORONTSY*) supported Russia's defensive war, but extremists sided with the INTERNATIONAL-ISTS. In 1917, the S.R. emerged as the largest political party, but their effectiveness was weakened by internal divergencies. One faction supported the PROVISIONAL GOVERNMENT of A. Kerensky, another favoured the MENSHEVIKS, and left-wingers sided with the BOLSHEVIKS. The support given to the Bolsheviks by the S.R. enabled the former to seize and retain power. But by Dec. 1917 the left-wingers had changed over to the opposition and formed a separate organization known as the Left Socialist Revolutionaries. In the CONSTITUENT ASSEMBLY (elected in Nov. 1917) the S.R. had more deputies (54 per cent) than all the other parties combined (including the Bolsheviks who had 20 per cent). The S.R. strongly opposed the BREST-LITOVSK TREATY with Germany. In July 1918, during the so-called Moscow Uprising, they staged an unsuccessful armed coup against the Bolsheviks (in which they also assassinated the German ambassador, W. Mirbach). Afterwards, the S.R. disintegrated as a party. Some joined the Bolsheviks, some turned to anarchism and others lost interest in political activity.

Socialist Unity Party of Germany (*Sozialistische Einheitspartei Deutschlands*) The ruling Communist Party in the [East] GERMAN DR. Its origin goes back to 1916 when the SPARTACUS LEAGUE (led by K. LIEBKNECHT and ROSA LUXEMBURG) was formed within the SOCIAL-DEMOCRATIC PARTY OF GERMANY. The S.L. founded the Communist Party of Germany (K.P.D.) on 1 Jan. 1919. After several setbacks, splits and reorganizations, the Party was outlawed by the Nazi regime from 1933 to 1945, but continued its activities underground and abroad. In June 1945, the K.P.D. was revived together with non-bourgeois parties, viz. the S.-D.P.G., the Christian Democratic Union of Germany and the Liberal Party of Germany. But in East Germany, under Soviet pressure, the S.-D.P.G. was soon (April 1946) forced to merge with the K.P.D. and the name of the S.U.P.G. was adopted. The Party's membership in the late 1970s was 2.1m. (of the total population of 16.8m.), which makes it the fifth largest Communist party in the world (after those of China, the USSR, Romania and Poland). It completely dominates the NATIONAL FRONT OF DEMOCRATIC GERMANY which is an alliance of all political parties in the country. The Party's formal source of power is the Congress, held every five years. Its highest policy-making bodies are the Central Committee, headed by the Party's First Secretary (E. Honecker since 1971), the Politburo, the Secretariat and the Control Committee. As elected at the 9th Party Congress in May 1976, the C.C. consisted of 145 full and 57 candidate members, the P. – 19 members, the S. – 12 members and the Control C. – 9 full and 7 candidate, members. The Party is given mass support by its subsidiary organizations, viz. Free German Youth (1.9m. members), the Ernst Thalmann Youth Pioneer Organization (1.2m. members), the Free German Trade Union Federation (7.8m. members) and the Democratic Women's League of Germany (1.3m. members). In foreign relations, the S.U.P.G. has been the most faithful executor of instructions from the Communist Party of the Soviet Union. The S.U.P.G.'s official regular publications include: *Neues Deutschland* (*New Germany*), a newspaper (1.1m. daily circulation); *Neuer Weg* (*New Way*), a fortnightly bulletin on party organization and current practice; *Einheit* (*Unity*), a monthly theoretical journal; *Junge Welt* (*Young World*), a daily organ of Free German Youth; and *Forum*, a fortnightly theoretical journal of Free German Youth.

Socialist Vanguard Party In Algeria, the legal front organization of the ALGERIAN COMMUNIST PARTY (since the latter was declared illegal in 1965).

Socialist Workers Party A small radical socialist party formed by the INTERNATIONAL SOCIALISTS OF GREAT BRITAIN in Dec. 1976 to broaden their political appeal and to provide 'the socialist alternative to the Labour Party'. It is the largest and most dynamic Trotskyite group in Britain, with a membership of about 4,000, and is committed to fighting unemployment and racialism. The Party's governing body is a Central Committee of 10 members and it publishes a weekly newspaper called *Socialist Worker*. The Party commands support mainly in the motor industry, on the waterfront, in railways, mining and among teachers and local government employees. It has a women's section, which publishes *Women's Voice* and which fights for women's liberation and socialism. It is one of the most active and extremist groups among women in Britain.

Socialist Workers' Party (in the USA) The best known Trotskyite party in the country, originally created in 1928, but its formal organization was established only in 1938 (now located in New York). Its membership is small (about 2,500) but quite active, especially in the publishing and electoral fields. It subscribes to TROTSKYISM, is highly critical of DEMOCRATIC CENTRALISM and party authoritarianism in China as well as the USSR, and is anti-Israeli. It has facilitated the formation of other Trotskyite groups in the country, such as the Workers' World Party, the Spartacus League and the Revolutionary Marxist Committee. In 1977, it admitted the R.M.C. to its own organization. It has a supporting youth group called the Young Socialist Alliance. The Party publishes *The Militant* (weekly), *International Socialist Review* (monthly) and *Young Socialist* (monthly).

Socialization In sociology, the process of shaping individuals' attitudes, values and conduct considered appropriate to their role as members of their society. The term itself in English had appeared by 1828, but the theory of s. dates only since the end of the 19th c., S. Freud (1856–1939), G. H. Mead (1863–1931) and C. H. Cooley (1864–1929) being its early exponents. Marxists attach special importance to s. for two reasons. 1. Guided by the principle of the PRIMACY OF SOCIAL INTEREST, they insist that individual persons should be 'de-privatized' and inculcated with such values and norms of social conduct that make them altruistic and well-adjusted members of their social group and society in general. 2. They see it as an essential process of inculcating Marxist ideals to ensure support for the Communist regime and to evolve the NEW COMMUNIST MAN. The main institutions of s. in the Socialist countries are the formal educational system, the communist children and youth organizations, (such as the PIONEERS and KOMSOMOL in the USSR), the Communist party, trade unions, social clubs, cultural societies and the (state owned) media (press, radio, television). Also CULTURAL REVOLUTION, INDOCTRINATION, RESOCIALIZATION.

Socialization of the Means of Production In Marxist political economy, the expropriation of private owners of land and capital by society, usually without compensation. The socialized means of production are then owned and utilized directly by the state or by a collective (co-operative workshop, collective farm and the like). The expression is applied to the Socialist countries while, in application to capitalism, the term NATIONALIZATION is used, implying compensation to previous owners. S. may apply to farming land, farm buildings and equipment, forests, urban land and buildings, mineral resources, industrial and commercial establishments, transport, banking, insurance and other assets which may yield income. S. of the m. of p. is considered essential by Communist regimes on the following grounds: 1. it removes a source of inequality, as private property is usually distributed unevenly;

2. it eliminates a source of inequality of personal income, as the ownership of the means of production usually yields (non-labour) income; 3. it removes the institution of privately hired labour and exploitation; 4. it deprives former capitalists of the foundation of their power; and 5. it is considered to be indispensable to effective central economic planning, as otherwise private owners would tend to undermine it. Although non-compensation is the rule in the Socialist countries, in some cases previous owners have been given some compensation viz. peasants joining collective farms, former owners continuing in managerial or specialist positions in the same establishments (especially in China) and foreign owners. In no Socialist country has complete socialization been achieved, as some private enterprise is still tolerated, even in the USSR. Land has been fully socialized only in Mongolia and the USSR, while in Poland and Yugoslavia over 80 per cent of the farming land is still privately owned. The s. of the m. of p. does not necessarily imply the expropriation of all private property. Even under FULL COMMUNISM private property is envisaged to exist with respect to personal effects (clothing, ornaments, books) and consumer durables (houses, furniture, household appliances, cars and the like).

Socialized Medicine a term used in capitalist countries, where health care is provided, or, at least administered and largely paid for by the state. The system may be contributory or non-contributory, but in each case the state bears at least a portion of the cost. Examples of s.m. are Medibank in Australia, Medicare in the USA and National Health Insurance in Britain. S.m. is usually opposed by the higher income groups, as the burden of taxation supporting the scheme is borne mostly by them and social distinctions are removed. The scheme is also opposed by most doctors, as they become state employees, or, otherwise their fees are subject to state control. In each Socialist country, complete medical care is provided by the state. However, private medicine is still tolerated, but fees charged privately are subject to state supervision.

Socialized Property SOCIALIZATION OF THE MEANS OF PRODUCTION.

Socialized Sector That part of the economy in the Socialist countries which is owned by society, as distinct from the private sector. The s.s. consists of state and co-operative enterprises (including collective farms). According to official statistics and taking the Socialist bloc as a whole, the share of the s.s. in total material production is 95 per cent. But, in Mongolia and the USSR, the proportion is almost 100 per cent, while in Poland and Yugoslavia, it is about 70 per cent.

Social Justice A sociological and ethical concept to denote fairness in the position of, and relations among, different social groups and individuals. Whether s.j. prevails in a particular society depends on the interpretation of fairness. Marxists emphasize that the concept of justice is not absolute, but varies from one social class to another and, further, historically from one period to another. The ruling classes endeavour to justify their privileged position by referring to the legal norms, established institutions (including religion) and prevailing customs. Thus, under SLAVERY, the accepted principle was 'to each according to his birth' (free or unfree), under FEUDALISM – 'to each according to his position' (determined by estates) and under CAPITALISM – 'to each according to his inherited or acquired position' (especially in relation to property and income). But to the slaves, serfs and proletarians those principles were or are grossly unfair, as they sanction social exploitation and oppression in one way or another. The lack of s.j. historically manifested itself in demands for social reforms, schemes of ideal communities, passive resistance, revolts, civil wars and revolutions. In the Marxist view, the precondition of s.j. is the abolition of the private ownership of the means of production, because the institution of private property not only creates inequality in the ownership of wealth, but also in income (as property yields income). Furthermore, private property gives power to the property owners as employers and rulers, who can support institutions (courts, police, armed forces) to enforce and preserve their privileged position. Communist leaders maintain that s.j. prevails in the Socialist countries where: 1. the means of production are socialized; 2. there is no exploitation of man by man; 3. there is equality of opportunity; 4. everybody has the same obligation to work according to his ability; and 5. social security and insurance provide protection 'according to needs', while distribution to the working population is 'according to work'. In practice, the prevalence of s.j. may be questioned, considering the existence of privileged groups (party elite, technocrats, top professionals), severe and arbitrary Party purges, the disregard for HUMAN RIGHTS, the persecution of dissidents, discrimination against members (and even their children) of the former upper and middle classes and the like.

Social Labour A Marxian term for labour performed in an organized society under the conditions of specialization, so that work by individual persons is mutually interdependent. The social nature of labour was emphasized by Marx (especially in *CAPITAL*, vol. I), irrespective of the social system. In a fully socialized economy, the social character of labour is direct and obvious. Although less apparent in a capitalist society, the labour of individual persons is not of private concern but is of social interest. In the case of private enterprise, labour is still social, but its social character manifests itself not in the process of production (where it represents PRIVATE LABOUR), but only in the market, in the sphere of exchange. Labour becomes increasingly social with the development of the PRODUCTION FORCES and the consequent extension of the DIVISION OF LABOUR and exchange. Marxists maintain that capitalism inevitably breeds serious contradictions deriving from the increasingly social character of labour and the restrictive and reactionary private ownership of the means of production and of private labour. On this account alone, capitalism must be replaced by socialism.

Socially-Indispensable Labour A concept introduced by Marx (in *CAPITAL*, vol. I), denoting the quantity of labour that is necessary from society's standpoint to produce an article under normal technical and social conditions prevailing at the time. The requirements are: 1. the article must be in demand; 2. the labour involved is assumed to require an average skill and intensity of application; 3. workers are equipped with the instruments of production appropriate to the technological level at the time; and 4. both past and current labour are included, i.e. labour previously embodied in fixed capital (i.e. AMORTIZATION) and circulating capital (raw materials and components) together with live labour (wages). S.-i.l. is the determinant of value in the Marxian sense. The VALUE of a product is determined not by the quantity of labour expended by each individual worker, but by the s.-i.l. If an article is produced by inefficient labour, it will not be approved (bought) in the market at that high price. With technological progress, the s.-i.l. time necessary for the production of a given article declines.

Socially-Indispensable Labour Time A Marxian term to describe the quantity of SOCIALLY-INDISPENSABLE LABOUR expressed in a unit of time that is normally required to produce a particular article.

Socially-Necessary Labour See SOCIALLY-INDISPENSABLE LABOUR.

Socially-Necessary Labour Time See SOCIALLY-INDISPENSABLE LABOUR TIME.

Social Market Economy A concept introduced by a neo-liberal West German economist A. Müller-Armack (*Soziale Markwirtschaft*), denoting a 'socially mildly-regulated' and 'socially-responsible' market economy. The term is widely used in the FR of Germany, to describe the economic system developed there in the 1950s and 1960s, noted for the freedom of enterprise, the operation of the market mechanism, competition and mild state intervention to prevent abuses and modify distribution in the interest of social justice. The supporters of the s.m.e. reject both the *LAISSEZ-FAIRE* market economy and the centrally planned economy. They stress that market processes, especially the market price mechanism, are basically indispensable to the most efficient utilization of resources, but they lead to socially unjust distribution. The latter must be corrected by the state in the form of monetary and fiscal instruments working with the market and not against it, supplemented with anti-monopoly legislation.

Social Mobility The movement of individuals or groups in society, thereby changing their relative social position. S.m. may be *vertical*, where it involves movement to higher or lower social status (usually associated with a change in property ownership, income, occupation, education or power), or *horizontal* where movement is merely from one social group to another of the same social ranking. The attitude to s.m. in the Socialist countries is complex. One of the charges levelled by them against the so-called antagonistic socio-economic formation (SLAVERY, FEUDALISM and CAPITALISM) is insufficient s.m. prevented or impeded by the ruling class utilizing law and police. But many of those who do manage to be socially promoted betray their previous lower class and identify themselves (if accepted) with the masters, feudal lords or the bourgeoisie. Under Socialism, after the seizure of power, the Communist regimes pursue the policies of rapid SOCIAL PROMOTION to ensure that the positions of power and influence are increasingly occupied by persons of worker or peasant background, displacing former bourgeois elements. There is also an upward social shift of the nation, made possible by rapid industrialization and all-round economic development. It is envisaged that under FULL COMMUNISM the question of vertical s.m. will disappear, but there will be increasing horizontal s.m., owing to the expected de-emphasis of the OCCUPATIONAL DIVISION OF LABOUR in favour of a wider variety of work performed by workers.

Social Norms Standards regulating the conduct of individuals or groups in a society. S.n. may be either *positive* – requiring certain responses or behaviour in relation to others, or *negative* – restraining persons or communities from particular types of acts. S.n. may be established by custom or by law and may relate to dress, the manner of walking in public places, work relations, driving vehicles, the use of public property and the like. S.n. are enforced by the pressure of public or group opinion or by legal sanctions. Marxists attach great importance to the setting and observance of s.n., in which the PRIMACY OF SOCIAL INTEREST should be reflected. They emphasize the changing nature of s.n., conditioned by the state of economic development and the class relations in force. The very concepts of 'good' and 'bad' vary according to the social class and, consequently, there may be contradictory s.n. (e.g. attitudes to strikes by professional associations and by industrial unions under capitalism). In general, the ruling class has a dominant influence over the setting of s.n., as it can use the state machinery and public media for their propagation and enforcement, in both capitalist and socialist countries.

Social Order See SOCIAL SYSTEM.

Social Ownership of the Means of Production Productive property owned by society (as opposed to private ownership) in the form of land and capital normally used for economic purposes. Social ownership may come into existence through either a public authority (national, provincial or local) buying out privately-held property in ordinary commercial transactions, or through NATIONALIZATION (forced expropriation against compensation to previous owners), or through SOCIALIZATION (as a rule no compensation). While the first two methods are typical of capitalist countries, the last one is the normal practice under Socialism. S.o. may embrace land, forests, water resources, urban sites and buildings, industrial, commercial and financial enterprises, banking and insurance, means of transport and various utilities. The extent of the s.o. of the m. of p. is generally small in capitalist countries (usually less than 20 per cent), while in the Socialist countries it ranges from 80 per cent to 100 per cent. In the latter countries, s.o. is considered to be of crucial importance to ensure social justice, the neutralization of former capitalists and the effectiveness of central economic planning. Social property is held either directly by the state or collectively by co-operative enterprises or farms.

Social Plan The official name applied to the ECONOMIC PLAN in Yugoslavia. The term is meant to indicate that the Plan is concerned with broad social objectives along the lines of WORKERS' SELF-MANAGEMENT, and not prescriptive in detail and binding on enterprises. The S.p. is not prepared and imposed by the state, but worked out directly by the organs of socio-political communities, ECONOMIC CHAMBERS and trade unions on the basis of self-management and mutual agreements.

Social Planning The sphere of public concern directed to the formulation of objectives and directions of the development of society and the methods and means of their implementation. It focuses on the problems of population policy, family planning, personal income, social services, education, cultural development, sport, holidays and various forms of entertainment considered to be desirable from society's point of view. Although s.p. is now carried on in most capitalist countries (especially in the affluent West), it is pursued on a much more comprehensive and systematic basis in the Socialist countries.

It is intermeshed with ECONOMIC PLANNING. But there is an inherent conflict between purely social and purely economic planning, as the former emphasizes the growth of consumption while the latter emphasizes saving and investment, necessary for the growth of production. While on ideological grounds the Communist regimes are committed to the extension of social welfare, a rapid growth of production at this stage of their economic development usually receives priority. In effect, the proportion of national income allowed for current consumption is usually lower than would be the case in a free market economy at the same stage of economic development. Consequently, at least in the past, s.p. in these countries was preoccupied with the reconciliation and even subordination of social welfare to accelerated economic development. In Yugoslavia, the term s.p. is used in a broader sense, embracing economic planning as well. Also SOCIAL ENGINEERING, SOCIO-TECHNICS.

Social Profit In Socialist enterprise and national income accounting, another term for GROSS PROFIT, i.e. before deductions are made from the total profits for the state budget, and intermediate levels of economic management. It is calculated by deducting materials, fuels etc. purchased from outside and wages from the enterprise's total receipts.

Social Profit Rate In modern Socialist enterprise accounting, the percentage ratio of SOCIAL PROFIT (also known as gross profit) to total assets (fixed and circulating) held. The s.p.r. is used for comparing the effectiveness of the utilization of assets among different branches of industry or the economy. But it is not a reliable indicator as prices in the Socialist countries are not necessarily efficiency (scarcity) prices.

Social Promotion, or Social Advancement The process of advancement for individuals or groups from lower to higher social classes, which may be indicated by higher income, greater power, higher cultural

545

standards or higher social prestige in general. S.p. may occur as a result of five different developments: 1. proceeding from lower to higher working age brackets and the usual promotion from lower to higher positions; 2. the accession of a left-wing government to power, replacing a right-wing regime in a capitalist democratic society, where the previously under-privileged social groups are given the equality of opportunity; 3. after a PROLETARIAN REVOLUTION, where the masses displace the BOURGEOISIE as the ruling class and the social security programme uplifts the lower strata; 4. rapid technological and economic progress, whereby heavy manual work and low-income and low-prestige occupations are eliminated, so that the lowest social strata are uplifted to the lower middle-class status. This is typical of higher stages of industrialization, irrespective of the social system; and 5. a substantial rise in educational levels (including the elimination of illiteracy) and cultural standards of the masses, made possible by a sympathetic government, and improving the occupational structure (affluence) of the working population.

'Social Quacks' A derogatory description applied by F. Engels in the English edition of *The COMMUNIST MANIFESTO* in 1888 to utopian socialists. There were a number of idealist middle-class writers in the 18th and 19th c. (such as G. B. MABLY, J. MESLIER, C. H. SAINT-SIMON, CH. FOURIER, and R. OWEN) who put forward schemes for an ideal society. Engels, together with Marx, first subjected these schemes to severe criticism in 1846 (in *The GERMAN IDEOLOGY*) and dismissed their UTOPIAN SOCIALISM for not having any solid foundations and a correspondence to reality. Instead, Engels and Marx called for a communist revolution based essentially on the materialist conception of history and the militancy of the proletariat.

Social Realism A term vaguely used in capitalist countries to describe the artistic movement emphasizing the representation of society's ordinary, real life and problems in literature, theatre, painting, sculpture and architecture, as contrasted with abstract or subjective impressionism. Some elements of s.r. can be traced back to the Middle Ages, but in its modern sense the concept was introduced in the middle of the 19th c., when the worker and peasant became respectable themes in art. In more recent times, s.r. has been represented by J. Amado (of Brazil), L. Aragon (France), B. Brecht (Germany), P. Neruda (Chile) and M. A. Nexo (Denmark). The term s.r. should not be used in application to the Socialist countries, as the appropriate designation in this case is SOCIALIST REALISM.

Social Relations Relations between individuals, groups and classes in society. To Marxist sociologists and philosophers, s.r. represent one of the most crucial spheres of human intercourse. They clearly distinguish between material and ideological s.r. They stress that MATERIAL PRODUCTION constitutes the basis of man's existence and development. Consequently, economic relations fundamentally condition all other relations – political, legal, cultural and moral. The character of s.r. depends on society's structure. In antagonistic class societies (SLAVERY, FEUDALISM and CAPITALISM), s.r. are strained and the inherent social contradictions are best resolved through revolutionary upheavals. Harmonious s.r. can prevail only in a CLASSLESS SOCIETY.

Social Rentability, or S.R. Rate In modern Socialist enterprise accounting, the percentage ratio of SOCIAL PROFIT to PRIME COST.

Social Requirements Fund That part of MATERIAL PRODUCTION in a Socialist economy which is not distributed in wages but is used for SOCIAL CONSUMPTION and for ACCUMULATION. It typically represents 45 per cent of the Socialist national income, more specifically called the NET MATERIAL PRODUCT.

Social Revolution A general term for RE-VOLUTION, PROLETARIAN REVOLUTION.

Social Revolutionaries A less commonly used term for SOCIALIST RE-VOLUTIONARIES (in Russia).

Social Security One of the bases for the provision of SOCIAL SERVICES. In Socialist terminology, s.s. is concerned with the provision of benefits in cash, kind or service to persons disabled from birth (blindness, deafness, infirmity) or by war. S.s. is financed from the state budget (not on a contributory basis) and is administered by specialized institutions. S.s. is regarded as a major step towards the Marxian ideal of distribution 'TO EACH ACCORDING TO HIS NEEDS' (as contrasted with 'to each according to his work'). S.s. differs from SOCIAL INSURANCE.

Social Services Benefits provided by society to persons in need to protect their minimum standard of living. These benefits may be in cash (periodical or lump-sum payments), in kind (medicines, artificial limbs, food in communal establishments, clothing, etc). or in services (medical, legal, cultural, housing, travel, entertainment, etc). Examples of common cash social benefits are child endowment, maternity allowance, sickness benefit, unemployment benefit, widow pension, old age pension, invalid pension, funeral allowance and scholarship. S.s. are provided by public authorities and sometimes by other organizations. They are financed either by the state out of general taxation or by contributions regularly paid by specified categories of people. S.s. represent a redistribution of national income from higher income groups (bearing the main brunt of progressive taxes) to lower income brackets (as s.s. are mostly open to, or taken advantage of by, the latter). Consequently, s.s. are not only conducive to greater social equality but also to the overall increase in social welfare (as the rich lose less, than the poor gain, in satisfaction). In capitalist countries, s.s. are best developed in the Scandinavian coun-

tries and the United Kingdom ('from the cradle to the grave'), while elsewhere they are on a more or less selective basis or non-existent. S.s. are developed on a most comprehensive and systematic basis in the Socialist countries, where the benefits provided are both wide-ranging and generous in relation to the *per capita* income levels attained. Generous s.s. are regarded not only as a matter of social ethics and an instrument of social equalization, but also as the avenue for the implementation of the Marxian ideal of distribution 'according to needs' (as distinct from the rule of 'according to work'). S.s. constitute the bulk of SOCIAL CONSUMPTION.

Social Significance A cultural conception referring to a social problem, particularly affecting the broad masses, brought out by the artist, writer, painter, sculptor, architect, or the performing arts producer, in creative works. The conception was developed in the USSR in the 1930s as the central element of SOCIALIST REALISM and PROLETARIAN ART, but the idea had appeared earlier (as discussed by Upton Sinclair in *Mammonart*, 1925). The opponents of the postulate of s.s. in art point out that such art is reduced to doctored naïve moralizing and ideological commercials, interfering with true artistic creativity.

Social State Another term used in some countries (notably in the FR of Germany) for the WELFARE STATE.

Social Status A person's position in society in relation to other persons, implying different degrees of social prestige. S.s. may be determined by property ownership, education, occupation, position held, income, race, religion, various privileges, responsibilities or disabilities. S.s. may be established by custom, current public opinion or by law. The concept has received a good deal of attention in Western sociology, from such thinkers as M. Weber (1864–1920) and R. Linton (1893–1953). The problem is naturally more relevant to a capitalist class society, noted for more or less HIERARCHICAL STRATIFI-CATION and wide-ranging social distinctions, than is typical under socialism. The likelihood of change in a person's s.s. is greater, the greater the SOCIAL MOBILITY. Although, in Marxist ideology, the idea of s.s. is generally identified with antagonistic socio-economic formations (SLAVERY, FEUDALISM, and CAPITALISM), experience shows that people in the Socialist countries, especially in Eastern Europe and the USSR, are acutely conscious of s.s. In these countries, party membership and the position in its hierarchy, bureaucrats, technocrats, professionals, holders of orders and other awards and distinctions are accorded high s.s., compared with unskilled labourers and peasants. It is envisaged that differences in s.s. will disappear only in a CLASSLESS SOCIETY, the ultimate goal of communism.

Social Stratification A hierarchical arrangement of social groups or SOCIAL CLASSES differing in social status with respect to wealth, power, income, education, occupation, cultural interests and achievements, and various privileges, responsibilities and disabilities. Birth, race, religion and nationality may also be contributing factors. The most rigid s.s. exists under the caste system, where it is sanctioned not only by law but also by religion and custom. S.s. exists, or existed, in striking forms also under SLAVERY, FEUDAL-ISM and CAPITALISM. In the case of open societies, SOCIAL MOBILITYto some extent obliterates social distinctions. Marxists condemn s.s. as socially unjust and attribute it primarily to the existence of the private ownership of the means of production, which inevitably leads to uneven distribution. They point out that ownership confers power and income, which the owners utilize through the state to protect their privileged position. In the Socialist countries, the term s.s. is not used in application to their societies, but the existence of social differentiation based on occupation and personal effort is conceded. However, it is possible to distinguish hierarchical social groups in these coun-

tries, as represented by the party elite, government bureaucracy, technocrats and successful professionals – in contrast to manual workers, unskilled labourers and peasants. Marx and Engels envisaged an ideal type of social organization, viz. a classless society, devoid of horizontal and even vertical social classes, which is expected to be achieved under FULL COMMUNISM.

Social Subsistence One of the basic concepts in Marxist ideology to denote the totality of the material conditions of life in society. Marx identified three critical conditions: 1. the geographical environment (location, climate, natural resources); 2. labour (density of population, natural increase, skills); and 3. the mode of production (consisting of PRODUCTION FORCES and PRODUCTION RELATIONS). Of the three, Marxists regard the mode of production to be the most important, because in their view the level and changes in the methods of production shape not only the material well-being of the population but also SOCIAL CONSCIOUSNESS. A proposition derived from HISTORICAL MATERIAL-ISM is that the material BASE determines the political, legal, social, cultural and psychological SUPERSTRUCTURE. But Marxists also point out that social development is not automatic, as man also influences the economic base and 'each generation forges its own destiny'.

Social System The complex of political, economic and social thinking, institutions and interrelationships peculiar to a group of nations at a particular historical stage, distinct from other systems. The crucial elements in a s.s. which lend themselves to fundamental differentiation are state power, property ownership, the organization of production, the distribution of national income, social structure and the legal establishment. Marx preferred the term 'socio-economic formation' and distinguished four major social systems in the historical sense, viz. PRIMITIVE COMMUN-ISM, SLAVERY, FEUDALISM and CAPITAL-ISM, to be followed by SOCIALISM and

FULL COMMUNISM. In the Marxist view, the most fundamental factor conditioning the nature of a s.s. is the material BASE embodying PRODUCTION FORCES and PRODUCTION RELATIONS. Developed on the base is the SUPERSTRUCTURE, embracing ideological, political, religious, moral, aesthetic and legal precepts, institutions, policies and practices. While most non-Marxists view the s.s. as a complementary and harmonious network of relations, Marxists stress their contradictory and conflicting nature. They further insist that while these contradictions and conflicts can be resolved in non-antagonistic s.s. (primitive communism, socialism, and communism), they are irreconcilable in antagonistic s.s. (slavery, feudalism, capitalism) and have to be resolved in violent, revolutionary ways.

Social Theory of Language Development LABOUR THEORY OF LANGUAGE DEVELOPMENT, MARRISM.

Social Unionism A basis of trade union thinking and practice which, in addition to its industrial pursuits directed towards the improvement of wages and other conditions of work, also includes broader social functions. These social functions may include: 1. the conduct of social activities for its members (dances, excursions, picnics, and cultural activities); 2. the provision of financial aid and personal care by members to other members and their families in case of need; 3. acting as a COUNTERVAILING POWER to large employers or employer associations to prevent exploitation of labour and other unfair practices of social consequence; 4. giving active support to the political wing of the labour movement and campaigning for social legislation or its further extension, in order to improve the political and economic position of the working class in society; 5. embarking on a more radical course directed towards a revolutionary transformation of the existing social system for the benefit of the working class; and 6. sometimes, in a wider sense, functioning as social microcosms, incorporat-ing not only workers but also employers and representatives of the state, concerning themselves with the interests of the whole society in particular branches. Examples of s.u. are medieval guilds, early trade unions (of the 18th and 19th c.), SYNDICALISM and CORPORATISM.

Social Value In Marxian terminology, the value of a product as determined by the SOCIALLY-INDISPENSABLE LABOUR embodied in it. The labour must involve an average skill and intensity using up-to-date equipment appropriate to the given stage of economic development and the product in question must be in demand as verified in the market. S.v. essentially refers to the *average* value and is distinct from the *individual* value of a product.

Society A large self-perpetuating group of persons linked by a network of institutions and various relationships. Traditionally, in the study of s. Western-liberal sociology has highlighted the importance of individualism on the one hand and co-operation on the other, while the Marxist approach has been preoccupied with the effect of s. on the individual and with class conflicts. In their analysis of s., Marxists emphasize that man is basically the most social of all living entities. His social mentality has been developed through living and working together in his struggle for material subsistence (food, shelter, and clothing), first by joint gathering and hunting and then by participating in the division of labour. Thus, it is the material BASE that determines the intellectual, political, social and legal SUPERSTRUCTURE in s. Marxism accepts the theory of the plasticity of human nature and insists that society is not a product of human nature (as humanists maintain) but an individual – whether good, bad or indifferent – is a product of s. As s. changes and develops, so does human nature. Consequently, to improve individual members of s., s. must first be improved. The most effective way of doing this in antagonistic societies (slavery, feudalism, and capitalism) is by REVOLUTION. As s. develops, contradictions appear sooner or later, irrespective of the social system. But in a Socialist s. they are not irreconcilable and can be rectified on a planned basis without a recourse to revolution.

Socio-Capitalism A stage of political, economic and social development beyond industrialized CAPITALISM towards SOCIALISM. The designation, also known as social capitalism and socialist capitalism, has been vaguely applied since the early 1950s to Great Britain, the Scandinavian countries, most other Western European countries, Australia, New Zealand, Canada and occasionally, the USA. S.-c. is basically capitalist, but it incorporates many elements of socialism, the precise combination and relations differing widely from one country to another. On the one hand, s.-c. is featured by the predominantly private ownership of the means of production, free enterprise, the market mechanism, the multi-party political system and democratic freedoms. On the other hand, s.-c. is noted for nationalized key industries and services (such as coal mining, iron, steel and defence industries, railways, air lines, banking, and insurance) and non-directive planning, but is opposed to the centralized, directive system of planning and management, proletarian revolution and the dictatorship of the proletariat. S.-c. is also characterized by a far-reaching REDISTRIBUTION OF NATIONAL INCOME, to reduce wide disparities in personal income and, to some extent, in property. This is achieved mainly by a highly progressive taxation of income and inherited property and the provision of wide-ranging social services (mostly for the benefit of the lower income groups). The implementation and administration of these schemes involves substantial state intervention. Revolutionary Marxists do not accept s.-c. as a solution to the basic problems of capitalism. In their view, the reforms represent a superficial patchwork amounting to OPPORTUNISM, still within the framework of capitalism, merely delaying the need for a proletarian revolution.

Socio-Cultural and Housing Fund In the Socialist countries, a fund maintained in enterprises and other entities employing labour for providing collective benefits to their personnel. These benefits may include reading rooms, entertainment, child care facilities for working mothers and factory housing for those in greatest need. The Fund is usually derived from enterprise profits with state regulations specifying what proportion and under what conditions the profits may be allocated. Great importance is attached to the Fund, as not only does it provide an incentive and a gesture in public relations, but it also constitutes distribution 'according to needs' (as distinct from that 'according to work').

Socio-Economic Formation One of the crucial concepts in Marxist HISTORICAL MATERIALISM, first analysed by Marx and Engels (in *THE GERMAN IDEOLOGY*). They distinguished four such formations, viz. PRIMITIVE COMMUNISM, SLAVERY, FEUDALISM and CAPITALISM, to be followed by SOCIALISM and FULL COMMUNISM. The development of society from one s.-e.f. to another is essentially determined by the material BASE, viz.: 1. PRODUCTION FORCES, i.e. the improvement of the means of production (especially tools, machinery, equipment); and 2. PRODUCTION RELATIONS (between owners and workers). Marx and Engels stressed that what is important is not so much *what* is produced but *how* it is produced. The material conditions of production in turn determine the intellectual, political, social, aesthetic, religious and legal SUPERSTRUCTURE, with all its institutions. The changeover from one formation to another is not accidental, but is governed by the LAW OF THE CONCORDANCE OF PRODUCTION RELATIONS WITH THE NATURE OF PRODUCTION FORCES. As the changes in the material base accumulate, in due time they necessitate a new superstructure. In antagonistic s.-e.f. (slavery, feudalism, and capitalism), due to the opposition of the privileged ruling classes, the necessary adjustments are held back and impede economic as well as social progress until the contradictions are resolved in a revolution, which then paves the way to a higher s.-e.f. In non-antagonistic s.-e.f. (primitive communism, socialism, and full communism) adjustments are gradual, even anticipatory, which (under socialism and communism) is facilitated by economic planning. In exceptional circumstances, it has been possible to skip a s.-e.f. Thus, Poland passed from primitive communism direct to feudalism and Mongolia from feudalism to socialism.

Socio-Economic Planning ECONOMIC PLANNING, SOCIAL PLANNING.

Socio-Economic System SOCIO-ECONOMIC FORMATION, SOCIAL SYSTEM.

Sociology The branch of knowledge concerned with the scientific study of the nature and development of human society, especially interaction between individuals and groups. The foundations of s. were laid down by non-Marxists, viz. A. Comte (1798–1857), H. Spencer (1820–1903), M. Weber (1864–1920) and E. Durkheim (1858–1917). From the start, Marxists adopted a critical attitude to s., describing it as a 'bourgeois pseudo-science', as it conflicted with HISTORICAL MATERIALISM. In their view, traditional s. was preoccupied with theorizing and demonstrating that the workers are inevitably destined to perform menial, physical labour, while the capitalists' mission is to guide and direct social processes – thus in effect seeking to prove the permanence of the capitalist social system. It is also claimed that the more recent Western s. advocates, or at least accepts, racial inequality and discrimination. Marx and Engels, naturally, approached the study of society and the laws of its development from a radical angle. On the basis of his analysis of socio-economic relations, Marx set out to prove that the development of society is determined not by ideas but by production methods and relations. Ever since, Marxists have maintained that it is the economic conditions that essen-

tially determine the political and cultural life of society, and that the individuals' behaviour is governed by their class interests. Marxists have also attacked Western s. for obscuring significant differences in society's characteristics in different historical periods. Marx, Engels and Lenin maintained that there are definite stages in the development of societies, which they called SOCIO-ECONOMIC FORMATIONS. They insisted that the task of s. should be to identify and explain the historical laws which govern the emergence, development and disappearance of particular social groups and their replacement by classes of a higher order. Although sociological studies continued in the USSR in the 1920s and in Eastern Europe in the latter 1940s, a period of repression followed up to the mid-1950s during which s. practically disappeared in universities and research institutes. The official view was that Marx, Engels, Lenin and Stalin had said all there was to say on s., thus further studies were pointless and indeed dangerous. However, since that time, s. has been gradually rehabilitated and some remarkable advances have been made, particularly in Poland (J. SZCZEPAŃSKI). The new approach has been (reluctantly) embraced by the authorities because s. is seen as a useful instrument in social planning for identifying and tackling social problems, improving the existing system and perfecting future society on a scientific basis. The authorities have found an increasing need for objective sociological studies in the Socialist countries because new forms of social stratification are emerging and social groups are becoming more diversified and increasingly complex, with conflicting interests raising new ideological implications. Modern Western methods of sociological enquiry offer a more useful means of understanding social development (in capitalist as well as socialist countries) in the modern technological age rather than in the traditional Marxist interpretation. Modern Socialist s. concentrates on empirical and quantitative studies, the analysis dwelling on such problems as delinquency, ethnic relations, internal migrations, leisure, social attitudes and motivation, social structure and time budgets. Research findings, even as published, suggest that the Socialist countries are subjected to similar social problems as in developed capitalist countries, and that socialism has not produced superior societies – free from stresses and conflicts – to the extent previously claimed. But although s. has become one of the most active fields of scientific enquiry, it has not been fully emancipated. It is still subject to various limitations and degrees in different Socialist countries. It appears that the authorities endeavour to use sociological research for providing continued ideological justification for the party rule, the perpetuation of socialism or communism and the suppression of publications of unpalatable findings. Modern developments in Socialist s., both in theoretical discussions and in applied research, have challenged the validity, or at least the applicability, of the dogmatic Marxist deductions under modern conditions created by the scientific and technical revolution. Some Western observers see the Socialist rehabilitation of s. as a force which may steer social management in the Socialist countries into more varied tolerant and humane forms. Also GEOGRAPHICAL DOCTRINE IN SOCIOLOGY, SOCIAL ENGINEERING, SOCIOLOGY OF KNOWLEDGE, SOCIO-TECHNICS, VULGAR SOCIOLOGISM.

Sociology of Knowledge A sphere of the science of knowledge (EPISTEMOLOGY) concerned with the study of the relation of social factors to systems of thought. Although this relationship had been acknowledged by some ancient and several modern thinkers, Marx gave it a much stronger, ideological interpretation and is commonly credited with almost being the creator of the doctrine. He emphasized that philosophical, political, religious, ethical, aesthetic and juridical ideas are conditioned by social group interests. Consequently, in class societies, knowledge is distorted, mostly consciously and

partly subconsciously. In antagonistic socio-economic formations (SLAVERY, FEUDALISM, and CAPITALISM), the content and direction of the development of knowledge is very largely determined by the exploiting classes in their efforts to provide apologetic justifications for the existing social system in force. In Marxist philosophy, knowledge is regarded to be very largely relative (RELATIVE TRUTH) and social conditioning further removes it from ABSOLUTE TRUTH. In the Marxist view, only in a CLASSLESS SOCIETY under full communism can the social distortion of knowledge disappear.

Socio-Technics A field of applied sociology concerned with the structural transformation of society and steering its development in desired directions. The term was established by Polish sociologists (such as A. Podgorecki in *Principles of Socio-Technics*, 1966) after W.W.II and is used in the Socialist countries in preference to SOCIAL ENGINEERING, once commonly employed in Western sociology. A socio-technician is concerned with scientific solutions, not setting objectives or making value judgments. He applies tested solutions not only from various branches of sociology but also from demography, education, psychology and economics. The development of s.-t. in the Socialist countries has been spurred by the following circumstances: 1. the traditional ideological suspicion of theoretical sociology; 2. the proliferation of practical social problems associated with the rapid industrialization of backward and agricultural societies and the consequent changing social structure and urbanization; and 3. the policy of social transformation along Marxist lines from capitalism to socialism and then full communism. There are three basic spheres of society's life to which s.-t. has so far been directed: education; public administration; and industrial relations. The implementation of the socio-technic schemes is facilitated in the socialist countries by the continuity of the government (ensured by the mono-party system), a very well developed state administrative machinery, central economic planning and the state ownership of the media (press, radio, television, cinema, theatre and other cultural institutions).

Sofia Rules (or Sofia Principle) Accords regulating the transmission of technology among the member countries of the COUNCIL FOR MUTUAL ECONOMIC ASSISTANCE. The S.R. were adopted at the second C.M.E.A. session in 1949, when it was agreed that the exchange, or unilateral transfer, of technology among the member countries was to be essentially free of charge (excepting the cost of reproduction of the documents and postage). The S.R. represent a practical expression of the accepted postulate of the 'EVENING OUT THE NATIONAL ECONOMIC LEVELS' in the member countries, whereby the less developed nations would, on balance, receive more technology than they had to contribute, thereby accelerating their economic development above the rates achieved in the more developed member nations. The S.R. were partly modified in 1971, so that in certain cases (especially when the cost of research and development is very high and when the recipient country clearly reaps substantial commercial benefits), the recipient has to make reasonable payment.

Solidarism A social movement which originated in the latter part of the 19th c. in Europe, emphasizing the need for and possibility of the solidarity of all social classes in a given community, society or nation. Its main exponents were E. Durkheim (1858–1917), L. Duguit (1859–1928) and Ch. Gide (1847–1932). This movement was sustained by social-democratic and moderate socialist parties and was supported by many intellectuals and by the churches. The advocates of s. rejected the inevitability of the CLASS STRUGGLE and maintained that the abuses of capitalism could be gradually removed by legislation and other reforms. They pressed for substantial state inter-

vention and far-reaching REDISTRIBUTION OF NATIONAL INCOME and wealth in favour of the lower social classes, together with workers' participation in the management and ownership of firms. In their view, these improvements of capitalism could ensure social harmony. Revolutionary Marxists have rejected s. as applied to capitalism, considering it anti-Marxist and engineered by the bourgeois stalwarts who fear the class war and proletarian revolution.

Solidarity (*Solidarność*, in Polish) The powerful free trade union in Poland and the only one in the Socialist bloc independent of the Communist party and the state. Sparked off by the increases in meat prices in July 1980, it originated as a co-ordinating committee of the unions striking or protesting against shortages, the authoritarianism of the privileged Party elite, the disregard of HUMAN RIGHTS and oppressive working and living conditions in general. It was officially recognized in late August 1980, when its demands were accepted in principle by the Government and was formally registered as an independent trade union in the following month. On 9 Oct. 1980, in a historical test-case, the Supreme Court ruled that the insistence of the Party's supremacy over S. was unconstitutional; but in Feb. 1981 it ruled against the registration of Rural Solidarity (to represent some 500,000 private farmers) as an independent trade union. S. has over 10m members (60 per cent of the labour force), co-ordinated by a Presidium of 18 headed by Lech Wałęsa (1943–), an electrician by trade, and its headquarters are in Gdansk. Although created by industrial workers, S. – for the first time in the Socialist bloc – has established a working relationship with the intellectual dissident groups, to mutual advantage. S. has, on the whole, followed a moderate course, fully aware of its precarious position, Polish economic problems and the watchful and critical Soviet leadership.

Solipsism

Solipsism (from Latin, *solus* meaning 'alone' and *ipse* denoting 'self') A philosophical theory according to which a man and his consciousness constitute the only existence, while everything else (including the rest of mankind) has no existence of its own except in the mind of that man. The main representatives of this theory were R. Descartes (1596–1650), J. Locke (1632–1704), I. Kant (1724–1804) and J. G. Fichte (1762–1814). Marxist philosophers reject s., regarding it as a by-product of IDEALISM, SUBJECTIVISM and INDIVIDUAL-ISM, totally opposed to MATERIALISM and the Marxist view of society. The Marxist critique of s. was presented by Lenin in *MATERIALISM AND EMPIRIO-CRITICISM.*

Solzhenitsyn, Aleksander (1918–) An outstanding Soviet writer and prominent campaigner for HUMAN RIGHTS in the USSR. During W.W.II he served in the Red Army with distinction and was decorated twice. After the war, he was sentenced to eight years in a forced labour camp (1945–53) and to four years of exile in Siberia on unspecified charges, but was subsequently (in 1957) rehabilitated as innocent. His first book, *One Day in the Life of Ivan Denisovich* (1962), was the first legally published book in the USSR (due to Khruschev's intervention) on the brutality in Soviet forced labour camps. None of his other books has been allowed to be published legally in the USSR, but they appeared in the West and have achieved great publicity and success, viz. *The First Circle* (1968); *Cancer Ward* (1968); *The Love Girl and the Innocent* (1969); *In the Interest of the Cause* (1970); *Stories and Prose Poems* (1971); *August 1914* (1971); *The Gulag Archipelago* (in three volumes, 1973, 1974 and 1976; *GULAG*; *A Letter to Soviet Leaders* (1974); *Lenin in Zurich* (1975); and *The Oak and the Calf* (1975). Of these *The Gulag Archipelago*, which he decided to publish in the West after the Soviet authorities seized it, immediately became a bestseller and has brought him most fame and widespread recognition. It is a poignant history of Soviet prison camps and an indictment of the inhuman Soviet distortion of Marxism, especially under Stalin. S. was expelled from the WRITERS' UNION OF THE USSR in 1969, exiled from his country in Feb. 1974 and deprived of Soviet citizenship by the decree of the Supreme Soviet of the USSR. His books won several prizes in the West in several countries and in 1970 he was awarded the Nobel Prize for Literature. In 1974, S. established a fund, derived from his royalties, to provide aid to Soviet dissidents. He was granted honorary US citizenship in the same year and, after having spent some time in West Germany, Norway and Switzerland, settled in the USA (Vermont).

Somali Socialist Revolutionary Party The ruling party in the Somali Democratic Republic. The Party subscribes to SCIENTIFIC SOCIALISM, but its Marxism is adapted to local conditions. It was founded in July 1976 as the country's only legal political party with the members of the former Supreme Revolutionary Council becoming members of the Party's Central Committee. The policy-making body of the S.S.R.P. is a five-man Political Bureau headed by the President of the Republic (Maj. Gen. M. Siad Barre) and the Party's Central Committee appoints ministers of the government. Up to Nov. 1977 the S.S.R.P. had been closely allied to and assisted by the USSR, but since that time the Soviets have changed sides and now support Ethiopia instead.

Sorel, Georges (1847–1920) A French engineer by education who became (at the age of 40) a philosopher and a theoretician of syndicalism and anarchism. Influenced by P. J. PROUDHON and K. MARX, S. attacked capitalism as a morally decadent social system. He stressed the need for proletarian struggle and advocated a violent transformation of society along syndicalist lines. He saw the GENERAL STRIKE as the basic weapon in the hands of the working class and attached a great inspirational role to myth in social movements. S. became a champion of A. Dreyfus, a Jewish army officer wrongly convicted of treason. S. was opposed to the peaceful and evolutionary interpretation of Marxism (as represented by E. BERNSTEIN and K. KAUTSKY) and the deterministic view of history. In his later years, S. turned away from SYNDICALISM in favour of ANARCHISM and even to monarchism. S. discarded UTOPIAN SOCIALISM, believing that only revolutionary action could lead to an ideal society and declared his support for the Bolshevik Revolution. His main works are: *The Socialist Future of the Syndicalists* (1901); *Reflections on Violence* (1908); *Illusions of Progress* (1908); *The Decomposition of Marxism* (1908); and *Studies on a Theory of the Proletariat* (1919).

Sorge, Friedrich Adolph (1828–1906) A German socialist and participant in the REVOLUTION OF 1848/49. For a time Sorge was a close friend of MARX and ENGELS and later became an organizer of the FIRST INTERNATIONAL in the United States.

Sotsial-Demokrat (*Social-Democrat*, in Russian) The central organ of the RUSSIAN SOCIAL-DEMOCRATIC LABOUR PARTY, published as an illegal newspaper from Feb. 1908 to Jan. 1917. Its places of publication were consecutively in Vilna, St. Petersburg (now Leningrad), Paris and Geneva. At one stage (in 1911) Lenin was its editor. In all, 58 issues appeared. In March 1917 *PRAVDA* became the central organ of the Bolshevik Party, but the *S.-D.* continued to be published after the October Revolution by the Moscow Soviet.

Sotsrealizm The abbreviated Russian form of *Sotsialistichesky realizm*, meaning SOCIALIST REALISM (in art).

South African Communist Party An illegal party which combines Marxist ideology with national and racial liberation. Although it is a non-racial party, its membership is dominated by the blacks. It was originally founded in 1921 as the Communist Party of South Africa, but was dissolved in 1950. Three years later the

Party was revived illegally under its present name. But most of its leaders operate from abroad – in the surrounding African countries and in Western and Eastern Europe. The Party's membership is estimated to be about 1,000 (the country's total population in 1978 was 26,800,000). The Party's organs are published irregularly: *Inkululeko – Freedom* and *African Communist* (edited in London but printed in East Germany).

South-East Asia Treaty Organization A defence pact created by the Treaty of Manila in 1954 on the initiative of the USA, directed against the Socialist countries (especially China) and communist subversion. Its membership, in addition to the USA, included Australia, France, New Zealand, Pakistan, the Philippines, Thailand and the United Kingdom. S.-E.A.T.O. was based in Bangkok and it was linked to C.E.N.T.O. and N.A.T.O. S.-E.A.T.O. lacked determination and strength and its effectiveness was further eroded by national differences, as was illustrated by the VIETNAM WAR. Pakistan withdrew from the Treaty in 1972, France followed in 1973 and the Organization was finally dissolved in June 1977 (but some of its functions have been taken over by the Association of South-East Asian Countries, founded in 1967).

Sovetskaya Rossiya (*Soviet Russia*, in Russian) The daily organ of the CENTRAL COMMITTEE OF THE CPSU of the RUSSIAN SOVIET FEDERATED SOCIALIST REPUBLIC, the SUPREME SOVIET and the COUNCIL OF MINISTERS OF THE USSR. It was founded in 1956 as an official Party and Government organ of the R.S.F.S.R., but its scope was extended after 1966 to cover the entire USSR. It is published in Moscow with a daily circulation of 3.2m. copies.

Soviet A Russian word for 'council' or 'committee', especially if elected by the common people and regarded as a symbol of government by the masses. The first S. appeared in 1905 as a factory strike committee in St Petersburg (later re-named

Leningrad). During the REVOLUTION OF 1905–07, 62 Soviets were elected in Russia, mostly on an industrial (rather than regional) basis, of which 47 were headed or influenced by the BOLSHEVIKS. The Soviets soon became militant and turned to revolutionary action, hence, they attracted increasing interest from the Bolsheviks. The Soviets reappeared in 1917 after the FEBRUARY REVOLUTION as SOVIETS OF WORKERS', PEASANTS' AND SOLDIERS' DEPUTIES, in which the Bolsheviks were most active with their slogan, 'All power to the Soviets'. The Soviets developed into a source of power and rivalled the PROVISIONAL GOVERNMENT, which they undermined, and were instrumental in installing the Bolsheviks into power in the October Revolution. Although at first the Bolsheviks were in a minority, they soon came to dominate the Soviets, especially the PETROGRAD SOVIET, whose Military Revolutionary Committee was used by Lenin as the co-ordinating centre for the GREAT OCTOBER SOCIALIST REVOLUTION. The second All-Russian Congress of the Soviets, which met on 25 Oct. 1917 and had a Bolshevik majority, approved the new Soviet regime and elected the Soviet of People's Commissars (Council of Ministers) headed by Lenin. After 1922, non-Bolsheviks were excluded from the Soviets at all levels. Until 1936, the Congresses of the Soviets were theoretically the highest source of power, but since that time they have been replaced at the Union level by the SUPREME SOVIET of the USSR, by Supreme Soviets at the Union Republic level and by regional and local Soviets. Today, there are about 50,000 local Soviets, organized on a hierarchical basis at different levels of public administration. They embrace over 2.0m. deputies, elected by equal and universal suffrage and by direct and secret ballot, of whom more than two-thirds are workers and peasants. The Soviets establish various local committees which involve some 25m. people. They suggest new legislation and supervise local affairs (education, the militia, local production, hospitals, water supply, transport and other public services). Although not all deputies elected are Party members (especially at lower levels), Party control or at least influence is assured in the Soviets at all levels.

Soviet Army The official name of the regular land armed forces in the USSR since 1947 (when it replaced the RED ARMY). It is described as the 'standing army of the workers and peasants' or the 'cadre army of the masses', which is supposed to exist until the stage of FULL COMMUNISM is reached. It is a highly professional armed force, organized largely along the traditional lines of military efficiency. Its important distinguishing feature is the dualism of military-political control, where ideological INDOCTRINATION and PATRIOTISM are integral parts of the system (*POLITRUK*). Over 93 per cent of the officer corps belongs to the COMMUNIST PARTY OF THE SOVIET UNION or *KOMSOMOL*. The strength of the S.A. in 1977 was as follows: 1,825,000 men (twice the size of the military manpower in the air force and navy combined) not counting reservists and paramilitary forces; 8 airborne divisions; 45 tank divisions; 115 motor rifle divisions; 1,200 surface-to-surface missile launchers; and 43,000 tanks.

Soviet Darwinism A term sometimes used to describe the Lamarckian version of the theory of evolution as put forward by Ch. Darwin, i.e. that acquired characteristics in plants, animals and humans are inheritable. The official Soviet view, reflected in MICHURINISM and LYSENKOISM, for a long time was that characteristics of living bodies are not exclusively a product of heredity, but also a product of the environment which can be controlled appropriately. That view, however, has been modified since the abandonment of Lysenkoism in the late 1950s, the official rehabilitation of MENDELISM and a revival of GENETICS. The previous official Soviet thinking was based on the acceptance of the principle of the inheritance of acquired characteristics indicated by Marx (in a letter to Engels, dated 7 Aug. 1866) and by Engels (in *DIALECTICS OF NATURE*).

Sovietization The policy and tactics of making the communist parties outside the USSR accept BOLSHEVISM and the Soviet patterns of party and state organization and practices, as opposed to other versions of communism. Originally, it was known as Bolshevization and acquired broader significance after the Fifth World Congress of the COMINTERN in 1924, when Stalin insisted that the member Communist parties condemn TROTSKYISM and support the line officially followed by the Soviet regime. The S. drive appeared in its extreme form in the East European countries during 1945–50 when, under Soviet pressure, Communist parties and leaders loyal to Moscow were installed in power. Communist parties were reorganized along Marxist-Leninist lines and state power was virtually monopolized in their hands. During this period S. proceeded typically in four stages in each satellite country (Bulgaria, Czechoslovakia, East Germany, Hungary, Poland and Romania): 1. under the leadership of the MUSCOVITES, the formation of a broad coalition government of various anti-fascist and anti-bourgeois parties developed, where the communists, usually in a minority, took control of the Ministry of the Interior (incl. militia and secret police), the armed forces and the media; 2. the elimination of the leadership of the oppositionist parties, especially peasant parties, accompanied by POLITICAL SHOW TRIALS; 3. the forced merger of the socialist and social-democratic parties with the communist party; and 4. purges of national communists not subservient enough to the USSR (or Stalin) and a drive against TITOISM. S. was also pursued in China in the 1930s in the areas controlled by the Chinese Communist Party. But by the 'DECLARATION OF SINCERE SOLIDARITY AND UNITY IN RESISTANCE TO THE ENEMY' in 1937, S. was largely suspended for the duration of war with Japan.

Soviet Man See NEW COMMUNIST MAN.

Soviet of Nationalities One of the two equal chambers of the legislature constituting the SUPREME SOVIET of the USSR. Its members are elected with a view to giving sufficient representation to Union Republics and other constituent nationalities. The total membership of the S.N. is 750 – 32 from each of the 15 Union Republics, 11 from each of the 20 Autonomous Republics, 5 from each of the 8 Autonomous Regions and 1 from each of the 10 National Areas.

Soviet of People's Commissars The official designation of the Council of Ministers in the USSR at All-Union, Union Republic and Autonomous Republic levels up to March 1946. The designation was introduced immediately after the October Revolution in 1917, to stress that the new government was established by the will of the Soviets (representing the masses) and that government departments were no longer headed by traditional bourgeois ministers, but by people's representatives. Since 1946, Soviet of Ministers (in Russian abbreviated to *Sovmin*) or Council of Ministers has been used instead, as the previous name caused confusion and misunderstanding among foreigners.

Soviet of the Union One of the two equal chambers of the legislature (the other being the SOVIET OF NATIONALITIES) in the SUPREME SOVIET of the USSR. It is elected every four years by citizens 18 years of age and over and consists of 767 deputies (one to 300,000 electors). It represents the common interests of the people, irrespective of their nationality, and roughly corresponds to the lower chamber of parliament in other countries.

Soviet Order No. 1 The first ordinance issued by the PETROGRAD SOVIET OF WORKERS' AND SOLDIERS' DEPUTIES at its first Joint Plenum on 1 March 1917 (O.-S.C.), lifting the obligation of the Petrograd troops to obey officers' orders. The Order was drafted by M. I. Sokolov, a MAKSIMALIST and a Bolshevik sympathizer, in a committee consisting of soldiers and one sailor. It also abolished saluting of officers off duty and gave power to soldiers' committees to control the distribution of all weapons. The Order was issued in reply to the Duma Committee, supporting the PROVISIONAL GOVERNMENT after the FEBRUARY REVOLUTION, which endeavoured to restore the old military discipline and use the Petrograd garrison for suppressing disorderly activities (especially by the Bolsheviks). But the Bolsheviks prevailed upon the P.S. for the inclusion of soldiers as deputies and to sanction the introduction of the elected Soldiers' Committees into all units. The Order decreed that soldiers would obey only the S.W.S.D. or their own Soldiers' Committees. It thus deprived the Duma, for the time being, of using the Petrograd garrison against the Bolsheviks and undermined military discipline in general.

Soviet Patriotism A concept applied to the form of PATRIOTISM developed in the USSR, claimed to be consistent with Marxist ideology. The official interpretation stresses its proletarian background made possible by the victory of the GREAT OCTOBER SOCIALIST REVOLUTION, the elimination of exploitation of man by man and the abolition of the oppression of national minorities. It is further held that S.p. combines national traditions with the ideological, social, economic and security interests of all the nationalities in the USSR and, by its cohesion and strength, serves the interests of international communism. Lenin himself (in 'On the National Pride of Great Russians', 1 Dec. 1914 and 'The Socialist Fatherland is in Danger', 21 Feb. 1918) was in favour of 'All-Russian' patriotism. But the cause of S.p. was developed to its peak under Stalin, especially during the GREAT PATRIOTIC WAR 1941–45 (highlighted in Stalin's *On the Great Patriotic War of the Soviet Union*, 1945). In 1944, the USSR introduced her national anthem, in which Soviet 'Fatherland' and victories are glorified (before that, the USSR used the *INTERNATIONALE*, the anthem of the COM-

INTERN). The opponents of communism, especially the Soviet version, point out that national patriotic feelings in the USSR are suppressed, as illustrated by discrimination against (incl. mass deportations of) Estonians, Latvians, Lithuanians, Jews, Kazakhs, Tartars, Ukrainians and others. Some see S.p., in fact, as a continuation of Tsarist CHAUVINISM and imperialism.

Soviet Russia A vague term which has been used in three different senses: 1. a short version of the RUSSIAN SOVIET FEDERATED SOCIALIST REPUBLIC, the largest of the 15 Union Republics in the USSR; 2. a short name for the Soviet state, including not only the R.S.F.S.R. but also other Republics, between 25 Oct. 1917 (the Bolshevik Revolution) and 30 Dec. 1922 (the official adoption of the present name of the country, the Union of the Soviet Socialist Republics); and 3. a colloquial name for the country under the Soviet regime since 25 Oct. 1917 (O.S.C.), irrespective of its official name (in contrast to Tsarist Russia).

Soviets of Workers', Peasants' and Soldiers' Deputies The councils or committees consisting of representatives elected by the popular vote which appeared in Russia after the FEBRUARY REVOLUTION OF 1917. They emerged as a rival source of power undermining the DUMA and the PROVISIONAL GOVERNMENT. Bolshevik representatives became the most active element in the S.W.P.S.D. and, with the aid of the LEFT SOCIALIST REVOLUTIONARIES, most Soviets became the carriers of the revolution. The Soviets held their Congresses, representing their highest level of authority, roughly twice a year (ALL-RUSSIAN CONGRESS OF SOVIETS). In the first Congress, held in Petrograd (now Leningrad) 3–24 June 1917, the Bolsheviks were in a minority, but gained a majority in the second Congress held on 25 Oct. 1917 which formally approved the Bolshevik seizure of power. In the events leading to the Bolshevik victory in the GREAT OCTOBER SOCIALIST

REVOLUTION, the PETROGRAD SOVIET, with its Military Revolutionary Committee, played the crucial part. In 1922, the A.-U.R.C.S. assumed the name of the All-Union Congress of Soviets.

Soviet Union An abbreviated form of the UNION OF THE SOVIET SOCIALIST REPUBLICS.

Sovkhoz A syllabic abbreviation in Russian of *Sovetskoe khoziaistvo*, meaning 'state farm'. All its means of production (land, farm buildings, equipment, improvements), and output belong to the state, and the persons working on it are state employees remunerated in wages. In contrast to *kolkhozes*, s. are mostly found on the confiscated land formerly owned by large landlords, in areas where *kolkhozes* are unsuccessful, in new farming regions (such as the VIRGIN LANDS) or are operated as experimental stations or model farms. In the late 1970s, there were about 18,000 s. in the USSR, each averaging about 13,000 hectares and embracing some 60 per cent of the farming area in the country.

Sovmin A syllabic abbreviation of *Sovet Ministrov*, in Russian meaning the 'Council of Ministers', which in March 1946 replaced the previous abbreviated designation *SOVNARKOM*. The S. consists of 73 members and is headed by a Chairman, i.e. Prime Ministers (N. A. Tikhonov). assisted by a First Vice-Chairman (I. V. Arkhipov), nine Vice-Chairmen, 62 Ministers (incl. Chairmen of the State Planning Commission, the State Construction Committee, the State Committee for Material and Technical Supply and the State Committee for Science and Technology) plus Chairmen of 12 other USSR Committees, 2 Chairmen of the State Bank and of the Central Statistical Board, and 15 Chairmen of the Union Republics' Councils of Ministers.

Sovnarkhoz The Russian syllabic abbreviation of *Sovet Narodnogo Khoziaistva*, meaning the 'Council of the National

Economy'. The S. system was first created in Soviet Russia after the October Revolution of 1917 within the framework of the Supreme Council of the National Economy (*VESENKHA*), which was in operation up to 1932. Then, economic administration was taken over by Ministries, each being responsible for a particular branch throughout the country. This led to over-centralization and bureaucratic waste. In 1957, Khrushchev revived the previous system of the S. on a distinctly regional basis. Under the new system, the powers and total number of Ministries were drastically reduced and much of their economic responsibility transferred to the *Sovnarkhozy*, which became organs of administration concerned with all industry and construction in their respective regions. But agriculture, transport and retail trade were outside their scope of authority. The work of the S. was supervised by the Council of Ministers in each Union Republic and by the 'USSR Council of the National Economy' established in Nov. 1962 (mainly to resolve disputes among the S.). The USSR C.N.E. was subordinated to the Supreme Council of the National Economy, created in March 1963. But the new system introduced cumbersome duplication and, after the fall of Khrushchev in Nov. 1964, it was abolished and the pre-1957 set-up was restored.

Sovnarkom The Russian syllabic abbreviation of *Sovet Narodnykh Komissarov*, meaning the 'Council of People's Commissars'. It was the official designation of the Council of Ministers in Soviet Russia and then the USSR from 1917 to 1946. Since March 1946 the S. has been replaced with the *SOVMIN* (*Sovet Ministrov*), meaning the 'Council of Ministers' to avoid misunderstanding among foreigners.

Sovznak The name of a currency issued by the Soviet Government over the period 1917–24. It was an abbreviated version of *Sovetsky znak*, meaning 'Soviet token' and was meant to replace the ROUBLE in a step towards the elimination of money. However, owing to the monetary chaos, inflation, and even hyperinflation (Dec. 1921–Jan. 1924), the *S.* was replaced by treasury notes, the name 'rouble' was rehabilitated and monetary discipline re-established.

Soyuz Pipeline Another name for the FRATERNITY (GAS) PIPELINE (*Soyuz* in Russian meaning 'fraternity').

Sozialistische Einheitspartei Deutschlands SOCIALIST UNITY PARTY OF GERMANY.

Space and Time Two concepts of philosophical importance which have been a subject of ideological controversy. In philosophical IDEALISM, s.a.t. are denied real existence and are regarded merely as creations of human consciousness. Similarly, in METAPHYSICS, the existence of matter is considered separate from its forms of existence, i.e. s.a.t. On the other hand, in Marxist HISTORICAL MATERIALISM and DIALECTICAL MATERIALISM, s.a.t. are treated as two basic and inseparable forms of existence of matter. Engels insisted (in *ANTI-DÜHRING*) that 'one cannot exist without the other'. Lenin (in *MATERIALISM AND EMPIRIO-CRITICISM*) argued that in this world there is nothing but 'moving matter', which as such must have the dimensions of s.a.t. Both Engels and Lenin emphasized that s.a.t. exist objectively, i.e. independently of man's consciousness and are infinite, i.e. space is endless and time is eternal. These propositions dispose of the need to have god, as there is neither a beginning (Creation) nor an end (Last Judgment).

Spanish Civil War (July 1936 – March 1939) Armed struggle between FASCISM and left-wing groups, in which the latter were defeated. At the elections of Feb. 1936, left-wing political parties (united electorally in the POPULAR FRONT) won a large majority and the Republican Government embarked upon far-reaching social reforms. A right-wing reaction (Nationalists), urged by high-ranking officers, landowners, industrialists and clergy and led by Gen. F. Franco, set out to overthrow the Republicans in favour of the Italian-style fascism. The Nationalists were given support by Fascist Italy and Nazi Germany in the form of some 100,000 volunteer troops, equipment and (German) air support. The Republicans were aided by Soviet advisers, the INTERNATIONAL BRIGADES and some supplies. But Stalin's emissaries and the Spanish Communists were preoccupied more with combating anarchists and syndicalists than with fighting the Nationalists. At a critical time, Stalin decided to withdraw supplies and advisers and Barcelona (the anarchist centre) fell in Jan. 1939 and Madrid two months later. The casualties during the Civil War totalled 1.0m. people. A fascist mono-party system was firmly established and left-wing political parties were subsequently suppressed for more than a quarter-century. Also FIFTH COLUMN.

Spanish Communist Party COMMUNIST PARTY OF SPAIN.

Spanish Socialist Workers' Party (*Partido Socialista de Obreros Españoles*) A large left-wing political party affiliated to the SECOND INTERNATIONAL. Originally founded in 1879, it is now the second largest political party in the country (after the Union of the Democratic Centre). The Party was suppressed by the fascist regime for more than a quarter of a century, following the SPANISH CIVIL WAR 1936–39. At the first parliamentary election since that time, in June 1977, it won 118 (of the 350) seats in the Congress of Deputies and 35 (of the 248) seats in the Senate in conjunction with its regional ally, the Catalan Socialist Party. The S.S.W.P. stands for far-reaching nationalization, the extension of social welfare, the separation of church from state and the removal of foreign military bases from Spain. It is considered to be to the left of the mainstream of Western socialism. The Party's Secretary-General is Felipe Gonzales, a labour lawyer.

Spartacus (died in 71 B.C.) A gladiator in ancient Rome who led several slave uprisings against the Roman state, oppression and exploitation. In one year of his triumph, he rallied some 50,000 slaves and defeated Roman armies in two battles. At one stage he was using the crater of Vesuvius as his headquarters. His units were defeated in the battle of Strongoli (in Calabria, southern Italy) by Roman legions in 71 B.C., in which S., together with 40,000 slaves were slain. About 6,000 of his supporters in central Italy were captured and crucified along the road from Capua to Rome. Although for centuries S. was villified first in Roman and then in other Western literature, Marxists have rehabilitated him since the middle of the 19th c. and have idealized him as the first revolutionary leader. In Germany, in 1916, revolutionary Marxists formed the SPARTACUS LEAGUE, the forerunner of the German Communist Party.

Spartacus League A revolutionary Marxist organization formed in Jan. 1916 within the SOCIAL-DEMOCRATIC PARTY OF GERMANY. It stemmed from the SPARTACUS LEAGUE INTERNATIONAL created in the preceding year and included K. LIEBKNECHT, ROSA LUXEMBURG, F. MEHRING and CLARA ZETKIN. The League was named after SPARTACUS, a militant slave leader in ancient Rome. The League published a radical bulletin called *Spartacus Letters*, edited by K. Liebknecht. The League was strongly opposed to the war and its leaders were imprisoned by the German authorities. In 1917, the S.L. joined the Independent Social-Democratic Party of Germany and later sought alliance with the victorious Bolsheviks. The League became the nucleus for the GERMAN COMMUNIST PARTY (founded on 1 Jan. 1919). There is also a S.L. in the USA today, a student wing of the INTERNATIONAL MARXIST GROUP affiliated to the FOURTH INTERNATIONAL.

Spartacus League International A left-wing group of German social-democrats in existence from March to Dec. 1915. It organized anti-war demonstrations and propaganda and published a bulletin under the same name, to which its leaders, incl. K. LIEBKNECHT and ROSA LUXEMBURG, contributed. From Jan. 1916, it adopted the name of the SPARTACUS LEAGUE which became the nucleus of the German Communist Party.

Special China List A version of the Western STRATEGIC EMBARGO introduced in 1952 in application to the PR of China, the DPR of [North] Korea and later extended to the DR of [North] Vietnam. The S.Ch.L. was a much stricter form of export control than that applied to the European Socialist countries. In fact some countries, notably the USA, for a time barred all trade with the Asian Socialist countries. The List was compiled by Chin-Com (China Co-ordinating Committee), established in Paris in 1952. In 1958, the S.Ch.L. was dropped by most Western countries, but not by the USA, Australia, Taiwan, R. of [South] Korea and R. of [South] Vietnam until the early 1970s.

Specialization See DIVISION OF LABOUR, OCCUPATIONAL DIVISION OF LABOUR.

Speculation Buying at low prices in anticipation of selling at substantially higher prices under the conditions of above-normal risk. The objects of s. may be commodities, shares or foreign exchange. There are two types of s. – one which leads to the evening out of prices and another to accentuating price discrepancies and fluctuations and is disruptive to the economy. Marxists are critical of s. regarding it as an inevitable feature of capitalist free enterprise, motivated by selfish private profit. Marx attributed s. to the concentration of capital and the DECLINING PROFIT RATE. In the Socialist centrally planned economies, uncertainty can be partly eliminated by state planning, where there is less scope for s. and private s. is illegal. In some Socialist countries, a colloquial term 'socialist s.' is used to describe the practice of hoarding materials beyond the legally permissible levels, owing to the uncertainty of deliveries and prevalent shortages, typical of SELLERS' MARKETS.

Speech LABOUR THEORY OF LANGUAGE DEVELOPMENT.

'Spirit of Capitalism' A phrase coined by the German sociologist, Max Weber (1864–1920), in his best known book *The Protestant Ethics and the Spirit of Capitalism* (1904–05). Its idea referred to entrepreneurship, hard work and thrifty habits carrying their own intrinsic rewards as features of 19th c. capitalism, particularly in Protestant countries. It was accepted that the accumulation of wealth was more moral than excessive consumption, which favoured rapid growth of capital and the development of capitalism.

Spontaneity A view held in the working class movement and shared by evolutionary Marxists that the emancipation of the working class from capitalist exploitation and domination can be achieved by the workers themselves spontaneously, as a matter of natural historical development. The supporters of this view refer to the Marxian doctrine of HISTORICAL MATERIALISM, according to which the development of society proceeds more or less automatically and independently of man's will from one stage to another, in response to the material conditions of production called the MODE OF PRODUCTION. The workers should concentrate their attention on industrial matters relying on trade unions and steering away from political activities, as the latter only slows down progress and their gains. Consequently, there is no need for a disciplined communist party and revolutionary action. This view was partly evident in the FIRST INTERNATIONAL and held predominantly in the SECOND INTERNATIONAL. However, s. is rejected by revolutionary Marxists, as exemplified by Lenin (in *What Is To Be Done?*, 1902), when he attacked ECONOMISM in the RUSSIAN SOCIAL-DEMOCRATIC LABOUR PARTY.

Spontaneous Materialism NATURAL MATERIALISM, SPONTANEITY.

Sportintern An international communist organization in existence from 1921 to 1935 for the purpose of winning sportsmen of proletarian background to the communist cause. The S. is a short international name derived from the Russian *Krasnyi Sportivnyi Internatsional*, meaning 'Red Sport International'. The S. was a section of the COMINTERN and was founded at the latter's third Congress in Moscow in July 1921. In addition to its general purpose, the S. recruited security guards for protecting communist meetings and leaders and for disrupting anti-communist demonstrations and rallies. At its peak of influence, in 1929, the S. had about 2.2m. members, mainly in the USSR (2.0m.), Czechoslovakia, Norway, France, Sweden, Argentina and Uruguay. Its official organ was *Der internationale Arbeiter – Sport (International Workers' Sport)*, published in Berlin. The S. was dissolved by the Comintern in 1935 in the interest of anti-fascist and anti-Nazi unity, represented politically by the POPULAR FRONTS.

Sputnik Russian word for 'travelling companion'. In popular usage, the term is applied to the artificial earth satellites, especially *Sputnik I, Sputnik II* and *Sputnik III* which the USSR launched on 4 Oct. 1957, 3 Nov. 1957 and 15 May 1958 respectively. *S. I*, the first artificial satellite launched in history, preceded the first US launching (*Explorer I*) by more than three months. In 1972, the member countries of the COUNCIL FOR MUTUAL ECONOMIC ASSISTANCE established *Intersputnik*, an organization based in Moscow and responsible for the operation of satellite communications.

SR Abbreviation for SOCIALIST REVOLUTIONARIES (in Russia).

Sri Lanka Communist Party An active party with widely fluctuating influence. It can trace its origin to 1935, when the Ceylon Equality Party was founded with

Trotskyite leanings, but was dissolved by the British colonial government in 1942. In the following year, the Ceylon Communist Party was founded with Stalinist leanings and in 1946 the C.E.P. was revived. In 1964 the C.C.P. split into pro-Soviet (majority) and pro-Chinese (minority) factions, while the C.E.P. changed its name to the Revolutionary C.E.P. In 1968, the two parties, together with the Social Democratic Freedom Party, created an electoral united front. At the 1970 elections, the communists won 19 (of the 187) seats and joined the coalition government of Mrs. Sirimavo Bandaranaike, leader of the S.D.F.P. After the name of the country was changed to Sri Lanka in 1972, it replaced 'Ceylon' in the official party designations, while the R.C.E.P. has now become the Lanka Sama Samaja Party. In the same year, the pro-Chinese faction formed the Communist Party of Sri Lanka (Marxist-Leninist). There are now three communist parties in the country, the S.L.C.P. being the largest with about 5,000 members (and the other two about 1,000 each). At the 1977 elections, although the communist polled 5 per cent of the votes cast, they won no parliamentary seats. The S.L.C.P. publishes two newspapers, *Samasama-jaya* (*Egalitarian Society*) and *Janadina* (*People's Daily*) and two bulletins, *Aththa* (*Torch*) and *Forward*.

SShA The abbreviation of the Russian name of the United States of America, viz. *Soedinennye Shtaty Ameriki.*

Stages of Growth Theory A theory put forward by the American economist W. W. Rostow (1916–), originally at Cambridge University in 1958 and subsequently developed further in his book *Stages of Economic Growth: The Non-Communist Manifesto* (1960). He distinguished six stages in the economic and social development of societies (with dates in application to England): 1. the traditional society (up to about 1650); 2. preconditions for take-off (1650–1783); 3.

take-off (1783–1802); 4. drive to maturity (1802–42); 5. economic maturity (1842–1935); and 6. the age of mass consumption (1935–). Rostow's theory was directed against Marxian SOCIO-ECONOMIC FORMATIONS. His point was that industrialization and technological progress must inevitably lead to affluence and produce similar institutions and mentality, irrespective of the existing political system. In his view, when the Socialist countries reach the 'age of mass consumption', the masses will become less militant and there will be no need for capitalism to be followed by socialism and communism.

Stakhanov, Alexei Grigorevich (1905–77) A Soviet miner who distinguished himself in the 1930s by a very high work performance. From 1927 on he worked in the Donets Basin coal mines and soon proved himself to be a hard-working and resourceful coal face miner. In one shift, in Aug. 1935, he cut 102 tons of coal (when the norm was 7 tons) and 227 tons in Sep. 1935. His work achievements, which were made possible by support from the authorities, were given widespread publicity, were embraced by the Party as a device for stepping up official work norms (especially during 1936–39) and led to the nationwide STAKHANOV MOVEMENT. There were rumours in the USSR at the time that S. was not a real worker but a fictitious person created by the Party to suit the Soviet state's campaign for raising output and productivity. But in fact he did exist. S. was admitted to the Party in 1936 (without the usual probationary period), elected deputy to the Supreme Soviet in 1937, but faded away from the public limelight after W.W.II. Similar 'Stakhanovites' were given official publicity in other branches of the economy in the USSR, viz. A. Kh. Busygin – in the vehicle industry, P. F. Krivonos – transport, V. S. Musinsky – timber industry, N. S. Smetana – footwear industry, E. V. and M. I. Vinogradova – textile industry, plus P. N. Angelina, K. A. Borin and M. S. Demchenko in agriculture.

Stakhanov (or Stakhanovite) Movement, or Stakhanovism A drive initiated by the authorities in the USSR in the mid-1930s, designed to raise the levels of output and labour productivity in the economy. It was named after A. G. STAKHANOV, an outstanding coalminer in the Donets Basin. An All-Union Stakhanov Conference was organized by the government in the Kremlin in Nov. 1935 which called for spreading S. to all major branches of the economy. In the same year, Stakhanovite schools began to be set up to cultivate work discipline, to teach the workers how to exceed and maximize production targets, how to avoid waste and how to improve quality. The Movement attained its highest intensity over the period 1936–39, when official norms were raised substantially (in 1936, 1937 and 1939), thus helping the implementation of the five-year plans. After W.W.II the term S.M. was not used but its idea is still carried on by the BRIGADES OF COMMUNIST LABOUR. The title of 'Stakhanovite' is still awarded to outstanding workers.

Stalin, Josip Vissarionovich (1879–1953) A Soviet leader and the dictatorial ruler of the USSR for a quarter of a century until his death. Born to a poor peasant family in Georgia (his father became a shoemaker), S.'s original name was J. V. Dzhugashvili. Sent to be educated for the priesthood, he was later expelled in 1899 for communist activities. He then turned into a professional revolutionary, was sent several times to Siberia and used different assumed names, including that of Stalin, from 1912 onwards. After the split in the RUSSIAN SOCIAL-DEMOCRATIC LABOUR PARTY in 1903, he sided with Lenin supporting the BOLSHEVIKS and in 1912 became the editor of PRAVDA. Although he participated in the GREAT OCTOBER SOCIALIST REVOLUTION, he played a minor role under Trotsky. After the Revolution, S. was appointed Commissar (Minister) for Nationalities. In 1922 he became the Party Secretary, the post he held till his death. He proved to be a skilful organizer and a cunning political manipulator. After Lenin's death (Jan. 1924) he gradually eliminated left-wing and right-wing rivals (led by TROTSKY and BUKHARIN, respectively) and further eliminated his critics and potential rivals in the GREAT PURGES of the 1930s. His dictatorial powers were further increased in 1941 when he became the Chairman of the Council of People's Commissars (Prime Minister), Chairman of the State Defence Committee and Generalissimo. Through his capable and ruthless leadership, he became identified by the Soviets and Western Allies as the architect of victories over Germany and of successful communist revolutions in Eastern Europe and, to some extent, in China and North Korea. After W.W.II. S. became an object of the PERSONALITY CULT and, after 1948, a symbol of the COLD WAR. He died in circumstances which are still shrouded in mystery. The quality, not the magnitude, of his impact on Soviet and world history has been a subject of controversy. Under his leadership, economic planning was introduced to great effect, the USSR was transformed from a backward agricultural country into a dynamic semi-industrial power, Nazi Germany was defeated and at least 10 other countries in Eastern Europe and Asia joined the Marxist community of nations. On the other hand, he was denounced as an unnecessarily cruel and paranoiac dictator, especially by Khrushchev (KHRUSHCHEV'S SECRET SPEECH), his indirect successor. S. was at first buried in LENIN'S MAUSOLEUM, but in 1961 his remains were removed to a grave along the Kremlin's wall nearby. S.'s major works are: *Marxism and the National and Colonial Question* (1912–13); *Problems for Leninism* (1926); *on Dialectical and Historical Materialism* (1938); *ON MARXISM AND LINGUISTICS* (1949); and *ECONOMIC PROBLEMS OF SOCIALISM IN THE USSR* (1952). Also DE-STALINIZATION, DOCTORS' PLOT, RE-STALINIZATION, STALINISM.

Stalingrad The official name of the Soviet city on the lower Volga, about 800 km. south-west of Moscow, from 1925 to

1961. During the Civil War, it was a scene of fighting between the Bolshevik and White armies (especially in 1918–19), where Stalin distinguished himself as one of the military organizers. The name S. replaced that of Tsaritsyn (originally founded in the 16th c.). From July 1942 to Feb. 1943, S. was the theatre of one of the fiercest and most decisive battles of W.W.II. where German, Romanian and Hungarian armies were encircled by G. Zhukov and defeated. The Battle of S. proved to be the turning point of the war on the Eastern Front. The city was almost completely destroyed, but magnificently rebuilt after the war. During the process of DE-STALINIZATION, in 1961 S. was renamed Volgograd, which in the late 1970s had 850,000 inhabitants. It is a major industrial centre, noted for metallurgical works, machine building, tractor works, shipbuilding, chemicals, food processing and woodworking.

Stalinism The dictatorial and repressive system of government, associated with the rule of J. V. STALIN in the USSR from 1929 to 1953. The term was never used officially in the USSR under Stalin, as he himself emphasized that the system he developed was Leninism. The term has been used in the West in a critical sense since the GREAT PURGES of the 1930s and in the USSR after the denunciation of Stalin in KHRUSHCHEV'S SECRET SPEECH in Feb. 1956. S. was noted for the following features: 1. the absolute and repressive DICTATORSHIP OF THE PROLETARIAT exercised by one person (Stalin); 2. the ruthless elimination of rivals in the top Party leadership and the elimination of actual or potential opposition leaders; 3. the extensive use of the secret police and terror (incl. FORCED LABOUR CAMPS); 4. the extreme disregard for human rights and the rule of law; 5. in the economic sphere, the CENTRALIZED DIRECTIVE SYSTEM OF PLANNING AND MANAGEMENT; 6. SOCIALISM IN ONE COUNTRY, as opposed to Trotsky's PERMANENT REVOLUTION; 7. the exploitation of foreign communist parties to serve the expedient interests of the USSR;

and 8. the PERSONALITY CULT. Also, DE-STALINIZATION, RE-STALINIZATION.

Stalin Prizes The official name given to the LENIN PRIZES over the period 1939–56.

Stalin's Constitution The Constitution of the USSR prepared under the guidance of STALIN in the atmosphere of the GREAT PURGES and adopted in 1936. Stalin described it as 'the most democratic constitution in the world'. It replaced the Soviet Constitution of 1922 (prepared under the guidance of Lenin) and in turn was replaced by that of 1976 Constitution (worked out under Brezhnev's guidance).

Stalin's Organs A colloquial term used in military circles for Soviet multiple, rapid-firing rocket launchers, employed during and after W.W.II. Their early version resembled male sexual organs, while in a more developed form the multiple barrels (about 40 in number) and the firing sound resemble church organs and their resonance. The term has been revived in Africa for the model 122 BM-21, supplied by the USSR to several African countries in the late 1970s.

Stambolysky, Aleksander (1879–1923) A Bulgarian revolutionary peasant leader, who established a republican government in his country over the period 1919–23 and introduced far-reaching agrarian and social reforms. Over the four years as Prime Minister, he exercised dictatorial powers and shifted the tax burden from the peasants to the urban classes. He was assassinated on 14 May 1923 in a successful right-wing coup. But his name survived in folk legends for many years.

Standing Committee A short name in China for the S.C. of the Central Committee of the CHINESE COMMUNIST PARTY. It is the top Party policy-making body, also described as the Politburo Standing Committee or sometimes as the Party Presidium. It consists of the five most senior Party leaders – the Chairman and four

Vice-Chairmen. Its members, as elected by the Central Committee at the 11th National Party Congress in August, 1977 are: HUA KUO-FENG (Chairman and Prime Minister); TENG HSIAO-PING (Deputy Prime Minister); Yeh Chien-Ying (Defence Minister); Li Hsien-mien; and Wang Tung-hsin. The Politburo, elected by the C.C. at the same Congress, had 23 full and 3 alternate members.

State, The A society's sovereign organ of administration, equipped with an administrative apparatus, police, courts and armed forces to maintain internal law and order and external security. In Western democracies, the s. is usually regarded as a neutral institution enforcing law and order, a guarantor and carrier of social justice and in particular, a protector of the weak and disadvantaged. But some view it as a dangerous political, economic and social institution threatening freedom and individualism. On the other hand, Marxists consider the s. as a passing historical phenomenon exploited by the ruling class to suppress other classes. Engels (in *The ORIGIN OF THE FAMILY, PRIVATE PROPERTY AND THE STATE*) concluded that the s. appeared as a consequence of the emergence of the private ownership of the means of production. Marx (in *A CONTRIBUTION TO THE CRITIQUE OF POLITICAL ECONOMY*) identified the s. with the dominant element of the SUPERSTRUCTURE critically conditioned by the stage of development of the material BASE. Historically, Marxists distinguish five major types of the s.: 1. the autocratic s. of slave society; 2. the aristocratic s. of feudal society; 3. the bourgeois democratic state under CAPITALISM; 4. the s. of the DICTATORSHIP OF THE PROLETARIAT under early SOCIALISM following the PROLETARIAN REVOLUTION; and 5. the 'STATE OF THE WHOLE PEOPLE' under developed socialism. As Lenin pointed out (in *The STATE AND REVOLUTION*), while the s. reaches the highest degree and extent of power under socialism (to fight internal counter-revolution and external attack from the hostile capitalist countries), FULL COMMUNISM will see the 'withering away' of the s. At that stage, society will advance 'from government over people to the administration of things' (Engels).

State and Revolution, The One of Lenin's best known books, written in Aug. – Sep. 1917. It consists of five chapters and represents a classical Marxist statement on the role of the state in different stages of society's development, especially under capitalism, socialism and communism. L. largely drew on the ideas of Marx and Engels and the revolutionary experience of 1848 and 1870 in France (in Part II he intended to discuss the lessons of the Revolution of 1905–07 and the February Revolution of 1917 in Russia, but the pressure of other work did not allow him). L. points out that the state emerged with the division of society into antagonistic social classes and that it became an instrument of oppression in the hands of the exploiting ruling class. He maintains that in the transition from capitalism to socialism, the bourgeois state must be destroyed in a violent PROLETARIAN REVOLUTION, to facilitate the construction of the socialist state. Under socialism, i.e. the lower phase of communism, the state becomes an instrument of the DICTATORSHIP OF THE PROLETARIAT for the elimination of the exploiting classes, for fighting COUNTER-REVOLUTION and for defending the new society from bourgeois attacks. The state will 'wither away' under FULL COMMUNISM, when the Marxian ideal of work and distribution is attained, viz. 'from each according to his work, to each according to his needs'. L.'s book was directed against both revisionists (who rejected the need for a violent revolutionary overthrow of the bourgeois state) and anarchists (who denied that there was a need for the state after the revolution).

State Capitalism A term used by Marxists to denote the different forms of state participation in the economy. 1. In developed capitalist countries, s.c. indicates substantial state intervention in economic activities, especially those involving key in-

566

dustries. Marxists do not welcome this involvement, as in their view the state still basically represents the ruling bourgeois class and s.c. merely delays the need for a proletarian revolution. The extreme case of s.c. is STATE MONOPOLY CAPITALISM. 2. In the early stages of socialism (after the proletarian revolution), s.c. refers to co-ownership of enterprises by the state and former private owners with the state becoming the dominant partner. *Elementary* s.c. refers to private shops handling the distribution of state-produced goods, while *advanced* s.c. involves the state ownership of capital with the proviso that former owners may act as managers. 3. In a critical sense, as used by Yugoslav communists, syndicalists and anarchists, s.c. indicates the replacement of private capitalism by the monolithic and ubiquitous state. The USSR is cited as the case in point. They emphasize that this system makes little difference to the worker, as he merely exchanges one type of capitalist for another.

State Committee for Material and Technical Supplies A Soviet state organization, concerned with the supply of intermediate products to enterprises and workshops. It was created in 1965 as the main instrument of inter-branch co-ordination. It controls all central distribution boards and distributes some 25,000 products through 21 central planning boards, employing about 600,000 persons.

State Council In China, the name of the extended Council of Ministers. In the late 1970s, it consisted of the Prime Minister, 10 Vice-Premiers, 28 Ministers and 110 Vice-Ministers. Under the 1975 Constitution, the number of specific functions was reduced from 17 to 5, viz.: 1. the issue of administrative measures, decrees and orders; 2. the co-ordination of policies involving different ministries, commissions and local state organs; 3. the drafting and implementation of the national economic plan; 4. the preparation of the state budget; and 5. the direction of state administration. In some European Socialist

countries (Bulgaria, the German DR, Poland and Romania), the S.C. is the top executive body of the parliament.

State Economic Commission (of the Council of Ministers of the USSR for Current Planning of the National Economy) *GOSEKONOMKOMISSIYA.*

State Economic Council (in the USSR) *GOSEKOMSOVET.*

State Defence Committee A powerful body in the USSR responsible for the conduct of W.W.II. It was created on 30 June 1941 (a week after the German attack) and was headed by Stalin himself. Its members were appointed by the Central Committee of the ALL-UNION COMMUNIST PARTY (OF THE BOLSHEVIKS), the PRESIDIUM OF THE SUPREME SOVIET and the COUNCIL OF PEOPLE'S COMMISSARS.

State Duma DUMA.

State Farms In the Socialist countries, farms owned and managed by the state. Those who work on s.f. are state employees receiving remuneration in wages. As such, they contrast with COLLECTIVE FARMS. S.f. were mostly formed from large estates formerly owned by large land-owners and are generally larger and more mechanized than collective farms (except in Bulgaria and the German DR). S.f. are more amenable to central planning than collective farms and many act as experimental stations or model farms. In the USSR, there are 18,000 s.f., each with (on the average) 13,000 hectares of land and 10,000 head of cattle. Ideologically, s.f. are considered to be superior to collective farms.

State Foreign Trade Monopoly The sole legal right of the state to conduct foreign trade to the exclusion of private enterprise. The monopoly is exercised, as a rule, by the ministry of foreign trade, while the actual export and import transactions are handled by relatively few and large FOREIGN TRADE CORPORATIONS.

Some designated enterprises may also be given permission to engage in exports or imports directly (especially in Czechoslovakia, the German DR, Hungary and Poland), but generally the s.f.t.m. is not infringed upon. The s.f.t.m. is enforced in all the Socialist bloc countries, except Yugoslavia where private entities may be licensed to engage in foreign trade (especially export). In most Socialist countries the s.f.t.m. is considered inevitable in view of the social ownership of the means of production (hence, foreign trade enterprises are socialized), central economic planning and the INSULATION OF DOMESTIC FROM FOREIGN MARKETS. The s.f.t.m. has also been introduced in Algeria, Burma and India.

State Intervention A term used in non-socialist countries for the active involvement of the state in the economic activities of the country. It is a reaction against *LAISSEZ-FAIRE* capitalism and may assume the following varied forms: 1. the modification of the operation of the market by influencing supply or/and demand in desired directions; 2. the maintenance of high levels of employment by ensuring sufficient spending; 3. the administration of social welfare programmes; 4. the maintenance of controls over prices and monopolies; 5. the promotion of economic stability by varying the size and timing of public investment; 6. the pursuit of protectionist policies to develop or safeguard manufacturing industries; 7. the pursuit of economic planning, usually of an indicative, non-compulsory type; and 8. the nationalization of key enterprises or industries. While in developed capitalist countries s.i. is directed mostly towards maintaining economic stability and high levels of social welfare, in less-developed areas it is aimed primarily at accelerating economic development, especially industrialization.

State Machinery Centres State enterprises in Poland, providing mechanical services and equipment to collective and private farms on a commercial basis. They are similar to the MACHINE-TRACTOR STATIONS which existed in the USSR up to the late 1950s. S.m.c. lend agricultural machinery, tractors, vehicles and implements, together with qualified operators, and repair and maintain machinery and other equipment owned by the farms. The centres charge fees for their services at levels controlled by the state. Their responsibility is to extend the mechanization of agriculture within the framework of the economic plan and, in particular, to utilize the available machinery and equipment in the most economical way. There are about 350 s.m.c. with some 700 branches. They played a greater role up to the late 1950s, when they were also concerned with providing agricultural education and prodding peasants to collectivization. But since that time some land has been de-collectivized and, today, over 80 per cent of agricultural land is privately farmed. In many districts AGRICULTURAL CIRCLES have taken over the function of the s.m.c.

State Monopoly Capitalism A description used by Marxists for capitalism in its higher stage of economic development, noted for substantial state participation in the operation of the economy in alliance with monopoly capital. In the leading capitalist countries it is also identified with IMPERIALISM. The concept of s.m.c. and its theoretical foundations were elaborated upon by Lenin (in *IMPERIALISM: THE HIGHEST STAGE OF CAPITALISM*). In the industrialized Western countries, the stage of s.m.c. began in the last quarter of the 19th c., became more pronounced in the 1930s and has spread further since W.W.II. Lenin described it as the basis for rescuing ailing capitalism by a far-reaching state involvement, especially in those spheres which private capitalists do not find profitable enough. In his view, s.m.c. is necessitated by the GENERAL CRISIS OF CAPITALISM, which is noted for wide fluctuations, unemployment, inflation and various abuses by unscrupulous groups. By providing cheap public utilities (subsidized by the exploited masses as taxpayers) and large military contracts, the state enhances the profits of private monopolies. Marxists do not regard the state involvement as a welcome step towards socialism, but as a bourgeois stratagem to delay the need and chance of a proletarian revolution. The collusive co-operation of the bourgeois state with industrial and financial monopoly capital is directed towards suppressing the rising power of the working classes, COLONIALISM, NEO-COLONIALISM and aggressive wars against NATIONAL LIBERATION MOVEMENTS. Also MILITARY-INDUSTRIAL COMPLEX, MONOPOLY, STATE CAPITALISM.

'State of the Whole People' The official designation of the form of state power in the USSR after the abandonment of the DICTATORSHIP OF THE PROLETARIAT, announced at the 22nd Congress of the CPSU in Oct. 1961. The concept is also used now in a more general sense to describe the stage of development of socialism after the former 'exploiting classes' are eliminated, so that there are no longer antagonistic class relations.

State Planning Commission A general name of the central economic planning and management authority in the Socialist countries. Its precise official name may differ from one country to another. For example, in Hungary it is known as the National Planning Office, in the DPR of Korea – the Economic Planning Board, in Poland – the Planning Commission Attached to the Council of Ministers, in the USSR – the *Gosplan* and in Yugoslavia – the Federal Committee for Social Planning. The S.P.C. plays the leading role in the management and development of the economy and its chairman is an *ex-officio* member of the Council of Ministers. It co-operates closely with all the economic ministries and other state commissions, bureaus etc. which may be of service or otherwise relevant in the preparation and implementation of the economic plan. There are five specific functions of a S.P.C.: 1. determination of the criteria of economic calculation underlying planning decisions; 2. determination and quantifi-

cation of the targets to be reached in short, medium and perspective plan periods; 3. co-ordination of the targets to ensure the internal consistency of the plans; 4. determination of the general appropriate methods to ensure plan fulfilment; and 5. current revision of targets and methods according to changing circumstances. The S.P.C. has to work within the guidelines laid down by the Communist party, but otherwise it enjoys vast powers and its preferences are deemed to reflect social needs (planners' sovereignty in lieu of CONSUMERS' SOVEREIGNTY).

State Price Planning Commission The main organ for price determination in the Socialist countries. In addition to price fixing, its function is to collect information on costs, the desired directions of economic and social development, provide advice to higher authorities (the Council of Ministers, the State Planning Commission) and other bodies, including enterprises, which have the power to set their own prices. It may also be concerned with determining the criteria and conditions for price fixing by other authorized entities. Its powers are in fact limited, as the crucial issues of price policies are determined by the Communist party, the Council of Ministers and the State Planning Commission.

State–Private Enterprises See JOINT STATE–PRIVATE ENTERPRISES.

State Secrets Information of political, economic, technical or scientific content which is prohibited by the state to be transmitted to, or to be sought by, unauthorized persons. There are severe laws in the socialist countries on s.s. As the scope of operation of the state is so wide and the militia and the secret service organs are very well developed, their effect on the lives of the people and on the operation of the economy is wide-ranging. This produces an atmosphere of suspicion and intimidation. The laws on the violation of s.s. were particularly harsh in the first two decades after W.W.II in the USSR and

Eastern Europe and still largely apply in the Asian Socialist countries. There have been three adverse effects of the s.s. laws: 1. the protection of incompetent personnel in high positions controlling the availability of information; 2. the use of secrecy laws as a means of political as well as private intimidation; and 3. the inhibition of technical and economic progress, owing to the limited availability of information (especially between the military-space and civilian sectors) at the enterprise level.

State Socialism A substantial extent of state participation in the operation, ownership of the means of production and directions of development of the economy. But the concept has different meanings in different contexts. 1. To liberal socialists, such as Fabians, it means the nationalization of key industries, economic planning and the provision of generous social welfare schemes by the state. 2. To anarchists and syndicalists, s.s. is an abhorrent alternative to capitalism, as they see the state as an instrument of oppression, irrespective of the social system. 3. The concept is also sometimes used in application to the Socialist countries ruled by Communist parties, where the role of the state is at its maximum. The critics of s.c. regard it as a misnomer. They point out that under capitalism the state is still a bourgeois institution and, as such, is incompatible with true socialism. In the socialist countries, the inclusion of the qualification 'state' is superfluous, as socialism inextricably involves the existence of the state and cannot be otherwise.

State Theory of Money A theory originally put forward by E. Knapp (1842–1926) and F. Bendixen (1864–1920) in Germany and Austria in the earlier part of this century, according to which the fundamental determinant of the nature and value of money is the state by virtue of its legislation and monetary policies. Although Marxists agree that the state alone should issue currency and create bank money for the benefit of society, they point out several weaknesses of the theory, viz.: 1. the legal tender of the currency is limited only to the sovereign territory of the state; 2. the state cannot control the purchasing power in capitalist market economies, as is also the case in the Socialist centrally planned economies; and 3. where the state fixes the gold parity of its currency, it is usually meaningless, unless it reflects the purchasing power of the currency in terms of gold in (private) international markets.

State Trading The conduct of trade by the state in competition with, or to the exclusion of, private trading entities. It may apply to wholesale, retail or foreign trade. S.t. is a rule in the Socialist countries where wholesale and foreign trade are almost completely carried on by the state through specially created trading enterprises for the purpose, while retail trade is less completely dominated by the state. But in Yugoslavia, large proportions of retail and foreign trade are conducted by private enterprise. S.t. was rare before W.W.II (it existed chiefly in the Scandinavian and some East European countries), but has spread since the war. In the Western countries, it is still rather exceptional, and where it does exist it is pursued in association with state monopolies (tobacco and alcoholic beverages) and in the marketing of some agricultural products (especially grains, in Australia, Canada and the USA). S.t. is now widely practised in less-developed countries, particularly in the export of certain staple products (such as cocoa, coffee, cotton and oil). In some of these countries, such as Algeria, Burma and India, all foreign trade has been nationalized.

Static Marxists Also known as 'dogmatic' M., those who faithfully accept the system of ideas, precepts and practices as embodied in the writings of K. Marx, without attempting to modify them to suit particular conditions. It contrasts with DYNAMIC M., OPPORTUNISM and REVISIONISM. Also DOGMATISM.

Statism ETATISM.

Strakhovka (literally 'the margin of safety', in Russian) A term used in the USSR for the precautionary hoarding of raw materials, semi-finished products and components by enterprises, owing to the uncertainty of allocation and the unreliability of deliveries. This practice was widespread, not only in the USSR, but also in other Socialist countries before the economic reforms of the 1960s when the system of incentives unwittingly encouraged it (in Poland, the practice was called *chomikarstwo*, literally meaning 'hamstering'). *S.* amounts to tied and idle resources and, as such, further accentuates shortages and causes bottlenecks. To discourage this practice, the USSR introduced CAPITAL CHARGES in 1964 (following the example of Yugoslavia in 1953 and Hungary in 1964).

Strategic Arms Limitation Talks Drawn-out negotiations between the USA and the USSR on the mutual curtailment of the major sophisticated offensive and defensive weapon systems. The idea of S.A.L.T. had been accepted by the two countries in early 1967, but the actual talks (prompted by the United Nations Conference on Disarmament) were begun in Helsinki in 1969. The negotiations, later described as S.A.L.T. I, led to an agreement concluded in May 1972, mildly limiting the arms race in terms of volume but not necessarily quality. The negotiations were then resumed under the name of S.A.L.T. II and, in Nov. 1974, general guidelines on ceilings were agreed upon in the VLADIVOSTOK ACCORDS. The S.A.L.T. II agreement was signed in Vienna in June 1979, according to which the total number of strategic missiles and bombers is to be reduced on each side from 2,400 to 2,250 by 1981. It is understood that S.A.L.T. III will be pursued in the future.

Strategic Curtain A term sometimes used to describe the Western STRATEGIC EMBARGO against the Socialist bloc, paralleling the IRON CURTAIN.

Strategic Deterrent Doctrine Also known as the 'doctrine of realistic deterrent', a proposition put forward by the US Department of Defense in 1971. This defence strategy, directed against the USSR and other WARSAW PACT countries, postulated that the USA concentrate on the development of strategic systems of weapons, especially multiple-head ballistic missiles and Polaris missiles. At the same time, other NATO countries were to see to a further development of conventional armed forces. In the Warsaw Pact countries, the S.D.D. was seen as a new phase of the ARMS RACE.

Strategic Embargo A system of controls administered by Western countries on exports embodying advanced technology to the Socialist bloc (Yugoslavia excepted). The S.E. was first introduced by the USA in 1947 and was later adopted by most Western and some less-developed countries. Their policies were shaped by the Consultative Group established in 1949 and based in Paris, consisting of ambassadors from 15 Western countries, the NATO countries, less Iceland, plus Japan. But the actual strategic lists were worked and revised by CO-COM, established in Paris in 1949. There were typically three 'lists' – Munitions, Atomic Energy and Industrial. Stricter controls were introduced in 1952 on exports to China, the DPR of [North] Korea and later, the DR of [North] Vietnam and Cuba. This Special China List was determined by CHIN-COM. At its height, during the Korean War (1950–53), the Embargo included over 1,000 categories of items representing some 40 per cent of the items entering world trade. The US version of the Embargo has always been stricter and covers more items. In 1957, the Special China List was dropped by most countries (but not the USA), and since that time, the Embargo has been gradually relaxed in some seven major revisions. Although nominally still in force, the Embargo is no longer a significant factor impeding East-West trade. The adverse effect on the Socialist countries has proved to be negligible, but below the expectations of its Western advocates.

Strategy and Tactics Two related concepts, the distinction between which is considered to be of great importance in Communist theory, policy and practice. S. is concerned with the broad and long-range objectives of the Party in its progressive march to FULL COMMUNISM. On the other hand, t. are directed towards dealing with particular situations as they arise and as such are more varied and fluctuating according to changing circumstances. Consequently, it is accepted that for the sake of expediency the party may from time to time resort to tactical retreats, seemingly contradicting long-run strategic objectives. Tactical zigzagging may evoke internal opposition within the party. Active opposition to current party policies is called DEVIATIONISM and is considered to be a serious breach of party discipline, which may lead to expulsion and even harsher penalties. Party tactics must not be confused with OPPORTUNISM and REVISIONISM.

Strike A stoppage of work by organized labour directed towards the improvement of working or social conditions. The s. is a weapon of the working class developed under capitalism during and after the Industrial Revolution in the 19th c. The s. may assume different forms: simple (when workers merely do not turn up for work); passive sit-in (when they turn up but do not work); and picketed (when they prevent strike-breakers from entering their work place). With respect to its purpose, a s. may be purely economic (wages, penalty rates, hours of work, membership, and physical conditions of work) or political (protest against government policies or social conditions). As to its extent, it may be single (affecting one trade union), multiple (several unions, including a SYMPATHY S.) or a GENERAL STRIKE. Evolutionary Marxists regard the s. as the principal instrument at the disposal of the working class for the improvement of the conditions of work as well as for the develop-

ment of socialism. On the other hand, revolutionary Marxists treat the s. as a weapon of the CLASS STRUGGLE under capitalism, postulating that the s. should not merely be economic, but primarily political in content. The official attitude in the Socialist countries is that in the context of the social ownership of the means of production strikes are pointless and damaging to the interests of the workers themselves. In most of them striking is illegal. However, it is known that serious strikes have occurred in Czechoslovakia, the German DR, Hungary, Poland, Romania and Yugoslavia. In the Chinese Constitution of 1975, Article 28 guarantees the freedom of striking but this freedom can be exercised under the conditions of 'discipline, centralism, the leadership of the Communist Party and the dictatorship of the proletariat'.

Structural Functional Analysis FUNCTIONALISM.

Structural Planning The new approach to economic planning in the more advanced Socialist countries, not based on the traditional branch-of-the economy approach, but preoccupied with selected broad technological goals or problems. It is essentially directed towards modernization, specialization, concentration, quality improvement, industrial co-operation, applied research and innovations. The aim is to change the structure of the economy in favour of the most advanced and efficient industries, involving electronics, automation, synthetics, light metals, precision engineering, nuclear developments, containerized transport and the like.

Struggle-Criticism Transformation An educational reform campaign in China during the GREAT PROLETARIAN CULTURAL REVOLUTION, initiated by Mao Tse-tung in July 1968. Its purpose was to explain the correct meaning of Mao's ideological line, the issues involved to the masses and to eliminate FACTIONALISM. The campaign was implemented by 'Mao Tse-tung Thought Propaganda Teams' and was guided by the following six post- ulates: 1. Establish courses for the study of Mao's thought; 2. Be vigilant against anti-Mao elements endeavouring to seize power; 3. Enlist the support of the masses in exposing Mao's enemies; 4. Identify and discredit class enemies; 5. While carrying on the ideological struggle, do not allow production to be adversely affected; and 6. Foster the alliance between the RED GUARDS and the PEOPLE'S LIBERATION ARMY and guard against the emergence of multiple centres of leadership.

Struggle for Existence One of the principles of evolution put forward by Ch. R. Darwin (1809–82) according to which there is natural rivalry among individual organisms and the species to survive. The principle implies a large number of organisms of differing characteristics within a species compared with the means of subsistence (caused by the relative overproduction of spores, seeds, and eggs). Consequently, those individuals with the most suited characteristics in relation to the given environment have the best chance of survival, reproduction and the transmission of their characteristics to subsequent generations. Marxists are rather critical of the Darwinian proposition in application to the social sphere. They point out that in a class society the poor, even though they may be physically and mentally superior, have a lesser chance of survival than the rich. The latter are better equipped economically to shelter their offspring which promotes the survival of the unfit. In the biological sphere T. D. LYSENKO held that the competitive s. for e. applied to inter-species not intra-species relations. Also NATURAL SELECTION, SOCIAL DARWINISM.

Struggle of Opposites See OPPOSITES.

Struve, Piotr Bernhardovich (1870–1944) A Russian economist, philosopher, political leader and the chief representative of LEGAL MARXISM. Although he was initially interested in Marxism, he later became increasingly conservative. In his best known work, *Critical Notes on the Problems of Economic Development in Russia* (1894), he attacked the theories and proposals of the liberal NARODNIKS and stressed the need for the capitalist development of Russia. He was also one of the first Russian writers who criticized the Marxian theory of value and the postulate of the proletarian revolution. He believed that all social problems could be solved within the existing social system by gradual reforms. S. joined the KADETS and was elected to the DUMA in 1906. He was opposed to the Bolsheviks and, after the Revolution, participated in a counterrevolutionary movement in the south. S. was a member of the government forces led by A. I. DENIKIN and P. N. WRANGEL. After its total collapse he emigrated. Lenin subjected the ideas of S. to a severe criticism (in *The Economic Content of Narodnism and Its Criticism in the Book by Struve*) and accused him of supporting REVISIONISM.

St. Simonism SAINT SIMON.

Student Power A general name given to the movement which arose in the 1960s among students in Western countries, directed against some features of developed capitalism, viz. CONSUMERISM, ELITISM, BUREAUCRACY, MONOPOLIES, MILITARY-INDUSTRIAL COMPLEXES, RACISM, IMPERIALISM and NEO-COLONIALISM. In contrast to the traditional domination of universities by conservative right-wing elements, the student movement of the 1960s was an explosive left-wing protest incorporating MARXISM, TROTSKYISM, MAOISM and ANARCHISM as its distinguishing elements. The peak of s.p. was reached during 1967–68 and was linked with the protest against the VIETNAM WAR. The most influential movements were the National Union of French Students, the Socialist Union of German Students and STUDENTS FOR A DEMOCRATIC SOCIETY in the USA. Its main leaders were D. Cohn-Bendit, J. Sauvageot and A. Geismar in France, R. Dutschke in West Germany, T. Ali in Britain, while in the USA its chief ideological exponent was H. MARCUSE. S.p. was a spontaneous movement, poorly co-ordinated, in many cases more adventurist and extremist than systematic and disciplined. Also ALTERNATIVE SYSTEM, NEW LEFT, NIGHT OF THE BARRICADES, TWENTY-SECOND OF MARCH MOVEMENT.

Students for a Democratic Society A loose left-wing political organization in the USA created in 1962. It was the most characteristic expression of the NEW LEFT and the main source of STUDENT POWER in the USA. Its peak influence was reached in the late 1960s and the early 1970s, when its activities were directed mainly against the American involvement in the VIETNAM WAR. But basically it was a spontaneous reform movement, highlighting the weaknesses of American society exemplifying developed capitalism, especially the inequalities in the distribution of wealth and income, the concentration of power in elites, the disregard for human rights, racism and a myopic preoccupation with material consumption. Its membership, as reported in 1972, was 40,000. The Society disappeared as an organization in the early 1970s, but its work has been continued by some 10 splinter associations.

Subbotnik In the USSR, a day's work done on a voluntary basis for public benefit outside normal working hours, usually on a designated Saturday (*subbota* in Russian meaning 'Saturday'). This practice was initiated on Saturday 12 April 1919 when Party members organized voluntary work on the Moscow-Kazan railway line with Lenin's active support. It has grown into a national yearly event on a Saturday, immediately preceding the anniversary of Lenin's birth (22 April). The proceeds from the work go to a special fund and, each year, the Central Committee of the CPSU, the Council of Ministers and the All-Union Central Council of Trade Unions determine the public purpose for which the money is to be used (such as schools, children's welfare, and foreign aid). On 21 April 1979, 150m.

workers participated and contributed 825m. roubles. Three-quarters of the proceeds that year were devoted to the Vietnamese.

Subjective Idealism One of the two main directions in philosophical idealism (the other being OBJECTIVE IDEALISM). It regards consciousness of the individual person as the essence of existence and rejects the reality of the world external to man's mind. Laws in the real world are interpreted as creations of the knowing subject as his reason ascribes them to nature. The best known exponents of this view were G. Berkeley (1684–1753) and J. G. Fichte (1762–1814). S.i. is inconsistent with MATERIALISM and is rejected by Marxist philosophers as unscientific, maintaining that images and impressions of the external world are reliable and convincing reflections of the real world. In their view, only through this process is man capable of acquiring true knowledge and scientifically formulating the laws of nature.

Subjective Interpretation of History INDIVIDUALIST INTERPRETATION OF HISTORY.

Subjective Method in Sociology A phrase applied by Marxists to that interpretation of the historical development of society which attributes the decisive part to outstanding personalities. This interpretation denies, or at least minimizes, the role of economic factors in determining social development and, as such, is inconsistent with HISTORICAL MATERIALISM. The main Marxist objection to the subjective approach is that it denies the possibility of and need for the proletarian revolution on the initiative of the masses. Instead, it relies on terror against individual leaders of the oppressing ruling class. The s.m. in s. was subscribed to by the NARODNIKS in Tsarist Russia, for which they were severely criticized by Lenin (in *What the 'Friends of the People' Are and How They Fight the Social-Democrats*, 1894). Lenin's views on the subject were later elaborated upon by Stalin (in *Anarchism or Socialism?*, 1906–07). Significantly, the s.m. in s. is related to the PERSONALITY CULT.

Subjective School of Bourgeois Economics A description applied by Marxists to the classical and neo-classical economic theories emphasizing the role of psychological factors in economic analysis and behaviour. The economists concerned include K. Menger (1840–1921), E. Böhm-Bawerk (1851–1914), F. Wieser (1851–1926) and V. Pareto (1848–1922). The main features of this school which have attracted Marxist criticism are: 1. MARGINAL UTILITY; 2. INDIVIDUALISM; and 3. its approach to VALUE, wages and profits in isolation from the social system.

Subjectivism A stand in philosophy attributing the decisive role to the mind of the individual and not to external reality governed by its own laws. As such, it contrasts with OBJECTIVISM. In Marxist philosophy, s. is identified with the extreme version of idealism (SUBJECTIVE IDEALISM), is opposed to MATERIALISM and OBJECTIVE REALITY, and is largely, but not completely, rejected on ideological grounds. In the theory of knowledge (EPISTEMOLOGY) s. is criticized for being preoccupied with subjective images rather than the real object; Marxists point out that if this approach is accepted, man is incapable of gaining knowledge outside the impressions and constructions in his mind. In AESTHETICS, Marxists stress, the s. of the artist divorces him from the masses and his art. This contrasts with SOCIALIST REALISM, which attempts to render art comprehensible to the common man. But in ETHICS, Marxist philosophers accept that the concepts and content of 'good' and 'bad' are not absolute but relative to the individual, social groups and the stage of social development. They also recognize that in sociology, the individual's judgment and scale of preferences are determined subjectively, largely by class interests.

Submergence Hypothesis A theoretical proposition purporting to explain the relations between capitalist and Socialist systems in terms of the complete elimination of one by the other. The theory was subscribed to by a number of specialists in the field from the late 1940s to the late 1950s, who were convinced that in the long run there was room for only one system in the world. Western exponents argued that capitalism must win, owing to its democratic freedoms, higher living standards (on the whole), greater wealth, more rapid technological progress and military superiority. This, they argue, contrasts with the political repression, depressed standards of living, and national opposition to either Soviet or Chinese domination in the East. On the other hand, Eastern spokesmen have little doubt that socialism will emerge victorious owing to the greater political cohesion, more effective party and social discipline, continuous full employment, stability, rapid economic development and social justice in the Socialist bloc. They in turn compare this with disunity, unemployment, strikes, inflation, racial problems and social antagonism in the capitalist world. Historical development so far has not lent support to the hypothesis and by 1960 it had been abandoned in favour of the DIVERGENCE THESIS (and later the CONVERGENCE THESIS).

Subsidiary Plots In the Socialist countries, a piece of land allowed to peasants in collective farms and, in a few cases, to urban dwellers and officials in remote areas for privately growing vegetables, potatoes, fruit trees and raising farm animals (cows, pigs, sheep, and poultry). They are also known as household p., individual p., personal p. and (incorrectly) private p. The ownership of land is generally vested in the state (or some other social entity), but the plotholder has a guaranteed right of utilizing the land for his own (approved) purposes. The size of the plots is regulated by the state and is usually less than one hectare, mostly 0.5 hectare. Similarly, the number of animals is regulated by the state. The produce can be used for direct consumption or for private sale in the local market. S. plots constitute from 1.5 per cent (in the USSR) to 10 per cent (in Bulgaria and Hungary) of total agricultural land. They are cultivated with great care and devotion (in contrast to the socialized farms) and are very productive. In the USSR, they contribute more than 25 per cent of the agricultural output (although occupying only 1.5 per cent of the cultivated area). In China, they represent 5 per cent of agricultural land but produce 30 per cent of all vegetables in most areas. S.p. are considered ideologically to be transitional, to disappear under FULL COMMUNISM. In China, under the TACHAI CAMPAIGN, s.p. have been abolished.

Subsistence Level A term used in classical and Marxist political economy for the minimum amount of goods and services needed by a worker to maintain his working capacity and reproduce it (i.e. by supporting a family). This level may vary geographically and historically, depending on natural and social conditions. In the Marxist theory of distribution, the s.l. is called 'indispensable labour', representing the lower limit of the VALUE OF LABOUR POWER, while the margin above is described as 'surplus labour'. In Marx's view, wages under capitalism tend to be depressed to the s.l., owing to the superior bargaining power of the employers and enhanced by the increasing substitution of capital for labour and the consequent pool of unemployment (RESERVE ARMY OF WORKERS). Also the IRON LAW OF WAGES.

Subsistence Theory of Wages IRON LAW OF WAGES.

Substantive Convertibility of Money MONETARY AND SUBSTANTIVE CONVERTIBILITY.

Sub-Structure BASE.

Subversive Activities Control Board An anti-communist governmental agency in the USA, established at the height of the Cold War by the MCCURRAN-WOOD IN-TERNAL SECURITY ACT of 1950. The Board's function is to determine whether a particular suspect organization, as indicated by the Attorney-General, is of the 'communist-action', 'communist-front' or 'communist-infiltrated' type. If it falls into any of these categories, the organization has to provide current details of its membership, the sources of its income and the purposes of its expenditure to the Department of Justice. The members of such registered organizations may be subjected to discrimination, especially with respect to Federal employment and grants. However, the Board has been recently inoperative, owing to the reluctance of the Attorney-General to request the maintenance or initiation of the registration of suspect organizations.

Successive Approximations Process See TRIAL AND ERROR METHOD OF PRICE DETERMINATION.

Sudanese Communist Party A small illegal party with a chequered history. It was founded in 1947, but due to several limitations it had to operate partly underground. Its peak of influence was reached in the late 1960s, when it had two ministers in the government. It attempted a coup in 1971, which failed and since that time it has suffered from several waves of repression. Its estimated membership in the late 1970s was 3,000 (compared with the country's population of 17,700,000). Owing to its proscription, it has sought to work through several legal front organizations. In 1975, it entered into a united National Front (with the Unionist Party and the Moslem Brotherhood). In its international orientation the Party has supported the Moscow line (but in 1965 pro-Chinese dissidents formed a separate faction).

Sun Yat-Sen University for the Toilers of China The name of the foreign division of the COMMUNIST UNIVERSITY FOR THE TOILERS OF THE EAST from 1925 to 1929.

Superstructure One of the fundamental Marxian concepts denoting the totality of

576

philosophical, ethical, cultural, political and legal ideas, attitudes and the associated network of institutions and organizations in society. The s. is considered to reflect the thinking and interests of the ruling class and, together with the material BASE, constitutes a SOCIO-ECONOMIC FORMATION. The s. is not directly involved in production, but both Marx (mainly in *A CONTRIBUTION TO THE CRITIQUE OF POLITICAL ECONOMY*) and later, Stalin (in *ON MARXISM AND LINGUISTICS*), were most insistent on the correct interpretation of the relation between the s. and the base, viz. 1. The s. is directly determined by the base, indirectly reflecting changes in the development of PRODUCTION FORCES after the latter are modified. This sequence is important to revolutionary Marxists who reject the view (which they call VULGAR MATERIALISM) that the s. is directly derived from production. Thus, a given s. exists in a relatively short historical period, during which a particular base operates. 2. The s. is not passive, but actively participates in the development of the base and society. In a class society, the s. usually impedes the progressive development of the base in the interest of the ruling class, while under Socialism it is utilized on a planned basis to respond and even anticipate desirable changes in the base. In the latter case, the state plays an important part.

Supreme Council of the National Economy *VESENKHA*.

Supreme People's Assembly (*Choe Ko In Min Hoe Ui*) The unicameral parliament in the DPR of [North] Korea, consisting of 579 deputies elected from a single unopposed list of candidates prepared by the DEMOCRATIC FRONT FOR THE REUNIFICATION OF THE FATHERLAND. The deputies were elected for five years up to the elections of Nov. 1977, but since that time they are elected for four years. The Assembly's permanently sitting executive body is the Standing Committee, consisting of a Chairman, a Vice-Chairman, a Secretary and 11 Members.

Supreme Soviet The highest formal source of state power in the USSR and in each of the 15 Union Republics. The institution of the S.S. was created in 1936, having replaced the CENTRAL EXECUTIVE COMMITTEE. It is elected for four years by citizens of 18 years and over. At the All-Union level, the S.S. consists of two equal-ranking chambers: 1. the *SOVIET OF THE UNION*, to which deputies are elected on the basis of general population (roughly, 1 deputy to 300,000 electors), totalling 767 deputies; 2. the *SOVIET OF NATIONALITIES* elected by the member Republics and Regions, totalling 750 deputies. Sessions of the S.S. are convened twice a year. Between sessions the parliamentary work is performed by Standing Commissions, of which there are 15 in each chamber. The chief executive body of the S.S. is the PRESIDIUM OF THE SUPREME SOVIET, headed by the President of the USSR (L. Brezhnev, also the Party's Secretary-General) and including 53 other top deputies. The sessions of the S.S. are very short (2–3 days in six months) and are held to ratify decrees issued or drafted by the Council of Ministers. Although the S.S. theoretically corresponds to parliament in most capitalist countries, the resemblance is nominal not substantive, as state policies originate in the CENTRAL COMMITTEE OF THE CPSU and the COUNCIL OF MINISTERS OF THE USSR. Moreover, many legislative acts do not come before the S.S. as its sessions are too short and infrequent. Therefore, the principle of unanimity of voting is typically observed. At the Union Republic level there is only one chamber, the Soviet of the Republic, but otherwise, parliamentary procedures are similar to those at the All-Union level.

Surplus Labour A Marxian term denoting that portion of total labour which is devoted to the creation of SURPLUS VALUE, i.e. over and above the subsistence level of wages of the workers employed in material production (called INDISPENSABLE LABOUR). S.l. (*s*) constitutes the exploitation of labour in material production and is measured by its relation to indispensable labour (v), or, in Marxian symbols, s/v. It is claimed that in a Socialist society, s.l. is not exploitative and, in value terms, is described as PRODUCT FOR SOCIETY (used by the state for investment, including the accumulation of stocks and the maintenance of the NON-PRODUCTIVE SPHERE).

Surplus Labour Time A concept introduced by Marx (in *CAPITAL*, vol. I) to denote that period of time which is over and above INDISPENSABLE LABOUR TIME. In the s.l.t. (in material production), the worker creates SURPLUS VALUE, which in a capitalist society is appropriated by the capitalist. Under Socialism, surplus value created in material production is called 'product for society' and is used by the state for investment (including increase in stocks) and the support of the NON-PRODUCTIVE SPHERE.

Surplus Product A description of SURPLUS VALUE in application to the Socialist countries, to avoid the implication of exploitation. It represents that portion of the total value which is over and above the legitimate cost of production, viz. depreciation, materials used and wages.

Surplus Value One of the most fundamental concepts in Marxian political economy and ideology, in application to capitalism. It is that portion of the total value which is created by hired labour not paid in wages but appropriated by the capitalist employer. As such, s.v. constitutes the exploitation of the producer (the worker) by a non-producer (the capitalist). S.v. appears in three forms constituting non-labour income in capitalist society, viz. rent, interest and profits, enjoyed by landowners, leaseholders, bankers, traders and employing entrepreneurial capitalists. The idea of s.v. first appeared in the classical French and English writings of CH. S. DE SISMONDI and W. Thompson (1785–1833). But it was Marx who analysed it in great detail (mainly in *CAPITAL*, vol. I) and gave it social and revolutionary connotations. In the Marxian formula of value,

$c + v + s$ (c = CONSTANT CAPITAL, v = VARIABLE CAPITAL, s = surplus value), the degree of exploitation is indicated by the ratio s/v, as labour alone can create value (the exploitation rate must not be confused with the profit rate, which is $s/(c-v)$. The exploitation rate depends on the length of the working day (over and above the INDISPENSABLE LABOUR TIME) and the intensity of work. The capitalist is able to appropriate s.v. owing to his superior bargaining power by virtue of his ownership of the means of production and the RESERVE ARMY OF WORKERS. The appropriation of s.v. by the capitalist is largely responsible for the IMMISERATION OF THE PROLETARIAT and the need for foreign markets. The concept of s.v. is central to the Marxian doctrine. With this ideological weapon, Marx and his followers were able to explain the LABOUR THEORY OF VALUE, constant and variable capital, cyclical fluctuations, the DECLINING PROFIT RATE, SOCIAL STRATIFICATION, the CLASS STRUGGLE, IMPERIALISM and the need for a PROLETARIAN REVOLUTION.

Surrealism An *avant-garde* left-wing artistic and literary movement which developed between the two world wars, mainly in France and then in other Western countries. S. was opposed to imposed rationality and saw man's exploration of his subconscious, uncontrolled by reason (incl. dreams, hallucinations, and hypnotic states), as answers to his artistic and social problems. Surrealist ideas are still influential in aesthetic theory and practice (incl. fashions, customs and advertising). Its leading representatives (L. Breton, L. Aragon and P. Edward) were contemptuous of the modern ultra-rational and institutionalized art, culture, morality and bourgeois society. Instead, they emphasized SPONTANEITY, MYSTICISM, INDIVIDUALISM and anarchical rebellion. Surrealists saw communism and the Bolshevik Revolution as a new vehicle for their artistic and social aspirations. Many of them joined the French Communist Party (in 1925) and established links with the Soviet Ministry of Education headed by A. V. LUNACHARSKY. They thought that the new social order in the USSR would give a chance to an artistic, cultural and social regeneration of mankind, in which artists, intellectuals and social reformers would play a leading and messianic role. However, both sides soon became disillusioned. The Communist parties found the surrealists too Bohemian, undisciplined and, in fact, too bourgeois by virtue of their background. At the same time, the surrealists were shocked by the Soviet regimentation of art, literature, thought and life from the mid-1920s onwards.

Survival of the Fittest NATURAL SELECTION, STRUGGLE FOR EXISTENCE.

Suslov, Mikhail Andreievich (1902–) A Soviet Party leader, recognized authority on Marxist-Leninist theory and an economist. He joined the Communist Party in 1921, supported Stalin against TROTSKY and ZINOVIEV in the 1920s and was elected to the Central Committee in 1941 and the Politburo in 1966. He graduated from the Plekhanov Institute of National Economy in 1928, the INSTITUTE OF RED PROFESSORSHIP in 1937 and was editor-in-chief of *Pravda* in 1949/50. S. attracted international attention when he pressed for the expulsion of Yugoslavia from the COMINFORM in 1948. He maintained a hardline stand in the Sino-Soviet dispute against the Chinese and established a reputation as an 'orthodox ideological watchdog', opposed to compromise and liberalization.

Sverdlov Communist University The first training institution at a post-secondary level for Party cadres and trade union leaders in the USSR. It was established in Moscow in July 1918 on the initiative of Y. M. Sverdlov, a Bolshevik leader, and was actively supported by Lenin. It was the highest Party educational establishment and was attached to the CENTRAL EXECUTIVE COMMITTEE. Its courses were gradually extended from 6 months to 4 years. When fully operational, it had

about 2,000 students. It also organized or supervised ancillary specialized educational institutions, viz. the Communist Correspondence University, the Communist Evening University, the Institute of Graduate Studies, and the Soviet and Party Evening School. In 1932, the S.C.U. was transformed into the Sverdlov Higher Communist Agricultural University (which, in 1935, was reorganized into the Sverdlov Higher School for Propagandists).

Swedish Communist Party It existed under this name from 1921 to 1967. Its main successor is the LEFT COMMUNIST PARTY.

Swing Credits A term often used in East–West trade involving BILATERAL TRADE. To allow for the irregular flow of exports and imports during the year, the partner countries undertake to grant each other credits, which are usually interest-free, to allow for the excess of imports over exports. These credits usually work to the advantage of the Socialist countries, whose imports tend to outstrip their exports. S.c. are usually interest-free up to 5–20 per cent of the value of the agreed annual import.

Swiss Party of Labour See PARTY OF LABOUR OF SWITZERLAND.

Swiss Social-Democratic Party See SOCIAL-DEMOCRATIC PARTY OF SWITZERLAND.

Switch Dealing A by-product of BILATERAL TRADE, characteristic of East–West trade and payments. A Western partner may agree to accept payment for its export to a Socialist country in goods the partner himself does not want. But a switch dealer, with his knowledge of the market and commercial contacts, may find a buyer or buyers for a consideration (a discount of up to 45 per cent). Vienna, Amsterdam, Geneva and Zurich are the main centres for s.d.

Sympathy Strike A stoppage of work by organized labour in support of the action taken by another trade union, usually in the same industry or craft. A s.s. may become a POLITICAL STRIKE or may even develop into a GENERAL STRIKE.

Syndicalism A working class movement based on a revolutionary philosophy which emphasizes the role of trade unions in the transformation of capitalism into an ideal society. The term means 'trade unionism' (from the French *syndicat*, meaning 'trade union') and was established by M. Latapie at a trade union congress in Amiens in Oct. 1906. S. arose in the latter half of the 19th c. in France and spread to other countries, especially Italy, Spain and several Latin American countries. It is based on the ideas of PROUDHON and G. SOREL. S. found its expression in modified forms in GUILD SOCIALISM in Britain and the INDUSTRIAL WORKERS OF THE WORLD in the USA. S. is opposed to the capitalist wage system, state power and nationalism. It advocates the organization of all workers into strong all-inclusive unions, direct industrial action by trade unions, boycotts, sabotage, strikes and, ultimately, a GENERAL STRIKE. It also favours the creation of producers' and consumers' co-operatives and the strengthening and development of working-class culture to the exclusion of bourgeois culture. S. aims for the overthrow of capitalism after which trade unions would assume administrative powers under self-government and co-ordinated by a central trade union federation. S. is strongly opposed to communism of the authoritarian Marxist-Leninist type, especially the MONO-PARTY SYSTEM OF GOVERNMENT and the DICTATORSHIP OF THE PROLETARIAT. Extreme forms of s. are represented by ANARCHO-SYNDICALISM and REVOLUTIONARY SYNDICALISM. Revolutionary Marxism rejects s., regarding it as a variant of PETTY BOURGEOIS SOCIALISM, which has no chance of success owing to its virtual disregard of political factors. S. reached its peak of popularity before W.W.I., but has declined under the impact of the success-

ful Bolshevik Revolution. Also INTERNATIONAL WORKERS' ASSOCIATION, WORKERS' OPPOSITION, WORKERS' PARTICIPATION, WORKERS' SELF-MANAGEMENT.

Synthesis In the Marxist philosophy of DIALECTICS, a product of the struggle of opposites, viz. the abstract concepts, thesis and antithesis. S. embodies elements of both, but usually one is dominant. S. itself contains the seed of further struggle and, in due time, resolves itself to repeat the process again. S. may be a product of gradual evolutionary changes or – if the opposing force is too strong and persistent – of a revolutionary leap. Development consists in a succession of syntheses, progressing from lower to higher stages.

Synthetic Incentive In Socialist economic practice, an inducement which rewards the worker for all the desirable achievements in one generalized type of incentive. Bonuses based on the profit of the enterprise where the worker is employed have come to be accepted as the best example. Maximum profit or profitability can be achieved if the workers (including the management) avoid waste, introduce innovations, ensure or improve quality, produce items for which there is demand, work to their best ability and produce the largest possible output at the most economic level. S.i. contrasts with specialized incentive, which rewards the worker for a narrowly defined specific achievement.

Syrian Communist Party (*al-Hizb al-Shuyu'i al-Suri*) A small, moderately influential party with a patchy history. It originated from the Lebanese People's Party founded in 1924, which operated underground in the last two years of French rule (1939–41). A separate group, the S.C.P., was formed in 1944, but its activities have been restricted from time to time. In 1971, it had two members in the government. The Party was legalized in 1972 by virtue of its co-operative participation in the National Progressive

Front. The Party has a membership of about 4,000 (in a population of 8,000,000 in 1978). During the 1977 elections, the Communists won 6 (of the 196) parliamentary seats. In its international orientation, the Party has supported the Moscow line. *Nidal al-Sha'b (People's Struggle)* is the Party's official organ, published fortnightly.

Szczecin Riots Violent unrest among workers in the Polish port of Szczecin in mid-December 1970, in protest against sharp increases in the prices of food and oppressive working and living conditions. At their height (17 December), the local headquarters of the POLISH UNITED WORKERS' PARTY were burned down by the rioters.

Szczepański, Jan (1913–) An outstanding Polish sociologist of international repute. From 1957 to 1968 he headed the Sociological Department in the Institute of Philosophy and Sociology of the Polish Academy of Sciences and became full professor in 1963. He was President of the International Sociological Association from 1966 to 1970 and greatly enhanced the international standing of Polish and East European SOCIOLOGY. He is an honorary member of the American Academy of Exact Sciences and the Humanities. In spite of the sensitive discipline he represents, he has a reputation for being able to 'get along' with the Communist regime. He has rendered invaluable service to sociology not only by rehabilitating it in the eyes of the regime, but also raising the level of sociological studies in Poland and other Socialist countries. His main publications (in Polish, unless otherwise indicated) are: *Structure of the Intelligentsia in Poland* (1960); *History of Sociology* (1961); *Sociological Problems of Higher Education* (1963, also in French and Hungarian); *Introduction to Sociology* (1963, also in Czech, Finnish, Hungarian and Russian); *Problems of Contemporary Sociology* (1965); *Sociology and Society* (1970, in Bulgarian); *Reflections on Education* (1973); *Changes in the Polish Community in the Process of Industrialization* (1973); (editor) *Studies in the Polish Class Structure* (28 vols); and (co-editor) *Social Problems of Work and Production* (1970, also in Russian).

T

Tachai Campaign A drive in Chinese agriculture to expand farming, based on wholly local resources and effort and relying on moral (as distinct from material) motivation. It was initiated by a PRODUCTION BRIGADE, called Tachai, in a PEOPLE'S COMMUNE in Shansi province. It abolished SUBSIDIARY PLOTS and PRODUCTION TEAMS and became noted for its 'three refusals', viz. not to accept 'money, food or materials' from outside. The T. brigade painstakingly terraced barren hillsides which, in 1963, were ruined by floods and refused to accept state aid to which it was entitled. The T. farm turned out to be very successful, showing high yields under difficult conditions and became a model farm. A slogan, 'Learn from Tachai' was launched by the authorities in 1964, at first largely directed against the policy of the THREE FREEDOMS AND ONE RESPONSIBILITY. A nation-wide emulation campaign was developed only in Oct. 1975, when the first 'Learn from Tachai' National Conference was held, at which HUA KUO-FENG outlined the programme of development of Tachai counties. The campaign was approved by Mao Tse-tung but was opposed by the GANG OF FOUR. It was planned that by 1980 one-third of China's 2,100 counties would adopt the T. system.

Taching Campaign A drive in Chinese industry emphasizing intensive work, self-reliance, revolutionary zeal and independence from foreign technology and assistance. It is named after a successful experiment on the Taching oilfield, in Heilungkiang province, after the withdrawal of Soviet aid in 1960. In that year, the 'Iron Man' Wang Ching-hsi, heading a drilling team of 1,205 men, opened a production well in five days of hard work under extremely adverse conditions in ice-bound Taching. A vast wilderness was soon transformed into a complex of oil rigs, refinery towers and China's largest producing oilfield, followed by a large modern farm and a mixture of rural-urban settlements. It has been developed into a model provincial community, embracing some 400,000 people and has also become a unit of government administration and a provincial Party branch. Mao Tse-tung hailed it as an example of 'agro-industrial social complex'. In early 1964, a 'Learn from Taching' slogan was launched, initiating an emulation campaign. Like its agricultural counterpart, the TACHAI CAMPAIGN, the T.C. was directed against the THREE FREEDOMS AND ONE RESPONSIBILITY.

Taft-Hartley Act In the USA, a well-known anti-strike law, passed by the Congress in 1947 on the initiative of Senator R. A. Taft and Congressman F. A. Hartley. In the name of law and order, the Act allows the employment of non-union labour during the cooling off period before the strike is permitted and bars union officials from belonging to the Communist Party. The critics of the Act see it as a calculated move on the part of the capitalist establishment to curb the power of 'Big labour' in its struggle with 'Big business'.

Tammerfors Conference The first conference of the Bolshevik faction of the RUS-

SIAN SOCIAL-DEMOCRATIC LABOUR PARTY held from 12 to 17 Dec. 1905. It was held at what was called at that time T. in Norway (now Tampere in Finland) at the height of the REVOLUTION OF 1905–07. At that Conference, Lenin and Stalin met for the first time.

Tanjug Abbreviation of *Telegrafska Agencija Nov Jugoslaviya*, meaning the Telegraphic News Agency of Yugoslavia. It is the state-owned official news agency with the exclusive right (since 1958) of distributing news in Yugoslavia. It is based in Belgrade and maintains reciprocal relations with all major news agencies in the Socialist as well as capitalist countries.

Tanzanian Socialism A brand of socialism being developed by President J. Nyerere, based on the traditional extended family participating in communal village enterprises. The foundation of T.s. was indicated in the Arusha Declaration of 1967, which provided for the nationalization of all major industries, banks, insurance companies, wholesale trade and foreign trade companies and the development of 'familyhood communal villages' (*ujamaa*). As of 1980, some 15m. people lived under *ujamaa* conditions. Luanga, a village of 2,500 inhabitants, is held as a model of T.s. Each family has a private plot of land, but participates in various communal farming, handicraft, trading and service pursuits. There is a village-owned furniture workshop, a smithy, a co-operative shop operated by women to sell milk and soft drinks, a child-care centre, a school, a clinic and a volunteer militia unit. Participation in communal enterprises is rewarded by 'points', which entitles each family to a corresponding share in profits.

Target In economic planning, a popular term for planned indicators laying down tasks to be achieved by enterprises during a specified period. A t. may consist in the minimum quantity of a particular product to be delivered to specified recipients, the saving of materials and power, and the

improvement in the quality of production, innovations, exports and profits. A t. may be directive (compulsory) or recommendatory. The fulfilment of a t. is all-important, as outputs of some enterprises become inputs of others and non-fulfilment may lead to BOTTLENECKS.

Target Pricing A term used in the Socialist planned economies to denote the flexible application of price mark-ups or mark-downs by the state to achieve desired social objectives. It involves the development of the economy in pre-determined directions, whereby the production and consumption of some items are encouraged and others reduced or phased out. T.p. is consistent with decentralization, the independence of enterprises and a greater consumers' freedom of choice. T.p. is one of the features of the flexible COMPLEX PRICE SYSTEM, introduced since the ECONOMIC REFORMS of the 1960s. This basis of pricing implies that prices do not necessarily reflect scarcity, market equilibrium or (Marxian) value.

TASS (abbreviation in Russian of *Telegrafnoe Agenstvo Sovetskogo Soyuza*, meaning Telegraphic Agency of the Soviet Union) The official state-owned press agency in the USSR providing domestic and foreign news and illustrations to domestic and foreign users. It was established in 1925, in succession to *ROSTA* (*Rossyskoe Telegrafnoe Agenstvo*, created in 1918). *T.* maintains about 500 regular correspondents in the USSR, plus about 100 abroad. In addition, it maintains working relations on a mutual exchange basis with more than 50 news agencies in the Socialist and capitalist countries.

Tatlinism Another term for the Russian version of CONSTRUCTIVISM, founded in 1913 by V. Tatlin (1885–1953), a Russian sculptor, painter and theatrical designer.

Tatzu-Pao The Chinese word for BIG-CHARACTER POSTER.

Taut Planning

Taut Planning

Taut Planning TIGHT PLANNING.

Taylorism The earliest scientific study of work management, initiated before W.W.I by an American engineer, F. W. Taylor (1856–1915), and further developed by F. B. Gilbreth (1868–1924), L. H. Gant (1861–1919), H. Emerson (1852–1931) and W. Kent (1851–1918). It is concerned with the principles of the scientific organization and administration of work on the basis of time and motion studies and a thorough preparation of work conditions. T. soon attracted the attention of many Marxists and trade union leaders, who adopted a highly critical attitude to it. In their view, under capitalism, T. leads to the intensification of work and a greater exploitation of labour and, as such, further exacerbates antagonism between labour and capital. Lenin described T. as 'a scientific method of squeezing out workers' sweat'. However, some methods of T. have been adopted in the Socialist countries, with STAKHANOVISM representing its extreme and crude form.

Team PRODUCTION TEAM.

Teamsters A colloquial name of one of the best known trade unions in the USA, viz. the International Brotherhood of Teamsters, Chauffeurs, Warehousemen and Helpers of America, or briefly, road transport workers. It has been in a position to exercise a good deal of power, owing to its large membership (over 1.0m.) and its ability to support other unions by withholding trucking. The union was founded in 1899 and has grown to be the largest trade union in the USA. It reached its peak of influence under Jimmy Hoffa, its President from 1957 to 1964 (who was murdered in 1978). It attracted some bad publicity, especially in the 1920s, as a powerful trade union without a sense of social responsibility which was dominated by corrupt and criminal elements, insensitive to public opinion. It was expelled from the *AFL-CIO* in 1957. In 1968, the T., together with the Auto Workers Union, formed the Alliance for Labor Action.

Technical Availability of Capital A general phrase in the Socialist countries, corresponding roughly to the Western concept of capital–labour ratio. It is expressed as a ratio of the value of productive fixed capital to the average size of employment. It is also known as capital reinforcement of labour, organic content of capital, productive outfit of live labour or simply, capital intensity.

Technical Coefficient of Costs In Socialist economic planning, a fractional figure showing the input-output relation applicable to a particular branch of the economy or a product relying on inputs from another branch, when inputs are expressed in value terms. If inputs are expressed in physical terms, the relation is known as the TECHNICAL COEFFICIENT OF PRODUCTION.

Technical Coefficient of Production A fractional figure indicating the input-output relation applicable to a particular industry or product. It is calculated by dividing input per output in physical terms and can be derived from the MATRIX OF INTER-BRANCH BALANCES. The quantity of input per unit of output depends on the technological level of production. The coefficient plays an important part in the allocation of resources.

Technical Composition of Capital TECHNICAL STRUCTURE OF CAPITAL.

Technical-Economic Plan Name typically given in the Socialist countries to the annual plan prepared by socialized enterprises and other economic organizations. Also known as the technical-industrial plan, it shows the details of the available capacities and the targets in physical terms, together with the means of their implementation. The main preoccupations of the t.-e.p. are: 1. increase in the volume of production; 2. the adaptation of the structure of production to demand; 3. the development of export; 4. the improvement of quality; 5. innovations; and 6. economies in the use of materials and labour. The t.-e.p. must be co-ordinated with similar plans of other supplying and recipient entities and be consistent with the overall national ECONOMIC PLAN.

Technical Structure of Capital In its modern usage in the Socialist countries, the relation between: 1. active capital, i.e. working equipment, embracing machinery, machine tools, instruments and other implements used in productive processes; and 2. passive capital, representing buildings. Compared with the situation in most Western countries, this ratio is rather low in the Socialist countries, owing to the latters' lower stage of economic development and harsher climatic conditions. Sometimes the term t.s. of c. is used vaguely instead of the ORGANIC STRUCTURE OF CAPITAL.

Techno-Bureaucracy A term commonly used in the Socialist countries for the state technical and economic establishment, dominated by technical and other experts, managers and state administrators. These persons constitute the new elite which exercises a great and increasing influence, by virtue of their power of decision-making over resources which, although socially owned, are effectively under the control of the techno-bureaucrats. Sometimes the term t.-b. is used instead of INTELLIGENTSIA, with an implication of disapproval.

Technocracy The social elite comprising technical decision-makers (engineers, scientists, managers and other professional specialists), dominating the whole society. The term is also used in a more profound sense denoting a doctrine of technological, economic, political and social content, according to which modern society should be increasingly run by technocrats in accordance with technical and economic rationality, irrespective of the social system in force. Its advocates maintain that the ills in our society are caused by politicians who make biased distorted decisions and that only technocrats are able to rise above the ideology and selfish interests of narrow social groups. They hold that technological changes automatically bring

about fundamental social and cultural readjustments and that the scientific and technical revolution is capable of solving all the basic social conflicts. The doctrine was developed in the USA in the 1930s, based on the ideas of T. Veblen (1857–1929) and J. Burnham (1905–) and spread to other industrialized capitalist countries. Marx himself underestimated the role of expertise and specialists in economic and social organization and management and referred critically to the 'fetishism of technology'. Revolutionary Marxists are opposed to this doctrine. In their view, it is too materialistic, devoid of ideology, implies the rule by an elite over the masses, denies the need for the class struggle, assumes that all the basic social problems under capitalism can be solved in a peaceful manner and negates the need for a proletarian revolution. As such, they regard the doctrine as an expedient bourgeois creation suited to the interests of capitalists, especially monopolies and multinational corporations. Also MANAGERIALISM, TAYLORISM.

Technological Curtain A term applied to that facet of the Western STRATEGIC EMBARGO which has been concerned with the barring of the flow of advanced technology to the Socialist countries, paralleling the IRON CURTAIN.

Teleological Planning GENETIC AND TELEOLOGICAL PLANNING.

Teleological Pricing Pricing designed to promote the achievement of desired objectives, as distinct from SCARCITY PRICES. The two types of t.p. are FUNCTIONAL PRICING and TARGET PRICING.

Teleology A philosophical theory according to which all existence and processes are governed by purposive or goal-oriented activity. The beginning of t. go back to Aristotle (384–322 B.C.), but among its modern exponents are R. B. Braithwaite (1900–) and E. Nagel (1901–). It is maintained that in all organisms there is a hidden aim, predetermining the development of plants and animals, which provides evidence of the existence of god. F. Engels (in *DIALECTICS OF NATURE*) rejected t., as being inconsistent with Marxism. Although DIALECTICAL MATERIALSIM implies that human activities are purposeful, it also insists that man's existence and behaviour are determined by objective factors, especially the material conditions of living.

Ten Days that Shook the World The title of the main work written in 1919 by John Reed (1887–1920), a radical American journalist. The book is a sympathetic account of the crucial events of the GREAT OCTOBER SOCIALIST REVOLUTION, concentrating on the period 16–26 Oct. 1917 (O.-S.C.). Lenin, in the introduction, described the book as a 'truthful and most vivid exposition of the events so significant to the comprehension of what really is the Proletarian Revolution and the Dictatorship of the Proletariat'. The author actually witnessed most of the historic events in Petrograd and identified himself with the cause of the Revolution. In 1919, he was a co-organizer of the Communist-Labor Party in the USA (re-named later the Communist Party of the USA). Reed died of typhus in Soviet Russia in 1920 and was buried in Red Square in Moscow (where a plaque in the Kremlin Wall commemorates him).

Teng Hsiao-P'ing (1904–) Versatile Chinese military and political leader noted for his distinguished and chequered career. Educated in France and the USSR, he became the chief of staff of the Chinese Red Army in 1930, participated in the LONG MARCH (1934–35) and then served as Political Commissar (*POLITRUK*) during the Sino-Japanese War (1937–45). After the Communist accession to power, he was appointed Minister of Finance (1953) and the Vice-Chairman of the National Defence Council (1954–67). Together with LIU SHAO-CH'I, he supported a moderate reformist course and was the chief architect of the liberal economic policy *San-zi Yi-pao* (THREE FREEDOMS AND ONE RESPONSIBILITY) and the LATER TEN

POINTS in the early 1960s. During the GREAT PROLETARIAN CULTURAL REVOLUTION, Teng became an object of attack and lost his posts. He was rehabilitated in 1973 and became the Chief of the General Staff of the PEOPLE'S LIBERATION ARMY and Vice-Premier in 1975, supported by CHOU EN-LAI. But Teng was again attacked by the GANG OF FOUR in 1975–76. However, in 1977 he was restored to the Party's Vice-Chairmanship and became senior Vice-Premier. Since Dec. 1978 his importance has been enhanced by the promotion of his supporters to several senior positions. He has initiated moves to guarantee the independence of the judiciary to endow the NATIONAL PEOPLE'S CONGRESS with legislative powers, to free the government from the excessive domination by the Party, to reduce government interference in the management of enterprises, to subsidize urban consumer prices and to raise state procurement prices payable to farms. He has proved to be resourceful and reasonable and commands widespread respect in China and abroad. Teng has a reputation for thorough knowledge of Marxist theory and international relations.

Ten Great Years Name given in China to the first ten years of the Communist rule 1949–59. It is also the title of the main Communist Chinese source book on that period, also published in English under the title *Ten Great Years: Statistics of the Economic and Cultural Achievements of the People's Republic of China* (Peking, Foreign Languages Press, 1960). There are 19 articles contributed by LIU SHAO-CH'I, CHOU EN-LAI, LIN PIAO, TENG HSIAO-P'ING and KANG SHENG. The same phrase, alluding to the Chinese precedent, was used in Ghana in a booklet, *Ten Great Years: 1951–60*, covering the first ten years of independence under the leadership of the left wing Prime Minister K. NKRUMAH, who had close relations with China's leaders.

Ten Guarantees Ten social safeguards provided in China by the more hard-working and efficient PEOPLE'S COM-MUNES to their members, in amounts guaranteeing a reasonable standard of living. They are as follows: 1. food; 2. clothing; 3. medical care; 4. housing; 5. maternity payment; 6. marriage allowance; 7. fuel for winter; 8. burial allowance; 9. haircuts; and 10. entertainment (theatre tickets). These benefits are provided under the condition that the economic situation of the commune allows it.

Ten Major (or Great) Relationships A significant speech delivered by MAO TSE-TUNG on 25 April 1956 in a conservative mood, stressing a moderate and pragmatic approach to economic organization and management in the construction of socialism in China. The speech represented a summarized compilation of views of agricultural and industrial leaders from the 34 sectors of the economy. It amounted to a rightist reaction against ideological extremism following the liberal mood of KHRUSHCHEV'S SECRET SPEECH two months earlier. Mao's speech was preoccupied with investment priorities and the *loci* of administrative power. He dwelt on ten crucial relationships noted for conflicting interests, viz. between: 1. manufacturing industries and agriculture; 2. industries in coastal and inland areas; 3. economic development and defence spending; 4. the state and enterprises; 5. central and local authorities; 6. the Han and minority nationalities; 7. the Party and non-party organizations; 8. revolution and counter-revolution; 9. right and wrong; and 10. China and other countries. However, the speech was published for the use of the masses for the first time only in Dec. 1976, after Mao's death, as a reaction against the adventurist policies pursued during the GREAT LEAP FORWARD and the GREAT PROLETARIAN CULTURAL REVOLUTION. The T.M.R. have become synonymous with economic commonsense, the efficient management of resources and a de-emphasis of ideological and political fervour in the interest of accelerated economic and technological development – the declared policy of HUA KUO-FENG.

Ten-Point Policy A programmatic statement issued by the Provisional Revolutionary Government of the Republic of South Vietnam on 1 April 1975, regarding the treatment of the Newly Liberated Areas by the Communist forces. The Ten Points were: 1. the complete replacement of the former bourgeois administration and political parties by the Communist revolutionary regime; 2. the protection of freedom and equality, irrespective of sex and religion; 3. national reconciliation and cohesion; 4. the maintenance of public order to protect people's safety, livelihood and property; 5. the administration of the assets of the previous government by the P.R.G.R.S.V.; 6. the normalization of operation of the economy in accordance with the national interest as viewed by the P.R.G.R.S.V.; 7. the promotion of primary production; 8. the eradication of bourgeois and foreign-influenced cultural, educational, technical and scientific institutions; 9. the provision of protection and assistance to the functionaries of the former regime (officers, soldiers, disabled troops, veterans, policemen and officials), provided they had proved their acceptance of the revolutionary cause or rendered service to it and the punishment of offenders against the revolutionary cause; and 10. the protection, of and reward to, foreigners who respect Vietnamese sovereignty and assist the South Vietnamese people.

Ten-Point Programme A policy statement in China announced by CHOU EN-LAI at the National People's Congress on 16 April 1962, emphasizing a reasonably uniform development of the major branches of the economy, economic commonsense and efficiency. It was a reaction against the Soviet-inspired emphasis on heavy industry (1953–57) and the adventurism of the GREAT LEAP FORWARD (1958–61). The Ten Points were: 1. increase in agricultural output, especially grains, cotton and oil-seeds; 2. a reasonable balance in the development of light and heavy industries, with due attention being paid to the production of basic consumer goods; 3. retrenchment of capital construction and the application of the available equipment, materials and manpower to the most urgent uses; 4. reduction of urban population by promoting resettlement and development in rural areas; 5. discipline in enterprise accounting and the release of idle resources; 6. discipline and improvement in the distribution of consumer goods; 7. discipline in the fulfilment of foreign trade targets; 8. readjustments in cultural, educational and scientific research; 9. reduction of waste in the use of resources; and 10. perfection of economic planning to ensure balanced development in the following order: agriculture, light industry, and heavy industry.

Ten-Year Communist-Annihilation Campaign A phrase applied to the period of open hostilities from 1927 to 1937 between the KUOMINTANG forces led by Chiang Kai-shek and the Chinese Communists later led by Mao Tse-tung. The Kuomintang campaign began after a period of Nationalist-Communist co-operation 1924–27, terminated by the death of Sun Yat-sen. The Campaign was marked by such events as the massacre of the Communists in 1927 and their re-grouping in the CHINGSHAN MOUNTAINS, the AUTUMN HARVEST UPRISING (1927), the formation of the CHINESE SOVIET RE-PUBLIC (1931), the LONG MARCH (1934–35) and the capture of Chiang Kai-shek by the Communists in 1937 to force him to lead China in the fight against the Japanese invaders. This was followed by the Kuomintang-Communist military co-operation over the period 1937–45.

Tesnyaks (*Tesnyaki* or *Tesny Sotsialisty*, in Bulgarian, meaning 'strict' or 'narrow' socialists) Early revolutionary Marxists in Bulgaria, whose activities and organization led to the foundation of the Bulgarian Communist Party. The T. emerged at the beginning of this century as a militant left-wing group in the Bulgarian Social-Democratic Party. In 1903 they formed a separate organization called the Workers Social-Democratic Party (Strict Socialists), thereby paralleling the BOLSHEVIKS who emerged in the Russian Social-Democratic Labour Party in the same year. The T. were led by D. Blagoyev (1856–1924), who had spent some time in Russia where he organized the BLAGOYEV GROUP. Other T. activists included G. Kirkov and V. Kolarov. The T. believed in strict Party discipline and tight organization with a core of devoted professional revolutionaries. They rejected compromise with 'broad' socialists (corresponding to the MENSHEVIKS) and any form of OP-PORTUNISM and REVISIONISM. The T. established two revolutionary organizations, viz. the General Workers' Trade Union (1904) and the Union of Workers' Social-Democratic Youth (1912). They also joined the SECOND INTERNATIONAL and opposed W.W.I as an imperialist war. In 1919, the W.S.-D.P. was reorganized to form the BULGARIAN COMMUNIST PARTY.

Testament of Lenin The political will left by LENIN, noted for its critical view of Stalin. Written in Dec. 1922 and supplemented in Jan. 1923 (about a year before Lenin's death), it outlined the guidelines for the development of the Party and communism in Soviet Russia. It also included a warning against Stalin's crudity and ruthlessness and a recommendation that he be removed from the Party's post of Secretary-General. Although Lenin referred favourably to the qualities of TROTSKY, he did not name him, or anyone else, as the successor to himself. The testament was dictated to Lenin's wife KRUPSKAYA, but in spite of her early efforts it was not published officially until 1956 (Stalin died in 1953). However, the content of the testament was leaked abroad and published in the West in 1924.

Thai United Socialist Front UNITED SOCIALIST FRONT OF THAILAND.

Thakin Than Tun (1915–68) A Burmese Marxist and guerrilla leader, who strove to develop a version of communism suited to the conditions in Burma. He became the Secretary-General of the Communist Party of Burma in 1947 (the anti-Soviet Trotskyite faction of the BURMA COMMUNIST PARTY). He followed Mao Tsetung's revolutionary strategy by concentrating on rural areas and relying mostly on the peasantry. During the civil war of 1948–50 he came to control most of Burma's countryside. His Party was outlawed by the central government in 1953 and he subsequently lost ground, especially after 1962 when the socialist military regime of Gen. U Ne Win embarked upon the reunification of the country and proclaimed the BURMESE ROAD TO SOCIALISM. By 1965, Thakin had lost most of the territory under his control to U Ne Win's forces, who were equipped with American and British weapons. After several successful operations, Thakin was killed in battle in 1968.

Thaw A term referring to the relaxation in East-West relations after the most frigid stage of the COLD WAR, i.e. the Korean War (1950–53). The term is also used to describe the modicum of liberalization in the European Socialist countries after Stalin's death (March 1953). The designation 't.' was first applied to the USSR, alluding to the book written by Ilya Ehrenburg (a Soviet journalist and propagandist turned semi-dissident), *Ottepel* (*The Thaw*, Moscow 1954), subsequently translated into Western languages. The t. also occurred in China, under the name of the 'HUNDRED FLOWERS' INTERLUDE.

Theism A religious doctrine propounding the existence of god supernaturally revealed to man. Unlike DEISM, t. postulates not only revelation and providence, but also divine intervention in human life. In Marxist philosophy, t. is treated even less seriously than deism and is rejected as one of the most extreme forms of philosophical IDEALISM.

Theology The science of religion concerned with the proof and forms of the existence of god. Marxism regards t. as a 'pseudo-science', based on IDEALISM and preoccupied with basically futile arguments. Also CHRISTIANITY, DEISM, THEISM.

Theology of Marxism CHRISTIANITY.

Theories of Location LOCATION THEORIES.

Theory and Practice The interrelations between these two phenomena are of fundamental importance in Marxist philosophy, in particular in the approach to KNOWLEDGE. This question was analyzed mainly by Engels (in *DIALECTICS OF NATURE*) and Lenin (in *MATERIALISM AND EMPIRIO-CRITICISM*). T.a.p. are regarded by them as a DIALECTIC unity, mutually supplementing each other. But in this process, PRACTICE is thought to be playing the decisive role, which reflects the Marxists adherence to the philosophy of MATERIALISM. T. is considered to be derived from p., amounting to generalizations of practical experience. P. is understood to consist of activities in the material sphere directed towards indispensable conditions of society's existence. Thus, there can be no t. without p., and only t. that is related to p. (serving society's needs) is of consequence.

Theory of Hieroglyphics HIEROGLYPHIC THEORY OF COGNITION.

Theory of Stages A theoretical proposition accepted by the advocates of ECONOMISM in Russia before W.W.I. The theory was outlined by E. D. Kuskova (1869–1958) in *Credo* (1899), who postulated that the working class movement, at least in the early stages, should steer away from the revolutionary political line and instead, concentrate on the improvement of labour's material working and living conditions by industrial and parliamentary actions. The theory envisaged progress in three stages: 1. strike actions;

2. the organization of all workers in trade unions and the creation of a central co-ordinating trade union body; and 3. parliamentary action to ensure the economic and political emancipation of the working class by peaceful reforms. The theory was rejected by both LENIN and PLEKHANOV as too short-sighted, too slow and thoroughly un-Marxist.

Theory of the Cyclical Development of Society See CYCLICAL DEVELOPMENT OF SOCIETY, THEORY OF.

Thermidor The name of the eleventh month in the revolutionary French calendar (from 19–20 July to 17–18 August, according to the Gregorian Calendar). In the later stage of the FRENCH REVOLUTION, on 27–28 July 1794, a right-wing group led by P. Barras overthrew the dictatorship of the left-wing JACOBINS led by M. F. I. Robespierre (who, together with his collaborators, were soon executed). Thus, political power was taken over by the Thermidorians, representing the interests of the BIG BOURGEOISIE, who three months later handed power over to the reactionary Directorate. The term T. is used by Marxists to describe the first stage of a counter-revolution, as a natural reaction on the part of the dispossessed bourgeoisie to defeat the proletarian revolution and restore capitalism.

Theses on Feuerbach A philosophical study written by K. MARX in 1845 and first published by F. Engels in 1888. The study contains eleven 'theses', or critical propositions, against the German philosopher L. FEUERBACH, thereby laying down foundations for the Marxist materialist philosophy. Marx attacked the previous approach to, and versions of, MATERIALISM (Feuerbach's included) which, in his view, had all been contemplative and speculative, ignoring the crucial role of practice (experience) as the basis of COGNITION and interrelation between man and nature.

Thesis, Antithesis and Synthesis Important philosophical concepts in the Marxist interpretation of the processes of development. These concepts, described as the 'triad', were borrowed by Marx and Engels from HEGEL. But they stressed that whilst in the Hegelian interpretation the threefold process is abstract and artificial (steeped in idealist philosophy), Marxism sees it as real with practical effects (reflecting materialist philosophy). Development is considered by Marxists to be proceeding in stages, each consisting of three phases. Inherent in each phenomenon (thesis) is its opposite (antithesis) producing a contradiction and struggle. In this process t. is partly destroyed by the a., but the latter itself is also modified in the secondary phase of negation (NEGATION OF THE NEGATION), leading to a new, higher phenomenon called s., embodying elements of both the t. and the a. The triad so understood has important social implications. Under capitalism, the bourgeoisie (thesis) brings forth the proletariat (antithesis) and in the process of the class struggle a new, higher social system emerges a CLASSLESS SOCIETY or COMMUNISM (synthesis).

Theses of the Fourth of April APRIL THESES

Thing-in-Itself A philosophical concept denoting existence independent of human consciousness, i.e. an object of pure thought, rational intuition, or a fact that cannot be known. The concept was introduced by I. Kant (1724–1804) in *Critique of Judgment* (1790), under the label 'noumenon', as distinct from 'phenomenon', which is known or can be perceived by human senses. Marxist philosophers reject Kant's interpretation, regarding it as idealistic and reactionary, designed to justify religion. According to DIALECTICAL MATERIALISM, there are no things-in-themselves divorced from reality; there is only a difference between what has come to be known and what is yet unknown, but will be known and confirmed by practice. The scope of the unknown is becoming gradually limited as a result of scientific and technical progress. Instrumental in this process are man's practical activities, especially those directed towards material production. Also PHENOMENOLOGY.

Thinking The process of revolving ideas in the mind, consisting in forming concepts, recollecting, exercising judgment, and reasoning. In philosophical IDEALISM, t. is identified with a supernatural entity, such as god or the absolute idea, independent of matter and physiological and practical activity. In the Marxist view, in accordance with MATERIALISM, t. is treated as the highest product of physiological activity of matter, viz. the matter organized in a particular pattern by the brain, in which molecular and chemical processes take place. Thinking derives directly from sensory experience and images, appearing in man's intercourse with nature in the process of practical human activities. Marxists insist that although physiological processes underlying human t. and psychological activities of animals are similar, man's t. is qualitatively higher and cannot be explained in terms of physiology alone. T. has emerged from social development, in which labour has become the critical and governing factor. Labour has necessitated the formulation of concepts and ideas, including their analysis and synthesis – themselves results of the abstract work of the brain (LABOUR THEORY OF ABSTRACT THOUGHT, LABOUR THEORY OF HUMANIZATION). The development of human t. has necessarily involved the development of language, which has become the means of social communication in the process of production and distribution. Marxism rejects the idealistic theory of pure t., such as that put forward by N. Marr (1865–1934), according to which t. is possible without language (LABOUR THEORY OF LANGUAGE DEVELOPMENT). Consequently, t. is considered by Marxists to be a social phenomenon coextensive with society's historical development, being both the latter's coincidental result and a factor facilitating further social development.

Third International Name given to the international Communist organization in existence from 1919 to 1943 and domi-nated by the USSR, as distinct from the FIRST INTERNATIONAL (1864–79), the SECOND INTERNATIONAL (1889–1919), the SECOND-AND-A-HALF INTERNATIONAL (1921–23) and the FOURTH INTERNATIONAL (1938–). The T.I. is better known as the COMINTERN.

Third Proletariat A colloquial name of the 'Polish Socialist Party' Proletariat, which was in existence in Russian Poland from 1900 to 1908 (as distinct from the FIRST P., 1882–87, and the SECOND P., 1888–93). It was a revolutionary working-class party and its objectives included independence for Poland, socialist propaganda and education, a proletarian revolution and the dictatorship of the proletariat, the separation of the church from the state and an eight-hour working day. In collaboration with the Russian revolutionaires, it organized a number of strikes and demonstrations in the main industrial centres of Poland during the REVOLUTION OF 1905–07. But its actions never reached large proportions. Its membership was about 1,000.

Third World A political and economic term introduced in the late 1950s for the world division other than the WEST (developed capitalist countries) and the SOCIALIST BLOC, viz. Africa (except South Africa), Asia (except Japan and the six Socialist countries) and Latin America. It embraces about 100 countries, constituting the following proportions of the world (as of the late 1970s): area – 48 per cent; population – 45 per cent; national income – 14 per cent; industrial output – 8 per cent; and foreign trade – 22 per cent. The T.W. is noted for the following features: 1. past domination by imperialist capitalist powers; 2. in international relations, steering a neutral or a middle course, but some of these countries more or less clearly aligning themselves with Western or the Socialist power blocs; 3. underdeveloped economies, with most populations being engaged in primitive agriculture and, in some cases, in mining; 4. low national income per head – about $700 in the late 1970s (compared with $5,000 in the West and $1,500 in the Socialist bloc); 5. early stages of social development, with feudal, semi-feudal or tribal relations prevailing in rural areas. According to Socialist estimates, the bourgeoisie typically constitutes 2–5 per cent, the urban proletariat 5–7 per cent, and the remainder representing socially unconscious rural masses; and 6. varied political structures with an increasing number of countries turning to socialism, in one form or another, and Marxist ideology.

Thirty-First of August Group An ultra-left rebellious political association active in southern China (especially in Canton) from Sep. 1966 to late 1968. It was formed by radical students following the second mass meeting of the RED GUARDS in Peking on 31 Aug. 1966. Its membership was small but militant. The Group attacked the Party's old bureaucratic establishment, especially its conservative front organization called the Rebellious Committee.

Thought Reform One of the forms of general INDOCTRINATION practised in China (known under the name of *Ssu-hsiang Kai-tsao*), applied especially to intellectuals in the early stages of Communist power. It involves a radical questioning of the individual's established views, considered officially to be 'bourgeois, selfish and decadent', and their adaptation by gradual persuasion to the ideals postulated by the Communist Party. It is less intense than BRAINWASHING, but psychologically broader in scope and more profound than SELF-CRITICISM. In South Vietnam, after the Communist takeover, it was practised under the name of 're-education'.

Three-Anti Campaign In China, a drive launched by Mao Tse-tung in Jan. 1952 against 'corruption, waste and bureaucratization'. It was prompted by the Chinese Communist Party's claim that it had discovered a well-organized attempt by commercial and industrial interests to corrupt the Party and government officials. The Campaign was most intense over the period 1953–56 and was aimed at reducing the power of the capitalists.

Three Balances Policy (*San Ping*, in Chinese) The popular description of the Unified Policy for State Financial and Economic Work, initiated by the Chinese Communist government in March 1950. The Policy aimed at the stabilization of prices and market equilibrium by concentrating on three spheres: 1. balancing the state budget; 2. balancing the supply of, with the demand for, the principal material resources; and 3. balancing the accounts of various government organizations. The Policy proved a great success when the inflationary and hyperinflationary pressures that had prevailed in the country in the preceding years were brought under control. The sequel to the T.B.P. was a radical currency reform in 1955 which effectively stabilized the Chinese currency and economy.

Three Bigs and Three Smalls Drive A campaign in China during the GREAT PROLETARIAN CULTURAL REVOLUTION, directed towards the replacement of 'big cities, big universities and big hospitals' with 'small towns, small colleges and small clinics'. The aim was to take education, health and other services and urban amenities to rural areas, even if it involved the lowering of standards. The emphasis in the drive was on practical application at the expense of theoretical preparation.

Three-Eight Working Style In China, the working fashion originally developed by the PEOPLE'S LIBERATION ARMY and popularized in the country at large in the 1960s. The name is derived from a maxim consisting of three mottoes and eight characters (in Chinese). The three mottoes are: 1. keep firmly to the correct political line; 2. be diligent and modest in work; and 3. ensure flexibility and mobility in strategy and tactics. The eight characters represent unity, alertness, earnestness and liveliness. The drive, prompted mostly by ideological considerations, began in May 1960 when, under the leadership of LIN PIAO, 120,000 army cadres were sent down to the 'basic units' (directly concerned with production, administration and cultural activities) to spread this working style throughout the country.

Three Fixes and One Substitution A scheme initiated by the Chinese Communist Party in the early 1960s, which consisted in the assignment of rural cadres to work and responsibilities in the countryside. The scheme postulated: 1. fixed labour bases; 2. reporting for duty at fixed hours; and 3. working for a fixed period of time each day. As to 'substitution', it involved learning the tasks of regular workers, so as to be prepared to replace them whenever necessary. The drive, which reached its peak in 1965, was administered by provincial Party authorities reporting to the central government.

Three Freedoms and One Responsibility (*San-zi Yi-pao*, in Chinese) A liberal New Economic Policy in China, in the early 1960s (especially 1961–62), emphasizing material incentives and freedom of enterprise. It was promoted by LIU SHAO-CH'I and supported by TENG HSIAO-P'ING and was noted for the following features: 1. freedom to increase the size of SUBSIDIARY PLOTS; 2. freedom to develop small enterprises for own profit; 3. freedom to develop free markets for privately grown or made products; and 4. responsibility for the cultivation or operation of one's private undertakings even though the assets may belong to a collective (such as a commune) and for individual accounting, including losses. This policy produced some good results, viz. it speeded up the economic recovery from the failures of the GREAT LEAP FORWARD and, in particular, enhanced the role and contribution of subsidiary plots to agricultural output in the face of the prevalent setbacks in socialized farming. But, it stimulated the re-emergence of the *KULAK* class. The policy was first attacked by Mao Tse-tung in 1963 and, in the following year, the Learn from Tachai campaign was launched (TACHAI CAMPAIGN), de-emphasizing material incentives and subsidiary plots.

Three Honests and Four Stricts A drive in China launched first in the early 1960s

and revived ten years later, emphasizing 1. honest people; 2. honest words; and 3. honest deeds, plus 1. strict demands; 2. strict organization; 3. strict behaviour; and 4. strict discipline. The drive has been associated with the TACHING CAMPAIGN and identified with the Maoist line, but was critically viewed by the GANG OF FOUR as not radical enough.

Three Ill Winds A phrase commonly used in the Communist Chinese terminology for 1. SUBJECTIVISM, 2. SECTARIANISM, and 3. excessive FORMALISM (the 'EIGHT-LEGGED ESSAY'). It was first launched by Mao Tse-tung in Feb. 1942 to 'rectify the Party's style of work'.

Three-in-one Combination A name applied by the REVOLUTIONARY REBELS in China, in early 1967, to the REVOLUTIONARY COMMITTEES, which were also described as a Three-way or Triple Alliance. The Committees were meant to constitute an alliance of three elements representing revolutionary masses: 1. Revolutionary Rebels (leaders of revolutionary organizations, RED GUARDS and other young people of revolutionary inclinations); 2. Revolutionary Party cadres; and 3. representatives of the PEOPLE'S LIBERATION ARMY. Although the three participating groups were nominally equal, the P.L.A. representatives soon came to dominate the Committees, because the other two elements had no coherent and disciplined organizations.

Three Internationals Three international organizations of the working class movement with conflicting objectives and policies which existed simultaneously in the early post-W.W.I period. They were: 1. the right-wing BERN INTERNATIONAL, 1919–23 (which claimed to be the successor to the SECOND INTERNATIONAL); 2. the Soviet-dominated Communist Third International, 1919–43 (the COMINTERN); and 3. the middle-of-the-road SECOND-AND-A-HALF INTERNATIONAL, 1921–23. In 1922 a Conference of the Three Internationals, was held in Berlin, arranged by the Second-and-a-Half International, in an effort to unite the international working class movement. Although some agreement was reached, co-operation lasted for only one year. In 1923, at a Conference in Hamburg, the Bern International and the Second-and-a-Half International agreed to merge and created the LABOUR AND SOCIALIST INTERNATIONAL which existed up to 1947, while the Third International was dissolved in 1943.

Three-Level Ownership A description sometimes applied to the form of social ownership in the Chinese PEOPLE'S COMMUNES, viz. the commune, the PRODUCTION BRIGADE and the PRODUCTION TEAM.

Three Magic Weapons A phrase used by Mao Tse-tung with reference to the strategic stages of the proletarian seizure and exercise of power: 1. the united front (communist collaboration with the bourgeoisie and peasantry); 2. the armed struggle (based on an independent source of communist armed units); and 3. party construction (consolidation and perpetuation of proletarian power exercised exclusively by the Communist party).

Three Old Articles Also known as the 'Three Constantly Read Articles', contributions written by Mao Tse-tung over the period 1938–45 dwelling on the essence of proletarian ethics required in a backward revolutionary society in the context of imperialism and world revolution. They are: 1. 'IN MEMORY OF NORMAN BETHUNE' (published on 21 Dec. 1939); 2. 'Serve the People' (8 Sep. 1944), a quasi-religious guide, exhorting leaders and masses to the pursuit of high ideals considered to be the destiny of the Chinese people – in particular, leaders must strive to save the suffering masses and, if necessary, die for the cause; and 3. 'The FOOLISH OLD MAN' (11 June 1945).

Three People's Principles Political and social guidelines laid down by Sun Yat-sen, China's social democratic leader, in the Manifesto of the First National Congress of the KUOMINTANG in 1924. They were: 1. national independence and interest; 2. democracy; and 3. social justice.

Three People's Solidarity Organization ORGANIZATION OF SOLIDARITY OF THE PEOPLES OF AFRICA, ASIA AND LATIN AMERICA.

Three Pillars of Bolshevism Three policy postulates of the BOLSHEVIKS in Tsarist Russia, calculated to gain popular support: 1. the abolition of monarchy in favour of a democratic republic; 2. the eight-hour working day; and 3. the distribution of large estates to the peasants. The demands were quite moderate by Bolshevik standards. After the seizure of power in Oct. 1917 Bolshevik policies became much more radical.

Three-Point Trade Formula Better known as the THREE PRINCIPLES OF SINO-JAPANESE TRADE.

Three Principles of Sino-Japanese Trade Three rules formulated by the Chinese Prime Minister, Chou En-lai in 1960, to govern trade between China and Japan. They were: 1. a trade agreement on a government-to-government basis; 2. contracts on an enterprise-to-enterprise basis; and 3. the export of specific items from China to Japan by specific arrangement. There were also three political conditions laid down, viz.: 1. the elimination of hostile attitudes in Japan towards Communist China; 2. the discontinuation of Japanese support for the two-Chinas policy; and 3. the promotion of the normalization of Sino-Japanese political relations. The acceptance of the principles led to the conclusion of the L – T AGREEMENT in 1962.

Three Reconciliations and One Reduction Charges made in China against the USSR in the Sino-Soviet dispute, originally formulated by Liu Ning-yi, Deputy Director of the Foreign Affairs Office of the State Council, in a speech to the NATION-

AL PEOPLE'S CONGRESS in 1964. The three reconciliations were: 1. peace with the imperialists; 2. peace with the reactionaries of various countries; and 3. peace with modern revisionists (incl. Yugoslavia). As to the reduction, it referred to the slowdown of the Soviet support of revolutionary struggles in the colonial and other exploited and oppressed countries.

Three Revolutions Three simultaneous campaigns proclaimed by the Vietnam Workers' Party (as the Communist party in North Vietnam was officially known then) in Hanoi in 1974, as a partial attempt to the reunification of North and South Vietnam. It involved: 1. revolution in the means of production (including radical improvements and the socialization of land and capital); 2. the revolutionization of the methods of production (especially radical improvements in technology); and 3. revolution in culture (especially re-education or thought reform).

Three-Seven Scheme A basis of mental-manual work applied in China during the GREAT PROLETARIAN CULTURAL RE-VOLUTION to cadres transferred from desk positions to the countryside. Owing to the shortages of labour in rural areas, the transferred cadres were required to engage mostly in manual labour: out of 10 days – seven in manual work and three in other activities. A variant of this scheme was the Two-Five pattern, where in each week five days were devoted to physical labour and two days to other activities.

Three Togethers A general principle adhered to in the Chinese PEOPLE'S LIBER-ATION ARMY, viz.: 1. work together; 2. eat together; and 3. live together. Work includes farm labour in which army units engage wherever they are stationed. During the GREAT PROLETARIAN CULTURAL REVOLUTION this principle was often applied to students and peasants in the Party's drive to promote COLLECTIVISM in the countryside.

Three-Way Alliance In China, another description of the THREE-IN-ONE COMBI-NATION.

Three Who Made a Revolution The title of a well-known book written by Bertram D. Wolfe and published in 1948 on LENIN, TROTSKY and STALIN. The book is a scholarly, authoritative and vividly written account of the three men's early lives, revolutionary activities and their role in the GREAT OCTOBER SOCIALIST REVOLUTION.

Three Worlds Theory An assertive proposition put forward by Mao Tse-tung in 1974, since that time elevated to a theory and published as a pamphlet, *Chairman Mao's Theory of the Differentiation of the Three Worlds as a Major Contribution to Marxism-Leninism* (1977). From the Chinese ideological and foreign policy standpoints, the world is seen as falling into three divisions (Worlds): 1. the two super-powers – the USA and the USSR; 2. the economically developed world – Western and Eastern Europe, Canada, Japan, Australia, New Zealand and South Africa; and 3. the Third World – Africa (except South Africa), Asia (including China, but excluding Japan) and all Latin America. The First World consists of imperialist super-powers, which are the common enemies of the world. Their rivalry will inevitably lead to a new world war. The USSR is described as a 'socio-imperialist country', a more likely source of world war than the USA as the latter's invincibility was shattered in Korea, Vietnam, Cambodia and Laos. The Second World has a dual character in that it stands in contradiction to both the First and the Third Worlds. On the one hand, it is oppressed and exploited by the imperialist super-powers, but on the other hand it oppresses and exploits the less-developed countries. For the sake of world peace, the Second World should join the Third World to fight the First World.

Tien An Men Incident A controversial affair involving many thousands of people which occurred in Tien An Men Square, the central public area flanked by the Great Hall of the People in Peking, on 5 April 1976. At the time, the affair was reported as a counter-revolutionary revolt engineered by TENG HSIAO-P'ING, in which the crowd went on a rampage destroying vehicles attacking militia and setting fire to a building. But the official version is that the report at the time was deliberately distorted by the GANG OF FOUR who at that time had control of the media and wanted to topple their chief enemy, Teng, who, in 1975, had assumed authority over the day-to-day work of the Central Committee of the Chinese Communist Party when CHOU EN-LAI fell ill (and died in Jan. 1976). In that capacity and by Mao's direction, Teng launched an attack on the Gang of Four. As officially asserted, and confirmed by HUA KUO-FENG, the incident was a public demonstration in tribute to the late Chou. To provoke the crowd, YAO WEN-YUAN (a member of the Gang of Four) gave orders to remove the wreaths presented by masses on the preceding day and spread the rumour that Chou had been the 'top capitalist roader'. Thus, the reaction from the crowd was allegedly directed against the opponents of Chou and Teng, not a revolutionary revolt against the government.

Tight Planning Also known as taut p., a system of economic planning noted for very high (ambitions) production targets in relation to the available resources. It is prompted by the determination to maximize rates of growth of production in quantitative terms, usually at the expense of quality. Central planners typically assume that the production capacities, as declared by enterprises, are understated, thus allowing stocks and reserves of materials and allocations of equipment to decrease quite low yet maintaining relatively high targets. As a result, there are prevalent shortages, deep SELLERS' MARKETS, recurring BOTTLENECKS and BLACK MARKETS. T.p. is characteristic of the CENTRALIZED DIRECTIVE SYSTEM OF PLANNING AND MANAGEMENT. It was common in the Socialist countries before the ECONOMIC REFORMS of the 1960s.

Time and Space See SPACE AND TIME.

Time Wages A basis of the calculation of wages which – given the worker's skill classification (wage rate) – depend on the period of work, viz. hour, day, week, month or year. Under this system, which contrasts with PIECEWORK WAGES, it is assumed that the value of the workers' services is proportional to the period of his work. It is implicitly assumed that work results are not directly dependent on the worker's effort, but rather on his qualifications and on the machinery, equipment or general working environment provided by the employer. In general, shorter periods (hour, week) are applied to less skilled manual or casual workers, while annual (or monthly or fortnightly) basis is applicable to professional, non-manual and permanent employees. On ideological grounds, Marxism favours t.w. rather than piecework w., especially in a capitalist economy, as the former are less likely to lead to sweated labour and exploitation. T.w. are also considered to be more conducive to workers' solidarity and equality and the employers' creation of more productive and congenial working conditions. In the Socialist countries, there is a tendency to replace piecework w. with t.w., and supplement them with incentives emphasizing collective (rather than individual) effort.

Timiriaziev, Kliment Arkadievich (1843–1920) A distinguished Russian scientist who supported Marxism and made substantial contributions to the interpretation of biological and social processes in accordance with the materialist philosophy acceptable to the BOLSHEVIKS. He became one of the leading exponents of Darwinism and the theory of evolution, ascribing the dominant role to the external environment. For his Marxist views, he was subjected to Tsarist persecution after 1894. He fully supported the October Revolution, the Bolshevik regime and defended the latter in the international scene. In biology, he rejected WEISMANNISM-MORGANISM and VITALISM in favour of PHOTOSYNTHESIS, stressing the role of opposites, causality and the possibility of changing species by an appropriate control of environmental factors. He laid down the early theoretical foundations for MICHURINISM and LYSENKOISM.

Tipping The practice of making small presents of money to workers providing personal services, such as waiters, cloakroom attendants, barbers, porters, postmen, guides, taxi drivers and the like. Originally, the tip was meant to be an extra payment for special service, but in many countries it has become a more or less automatic practice and even an entitlement going with the job and enforced by custom. Labour leaders and social reformers have traditionally been against t. on the following grounds: 1. it is degrading to labour; 2. it provides an excuse for employers to keep wages down; 3. it introduces an element of inequality among workers not necessarily related to their skill, responsibility or disadvantageous working conditions and, furthermore, some workers are in a better position to receive higher tips than others; and 4. it may be looked upon as a type of bribery which leads to differentiated service with the low-income customers being penalized. There have been special efforts in some countries (such as Australia) to abolish t. T. is still common in most Socialist countries, which is explained largely by the low levels of planned personal income. But it is officially frowned upon as a capitalist survival and assumed that it will disappear in the long run.

Tito (original name **Josip Broz**) (1892–1980) An outstanding Yugoslav Communist leader, military commander and statesman. He joined the Social-Democratic Party in 1910 and became a Communist. Recruited into the Austrian army in W.W.I he was forcibly sent to the Russian front (in 1915) where he was taken prisoner of war. He then participated in the Bolshevik Revolution (in Siberia) and returned to Yugoslavia where he joined the illegal Communist Party of Yugoslavia. He spent several terms in prison and in 1934 assumed the name of T. From then on he was active in the international Communist movement including the organization of the INTERNATIONAL BRIGADES for the Spanish Civil War on behalf of the COMINTERN. He survived the GREAT PURGES in the USSR in the late 1930s, when the entire leadership of the C.P.Y. was eliminated, became the Party's Secretary-General in 1937 and returned to Yugoslavia in the following year. During W.W.II he led the left-wing resistance against the German occupying forces with a much greater success than his right-wing rival D. MIHAJLOVIĆ. T. became Marshal and enjoyed support not only from the USSR, but also (especially military supplies) from Britain and the USA. In addition to the Germans, he fought the Italians, monarchists, Croats and the church establishment. After the war, having ruthlessly eliminated all opposition, T. was Prime Minister in 1945–53. After Jan. 1953, he became the country's President, in addition to his top position in the Party. Although he cautiously cooperated with the USSR for several years after W.W.II, in 1948 he defied Stalin's dictatorship in the international Communist movement and, as a result, Yugoslavia was expelled from the COMINFORM in that year. With solid domestic support and Western (especially US) economic aid, T. emerged victorious and an acknowledged world statesman. In 1955, KHRUSHCHEV went to Belgrade seeking reconciliation with T., thereby conceding Stalin's error. He was very active in international politics until his death and was (as of 1979) the longest surviving W.W.II leader. The version of communism developed in Yugoslavia since 1948 has come to be known as TITOISM.

Titoism A type of communism developed in Yugoslavia after TITOS's break with Stalin in 1948. The term was first introduced in the USSR and China in a critical sense, synonymous with nationalistic revisionism disloyal to the international Communist movement. In the West, T. became identified with national communism and independence from Moscow in domestic, as well as foreign policies. Although explicitly subscribing to a neutral line in the East-West conflict, T. is still loyal to Marxism, is careful not to offend smaller Socialist countries and attaches great importance to foreign trade, especially with the West. In domestic policies, T. involves: 1. a mono-party system but allowing greater personal freedom than in other Socialist countries; 2. the social ownership of the means of production, in practice exercised by WORKERS' COUNCILS and not by the state; 3. considerable decentralization of economic planning and management; 4. substantial operation of the market mechanism (MARKET SOCIALISM); and 5. considerable freedom of enterprise, including private enterprise, especially in agriculture, small-scale industry and services.

Tkachev, Pyotr Nikitich (1844–86) A Russian revolutionary and one of the leading theoreticians of NARODNISM. He co-operated with S. NECHAYEV, was arrested for revolutionary and terrorist activities and escaped to Switzerland, where he collaborated in editing the revolutionary journals *VPERED!* and *Nabad* (*Tocsin*). T. advocated immediate revolution, to be carried out by a tightly organized secret fraternity of professional conspirators. He was contemptuous of the masses ('uncivilized mob') as a revolutionary force, but thought they could be useful in disrupting and destroying the existing establishment. He differed with the anarchists in that he attached crucial importance to the seizure of state power and the transformation of society 'from above'. His ideas influenced Engels and some were adopted by *NARODNAYA VOLYA* (in its terrorist activities) and later by Lenin. T. died insane in Paris.

To each according to his birth A Marxist expression for the principle of distribution of personal income and property according to the social class to which a person is born. This is claimed to be typical of societies where SOCIAL CLASSES are clearly defined by law or custom and where there is no SOCIAL MOBILITY, as exemplified by the caste system and slavery.

To each according to his needs 'FROM EACH ACCORDING TO HIS ABILITY, TO EACH ACCORDING TO HIS NEEDS'.

To each according to his work A principle of distribution of personal income dependent on the quantity and quality of work performed, not on a person's needs. Its full statement is 'from each according to his ability, to each according to his work'. It is also known as the Leninist principle of distribution and was adopted in Soviet Russia in 1921, to be applicable during the stage of socialism transitional to full communism. Distribution 'according to work' is based on the following assumptions and practices: 1. labour is the only socially legitimate source of personal income (except social security); 2. for remuneration purposes, work in MATERIAL PRODUCTION and in the NON-PRODUCTIVE SPHERE is treated alike; 3. standard wage scales are differentiated according to the quality and intensity of work or occupation; 4. bonuses payable to workers by enterprises are based on their performance and, similarly, overtime work is remunerated accordingly; and 5. the total wage fund and average earnings are set independently on a centrally planned basis. In actual practice, personal income in the socialist countries is partly based on the principle 'according to needs', in the form of SOCIAL CONSUMPTION.

Togliatti, Palmiro (1893–1964) An Italian Communist leader, who dominated the Italian Communist Party for four decades until his death and was active in the international Communist movement. He joined the Italian Socialist Party in 1914 and later was a co-founder of the ITALIAN COMMUNIST PARTY in 1921 with

A. GRAMSCI. He was elected to the Party's Executive Committee in 1922 and became its Secretary-General in 1927. He also became a member of the Executive Committee of the COMINTERN in 1925 and served on its Secretariat from 1935 to 1937. T. was arrested several times for anti-fascist activities, spent many years in exile (mostly in France and the USSR) and participated in the SPANISH CIVIL WAR. After his return from the USSR in 1944, he became Deputy Premier 1944–47 and Minister for Justice and led the Italian Communists in the Italian parliament up to 1948. He proved to be a capable Party administrator and developed the I.C.P. into the largest communist party in the capitalist world. After the TWENTIETH CONGRESS OF THE CPSU in Feb. 1956, he became an influential advocate of DE-STALINIZATION in the international Communist movement, pressing for independence of each national Communist party, and he popularized the concept of POLYCENTRISM. His ideas on the international Communist movement were systematized in the YALTA MEMORANDUM, which he produced in a Soviet hospital at Yalta shortly before his death. T. can be considered as an early forerunner of EUROCOMMUNISM. The Soviet Government commemorated his name in 'Togliattigrad', on the Volga where the Volga Automotive Works were constructed by Fiat 1967–70, as a tribute to his leadership, services to the international communist movement and Italian technology.

Tolkach (plural *tolkachi*) A Russian term meaning 'pusher', 'expediter' or even 'conjurer'. It is used colloquially in the USSR to describe a person employed by an enterprise to secure badly needed supplies of materials, components or equipment which are difficult to obtain through regular channels. A *t.* is typically employed in the supply department of a plant, but usually travels throughout the country, looking for scarce and urgently needed items. Such items may not be otherwise obtainable, either because of failures or delays in the official supply network or because of the unconventional nature of the items not included in the normal supply lists. Yet, such items are indispensable to the fulfilment of targets. A *t.* uses his own ingenuity, including personal visits to appropriate producing, importing enterprises or warehouses, threats, bribes and the like. Although frowned upon by the authorities, the *t.* is tolerated as, on the whole, he performs a useful function in the cumbersome supply system. A *t.* is more respectable than a *BLAT*.

Tolstoy, Lev Nikolaievich (1828–1910) A prominent Russian writer and social reformer of aristocratic descent (a count). In his later writings, he concentrated on exposing the weaknesses and injustice in the existing Russian society, the arbitrary power of the state and of the church hierarchy, the encroachments on personal freedom and the ill-treatment and exploitation of peasants. He advocated a patriarchal peasant community as a model for a better society and exerted a great moral influence on many social reformers, including Mahatma Gandhi in India. Although Marxists showed interest in his courageous and altruistic stand, they regarded his views and activities as utopian and anti-revolutionary. T.'s most famous works were *War and Peace* (1865, 1869) and *Anna Karenina* (1877).

Tonkin Gulf Resolution An Act of the US Congress passed in Aug. 1964 authorizing the US President to take 'all necessary steps, including the use of armed forces' to prevent further communist aggression in South-East Asia. It was specifically directed against the North Vietnamese attack on American vessels in the Gulf of Tonkin, regarded as international waters. On the basis of this resolution, President L. B. Johnson ordered the bombing of military bases in North Vietnam, beginning in 1965, and stepped up US military aid to South Vietnam. The T.G.R. produced an adverse reaction all over the world and was repealed by President R. M. Nixon on 12 Jan. 1971.

Tourist Exchange Rate The exchange rate administered in some Socialist countries (Albania, Bulgaria, Czechoslovakia, Hungary, Poland, and Romania) in application to foreign tourists exchanging hard currencies into Socialist currencies. This rate is more favourable to foreigners than the BASIC EXCHANGE RATE applied in visible trade. For example, in Romania as of late 1978, the basic exchange rate to US$1.00 was 4.47 lei, while the t.e.r. was 12.00 lei. The respective rates for Bulgaria were 0.88 and 1.32 lev, Czechoslovakia – 5.35 and 9.36 koruny, and Poland – 3.16 and 31.62 zlotys. The t.e.r. is meant to be related to RETAIL PRICES (the cost of living, which affects tourists), while the basic exchange rate is supposed to reflect PRODUCER PRICES.

TOZ Abbreviation in Russian of *Tovarishestvo dlya Sovmestnoi Obrabotki*, meaning Association for the Collective Cultivation of Land. It was the simplest form of collective farming in the USSR, originally created in 1918 out of former private estates and later transformed into *ARTEL* and fully-fledged *KOLKHOZ*. *TOZ* was a transitional mixture of private and co-operative farming. Land was held by individual peasants, farm buildings, livestock and minor implements were privately owned, as well as the produce, which could be sold in private markets (after taxes and/or compulsory deliveries to the state). But the major items of farm equipment, especially machinery and vehicles, were collectively owned. Major farm operations were undertaken on a collective basis. These entities were similar to the AGRICULTURAL CIRCLES in Poland in existence now.

Trade Agreement A formal accord between governments (usually involving the Ministries of Foreign Trade on each side) or some semi-official bodies (in the absence of diplomatic relations) on commercial exchanges covering medium-term periods, of two to five years. It is the typical basis for the conduct of foreign trade in the Socialist countries, as it facilitates economic planning. A t.a. usually specifies provisions for trade representation, the classes of goods to be exchanged and the tariffs to be applied. It may also include the agreed form of payment or may be supplemented with a separate payment agreement. A t.a. is more detailed and definite if concluded with another Socialist country than with a capitalist country. A t.a. is less formal and covers a shorter period than a trade treaty and generally does not require parliamentary ratification (while a trade treaty does), but it is less specific and covers a longer period than a TRADE PROTOCOL.

Trade Protocol A formal agreement typically concluded by a Socialist country, specifying the goods to be exchanged with another country in the next 12 (occasionally less or more) months. A t.p. is more specific than a trade agreement and, in fact, is supplementary to the latter. If the partner is a capitalist country, it merely means that the latter country undertakes to issue import and export licences to the entities trading with the Socialist country in question to the amount agreed on, but it does not guarantee reaching the quotas or totals agreed upon in the protocol.

Trades Union Congress The highest co-ordinating organization of British trade unions, based in London and embracing some 170 affiliated unions with about 9.0m. members. It was founded in Manchester in 1868 and has developed into a large federation, with permanent staff and certain limited powers over its affiliated bodies. The affiliated unions are, in general, national in scope and mostly involve manual or lower-paid workers (there are about 1.5m. trade unionists not affiliated to the T.U.C.). There has been close co-operation between the T.U.C. and the LABOUR PARTY, which it helped establish (in 1900 under the name of the Labour Representative Committee, in 1906 renamed the Labour Party). The policy of the T.U.C. is determined by the General Council, elected by industrial groups.

Trade Unions Mass organizations of workers, especially in industry, for the protection and advancement of their economic and social interests. They first developed largely in response to the Industrial Revolution in the leading capitalist countries, especially in the five decades before W.W.I. Traditionally, t.u. have been preoccupied with improvement in the material conditions of work (wages, hours, and amenities) within the framework of capitalism. But radical union leaders and social reformers have pressed for a more far-reaching approach, embracing political action directed to the evolutionary or revolutionary creation of a socialist society, as exemplified by GUILD SOCIALISM, SYNDICALISM and the idea of a GENERAL STRIKE. Marx and, especially, Lenin emphasized the decisive importance of the political working class movement and regarded t.u. to be secondary or even delaying the need for a proletarian revolution. In the Socialist countries, t.u. are a curious mixture of survivals from the past and modern adaptations to the needs of the state. In some respects, they are reminiscent of medieval guilds in that they embody the employer (representative of the state) and the employees (workers), organize educational and recreational activities and, in some countries (as in the USSR), administer social insurance funds. In some ways they are like the unions of the advanced capitalist countries, in that they endeavour to safeguard the interest of the workers against the management and send elected representatives to the national trade union congresses. But their most distinctive feature is that, while providing protection against management and bureaucracy, they cooperate with the employer, the state, and assist in the implementation of the economic plan on the labour front. The unions are organized on a vertical, industrial basis, i.e. according to the branches of industry, although there is also regional co-ordination. The pyramid in each country is headed by the Central Council of Trade Unions consisting of representatives who, like other trade union leaders,

are elected. The membership of unions is voluntary and it includes both workers and persons of managerial status. Except SOLIDARITY, the independent Polish trade union created in 1980, the party and state control of trade unions is assured. The election of union officials is usually arranged by the Communist party and higher positions are mostly occupied by party members. Lenin himself described trade unions as a 'school for communism' and 'transmission belts' for the party economic programme to the working masses. The recent economic reforms appear to be providing a new challenge to Socialist trade unions. The profit criterion, the growing power of technocracy and the strengthened position of the managers are creating new conflicts, such as the threat of dismissal of inefficient and redundant labour, the closing down of unprofitable factories and the need for stricter work discipline. This tends to reduce ordinary workers to a similar position, in some respects, as in capitalist countries. There is evidence to suggest that some Socialist leaders would like to see the party divorced from industrial conflicts. They think that trade unions should take over the responsibility and become genuine guardians of workers' interests at the enterprise level. Also CRAFT UNIONS, INDUSTRIAL UNIONISM, INTERNATIONAL CONFEDERATION OF FREE TRADE UNIONS, WORLD CONFEDERATION OF LABOUR, WORLD FEDERATION OF TRADE UNIONS.

Tragic Dialectics A pessimistic reinterpretation of Hegelian DIALECTICS, put forward by a German neo-Kantian philosopher, A. Liepert (1878–1946) in *Foundations of Dialectics* (1929). According to Liepert, dialectic contradictions are permanently antagonistic and are insoluble, i.e. antagonisms between existing situations and situations as they ought to be are eternal. Marxist philosophers reject t.d., as in their view it is too static, ignores dynamic development and overlooks the possibility of NON-ANTAGONISTIC CONTRADICTIONS under socialism.

Transferable Rouble The collective abstract currency introduced by the member countries of the COUNCIL FOR MUTUAL ECONOMIC ASSISTANCE in 1964 for settling mutual payments. It is also described as the 'clearing' or 'conversion' rouble. Its assigned function is to act as an instrument of progressive extension of MULTILATERAL TRADE AND PAYMENTS in the C.M.E.A. and perhaps beyond. But so far, it is not convertible into (capitalist) hard currencies, nor automatically transferable among the member countries. The t.r. is distinct from the Soviet rouble in internal circulation in the USSR. Although originally the official gold parity of both was the same (0.987412 gramme of fine gold), since 1973, in some types of transactions, 1.00 t.r. has been equivalent to 1.20 internal Soviet roubles. The t.r. can be created only by the export of goods and services to the member countries or by the extension of credit by the INTERNATIONAL BANK FOR ECONOMIC CO-OPERATION or the INTERNATIONAL INVESTMENT BANK, as agreed in co-ordinated plans and contracts. In several respects, the t.r. resembles the Special Drawing Rights of the International Monetary Fund, but, unlike the latter, it is not dependent on the value of the national currencies or economic fluctuations. The essence of the t.r. is that a credit balance can be transferred for spending in another member country, providing that it is done on a mutually agreed planned basis. There has been a progressive extension of transferability in this sense since 1964.

Transformation of Commodities In the Marxian framework by reference to a capitalist market economy, the process of the production of goods in its successive phases. Productive money capital (in the form of CONSTANT CAPITAL and VARIABLE CAPITAL) is used to purchase the means of production and LABOUR POWER. The resources acquired are used to produce new commodities. The commodities are then sold in the market for money, whereby their value (production costs and SURPLUS VALUE) is realized.

Transformation of Value In the Marxian analysis of capitalist production, the forms of value created by labour, viz. the conversion of VALUE into PRODUCTION PRICE, of SURPLUS VALUE into PROFIT and of profit into average profit (AVERAGE PROFIT RATE).

Transformation Problem In Marx's analysis of circulation (i.e. distribution), the process of conversion of value into prices. It is one of the most controversial questions in the Marxian treatment of production, the creation of value and exploitation under capitalism, where Marx is considered to be inconsistent or virtually discarding the LABOUR THEORY OF VALUE. The t.p. arises from the differing ORGANIC STRUCTURE OF CAPITAL in different branches of the economy, the deviation of market prices from VALUE and the tendency for the equalization of the RATE OF EXPLOITATION and the SOCIALLY-NECESSARY LABOUR embodied in commodities ($c + v + s$, i.e. CONSTANT CAPITAL, VARIABLE CAPITAL and SURPLUS VALUE). This is the essence of Marx's labour theory of value and the theory of surplus value, expounded by him in *CAPITAL*, vol. I. The differing organic structure of capital (capital-labour ratio) in different forms of production results in differing rates of surplus value, ie the same amounts of capital produce different amounts of surplus value, depending on the share of live labour in different industries. But the profit rate tends to be equalized owing to capitalist competition aiming at profit maximization, which is achieved by the flow of investment capital from low-profit to high-profit industries. This means that market prices of different commodities do not correspond to the socially-indispensable labour embodied in them. Marx attempted to gloss over this inconsistency in vol. III, ch. 9 of *Capital*, by constructing a table showing the transformation process for five industries with differing organic structures of capital. Here he introduced the concept of PRODUCTION PRICE (production cost *plus* the average profit rate). Marx argued that the market price oscillated around production price and that the former corresponded to the latter only where the organic structure of capital happens to be average for the economy. He further reasoned that the sum of prices in the economy was equal to their values and that total profit in the economy was equal to the total surplus value. Apparently, Marx himself was not satisfied with his analysis of the transformation process, and one wonders if he would not have re-written it had he edited the volume himself (vol. III was prepared for publication by Engels and appeared in 1894, 11 years after Marx's death).

Transgas FRATERNITY PIPELINE.

Transideological Collaboration A term describing various forms of co-operation between capitalist and Socialist enterprises, institutions and governments, in spite of the continued persistence of basic ideological differences. The term was first introduced by H. V. Perlmutter, an American economist, in 1969 by reference to joint East-West ventures. This trend has become evident since the early 1960s, as exemplified by capitalist-socialist INDUSTRIAL CO-OPERATION, joint financing and mutual participation in the work of the same international organizations. T.c. does not necessarily presuppose, although it does not exclude, the possibility of CONVERGENCE. Such collaboration is feasible and workable, even if basic ideological differences persist.

Transitional Period A Marxist concept applied to the changeover from capitalism to communism, more specifically from the PROLETARIAN REVOLUTION to FULL COMMUNISM, during which the remaining antisocial features of CAPITALISM are eliminated. The idea of the t.p. has been a controversial question among Marxists. Marx himself thought that it would be quite short (several years), but practical experience in the USSR and other Socialist countries has demonstrated that it may involve a period extending over several generations. The t.p., also described in

Marxist theory as SOCIALISM or the 'lower phase of communism', is characterized by the persistence of some private enterprise, material incentives ('FROM EACH ACCORDING TO HIS ABILITY, TO EACH ACCORDING TO HIS WORK'), rapid industrialization, the operation of the market mechanism in selected spheres and coexistence with the hostile capitalist countries. The widely differing views on the strategy and tactics of the t.p. have led to disunity in the international communist movement and its different versions, as exemplified by CASTROISM, EUROCOMMUNISM, MAOISM, OWN PATH TO SOCIALISM, STALINISM, TITOISM and TROTSKYISM.

Transitional Programme The strategy and tactics applicable during the 'TRANSITIONAL PERIOD', from the proletarian revolution to FULL COMMUNISM. More specifically, the term is applied to the central theme in the controversy between TROTSKY and STALIN in the USSR in the 1920s. Trotsky favoured democratic processes in the organization and operation of the Communist Party, the participation of the masses in decision-making, the elimination of market relations, SOCIALIST INTERNATIONALISM and PERMANENT REVOLUTION in domestic and foreign policies. On the other hand, Stalin urged bureaucratic controls, the ruthless elimination of the opposition, SOCIALISM IN ONE COUNTRY and peaceful coexistence with capitalist countries. In 1938, Trotsky elaborated on his strategy and tactics in a study, *Death Agony of Capitalism and the Coming Tasks of the Fourth International*, which is commonly known as the T.P. It was adopted at the founding Conference of the FOURTH INTERNATIONAL on 2 Sep. 1938 at Perigny (near Paris) as its primary guide.

Transition from Capitalism to Socialism In Marxist ideology, the period from the proletarian seizure of power from the bourgeoisie to the construction of the communist society. The strategy, tactics and practices to be applied in this stage have been a subject of controversy among

Marxist thinkers and policy makers ever since the formation of the First International in 1864. After renewed heated discussions in the 1950s, the leading communist parties held two important meetings on the question in Nov. 1957 (attended by 12 ruling parties which issued the MOSCOW DECLARATION) and in Dec. 1960 (attended by 81 Parties, including the Chinese Communist Party). The accepted guidelines which emerged from the two meetings were: 1. the seizure of power by the proletariat led by a well disciplined and tightly organized Communist party; 2. the institution of the DICTATORSHIP OF THE PROLETARIAT; 3. the alliance of the industrial working class with peasants and other groups of the working masses; 4. the SOCIALIZATION OF THE MEANS OF PRODUCTION; 5. the gradual socialization of agriculture; 6. planned economic development directed to the construction of socialism and communism; 7. the pursuit of the Socialist revolution in the sphere of ideology and culture and the creation of a large intelligentsia dedicated to the cause of socialism; 8. the abolition of discrimination among different nationalities and the cultivation of fraternal co-operation among different nations; 9. the defence of Socialist achievements against external aggressors as well as internal enemies; and 10. the solidarity of the working classes of the Socialist country with the working classes of other countries. (SOCIALIST INTERNATIONALISM). It was also emphasized in these declarations that the above general principles can be implemented by different methods and in different forms, according to the specific economic, political, social and cultural conditions existing in each country and the mentality of its people. In other words, the declarations clearly conceded the possibility of the nations' OWN PATHS TO SOCIALISM. The question of the transition has been widely discussed further by Western Marxists, especially since the mid-1960s, the prevailing feature of which has been a noteworthy DERADICALIZATION of the communist programmes. Also EUROCOMMUNISM, TWO-ROADS CONFLICT.

Transmission Belt A term appearing in communist usage in two different contexts. Lenin described trade unions under socialism (specifically in the USSR in the early 1920s) as a 't.b.' for the state economic policies, viz. facilitating the fulfilment of targets and the implementation of social policies. He emphasized that in a Socialist society there was no basic conflict between workers and the state, as the latter represented the workers and the employing entities were owned in one form or another by the workers. The expression also came into use in capitalist countries in the 1930s in application to communist front organizations. They were nominally non-communist but were indirectly used or infiltrated by communists. Those organizations were engaged in activities favouring the communist cause or carrying out communist programmes without arousing the suspicion of the general public, or coming into conflict with anti-communist legislation (as exemplified by the American League for Peace and Democracy in the 1930s and the INTERNATIONAL COMMUNIST FRONT ORGANIZATIONS since W.W.II).

Trans-Siberian Railway The railway line linking the European USSR (Chelyabinsk in the Ural Mountains) across southern Siberia with the Pacific coast (Vladivostok). It is the longest rail link in the world (7,400 km.). It was built between 1891 and 1904, with the eastern end running across Manchuria, but later (by 1916) extended to run entirely on Russian territory. During the FOREIGN INTERVENTION (1918–22) it was occupied for a time by the Czech Legion and was used by British, French and Japanese troops. Under the Soviet regime, the T.-S.R. was substantially improved i.e., another track was constructed during W.W.II, the speed capacity has been raised from 35–50 to 90–100 km.p.h. and it has been almost wholly electrified. The railway has proved to be of great economic and defence value and has contributed substantially to the development of southern Siberia. The journey from Moscow to Vladivostok

(9,300 km) takes seven days, but for foreigners (to whom Vladivostok is barred for security reasons) it takes longer, as they have to travel to Nakhodka, some 100 km. further east.

Treason Trials The political show trials in the USSR which took place over the period 1936–38, mostly involving senior Party leaders, government officials and army officers inconvenient to Stalin. The initial excuse for the trials was the assassination of S. M. KIROV, whose death was probably engineered by Stalin himself. The Public Prosecutor was A. Y. Vyshinsky (ex-Menshevik and Minister for Foreign Affairs 1949–53, at the height of the Cold War), while the administrative support was provided by the NKVD under the terrorist direction of N. I. YEZHOV. The trials, unmistakingly from the start, were undertaken to 'prove' the defendants to be guilty of treason, in particular of plots, political assassinations, sabotage, espionage and conspiracy with Germany and Japan to dismember the USSR. The T.T. represented attempts to justify legally the GREAT PURGES and to eliminate actual and potential opposition to Stalin's rule by terror. New perfected methods of psychological and medical conditioning and torturing were applied to the accused, who, almost without exception, publicly testified against themselves and 'confessed' to the most incredible crimes. There were four distinct trials: 1. 19–24 Aug. 1936, involving many OLD BOLSHEVIKS, such as L. B. KAMENEV and G. E. ZINOVIEV (who in the early 1920s helped Stalin against Trotsky); 2. 23–30 Jan. 1937, which included K. RADEK and Y. Pyatakov (Lenin's colleague in the October Revolution); 3. 4–10 June 1937, a secret trial involving senior army officers, including Marshal M. N. TUKHACHEVSKY; and 4. 2–13 March 1938, directed against the RIGHT OPPOSITION, including N. BUKHARIN, A. RYKOV and G. G. YAGODA. L. D. TROTSKY was tried *in absentia*, as he was in Mexico at the time, and was sentenced to death (he was murdered in 1940, almost certainly by Stalin's agent). At least 55

defendants appeared before tribunals and almost all were found guilty and shot. World public opinion regarded the T.T. as a travesty of liberty, justice and humanity. The sham trial procedures were later brought to light in KHRUSHCHEV'S SECRET SPEECH in 1956, after which some of the victims were subsequently rehabilitated.

Tred A labour unit of value proposed in Soviet Russia during WAR COMMUNISM. The idea was worked out by the prominent Soviet economist S. Strumilin, as part of his plan to abolish money, including its function as a measure of the production (scarcity). *T.* is a syllabic abbreviation of Russian words *trudovaya edinitsa* (labour unit). *T.* was to represent the value of a product made during a normal day by a worker in a reasonably efficient manner (according to the officially laid-down norms). Also *DOV*.

Trial and Error Method of Price Determination The process of successive approximations of prices by the state in a liberal, largely decentralized, socialist economy. This method was first suggested by E. BARONE in 1908, with some later additions by F. M. Taylor in 1928. But a more systematic analysis and in a broader context of economic calculation was presented by O. LANGE in the late 1930s (especially in *Review of Economic Studies*, 1936, 1937), with whom the method has been commonly identified ever since. In reply to the Western critics of collectivism (L.v. Mises, F.v. Hayek and L. Robbins), Lange conceded the need for a rational, essentially scarcity-governed price system. But he denied that only a private enterprise market economy was capable of providing efficient prices. He reasoned that in a socialist economy the Central Planning Board could establish 'accounting' or 'shadow' prices of the socialized resources, which could perform the same calculating and co-ordinative functions as conventional prices in a competitive capitalist market economy; in fact better, because the socialist state could take social (as distinct from private) cost-benefit into account. The method involves the following steps: 1. the state determines the money income of the population; 2. consumer goods are produced in accordance with the CONSUMER'S FREEDOM OF CHOICE; 3. the prices of consumer goods are set by the state at the minimum average cost levels, periodically readjusted to ensure equilibrium between market demand and state supply; 4. the socialized resources are assigned initial (historical or roughly estimated) prices; 5. the managers of socialized enterprises strive to maximize profits by producing at levels where marginal cost is equal to marginal revenue (i.e. to average revenue or price, which is given); 6. if the enterprises' demand for resources reveals shortages or surpluses, the state raises or lowers the prices of the resources concerned, so as to re-establish equilibrium in the factor market; and 7. prices are periodically altered in response to changing demand and supply conditions, to ensure market equilibrium and taking account of social cost-benefit considerations. Many Marxist economists, not only in the USSR and later in other Socialist countries, but also in the West (such as M. Dobb), rejected the postulate of the market equilibrium under socialism, especially the t.-a.-e.m. of achieving it. The method as proposed by Lange and other Western economists has never been applied in practice in any Socialist centrally planned economy, except in modified forms in Yugoslavia and Hungary.

Tricon, Tricontinental Abbreviated form of the Tricontinental Solidarity Organization, formally known as the ORGANIZATION OF SOLIDARITY OF THE PEOPLES OF AFRICA, ASIA AND LATIN AMERICA.

Trinity Formula An expression used by Marx (in CAPITAL, vol I) for the three factors of production and their remunerations as the essence of capitalist production. In the work cited, he said: 'The trinity formula ... comprises all the secrets of the social production process. The trinity formula reduces itself more specifically to

the following: capital INTEREST, land GROUND RENT, labour WAGES ...'.

Triple Alliance In China, another name for the THREE-IN-ONE COMBINATION.

Troika A Russian term meaning 'the three' or 'threefold', which has come to have at least three different meanings. Originally, in Russia, it meant a fast, light carriage drawn by three horses, in common use up to the middle of the 19th c. for carrying mail, but since that time used mostly for sporting purposes. Under Stalin *T.* was a Committee of Three directing the Soviet secret police and the administration of justice. It had the authority of holding secret trials and the power to sentence the guilty to exile, imprisonment or death. The Committee was abolished after the removal of BERIA in 1953. The term was also used by the Soviet leaders in the forum of the United Nations. In 1961 KHRUSHCHEV proposed a radical reform of the UN by establishing a *T.* - a Secretariat of Three, consisting of three Secretaries representing the three world divisions: the Developed Capitalist World (the West); the Socialist bloc; and the Third World (less-developed countries).

Trotsky (also spelt Trotskii, Trotski), **Lev Davidovich** (1879–1940) A Soviet revolutionary leader, a brilliant writer, orator and organizer, one of the *THREE WHO MADE A REVOLUTION* and one of the most controversial figures in the international communist movement. The son of a Jewish farmer in the southern Ukraine, he became a revolutionary as a student at the age of 18 and was constantly harassed by the Tsarist police. Between 1902 and 1917 he carried on his revolutionary activities mostly abroad (England, Germany, Austria, Switzerland, France and the USA). He first met Lenin in London in 1902 and collaborated with him in the publication of *ISKRA*. In 1904, he abandoned his family name of Bronstein and assumed T. instead (his gaoler in Odessa). He actively participated in the REVOLU-

TION OF 1905–07 and led the Soviet of Workers' Deputies in St Petersburg (now Leningrad), the first SOVIET ever established. At the time of the split in the RUSSIAN SOCIAL-DEMOCRATIC LABOUR PARTY in London in 1903, T. opposed Lenin for his authoritarian and intolerant programme and became a leading MENSHEVIK. But after his return to Russia in May 1917, he accepted Lenin's APRIL THESES as an expression of his own theory of PERMANENT REVOLUTION and joined forces with him thereafter. In July 1917, T. became the Chairman of the PETROGRAD SOVIET. It was his organizing ability that was responsible for the success of the GREAT OCTOBER SOCIALIST REVOLUTION. As the People's Commissar (Minister) for Foreign Affairs (1917–18), he negotiated the BREST-LITOVSK TREATY and, as the People's Commissar for War, he created the RED ARMY, successfully defended Soviet power during the Civil War 1918–20 and pressed for the MILITARIZATION OF LABOUR. He was also active in the COMINTERN, which he regarded as an instrument of spreading the revolution to the capitalist world, without which he saw little chance of the Soviet regime surviving. T. was the first Marxist leader to suggest that a revolution could occur in underdeveloped areas and then be carried to industrialized nations. He advocated the use of the USSR as the springboard for the world revolution. T. pressed for democratic processes in the Party, in which he led the LEFT OPPOSITION (1923–27) and came into insurmountable conflict with STALIN. Although the most obvious candidate to succeed Lenin (who died in Jan. 1924), T. fell victim to Stalin's superior cunning and ruthlessness and was gradually stripped of his offices, expelled from the Party (1927), deported to Alma-Ata (1928), expelled from the USSR (1929) and deprived of Soviet citizenship (1932). He lived in Turkey (1929–32), France (1933–35), Norway (1935–36) and Mexico (1936–40). After several attempts at creating an alternative to Comintern, he founded the FOURTH INTERNATIONAL in 1938, based in Paris. At Stalin's TREASON TRIALS (1936–38), T. was accused of directing subversive activities against the Soviet regime, tried *in absentia* in March 1938 and sentenced to death. T. died in Mexico City on 21 Aug 1940 as a result of wounds inflicted on him by his close associate in the Fourth International, Ramon Mercader (*alias* Frank Jackson, Jacque Murnard), almost certainly on Stalin's orders. T.'s main publications were: *Our Political Tasks and Organizational Questions* (1904); *Results and Prospects* (1906); *Our Revolution: Essays on the Working-Class and International Revolution 1904–17* (1918); *Terrorism and Communism* (1920); *How the Revolution Armed Itself* (1923–25); *Lenin* (1924); *Permanent Revolution* (1930); *My Life* (1930); *Problems of the Chinese Revolution* (1932); *History of the Russian Revolution* (1931–33, in three volumes); *The Stalin School of Falsification* (1932); *The Revolution Betrayed* (1937); and *Death Agony of Capitalism and the Coming Tasks of the Fourth International* (1938).

Trotskyism (also spelt Trotskiism) A major version of Marxism propagated by L. D. TROTSKY and his followers. The term was first applied by Stalin and his supporters in a critical sense in 1924, but became well established outside the USSR in the 1930s. The basic doctrine of T. is contained in Trotsky's PERMANENT REVOLUTION and is further summarized in his *Death Agony of Capitalism and the Coming Tasks of the Fourth International* (1938), commonly known as the Transitional Programme. The distinguishing tenets of T. are: 1. the victory of the socialist revolution and communism can be achieved only by a simultaneous process in different countries; 2. although a revolution can begin in a backward agricultural country, it must be carried – by force if necessary – to industrialized countries which are in the best position to build communism; 3. the policy of coexistence must be condemned, as it amounts to ideological timidity and is inconsistent with the Permanent Revolution; 4. the revolution must be pursued primarily by the industrial workers as neither the bourgeoisie can be trusted, nor can the peasantry be relied upon; 5. the revolutionary process must be continuous and designed to destroy gradually the capitalist heritage, values and institutions – the mere nationalization or socialization of the means of production is not enough; 6. NATIONALISM and PATRIOTISM are essentially restrictive and must be subordinated to SOCIALIST INTERNATIONALISM and world revolution; 7. the principle of the democratic processes in the organization and operation of the Communist party must be strictly observed, to avoid excessive centralism and unscrupulous manipulation by individual leaders; 8. there is a danger in the growth of the party and state bureaucracy, as it becomes increasingly divorced from the masses, tends to develop into a privileged elite and can be used by unscrupulous elements for narrow group interests; and 9. with the socialization of the means of production, the elimination of market relations and the institution of economic planning, objective economic laws cease to exist under socialism. Instead, labour, through central economic planning, becomes the master of its own destiny. Officially, T. has always been regarded by the Soviet leaders as a petty bourgeois heresy amounting to COUNTER-REVOLUTION. It has been further accused philosophically of MECHANISTIC MATERIALISM and IDEALISM. Although backed up by a doctrine appealing especially to young militant idealists, T. is not sufficiently clear-cut on strategy and tactics and, as a movement, has fragmented into a number of associations and factions (especially during 1951–54, 1961–65 and 1971–75). In Britain alone, over the period 1932–78, at least 25 different Trotskyite groups can be identified. T. has never enjoyed significant appeal in the Socialist countries, but has aroused considerable interest in some Western and less-developed countries (particularly in Britain, France, Italy, Spain, the USA, Argentina, Bolivia, Brazil, Peru and Venezuela).

Trotskyite, Trotskyist (also spelt Trotskiite, Trotskiist, Trotskite, Trotskist) Used as an adjective and noun, pertaining to or a follower of L. D. TROTSKY or TROTSKYISM.

Trud (*Labour*, in Russian) The daily organ of the ALL-UNION CENTRAL COUNCIL OF TRADE UNIONS in the USSR. It first appeared in 1921 and concentrates on Soviet unionism, industrial problems, labour productivity, the impact of new technology on labour and the international aspects of trade unionism and labour problems. Its head office is in Moscow but it is also printed in 32 other cities in the USSR. Its total daily circulation now exceeds 5m copies. T. also publishes a weekly supplement called *Novoie vremya* (*New Times*), devoted to international affairs appearing not only in Russian, but also in Czech, English, French, German, Polish and Spanish.

Trudoviks (or *Trudoviki*) Literally 'toilers' in Russian, a political group consisting of peasant deputies and some intellectuals in the State DUMA in Russia. They advocated the creation of medium-sized farms to be worked by peasants and their families, pressed for decentralization and the strengthening of local government, constitutional monarchy and universal suffrage and were opposed to racial discrimination. During W.W.I they supported the war effort (unlike the Bolsheviks) and the FEBRUARY REVOLUTION. A. F. KERENSKY was among their leaders.

Truman Doctrine A political declaration formulated by the US President Harry S. Truman on 12 March 1947 in the Congress, pledging American economic and military support to foreign governments against serious internal communist threats. The aid was offered in the first instance to Greece and Turkey, but was soon broadened to include any country in the capitalist world. To this effect, President Truman asked the Congress to appropriate $400m, which was later raised several times. It provided the basis for the policy of CONTAINMENT and became one of the instruments of the COLD WAR. The Communist regimes interpreted the doctrine as an attempt to intervene in the internal affairs of other countries, stem the march of inevitable progressive forces, oppose NATIONAL LIBERATION MOVEMENTS in colonial and other dependent areas and the virtual rejection of peaceful COEXISTENCE. The T.D. was replaced by the Eisenhower Doctrine in 1957 (DULLES-EISENHOWER DOCTRINE).

Truth In philosophy, correspondence of belief to fact which contrasts with falsity. The different approaches to the nature of t. are reflected in coherence, correspondence, performative, pragmatic, semantic and other theories. Marxist philosophers, subscribing as they do to MATERIALISM, define t. as a correspondence of impressions, images, concepts or ideas to their objects, or a concordance of thought with OBJECTIVE REALITY. In METAPHYSICS, t. is treated as the final result of cognition and consequently, absolute and immutable. On the other hand, Marxist DIALECTICAL MATERIALISM regards the process of truth-pursuit (cognition) as a historical process – from ignorance to the cognition of individual objects, then to wider and deeper knowledge. Marx (in THESES ON FEUERBACH) and Lenin (in *MATERIALISM AND EMPIRIO-CRITICISM*) pointed out that PRACTICE, especially man's activities associated with production and social and revolutionary pursuits, is the only final test of t. Until t. is absolute, it is essentially relative. This approach to t. reflects the Marxist adherence to HISTORICAL MATERIALISM and SELF-MOVEMENT. To orthodox Marxists, the insistence (by E. MACH) on human impressions and experience (SOLIPSISM, and EMPIRIO-CRITICISM) as the criterion of t. is not acceptable, as they are considered to be subjective. Also ABSOLUTE T., CONCRETE T., ETERNAL T., OBJECTIVE T., RELATIVE T.

TsK KPSS Transliterated abbreviation of Russian *Tsentral'nyi Komitet Kommunisticheskoi Partyi Sovetskogo Soyuza*, meaning CENTRAL COMMITTEE OF THE COMMUNIST PARTY OF THE SOVIET UNION.

T.U.C. A commonly used abbreviation for the TRADES UNION CONGRESS (in Britain).

Tudeh Party The Communist Party of Iran (literally, the 'Party of the Masses'). Founded in 1920 under the name of the Communist Party of Iran, it was proscribed in 1931 and for the next decade operated underground, with most of its leaders in exile (especially the USSR). In 1941 the communist movement reappeared in the open under its present name. It soon became the largest political party in the country, with more than 400,000 members and three Ministers in the Government. Following an unsuccessful assassination attempt on the Shah's life by a Party member in 1947, the Party was banned for two years. It was banned again in 1954 but operated underground, directed by leaders in exile based mostly in West and East Berlin. The Party has followed a pro-Soviet orientation. Its membership is estimated to be about 2,000 (the country's population being 35m). But there are other Marxist groups, believed to have more than 20,000 adherents, in particular the Revolutionary Tudeh Party, the Organization of Marxist Leninists (Maoist), the Guerilla Organization of the Devotees for the People and others. In the Iranian upheavals of 1978–79, the T.P. adopted a strongly anti-Shah stand, pressed for a more radical line and resorted to extremist and violent activities.

Tukhachevsky, Mikhail Nikolaievich (1893–1937) A Russian army officer of noble descent, a communist and Marshal of the Soviet Union. He joined the Bolsheviks in 1918 and immediately helped organize the RED ARMY. He distinguished himself during the Civil War fighting the Czech Legion, Kolchak's White army and other opponents of the Soviet regime. He supported Trotsky's idea of the PERMANENT REVOLUTION and, during the Soviet-Polish War (1919–20), urged the spread of the communist revolution to Central and Western Europe by the force of arms. Over the period 1925–28, he was Chief of the General Staff and in 1935 was promoted to the rank of Marshal of the Soviet Union. But he fell victim in Stalin's GREAT PURGES. In 1937 he was accused of being a leader of a military conspiracy, was tried in the third, secret Treason Trial (June 1937) and shot. An extensive and arbitrary purge among senior army officers followed. In 1956, it was officially conceded that T. had not been guilty of the charges and was formally rehabilitated after the 22nd Party Congress in 1961.

Tupamaros Fanatical left-wing urban guerillas in Uruguay, resorting to extremist activities (incl. kidnapping and assassination) to provoke armed insurrection against the ruling regime. The movement was founded by Raúl Sendic (a former law student) in the early 1960s and its first armed raid was staged in July 1963. The name T., adopted in 1964, is derived from Tupac Amaru (1742–81), an Inca leader, social reformer and intellectual who was executed after an unsuccessful uprising against the Spanish rule. T. is used as a short name for the National Liberation Movement which adopted its Constitution in 1966. At first the T. attracted mostly young and well educated radicals and became most active in Montevideo during 1969–72 (especially in 1970/71 when they kidnapped several foreign diplomats). The movement has gained supporters in other South American countries, particularly in Argentina and Bolivia. The T. developed a most intricate organization (including underground bases, tunnels and escape routes), regarded by some radicals as the new model for the revolutionary movement. Although the T. are aware of the successful revolutionary experience in China and Cuba (CASTROISM, MAOISM), they do not favour the countryside as the starting base for a social revolution under South American conditions. The failure of several rural uprisings, especially the venture led by GUEVARA in Bolivia in 1967, has evoked some popular support for their strategy. The T. suffered a serious defeat by the Uruguayan army in 1972 when about 1,000 (some one-third of their total number) were arrested, including the wounded Sendic. In a repressive campaign, the government captured most of the members and their leaders and prohibited the use of the term T. in print. But the T. have continued as an organization, even though in 1974 two competing groups emerged within the movement.

Turkish Communist Party (*Türkiye Komunist Partisi*) A small, insignificant party, banned for more than half a century, being the only illegal communist party in Europe. Its beginnings go back to 1918, when an Executive Committee of the Turkish Socialist-Communists was created in Moscow, which two years later moved to Baku and assumed the name of the T.C.P. In the same year, its leaders founded another illegal group in Istanbul under the same name, while legally another group emerged called the People's Communist Party of Turkey. But the latter was banned too in 1922 and its members joined the T.C.P. An attempt in 1946 to create the Turkish Socialist Workers' and Peasant Party as a legal communist front organization proved unsuccessful as it was banned in the same year. The T.C.P. has continued operating underground, but with little impact on the country's political and social life. Its leaders are mostly in exile in Eastern Europe. The Party's membership is probably 2,000, but it claims 26,000 adherents (of the country's total population of 43m in 1978). In its international orientation, the Party has consistently followed the pro-Soviet line.

Turnover Tax A term peculiar to the Socialist centrally planned economies, roughly corresponding to the sales (or purchase) tax in capitalist countries. It was first introduced in the USSR in 1931 and was later adopted by other Socialist countries as well. It is a type of an indirect tax added to the producer (or wholesale) price and is mostly collected by trading enterprises at the wholesale level. The tax is employed not only for raising state revenue, but also – and more importantly – for regulating the demand for and (to a lesser degree) the supply of consumer goods and services. In some countries (such as Romania) it may also be imposed on producer goods (i.e. the cost is borne by the socialized enterprises in the first instance). In capitalist market economies the level of the retail price depends on the indirect tax, i.e. changes in the latter usually lead to a corresponding change in the retail price. But under Socialism, it is the size of the t.t. that is typically determined by the postulated levels of the RETAIL PRICE and the PRODUCER PRICE. The rates of the t.t. are highly differentiated, reflecting different elasticities of consumer demand for different products and the macrosocial preferences of the state. The t.t. is an instrument for insulating production from consumption and enables the administration of a TWO-TIER PRICE SYSTEM.

Tutti-Frutti Communism A colloquial term which originated in Italy ('All-fruit mixture Communism'), after Krushchev's admission in 1956 of the possibility of countries taking their OWN PATH TO SOCIALISM and Togliatti's popularization of the concept of POLYCENTRISM in 1957 in the international Communist movement. These facts were acknowledged formally at the Conference of the 81 Communist and Workers' Parties in Nov. 1960 in the MOSCOW STATEMENT.

Twelve Rules Instructions issued by the Central Committee of the Chinese Communist Party in 1960 to the rural PEOPLE'S COMMUNES, which consisted of 12 points: 1. the commune is to be characterized by a three-level ownership, viz. the commune, PRODUCTION BRIGADE and PRODUCTION TEAM. 2. oppose EQUALITARIANISM and the random transfer of manpower and materials; 3. strengthen the basic ownership of the production brigade which is to be the hub of the operation; 4. retain minor partial ownership of the production

team; 5. allow the commune members to operate private SUBSIDIARY PLOTS; 6. as far as possible, increase the incomes of about nine-tenths of the commune members by deducting less from, and distributing more to, them; 7. Implement the principle 'from each according to his ability, to each according to his work' (personal income is to account for 70% and social services for 30% of total consumption); 8. economize labour by allowing not more than 3% to be engaged in management, administration and control; 9. administer the rationing of grain strictly and economize food in public catering; 10. reactivate rural trade fairs on a planned basis; 11. observe the prescribed guidelines on the distribution of time between work and rest, and allow male commune members to have four and female members six days off per month; 12. provide leadership to the rectification and readjustment drive in the commune. The T.R. represented a turn towards a more liberal policy, strengthening material incentives and the line favoured by LIU SHAO-CH'I, but opposed by MAO TSE-TUNG.

Twentieth Congress of the Communist Party of the Soviet Union One of the most crucial Communist Party's Congresses ever, held in Moscow from 14 to 25 Feb. 1956. It was attended by 1,436 delegates representing 6,795,000 CPSU members and including guest delegates from 55 foreign Communist parties. The Congress made history for six events of far-reaching consequences. 1. In KRUSHCHEV'S SECRET SPEECH, Stalin was denounced for his arbitrary and unnecessarily cruel acts and the abuse of power. 2. The PERSONALITY CULT was condemned, and instead, the principle of SOCIALIST LEGALITY and democratic processes were reaffirmed. 3. DOGMATISM in the interpretation of Marxism-Leninism was rejected, especially in establishing the general party line and relations between different Communist parties. 4. The possibility of different approaches to the establishment and construction of socialism was conceded, not necessarily that pioneered by the CPSU

(OWN PATH TO SOCIALISM). 5. The desirability of peaceful COEXISTENCE between countries with different social systems was declared and an offer was made to this effect by the USSR. 6. Major wars were proclaimed to be no longer unavoidable owing to the strength of the socialist bloc and the destructiveness of the atomic weapons. Although the major decisions made at the Congress were hailed with satisfaction in most socialist countries and in the West, Stalinists and later the Chinese Communist Party attacked the resolutions as revisionist and too accommodating to capitalism.

Twenty-five Thousanders A popular description of the 25,000 enthusiastic and trusted industrial workers sent by Stalin in 1930 to the rural areas for carrying out a rapid COLLECTIVIZATION of farming in the USSR. They hardly had any knowledge of agriculture and three-quarters of them were devoted Party members. Their actions were noted for excessive zeal and striking hostility to the *KULAKS*. Even Stalin commented on their enthusiasm, 'DIZZY WITH SUCCESS'.

Twenty-one Conditions of Admission to the Comintern The terms of admission of a Communist Party to the Third International (the COMINTERN), prepared by Lenin and adopted by the second Congress of the Comintern in Petrograd (now Leningrad) in 1920. They were also known as the Twenty-One Points or the Twenty-One Terms, and were more stringent than the Fifteen Points formulated in 1919. The Conditions amounted to very strict rules of Party organization and discipline, patterned on the RUSSIAN COMMUNIST PARTY (OF THE BOLSHEVIKS) and were described as an instrument of the Bolshevization of foreign Communist Parties. In effect, the admitted national communist parties became sections of the Comintern, in which the majority of voting members were Bolsheviks or foreign Communists resident in Soviet Russia. Those opposed to the T.-O.C. were eliminated from the Comintern. The main

Conditions in a summarized form were: (a) inclusion of 'Communist' in the official name of the Party; (b) dismissal of reformists and centrists from responsible positions in the Party; (c) subordination of Communist deputies to the Party's Central Committee and the removal of unreliable elements from parliamentary representation; (d) pursuit of daily propaganda and agitation in the armed forces and in the countryside; (e) obligation to pursue legal as well as illegal (incl. armed) activities towards a PROLETARIAN REVOLUTION; (f) strict Party discipline; (g) systematic purging of the Party of petty bourgeois elements; (h) DEMOCRATIC CENTRALISM in Party organization and operation as well as in the Comintern; (i) systematic Communist infiltration of trade unions, co-operatives and other working class organizations; (j) support to red trade unions against YELLOW UNIONS; (k) repudiation of the INTERNATIONAL FEDERATION OF FREE TRADE UNIONS and of the International Labour Organization; (l) at least two-thirds majority in the Party supporting entry into the Comintern; (m) expulsion of the Party members opposed to the T.-O.C; (n) implementation of all resolutions of the Comintern; (o) acceptance of the principle of the DICTATORSHIP OF THE PROLETARIAT; (p) aid to the USSR in fighting COUNTER-REVOLUTION; (q) support of NATIONAL LIBERATION MOVEMENTS in colonies and other dependencies; and (r) adherence to the principle of PROLETARIAN INTERNATIONALISM.

Twenty-second of March Movement A movement initiated in Paris on 22 March 1968, which included university and secondary school students and other left-wing groups opposed to the US presence in France, US participation in the VIETNAM WAR, IMPERIALISM, inflexible university administration and the capitalist system in general. It was led by a Franco-German student, Daniel Cohn-Bendit. Its members also called themselves ENRAGÉS. The Movement was the main force behind the FRENCH STUDENT REVOLUTION OF MARCH–MAY 1968.

Twenty-sixth of July Movement A reformist left-wing and anti-foreign movement in Cuba initiated on 26 July 1953, the date of the MONCADA OPERATION, and led by F. CASTRO. It was specifically directed against the corrupt right-wing dictatorial regime of President F. Batista and American domination. At first the Movement was patronized mostly by students and some intellectuals (who formed a Revolutionary Directorate), but it gradually gained support among peasants and workers. Its two major operations in 1953 and 1956 ended in failure, but secret training camps (especially in the Maestra Mountains) improved the members' guerilla fighting capacity. The Movement at first kept aloof of the Socialist People's Party (the country's communist party), but cooperation began in 1958. In the same year, Batista's attack against the guerillas' bases ended in failure. The Movement then turned to the attack, occupied the capital city in Feb. 1959 and seized power in the following July. In May 1961, the Revolutionary Directorate and the Socialist People's Party merged with the T.-S.M. and formed the United Party of the Socialist Revolution (which in Oct. 1965 assumed the name of the COMMUNIST PARTY OF CUBA).

Two-and-a-half International SECOND-AND-A-HALF INTERNATIONAL.

Two-and-a-half Wars Doctrine, One-and-a-half Wars Doctrine Name of the US military thinking in the 1960s, which postulated that the US military potential should be such as to be able to wage two and a half wars simultaneously on different continents. In that conception, the Vietnam War was taken as one-half of a war. The reverses in Vietnam forced the US Government to revise the ambitious doctrine to one-and-a-half wars, while other wars were to be waged by the countries supporting the USA (Europeanization, Vietnamization, and Koreanization) the USA supplying military equipment.

Two combine into one vs One divides into two Controversy ONE DIVIDES INTO TWO VS. TWO COMBINE INTO ONE CONTROVERSY.

Two-Five Scheme THREE-SEVEN SCHEME.

Two-legs Policy WALKING ON TWO LEGS.

Two-roads conflict The left-wing and right-wing lines of policy within the Chinese Communist Party which emerged during 1958–66 concerning the strategy and tactics of the transition from capitalism to communism. They were represented by the factions led by MAO TSE-TUNG and LIU SHAO-CH'I, respectively. Mao's faction accused Liu's group of following the capitalist road (CAPITALIST ROADER), its complacency, bureaucratization, technocratization and self-interest, which was bound to lead to the restoration of capitalism. The former stressed ideology, the primacy of politics over economics ('POLITICS IN COMMAND'), enthusiasm, moral incentives, manual labour, the CONTINUING REVOLUTION and the masses' participation in a rapid and uncompromising march to FULL COMMUNISM. The latter, not as intensely and explicitly, emphasized or at least tolerated pragmatism, economic commonsense, material incentives, rapid economic and technological development, orderly and conservative administration and elitism. The conflict developed into a life-or-death struggle and came into the open in 1966 with the outbreak of the GREAT PROLETARIAN CULTURAL REVOLUTION, when the right-wing group was defeated.

Two-tier Price System The practice of state administration of two levels of prices for the same products, viz. PRODUCER PRICES and RETAIL PRICES, the latter being maintained at a much higher level than the former. The two levels can move independently of each other by the state's flexible manipulation of TURNOVER TAXES.

U

Ulbricht, Walter (1893–   ) East German Communist leader and statesman, who dominated the political and social scene in the GERMAN DR in the 1950s and 1960s. Born to a poor working-class family, he joined the SPARTACUS LEAGUE in 1918 and the COMMUNIST PARTY OF GERMANY when it was founded in the following year. He became the Party Secretary in 1925 and served as a Communist deputy in the Reichstag from 1928–1933. He then left Germany, lived in the USSR from the 1938–1945 and, over the period 1938–43, represented the C.P.G. in the COMINTERN. Having returned to East Germany with the Soviet troops, he organized support for the Soviet occupation and administration. He played a leading role in the amalgamation of the C.P.G. with the Socialist Party of Germany creating the SOCIALIST UNITY PARTY OF GERMANY in 1946. He was a member of the party's Political Bureau 1946–50 and from 1950 he was Secretary-General of the Party's Central Committee. He was also Prime Minister from 1949–1960 and Chairman of the State Council from 1960 to May 1971, when he resigned (succeeded by E. Honecker). U. gained an unpopular reputation for his Stalinist methods and inflexible policies, including the construction of the BERLIN WALL in 1961.

Ulbricht Doctrine A cautious and conditional policy of *détente* of the [East] GERMAN DR towards the FR of [West] Germany, acceptable to the East European countries and the USSR and formulated by W. ULBRICHT in early 1967. The doc-trine was subsequently endorsed at a Conference of Foreign Ministers of Bulgaria, Czechoslovakia, the German DR, Hungary, Poland and the USSR in Feb. 1967. As a condition of *détente*, the doctrine insisted that the FR of Germany must extend diplomatic recognition to the German DR, accept East-West German frontiers as inviolable and renounce all nuclear weapons. In the same spirit, treaties were subsequently concluded between the signatories to the Conference, embodying assurances of support to the German DR and the security of her borders. Only Romania adopted a neutral non-committal stand.

Ultimatists A radical group in the Bolshevik faction of the RUSSIAN SOCIAL-DEMOCRATIC LABOUR PARTY before W.W.I. The group insisted that an ultimatum be sent to the Bolshevik deputies in the Tsarist DUMA with a condition that they be recalled if the instructions in the ultimatum were rejected. The U. were left Communist oppositionists to Lenin's decision in 1905 of having Bolshevik deputies in the Duma at least for propaganda purposes. The U. demanded that the deputies adopt a more radical revolutionary line.

Ultra-Democracy An extreme form of political equality parallel to ABSOLUTE EQUALITARIANISM in the economic and social sphere. The idea is rejected by MARXISM-LENINISM, as u.-d. is opposed to the accepted principle of DEMOCRATIC CENTRALISM. The concept of u.-d. was widely discussed in China during the GREAT PROLETARIAN CULTURAL RE-

614

VOLUTION. But Mao Tse-tung finally denounced it in 1972 (in 'On Ultra-Democracy' in *FIVE MOST READ ARTICLES*) by reference to the Chinese Communist Party and the People's Liberation Army. He stated that u.-d. 'damages or even completely wrecks the Party organization . . . undermines the Party's fighting capacity and constitutes the petty bourgeoisie's individualistic aversion to discipline'.

Ultra-Imperialism A concept put forward by K. KAUTSKY in 1914 to denote a peaceful and extreme exploitation of weaker and poorer nations by the financial oligarchies of the imperial powers. In Kautsky's view, u.-i. represents a higher stage of IMPERIALISM, which inevitably replaces rivalry among the national banking and financial interests. He based his proposition on Marxist DIALECTICAL MATERIALISM, arguing that collusion among imperialist powers is a logical development, whereby MONOPOLY CAPITALISM in each imperialist country would degenerate into universal monopoly capitalism. He thought that this development would have favourable effects, as wars would no longer be inevitable and, furthermore, u.-i. would pave the way for a world-wide planned economy. Lenin strongly disagreed with this interpetation (in *The Proletarian Revolution and the Renegade Kautsky*, 1918), describing Kautsky's contention as a misinterpretation of Marxian DIALECTICS and HISTORICAL MATERIALISM. Lenin insisted that the greed and pride of the national oligarchies precluded peaceful collusion and that imperialism must necessarily breed wars.

Ultra Leftists Extremist radicals headed by CH'EN PO-TA and LIN PIAO in China during the GREAT PROLETARIAN CULTURAL REVOLUTION. They placed politics first, the economy second, and emphasized self-reliance, national self-sufficiency and Chinese ingenuity. They were against the possession of books and objects which could be regarded as bourgeois, practising religion, maintaining foreign contacts, the wearing of smart or unconventional clothing, eating expensive foods, and the preservation of traditional literature, art and music. They were attacked even by Mao's establishment as hotheads and adventurers. The U.L. became isolated, lost their cause during the G.P.C.R. and were destroyed as a group after the 1971–72 campaign against them.

Ulyanov, Vladimir Ilyich The original name of V. I. LENIN up to 1895. Before he adopted the name Lenin, he had used such assumed names as Tulin, Karpov, Meyer, Starik, Ilyin and others. He apparently made up the name Lenin from Ilyin (his father's first name) and Ulyan (his father's abbreviated surname).

Umbrella Trade Agreement A medium or long-term commercial agreement entered into by a Socialist centrally planned economy with a capitalist country. It is phrased in general terms covering broad categories of goods to be exchanged and such conditions as tariff levels, the method of payment and the exchange of trade missions. As a rule, the agreement is not legally binding and does not prescribe the goods to be exchanged in terms of quantity, delivery dates and prices. An u.t.a. is typically supplemented with annual TRADE PROTOCOLS which are more specific and detailed.

Un-American Activities A phrase officially used in the USA for anti-democratic activities by Americans, in particular if they are in support of fascism or (especially) communism. In 1938, a Committee on Un-American Activities was created temporarily in the House of Representatives. The Committee was made permanent in 1945 and was known under its abbreviated version as HUAC (The House Un-American Activities Committee). Although it first intended to enquire into loyalty and security matters, it later exceeded its originally intended function and achieved notoriety, especially during the COLD WAR in the 1950s, for inquisitorial methods, the harassment of individuals, character assassination and 'witch hunts'. It came to be identified with McCARTHYISM. In 1969, the name of the Committee was changed to House Committee on Internal Security and its methods have become more moderate.

Underdeveloped countries LESS-DEVELOPED COUNTRIES, THIRD WORLD.

Under-Structure BASE.

Unemployment A situation in the labour market noted for the inability of finding employment, or at least where the number of persons registered as unemployed substantially exceeds the number of vacancies. According to its causes, u. may be cyclical, structural or frictional. Marxists have traditionally identified u. with capitalism. Marx (in CAPITAL, vol. I) argued that the market mechanism and private ownership of the means of production naturally lead to the RESERVE ARMY OF WORKERS which is indispensable to the normal functioning of a capitalist economy. He further explained that the level of u. increases with the rising OR-GANIC STRUCTURE OF CAPITAL (capital-labour ratio). U. is further caused by the growing power of monopoly capital which eliminates small producers. In the socialist centrally planned economies there is virtually no u., except temporary frictional u., in fact most of them suffer from shortages of labour. Yugoslavia is a conspicuous exception where, since the mid-1960s, u. has ranged from 6 to 10 per cent. Proposals by some economists in other Socialist countries to improve labour discipline and productivity by creating small pools of u. have been consistently rejected on ideological, ethical and social grounds.

Uninterrupted Revolution CONTINUING REVOLUTION, PERMANENT REVOLUTION.

Union for Radical Political Economics A scholarly association in the USA, founded in 1968 and based at the University of Michigan, for the radicalization of economics, especially as it is taught and practised at universities and colleges. Its membership, about 1,800, consists of academics teaching in tertiary institutions, students, government employees, private researchers and NEW LEFT organizations. It prepares new courses for POLITICAL ECONOMICS, sponsors regional and national conferences and, in general, aims at promoting studies on alternative economic systems. It publishes a newsletter (appearing 4–6 times a year), *Review of Radical Political Economics* (quarterly) and OCCASIONAL PAPERS.

Union of Militant Atheists LEAGUE OF MILITANT ATHEISTS.

Union of Polish Patriots in the USSR A political organization set up in Moscow in March 1943 by Polish Communists with the support of the Soviet Government. It was led by Wanda Wasilewska, Z. Berling, B. Drobner and others. It aimed at representing the Poles in the USSR, liberating Poland from the German occupation and establishing a communist regime allied to the USSR. It facilitated the organization of the Polish Army in the USSR and, by the end of 1944 had established offices in 48 cities and 97 regional centres in the USSR and claimed 50,000 members. The Union became a puppet of the Soviet authorities and provided a nucleus of the communist regime in Poland. In July 1944, in defiance of the Polish government-in-exile in London, it declared its full support to the Soviet-controlled Home National Council in Poland, with which it jointly formed the Polish Committee of National Liberation. From then on, up to its dissolution in Aug. 1946, it assisted in the repatriation of the Polish population from the USSR.

Union of Soviet Writers WRITERS' UNION OF THE USSR.

Union of Struggle for the Liberation of the Working Class LEAGUE OF STRUGGLE FOR THE LIBERATION OF THE WORKING CLASS.

Union of the Soviet Socialist Republics (*Soyuz Sovetskikh Sotsialisticheskikh*

Respublik) The first country in the world where a successful PROLETARIAN REVOLUTION was carried out and a Marxist regime established. It is a successor to the Russian Empire which was noted for a semi-feudal society, autocratic Tsarist government and a backward agricultural economy. Following some two decades of social and revolutionary unrest and defeats in W.W.I, Tsar NICHOLAS II was deposed in the FEBRUARY REVOLUTION OF 1917 and, after the initial turmoil, a moderate socialist government was formed headed by A. F. KERENSKY. But it was not accepted by the BOLSHEVIKS, who eight months later, led by V. I. LENIN seized power in the GREAT OCTOBER SOCIALIST REVOLUTION. The new government, called the Council of People's Commissars, immediately embarked on the socialization of land, industry, banking and transport. With the creation of the GOSPLAN in 1920 it pioneered economic planning, especially after the introduction of the first FIVE-YEAR PLAN in 1928. Following the period of WAR COMMUNISM and the FOREIGN INTERVENTION, the Soviet regime was firmly established and the official name of the country, the USSR, was adopted in Dec. 1922. After annexations during and after W.W.II, the country's size was increased to 22,402,000 sq. km., making it the largest country in the world (one-seventh of the world's land area) and its population in 1978 stood at 258,700,000. The first Soviet Constitution was adopted in Jan. 1924 (replacing that of July 1918 for the Russian Soviet Federated Socialist Republic), followed by that of Dec. 1936 which, in turn, was replaced by the Constitution of Oct. 1977. The highest formal organ of state power is the SUPREME SOVIET OF THE USSR, headed by President (L. I. BREZHNEV), who is the formal head of state. The executive and administrative power is exercised by the COUNCIL OF MINISTERS OF THE USSR, headed by a Chairman i.e. Prime Minister (A. N. KOSYGIN), formally accountable to the Supreme Soviet. But effective power rests with the COMMUNIST PARTY OF THE SOVIET UNION, especially its POLITBURO, headed by the Secretary-General of the Party's Central Committee (L. I. Brezhnev). The country now (since 1956) consists of 15 Union Republics, theoretically independent and free to secede, viz. the RUSSIAN SOVIET FEDERATED SOCIALIST REPUBLIC (constituting 76 per cent of the country's area and 56 per cent of its population) and the following Soviet Socialist Republics: Armenian; Azerbaijan; Byelorussian; Estonian; Georgian; Kazakh; Kirghiz; Latvian; Lithuanian; Moldavian; Tadzhik; Turkmen; Ukrainian; and Uzbek. The country's administrative subdivisions include 20 AUTONOMOUS REPUBLICS, 8 AUTONOMOUS REGIONS, 10 National Areas (*Krai*), 6 Territories and 117 Provinces (*Oblast*).

Union Shop CLOSED SHOP.

United Front A general term used in communist political phraseology to describe various forms of co-operation in a particular country between the communist party (whatever its official name may be) and other left-wing parties (socialists, radicals, populists, social democrats, christian socialists and the like), representing the interests of the working class. In general, revolutionary Marxists are opposed to collaboration with non-communist parties even if they represent the working class and accuse them of OPPORTUNISM, REVISIONISM and delaying the need for the PROLETARIAN REVOLUTION. But in exceptional cases, collaboration in u.f. is acceptable. The desirability of such collaboration was first indicated by COMINTERN at its third Congress in Moscow in June–July 1921. A u.f. may mean POPULAR FRONT, such as that in the 1930s in France, Spain and Chile against fascism or other extreme forms of capitalism. A modified version of the u.f. is EUROCOMMUNISM. A u.f. may also mean electoral solidarity among workers of different political persuasions voting against right-wing parties and not co-operating with opportunist leaders in left-wing parties who compromise too much ('united front from below').

In a different setting, viz. in the Socialist countries, a u.f. may mean a Communist-dominated coalition, in which Communists may be in a minority or need wider popular support if their position is not strong enough. This was particularly the case in the East European countries and China soon after the Communist seizure of power, where the Communist parties tolerated non-bourgeois political parties in patriotic, people's or national electoral fronts, provided such parties accepted the communist leadership. In most Socialist countries, electoral fronts have been retained as a proof of the democratic multi-party system, as is exemplified by the DEMOCRATIC FRONT FOR THE REUNIFICATION OF THE FATHERLAND (in the DPR of Korea), the FATHERLAND FRONT (in Bulgaria), the FRONT OF THE NATION'S UNITY (Poland), the NATIONAL FRONT OF DEMOCRATIC GERMANY (German DR), the NATIONAL UNITED FRONT (China) and the PATRIOTIC PEOPLE'S FRONT (in Hungary).

United Front from Above A type of UNITED FRONT which is imitated and dominated by the Communist party in a particular country. The phrase was applied mostly to the situation in the East European countries and China in the early stages of the Communist takeover during and after W.W.II. It consisted in the forced mergers of the Socialist and populist (peasant) parties with the Communist party and common electoral and parliamentary policies under Communist leadership. Such united fronts did not arise 'from below' (widespread popular support), but were imposed 'from above' by the secret police and (in Eastern Europe) by Soviet political and military pressure.

United Institute for Nuclear Research JOINT INSTITUTE FOR NUCLEAR RESEARCH.

United Socialist Front of Thailand A type of an integrated UNITED FRONT of six leftwing political parties which legally existed up to the right-wing coup of Oct. 1976. It drew its support mainly from small peasants, craftsmen and white-collar workers, especially in the north-eastern part of the country adjacent to Laos. Its programme included the abolition of anti-communist laws, radical land reforms, the nationalization of key industries, the withdrawal of US forces and the normalization of relations with China. At the 1975 elections, the Front won 12 (of the 271) seats in the House of Representatives. But its impact in the country's politics was never great.

Universal Entitlement A modern term used in the West, postulating the right of every citizen to the equality of opportunity, employment, job satisfaction, health care and leisure. It is assumed that in a reasonably developed economy, it is the responsibility of the state to ensure the implementation of these rights. The concept is associated with the NEW POLITICAL ECONOMY.

University for the Western National Minorities COMMUNIST UNIVERSITY FOR THE WESTERN NATIONAL MINORITIES.

Unproductive Sphere NON PRODUCTIVE SPHERE.

Uravnilovka An economic term often used in the USSR in the 1920s, meaning 'equalization' (in respect to personal income). There were many experiments with *U.* during the period of War Communism (1918–20). But with the introduction of the NEW ECONOMIC POLICY in 1921 and the application of the Leninist principle, 'from each according to his ability, to each according to his work', *U.* was often disregarded and implicitly rejected. Stalin, in his famous 'U. speech' in 1931, condemned the equalization of wages of industrial and agricultural workers as 'petty bourgeois deviation'.

Urban-Rural Contradiction RURAL-URBAN CONTRADICTION.

Use-Value A Marxist concept borrowed

from the early classical economists, denoting the usefulness of material objects or capacity to satisfy human wants. U.-v. is usually different from VALUE and from EXCHANGE-VALUE. U.-v. occupies an important place in Marx's political economy (especially in *CAPITAL*, all three volumes). Marx stated that u.-v. is the basic element of capitalist wealth and he rejected the idea that the u.-v. of a commodity can be adopted as a measure of value. In accordance with the LABOUR THEORY OF VALUE, he stressed that an article may have a greater u.-v. than value, if demand for it is high, even though little or no SOCIALLY-INDISPENSABLE LABOUR was expended on it. At the same time, u.-v. may be lower than exchange-value in the case of monopolistically restricted products resulting in artificially high prices. U.-v. is a historically conditioned phenomenon, as new uses are discovered and others are phased out, depending on man's knowledge and technology. At the same time, in reply to his critics that he neglected the role of demand in his value analysis, Marx pointed out (in *CAPITAL*, vol. III) that the condition of the socially-indispensable labour takes care of the demand side as well (in addition to the cost of production).

USSR The English abbreviation of the UNION OF THE SOVIET SOCIALIST REPUBLICS, corresponding to the Russian abbreviation SSSR or (in cyrillic alphabet) CCCP.

Usury Excessive interest charged by the lender to the borrower. The appearance of u. goes back to ancient times when the credit involved was usually used for direct consumption purposes. It is interesting to note that most religions as well as Marxism have condemned u. Marxists emphasize that u. is a result of social stratification and constitutes a more blatant form of exploitation (SURPLUS VALUE) than INTEREST. But they concede that capitalism, with its developed money and capital markets, has made the elimination of u. possible. However, they insist that u. still

exists in capitalist countries even today: 1. in less-developed countries, where lenders take advantage of the scarcity of capital and the plight of the non-propertied classes; and 2. in the West where, owing to a greater risk factor, banks and finance companies charge higher interest rates to smaller business firms and individual craftsmen (than to big companies and multinational corporations) and to improvident consumers (on hire purchase loans).

Utilitarianism A philosophical and ethical doctrine according to which individual or social benefit is the most appropriate criterion of human conduct. U. became a feature of the French and British Enlightenment of the 18th and 19th c. Utilitarians, such as J. Bentham (1784–1832) and J. S. Mill (1806–73), insisted that the greatest happiness of society should be the objective of human activities. This could be achieved by 'rational egoism', i.e. a judicious combination of individual and society's interests. The Marxist evaluation of u. is favourable to the extent that it constituted a reaction against religion and feudal mentality. But Marxists point out that u. has served the interests of the BOURGEOISIE, which, owing to its ownership of wealth, better education and insatiable greed, is in a better position to pursue utilitarian objectives than the PROLETARIAT, usually at the latter's expense. U. has been attacked as a product of philosophical IDEALISM steeped in SUBJECTIVISM, on the one hand, and a convenient onesided theory emphasizing egoistic material pursuits disregarding ideological considerations, on the other.

Utility The capacity to satisfy human wants. It is one of the contentious questions in the bourgeois-Marxist controversy on value. According to the PSYCHOLOGICAL SCHOOL OF BOURGEOIS ECONOMICS, opposed to the Marxian LABOUR THEORY OF VALUE, u. determines value and the diminishing MARGINAL UTILITY explains consumer behaviour. The consumer maximizes his total u. in accordance with his income, viz. he spends in such a way that marginal utilities of individual products are proportional to their market prices, so that the marginal u. of each product is equal to its price multiplied by the marginal u. of money. The extreme importance attached to u. was represented by the UTILITY THEORY OF THE UPPER SOCIAL CLASS, justifying the existence of a privileged and elitist social class. The Marxist reaction to this interpretation is as follows: 1. it relies on the subjective valuation of u. and, as such is allied to the doctrine of SUBJECTIVISM and philosophical IDEALISM; 2. neither total nor marginal u. of a consumer can be quantitatively measured and, by the same token, interpersonal comparisons of u. are impossible; and 3. the bourgeois interpretation contains convenient and apologetic arguments calculated to destroy the Marxist theory of value and the justification for social equality. Although Marx (mainly in *CAPITAL* vol. I) attributed VALUE essentially to labour, he did not altogether disregard u. in the process. He insisted that to have value, a product must contain SOCIALLY-INDISPENSABLE LABOUR, i.e. only that expended labour for which there is demand, expressed by buyers in the market. 'Nothing can have value, without being an object of utility. If the thing is useless, so is the labour contained in it. . . . Therefore, if an article loses its utility, it also loses its value'.

Utility Theory of the Upper Social Class A theoretical proposition put forward by an English mathematical social scientist, F. Y. Edgeworth (1845–1926) in *Mathematical Psychics* (1881). He held that persons born to higher social classes had greater needs, on the one hand, and a greater capacity for enjoyment, on the other. Therefore, they should have higher incomes than the PROLETARIAT, in order to enable them to consume more than the average person in society. The higher satisfaction achieved by the upper class means that society as a whole achieves a higher level of well-being than would be possible in the case of an egalitarian socie-

ty. This theory never commanded wide acceptance even in the West, and Marxists have never treated it seriously.

Utopian Socialism So named after T. More's *Utopia* (1516) exemplifying idealistic socialism divorced from reality and impossible to achieve in practice. It embraces several theories of the socialist transformation of society in peaceful, evolutionary ways and can be regarded as an earlier stage of socialist ideology, put forward by idealist intellectuals, before deep class conflicts had developed in capitalist society. U. socialists on the whole agreed that capitalism led to exploitation and the IMMISERATION OF THE WORKING CLASS, chaotic competition and a waste of human labour. But even later u. socialists, of the 19th century (such as N. G. CHERNYSHEVSKY, C. FOURIER, R. OWEN, C. H. SAINT-SIMON) – although clearly aware of the antagonistic class conflicts – did not accept social violence and, in fact, did not believe that the working class was capable of becoming a well organized power to achieve socialist objectives by force. They believed that the ideal society could be gradually and peacefully evolved by appealing to reason and conscience, (rather than class hatred), publicity, persuasion and legislation. They advocated the establishment of ideal communities to serve as models for further development. In this process, they were prepared to rely on voluntary action and state measures to achieve the disappearance of private property and inequalities between social classes (especially between the rural and urban population). U.s. contrasts with SCIENTIFIC S., advocated by Marx (in POVERTY OF PHILOSOPHY) and Engels (especially in *Socialism: Utopian and Scientific*, 1880) and their revolutionary followers. Engels derided u. socialists (such as Fourier, Morelly, Owen and Saint-Simon) calling them naïve, abstract and impractical dreamers, and emphasized the need for basing the socialist movement on the working masses which alone are capable of introducing a new social order. Other Marxists attacked u. socialists for their lack of confidence in the proletariat and treating it as a helpless and defenceless class which had to be pitied and helped paternalistically. Engels (in the 'Preface' to English edition of THE COMMUNIST MANIFESTO, published in 1888) described u. socialists as 'social quacks'. It may be observed here that the Marxist vision of the perfect society, FULL COMMUNISM, can also be regarded as unrealistic and as such u. (as illustrated by more than 60 years of experience in the USSR).

V

Value One of the most controversial economic concepts of fundamental ideological consequence. The capitalist economic theory attributes v. to UTILITY or scarcity as indicated by the market, determined directly by the forces of demand and supply. In Marxist economic analysis, these interpretations are rejected and, instead, v. is explained by the LABOUR THEORY OF VALUE. V. is attributed to SOCIALLY-INDISPENSABLE LABOUR embodied in the COMMODITY. V., according to Marx (as explained in *CAPITAL*, vol. I), appears wherever there is production and exchange of commodities under market conditions. The well-known Marxian formula for v. is $c+v+s$, where c = CONSTANT CAPITAL, v = VARIABLE CAPITAL and s = SURPLUS VALUE. Marx insisted that the v. of the product is determined during the process of production, before the product enters the market as a commodity. The market price oscillates around v., but is not necessarily indicative of v., Marx also employed two related concepts: 1. USE-VALUE, the qualitative capacity of a product to satisfy human wants (indicating a subjective relation between man and commodities); and 2. EXCHANGE-VALUE, the market price at which a commodity is bought and sold in the market (indicating a social relation between man and man). The Marxist theory of v. is one of the weaknesses of the Marxist political economy. It denies value to non-labour factors of production, notably land (in so far as it is not a product of labour), and denies a value-creating capacity to land and capital. Furthermore, Marx himself appears to be confused on the subject of v. In his work, *A CONTRIBUTION TO THE CRITIQUE OF POLITICAL ECONOMY*, he assigned different meanings to v. and exchange-value compared to those in *Capital*, vol I. In *Capital*, vol. III, by introducing the concept of the PRODUCTION PRICE, he virtually abandoned the labour theory of value (TRANSFORMATION PROBLEM). In the Socialist centrally planned economies, the Marxian theory of v. has never been consciously applied either in the pricing of producer goods, consumer goods (RETAIL PRICES) or in the allocation of resources. The ECONOMIC REFORMS in the European socialist countries in the 1960s and the development of OPTIMAL PLANNING represent further departures from the Marxian v.

Value Forms A concept used by Marx (in *CAPITAL*, vol. I) to denote different types of EXCHANGE-VALUE, i.e. for how much a given commodity can be exchanged. V.f. reflect the stage of economic and social development. The earliest type of the v.f. was *occasional barter* between two parties, when a given quantity of one article was exchanged for an agreed quantity of another. In the next stage, the exchange becomes *regular*, with the value of one product in terms of another being known and accepted. In the *fully developed* v.f., the value of one article is expressed in terms of a large number of other articles. A higher stage is reached when one article in common demand, portable and easily stored (cattle, shells, silver, and gold etc.), is used as a *universal equivalent* and becomes intrinsic money. The highest v.f. is represented by *token money*, in which prices are expressed and which represents a claim on real values.

Value-in-Exchange EXCHANGE-VALUE.

Value of Labour Power A Marxian concept to denote the mode in which LABOUR POWER is realized, viz. in the form of wages. It consists of two elements: 1. the minimum subsistence for the maintenance and reproduction (including training) of the worker's household; and 2. historical loading, corresponding to the stage of economic and social development, the accepted standard of living, the current state of prosperity and the situation in the labour market. The v. of l.p. is differentiated according to the workers' skill and bargaining power, but at any rate it is lower than the VALUE created by the worker in the process of production. In a capitalist society the worker is exploited by the capitalist to the extent of SURPLUS VALUE.

Value Structure of Capital In Marxian economic terminology, the ratio of the value of the means of production and the VALUE OF LABOUR POWER. This ratio basically depends on the level of technology and increases with technological progress. The v.s. of c. rises slower than the TECHNICAL STRUCTURE OF CAPITAL, owing to the increasing productivity of labour in producing the means of production and their consequent declining value.

Vanguardism One of the features of revolutionary Marxism-Leninism, postulating the need for a highly disciplined communist party led by devoted professional revolutionaries to act as the vanguard of the working class movement. The idea of v. in Russia goes back to at least P. N. TKACHEV, but its most influential and successful advocate was Lenin. In its extreme sense, v. may mean elitist left adventurism, which ignores the need for participation by the masses in revolutionary activities, asserting that the vanguard by it-

self can carry out a proletarian revolution and achieve socialism.

Variable Capital An important concept in Marxian ideology, in particular in the analysis of VALUE, developed by Marx (in *CAPITAL*, vol. I). In the process of production, v.c. is used to buy LABOUR POWER and is one of the three components in Marx's formula for value, $c+v+s$ (c = CONSTANT CAPITAL, meaning fixed capital and materials used; v = variable capital, or simply wages; s = SURPLUS VALUE). V.c. is that part of capital that undergoes variation in the sense that not only does it replace itself (in the form of the VALUE OF LABOUR POWER) but it also creates new value (surplus value). On the other hand, constant capital can only transfer its value with the aid of labour to another commodity, but cannot create new value. The relation between constant capital and v.c. (c/v) is called in Marxian economics the ORGANIC STRUCTURE OF CAPITAL (meaning capital-labour ratio). According to Marx, technical progress leads to a faster growth of constant capital than of v.c. (i.e. increasing organic structure of capital), which contributes to the IMMISERATION OF THE WORKING CLASS. The relation of surplus value to v.c. represents the rate of exploitation.

Varna Methodology Also known as the Varna Model Regulation, the method of calculating consistent conversion coefficients for the keeping and settlement of accounts in jointly established enterprises by the member countries of the COUNCIL FOR MUTUAL ECONOMIC ASSISTANCE. The V.M. was approved at the 25th Session of the Standing Commission for Currency and Finance in Oct. 1973, when it replaced the BERLIN METHOD. The agreement specifies that the initial value of the project is to be calculated in the national currency in accordance with the local prices of the country in which the entity is located. Using laid down complicated formulae, the values, including profits, are then converted into TRANSFERABLE ROUBLES. The methodology is orientational, not necessarily binding, and the interested parties are free to negotiate the actual exchange rates according to the type of operations. Owing to the widely differing national price structures and the methods used in determining different types of prices in each member country, the V.M. has provided only a moderately successful solution to the CMEA exchange rate problems.

VAZ Russian abbreviation of *Volzhsky Avtomobilnyi Zavod*, meaning Volga Automobile Works, situated at Togliattigrad on the middle Volga. The abbreviation is used to prefix all vehicle models made at the Works (such as VAZ-2102, based on Fiat 124). The plant was constructed by Fiat of Italy over the period 1967–70 and is the largest factory in the Soviet motor vehicle industry, 2km. long, embracing 157 automatic machine lines together with 16,000 units of equipment and producing 800,000 vehicles a year, viz. *Zhiguli* (also known abroad as the LADA).

VEB The commonly used abbreviation in the [East] German DR for a socialized industrial or commercial enterprise operating as an independent accounting entity. It stands for *Volkseigener Betrieb*, meaning People's Own Enterprise.

Vecheka A Russian syllabic abbreviation for *Vserossyskaya Cherezvychainaya Komissiya Borbe s Kontrrevoliutsiei i Sabotazhem*, meaning the All-Russian Extraordinary Commission for Combating Counter-Revolution and Sabotage, which existed in Soviet Russia from Dec. 1917 to Feb. 1922, more commonly known as the *CHEKA*.

VEG the East German commonly used abbreviation for *Volkseigenes Gut*, literally meaning People's Own Estate, or simply STATE FARM. There are about 660 *VEG* in the German DR, covering 425,000 hectares or 6.7 per cent of the total farming land in the country.

Vernalization (*Yarovizatsiya*, in Russian) The scientific process of breaking the rest period of seeds by soaking them in water then freezing them, so that the seeds germinate earlier in spring and the plants ripen much earlier. The discovery of this process is widely attributed to T. D. LYSENKO, a Soviet biologist, as his most valuable contribution to AGROBIOLOGY in application to wheat. He described the process in 1928 and also claimed that the effects of v. were inheritable. He used the principle of v. as one of his arguments for undermining the Western science of GENETICS. However, his discovery was not new, as the process (in application to wheat) had been known in the USA as early as 1837, but was abandoned owing to the development of new varieties of spring wheat.

Vertical Co-production A form of industrial production co-operation often practised between capitalist firms and Socialist enterprises, whereby one partner specializes in the production of parts, sub-assemblies, etc. involving earlier stages of production which are technologically less advanced than the other partner. The articles so produced are exchanged on a systematic basis and either both partners, or occasionally one, may be responsible for the final assembly of the complete product. The Socialist countries are against this type of industrial co-operation with the West, as it reduces them to an inferior position and does not enable a transfer of advanced Western technology to the East. Instead they favour HORIZONTAL CO-PRODUCTION.

Vertical Foreign Trade Trade between countries where primary products (such as food, raw materials, fuels) of one country are exchanged for highly processed and valuable manufactures of another country. This structure of trade is typical of exchanges between economically undeveloped and highly developed nations. The Socialist countries are critical of v.f.t., as it represents an exploitation of poorer and weaker countries by richer industrialized nations, amounting to NON-EQUIVALENT EXCHANGE and tending to perpetuate the existing international division of labour. Instead, they favour the development of *horizontal* foreign trade, whereby the goods traded between the countries embody about the same degree of processing. In general, Socialist foreign trade is largely vertical in exchanges with the West and the Third World, but the position of the Socialist countries is reverse in each case.

Vertical Planning and Management Another designation for HIERARCHICAL PLANNING AND MANAGEMENT.

Vertical Unionism A basis of trade union membership where unskilled, semi-skilled and highly skilled workers belong to the same union. It may embrace all types of employees in a large firm or an industry. It is also known as INDUSTRIAL UNIONISM and is considered by Marxists to be ideologically preferable to (exclusive) craft unions.

Vesenkha The commonly used Russian abbreviated form of *Vysshyi Sovet Narodnogo Khoziaistva*, meaning the Supreme Council of the National Economy. It was created by the Soviet Government in Dec. 1917, and was made directly responsible to it as the chief controlling body for economic affairs, in particular, for the socialization and administration of industry. Its control and administration were exercised through Heading Departments (*Glavki*), corresponding to each major industry and regional economic councils. The greatest influence exerted by *V.* was during WAR COMMUNISM (1917–20). In 1932, *V.* was abolished and its functions were taken over by three People's Commissariats – for heavy, light and timber industries established at the same time. The Council was restored under a similar name, *Vesenkha USSR*, in March 1963 to co-ordinate industry and construction on a national scale, but was abolished in Oct. 1965.

Vienna (or Viennese) International A short name for the SECOND-AND-A-HALF

INTERNATIONAL, or the International Working Union of the Socialist Parties, created in Vienna in Feb. 1921 and dissolved in May 1923.

Viet Cong (full name: *Viet Cong San*) A colloquial name for the South Vietnamese communist guerrillas during the VIETNAM WAR. V.C. units were initially formed in 1957 by the former members of the VIET MINH who remained in or returned to South Vietnam. The V.C. at first engaged in minor terrorist activities, but soon turned to guerrilla-style military actions. In 1960 the NATIONAL LIBERATION FRONT OF SOUTH VIETNAM was formed embodying the V.C. From then on, the members of the Front rejected the term V.C., but due to popular usage in South Vietnam as well as outside the country, the description V.C. continued to be used.

Viet Minh The abbreviated form of *Viet Nam Doc Lap Dong Minh Hoi*, meaning the Revolutionary League for the Independence of Vietnam. It was a Marxist-Leninist revolutionary political organization, founded by HO CHI MINH in Kwangsi, South China, in 1941 for the liberation of Vietnam from the Japanese and the French. Although ostensibly claiming to be a united front, it was in practice dominated by communists, determined to transform the Vietnamese society along socialist lines under a Marxist regime. It was essentially a highly indoctrinated and devoted guerrilla force. After a nine-year war against the French 1946–54, the V.M finally scored a brilliant victory at DIEN BIEN PHU under the command of General VO NGUYEN GIAP in May 1954. In Sep. 1955, the V.M. political and military wings were re-formed into a broader organization called *Liet Viet* (Fatherland Front) to promote unification with South Vietnam. Those who remained in, or returned to, South Vietnam later became known as the VIET CONG.

Vietnam Communist Party (*Dang Cong san Viet Nam*) the ruling party in the Socialist Republic of VIETNAM. Its beginnings go back to the 1920s, when three communist groups emerged – Marxist-Leninist, Trotskyite and local national. On the instructions from the COMINTERN to HO CHI MINH, the three groups were merged and the Communist Party of Indochina was created in Hong Kong in 1930. In 1941, it was re-formed in Kwangsi in South China by HO CHI MINH and called the League for the Independence of Vietnam (Viet Minh), which in turn was further reorganized in 1951, its membership broadened and re-named the Vietnam Workers' Party. After the partition of Vietnam along the 17th Parallel into North and South Vietnam in 1954, the Party became the driving force for a re-unification under communist rule. As part of this drive, in the South in Dec. 1960, the National Liberation Front of South Vietnam was created, popularly known as the Viet Cong. In 1969, Ho Chi Minh died and Le Duan succeeded to the Party's leadership. After the victorious VIETNAM WAR, North and South Vietnam were officially reunited in July 1976 as the Socialist Republic of Vietnam and the V.W.P. and the N.L.F.S.V. were merged in Dec. 1976 to form the V.C.P. About 50 per cent of all Party cadres of the North (some 400,000) was sent to the South to assist and supervise the socialist transformation. Up to 1977 the Party had pursued a neutral line in the international communist movement but since that time, owing to the deterioration of Vietnam's relations with China, a pro-Soviet orientation has been adopted. The Party's membership, as claimed at its 4th Congress in Dec. 1976, was 1,534,000 (of the total population of 51,152,000). The Party's highest source of power is the Congress, normally held every four years, but power is concentrated in the Party's Politburo headed by the Party's Secretary-General (Le Duan). At the Party's 4th Congress in Dec. 1976 the following Party top organs were elected: the Central Committee – 101 full and 32 alternate members (the previous respective figures had been 47 and 25); the Secretariat – 9 members; the Politburo – 14 full and 3 alternate mem-

bers; and the Control Committee – 11 members. The Party's main mass support organizations are the General Confederation of Trade Unions and the Ho Chi Minh Youth Union. The Party's main publications are: *Nhan Dan* (*People*), a daily; *Tap Chi Cong San* (*Communist Review*), a monthly theoretical journal; *Tap Chi Quan Do Nhan Dan* (*People's Army Studies*), a monthly military journal; *Tien Phong* (*Vanguard*), organ of the Ho Chi Minh Youth Union; *Lao Dong* (*Workers*) a weekly organ of the General Confederation of Trade Unions; and *Cuu Quoc* (*National Salvation*), the official organ of the NATIONAL UNITED FRONT.

Vietnam, Socialist Republic of (*Cong Hoa Xa-Hoi Chu-Nghia Viet Nam*) A medium-sized country in South-East Asia, ruled by the COMMUNIST PARTY OF VIETNAM, embracing an area of 336,000 sq. km. and a population of 49,100,000 (in 1978). It was formerly a part of the French dependency of Indochina, but in 1945 the country was proclaimed the Democratic Republic of Vietnam by HO CHI MINH. After the war with the French in 1946–54, which ended in the French defeat at DIEN BIEN PHU in May 1954, by the GENEVA AGREEMENTS, V. was divided along the 17th Parallel into the Communist-ruled Democratic Republic of North V., with its capital in Hanoi, and the capitalist-ruled Republic of South V., with Saigon as its capital. The Communist regime soon embarked upon a reunification campaign. In 1960, the National Liberation Front of South Vietnam was founded in the South which created the guerrilla fighting force, the Viet Cong San, better known as the Vietcong, largely trained and equipped by the D.R.V. At the same time, the USA provided increasing support to the South in the form of advisers, equipment and troops which, by the early 1970s, had exceeded 540,000. Following the protracted PARIS PEACE TALKS and US defeats against the background of the incapacity of the South Vietnamese regime, a cease-fire agreement was signed in Jan. 1973. It was followed by the withdrawal of foreign troops and the collapse of the South Vietnamese Government in April 1975. On 2 July 1976, the S.R. of V. was officially proclaimed by the first NATIONAL AS-SEMBLY, elected from both the North and the South in the preceding April, as a reunified country with Hanoi as its capital. The Vietnam Workers' Party (created in the North in 1951) was reorganized to include South Vietnamese communists and, in Dec. 1976 was renamed the Com-munist party of Vietnam. In 1977, the S.R.V. was admitted to the United Na-tions, the International Monetary Fund, the Asian Development Bank and also to the COUNCIL FOR MUTUAL ECONOMIC AS-SISTANCE. During 1977–78, the country became involved in a dispute with China and the Vietnamese regime decided to adopt a pro-Soviet orientation. It also adopted an aggressive stand towards the Kampuchean regime of Pol Pot and instal-led a new Communist regime convenient to itself. In Feb.–Mar. 1979, China tem-porarily invaded four northern provinces of V. 'to teach Vietnam a lesson'. As a consequence, there has been a large-scale exodus of refugees from V., especially those with Chinese backgrounds.

Vietnam War Also described as the Thirty-Year War, the protracted re-volutionary war for the national libera-tion, reunification and the social transfor-mation of Vietnam, which lasted from 1944 to 1975. Following the Marxist clas-sification, it fell into two stages. 1. *The national revolutionary war, 1944–54*, in which national bourgeois elements joined with the communists to drive out the Japanese and French imperialists. The main fighting force was the VIET MINH established by HO CHI MINH. After some actions against the Japanese, the Demo-cratic Republic of Vietnam was pro-claimed on 2 Sep. 1945. But the French efforts to re-establish their rule (in all Indochina) led to a protracted struggle from 1946 to 1954, which ended in the defeat of the French at DIEN BIEN PHU in May 1954. By the GENEVA AGREEMENT of July 1954, Vietnam was divided along the 17th Parallel into the communist-ruled North (D.R. of V.) and the bourgeois-ruled South (Republic of V.). 2. *The Socialist revolutionary war, 1955–75* – waged by the communists against the bourgeois establishment in South V. later supported by the USA and its co-partners Australia, South Korea, New Zealand the Philippines and Thailand. In 1955, the Fatherland Front was created in the North for the reunification with the South under the Communist regime. Two years later the VIET CONG units began to be formed in South V. and the NATIONAL LIBERATION FRONT OF SOUTH VIETNAM was estab-lished in 1960, bringing different in-surgent groups (incl. the Viet Cong) to-gether. After 1964, N.V. stepped up assis-tance to the South Vietnamese guerillas, in which China, the USSR and the East European countries also played important parts. At the same time, the USA also stepped up her support for the South Vietnamese regime. During its peak in 1968, the USA was using 543,000 troops (two-thirds of her land forces) and cost the USA $382,000m. The US co-partners supplied 63,000 troops and the South Vietnamese force totalled 1,200,000 troops plus 200,000 police. During the V.W., over the territory of S.V. alone, seven times more bombs and missiles were deployed than during W.W.II on all the fronts. Over 350,000 civilians were killed and 1,500,000 were wounded, 1,000,000 women were widowed, 1,500,000 chil-dren were orphaned and 60 per cent of the villages were destroyed. To end the war the PARIS PEACE TALKS were initiated in 1967 and, in mid-1969, US and other foreign troops began to withdraw. In Jan. 1973 a cease-fire agreement was signed, but various operations continued till 30th April 1975 when the Provisional Re-volutionary Government of the Republic of S.V. took over power from the col-lapsed South Vietnamese Government. The reunification of Vietnam under com-munist leadership was formally pro-claimed on 2 July 1976 when the Socialist Republic of Vietnam was officially created. The V.W. was the first war that

627

the USA lost in its history. It also demonstrated that ideological indoctrination, strict discipline, and ruthless guerrilla tactics can be more effective in modern warfare than economic, technical and military superiority.

Virgin Lands (*Tselina*, in Russian) Unoccupied or uncultivated areas in the USSR, otherwise considered suitable for agricultural purposes. They include lands in the lower eastern Volga region, the Urals, the North Caucasus, Kazakhstan, Southern Siberia and the Far East. A ten-year reclamation campaign was initiated by KHRUSHCHEV in 1953 to put the V.L. of the southern Urals, north Kazakstan and western Siberia under cultivation. This was done in order to expand the Soviet grain output. It involved a priority allocation of investment and a drive to attract young people from the European USSR. But owing to erratic rainfall, unpredictable early frosts and remoteness, the scheme has proved only a limited success.

Vitalism A philosophical and biological doctrine attributing life processes to an inherent non-material force, controlling the physical and chemical behaviour of organisms. All actions and reactions in living organisms are understood to be guided in purposive and harmonious processes in response or adaptation to the environment. Aristotle (384–322 B.C.) called this vital force *entelechy* (force at the root of the development of the matter) and G. W. Leibnitz (1648–1716) identified it with *monads* (self-acting independent spiritual entities). Among other exponents of v. were H. Bergson (1859–1941) and H. Driesch (1867–1940). V. has met with scepticism from most biologists, especially since the development of organic chemistry and the theory of evolution in the 19th c. Marxist thinkers (especially Marx, Engels and Timiriaziev) reject v., treating it as a product of philosophical IDEALISM, further embraced by the supporters of religion. Instead, life processes are viewed as a product of a long historical development

shaped by natural selection, where the law of the transformation and conservation of energy plays the central role.

Vladivostok Accords Also known as V. Guidelines or V. Ceilings, an understanding reached between the USA and the USSR at the summit meeting of President G. Ford and Party Secretary-General L. Brezhnev in Vladivostok in Nov. 1974 for ceilings on the number of strategic delivery vehicles and launchers. It was agreed to limit the overall number of strategic delivery vehicles, including long-range bombers to 2,400, of which 1,320 could be armed with multiple warhead missiles known as MIRV (Multiple Independently-targeted Re-entry Vehicles). The V.A. became the starting point for the second-round of the STRATEGIC ARMS LIMITATION TALKS, or SALT II.

Vlassovites During W.W.II, Soviet soldiers disenchanted with Stalinism who were fighting on the German side. They were led by Gen. A. A. Vlassov, who surrendered to the Germans in the Volkhov area in 1942 and who later organized a brigade collaborating with the German army. The Soviet Government treated V. as traitors and counter-revolutionaries. Vlassov was captured by the Soviet forces in Germany in 1945 and executed the following year.

Vneshtorgbank The commonly used abbreviated form for *Vneshtorgovyi Bank* in the USSR, meaning the Bank of Foreign Trade. It was founded in 1922, but until 1961 it operated virtually as a department of the GOSBANK. Since that time, its independence has increased substantially, especially since 1964 when all the *Gosbank's* correspondent accounts with foreign commercial banks were transferred to the V. The V. is responsible for all foreign payments, except those involving foreign tourists and other foreigners in the USSR, which are still handled by the *Gosbank*. The V.'s total assets in the late 1970s amounted to 20,000m. roubles (about $27,000m.). The V. is a shareholder in the following Soviet banks located in the capitalist world: Bank Russo-Iran (Teheran); Banque Commerciale pour l'Europe du Nord (Paris); Banque Uni Est–Ouest (Luxembourg); Donau Bank (Vienna); Moscow Narodny Bank (London); Ost–West Handelsbank (Frankfurt/M); and Wozchod Handelsbank (Zurich). The *V.*, through its affiliate in Zurich, now provides the facility of numbered accounts to capitalist depositors, with banking secrecy unconditionally guaranteed to all customers.

Volkskammer (People's Chamber) The unicameral parliament in the [EAST] GERMAN DR, consisting of 500 deputies elected for five years. It is the supreme formal organ of state power in the country, consisting of two types of members: 434 members are elected by citizens of 18 years of age and over by universal and secret ballot, from a single list of candidates prepared by the NATIONAL FRONT OF DEMOCRATIC GERMANY dominated by the SOCIALIST UNITY PARTY OF GERMANY; and 66 members are nominees of the City Assembly of East Berlin (without voting power). The *V.* elects a permanent executive body called the Council of State (*Staatsrat*) of 25 members headed by a Chairman, who is the formal Head of State.

Voluntarism A philosophical doctrine according to which the human will is free and the basic, decisive driving force in nature and social development. Its main exponents were such thinkers as D. Hume (1711–76), I. Kant (1724–1804), F. Nietzsche (1844–1900) and A. Schopenhauer (1788–1860). Voluntarists assume the primacy of will in its different manifestations over reason and stress irrational elements in human behaviour. They also deny the existence or minimize the role of objective laws of development independent of human will. In a sense, v. was implicitly embraced by some Socialist (especially Soviet) economists, lawyers and philosophers, who believed that the socialist state could abolish some economic laws and replace them with others as it thinks fit, thus identifying legal enactments with economic laws. On the whole, Marxists are strongly opposed to v. which is described as the 'fabrication of, reactionary idealists'. Marxist philosophers maintain that the course of history is determined not by will and dominant personalities but by the objectively necessary laws of social development (OBJECTIVE REALITY). These laws, as Marx argued, operate irrespective of the human will. V. has been officially condemned by the Socialist regimes because its acceptance would: 1. create the possibility of arbitrary decision-making; 2. make pointless the prediction of economic and social developments and taking appropriate measures on a planned basis; 3. legitimize the doctrine of divine predestination, making man dependent on God's will; 4. justify the oppression of the working masses by the ruling elite (exercising its powerful anti-social will); and 5. negate the inevitability of the breakdown of capitalism (as it could be arrested by will and great men). In practice, there were cases of the resurgence of v. in the Socialist countries, especially under the PERSONALITY CULT of Stalin and Mao Tse-tung.

Vo Nguyen Giap (1912–) A distinguished Vietnamese military and political leader. He was educated as a lawyer but for a time worked as a history teacher. He joined the Communist party in the early 1930s, helped organize the VIET MINH against the Japanese during W.W.II and then against the French. In 1946, Giap became the Commander-in-Chief of the Viet Minh army and, under his leadership, the French were defeated at DIEN BIEN PHU in May 1954. In his military and political thinking, he regarded the peasantry to be the chief revolutionary base, but favoured the adventurous approach of GUEVARA rather than Marxian, Soviet or Maoist prescriptions. Giap was the chief architect of victories in South Vietnam during the VIETNAM WAR, became a full member of the Party's Politburo, Minister of Defence and Deputy Prime Minister in the unified SR of Vietnam. He is reputed to be an outstanding organizer and a conscientious *APPARATCHIK* in the Party hierarchy. Although he proved himself to be a master of guerrilla warfare and an outstanding and resourceful tactician, he is not regarded as a great strategist. His publications, *People's War, People's Army, Big Victory* and *The Great Task*, do not embody any new principles.

Voprosy filosofy *(Problems of Philosophy,* in Russian) The leading Soviet journal of philosophy, published monthly by the Institute of Philosophy of the Academy of the Sciences of the USSR. Its publication began in 1947, having replaced *Podznamenem Marksizma (Under the Banner of Marxism,* which appeared from 1922 to 1944). *V.f.* reflects the official Soviet view in conformity with MARXISM–LENINISM, concentrating on the current interpretation of philosophical issues, together with the criticism of non-Marxist philosophy and sociology. The journal also includes general articles on social and political theory and is regarded as a scholarly periodical of wider interest. Its circulation exceeds 110,000 copies.

Vorwärts! *(Forward!)* A left-wing German newspaper. It was originally published by the German exiles in Paris in the early 1840s, to which Marx and Engels contributed. But its publication lapsed after the French Government, prodded by the Prussian Government, expelled the paper's contributors from France. The newspaper reappeared in Germany in 1876 as a Marxist paper under the editorship of W. LIEBKNECHT, with Engels contributing a few articles. It became the organ of the SOCIAL-DEMOCRATIC PARTY OF GERMANY after the latter was established in 1890 and adopted a moderate course under the editorship of K. KAUTSKY. The newspaper continued its publication until Hitler came to power in 1933 when it was suspended. But it continued to appear under the title *Neuer Vorwärts (New Forward)* in Prague and Paris until 1939. Its publication was resumed in West Germany in 1948 as the central organ of the S.D.P. of West G., but reverted to its original title *V.* in 1955 which now appears weekly in Bad Godesberg (near Bonn).

Vpered *(Forward,* in Russian) Left-wing Russian publications before W.W.I, with a varied history. 1. *Vpered!* – an organ of the NARODNIKS irregularly published as a theoretical journal and commentary in Zurich in 1873 and then in London 1874–77. It concentrated on the international workers' movement and current developments in Russia. 2. *Vpered!* – a newspaper organ of the Narodniks published fortnightly in London over the period 1875–76 (48 issues in all). It concentrated on the popularization of populist ideas and sought to reconcile Marxists and anarchists in the FIRST INTERNATIONAL. 3. *Vpered* – the first Bolshevik weekly newspaper, which appeared from 4 Jan. to 18 May 1905 (18 issues in all). It was founded as a counter to *ISKRA* which had been taken over by the MENSHEVIKS in 1903 (and followed a moderate line). The name *V.* was suggested by Lenin and its editorial board which, in addition to Lenin, included A. V. LUNACHARSKY, V. V. Vorovsky and N. KRUPSKAYA as secretary. *V.* appeared in Geneva, followed a left revolutionary line in the spirit of the old *Iskra* and was succeeded in 1905 by PROLETARY. 4. *Vpered* – a daily Bolshevik newspaper published legally in St Petersburg (now Leningrad) in June 1906 (only 17 issues appeared). It was edited by Lenin and was later replaced by *Ekho*. 5. *Vpered* – a literary, cultural, political and philosophical journal published irregularly in Geneva 1909–17 by dissident Bolsheviks called the *OTZOVISTS* and later the VPEREDISTS.

Vpered Group, Vperedists Dissident Bolsheviks who emerged in the RUSSIAN SOCIAL-DEMOCRATIC LABOUR PARTY and established a separate faction, opposed to Lenin's authoritarianism, in Capri in Dec. 1909. The Group clustered around the intellectualist anti-Bolshevik journal called *VPERED*, and included *OTZOVISTS*, UL-

TIMATISTS and followers of GOD-SEEKING. It was led (at first) by A. A. BOGDANOV and G. A. Alekinsky. Among its notable members were A. V. LUNACHARSKY, V. R. Menzhinsky, A. V. Sokolov and (at one stage) A. M. GORKY. The *Vperedists* insisted on the freedom of factionalism in the R.S.-D.L.P., maintained their own schools in Capri and Bologna, but ceased their activities by the end of 1913 and disappeared as an identifiable group after the February Revolution of 1917.

VSNKh *VESENKHA.*

Vulgar Marxism A general term used by Lenin and dogmatist Marxists for simplified and misinterpreted Marxism, conveniently adapted to specific situations or conditions. They describe it as a caricature of Marxism or a product of 'naïve fanaticism' by 'myopic, half-educated intellectuals', especially left-wing Marxists. Specific aspects of v.M. are MECHANISTIC MATERIALISM, VULGAR MATERIALISM, VULGAR POLITICAL ECONOMY and VULGAR SOCIOLOGISM.

Vulgar Materialism A description used by Engels and Lenin for the simplified interpretation of philosophical MATERIALISM. It was initiated by a French philosopher F. Cabanis (1757–1808) and developed by the German philosophers L. Büchner (1824–99), J. Moleschott (1822–93) and C. Vogt (1817–95) in the 1850s. V. materialists, aware of the great discoveries in natural sciences, recognized matter as the only reality, regarded thinking as a secretion of the brain and explained human attitudes and behaviour by purely natural conditions, viz. the physical environment, climate, diet, and the like. They were opposed to philosophical idealism and religion. Although Engels (in *ANTI-DÜHRING*) acknowledged their contribution to the popularization of natural scientific laws and atheism, he attacked them for the following: 1. they rejected the active part played by consciousness; 2. they ignored the role of the dialectic struggle of opposites in the process of develop-

ment; 3. they believed that natural laws also apply to social development; 4. they over-stressed the role of hereditary differences which they accepted as a justification of social differentiation; and 5. they rejected the need for developing philosophy as a science. He described their version of materialism as 'cheap materialism' and its exponents as 'vulgarizers' and 'itinerant preachers'.

Vulgar Political Economy A description used by Marx (mainly in *CAPITAL*, vol. III) for bourgeois economics as it developed in the latter part of the 19th c. in contradiction to Marxian economic and social analysis. Although Marx accepted (in fact borrowed) many ideas of ADAM SMITH and DAVID RICARDO, he attacked J. B. Say (1767–1832), F. Bastiat (1802–50), T. R. Malthus (1766–1834), J. S. MILL (1806–73), J. R. MACCULLOCH (1789–1864), N. Senior (1790–1864) and others as misinterpreters and distortionists of the earlier classical contributions. The vulgarization of economic thought, in his view, consisted in the separation of economic theory from the analysis of social production relations and in the assumption that the economic principles so deduced represented immutable universal laws applicable to any social system. The main specific targets of Marx's criticism were: 1. the acceptance of production cost, utility, scarcity and the market price as bases of value (and the consequent rejection of the LABOUR THEORY OF VALUE; 2. the treatment of land, capital and entrepreneurship as factors of production and the acceptance of rent, interest and profit as legitimate sources of personal income; 3. the disregard of exploitation, economic crises, the growth of monopolies, unemployment and the immiseration of the working class; and 4. the proposition that the operation of the competitive market mechanism is conducive to harmony, general economic equilibrium and maximum social welfare. V.p.e. was considered by Marx to be anti-scientific and an apologetic systematization of political economy to justify capitalism as an eternal social system. In a broader sense, dogmatic Marxists today apply the label of v.p.e. to Western economics, including post-classical developments.

Vulgar Sociologism A term popularized in the USSR in the 1930s to denote a simplified, naïve and enthusiastic approach to Marxist sociology, which appeared after the Bolshevik Revolution, especially in history, art and literature. Lenin regarded the essence of v.s. as a 'caricature of Marxism', socially anomalous and detrimental to the cause of communism in the long run. V.s. arose mostly among left-wing radicals who rejected pre-revolutionary traditions and culture (including cultural movements and societies, literary works, paintings, and museums), which were regarded as useless or at best an expedient 'cemetery'. V. sociologists were preoccupied with demonstrating the 'servility' of artists and with detecting anti-proletarian elements in current cultural activities. Officially, v.s. was regarded as a natural and inevitable initial reaction against the past which, although well meant and genuine, was fanatical, anarchical, undisciplined, excessively extremist and inconsistent with Party policies. V.s. virtually disappeared in the USSR after the GREAT PURGES 1936–38. But it has survived and in this form is sometimes referred to officially as 'sociological recedivism', and has been mostly associated with left-wing communism.

V.U.R.S. A Russian military abbreviation of *Vozdushnyi Upravlenyi Reaktyvnyi Snaryad*, corresponding to G.A.R. in English (Guided Aircraft Rocket).

W

Wade-Giles System One of the ways of spelling Chinese words in English, invented by the two English linguists in the 19th c. It is only a vague approximation of the Chinese sounds. From Jan. 1979 the Chinese authorities have introduced a new basis of transliteration into English called *PINYIN*, (meaning 'phonetic spelling'). Thus, 'Mao Tse-tung' is the traditional W.-G.s. of spelling, but according to *Pinyin* its spelling should be 'Mao Zedong'.

Wage Fund In a Socialist centrally planned economy at the national level, that portion of national income or production, in value terms which is allowed to be paid in wages (including salaries and bonuses). The w.f. is determined on a planned basis in the economic plan and corresponds to the goods and services produced and allowed for PRIVATE CONSUMPTION plus expected personal savings. The w.f. is set at such a size which, together with the fixed retail price level, ensures the postulated amount of ACCUMULATION in the plan. In addition, at the microeconomic level, w. funds are determined fo each employing entity. The w.f. may be subdivided into personal and impersonal funds. The latter includes benefits to the enterprise workers concerned in the form of collective or group amenities (which is usually determined by the enterprises themselves, not by central planners).

Wage Fund Theory A theory first put forward by ADAM SMITH (1723–90) and later elaborated by other early British classical thinkers in the early decades of the 19th c., especially Jeremy Bentham (1748–1832). According to the theory, in any economy there is a fixed portion of total national income available to the working class for consumption, more or less at the subsistence level. The theory had considerable social implications as far as wage increases were concerned. If a labour group succeeded in obtaining higher wages, it could be achieved only at the expense of the workers themselves, viz. 1. wages of other workers would be reduced; 2. prices of the products concerned would increase, thereby reducing real wages of all workers (and the rest of the community); and 3. unemployment would result, as employers would discharge less efficient labour (whose marginal product is below the new wage). The theory attracted the attention of K. Marx, who attacked it in *CAPITAL*, vol. I. He pointed out that the earnings of the working class must not be treated as a fixed quantity, but as a stream of income corresponding to the flow of production. Higher wage payments could be achieved not only from greater production, but also from the reduction of the excessive income of the BOURGEOISIE. He considered the theory as a convenient bourgeois justification of the existence of poverty among workers and the futility of trade unionism and industrial action.

Wage-Labour A term used by Marx and Engels (e.g. in *THE COMMUNIST MANIFESTO*) to describe the PROLETARIAT, whose only source of income is the sale of its labour to the property-owning BOURGEOISIE. Owing to competition among the workers, accentuated by the

633

RESERVE ARMY OF WORKERS, wages tend to be close to the subsistence level, i.e. barely sufficient to support the worker and his immediate family.

Wages Remuneration for work performed by labour, hired by an employer who may be a private capitalist, a firm or the state. W. appear both in capitalist market economies and under Socialist economic planning, but in each case are determined differently and have a different social content. According to Marx (*Paris Manuscripts of 1844* and *CAPITAL*, vol. I), under capitalism w. represent the price of LABOUR POWER, being governed by the supply of and demand for labour in the market and the consequent bargaining power of the worker. In the struggle between the employing capitalist (owning the means of production) and the worker (who for survival has to sell his labour to the capitalist employer), the balance of power is indisputably in favour of the former, so that he exploits the worker to the extent of SURPLUS VALUE. Under socialism, w. are interpreted as essentially representing the worker's share in the total production of society. In general, w. are governed by the worker's quantity and quality of work, i.e. the Leninist principle 'TO EACH ACCORDING TO HIS WORK'. Specifically the following considerations are taken into account: 1. relevant formal qualifications; 2. experience; 3. responsibility; 4. physical conditions of work; and 5. supply and demand conditions in a particular occupation or locality.

Wagner, Adolph (1835–1917) A German professor of economics who supported the social-legal school of POLITICAL ECONOMY and STATE SOCIALISM. MARX's criticism of Wagner's economics, *Notes on Adolph Wagner*, (1879–80) have recently been shown to reveal insights to Marx's methodology and approach to political economy.

Walking on Two Legs A policy of economic development in China, in which indigenous traditional methods and small-scale local production are accorded about the same priority as large-scale modern industry based on foreign technology. The policy, whose name was coined by Mao Tse-tung, was launched in 1957 as part of the GREAT LEAP FORWARD and was formally approved at the Congress of the Chinese Communist Party in May 1958. It is essentially a compromise amounting to a departure from the previously followed Soviet model, which had emphasized the development of heavy industry under centralized control, in favour of local initiative, self-reliance and decentralization. Large-scale production relying on foreign technology is limited to oil processing, synthetics, chemical fertilizers, quality steel and heavy engineering. The policy is conditioned by the following considerations: 1. the scarcity of capital for large-scale projects, paralleled by the abundance of underutilized labour, especially in rural areas; 2. shorter periods of the immobilization of resources in small-scale projects, especially if based on local materials and manpower; 3. the meagre and overburdened transport facilities, favouring local self-sufficiency; 4. in the lower stage of economic development, the sheer growth in the volume of output is considered to be more important than the quality and efficiency of production; and 5. national pride, reaction against the Soviet strategy and, in general, contempt for foreign methods. The policy is not conducive to modernization, the economies of scale and a rapid growth of productivity. It has been de-emphasized under the regime of HUA KUO-FENG.

Wall Posters An important means of PROPAGANDA employed by communists, especially in the socialist countries. They are mostly aimed at the urban population, owing to the concentration of population and the possibility of being read or interpreted to the illiterates. W.p. are relatively cheap and easy to display and can be used to support current drives and campaigns in the implementation of party and state policies. They may be displayed in suitable street locations, factories, offices, schools, clubs, means of transport and the like. W.p. have reached the highest degree of development in China, especially in the form of the BIG-CHARACTER POSTERS.

Wang Hung-wen (1937–   ) A Chinese Communist leader who figured prominently in the GREAT PROLETARIAN CULTURAL REVOLUTION as a representative of the REVOLUTIONARY REBELS and a protégé of Mao Tse-tung. However, he was stripped of his posts in 1976. In 1967 he formed the WORKERS' REVOLUTIONARY REBEL GENERAL HEADQUARTERS in Shanghai and became Vice-Chairman of the Shanghai Revolutionary Committee the following year. He was appointed the Party Secretary in Shanghai in 1971, Political Commissar in the People's Liberation Army in 1972 and in the following year he became the Vice-Chairman of the Chinese Communist Party and a member of the STANDING COMMITTEE of the Politburo of the C.C.P. Wang was the most senior member of the GANG OF FOUR. He was arrested in Oct. 1976, stripped of his posts, expelled from the Party in July 1977. After the public trials of Dec. 1980–Feb. 1981 he was sentenced to life imprisonment.

War Organized hostilities between two large opposing interests, involving armed forces and systematic violence. The Marxist view of w. is that it is basically a social phenomenon, a consequence of private property, social classes, the state, the uneven distribution of resources and differing stages of economic development. W. is regarded as a continuation of politics by a particular social class resorting to violent means. Marxism distinguishes between just and unjust wars. The former includes the armed struggle against the exploiting ruling class, defence against an imperialist attack and a war of national liberation, all of which are considered to be justified. Unjust wars are wars of aggression aimed at the subjugation of another nation or social class for the sake of exploitation and, consequently, are regarded to be anti-social and immoral, and as such are rejected. In several respects, there is a smaller predisposition for wars in the Socialist than in the capitalist countries. Marxism is opposed to militant NATIONALISM, IMPERIALISM and COLONIALISM. The pressure of private vested interests attracted to profits in military production is absent, full employment is maintained by economic planning with no need for military spending, heavy military spending is more clearly seen to be reducing social welfare programmes and the capacity of progress to FULL COMMUNISM. At the TWENTIETH CONGRESS OF THE CPSU in 1956, it was conceded that wars under imperialism, as well as between capitalist and Socialist countries, were no longer inevitable. It was also conceded that in some capitalist countries it was possible to arrive at Socialism by peaceful parliamentary methods. At the Twenty-Second Congress of the CPSU in 1961, the postulate of the DICTATORSHIP OF THE PROLETARIAT in the USSR was dropped in favour of the 'state of the whole people'. Marxists generally assume that after the disappearance of capitalism in the world, the state will 'wither away' and the sources of w. will be eliminated once and for all.

War Communism The three-year period of civil war and the FOREIGN INTERVENTION in Soviet Russia, following the GREAT OCTOBER SOCIALIST REVOLUTION of 1917. It was noted for battles between the Soviet and White armies, the latter to varying extent supported by American, British, Czech and French troops, the war with Poland, campaigns against the secessionist movement in the Ukraine, Armenia, Georgia and other parts of the former Russian empire and the struggle against the COUNTER-REVOLUTION in general. In the economic sphere, the Soviet Government pressed on with the socialization of farming and industry, established a highly centralized system of economic administration and resorted to the compulsory requisitioning of food from richer peasants. There was also a prohibition of private trading, the rationing of food in urban areas, the payment of most wages in kind, rapid inflation and an attempt to abolish money. W.C. was followed by the NEW ECONOMIC POLICY initiated in March 1921.

Warsaw Pact A military alliance with its headquarters in Warsaw, embracing the USSR, Bulgaria, Czechoslovakia, the German DR, Hungary, Poland and Romania (Albania was a member up to 1961 after which it ceased to participate in its activities and formally withdrew in Sep. 1968). The Pact was signed on 15 May, 1955 as a consequence of the admission of the FR of [West] Germany to the NORTH ATLANTIC TREATY ORGANIZATION. The W.P. obliges its member countries to provide mutual military assistance in the case of 'an armed attack in Europe on one or several of the signatory states'. The posts of the Commander-in-Chief and of the Chief of Staff have invariably been in the Soviet hands. The USSR constitutes four-fifths of the Pact's military strength and is in the exclusive possession of nuclear weapons. In 1978 the W.P. had 4,750,000 in the armed forces (NATO had 4,820,000), of which combat manpower represented 1,350,000 (NATO – 1,190,000), plus 5,150,000 reservists (NATO – 5,200,000), 27,200 main battle tanks in Europe (NATO – 11,000) and 5,600 tactical aircraft in Europe (NATO – 3,300). Like NATO, the W.P. has had its internal problems. There has been dissatisfaction with the complete Soviet domination of the alliance and opposition to the use of forces against a member country (as illustrated by the HUNGARIAN UPRISING of 1956 and the INVASION OF CZECHOSLOVAKIA in 1968).

WCL WORLD CONFEDERATION OF LABOUR.

Weatherman Underground Organization An illegal revolutionary movement in the USA committed to Marxism-Leninism and advocating the destruction of the established social order by violence. Its members, mostly left-wing students, call themselves Weathermen, derived from the line composed by Bob Dylan, 'You don't need a weatherman to know which way the wind blows'. The organization has been developed by the militant faction of the STUDENTS FOR A DEMOCRATIC SOCIETY and engaged in subversive activities, armed attacks and bombings (directed against police stations, court buildings and universities). Its leaders were involved in the Chicago riots and the organization was declared illegal in 1967. It has co-operated with a communist group called the Prairie Fire Distributing Committee. The W.U.O. preached support for revolutionary movements in China, Cuba, Vietnam and the Middle East (especially the Palestine Liberation Organization). The W.U.O. has declined in its fervour and size since the early 1970s and was further weakened by a split in 1977.

Webb, Sidney James (1859–1947) and **Beatrice Potter** (1858–1943) English socialist thinkers, social reformers and the most prominent exponents of FABIANISM, who exerted considerable influence on British social thought and the labour movement along moderate lines. They were the chief founders of the Fabian Society (1884) and the London School of Economics (1895). They were also active in social and political circles and contributed several studies which became classics in their fields. S.J.W. served on the London County Council (1892–1910), was a member of the Royal Commission on Trade Union Law (1906), the Labour Party Executive (1915–25) and was elected to Parliament (in 1922). B.P.W. participated in pioneering the social survey as a member of the Royal Commission on the Poor Law. Their sympathetic view of the Bolshevik Revolution and Soviet reforms contributed considerably to the cultivation of support for the Soviet regime in Britain and in other countries, especially after their visit to the USSR in 1922. Their main joint works were: *History of Trade Unionism* (1894); *Industrial Democracy* (1897); *A Constitution of the Socialist Commonwealth of Great Britain* (1920); *The Decay of Capitalist Civiliza-*

tion (1923); and *Soviet Communism: A New Civilization* (1935). S.J.W. also contributed to the *Fabian Essays* (1889) and B.P.W. wrote *The Co-operative Movement in Great Britain* (1891), *My Apprenticeship* (1926), *Methods of Social Study* (1932) and *Our Partnership* (1948).

Weismannism-Morganism The description used in Soviet biological studies critical of Western GENETICS. W.-M. emerged in the four decades preceding the Bolshevik Revolution of 1917 and denies the role of the environment in the variety and development of species. The description is derived from A. Weismann (1834–1914), a German biologist who developed the theory of embryonic plasma and T. H. Morgan (1886–1945), an American Nobel prizewinner who formulated the chromosome theory of heredity. W.-M. accepts Mendel's theory of heredity via genes, which Morgan located in the chromosomes of the sperm, and rejects the possibility of dropping the suppressed, or inheriting the acquired, characteristics. It explains the variety of species essentially by changes in the combinations of otherwise immutable genes. The appearance of qualitatively new species is attributed to sudden and unknown (supernatural) causes. W.-M. found supporters among many Soviet biologists, such as N. P. Dubinin, Yu. A. Filipchenko, A. S. Serebrovsky, I. I. Shmalhauzen and A. R. Zhebrak. But it was strongly attacked in the USSR in the 1930s and 1940s as a bourgeois reactionary doctrine serving the interests of the exploiting classes, which aided the development of EUGENICS. It was also accused of philosophically being akin to METAPHYSICS, Kantism, MACHISM, PRAGMATISM and VITALISM, thus being inconsistent with MATERIALISM. W.-M. was condemned at the Conference of the All-Russian Academy of Agricultural Sciences in July-Aug. 1948. Opposed to W.-M. were the officially accepted biological schools, MICHURINISM and LYSENKOISM, which emphasized the part played by the external material environment in the alteration of species, the inheritance of

acquired characteristics and thus, the possibility of planned improvement of plant, animal and human organisms. Following the scientific plight of Lysenkoism after the late 1950s and the regeneration of Soviet genetics, the label W.-M. was dropped in Soviet scientific, as well as ideological, discussions.

Weitling, Wilhelm (1808–71) An early German moderate socialist, whose ideas attracted the attention of Marx and Engels. Although a tailor by occupation, he engaged in intellectual pursuits and became a socialist through biblical studies. He advocated an idealist egalitarian society to be achieved by parliamentary methods. Persecuted for his revolutionary ideas, he fled to Paris, where he joined the LEAGUE OF THE JUST in 1838. W. participated in the unsuccessful REVOLUTION OF 1848 and then emigrated to the USA, where he organized a Workers' Union. His writings (in German), rather naïve and lacking consistency, included *Humanity: As It Is and Should Be* (1839) and *Guarantees of Harmony and Freedom* (1845).

Welfare State A concept applied to a non-socialist country with a government which provides comprehensive social security 'from the cradle to the grave', in such forms as free or virtually free medical services, hospitalization, maternity allowances, child endowment, unemployment benefit, old age pensions, funeral expenses and special benefits for the handicapped and otherwise underprivileged. The idea of the w.s. represents a departure from *LAISSEZ-FAIRE* capitalism, recognizes the need for intervention by the state as a neutral and supra-class institution, in the form of social legislation and the redistribution of national income from the higher to the lower income groups. Although the w.s. is usually associated with the nationalization of some key industries and services, otherwise the champions of the w.s. reject the complete socialization of the means of production, the mono-party system of government and the dictatorship of the proletariat. The idea of the w.s. was first developed and implemented in Britain (especially under the Labour Party Government during 1945–51). Scandinavian countries and most other Western European nations, Australia, New Zealand, Canada and several other rich developed countries have also adopted similar social welfare programmes. The conservative critics have attacked the w.s., describing it as the 'social warfare state', representing creeping socialism and communism, leading to fiscal irresponsibility, the blunting of incentives and the destruction of private initiative. Although it may appear surprising, revolutionary Marxists have also attacked the w.s. as created in capitalist countries. They regard it as an 'apologetic attempt to rescue the ailing capitalist social system' from its inevitable doom, merely delaying the need for a proletarian revolution.

'We'll Bury You' A phrase used by KHRUSHCHEV when he addressed Western ambassadors at a reception in the Kremlin on 17 Nov. 1956. Although the meaning of the phrase attributed to him in the West was 'we'll kill you' or 'we'll destroy you', it appears to have been a misrepresentation, and indeed he himself denied that implication. In the Russian colloquial parlance, the phrase means 'We'll be present at your funeral', i.e. given peaceful coexistence and competition, communism will outlive capitalism.

Westphalen, Jenny von (1814–81) The maiden name of K. Marx's wife who was his childhood friend and whom he married in 1843 (just before he went into exile in Paris). She came from a well-to-do family and her older brother had been Minister of the Interior in Prussia (1850–58). As Marx's wife, after her dowry was spent, she lived in abject poverty, lost three of her six children because of malnutrition and a lack of medical attention and died of cancer in 1881, two years before her husband's death. Yet she remained his loyal wife to the last, following him in exile to Paris, Brussels and London. One of their daughters, Laura, married P. LAFARGUE, both of whom died in a mutual suicide pact.

WFDY WORLD FEDERATION OF DEMOCRATIC YOUTH.

WFTU WORLD FEDERATION OF TRADE UNIONS.

What Is To Be Done? A book written by Lenin in 1901–02 and first published in Stuttgart in March 1902. It was directed against peaceful, evolutionary Marxism in the international working class movement. Instead, Lenin postulated a revolutionary approach to the transformation of society, spearheaded by a tightly organized, disciplined and devoted communist party. He attacked the PARLIAMENTARY ROAD TO SOCIALISM and ECONOMISM advocated by moderate social-democratic parties, accusing them of OPPORTUNISM. He stressed the need for developing CLASS CONSCIOUSNESS in the proletariat and the importance of revolutionary theory in guiding the communist parties and the international working class movement. Lenin did not regard trade union activities to be sufficient to lead to socialism, as they were too preoccupied with immediate improvement in material conditions of work to overthrow capitalism. Lenin's book reflected two opposed strategies in the RUSSIAN SOCIAL-DEMOCRATIC LABOUR PARTY which led to a split in 1903 – the revolutionary Marxists called BOLSHEVIKS who adopted Lenin's strategy, and the moderate evolutionary Marxists called MENSHEVIKS. In reply to Lenin's book, PLEKHANOV (the leading Menshevik) wrote *What Is Not To Be Done*. It may be added that N. G. CHERNYSHEVSKY, whom Lenin acknowledged as the precursor of Russian revolutionaries, also wrote a book *What Is To Be Done* (1862), which was a literary piece presenting a vision of the future ideal socialist society, including emancipated women.

White In the political sense, the colour

identified with anti-communism, implying purity, harmony and the absence of violence, as opposed to RED. In Tsarist Russia, the terms 'w. linings' or 'whites' were applied to the university students who came from wealthy and aristocratic families, as they wore silk linings on their expensive uniforms. After the October Revolution, the Bolsheviks used the description 'W.' with a defamatory connotation in application to the Tsarist and other counter-revolutionary troops fighting the RED ARMY and the Soviet regime in general. The WHITE GUARDS were the elite Tsarist armed units and the White Terror referred to the reprisals against Bolshevik officials and communist sympathizers in the areas temporarily controlled by the Tsarist armed units.

White Guards The name given by the Bolsheviks to the elitist volunteer armed units during the Russian Civil War (1917–21) who fought against the RED ARMY to restore the Tsarist regime. They constituted the main counter-revolutionary force which, by 1922, had been defeated or scattered by the Soviet regime.

White-haired Girl, The Originally a play written by Ho Ching-chih and Ting Ni and first presented on stage in Yenan in 1945, which has come to occupy an important position in Chinese communist literature and ideology. It is a sentimental story about a peasant girl who was raped by a landlord and made pregnant. She then ran away to live in haunted caves. She survived by pretending to be a ghost in a mountain temple frightening local peasants into making offerings of food to the ghost with the white hair. After the communist victory, she was rescued by a handsome guerrilla leader. The play, which was awarded Stalin's Prize in 1952, was adapted by CHIANG CH'ING (Mao's wife) to ballet in the early 1960s and widely employed during the GREAT PROLETARIAN CULTURAL REVOLUTION to revolutionize ideas and attitudes stemming from the old social relations. In the ballet,

Wholesale Price In Socialist economic practice, PRODUCER PRICE *plus* the wholesale margin, or RETAIL PRICE *minus* the retail margin and the turnover tax (or, plus the subsidy). The w.p. can move independently of the retail price, owing to the flexible manipulation of the turnover taxes and subsidies by the state.

the girl's sufferings under the old regime are highlighted, but the peasants' superstitions are played down. The girl is also depicted as a participant in the communist struggle, in order to convey the idea of the equality of the sexes.

Withering Away of the State One of the features of the ideal society under FULL COMMUNISM, postulated by Marx and Engels. The idea was first put forward by Marx in 1846 (in *The POVERTY OF PHILOSOPHY*) and then elaborated upon by Engels in 1878 (in *ANTI-DÜHRING*). They argued that the state was still necessary under SOCIALISM, the transitional phase to full communism which, in their view, would probably take less than a decade. Their view differed from ANARCHISM in which the immediate abolition of the state is postulated. In no socialist country have steps been taken to phase out the state. In the oldest of them, the USSR, the power of the state was in fact greatly increased ten years after the Bolshevik Revolution. The Soviet state is still the most coercive and powerful state in the world. In defending the persistence of the state in the USSR, Stalin argued that the thesis of Marx and Engels was applicable to the situation where proletarian revolutions occur and are successful in all countries. Under the conditions of SOCIALISM IN ONE COUNTRY or only in a few countries, the state must be developed into a powerful machine to defend socialism against CAPITALIST ENCIRCLEMENT and further be employed to spread the revolution to capitalist countries until capitalism is completely eliminated.

Women, Community of 'COMMUNITY OF WOMEN'.

Women's International Democratic Fed-

eration An INTERNATIONAL COMMUNIST FRONT ORGANIZATION created in Dec. 1945. It was initiated by the communist-controlled Union of French Women at the founding congress in Paris, in which women's organizations, mostly communist-controlled, from some 40 countries participated. The Federation was expelled from France in 1951 and its headquarters were moved from Paris to East Berlin in the same year. Its highest level of authority is the Congress (held every four years) which elects a Council (meeting once a year). The latter elects a Bureau (meeting twice a year) and the working Secretariat. In the late 1970s, the Federation claimed 123 affiliated national organization plus individual women in 109 countries, totalling 200m. members. But no non-communist women's organizations of any consequence have joined. However, the W.I.D.F. endeavours to maintain contacts with non-affiliated women's groups through its International Liaison Bureau (with its head office in Copenhagen and a secretariat in Brussels). The Federation also has a consultative status with UNESCO and the ILO. The W.I.D.F. aims to unite women irrespective of their political views, nationality, race and religion, to defend women's rights as citizens, mothers and workers, to protect children and to work towards world peace. It publishes a quarterly called *Women of the Whole World*, published in six languages (Arabic, English, French, German, Russian and Spanish) and *Documents and Information*, appearing irregularly.

Work In classical Marxist thought, human activity directed to the production of USE-VALUE, i.e. products for consumption. It is thus distinct from LABOUR (which is directed to the creation of exchange-value, i.e. products for sale).

Work Co-operative A type of CO-OPERATIVE ENTERPRISE based on the personal labour of its members, who are thus employers, co-managers and employees at the same time. Each member may contribute a share to the jointly owned assets, receive current remuneration for his work and, in addition, participate in the net income and share in the losses on an equal basis or to the maximum of his capital contribution. There are two categories of the w.c.: 1. *workers' producer c.* – where the members own the assets and output of the enterprise on a collective basis (the more common variant); and 2. *labour contracting c.* – where the means of production, as well as the output, belong to the state or some other entity, but the co-operative workers share in the proceeds received from the principal. The idea of the w.c. was first developed in Western Europe in the 19th c. by J. L. BLANC and CH. FOURIER and applied in practice in France and Italy. Although Marx praised the schemes as worthwhile social experiments, he did not treat them seriously as a real solution to social problems. In the Socialist countries, w.c. were quite important soon after the communist accession to power (LENIN'S SCHEME FOR CO-OPERATIVE AGRICULTURE), but today they are limited to the less important spheres (agriculture, small-scale industry, and consumer services) and their members are usually worse off than workers in the state sector.

Work-day Unit A measure of work performed in a COLLECTIVE FARM by individual members, used as the basis for the distribution of personal income (in state farms, workers are paid ordinary wages, like factory workers). The system was first introduced in the USSR in 1931 (under the name of *trudoden*) and has been adopted in its essence in other Socialist countries as well. The w.-d.u. represents a day's work by one person, of average intensity and complexity. The least skilled work is generally taken as 0.5 w.-d.u. and the most skilled work – as 2.5. These and intermediate coefficients are used to multiply the time actually spent at work. A minimum, or a norm, expected from each member may also be established, typically ranging from 50 to 100 w.-d.u. a year, in order to prevent members from spending too much time on their SUBSIDIARY PLOTS.

The total number of w.-d.u. in a year is regarded as the member's contribution to the farm's results. The member is paid accordingly in money and in kind as well. The payment per w.-d.u. for the year is arrived at by dividing the portion of the farm's income allocation for personal distribution by the total number of the w.-d.u. worked. The average is then multiplied by the number of the w.-d.u. performed by the worker concerned. The system has been largely abandoned in most Socialist countries in favour of payment in money with a guaranteed minimum income to each member or family, as illustrated by the Model Statute for Collective Farms adopted in the USSR in 1969.

Work Discipline The totality of the worker's explicit and implicit obligations deemed necessary in employer-employee or collective work relations. These obligations may be either imposed by law, economic necessity, commonly accepted as moral sanctions, or may be voluntarily formulated and observed on the initiative of the workers themselves. The Marxist view of w.d. under capitalism is that of a matter of effective economic compulsion, where the worker has to sell his labour and remain in employment to survive, as the means of production are owned by the capitalists and w.d. is largely enforced by the threat of unemployment (RESERVE ARMY OF WORKERS). It is claimed that in the Socialist countries, where the workers own the working establishments and participate in their operation and control, the approach to w.d. is different in that it relies more on civic responsibility rather than crude economic compulsion. But continuous full employment and generous social security has led, in the past, to lax working habits. Consequently, the authorities, in co-operation with trade unions, have formulated mandatory and informal labour codes to promote better w.d. They typically insist on the following: 1. punctual attendance at work in a fit work condition; 2. active performance of the tasks handed out by superiors in accordance with the existing legislation, work agreements and social interest in general; 3. proper maintenance and protection of social property in the workplace; 4. observance of safety and sanitary regulations; 5. co-operation with other members of the working establishment; and 6. appreciation of the commonly accepted rule under socialism, 'He who does not work, shall not eat.' The workers, including the managerial personnel, are expected to participate in SOCIALIST COMPETITION and emulation campaigns to achieve socially desired targets and improve work performance. Negligence at work or wilful damage to the socialized property is treated seriously, whereby the guilty person is liable to the restitution of the damage out of his income, or may be punished by demotion or even imprisonment.

Worker A person engaged in the production of goods or services for the satisfaction of human wants and who does not privately own the means of production involved. In its narrow sense, the term refers to a manual factory worker (blue collar w.), but in its wider meaning, it refers to non-manual employees with less than university or vocational secondary education (including white collar w.). The term w. appeared in common usage during the Industrial Revolution in the early 19th c. in application to hired industrial labour and implied a toiler who had to sell his labour to survive. It may be mentioned that in several East European languages (Bulgarian, Croat, Polish, Russian, Serbian, Slovak and Ukrainian) the term w. is derived from the ancient Slavonic root *rab* or *rob*, meaning slave or slave labourer. Marx and Engels, more clearly than anybody else before, recognized the w. as not only the unjustly exploited member of the capitalist society, but also as a member of the proletariat, the largest social class and potentially (i.e. when class-conscious) the most dynamic and militant element capable of overthrowing capitalism. Under Socialism, workers are regarded as the most important social class (ahead of the peasants and intelligentsia), the mainstay of communist power.

Workers' and Peasants' Inspectorates Offices of popular control in Soviet Russia established on the initiative of Lenin in 1919 (they were popularly known as *Rabkrin*, an abbreviated form of *Raboche-Krestyanskaya Inspektsiya*). They were meant to exercise restraint on the power of bureaucracy, detect inefficiency and corruption by 'scrutiny from below' and give satisfaction to the ordinary masses participating in social administration. In 1920, the W.P.I. were reorganized into the Worker and Peasant Commissariat (Ministry), with Stalin as its first Commissar. The W.P.C. continued to operate until 1934 when it was transformed into the Commission of Soviet Control. After W.W.II, the W.P.C. was renamed the Ministry of State Control.

Workers' and Peasants' Red Army The initial name in Soviet Russia of the RED ARMY.

Workers' Aristocracy LABOUR ARISTOCRACY.

Workers' Brigade PRODUCTION BRIGADE.

Workers' Councils In Yugoslav enterprises, boards elected by the workers, vested with the power of decision-making on crucial issues, such as the hiring of managerial staff, the structure of output, prices, borrowing, investment and the allocation of income. W.C. were introduced in 1949, legally formalized in 1950 and, by 1952, were commonly found in the non-agricultural sector. They have become the main and characteristic element of Yugoslav WORKERS' SELF-MANAGEMENT. Each socialized economic organization (including non-commercial entities, such as hospitals), now called the BASIC ORGANIZATION OF ASSOCIATED LABOUR, is required to elect a W.C. by secret ballot to serve for two years, one half of whom are replaced every year. The number of elected members ranges from 15–120, but 20–30 is typical, while in small B.O.A.L. all members may constitute a W.C. Within the rules laid down by the state, each W.C. adopts a constitution which provides a basis for the operation of the enterprise to suit local conditions. If the W.C. is large, it selects an inner body called the Board of Management, consisting of 3–11 members. The enterprise director (general manager) is appointed by the W.C. in accordance with the rules established by the state. By the same token, the director may suspend the decision of the W.C. if they are not consistent with the state law. Before 1971, each enterprise had one W.C., but since the reform in that year, enterprises with subsidiaries have multiple W.C. About one-fifth of the 7,800 Yugoslav enterprises have more than one W.C. A large entity creates a central W.C. with representatives from each subsidiary W.C. Private firms, including farms (which may employ no more than five persons) are exempt from having to elect W.C. A similar system was introduced temporarily in Poland (1956–58), Hungary (1968) and Czechoslovakia (1968–69), but it has never developed further to provide a viable basis for workers' self-management as in Yugoslavia.

Workers' Defence Committee A dissident association in Poland founded in June 1976, following protests, strikes and riots against oppressive living and working conditions. The purpose of the Committee is to represent the interests of the strikers and protesters harassed and imprisoned by the communist regime.

Workers' Fatherland, Workers' State Sympathetic descriptions used for the UNION OF THE SOVIET SOCIALIST REPUBLICS, especially before the end of W.W.II. They were used not only in the USSR, but also by workers in capitalist countries. The USSR was treated as a special country of interest to workers anywhere on the following grounds: 1. it was the only country in which a proletarian revolution against tremendous odds had been successfully staged with the workers' retaining power; 2. it was the only safe base of the international working class movement and the haven for persecuted communist leaders and revolutionaries; 3. it was the centre of the Communist International, from which the communist parties as sections of the COMINTERN were guided, assisted and prepared for proletarian revolutions; and 4. Stalin developed the idea of Soviet PATRIOTISM, which he regarded to be consistent with SOCIALIST INTERNATIONALISM. However, the FORCED LABOUR CAMPS, the treacherous attacks against Poland (1939) and Finland (1939–40) and the annexation of the Baltic states and Polish, Czechoslovak, Romanian, Mongolian and Japanese territories during and after W.W.II dimmed the workers' fascination for the USSR. Since W.W.II the descriptions have hardly been used.

Workers' International Relief (*Mezhrabpom* in Russian, abbreviated from *Mezhdunarodnaya Rabochiya Pomoshch*) A short-lived international front organization of the COMINTERN. W.I.R. was founded in Berlin in Sep. 1921 for the purpose of enlisting the support of the communist parties and other left-wing organizations in capitalist countries to contribute to the relief efforts in the USSR. In spite of its enthusiastic beginnings, it never achieved much success. It managed to establish active affiliates in only a few countries (especially in Germany), but after the famine in the USSR was over in 1925, its efforts declined. It was formally dissolved by the Comintern in Oct. 1935.

'Workers of All Lands, Unite!' The challenging call to the international working class movement, concluding THE *COMMUNIST MANIFESTO*, prepared by Marx and Engels, originally in German in 1848. The slogan is also rendered in English as 'Workers of all countries, unite' and 'Proletarians of all lands, unite'.

Workers' Opposition A syndicalist faction (consisting of trade unionists) in the RUSSIAN COMMUNIST PARTY (OF THE BOLSHEVIKS) in existence during 1920–22 which opposed Lenin's plan for state control of the economy based on the principle of DEMOCRATIC CENTRALISM. Instead, it

advocated that economic administration be handed over to the All-Russian Congress of Producers to be established for the purpose. The label of the W.O. was coined by Lenin who saw its scheme as an anarcho-syndicalist threat to his system of centralized state administration. The group, led by ALEXANDRA M. KOLLONTAI, S. P. Medvedev and A. G. Shlyapnikov (Labour Commissar in the Soviet Government), was against the bureaucratic domination of the economy by the Party and the State and insisted that the economic processes should be managed by trade unions. The W.O. was condemned by the Party majority at the 10th Congress of the R.C.P.(B). in March 1921. Furthermore, two resolutions were pushed through by Lenin, banning FACTIONALISM and giving power to the Central Committee to expel the offenders. The members of the W.O. continued to voice its views for another year, but with little popular support. Most of them, with the notable exception of A. M. Kollontai, disappeared in the GREAT PURGES of the 1930s.

Workers' Participation A term used in industrial relations to denote the involvement of all employees in decision-making – either personally or through their elected representatives – on matters affecting them at work. The term is mostly used in application to capitalist countries, where w.p. may also involve the ownership of shares in the companies concerned. W.p. has reached considerable development in Denmark, the FR of [West] Germany, the Netherlands, Norway and Sweden and to a lesser extent in several other Western European countries. Workers' representatives sit on the boards of directors and management committees and attempt to bridge the traditional gap between the management and ordinary workers. But the system has been developed to its greatest extent in Yugoslavia, where it is known under the name of WORKERS' SELF-MANAGEMENT, exercised through the elected WORKERS' COUNCILS. Although the means of production are formally owned by the state, they are controlled and utilized by the workers teamed up in the BASIC ORGANIZATIONS OF ASSOCIATED LABOUR. There were attempts to develop w.p. along similar lines in the USSR (up to the early 1930s), Poland (1956–58), Hungary (1968), Czechoslovakia (1968–69) and China (1966–76). But in each case, the attempts have been followed by the strengthening of the traditional authoritarian forms of operating socialized enterprises, even though concessions to trade unions are occasionally made and the workers' active interest and involvement in enterprise activities are encouraged. The most systematic approach to w.p. is advocated by GUILD SOCIALISM and SYNDICALISM.

Workers' Revolutionary Party The largest Trotskyite organization in Great Britain and the main rival to the leadership of the Communist movement in the country. It follows the orthodox version of TROTSKYISM and is affiliated to the FOURTH INTERNATIONAL (United Secretariat). It was formed in Nov. 1973 as a reorganized successor to the SOCIALIST LABOUR LEAGUE (established in 1959). The Party's main base of influence is in industrial unions and some professions, especially mining, engineering, the docks and the theatre (Vanessa Redgrave being among its members). It co-operates closely in the industrial field with the All Trades Union Alliance. The Party's claimed membership is 2,000 plus 20,000 in its youth arm, the Young Socialists (the largest Marxist youth organization in Great Britain). Although it has contested general elections, it has not gained any parliamentary seats. The Party has suffered from internal instability. Some of its members were expelled in 1974 and created the WORKERS' SOCIALIST LEAGUE and some resigned in 1975 and formed a new quasi-Trotskyite group called the INTERNATIONAL COMMUNIST LEAGUE. The W.R.P. publishes a daily newspaper, *Newsline* (which replaced *Workers' Press*) and a quarterly journal, *Fourth International*.

Workers' Revolutionary Rebel General Headquarters An organization established in Shanghai in Jan. 1967 by the left-wing supporters of the GREAT PROLETARIAN CULTURAL REVOLUTION. It immediately took over power from the established conservative Party leadership in Shanghai. It also acted as a co-ordinating centre for several left-wing revolutionary groups in the Shanghai region. The organization and its extremist actions received enthusiastic support from Mao Tse-tung who praised it for practising EXTENSIVE DEMOCRACY.

Workers' Self-Management A description applied in the Socialist countries to the control and operation of socialized enterprises. It is more advanced and systematic than workers' participation applicable mostly in capitalist economies. The idea of w.s.-m. goes back to the experiments with idealistic communities in the 19th c. (COMMUNITARIANISM) and to GUILD SOCIALISM and SYNDICALISM. But its most systematic and lasting application has found its expression in Yugoslavia, the country to which the term w.s.-m. is mostly applied nowadays. It is an example of economic decentralization, a reaction against the CENTRALIZED DIRECTIVE SYSTEM OF PLANNING AND MANAGEMENT which had prevailed in the country before 1950. W.s.-m. was formally introduced in Yugoslavia in 1950 and further extended and improved by the reforms of 1952, 1965 and 1971. The means of production, although formally owned by the state, are placed at the disposal of the workers economically linked in the BASIC ORGANIZATIONS OF ASSOCIATED LABOUR. The latter may be productive enterprises or service enterprises, institutions, government departments and other work entities outside agriculture and private firms employing five or less persons. The workers in each B.O.A.L. elect a WORKERS' COUNCIL (typically of 20–30 representatives) for two years which, if large, may create an inner body known as the Management Board (usually from 3–11 members). The W.C. or the M.B. appoints the B.O.A.L.'s chief executive officer called the 'director' (general manager) in accordance with the regulations laid down by the state. The W.C. has the power to determine the local labour code, the composition of production of goods and/or services, the size and directions of investment, borrowing and lending operations, prices, current income payments, the distribution of residual profits and the provision of socio-cultural amenities. Although in other Socialist countries lip service is paid to w.s.-m., it is nowhere as well developed as in Yugoslavia. Factory committees elected by the workers, trade unions and local authorities are involved in the operation of the socialized enterprises, but mostly in advisory or surveillance capacities. Genuine w.s.-m. was introduced in Poland by the legislation of 1956–58, but the actual incidence of the enterprises operating under the system is limited. The attempts in Hungary (1968) and Czechoslovakia (1968–69) were short-lived. W.s.-m. of a sort was popularly tried in China during the GREAT PROLETARIAN CULTURAL REVOLUTION (1966–68) and further experimented with until Mao Tsetung's death (1976), but has been largely abandoned by the regime of HUA KUO-FENG since 1977. W.s.-m. may be said to prevail in all the Socialist countries in the co-operative sector, craftsmen CO-OPERATIVES in small-scale industry and services, COLLECTIVE FARMS and COMMUNES.

Workers' Socialist League In Great Britain, a small Trotskyite group of several hundred members, basing its programme entirely on Trotsky's TRANSITIONAL PROGRAMME. It was founded in Dec. 1974 by the 200 or so members expelled from the WORKERS' REVOLUTIONARY PARTY. Its leader is Alan Thornett (popularly known to members as 'The Mole'). The League campaigns for greater democracy in the labour movement and publishes a weekly called *Socialist Press*.

Work Ethics See WORK DISCIPLINE.

Working Class The social class deriving its livelihood from employment outside agriculture and the professions. The core of the w.c. are industrial workers, workers employed in construction, fishing, forestry, transport, communications and trade. The overlapping craftsmen, white-collar workers, servants, itinerant workers and the unemployed (if any) are also included. The w.c. is one of the three main social classes, whether under capitalism (in addition to the BOURGEOISIE and the peasantry) or SOCIALISM (in addition to the peasantry and the INTELLIGENTSIA), but its nature and role differ under each system. In a capitalist society, as interpreted by Marxists, the w.c. is deprived of the means of production. To survive it has to sell its labour to the capitalists who own the means of production and who are supported from the SURPLUS VALUE created by the workers. Both economically and politically, the w.c. or the proletariat are dominated by the ruling class – the bourgeoisie. Economic development inevitably leads to the expansion of the w.c. which, when it becomes class conscious, becomes capable of overthrowing capitalism in a PROLETARIAN REVOLUTION. It then seizes political power, which is exercised by the Communist party under the conditions of the dictatorship of the proletariat. In alliance with the peasantry and intelligentsia, the w.c. is the main driving force in building socialism and then, communism. In the final stage of social development, differences between physical and mental and between rural and urban labour will disappear and a CLASSLESS SOCIETY will emerge under FULL COMMUNISM. At the beginning of the 19th c. the industrial w.c. constituted less than 5m. or 0.5 per cent of the world's population, but by 1980 the world figures had risen to some 700m., or 15 per cent (30 per cent in developed countries).

Working Day A concept of economic and legal importance analysed by Marx (in *CAPITAL*, vol. I), which he defined as 'the sum of INDISPENSABLE LABOUR and SURPLUS LABOUR, i.e. of the periods of time during which the workman replaces the value of his LABOUR POWER and produces the SURPLUS VALUE'. The maximum length of the w.d. is limited by the physical and mental capacity of the worker, but its actual duration is determined by the productivity of labour, the bargaining power of labour, the prevailing moral attitudes, the social system in force and economic and political circumstances at a particular time. At the height of the Industrial Revolution in England, the w.d. reached 16 hours, but has since been halved. The demand for an eight-hour w.d. was formulated by the FIRST INTERNATIONAL in 1866 and was first officially won in Victoria (Australia) in 1883 (in 1916 in the USA). The eight-hour w.d. was accepted as a rule by the Soviet Government in one of its first decrees in 1917 and by the HUNGARIAN SOVIET REPUBLIC in 1919. It was also mentioned in the Treaty of Versailles (Article 427) and embodied in the international Convention No. 1 of the International Labour Organization in 1919. As in capitalist countries, the w.d. under socialism is not fully remunerated in wages. In the Socialist countries, the w.d. consists of two periods: 1. that part during which the worker creates value equivalent to his wage, known as the PRODUCT FOR ONESELF; and 2. the remaining part during which he creates value to support SOCIAL CONSUMPTION and other macrosocial needs (including investment), known as the PRODUCT FOR SOCIETY.

Work Norms Formally laid-down rules, specifying the length of time normally needed for the performance of particular task(s) or the quantity of output to be normally achieved in a unit of time under given conditions in the entities of employment. The system of w.n. is very well developed in the socialist countries for the following reasons: 1. they have been found necessary owing to continuous full employment, generous social security and the absence of private enterprise; 2. they contribute to WORK DISCIPLINE; 3. they facilitate economic planning; and 4. they are used as a basis for calculating wages and bonuses. W.n. can be established by two methods. Statistical w.n. are based on past statistical records, while analytical (or technical) w.n. are arrived at by a thorough examination of the production capacity of the work place, a detailed analysis of the technical processes involved and the specification of separate tasks to be performed in the prescribed manner and sequence. W.n. may be laid down by the local plant, the relevant branch association, ministry or the state planning commission, in the last case, applicable to the whole economy.

World Anti-Communist League An organization based in Seoul (South Korea) directed against communism. It was originally founded in 1954 as the Asian People's Anti-Communist League, but was broadened at its 12th Conference in Nov. 1966 into the W.A.-C.L. Its objectives include the elimination of communism and other forms of totalitarianism, the protection of HUMAN RIGHTS and safeguarding the self-determination of all peoples. It embraces 12 international, 6 regional and 74 national anti-communist associations in 68 non-socialist countries, including Australia, Brazil, Canada, France, India, Indonesia, Japan, Sweden, the UK, the USA and 6 'subjugated nations in exile', viz. Bulgaria, Byelorussia, Croatia, Lithuania, Romania and the Ukraine. The League holds annual conferences on communist and anti-communist affairs and publishes a quarterly, *WACL Bulletin* and a monthly, *WACL Newsletter*. The activities of the League have produced little effect, especially in recent years.

World City, World Village Concepts coined by LIN PIAO, the former symbolizing the capitalist rich industrial nations, while the latter refer to the poor undeveloped agricultural countries. Lin employed the terms in summer 1965, when he called on Japan to join China in her efforts to 'liberate the W.V.' from the exploitation by the W.C. He also alluded to Mao Tse-tung's revolutionary strategy, whereby the revolution begins in the countryside and then engulfs the cities.

World Confederation of Labour An international working class organization based in Brussels, subscribing to religious ideals. It was originally founded in The Hague in 1920 under the name of the INTERNATIONAL FEDERATION OF CHRISTIAN TRADE UNIONS, but at its 16th Congress in Luxemburg in Oct. 1968, it broadened its function to appeal to non-Christian countries as well and changed its name to the W.C.L. Its membership includes national trade union and other labour confederations in 75 non-socialist countries, with the conspicuous exception of Sweden, the UK and the USA. Its declared aims are to defend workers' interests and to develop human society united in freedom, labour dignity, justice and fraternity, irrespective of creed, race, nationality and sex. It is guided by the Universal Declaration of Human Rights and the United Nations Charter. In addition to its co-ordinating functions, it represents its affiliated bodies in such international institutions as the Council of Europe, the EEC, ILO, OECD, UNCTAD, UNESCO and UNIDO. It organizes conferences and the training of labour leaders and technical specialists for African, Asian and Latin American countries. It publishes a bimonthly, *Labour* (in Dutch, English, French, German and Spanish) and other regular and occasional literature. The W.C.L. holds its Congress every four years, which elects the Confederal Board. The latter appoints a Council every year, plus eight Permanent Committees for specialized responsibilities. The W.C.L. competes in the international labour movement with the conservative INTERNATIONAL CONFEDERATION OF FREE TRADE UNIONS and the Communist-dominated WORLD FEDERATION OF TRADE UNIONS.

World Council of Churches An international organization with pro-communist sympathies for the promotion of co-operation among all churches, of religious studies and missionary work. It was founded in Amsterdam in 1948 and its Secretariat is located in Geneva. With it are affiliated 286 church bodies in over 100 countries – both capitalist (including Canada, France, the FR of Germany, India, Indonesia, Italy, Japan, Sweden, Switzerland, the UK and the USA) and Socialist (Czechoslovakia, Hungary, Poland, Romania and Yugoslavia). The W.C.C. has been accused in the West, especially since the early 1970s of: 1. giving the Marxist movement a Christian justification; 2. revolutionary pro-communist and anti-Western politics; 3. supporting left-wing terrorist activities against former colonial powers (especially in Africa); and 4. spreading 'fraudulent gospel' in general. The W.C.C. carries on an extensive publications programme, including *Ecumenical Press Service* (bi-weekly), *Ecumenical Review* (quarterly), *Inter-Church Aid Newsletter* (monthly), *International Review of Missions* (quarterly), *One World* (monthly), *Risk* (quarterly) and *Study Encounter* (quarterly).

World Council of Peace WORLD PEACE COUNCIL.

World Federation of Democratic Youth An INTERNATIONAL COMMUNIST FRONT ORGANIZATION, founded in London on 10 Nov. 1945 with its headquarters now in Budapest. It aims to promote co-operation among international youth organizations and a closer international understanding among young people. It campaigns for peace and is against RACISM, COLONIALISM, NEO-COLONIALISM and MILITARISM. As part of the pursuit of its objectives, it celebrates 10 November each year as International Solidarity Day. The Federation is headed by the Executive Council and its permanent Bureau. In addition, there are several specialized Committees, such as International Tourism and Exchange, Sports Committee and the Youth Rights Committee. The W.F.D.Y. organizes youth festivals, seminars and voluntary work camps and publishes *WFDY News* (monthly), *World*

Youth (quarterly) and occasional specialized bulletins. The Federation claims to represent 257 affiliated organizations in 115 countries with a combined membership of 150m. All the socialist countries are represented except Yugoslavia (which resents the Soviet domination), while China and Cuba have boycotted it on occasions for not being revolutionary enough. Most capitalist countries are also represented with some exceptions, such as the FR of Germany and the USA.

World Federation of Scientific Workers An INTERNATIONAL COMMUNIST FRONT ORGANIZATION based in London. It was created in July 1946 on the initiative of the British Association of Scientific Workers, but communist sympathizers soon took over the leadership of the Federation. Soviet scientists began to be represented only after 1951. Its function is to provide a liaison among organized scientific workers to safeguard scientific rights, to improve working conditions, to promote peaceful applications of scientific discoveries and to oppose nuclear weapons. The Federation's highest level of authority is the General Assembly holding a Congress every three years, which elects an Executive Council of 35, but the day-to-day work is carried on by a Bureau. The membership of the W.F.S.W. includes national associations of scientific workers totalling 300,000 in 28 countries, both Socialist and capitalist. The Federation organizes international symposiums and publishes a quarterly, *Scientific World* (in Arabic, Czech, English, French, German, Russian and Spanish) and occasional reports on major scientific problems of ideological and propagandist content.

World Federation of Teachers' Unions An INTERNATIONAL COMMUNIST FRONT ORGANIZATION based in Prague and affiliated to the WORLD FEDERATION OF TRADE UNIONS. The W.F. of Teachers' U. was founded in Paris in 1946 with its initial headquarters there, but was expelled from France in 1951 for subversive activities and moved its base to Vienna (in the Soviet sector). It was expelled again in 1956 and finally established its base in Prague in 1959. Its membership includes 52 teachers' unions totalling 13m. members in 41 countries – all the socialist countries, except Yugoslavia, and mostly less-developed countries (Canada, France, the FR of Germany, Italy, the UK and the USA are not members). The Federation aims at improving teachers' working conditions, cultivating solidarity and democracy among teachers, and facilitating adjustments in education consequent upon scientific and technological developments. It also works towards international understanding and peace and campaigns against colonialism and militarism. It publishes *Information Bulletin* eight times a year (in Arabic, English, French, German, Russian and Spanish) and a quarterly, *Teachers of the World* (in English, French, German and Spanish).

World Federation of Trade Unions An INTERNATIONAL COMMUNIST FRONT ORGANIZATION with its headquarters in Prague. It was founded at the World Trade Union Congress in Paris in Oct. 1945. But during 1947–49, differences emerged between communist and non-communist elements. Many Western trade unions left the W.F.T.U. (including the AMERICAN FEDERATION OF LABOUR and the British TRADES UNION CONGRESS) and, in Nov. 1949, created the INTERNATIONAL CONFEDERATION OF FREE TRADE UNIONS (based in Brussels). In addition, there is also the Christian-dominated WORLD CONFEDERATION OF LABOUR (also based in Brussels). In 1949, the W.F.T.U. established a special International Fund to provide financial assistance for communist-led strikes. During the most frigid stage of the Cold War 1949–53, it conformed to Stalinist policies. The Federation's original headquarters were in Paris, but the organization was expelled in 1951 for subversive work and moved to Vienna. After another expulsion in 1956 they were finally moved to Prague. In addition, the W.F.T.U. has representatives in Geneva, Paris and Norwalk (USA). The Federation is still the largest trade union organization in the world, embracing 70 international and national trade union associations in 70 countries. Almost all the socialist countries are members (Yugoslavia being conspicuous for her absence). Among the 56 non-socialist countries represented are Argentina, Austria, Bangladesh, Brazil, Finland, France, India, Indonesia, Pakistan and the Philippines. The combined membership of the affiliated organizations is over 160m., nine-tenths in the socialist countries (110m. in the USSR alone). The W.F.T.U. is the only international communist front organization enjoying status with the United Nations, the Economic and Social Council, the Food and Agriculture Organization, the INTERNATIONAL LABOUR ORGANIZATION and UNESCO. The main organ of authority of the W.F.T.U. is the World Trade Union Congress, held every four years, which elects a General Council, meeting at least once a year. The latter elects a Bureau (consisting of a President, a General Secretary and members representing different continents), which meets three times a year. The W.F.T.U.'s objectives include the consolidation and unification of the international trade union movement, irrespective of race, religion, nationality and political views, the protection and improvement of economic conditions and social rights of organized labour, assistance in organizing trade unions in less-developed countries, the exchange of information and the cultivation of CLASS CONSCIOUSNESS of trade union members. It also supports the peace movement, co-operating with the WORLD PEACE COUNCIL. The Federation publishes a weekly, *Flashes on the Trade Union World* (in Arabic, English, French, Russian and Spanish), a monthly, *World Trade Union Movement* (in Arabic, English, Finnish, French, German, Japanese, Romanian, Russian and Spanish) and occasional reports, pamphlets and posters.

World Marxist Review A monthly theoretical and information journal of the 'Communist and Workers' Parties', now published monthly in Toronto (by Progress Books). The publication began in Sep. 1958 in Prague, but since Oct. 1964 it has been appearing in Toronto. The *Review* is the North American edition of *Problems of Peace and Socialism* (which in the past also appeared as *Peace, Freedom and Socialism*), published in Prague in 34 languages, in 57 national editions and distributed in 145 countries. Its editor is K. Zarodov, a Russian Marxist hardliner (ZARODOV DOCTRINE), who is assisted by an Editorial Board representing 58 socialist and non-socialist countries. The journal, from its Prague headquarters, also organizes international conferences on the exchange of experience and information and new directions of development in the theory and practice affecting the international communist movement.

World Peace Council An INTERNATIONAL COMMUNIST FRONT ORGANIZATION based in Helsinki. It originated from the World Congress of Intellectuals for Peace, held in Wrocław (Poland) in Aug. 1948, at which Professor F. Joliot-Curie was the most prominent participant. The W.P.C. was created at the second World Peace Congress in Warsaw in Nov. 1950, having replaced the World Peace Committee elected at the first World Congress of the Partisans of Peace in Paris-Prague, March 1949. Although originally the W.P.C. was based in Paris, it was expelled in 1951 by the French Government for communist propaganda. In 1954 its seat was established in Vienna, from where it was expelled again (however, it changed its name to the International Institute for Peace and remained there as a subsidiary organization). In 1968, the headquarters of the W.P.C. were permanently established in Helsinki. The peace movement was supported by the COMINFORM and was prompted by the COLD WAR (after 1946), the creation of the NORTH ATLANTIC TREATY ORGANIZATION (1949), the Korean War (1950–53) and the development of nuclear weapons. The affiliated membership of the W.P.C. (as of Jan.

1977) includes 70 international and 220 national peace organizations and over 600 individuals recommended by national groups as supporters of peace, in more than 100 countries. The W.P.C. maintains an active publication programme, notably, *New Perspectives*, quarterly (in English and French) and *Peace Courier*, fortnightly (in English, French, German and Spanish).

Wozchod Handelsbank (Western Commercial Bank, in German) The Soviet-owned bank in Zurich, founded in 1966 by the *VNESHTORGBANK* and several Soviet foreign trade enterprises. Its main function is to finance Soviet-Western trade, but in addition it finances other socialist countries' trade with the West as well, and handles Soviet gold sales in Western Europe (having largely replaced the MOSCOW NARODNY BANK in this function since the early 1970s). The W.H. also acts as an agent of the *Vneshtorgbank* in the West for numbered bank accounts which can be maintained by capitalist depositors with hard currencies (safety and secrecy unconditionally guaranteed).

Wrangel, Peter Nikolaievich (1878–1928) A Russian Tsarist general who during the Civil War 1918–20 became one of the leaders of the White Armies fighting the Bolsheviks in the Ukraine. He gave sympathetic support to the KORNILOV REBELLION in order to overthrow the PETROGRAD SOVIET. He commanded a cavalry corps in the Volunteer Army of General A. I. DENIKIN 1918–19, but disagreed with him on strategic and political questions. After the failure of Denikin's offensive June-Oct. 1919, he was appointed Commander-in-Chief of the counter-revolutionary forces in April 1920. His efforts to win the support of the peasants, Cossacks and Western allies had a limited success. His forces were routed by the RED ARMY under M. V. FRUNZE in the south-western Ukraine, June-Nov. 1920. He efficiently organized the evacuation of 150,000 White Army personnel and refugees from the Black Sea ports. He

moved to Belgium where he died in 1928. There are several geographical features in the eastern USSR and in Alaska named, not after General P.N.W., but after F.P.W. (1796–1870), a distinguished Russian navigator.

Writers' Union of the USSR A national organization associating Soviet writers, with corresponding organizations at the Union Republic level. It was founded by the decision of the Central Committee of the ALL-UNION COMMUNIST PARTY (OF THE BOLSHEVIKS) in 1932, as a new move to ensure that the writers participate in the government's drive to proletarianize literature. The two previously existing literary groups, the *RAPPISTS* and the *POPUTCHIKI*, were dissolved and became members of the Union. At its second Congress in 1934, the Union adopted SOCIALIST REALISM as the binding code of its members. There has always been opposition within the Union to excessive conformity limiting free, creative activities of the writers. In spite of some liberalization after Stalin's death (1953), the writers' creative freedom is still circumscribed. Among those expelled from the Union were B. Pasternak (in 1958, for *Doctor Zhivago*) and A. SOLZHENITSYN (in 1969, for dissident activities).

Wuchan Resolution A policy-decision made by the Central Committee of the Chinese Communist Party, in a document entitled 'About Some Questions in Relation to People's Communes'. At its meeting in Wuchan (located in the province of Hupeh in central eastern China) on 10 Dec. 1958, it revoked payment in communes according to needs in favour of the rule 'according to work'. The Resolution was highly critical of Party cadres and, indirectly, of Mao Tse-tung for the manner in which the PEOPLE'S COMMUNES were being established during the GREAT LEAP FORWARD. They were charged with having committed serious errors, such as the use of military methods to organize production, the forced collectivization of personal household effects and the failure to distribute income according to the socialist principle 'TO EACH ACCORDING TO HIS WORK'. The W.R. was further supplemented with the LUSHAN RESOLUTION of Aug. 1959. Indirectly, the criticism was levelled against Mao and his stalwarts as initiators of the Great Leap. Soon afterwards, Mao decided to step down as the Chairman of the PR of China in favour of LIU SHAO-CH'I.

Wuhan Incident An event involving the RED GUARDS, a military commander and the Chinese Communist Party at the height of the GREAT PROLETARIAN CULTURAL REVOLUTION in mid-1967, which almost brought China to the brink of anarchy. In mid-July 1967, Mao Tse-tung sent a high-level mission, headed by Hsieh Fu-chih and Wang Li, to Wuhan (capital of the Hupeh Province in central east China) urging the Regional Military Command to accept REVOLUTIONARY REBELS over the conservative elements and, thereby, reverse its earlier decision. But the commanding officer, Chien Tsai-tao and other military leaders, refused and instigated a demonstration in support of the conservative faction, during which the two officials from Peking were detained and beaten up. The Maoist faction in Peking reacted strongly, secured the release of the two officials, ordered the offending military commanders to report to Peking, humiliated them publicly and dismissed them. Furthermore the CULTURAL REVOLUTION GROUP, to prevent similar 'mutinous acts' by army units, prevailed upon Mao in Aug. 1967 to authorize the arming of selected Red Guard and Revolutionary Rebel groups to defend themselves in the pursuit of the Cultural Revolution. It led to excesses and, finally, Mao had to exercise moderation in the revolutionary activities to restore order.

X

Xin Hua (New China, in Chinese) The official news agency in the PR of China, known in English as the New China News Agency. It was founded in 1937 and is the chief source of domestic and the exclusive channel of international news for the domestic press. It also releases official announcements of policy statements and material for newspapers, radio and television in 12 Chinese dialects and 11 foreign languages. *X.H.* is attached to the State Council and has two major subsidiaries – the China Press Agency, for transmitting a daily news file to both domestic and international listeners, and the China News Agency which provides news to Overseas Chinese newspapers, magazines and periodicals (especially those in Hong Kong and Macao). *X.H.* has over 1,500 offices throughout China and some 70,000 part-time reporters. It also maintains offices in foreign countries, some of which have been accused of subversive activities and spying (as was the case in Cambodia, Kenya and the Central African Republic).

Y

Yagoda, Genrikh Grigorievich (1891–1938) A Bolshevik revolutionary and the chief of the Soviet secret police before W.W.II. He became a Bolshevik in 1907 and, after the October Revolution of 1917, joined the CHEKA, became the deputy chief of the OGPU in 1924 and the chief of the NKVD ten years later. In this capacity, he greatly expanded the FORCED LABOUR CAMPS and organized the first TREASON TRIAL (Aug. 1936). But because of his previous association with the RIGHT OPPOSITION and insufficient ruthlessness, he was removed by Stalin in Sep. 1936 (and replaced by N. I. YEZHOV). In April 1937, he was arrested, tried for treason, together with BUKHARIN and RYKOV, and was executed in the following year.

YAK The Soviet abbreviation for piston or jet-engined fighter and passenger aircraft, designed by A. S. Yakovlev (1906–), a distinguished Soviet aircraft designer and military engineering leader.

Yalta Conference An important meeting of the leaders of the three Allied Powers at Yalta in the Crimean Peninsula in the latter stages of W.W.II mainly on the final defeat and treatment of Germany. The Conference took place from 4 to 11 Feb. 1945 and was attended by J. V. Stalin, F. D. Roosevelt and W. Churchill, aided by their foreign ministers, chiefs of staff and various advisers. It was agreed that the Allied administration would be established for defeated Germany with joint headquarters in Berlin (to which France would also be invited), that the USSR would take over eastern Poland and the latter would be 'compensated for' with German territories, that the USSR would have a free hand in Eastern Europe and that the USSR would enter war against Japan and be rewarded with southern Sakhalin, the Kuril Islands and special rights in Manchuria. It was also decided to prepare the United Nations Charter and hold trials of the war criminals. Most of the content of the Conference was kept secret at the time and some of it has not been implemented in the friendly spirit originally intended. The chief beneficiary of the Y.C. was the USSR and later it became a symbol of US and British capitulation to Stalin.

Yalta Group See RIGA AND YALTA GROUPS

Yalta Memorandum Ideological precepts preapred by P. TOGLIATTI while on holidays at Yalta and in the Crimea, shortly before his death and published posthumously in Aug. 1964. The Y.M. dwelt on the international communist movement and was written in the form of an address to KHRUSHCHEV. It contained critical observations on the tactics of the Communist Party of the Soviet Union in relation to the Chinese Communist Party. Togliatti called for greater independence of the communist parties and a flexible interpretation of Marxism.

Yang Hsien-chen (1899–) A leading Chinese Marxist philosopher, former President of the Higher Party School who, owing to differences in philosophical interpretation with Mao Tse-tung, was removed from his position of influence. Y. attended the COMMUNIST UNIVERSITY FOR THE TOILERS OF THE EAST in Moscow in the 1920s and spent several years in the USSR, working for the COMINTERN and the Soviet Foreign Languages Press as a translator and propagandist of Marxist ideas. He participated in the Sino-Japanese War and, after the communist seizure of power in 1949, became active in Party propaganda work and philosophical societies, served as a deputy to the National People's Congress in 1954–64 and, in 1956, was elected to the Central Committee of the Chinese Communist Party. In the early 1950s, he became Vice-President of the Marx-Lenin Institute (attached to the CC of the CCP) for the theoretical training of higher Party cadres. In 1955 he was appointed President of the Institute and its name was soon changed to the Higher Party School. While there, he was contributing to Marxist philosophical thought and formulated his most famous principle, Two Combine into One, in accordance with the traditional Marxist dialectics concerning the resolution of CONTRADICTIONS. But Mao attacked him sharply in 1964 and put forward the opposite thesis, viz. One divides into Two, which developed into the 'ONE DIVIDES INTO TWO VERSUS TWO COMBINE INTO ONE CONTROVERSY'. Mao described Yang's stand as 'revisionist', 'undermining the proletarian outlook', 'reactionary' and 'pro-Soviet'. Yang was removed from the Presidency of the School in the early 1960s and lost other posts and functions of influence.

Yao Wen-yuan (1923–) A Chinese journalist, Party ideologist and politician noted for left extremism, who lost influence under the regime of Hua Kuo-feng. Yao was a member of the CULTURAL RE-VOLUTION GROUP in the late 1960s and of the GANG OF FOUR in the early 1970s. He was a prominent activist in the power struggle and a contributor to the Party's theoretical organ HUNG-CH'I urging the 'intensification of the dictatorship of the proletariat'. According to the present offi-

cial version, he was the leading figure behind the distortion of the events known as the TIEN AN MEN INCIDENT in April 1976. He was expelled from the Party in July 1977, tried in 1980–81 and sentenced to 20 years imprisonment.

Yellow International A colloquial critical term applied by revolutionary Marxists to the INTERNATIONAL FEDERATION OF TRADE UNIONS, which existed from 1919 to 1945 and sometimes to the INTERNATIONAL CONFEDERATION OF FREE TRADE UNIONS created in 1949. In the Marxist view, the Y.I. – in contrast to the Red International of Labour Unions (THE PRO-FINTERN) and the WORLD FEDERATION OF TRADE UNIONS – stood or stands for collaboration between trade unions and employers, is opposed to the CLASS STRUGGLE and the PROLETARIAN REVOLUTION as the means of achieving an ideal society. Also YELLOW UNIONS.

Yellow Unions A Marxist term for trade unions whose leaders pursue a policy of class collaboration and co-operate with employers. The term originated in France (*syndicats jaunes*) in 1887, when, during a strike at Montceau-les-Mines, employers managed to organize a labour union to break the strike. The union held a meeting in a hall where windows were patched with yellow paper to repair the glass previously broken by the striking workers. The term was later applied to the national trade unions which belonged to the INTERNATIONAL FEDERATION OF TRADE UNIONS (1919–45) in contrast to the Red International of Labour Unions (the PROFINTERN).

Yemeni Socialist Party The ruling Communist party in the People's Democratic Republic of YEMEN. It is the successor to the National Front and held its first Congress in 1978. The Party claims to be Marxist-Leninist and is committed to 'scientific socialism adapted to local conditions'. It is controlled by Central Committee of 78 members, plus 14 substitute members, headed by the Secretary-General (Abdul Fattah Ismail).

Yemen, People's Democractic Republic
of the (*Jumhouriyyat al-Yemen al-
Dimuoraaiyya esh-Sha'biyya*) A country
in the southern Arabian Peninsula, occupying the former Aden Protectorate. Its
area is 287,680 sq. km., the population is
1,850,000 (in 1978) and the capital is
Aden. The country separated from the
[North] Yemen in 1967, nationalized
most foreign capital (except a British Pet-
roleum refinery) in 1969 and adopted its
present name and a new Constitution in
1970. The country is ruled by a quasi-
Marxist regime representing the YEMENI
SOCIALIST PARTY, successor to the National Front (which had replaced the National Liberation Front). The P.D.R.Y.
has established close ties with the USSR
and China from which it has been receiving military and technical aid. On the
other hand, the [North] Yemen Arab Republic has been aided by the USA and
Saudi Arabia. In another attempt to unify
the two Yemens, the P.D.R.Y. - aided by
the Soviets, Cubans and East Germans –
attacked North Yemen in Feb. 1979. But
an uneasy truce was agreed upon in March
1979 by the intervention of other Arab
states, with a view to reunification.

Yenan The headquarters of the Chinese
Communists from 1935 to 1949, situated
in north central China. It is a town, also
known as Fushih, on the south bank of the
Yen River (a tributary of the Hwang-ho
River) in the northern province of Shensi,
about 800km. south-west of Peking. The
town is situated in the fertile loess high-
lands noted for its caves and surrounded
by rugged mountains and semi-deserts.
The Communists reached it in Oct. 1935
after the LONG MARCH. Consequently, its
population increased from 6,000 to over
50,000. Y. became the capital of the
Shensi-Kansu-Ningsia Border Area, controlled by the Chinese Communist Party,
with its own strict, uncorrupt administration and currency. It was used as the base
for launching operations against the
Japanese and extending the areas under
Communist control. After W.W.II, following the all-out offensive by the

Nationalist Government of Chiang Kai-
shek against the Communists, Y. was captured by the Kuomintang forces in March
1947, but recaptured by the Communists
in April 1948. After the Communist victory on the mainland and the proclamation of the PR of China on 1 Oct. 1949, the
seat of the Communist regime was moved
to Peking.

Yezhov, Nikolai Ivanovich (1894–1939)
A Soviet Party official and chief of the
secret service. He joined the Bolsheviks in
1917, became a *POLITRUK* in the Red
Army and began specializing in Party personnel and security work. As Stalin's protégé, he was elected to the Party's Central
Committee in 1934 and, for his ruthless
efficiency, was appointed the chief of the
NKVD in Sep. 1936 (replacing YAGODA).
Under Yezhov, Stalin's GREAT PURGES
reached their unprecedented peak of terror known as the YEZHOVSHCHINA. After
the Purges, Y. was removed from his post
in Dec. 1938 (succeeded by BERIA) and
disappeared in the following year. According to conflicting unofficial reports,
he was either shot without trial, committed suicide or died insane.

Yezhovshchina or **Yezhovism** Colloquially used terms for the period of the secret
police terror in the USSR, when N. I.
YEZHOV was the Commissar for Internal
Affairs and chief of the secret police, the
NKVD, from Sep. 1936 to Dec. 1938. The
first Treason Trial, 19 – 24 Aug. 1936 had
been organized by YAGODA, but Stalin did
not regard him ruthless enough and had
him replaced by Yezhov. Under Yezhov,
the GREAT PURGES reached their peak,
which resulted in mass executions and imprisonment of Party, military and administrative leaders, diplomats, various
government officials and foreign communist leaders resident in the USSR at the
time. Unofficial estimates place the
casualties of Y. at 1m. executed (incl.
Yagoda) and 2m. deaths in the FORCED
LABOUR CAMPS. At the time of Yezhov's
replacement by BERIA in Dec. 1938, there
were 9m. inmates in the forced labour

camps. Also MOSCOW TRIALS, TREASON TRIALS.

Young Hegelians Another description for Left Hegelians or the HEGELIAN LEFT (to which Marx and Engels temporarily belonged as students).

Young Socialists A description referring to three different left-wing associations of young people. 1. A short-lived fraternity of young intellectuals (writers, artists, and students), in the SOCIAL-DEMOCRATIC PARTY OF GERMANY, which emerged in 1890. They entertained idealistic socialist ideas, but had little in common with the working class and were not interested in revolutionary action. They were expelled from the Party at its Congress in Erfurt in 1891. 2. A Trotskyite youth organization in Great Britain, affiliated to the WORKERS' REVOLUTIONARY PARTY of Great Britain, established in 1973. The Y.S. claim a membership of 20,000 which makes them the largest Marxist youth organization in Great Britain. Its organ is *Keep Left*. 3. A Trotskyite youth organization within the [Labour Party] in Great Britain. In its programme, 'British Perspectives and Tastes' it aims "to penetrate every constituency party in the country" with Trotskyites. It is also known as the Militant Tendency and publishes a weekly, *Militant*.

Yugoslav Communist Party LEAGUE OF COMMUNISTS OF YUGOSLAVIA.

Yugoslavia, Socialist Republic of (*Socijalistička Federativna Republika Jugoslavija*) A medium-sized country in southeastern Europe of 255,800 sq. km. and 22.0m. inhabitants (in 1978), ruled by the League of Communists of Yugoslavia under a mono-party system of government. Y. is a federal state embracing six Republics: Bosnia-Herzegovina; Croatia; Macedonia; Montenegro; Serbia; and Slovenia, plus the autonomous provinces of Kosovo and Vojvodina. Before W.W.II, Y. was a monarchy and the Communist Party of Yugoslavia (as it was called then) was illegal. After the German and Italian invasion in 1940, two separate resistance movements emerged – the right-wing *Chetniks* led by D. MIHAJLOVIĆ and the Communist *Partisans* led by J. TITO. The *Partisans* performed better, commanded a wider popular appeal and, from 1943 on, Allied (British) military aid was diverted away from the *Chetniks* to support the *Partisans*. After the war, Tito immediately organized a Communist-dominated People's Front and the country was proclaimed the People's Republic of Yugoslavia, but that name was replaced in 1963 by the S.R. of Y. Stalin's differences with Tito led to the expulsion of the Communist Party of Yugoslavia from COMINFORM in June 1948. Y. received massive American and other Western aid and turned to liberal economic reforms which have made her a model of MARKET SOCIALISM and WORKERS' SELF-MANAGEMENT. The Government has endeavoured to pursue a policy of non-alignment and, after Stalin's death (March 1953), relations began to improve with the USSR, as confirmed in the BELGRADE DECLARATION (June 1955). Y. was accorded an associate status in the COUNCIL FOR MUTUAL ECONOMIC ASSISTANCE in Sep. 1964 and, in June 1973 signed a non-preferential trade agreement with the European Economic Community. In 1974, a new (the third after W.W.II) Constitution was adopted (replacing that of 1963). The highest legislative power is vested in the FEDERAL ASSEMBLY. But effective power is exercised by the LEAGUE OF COMMUNISTS OF YUGOSLAVIA, effectively aided by the SOCIALIST ALLIANCE OF THE WORKING PEOPLE OF YUGOSLAVIA, a united front dominated by the L.C.Y.

Z

Zarodov Doctrine A term used in the West for the hardline tenets on the international Communist movement held and publicized by Konstantin Zarodov, a Soviet expert on the communist parties outside the USSR and the editor of *Problemy mira i sotsializma* (*Problems of Peace and Socialism*), also appearing in English under the title *WORLD MARXIST REVIEW*. The Z.D. is opposed to the peaceful and evolutionary PARLIAMENTARY ROAD TO SOCIALISM and EUROCOMMUNISM. It is also against close co-operation between the Communist parties on the one hand, and social-democratic and moderate socialist parties and groups on the other, as it leads to compromises and departures from Marxist ideals. If there is such a collaboration, it must be under Communist dominance because, as Zarodov said, 'Majority is not an arithmetical but a political concept'. Instead, the Doctrine emphasizes the historic mission of the proletariat, revolutionary strategy and the need for direct action, including violence.

Zasulich (also known as **Zasulica** or **Sassoulitch**), **Vera** (1851 – 1919) A Russian revolutionary active in NARODNISM, who later sided with the MENSHEVIKS rather than the Bolsheviks. She participated in the assassination of Gen. F. F. Triepov in Jan. 1878 but was freed. In the following year, she joined the *CHORNYI PEREDEL* and two years later, the EMANCIPATION OF LABOUR GROUP, but she was opposed to individual terror. She then lived mostly in Switzerland up to 1905, where she served on the editorial board of *ISKRA* and translated the works of Marx and Engels into

Russian. After the split in the RUSSIAN SOCIAL-DEMOCRATIC LABOUR PARTY in 1903, she supported PLEKHANOV and became one of the leading Mensheviks. She did not participate in the Bolshevik Revolution of 1917.

Zemlya i Volya (Land and Freedom, in Russian) A secret Russian revolutionary organization formed in 1861/62, as a merger of two revolutionary groups in St Petersburg (now Leningrad) and London. Its ideological leader was N. G. CHERNYSHEVSKY and its revolutionary programme (*What People Need*) was prepared by N. P. OGARIOV. The programme demanded land for peasants, political freedom for all and the abolition of the state, to be achieved by a peasant revolution. The organization published *KOLOKOL* and *Svoboda* (*Liberty*). *Z.i.V.* was dissolved in 1864, but the revolutionary tradition it created lived on and led to the formation of similar organizations. It was revived in 1876, but after three years' existence it split into *CHORNYI PEREDEL* (*Land Distribution Group*) and *NARODNAYA VOLYA* (*People's Freedom*).

Zetkin, Clara (1857 – 1933) One of the most outstanding women in the German and international communist movement. Of German descent (*née* Eisner), she married a Russian revolutionary Osip Z., through whom she was converted to Marxism and, in 1881 joined the Social-Democratic Party of Germany (illegal at the time). She was a founding delegate to the SECOND INTERNATIONAL, participated in the INTERNATIONAL SOCIALIST

657

Zhdanov, Andrei Aleksandrovich

WOMEN'S CONGRESS (of which she became the Secretary-General) in 1907 and from 1907 to 1917 she served on the Executive Committee of the SOCIAL-DEMOCRATIC PARTY OF GERMANY, where she co-operated closely with another left-winger, ROSA LUXEMBURG. C.Z. was active in the Marxist opposition to W.W.I (for which she was imprisoned later) and, in 1916, together with K. LIEBKNECHT and Rosa Luxemburg, participated in the foundation of the SPARTACUS LEAGUE (the forerunner of the German Communist Party). In 1921 she became a member of the EXECUTIVE COMMITTEE OF THE COMMUNIST INTERNATIONAL and also headed the INTERNATIONAL WOMEN'S SECRETARIAT. She was also a deputy to the German *Reichstag* and presided over its last opening in 1932 before its destruction by fire. In her last years she lived in the USSR and died in a Soviet clinic.

Zhdanov, Andrei Aleksandrovich (1896 – 1948) A prominent Bolshevik Party leader, a leading theoretician and exponent of MARXISM-LENINISM and SOCIALIST REALISM under Stalin and a capable organizer active in the Soviet and international communist movement. He joined the Bolsheviks in 1915 and in 1917 participated in the Revolution in the Urals. After the assassination of S. M. KIROV in 1934, he became the chief of the Leningrad Party Organization (until 1944). Also, in 1934, he was elected a secretary of the Central Committee of the ALL-UNION COMMUNIST PARTY (OF THE BOLSHEVIKS) and, in 1939, became a full member of the Politburo. He became the chief elaborator of Lenin's PARTY-MINDEDNESS in philosophy, literature and art and, as a writer, speaker and organizer, contributed substantially to the development of Soviet culture and patriotism. After W.W.II he organized ruthless campaigns against the 'bourgeois survivals' and influence in Soviet thought and intellectual circles. The system of ideas and practices in the ideological, cultural and aesthetic fields pursued by him became known as *Zdanovshchina*. He advocated a

hard line in the international communist movement and was Stalin's spokesman in the COMINFORM (founded in 1947). At that time, he was regarded as Stalin's prospective successor to the Party leadership. His sudden death in 1948, in the prime of his leadership powers, occurred in mysterious circumstances.

Zhdanovshchina The system of ideas and practices associated with the writings and activities of A. A. ZHDANOV in the sphere of ideology, culture, literature and art.

Zhiguli The name of the Soviet passenger car produced since 1970 at the Volga Automobile Works in Togliattigrad. The car's name comes from the Zhiguli Hills, on the right bank of the Volga near Togliattigrad, noted in folk legends as a hideout in the 17th c. during a peasant uprising led by Stepan Razin. Because of the difficulties associated with pronunciation, spelling and uncomplimentary meanings in foreign languages, its name for export has been changed to Lada. The plant (named after the late Italian Communist Party leader, P. TOGLIATTI), was constructed by Fiat during 1967–70, where 800,000 vehicles of this type are produced annually. The vehicle is based essentially on the Fiat 124, but has been adapted to the harsher Soviet climatic and road conditions. It is now produced in several models all of them are identified by the prefix *VAZ*, abbreviated from *Volzhsky Avtomobilnyi Zavod*, meaning Volga Automobile Works. The first model was the *VAZ*-2101, a five-seater weighing 890kg., with a power rating of 62 HP and a maximum speed of 140km.p.h.

Zhongda THIRTY-FIRST OF AUGUST GROUP (in China).

Zhukov, Georgy Konstantinovich (1896 – 1974) A distinguished Soviet military leader and Bolshevik. Of peasant background, he joined the RED ARMY in 1918 and the Bolshevik Party in the following year. He distinguished himself during the GREAT PATRIOTIC WAR 1941–45, first as the commanding officer of the Leningrad Front, then in the Battles of Stalingrad and Kursk, he planned several defensive and offensive campaigns and his Byelorussian Front Army took Berlin. On 8 May 1945, he accepted the surrender of Nazi Germany and headed the Soviet military occupation of East Germany 1945–46. He was identified as the most popular war hero in the USSR, to which Stalin did not take kindly and relegated him to minor posts. After Stalin's death (March 1953), Zh. became a member of the Central Committee of the CPSU, of the Party Presidium (now called the Politburo) and also the Minister of Defence (1955–57). In Oct. 1957 he was stripped of his posts on the grounds of opposing Party control of the armed forces and indulging in a personality cult. He retired from public life thereafter.

Zimmerwald Conference An international socialist meeting held at Zimmerwald, a small town in western Switzerland, south of Bern, in Aug. 1915. It was attended by 38 delegates of the socialist parties representing 11 countries: Bulgaria; France; Germany; Italy; the Netherlands; Norway; Poland; Romania; Russia; Sweden; and Switzerland. The main theme of the Z.C. was the discussion of the attitude of the SECOND INTERNATIONAL to W.W.I. Among the participants was Lenin, around whom a group of extremists formed the so-called Zimmerwald Left, also known as the Internationalists. They pressed for the transformation of the 'imperialist' war into a civil war and a proletarian revolution. But the majority of the delegates were moderates, representing CENTRISM, and favoured peace. When Lenin put forward his 'Theses' calling upon socialists to work towards the defeat of their own nations, the majority turned against him. In the following month Lenin, supported by eight delegates, organized a sequel conference which adopted his theses.

Zimmerwald Left A group of left-wing socialists, also known as the Internationalists, led by Lenin who, as a minority, opposed CENTRISM at the ZIMMERWALD CONFERENCE in Aug. 1915. The Z.L. pressed for a more radical programme and introduced a draft resolution (Lenin's 'Theses') condemning imperialist wars and criticizing the socialist parties of the belligerent countries for not opposing the war. The Z.L. also participated in the Second International Socialist Conference during W.W.I in April 1916 (KIENTAL CONFERENCE), where it gained a stronger position.

Zinoviev (original name **Radomysl'sky**), **Grigory Evseievich** (1883–1936) A leading Russian Party official and politician, prominent in the international communist movement, who fell victim in the Stalin-Trotsky rivalry. He joined the RUSSIAN SOCIAL-DEMOCRATIC LABOUR PARTY in 1901 and, at the time of the split in 1903, sided with Lenin and became one of the leading BOLSHEVIKS. During W.W.I, Z. was one of the leading INTERNATIONAL-ISTS and, in April 1917, accompanied Lenin from Switzerland to Petrograd in the sealed train across Germany. Z. at first opposed Lenin's idea of an armed coup, but later supported him and became one of his chief lieutenants. After the October Revolution of 1917, he at first reacted strongly against the exclusion of the non-Bolsheviks from the government. He became chairman of the PETROGRAD SOVIET, then was appointed chairman of the EXECUTIVE COMMITTEE OF THE COMMUNIST INTERNATIONAL (1919–26) and, during Lenin's illness 1923–24, was a member of the ruling *troika* (together with KAMENEV and STALIN). At that stage, Z. took Stalin's side against TROTSKY. But in 1926, he joined Trotsky against Stalin, for which he was expelled from the Politburo in June 1926 and from the Party in Nov. 1927. After a recantation of his 'errors', he was readmitted to the Party in the following year, held several important posts, but Stalin still doubted his loyalty. In Oct. 1932, Z. was again expelled from the Party and, although he recanted his errors again, he was later sentenced in a secret trial to 10 years' imprisonment in Jan. 1935. At the first open MOSCOW TRIAL of the Trotskyites-Zinovievites in Aug. 1936, Z. was sentenced to death for 'treason' and executed immediately.

Zionism A Jewish nationalist movement on the international scale which emerged towards the end of the 19th c. It recruited its supporters mainly from the middle classes and some sections of the working class. Its aim was to establish a sovereign national state in Palestine. After the creation of Israel in 1948, Z. has continued its activities, postulating that all Jews, in whichever country they live, form part of one world community owing its loyalty to Israel. Z. in the international arena is pursued by the World Zionist Organization, founded at its first Congress in Basel in 1897, now directed from Israel with International Secretariats in Geneva, London, New York and Paris. There are 39 national Zionist federations which are affiliated with it, representing 44 countries, all of which are non-Socialist, except Cuba. Marxists have, on the whole, adopted a critical view of Z., regarding it historically separate from the international working class struggle, petty bourgeois, chauvinistic, steeped in Talmudist elitist religion and, furthermore, supportive of US 'imperialist policies' in Africa and Asia. As such Z. is considered to be inconsistent with Marxist ideals and the international communist movement. Zionist activities are prohibited in virtually all Socialist countries.